STEAM LOCOMOTIVES OF THE GREAT NORTHERN RAILWAY

Kenneth R. Middleton
Norman F. Priebe

Great Northern Railway Historical Society

STEAM LOCOMOTIVES OF THE GREAT NORTHERN RAILWAY

Published by the Great Northern Railway Historical Society, Philip W. Gjevre, Publications Officer

Printed by Spectra Print Corporation, Stevens Point, WI
Kay Ausloos, Graphic Designer

Printed on 70# Gusto Satin Text
Typeset in Bodoni and Arial
Printed and Bound in the USA

Library of Congress Control Number: 2010910387
ISBN 978-0-615-38759-8

First Printing

R-1 Raw Power for a Raw Day

Seattle Washington 1941. It's a raw autumn day in the Pacific Northwest. The rain has turned to a cold mist as one of Great Northern's huge R-1 class 2-8-8-2's takes an eastbound train along Seattle's Railroad Avenue. Track workers quitting for the day don't give the big machine much attention as the train eases down the wet rails. The Great Northern Railway built these mammoth locomotives in their Hillyard, Washington locomotive shops. The 2043 was built in 1928 and was the last of the R-1 class. These locomotives weighed in at 963,000 lbs., had four 28" X 32" cylinders and posted an astonishing 142,000 lbs. of starting tractive force. Behind the tender, 2043 has 97 cars and

5,183 tons of train moving along the Seattle waterfront. The locomotive will take the train up the Cascades to Skykomish, Washington where electric locomotives will take over to drag the train through the 7.8-mile long Cascade tunnel.

Gilbert H. Bennett, renowned Lehi, Utah, locomotive illustrator, has captured the majesty of the great steam locomotives of the 30's and 40's in his latest exclusive original painting for Miner's collection. Bennett is appreciated worldwide for his meticulous detail in railroad paintings.

Acknowledgements

Any endeavor such as this requires input from many more people than just the authors. This work is the culmination of many years of research conducted by many people. Foremost among these is the late Norman C. Keyes, Jr., who worked for many years with the authors to develop the basic steam locomotive roster, an extract from which was published in Railroad History Volume 143, originally published by the Railway and Locomotive Historical Society in 1980 and later reprinted at the request of the Great Northern Railway Historical Society (GNRHS) in 1989. Norm spent many hours at Burlington Northern headquarters conducting research which contributed to the development of this book. We would also like to thank his wife, Helen, for passing along many of Norm's notes and research materials to us.

Cassandra Middleton has spent hours of her time copying records at the Minnesota Historical Society, Burlington Northern and in the GNRHS Archives which have greatly contributed to the completion of this work.

Walter F. Becker was an early researcher whose work was very helpful. Jeanette Priebe aided with the proof reading.

Many officers and employees of the former Great Northern Railway contributed.

From the Great Northern Motive Power Department, we acknowledge Lambert M. (Bert) Baker, who provided roster data and information about the early design of the O-8 class, Howard S. (Sam) Silver for the details of the N-3 design and R. E. (Dick) Johnson, GN and BN Director, Mechanical Engineering, retired, for information regarding the testing of the N-3 and O-8 class locomotives.

Carl Olson and Dick Scott of the GN Valuation Engineering department are acknowledged for allowing early access to the Unit Record of Property Changes - Equipment, Account 51, Steam Locomotives. Reginald Spoo also provided access to BN computer records and the Change Number Record Accounts. Frank Perrin of the GN Public Relations Department provided photographs and arranged many of the contacts.

Robert Downing, Thomas Lamphier, G. R. Nelson, Richard J. Foster and Don Holmgren provided operations data. Mr. Downing also provided information on the GN's use of coal. Numerous locomotive engineers and firemen were interviewed over the years that contributed valuable information.

The reference library staff at Minnesota Historical Society provided a great deal of help over the years in accessing the Great Northern collection held by that agency. We especially want to thank John M. Wickre from the early years and most recently, Ruth Bauer Anderson. Deirdre K. Shaw, archivist at the National Park Service Museum, West Glacier, Montana, and Eileen McCormick, former reference librarian at Hill Reference Library were very helpful. The staff of numerous regional historical societies and libraries gave assistance, especially the Kandiyohi Historical Society museum, Willmar, MN; Stearns History Museum and Research Center, St. Cloud, MN and the Ottertail County Historical Society, Fergus Falls, MN.

Stuart Holmquist provided access to the photographs now held by the Great Northern Railway Historical Society (GNRHS). Duane Amdahl, Doug Complin and John Thomas assisted with research from the GNRHS Great Northern Authority for Expenditure (AFE) file collection in St.Paul, MN.

Several other individuals contributed data without which this book would be quite incomplete. Al Deutscher provided information aiding the branch pipe heater study. George Fischer provided access to the Alex Colville notebook. Lawrence Hargis furnished data from the H.K. Porter Company. Robert LeMassena provided articulated locomotive data and photos. Dennis L. Lutz gave us access to his 1941 Locomotive Cyclopedia. The 1943 locomotive diagram set was obtained from Ray Norton. Father Dale Peterka gave permission to use material from a number of GNRHS Reference Sheets he authored in several chapters of this work. Mike Miller and Robert Solinger provided buried locomotive data. Stan Townsend helped in obtaining information about locomotives sold to the Spokane, Portland and Seattle Railway. Joel Weeks drew the superheater diagram. Mark Wilkouski provided data on the use of GN O-1's on the Atchison, Topeka and Santa Fe.

We thank Gil Bennett, the artist, and the Miner Enterprises Corporation for allowing reproduction of the painting used as the frontispiece. Jennifer Gaydos of Miner Enterprises made arrangements to use the Bennett painting.

We also acknowledge the many photographers, several since deceased, collectors and agencies that provided photographs or permission to use photographs for this publication. In addition to the former Great Northern Railway, the direct contributors include Walter Ainsworth (Warren Wing, W. C. Whittaker, R. W. Johnston and part of the Rail Photo Service collections), ALCO Historic Photos, Allen County Historical Society, Eric Archer, Richard Bartholow, Douglas C. Bemrich, Bruce Black, Joe Collias, William Cornwell, the Douglas County Historical Society, Milton Drefke, Jack Dykstra, Jack W. Farrell, Albert Farrow, George Fischer, General Steel Castings Corporation, Henry R. Griffiths, Hugh Grinnell, Don Gruber, Jerrold F. Hilton, Connie Hoffman, Inland Empire Railway Historical Society, Martin Johnson, R. E. Johnson, Skip Nelson for the Hoff-Nelson collection, Ed Kanak, Bob Kelly, Stan Kistler, The Library of Congress, John Luecke, Stan Mailer, John Malven, James C. Mattson, Warren McGee, the Minnesota Historical Society, the Minnesota Transportation Museum, the Montana Historical Society, the National Park Service, Cordell R. Newby, R. V. Nixon, Frank North, the Northwest Montana Historical Society Kalispell Museum, Gary Oliver of GTC collectibles (Stan Styles and Bordertown collections), the Ottertail County Historical Society, Fr. Dale Peterka, Jack Porzig, J.R. Quinn, William Raia (Charles T. Felstead collection), the Railroad Museum of Pennsylvania (PHMC), Maynard Rikerd, Ben Ringnalda, the Siouxland Historical Railroad Association, the Stearns History Museum, Harold K. Vollrath, James R. Vyverberg, Charles E. Winters, and F. G. Zahn.

Several people have made significant contributions to the publication of this book. Philip K. Webb has artfully managed to prepare the graphics for this publication. Kay Ausloos, the graphic designer at Spectra Print, has done the typesetting, layout and map revision. John and Beverly Tracy provided the substantial initial financial contribution to enable the production of this book. Phil Gjevre provided the initiation of the final drive to get the book written and support with getting it published.

Kenneth R. Middleton
Norman F. Priebe

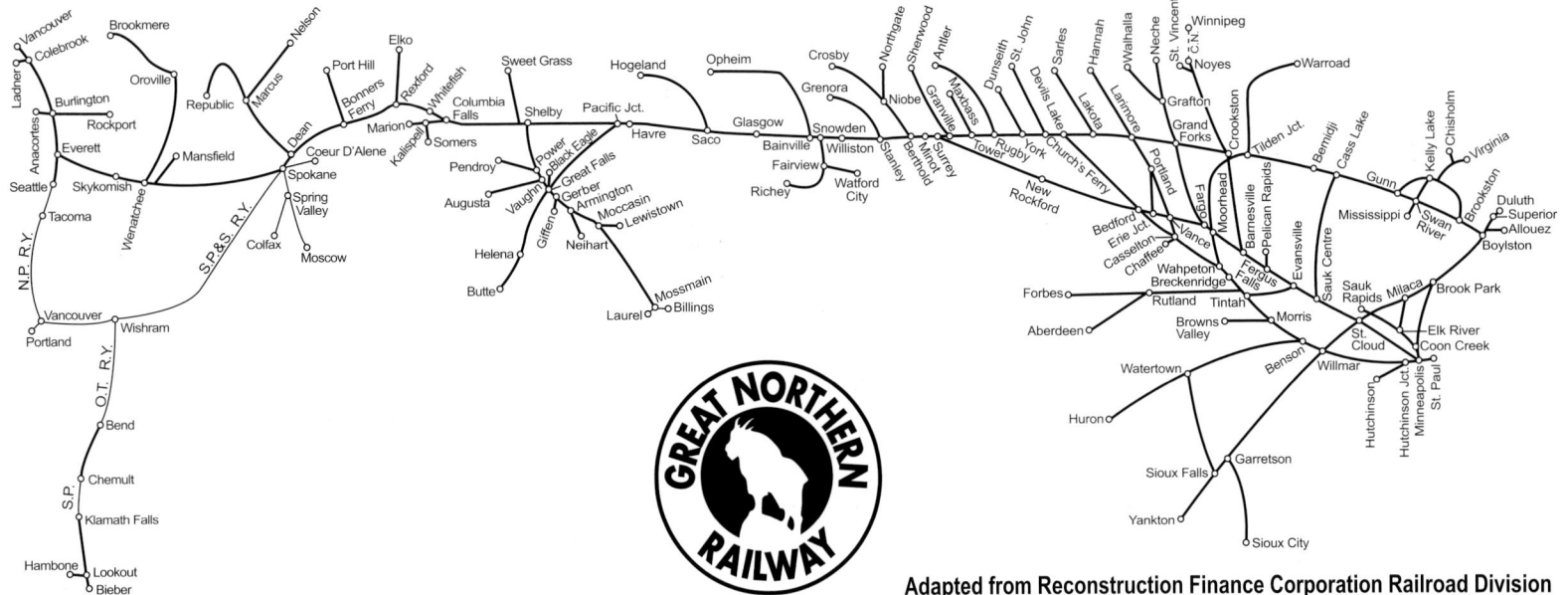

Adapted from Reconstruction Finance Corporation Railroad Division

TABLE of CONTENTS

Acknowledgements 4

Foreword 6

1 A Brief Early Corporate History 7

2 Great Northern Steam
Locomotive Class Systems 19

3 The Great Northern Steam Locomotive....................25

4 The Great Northern Engine Reweigh Rate Case 41

5 Class A 0-6-0 Six-Wheel Switcher.........................43

6 Class B 4-4-0 American Standard..........................57

7 The First Class C 0-4-0 Four-Wheel Switcher 79

8 Class C 0-8-0 Eight-Wheel Switcher......................82

9 Class D 2-6-0 Mogul 95

10 Class E 4-6-0 Ten-Wheeler 105

11 Class F 2-8-0 Consolidation 131

12 Class G 4-8-0 Mastodon 151

13 Early Class H 4-6-2 Pacific 159

14 Class H 4-6-2 Pacific (Rebuilt Classes).................171

15 Class J 2-6-2 Prairie 186

16 Class K 4-4-2 Atlantic 195

17 Class L 2-6-6-2 Articulated.................................201

18 Class M 2-6-8-0 Articulated.................................209

19 Class N 2-8-8-0 Articulated and
Class R 2-8-8-2 Glacier Park 219

20 Early Class O 2-8-2 Mikado 249

21 Class O-5 and O-6 2-8-2 Mikado Rebuilds 281

22 Class O-7 and O-8 2-8-2 Mikado Rebuilds 294

23 Class P 4-8-2 Mountain......................................310

24 Class Q 2-10-2 Santa Fe.....................................327

25 Class S 4-8-4 Empire Builder..............................340

26 Class Z-6 4-6-6-4 Challenger.............................359

27 Miscellaneous Steam Locomotives 363

28 Experimental & Proposed Locomotive Designs ...369

29 Roster Preface and Abbreviations 377

30 Predecessor and Subsidiary
Steam Locomotive Roster 381

31 Great Northern Steam Locomotive Roster............407

32 Great Northern Steam Locomotive
Tender Roster..461

33 Great Northern Steam Locomotive
Roster Notes...507

34 Known Tender Assignments 519

35 References for the Rosters...................................535

Bibliography 537

Indices 541

Foreword

This book had its start in the 1960's, inspired by the likes of Kratville and Ranks' in-depth study of Union Pacific motive power, first published in 1958. Because of its long gestation, the authors acknowledge this book is late. Most of the principal class 1 railroads have already had the story of their steam locomotives told. The Great Northern's story also needs to be told. The GN was a leader in steam innovation and produced many notable designs. In addition, the Great Northern was a prolific builder and re-builder of its own locomotives, and maintained locomotive shops at five locations.

However in the later years of steam, the GN's efforts were overshadowed by designs such as the Northern Pacific, Santa Fe and Union Pacific 4-8-4's, the Santa Fe's remarkable 2-10-4, the NP and DM&IR 2-8-8-4, and the Union Pacific 4-8-8-4, as well as numerous 4-6-6-4 designs. But the reason for this was another example of the Great Northern's forward vision. During 1939 the road committed to diesel power, and the remarkable locomotives they developed after that time were simply overshadowed by the large number of spectacular modern steam locomotives built by the roads that stayed with steam so much longer.

The text attempts to present an in-depth history of the locomotives and their development over time both collectively and individually. An example of new information found was the previously unremarked branch pipe heater. Along the way the authors hope to have dispelled a few myths.

One item deliberately avoided was mention of the installation of automatic train control equipment. Due to an ICC ruling, locomotives on the "High Line" were required to have this apparatus between 1925 and 1932, approximately. The authors felt this was a signaling issue, not a locomotive issue, and no mention is made of it in the text.

Because present-day readers may not be as familiar with the operation of the steam locomotive as they would have been fifty years ago, a small amount of tutorial material was included in Chapter 3.

The roster has been completely revised and much additional information has been added since an earlier version was published in Railroad History Vol. 143. It is now in strict numerical order. This will allow the reader to find a locomotive by number alone, without having to know the class. There is, however, a class to number cross-index in Chapter 29. Additionally, numerous corrections have been made since it was last published.

What made this project possible, even though or perhaps why it took over 40 years to complete, was the large amount of information available. The Great Northern graciously permitted research of the Valuation Engineering Department records at St. Paul beginning in 1965. After merger, records became available at the Minnesota Historical Society, the archives of the Great Northern Railway Historical Society (GNRHS) and the Hill Reference Library, all located at St. Paul, Minnesota. Great Northern archives, which had been transferred from Burlington Northern to the Minnesota Historical Society, became available to the public in 1974. In 1983 the authors were given access to the Great Northern and Burlington Northern Change Number Record Accounts by the Burlington Northern Valuation Engineering Department. In 1984 Burlington Northern donated the Authority for Expenditure (AFE) files to GNRHS. Recently the James and Louis Hill collections at the Hill Reference Library have been moved to the Minnesota Historical Society. We do not know if any of the other railroad material there was transferred or not. For the interested historian, note that we have not uncovered all there is to know about Great Northern steam. There is much more to learn, and many files not yet read may have answers to present questions and possibly new information as yet unknown.

In a number of chapters, and especially the roster chapters, parenthetical numbers [e.g. "(1)" and "(2)"] are used. These parenthetical numbers are used to indicate sequence. 1050(1), for example, would be the first engine to carry the number 1050, while 1050(2) would be the second to carry that number. Note that these parenthetical numbers were not used by the Great Northern or its predecessors, but have been assigned by the authors for clarity.

A note on the citations from the Minnesota Historical Society is in order. The MHS index system was changed during the course of research for this book. We have converted many of the citations to the new system, but some early research remains with citations to the old system. These source citations may be cross-referenced to the new system at the MHS library.

The William Crooks, Great Northern's pioneer locomotive, is shown here at St. Paul, Minnesota, after being readied for an exhibition trip to the Chicago Railroad Fair of 1948/1949. Courtesy of the Corrin collection.

Chapter 1

A Brief Early Corporate History

While a book devoted to a railroad's locomotives cannot possibly also include a complete corporate history, some mention of the history is necessary for an understanding of the motive power requirements of the road. This brief history is intended only for that purpose. For more detailed historical information on the Great Northern Railway, the authors suggest *The Great Northern Railway, A History*, by Ralph W. Hidy, Muriel E. Hidy, and Roy V. Scott with Don L. Hofsommer (Harvard Business School Press, 1988). Further reading might also include *James J. Hill & the Opening of the Northwest*, by Albro Martin (Oxford University Press, 1976); *James J. Hill, Empire Builder of the Northwest*, by Michael Malone (University of Oklahoma Press, 1996); and *The Saint Paul & Pacific Railroad*, by Augustus J. Veenendaal, Jr. (Northern Illinois University Press, 1999). A complete, but not detailed, list of Great Northern predecessors and fully controlled subsidiaries follows at the end of this chapter.

Great Northern's first predecessor, the Minnesota and Pacific Railroad Company, was incorporated on May 22, 1857, by an act of the legislature of the Territory of Minnesota, to construct, operate, and maintain a railway line from Stillwater, MN, via St. Paul and St. Anthony, to Breckenridge, MN; and also a branch from St. Anthony, via St. Cloud, to St. Vincent, MN. The company was sold on June 23, 1860, to the State of Minnesota, which held the property until March 8, 1861, at which time by a special legislative act, the company's property was restored. No line was ever constructed, though rolling stock (including two locomotives) was purchased. The conditions of the restoration were not complied with, and the property was again forfeited to the state. On March 10, 1862, an act of the legislature incorporated The St. Paul and Pacific Railroad Company (StP&P) and conferred the property and rights of the Minnesota and Pacific (except between Stillwater and St. Paul) to it. At this time, the roadbed and bridges had been constructed, but no rail laid, on some 62 miles of line from St. Anthony toward Watab and St. Cloud.[1]

In 1862, the StP&P completed a railway line from St. Paul to St. Anthony (now a part of Minneapolis), MN, about 10 miles. Owing to financial difficulties, the First Division of the St. Paul and Pacific Railroad Company was incorporated on February 6, 1864, and the parent St. Paul & Pacific transferred part of its charter rights to the First Division. Later that year, construction (under the auspices of the First Division) was completed from St. Anthony westward to Elk River, MN, about 30 miles. By 1867, the road had reached as far west as Sauk Rapids, MN (near St. Cloud), for a total of about 75 miles. This portion of the road was termed the "Branch Line," while the "Main Line," which had been proposed to run west from Minneapolis to Breckenridge, MN (and to which the First Division had also received the charter rights), had not yet been constructed.

This view of Aneta, ND, shows the GN depot and elevator.
Photograph by Pitsch from the Hoffman collection.

Work on the "Main Line" was begun in 1867, and the line was completed from Minneapolis to Breckenridge, MN, about 205 miles, in 1871. This was the last portion of the line constructed by the First Division.

Control of both of these two companies rested with two brothers, E. B. Litchfield and E. Darwin Litchfield. On December 9, 1870, the Litchfields made an agreement with the Northern Pacific Railroad Company (NP) under which the two St. Paul & Pacific companies were placed under NP Control. The NP failed to comply with certain terms of the contract (largely due to its own corporate failure), E. B. Litchfield sued, and he recovered the stock of the First Division.

When the stock of the First Division was returned to Litchfield, control of much of the stock of the St. Paul & Pacific Railroad Company apparently still rested with the NP. However, this situation soon changed. In 1872, the St. Paul and Pacific began construction of two branch lines. One was an extension of the First Division "Branch Line," intended to extend westward from St. Cloud to the Red River Valley, and then northward along the valley to St. Vincent, near the Minnesota-Manitoba border (about 310 miles). The other line was to extend northward from Watab (near St. Cloud) to Brainerd, MN (about 60 miles). In order to finance this construction, bonds were issued by the First Division, most of which were sold in Holland.[2]

Slightly over 100 miles of the St. Vincent Extension were completed in 1872.[3] Construction stopped, the company defaulted on interest payments, and bankruptcy was declared. The hiatus would last six years. Accordingly, in 1873 the bondholders brought suit against the St. Paul & Pacific, the First Division, and the Northern Pacific.[4] As a result of this suit, Jesse P. Farley was appointed Receiver of the St. Paul and Pacific Railroad Company. Due in part to local sentiment against the primarily Dutch bondholders, a receiver was not named for the First Division. The First Division did run into problems, though, as about this time it was unable to meet interest payments on the bond issue, thus enabling the bondholders to take control of the company. Operation of the two roads apparently thus continued as essentially one road.[5]

In 1877, Farley managed to complete a link between Breckenridge (on the "Main Line") and Barnesville, MN (on the "St. Vincent Extension"), about 33.5 miles. This was done, however, under the name of the Red River and Manitoba Railroad Company. This was a very important link at the time, for it would allow traffic to St. Vincent, a land grant condition, before the Branch Line could be completed to Barnesville.

James J. Hill and his associates Donald A. Smith, Norman W. Kittson, and George Stephen, gained control of the Dutch bonds March 13, 1878,[6] and immediately resumed construction of both the Branch Line and the St. Vincent Extension in order to reach Alexandria and St. Vincent by December as required by the Minnesota legislature. Having this control permitted Hill to have a strong influence on Farley, and although he may have overstepped his bounds, Hill actually pushed Farley aside in September, to expedite the construction of the vital St. Vincent line.[7]

As a result both lines were completed on time, to Alexandria on November 5, and to St. Vincent on November 10, 1878. While construction was being continued, a good deal of financial maneuvering was also taking place. During 1878, James J. Hill and his associates Donald A. Smith, Norman W. Kittson, and George Stephen were acquiring control of both the St. Paul and Pacific Railroad Company and the First Division. A cash settlement was arranged with E. B. Litchfield whereby Hill and associates acquired control of the stock of the First Division. An arrangement with the Northern Pacific, under which the NP apparently received trackage rights from Sauk Rapids to St. Paul as well as receiving the incomplete Brainerd Extension, gave the associates control of the stock of the St. Paul and Pacific Railroad Company. The agreement with the Dutch bondholders allowed Hill and associates to acquire the outstanding bonds, to be paid for in either cash or securities. After their acquisition of control in the companies, both the St. Paul and Pacific Railroad Company and the First Division were sold at a foreclosure sale on May 10, 1879 to the associates (personally), thus allowing retirement of the St. Paul and Pacific and First Division securities.[8] On June 14, 1879, the associates transferred the property to a new corporation under their control, the St. Paul, Minneapolis and Manitoba Railway Company (StPM&M).

The St. Paul, Minneapolis and Manitoba Railway Company had been organized on May 23, 1879, by James J. Hill and his associates to take over the StP&P lines purchased by them at the foreclosure sale. On June 21, 1879, the St. Paul, Minneapolis & Manitoba (or simply the Manitoba, as it came to be known) purchased two additional companies. One of these was The Red River and Manitoba Railroad Company, which had built the 33.5 mile railway line between Barnesville and Breckenridge, MN, connecting the two St. Paul & Pacific lines.

The other was the Red River Valley Railroad Company, which had constructed a line running from Crookston (on the StP&P St. Vincent line) to East Grand Forks, MN (about 24 miles).[9]

The StPM&M soon embarked upon a program of building extensions and branch lines, and also continued to purchase smaller lines. In 1879, the old Red River Valley line was extended west through Grand Forks, ND. In 1882, a line extending across the Red River from Moorhead (a point reached by a purchased line), MN, to Fargo ND, and on north via Grand Forks to the International Boundary near Neche, ND (about 155 miles) was completed. The line from Grand Forks was extended westward and by the end of 1882 had reached one mile west of Bartlett, ND.

During the years 1883, 1884, and 1885, the StPM&M continued its policies of branch-line construction, and also continued to purchase small adjoining lines. This time period saw the road's first extension toward Lake Superior as well.

The period from January 1, 1886, until February 1, 1890, was a time of great expansion for the Manitoba. In 1886, the first construction steps were taken toward making the future Great Northern a transcontinental railroad. In that year, construction started west across the prairie from Devils Lake, reaching to slightly west of Minot, ND (about 120 miles). During 1887, 545 more miles of line were completed from Minot to Sun River (near Great Falls), MT. While the Manitoba continued to construct branch lines, no more major construction was initiated for several years. During this period, the mainline was completed westward into Montana, and numerous branches were constructed in North Dakota and Minnesota. In addition, some smaller roads were purchased. On February 1, 1890, though, the entire property of the St. Paul, Minneapolis & Manitoba was leased to the Great Northern Railway Company.[10]

The Montana Central Railway Company was incorporated on January 26, 1886. James J. Hill advanced funds for the initial surveys and construction of the road, and on May 9, 1887, he received all of the company's stock and essentially half of its outstanding bonds in return. On August 19, 1887, he assigned these securities to the St. Paul, Minneapolis and Manitoba Railway Company. In 1887, the Montana Central completed a line from the StPM&M terminus at Sun River to Helena, MT, about 96 miles. In 1888, this line was extended from Helena southwestward to Butte, MT, about 73 more miles. A branch was constructed from Great Falls southeast to Sand Coulee, MT (about 15 miles), during this same year, as well as a number of smaller spurs. On February 1, 1890, the Montana Central, along with the StPM&M, was leased to the Great Northern Railway Company. In 1891, the road built a line from Gerber (Allen) to Neihart, MT, about 56 miles.

The lease of the StPM&M to the GN triggered the completion of the transcontinental mainline (which was still actually owned by the Manitoba), and from 1891 through 1893, the GN pushed the line west from Pacific Junction (near Havre, MT), to Lowell (near Everett), WA, a total of just over 820 miles. The line crossed the Rocky Mountains through Marias Pass, the lowest elevation crossing of any of the northern transcontinental routes. It did not fare so well crossing the Cascades, as a series of switchbacks were needed for the crossing until the first Cascade Tunnel was completed in 1900. Additional branch lines were constructed, as was Hill's fashion, during this time, and some smaller companies purchased. Also, a section of line north of the original mainline, running from Jennings, MT, north to Rexford, and then southeast to Columbia Falls, MT (bypassing Kalispell on the old mainline) was constructed from 1901 through 1904 by the Montana and Great Northern Railway Company. This trackage was purchased by the

The engine crew poses at the front of F-1 No. 534. Hoffman collection.

StPM&M (for use by the Great Northern) on May 17, 1905.

From February, 1890, until November 1, 1907, the StPM&M continued to construct branch lines throughout the region it served. During this time, of course, it was leased to and operated by the Great Northern. It also purchased several smaller roads. Its chief accomplishment, however, was the construction of the Pacific Extension to the West Coast. This completed the transcontinental line which James J. Hill had envisioned.

Another subsidiary, the Eastern Railway Company of Minnesota (EM) was incorporated on August 13, 1887, through transfer of certain rights of the Minneapolis & St. Cloud Railroad Company. On January 12, 1888, the EM was consolidated with The Lake Superior & South Western Railway Company (of Wisconsin), but retained the former name. By this consolidation, the Eastern of Minnesota acquired industrial trackage, land, elevators, and dock facilities at West Superior, WI, all of which had been financed by the StPM&M. Later in that year a railway line from Hinckley, MN, to West Superior, WI (69.78 miles), was completed.[11]

The EM acquired a number of lines, including in 1898 the Duluth, Superior and Western Railway Company (DS&W). The DS&W owned a line from Deer River, MN, to the St. Louis River (near Cloquet, MN), 99.78 miles. In conjunction with this purchase, a line was constructed by the Eastern of Minnesota between Deer River and Fosston, MN

M-1 mallet articulated engine drawing 120 ore cars at Hibbing MN.
Photograph by Aubin from the Hoffman collection.

(98.59 miles).[12]

On May 1, 1899, the EM purchased the Duluth, Mississippi River and Northern Railroad Company, which owned 49.47 miles of roadway between Hibbing and Mississippi, MN, and a line from Hibbing to Dewey Lake.[13] After September 19, 1899, the Chisholm to Dewey Lake line was leased to the Swan River Logging Company (and was sold to the Swan River by GN in 1909).[14] During 1899 the company also constructed 87.53 miles of trackage from Boylston, WI, to Cloquet, MN, and 64.72 miles of line between Hinckley and Fridley, MN. On March 27, 1900, 5.87 miles of road (between New Duluth, MN, and Saunders, WI) was purchased from the Superior Belt Line and Terminal Railway Company. In 1900, the Eastern of Minnesota also began constructing a number of lines in the Iron Range area. This construction continued until the company was ultimately purchased by the Great Northern. In 1901, 46.49 miles of roadway were constructed between Brookston and Ellis, MN. On July 6, 1902, the EM purchased a line from Barclay Junction (near Hibbing) to Virginia, MN, from the Swan River Logging Company.[15]

On May 1, 1902, the property of the Eastern of Minnesota was leased to the Great Northern Railway Company.

Several subsidiaries constructed railway lines along the Pacific coast. The Seattle and Montana Railroad Company was incorporated under the laws of the State of Washington on March 29, 1898. On March 30, 1898, this company purchased the property of the Seattle and Montana Railway Company, consisting of a line from Seattle to a connection with the Fairhaven and Southern Railroad near Burlington, WA (78.20 miles). On this same date, the property of the Fairhaven and Southern Railroad Company was purchased. The Fairhaven & Southern property included a line from Sedro-Woolley to Blaine, WA (40.80 miles) and a line from Fairhaven and Southern Junction at Sedro-Woolley to Cokedale, WA (16 miles). On February 1, 1902, the property of the Seattle and Northern Railway Company, consisting chiefly of a line from Anacortes to Rockport, WA (55.34 miles), was purchased. In 1902 a line was constructed from Fairhaven to Belleville, WA (18.82 miles). The line was leased to the Great Northern prior to its sale. As a result of track changes and abandonments, the Seattle and Montana Railroad Company owned 191.89 miles of railway line on July 1, 1907, the date it was sold to the Great Northern Railway Company.[16]

The Willmar and Sioux Falls Railway Company (WSF) was incorporated under Minnesota law on March 11, 1886, and after July, 1888, was controlled by the Saint Paul, Minneapolis and Manitoba

Railway Company.[17] In 1888 the WSF completed a railway line from Willmar, MN, to Sioux Falls, SD (146.91 miles).[18] On July 27, 1893, the WSF purchased the Sioux Falls, Yankton and South Western Railway Company, which owned a line 58 miles long from Sioux Falls to Yankton, SD (construction funds for this line had been advanced by the Great Northern).[19] As of January 1, 1900, the WSF began operation of the Sioux City and Western Railway Company line (though the actual date of the lease was February 24, 1900). The Sioux City and Western owned a line from South Sioux City to O'Neill, NE (128 miles).[20] On January 15, 1900, the WSF purchased the Sioux City and Northern Railway Company, which owned a line from Garretson, SD, to Sioux City, IA (96 miles). The Sioux Falls Terminal Railroad Company, which owned terminal facilities and 3.02 miles of trackage at Sioux Falls, SD, was purchased by the Willmar and Sioux Falls on April 1, 1900. On July 7, 1907, the entire property of the WSF was sold to the Great Northern Railway Company.[21] The lease for the Sioux City and Western was assigned to the Chicago, Burlington and Quincy Railroad Company (CB&Q) on October 31, 1907. This part of the road was sold to the CB&Q on December 1, 1908.[22]

The Spokane Falls and Northern Railway Company (SF&N) was incorporated on April 14, 1888, in the interests of D. C. Corbin and associates. In 1889 and 1890, the SF&N constructed a line from Spokane north to Little Dalles, WA (124.05 miles). This was extended to Northport, WA (6.40 miles), in 1892,[23] and in 1899 was extended to reach GN tracks at Spokane.[24] D. C. Corbin also controlled the Nelson & Fort Sheppard Railway Company, the Red Mountain Railway Company, and the Columbia and Red Mountain Railway Company, all of which were operated in close conjunction with the SF&N.[25]

Sometime prior to July 1, 1898, the Northern Pacific Railroad Company acquired practically all the outstanding capital stock and all of the outstanding bonds of the SF&N. It sold these to the Great Northern Railway Company on July 1, 1898, and the GN maintained control thereafter.[26] From the time of the acquisition by the GN of the Spokane Falls & Northern Railway System (as it was called) until 1907, the property was operated independently of the GN. The GN also operated the Washington and Great Northern Railway Company and the Vancouver, Victoria & Eastern Railway and Navigation Company as part of the SF&N system.[27] On July 1, 1907, the property of the Spokane Falls and Northern Railway Company was purchased

This early photograph shows one of the L-1 Mallet compound engines, probably shortly after delivery. Note that the hinged coal bunker on the tender is slightly raised. Spokane Post Card Company, Spokane, WA. Hoffman collection.

outright by the GN, and from that time on it was operated as a part of the parent company.[28]

The Great Northern Railway Company was originally incorporated under an act of the Territorial legislature of Minnesota on March 1, 1856, as the Minneapolis and St. Cloud Railroad Company (M&StC). Under an act of February 28, 1865, the name of the corporation was changed to the Minneapolis & St. Cloud Railroad Company. This act, and subsequent ones, authorized and empowered the company to consolidate any portion of its road and property and to consolidate the whole or any portion of each organized branch or main and branch line railroad, also the property, rights, powers, franchises, grants, and effects pertaining to such roads, with the rights, powers, franchises, grants, and effects of any other railroad either within or without the then Territory or future State of Minnesota, that was then chartered or which might be organized, and with the consent of any such State, become a part owner thereof; also to change its name or that of any of its branches or divisions.[29]

The company's capital stock was acquired by the St. Paul, Minneapolis and Manitoba Railway Company in March 1881, in connection with repayment of expenditures already made on the property. A line was then constructed by the StPM&M for the M&StC from St. Cloud to Hinckley, MN, about 66.5 miles. This constructed road and part of the charter rights were sold to the StPM&M on April 23, 1883. On August 13, 1887, right to construct and operate a road from Hinckley, MN, to a point at or near the mouth of the St. Louis River was transferred to the Eastern Railway Company of Minnesota.[30]

On September 18, 1889, when it owned no physical property, the name of the Minneapolis & St. Cloud Railroad Company was changed to the Great Northern Railway Company.[31] It leased the property of the St. Paul, Minneapolis and Manitoba Railway Company and any thereafter constructed by it on February 1, 1890. The Montana Central was leased on the same date. On May 1, 1902, the Great Northern leased the property of the Eastern Railway Company of Minnesota for a period of 99 years. On July 1, 1907, the properties of the Eastern of Minnesota, Montana Central, Seattle and Montana Railroad, the Willmar & Sioux Falls, and the Spokane Falls and Northern were purchased outright by the GN.[32] Having served its purpose in constructing James J. Hill's railroad empire, the St. Paul, Minneapolis & Manitoba was sold to the Great Northern Railway Company on November 1, 1907.[33]

Though many of the Great Northern-owned lines had been leased to and operated by the GN for some years, it was not until 1907 that most of these lines were actually consolidated under the name of the Great Northern Railway Company. The Great Northern had begun to construct railroad lines under its own name as early as 1902, though the majority of new construction was still done by the subsidiary companies. The year 1907 saw the Great Northern actually gel as a complete system.

The number of divisions and the division points on the GN changed over the course of time, and a description is beyond the scope of this work. However, division assignments of the steam locomotives on the roster during different years can be found in Great Northern Railway Historical Society Reference Sheets 4 (1954), 15 (1936), 19 (1942) and 23 (1949).

The Great Northern continued in operation until March 2, 1970, when along with the Spokane, Portland & Seattle Railway Company, Northern Pacific Railway Company, and Chicago, Burlington & Quincy Railroad Company, it was merged to become Burlington Northern Incorporated.[34]

Notes:

1. ICC Valuation Report [Decisions of the Interstate Commerce Commission of the United States (Valuation Reports), Report of the Commission, U.S. Government Printing Office, Washington, DC, Volume 133 (July-November, 1927). It was submitted October 23, 1925 and 'decided' July 11, 1927. It covers the valuation of the Great Northern Railway Company as of June 30, 1915.], p. 255.
2. Albro Martin, *James J. Hill and the Opening of the Northwest*, p. 120, Oxford University Press, New York, 1976.
3. Jack Porzig and Stan Townsend, Great Northern Railway Historical Society Reference Sheet No. 78, "Great Northern Historic Track Laying Record," March 1983.
4. *The Railroad Gazette*, Volume 5, p. 55 (February 8, 1873)
5. Albro Martin, op. cit., pp. 120-121.
6. Augustus J. Veenendaal, Jr., *The Saint Paul & Pacific Railroad*, p. 120, Northern Illinois University Press, DeKalb, 1999.
7. Albro Martin, op. cit., p. 163.
8. Ibid.
9. ICC Valuation Report, op. cit., pp. 183, 187.
10. Ibid., p. 186.
11. Ibid., p. 263.
12. Ibid., p. 270.
13. Ibid., p. 275.
14. Norman C. Keyes, Jr., personal communication to Kenneth R. Middleton dated February 22, 1976.
15. ICC Valuation Report, op. cit., pp. 189, 276-277.
16. Ibid., p. 279.
17. Ibid., p. 287.
18. Jack Porzig and Stan Townsend, op. cit.
19. ICC Valuation Report, op. cit., p. 184.
20. W. W. Baldwin. Corporate History of the Chicago, Burlington & Quincy Railroad Company and Affiliated Companies (As of date June 30, 1917), p. 405ff.
21. ICC Valuation Report, op. cit., p. 184.
22. W. W. Baldwin, op. cit.
23. ICC Valuation Report, op. cit., pp. 311-315.
24. Jack Porzig and Stan Townsend, op. cit.
25. John Fahey, *Inland Empire, D.C. Corbin and Spokane*, University of Washington Press, Seattle, WA, 1965.
26. ICC Valuation Report, op. cit., pp. 311-315.
27. Great Northern Railway Company Annual Report No. 15 (June 30, 1904).
28. ICC Valuation Report, op. cit., pp. 311-315.
29. Ibid., p. 183.
30. Ibid., p. 237.
31. Ibid., p. 183.
32. Ibid., pp. 183-184.
33. Ibid., p. 183.
34. Ralph W. Hidy, Muriel E. Hidy, Roy V. Scott, and Don L. Hofsommer, *The Great Northern Railway: a History*, pp. 301-304, Harvard Business School Press, Boston, MA, 1988.

The Great Northern Railway Company
Predecessors and Fully-Controlled Subsidiaries

Since there were numerous companies, some of which are not well known, that became part of the Great Northern, a list of those companies with a brief history of each is presented here.

* Indicates that the predecessor or subsidiary company is known to have operated its own steam locomotives.

Aberdeen, Fergus Falls and Pierre Railroad Company	Incorporated 4/19/1886	Partially completed a line from Aberdeen, South Dakota, to Rutland, North Dakota. Sold to St. Paul, Minneapolis & Manitoba 12/30/1886.
The Allouez Bay Dock Company*	Incorporated 4/7/1903	Leased real estate, ore docks, and trackage from Duluth, Superior and Western Terminal 6/1/1903, which it purchased outright 8/1/1908. Sold to GN 4/22/1913.
Austin and Mankato Railroad Company	Incorporated 1/28/1880	Owned no property. Consolidated with St. Cloud, Mankato & Austin 11/22/1881.
Barnesville and Moorhead Railway Company	Incorporated 8/10/1880	Constructed a line from Barnesville to Moorhead, Minnesota. Sold to St. Paul, Minneapolis & Manitoba 10/29/1880.
Bedlington & Nelson Railway Company	Incorporated 1893	Controlled by the Kootenay Railway & Navigation Company. Constructed a line from the International Boundary to Kuskonook, British Columbia in 1899 and 1900. Came under GN control 1900. During the reporting year ending 6/30/1911 the GN liquidated the stock of the parent company and took over operation of the railroad. Part of the line was abandoned in 1913 and the remainder in 1916.
Billings & Northern Railroad Company	Incorporated 4/10/1902	Originally controlled by the CB&Q, but control passed to GN 3/1906. Partially completed a line from Laurel to Armington, Montana. Sold to GN 7/1/1907.
Brandon, Devils Lake & Southern Railway Company*	Incorporated 7/17/1905	Constructed a line between Rock Lake and Hansboro, North Dakota, operated by Farmers' Grain & Shipping Company. Sold to GN 11/3/1943.
Brandon, Saskatchewan & Hudson's Bay Railway Company	Incorporated 1903	Wholly owned by GN. Constructed a line from the International Boundary at St. John, North Dakota, to Brandon, Manitoba, 1905-06. Purchased a line from the international boundary to Morden from the Manitoba Great Northern Railway in 1928. Abandoned 1936.
Casselton Branch Railroad Company	Incorporated by NP 8/26/1880	Line constructed between Casselton and Mayville, North Dakota. Sold to the St. Paul, Minneapolis & Manitoba 8/25/1883.
Coeur d'Alene and Spokane Railway Company, Limited	Incorporated 10/20/1902	Constructed a 600V DC electric railway line from Spokane, Washington, to Coeur d'Alene, Idaho, with an extension to Hayden Lake, Idaho. Consolidated with other companies for operation by the Spokane and Inland Empire Railroad Company on June 30, 1907. Sold to Spokane and Inland Empire 2/13/1908.
Columbia and Puget Sound Railroad Company	Incorporated 11/26/1880	Purchased the Seattle & Walla Walla 11/30/1880. Constructed additional narrow-gauge lines near Renton, Washington, converted to· standard gauge late 1897. Sold to Pacific Coast Company 11/6/1897.
Columbia and Red Mountain Railway Company*	Incorporated 1/25/1895	Constructed a line from Northport, Washington, to the international boundary and a junction with the Red Mountain. Control acquired by GN 8/8/1898; sold to GN 7/1/1907.
The Crow's Nest Southern Railway Company.	Chartered 4/24/1901	Constructed a line from the International Boundary near Gateway, Montana, to Michel, British Columbia. Apparently wholly owned by GN from its inception. The portion north of Elko, British Columbia was abandoned in 1926. The remainder, along with its U.S. connection to Rexford, Montana, was abandoned in 1936.
Dakota and Great Northern Railway Company	Incorporated by GN 6/21/1900	Constructed branch lines in North Dakota from Aneta to Devils Lake; Berthold to Crosby; Bottineau to Antler; Granville to Sherwood; Lakota to Sarles; York to Dunseith; and Towner to Maxbass. Sold to GN 7/1/1907.
Duluth and Winnipeg Railroad Company*	Incorporated 2/11/1878	Road constructed between Cloquet and Deer River, Minnesota, 1890-92. Sold to Duluth, Superior & Western 11/27/1896.
Duluth and Winnipeg Terminal Company	Incorporated 6/13/1892	Owned an ore dock at Superior, Wisconsin, and about one mile of track. Sold to Duluth, Superior & Western Terminal 5/15/1897.

Duluth, Mississippi River and Northern Railroad Company*	Incorporated 3/21/1892	Operated a line between Mississippi River and Hibbing, Minnesota, constructed by Swan River Logging Co. During 1897 extended the line from Hibbing to Chisolm, Minnesota. Sold to Eastern of Minnesota 5/1/1899.
Duluth, Superior and Western Railway Company*	Incorporated 9/24/1896	Took over the property of the Duluth & Winnipeg. Sold to Eastern of Minnesota 6/23/1898.
Duluth, Superior and Western Terminal Company*	Incorporated 7/22/1897	Took over the property of the Duluth & Winnipeg Terminal Company. Constructed two additional ore docks and acquired trackage from the Superior Belt Line & Terminal Railway. Leased the ore docks and original trackage to Allouez Bay Dock Co., and new trackage to GN 6/1/1903. Properties sold to lessees 8/1/1908.
Duluth Terminal Railway Company	Incorporated 8/11/1887	Constructed 1.8 miles of line in Duluth. Leased to GN 1921 or 1922; sold to GN 12/31/1928.
Duluth, Watertown and Pacific Railway Company	Incorporated 8/21/1885	Constructed a line from Watertown to Huron, South Dakota. Controlled by St. Paul, Minneapolis & Manitoba and by GN. Sold to GN 7/1/1907.
Eastern Railway Company of Minnesota*	Incorporated 8/13/1887	Constructed lines from Hinckley, Minnesota, to West Superior, Wisconsin; Deer River to Fosston, Minnesota; Boylston, Wisconsin, to Cloquet, Minnesota; and Hinckley to Fridley, Minnesota. Trackage also constructed in the Iron Range area, and several roads acquired by purchase. Leased to GN 5/1/1902; purchased by GN 7/1/1907.
Everett & Cherry Valley Traction Company	Incorporated 8/31/1907	Constructed a line from Monroe to Carnation (later Tolt), Washington, turned over to GN upon completion. Sold to GN 6/21/1912.
Fairhaven and Southern Railroad Company*	Incorporated 11/27/1888	Constructed lines between Sedro-Woolley and Blaine, Washington, and Sedro-Woolley and Cokedale, Washington. Sold to Seattle and Montana Railroad Co. 3/30/1898.
Farmers' Grain & Shipping Company*	Incorporated 10/11/1902	Operated a line between Devils Lake and Starkweather, North Dakota, constructed by the Devils Lake and Northern Railway Company. FG&S controlled by GN through the Brandon, Devils Lake & Southern. Additional trackage constructed from Starkweather to Rock Lake, North Dakota. Sold to GN 11/23/1943.
Glacier Park Hotel Company	Incorporated 5/13/1914	Purchased line between Marion and Hubbard, Montana, from Somers Lumber Company 12/31/1940. Sold line to GN 6/15/1942. Name changed to Glacier Park Company 5/27/1943, a GN subsidiary which was sold in 1960.
The Great Falls and Canada Railway Company	Incorporated 10/3/1889	Constructed a three-foot-gauge line between Great Falls and the International Boundary at Sweet Grass, Montana. Sold to Montana and Great Northern 8/1/1901, and conversion to standard gauge completed 1/4/1903.
Great Falls and Teton County Railway Company	Incorporated 9/12/1912	With financial advances from GN, constructed a line from Power to Bynum, Montana. Operated by GN after completion, and purchased 11/16/1914 (per Interstate Commerce Commission records) or 12/31/1928 (per GN records).
Great Northern Railway Company*		Name changed from Minneapolis & St.Cloud Railroad Company 9/18/1889. Leased the properties of the St. Paul, Minneapolis & Manitoba and the Montana Central for operation 2/1/1890. Numerous other properties acquired by lease and/or sale, and the system gradually developed into a transcontinental, the northernmost in the United States. Merged into Burlington Northern 3/2/1970.
Great Northern Terminal Railway Company	Incorporated 1/3/1917	Operated by GN prior to its sale to GN 12/31/1928.
Idaho Central Railway Company	Incorporated 9/15/1909	Purchased the property of the Panhandle Electric Railway & Power Company 10/19/1909. Name changed to Spokane, Coeur d'Alene and Palouse Railway Company 12/11/1926.
Inland Empire Railroad Company	Incorporated 1/3/1920	Took over one-fourth of the defunct Spokane and Inland Empire, a line running between Spokane, Washington, and Moscow, Idaho, and between Spring Valley and Colfax, Washington. Sold to Spokane, Coeur d'Alene and Palouse 11/26/1926.
Inland Empire Railway Company	Incorporated 1/15/1906	Name changed to Spokane and Inland Empire Railroad Company 11/7/1906.
International Navigation & Trading Company	Incorporated 10/10/1895	Incorporated as the International Trading Company Limited, with name changed shortly thereafter. Operated two sternwheeler vessels on Kootenay Lake in southern British Columbia. Control passed to the Kootenay Railway & Navigation Company in 1898.

Iowa and Great Northern Railway Company	Incorporated 1/23/1905	Constructed extensive terminals (but no trackage) in Woodbury County, Iowa. Sold to GN 6/30/1910.
Kaslo and Slocan Railway Company	Incorporated 1892.	James J. Hill and the GN financed construction of the three-foot gauge line between Kaslo and Sandon, British Columbia. GN acquired control in 8/1896 and in 1898 the company's debentures and stocks were transferred to the Kootenai Railway & Navigation Company. A 1910 fire destroyed most of the line, and it was sold to a syndicate of Kaslo citizens on May 27, 1911. It was then transferred to the Canadian Pacific Railway on May 13, 1912.
The Kettle River Railroad Company	Incorporated 8/26/1886	Acquired or constructed line between Sandstone and Kettle River, Minnesota. The Northern Pacific had advanced funds for the road's construction, and the Eastern of Minnesota acquired control in 9/1891 by purchasing the company's stock. The Eastern of Minnesota transferred its investment in the capital stock to its investment in road and equipment 6/30/1893.
Kootenay Railway & Navigation Company	Incorporated 8/8/1898	GN turned over the debentures and stocks of the Kaslo and Slocan Railway to this company in 1898. The property of the International Navigation & Trading Company was obtained through an exchange of debentures and stock in 1898. This company also controlled the Bedlington & Nelson and the Kootenai Valley. On 6/20/1900 the directors of the GN agreed to guarantee the principal and interest on the debentures of this company, which operated sternwheel vessels on Kootenai Lake in British Columbia. Due to business declines, in 1910 all debentures were acquired by the GN and the issue cancelled. The stocks and bonds were delivered to the GN in 3/1911 and the affairs of the Kootenay Railway and Navigation Company closed out.
Kootenai Valley Railway Company*	Incorporated 10/19/1898	Controlled by the Kootenay Railway & Navigation Company. Constructed a line from Bonner's Ferry to Port Hill, Idaho, in conjunction with the Bedlington & Nelson. GN acquired control in 1911 as a result of liquidating the Kootenay Railway & Navigation Company. Leased to GN 7/1/1911; sold to GN 8/8/1913.
The Lake Superior & South Western Railway Company (of Wisconsin)	Incorporated 8/6/1885	Controlled by the StPM&M from its inception. Property consisted primarily of real estate and docks at West Superior, Wisconsin. Consolidated with Eastern of Minnesota 1/12/1888.
Manitoba Great Northern Railway Company		Wholly-owned subsidiary of GN which purchased lines formerly owned by the Midland Railway Company of Manitoba 7/1/1909. In 1926 and 1927 the line from near Neche, North Dakota, to Portage la Prairie, Manitoba, was abandoned. In 1928 the line from near Walhalla, North Dakota to Morden, Manitoba, was sold to the Brandon, Saskatchewan and Hudson's Bay Railway Company.
The Midland Railway Company of Manitoba*		Jointly owned by GN and NP. Constructed a line northward from Neche, North Dakota, to Portage la Prairie, Manitoba, and from near Walhalla, North Dakota to Morden, Manitoba 1906-07. Trackage rights apparently obtained over CN into Winnipeg. Property transferred to Manitoba Great Northern 7/1/1909.
Minneapolis and Northwestern Railroad Company	Incorporated 2/5/1878	Incorproated as a subsidiary of the Minneapolis & St. Louis. Constructed a line from Minneapolis to St. Cloud, Minnesota, on the west side of the Mississippi River, which was sold to the St.Paul, Minneapolis & Manitoba 4/23/1883.
Minneapolis and St. Cloud Railroad Company	Incorporated 3/1/1856	Name changed to Minneapolis & St. Cloud Railroad Company 2/28/1865.
Minneapolis & St. Cloud Railroad Company		Name changed from Minneapolis and St. Cloud Railroad Company 2/28/1865. Constructed a line from St. Cloud to Hinckley, Minnesota, which was sold to StPM&M 4/23/1883. Name changed to Great Northern Railway Company 9/18/1889.
Minneapolis Belt Line Company	Incorporated 5/14/1917	Operated by GN prior to its purchase by GN 12/31/1928.
Minneapolis, Lyndale and Minnetonka Railway Company	Incorporated 6/21/1878	Incorporated as Lyndale Railway Company. Name changed 2/9/1881. Sold 53 miles of trackage (Hutchison to vicinity of Wayzata, Minnesota) to the St. Paul, Minneapolis & Manitoba 12/1/1886.
Minneapolis Union Railway Company	Incorporated 12/1/1881	Constructed the Stone Arch Bridge over the Mississippi River 1883. Sold to GN 7/1/1907.
Minneapolis Western Railway Company*	Incorporated 10/29/1884	Came under GN control about 1890. Constructed some trackage in Minneapolis and a bridge across the Mississippi River. Leased to GN about 1922; purchased by GN 12/31/1928.
Minnesota and Dakota Northern Railroad Company	Incorporated 3/4/1879	Constructed a line between Moorhead and Halstad, Minnesota, with funds advanced by the St. Paul, Minneapolis &: Manitoba. Before completion, line sold to the StPM&M 11/24/1883.

Minnesota and Great Northern Railway Company	Incorporated 3/31/1904	Constructed a line between Thief River Falls and Greenbush, Minnesota, and partially completed a line between Greenbush and Warroad, Minnesota. Sold to GN 7/1/1907.
Minnesota Northern Railroad Company	Incorporated 2/5/1878	Name changed to Northern Pacific, Fergus Falls and Black Hills Railway Company 4/18/1881.
Minnesota and Pacific Railroad Company*	Incorporated 5/22/1857	Incorporated to construct lines from Stillwater to Breckenridge, Minnesota, and from St. Anthony to St. Vincent, Minnesota. No lines built. Company sold 6/23/1860 to the State of Minnesota, returned 3/8/1861, and again repossessed by the state. Rights and property conferred to The St.Paul and Pacific Railroad Company 3/10/1862.
The Montana Central Railway Company*	Incorporated 1/26/1886	Controlled nearly from its inception by J.J. Hill. Constructed a line from Sun River (near Great Falls) to Butte, Montana, with several branches and spurs. Leased to GN 2/1/1890; sold to GN 7/1/1907.
Montana Eastern Railway Company	Incorporated 11/23/1912	Incorporated to construct a line from Lewiston, Montana, through a point near Fairview, Montana, to New Rockford, North Dakota. Portions of line built, but application to the ICC for completion denied in 1927. Application resubmitted in 1929, withdrawn in 1930 due to the depression. Sold to GN 12/31/1928.
Montana and Great Northern Railway Company	Incorporated 6/6/1901	Purchased narrow-gauge line between Great Falls and the International Boundary at Sweet Grass, Montana, from Great Falls and Canada 8/1/1901. Conversion to standard gauge completed 1/4/1903. Also constructed a line from Columbia Falls via Rexford to Jennings, Montana, 1902-04. Portion of the road sold to St. Paul, Minneapolis & Manitoba 5/17/1905; remainder sold to GN 7/1/1907.
Montana Western Railway Company*	Incorporated 5/3/1909	Constructed a line between Conrad and Valier, Montana. Control acquired by GN 1912; sold to GN 1/12/1970 (but line had been abandoned 1/10/1970).
Moorhead and South Eastern Railway Company	Incorporated 9/15/1884	Constructed a line between Moorhead and Wahpeton, Minnesota. Sold to St. Paul, Minneapolis & Manitoba 1/28/1891.
Nebraska and Western Railway Company		See Pacific Short Line.
The Nelson & Fort Sheppard Railway Company*	Incorporated 4/20/1891	Constructed a line from a connection with the Spokane Falls & Northern at the International Boundary north to Troup Junction, British Columbia. Operated as a portion of the Spokane Falls & Northern system. Control passed to GN in 1898. Operated by GN after 7/1/1898; sold to GN 1/1/1945.
The New Westminster Southern Railway Company	Incorporated 4/7/1887	Constructed a line between Blaine, Washington, and Port Kells and Brownsville, British Columbia, 1890-91. Company control acquired by GN about 1908. Most of this abandoned 1915-19. The line from Brownsville to Port Kells was sold to the Canadian Northern Pacific Railway in 1916. Remainder of corporation sold to Vancouver, Victoria & Eastern 12/31/1924.
Northern Pacific, Fergus Falls and Black Hills Railway Company	Incorporated 4/18/1881	Portion of the road between Fergus Falls and Pelican Rapids, Minnesota, sold to the St. Paul, Minneapolis & Manitoba 11/28/1882.
Pacific Coast Company	Incorporated 11/29/1897	Incorporated to reorganize the Oregon Improvement Company, including the Columbia & Puget Sound, which had been purchased on its behalf on 11/6/1897. The line ran from Seattle to Franklin, Washington. Much of the line abandoned between 1921 and 1944. Sold to GN 10/31/1951.
Pacific Short Line*		Comprised of a group of firms that were to construct a line projected to connect Sioux City, Iowa, and Ogden, Utah. The line in Nebraska, built by the Nebraska and Western Railway Company (incorporated 3/11/1889), was the only link even partially completed – Covington (South Sioux City) to O'Neill, Nebraska, in 1890. The Wyoming portion was to have been constructed by the Wyoming and Eastern Railway Company, the Utah portion by the Salt Lake Valley and Eastern Railway Company. The Wyoming Pacific Improvement Company was intimately involved with the Pacific Short Line, though the legal relationship is unclear. The contracts for construction of the road were let by that company, and the locomotives were ordered by it. The Nebraska and Western was transferred to the Sioux City, O'Neill & Western 1/1/1892, and apparently operated in close conjunction with the Sioux City & Northern.
Panhandle Electric Railway & Power Company	Incorporated 1908	Sold to Idaho Central 10/19/1909.
Park Rapids and Leech Lake Railway Company	Incorporated 10/6/1897	Constructed a line between Park Rapids and Leech Lake, Minnesota, which was leased to GN upon completion in 1899. Sold to GN 7/1/1907.

Penticton Railway Company		Apparently chartered in British Columbia by GN to construct a line probably between Penticton and vicinity of Oliver (?), British Columbia. No roadway ever constructed, though trackage rights may have been acquired through this company over the Kettle Valley Railway.
Red Mountain Railway*	Incorporated 4/12/1893	Controlled by Spokane Falls & Northern. Constructed a line from the International Boundary, where it connected with the Columbia & Red Mountain, to Rossland, British Columbia. Control acquired by GN in 1898; operated by GN after 7/1/1907. Trackage abandoned 1922. Property sold to the Washington and Great Northern Townsite Company 6/30/1922.
Red River and Lake of the Woods Railway	Incorporated 4/3/1882	Constructed a line between Shirley and St. Hilaire, Minnesota. Sold to St. Paul, Minneapolis & Manitoba 7/11/1883.
The Red River and Manitoba Railroad Company	Incorporated 8/13/1877	Constructed a line from Breckenridge through Barnesville, Minnesota, to a connection with the St. Paul & Pacific. Apparently operated by StP&P after completion. Sold to St. Paul, Minneapolis & Manitoba 6/21/1879.
Red River Valley and Western Railroad Company	Incorporated 7/18/1893	Constructed a line between Addison and Rita (Chaffee), North Dakota. Sold to St. Paul, Minneapolis & Manitoba 10/28/1893.
Red River Valley Railroad Company	Incorporated 6/12/1875	Constructed a line between Crookston and East Grand Forks, Minnesota. Sold to St. Paul, Minneapolis & Manitoba 6/21/1879.
St. Cloud and Lake Traverse Railway Company	Incorporated 5/1/1880	Constructed a line between Morris Junction and Browns Valley, Minnesota. Sold to St. Paul, Minneapolis & Manitoba 10/29/1880.
St. Cloud, Mankato & Austin Railroad Company	Incorporated 2/28/1865	Consolidated with the Austin & Mankato 11/22/1881. Constructed a line from St. Cloud to Willmar, Minnesota. Sold to St. Paul, Minneapolis & Manitoba 5/24/1886.
The St. Paul and Pacific Railroad Company*	Incorporated 3/10/1862	Incorporated to take over the rights and property of the Minnesota and Pacific. The First Division of the St. Paul and Pacific Railroad Company (incorporated 2/6/1864) received certain rights of the St. Paul & Pacific. For all practical purposes the two companies were operated as one. Lines constructed from St. Paul northwest to St. Cloud and westward via Willmar to Breckenridge, Minnesota. After control obtained by J.J. Hill, a line was constructed west from St. Cloud via Barnesville to St. Vincent, Minnesota. Both companies sold to the St. Paul, Minneapolis & Manitoba 6/14/1879.
The St. Paul, Minneapolis and Manitoba Railway Company*	Incorporated 5/23/1879	Incorporated to take over the lines of the St. Paul & Pacific. The StPM&M continued to expand and purchase smaller lines, eventually developing most of what was to become the GN in Minnesota, North Dakota, and Montana. Property of the StPM&M leased to GN 2/1/1890; sold to GN 11/1/1907.
Sauk Center Northern Railway Company	Incorporated 2/23/1881	Constructed a line from Sauk Center to Eagle Bend, Minnesota. Sold to St. Paul, Minneapolis & Manitoba 4/23/1883 and 11/24/1883.
Seattle and Montana Railroad Company*	Incorporated 3/29/1898	Incorporated to purchase the property of the Seattle and Montana Railway Company and the Fairhaven & Southern. Purchased the Seattle & Northern 2/1/1902. Constructed a line from Fairhaven to Belleville, Washington, 1902. Purchased the property of the Union Wharf Company of Anacortes 5/26/1906. Sold to GN 7/1/1907.
Seattle and Montana Railway Company*	Incorporated 3/7/1890	With GN funds, constructed a line from Seattle to vicinity of Burlington, Washington. Sold to Seattle & Montana Railroad Co. 3/30/1898.
Seattle and Northern Railway Company*	Incorporated 8/9/1888	Constructed a line from Anacortes to Rockport, Washington. Sold to Seattle & Montana 2/1/1902.
Seattle and Walla Walla Railroad and Transportation Company	Incorporated 7/23/1873	Incorporated to construct a three-foot-gauge line from Seattle to Walla Walla. Very little construction completed. Sold and reorganized as the Seattle and Walla Walla Railroad Co. 11/8/1876.
Seattle and Walla Walla Railroad Company		Reorganized from Seattle and Walla Walla Railroad and Transportation Co. 11/8/1876. Constructed a three-foot-gauge line from Seattle through Renton to Newcastle, Washington. Reincorporated as the Columbia & Puget Sound Railway Company 11/26/1880.
The Sioux City and Northern Railroad Company*	Incorporated 10/3/1887	Constructed a line from Garretson, South Dakota, to Sioux City, Iowa. Sold to the representatives of the bondholders 12/12/1899, and after 1/1/1900 operated by the Willmar & Sioux Falls, which purchased it outright on 1/15/1900.

The Sioux City and Western Railway Company*	Incorporated 5/29/1899	Incorporated to take over the property of the Sioux City, O'Neill & Western, which it purchased 6/28/1899 and began operating 6/30/1899. Operated by the Willmar & Sioux Falls after 1/1/1900. GN took over operation of this original portion of the SC&W 7/1/1907. SC&W completed a line from Laketon to Ashland, Nebraska, 1905-06; apparently operated by Chicago, Burlington & Quincy. CB&Q began operating the entire SC&W 11/1/1907 and purchased it 12/1/1908.
The Sioux City, O'Neill and Western Railway Company*	Incorporated 10/27/1891	Incorporated to purchase a line owned by the Nebraska & Western (Pacific Short Line). Sold to the Sioux City & Western 6/28/1899.
Sioux City Terminal Railroad and Warehouse Company	Incorporated 10/23/1889	Obtained rights of way in Sioux City, Iowa, as well as constructing a depot, warehouse, and a small amount of trackage there. Conveyed to Union Terminal Railway Company 6/22/1900.
Sioux Falls Terminal Railroad Company		Name changed from South Sioux Falls Railroad and Rapid Transit Company 3/28/1890. Owned some trackage in the Sioux Falls, South Dakota, area. Sold to Willmar & Sioux Falls 4/1/1900.
Sioux Falls, Yankton and South Western Railway Company	Incorporated 7/23/1889	Constructed a line from Sioux Falls to Yankton, South Dakota. Sold to Willmar & Sioux Falls 7/27/1893.
Somers Lumber Company*	Incorporated 9/28/1900	Originally incorporated as the John O'Brien Lumber Company to supply ties for the GN. Sawmill and tie plant at Somers, Montana, purchased by GN 1906, and on 11/11/1907 changed the name to Valley Lumber Company. Due to a conflict in names, about a month later the name was changed to Somers Lumber Company. Trackage standard-gauged in the mid-1920's. Operation of the GN branch line serving the tie-treating plant also turned over to the Somers Lumber Co. 1/1/1930. Built a line from Marion to Hubbard, Montana, 12/1935. A corporate rearrangement in 1941 made the Somers Lumber Company the Somers Lumber Division of the Glacier Park Company, a GN and later BN subsidiary. The sawmill portion was shut down in 1949, leaving only the tie plant in operation.
South Dakota Central Railway Company*	Incorporated 9/27/1902	Constructed a line between Watertown and Sioux Falls, South Dakota. Sold to Watertown & Sioux Falls 6/28/1916.
South Sioux Falls Railroad and Rapid Transit Company	Incorporated 12/17/1888	Name changed to Sioux Falls Terminal Railroad Company 3/28/1890.
Spokane and Eastern Railway and Power Company	Incorporated 1/3/1920	Incorporated to take over three-fourths of the defunct Spokane and Inland Empire Railroad Company (that portion of the line between Spokane, Washington, and Coeur d'Alene, Idaho operating on 600 V DC). A portion of this company (the Spokane city streetcar operation) was sold to the Spokane City Railway Company 3/22/1922. The remainder (including the locomotives) sold to the Spokane, Coeur d'Alene and Palouse 11/26/1926.
Spokane and Inland Empire Railroad Company		Name changed from Inland Empire Railway Company 11/7/1906. Purchased Spokane Terminal Co. 11/27/1906. Purchased Spokane & Inland Ry. Co.; Coeur d'Alene and Spokane Ry. Co., Ltd.; and Spokane Traction Company 2/13/1908. Constructed lines from Moran to Colfax, Washington; from Spring Valley, Washington, to Moscow, Idaho; and numerous branches and spurs. One-fourth of the road's property sold to the Inland Empire Railroad Company and three-fourths to the Spokane and Eastern Railway and Power Company 11/1/1919.
Spokane & Inland Railway Company		Name changed from Spokane Interurban System 1/10/1905. Constructed a line between Spokane and Moran, Washington. Sold to the Spokane and Inland Empire Railroad Company 2/13/1908.
Spokane and Montrose Motor Railroad Company	Organized 3/9/1888	Transferred to Spokane Traction Co. 1903.
Spokane City Railway Company	Incorporated 5/8/1922	Purchased a portion of the property of the Spokane and Eastern Railway and Power Co. 3/22/1922.
Spokane, Coeur d'Alene and Palouse Railway Company		Name changed from Idaho Central Railway Company 12/11/1926. Acquired the properties of the Spokane and Eastern Railway and Power Co. and the Inland Empire Railroad Co. 11/26/1926. Sold to GN 5/1/1943.
The Spokane Falls and Northern Railway Company*	Incorporated 4/14/1888	Constructed a line from Spokane to Northport, Washington. Control acquired by GN 7/1/1898, but operation kept separate until GN purchase 7/1/1907.

Spokane Interurban System	Incorporated 12/17/1904	Name changed to Spokane & Inland Railway Company 1/10/1905.
Spokane Terminal Company	Incorporated 3/1/1905	Sold to Spokane and Inland Empire Railroad Company 11/27/1906.
Spokane Traction Company	Incorporated 2/18/1903	Sold to Spokane and Inland Empire Railroad Company 2/13/1908.
Superior Belt Line and Terminal Railway Company		Name changed from Superior Terminal and Belt Line Railway Company 11/9/1891. Constructed line from New Duluth, Minnesota, to Saunders, Wisconsin, sold to Eastern of Minnesota 3/27/1900. Also constructed line from Belt Line Junction to Saunders, sold to Duluth, Superior & Western Terminal Co. 4/18/1900.
Superior Terminal and Belt Line Railway Company	Incorporated 8/29/1890	Name changed to Superior Belt Line and Terminal Railway Company 11/9/1891.
Swan River Logging Company, Ltd.	Incorporated 6/28/1898	Constructed the line of the Duluth, Mississippi River & Northern between the Mississippi River and Hibbing, Minnesota. The Eastern of Minnesota apparently bought a branch line of the Swan River Logging Co. between Barclay Junction and Virginia, Minnesota, 1/6/1902.
The Union Terminal Railway Company.	Incorporated 6/22/1900	Incorporated to acquire the property of the Sioux City Terminal Railroad and Warehouse Company. Sold to GN 7/1/1910.
The Union Wharf Company of Anacortes	Incorporated 1/22/1892	Constructed a wharf (which later collapsed) and warehouse at Anacortes, Washington. Sold to Seattle and Montana Railroad Company 5/26/1906.
Vancouver, Victoria & Eastern Railway and Navigation Company	Incorporated 5/8/1897	Constructed lines in British Columbia connecting with the old Spokane Falls & Northern trackage in Washington 1902-06. Bought the properties of the Victoria Terminal Railway and Ferry Company and the Vancouver, Westminster & Yukon Railway 11/7/1907 and 3/26/1908, respectively. Built a connecting line 1907-16 across southern British Columbia between a point on the International Boundary near Chopaka, Washington, to the old VTR&F terminal at Cloverdale, British Columbia (included trackage rights over the Kettle Valley Railway Company). Line also constructed from New Westminster, British Columbia, to Blaine, Washington. Portions abandoned between 1920 and 1935. In 1944, the Canadian government permitted the GN to operate directly into Canada, and the road was purchased by the GN 12/31/1944.
Vancouver, Westminster and Yukon Railway Company*	Incorporated 1897	Constructed a line between Vancouver and New Westminster, British Columbia. Sold to Vancouver, Victoria & Eastern 3/26/1908.
Victoria & Sidney Railway Company*	Incorporated 4/23/1892	Constructed a line between Victoria and Sidney, British Columbia. Came under control of GN 10/5/1902. Discontinued operations 4/30/1919; tangible assets liquidated 11/1922.
Victoria Terminal Railway and Ferry Company*	Incorporated 5/11/1901	Constructed a line between Blaine, Washington, and Mud Bay, British Columbia, and between Cloverdale and Ladner, British Columbia. Sold to Vancouver, Victoria & Eastern 11/7/1907.
Wadena and Park Rapids Railroad Company	Incorporated 6/4/1883	Constructed a line from Eagle Bend to Park Rapids, Minnesota. Sold to St. Paul, Minneapolis & Manitoba 8/1/1891.
Washington and Great Northern Railway Company	Incorporated 6/21/1901	Constructed a number of GN branch lines in Washington which were operated as part of the Spokane Falls & Northern system. Sold to GN 7/1/1907.
Watertown and Sioux Falls Railway Company*	Incorporated 6/24/1916	Incorporated to acquire the property of the South Dakota Central, which it did on 6/30/1916. Locomotives were incorporated into GN's class system by about 1918, and GN began operating the road in 1922. Sold to GN 12/31/1928.
The Willmar and Sioux Falls Railway Company*	Incorporated 3/11/1886	Constructed a line between Willmar, Minnesota, and Sioux Falls, South Dakota. Purchased Sioux Falls, Yankton & South Western 7/27/1893; leased the Sioux City & Western as of 1/1/1900; purchased Sioux City & Northern 1/15/1900; and Sioux Falls Terminal 4/1/1900. Sold to GN 7/1/1907.
Wyoming Pacific Improvement Company		See Pacific Short Line.

Passing a Freight near Summit, Mont. Gt. Northern, Ry.

Passing a freight near Summit, MT. Published by Oakes Photo, Seattle, WA. Hoffman collection.

Chapter 2
Great Northern Steam Locomotive Class Systems
The Old Class System

The old class system of the Great Northern Railway, in use up until October, 1903, was apparently a holdover from the very early years of the St.Paul, Minneapolis and Manitoba Railway. It was probably set up shortly after the acquisition of the St.Paul and Pacific by Hill and his associates. The pattern used would seem to point to a date in early 1882 for its founding, which includes the first 21 (or possibly the first 23) classes. These classes seem to have been set up by manufacturer. With one exception (possibly explained below), the order of the class numbers assigned to a manufacturer's locomotives would seem to be the order in which the manufacturers first supplied locomotives to the road. Thus Smith & Jackson, who provided the first two locomotives, probably received the first two classes. Norris, or some other builder, the second provider, would have received the next block of classes (or single class), though this was apparently modified as the scheme was worked out. A hypothetical arrangement of the first 23 classes, with explanations as to why they have been placed in this order, follows. Certain of these class numbers were later reused, and these are so indicated by the (1) following the class number.

Class	Numbers	Manufacturer	Whl. Arrgt.	Date
1	StPM&M 1	Smith & Jackson	4-4-0	1861
2(1)	StPM&M 2	Smith & Jackson	4-4-0	1861

These two locomotives, which may have been similar upon delivery, are placed in separate classes since they are believed to not have been identical, and had undergone extensive repairs with different outcomes by 1869. Thus the locomotives were certainly different at the time the class system was set up. Further evidence might be cited in the fact that No. 2, the *Edmund Rice*, was scrapped in 4/1887. The locomotives which were later known to have been placed in Class 2 were Hinkley 0-6-0's which were built in 8/1888. This is most likely a case of the class number having been reused once it was vacated.

Class	Numbers	Manufacturer	Whl. Arrgt.	Date
3	StPM&M 3	Brooks	0-4-0	1879
4	StPM&M 87-89	Brooks	0-4-0	1881

These classes would seem to be the exception to the lumping of locomotives into class blocks by manufacturer and date received. However, it might be remembered that at the time of the acquisition of the StP&P by the StPM&M, the number 3 was apparently vacant. Shortly thereafter, StPM&M No. 51(1) was moved into this number, and may have also been accorded the class which would have gone with StP&P No. 3. Being the next locomotive received after the *Crooks* and the *Rice*, StP&P No. 3 would have logically been placed in Class 3.

This is, of course, an attempt to explain away a discrepancy, but Class 3 might be an instance of "reuse" of a class which had not actually been used the first time.

Once the decision to use Class 3 for a Brooks locomotive had been made, the other Brooks engines on the roster at the time were given the next class number, Class 4. It is unlikely that StPM&M No. 4 was ever in this class. The Brooks 0-4-0's are known to have been in Class 4 by 1891[1], and these are probably the only type engines to ever occupy Class 4. StPM&M No. 4, a Souther 4-4-0, was sold in 1882, probably just prior to the setting up of the class system. Had StPM&M No. 4 been placed in Class 4 (i.e., had the system been set up earlier), then for a period of about one year (from the delivery of StPM&M Nos. 87-89 in 1881 until the sale of StPM&M No. 4 in 1882), either Class 4 contained some quite dissimilar locomotives, or the Brooks 0-4-0's were in another class. Both of these possibilities seem to lack any substantiation. This might, in fact, be one of the strongest bits of evidence that the class system was designed in 1882.

StPM&M Nos. 187-193, also Brooks 0-4-0's, were probably not placed in Class 4 immediately upon their receipt. If it is assumed that after 1882 class numbers were merely assigned to locomotives as they arrived from the builders, these locomotives would fit in chronologically as Class 31. Apparently at some later date (probably about 1887), it was decided that these locomotives were similar enough to StPM&M Nos. 87-89 to be placed in Class 4, and they were moved. This then left Class 31 vacant, but it was reused for Rogers-built 0-6-0's which began arriving in 1887. This would explain why Class 31 does not appear to fit into sequence chronologically. The Rogers 0-6-0's were actually Class 31(2).

Class	Numbers	Manufacturer	Whl. Arrgt.	Date
5(1)	StPM&M 6, 7	Norris	4-4-0	1865

Norris, being the next builder in sequence after Smith & Jackson, was given the next class after the "inserted" Brooks locomotives. StPM&M Nos. 6 and 7 were scrapped in 11/1888. Locomotive No. 16, a Danforth 4-4-0, was moved into Class 5 from Class 6 late in 1891 or early in 1892 (as indicated by Machinery Department Annual Reports).[2] Here again, the time the class was vacated correlates well with its known reuse.

Class	Numbers	Manufacturer	Whl. Arrgt.	Date
6	StPM&M 5	Danforth	4-4-0	1866
7(1)	StPM&M 12-14	Danforth	4-4-0	1869
8(1)	StPM&M 15	Danforth	4-4-0	1870
9(1)	StPM&M 16	Danforth	4-4-0	1870

This locomotive was probably the original member of Class 6, though locomotives 15 and 16 were later included (16 only to be removed again and placed in Class 5). Later on, this class became a catch-all for many early 4-4-0's which were left on the roster and had been rebuilt with smaller drivers for switching duty.

Here again, these locomotives probably made up the original Class 7, though there were later changes. Locomotives 12 and 13 were placed in Class 8 for a time beginning in 1891 or 1892.[3] All three locomotives eventually found their ways to Class 6. Class 7 was eventually reused for Brooks 0-6-0's which were built from 1892 to 1898.

Classes 8 and 9 were vacant in 1891,[4] but later reused (probably more than once). Locomotives 15 and 16 are arbitrarily placed here due to their builder and date built. The reason why they might have been split into separate classes is not known, but the class assignments of the other locomotives at the time would seem to indicate that this was probably the case.

Class	Numbers	Manufacturer	Whl. Arrgt.	Date
10(1)	StPM&M 8	Mason	4-4-0	1867
11(1)	StPM&M 9, 11	Mason	4-4-0	1868, 1869
12(1)	StPM&M 10	Mason	4-4-0	1868

Assignment of the Mason locomotives to these classes is based upon the 1891 Machinery Department Annual Report.[5] Two of these locomotives were sold before the GN renumbering in 1899, and the others were placed in "catch-all" Class 6. Once these classes were vacated, all were reused.

Class	Numbers	Manufacturer	Whl. Arrgt.	Date
13	StPM&M 17-19, 24-26	Pittsburgh	4-4-0	1870, 1875
14	StPM&M 68-77	Pittsburgh	4-4-0	1880
15	StPM&M 67(2), 78-86	Pittsburgh	4-4-0	1881

For the most part, these classes remained relatively stable, though No. 17 was transferred to Class 6 for reasons unknown.

Class	Numbers	Manufacturer	Whl. Arrgt.	Date
16	StPM&M 47-50	Baldwin	4-4-0	1871, 1879
17	StPM&M 20-23	Baldwin	4-4-0	1871
18	StPM&M 51(2), 52-66	Baldwin	4-4-0	1880

These may not have been the specific locomotives in these three classes at the time of inception of the system, but these locomotives listed were probably in one of the three Baldwin classes. It is probable that there was some shuffling between these three classes as the locomotives were modified. The specific locomotive assignments for the individual locomotive classes were derived from the 1891 Machinery Department Annual Report.[6] It would seem more logical if the older locomotives (Nos. 20-23) had been placed in Class 16, with Nos. 47-50 in Class 17, but there is no evidence at present that this was ever the case.

Class	Numbers	Manufacturer	Whl. Arrgt.	Date
19	StPM&M 27-42	Rogers	4-4-0	1878
20	StPM&M 43, 44	Rogers	4-4-0	1879
21	StPM&M 45, 46	Rogers	2-6-0	1879
22	StPM&M 90-93	Rogers	0-4-0	1882
23	StPM&M 94(1), 95(1)	Rogers	4-4-0	1882

These classes appear to have been fairly stable. Classes 22 and 23 were probably either the highest class numbers used at the inception of the class system, or the first class numbers used for newly received locomotives.

From about 1882 on, the class system seems to have taken a different direction. After this time, it would appear that new locomotives were assigned a class as they were obtained by the railroad. This could have been done at the time of the initial order to the manufacturer, at the time of receipt of the locomotives, at the time an A.F.E. was written to authorize their purchase, or at the whim of whoever was actually given the responsibility for assigning class numbers. At any rate, from Class 21 on, the class numbers correlate very well with the purchase dates for the locomotives, however they may have been determined. Apparent exceptions can be explained by the fact that as classes became vacant, the class numbers were reused. Also, when new locomotives were acquired which were deemed similar to an older class already on the roster, these new locomotives were often given the same class number with a letter suffix.

In addition to the St.Paul, Minneapolis and Manitoba locomotives, all the locomotives of the Great Northern-related system were assigned class numbers within this system. This system was not, of course, united until the massive renumbering which began in 1899. The remainder of the old classes (i.e. those which were not in existence at the beginning of the system) are listed below in order. The numbers used are those that the engines carried when they were incorporated into the class system as they were purchased new from builders or acquired with purchased companies.

Class	Numbers	Manufacturer	Whl. Arrgt.	Date
2(2)	StPM&M 232, 233	Hinkley	0-6-0	1888
2A	SC&N 7, 9	Rogers	0-6-0	1890

Class 2(1) had apparently been vacated by the time (1888) the Hinkley 0-6-0's were received, probably due to the scrapping of StPM&M No. 2. The Hinkley locomotives were used to fill the vacancy. When the Sioux City & Northern engines were incorporated into the classification and numbering scheme of the GN, its 0-6-0's were apparently deemed similar enough to the Hinkley engines to be placed in the suffix class 2A.[7]

Class	Numbers	Manufacturer	Whl. Arrgt.	Date
5(2)	StPM&M 16	Danforth	4-4-0	1869

After considerable shuffling among the classes of early locomotives, StPM&M No. 16 was placed in Class 5(2) in late 1891 or early 1892.[8] StPM&M Nos. 6 and 7, probably the original occupants of Class 5(1), had been scrapped in 11/1888, leaving the class vacant.

Class	Numbers	Manufacturer	Whl. Arrgt.	Date
7(2)	MC 25, 26; EM 5-8; GN 250(1), 251(1), 253, 254, 255(1)-258(1)	Brooks	0-6-0	1892-1895
7A	GN 70-72	Rogers	0-6-0	1900
7A	GN 73-82	Rogers	0-6-0	1903

In the reshuffling of older locomotives, the original occupants of Class 7(1) were moved to other classes, eventually ending up in Class 6. The vacancy created in Class 7 was filled with Brooks 0-6-0's. Later 0-6-0 locomotives were placed in the suffix Class 7A by the GN.[9]

The Great Northern Flyer *was GN's premier transcontinental train from 1899 to 1905. Published by Charles E Morris, Chinook, MT. Hoffman collection.*

Class	Numbers	Manufacturer	Whl. Arrgt.	Date
8(2)	StPM&M 12, 13	Danforth	4-4-0	1868
8(3)	MC 9(2), 27, 28	Brooks	0-6-0	1898
8A	EM 88, 89	Brooks	0-6-0	1900
9(2)	StPM&M 9	Mason	4-4-0	1868
9(3)	DS&WT 1,2; EM 58, 59	Brooks	0-6-0	1899
10(2)	F&S 1, 2	Schenectady	4-6-0	1889
11(2)	SC&N 1-4, 8, 10	Rogers	4-4-0	1889-1890
11(2)	SC&W 13	Rhode Island	4-4-0	1889
12(2)	S&N 1, 2	New York	4-4-0	1890

StPM&M Nos. 9, 12, and 13 were removed from their original classes and placed into Classes 8(2) and 9(2) in late 1891 or early 1892.[10] Class 8(2) was vacated when StPM&M Nos. 12 and 13 were placed in Class 6. StPM&M No. 9 was sold in 1898, thus vacating Class 9(2). Both Classes 8 and 9 were then filled with 0-6-0's. Eastern of Minnesota Nos. 88 and 89 were close enough to the Class 8(3) engines to be placed in Class 8A. Classes 10(1), 11(1), and 12(1) had all been vacated either by the sale or reclassification of their locomotives. The Fairhaven and Southern engines were used to fill Class 10(2), probably in the mid-1890's. Classes 11(2) and 12(2) were filled with locomotives acquired from purchased roads about 1900.[11]

Class	Numbers	Manufacturer	Whl. Arrgt.	Date
24	StPM&M 100-124	Baldwin	4-4-0	1882
24A	StPM&M 118, 120-124	Baldwin	4-4-0	1882

A number of the locomotives originally in Class 24 (StPM&M Nos. 117-124) were later moved to Classes 18 and 24A, for reasons which are not absolutely certain. Those locomotives moved to Class 18 apparently received smaller drivers, though. The engines moved to Class 24A may have been different enough (diagrams indicate a considerably different type of boiler) from the start to justify merely placing them in a new class. Class 24A probably was not set up until about 1900.

Class	Numbers	Manufacturer	Whl. Arrgt.	Date
25	StPM&M 125-133	Schenectady	4-4-0	1882
26	StPM&M 134-139	Rhode Island	4-4-0	1882
27(1)	StPM&M 140-142, 143(1)-144(1)	Taunton	4-4-0	1882
27(2)	SC&N 5, 6	Rogers	4-6-0	1890
27A	SC&W 15	Rhode Island	4-6-0	1890
27B	EM 991	Brooks	4-6-0	1898
27C	SC&W 16-18	Rhode Island	4-6-0	1890

Classes 25, 26, and 27(1) were apparently filled in order as the locomotives were acquired. Class 27(1) was vacated by the sale of the Taunton engines to the Mason City & Fort Dodge in 1886 and 1892. It was filled with Sioux City & Northern engines acquired about 1900. Classes 27A, 27B, and 27C were apparently considered similar enough to the Class 27(2) engines to be classified in this manner.[12] These lettered classes were probably set up about 1900.

GN 1977, a Class M-2 2-6-8-0, was photographed at Kelly Lake in 1949. Photographer is unknown. Hoffman collection.

Class	Numbers	Manufacturer	Whl. Arrgt.	Date
28	StPM&M 145-149	Grant	4-4-0	1882
29	StPM&M 150-151	Brooks	4-4-0	1882
30	StPM&M 152-186	Brooks	4-4-0	1882
31(1)	StPM&M 187-193	Brooks	0-4-0	1882
31(2)	StPM&M 94(2)-97(2), 98, 99, EM 1-3	Rogers	0-6-0	1887-1888

Classes 28, 29, 30, and 31(1) were again filled in order as new locomotives were acquired. At some time prior to 1887, though, it was apparently decided that StPM&M Nos. 187-193 were similar enough to StPM&M Nos. 87-89 to be placed in Class 4 with them. This vacated Class 31, which was then filled with the Rogers 0-6-0's.[13]

Class	Numbers	Manufacturer	Whl. Arrgt.	Date
32	StPM&M 194-196	Brooks	0-6-0	1882
33	StPM&M 197-206	Rhode Island	4-4-0	1882-1883
34	StPM&M 207-225	Rogers	4-4-0	1887
34A	EM 101-105	Rogers	0-4-0	1888-1889
35	StPM&M 300-321, 322(1)-324(1), 322(2), 323(2), 325	Rogers	2-6-0	1887-1888
36	StPM&M 324(2), 326-347, EM 201-210	Rogers	2-6-0	1887-1888
36A	SC&W 14	Rhode Island	2-6-0	1890
36B	EM 297	Baldwin	2-6-0	1892

Classes 32, 33, 34, 35, and 36 were filled with new locomotives as they were acquired. Classes 34A, 36A, and 36B were filled (probably about 1900) with locomotives which were apparently similar enough to previously owned engines to be placed in suffix classes.

Class	Numbers	Manufacturer	Whl. Arrgt.	Date
37(1)	GN 400(1)-409(1)	Brooks	4-8-0	1891
37(2)	GN 351(1)-361(1), 361(2), 362, 363(1)-365(1), 363(2)-365(2), 366-370, EM 250-255	Brooks	2-6-0	1893, 1895
38	GN 400(1)-414(1), 410(2)	Brooks	4-8-0	1893-1895

Great Northern Nos. 400(1)-409(1) were apparently received as Class 37(1). Shortly afterward, though, the GN began rebuilding them with a different cylinder size and they were apparently placed into Class 38 as they were rebuilt. This left Class 37 vacant, and it was filled with Brooks 2-6-0's.

Class L-2 No. 1806 was one of GN's smaller Mallet compounds. Published by W.M. Chase, Willmar, MN. Hoffman collection.

Class	Numbers	Manufacturer	Whl. Arrgt.	Date
39	GN 450(1)-480(1), 481-499, 500(2)-504(2), 505-515	Brooks	2-8-0	1892-1895
40	GN 500(1)-504(1)	Baldwin	2-8-0	1892
41	EM 600-601	Baldwin	4-6-0	1892
42	GN 650-699	Brooks	4-6-0	1893
43	EM 256-260, GN 371-377, 378(1)-392(1)	Brooks	2-6-0	1896-1897
44	MC 100-107	Brooks	4-8-0	1897-1898
45	EM 300-319	Brooks	4-8-0	1898
45A	GN 770-779	Brooks	4-8-0	1900
46	EM 150-157	Brooks	4-6-0	1898
47	GN 900-909	Rogers	4-6-0	1899
48	GN 720-769	Rogers	4-8-0	1899-1900
49	GN 1050(1)-1052(1), 1053-1069	Rogers	4-6-0	1900-1904
50	GN 1100-1109	Rogers	2-8-0	1901
50A	GN 1130-1139	Cooke	2-8-0	1901
50B	GN 1110-1129	Brooks	2-8-0	1901
51, 51A	GN 1140-1159, 1160(2)-1164(2), 1165-1194, 1195(2)-1199	Rogers	2-8-0	1901-1903
51B	GN 1300-1324	Brooks	2-8-0	1903
52	GN 1160(1)-1164(1)	Rogers	2-8-0	1901
53	GN 925-939	Rogers	4-6-0	1902

The Modern Steam Locomotive Class System

The final Great Northern classification scheme was adopted in October, 1903, as indicated by correspondence found at the Minnesota Historical Society.[15]

Class designations for steam locomotives were as follows:

Class	Whl. Arrgt.
A	0-6-0
B	4-4-0
C(1)	0-4-0
C(2)	0-8-0
D	2-6-0
E	4-6-0
F	2-8-0
G	4-8-0
H	4-6-2
J	2-6-2
K	4-4-2
L	2-6-6-2 (2-6-8-0's were also in Class L for a short time)
M	2-6-8-0
N	2-8-8-0
O	2-8-2
P	4-8-2
Q	2-10-2
R	2-8-8-2
S	4-8-4
Z-6	4-6-6-4

With the exceptions of Classes 45A, 50A, and 50B, these classes were all apparently filled in order as new locomotives were purchased. These three suffix classes were considered similar enough to Classes 45 and 50 to be classified in this manner. The identity of the locomotives in Class 51 (vs. those in 51A) is uncertain at present, though a locomotive diagram does exist showing Nos. 1150-1154 as being in Class 51.[14] The reason for their separation is also unknown, since both were later lumped together in Class F-8. The locomotives in Class 51B were somewhat different, no doubt justifying the use of a suffix class. These classes were again assigned as new locomotives were received. Class 53 was apparently the highest number class used in the Old Class system.

Classes A, B, and D through G were already on the roster at the time of the adoption of the new class system. It is the authors' opinion that Class C was originally planned for a number of 0-4-0's still on the system. These were disposed of at about the same time as the initiation of the new class system, but were probably still on the roster when it was being designed. The reason for placing 0-8-0's in Class C, even though they were not on the roster until several years after the beginning of the new class system, is uncertain. The classes from H onward were assigned sequentially as new wheel arrangements appeared on the roster. The letter "I" was omitted from the system.

Notes:

1. Annual Report, Machinery Department, StPM&M Ry., June 30, 1891 (Minnesota Historical Society GN Presidents Subject Files)
2. Annual Report, Machinery Department, StPM&M Ry., June 30, 1891 and Annual Report, Machinery Department, June 30, 1892 (Minnesota Historical Society GN Presidents Subject Files).
3. Ibid., 1891 and 1892.
4. Ibid., 1891.
5. Ibid., 1891.
6. Ibid., 1891.
7. Great Northern Ry. Line Locomotive Equipment List (Diagrams), 1900.
8. Op. cit., 1891 and 1892.
9. Op. cit., 1900.
10. Op. cit., 1891 and 1892.
11. Op. cit., 1900.
12. Op. cit., 1900.
13. Op. cit., 1900.
14. Minnesota Historical Society GN Vice-President Operating File 40, Part 2.
15. F.E. Ward, memo to G.T. Slade dated October 24, 1903 (Minnesota Historical Society 132.B.16.5B,GN 40-16).

It is likely, although it has not been confirmed, that the GN first began the use of the Worthington BL feedwater heater with the construction of the H-5 class engines. No. 1350, the first one with a completion date of July 8, 1921, is shown with the device mounted behind its single New York air pump, at Portland, OR, on December 27, 1946. Wilbur C. Whittaker photograph from the Collias collection, now part of the GNRHS collection.

Chapter 3

The Great Northern Steam Locomotive

In the days of steam, each railroad developed its own unique version of the steam locomotive. There was little standardization outside of wheel arrangements and accessories. The Great Northern was no exception. In this chapter the features that defined the Great Northern steam locomotive are briefly described.

Belpaire Firebox

The firebox side and crown sheets must be suspended inside the boiler shell. This is done with staybolts. (The improved, flexible staybolts began replacing rigid bolts in 1912.) There were generally two ways to do this. The radial stay configuration is the most common. Here, rows of staybolts are placed radially between the curved firebox sheets and the boiler shell. The alternative was the Belpaire firebox. It had a flat crown sheet and the staybolts were arranged both horizontally and vertically to support it.[1] The near rectangular shape resulted in prominent shoulders at the top of the firebox. The advantage of the Belpaire was greater firebox heating surface area, the disadvantage was greater weight. The Belpaire design was a distinguishing feature of most Great Northern locomotives, and was first introduced to the GN by the Brooks Locomotive Works on the G-1 class in 1891. After that only a few GN locomotives, probably influenced by USRA designs, carried radial stay fireboxes. The Pennsylvania Railroad was the only other North American system to use the Belpaire as extensively as did the Great Northern.

Mechanical Stokers and Oil Burners

The mechanical stoker came to the GN in 1916 with an order of O-1 Mikados received that year. This was quite a few years after the delivery of other engines large enough to need mechanical stoking, including such monsters as the L-Class 2-6-6-2's, M-1 2-6-8-0's and N-1 2-8-8-0's. The GN began retrofitting its larger engines with mechanical stokers in 1917. The Street stoker, from the Locomotive Stoker Company, was used considerably early on, shifting to that company's Duplex stoker when it became available.[2] The Standard Stoker Company's model B-K was being installed by 1930.[3] The GN was long an advocate of using fuel oil instead of coal whenever it could. Until the latter years of steam locomotive operation, the western divisions used oil while the eastern divisions used coal, and it was a common practice to change the engines back and forth from one fuel to another as they were reassigned to different divisions. This necessitated considerable work removing and installing stokers. By 1951 all of the GN engines burned oil.[4]

These views show the engineer's and fireman's side non-lifting injectors on the 1355, a class H-5 4-6-2. Note the custom "GN" cast into the body. Photographs by Norman F. Priebe.

Live Steam Injector

The basic injector was the live steam injector. There are two types, the lifting injector and the non-lifting injector. The lifting injector has the ability to draw water up from the source, as well as inject it into the firebox. Because of this it is located high on the boiler, either just inside or outside the front of the cab. Except for a few early engines such as the D-2 and D-4 classes, and those that were obtained from other companies, the GN did not use this type. Instead, the GN preferred the non-lifting injector, and applied it to the vast majority of its power. This type could not lift water and was located below the lowest point of the tender waterline.

When a live steam non-lifting injector was the only type used on a locomotive, there were two installed, one on each side, located under the cab. If a feedwater heater or other feedwater heating device was used, it replaced one live steam injector. The GN obtained these injectors from many companies, and at least one provided them with a custom "GN" cast into the body.

The Branch Pipe Heater, Exhaust Steam Injectors and Feedwater Heaters

Introducing heated water into a locomotive boiler results in expending less energy to heat the water once it is in the boiler. Over the years, Great Northern used a number of different devices to heat feedwater for locomotives. All of these involved using low pressure steam exhausted from the cylinders to heat the feedwater.

Probably the earliest of these devices was the branch pipe heater. The branch pipe heater was also known on the GN as a Kelly feedwater heater (William Kelly was GN's General Superintendent of Motive Power from about 1920 to 1935). While complete details have not been found, it can be determined it was a device for heating the water in the feedwater delivery pipe leading from the injector to the check valve. This pipe was called the branch pipe on the Great Northern and Northern Pacific, though on other roads the term branch pipe was used for other parts of the locomotive. The device replaced the normal branch pipe, and was in effect a closed form feedwater heater built around the branch pipe. Locomotive exhaust steam was used to provide the heat, and after passing through the heater, was exhausted into the tender.[5] What is known from the documentation that has been found is that the heater was constructed in different ways.[6] They all apparently used 6 or 8 inch gas pipe for the casing. The cores differed, with some heaters using a core of gas pipe, one pipe per heater. Others used 1¼-inch copper tubing, four tubes per heater. Another had a single copper tube in the heater. Still another variation had five copper tubes per heater, but it was eventually replaced with one common gas pipe on at least one locomotive. The heater was a strictly homemade affair, assembled in the GN shops.

Performance of the heater would be limited by the small diameter steam pipe couplings, the low incoming steam temperature relative to that of the live steam operating the injector and by the limited surface area that could be obtained in the branch pipe. At least 90 of these devices were installed by 1930. The branch pipe heater has seldom been photographed.

This view shows the non-lifting injector under the cab, and the starting valve in front of the cab, for the fireman's side of class O-8 No. 3396. Photograph by Ernest Lehmann.

Class O-1 Mikado No. 3122 is at Pasco, WA, leased to the SP&S in 1932. The casing around the fireman's side delivery pipe in this view is the branch pipe heater. Note also the associated exhaust drain pipe running to the tender tank. Photograph from the C. W. Jernstrom Collection.

1724 has a smaller, size No. 11 Sellers exhaust steam injector. This H-6 Pacific was photographed by D. H. Roberts at Portland, OR, on May 1, 1947. Collection of William Raia.

The Elesco exhaust steam injector beneath the firebox on the engineer's side is quite prominent. P-2 No. 2513 was photographed at Minot in 1947. Collection of J. R. Quinn.

Great Northern installed exhaust steam injectors on many of its locomotives. Two principal types were used, and they were normally installed on the engineer's side of the locomotive beneath or in front of the cab, heating the water going into the check valve on the right side. One was the Elesco exhaust steam injector, produced by The Superheater Co., and the other was the Sellers exhaust steam injector. During operation of the locomotive, exhaust steam from the cylinders was used to heat the water going into the check valve. When the engine was not operating (i.e. when the throttle was closed), live steam from the turret could be used to heat the feedwater. These are sometimes referred to as "poor man's feedwater heaters."[7]

From the mid-1920's on, some of Great Northern's steam locomotives began to be equipped with feedwater heaters. Feedwater heaters can be classified as either "open" (where the feedwater comes in direct contact

New N-3 No. 2024, at Superior after rollout, displays its Sellers exhaust steam injector. Note the valve in the exhaust steam supply line, not present in the Elesco design. Great Northern records indicate the Sellers exhaust steam injector was out of production by 1943. Great Northern Railway photograph.

This close up view of an Elesco exhaust steam injector is on No. 3250, a class O-4. Photograph by Norman F. Priebe.

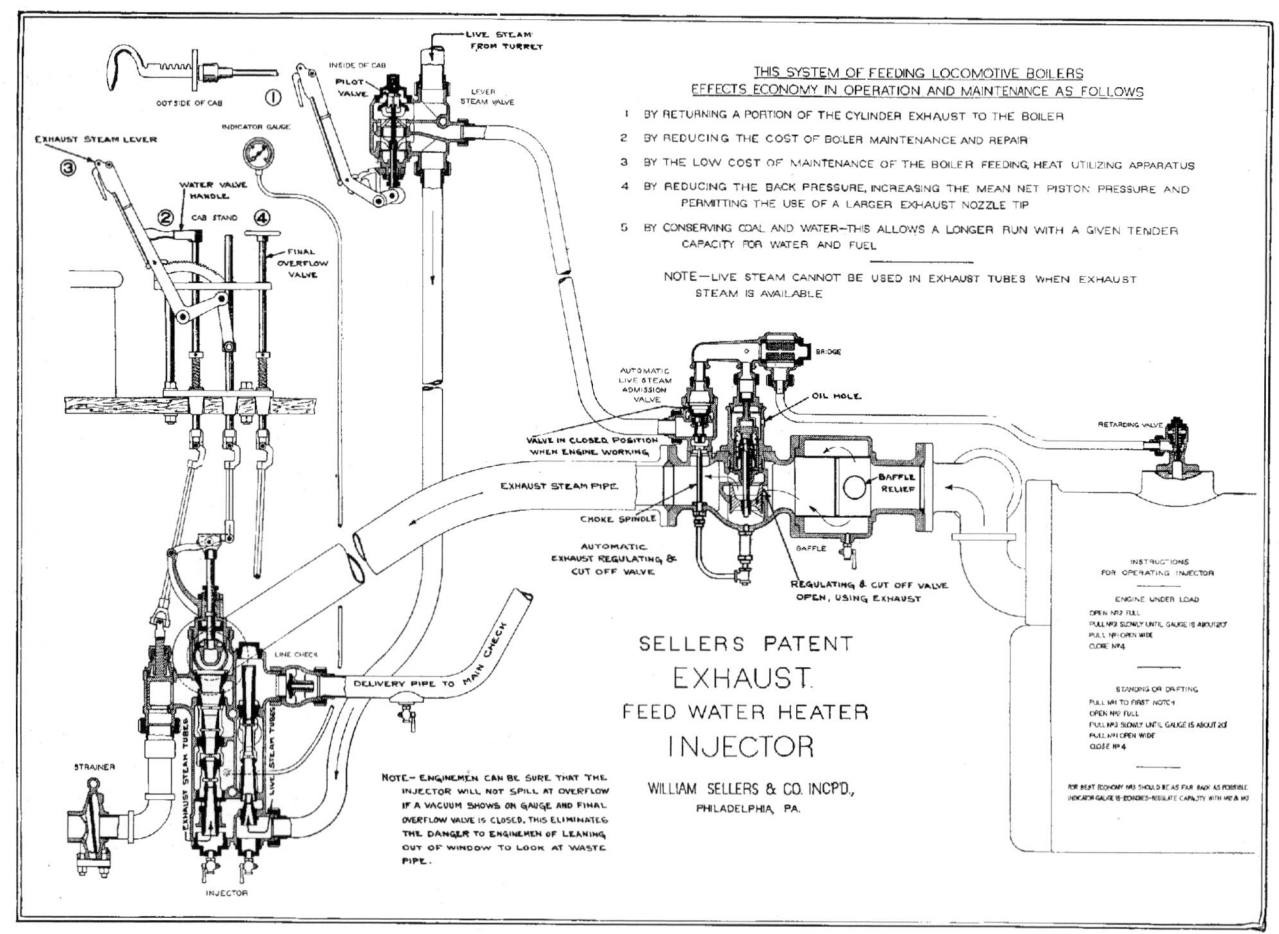

This Sellers drawing clearly shows the separation of the related valves from the body of the injector. Courtesy the Sellers Company.

with exhaust steam) or "closed," where there is no direct contact. Closed systems were claimed to have an advantage in that lubricants and dirt from the exhaust steam could not be introduced into the boiler. The closed system used by GN was the Elesco feedwater heater, though it was relatively uncommon, having been used on only a few O-1 Mikados. The Elesco feedwater heater was of prominent appearance, having a large cylindrical tank mounted in front of the stack. The tank contained small tubes for the water to flow through. The tubes were surrounded with exhaust steam coming from the cylinders or with live steam from the turret when the exhaust was not operating.[8]

Once efficient oil separators had been developed, the open feedwater heaters became more popular, and indeed most of GN's feedwater heaters were of this type. Developed by the Worthington Pump and Machinery Co., these feedwater heaters used a spray to mix the feedwater with exhaust steam. The device was a large combined unit including both pumps and the spray heater in one assembly. A large line from the exhaust steam chest on each side of the engine provided the exhaust steam used in the process. Many GN locomotives of different classes received the first type developed, the BL feedwater heater. Worthington's designation for these units varied as the design evolved. The BL was the earlier, "flat-bottomed" model. The later BL-2 was the "step-bottomed" model. In the great majority of cases, the Worthington feedwater heaters were mounted on the fireman's side of the engine, the notable exception being the N-2 class, where they were mounted on the engineer's side. The Great Northern first used the BL on the H-5 construction in 1921. The road began using the type BL-2 after it became available, beginning in 1925 on the class P-2, Q-1 and N-2 locomotives. However, all of these examples also received some of the BL model. After that, the road used either type indiscriminately, in sizes ranging from the No. 3 to the No. 4½.

No. 3052 was one of ten O-1's to receive the closed system Elesco feedwater heater. This view shows the engineer's side piping. The locomotive is on the Sioux City line local, No. 576 at Marshall, MN, August 1950. Photograph by Norman F. Priebe.

This view of 3106, one of the last group of O-1s received, clearly shows the fireman's side of the Elesco feedwater heater. Note the piping and the pump, located under the running board behind the air pumps. This engine is also equipped with a booster on the trailing truck. Taken at Minneapolis in the late 1930's. Robert Graham photograph from the collection of William Raia.

The P-2 and the Q-1 class were shipped from Baldwin without feedwater heaters. The GN began installing them in 1925. The earliest view found is of an installation of a Worthington BL-2 model on the 2512, taken before 1929, while it still had its retractable smoke hood. Later this was changed to an older BL model. Collection of Norman F. Priebe.

This late view of 2512 shows that it carried an older BL Worthington near the end of its service. It was photographed by Ted Gay at Minot, ND, on October 5, 1952. Collection of Norman F. Priebe.

The 2514 received a BL-2 while the 2515 received a BL. Many other of the P-2's received exhaust steam injectors. The 2514 is at Fargo, ND, in November, 1954. Photograph by Carl Ulrich from the collection of William Raia.

The 2515, with the older BL model Worthington is at St. Paul in 1946. Photograph by Bob Graham.

Q-1 No. 2124 at Klamath Falls, OR, in August 1951, carried a Worthington BL feedwater heater. So did No. 2126. Bob Graham collection.

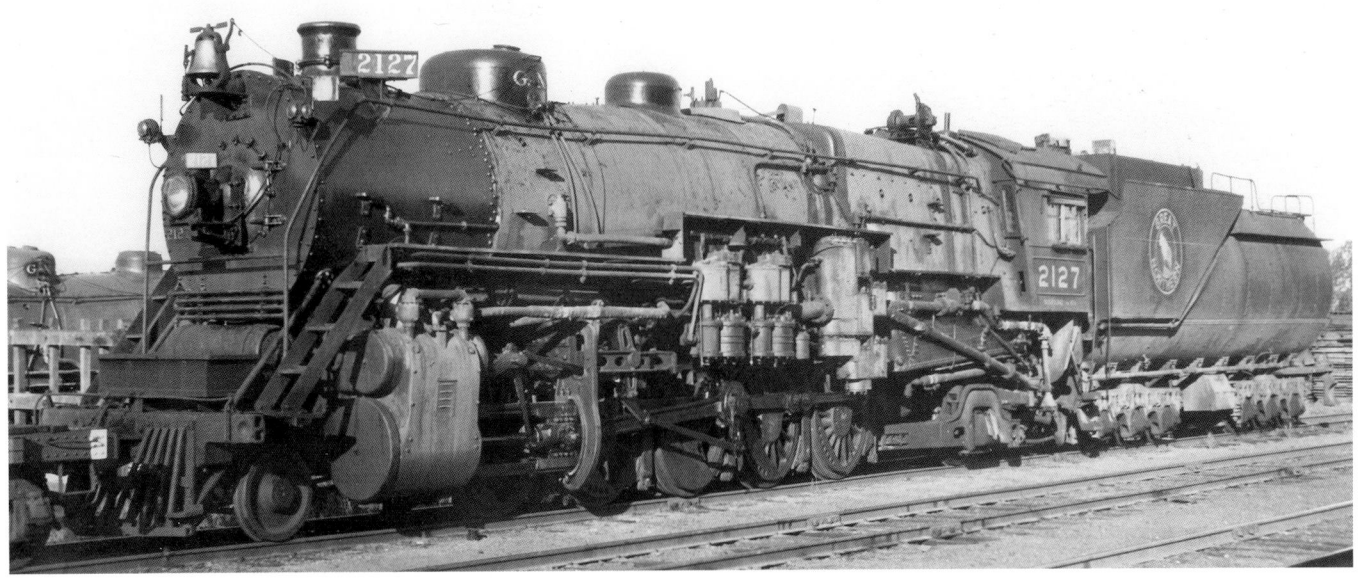

Other Q-1's carried the BL-2 model, such as the 2127, also at Klamath Falls, in June of 1949. Collection of Harold K. Vollrath.

The 3071 also received a large BL Worthington. This view of the original installation shows how access to the boiler check valve was obstructed by the air pump piping. This was eventually corrected. Unusual on the GN, this engine still has its original tender, though it has been rebuilt to Style 64 with a 10,000 gallon water capacity. The engine was photographed at Minneapolis, MN, on July 18, 1938, by R. Graham. Collection of William Raia.

The only GN Mikado to receive a type SA Worthington feedwater heater was the class O-1 3033. This view illustrates the engineer's side piping. Shown under tow from Sioux City, IA, to Willmar, MN, the 3033 is at Marshall, MN, in June 1951. Photograph by Norman F. Priebe

The mass of piping on the smokebox side leads to the Worthington SA feedwater heater located in front of the stack. While the more common industry practice was to mount the pump on the left side of the engine, it appears that GN typical installation placed the pump on the deck beneath the air pumps. Note that this engine is also equipped with a booster engine, indicated by the pipes and elbows beneath the cab. The photograph was taken at Portland, OR, in April 1950. Collection of Harold K. Vollrath.

The Worthington Type S feedwater heater was developed with separate pumps and spray chamber in the early 1930's to increase the water delivery capacity. Piping connections to the heater were usually made inside the smokebox.[9] The type S is known to have been used on three or four N-2's and a single O-1. It looked like a small box in front of the stack, with a pump mounted on the engineer's side beneath the running board. The Worthington Type SA feedwater heater was developed later, and was installed on relatively few GN locomotives (one or two O-1's, a few Q-1's and the Z-6's). It had a higher water output than the Type S. It used a float valve in the heater so the steam to operate the cold water pump was controlled by the water level in the heater. Thus, it had two smaller pipes coming out of the top – a small air vent and drain to release air that accumulated in the heater. It looked similar to the Type S except for the vent and drainpipes, and the fact that more of the piping was normally outside the smokebox on the SA.[10]

This view of the fireman's side of 3033 with a SA Worthington is at St. Paul, MN, in July 1940. Collection of Harold K. Vollrath.

This view shows the fireman's side piping for the SA on the 3033 while at Minneapolis on September 19, 1947.
Note the pipe routing has changed between the two dates. Photograph by K. L. Zurn from the collection of William Raia.

Superheating Steam and Superheaters

Early steam locomotives used what is called "saturated steam" to operate the cylinders. This steam was created by simply boiling the water with heat passing from the firebox through flues to the smokebox. The steam was collected in the steam dome and passed through the dry pipe to the steam pipes (or branch pipes) to the valves and cylinders. Saturated steam is steam that is at the minimum temperature for steam to exist at a given pressure. Even the slightest cooling will cause water droplets to form in it. When such steam is admitted to the cylinder, it meets the cylinder walls, the temperature of which is less than that of the entering steam, and some of the steam condenses. As the piston proceeds on its stroke and expansion occurs, some of the steam initially condensed will be re-evaporated. The cylinder, therefore, goes through a process of alternately cooling and reheating, resulting in condensation and re-evaporation, causing losses in efficiency.[11] Locomotive boilers could produce saturated steam having a temperature of about 400°F at typical boiler pressures.[12]

To reduce the loss of efficiency of operating with saturated steam, devices called superheaters were developed. A superheater consists of a series of tubes and headers through which the steam passes to raise its temperature. The first superheated locomotives received by the Great Northern were part of an order of ten 4-4-2's, twenty 4-6-2's and fifty 2-6-2's received in 1906. One of each type was obtained from the builder (Baldwin Locomotive Works) with a superheater installed. It is interesting that references disagree about the type of superheater in these locomotives. Information in the trade press of the time indicated that the engines had Baldwin superheaters.[13] However, later information stated that the engines had Schmidt superheaters.[14]

The Baldwin superheater was located entirely within the smokebox, and consisted of two cast steel headers which were cored with passages and walls. The headers were connected by a large number of curved tubes which followed the contour of the smokebox shell. The steam passed down in the rear of the smokebox through one set of tubes, then up through another into the lower header. It then passed up and down again through a forward set of tubes, and then from the lower header to the saddle. The tubes were heated by gases from the fire tubes. It was not possible to obtain a very high degree of superheat with this type heater. Diagrams of the 4-6-2 and 2-6-2 indicate that by 1914, these engines did have Schmidt superheaters, so the real story may be that the engines were delivered with Baldwin superheaters which were then replaced by Schmidt superheaters.

Dr Wilhelm Schmidt of Kassel, Germany, developed the first successful superheater. Great Northern used three types of Schmidt superheater. The Schmidt Type A superheater included a top header in the smokebox and a system of tubular elements extending back into the flues. Each superheater element consisted of four tubes, or elements, (two loops of two tubes each connected by tube ends with return bends), which were placed in enlarged boiler flues. In passing through the superheater, the steam enters the saturated steam compartment from the dry pipe and makes two passes through the units toward the firebox and back again, during which it is subjected to the relatively intense heat of the furnace gases direct from the firebox. The steam then returns to the header, going through the superheated steam compartment, from which it continues to the cylinders through the steam pipes and steam chests.[15] Superheaters have the ability to increase the temperature of the steam from the 400° F of saturated

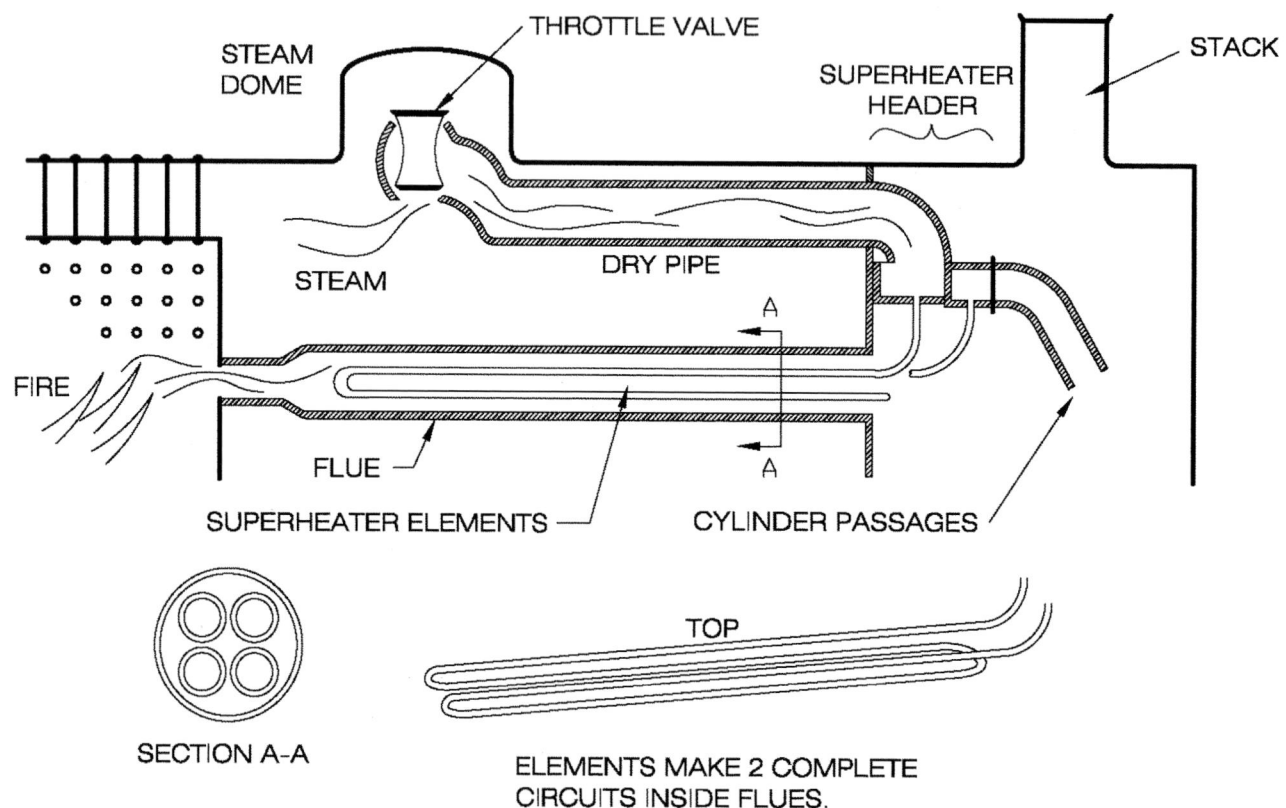

TYPE-A SUPERHEATER

This diagram shows the basic components of a Schmidt Type A or H-4 superheater. Redrawn by Joel Weeks from an original by Douglas C. Bemrich.

steam to about 700° F.[16] Superheated steam has a larger volume and greater total heat value (energy) per unit mass, and thus increases the efficiency of the locomotive.[17] A number of GN engines had Schmidt type H-4 superheaters, which were similar to the Type A.

The Schmidt Type E superheater was similar in function to the Type A, but had only a single loop of two tubes (elements) within a larger number of boiler flues. For example, the H-4 locomotives, with a Schmidt Type A superheater, had 160 2¼" flues and 32 5½" flues, the latter being the ones containing the superheater elements. The R-2 engines, with Schmidt Type E superheaters, had 88 2 ½" flues and 281 3 ½ " flues, the latter again being the ones with superheater elements.

At least one GN locomotive (H-3S 1430) is listed on diagrams as having a Halen superheater (later replaced with a Schmidt). A number of GN's smaller locomotives (parts of Classes G-3, F-6 and F-8) were equipped with H&D superheaters. Judging from the size and number of flues, these were probably similar to the Schmidt Type A.

During the early years of superheater use, Great Northern developed two types of superheater. One was called Great Northern Old Style (abbreviated O. S. on diagrams), and the other was called Great Northern New Style (abbreviated N. S. on diagrams). Both seem to have a small number of large flues, presumably having four elements, with a large number of small flues, much like the Schmidt Type A. Evidently the Old Style superheaters had elements in flues in the lower part of the boiler, and these flues were prone to getting plugged by cinders. The New Style had the elements in the middle and upper part of the boilers.[18] The trade press at the time called the Great Northern (both O. S. and N. S.) superheaters "Emerson superheaters." [19, 20] George H. Emerson was Great Northern's Superintendent of Motive Power in the early years of the Twentieth Century, later becoming General Manager and remaining with the company until 1917. "Emerson" superheater was most likely an alternate name, indicating the GN superheaters were actually designed by Mr. Emerson.

A much later Great Northern superheater design was the Type HA. This was designed by Howard Silver, designer of the N-3, specifically for that engine. It was basically designed to fit in the same 5 ½ inch flue as a Schmidt Type A, but with the novel feature that the incoming and return pipes are concentric with each other, greatly increasing the surface exposed with two passes of the steam instead of four. While installed only in the N-3, it was described in the 1941 Locomotive Cyclopedia.[21] See Chapter 19 for more information.

Great Northern installed superheaters in many of its older locomotives in its own shops. These locomotives received an "S" suffix to their class designation. For example, a C-3 which had been superheated became a Class C-3S locomotive. An "S" was also placed on the cab side of superheated locomotives following the class number in the cab side data.

Installation of superheaters made other modifications to the locomotives necessary. Superheating necessitated the installation of piston valves. Slide valves were inefficient with superheated steam in that they dragged due to increased friction, resulting in poor distribution of steam and rapid wearing of the valve and seat. Balanced piston valves reduced friction and provided for better steam distribution.[22]

When superheated, a number of the GN's older engines with slide valves (Classes H-2S, J-1S and J-2S) were retrofitted with a smaller piston valve made to fit within the dimensions of the original slide valve chamber. Called the Heron valve, it was developed by J. C. Heron, Superintendent of Dale Street Shops.

Some of the early engines purchased with superheaters also had inside steam pipes in the cylinder block (examples include the

The inside of the smokebox of GN H-5 1355 clearly shows the two sizes of flues, the larger of which would contain the superheater elements. Photograph by Douglas C. Bemrich.

H-4 4-6-2's and the first two orders of O-1's). This was found to be a problem with the high temperatures reached by superheated steam. The expansion and contraction of the inside steam pipes resulted in breaking of the cylinder castings. To remedy this situation, GN installed outside steam pipes which ran from the steam pipe in the smokebox through the smokebox to the steam chest. By applying outside steam pipes, the breakage was overcome, but GN also found that they could use cylinders that already had cracked steam passages by filling these passages with cement when the outside steam pipes were installed. In fact, it was sometimes necessary to remove engines from service because the cylinders became so badly cracked when they had inside steam pipes.[23]

Walschaert valve gear

The early Great Northern locomotives had the standard valve gear of the day, the Stephenson type. It suffered from two problems: the number of joints and accessibility. The wear on the joints would introduce large errors in the position of the valves as time went on.[24] This was compounded by the fact that all the levers were inside the frame, under the locomotive, making it difficult to adjust. The Walschaert design had been in existence since before 1876, but did not gather a following in the United States until after its application to the pioneer

0-6-6-0 of the Baltimore and Ohio, completed in 1904.[25] By this time the railroads were eager for change and the Walschaert valve gear was rapidly accepted. The GN began to change in 1906, and never looked back. After a period, there were other competing designs to the Walschaert. They were the Baker, Southern and Young designs. The GN received five class O-1's (3140 to 3144) with Southern valve gear during WW I, as dictated by the USRA. The GN eventually changed them to Walschaert between 1933 and 1943.

Cab

In the older diagram books there are a large number of cab styles called out. The authors have never found a definition of all these types. All GN steel cabs except the earliest ones had a border of 1-inch half round iron framing the area for the cab-side number. As time went on, and the switch to all-steel cabs was completed, the standard design became one with a perpendicular front wall, the so-called "square cab".

At the time of the building of the R-1 class, a change was made to a slanted front, parallel to the boiler backhead. The earlier O, the P-2 and the Q-1 classes were eventually retrofitted with this style slant front cab. A very few H-class engines were also changed. Note that the first slant-cabs applied to the P-2s had an extra window.

Later, at the time of the design of the N-3, a streamlined cab was designed and applied to the H-5 and N-3 classes. This cab slanted to the back as it went from bottom to top, a true streamlined design. The earlier slant front slanted back from top to bottom, which would not allow air to move past the junction with the running board, except by moving to the outside, causing turbulence. Despite the improved air stream flow, the streamlined cab did not gain acceptance and was eventually replaced on all of the N-3's, although it remained on a few H-5's.

The setting back of cabs was done frequently on the Great Northern as time went on. Some say it was to allow for a different type stoker, other factors might have included enlarging the cramped space in some cabs. A most vexing problem is determining if this was done in association with installing slant front cabs or not. The URPC only calls out the "set cab back" operation and says nothing about installing slant front cabs. However, by the time most engines were noted as having their cab set back, they also had gained a slant front cab.

It is important to note that the GN did not alter the original erecting drawings when a cab was set back. Therefore, the actual length of an engine with a set back cab was longer than indicated on its erection drawing. Locomotive diagrams are of no help, as they do not include the superstructure length. A modeler that did not make his own measurements would have to estimate the distance of the set back from photographs. The authors offer their opinion that it amounted to approximately 18 inches.

The 3140 is shown outside Hillyard shops in September 1934, undergoing rod work. The engine still had its Southern Valve Gear at the time. It also has a branch pipe heater, newly installed in June. Photo from the collection of Robert W. Johnston.

Stack

Starting about the time of the construction of the Q-2 class, the GN developed a series of similar standard cast smoke stacks that it used on the majority of its home-built locomotives and to replace stacks of commercially-built engines as they wore through from cinder erosion. The exception to this were the R-1 and R-2 classes, which had different, much shorter stacks visible on the outside of the smokebox.

The Great Northern Headlight

The GN began to install electric headlights in approximately 1910, the first ones being arc lamps. All railroads were required by law to have incandescent electric headlights by 1920, and the GN began to install them in 1919. These were in sheet iron housings, many likely converted from the earlier arc lamps.

In 1921, the GN adopted a cast steel headlight casing manufactured by Pyle-National for its incandescent bulb electric headlights. This unique design quickly became the standard. Nothing like it has been seen on other railroads, except on subsidiary Spokane Portland and Seattle. Use of a smaller cast design for switchers began in 1918 with the delivery of the C-1 class engines.

The class O-3 and O-4 engines were the last engines delivered before the GN standard design was adopted. Much later, one Z-6 engine arrived from the SP&S with a GN headlight and one with a NP headlight. Good evidence that the SP&S remained in charge of the maintenance of these units was that soon after the sale of these units to the GN, the GN headlight was replaced with an NP style.

Electric Train Indicators

After the Great Northern completed its Inside Gateway through Oregon, part of the route was over a portion of the Southern Pacific Railway, via trackage rights. Electric Train Indicators, commonly called illuminated number boards, were required to conform to Southern Pacific operating rules. On the SP as well as on the Union Pacific, the locomotive was required to display the train number.

Installation on Great Northern locomotives began in 1928. The 3304 may have had them installed even earlier, as it had its set removed for use in work done under AFE 36721. The first engines authorized to receive them under this AFE were the 1097, 1098 and 1099.[26] They were followed by the 1096, 1100, and 1102.[27] The next batch were authorized in 1932 and applied to 1098 (a repeat that hadn't been completed earlier), 1712, 1713, 3113, 3120, 3123, 3350, 3351, 3355, and 3356.[28] Later the same year 3117 was also authorized.[29] According to at least one photograph, these indicators were installed before the end of 1931.

Then the installation stopped. Those receiving the device were "sufficient engines for the present business."[30] For twelve years the indicators were used only on the Klamath Division engines and engines assigned to the Oregon Trunk, running between Wishram, Washington and Klamath Falls, Oregon. However, in 1943, the GN decided to put them on all of its engines, not to display train numbers, but as an engine number display that was easier to see at night.

The process took several years and AFE's were issued in 1943 and 1944.[31] While this was intended to be a universal application, there were some curious omissions, among them, several class O-8 locomotives. The installation ceased in 1946.

Air Pumps

The common knowledge regarding Great Northern air brake equipment is that the road ordered all of its air brake apparatus from the New York Air Brake Company. The authors have found nothing to refute this. The large number of No. 5 New York duplex air brake pumps installed on the steam engines supports this assertion. The Westinghouse look-alike duplex pumps, the ones called "8 ½ inch" by the Great Northern, were reported to also have been supplied by New York Air Brake. It is possible the New York company had license rights from Westinghouse.

The Great Northern was renowned for its mounting of air pumps on the smoke box front of most of its larger engines. The practice was introduced with the R-1 class in 1925, and every engine class since then had them so mounted. Some of the Q-1 class, and all of the O-3 class were retrofitted, but the P-2's, when given two New York pumps in place of the single original equipment "Westinghouse" type, had them placed on the pilot deck. This was the only case of a pilot deck installation on the Great Northern.

Steam Locomotive Paint Scheme

During the classic steam era, the boiler jackets of Great Northern steam locomotives were painted green. Builders photos of locomotives from as early as 1891 indicate that the color of the boilers were much lighter than the cabs of the locomotives. This was the likely beginning of Great Northern's classic green boilers. In 1919, the brand of paint used was Niles Jacket Enamel.[32] There is evidence that later on the passenger engines and freight engines used different shades of green. The passenger engines were painted with "Deluxe Green jacket enamel" (perhaps intended to mean Dulux by DuPont) while the freight engines were painted with "Locomotive Green jacket enamel" supplied by Patterson-Sargent.[33] Those who remember seeing these engines when they were operating have indicated that the passenger engines were a somewhat darker, richer green than the freight engines. The domes, running gear, the walkways and boiler beneath the walkways, domes and cab were painted black. The cabs were black.

The cab roof was painted black in the original scheme. The mineral red roof was a later addition to the paint scheme, but the exact date of introduction has not been determined.[34] Interviews with Cascade Division old-timers state that they could never remember cab roofs painted red on either the Spokane or Cascade Divisions.[35] Later color photography also shows black roofs on engines painted by the Hillyard shops. On the other hand, Mesabi Division (Superior shops) seems to have been the most prolific user of mineral red for roofs, even switching to Omaha Orange after diesels were on the property, as supplies of the mineral red apparently became less abundant.

The smokebox, including the smokestack (the smokestack was always painted the same color as the smokebox) and firebox beneath the running boards were painted with graphite in most cases, though on some freight engines the firebox may have been black. The graphite could vary from charcoal gray (almost black) to medium gray. Dixon Graphite was the brand used in 1919.[36] A variation on graphite smokeboxes was introduced in the late 1920's by William Lowney, the roundhouse foreman at Whitefish. He believed the engines needed greater visibility at grade crossings in the forests, and introduced the bright aluminum smokebox to engines on the Kalispell Division.[37] This feature was predominant during the 1930's but photographs show it disappeared during World War II.

The domes were black except where the center of the older fluted domes, (with the "G.N." on it) was painted jacket green, an almost universal feature. In this case, the fluted base and top would be black. Occasionally this pattern would be reversed, particularly on the earliest examples. The un-jacketed Belpaire firebox shoulders were black.

An interesting variation on the S-2 was the drive wheels were also painted jacket green.[38]

The rods were polished and oiled. The cylinder jackets in most cases were also green, with the remainder of the cylinder block being painted black. In some cases, the entire cylinder block, including the jacket, was painted black. The cylinder and valve head covers on at least some passenger locomotives were brushed nickel.

The 1930's saw a period where the green jacket paint was not applied, apparently as a cost-saving measure. In 1949, the Great Northern introduced the final period of black-painted jackets.[39] This conversion was supposed to be finished by 1950 but in 1951 Hillyard painted 2 or 3 more in green. Even with black paint, GN continued to apply graphite to the smokebox and firebox of most engines, but some were painted black also. A few black engines still had red cab roofs.

Perhaps the most overlooked color detail was the bell. Although the exterior of the bell remained in its natural brass, the interior was painted vermilion.[40]

The historical color of the lettering on both engine and tender was white, with the heralds being white and red. One source stated that aluminum lettering was not introduced until WWII, since it could be seen more easily during blackouts due to its higher reflectivity.[41] Aluminum was also applied to the herald during this period. Once engines began to be painted all black, the war was over and some shops, but not all, reverted to applying white lettering.

Stenciling

By 1892, the locomotives of the St.Paul, Minneapolis and Manitoba began to be lettered as Great Northern engines. At this point the engines were lettered "Great Northern" on the cab sides and on the faring of the tender tank.

There was an engine number on the sand dome and large numbers on the tender tank. The name of the owning road (e.g. "G.N.Ry.") was painted in small letters below the large tender number.

About 1903 lettering was removed from the tender sides. The cab still had "Great Northern" but also a large engine number (see builders photograph of GN 1323 in Chapter 11).

By 1906, the cab contained only the engine number with a small "G.N.Ry." beneath the number. This was the style in which the H-2/K-1/J-1 were delivered. By 1908, the cab lettering had reached the modern state, with the standard cab side data beneath the number, and the initials "G.N." appearing on the sand dome. There was still no lettering on the tender sides. Then in 1912 the N-1's were delivered with a rectangular herald on the tender side. This continued until

1918, although a "Goat Sign" was apparently painted on the tenders of passenger engines on the "coast lines" in 1917.[42] It is unknown how similar or dissimilar this may have been to the later heralds. Then in 1920 and 1923, locomotives were delivered with "Great Northern" lettered on the tender. The "Great Northern" lettering on the tenders lasted on some engines at least until 1932, but also there were a number of engines operating at this time with no lettering on the tender sides. Then in 1925 the R-1's were delivered with the "facing goat" herald, which had the goat encircled by the words "Great Northern." In the late 1930's, GN switched to the "side-facing goat" herald, on which there was a side profile of the goat still encircled by the words "Great Northern". In 1948, the herald used on the steam locomotives was changed again. The profile goat was retained, but it was now encircled with the words "Great Northern Railway". This herald had been first applied to the new diesels starting in 1938, and ten years later to the steam locomotives as they were repainted. The steamers were still painted with the green boiler jacket at this time. It was the most common herald on locomotives after they were painted black, although the previous herald was also seen on black engines.

A late variation on the last version of the goat herald was to face the goat to the right when applied on the engineer's side of the locomotive. This was to always have the goat looking forward, and the GN motor truck division may have initiated the practice.

Cab Side Data

During the "modern" steam locomotive period, Great Northern's steam locomotives carried statistical data about the locomotives on their cab sides, beneath the large locomotive number (or "cab number" in this discussion). The earliest evidence of this data found to date by the authors appears in builder's photographs of the Class H-4 and E-14 locomotives, which were received by the GN in 1909. The data consisted of the following (using Class F-1 as an example):

F1 S 55 120 22/26 89

The above data elements found on the cab sides of GN steam locomotives represent the following:

F1   Locomotive Class
S   Superheated
55   Driver diameter over the tires in inches
120 Engine weight on drivers in thousands of pounds
22/26 Cylinder diameter in inches/cylinder stroke in inches (often referred to as "Bore and Stroke")
89   Per cent working pressure, i.e. the ratio of the mean effective pressure (MEP) to the boiler pressure.[43]

These heralds are the ones used on Great Northern's steam locomotives.

In actual practice, however, this system was much less straightforward than it appears, and the data took many different forms. While the following are generalizations, exceptions to almost all of these statements can be found. In the earlier years, periods were painted between each of the data elements. Sometimes the data was bunched rather tightly, and sometimes it was quite spread out.

The "S", of course, was only present if the individual locomotive was in fact superheated. In many classes only some of the locomotives were superheated. In this case, only the superheated locomotives would be lettered with the "S", and this was done with relative consistency. In cases where the entire class was superheated (the more modern locomotives), it seems as though some locomotives were lettered with the "S" and some without.

Weight on drivers tended to increase as the locomotive aged (or as a result of reweighing – see Chapter 4), and in many cases different numbers can be found on various locomotives in the class. In some cases, photographs of specific individual locomotives provide evidence that the data had been updated or changed from one time to another. Evidence in general indicates that this number was rounded down to the next 1,000 pounds, though there were exceptions.

Cylinder dimensions sometimes varied within a class. For example, in those classes having both superheated and non-superheated locomotives, the cylinder dimensions of the superheated locomotives were commonly different from those of the non-superheated locomotives. In some cases (for example Class Q-1) the cylinder dimensions were actually changed during the service lives of the locomotives.

The percent working pressure (defined above) is probably the most confusing part of the data. For the most part, this data element was not used until probably sometime in the 1940's. It sometimes varied within a class. It was usually only carried to one decimal place, but sometimes two were used. It was also fairly common for the numbers after the decimal to be a smaller size than those before the decimal.[44]

Tenders

The Great Northern used an unusual rectangular tender for its earlier coal burning engines. The design was first seen in 1909 on deliveries from Baldwin. Lima also delivered this style of tender on the H-4 and P-1 in 1914. This tender had a steam-operated tilting coal bunker that would move coal forward as it was raised. Commonly called the

An example of the cab side on a smaller superheated locomotive is shown at Great Falls, MT, in 1945. Note the periods separating each element, which were not consistently applied to GN locomotives. A W. J. Pontin (Rail Photo Service) photograph from the collection of Norman F. Priebe.

"grape-arbor" tender, the so-called grape arbor was a structural cross-brace, that along with one or two stiffeners on each side, helped keep the bunker from spreading while raised. Once stokers came into use, the stoker screw made this device unnecessary.

The Great Northern's affinity for the Vanderbilt tender deserves a brief mention. After 1920 all tenders ordered or built by the Great Northern were of the Vanderbilt type. The single exception was the Z-6 class, which was a Northern Pacific design that the GN was required to purchase from the Spokane Portland and Seattle.

Tender details are presented throughout the book, especially in Chapters 32 and 34.

The Great Northern Shops

In the steam era the Great Northern maintained five large locomotive shops that were capable of any work from heavy repairs to complete locomotive construction. They were Dale Street, located at St. Paul, MN; Superior, located at Superior, WI; Great Falls, located at Great Falls, MT; Hillyard, located near Spokane, WA; and Delta, located

Class N-1 No. 2001 demonstrates the GN's unique coal-forwarding tilting bunker at Hillyard, WA, on October 10, 1914. Robert Johnston Collection, courtesy Bob Kelly.

near Everett, WA. The Great Falls shop was closed briefly during the depression, and was closed permanently in favor of a new diesel shop at Havre, MT, at the beginning of the diesel era. Likewise, the Delta shop was closed at the beginning of the diesel era. There was another locomotive shop at Devils Lake, ND that was closed shortly after 1927.

Steam Era Motive Power Principals

These were the men who defined the Great Northern steam locomotive. There are gaps in the record, so someone may have been omitted. Consequently, there is also some uncertainty with the date spans. During the steam era, the titles of the top motive power men changed from time to time. The following list includes the titles Superintendent of Motive Power and General Superintendent of Motive Power (GSMP), but not assistant Superintendent of Motive Power. One mechanical engineer covers a period where no motive power superintendents could be found. The list is ended at the point where M. B. Crowley became a superintendent in 1958. From 1954 on the duties formerly performed by the GSMP were performed by the Chief Mechanical Officer.[45]

J. O. Pattee, Superintendent of Motive Power – 1892
(MHS GN Presidents Subject File 975.)
Max Toltz, Mechanical Engineer - 1901
George H. Emerson, General Superintendent of Motive Power – 1903-1909
(AFE 10291, MHS 132.B.16.10(F) GN File 42-11).
A. C. Deverell, General Superintendent of Motive Power – 1910-1920 (St. Paul)
(AFE 16844, AFE 12641)

R. D. Hawkins, General Superintendent of Motive Power – 1910-1917 (St. Paul)
(AFE 1661, MHS 132.B.16.10(F), GN File 42-11).
William Kelly, General Superintendent of Motive Power – 1920-1935
(AFE 14507, AFE 50058)
Henry Yoerg, Superintendent of Motive Power – 1920-1932 (St. Paul)
(AFE 19750, AFE 46484).
General Superintendent Motive Power – 1935-1942
(AFE 51290, AFE 64359)
J. J. Dowling, Superintendent of Motive Power – 1920-1928 (Spokane)
(AFE 15435, AFE 35872)
T. J. Clark, Superintendent of Motive Power - 1930-1934 (Spokane)
Alex Colville, Superintendent of Motive Power - 1940–1942 (Spokane)
Superintendent of Motive Power, Steam, July 1, 1942-1953 (Spokane)
(Announcement, I. G. Pool, GSMP, July 1, 1942. Collection of Don Colville.)
Ira G. Pool, General Superintendent of Motive Power - 1942-1949
(AFE 65757, AFE 77762)
John L. Robson, Superintendent of Motive Power, Diesel - July 1, 1942 - February 23, 1950, (St. Paul).
(Announcement, I. G. Pool, July 1, 1942, collection of Don Colville.)
General Superintendent of Motive Power - 1950-1953 (AFE 78972)
Chief Mechanical Officer (CMO) - 1954 –1958
J. H. Heron, Superintendent of Motive Power - 1950 – 1956 (St. Paul)
CMO, 1958 – 1959
R. A. Smith, Superintendent of Motive Power - 1954 – 1958 (Spokane)

Notes:

1. Alfred W. Bruce, 1952. *The Steam Locomotive in America*, Bonanza Books, New York.
2. L. V. Stevens, Locomotive Stoker Co. to W. R. Wood, Nov. 20, 1924. Valuation Dept. Correspondence File, No. 125, Authors collection.
3. F. R. Roach, The Standard Stoker Company to F. I. Plechner, Nov. 21, 1930. Valuation Dept. Correspondence File, No. 125, Authors collection.
4. GN Valuation Department Correspondence File, No. 125. Authors collection.
5. Great Northern Railway Authority for Expenditure (AFE) 41367, June 6, 1929. Drawing UF 1256 referenced, but not in file. AFE 39238 approved 2-2-1929, work done Sept 1927, January 1928, June 1928. GNRHS
6. Memo, J. M. Hurley to J. R. W. Davis, March 12, 1929 attached to AFE 39238. GNRHS
7. Linn H. Westcott (Ed.), 1960. *Model Railroader Cyclopedia Volume 1 – Steam Locomotives*. Kalmbach Publishing Company, Milwaukee.
8. Ibid.
9. Ibid.
10. Ibid.
11. Llewellyn V. Ludy, 1920. *Locomotive Boilers and Engines*, American Technical Society, Chicago. (On line at San Diego Railroad Museum website: http://www.sdrm.org/faqs/boiler/title.html)
12. Westcott, op. cit.
13. *Railroad Gazette*, October 26, 1906, Vol. 41, No. 17, p. 371
14. Paul T. Warner, 1925. "The Great Northern Railway and Its Locomotives", *Baldwin Locomotives*, January 1925.
15. Roy V. Wright (Ed.), 1930. *Locomotive Cyclopedia of American Practice*, Ninth Edition – 1930, Simmons-Boardman Publishing Company, New York.
16. Westcott, op. cit.
17. Ludy, op. cit.
18. Great Northern Railway AFE 22222 (personal communication from Duane Amdahl to Kenneth R. Middleton dated March 19, 2008).
19. "Mikado Locomotives for the Great Northern", *Railway Age Gazette*, Vol. 51, No. 24, p.1214 (December 15, 1911)
20. "Mikado Type Locomotives for the Great Northern Ry.", *Railway Review*, Vol. 60, No. 1, p. 3 (January 6, 1917).
21. Roy V. Wright (Ed.), 1941. *Locomotive Cyclopedia of American Practice*, Eleventh Edition – 1941. Simmons-Boardman Publishing Company, New York.
22. Great Northern Railway AFE 13522, approved April 30, 1920

23. Great Northern Railway AFE 16489, approved January 24, 1921
24. Angus Sinclair, 1907. *Development of the Locomotive Engine*, Annotated edition, by John H. White, Jr., 1970, M.I.T. Press, Cambridge
25. Bruce, op. cit.
26. AFE 36721 approved April 2, 1928. GNRHS.
27. AFE 37293, approved June 21, 1928 for 1096, AFE 37704, approved Sept. 4, 1928 for 1100, and AFE 40379, approved August 19, 1929 for 1102. GNRHS.
28. AFE 44242, approved June 1, 1931. GNRHS.
29. AFE 45908, approved June 24, 1932. GNRHS.
30. Ibid.
31. AFE 67224, approved August 28, 1943, AFE 68648, approved April 20, 1944 and AFE 69514, approved September 20, 1944. GNRHS.
32. A. C. Deverell to J. M. Gruber, March 19, 1919. GN files MHS
33. Alex Colville, undated. Shop Foreman's Notebook.
34. CMO-office, Statement, Painting of Steam Locomotives, March 30, 1964
35. George E. Fischer, personal communication to N. F. Priebe, January 16, 1974
36. J. M. Gruber to A. C. Deverell, February 12, 1919. GN files MHS
37. Related by R. E. Johnson and George Wier to N. F. Priebe
38. Donald R. Sease, to R. E. Johnson, October 21,1961, relating memories of steam from the 1940's.
39. Martin Evoy III, Norman C. Keyes, Jr., W.A. McGinley, Wolfgang F. Weber and the Minnesota Historical Society, 1977. "Great Northern Equipment Color Schemes." Fraternal Order of Empire Builders Reference Sheet No. 28. See also Alex Colville, op. cit. (Note the disagreement on date.)
40. CMO op. cit.
41. George T. Wier, personal communication to N. F. Priebe, November 26, 1973
42. Great Northern Railway Authority for Expenditure (AFE) 3784, approved December 12, 1916.
43. Norman C. Keyes, Jr., personal communication to Kenneth R. Middleton, March 7, 1974
44. Kenneth R. Middleton, 2006. "Great Northern Steam Locomotive Cab Side Data," Great Northern Historical Society Reference Sheet 334.
45. The primary source of this information was the collection of "The Official List of Officers, Stations and Agents", at the Minnesota Historical Society. This set spans the volumes from No. 7 to the end, but has gaps up to 1917. Substantiating sources are given at each entry.

The heavy O-8 class was the type likely to have triggered the reweigh grievance.
Here is 3379, the O-8 class engine weighed, at Minneapolis in 1956. Photo by Bob Vierkant.

Chapter 4

The Great Northern Engine Reweigh Rate Case

After World War II, Great Northern enginemen became aware that many of their engines did not perform according to their stated weight. Rather, they behaved as heavier engines. This was of major concern since engine weights were used as the basis of their pay. It has been said, so far unproven, they weighed an O-8 themselves for proof. The first record of a problem was in a letter dated Feb. 9, 1946.[1] This letter pointed out that a precedent for how far back retroactive pay was entitled was established by earlier cases (see below) as no farther than the date the request for reweighing was first made, and refers to an earlier letter from December, 1945. In light of the outcome, we judge the first request to reweigh GN locomotives was made in 1945.

A grievance was filed that became the BLE Strike Docket Case No. 50. The previous weight grievance cases with other railroads that were cited in this case are listed below. They were National Railroad Adjustment Board:

Award No. 53, Docket No. 102, Chicago Burlington and
  Quincy, 1935
Award No. 338, Docket No. 244, Colorado and Southern 1935
Award No. 2730, Docket No. 5252, Wabash Ry. Co., 1938
Award No. 7625, Docket No. 14724, Texas and Pacific, 1943

These cases also established the precedent that permitted the weighing of just one representative engine in each class. The settlement was dated September 11, 1950. The dates of the official reweighing were not recorded on the documentation received, but it is believed to have been done some time in 1948, judging from the retroactive pay period termination date. The outcome for the enginemen allowed retroactive compensation from July 1, 1945 through December 1, 1948.

The outcome for the bridge department was that they had to re-examine the Cooper Ratings of all the Railway's bridges in light of the new heavier engine weights. The outcome for the motive power department was that they had to re-do the locomotive diagram book. The new weights first appeared on the locomotive diagrams in November 1948. And the outcome for the locomotive historian was the necessity to be aware of these changes and use specifications from November 1948 or later to have correct engine weights.

Note that this book contains locomotive diagrams from many eras. Only diagrams dated November 1948 or later reflect the correct weights for the reweighed engine classes, as shown in the following table.

LOCOMOTIVE CLASSES WEIGHED, WITH ORIGINAL AND NEW WEIGHTS
Weight is in Pounds

Class	Old Weight on Drivers	New Weight on Drivers	Engine No. Weighed	Comments
F-8 Oil	180,000	192,000	1150	
F-8 Coal	180,000	195,000	1188	
H-4 Oil	152,000	176,000	1450	Loco. Diagram differs
H-5 Coal	164,950	180,000	1366	
H-5 Oil	165,000	176,000	1372	
H-6 Oil, booster	218,260	227,800	1714	Loco. Diagram shows same
H-6 no booster	161,580	169,000		as without booster
H-7 Oil, booster	226,200	250,000	1376	Loco. Diagram shows a decrease to 189,000
N-3 Coal	459,200	542,000	2010	
O-1 Coal	229,000	242,000	3047	
O-1 Oil, booster	291,700	300,400	3144	Loco. Diagram shows same as without booster
O-1 no booster	229,000	236,000		
O-3 Coal	239,000	246,000	3205	
O-4 Oil	242,800	254,000	3220	
O-4 Coal	242,800	262,000	3254	
O-6 Oil	268,100	260,000	3364	This weight decreased
O-8 Oil	280,000	325,000	3379	
Q-1 Coal, booster	403,620	432,500	2109	Loco. Diagram differs
Q-1 Coal, no booster	342,490	367,000		
Q-1 Oil, booster	403,620	419,500	2119	
Q-1 Oil, no booster	342,490	356,000		
Q-2 Coal	290,000	321,000	2178	
Q-2 Oil, booster	354,600	383,500	2179	
Q-2 Oil, no booster	290,000	314,000		
R-1 Oil	532,000	555,000	2041	
R-2 Oil	544,000	592,000	2056	
S-1 Oil	271,000	301,000*	2551	New wt. 283,000*
C-1 Coal	232,600	253,200	812	
C-1 Oil	233,000	245,640	815	

* The actual new weight for the S-1 was 283,000 pounds. Since this weight did not quite come up to that of similar sized locomotives, for purposes of pay rate equality the weight was bumped up slightly to put the S-1 with the O-8 and Q-class engines. Thus the cryptic note on the diagram sheet for the S-1 after November, 1948: "Wt. on drivers and cab stenciled for rate making purposes 301000 lbs. as per verbal agreement of 8-12-48."

The P-2 and S-2 classes were not shown in the table provided. That they were reweighed is shown by increased weights on locomotive diagrams of 1948 and later.

P-2 Oil	242,000	265,000
S-2 Oil	247,300	257,000

Differences, except for the S-1 class, between these results and the numbers used by the motive power department cannot be explained by the information available.

Notes:

The information related in this chapter was provided by M. L. Glover, who was Vice Chairman of the Brotherhood of Locomotive Engineers, Burlington Northern, St. Paul, at the time the information was provided, in 1982.

1. M. C. Anderson to A. F. Kummer, BLE, St. Paul, MN. February 9, 1946, File E-1(j).

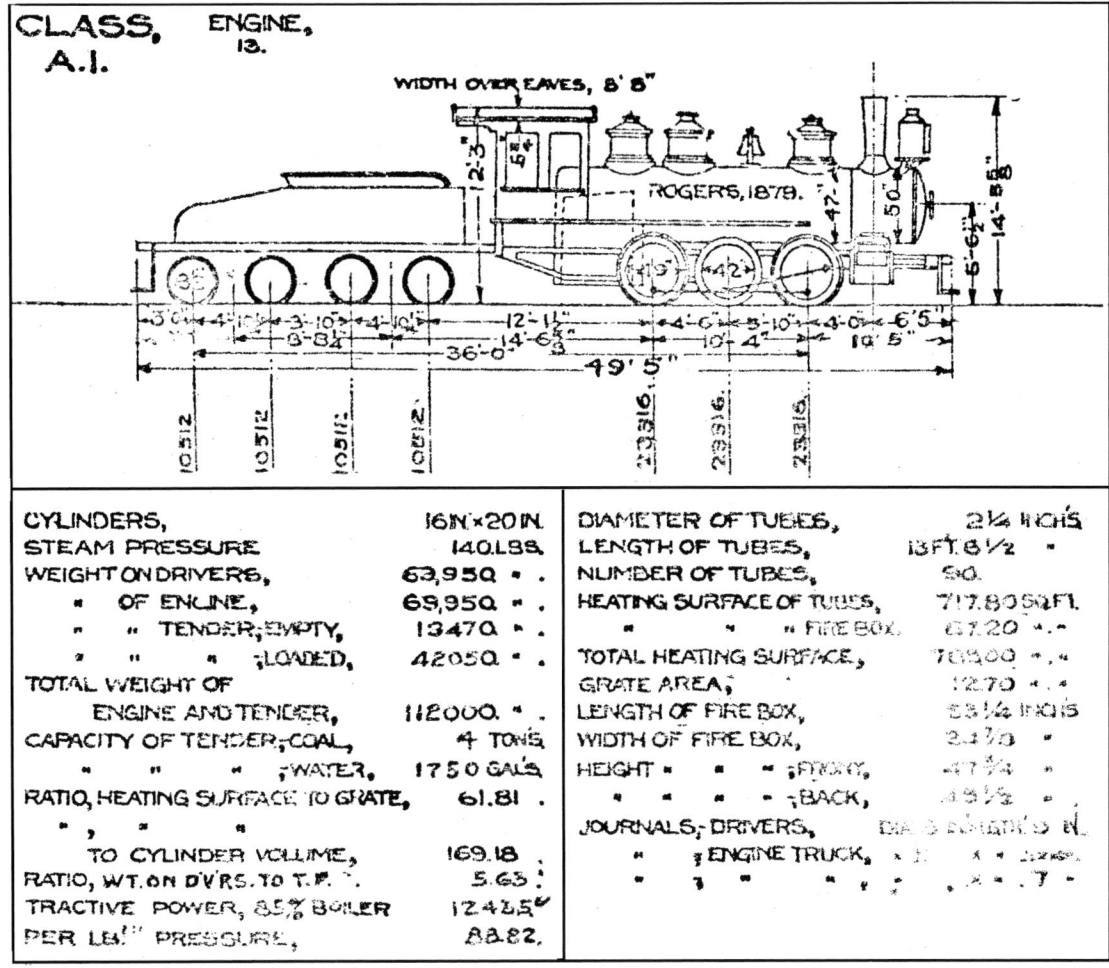

CYLINDERS,	16IN×20IN.	DIAMETER OF TUBES,	2¼ INCHS
STEAM PRESSURE	140.LBS.	LENGTH OF TUBES,	13FT.8½ "
WEIGHT ON DRIVERS,	63,950 " .	NUMBER OF TUBES,	90.
" OF ENGINE,	69,950 " .	HEATING SURFACE OF TUBES,	717.80SQFT.
" " TENDER; EMPTY,	13470 " .	" " " FIRE BOX,	67.20 " .
" " " ;LOADED,	42050 " .	TOTAL HEATING SURFACE,	785.00 " .
TOTAL WEIGHT OF		GRATE AREA,	12.70 " .
ENGINE AND TENDER,	112000. " .	LENGTH OF FIRE BOX,	63¼ INCHS
CAPACITY OF TENDER;COAL,	4 TONS	WIDTH OF FIRE BOX,	24⅞ "
" " " ;WATER,	1750 GALS	HEIGHT " " " ;FRONT,	47¾ "
RATIO, HEATING SURFACE TO GRATE,	61.81 .	" " " " -;BACK,	49½ "
" , " "		JOURNALS; DRIVERS,	
TO CYLINDER VOLUME,	169.18 .	" ; ENGINE TRUCK,	
RATIO, WT. ON D'V'RS. TO T.P.,	5.63 :		
TRACTIVE POWER, 85% BOILER	12435		
PER LB. PRESSURE,	88.82.		

Chapter 5
Class A 0-6-0 Six-Wheel Switcher

The Great Northern Railway and its predecessors and subsidiaries had already acquired many locomotives of the 0-6-0 wheel arrangement by the time the new class system was implemented. That the majority of the A classes were of older design can be noted by the fact that only the GN Class A-10 and A-11 0-6-0's had piston valves. That the A-10's had them is not noted on the diagram sheet but is visible in photographs. Only Class A-11 was superheated.

Class A-1

Those assigned to Class A-1 had been members of Old Class 21, and were the last locomotives received by the St.Paul & Pacific. These locomotives, StP&P 45 and 46, were actually received from the Rogers Locomotive Works in April 1879 as 2-6-0's, and were listed in the 1891 Annual Report of the Machinery Department (ARMD) as "Mogul Switch" engines.[1] They had 16-inch by 20-inch cylinders and 46-inch drivers. They are listed in the ARMD as having a total engine weight of 67,250 pounds, of which 60,000 pounds were on the drivers. At some time between June 30, 1892 (the date the 1892 ARMD was issued) and 1900 (the date of the earliest GN locomotive diagrams known to the authors), the lead trucks were removed. About 1896 the drivers were increased in size to 49 inches, giving a tractive effort of 12,435

pounds. The engines had been passed along to the St.Paul, Minneapolis & Manitoba as its numbers 45 and 46, and later became GN 45 and 46. As part of the major renumbering in 1899, these engines became GN 12 and 13. Number 12 was sold in 1902, technically before it became a member of Class A-1. No. 13 lasted until 1917. No photographs of these engines are known by the authors to exist, but diagrams indicate that they had straight boilers with a 50-inch smokebox diameter and flanged domes (two sand domes plus the steam dome).

Class A-2

Class A-2 had been received from Hinkley Locomotive Works in 1888 as StPM&M 232 and 233. The engines were delivered with 17-inch by 24-inch cylinders and 51-inch drivers, with engine weights of 83,000 pounds. They were in Old Class 2(2nd). In 1893 No. 232 was sold to the Seattle & Montana Railway (one of GN's "Coast Lines"), where it retained its same number, and it was later transferred to the Seattle & Montana Railroad Company. About 1895 the driver diameter was reduced to 49 inches. In the 1899 renumbering, the two locomotives became GN 30 and 31. Both left the roster in 1915. Diagrams show them with straight boilers having a smokebox diameter of 54 inches, and flanged domes (again with two sand domes).

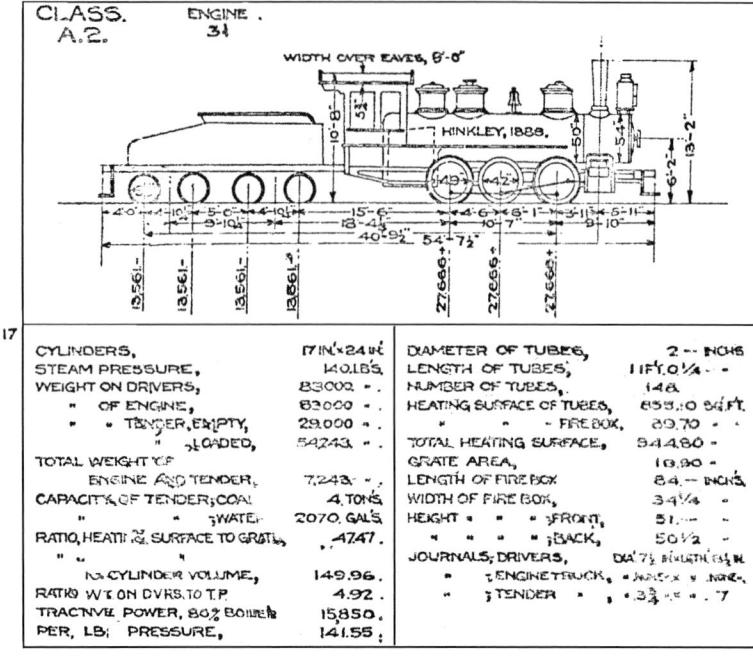

CLASS. A.2.   ENGINE. 31

WIDTH OVER EAVES, 8'-0"

HINKLEY, 1888.

CYLINDERS,	17 IN.x 24 IN.	DIAMETER OF TUBES,	2 -- INCHS
STEAM PRESSURE,	140 LBS.	LENGTH OF TUBES,	11 FT. 0 1/4 - -
WEIGHT ON DRIVERS,	83000 ".	NUMBER OF TUBES,	148
" OF ENGINE,	83000 ".	HEATING SURFACE OF TUBES,	855.0 SQ. FT.
" " TENDER, EMPTY,	29,000 ".	" " - FIRE BOX,	89.70 - .
" ; LOADED,	54243 ".	TOTAL HEATING SURFACE,	944.80 -
TOTAL WEIGHT OF		GRATE AREA,	18.90 -
ENGINE AND TENDER,	7,243 ".	LENGTH OF FIRE BOX	84. -- INCHS.
CAPACITY OF TENDER; COAL,	4. TONS	WIDTH OF FIRE BOX,	34 1/4 -
" " ; WATER,	2070. GALS	HEIGHT " " ; FRONT,	51. -
RATIO, HEATING SURFACE TO GRATE,	.4747.	" " " ; BACK,	50 1/2 -
" "		JOURNALS; DRIVERS,	DIA 7 1/2 LENGTH 8 1/2 IN.
" CYLINDER VOLUME,	149.96 .	" ; ENGINE TRUCK,	. 3/4 x 1/4 -- .
RATIO WT ON DVRS. TO T.P.	4.92 .	" ; TENDER " .	3/4 " " . 7
TRACTIVE POWER, 80% BOILER	15,850.		
PER. LB; PRESSURE,	141.55 ;		

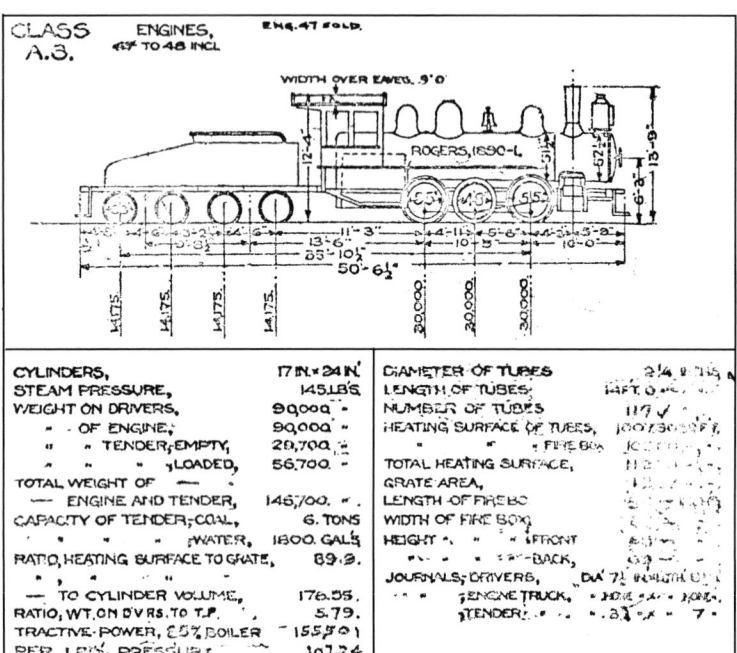

CLASS A.3.   ENGINES, 47 TO 48 INCL.   ENG. 47 SOLD.

WIDTH OVER EAVES, 9'0"

ROGERS, 1890-L.

CYLINDERS,	17 IN.x 24 IN.	DIAMETER OF TUBES	2 1/4 x 7/8
STEAM PRESSURE,	145 LBS.	LENGTH OF TUBES;	11 FT. 0 1/4 ".
WEIGHT ON DRIVERS,	90000 ".	NUMBER OF TUBES	117
" OF ENGINE,	90,000 "	HEATING SURFACE OF TUBES,	100730 SQ. FT.
" " TENDER, EMPTY,	29,700 ".	" " - FIRE BOX,	90.90
" " ; LOADED,	56,700. -	TOTAL HEATING SURFACE,	1129.0
TOTAL WEIGHT OF		GRATE AREA,	13.43
ENGINE AND TENDER,	146,700. ".	LENGTH OF FIRE BOX	84.
CAPACITY OF TENDER; COAL,	6. TONS	WIDTH OF FIRE BOX	34 1/4
" " ; WATER,	1800. GALS	HEIGHT " " ; FRONT,	51.
RATIO, HEATING SURFACE TO GRATE,	89.3.	" " " ; BACK,	50 1/2
" "		JOURNALS; DRIVERS,	DIA 7 1/2 LENGTH 8 1/2 IN.
" TO CYLINDER VOLUME,	176.55 .	" ; ENGINE TRUCK,	. 3/4 x 4 .
RATIO; WT. ON DVRS. TO T.P.	5.79 .	; TENDER;	. 3/4 x 7
TRACTIVE POWER, 85% BOILER	15530		
PER. LB; PRESSURE.	107.24		

Class A-3

The two members of Class A-3 had been built by Rogers in 1890 and 1891 as Sioux City & Northern 7 and 9. They had 17-inch by 24-inch cylinders and 56-inch drivers. Engine weights were 85,000 pounds When the Sioux City & Northern was sold to the Willmar & Sioux Falls in 1900, these locomotives were included in the sale. They were renumbered as Willmar & Sioux Falls 47 and 48 and placed in Old Class 2A. They came to the Great Northern, as 47 and 48, with the Willmar & Sioux Falls in 1907. One was sold and the other scrapped in 1918. No photographs are known by the authors to exist. Diagrams show them with straight boilers having a smokebox diameter of 52½ inches and rounded style domes.

Class A-4

There were three locomotives in Class A-4. These had originally been acquired by the StPM&M in 1882 as its 194-196, Class 32. No. 195 was sold to the Minneapolis Western in 1891, but in 1899 all three of the engines were renumbered as GN 27-29. They were quite small, with 17-inch by 24-inch cylinders, 49-inch drivers (though photographic evidence indicates that at least one had its driver diameter reduced to 42 inches) and weights on drivers of only 67,050 pounds All were sold or scrapped in the late teens. Like the other early 0-6-0's, diagrams show them as having straight boilers with 50¾-inch smokebox fronts and flanged domes.

Class A-5 (1st)

Class A-5 was used twice. The members of A-5(1st) were Old Class 31(2nd) engines. They had been purchased from Rogers in at least three different orders. The first order of six engines was received in 1887 as StPM&M 94-99. In 1888 six more locomotives were received by the StPM&M and numbered as 226-231. That same year the Eastern of Minnesota (EM) received an order of three that were numbered as its 1-3. These engines all had 18-inch by 24-inch cylinders and 49-inch drivers, and weighed in at 86,450 pounds In 1892, StPM&M 98 was sold to the Minneapolis Western as its No. 1. In 1893 StPM&M 99 was sold to the Eastern of Minnesota and became EM 4. Almost immediately

Class A-2 No. 30 is shown at Bellingham, Washington in 1906. Note the shield over the valve linkage. Collection of William Bissinger.

upon receipt, StPM&M 226 and 227 were sold to the Montana Central (MC) and became MC 14 and 15. The major renumbering of 1899 brought them back into one number series as 32-46, although 37 and 40-42 were still technically Eastern of Minnesota locomotives. Diagrams indicate their appearance was similar to the other early 0-6-0's, with flanged domes and straight boilers.

Class A-5 (2nd)

A-5(2nd) had only two members, GN 32 and 33. These were originally D-5 2-6-0's built by Brooks Locomotive Works in 1896 as GN 379 and 376, respectively. In 1899 they had become 458 and 455, respectively. These had 19-inch by 26-inch cylinders and 55-inch drivers. In 1925 and 1926, respectively, the two engines had their lead trucks removed at GN's Jackson Street (St.Paul, MN) Shops, thus placing their entire engine weight of 126,000 pounds on the drivers. A locomotive diagram dated January 1, 1926, indicates that there may have been plans to convert a third engine, but this was apparently not done. Both A-5's left the roster in 1929. GN 32 was sold to the Midland of Manitoba, where it became 3. GN 33 was simply retired in 1929. The authors know of no photos showing these engines in their switcher configuration.

Class A-6

Class A-6 contained four locomotives, which had been in Old Class 9(3rd). These were products of Brooks, built in 1899. Two of the locomotives were delivered as Duluth, Superior and Western Terminal Company (DS&WT) 1 and 2. The other two were delivered as Eastern of Minnesota 58 and 59. The builders photograph of EM 58 shows an interesting closed cab and a Belpaire firebox. The engines had 18-inch by 26-inch cylinders with 49-inch drivers. Engine weights were 109,400 pounds. The DS&WT and EM engines became GN 56-59 in 1903 and 1902, respectively. Then in 1909 the former DS&WT engines (now GN 56 and 57) were sold to the Allouez Bay Dock Company and renumbered as its 1 and 2. These came back to GN in 1913 as 378 and 379. All four locomotives were sold in 1926.

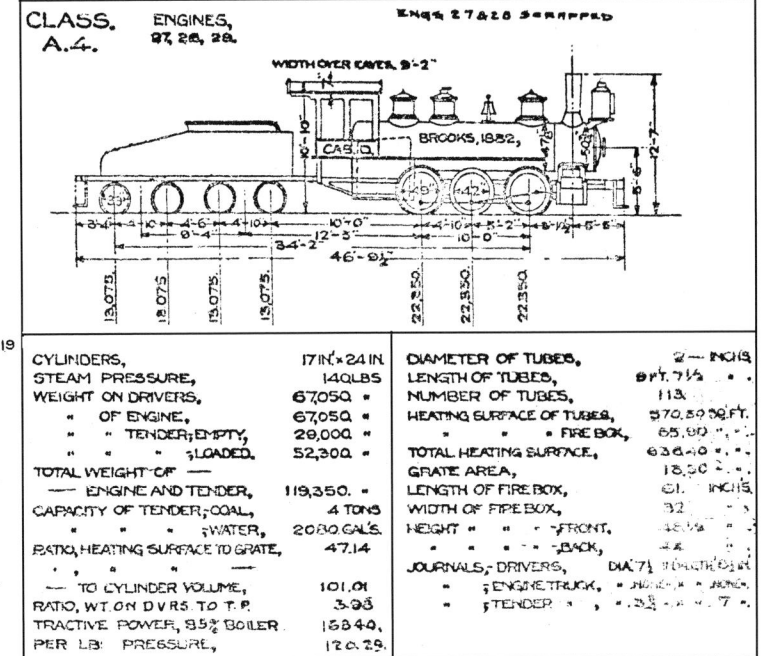

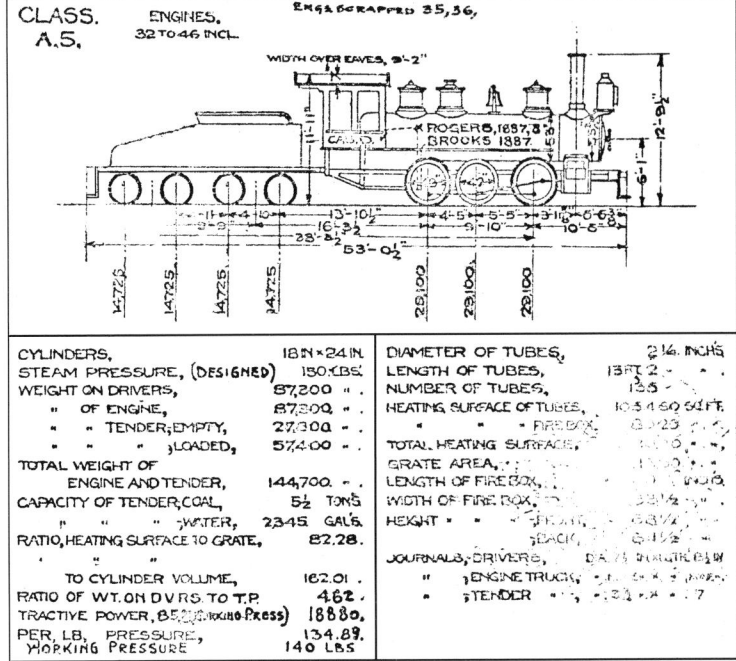

A proud crew posed with A-4 class No. 29 at Spokane in 1911. Note that the stenciling on the cab side shows a driver diameter of 42 inches. Collection of R.E. Johnson.

StPM&M 98 was built by Rogers in 1887 as a member of Old Class 31(2nd). In 1903 it became a Class A-5 engine. ALCO Historic Photos.

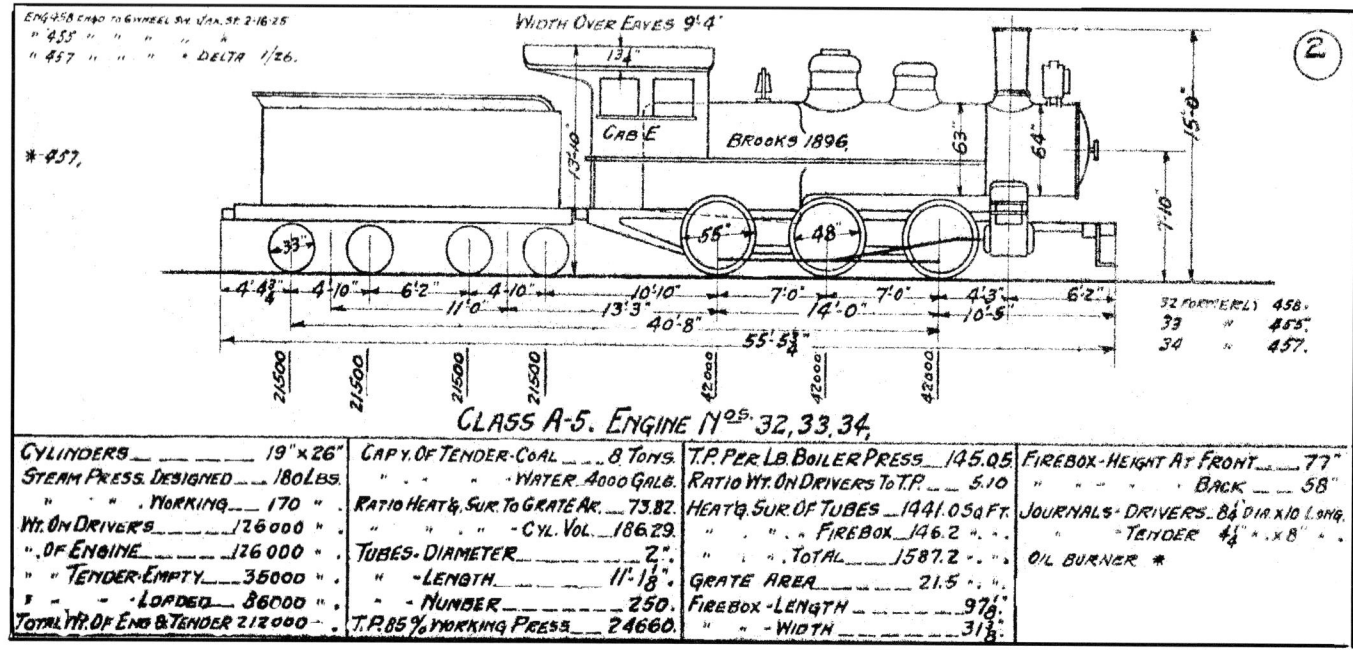

CLASS A-5. ENGINE NOS. 32, 33, 34.

CYLINDERS _____ 19"x26"	CAP'Y. OF TENDER-COAL __ 8 TONS.	T.P. PER LB. BOILER PRESS __ 145.05	FIREBOX-HEIGHT AT FRONT ___ 77"
STEAM PRESS. DESIGNED ___ 180 LBS.	" " " -WATER_ 4000 GALS.	RATIO WT. ON DRIVERS TO T.P. __ 5.10	" " -BACK ___ 58"
" " WORKING ___ 170 "	RATIO HEATG. SUR. TO GRATE AR. _ 73.82	HEATG. SUR. OF TUBES __ 1441.0 SQ FT.	JOURNALS-DRIVERS 8¼ DIA. X10 LONG.
WT. ON DRIVERS _____ 126000 "	" " " -CYL. VOL. _ 186.29.	" " " FIREBOX _ 146.2 " "	" -TENDER 4½" " X 8 " "
" OF ENGINE _____ 126000 "	TUBES-DIAMETER _____ 2".	" " " TOTAL __ 1587.2 " ."	OIL BURNER *
" TENDER-EMPTY __ 35000 "	" -LENGTH _____ 11'-1⅛"	GRATE AREA _____ 21.5 " "	
" " -LOADED _ 86000 "	" -NUMBER _____ 250	FIREBOX-LENGTH _____ 97⅝"	
TOTAL WT. OF ENG & TENDER 212000 "	T.P. 85% WORKING PRESS __ 24660.	" " -WIDTH _____ 31⅛"	

Eastern of Minnesota No. 58, later a member of Class A-6, had an early version of the all-weather cab. ALCO Historic Photos.

Class A-7

Class A-7 locomotives had originally been in Old Class 7(2nd). They were received in three orders from Brooks. The first order of eleven locomotives was received in 1893. They were received as Montana Central 25 and 26, and GN 250-258. No. 258 was exhibited at the Columbian Exposition prior to being delivered to GN. Five of these engines (Nos. 252-256) were sold to the Butte, Anaconda & Pacific before they were a year old. The remaining two orders were purchased by the Eastern of Minnesota. Each order was for two locomotives, with an 1895 order for EM 5 and 6, and an 1898 order for EM 7 and 8. In 1899 the GN engines became 60-63 and the Eastern of Minnesota engines became 66-69. The Montana Central engines became GN 64 and 65 about 1900. The engines had 19-inch by 26-inch cylinders and 49-inch drivers. These were the first 0-6-0's on the Great Northern to have Belpaire fireboxes, and were received with rounded style domes. Engine weights were 114,700 pounds. GN 60 was sold to Somers Lumber Company, Great Northern's tie production plant, in 1930 and became Somers S4. It was ultimately sold to the federal government in 1939. The other locomotives were sold or retired in the late 1920's and 1930's. The final holdout, GN 64, was retired in 1937.

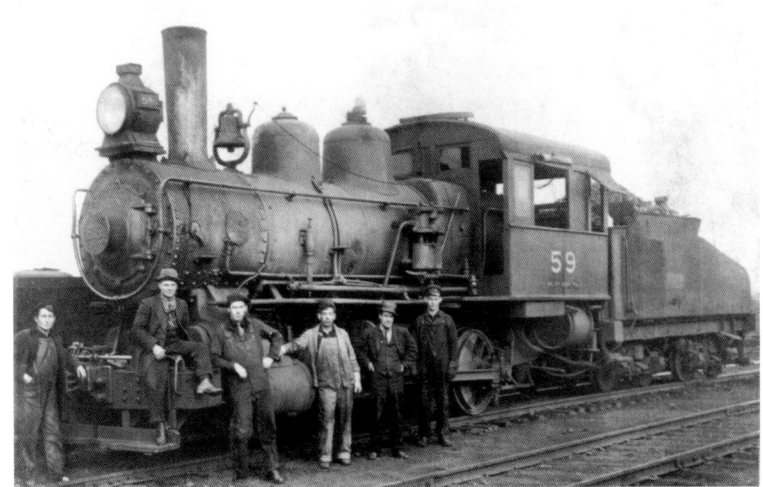

The long cab on GN 59 has been rebuilt without side doors. The engine is shown at Allouez yard in 1917. Collection of Norman F. Priebe.

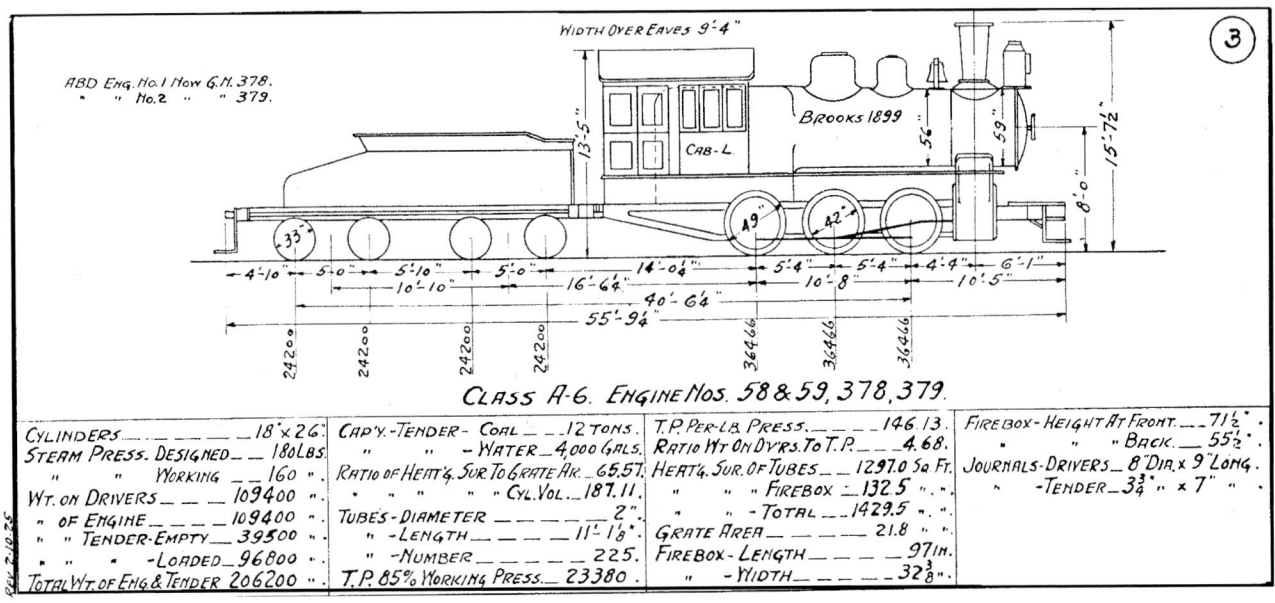

CLASS A-6. ENGINE NOS. 58 & 59, 378, 379.

CYLINDERS 18" x 26"	CAP'Y - TENDER - COAL 12 TONS	T.P. PER-LB. PRESS. 146.13	FIREBOX - HEIGHT AT FRONT 71½"
STEAM PRESS. DESIGNED 180 LBS	" " - WATER 4,000 GALS	RATIO WT ON DVRS. TO T.P. 4.68	" " BACK 55½"
" " WORKING 160	RATIO OF HEAT'G SUR. TO GRATE AR. 65.57	HEAT'G SUR. OF TUBES 1297.0 SQ FT	JOURNALS-DRIVERS 8" DIA x 9" LONG
WT. ON DRIVERS 109400 "	" " - CYL. VOL. 187.11	" " FIREBOX 132.5 " "	" -TENDER 3¾" x 7" "
" OF ENGINE 109400 "	TUBES - DIAMETER 2"	" " - TOTAL 1429.5 " "	
" TENDER-EMPTY 39500 "	" -LENGTH 11'-1⅛"	GRATE AREA 21.8 "	
" " -LOADED 96800 "	" -NUMBER 225	FIREBOX - LENGTH 97 IN.	
TOTAL WT. OF ENG & TENDER 206200 "	T.P. 85% WORKING PRESS. 23380	" - WIDTH 32⅜"	

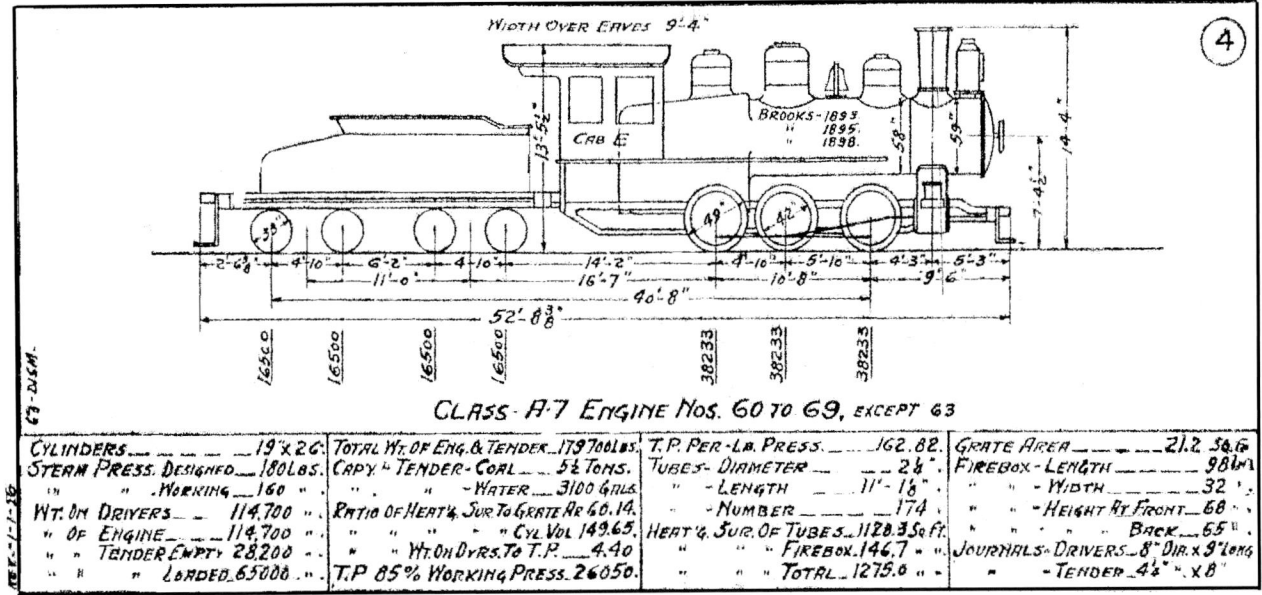

CLASS A-7 ENGINE NOS. 60 TO 69, EXCEPT 63

CYLINDERS 19" x 26"	TOTAL WT. OF ENG. & TENDER 179700 LBS	T.P. PER-LB. PRESS. 162.82	GRATE AREA 21.2 SQ.G
STEAM PRESS. DESIGNED 180 LBS	CAP'Y - TENDER - COAL 5¼ TONS	TUBES - DIAMETER 2¼"	FIREBOX - LENGTH 98 IN
" " WORKING 160	" " - WATER 3100 GALS	" - LENGTH 11'-1⅛"	" - WIDTH 32 "
WT. ON DRIVERS 114,700 "	RATIO OF HEAT'G SUR. TO GRATE AR 60.14	" - NUMBER 174	" - HEIGHT AT FRONT 68 "
" OF ENGINE 114,700 "	" " - CYL. VOL 149.65	HEAT'G SUR. OF TUBES 1128.3 SQ FT	" - BACK 55 "
" TENDER EMPTY 28,200 "	" WT. ON DVRS. TO T.P. 4.40	" " FIREBOX 146.7 " "	JOURNALS-DRIVERS 8" DIA x 9" LONG
" " LOADED 65000 "	T.P. 85% WORKING PRESS. 26050	" " TOTAL 1275.0 "	" - TENDER 4½" x 8"

Eastern of Minnesota No. 8, which became Class A-7 engine 69, sits on a turntable at Dunkirk, NY, prior to its delivery. ALCO Historic Photos.

No.65, a class A-7, is shown at St. Paul in April 1922. Collection of Harold K. Vollrath.

Somers Lumber Company S4 was formerly GN 60, received from Brooks in 1893. GNRHS Collection.

GN No. 72 was delivered in 1900 as part of Old Class 7A, and later became part of Class A-8. Collection of Harold K. Vollrath.

Class A-8 No. 71, likely shown at Minneapolis, still maintains the same lines as when built, but has received a standard GN switcher headlight, has had the air pump moved to the fireman's side, and has a slightly enlarged coal bunker. GNRHS Collection.

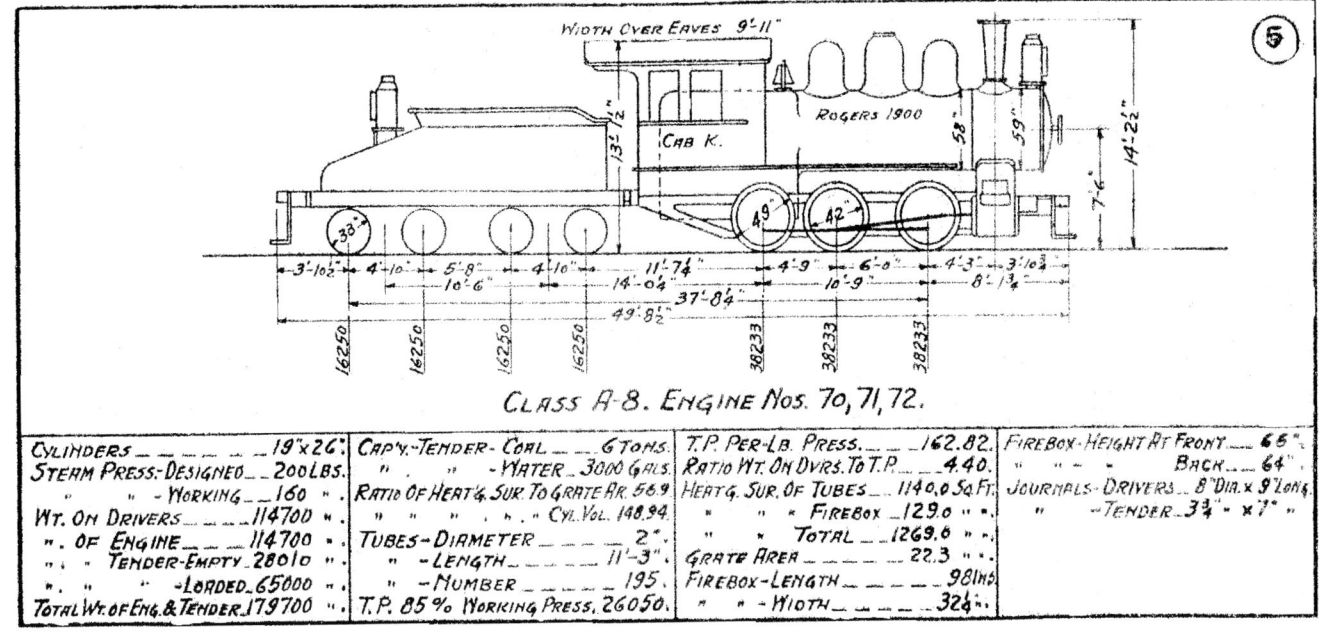

CLASS A-8. ENGINE NOS. 70, 71, 72.

CYLINDERS _ _ _ _ _ 19"x26"	CAP'Y- TENDER- COAL _ _ _ 6 TONS.	T.P. PER-LB. PRESS. _ _ 162.82.	FIREBOX-HEIGHT AT FRONT _ _ 65"
STEAM PRESS- DESIGNED _ _ 200 LBS.	" . _ WATER _ 3000 GALS.	RATIO WT. ON DVRS. TO T.P. _ 4.40.	" - BACK _ _ 64"
" -WORKING _ _ 160 "	RATIO OF HEAT'G. SUR. TO GRATE AR. 56.9	HEAT'G. SUR. OF TUBES _ _ 1140.0 SQ.FT.	JOURNALS-DRIVERS _ 8"DIA.x 9"LONG.
WT. ON DRIVERS _ _ _ _ 114700 "	" " CYL. VOL. 148.94	" " FIREBOX 129.0 " .	" -TENDER 3¾"- x 7" "
" . OF ENGINE _ _ _ _ 114700 "	TUBES-DIAMETER _ _ _ _ 2"	" " TOTAL _ 1269.0 " "	
" . " TENDER-EMPTY 28010 "	" - LENGTH _ _ _ _ 11'-3"	GRATE AREA _ _ _ _ 22.3 " "	
" . " -LOADED 65000 "	" -NUMBER _ _ _ _ 195	FIREBOX-LENGTH _ _ _ _ 98 INS.	
TOTAL WT. OF ENG. & TENDER 179700 "	T.P. 85% WORKING PRESS. 26050.	" - WIDTH _ _ _ _ 32¼"	

Class A-8

Three locomotives from Rogers, originally placed in Old Class 7A, comprised Class A-8. These were built in 1900 as GN 70-72. These engines had clean lines and were by far the largest 0-6-0's yet received by the Great Northern, with engine weights of 137,000 pounds and a tractive effort of 26,050 pounds Diagrams indicate that the weight may have been decreased in later life, though this could also be a drafting error. They had 19-inch by 26-inch cylinders and 49-inch drivers. A 1936 assignment roster shows them as assigned to the Willmar Division, probably indicating that they were used in the Twin Cities area.

Class A-9

Class A-9 was the largest class of 0-6-0's on the Great Northern, with a total of 76 locomotives in the group. They came closest to being the "standard" 0-6-0's on the GN, and were used on all divisions throughout the system. The engines were received in six different orders, the first ten arriving from Rogers in 1903 as 73-82. These (and the following orders) had 19-inch by 26-inch cylinders and 49-inch drivers when delivered. In 1905 six additional locomotives, 83-88, were received from Alco-Rogers. Great Northern itself built the next ten locomotives, numbered as 14-23, in 1906. In 1907 Baldwin delivered twenty additional A-9's. These were numbered as GN 2-11, 52-55, and 89-94. Great Northern's Dale Street (St.Paul) Shops completed ten more in 1907, numbered as 1, 12, 24-26, 49-51, 56 and 57. The final twenty locomotives were delivered by Baldwin in 1912 as 380-399. Diagrams indicate that when received, the engine weights were 135,000 pounds. With the 49-inch drivers, the tractive effort was 28,490 pounds, but many of the locomotives were rebuilt during their service lives with 52-inch drivers, which decreased the tractive effort to 26,850 pounds. Total weights increased during the engines' service lives, ultimately reaching 142,800 pounds (for the engines with 49-inch drivers) and 147,000 pounds (for those with 52-inch drivers).

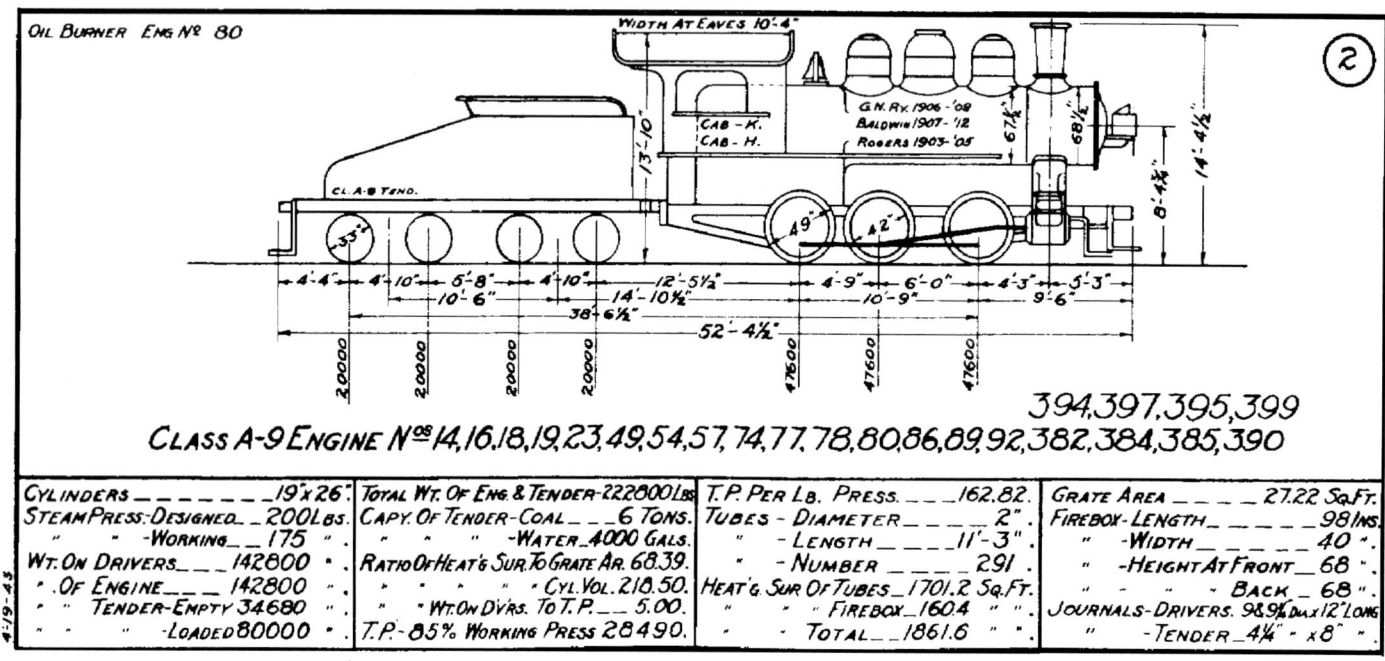

CLASS A-9 ENGINE Nos 14,16,18,19,23,49,54,57,74,77,78,80,86,89,92,382,384,385,390

CYLINDERS _____ 19"x 26"	TOTAL WT. OF ENG. & TENDER-222800 Lbs.	T.P. PER LB. PRESS. ____162.82.	GRATE AREA _____ 27.22 Sq.Ft.
STEAM PRESS-DESIGNED __200 Lbs.	CAP'Y. OF TENDER-COAL ___ 6 TONS.	TUBES - DIAMETER _____ 2".	FIREBOX-LENGTH _____98 INS.
" - WORKING__ 175 ".	" " " -WATER 4000 GALS.	" -LENGTH ____ 11'-3".	" -WIDTH ____ 40 ".
WT. ON DRIVERS___ 142800 ".	RATIO OF HEAT'G. SUR. TO GRATE AR. 68.39.	" -NUMBER ____ 291.	" -HEIGHT AT FRONT__ 68 ".
" OF ENGINE___ 142800 ".	" " " " CYL. VOL. 218.50.	HEAT'G. SUR. OF TUBES 1701.2 Sq.Ft.	" " " BACK _ 68 ".
" " TENDER-EMPTY 34680 ".	" WT. ON DVRS. TO T.P. 5.00.	" " FIREBOX 160.4 " ".	JOURNALS-DRIVERS 9 & 9¼ DIA x 12" LONG.
" " -LOADED 80000 ".	T.P.-85% WORKING PRESS 28490.	" - TOTAL__1861.6 " ".	" -TENDER 4¼" - x 8" ".

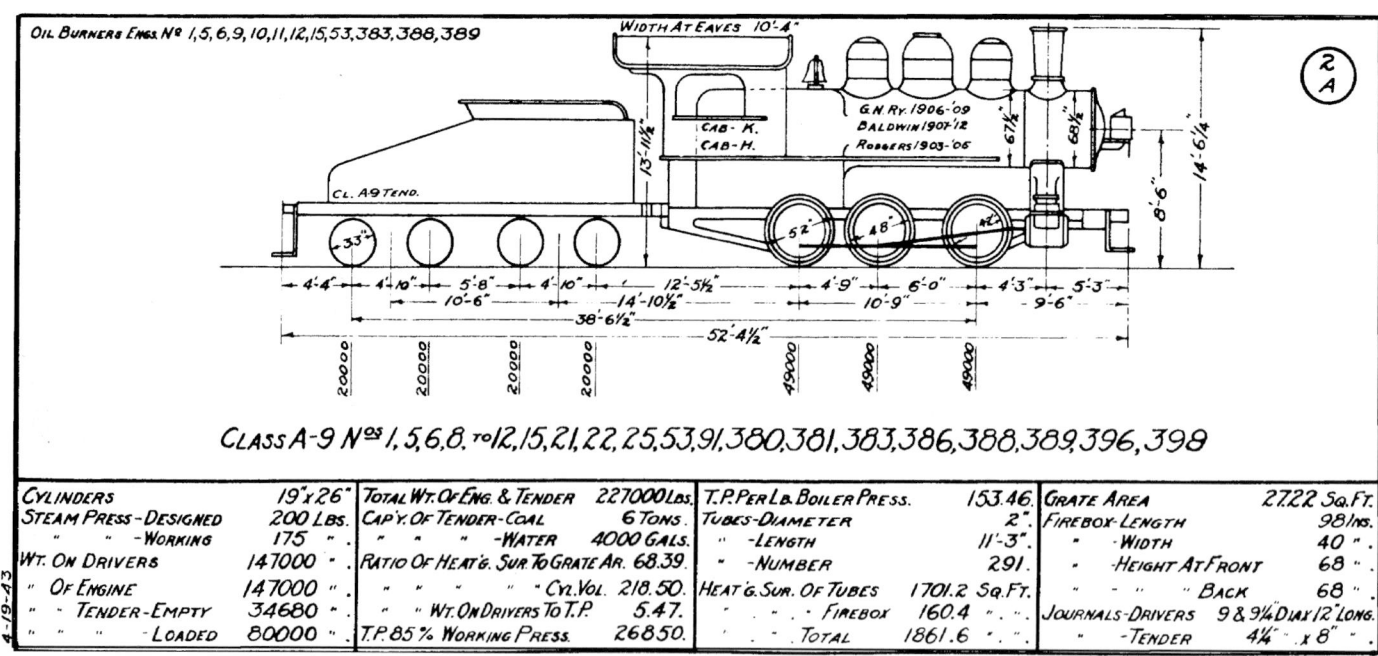

CLASS A-9 Nos 1,5,6,8, To 12,15,21,22,25,53,91,380,381,383,386,388,389,396,398

CYLINDERS 19"x 26"	TOTAL WT. OF ENG. & TENDER 227000 Lbs.	T.P. PER LB. BOILER PRESS. 153.46.	GRATE AREA 27.22 Sq.Ft.
STEAM PRESS-DESIGNED 200 LBS.	CAP'Y. OF TENDER-COAL 6 TONS.	TUBES-DIAMETER 2".	FIREBOX-LENGTH 98 INS.
" " -WORKING 175 ".	" " " -WATER 4000 GALS.	" -LENGTH 11'-3".	" -WIDTH 40 ".
WT. ON DRIVERS 147000 ".	RATIO OF HEAT'G. SUR. TO GRATE AR. 68.39.	" -NUMBER 291.	" -HEIGHT AT FRONT 68 ".
" OF ENGINE 147000 ".	" " " " CYL. VOL. 218.50.	HEAT'G. SUR. OF TUBES 1701.2 Sq.Ft.	" BACK 68 ".
" - TENDER-EMPTY 34680 ".	" WT. ON DRIVERS TO T.P. 5.47.	" " " FIREBOX 160.4 " ".	JOURNALS-DRIVERS 9 & 9¼ DIA x 12" LONG.
" " -LOADED 80000 ".	T.P. 85% WORKING PRESS. 26850.	" " TOTAL 1861.6 " ".	" -TENDER 4¼" x 8" ".

Class A-9 engine 28 was photographed at Minneapolis on July 19, 1940. John Westphal photograph from the John Luecke Collection.

No. 78 still has a wood pilot beam and No. 2 air pump in this 1930's scene taken at Minneapolis.
Robert Graham photograph from the collection of William Raia.

GN No. 1 was photographed at Vancouver, BC, in October 1939. It shows the steam dome
cover with the slight bulge at the base. Collection of Harold K. Vollrath.

GN No. 5 was photographed at Spokane, in 1939. It shows the steam dome cover with the slightly flared base. Collection of Norman F. Priebe.

*GN No. 15 shows the straight steam dome cover, and was photographed at
Vancouver, BC, on October 6, 1943. Stan F. Styles Collection of GTC Collectibles.*

Engine 385, with a larger No. 5 air pump, was photographed at Williston, ND, in 1940. GNRHS Collection.

What appears to be a "builders photograph" of A-9 386 provides a nice view of the rear of the tender. Great Northern Railway photograph from the collection of Wolfgang Weber.

No. 395, a Baldwin engine built in 1912, is seen at Fargo, ND, in 1945. GNRHS Collection.

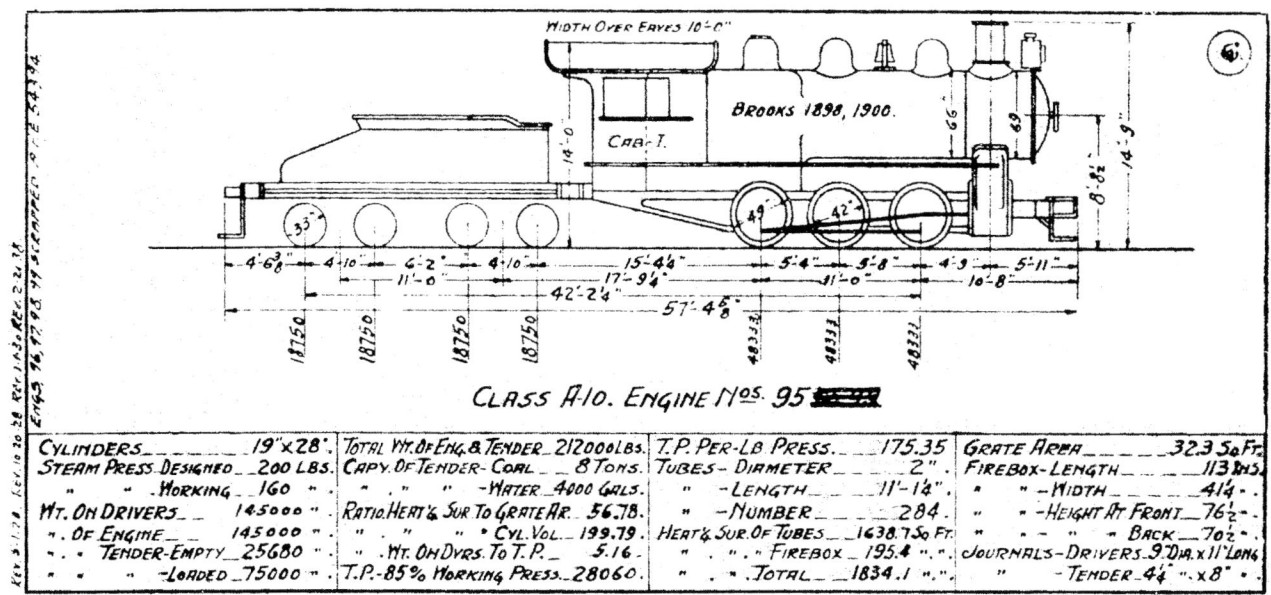

CLASS A-10. ENGINE NOS. 95 ~~~~~

CYLINDERS __ 19"x28".	TOTAL WT. OF ENG. & TENDER 212000 LBS.	T.P. PER-LB PRESS. __ 175.35	GRATE AREA __ 32.3 SQ.FT.
STEAM PRESS. DESIGNED __ 200 LBS.	CAPY. OF TENDER-COAL __ 8 TONS.	TUBES-DIAMETER __ 2".	FIREBOX-LENGTH __ 113 INS.
" . " -WORKING __ 160 "	" . " -WATER _4000 GALS.	" -LENGTH __ 11'-1¼".	" -WIDTH __ 41¼"
WT. ON DRIVERS __ 145000 "	RATIO. HEAT'G SUR. TO GRATE AR. _ 56.78.	" -NUMBER __ 284.	" -HEIGHT AT FRONT _76½"
" . OF ENGINE __ 145000 "	" . " . " CYL. VOL. _199.79	HEAT'G SUR. OF TUBES __1638.7 SQ.FT.	" -BACK __ 70½"
" . TENDER-EMPTY __ 25680 "	" . WT. ON DVRS. TO T.P. _ 5.16.	" . " . FIREBOX _ 195.4 "	JOURNALS-DRIVERS 9"DIA.x11"LONG
" . " -LOADED _ 75000 "	T.P.-85% WORKING PRESS. _28060.	" . " . TOTAL __ 1834.1 " " .	" -TENDER 4¼" x 8".

*Class A-10 engine 27, sublettered for the Montana Central, became GN 86(2nd) in 1899, and then GN 96(2nd) in 1905.
The arched cab windows are somewhat unusual for the Great Northern. ALCO Historic Photos.*

*While not noted on diagrams, A-10 No. 98 appears to have piston valves in this photograph
at an unknown date and location. Collection of James R. Vyverberg.*

*Number 30 is at Minneapolis in July 1934. While the A-11 class had piston valves, they still had the obsolete
Stephenson valve gear, despite being constructed in 1916. Collection of Kenneth R. Middleton.*

It is interesting that three different shapes of steam dome covers were used with the A-9's. Nearly all of the photographs seen by the authors of locomotives purchased from other builders (one exception was found) show steam dome covers that "flare" into the boiler with a gradual curve. However, the engines built by GN in 1906 and 1907 show two different types of domes. Some show a steam dome cover with a slight bulge at the base, while others show dome covers that are quite straight, contacting the top of the boiler at nearly a 90-degree angle. A number of physical modifications were made to the locomotives during their service lives. Somewhat more than half of the engines received a second No. 2 New York air pump in the mid to late 1920's. It might be noted that some of the A-9's had the air pumps on the fireman's side,

and others on the engineer's side. In the 1930's and 1940's, thirteen of these then had the double pumps replaced with a single No. 5 air pump. A few received steel pilot beams from 1918 through 1926. Many of the engines that had not been scrapped by the late 1930's received either Baldwin, Alco or Ragonnet power reverse gear. In the mid to late 1940's, many of the remaining engines received either Nathan or Barco low water alarms.[2]

Most of the A-9's lasted until the late 1940's or early 1950's, when they were replaced with diesel-electric switchers. In 1944, GN renumbered it's diesel locomotives from the 5000-series to lower numbers and four of the A-9's in the 73-94 series were renumbered as 26-29 to clear numbers for EMD SW-1's. In 1950, six more were renumbered into

No. 31 served the GN until after World War II. However, this view gives the impression there was a surplus of smaller power at the time. The locomotive is at Minneapolis in early summer of 1937. GNRHS Collection.

A-11 31, acquired from the Arthur Iron Mining Company (a Great Northern Iron Ore Property), is at Minneapolis in 1940. Collection of Norman F. Priebe.

390-series numbers which had been vacated by scrapping. These were renumbered from the 1-12 and 14-26 series to clear numbers for Alco-GE S-12's and GMD/EMD SW-9's. It is interesting to note that the number 13 was skipped in the A-9 numbering sequence, but this was done because there was still an A-1 locomotive occupying that number when the A-9's were received.

Class A-10

The A-10 locomotives were built by Brooks. The first three were constructed in 1898 as Montana Central 9, 27 and 28 and were originally in Old Class 8(3rd). The final two were received in 1900 as Eastern of Minnesota 88 and 89, and were placed in Old Class 8A. All had 19-inch by 28-inch cylinders, 49-inch drivers and engine weights of 137,000 pounds The Montana Central locomotives were renumbered as GN 85-87 about 1900. All five of the locomotives were renumbered as GN 95-99 in 1905. In 1936 all of them were assigned to the Willmar Division, probably indicating use in the Twin Cities terminals. Most received steel pilot beams from 1918-1920.[3] While the diagrams do not list these engines as having piston valves (which

the diagrams normally would have during the time these engines were used), photographs show what appear to be piston valves. They were retired and scrapped in the late 1930's.

Class A-11

The final six-coupled switchers on the Great Northern were numbers 30 and 31, classified as A-11. These had been constructed by Lima Locomotive Works in 1916 as part of an order of eight locomotives constructed for "Great Northern Iron Ore Properties" (GNIOP) as numbers 201-208.[4] Great Northern New Equipment Registers indicate that 30 was originally Grant Iron Mining Company 203, while 31 was originally Arthur Iron Mining Company 204. The locomotives were acquired by the GN in 1917. The disposition of the remaining six GNIOP locomotives is unknown. The A-11 locomotives had 20-inch by 24-inch cylinders, 49-inch drivers, and engine weights of 130,000 pounds They were clean-lined engines with radial stay fireboxes and piston valves. These engines were both assigned to the Willmar division. No. 30 was scrapped in 1939, while No. 31 was sold to the Midland Railway Company of Manitoba in 1946.

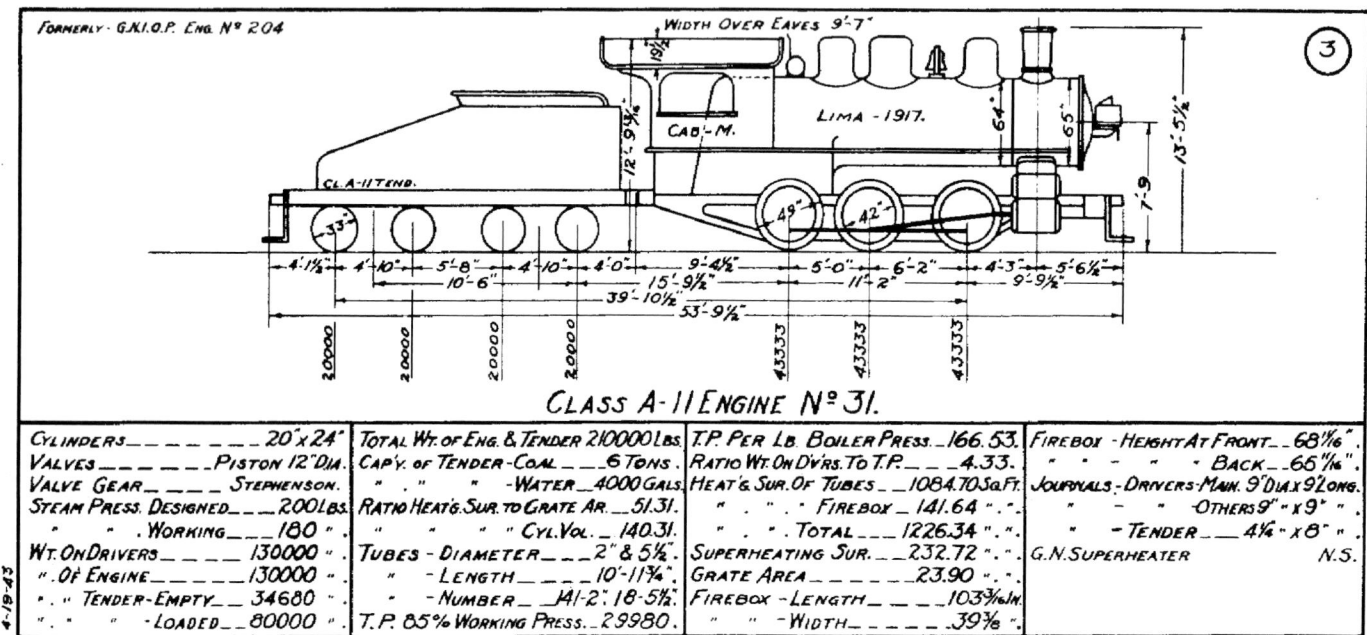

CLASS A-11 ENGINE Nº 31.

CYLINDERS _ _ _ _ _ _ _ 20"x 24"	TOTAL WT. OF ENG. & TENDER 210000 Lbs.	T.P. PER LB. BOILER PRESS. _ 166.53.	FIREBOX - HEIGHT AT FRONT _ _ 68¹¹⁄₁₆".
VALVES _ _ _ _ _ _ PISTON 12"DIA.	CAP'Y. OF TENDER-COAL _ _ _ 6 TONS.	RATIO WT. ON DVRS. TO T.P. _ _ _ 4.33.	" - " - " - BACK _ _ 65¹¹⁄₁₆".
VALVE GEAR _ _ _ _ STEPHENSON.	" . " " -WATER _ 4000 GALS.	HEAT'G. SUR. OF TUBES _ _ 1084.70 SQ.FT.	JOURNALS - DRIVERS-MAIN. 9"DIA x 9"LONG.
STEAM PRESS. DESIGNED _ _ _ 200 LBS.	RATIO HEAT'G. SUR. TO GRATE AR. _ 51.31.	" . " . " FIREBOX _ 141.64 ".."	" - " - OTHERS 9" x 9" ".
" - " . WORKING _ _ _ 180 ".	" " " " CYL. VOL. _ 140.31.	" . " . " TOTAL _ _ _ 1226.34 ".".	" - " - TENDER _ _ 4¼" x 8" ".
WT. ON DRIVERS _ _ _ _ _ 130000 ".	TUBES - DIAMETER _ _ _ 2" & 5½".	SUPERHEATING SUR. _ _ 232.72 ".".	G.N. SUPERHEATER _ _ N.S.
" .OF ENGINE _ _ _ _ _ 130000 ".	" - LENGTH _ _ _ _ 10'-11¾".	GRATE AREA _ _ _ _ _ 23.90 ".".	
". " TENDER-EMPTY _ _ 34680 ".	" - NUMBER _ _ 141-2". 18-5½".	FIREBOX - LENGTH _ _ _ _ 103³⁄₈ IN.	
" . " " -LOADED _ _ 80000 ".	T.P. 85% WORKING PRESS. _ 29980.	" " -WIDTH _ _ _ _ _ 39⅜ ".	

Notes:

1. Great Northern Railway Annual Report, Machinery Department, June 30, 1891.
2. Great Northern Railway Company Equipment Completion Report and Unit Record of Property Changes – Equipment (URPC).
3. Ibid.
4. William D. Edson and John H. White, "Lima Locomotive Works," The Railway and Locomotive Historical Society Bulletin No. 123, pp. 81-102, October 1970

This early view of the Wm. Crooks was taken at Elk River, MN in 1864 and illustrates the original shotgun (straight) boiler. Great Northern Railway.

Chapter 6
Class B 4-4-0 American Standard

The American Standard 4-4-0 wheel type was by far the most common among GN's predecessor roads. In fact many 4-4-0's were acquired and then sold before they ever actually received a B classification. Consequently, rather than treating these locomotives in order of B classes, they will be addressed in chronological order of their acquisition. It should also be noted that none of the B class locomotives were purchased by the Great Northern – all were inherited from predecessors. Also, none had Belpaire fireboxes. All of the St.Paul & Pacific (StP&P) locomotives were wood burners. These early locomotives also used crosshead-driven water pumps to introduce

water into the boiler. Shortly after the St.Paul, Minneapolis & Manitoba (StPM&M) took over the StP&P, it began converting the locomotives to coal burners and replacing water pumps with injectors. Entries in the Historic Engine Record indicate that the conversion to coal burning was well under way by late 1880, and the replacement of pumps with injectors by 1881.

The following table lists the various B classes on the roster after October 1903. It also gives their old class numbers and the numbers of the locomotives assigned to them. As one can see, the B classes were not applied in either chronological order or in order of the old classes.

Class	Old Class	Modern Numbers	Original Numbers	Builder	Date Built
B-1	5(2nd)	240	StP&P 16	Danforth	1869
B-2	6, 17	11/244, 243	StP&P 17, NP 20(1)	Pittsburgh, Baldwin	1870, 1871
B-3	13	241, 242, 248	StP&P 18, 19, 26	Pittsburgh	1870, 1875
B-4	16	245, 249, 250, 252	NP 22(1), [StP&P 47, 48, 50]	Baldwin	1871, 1879
B-5	19	255, 256, 259, 262, 265, 266	StP&P 27, 28, 31, 34, 39, 40	Rogers	1878
B-6	11(2nd)	232-237, 238	SC&N 1-4, 8, 10, PSL 13	Rogers, Rhode Island	1890, 1889
B-7	12(2nd)	139	S&N 2	New York	1890
B-8	14	288-293	StPM&M 72-77	Pittsburgh	1880
B-9	15	187-189, 191-195	StPM&M 67, 78, 79, 81-85	Pittsburgh	1881
B-10	18	268-272, 274, 281, 282	StPM&M 67, 117, 53-55, 58, 64, 65	Baldwin	1880-1882
B-11(1st)	20	294	StP&P 43	Rogers	1879
B-11(2nd)	---	141, 142	SF&N 6, 5	Baldwin	1890
B-12	23	143, 144	StP&D 16, 17	Rogers	1882
B-13	24	100-104, 106, 107, 109-111, 113	StPM&M 100-104, 106, 107, 109-111, 113	Baldwin	1882
B-14	24	117-120, 122-124	StPM&M 52, 118, 62, 120. 122-124	Baldwin	1880-1882
B-15	25	125-133	StPM&M 125-133	Schenectady	1882
B-16	26	135-138	StPM&M 135-138	Rhode Island	1882
B-17	28	145, 147, 149	StPM&M 145, 147, 149	Grant	1882
B-18	29	150, 151	StPM&M 150. 151	Brooks	1882
B-19	30	152-186	StPM&M 152-186	Brooks	1882-1883
B-20	33	197-206	StPM&M 197-206	Rhode Island	1882-1883
B-21	34	207-225	StPM&M 207-225	Rogers	1887
B-22	34A	226-230	EM 101-105	Rogers	1888-1889
B-23	---	231	N&FS 7	Baldwin	1893

The Wm. Crooks *is shown here at the end of its service life at Havre, MT, in 1900. This may be the earliest photo to show the wagon-top boiler now installed. It would be restored in 1908 to honor James J. Hill. Minnesota Historical Society.*

The earliest 4-4-0's were of course the *Wm. Crooks* and the *Edmund Rice*, originally acquired by the Minnesota and Pacific in 1861. The original specifications for the *Wm. Crooks* and *Edmund Rice* have not been found. The locomotives were similar when received, both being 4-4-0 American type engines having straight boilers, and built by the same manufacturer at nearly the same time. If they were in fact identical (as some have speculated), then it is far more likely the cylinder dimensions of both were originally 12 by 22 inches, rather than 14 by 22 inches. The earliest document found, an 1867 report of the St. Paul and Pacific, does not show the locomotives as identical. In 1865 the *Rice* had already undergone major repairs. By May 1867 the *Rice* had 54-inch drivers, 14 by 22-inch cylinders and weighed 8,000 pounds more than the *Crooks*. The *Crooks* had 12 by 22-inch cylinders and 60-inch drivers. The *Crooks* had received minor repairs by that date, and then received major repairs in 1869, following the June 1867 fire. The *Crooks* received a new wagontop boiler in 1881 and by that time had 63-inch diameter drivers. It received a straight stack in 1887. At some time during its service life, the *Edmund Rice* was apparently renamed *Sarachet*. Both locomotives remained on the roster until the StP&P was acquired by the St. Paul, Minneapolis & Manitoba (StPM&M) on June 14, 1879. It should be noted that driving wheel

diameters are the authors' best estimates of the original diameters. Shop records indicate that the tires were turned periodically and large amounts of metal (nearly an inch in some cases) were removed during this process. These shop records commonly list driver diameter over the tires in fractional measurements (e.g. 62 13/16 inches).

When the early class system was implemented, the *Crooks* was placed in Class 1 and the *Rice* was most likely placed in Class 2(1st). The *Rice* was scrapped in 1887, while the *Crooks* went on to become Great Northern No. 1, ultimately being rebuilt as an exhibition engine. For further information on the *Crooks* and the *Rice*, please consult "Iron Brothers – The Crooks and the Rice" by Walter F. Becker (originally published in the Railway and Locomotive Historical Society *Bulletin No. 107*, October 1962; later reprinted by the Great Northern Railway Historical Society as Reference Sheet No. 198, March 1993).

In 1863, the StP&P acquired its third locomotive, the *Minnesota* (No. 3). This was another 4-4-0 with 12-inch by 22-inch cylinders and 56-inch drivers. The locomotive had been built by Norris Locomotive Works of Philadelphia, and may well have been acquired used. At some time during its service life the name was changed to *B. L. Drake* and later *Pacific*. The disposition of this locomotive is unknown, as it left the roster before the StP&P was acquired by the StPM&M, the

StP&P No. 2, the Edmund Rice, *on the original bridge across the Mississippi River at St. Cloud, MN, on September 4, 1877. Photo by N. J. Trenham, Courtesy of the Stearns History Museum.*

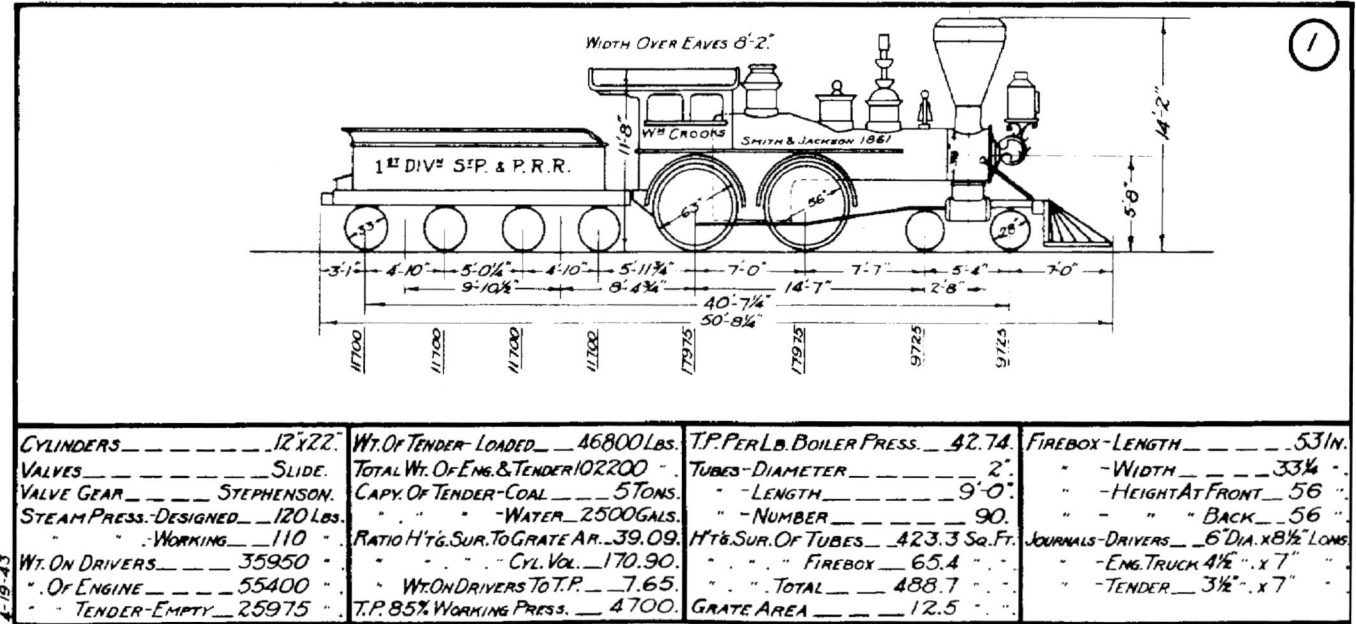

CYLINDERS	12"x22"	WT. OF TENDER-LOADED	46800 Lbs.	T.P. PER LB. BOILER PRESS.	42.74	FIREBOX-LENGTH	53 IN.
VALVES	SLIDE.	TOTAL WT. OF ENG. & TENDER	102200 "	TUBES-DIAMETER	2".	" -WIDTH	33¾ "
VALVE GEAR	STEPHENSON.	CAPY. OF TENDER-COAL	5 TONS.	" " -LENGTH	9'-0".	" -HEIGHT AT FRONT	56 "
STEAM PRESS.-DESIGNED	120 Lbs.	" " -WATER	2500 GALS.	" " -NUMBER	90.	" " -BACK	56 "
" " -WORKING	110 "	RATIO H'T'G.SUR. TO GRATE AR.	39.09.	H'T &.SUR. OF TUBES	423.3 Sq. Ft.	JOURNALS-DRIVERS	6" DIA. x 8½" LONG
WT. ON DRIVERS	35950 "	" " " -CYL. VOL.	170.90.	" " " FIREBOX	65.4 " "	" -ENG. TRUCK 4½". x 7"
" " OF ENGINE	55400 "	WT. ON DRIVERS TO T.P.	7.65.	" " " TOTAL	488.7 " "	" -TENDER 3½". x 7"
" " TENDER-EMPTY	25975 "	T.P. 85% WORKING PRESS.	4700.	GRATE AREA	12.5 " "	

only StP&P locomotive to do so. This engine is believed to have been lost to quicksand in the Cedar Lake region of western Minneapolis during the construction of the StP&P.[1] The Historical Engine Record attributes the loss to an accident, without details.[2] As a result of the early departure of StP&P 3 from the roster, the authors do not believe this locomotive ever received a class number. The authors are not aware of any photographs or drawings of StP&P 3.

Local lore also has locomotives lost in mud or quicksand during construction at Howard Lake, MN, at Schinghamer Lake, west of Avon, MN and at "Happy Hollow" between Richmond and Roscoe, MN, but GN records found to date show no such loss. Perhaps the engines were owned by contractors or the Northern Pacific.

A fourth locomotive, the *Itasca*, No. 4, was acquired used from the Dayton & Union Railroad in early 1865. It had 14-inch by 20-inch cylinders and only 48-inch drivers (at least by 1880), with an engine weight of 48,000 pounds. It had been built by John Souther. It was sold in 1882, and probably did not receive a class number. This locomotive was built following English conventions and featured an outside frame.

The *Anoka*, No. 5, was built by the Danforth Locomotive and Machine Co. in 1866. This American type had 16-inch by 22-inch cylinders, 60-inch drivers, a wagon-top boiler and a weight of 66,000 pounds, thus being the largest locomotive yet received. This engine was most likely original member of Class 6, which later became more of a catch-all class for engines rebuilt with smaller drivers for switching service. It was renumbered as 4 in the major locomotive renumbering of 1899, and was sold in 1902, thus never receiving a modern class number.

Locomotive Nos. 6 and 7 (*St. Paul* and *St. Cloud*) were built in 1865, but not placed in service until 1866. Great Northern documents indicate that they were built by Norris Locomotive Works. While they probably were delivered with 16-inch by 22-inch cylinders, the 1880 Historic Engine Record indicates that by 1880 No. 6 had 16-inch by 24-inch cylinders, No. 7 had 16-inch by 22-inch cylinders, and both had 60-inch drivers. They weighed approximately 64,000 pounds. These were probably placed in Class 5(1st), but were both sold in 1888 before they could receive a modern class number. In September of 1867 StP&P No. 8, the *Geo. L. Becker* (named for the president of the First Division

This photo of St. P&P No. 4 (Itasca) at St. Paul is undated. Note the outside frame and that it did not have a pilot. Collection of Jerrold F. Hilton.

The Anoka, StP&P 5, is shown in its glory days before it was rebuilt with 49-inch drivers for switching service. R.V. Nixon Collection.

company), was built by Mason Machine Works as its construction number 270. This 4-4-0 had 14-inch by 22-inch cylinders, 63-inch drivers and a total engine weight of 57,600 pounds. It was placed in Class 10(1st), but was dismantled in 1893 without receiving a modern class. The authors are not aware of any photographs or drawings of StP&P 6, 7 or 8.

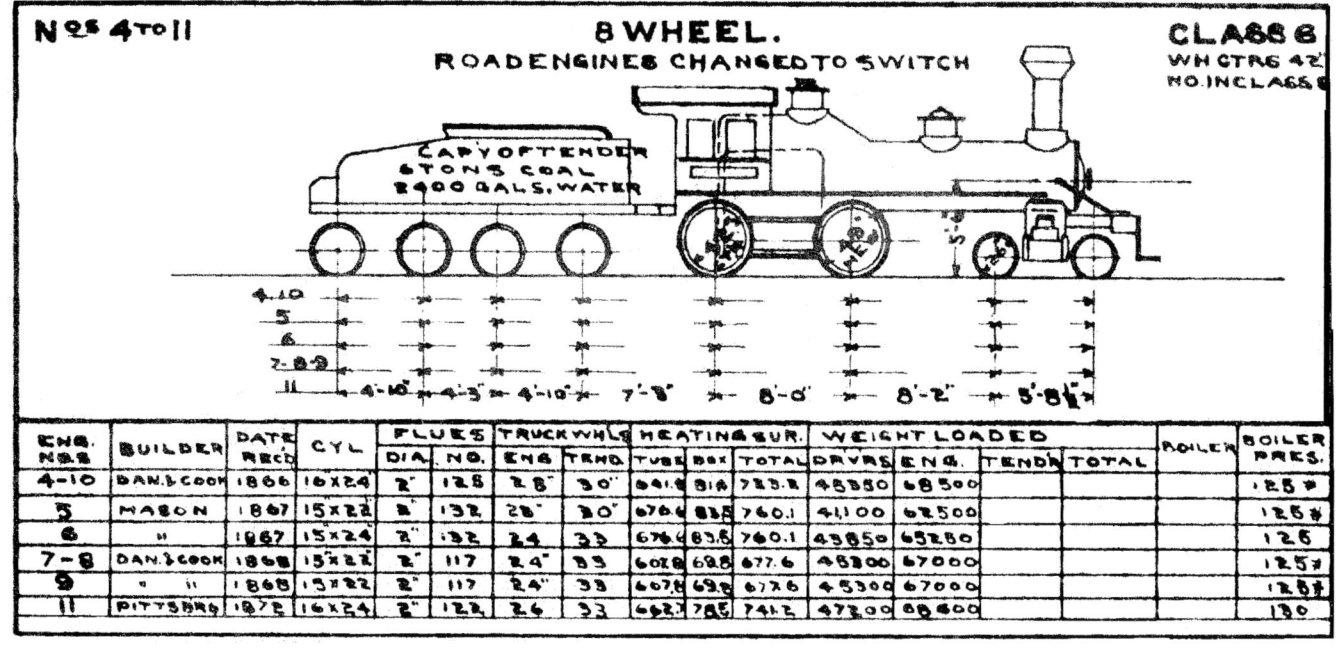

ENG. NOS	BUILDER	DATE REC'D	CYL	FLUES DIA.	FLUES NO.	TRUCK WHLS ENG	TRUCK WHLS TEND	HEATING SUR. TUBE	HEATING SUR. BOX	HEATING SUR. TOTAL	WEIGHT LOADED DRVRS	WEIGHT LOADED ENG	WEIGHT LOADED TEND'R	WEIGHT LOADED TOTAL	BOILER	BOILER PRES.
4-10	DAN. & COOK	1866	16×24	2"	125	28"	30"	641.8	81.4	723.2	45350	68500				125#
5	MASON	1867	15×22	2"	132	28"	30"	676	83.6	760.1	41100	62500				125#
6	"	1867	15×24	2"	132	24	33	676	83.6	760.1	43850	65280				125
7-8	DAN. & COOK	1868	15×22	2"	117	24"	33	608	69.8	677.6	45300	67000				125#
9	" "	1868	15×22	2"	117	24"	33	607.6	69.8	677.6	45300	67000				125#
11	PITTSBRG	1872	16×24	2"	122	26	33	662.7	78.5	741.2	47300	68600				130

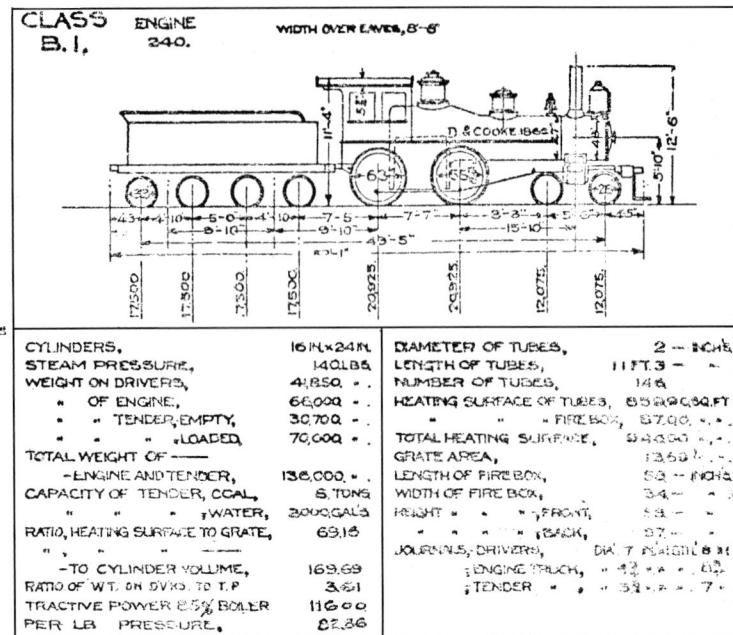

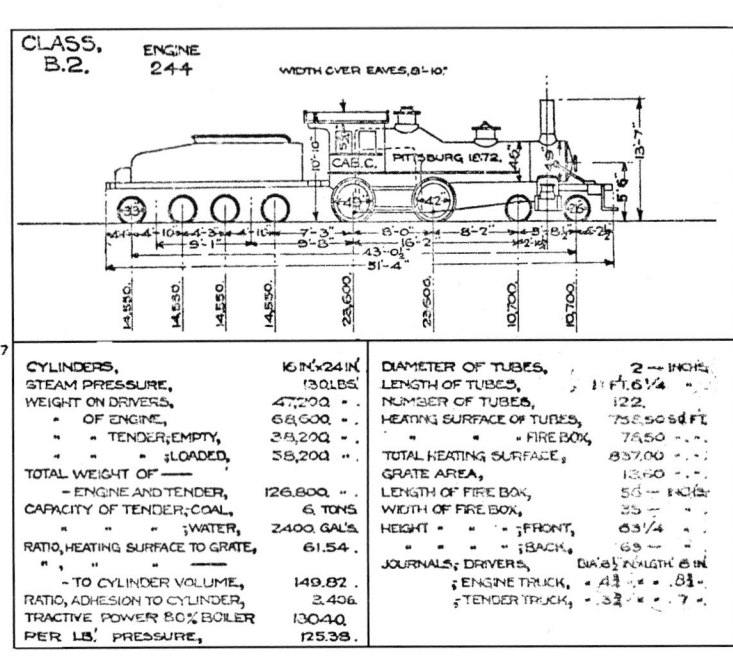

Two additional StP&P locomotives were built by Mason in 1868. No. 9, the *F. R. Delano* (superintendent of the StP&P), was built in May 1868 as construction number 279. It had 15-inch by 24-inch cylinders, 63-inch drivers and a weight of 62,750 pounds. No. 10, the *Jared Benson* (an StP&P director), was built in July 1968 with 15-inch by 22-inch cylinders, 63-inch cylinders and a weight of 60,000 pounds. A fourth Mason engine, the *Jud Rice* (No. 11), was not received until 1869. It had 15-inch by 24-inch cylinders, 63-inch drivers and a weight of 62,750 pounds. Nos. 9 and 11 were placed in Class 11(1st) while No. 10 was placed in Class 12(1st). No. 9 was sold in 1898, while Nos. 10 and 11 became 5 and 6 in the 1899 renumbering. All three were rebuilt in the early 1890's with smaller drivers for switching. No. 9 was moved at this time to Class 9(2nd) while the other two were moved to Class 6, by that time a catch-all for a number of dissimilar American types rebuilt with low drivers for switching. None of these engines lasted long enough to receive modern class numbers. Photographs or diagrams of these engines have not been found.

The StP&P turned to Danforth for its next order, three locomotives obtained during 1868. Nos. 12, 13 and 14 (the *Wayzata, Willmar* and *Litchfield*) were again 4-4-0's. These engines had 15-inch by 22-inch cylinders, 63-inch drivers and weighed 64,500 pounds. They were placed in Class 7(1st) with the implementation of the class system. However, in they early 1890's these engines were rebuilt with 49-inch drivers for switching and were moved to Class 6. In 1899 they were renumbered as 7, 8 and 9. All were scrapped or sold before receiving modern class designations.

Two additional Danforth locomotives were built in 1869. No. 15 (*H. Trott*, named for the company's land commissioner) and No. 16 (*Kerkhoven*, named after an Amsterdam stockbroker) were 4-4-0's with 16-inch by 24-inch cylinders, 63-inch drivers and weights of 66,000 pounds. These engines were probably placed in Class 8(1st) and 9(1st) when the class system was implemented. In 1891 No. 15 was rebuilt with smaller drivers and moved to Class 6. It was renumbered as 10 in 1899 and sold in 1902. No. 16 was renumbered as 240 in 1899, remaining as a road service engine. In late 1903 No. 240 became the sole member of Class B-1. No photographs of these engines are known to the authors.

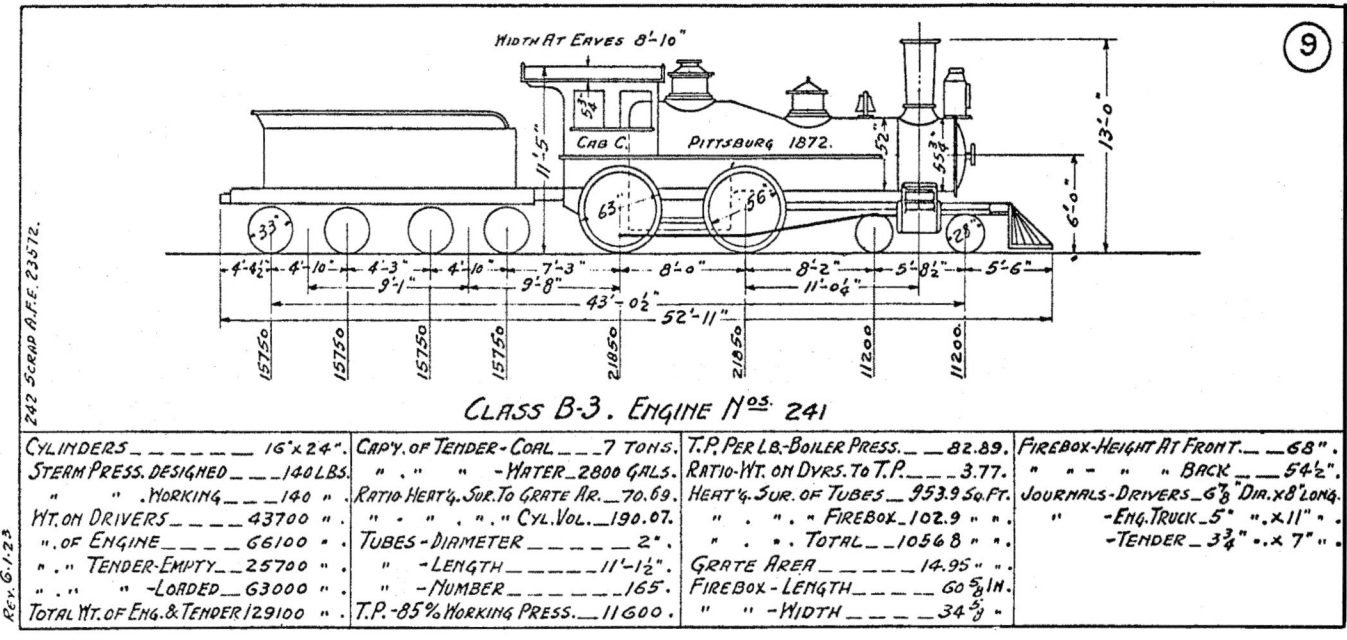

The next locomotive order, built in 1870, went to the Pittsburgh Locomotive and Car Works. Nos. 17-19 (*Chippewa*, *Hancock*, and *C. N. Parker*) had 16-inch by 24-inch cylinders, 63-inch drivers and weighed 66,100 pounds. No. 17 was rebuilt with smaller drivers in 1893 and moved to Class 6. In 1899 it was renumbered as 11, and in 1907 as 244. Nos. 18 and 19 were renumbered as 241 and 242 in 1899. In 1903 No. 244 was placed in Class B-2. Nos. 241 and 242 became Class B-3 engines.

Four locomotives built in 1871 had been ordered by the Northern Pacific, but were diverted to the St. Paul & Pacific (the StP&P was temporarily under NP control at the time). Nos. 20-23 were built by Baldwin Locomotive Works and were received in December 1871. These engines had 15-inch by 24-inch cylinders, 63-inch drivers and weights of 68,800 pounds when delivered. No. 22 was rebuilt prior to 1880 with 16-inch by 24-inch cylinders. Only one of these locomotives (No. 22) was known to be named, as *J. H. Randall*. Whether this is truly the case or whether the names of the other locomotives have simply been lost is unknown. When the class system was implemented, Nos. 20, 21 and 23 were placed in Class 17 while No. 22 was placed in Class 16. In 1899 they were renumbered as 243-246. While 244 and 246 did not last until 1903, 243 became a member of Class B-2 in that year. No. 245 was placed in Class B-4.

No. 241, built by Pittsburgh in 1870 and originally named Hancock, *lasted until 1926. This Class B-3 engine is at Grand Forks, ND, near the end of its life but still in good condition. Great Northern Railway, Carl L. Ulrich Collection.*

We are fortunate to have both the engineer's and fireman's side views of the 241. Here it is at Grand Forks in February 1924. Collection of Harold K. Vollrath.

Three additional locomotives (Nos. 24-26) were obtained in 1875, this time from Pittsburgh Locomotive and Car Works. They had 16-inch by 24-inch cylinders and 63-inch drivers, with engine weights of 72,700 pounds, the heaviest engines yet received. No evidence has been found that these engines carried names. They were placed in Class 13. No. 25 was scrapped in 1898, while Nos. 24 and 26 were renumbered as GN 247 and 248 in 1899. No. 247 was rebuilt as a weed burner in 1902. In 1903 No. 248 was placed in Class B-3. No photographs of these engines are known to exist.

With the massive construction effort to complete the StP&P, the largest locomotive order placed by that road was given to Rogers Locomotive Works. Sixteen locomotives, Nos. 27-42, were delivered from June through October of 1878. These engines, again 4-4-0's, had 16-inch by 24-inch cylinders, 58-inch drivers and weighed 66,170 pounds each. No. 38 was also named *G. W. Turner*. Whether the others were unnamed or the names have been lost is unknown to the authors. These engines were placed in Class 19 and later had their driver

Class B-3 No. 241 had a remarkably long service life of 56 years. It still appeared in good condition in this view at Grand Forks, ND, with a few years left to go. Great Northern Railway.

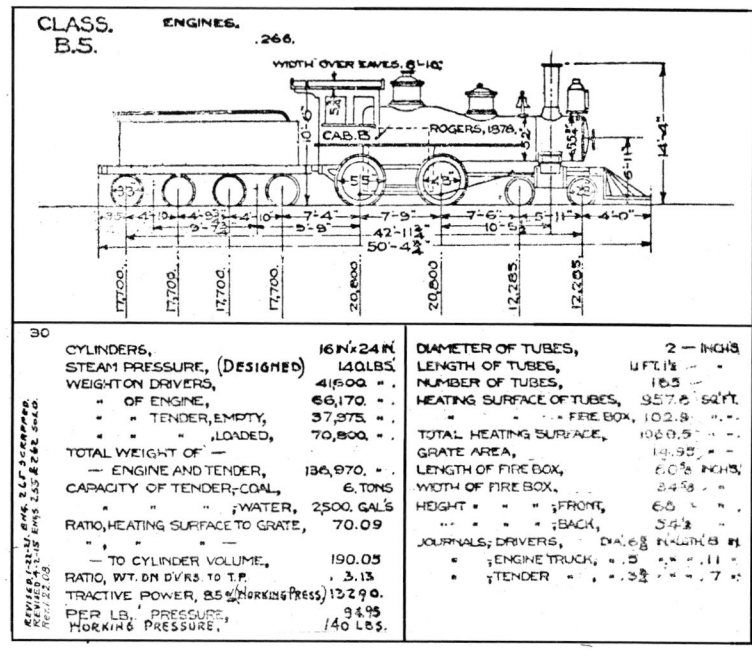

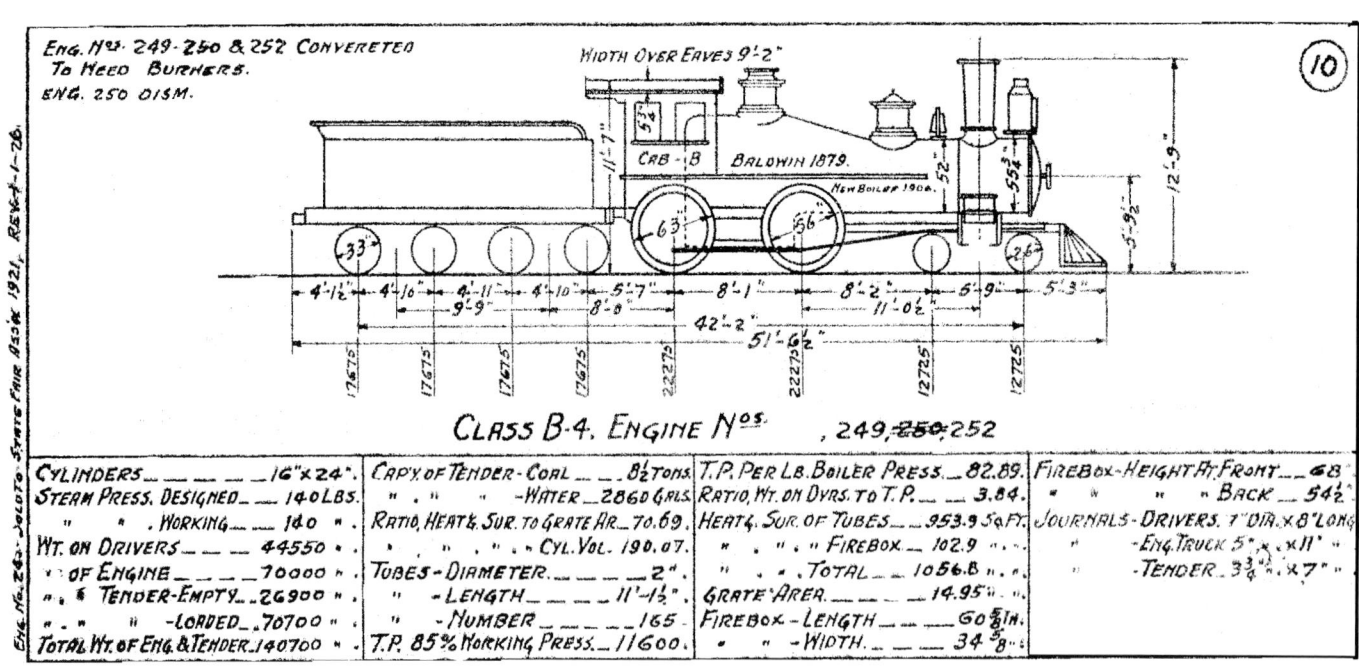

Baldwin-built number 23 was power for the excursion train ready to depart Crookston, MN, for Devils Lake, ND, to celebrate completion of the line to that point on July 4, 1883. It was twelve years old at the time. Collection of Harold K. Vollrath.

StP&P 38, G. W. Turner, *was built by Rogers in 1878. ALCO Historic Photos.*

StPM&M 35 was photographed at Melrose, MN, in April 1880. This engine later became GN 263, a member of Class B-5. Collection of William Bissinger.

diameters reduced to 55 inches. They served for many years with both the StPM&M and the Great Northern. While three (Nos. 37, 38 and 42) were scrapped before the 1899 renumbering, the rest became GN 255-267. Those remaining on the roster in late 1903 were placed in modern Class B-5.

In January 1879, the final locomotives received by the StP&P arrived. Two of these were 4-4-0's from Rogers. Nos. 43 and 44 had 16-inch by 24-inch cylinders, 58-inch drivers and weighed 70,300 pounds. In the 1890's the driver diameter was reduced to 55 inches. They were placed in Old Class 20. In 1899 they were renumbered as GN 294 and 295. While 295 was scrapped in 1902, the 294 was placed in modern Class B-11(1st).

A final order of four American Standard locomotives had been placed by the StP&P, but these were not delivered until November 1879, and therefore were delivered to the StPM&M. These were produced by Baldwin and had 16-inch by 24-inch cylinders, 63-inch drivers and weighed 70,000 pounds each. They had been ordered as StP&P Nos. 47-50, but were delivered as StPM&M 47-50. These were apparently deemed similar enough to StP&P/StPM&M No. 22 to be placed with it in Class 16. In 1899 they were renumbered as GN 249-252. The three remaining on the roster in late 1903 were placed in modern Class B-4 along with the former StP&P 22. No photographs are known to exist.

The StPM&M soon began ordering its own locomotives. Their program of building extensions and branch lines and purchasing smaller railway lines (at least some of which it had financed) required more motive power. From March through May of 1880 16 new 4-4-0's, later placed in Class 18, were received. These were numbered as 52-67, and had 17-inch by 24-inch cylinders, 58-inch drivers and weighed approximately 70,000 pounds These engines had also been built by Baldwin. Shortly after their receipt, No. 67 was renumbered as 51(2nd), filling a vacant number originally received by an 0-4-0. Two of these locomotives (52 and 62) were rebuilt with 63-inch drivers and moved to Class 24A. The remainder had the driver size reduced to 55 inches. The two locomotives with 63-inch drivers were renumbered as 117 and 119 in 1899, and were placed in Class B-14 in 1903. The other 14 were renumbered as 268, 270-278, and 280-283 in 1899, and placed in Class B-10 in 1903. It is interesting to note that Great

Northern records indicate that six of these locomotives (as well as several from other classes) were "Sold to B&O RR" in 1900, though no evidence of them on the Baltimore & Ohio has yet turned up. One of this class (No. 282) had its driver size increased to 63 inches in 1918. The authors know of no photographs of these engines.

The StPM&M turned to Pittsburgh Locomotive and Car Works for its next two locomotive orders. Nos. 68-77, later placed in Class 14, were received in August and September 1880. They had 17-inch by 24-inch cylinders, 58-inch drivers and weighed 73,400 pounds In the 1890's the driver diameter was reduced to 55 inches, and in 1899 they were renumbered as 284-293. In 1903 those remaining on the roster were assigned Class B-8. One of these locomotives, No. 290, received 63-inch drivers and spent part of its service life in Canada on the Victoria Terminal Railway and Ferry Company and the Victoria and Sidney.

Pittsburgh 4-4-0's 67(2nd) (numbered to fill in a blank number) and 78-86, later placed into Class 15, were received from March through May of 1881. They had 17-inch by 24-inch cylinders, 63-inch drivers and weighed 74,800 pounds In 1899 they were renumbered as 187-196. Those still on the roster were placed in Class B-9 in 1903, and received new boilers from 1905 to 1907. The last surviving members of the class were assigned to the Willmar, Dakota, Butte and Minot Divisions.

1882 turned out to be a banner year for StPM&M locomotive orders, as over 70 American Standard locomotives were received. 94 and 95, built by Rogers for the St.Paul and Duluth, a Northern Pacific subsidiary, as its Nos. 16 and 17, were apparently diverted to the StPM&M. Rogers records show them as having been completed in February 1882, and Great Northern records show them as having been received in March 1882. They had 17-inch by 24-inch cylinders, 63-inch drivers, weighed 77,500 pounds and were placed in Class 23. These engines were renumbered as 143 and 144 in 1887, and later were placed in Class B-12. No photos are known to exist.

Two 4-4-0's, Nos. 96 and 97, were received from Taunton Locomotive Manufacturing Company in late May 1882. They were placed in Class 27(1st) and had 17-inch by 24-inch cylinders, 63-inch driving wheels and weighed 78,100 pounds. Immediately upon delivery, they were renumbered as 140 and 141. Three additional Class 27(1st)

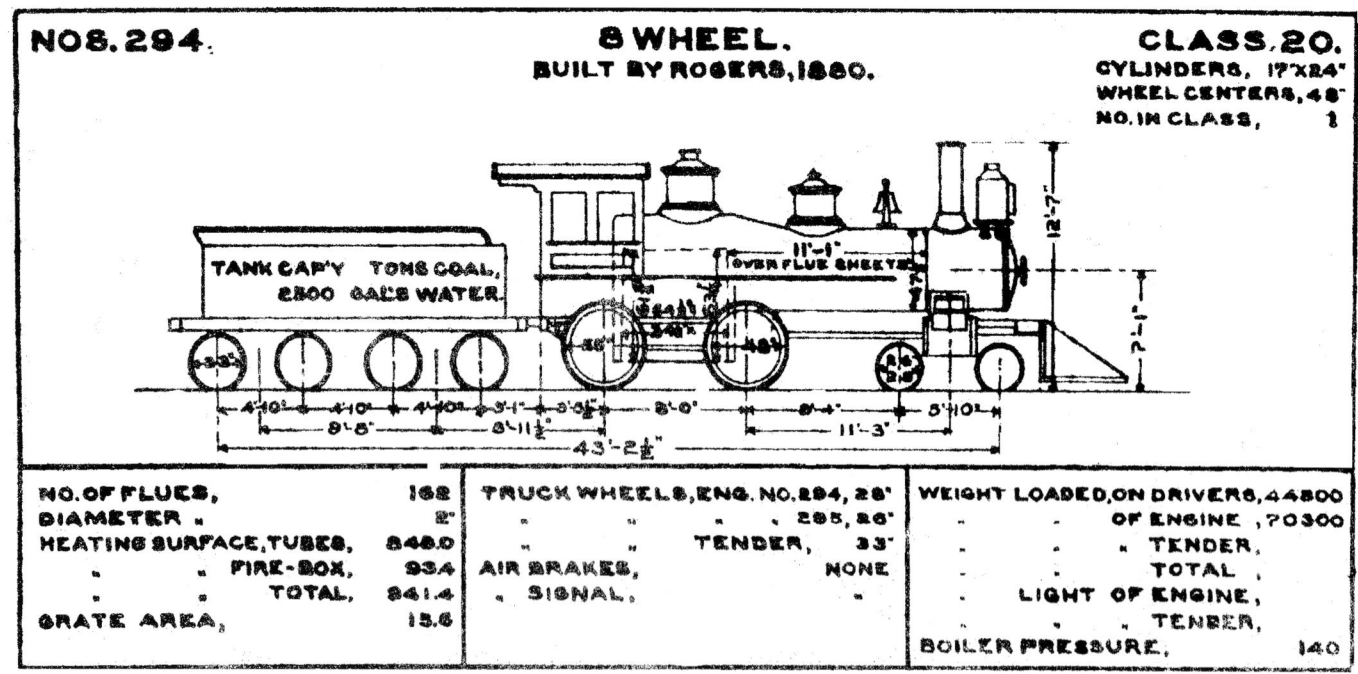

NOS. 294.	8 WHEEL. BUILT BY ROGERS, 1880.	CLASS, 20. CYLINDERS, 17"X24" WHEEL CENTERS, 48" NO. IN CLASS, 1

NO. OF FLUES,	168	TRUCK WHEELS, ENG. NO. 294, 26"		WEIGHT LOADED, ON DRIVERS, 44800	
DIAMETER "	2"	" " " 295, 26"		" " OF ENGINE , 70300	
HEATING SURFACE, TUBES,	848.0	TENDER, 33"		" " " TENDER,	
" " FIRE-BOX,	93.4	AIR BRAKES,	NONE	" " TOTAL,	
" " TOTAL,	941.4	" SIGNAL,		LIGHT OF ENGINE,	
GRATE AREA,	15.6			" " " TENDER,	
				BOILER PRESSURE,	140

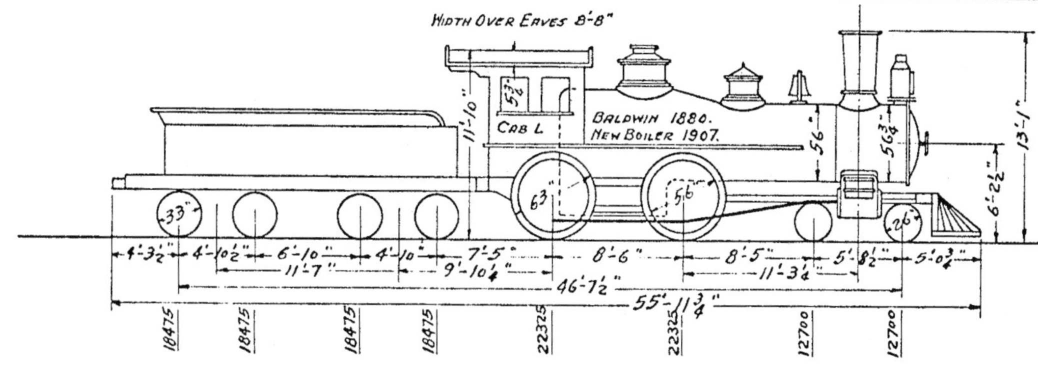

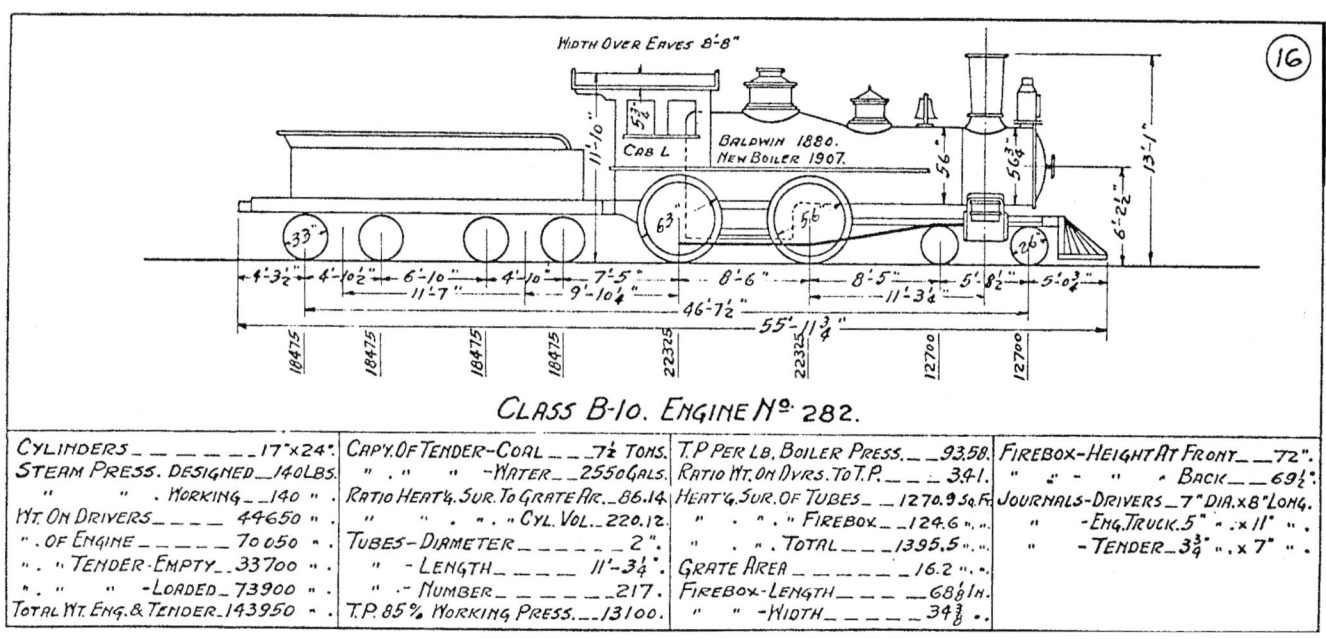

CLASS B-10. ENGINE No. 282.

Cylinders — 17"×24".	Cap'y. of Tender-Coal — 7½ Tons.	T.P. per Lb. Boiler Press. — 93.58.	Firebox-Height at Front — 72".
Steam Press. Designed — 140 Lbs.	" " " -Water — 2550 Gals.	Ratio Wt. on Dvrs. to T.P. — 3.41.	" " " -Back — 69½".
" " Working — 140 " .	Ratio Heat'g. Sur. to Grate Ar. — 86.14	Heat'g. Sur. of Tubes — 1270.9 Sq.Ft.	Journals-Drivers — 7" Dia.×8" Long.
Wt. on Drivers — 44650 " .	" " " Cyl. Vol. — 220.12.	" " " Firebox — 124.6 " " .	" -Eng. Truck 5" " ×11" " .
" of Engine — 70050 " .	Tubes-Diameter — 2".	" " " Total — 1395.5 " " .	" -Tender — 3¾" " ×7" " .
" " Tender-Empty — 33700 " .	" -Length — 11'-3¼".	Grate Area — 16.2 " " .	
" " " -Loaded — 73900 " .	" -Number — 217.	Firebox-Length — 68⅛ In.	
Total Wt. Eng. & Tender — 143950 " .	T.P. 85% Working Press. — 13100.	" -Width — 34⅜ " .	

Eng. Nos ~~288~~ & 289 Have 63" Drivers and 30" Eng. Tr. Wheel.

Eng. 291 Dismantled A.F.E. 24363. A.F.E. 27841.
Eng. 288

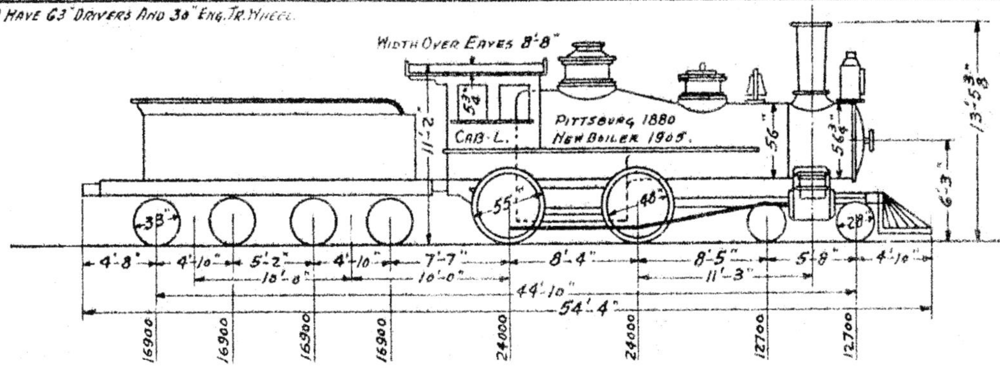

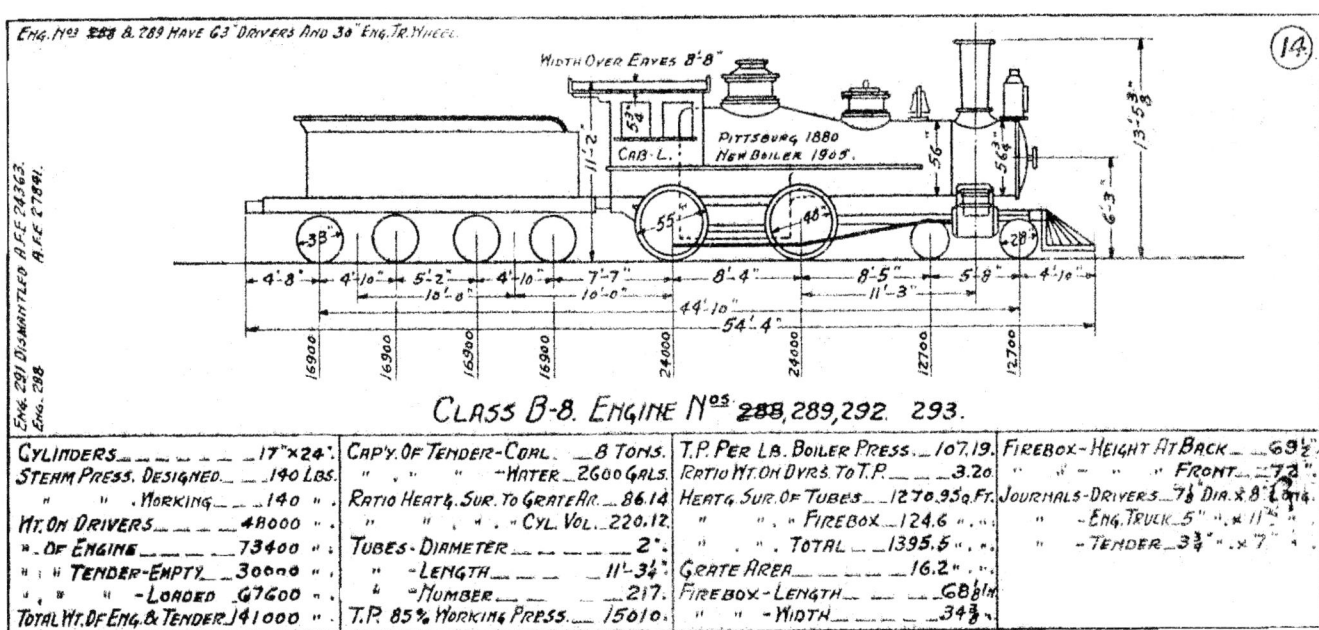

CLASS B-8. ENGINE Nos ~~288~~, 289, 292. 293.

Cylinders — 17"×24".	Cap'y. of Tender-Coal — 8 Tons.	T.P. per Lb. Boiler Press. — 107.19.	Firebox-Height at Back — 69½".
Steam Press. Designed — 140 Lbs.	" " " -Water — 2600 Gals.	Ratio Wt. on Dvrs. to T.P. — 3.20.	" " " Front — 72".
" " Working — 140 " .	Ratio Heat'g. Sur. to Grate Ar. — 86.14	Heat'g. Sur. of Tubes — 1270.9 Sq.Ft.	Journals-Drivers — 7⅛" Dia.×8" Long.
Wt. on Drivers — 48000 " .	" " " Cyl. Vol. — 220.12.	" " " Firebox — 124.6 " " .	" -Eng. Truck 5" " ×11" " .
" of Engine — 73400 " .	Tubes-Diameter — 2".	" " " Total — 1395.5 " " .	" -Tender — 3¾" " ×7" " .
" " Tender-Empty — 30000 " .	" -Length — 11'-3¼".	Grate Area — 16.2 " " .	
" " " -Loaded — 67600 " .	" -Number — 217.	Firebox-Length — 68⅛ In.	
Total Wt. of Eng. & Tender — 141000 " .	T.P. 85% Working Press. — 15010.	" -Width — 34⅜ " .	

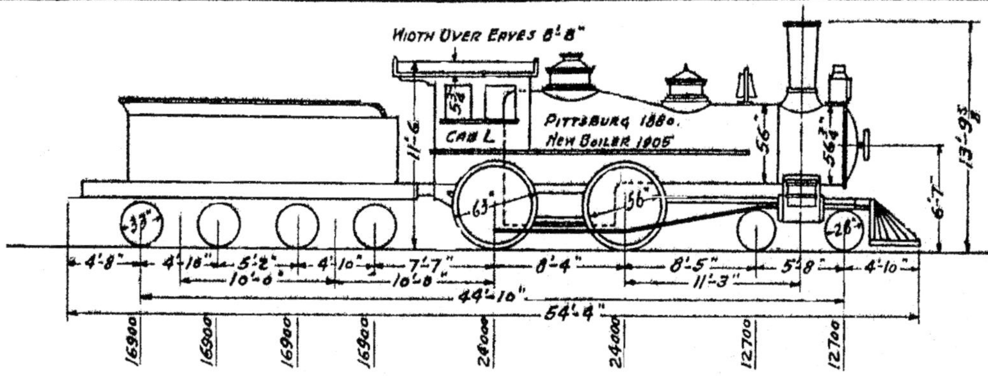

CLASS B-8. ENGINE No. 290. OIL BURNER.

Cylinders — 17"×24".	Cap'y. of Tender-Coal — 8 Tons.	T.P. per Lb. Boiler Press. — 93.58.	Firebox-Height at Front — 72".
Steam Press. Designed — 140 Lbs.	" " " -Water — 2600 Gals.	Ratio Wt. on Dvrs. to T.P. — 3.66.	" " " -Back — 69½".
" " Working — 140 " .	Ratio Heat'g. Sur. to Grate Ar. — 86.14.	Heat'g. Sur. of Tubes — 1270.9 Sq.Ft.	Journals-Drivers — 7⅛" Dia.×8" Long.
Wt. on Drivers — 48000 " .	" " " Cyl. Vol. — 220.12.	" " Firebox — 124.6 " " .	" -Eng. Truck 5" " ×11" " .
" of Engine — 73400 " .	Tubes-Diameter — 2".	" " Total — 1395.5 " " .	" -Tender — 3¾" " ×7" " .
" " Tender-Empty — 30000 " .	" -Length — 11'-3¼".	Grate Area — 16.2 " " .	
" " " -Loaded — 67600 " .	" -Number — 217.	Firebox-Length — 68⅛ In.	
Total Wt. of Eng. & Tender — 141000 " .	T.P. 85% Working Press. — 13100.	" -Width — 34⅜ " .	

Rev. 2.14.22.

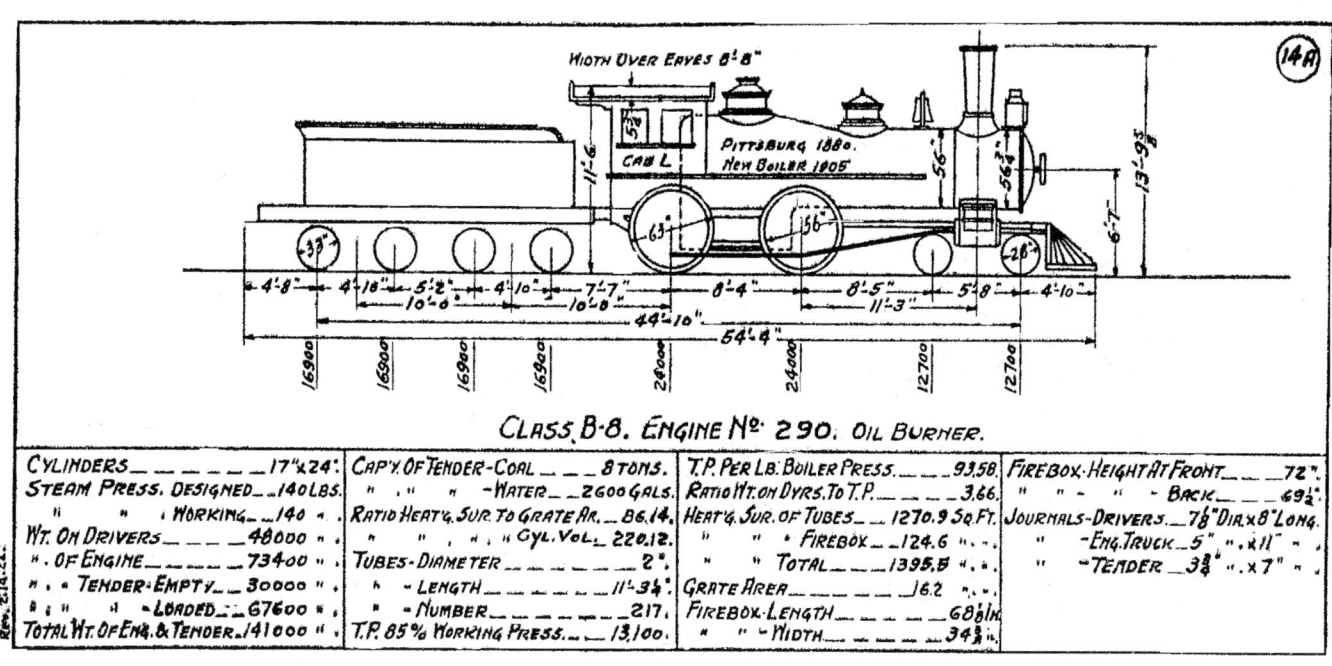

4-4-0's were received from Taunton in July 1882. They had the same dimensions as the two locomotives received in May. The July order engines were numbered as 142-144. All five of these locomotives were sold to the Mason City & Fort Dodge, three in 1886 and two in 1892.

Schenectady Locomotive Works provided 9 Class 25 locomotives, Nos. 125-133, in early 1882. These had the common place 17-inch by 24-inch cylinders and 63-inch drivers, and weighed 75,150 pounds. In 1903 they were placed in Class B-15. Most later received new boilers, and some lasted until the late 1930's. The final three, retired in 1937, were assigned to the Dakota Division.

Baldwin supplied 27 4-4-0's in 1882, all delivered in May of that year. These had 17-inch by 24-inch cylinders and 63-inch drivers, but actually fell into two different groups. Nos. 100-114 weighed 76,650 pounds and had wagontop boilers, while Nos. 115-124 weighed 72,700

This high angle view of the fireman's side of oil-burning B-8 No. 290 was taken at Everett, Washington on June 9, 1920. J. Foster Adams photograph from the GNRHS Collection.

The engineer's side view of No. 290 was taken at New Whatcom, WA, in 1900. Collection of Harold K. Vollrath.

pounds and had straight boilers. All were initially placed in Class 24. However, two of the lighter engines (117 and 119) later received 55-inch drivers and were moved to Class 18. These two locomotives were renumbered as 269 and 279 in 1899. No. 269 was placed in Class B-10 in 1903, while 279 was sold to the B&O. The remaining light locomotives kept the original 63-inch drivers and were moved to Class 24A about 1900. These were placed in Class B-14 in 1903. The heavier engines were placed in Class B-13. One of these, No. 103, a Spokane Division engine, was renumbered as GN 219 in 1944 to clear the number for an NW-2 being renumbered from the 5300-series. No. 219 lasted until July 1947.

Rhode Island Locomotive Works built six Class 26 4-4-0's (Nos. 134-139) in 1882, which were a little larger than the previous orders. They had 17-inch by 24-inch cylinders, 64-inch drivers and weighed 86,500 pounds Two of these were sold to the Butte, Anaconda & Pacific in 1893. The remaining engines were placed in Class B-16 in 1903.

B-9 192 was built in 1881, but received a new boiler in 1905. The engine is shown at St.Cloud, MN, in November 1938. It is less that a year from scrapping. Warren R. McGee photograph courtesy Railroad Museum of Pennsylvania (PHMC).

No. 192 was still in passenger service at St. Cloud early in 1938. GNRHS Collection.

B-9 193 still seems to be in immaculate condition in February 1924 at Grand Forks, ND, even though the main rods are missing. The locomotive was not retired until 1938. Railroad Museum of Pennsylvania (PHMC).

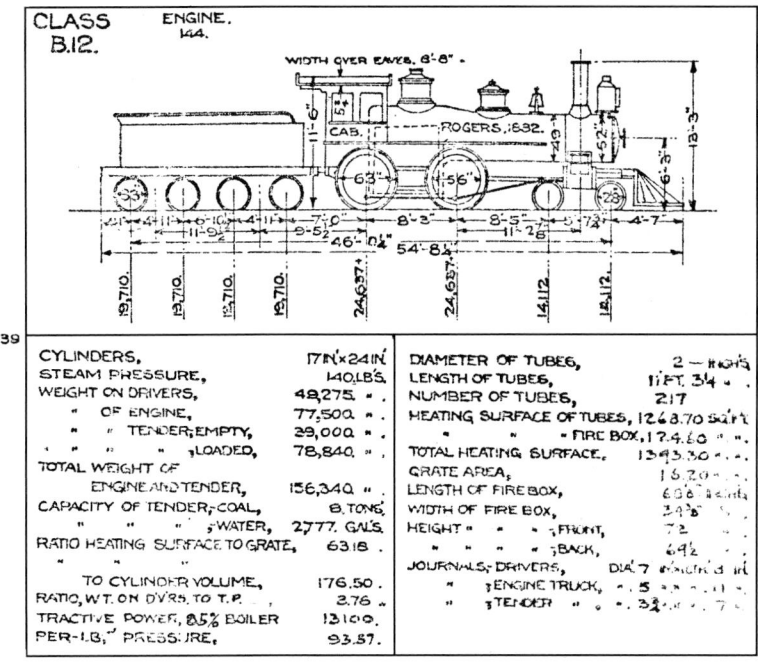

CYLINDERS,	17IN×24IN.	DIAMETER OF TUBES,	2 - INCHS
STEAM PRESSURE,	140.LBS.	LENGTH OF TUBES,	11 FT. 3¼ "
WEIGHT ON DRIVERS,	49,275 "	NUMBER OF TUBES,	217
" OF ENGINE,	77,500 "	HEATING SURFACE OF TUBES,	1268.70 SQ.FT.
" " TENDER; EMPTY,	29,000 "	" " FIRE BOX,	124.60 " "
" " ,LOADED,	78,840 "	TOTAL HEATING SURFACE,	1393.30 " "
TOTAL WEIGHT OF		GRATE AREA,	16.20 " "
ENGINE AND TENDER,	156,340 "	LENGTH OF FIREBOX,	69.6 INCHS
CAPACITY OF TENDER; COAL,	8. TONS.	WIDTH OF FIRE BOX,	34⅜ "
" " ; WATER,	2777. GALS.	HEIGHT " " ; FRONT,	72 "
RATIO HEATING SURFACE TO GRATE,	63.18 "	" " " ; BACK,	69½ "
		JOURNALS; DRIVERS,	DIA 7 INCHS LG 8 IN
TO CYLINDER VOLUME,	176.50 "	" ; ENGINE TRUCK,	" 5 " " " "
RATIO, WT. ON DVRS. TO T.P. ,	3.76 "	" ; TENDER,	" 3¾ " " " 7 "
TRACTIVE POWER, 85% BOILER	13100.		
PER-LB." PRESSURE,	93.57.		

CLASS B.12. ENGINE. 144.

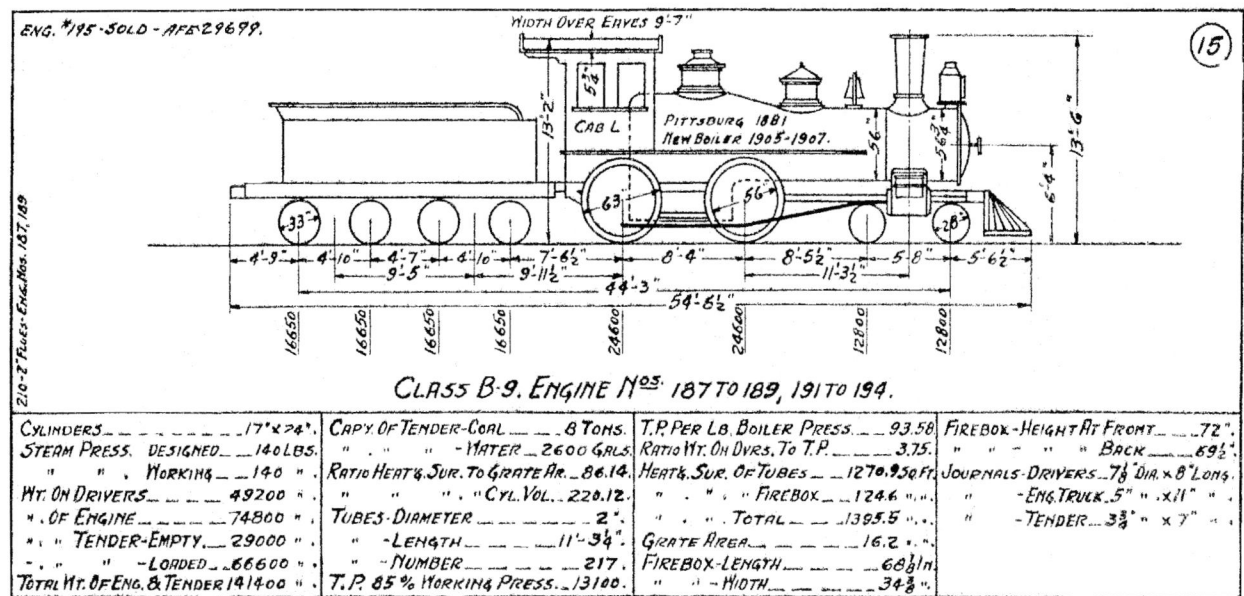

CLASS B-9. ENGINE N°S. 187 TO 189, 191 TO 194.

CYLINDERS	17"×24".	CAP'Y OF TENDER-COAL	8 TONS.	T.P. PER LB. BOILER PRESS.	93.58	FIREBOX-HEIGHT AT FRONT	72".
STEAM PRESS. DESIGNED	140 LBS.	" " -WATER	2600 GALS.	RATIO WT. ON DVRS. TO T.P.	3.75.	" " BACK	69½".
" " WORKING	140 "	RATIO HEAT'G SUR. TO GRATE AR.	86.14.	HEAT'G. SUR. OF TUBES	1270.95 SQ.FT.	JOURNALS-DRIVERS	7⅛"DIA × 8"LONG.
WT. ON DRIVERS	49200 "	" " " CYL. VOL.	220.12.	" " " FIREBOX	124.6 " "	" -ENG.TRUCK	5 " × 11 "
" OF ENGINE	74800 "	TUBES-DIAMETER	2".	" " TOTAL	1395.5 " "	" -TENDER	3¾ " × 7 "
" " TENDER-EMPTY	29000 "	" -LENGTH	11'-3¼"	GRATE AREA	16.2 " "		
" " -LOADED	66600 "	" -NUMBER	217	FIREBOX-LENGTH	68⅝ IN.		
TOTAL WT. OF ENG.& TENDER	141400 "	T.P. 85% WORKING PRESS.	13100.	" -WIDTH	34⅜ "		

ENG. #195-SOLD-AFE 29699. WIDTH OVER EAVES 9'-7" PITTSBURG 1881 NEW BOILER 1905-1907. (15)

210-2"FLUES-ENG. NOS. 187, 189

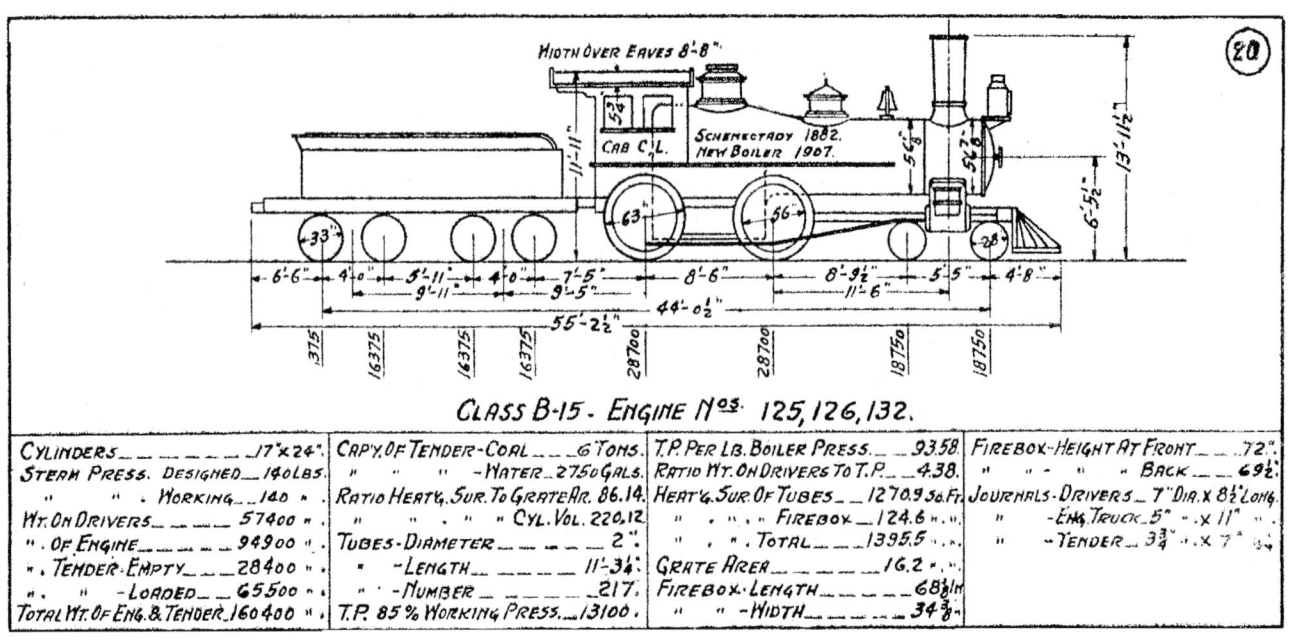

CLASS B-15 - ENGINE Nos. 125, 126, 132.

CYLINDERS ___17"x24".	CAP'Y. OF TENDER-COAL ___6 TONS.	T.P. PER LB. BOILER PRESS. ___93.58	FIREBOX-HEIGHT AT FRONT ___72".
STEAM PRESS. DESIGNED___140 LBS.	" " -WATER_2750 GALS.	RATIO WT. ON DRIVERS TO T.P. ___4.38	" " " BACK___69½
" " WORKING___140 "	RATIO HEAT'G. SUR. TO GRATE AR. 86.14	HEAT'G. SUR. OF TUBES ___1270.9 SQ.FT.	JOURNALS-DRIVERS ___7" DIA. x 8½ LONG
WT. ON DRIVERS___57400 "	" " " CYL. VOL. 220.12	" " " FIREBOX ___124.6 "	" -ENG. TRUCK 5" " x 11"
" OF ENGINE___94900 "	TUBES-DIAMETER ___2".	" " " TOTAL ___1395.5 "	" -TENDER 3¾" " x 7" "
" TENDER-EMPTY___28400 "	" -LENGTH ___11'-3¼"	GRATE AREA ___16.2 "	
" " -LOADED ___65500 "	" -NUMBER ___217	FIREBOX-LENGTH ___68⅛ IN.	
TOTAL WT. OF ENG. & TENDER. 160400 "	T.P. 85% WORKING PRESS. ___13100	" " -WIDTH ___34⅜ "	

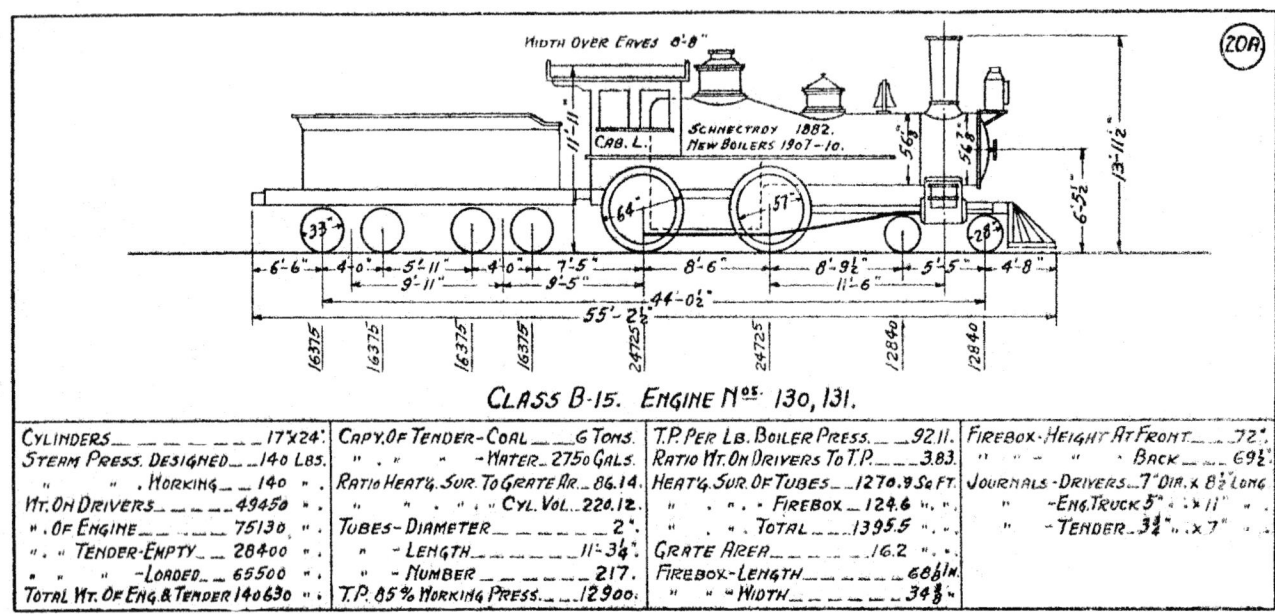

CLASS B-15 - ENGINE Nos. 130, 131.

CYLINDERS ___17"x24".	CAP'Y. OF TENDER-COAL ___6 TONS.	T.P. PER LB. BOILER PRESS. ___92.11	FIREBOX-HEIGHT AT FRONT ___72".
STEAM PRESS. DESIGNED___140 LBS.	" " -WATER_2750 GALS.	RATIO WT. ON DRIVERS TO T.P. ___3.83	" " " BACK___69½
" " WORKING___140 "	RATIO HEAT'G. SUR. TO GRATE AR. 86.14	HEAT'G. SUR. OF TUBES ___1270.9 SQ.FT.	JOURNALS-DRIVERS ___7" DIA. x 8½ LONG
WT. ON DRIVERS___49450 "	" " " CYL. VOL. 220.12	" " " FIREBOX ___124.6 "	" -ENG. TRUCK 5" " x 11"
" OF ENGINE___75130 "	TUBES-DIAMETER ___2".	" " " TOTAL ___1395.5 "	" -TENDER 3¾" " x 7" "
" " TENDER-EMPTY___28400 "	" -LENGTH ___11'-3¼"	GRATE AREA ___16.2 "	
" " -LOADED ___65500 "	" -NUMBER ___217	FIREBOX-LENGTH ___68⅛ IN.	
TOTAL WT. OF ENG. & TENDER 140630 "	T.P. 85% WORKING PRESS. ___12900	" " -WIDTH ___34⅜ "	

B-15 125 was photographed in 1922 at Devils Lake, ND, pulling a tender from a much later locomotive class. J. Foster Adams photograph from the GNRHS Collection

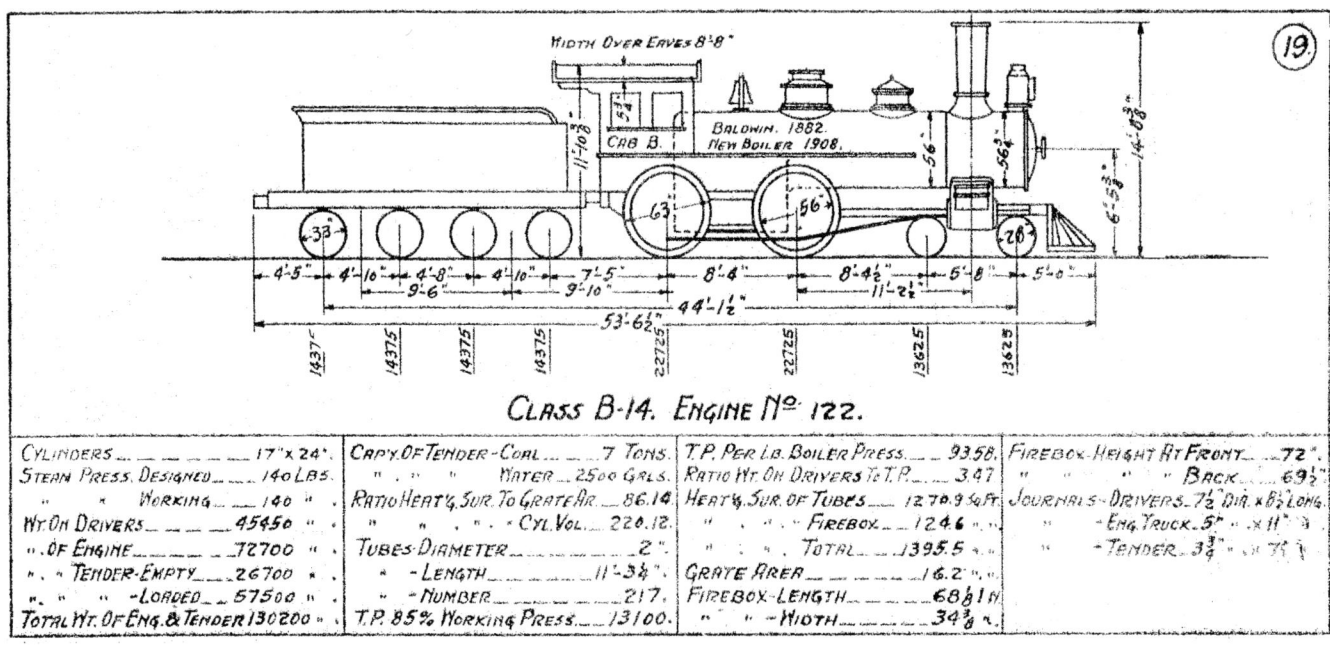

CLASS B-14. ENGINE Nº 122.

CYLINDERS _ _ _ _ _ _ _ 17"x24".	CAP'Y. OF TENDER-COAL _ _ 7 TONS.	T.P. PER LB. BOILER PRESS. _ 93.58.	FIREBOX-HEIGHT AT FRONT _ _ 72".
STEAM PRESS. DESIGNED _ _ 140 LBS.	" " " WATER _ 2500 GALS.	RATIO WT. ON DRIVERS TO T.P. _ 3.47.	" " " BACK _ _ 69½".
" " WORKING _ _ 140 "	RATIO HEAT'G. SUR. TO GRATE AR. _ 86.14	HEAT'G. SUR. OF TUBES _ _ 1270.9 SQ.FT.	JOURNALS-DRIVERS 7½" DIA. x 8½" LONG.
WT. ON DRIVERS _ _ _ _ 45450 "	" " " " CYL. VOL. 220.12	" " " FIREBOX _ _ 124.6	" -ENG.TRUCK. 5" " x 11" "
" .OF ENGINE _ _ _ _ 72700 "	TUBES-DIAMETER _ _ _ _ _ 2".	" " " TOTAL _ _ 1395.5 " "	" -TENDER _ 3¾" " x 7" "
" " TENDER-EMPTY _ 26700 "	" -LENGTH _ _ _ _ 11'-3¾"	GRATE AREA _ _ _ _ _ 16.2 " "	
" " " -LOADED _ 57500 "	" -NUMBER _ _ _ _ _ 217.	FIREBOX-LENGTH _ _ _ _ 68 3/8 IN	
TOTAL WT. OF ENG. & TENDER 130200 "	T.P. 85% WORKING PRESS. _ 13100.	" " -WIDTH _ _ _ _ 34 3/8 "	

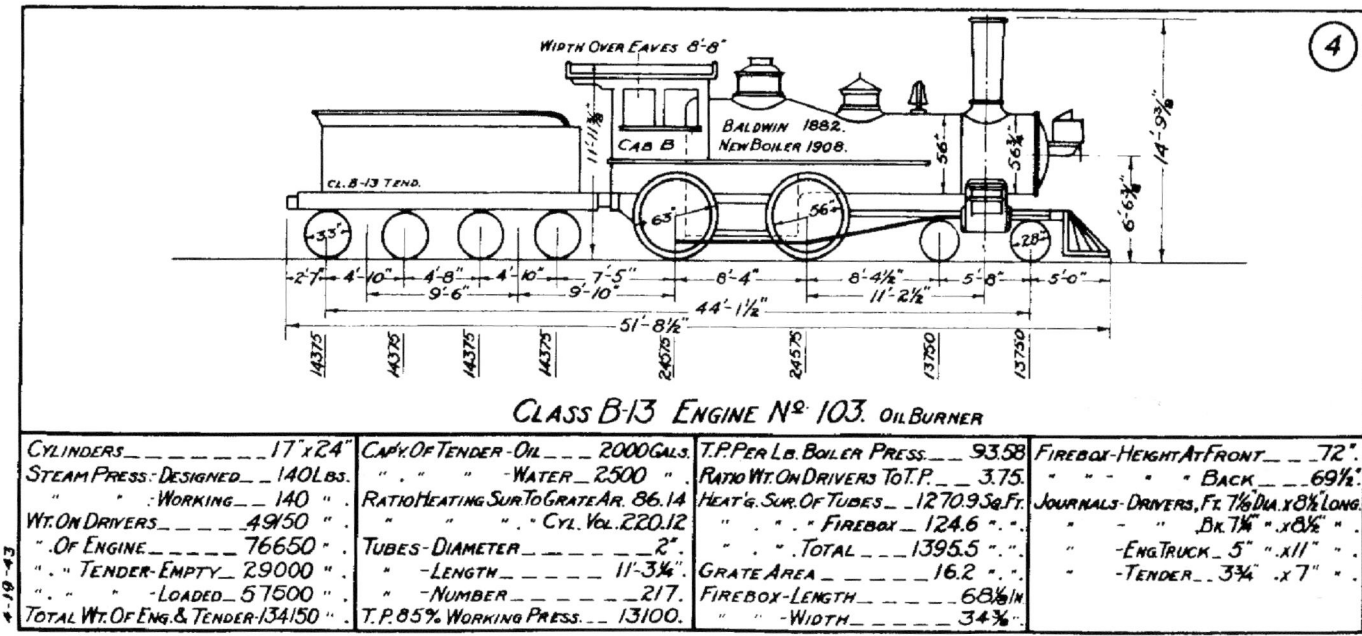

CLASS B-13 ENGINE Nº 103. OIL BURNER

CYLINDERS _ _ _ _ _ _ 17"x24".	CAP'Y. OF TENDER-OIL _ _ 2000 GALS.	T.P. PER LB. BOILER PRESS. _ _ 93.58.	FIREBOX-HEIGHT AT FRONT _ _ _ 72".
STEAM PRESS.-DESIGNED _ _ 140 LBS.	" " -WATER _ 2500 "	RATIO WT. ON DRIVERS TO T.P. _ _ 3.75.	" " " BACK _ _ _ 69½".
" " :WORKING _ _ 140 "	RATIO HEATING SUR. TO GRATE AR. 86.14	HEAT'G. SUR. OF TUBES _ 1270.9 SQ.FT.	JOURNALS-DRIVERS, FT. 7½" DIA. x 8½" LONG.
WT. ON DRIVERS _ _ _ 49150 "	" " " CYL. VOL. 220.12	" " " FIREBOX _ 124.6 " "	" " BK. 7½" " x 8½" "
" .OF ENGINE _ _ _ _ 76650 .	TUBES-DIAMETER _ _ _ _ 2".	" " " TOTAL _ _ 1395.5 " "	" -ENG.TRUCK _ 5" " x 11" "
" " TENDER-EMPTY _ 29000 "	" -LENGTH _ _ _ _ 11'-3¾"	GRATE AREA _ _ _ _ 16.2 " "	" -TENDER _ _ 3¾" " x 7" "
" " " -LOADED _ 57500 "	" -NUMBER _ _ _ _ 217.	FIREBOX-LENGTH _ _ _ _ 68 3/8 IN	
TOTAL WT. OF ENG. & TENDER-134150 "	T.P. 85% WORKING PRESS. _ _ 13100.	" " -WIDTH _ _ _ _ 34 3/8 "	

Engine 103, a member of Class B-13, still looks to be in good condition when photographed at Hillyard, WA, in July 1940. Collection of Harold K. Vollrath.

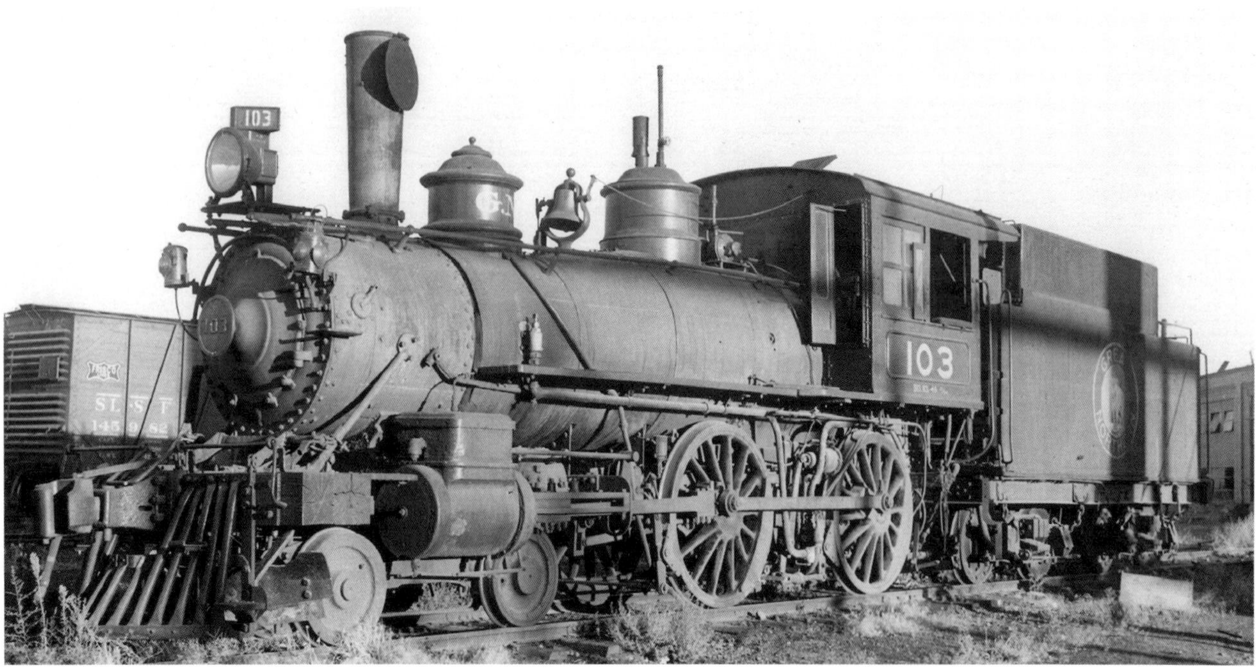
103
103

This fireman's side view of B-13 103 was taken at Hillyard, WA, on an unknown date. The engine was given No. 219 on March 4, 1944. GNRHS Collection.

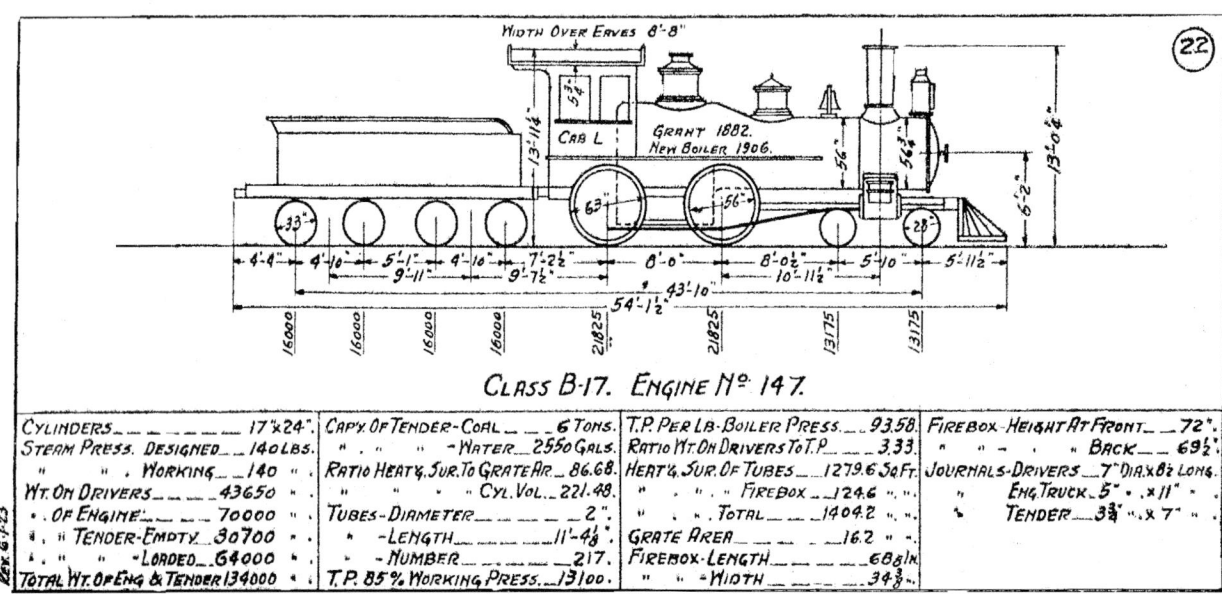

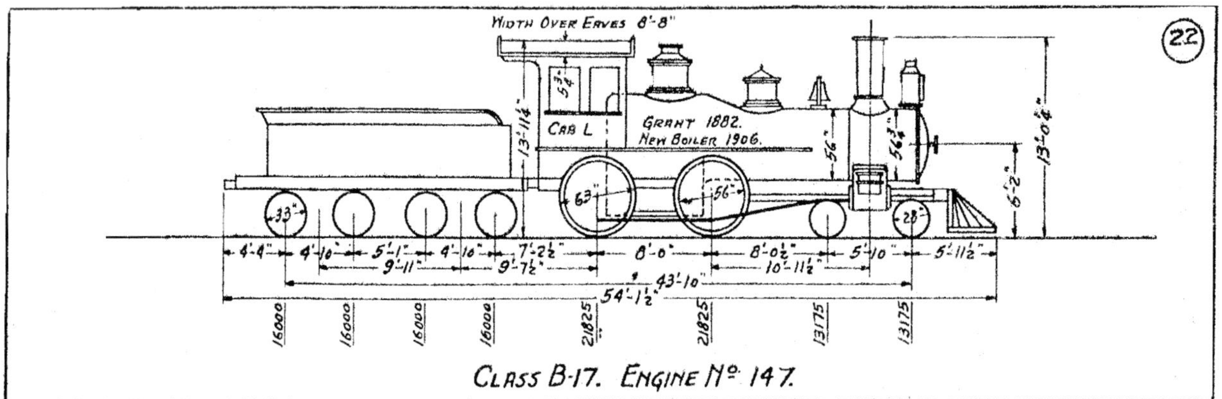
WIDTH OVER EAVES 8'-8"
22
CAB L
GRANT 1882.
NEW BOILER 1906.
4'-4" 4'-10" 5'-1" 4'-10" 7'-2½" 8'-0" 8'-0½" 5'-10" 5'-11½"
9'-11" 9'-7½" 10'-11½"
43'-10"
54'-1½"
16000 16000 16000 16000 21825 21825 13175 13175

CLASS B-17. ENGINE No. 147.

CYLINDERS — 17"x24".	CAP'Y OF TENDER-COAL — 6 TONS.	T.P. PER LB-BOILER PRESS. — 93.58.	FIREBOX-HEIGHT AT FRONT — 72".
STEAM PRESS. DESIGNED — 140 LBS.	" " " -WATER — 2550 GALS.	RATIO WT. ON DRIVERS TO T.P. — 3.33.	" " " BACK — 69½".
" " WORKING — 140 "	RATIO HEAT'G. SUR. TO GRATE AR. — 86.68.	HEAT'G. SUR. OF TUBES — 1279.6 SQ. FT.	JOURNALS-DRIVERS — 7" DIA. x 8½ LONG.
WT. ON DRIVERS — 43650 "	" " " " CYL. VOL. — 221.48.	" " " FIREBOX — 124.6 " "	" ENG. TRUCK — 5" " x 11" "
" OF ENGINE — 70000 "	TUBES-DIAMETER — 2".	" " " TOTAL — 1404.2 " "	" TENDER — 3¾" " x 7" "
" " TENDER-EMPTY — 30700 "	" -LENGTH — 11'-4⅛".	GRATE AREA — 16.2 " "	
" " " -LOADED — 64000 "	" -NUMBER — 217.	FIREBOX-LENGTH — 68⅛ IN.	
TOTAL WT. OF ENG. & TENDER 134000 "	T.P. 85% WORKING PRESS. — 13100.	" " -WIDTH — 34⅜ "	

REV. 6-1-23

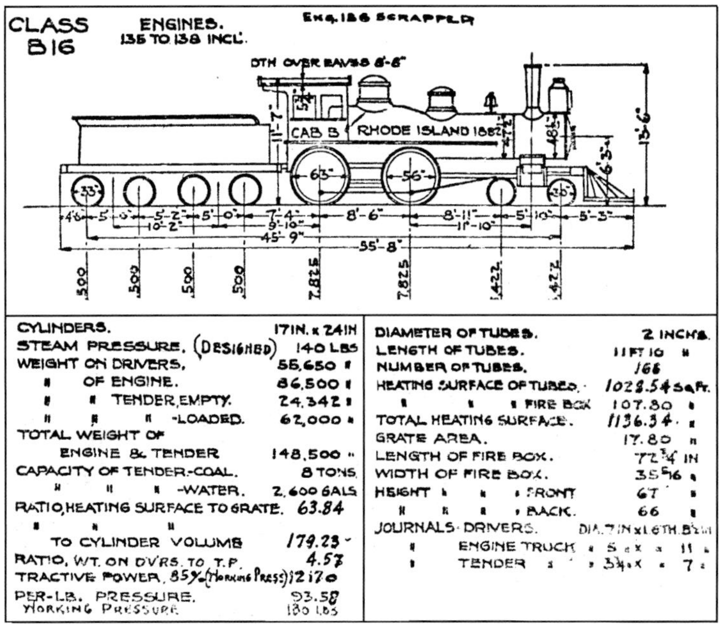
CLASS B16
ENGINES. 135 TO 138 INCL.
ENG. 136 SCRAPPED
WIDTH OVER EAVES 8'-8"
CAB B
RHODE ISLAND 1882
4'6" 5'-0" 5'-2" 5'-0" 7'-4" 8'-6" 8'-11" 5'-10" 5'-3"
10'-2" 9'-10" 11'-10"
45'-9"
55'-8"
500 500 500 500 7,825 7,825 1,422 1,422

43

CYLINDERS. 17 IN. x 24 IN	DIAMETER OF TUBES. 2 INCHES.
STEAM PRESSURE. (DESIGNED) 140 LBS	LENGTH OF TUBES. 11 FT 10 "
WEIGHT ON DRIVERS. 55,650 "	NUMBER OF TUBES. 168
" OF ENGINE. 86,500 "	HEATING SURFACE OF TUBES. 1028.54 SQ. FT.
" " TENDER, EMPTY. 24,342 "	" " " FIRE BOX 107.80 "
" " " -LOADED. 62,000 "	TOTAL HEATING SURFACE. 1136.34 "
TOTAL WEIGHT OF ENGINE & TENDER 148,500 "	GRATE AREA. 17.80 "
CAPACITY OF TENDER-COAL. 8 TONS	LENGTH OF FIRE BOX. 72¾ IN
" " " -WATER. 2,600 GALS	WIDTH OF FIRE BOX. 35 5/16 "
RATIO, HEATING SURFACE TO GRATE. 63.84	HEIGHT " " " FRONT 67 "
" " " TO CYLINDER VOLUME 179.23	" " " " BACK. 66 "
RATIO, WT. ON DV'RS. TO T.P. 4.57	JOURNALS-DRIVERS. DIA. 7 IN x LGTH. 8½ IN
TRACTIVE POWER, 85% (Working Press) 12170	" ENGINE TRUCK " 5 " x " 11 "
PER-LB. PRESSURE. 93.58	" TENDER " " 3¾ " x " 7 "
WORKING PRESSURE 180 LBS	

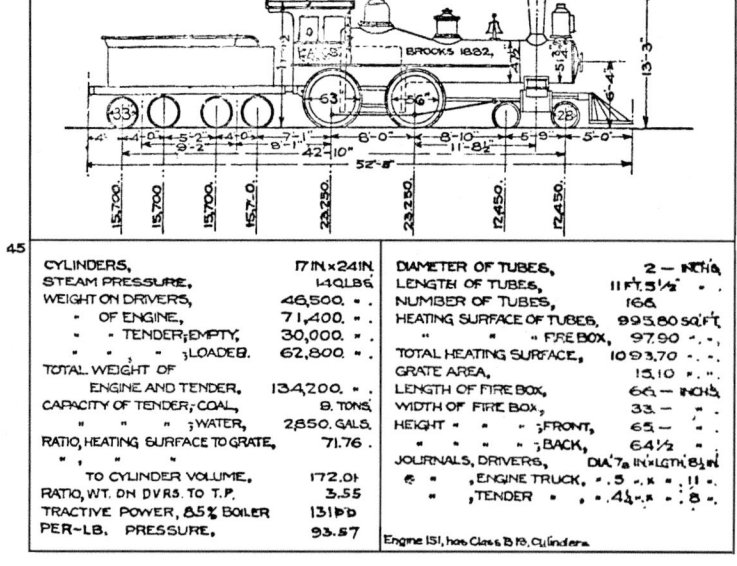

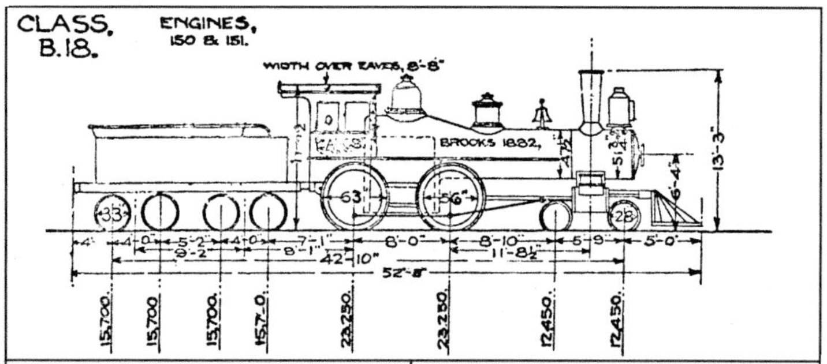
CLASS. B.18.
ENGINES, 150 & 151.
WIDTH OVER EAVES, 8'-8"
BROOKS 1882.
4' 4'-0" 5'-2" 4'-0" 7'-1" 8'-0" 8'-10" 5'-9" 5'-0"
9'-2" 8'-1" 11'-8½"
42'-10"
52'-8"
15,700 15,700 15,700 15,700 23,250 23,250 12,450 12,450

45

CYLINDERS, 17 IN. x 24 IN.	DIAMETER OF TUBES, 2 — INCHES
STEAM PRESSURE, 140 LBS.	LENGTH OF TUBES, 11 FT. 5½" "
WEIGHT ON DRIVERS, 46,500. "	NUMBER OF TUBES, 166
" OF ENGINE, 71,400. "	HEATING SURFACE OF TUBES, 995.80 SQ. FT.
" " TENDER; EMPTY, 30,000. "	" " " FIRE BOX, 97.90 "
" " " ; LOADED. 62,800. "	TOTAL HEATING SURFACE, 1093.70 "
TOTAL WEIGHT OF ENGINE AND TENDER, 134,200. "	GRATE AREA, 15.10 "
CAPACITY OF TENDER; COAL, 8. TONS	LENGTH OF FIRE BOX, 66 — INCHES
" " " ; WATER, 2850. GALS.	WIDTH OF FIRE BOX, 33 — "
RATIO, HEATING SURFACE TO GRATE, 71.76	HEIGHT " " " ; FRONT, 65 — "
" " " TO CYLINDER VOLUME, 172.01	" " " " ; BACK, 64½ "
RATIO, WT. ON DVRS. TO T.P. 3.55	JOURNALS, DRIVERS, DIA. 7⅛ IN. x LGTH. 8½ IN.
TRACTIVE POWER, 85% BOILER 131 lbs	" " , ENGINE TRUCK, " 5 " x " 11 "
PER-LB. PRESSURE, 93.57	" , TENDER " " 4½ " x " 8 "
	Engine 151, has Class B 19, Cylinders

Class B-17 engine 148 and its crew were photographed at an unknown location on an unknown date. Collection of William Bissinger.

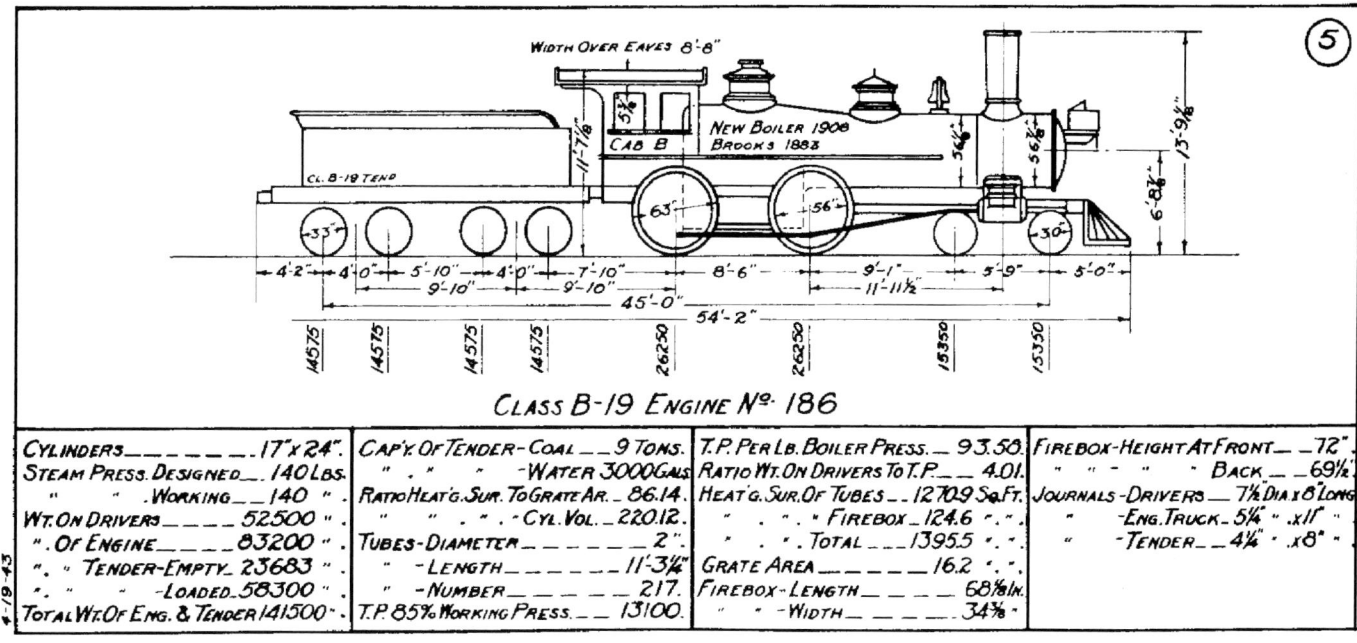

Class B-19 Engine No. 186

CYLINDERS _____ 17"x 24".	CAP'Y. OF TENDER-COAL __ 9 TONS.	T.P. PER LB. BOILER PRESS. __ 93.50.	FIREBOX-HEIGHT AT FRONT __ _72".
STEAM PRESS. DESIGNED __ 140 LBS.	" . " " -WATER 3000 GALS	RATIO WT. ON DRIVERS TO T.P. __ 4.01.	" " - " · BACK. __ 69½".
" " . WORKING __ 140 ".	RATIO HEAT'G. SUR. TO GRATE AR. _ 86.14.	HEAT'G. SUR. OF TUBES __ 1270.9 SQ. FT.	JOURNALS-DRIVERS __ 7½ DIA x 8"LONG
WT. ON DRIVERS _____ 52.500 ".	" . " . CYL. VOL. 220.12.	" . ". " FIREBOX. 124.6 ". ".	" -ENG. TRUCK- 5¼ " . x 11"
". OF ENGINE _____ 83200 ".	TUBES-DIAMETER _____ 2 ".	" . ". " TOTAL __ 1395.5 ". ".	" -TENDER __ 4¼ " . x 8" .
". " TENDER-EMPTY. 23683 ".	" -LENGTH _____ 11'-3½"	GRATE AREA _____ 16.2 ". ".	
". " " -LOADED. 58300 ".	" -NUMBER _____ 217.	FIREBOX-LENGTH _____ 68⅛IN.	
TOTAL WT. OF ENG. & TENDER 141500 ".	T.P. 85% WORKING PRESS. __ 13100.	" -WIDTH _____ 34⅜".	

B-19 No. 162 was photographed at Lakota, ND. This is believed to be a J. Foster Adams photograph taken on June 22, 1922. GNRHS collection.

In July 1882 the StPM&M received an order of five 4-4-0 locomotives from Grant Locomotive Works, and two from Brooks. The Grant locomotives, Nos. 145-149, with 17-inch by 24-inch cylinders, 63-inch drivers and weights of 70,000 pounds, were placed in Class 28. One of these had an interesting history. No. 147 was sold to the Duluth, Superior & Western in 1897, but the DS&W was then acquired by the Eastern Railway Company of Minnesota, and No. 147 came back to the GN when that road was absorbed. The Grant engines were placed in Class B-17 in 1903. The Brooks engines, numbered as 150 and 151 and placed in Class 29, had 17-inch by 24-inch cylinders, 64-inch drivers and weighed 71,400 pounds The Brooks engines were ultimately placed in Class B-18.

Twenty more 4-4-0's were received from Brooks in late 1882. They had the standard 17-inch by 24-inch cylinders and 63-inch drivers. They weighed 83,200 pounds and were placed in Class 30 and carried numbers 152-171. This was only a partial order, as fifteen more identical engines (172-186) were received in early 1883. In 1903 these

were placed in Class B-19. Many of these received new boilers during their service lives. Members of the class lasting into the 1930's were assigned to the Dakota (4 engines), Minot (1 engine) and Willmar (1 engine) Divisions. The last surviving member of this class, No. 186, a Willmar Division engine, lasted long enough to be renumbered as 220 in 1944, to clear the number for a newly ordered EMD NW-5 diesel. This last B-19 wasn't sold until January 1947.

Besides the Brooks Class 30 4-4-0's, only ten locomotives were received in 1883 (two actually arrived on December 28, 1882). These 4-4-0's were numbered as 197-206, came from Rhode Island and were placed in Class 33. They had 18-inch by 24-inch cylinders, 63-inch drivers and weighed 90,900 pounds These were placed in Class B-20 in 1903. The last three engines were assigned to the Willmar, Kalispell and Dakota Divisions.

In 1883, the slowing economy slipped into recession. The Manitoba lowered its freight rates and reduced its dividend in 1884. By the mid-1880's, conditions had begun to improve and James J. Hill began

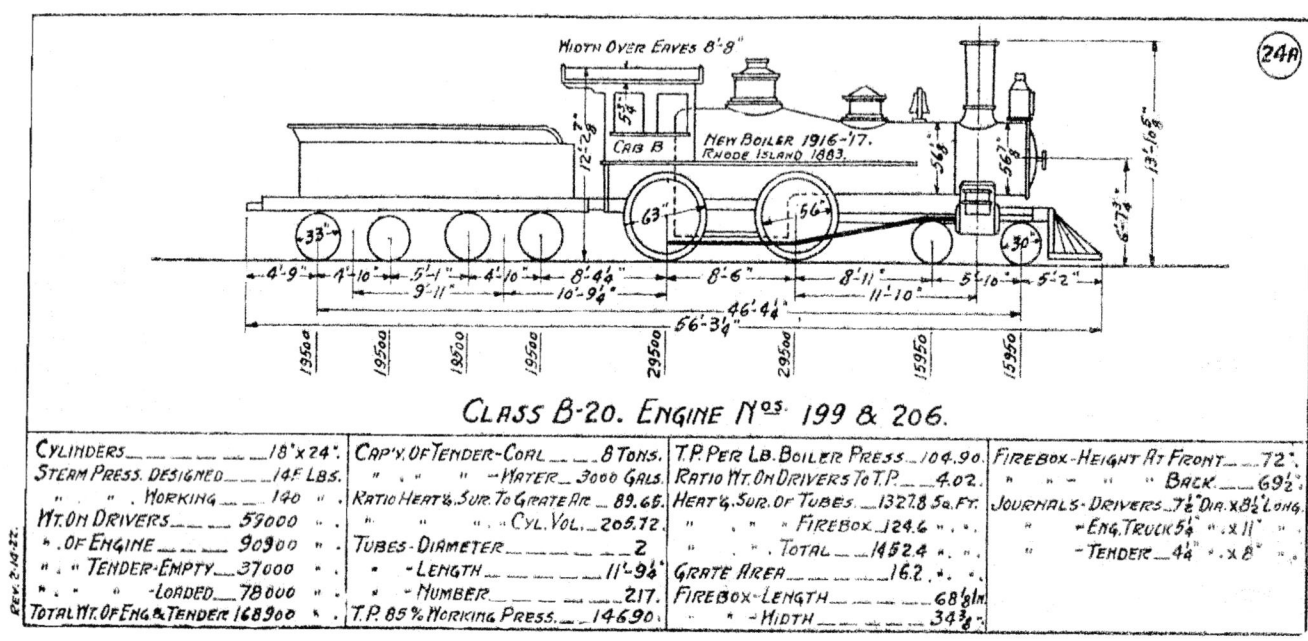

B-20 199 is seen at Spokane in 1938 with a modern headlight and a tender with a raised water hatch. H. Miller photograph from the collection of William Raia.

considering westward expansion. In 1886 construction started west of Devils Lake, and by 1887, the StPM&M was back in the market for locomotives.

The first road engines of 1887 were 19 4-4-0's from Rogers. These Class 34 engines, Nos. 207-225, had 18-inch by 24-inch cylinders, 63-inch drivers and weighed 94,100 pounds Five of these locomotives were sold to the Montana Central in 1888, but returned to the GN with their original numbers. In 1903 they were placed in Class B-21. Those which lasted until the late 1930's and beyond were assigned to the Willmar and Dakota Divisions. One of these, No. 214, a Willmar Division engine, was not sold until 1949, becoming the last 4-4-0 on the GN.

The final order of American Standard locomotives placed by any of the Great Northern "family" roads was received in late 1888 and

Still appearing to be well-maintained, Class B-21 engine 209 was photographed at St.Cloud, MN, in August 1931. Collection of Harold K. Vollrath.

While 202 is also a member of Class B-20, its appearance is markedly different from that of 199, though part of this is because of its earlier date. The engine still has an old style headlight, and also has an oil bunker in the tender. This engine has the original boiler, with a marked conical section that forces the steam dome up against the cab. Engine 199, shown on the opposite page, received a new boiler in 1917. No. 202 was at Everett, WA, on June 9, 1920. J. Foster Adams photograph from the GNRHS Collection.

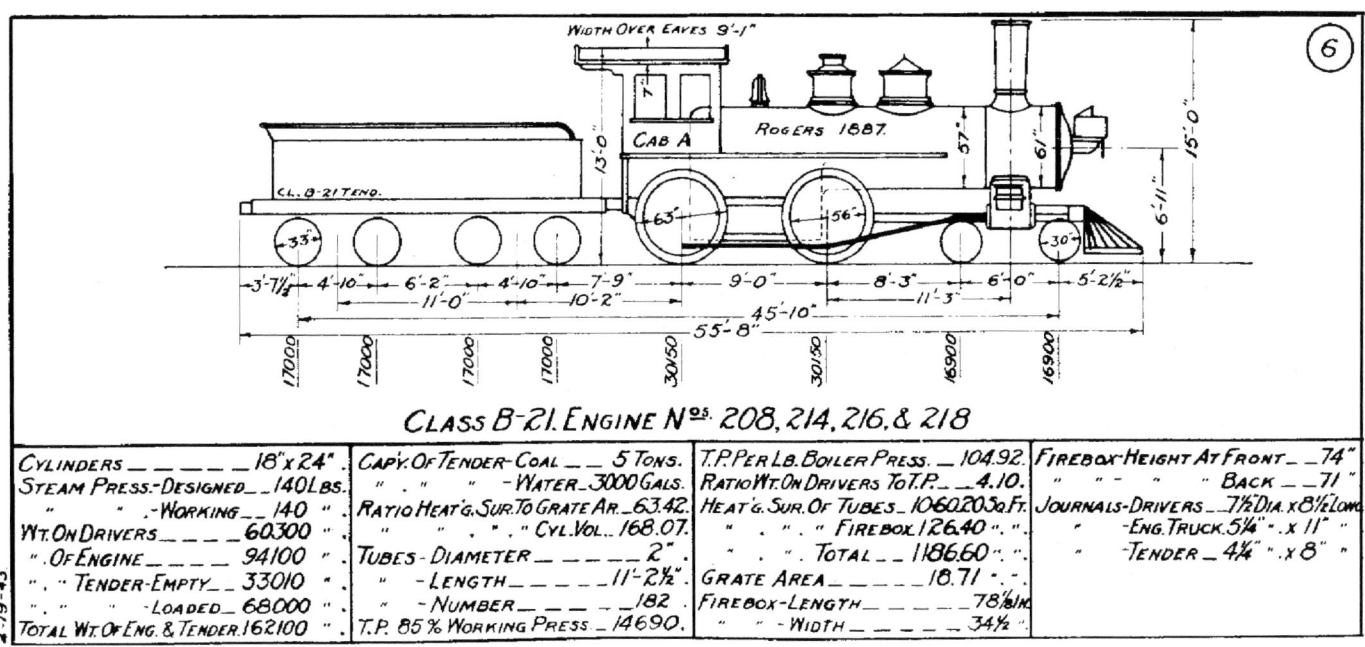

CLASS B-21. ENGINE Nos. 208, 214, 216, & 218

CYLINDERS ___ 18"x24"	CAPY. OF TENDER-COAL __ 5 TONS.	T.P. PER LB. BOILER PRESS. __ 104.92	FIREBOX-HEIGHT AT FRONT __ 74"
STEAM PRESS.-DESIGNED __ 140 LBS.	" " " -WATER 3000 GALS.	RATIO WT. ON DRIVERS TO T.P. __ 4.10.	" " - " BACK __ 71 "
" " .-WORKING __ 140 "	RATIO HEAT'G. SUR. TO GRATE AR. _63.42.	HEAT'G. SUR. OF TUBES _ 1060.20 SQ. FT.	JOURNALS-DRIVERS __ 7½ DIA. x 8½ LONG.
WT. ON DRIVERS ___ 60300 "	" " . " . " CYL. VOL. 168.07.	" . " " FIREBOX 126.40 ". ".	" -ENG. TRUCK. 5¼ " . x 11 "
" . OF ENGINE ___ 94100 "	TUBES-DIAMETER ___ 2 ".	" . " " TOTAL __ 1186.60 ".	" -TENDER __ 4¼ " . x 8 "
" . " TENDER-EMPTY __ 33010 "	" -LENGTH ___ 11'-2½ "	GRATE AREA ___ 18.71 ". .	
" . " " -LOADED __ 68000 "	" -NUMBER ___ 182	FIREBOX-LENGTH ___ 78⅛ IN.	
TOTAL WT. OF ENG. & TENDER. 162100 "	T.P. 85% WORKING PRESS __ 14690.	" -WIDTH ___ 34½	

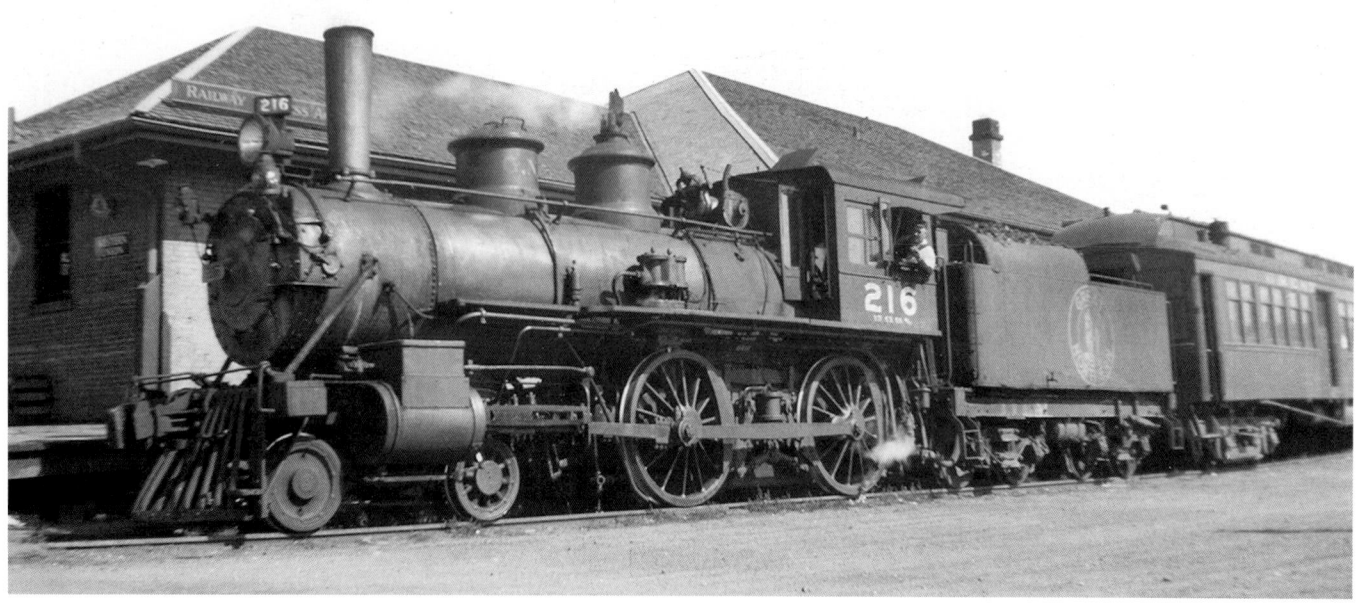

B-17 engine 216, at age fifty, still appears in good condition. It was photographed in 1937 at Fergus Falls, MN. Warren R. McGee.

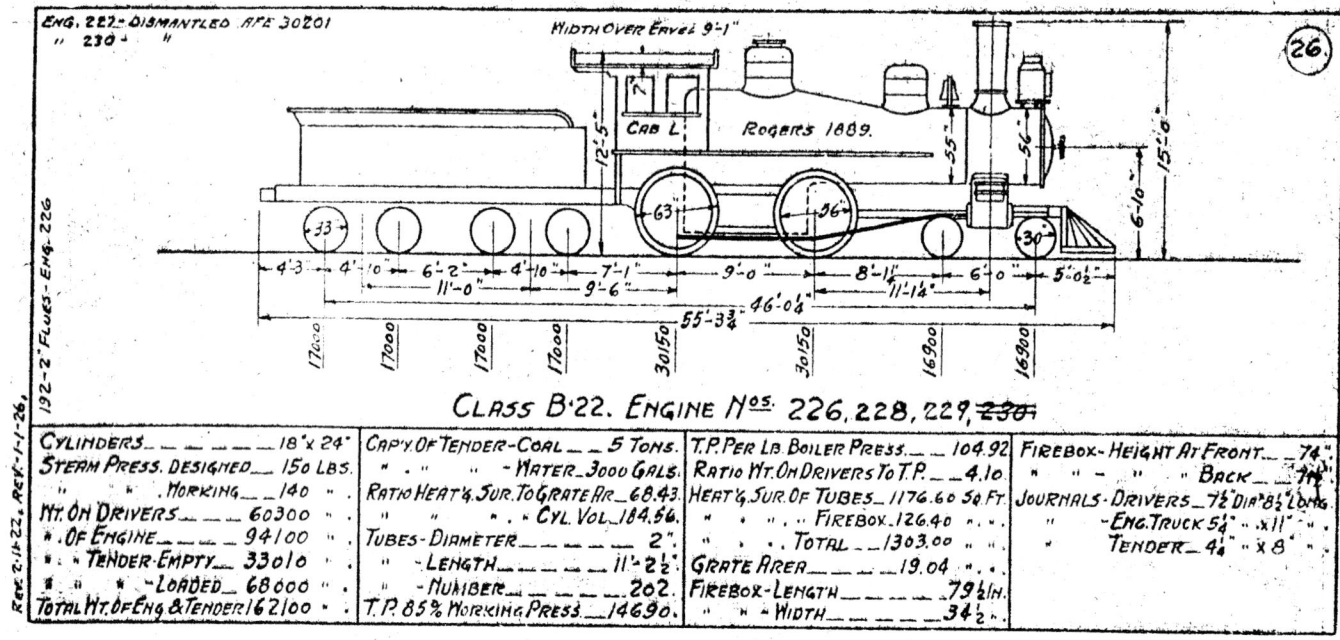

CLASS B-22. ENGINE Nos. 226, 228, 229, 230

CYLINDERS ___ 18" x 24"	CAP'Y OF TENDER-COAL ___ 5 TONS.	T.P. PER LB BOILER PRESS. ___ 104.92
STEAM PRESS. DESIGNED ___ 150 LBS.	" " " -WATER 3000 GALS.	RATIO WT. ON DRIVERS TO T.P. ___ 4.10
" " WORKING ___ 140 "	RATIO HEAT'G SUR. TO GRATE AR. ___ 68.43	HEAT'G SUR. OF TUBES ___ 1176.60 SQ. FT.
WT. ON DRIVERS ___ 60300 "	" " . CYL. VOL. 184.56.	" " .. FIREBOX 126.40 " "
" OF ENGINE ___ 94100 "	TUBES-DIAMETER ___ 2".	" " .. TOTAL ___ 1303.00 " "
" - TENDER-EMPTY 33010 "	" -LENGTH ___ 11'-2½"	GRATE AREA ___ 19.04 " "
" " " LOADED 68000 "	" -NUMBER ___ 202.	FIREBOX-LENGTH ___ 79½ IN.
TOTAL WT. OF ENG. & TENDER 162100 "	T.P. 85% WORKING PRESS. ___ 14690.	" - WIDTH ___ 34½ "

FIREBOX-HEIGHT AT FRONT ___ 74"
" " - " BACK ___ 74"
JOURNALS- DRIVERS 7½" DIA 8½" LONG
" -ENG. TRUCK 5¼" x 11"
TENDER ___ 4¼" X 8"

The Eastern Railway Company of Minnesota received No. 105 from Rogers in 1899. It ultimately became GN 230, a member of Class B-22. ALCO Historic Photos.

No. 226 of Class B-22 was photographed in front of the Jackson Street Roundhouse (St.Paul, MN) about 1918. Minnesota Transportation Museum Archives.

Engine 228, also a member of Class B-22, has received a steel cab and side board extensions on the tender by the time it was photographed on June 17, 1922, at Minneapolis. J. Foster Adams photograph from the collection of Kenneth R. Middleton.

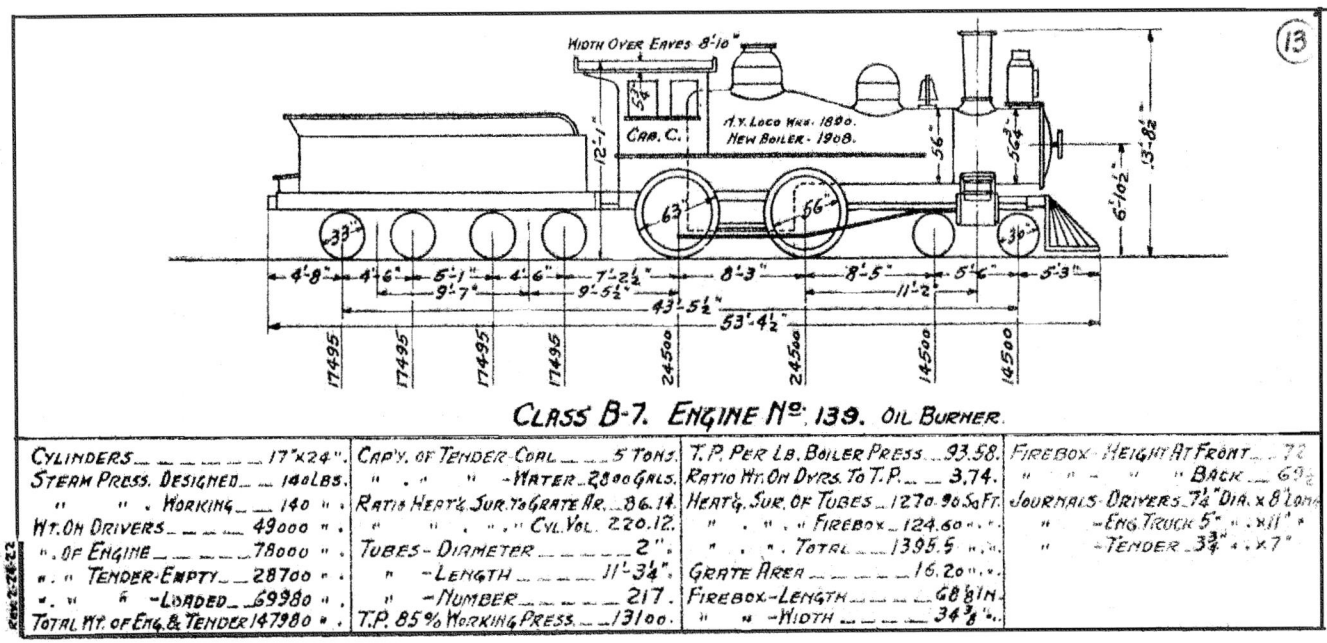

CLASS B-7. ENGINE Nº 139. OIL BURNER.

CYLINDERS ___ 17"x24".	CAP'Y. OF TENDER-COAL ___ 5 TONS.	T.P. PER LB. BOILER PRESS ___ 93.58.	FIREBOX-HEIGHT AT FRONT ___ 72
STEAM PRESS. DESIGNED ___ 140 LBS.	" " " -WATER 2800 GALS.	RATIO HT. ON DVRS. TO T.P. ___ 3.74.	" " " BACK ___ 69
" " " WORKING ___ 140 " .	RATIO HEAT'G SUR. TO GRATE AR. ___ 86.14.	HEAT'G. SUR. OF TUBES ___ 1270.90 SQ.FT.	JOURNALS-DRIVERS 7¼" DIA. x 8" LONG
WT. ON DRIVERS ___ 49000 " .	" " " " CYL. VOL. 220.12.	" " " FIREBOX ___ 124.60 " .	" -ENG. TRUCK 5" " x11" "
" . OF ENGINE ___ 78000 " .	TUBES-DIAMETER ___ 2".	" " " TOTAL ___ 1395.5 " "	" -TENDER 3¾" " x 7"
" " TENDER-EMPTY ___ 28700 " .	" -LENGTH ___ 11'-3¾".	GRATE AREA ___ 16.20 " .	
" " " -LOADED 69980 " .	" -NUMBER ___ 217.	FIREBOX-LENGTH ___ 68 8/8 IN.	
TOTAL WT. OF ENG. & TENDER 147980 " .	T.P. 85% WORKING PRESS. ___ 13100.	" " -WIDTH ___ 34 ½ " .	

Rare class B-7, No.139, is shown approaching the Ballard, WA, station, powering the eastbound Skykomish passenger local No. 278. Ballard is a northern suburb of Seattle. The date was June 3, 1924. From the Warren Wing collection, courtesy of Walter Ainsworth.

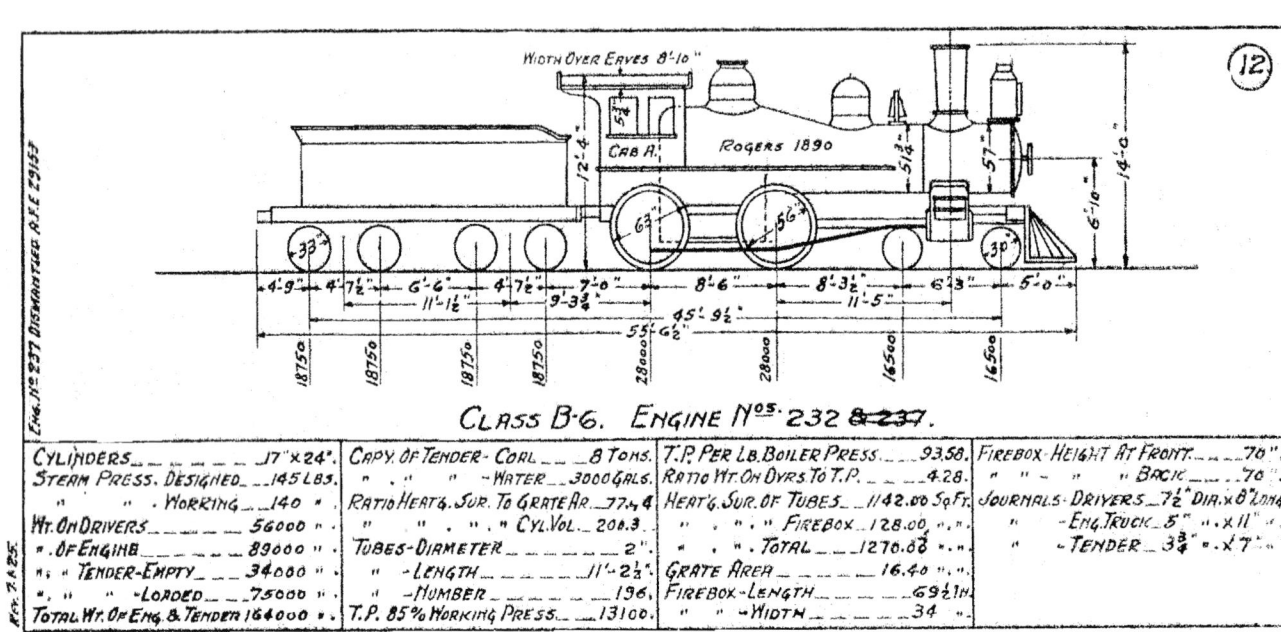

CLASS B-6. ENGINE Nos. 232 & 237.

CYLINDERS _____ 17"x24".	CAP'Y. OF TENDER- COAL ___ 8 TONS.	T.P. PER LB. BOILER PRESS. ___ 93.58.	FIREBOX- HEIGHT AT FRONT ___ 70".
STEAM PRESS. DESIGNED __ 145 LBS.	" " " -WATER ___ 3000 GALS.	RATIO WT. ON DVRS TO T.P. ___ 4.28.	" " " " BACK ___ 70".
" " -WORKING __ 140 "	RATIO HEAT'G. SUR. TO GRATE AR. 77.4	HEAT'G. SUR. OF TUBES ___ 1142.00 SQ.FT.	JOURNALS- DRIVERS_ 7½" DIA. x 8" LONG.
WT. ON DRIVERS _____ 56000 "	" " " " CYL.VOL. 208.3.	" " " FIREBOX __ 128.00 " "	" -ENG. TRUCK- 5 " " x11"
" OF ENGINE _____ 89000 "	TUBES- DIAMETER _____ 2"	" " " TOTAL ___ 1270.00 " "	" -TENDER _ 3¾" " x 7 "
" " TENDER-EMPTY __ 34000 "	" -LENGTH _____ 11'-2½"	GRATE AREA _____ 16.40 "	
" " " -LOADED __ 75000 "	" -NUMBER _____ 196.	FIREBOX- LENGTH _____ 69½ IN.	
TOTAL WT. OF ENG. & TENDER 164000 "	T.P. 85% WORKING PRESS. __ 13100.	" -WIDTH _____ 34 "	

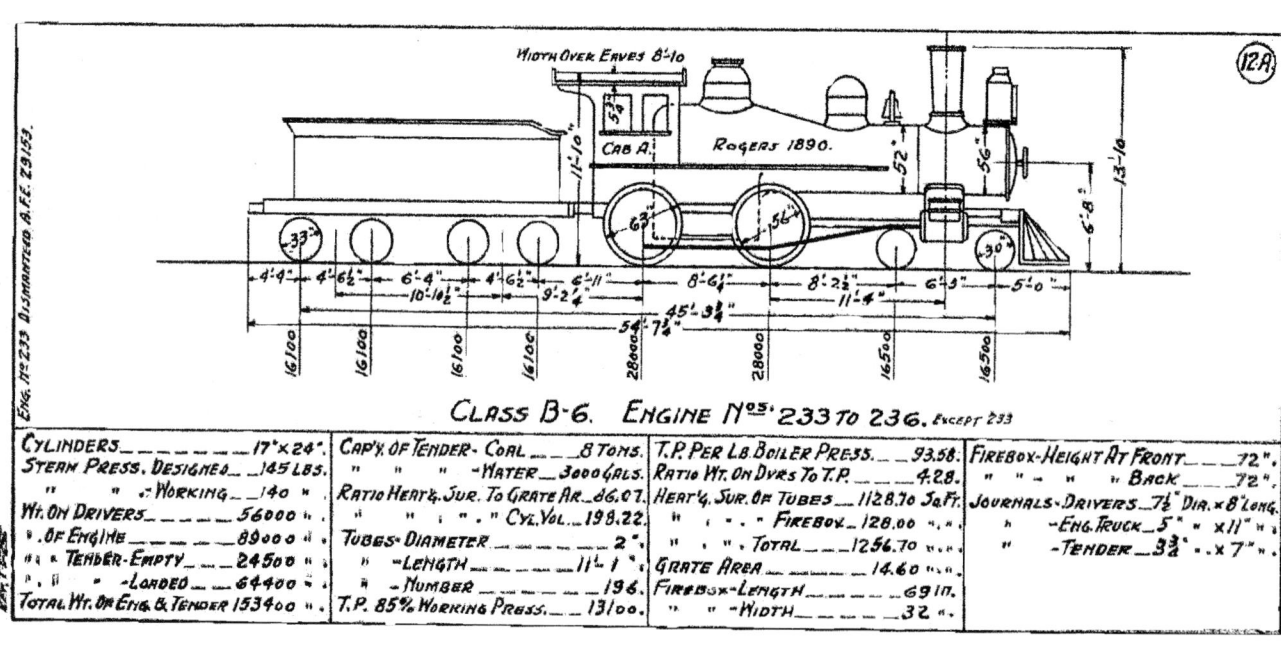

CLASS B-6. ENGINE Nos. 233 TO 236. EXCEPT 233

CYLINDERS _____ 17"x24".	CAP'Y. OF TENDER- COAL ___ 8 TONS.	T.P. PER LB BOILER PRESS. ___ 93.58.	FIREBOX- HEIGHT AT FRONT ___ 72".
STEAM PRESS. DESIGNED __ 145 LBS.	" " " -WATER ___ 3000 GALS.	RATIO WT. ON DVRS TO T.P. ___ 4.28.	" " " " BACK ___ 72".
" " -WORKING __ 140 "	RATIO HEAT'G. SUR. TO GRATE AR. 86.07.	HEAT'G. SUR. OF TUBES ___ 1128.70 SQ.FT.	JOURNALS- DRIVERS_ 7½" DIA. x 8" LONG.
WT. ON DRIVERS _____ 56000 "	" " " " CYL.VOL. 198.22.	" " " FIREBOX __ 128.00 " "	" -ENG. TRUCK- 5 " " x11"
" OF ENGINE _____ 89000 "	TUBES- DIAMETER _____ 2"	" " " TOTAL ___ 1256.70 " "	" -TENDER _ 3¾" " x 7 "
" " TENDER-EMPTY __ 24500 "	" -LENGTH _____ 11'-1"	GRATE AREA _____ 14.60 "	
" " " -LOADED __ 64400 "	" -NUMBER _____ 196.	FIREBOX- LENGTH _____ 69 IN.	
TOTAL WT. OF ENG. & TENDER 153400 "	T.P. 85% WORKING PRESS. __ 13100.	" -WIDTH _____ 32 "	

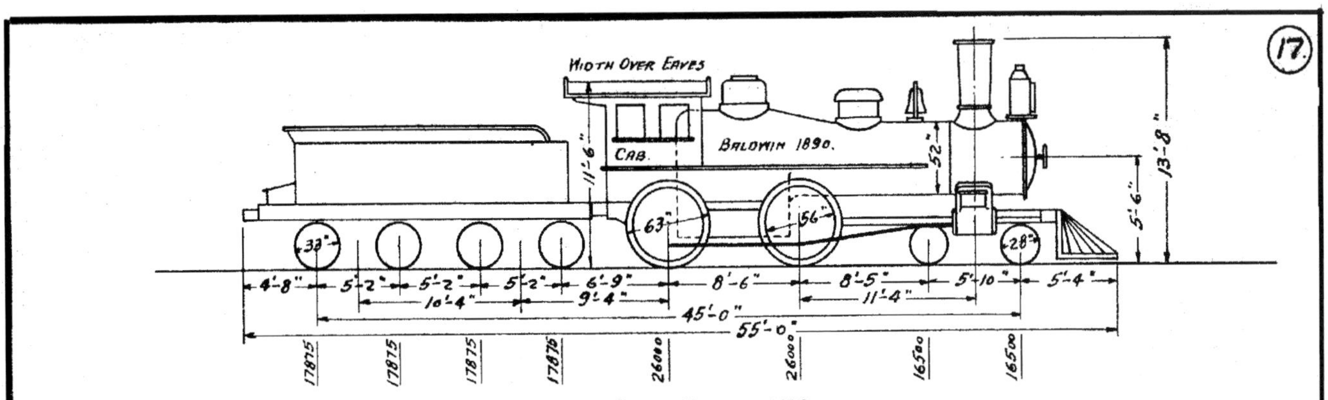

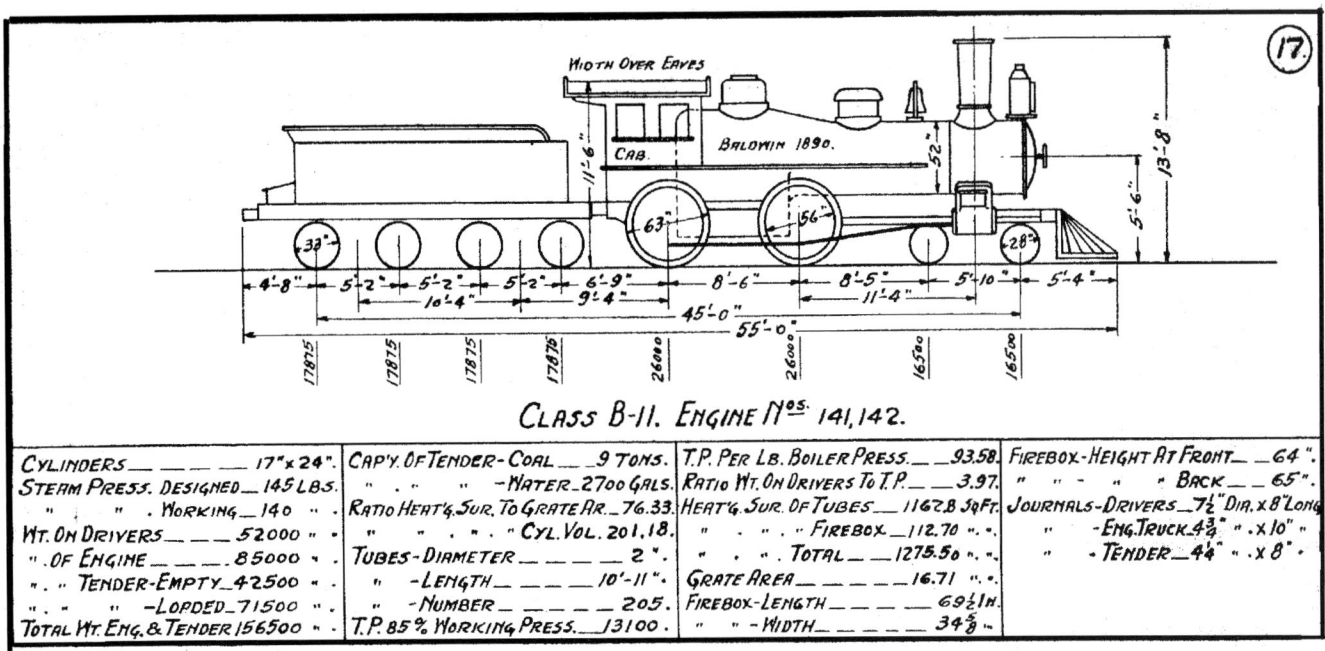

CLASS B-11. ENGINE Nos. 141, 142.

Cylinders ________ 17"x 24".	Cap'y. of Tender-Coal ___ 9 Tons.	T.P. per Lb. Boiler Press. ___ 93.58.	Firebox-Height at Front ___ 64".
Steam Press. Designed ___ 145 Lbs.	" " " -Water _ 2700 Gals.	Ratio Wt. on Drivers to T.P. ___ 3.97.	" " - " " Back ___ 65".
" " . Working ___ 140 " .	Ratio Heat'g. Sur. to Grate Ar. _ 76.33.	Heat'g. Sur. of Tubes ___ 1162.8 Sq.Ft.	Journals-Drivers _ 7½" Dia. x 8" Long
Wt. on Drivers ______ 52000 " .	" " " . " Cyl. Vol. 201.18.	" " " . " Firebox ___ 112.70 " . " .	" -Eng. Truck 4¾" " . x 10" "
" . of Engine ______ . 85000 " .	Tubes-Diameter ________ 2".	" " " . Total ___ 1275.50 " . " .	" - Tender _ 4¼" " . x 8" .
" . " Tender-Empty _ 42500 " .	" -Length ________ 10'-11".	Grate Area ________ 16.71 " . " .	
" . " " -Loaded _ 71500 " .	" -Number ________ 205.	Firebox-Length ________ 69½ In.	
Total Wt. Eng. & Tender 156500 " .	T.P. 85% Working Press. ___ 13100.	" " -Width ________ 34⅝ "	

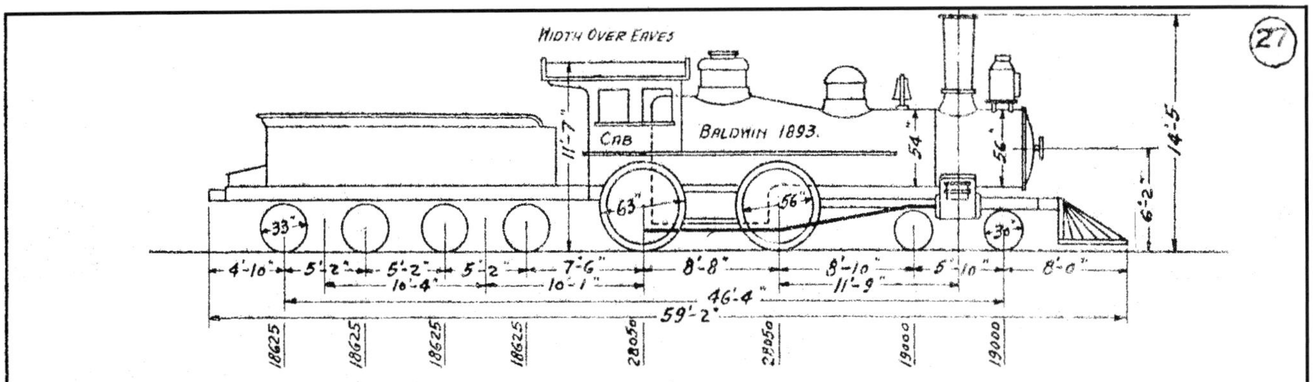

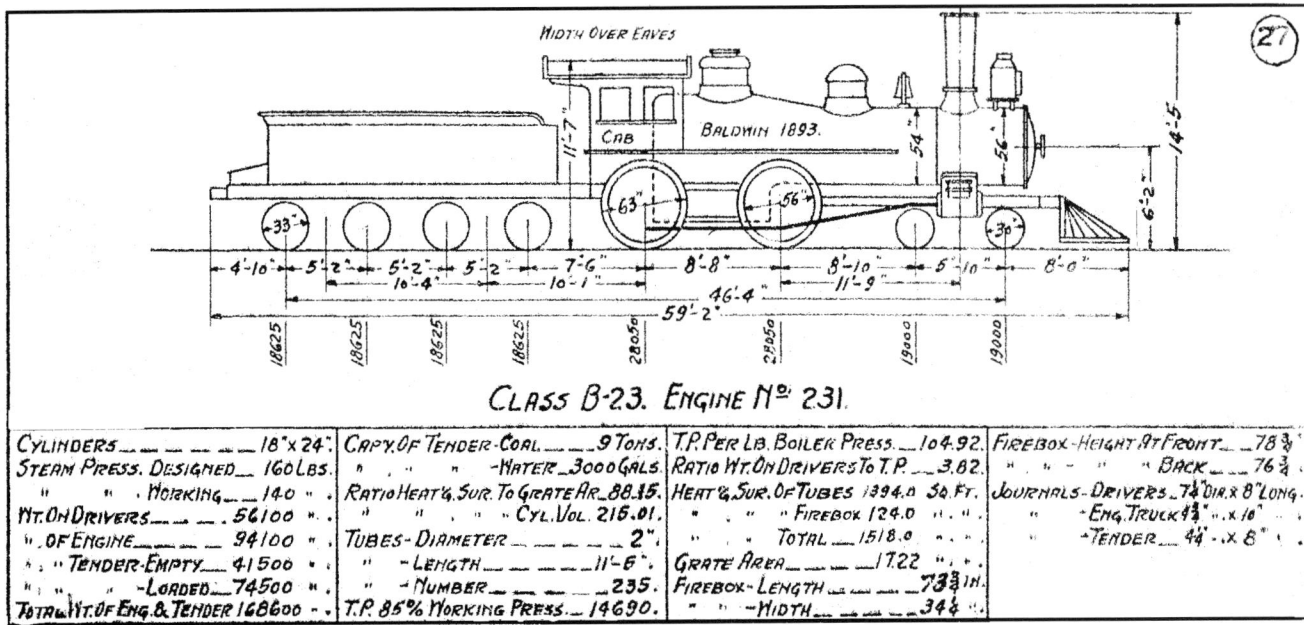

CLASS B-23. ENGINE No. 231.

Cylinders ________ 18"x 24".	Capy. of Tender-Coal ___ 9 Tons.	T.P. per Lb. Boiler Press. ___ 104.92.	Firebox-Height at Front ___ 78⅞
Steam Press. Designed ___ 160 Lbs.	" " " -Water _ 3000 Gals.	Ratio Wt. on Drivers to T.P. ___ 3.82.	" " - " " Back ___ 76¾ .
" " . Working ___ 140 " .	Ratio Heat'g. Sur. to Grate Ar. _ 88.15.	Heat'g. Sur. of Tubes 1394.0 Sq. Ft.	Journals-Drivers _ 7¼" Dia. x 8" Long.
Wt. on Drivers ______ 56100 " .	" " " " Cyl. Vol. 215.01.	" " " Firebox 124.0 " . " .	" -Eng. Truck 4¼" " . x 10" .
" . of Engine ______ 94100 " .	Tubes-Diameter ________ 2".	" " " Total ___ 1518.0 " . " .	" -Tender ___ 4¼" . x 8" .
" . " Tender-Empty ___ 41500 " .	" -Length ________ 11'-6".	Grate Area ________ 17.22 " . " .	
" " " -Loaded ___ 74500 " .	" -Number ________ 235.	Firebox-Length ________ 73¾ In.	
Total Wt. of Eng. & Tender 168600 " .	T.P. 85% Working Press. ___ 14690.	" " -Width ________ 34¼ " .	

Spokane Falls & Northern No. 7 was built for the Nelson & Fort Sheppard (a Canadian Spokane Falls & Northern subsidiary) in 1893. It became GN 231, the only member of Class B-23. Fred Jukes photograph from the Inland Empire Railway Historical Society Collection.

early 1889. Five Rogers locomotives were received by the Eastern of Minnesota Railway (EM) as its Nos. 101-105. These had 18-inch by 24-inch cylinders, 63-inch drivers, and weights of 94,100 pounds About 1900 they were renumbered as EM 226-230, ultimately coming to the GN with these numbers. These were purchased as Class 34A, but in 1903 became Class B-22 engines. The last survivor, No. 228, was assigned to the Dakota Division.

An "orphan" 4-4-0 was acquired by GN when subsidiary Seattle and Montana Railroad Company purchased the Seattle and Northern Railway Company in 1902. Seattle and Northern No. 2 had been built by New York Locomotive Works in 1890. It had 17-inch by 24-inch cylinders, 63-inch drivers, and weighed 78,000 pounds. It was placed in Class 12(2nd) and in late 1902 it was renumbered as Seattle and Montana Railroad No. 139. It kept that number when GN purchased the Seattle and Montana Railroad in 1907. In 1903 it was placed in Class B-7. It received a new boiler in 1908, but was destroyed by a boiler explosion in 1930.

Seven additional 4-4-0's were acquired when the GN purchased the Willmar and Sioux Falls (WSF) Railway (controlled from its beginning by StPM&M and GN) in 1907. Six of these had been built in 1890 by Rogers for the Sioux City and Northern Railway (SC&N). They had originally been built as SC&N 1-4, 8 and 10, and became WSF 232-237 in 1900 and 1901 as a result of the purchase of the SC&N by the WSF. One (No. 238) had been built for the Pacific Short Line by Rhode

Island as its No. 13 in 1889. After a couple reorganizations the Pacific Short Line had become the Sioux City and Western Railway, which was leased by the Willmar and Sioux Falls in 1900. Despite the different manufacturers, all seven of these locomotives were placed in Class 11(2nd). In 1903 these engines were placed in Class B-6. The former Sioux City and Western lines were sold to the Chicago, Burlington and Quincy in 1907, and No. 238 went to the CB&Q as part of the sale.

The Sioux City and Northern had also acquired two used 4-4-0's from the Chicago, St. Paul, Minneapolis & Omaha. These were CStPM&O 220 and 221, which had originally been built as Sioux City & St. Paul Nos. 4(1) and 1, respectively.[3] They were purchased used by the SC&N in 1890 and numbered as 11 and 12. SC&N 11 was sold before January 1, 1900, when the Willmar & Sioux Falls took over SC&N operations.[4] SC&N 12 was scrapped in 1902 without ever receiving a GN number.[5] Since there never was a GN 239, one might speculate that that number had been reserved for SC&N 12.

The final three 4-4-0's acquired by the Great Northern were received when the GN took over the Spokane Falls and Northern Railway (SF&N) system in 1907. The SF&N owned two 4-4-0's, Nos. 5 and 6, which had been built by Baldwin in 1890. These were renumbered as GN 142 and 141, respectively, and were placed in Class B-11(2nd). The Nelson & Fort Sheppard Railway Company, a Canadian subsidiary of the SF&N, owned a single 4-4-0, its No. 7. This locomotive became GN 231 and was placed in Class B-23.

B-6 232 was originally delivered as Sioux City & Northern No. 1 in 1890. It was photographed at Grand Forks in 1922. J. Foster Adams photograph from the GNRHS Collection.

Notes:

1. Lambert M. Baker, *The St. Paul and Pacific Railroad, a Minnesota Pioneer*, Minneapolis, unpublished manuscript dated 1967.
2. Great Northern Historical Engine record, 1880 – 1900. Photocopy courtesy Helen Keyes.
3. Roy W. Carlson (Ed.), Chicago, St. Paul, Minneapolis & Omaha roster. *Midwest Railroader, the Complete Roster Journal*, No. 41 (March 1964).
4. "Historical Record of S. C. and N. and Sioux City and Western, January 1. 1900," found with Great Northern Historic Car Records (Minnesota Historical Society).
5. Historic Engine Record. *op cit.*

The first locomotive received by the St, Paul, Minneapolis & Manitoba was this 0-4-0. It was almost immediately renumbered as StPM&M 3 to fill a vacant number. GNRHS collection.

Chapter 7
The First Class C 0-4-0 Four-Wheel Switcher

When the modern class system was implemented in October 1903, it is the authors' opinion that Class C was planned for a number of 0-4-0's still on the roster when the class system was being developed. However, these were sold on dates earlier than any documentation of specific class assignments have been found. The later assignment to Class C of the 0-8-0's that the GN began acquiring in 1918, meant that Class C was vacant for nearly 15 years.

The first 0-4-0 acquired by Great Northern's predecessors was StPM&M 51, received from Brooks Locomotive Works in October 1879. It had 14-inch by 22-inch cylinders, 49-inch drivers and weighed 49,000 pounds Shortly after delivery it was renumbered as 3, to fill a vacant number inherited from the StP&P. It was placed in Old Class 3, and was scrapped in June 1901.

Three more 0-4-0's were acquired in 1881 from Brooks as Nos. 87-89. These had 15-inch by 24-inch cylinders, 49-inch drivers and weights of 53,900 pounds. They were the first to be placed in Class 4. These were renumbered as GN 14, 15 and 16 in the major renumbering of 1899. One of these, No. 15, was not scrapped until September 1903, while another, No. 16, was actually not sold until May 1904, making it a prime candidate for being a Class C locomotive.

In 1882, four 0-4-0's were received from Rogers Locomotive Works. These were numbered as StPM&M 90-93, had 15-inch by 24-inch cylinders, 49-inch drivers, and weighed 62,000 pounds They were placed in Class 22. In 1899 they were renumbered as GN 17-20. Three of these were not scrapped until 1902.

In August 1882, seven more 0-4-0's were received by the StPM&M. These were numbered as 187-193. They had 15-inch by 24-inch cylinders, 49-inch drivers, and weighed 53,900 pounds The authors believe that these were originally placed in Class 31(1st), but prior to 1887 they were moved to Class 4. One of these, StPM&M 147, was sold to the Minneapolis Western as its first No. 1 in 1891, but was returned as No. 187 in 1892. No. 189 was wrecked at Barnesville, MN, in 1897, but the other four were renumbered as GN 21-26 in 1899. Two of these, 21 and 22, were not scrapped until 1903.

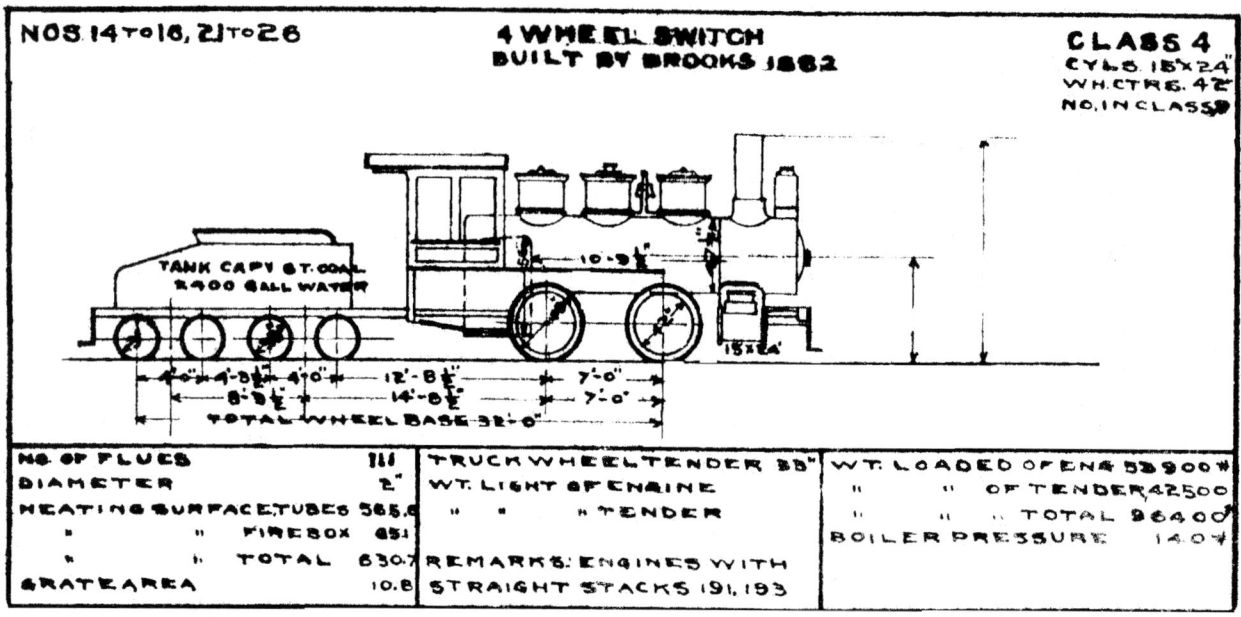

| NOS. 14 TO 16, 21 TO 26 | 4 WHEEL SWITCH BUILT BY BROOKS 1882 | CLASS 4 CYLS. 15X24" WH. CTRS. 42" NO. IN CLASS 9 |

NO. OF FLUES	111	TRUCK WHEEL TENDER 33"		WT. LOADED OF ENG. 53 900 #	
DIAMETER	2"	WT. LIGHT OF ENGINE		" " OF TENDER 42500	
HEATING SURFACE TUBES	585.6	" " " TENDER		" " " TOTAL 96400	
" " FIREBOX	45.1			BOILER PRESSURE 140 #	
" " TOTAL	630.7	REMARKS: ENGINES WITH			
GRATE AREA	10.8	STRAIGHT STACKS 191, 193			

Upon the arrival of the huge Brooks Class 44 4-8-0 type in 1897, a "largest and smallest" view was arranged with 4-8-0 No. 100 and 0-4-0 Class 4 No. 89 at Great Falls. Both were built by Brooks, and both were considered Great Northern locomotives at the time, but the 100 was owned by the Montana Central and the 89 was owned by the Minneapolis, St. Paul and Manitoba. As No. 16, the 89 may have been the sole occupant of the first class C. The 100 went on to become GN class G-5 No. 800, the 89 was sold in 1904 and the photographer went on to spend a lifetime at Dale Street shops in St. Paul. Photograph by William H. Fowler from the collection of Jerrold F. Hilton.

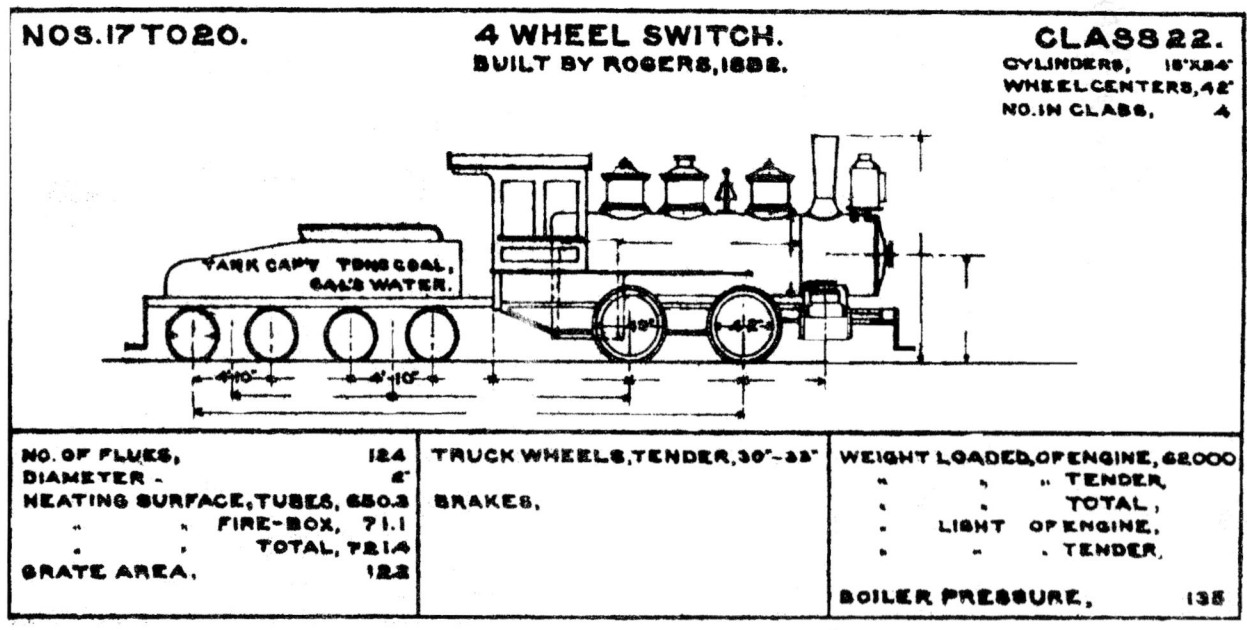

| NOS. 17 TO 20. | 4 WHEEL SWITCH. BUILT BY ROGERS, 1882. | CLASS 22. CYLINDERS, 15"X24" WHEEL CENTERS, 42" NO. IN CLASS, 4 |

NO. OF FLUES,	124	TRUCK WHEELS, TENDER, 30"-33"	WEIGHT LOADED, OF ENGINE, 62,000
DIAMETER -	2"		" " " TENDER,
HEATING SURFACE, TUBES,	650.3	BRAKES,	" " TOTAL,
" " FIRE-BOX,	71.1		" LIGHT OF ENGINE,
" " TOTAL,	721.4		" " TENDER,
GRATE AREA,	12.2		
			BOILER PRESSURE, 135

StPM&M 191 was built by Brooks in 1882, and eventually became GN 24(2nd), a member of Class 4. All of the
Manitoba/GN 0-4-0's had straight boilers and flanged domes. None had Belpaire fireboxes. Minnesota Historical Society.

Another view of a class 4 is No. 192 on June 12, 1887. The location is unknown. The size of
successive 0-4-0's increased only slightly over the first 0-4-0, No. 51. Minnesota Historical Society.

Class C-3 No. 883 is at work at Seattle King Street Station, shown handling NP train 408. The date is February 1951. Photograph by James Mattson.

No. 787 was one of the C-4 class engines that was not superheated. It is unusual among the C-4 class for having Walschaert valve gear. It and the 789 shown below also share a taller than usual profile. Despite the diagrams that show all C-4's and parent F-8's with the same height over the cab, a picture of the 787 back to back with the 1158 on a scrap line, without tenders, clearly shows the 787 to be taller by far than the F-8. Exact dimensions are not available. This view is at Minneapolis during July 1940. Photograph from the Robert W. Johnston Collection, courtesy of Walter Ainsworth.

Number 789 was another of the non-superheated C-4 engines, retaining its slide valves. The cab on this locomotive was much shorter front to back than that of 787. As with many of the C-4 engines, an F-8 tender was retained but the coal bunker sides were cut down and new sides added further inboard to improve visibility during switching operation. No. 789 was photographed at Minneapolis during 1937. Robert Graham photograph from the GNRHS collection, courtesy of Fr. Dale Peterka.

It looks as though the rods on engine 813 are being oiled. The engine was photographed at Minot in July 1938. The completely black cylinder block was fairly common on Minot Division engines. George Harris photograph from the collection of Norman F. Priebe.

Chapter 8

Class C 0-8-0 Eight-Wheel Switcher

Class C-1

Until 1918, switching chores on the Great Northern Railway were handled by several classes of 0-6-0's, elderly 4-4-0's which had been rebuilt with low (49 to 55-inch) drivers, and, in the early days, a small number of 0-4-0's. Due to increasing train weights and the resultant need for heavier switching service, an order was placed with Baldwin in 1918 for forty 0-8-0 switchers, designated Class C-1 upon their arrival. These locomotives were delivered as Nos. 810 through 849, and kept these numbers throughout their service lives. They had the common (at least for the GN) 55-inch drivers and 26-inch by 28-inch cylinders. They were equipped with Walschaert valve gear and piston valves. As delivered, they operated at a boiler pressure of 200 psi (design pressure was 210 psi) with a total weight of 232,600 pounds (all on the drivers, of course) and a tractive effort of 58,500 pounds. Tender capacities were 12 tons of coal and 6,000 gallons of water. They had Great Northern New Style superheaters. The last of the C-1's were delivered in early 1919, which allowed the GN to avoid buying the USRA 0-8-0 switcher whose construction began as the C-1's were completed.

The external appearance of these locomotives changed remarkably little during their service lives. The alterations consisted primarily of minor piping changes. Many of them received a second air pump, including at least Nos. 810-812,817-819,822,829-831,836-837,840-841,843 and 845. (Note that Nos. 814, 820, 821, 826, 832-834, 838, 842, 846 and 848 apparently never had a second pump installed.) Unlike most other GN steam locomotives, each Class C-1 locomotive operated with a Class C-1 tender until it went to the scrap line. Some of the locomotives were converted to oil burners, beginning with Nos. 820 and 838, which were converted before 1926. During, or shortly after, World War II all but fifteen of them were converted to oil.

The coal burners remaining were Nos. 810-812, 818, 819,822,829-831,836,837,839,841,845 and 849. At this same time, working steam pressure was raised to 210 psi, increasing tractive effort to 61,430 lbs. As a result of the reweigh case (see Chapter 4), weight on drivers was increased to 253,200 lbs. (coal burners) or 245,640 lbs. (oil burners). In the mid to late 1940's, the engines received mechanical lubricators and either Nathan or Barco low water alarms.[1] By 1951 all of the C-1's had been converted to burn oil. Another cosmetic change was the installation of window vestibules on the cabs of many locomotives during the late 1940's or early 1950's. The GN called them cab storm windows. Nos. 821, 826 and 832 acquired some unique piping modifications in February 1952 so that they could be operated with the Bros Sno-Melter (No. X-1620) acquired that year.

While the C-1's certainly never had the beauty or glamour of the P-2 or S-2 passenger locomotives, it is noteworthy that these "lowly" 0-8-0's outlasted nearly all their more publicized sisters. With two exceptions – 812 and 844 – the C-1 class survived intact until December 1957, when the first twelve locomotives were retired. Even after retirement, the entire class but one sat in the Superior deadline until they went to the cutting torch en masse in 1962 and 1963.

Class C-2

The remaining classes of 0-8-0's on the Great Northern were Consolidations from which the engine trucks had been removed, thus placing the entire engine weight on the drivers. It seems likely that the GN found itself with an excess of 2-8-0's after it began receiving the heavier and more powerful 2-8-2's, and had begun using them as switchers. A January 12, 1926, memo from William Kelly to C.O. Jenks stated "These engines switching as a consolidated engine, take the F-6

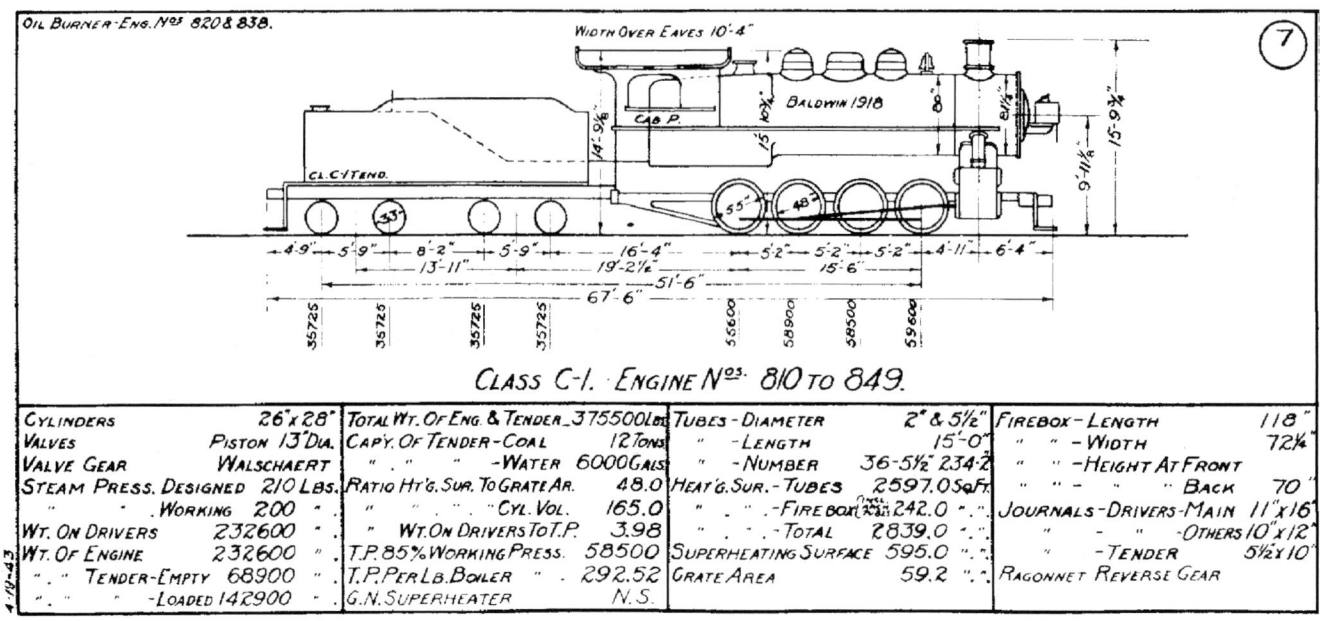

OIL BURNER ENG. Nos. 820 & 838.

CLASS C-1. ENGINE Nos. 810 to 849.

CYLINDERS	26" x 28"	TOTAL WT. OF ENG. & TENDER	375500 Lbs.	TUBES - DIAMETER	2" & 5½"	FIREBOX - LENGTH	118"

CYLINDERS	26"x28"	TOTAL WT. OF ENG. & TENDER	375500 Lbs.	TUBES - DIAMETER	2" & 5½"	FIREBOX - LENGTH	118"
VALVES	PISTON 13"DIA.	CAPY. OF TENDER - COAL	12 Tons	" - LENGTH	15'-0"	" - WIDTH	72¼
VALVE GEAR	WALSCHAERT	" " " - WATER	6000 Gals	" - NUMBER	36-5½" 234-2"	" - HEIGHT AT FRONT	
STEAM PRESS. DESIGNED	210 LBS.	RATIO HT'G. SUR. TO GRATE AR.	48.0	HEAT'G. SUR. - TUBES	2597.0 Sq.Ft.	" " " BACK	70"
" " WORKING	200 "	" " " " CYL. VOL.	165.0	" " - FIREBOX	242.0 "	JOURNALS - DRIVERS - MAIN	11"x16"
WT. ON DRIVERS	232600 "	WT. ON DRIVERS TO T.P.	3.98	" " - TOTAL	2839.0 "	" " - OTHERS	10"x12"
WT. OF ENGINE	232600 "	T.P. 85% WORKING PRESS.	58500	SUPERHEATING SURFACE	595.0 "	" - TENDER	5½"x10"
" " TENDER - EMPTY	68900 "	T.P. PER LB. BOILER "	292.52	GRATE AREA	59.2 "	RAGONNET REVERSE GEAR	
" " " - LOADED	142900 "	G.N. SUPERHEATER	N.S.				

C-1 No. 820 was photographed in Glacier Park paint with the facing goat herald at Hillyard in July 1938. Wilbur C. Whittaker photograph from the Collias/GNRHS Collection.

C-1 No. 825 was photographed backing a train at Great Falls, MT, in August 1946. The device atop the engineer's side of the firebox is a Nathan low water alarm. Collection of Harold K. Vollrath.

The 815 was one of many GN switchers equipped with cab storm windows. This permitted the engineer and fireman to peer out beyond the confines of the cab wall for signals from switchmen with the window shut in cold weather. Also, from time to time C-1's would be fitted with classification lamps to permit running out on the road, as shown here at Grand Forks, ND, in October 1954. Eric Archer collection.

The 828 was another engine with cab storm windows Engines without these devices invariably had sun awnings installed in the summer. The engine is shown at Minneapolis, MN, in September 1956. Bob Vierkant photograph from the collection of Norman F. Priebe.

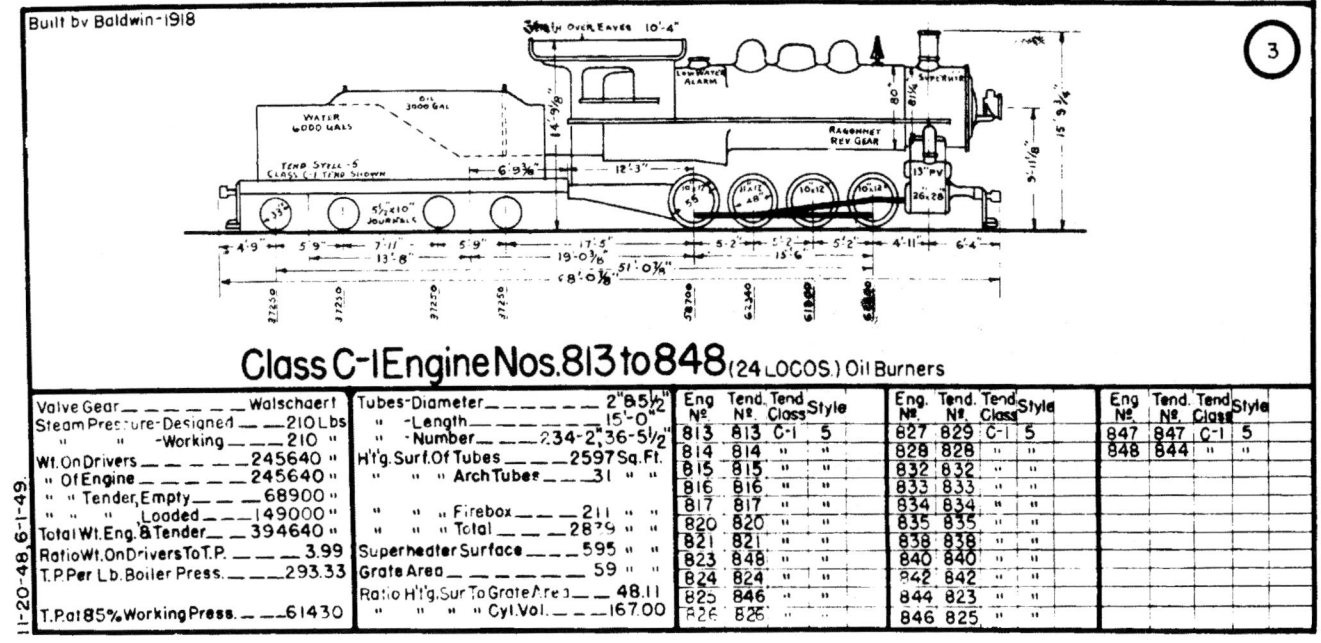

Class C-1 Engine Nos. 813 to 848 (24 LOCOS.) Oil Burners

Spec	Value		Spec	Value	Eng N̊.	Tend. N̊.	Tend. Class	Style		Eng N̊.	Tend. N̊.	Tend. Class	Style		Eng N̊.	Tend. N̊.	Tend. Class	Style
Valve Gear	Walschaert		Tubes-Diameter	2" & 5½"	813	813	C-1	5		827	829	C-1	5		847	847	C-1	5
Steam Pressure-Designed	210 Lbs		" -Length	15'-0"	814	814	"	"		828	828	"	"		848	844	"	"
" -Working	210 "		" -Number	234-2" 36-5½"	815	815	"	"		832	832	"	"					
Wt. On Drivers	245640 "		H't'g. Surf. Of Tubes	2597 Sq. Ft.	816	816	"	"		833	833	"	"					
" Of Engine	245640 "		" " Arch Tubes	31 "	817	817	"	"		834	834	"	"					
" Tender, Empty	68900 "				820	820	"	"		835	835	"	"					
" " Loaded	149000 "		" " Firebox	211 "	821	821	"	"		838	838	"	"					
Total Wt. Eng. & Tender	394640 "		" " Total	2839 "	823	848	"	"		840	840	"	"					
Ratio Wt. On Drivers To T.P.	3.99		Superheater Surface	595 "	824	824	"	"		842	842	"	"					
T.P. Per Lb. Boiler Press.	293.33		Grate Area	59 "	825	846	"	"		844	823	"	"					
			Ratio H't'g. Sur. To Grate Area	48.11	826	826	"	"		846	825	"	"					
T.P. at 85% Working Press.	61430		" " " Cyl. Vol.	167.00														

Built by Baldwin-1918

1-20-48, 6-1-49

*As with the 836, shown at Superior, August 1949, the majority of C-1's with two air pumps were on the Mesabi Division.
R. J. Foster photograph from the Collias/GNRHS collection.*

No. 829 was photographed at Superior, WI, in August 1949. Collection of Frank North.

*C-1 826 is shown at Minneapolis in August 1952. The piping coming down and forward from the steam dome is the
connection to be used when operating the Bros Sno-Melter. Collection of Harold K. Vollrath.*

At Minneapolis, August 14, 1955, the hostler is getting the 814 ready for another shift of switching. This engine had a Barco low water alarm, located between the rear sand dome and the steam dome, well illustrated in this view. Bob Vierkant photograph from the collection of Norman F. Priebe

C-2S 854 was superheated when it was still a Class F-6 Consolidation. It is shown at Minneapolis on April 30, 1939. The tender is carried by arch bar trucks, also used by the C-1 class tenders. This tender, probably with only a 6,000 gallon water capacity, was replaced before the engineer's side photograph was taken. Robert Graham photograph from the collection of William Raia.

The engineer's side of the 854 is shown as it switches passenger equipment at St. Paul Union Depot on September 14, 1946. The 854 ended its career at Sioux City, IA. It kept this tender, a Style 18 F-8 tender with an 8,000 gallon water capacity, until it was retired in 1950. Stan Styles Collection of GTC Collectibles.

and F-9 for instance, carry about 16,000 to 17,000# on the front truck. We remove the truck and place the weight on the drivers. This enables us to bore the cylinders out one inch larger and increase the tractive power on the F-6 and F-9 from 41,540# to 45,800# so you can see what a great advantage this is to us in handling heavy trains that we have to handle at the different terminals."[2]

Class C-2 locomotives were converted from F-6 2-8-0's, with the first ones, 850 and 851, completed in May 1925. By October 1928, the entire class of twenty F-6 locomotives had been converted to C-2's and numbered as 850-869. Fifteen of the F-6's had been superheated prior to their conversion to 0-8-0's, and these locomotives retained their superheaters during the reconstruction. The non-superheated locomotives in Class C-2 were 850, 851, 852, 857 and 858. These locomotives had 21-inch by 32-inch cylinders, a 1 inch larger diameter than the F-6's. GN 859 (formerly F-6 1116) had the same size cylinders as the-non superheated engines. The remaining superheated engines, however, had 23½-inch by 32-inch cylinders, which they had received

when they were superheated as F-6's. All the C-2's retained the 55-inch drivers of the F-6 Consolidations. The superheated locomotives were designated as "C-2S" by Great Northern. Assignment rosters indicate that the C-2's were assigned to the eastern divisions (Minot, Willmar and Dakota).

Class C-3

The Class C-3 engines (875-899) were rebuilt from F-9 Consolidations. The first one, GN 875, was converted in March 1925, and by mid-1928 all 25 of the F-9's had been converted to switchers. Only twelve of the F-9's had been superheated, but these retained their superheaters during the rebuild. Unlike the C-2's, which were all converted at Dale Street, the work of converting the F-9's was done mostly at Hillyard, with a few at Great Falls. Like the non-superheated C-2's, the C-3's had their cylinders bored out to 21 inches, but they also kept their 32-inch stroke. Ten of the F-9's had received 21-inch by 32-inch cylinders at the time of superheating, and they retained

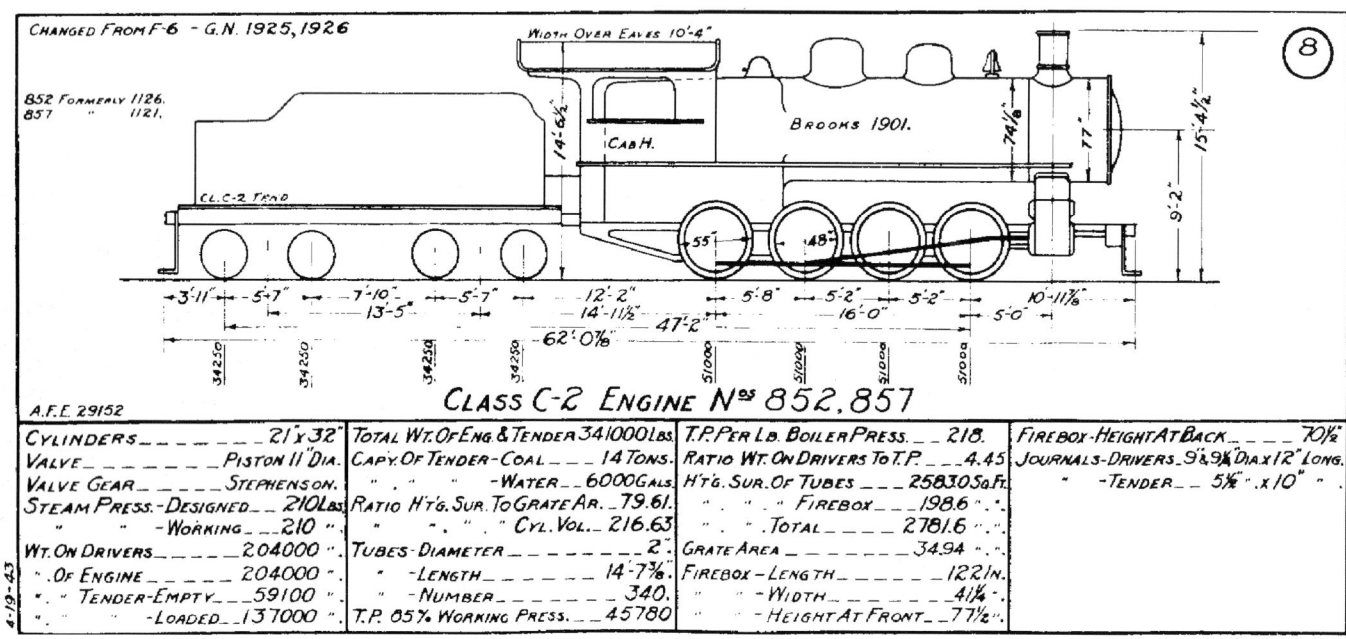

CLASS C-2 ENGINE Nos 852, 857

CYLINDERS — 21"x 32"	TOTAL WT. OF ENG. & TENDER 341000 Lbs.	T.P. PER LB. BOILER PRESS. — 218.	FIREBOX-HEIGHT AT BACK — 70½"
VALVE — PISTON 11" DIA.	CAP'Y. OF TENDER-COAL — 14 TONS.	RATIO WT. ON DRIVERS TO T.P. — 4.45	JOURNALS-DRIVERS 9 & 9½ DIA x 12" LONG.
VALVE GEAR — STEPHENSON.	" . " -WATER — 6000 GALS.	H'T'G. SUR. OF TUBES — 2583.0 Sq.Ft.	" -TENDER — 5½" . x 10" ".
STEAM PRESS.-DESIGNED — 210 Lbs.	RATIO H'T'G. SUR. TO GRATE AR. — 79.61	" . " . FIREBOX — 198.6 ". ".	
" -WORKING — 210 ".	" . " . " CYL. VOL. 216.63	" . " . TOTAL — 2781.6 ". ".	
WT. ON DRIVERS — 204000 ".	TUBES-DIAMETER — 2".	GRATE AREA — 34.94 ". ".	
" . OF ENGINE — 204000 ".	" -LENGTH — 14'-7⅞".	FIREBOX-LENGTH — 122 IN.	
" . " TENDER-EMPTY — 59100 ".	" -NUMBER — 340.	" -WIDTH — 41¼".	
" . " " -LOADED — 137000 ".	T.P. 65% WORKING PRESS. — 45780	" -HEIGHT AT FRONT — 77½".	

A.F.E. 29152

CHANGED FROM F-6 - G.N. 1925, 1926
852 FORMERLY 1126.
857 " 1121.
WIDTH OVER EAVES 10'-4"
BROOKS 1901.

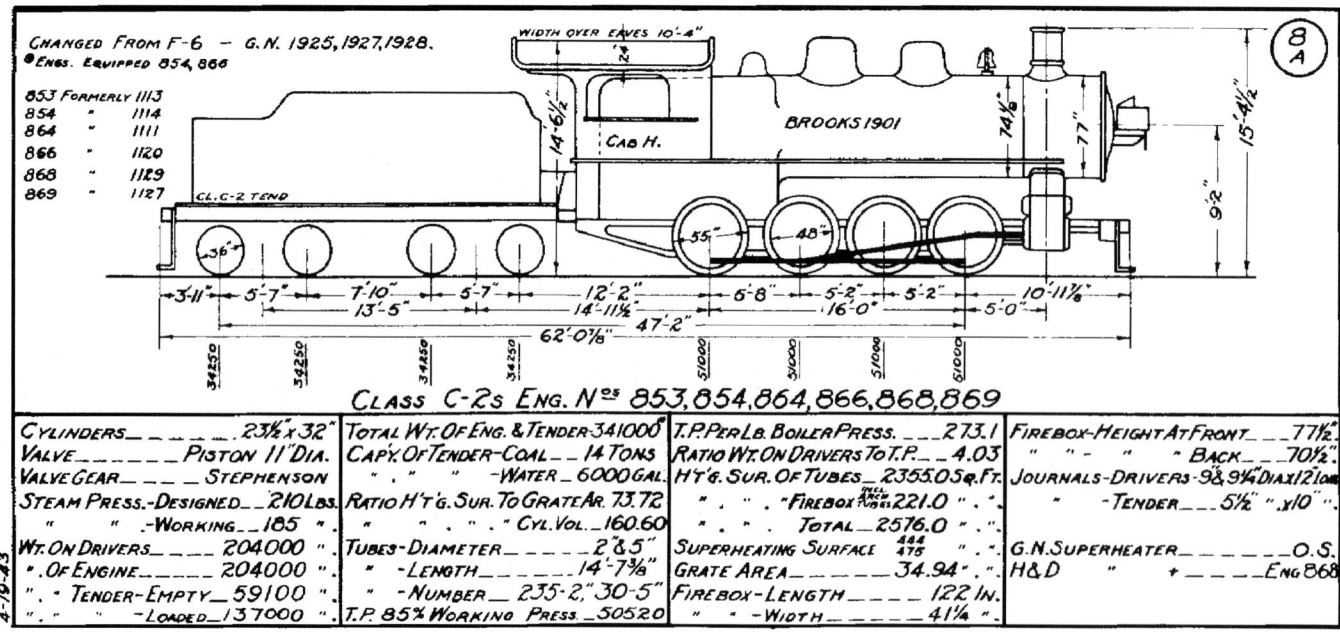

CLASS C-2s ENG. Nos 853, 854, 864, 866, 868, 869

CYLINDERS — 23½ x 32"	TOTAL WT. OF ENG. & TENDER 341000	T.P. PER LB. BOILER PRESS. — 273.1	FIREBOX-HEIGHT AT FRONT — 77½"
VALVE — PISTON 11" DIA.	CAP'Y. OF TENDER-COAL — 14 TONS	RATIO WT. ON DRIVERS TO T.P. — 4.03	" " " " BACK — 70½".
VALVE GEAR — STEPHENSON	" . " -WATER — 6000 GAL.	H'T'G. SUR. OF TUBES — 2355.0 Sq.Ft.	JOURNALS-DRIVERS 9 & 9½ DIA x 12 Long.
STEAM PRESS.-DESIGNED — 210 Lbs.	RATIO H'T'G. SUR. TO GRATE AR. 73.72	" . " . FIREBOX 221.0 ". ".	" -TENDER — 5½" . x 10" .
" " -WORKING — 185 ".	" . " . " CYL. VOL. 160.60	" . " . TOTAL — 2576.0 ". ".	
WT. ON DRIVERS — 204000 "	TUBES-DIAMETER — 2 & 5"	SUPERHEATING SURFACE 475 ". ".	G.N. SUPERHEATER — O.S.
" . OF ENGINE — 204000 ".	" -LENGTH — 14'-7⅞"	GRATE AREA — 34.94 ". ".	H & D " + — ENG 868.
" . " TENDER-EMPTY 59100 ".	" -NUMBER — 235-2", 30-5"	FIREBOX-LENGTH — 122 IN.	
" . " " -LOADED — 137000 ".	T.P. 85% WORKING PRESS. — 50520	" -WIDTH — 41¼".	

CHANGED FROM F-6 - G.N. 1925, 1927, 1928.
ENGS. EQUIPPED 854, 866
853 FORMERLY 1113
854 " 1114
864 " 1111
866 " 1120
868 " 1129
869 " 1127
WIDTH OVER EAVES 10'-4"
BROOKS 1901.

The 856 is resting between jobs at Minneapolis on August 12, 1946. The tender has been fitted with two different truck designs: one Andrews and one Bettendorf. Robert Graham photograph from the collection of William Raia.

C-2S 863 was photographed hiding behind a pole at Minot, ND, in July 1938. This engine remained at Minot until after WWII, after which it went to the Willmar Division until it was scrapped in 1952. George Harris photograph from the collection of Norman F. Priebe.

C-2S 864 was photographed at Minot, ND, on August 29, 1949. All C-2 class engines shown here had been superheated. Collection of Cordell R. Newby.

this cylinder size during rebuilding. Two of the F-9's had received 23½-inch by 32-inch cylinders when superheated, and these also kept the same dimensions at rebuilding. All retained their 55-inch drivers. The superheated engines were designated as "C-3S." Unlike the C-2's, the C-3's were used primarily on Lines West, with assignments to the Butte, Kalispell, Spokane and Klamath Divisions.

Class C-4

The eleven members of Class C-4 were all originally built as F-8 Consolidations. However, the first of these (GN 870, later renumbered as 780) was rebuilt from 2-6-8-0 1999, which had in fact been rebuilt from F-8 1254. The justification stated that "Engine 1999 requires tires, flues and other work. It is the only engine of its class and cannot be simplified. By scrapping the front end, back end…can be converted into a good superheated switch engine."[3] Six of the remaining engines were completed from 1928 through 1930, while the last four were not converted until 1937. The second engine converted was originally numbered as 871, but in 1929 was changed to 781. The C-4's ultimately filled the number block of 780-790. Nos. 780, 781, 782 and 783 had

all been superheated prior to the conversion. Number 780 had 20-inch by 32-inch cylinders. The remaining three had 23½-inch by 32-inch cylinders. One locomotive, No. 785, was superheated and received piston valves at the time of conversion, and it had 21-inch by 32-inch cylinders. The superheated engines were designated "C-4S" by GN. All kept their 55-inch drivers when rebuilt. The 1937-built engines had elevated cabs, with the last two also being narrower. Most of the C-4's were assigned to the Willmar Division, but two were assigned to the Dakota and one the Spokane Division. Tender assignments for the C-4's seem to have consistently been either Style 17 (6,000 gallons water) or Style 18 (8,000 gallons water) Class F-8 tenders, though they commonly had the coal bunkers cut down for better vision during switching operations.

Class C-5

Class C-5 had only four members, which were converted from F-5 Consolidations in 1929 and 1930. All four (numbered as 870-873) retained the 20-inch by 32-inch cylinders and 55-inch drivers from the F-5's. None of these engines had superheaters. All were assigned to the Spokane Division.

C-3 876, one of the non-superheated members of the class, is being backed off the turntable at Interbay in Seattle, WA, some time prior to 1949. Note the unusual sloped sides on the tender bunker. GNRHS Collection.

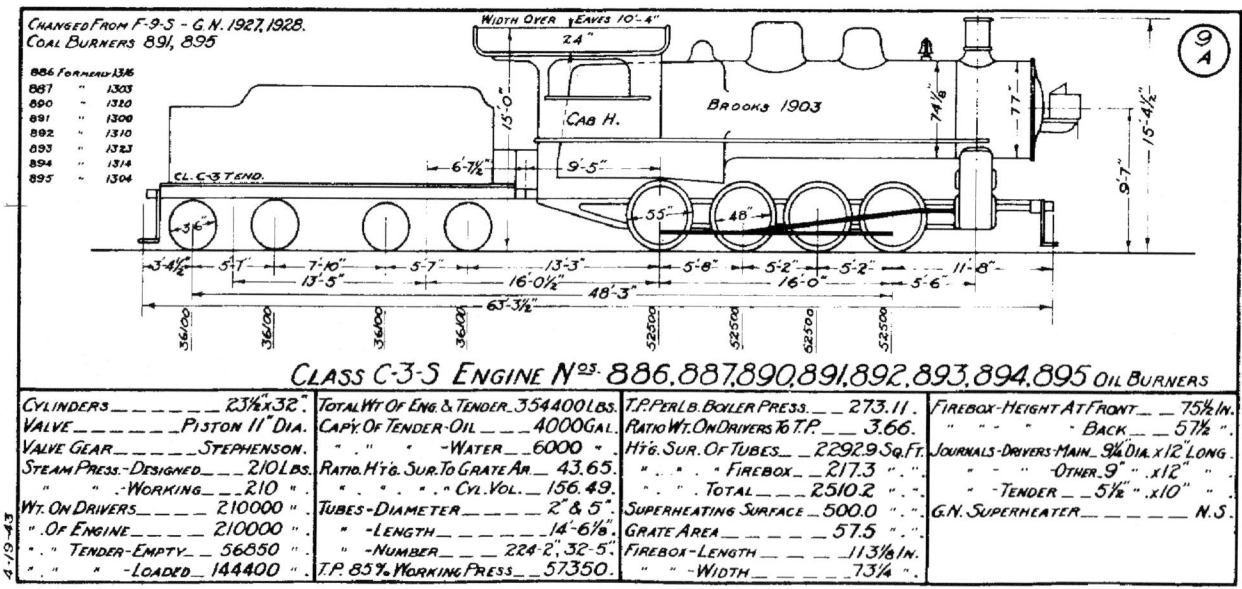

C-3 879 was photographed on an unknown date, probably at Klamath Falls, OR.
Wilbur C. Whittaker photograph from the R. W. Johnston collection of Walter Ainsworth.

Converted from F-6S 1316 in 1927, C-3S No. 886 was photographed at Bieber, CA, in 1941.
Wilbur C. Whittaker photograph from the collection of Walter Ainsworth.

This view of the fireman's side of C-3S 886 was taken at Hillyard, WA, in 1935. GNRHS Collection.

C-4S 780 simmers in the snow at St.Cloud, MN, in 1940. The engine was originally F-8 1254, but was rebuilt to the M-2(1) 2-6-8-0 in 1910. Then in 1926 the front engine of the articulated was scrapped, and the engine converted to an 0-8-0. Warren R. McGee.

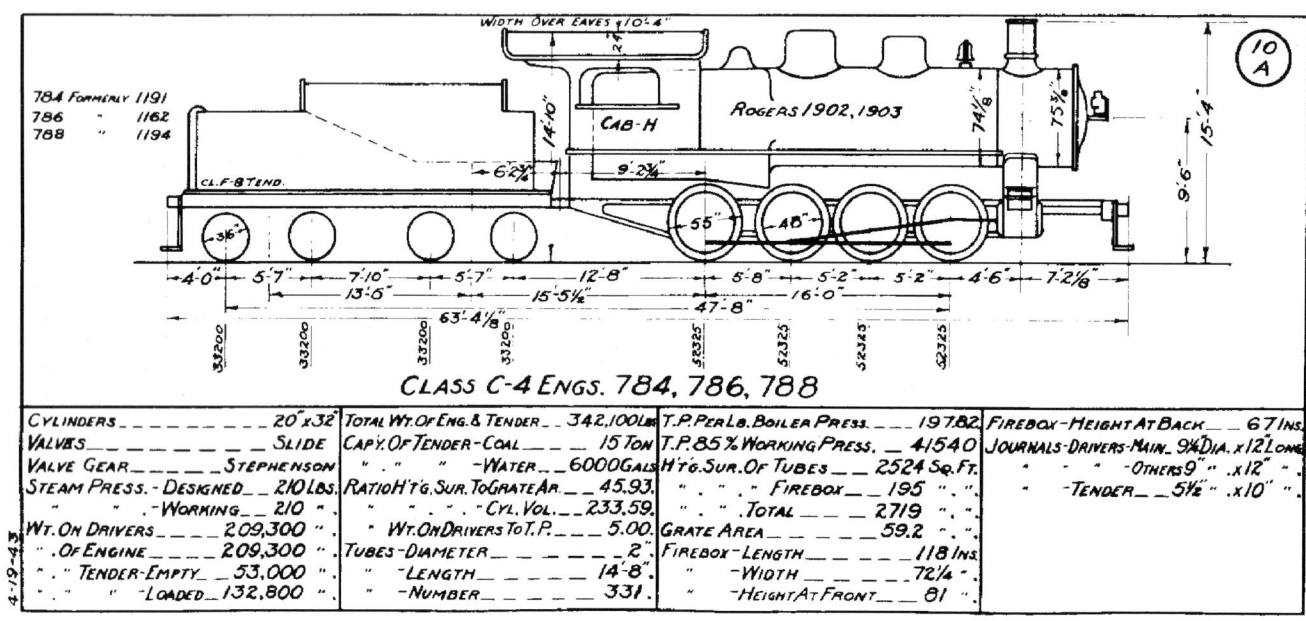

CLASS C-4 ENGS. 784, 786, 788

CYLINDERS _ _ _ _ _ _ _ _ 20"x32"	TOTAL WT. OF ENG. & TENDER _ _ 342,100 LBS.	T.P. PER LB. BOILER PRESS. _ _ _ 197.82	FIREBOX-HEIGHT AT BACK_ _ _ 67 INS.
VALVES _ _ _ _ _ _ _ _ SLIDE	CAPY. OF TENDER-COAL _ _ _ 15 TON	T.P. 85% WORKING PRESS. _ _ 41540	JOURNALS-DRIVERS-MAIN_ 9¼ DIA. x12 LONG
VALVE GEAR_ _ _ _ _ STEPHENSON	" " -WATER _ _ 6000 GALS	H'T'G. SUR. OF TUBES _ _ _ 2524 SQ.FT.	" " -OTHERS 9" " .x12" "
STEAM PRESS.-DESIGNED_ _ 210 LBS.	RATIO H'T'G. SUR. TO GRATE AR._ _ 45.93.	" " . " FIREBOX_ _ 195 " . "	" -TENDER_ 5½" .x10" "
" " .-WORKING_ _ 210 "	" " . " . " CYL. VOL._ _ 233.59.	" " . " TOTAL _ _ _ 2719 " . "	
WT. ON DRIVERS_ _ _ _ 209,300 "	" WT. ON DRIVERS TO T.P. _ _ _ 5.00.	GRATE AREA _ _ _ _ _ 59.2 " . "	
" .OF ENGINE _ _ _ 209,300 "	TUBES-DIAMETER _ _ _ _ _ _ 2"	FIREBOX-LENGTH _ _ _ _ _ 118 INS.	
" " TENDER-EMPTY _ 53,000 "	" -LENGTH _ _ _ _ _ _ 14'-8"	" -WIDTH _ _ _ _ _ 72¼ "	
" " -LOADED_132,800 "	" -NUMBER _ _ _ _ 331.	" -HEIGHT AT FRONT_ _ 81 "	

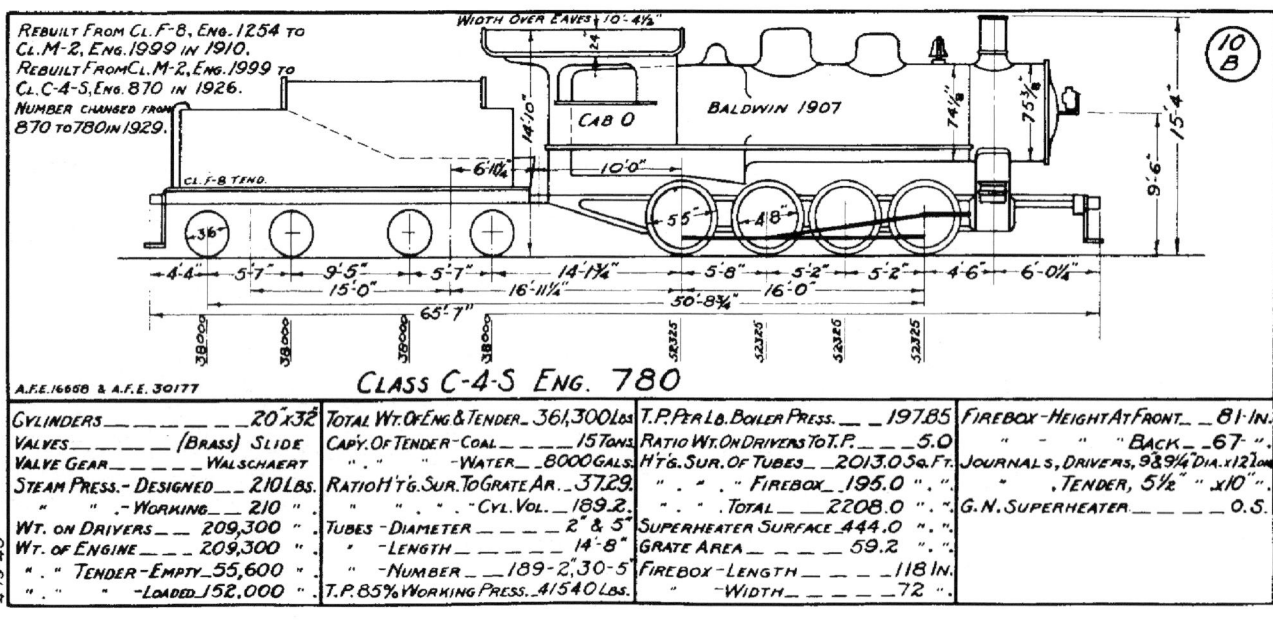

CLASS C-4-S ENG. 780

CYLINDERS _ _ _ _ _ _ _ 20"x32"	TOTAL WT. OF ENG. & TENDER_ 361,300 LBS.	T.P. PER LB. BOILER PRESS. _ _ _197.85	FIREBOX-HEIGHT AT FRONT_ _ 81 IN.
VALVES_ _ _ _ _ (BRASS) SLIDE	CAPY. OF TENDER-COAL _ _ _ 15 TONS	RATIO WT. ON DRIVERS TO T.P._ _ _ 5.0	" " BACK_ _ 67 ".
VALVE GEAR_ _ _ _ _ WALSCHAERT	" " -WATER_ _ 8000 GALS	H'T'G. SUR. OF TUBES_ _ 2013.0 SQ.FT.	JOURNALS, DRIVERS, 9¼" x12 LONG
STEAM PRESS.-DESIGNED_ _ 210 LBS.	RATIO H'T'G. SUR. TO GRATE AR._ _ 37.29	" " . " FIREBOX_ 195.0 " . "	" . TENDER, 5½" .x10"
" " .-WORKING_ _ 210 "	" " . " . " CYL. VOL._ _189.2.	" " . " TOTAL _ _ 2208.0 " . "	G.N. SUPERHEATER _ _ _ _ O.S.
WT. ON DRIVERS_ _ 209,300 "	TUBES -DIAMETER _ _ _ _ 2" & 5"	SUPERHEATER SURFACE 444.0 " . "	
WT. OF ENGINE _ _ 209,300 "	" -LENGTH _ _ _ _ _ 14'-8"	GRATE AREA _ _ _ _ 59.2 " . "	
" TENDER-EMPTY 55,600 "	" -NUMBER _ _ 189-2",30-5"	FIREBOX-LENGTH _ _ _ _ 118 IN.	
" " -LOADED_152,000 "	T.P. 85% WORKING PRESS. 41540 LBS.	" -WIDTH _ _ _ _ _72 "	

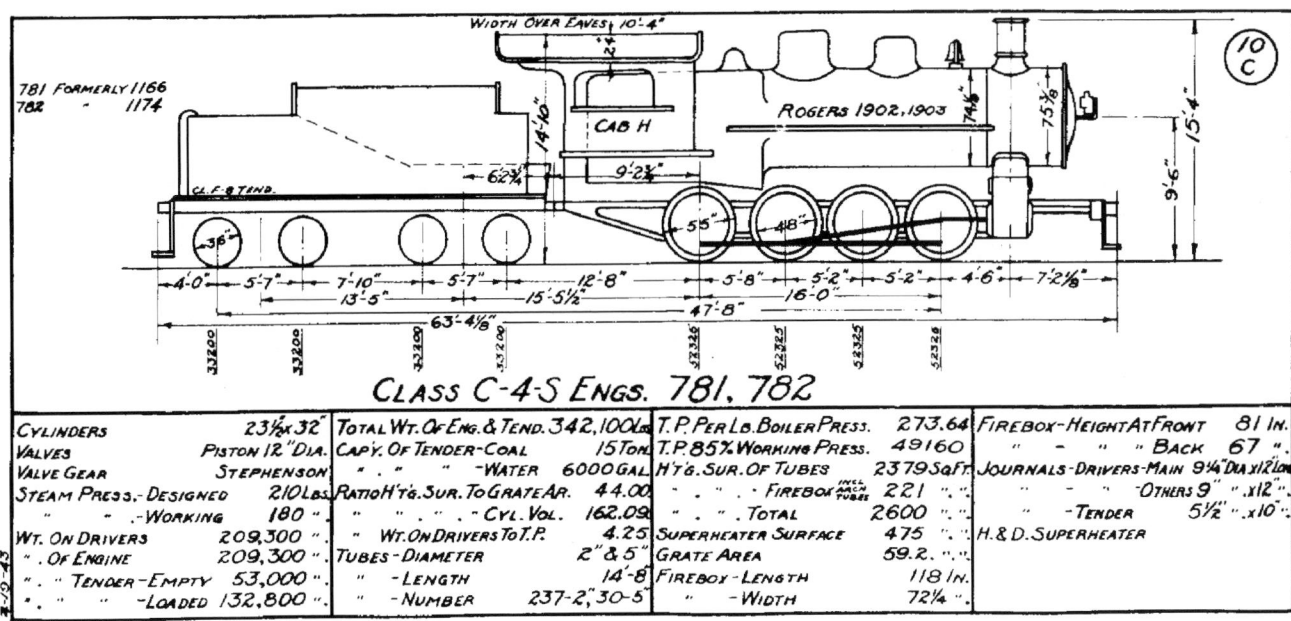

CLASS C-4-S ENGS. 781, 782

CYLINDERS	23½ x 32	TOTAL WT. OF ENG. & TEND.	342,100 Lb.	T.P. PER LB. BOILER PRESS.	273.64	FIREBOX - HEIGHT AT FRONT	81 IN.
VALVES	PISTON 12" DIA.	CAP'Y. OF TENDER - COAL	15 TON	T.P. 85% WORKING PRESS.	49160	" - " - " BACK	67 "
VALVE GEAR	STEPHENSON	" . " " - WATER	6000 GAL	H'T'G. SUR. OF TUBES	2379 Sq. Ft.	JOURNALS - DRIVERS - MAIN 9¼ DIA. x 12 Lg.
STEAM PRESS. - DESIGNED	210 Lbs	RATIO H'T'G. SUR. TO GRATE AR.	44.00	" . " " FIREBOX INCL. TUBES	221 "	" " - OTHERS 9 " x 12
" . " - WORKING	180 "	" . " " - CYL. VOL.	162.09	" . " . TOTAL	2600 "	" - TENDER 5½ " x 10 "
WT. ON DRIVERS	209,300 "	" WT. ON DRIVERS TO T.P.	4.25	SUPERHEATER SURFACE	475 "	H. & D. SUPERHEATER
" . OF ENGINE	209,300 "	TUBES - DIAMETER	2" & 5"	GRATE AREA	59.2 "	
" . " TENDER - EMPTY	53,000 "	" - LENGTH	14'-8"	FIREBOX - LENGTH	118 IN.	
" . " " - LOADED	132,800 "	" - NUMBER	237-2", 30-5"	" - WIDTH	72¼ "	

The piston valves of C-4S 782, rebuilt from F-8S 1174, are clearly visible since they are directly above the cylinders. The engine was photographed in Minneapolis on October 9, 1946. Collection of William Raia.

C-4S 785 was superheated at the time it was rebuilt from a Consolidation. However, the valves were replaced with Heron piston valves rather than cylindrical piston valves. Heron valves were designed to operate in the square slide valve chests. The engine was photographed in Spokane, WA, on June 8, 1946. Ron Nixon photograph from the Wilbur C. Whittaker collection, courtesy of Eric Archer.

C-5 871 is under steam at Hillyard, WA, in the 1940's. Don Vang Collection.

No. 872, another member of Class C-5, was photographed at Tacoma, WA, in March 1947. This view shows the fireman's side. Collection of Norman F. Priebe.

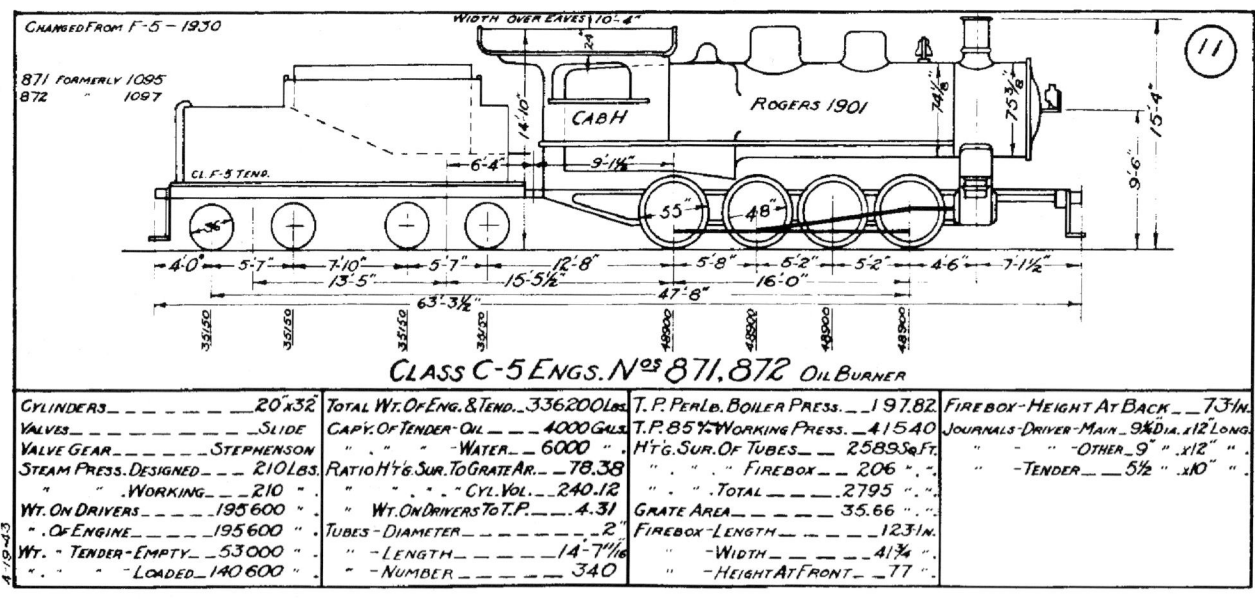

CYLINDERS	20"x32"	TOTAL WT. OF ENG. & TEND.	336200 Lbs.	T.P. PER LB. BOILER PRESS.	197.82	FIREBOX - HEIGHT AT BACK	73 IN.
VALVES	SLIDE	CAP'Y. OF TENDER - OIL	4000 Gals.	T.P. 85% WORKING PRESS.	41540	JOURNALS - DRIVER - MAIN 9¾ Dia. x 12 Long.
VALVE GEAR	STEPHENSON	" - WATER	6000	HT'G. SUR. OF TUBES	2589 Sq. Ft.	" - OTHER 9" x 12"
STEAM PRESS. DESIGNED	210 Lbs.	RATIO H'T'G SUR. TO GRATE AR.	78.38	" " FIREBOX	206 " .	" - TENDER 5½" x 10"
" . WORKING	210 " .	" " " CYL. VOL.	240.12	" " TOTAL	2795 " ."	
WT. ON DRIVERS	195600 " .	WT. ON DRIVERS TO T.P.	4.31	GRATE AREA	35.66 " . " .	
" . OF ENGINE	195600 " .	TUBES - DIAMETER	2"	FIREBOX - LENGTH	123 IN.	
WT. - TENDER - EMPTY	53000 " .	" - LENGTH	14-7"¹¹⁄₁₆	" - WIDTH	41¾ "	
" . " - LOADED	140600 " .	" - NUMBER	340	" - HEIGHT AT FRONT	77 " .	

Notes:

1. Great Northern Unit Record of Property Changes – Equipment.
2. Great Northern Authority for Expenditure 30741.
3. Great Northern Authority for Expenditure 30177.

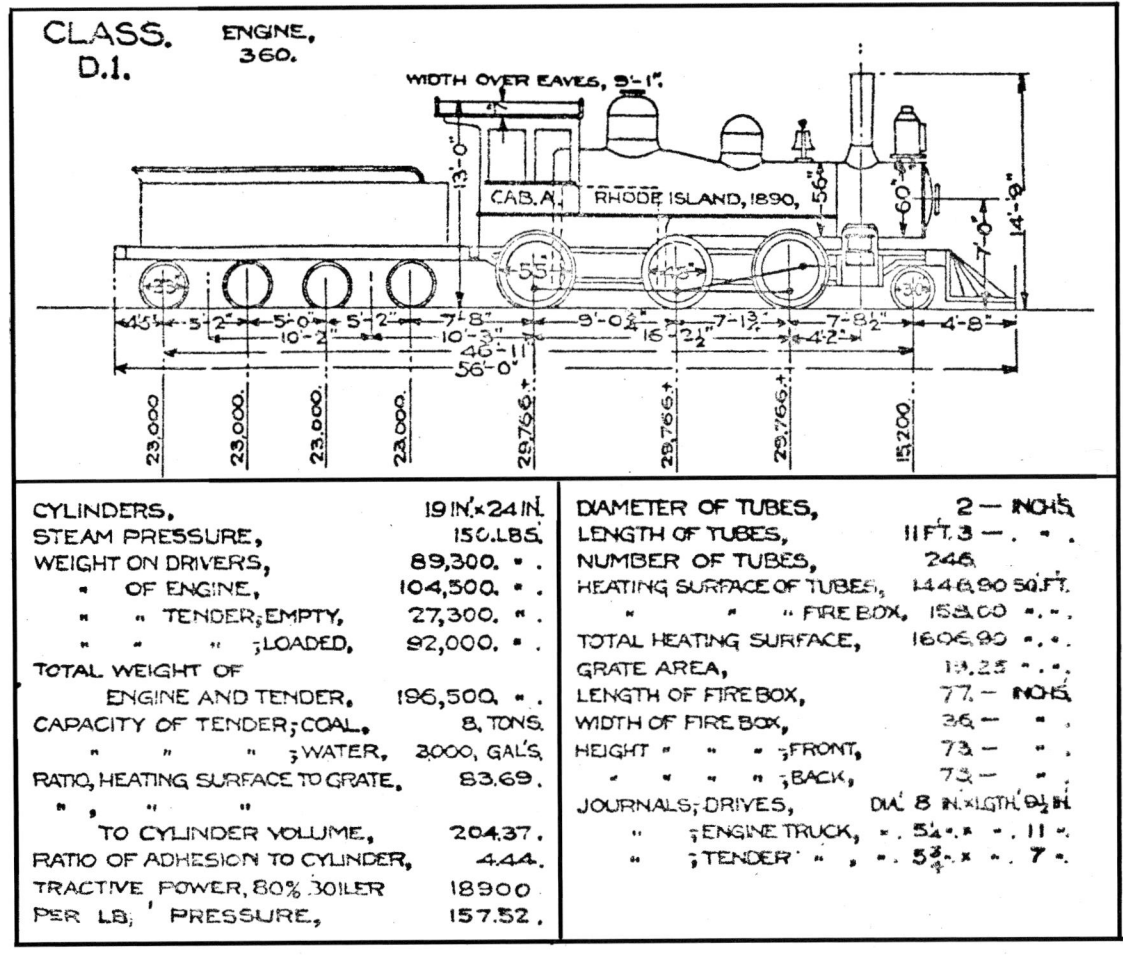

CYLINDERS, 19 IN. x 24 IN.	DIAMETER OF TUBES, 2 — INCHS
STEAM PRESSURE, 150.LBS.	LENGTH OF TUBES, 11 FT. 3 — . .
WEIGHT ON DRIVERS, 89,300. . .	NUMBER OF TUBES, 246.
" OF ENGINE, 104,500. . .	HEATING SURFACE OF TUBES, 1446.90 SQ.FT.
" " TENDER; EMPTY, 27,300. " .	" " " FIRE BOX, 158.00 . .
" " " ;LOADED, 92,000. . .	TOTAL HEATING SURFACE, 1606.90 . . .
TOTAL WEIGHT OF	GRATE AREA, 19.25 . . .
ENGINE AND TENDER, 196,500. . .	LENGTH OF FIREBOX, 77. — INCHS
CAPACITY OF TENDER; COAL, 8, TONS.	WIDTH OF FIRE BOX, 36 — " .
" " " ;WATER, 3,000, GAL'S.	HEIGHT " " " ;FRONT, 73 — " .
RATIO, HEATING SURFACE TO GRATE, 83.69 .	" " " " ;BACK, 73 — " .
" , " "	JOURNALS; DRIVES, DIA' 8 IN. x LGTH' 9¼ IN
TO CYLINDER VOLUME, 204.37 .	" ;ENGINE TRUCK, " . 5¼ . . . 11 ".
RATIO OF ADHESION TO CYLINDER, 4.44 .	" ;TENDER " , . . 5⅜ . x . 7 .
TRACTIVE POWER, 80% BOILER 18900	
PER LB; ' PRESSURE, 157.52 .	

Chapter 9
Class D 2-6-0 Mogul

Class D-1(1st)

The original Class D-1 had only one member. It had been built by Rhode Island in 1890 for the Pacific Short Line, an ambitious project to build a line from Sioux City, Iowa, to Ogden, Utah, which only got as far west as O'Neill, Nebraska. It was fairly small, with 19-inch by 24-inch cylinders and 55-inch drivers, and was numbered Pacific Short Line 14. The Pacific Short Line went through several bankruptcies, and was reincarnated as the Sioux City O'Neill & Western, and then the Sioux City & Western. The Sioux City & Western was ultimately purchased by the Hill-controlled Willmar & Sioux Falls, which renumbered the engine as 360 and placed in Class 36A. The engine became GN 360 when the Willmar & Sioux Falls was incorporated into the GN in 1907. However, in late 1907, GN management realized that a short line to O'Neill, Nebraska, wasn't that vital to them, and leased the line, including the rolling stock, to the Chicago, Burlington & Quincy. GN 360 was delivered to the CB&Q about 1908. The authors know of no photographs of this engine, but diagrams indicate that it had a wagontop boiler with radial stay firebox.

Class D-1(2nd)

On July 1, 1907, the Great Northern purchased The Spokane Falls and Northern Railway Company (SF&N), and with it acquired three tiny 2-6-0's, SF&N 1-3. A fourth identical locomotive, SF&N 4, had been transferred to the Vancouver, Westminster and Yukon, a Canadian GN subsidiary, about 1904. The engines had 18-inch by 24-inch cylinders, 55-inch drivers and weighed only 90,000 pounds They had been purchased from Baldwin in 1889. In 1908 all four were renumbered as GN 477-480, and placed in Class D-1(2nd), the original Class D-1 now belonging to the Burlington. All were sold for scrap in 1926.

Class D-2

The Saint Paul, Minneapolis and Manitoba acquired its first 2-6-0 locomotives in 1887. These were the first road locomotives ordered for the system that were not 4-4-0's. The locomotives were built by Rogers and had 19-inch by 24-inch cylinders and 55-inch drivers. Twenty-five of these locomotives were received in 1887. The engines, numbered as 300-324, weighed only 105,040 pounds, of which 87,290 was on the drivers. They had straight-top boilers. Three of these were sold very quickly to the Montana Central. The Manitoba received twenty-three more in 1888, with three more arriving in 1889. Ten were built for the Eastern of Minnesota (Nos. 201-210) in 1888. Several engines from the 1888 receipts also went to the Montana Central, and one was sold to the Seattle & Montana Railway, one of GN's "Coast Lines." The diagrams show these engines as having fluted domes, but photographic evidence indicates that only the 1887 order did, while photographs of the 1888 and 1889 deliveries show smooth dome covers. For some

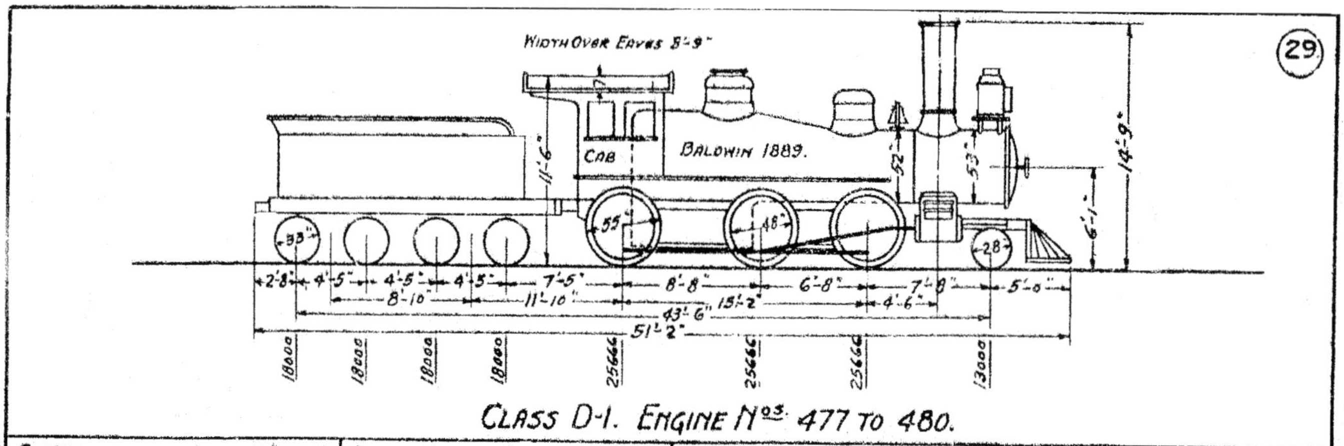
WIDTH OVER EAVES 8'-9"
29
CAB
BALDWIN 1889.
14'-9"
11'-6"
6'-1"
52"
53"
55"
48"
33"
28"
2'-8" 4'-5" 4'-5" 4'-5" 7'-5" 8'-8" 6'-8" 7'-8" 5'-0"
8'-10" 11'-10" 13'-2" 4'-6"
43'-6"
51'-2"
18000 18000 18000 18000 25666 25666 25666 13000
CLASS D-1. ENGINE Nos. 477 TO 480.

CYLINDERS 18" x 24"	CAPY. OF TENDER-COAL 9 TONS.	T.P. PER LB. BOILER PRESS. 120.17.	FIREBOX-HEIGHT AT FRONT 66".
STEAM PRESS. DESIGNED 145 LBS.	" " " -WATER 3000 GALS.	RATIO WT. ON DRIVERS TO T.P. 4.58.	" " " BACK 67".
" " WORKING 140 " .	RATIO HEAT'G. SUR. TO GRATE AR. 75.78.	HEAT'G. SUR. OF TUBES 1148.72 SQ. FT.	JOURNALS-DRIVERS 7¼" DIA. x 8" LONG.
WT. ON DRIVERS 77000 " .	" " " " CYL. VOL. 181.82.	" " " FIREBOX 134.98 " " .	" -ENG. TRUCK 4⅜" " x 10" " .
" OF ENGINE 90000 " .	TUBES-DIAMETER 2".	" " TOTAL 1283.70 " " .	" -TENDER 4¼" " x 8" " .
" " TENDER-EMPTY 42000 " .	" -LENGTH 11'-0".	GRATE AREA 16.94 " " .	
" " " -LOADED 72000 " .	" -NUMBER 201.	FIREBOX-LENGTH 71¾ IN.	
TOTAL WT. OF ENG. & TENDER 162000 " .	T.P. 85% WORKING PRESS. 16820.	" " -WIDTH 34 " .	

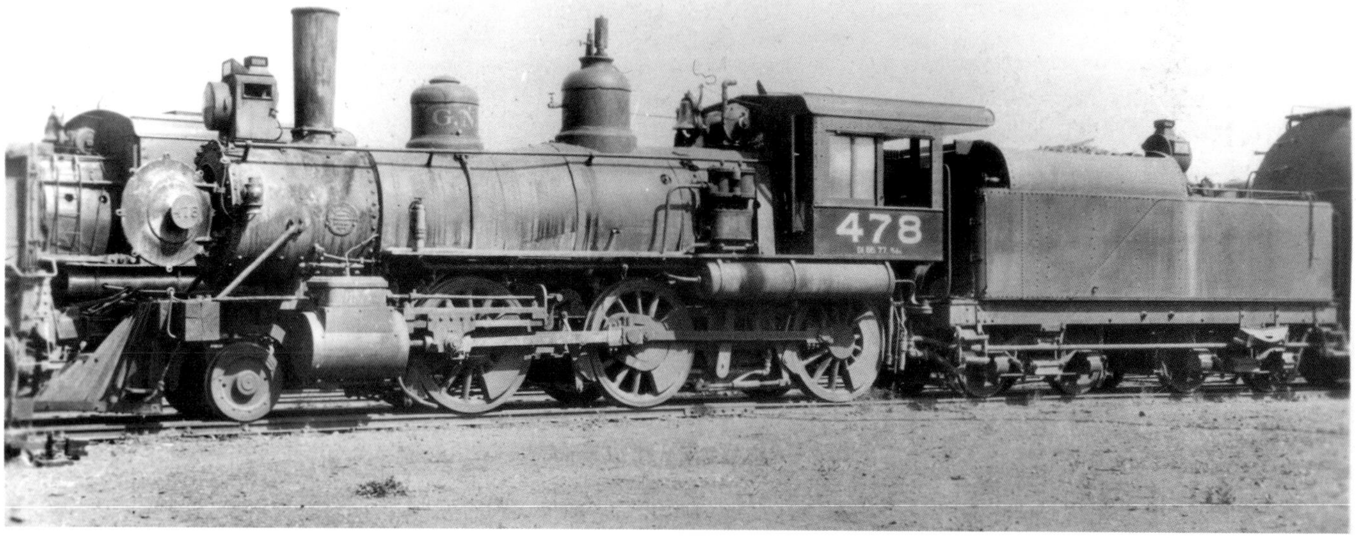
478
Diminutive Class D-1(2nd) No. 478 was purchased by the Spokane Falls and Northern in 1889. In this June 1924 view, taken at Spokane, WA, the engine still has a wooden pilot and an older style headlight. Collection of Harold K. Vollrath.

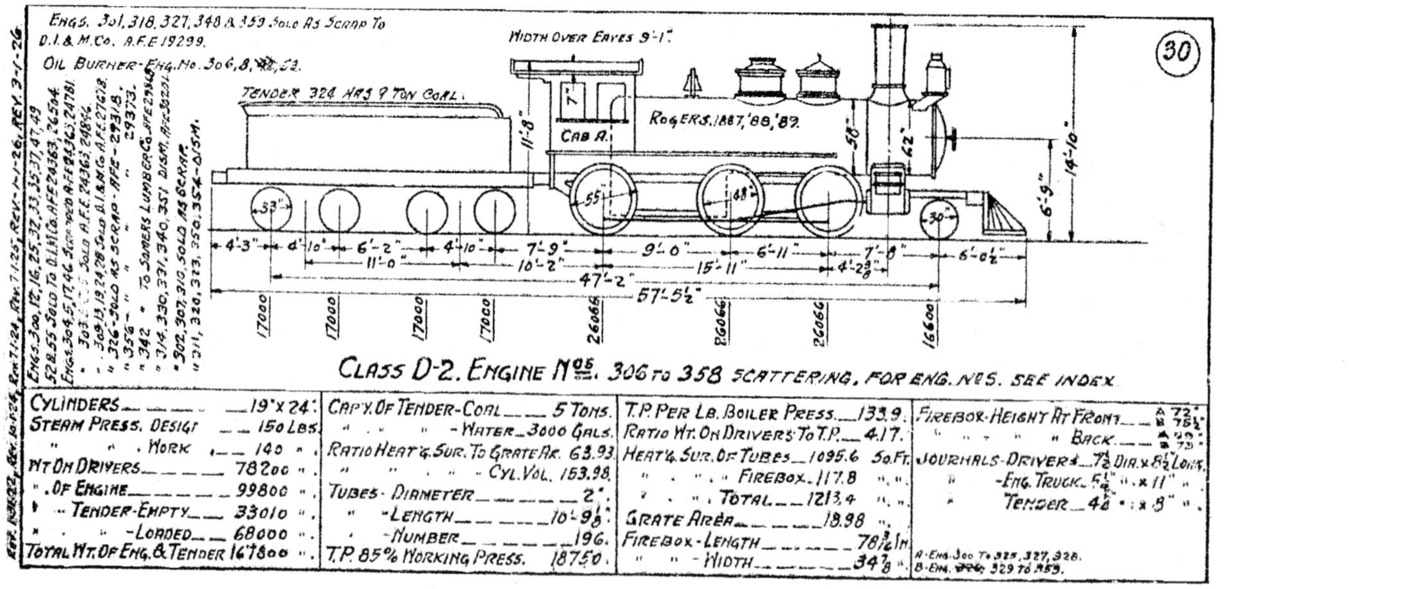
ENGS. 301, 318, 327, 348 & 359 SOLD AS SCRAP TO D.I. & M. CO. A.F.E. 19299.
OIL BURNER-ENG. No. 306, 8, 52.
TENDER 324 HAS 9 TON COAL.
WIDTH OVER EAVES 9'-1"
30
CAB A.
ROGERS, 1887, '88, '89.
14'-10"
11'-8"
6'-9"
58"
62"
55"
68"
33"
30"
4'-3" 4'-10" 6'-2" 4'-10" 7'-9" 9'-0" 6'-11" 7'-8" 6'-0½"
11'-0" 10'-2" 15'-11" 4'-2⅜"
47'-2"
57'-5½"
17000 17000 17000 17000 26066 26066 26066 16600
CLASS D-2. ENGINE Nos. 306 TO 358 SCATTERING. FOR ENG. NOS. SEE INDEX

CYLINDERS 19" x 24".	CAPY. OF TENDER-COAL 5 TONS.	T.P. PER LB. BOILER PRESS. 133.9.	FIREBOX-HEIGHT AT FRONT A 72", B 75½"
STEAM PRESS. DESIG. 150 LBS.	" " " -WATER 3000 GALS.	RATIO WT. ON DRIVERS TO T.P. 4.17.	" " " BACK A 69", B 73"
" " WORK 140 " .	RATIO HEAT'G. SUR. TO GRATE AR. 63.93.	HEAT'G. SUR. OF TUBES 1095.6 SQ. FT.	JOURNALS-DRIVERS 7½" DIA. x 8½" LONG.
WT. ON DRIVERS 78200 " .	" " " " CYL. VOL. 153.98.	" " " FIREBOX 117.8 " " .	" -ENG. TRUCK 5¼" " x 11" " .
" OF ENGINE 99800 " .	TUBES-DIAMETER 2".	" " TOTAL 1213.4 " " .	" TENDER 4¼" " x 8" " .
" TENDER-EMPTY 33010 " .	" -LENGTH 10'-9⅛".	GRATE AREA 18.98 " .	
" " -LOADED 68000 " .	" -NUMBER 196.	FIREBOX-LENGTH 78⅜ IN.	A-ENG. 300 TO 325, 327, 328.
TOTAL WT. OF ENG. & TENDER 167800 " .	T.P. 85% WORKING PRESS. 18750.	" " -WIDTH 34⅞ " .	B-ENG. 329 TO 359.

reason unknown to the authors, some of these were placed in Class 35 and some in Class 36. After the MC and EM engines were incorporated into GN's numbering system about 1900, the entire number series ran from 300 to 359. With the implementation of the new class system, all sixty (both Classes 35 and 36) were placed in Class D-2. As relatively light power, the D-2's apparently became obsolete fairly early, and all but one were sold prior to or during the 1920's. One of these engines, No. 341, was sold to the Brandon, Devils Lake and Southern in 1906,

and then became Farmers' Grain & Shipping No. 4. A diagram has been found indicating that it was proposed to return the locomotive to the GN, as 341, in 1927. It was to have been classified as a D-8, but apparently was scrapped before the transfer took place. GN 342 was sold to the Somers Lumber Company in 1925, and was the only engine to outlast the 1920's, being dismantled in February 1930.

StPM&M No. 324, from the first order that ultimately became D-2's, shows flanged domes and a diamond stack in its builders photograph. ALCO Historic Photos, GNRHS collection.

In this undated view of D-2 300 from North Dakota, the stack and headlight have both been replaced, the cylinder head cover has been removed, and bars have been used to increase the coal capacity of the tender. Collection of Norman F. Priebe.

Class D-3(1st)

The first Class D-3 also had only one locomotive, which had an interesting history. In July 1892 Baldwin Locomotive Works built two small 2-6-0's, numbered 6 and 7, for the Duluth and Winnipeg Railroad Company, which had a railway line running between the Saint Louis River (near Cloquet, Minnesota) and Deer River, Minnesota. These engines had 18-inch by 24-inch cylinders, 57-inch drivers, and weighed 107,000 pounds. In 1894, No. 7 was transferred to the Duluth, South Shore and Atlantic. No. 6, along with the rest of the Duluth and Winnipeg, was sold to the Duluth, Superior and Western Railroad Company on December 1, 1896, where it became number 200. The

Duluth, Superior and Western was in turn purchased by the Eastern Railway Company of Minnesota on June 22, 1898. The little Mogul was renumbered as Eastern of Minnesota 297 and placed in Class 36B. With the introduction of the new class system in 1903, what was now Great Northern 297 became the sole member of Class D-3(1st). In 1905 the engine was sold to the Farmers' Grain and Shipping Company, a GN subsidiary, where it became No. 3. Its return to GN, as No. 430, to be placed in Class D-7, was proposed about 1927. However, the locomotive was apparently scrapped before it could be returned. No photos of this engine are known to exist but diagrams show a straight boiler with radial stay firebox and flanged domes.

Engine 345, from an 1889 order for D-2's, has tall, smooth domes, much different from the flanged domes of the first order. The photo was taken at Minnetonka Beach, MN. Collection of William Bissinger.

While No. 357 is near the scrapper's torch, with its headlight, air pump and other parts missing, it shows different styles of domes, and also an interesting use of wood sideboards to increase the coal capacity of its tender. The tender is reversed and not coupled to the engine. This photograph is the latest view of a D-2 found, at Great Falls. MT, likely taken the summer of 1925. Collection of Harold K. Vollrath.

Class D-3(2nd)

The vacant Class D-3 was reused in 1921. At that time the locomotives of the Watertown and Sioux Falls (W&SF) were incorporated into the GN numbering and classification system. The sole occupant of Class D-3(2nd) was W&SF 13, which became GN 432. This engine was originally built by Baldwin in 1901 for the Kanawha and Michigan, and was apparently sold to the South Dakota Central (SDC) between 1908 and 1911. When the SDC was sold to the W&SF in 1916, this engine became W&SF 13. The engine had 18-inch by 24-inch cylinders, 55-inch drivers and weighed 119,000 pounds. It was scrapped in 1926. No photographs of this engine are known to exist.

Class D-4

The locomotives which were ultimately the members of Class D-4 were built by Brooks in two orders. The first fifteen locomotives were delivered as GN 351-365 in 1893. These had 19-inch by 24-inch cylinders, 55-inch drivers, and engine weights of 118,000 pounds, and were placed in Class 37(2nd). They were the first Moguls on the Great Northern to have Belpaire fireboxes. One of these went to the Montana Central within weeks of its delivery to GN, and three were renumbered as Butte, Anaconda and Pacific locomotives within days of their receipt. One of the Butte, Anaconda and Pacific locomotives was sold to the Oregon Railway and Navigation Company in 1906, and then was sold to the Montana Western (as its No. 10) in 1916. Fifteen identical engines were received in 1895, numbered as GN 361 and 363-370, and Eastern of Minnesota 250-255. In the major renumbering of 1899, these engines became Nos. 400-426, and in 1903 were placed in Class D-4. One was sold to the Spokane, Portland and Seattle in 1924, but all the remainder, except for the Montana Western engine, were scrapped in the mid-1920's.

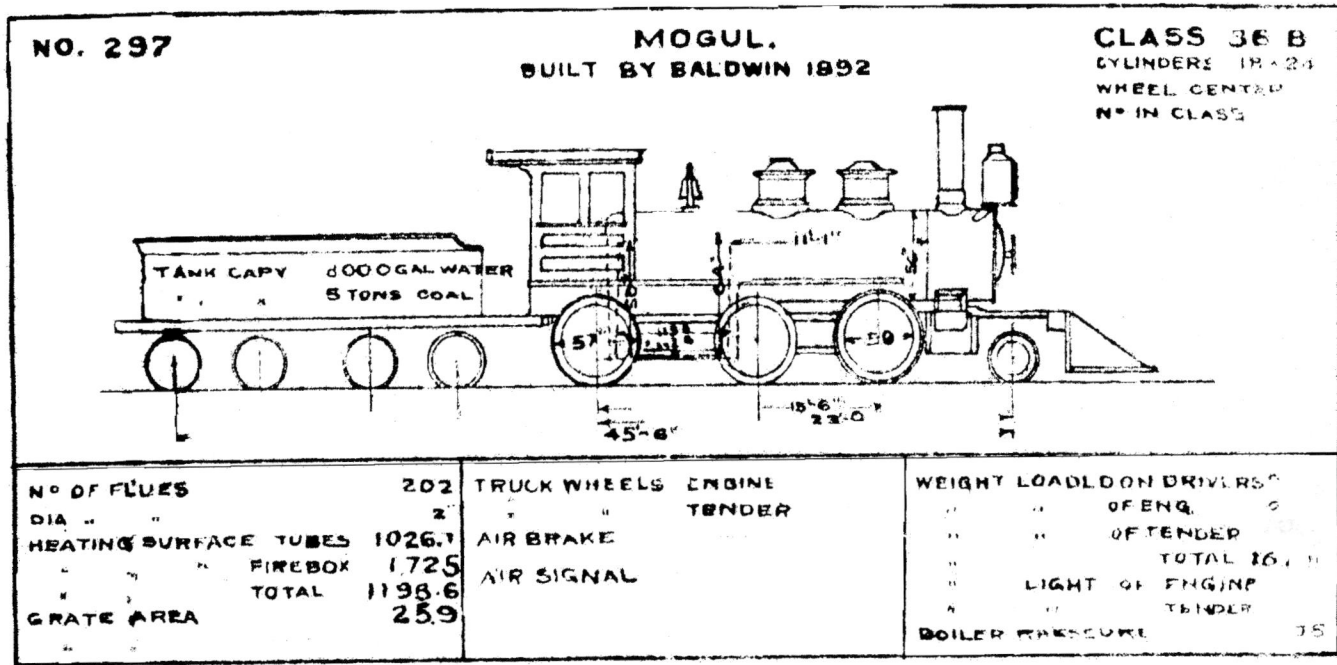

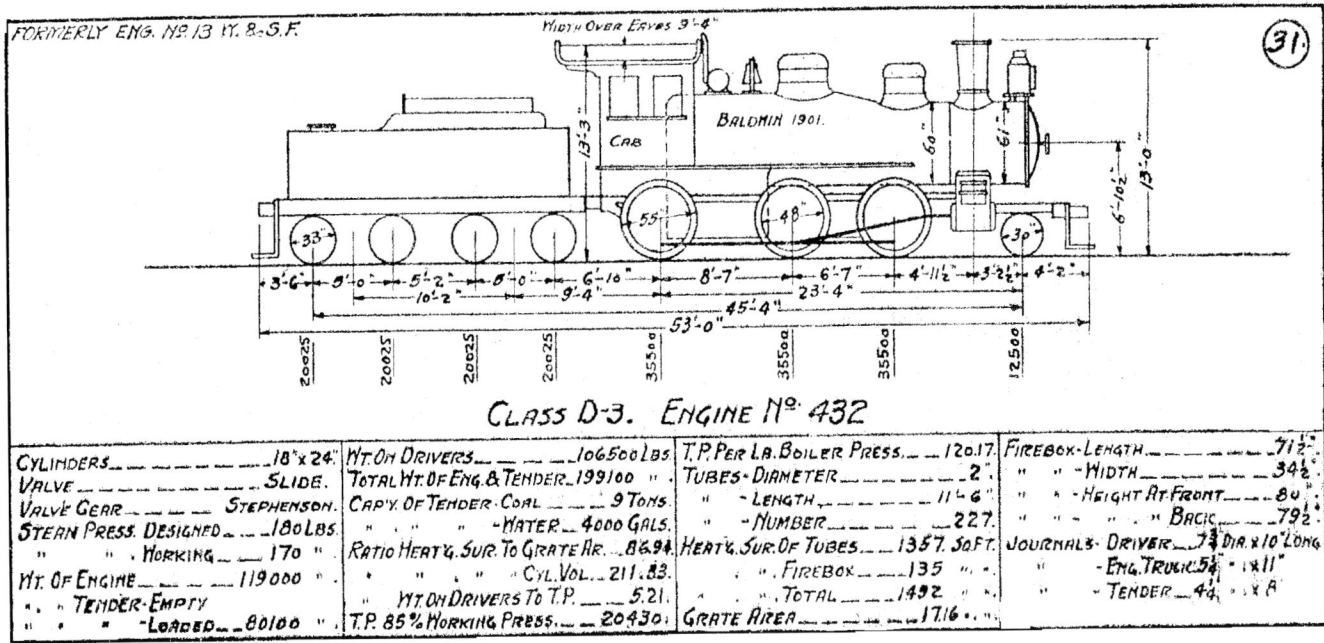

CLASS D-3. ENGINE Nº 432

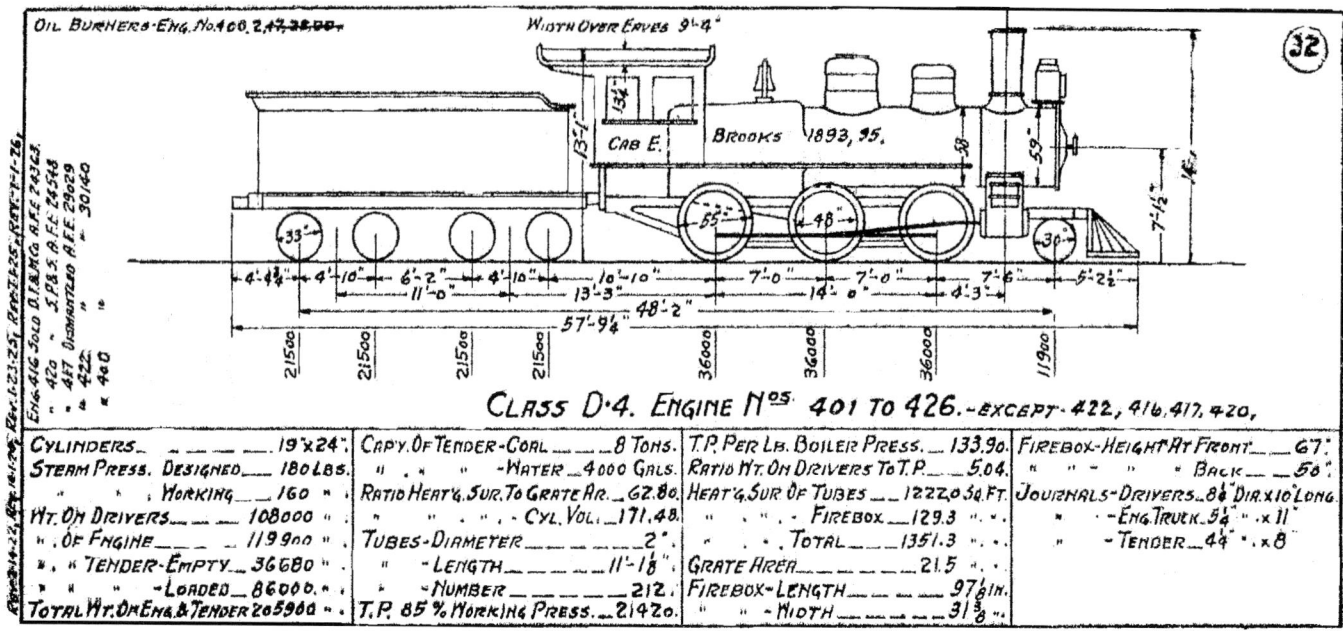

CLASS D·4. ENGINE Nᵒˢ 401 TO 426. - EXCEPT· 422, 416, 417, 420,

CYLINDERS ___ ___ ___ 19"x24".	CAP'Y. OF TENDER-COAL ___ 8 TONS.	T.P. PER LB. BOILER PRESS. ___ 133.90.	FIREBOX-HEIGHT AT FRONT ___ 67".
STEAM PRESS. DESIGNED ___ 180 LBS.	" ___ "-WATER ___ 4000 GALS.	RATIO WT. ON DRIVERS TO T.P. ___ 5.04.	" " " BACK ___ 56".
" , WORKING ___ 160 "	RATIO HEAT'G. SUR. TO GRATE AR. ___ 62.80.	HEAT'G. SUR. OF TUBES ___ 1222.0 SQ. FT.	JOURNALS-DRIVERS..8¼ DIA.x10"LONG.
WT. ON DRIVERS ___ 108000 "	" " ". CYL. VOL. ___ 171.48.	" " . FIREBOX ___ 129.3 " . " .	" -ENG. TRUCK..5½ " . x 11"
" . OF ENGINE ___ 119900 "	TUBES-DIAMETER ___ 2".	" " . TOTAL ___ 1351.3 " . " .	" -TENDER __ 4¼ " . x 8"
" . " TENDER-EMPTY ___ 36680 "	" -LENGTH ___ 11-1⅛"	GRATE AREA ___ 21.5 " . " .	
" . " " -LOADED ___ 86000. "	" -NUMBER ___ 212.	FIREBOX-LENGTH ___ 97⅝IN.	
TOTAL WT. ON ENG. & TENDER 205900 ".	T.P. 85 % WORKING PRESS. ___ 21420.	" -WIDTH ___ 31⅝".	

Great Northern 351(1st) later became D-4 No. 400. ALCO Historic Photos. See below for a photograph as No. 400.

No. 400, the same engine shown above as 351, was photographed in Portland, OR, probably in the 1920's (it was sold for scrap in 1926).
The engine has apparently been fitted for switching duty, as it has a switcher tender and footboards on both the pilot and tender. GNRHS Collection.

No. 408, photographed at St.Paul in 1922, has two different styles of headlights and has received footboards on both the pilot and tender. GNRHS Collection.

The last surviving member of Class D-4 was Montana Western 10, shown here at Conrad, MT, in April 1933. It was originally GN 364(1st), sold to the Butte, Anaconda and Pacific in 1893. It passed through the ownership of three other companies before ending up on the Montana Western. The engine has been fitted up with a fairly modern-looking boiler tube pilot and has had a second sand dome added. Collection of Harold K. Vollrath.

Class D-5

The largest Moguls owned by GN were received in 1896 as GN 371-382. These had 19-inch by 26-inch cylinders, 55-inch drivers, and weighed 130,000 pounds. They were placed in Class 43. These were delivered with "the Brooks Company's patent improved Belpaire wagon top" boilers.[1] Fifteen identical locomotives (GN 383-392 and Eastern of Minnesota 256-260) were received in 1897. In 1899 they were renumbered as GN 450-476, and in 1903 they were placed in Class D-5. Being larger than the other 2-6-0's on the system, some of these engines survived longer than the other Moguls. Two were converted to A-5 0-6-0's in the mid-1920's. Four of them (452, 455, 460 and 466) received a second No. 2 air pump from 1925-1927, though these engines were not among the last survivors of the class. While many of the others were scrapped in the late 1920's, four of them survived until 1937, and two until 1940. The last four survivors were assigned to the Spokane Division, and were all oil burners.

GN 371, received from Brooks in September 1896 later became D-5 No. 450(2nd). Collection of William Bissinger.

D-5 No. 450 is the same engine as shown in the previous builders photograph, but some 30 plus years later.
The engine was photographed at Tacoma, WA, on July 19, 1932. Charles E. Winters Collection.

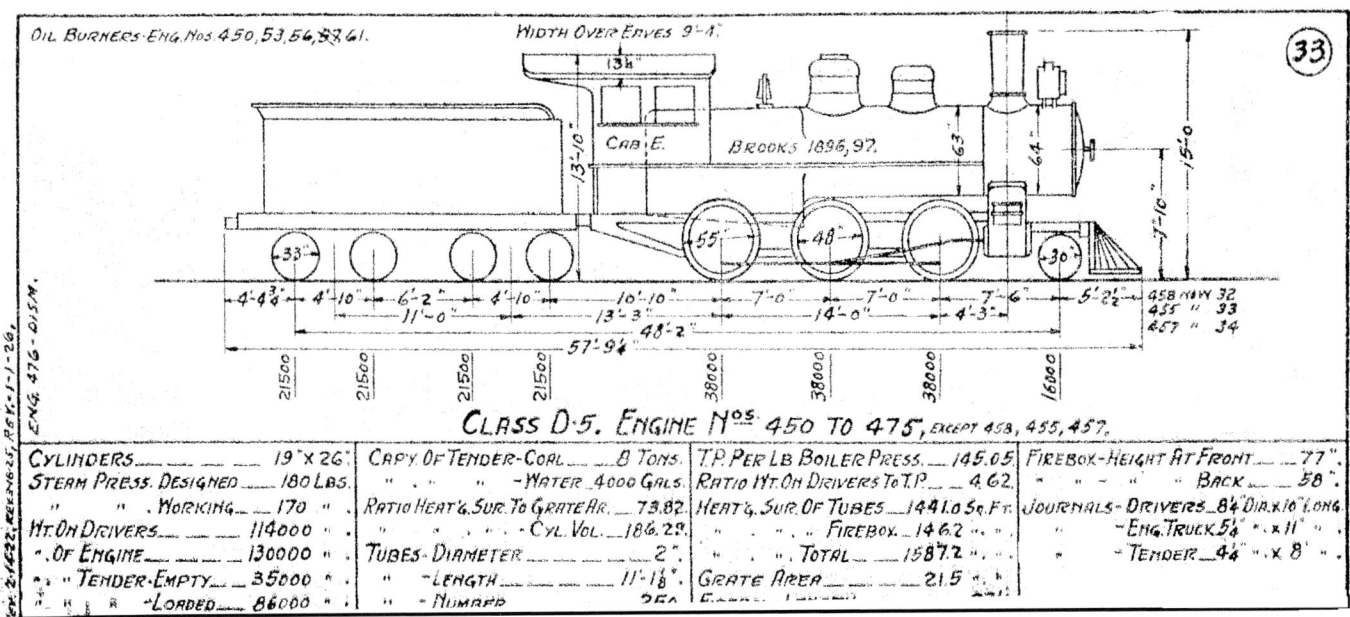

OIL BURNERS-ENG. Nos. 450,53,56,57,61. WIDTH OVER EAVES 9'-4". (33)

CAB E. BROOKS 1896,97.

CLASS D-5. ENGINE Nos 450 TO 475, EXCEPT 453, 455, 457.

CYLINDERS ____ 19"x 26"	CAP'Y OF TENDER-COAL ____ 8 TONS.	T.P. PER LB BOILER PRESS. ____ 145.05	FIREBOX-HEIGHT AT FRONT ____ 77"
STEAM PRESS. DESIGNED ____ 180 LBS.	" " " -WATER 4000 GALS.	RATIO WT. ON DRIVERS TO T.P. ____ 4.62	" " " BACK ____ 58"
" " WORKING ____ 170 "	RATIO HEAT'G SUR. TO GRATE AR. ____ 73.82	HEAT'G SUR. OF TUBES ____ 1441.0 Sq. Ft.	JOURNALS-DRIVERS 8¼"DIA. x 10"LONG.
WT. ON DRIVERS ____ 114000 "	" CYL. VOL. ____ 186.29	" " " FIREBOX ____ 146.2 "	" -ENG. TRUCK 5¼" " x 11"
" " OF ENGINE ____ 130000 "	TUBES-DIAMETER ____ 2".	" " " TOTAL ____ 1587.2 " "	" -TENDER ____ 4¼" " x 8" "
" " " TENDER-EMPTY ____ 35000 "	" -LENGTH ____ 11'-1⅛"	GRATE AREA ____ 21.5 " "	
" " " -LOADED ____ 86000 "	" -NUMBER ____ 250		

D-5 No. 453 wasn't scrapped until 1940, the next to last of its class. Assigned to the Spokane Division, it has been converted to an oil burner, and has a large bunker in the tender. It is shown here at Vancouver, BC, in 1927. Bordertown Collection of GTC Collectibles.

GN 461, the other D-5 survivor until 1940, was also an oil-burning Spokane Division engine. It has received footboards on the pilot. It is shown at Vancouver, BC, in April 1935. Collection of Harold K. Vollrath.

Class D-6

Two additional W&SF 2-6-0's were placed in Class D-6, even though they were not identical. W&SF 11 (formerly SDC 11) became GN 430 in 1921. It had been produced at Alco's Schenectady works in 1902, and had 19-inch by 24-inch cylinders, 55-inch drivers and a weight of 114,500 pounds. W&SF 12, an Alco-Schenectady 1906 product (formerly SDC 12) became GN 431. It also had 19-inch by 24-inch cylinders and 55-inch drivers, but was considerably heavier with a weight of 126,900 pounds. Both of these had apparently been purchased used by the SDC, but neither their original numbers or construction numbers are known. No photographs are known to exist.

Additional Early 2-6-0's

Several other 2-6-0 locomotives were owned by GN predecessors, but were never placed in either of GN's class systems. In 1899 the Eastern of Minnesota acquired the Duluth, Mississippi River and Northern Railroad Company, which at various times had owned eight Moguls. These were built by Porter and Brooks from 1892 through 1898, but apparently were sold before the Eastern of Minnesota acquisition. The Victoria & Sidney Railway Company, which came under GN control in 1902, owned a single 2-6-0, built by the Canadian Locomotive Company in 1902. It was sold about the time the line was abandoned, but never received a class designation.

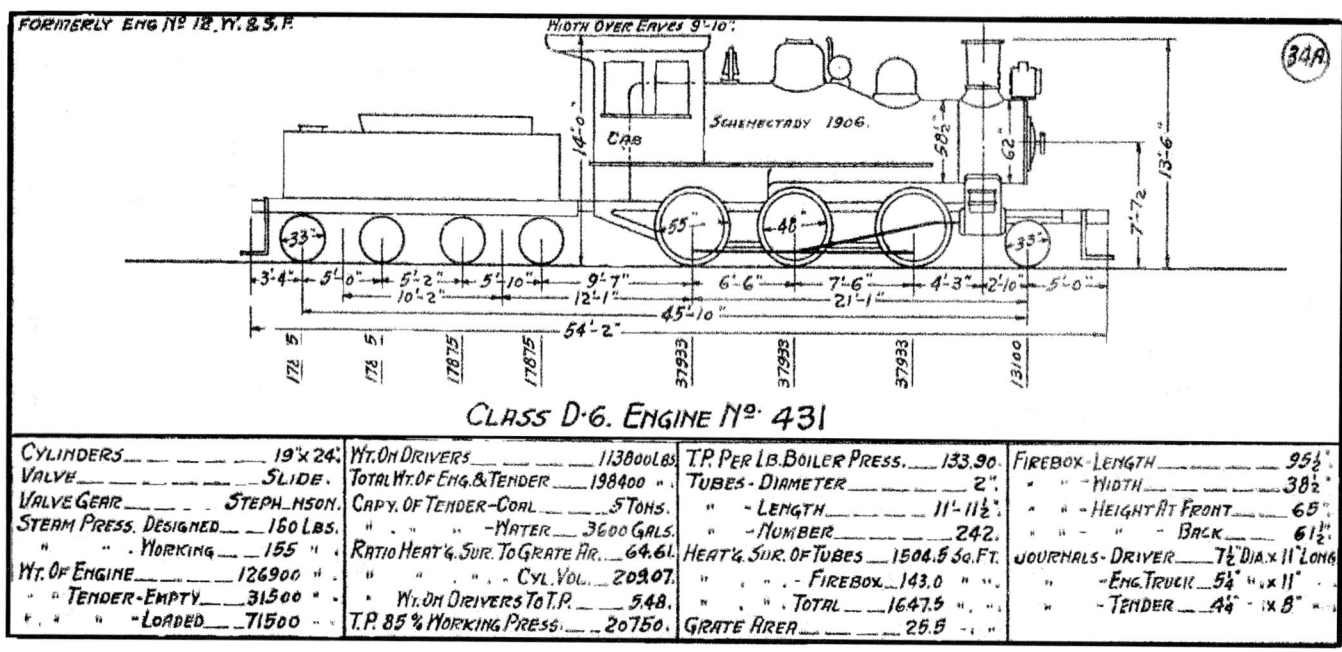

CLASS D-6. ENGINE No 431

CYLINDERS 19"x24"	WT. ON DRIVERS 113800 LBS	T.P. PER LB. BOILER PRESS. 133.90	FIREBOX - LENGTH 95½"
VALVE SLIDE	TOTAL WT. OF ENG. & TENDER 198400 "	TUBES - DIAMETER 2"	" - WIDTH 38½"
VALVE GEAR STEPHENSON	CAP'Y. OF TENDER - COAL 5 TONS	" - LENGTH 11'-11½"	" - HEIGHT AT FRONT 65"
STEAM PRESS. DESIGNED 160 LBS	" " " - WATER 3600 GALS	" - NUMBER 242	" " - BACK 61½"
" " WORKING 155 "	RATIO HEAT'G. SUR. TO GRATE AR. 64.61	HEAT'G. SUR. OF TUBES 1504.5 SQ. FT.	JOURNALS - DRIVER 7½" DIA. x 11" LONG
WT. OF ENGINE 126900 "	" " " CYL. VOL. 209.07	" " - FIREBOX 143.0 " "	" - ENG. TRUCK 5¼" " x 11"
" TENDER - EMPTY 31500 "	" WT. ON DRIVERS TO T.P. 5.48	" " TOTAL 1647.5 " "	" - TENDER 4½" " x 8" "
" " " - LOADED 71500 "	T.P. 85% WORKING PRESS. 20750	GRATE AREA 26.5 " "	

Class D-5 engine 452 was photographed at Grand Forks, ND, in February 1924. It's apparently in passenger or mixed train service. Judging from the ice on the side of the tender, it looks as though it was overfilled with water. Collection of Harold K. Vollrath.

Notes:
1. *The Railroad Gazette*, Vol. 28 (October 23, 1896).

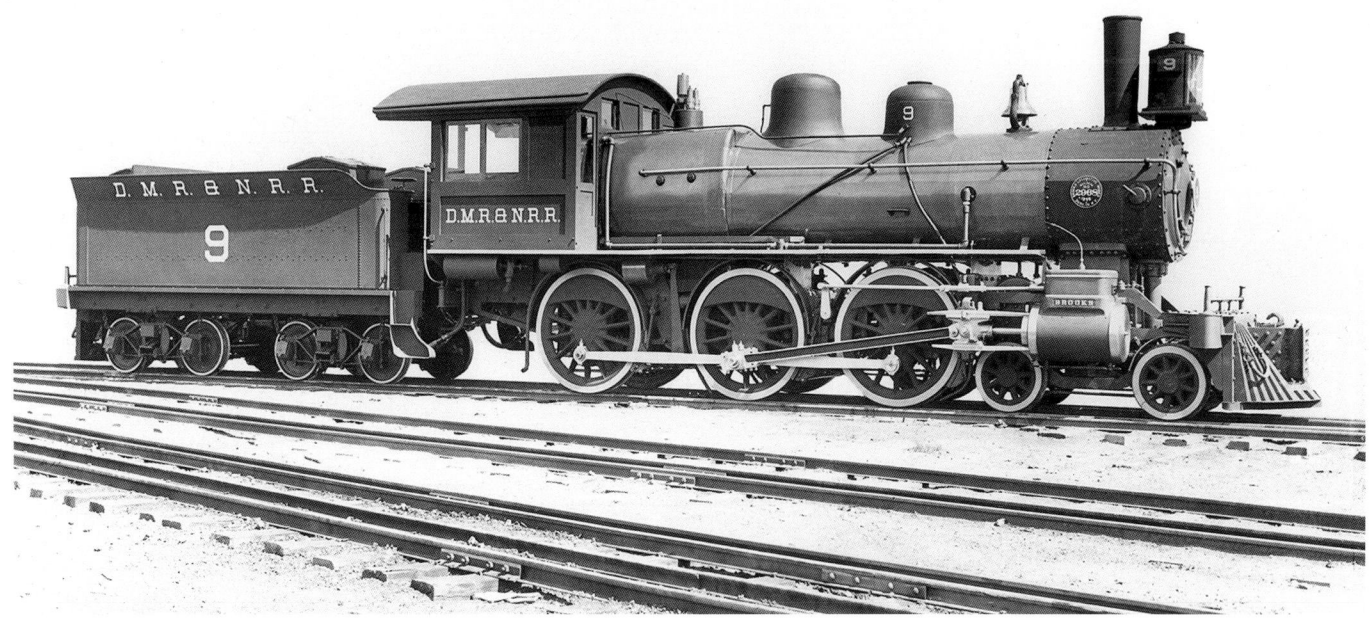

Duluth, Mississippi River and Northern No. 9 eventually became Eastern of Minnesota 991. ALCO Historic Photos.

Chapter 10
Class E 4-6-0 Ten-Wheeler

Early 4-6-0's

Only one 4-6-0 on the Great Northern system did not receive a Class E designation. This engine had been built in 1898 by Brooks for the Duluth, Mississippi River and Northern Railroad (DMR&N), and was the only locomotive from that road that ever received a GN number. The engine was originally built as DMR&N 9 and had 18-inch by 24-inch cylinders and 63-inch drivers, with an engine weight of 127,800 pounds. The Eastern of Minnesota (EM) purchased the DMR&N in 1899, renumbered the engine as EM 231 in that same year, and classified the locomotive as 27B. In 1902 it was renumbered as EM 991, but sold a few months later for reasons unknown to the authors. It eventually found its way to the St.Louis-San Francisco Railway.

Class E-1

The two members of Class E-1 were originally built for the Sioux City and Northern Railroad (SC&N) in 1890. They were constructed by Rogers, and had 18-inch by 24-inch cylinders, 55-inch drivers, and engine weights of 100,000 pounds. When the SC&N was purchased by the Willmar and Sioux Falls Railway in 1900, the engines were renumbered as 992 and 993, numbers they kept after coming to the GN in 1907. These were the smallest Ten-Wheelers on the GN, and they were among the first to be sold, in the mid-1920's. No photos of these engines are known to exist.

Class E-2(1st)

The original members of Class E-2 also had a Sioux City connection. They had been built by Rhode Island in 1899 for the Pacific Short Line as Nos. 10-12. Nos. 10 and 11 had originally been intended to go to the Macon Construction Company, but were apparently diverted to the Pacific Short Line. They were fairly small, having 18-inch by 24-inch cylinders, 56-inch drivers, and weights of only 102,800 pounds. They were transferred to the Sioux City, O'Neill and Western (SCO&W) Railway in 1891, and at some time while on the SCO&W were renumbered as 14-16. This was likely done because the SCO&W was at that time controlled by the same individuals who owned the SC&N. The roads were probably operated in conjunction, but the SC&N already had locomotives numbered as 10-12. In 1899 the bankrupt SCO&W was reorganized as the Sioux City and Western (SC&W), and almost immediately was leased by the Willmar and Sioux Falls (WSF), a GN subsidiary. The engines were renumbered as 994-996 and assigned Class 27C. The GN purchased the WSF in July 1907, but the SC&W had still only been leased rather than purchased by the WSF. In November 1907 the SC&W lease was assigned to the Chicago, Burlington & Quincy, and shortly thereafter the locomotives were turned over by the GN. No photos of these engines have been found.

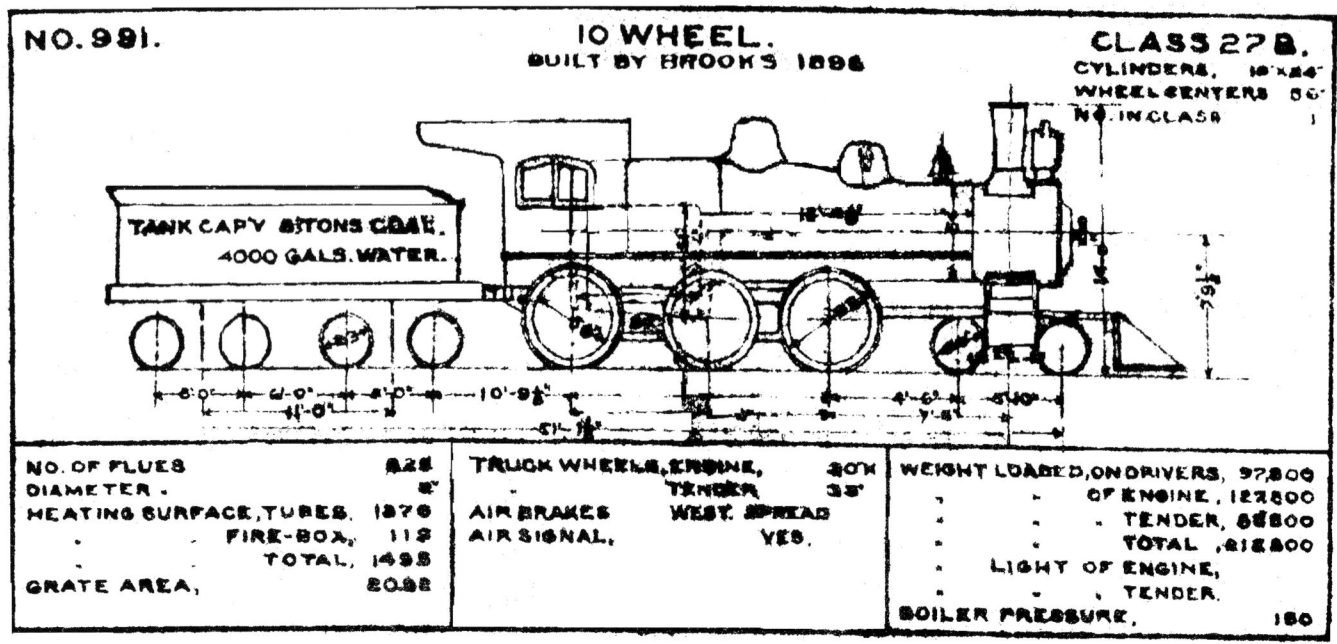

NO. 991.   **10 WHEEL.**   **CLASS 27B.**
BUILT BY BROOKS 1896
CYLINDERS, 18"×24"
WHEEL CENTERS 56"
NO. IN CLASS 1

TANK CAP'Y 8 TONS COAL.
4000 GALS. WATER.

NO. OF FLUES	225	TRUCK WHEELS, ENGINE,	30"	WEIGHT LOADED, ON DRIVERS,	97,800
DIAMETER	2"	TENDER	33"	" " OF ENGINE,	127,800
HEATING SURFACE, TUBES,	1376	AIR BRAKES	WEST. SPREAD	" " " TENDER,	85,800
" " FIRE-BOX,	112	AIR SIGNAL,	YES.	" " " TOTAL,	213,800
" " TOTAL,	1498			" LIGHT OF ENGINE,	
GRATE AREA,	20.98			" " TENDER,	
				BOILER PRESSURE,	150

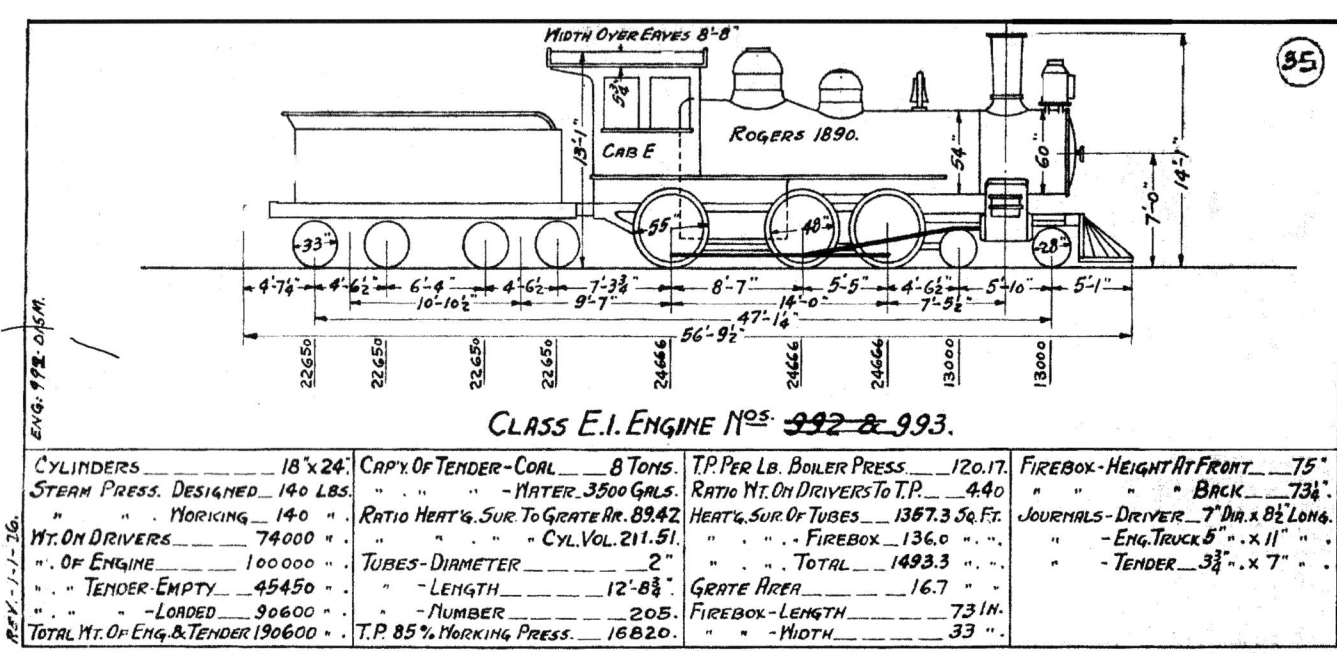

WIDTH OVER EAVES 8'-8"
CAB E   ROGERS 1890.

ENG: 992-0|5M.
REV-1-1-26.

CLASS E.1. ENGINE Nos. 992 & 993.

CYLINDERS	18"×24"	CAP'Y. OF TENDER–COAL	8 TONS	T.P. PER LB. BOILER PRESS.	120.17	FIREBOX–HEIGHT AT FRONT	75"
STEAM PRESS. DESIGNED	140 LBS.	" " –WATER	3500 GALS.	RATIO WT. ON DRIVERS TO T.P.	4.40	" " " BACK	73¼"
" " WORKING	140 "	RATIO HEAT'G. SUR. TO GRATE AR.	89.42	HEAT'G. SUR. OF TUBES	1357.3 SQ. FT.	JOURNALS–DRIVER	7" DIA. × 8½" LONG
WT. ON DRIVERS	74000 "	" " " CYL. VOL.	211.51	" " " FIREBOX	136.0 " "	" –ENG. TRUCK 5" " × 11"	
" OF ENGINE	100000 "	TUBES–DIAMETER	2"	" " " TOTAL	1493.3 " "	" –TENDER 3¾" " × 7"	
" " TENDER–EMPTY	45450 "	" –LENGTH	12'-8¾"	GRATE AREA	16.7 " "		
" " –LOADED	90600 "	" –NUMBER	205	FIREBOX–LENGTH	73 IN.		
TOTAL WT. OF ENG. & TENDER	190600 "	T.P. 85% WORKING PRESS.	16820	" –WIDTH	33 "		

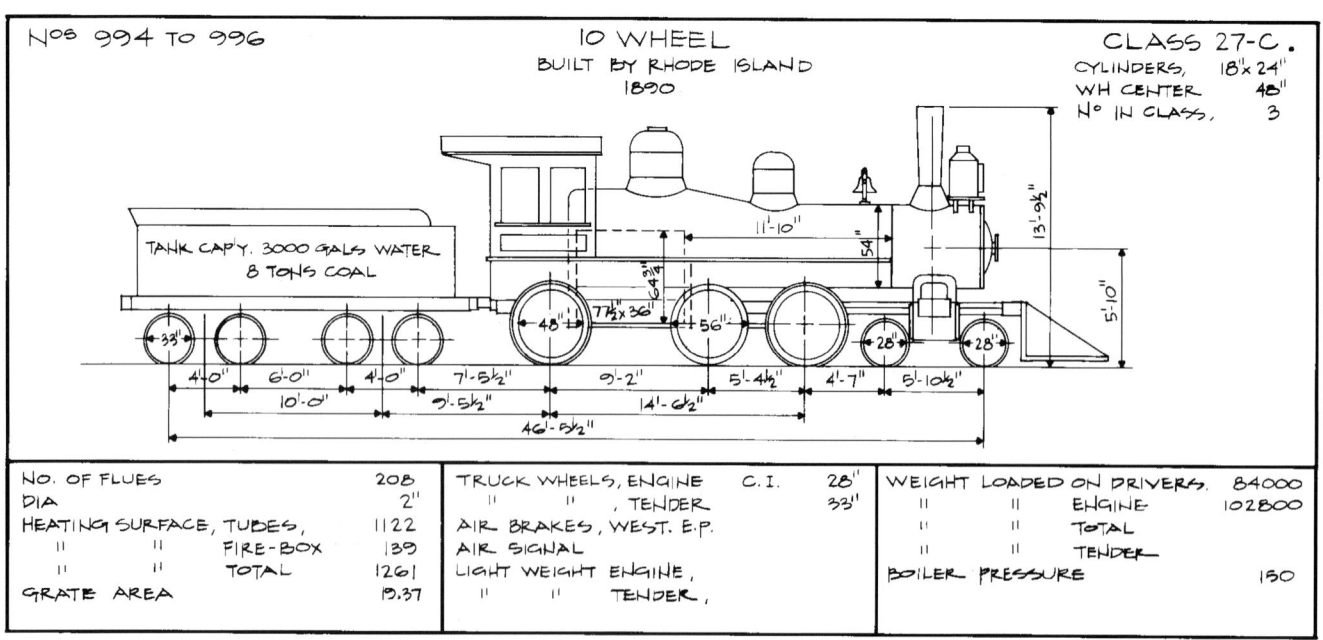

Nos 994 TO 996   **10 WHEEL**   **CLASS 27-C.**
BUILT BY RHODE ISLAND
1890
CYLINDERS, 18"×24"
WH CENTER 48"
No IN CLASS, 3

TANK CAP'Y. 3000 GALS WATER
8 TONS COAL

NO. OF FLUES	208	TRUCK WHEELS, ENGINE C.I.	28"	WEIGHT LOADED ON DRIVERS.	84000
DIA	2"	" " , TENDER	33"	" " ENGINE	102800
HEATING SURFACE, TUBES,	1122	AIR BRAKES, WEST. E.P.		" " TOTAL	
" " " FIRE-BOX	139	AIR SIGNAL		" " TENDER	
" " " TOTAL	1261	LIGHT WEIGHT ENGINE,		BOILER PRESSURE	150
GRATE AREA	19.37	" " TENDER,			

Class E-2(2nd)

In 1921, Class E-2 was reused for two Ten-Wheelers acquired along with the Watertown and Sioux Falls (W&SF) Railway. These were built in Alco's Brooks works in 1915 as South Dakota Central 16 and 17, and became W&SF 16 and 17 when it took over the South Dakota Central. The two engines were not identical, but were placed in the same class. They both had 18-inch by 24-inch cylinders and 60-inch drivers. The engine weights were 130,000 pounds for the former SDC 16 and 135,500 pounds for the former SDC 17. These engines had radial stay fireboxes. They were renumbered as GN 910 and 911 in 1921. At some time during their service lives, No. 910 received 63-inch drivers and No. 911 received 61-inch drivers. By the mid-1930's they had been moved to the Mesabi Division, where they apparently spent most of their days. Both were equipped with Class E-15 tenders, and both were sold for scrap in 1949.

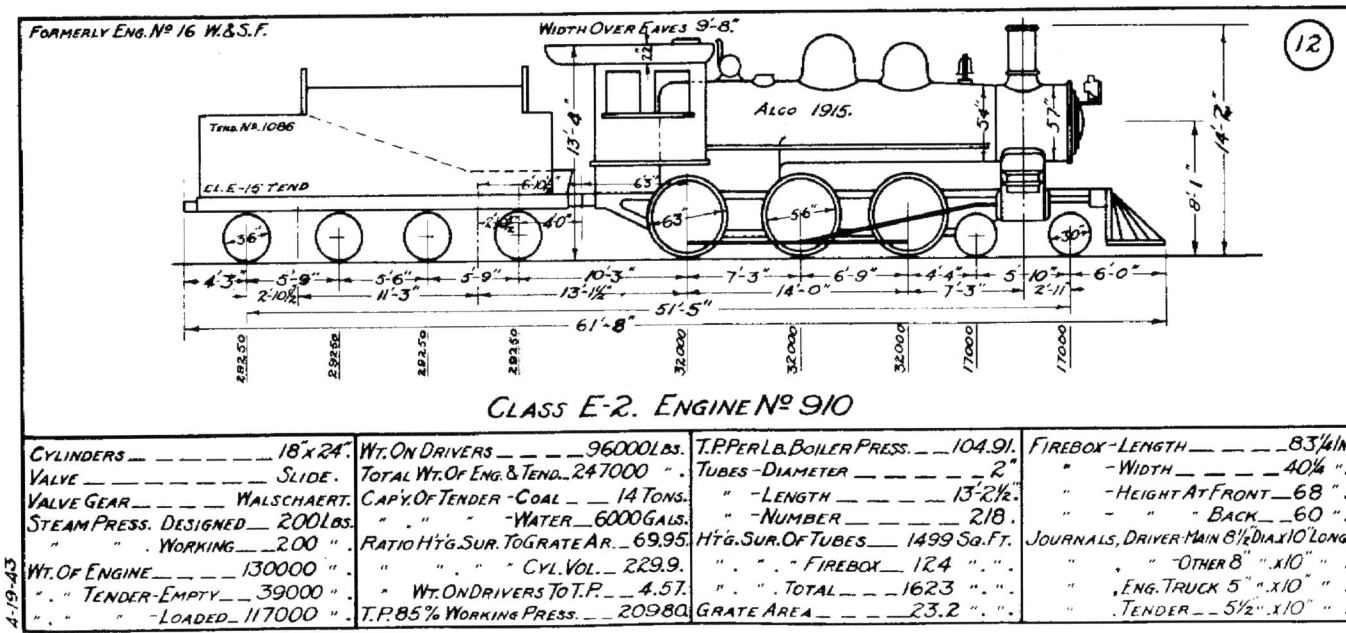

CLASS E-2. ENGINE Nº 910

CYLINDERS _ _ _ _ _ _ _ 18"x24".	WT. ON DRIVERS _ _ _ _ 96000 LBS.	T.P. PER LB. BOILER PRESS. _ _ 104.91.	FIREBOX - LENGTH _ _ _ _ _ 83¼ IN.
VALVE _ _ _ _ _ _ _ _ _ SLIDE.	TOTAL WT. OF ENG. & TEND. 247000 ".	TUBES - DIAMETER _ _ _ _ _ _ 2"	" - WIDTH _ _ _ _ _ 40¼ ".
VALVE GEAR _ _ _ _ WALSCHAERT.	CAP'Y. OF TENDER - COAL _ _ 14 TONS.	" - LENGTH _ _ _ _ _ 13-2½.	" - HEIGHT AT FRONT _ 68 ".
STEAM PRESS. DESIGNED _ _ 200 LBS.	" ." " - WATER_ 6000 GALS.	" - NUMBER _ _ _ _ _ 218.	" - " " BACK _ _ 60 ".
" " . WORKING _ _ 200 ".	RATIO HT'G. SUR. TO GRATE AR. 69.95.	HT'G. SUR. OF TUBES _ _ _ 1499 SQ. FT.	JOURNALS, DRIVER-MAIN 8½ "DIA.x 10"LONG
WT. OF ENGINE _ _ _ _ 130000 ".	" " . " CYL. VOL. _ 229.9.	" . " . FIREBOX _ _ 124 ". ".	" , -OTHER 8 " . x 10 " .
". " TENDER- EMPTY _ _ 39000 ".	" WT. ON DRIVERS TO T.P. _ 4.57.	" . " . TOTAL _ _ 1623 ". ".	, ENG. TRUCK 5 " . x 10 " .
". " " - LOADED _ 117000 ".	T.P. 85% WORKING PRESS. _ _ 20980	GRATE AREA _ _ _ _ 23.2 ". ".	. TENDER _ _ 5½ " . x 10 ".

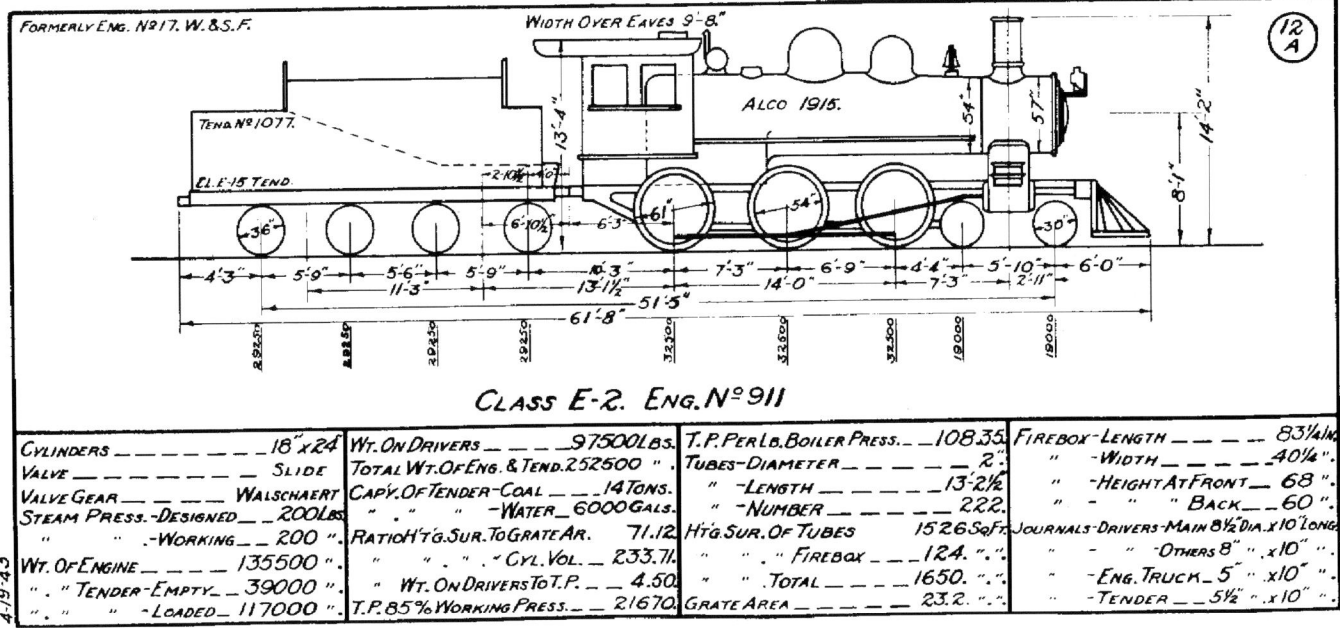

CLASS E-2. ENG. Nº 911

CYLINDERS _ _ _ _ _ _ 18"x24	WT. ON DRIVERS _ _ _ _ 97500 LBS.	T.P. PER LB. BOILER PRESS. _ _ 108.35	FIREBOX - LENGTH _ _ _ _ _ 83¼ IN.
VALVE _ _ _ _ _ _ _ _ SLIDE	TOTAL WT. OF ENG. & TEND. 252500 ".	TUBES - DIAMETER _ _ _ _ _ 2"	" - WIDTH _ _ _ _ _ 40¼ ".
VALVE GEAR _ _ _ _ WALSCHAERT	CAP'Y. OF TENDER - COAL _ _ _ 14 TONS.	" - LENGTH _ _ _ _ _ 13-2½	" - HEIGHT AT FRONT _ 68 ".
STEAM PRESS. - DESIGNED _ _ 200 LBS	" . " " - WATER _ 6000 GALS.	" - NUMBER _ _ _ _ _ 222.	" - " " BACK _ _ 60 ".
" " . - WORKING _ _ 200 ".	RATIO HT'G. SUR. TO GRATE AR. 71.12	HT'G. SUR. OF TUBES _ _ 1526 SQ. FT.	JOURNALS - DRIVERS - MAIN 8½ DIA.x 10"LONG
WT. OF ENGINE _ _ _ _ 135500 ".	" " . " CYL. VOL. _ 233.71.	" . " . FIREBOX _ _ 124 . " . ".	" - " - OTHERS 8 " . x 10 " .
". " TENDER - EMPTY _ _ 39000 ".	" WT. ON DRIVERS TO T.P. _ 4.50.	" . " . TOTAL _ _ _ 1650. " . ".	- ENG. TRUCK _ 5 " . x 10 " .
". " " - LOADED _ 117000 ".	T.P. 85% WORKING PRESS. _ _ 21670	GRATE AREA _ _ _ _ 23.2 " . ".	- TENDER _ _ 5½ " . x 10 ".

Both sides of SDC No. 16 were photographed at the time of completion at the Alco-Brooks works in 1915. It became one of two Class E-2(2nd) locomotives. ALCO Historic Photos (engineer's side), GNRHS Collection (fireman's side).

E-2(2nd). 910 was photographed at Sioux Falls, in the mid 1920's, on what was likely the same but unknown date as No. 3149. It had W&SF sub-lettering on cab, since it was not yet completely merged into the GN system. There was very little physical change to the engine since its construction. George Sittig collection.

The 910 was photographed in Bemidji in 1937. It still has the W&SF sub lettering on the cab, even though it was now a GN engine. Assigned to the Mesabi Division by this time, the 910 and 911 powered trains 105 and 106 between Sauk Centre and Bemidji, MN. Collection of Harold K. Vollrath.

E-2(2nd) 911, with "WSF" sub-lettering on the cab and what appears to be fresh paint, was photographed at St.Paul on June 17, 1922. J. Foster Adams Photograph from the collection of Kenneth R. Middleton.

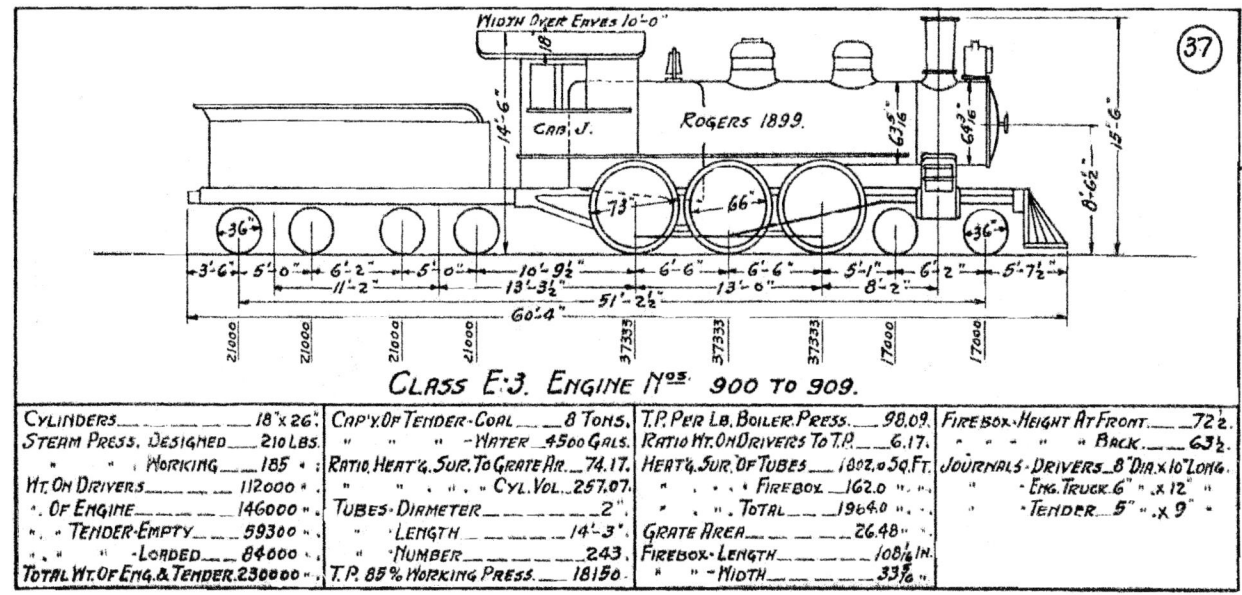

CLASS E-3. ENGINE Nos. 900 TO 909.

CYLINDERS 18"x26"	CAP'Y. OF TENDER-COAL 8 TONS.	T.P. PER LB. BOILER PRESS. 98.09.	FIREBOX-HEIGHT AT FRONT 72 2.
STEAM PRESS. DESIGNED 210 LBS.	" " " -WATER 4500 GALS.	RATIO WT. ON DRIVERS TO T.P. 6.17.	" " " BACK 63½.
" " WORKING 185 "	RATIO. HEAT'G. SUR. TO GRATE AR. 74.17.	HEAT'G. SUR. OF TUBES 1802.0 SQ.FT.	JOURNALS-DRIVERS 8"DIA.x10"LONG.
WT. ON DRIVERS 112000 "	" " " CYL. VOL. 257.07.	" " " FIREBOX 162.0 " "	" - ENG. TRUCK 6 " x 12"
" OF ENGINE 146000 "	TUBES-DIAMETER 2"	" " " TOTAL 1964.0 " "	" -TENDER 5 " x 9 "
" " TENDER-EMPTY 59300 "	" LENGTH 14'-3"	GRATE AREA 26.48"	
" " " -LOADED 84000 "	" NUMBER 243	FIREBOX-LENGTH 108½ IN.	
TOTAL WT. OF ENG. & TENDER 230000 ".	T.P. 85% WORKING PRESS. 18150	" " -WIDTH 33⅞	

The E-3's were delivered with an interesting clerestory roof. ALCO Historic Photos.

E-3 engine 901 is apparently undergoing an experiment, as it is equipped with two types of headlight, one in the normal position and one on the pilot deck. This would place the date around 1910. Collection of Ben Ringnalda.

No. 903 has lost its clerestory roof and has had one of its lead truck wheels replaced with a spoked wheel, but still has a wooden pilot. It was photographed at St. Paul in 1919. The man in front of this E-3 engine appears to be dumping ashes into a pit. Collection of Harold K. Vollrath.

Class E-3

The E-3 locomotives were not constructed until 1899, when they were produced by Rogers. There were ten of them, numbered as 900-909 and originally placed in Class 47. They had 18-inch by 26-inch cylinders, 73-inch drivers (as large as any of GN's 4-6-0's), Belpaire fireboxes, and weighed 146,000 pounds. These were the fast passenger locomotives of their day, and some of their exploits have been described in earlier publications.[1] Most were scrapped by the early 1930's, but two (903 on the Willmar Division and 908 on the Minot Division) lasted until 1938, and one (907 on the Willmar Division) lasted until 1939.

Engine 904 was photographed leaving Devils Lake, ND, on June 22, 1922. This E-3 is on train No.10 which departed at 1:50 pm. J. Foster Adams Photograph from the collection of Kenneth R. Middleton.

When photographed at Minneapolis in May 1938, No. 907 was the last remaining member of Class E-3. It would be retired the next year at the age of 40. Collection of Harold K. Vollrath.

Class E-4

The two Class E-4 engines were acquired second-hand. They had originally been built for the Fairhaven and Southern (F&S) as its Nos. 1 and 2 by Schenectady in 1889. They had wagontop boilers with radial stay fireboxes. They had 55-inch drivers and only weighed 100,800 pounds. When the F&S was taken over by the Seattle and Montana Railroad, one of GN's "Coast Lines," they became Nos. 298 and 299 and were placed in Class 10. They kept these numbers when formally acquired by the GN. Engine 299 was sold in 1911 to the Waterville Railway, where it lasted until 1935. Engine 298 was scrapped in 1923.

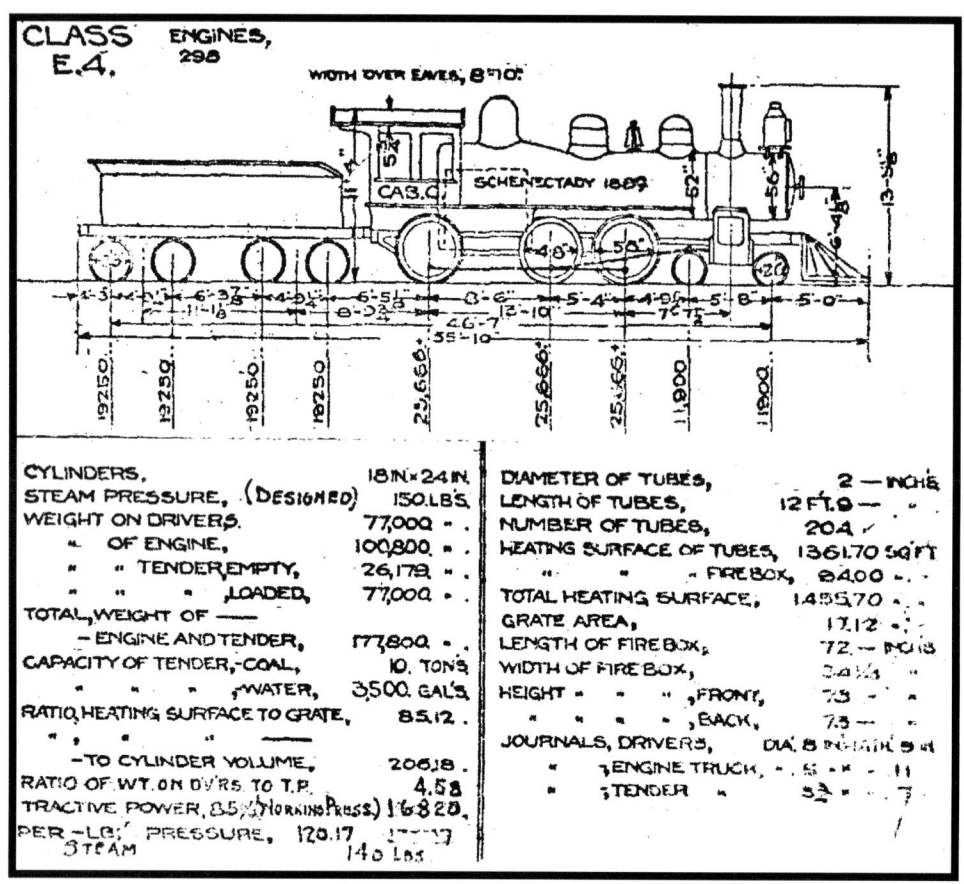

Engine No. 2, still sub-lettered for the Fairhaven and Southern on the tender, was photographed along GN's coast line. The date would be sometime between 1891, when the road came under James J. Hill's control, and 1898, when the F&S was merged into the Seattle and Montana Railroad Company. Photograph by Fred Jukes from the collection of William Bissinger.

Class E-5

Class E-5 was comprised of a single locomotive, which had been built by Rhode Island in 1890 as Pacific Short Line (PSL) 15. When the engine was eventually acquired by the Willmar and Sioux Falls in 1900 it was placed in Class 27A and given number 997. It had 55-inch drivers and weighed only 105,800 pounds. Like the other PSL locomotives acquired by the GN, it was transferred to the Burlington in 1908 with the Sioux City, IA, to O'Neill, NE, branch line. No photos of this engine are known to exist.

Class E-6

Great Northern itself purchased the E-6 locomotives, which were acquired from Rogers in 1902. They were numbered as 925-939 and originally placed in Class 53. They had relatively low 63-inch drivers, and weighed 152,000 pounds. The lower drivers did, however, provide increased tractive effort. Most of them lasted in branch line service until the 1940's and 1950's, though 938 was sold to the Pacific & Eastern in 1910, ultimately becoming SP&S 159. With the exception of 925, a Spokane Division engine, and 937, assigned to the Butte Division, most of them were assigned to the eastern divisions of the railroad. The 925 was the only oil burner. Several of them (925, 926, 927, 931, 933, 937) received power reverses from 1938 to 1948. A few (927, 929-931, 933, 937, 939) received Barco low water alarms in the mid-1940's, and three (926, 933 and 935) even received electric train indicators in 1945-1946. Since the original E-6 tenders carried only 6,000 gallons of water, nearly all of the engines received larger tenders.

Class E-7

The locomotives which later became E-7's were purchased in 1893 to handle transcontinental passenger trains.[2] The twenty locomotives, numbered as 650-669 had 72-inch drivers and weighed 138,000 pounds. They were placed in Class 42. They had straight boilers and the normal by now Belpaire firebox. During the 1899 renumbering they

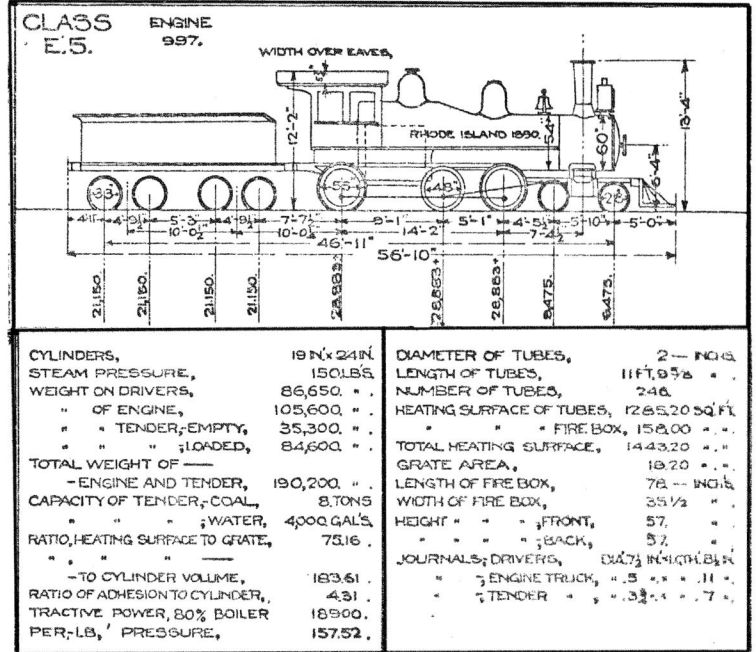

CYLINDERS,	19 IN x 24 IN.	DIAMETER OF TUBES,	2 — NO.1.
STEAM PRESSURE,	150 LBS.	LENGTH OF TUBES,	11 FT. 9⅝ " .
WEIGHT ON DRIVERS,	86,650. " .	NUMBER OF TUBES,	246.
" OF ENGINE,	105,600. " .	HEATING SURFACE OF TUBES,	1285.20 SQ FT.
" " TENDER, EMPTY,	35,300. " .	" " " FIRE BOX,	158.00 " . " .
" " " ; LOADED,	84,600. " .	TOTAL HEATING SURFACE,	1443.20 " . "
TOTAL WEIGHT OF —		GRATE AREA,	18.20 " . "
— ENGINE AND TENDER,	190,200. " .	LENGTH OF FIRE BOX,	78 — INCHES
CAPACITY OF TENDER, COAL,	8. TONS	WIDTH OF FIRE BOX,	35½ " .
" " " ; WATER,	4000 GAL'S.	HEIGHT " " ; FRONT,	57, " .
RATIO, HEATING SURFACE TO GRATE,	75.16 .	" " " ; BACK,	52, " . " .
" " " " " ,	.	JOURNALS; DRIVERS,	8 x 7½ IN. LGTH B 8 K
— TO CYLINDER VOLUME,	183.61 .	" " ; ENGINE TRUCK,	" . 5 " . " . 11 " .
RATIO OF ADHESION TO CYLINDER,	4.31 .	" " ; TENDER " , " . 3⅞ " . " . 7 " .
TRACTIVE POWER, 80% BOILER	18900.	.
PER LB,' PRESSURE,	157.52 .	

became GN 950-969. The driver size was later increased to 73 inches. One of these, GN 957, received 63-inch drivers some time between 1900 and 1912, and was placed in Class E-11. The drivers of 957 were changed back to 73 inches and it was returned to Class E-7 in 1912. One of the E-7's, No. 959, was singled out in 1926 for setting a record of 293,329 miles since its last shopping. It was stated "Either the Great Northern has some really remarkable locomotives, or at least they must follow some unusual methods for maintaining them, or they could not get practically 300,000 miles service out of an engine between shoppings. However, the record is authentic, and will no doubt stand for some time before it is bettered."[3] Apparently, though, these rather small but high-drivered engines were no longer needed, and all were scrapped in the mid-1920's. Perhaps 959 was run for that many miles because it was bound for the scrap yard.

Engine 299, the same engine as in the previous photograph, has received barred side extensions to increase coal capacity and has different style headlights on the engine and tender. It is shown here at Burlington, WA, in 1902. It was one of only two members of Class E-4. Collection of William Bissinger.

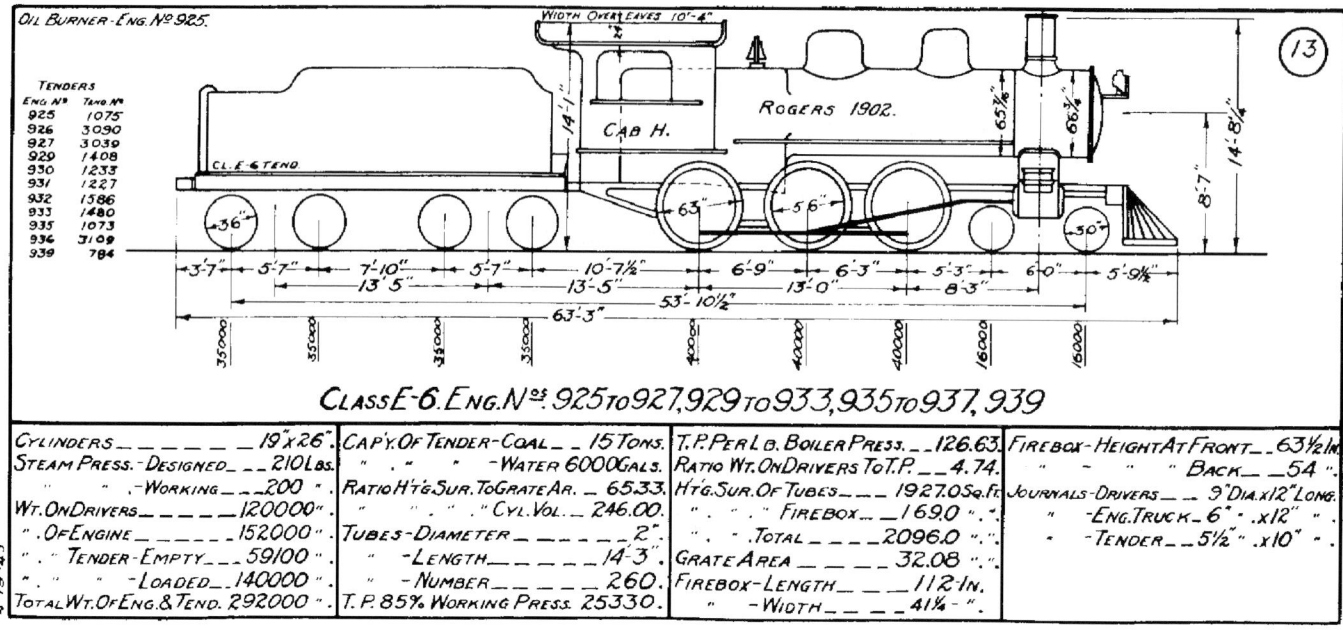

CYLINDERS _____ 19"x26".	CAP'Y. OF TENDER-COAL __ 15 TONS.	T.P. PER L B. BOILER PRESS. __ 126.63	FIREBOX-HEIGHT AT FRONT __63½ In.
STEAM PRESS.-DESIGNED __ 210 Lbs.	" " " -WATER 6000 GALS.	RATIO WT. ON DRIVERS TO T.P. __ 4.74.	" - " " BACK __ 54 ".
" " -WORKING ___ 200 ".	RATIO H'TG.SUR. TO GRATE AR. _ 65.33.	H'TG.SUR. OF TUBES ___ 1927.0 Sq.ft.	JOURNALS-DRIVERS __ 9"Dia.x12"Long.
WT. ON DRIVERS _____ 120000 ".	" " " CYL. VOL. _ 246.00.	" " " FIREBOX __ 169.0 ".	" -ENG.TRUCK- 6" - x12 " ".
" .OF ENGINE _____ 152000 ".	TUBES-DIAMETER _____ 2".	" " .TOTAL ___ 2096.0 ".	" -TENDER __ 5½" - x10" ".
" . TENDER-EMPTY ___ 59100 ".	" -LENGTH _____ 14-3".	GRATE AREA _____ 32.08 ".	
" " -LOADED _ 140000 ".	" -NUMBER _____ 260.	FIREBOX-LENGTH ___ 112 In.	
TOTAL WT. OF ENG. & TEND. 292000 ".	T.P. 85% WORKING PRESS. 25330.	" -WIDTH ___ 41¼ - ".	

The only oil burner among the E-6 class, and one of two stationed on Lines West was the 925. It is shown here at Leavenworth WA, June 10, 1946. The engine was scrapped one year after this photograph was taken. Photograph by R. V. Nixon.

Engine 926 is shown here at Minneapolis, MN, before World War II. It has no snowplow in this photograph, and is pulling what is probably a Style 62 O-1 tender. R. J. Foster Photograph from the collection of William Raia.

E-6 No. 926 was photographed at Milaca, MN, in 1947 bearing a snow plow and electric train indicators.
The tender is a Style 61 tender delivered with O-1 3090. Wilbur C. Whittaker Collection.

GN 927 was the last surviving E-6. The engine had been a regular on trains 31 and 32 between Willmar and Sandstone at the time.
It was photographed by Robert Graham on September 27, 1949, at Minneapolis, MN. Collection of Cordell R. Newby.

The engineer's side of E-6 932 was photographed at the water column in Minneapolis, MN, on April 20, 1935 with a tender having arch bar trucks. Collection of William Raia.

Carrying what was probably a J-2 tender, the 932 is shown at Minneapolis on July 17, 1946. By 1949, the last two E-6 class engines were on the eastern ends of the Willmar and Mesabi Divisions. The 932 was not one of them, being scrapped in 1947. John Westphal collection of the John Luecke Collection.

The last assignment for E-6 933 was on the Hutchinson, MN, local, trains 60 and 61. It held this job for many years, from the 1930's until late 1948, and was a precursor for the long tenure of diesel 186 on this job. As a child, one of the authors viewed this "giant" with much awe as it roared past his grandfather's home. It is shown at Minneapolis in July 1940. Collection of Norman F. Priebe.

The plow on the 935 was different than shown on 926. Plows were designed and built by the local shop crews. There was no standard. The E-6 engine carries a Style 13 Class E-15 tender. There is little to tell that this photograph was taken in 1926 instead of 1949. The engine is at Minneapolis. Photograph by Chesney (RPS) from the collection of Norman F. Priebe.

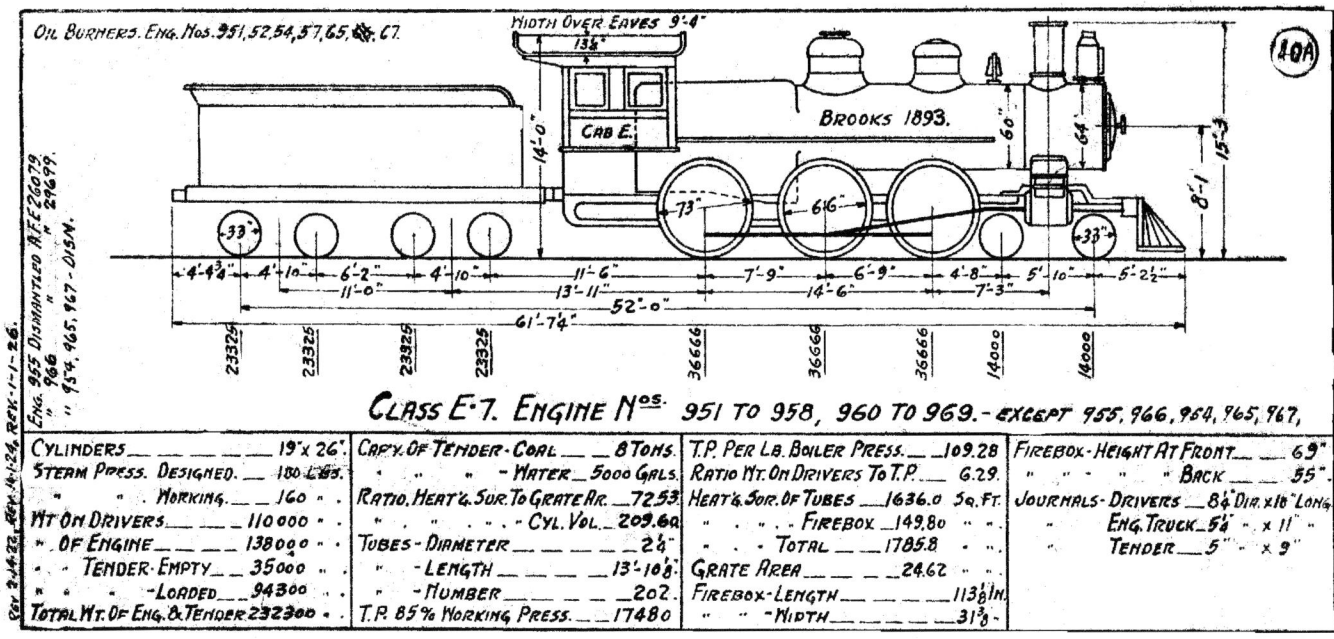

CYLINDERS	19"x 26"	CAP'Y. OF TENDER - COAL	8 TONS	T.P. PER LB. BOILER PRESS.	109.28	FIREBOX - HEIGHT AT FRONT	69"
STEAM PRESS. DESIGNED	180 LBS	" " " - WATER	5000 GALS	RATIO WT. ON DRIVERS TO T.P.	6.29	" " " BACK	55"
" " WORKING	160 "	RATIO, HEAT & SUR. TO GRATE AR.	72.53	HEAT & SUR. OF TUBES	1636.0 Sq. Ft.	JOURNALS - DRIVERS	8¼ DIA. x 10" LONG
WT. ON DRIVERS	110 000 "	" " " CYL. VOL.	209.60	" " FIREBOX	149.80 " "	ENG. TRUCK 5½" x 11"
" OF ENGINE	138 000 "	TUBES - DIAMETER	2¼"	" " TOTAL	1785.8 " "	TENDER 5 " x 9"
" " TENDER - EMPTY	35 000 "	" - LENGTH	13'-10⅛"	GRATE AREA	24.62 " "	
" " - LOADED	94300 "	" - NUMBER	202	FIREBOX - LENGTH	113⅛ IN.	
TOTAL WT. OF ENG. & TENDER	232300 "	T.P. 85% WORKING PRESS.	17480	" - WIDTH	31⅜ "	

CLASS E-7. ENGINE Nᵒˢ· 951 TO 958, 960 TO 969.- EXCEPT 955, 966, 964, 965, 967,

GN 650, all shiny and polished, posed for its builders photograph in 1893. In 1899 it became No. 950, and in 1903 was placed in Class E-7. ALCO Historic Photos.

E-7 954 sits at the train shed in Tacoma, WA, in July 1923. It looks as though extensions for increasing coal capacity had been put on the tender, but there is now an oil bunker in place. Collection of Harold K. Vollrath.

The 960, shown here on the Mansfield branch in Washington State on February 19, 1919, was also an oil burner. Collection of R . E . Johnson.

E-7 965 is shown making a station stop at Blanchard in 1911. Warren Wing photograph from the collection of Walter Ainsworth.

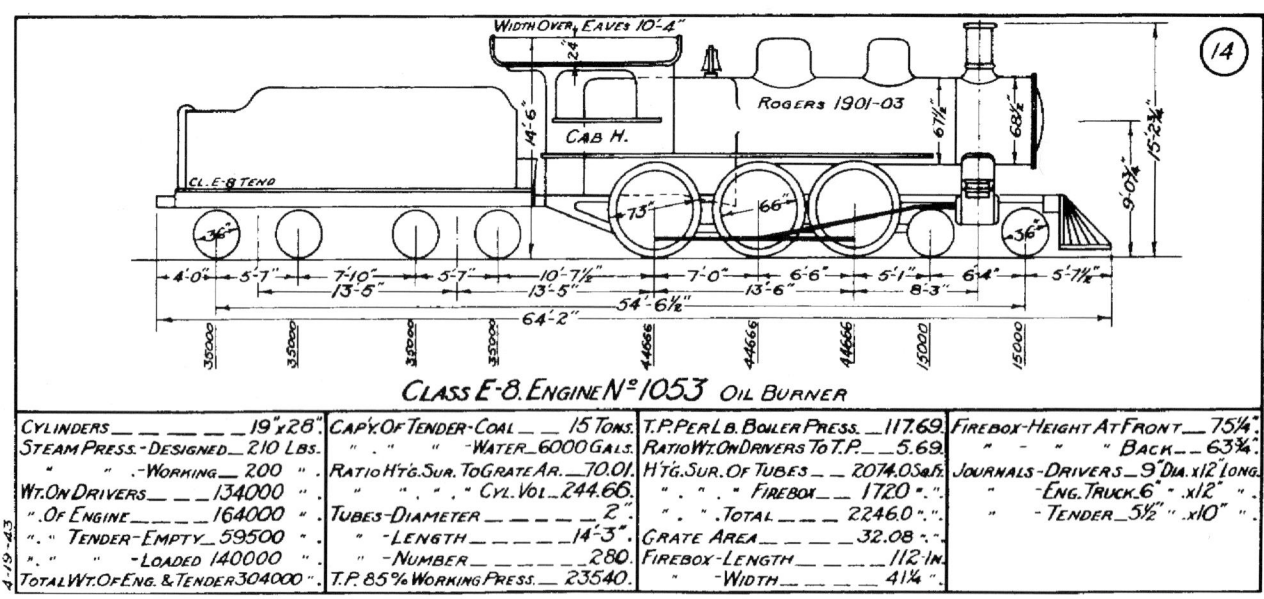

CLASS E-8. ENGINE Nº 1053 OIL BURNER

CYLINDERS __ __ __ 19"x28"	CAP'Y. OF TENDER-COAL __ __ 15 TONS.	T.P. PER LB. BOILER PRESS. __ 117.69	FIREBOX-HEIGHT AT FRONT __ 75¼"
STEAM PRESS.-DESIGNED__210 LBS.	" " " -WATER_6000 GALS.	RATIO WT.ON DRIVERS TO T.P. __ 5.69.	" " " BACK__ 63¾"
" " .-WORKING__200 "	RATIO H'TG.SUR.TO GRATE AR.__70.01.	HTG. SUR. OF TUBES __ __ 2074.0 sq ft.	JOURNALS-DRIVERS_9" DIA. x12" LONG.
WT. ON DRIVERS __ __ 134000 "	" " . " CYL. VOL __ 244.66.	" . " FIREBOX __ 172.0 " ".	" -ENG. TRUCK 6 " - x12 "
" .OF ENGINE__ __ __ 164000 "	TUBES-DIAMETER __ __ __ 2"	" . " TOTAL __ __ 2246.0 " ".	" -TENDER 5½ " " x10 "
" . " TENDER-EMPTY_59500 "	" -LENGTH __ __ __ 14'-3".	GRATE AREA __ __ __ 32.08 " ".	
" . " -LOADED 140000 "	" -NUMBER __ __ __ 280.	FIREBOX-LENGTH __ __ 112-IN.	
TOTAL WT. OF ENG. & TENDER 304000 ".	T.P. 85% WORKING PRESS.__23540.	" -WIDTH __ __ __ 41¼ "	

Class E-8

In 1901 and 1902, ten 4-6-0's were received from Rogers, numbered as 1050-1059. These were the heaviest high-drivered (73-inch) Ten-Wheelers yet received, with weights of 164,000 pounds. They were placed in Class 49 and were later reclassified as Class E-8. They had straight boilers with Belpaire fireboxes. Ten identical locomotives, numbered as 1060-1069, were received in 1904. In 1910, 1050-1052 were renumbered as 1070-1072 to clear numbers for Class E-14 locomotives on order for that year. All but two were scrapped by 1934, but engine 1063 lasted until 1941 on the Mesabi Division, and 1053 remained in use on the Kalispell Division until 1947.

Class E-9

The locomotives placed in Class E-9 had been received in 1892 from Baldwin. They were numbered 600 and 601 and were placed in Class 41. They were Vauclain compounds, with one high and one low pressure cylinder, placed one above the other, on each side of the locomotive. The high pressure cylinders were 14 inches by 24 inches, and the low pressure cylinders were 24 inches by 24 inches. The driver diameter was 69 inches. The total engine weight was 134,600 pounds.[4] At some time prior to 1900, they were rebuilt to simple engines with cylinder dimensions of 20 inches by 24 inches. In 1899, they were renumbered as 998 and 999. Both were retired in 1929 and scrapped in 1932.

While most builders photographs of steam locomotives were taken with the side rods down, this photograph of E-8 1059 is an exception. ALCO Historic Photos.

GN 1053, a Kalispell Division engine, was the last survivor of Class E-8. It was photographed in Great Falls, MT, on May 29, 1926. Railroad Museum of Pennsylvania (PHMC).

The fireman's side of the 1053 was captured in this view at Columbia Falls, MT, in March 1936. It was on train 243, one of the trains to Kalispell, and is pinch-hitting for a motor car. Within a few years the engine would be on the Dakota Division. Photograph by R. V. Nixon.

This is E-8 1054 with a rectangular herald when still used, in August 1908. It is at Vancouver, WA. Photograph from the collection of Harold K. Vollrath, courtesy of Eric Archer.

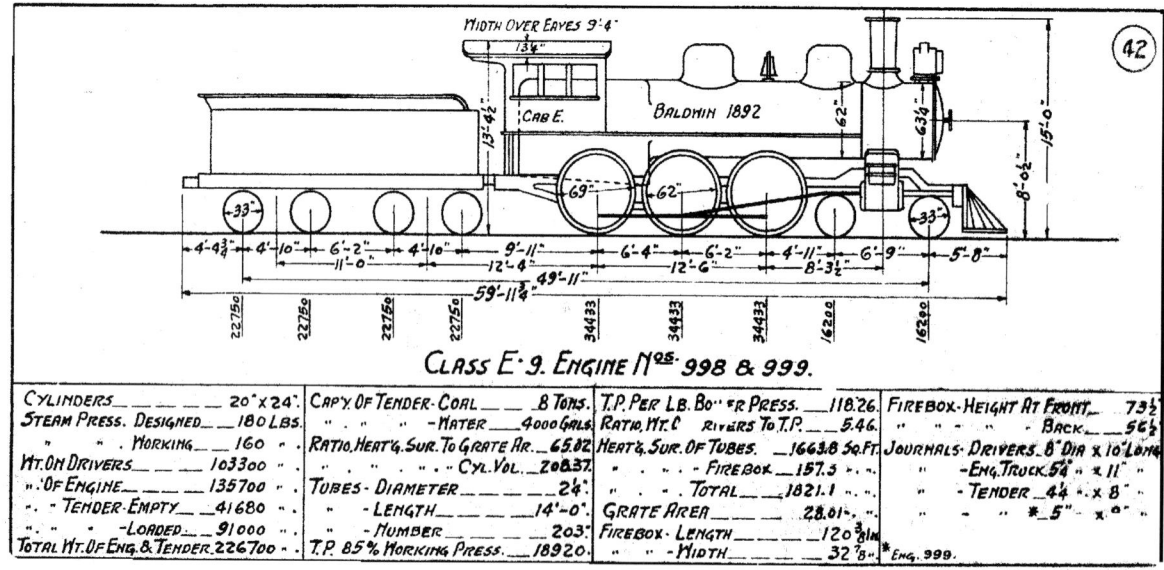

CLASS E-9. ENGINE Nos. 998 & 999.

CYLINDERS __ 20"x 24".	CAP'Y OF TENDER-COAL __ 8 TONS.	T.P. PER LB. BOILER PRESS. __ 118.26.	FIREBOX-HEIGHT AT FRONT __ 73½
STEAM PRESS. DESIGNED __180 LBS.	" " -WATER __ 4000 GALS.	RATIO. WT. C DRIVERS TO T.P. __ 5.46.	" " - BACK __ 56½
" " . WORKING __ 160 ".	RATIO. HEAT'G SUR. TO GRATE AR. __ 65.82.	HEAT'G. SUR. OF TUBES. __ 1663.8 SQ.FT.	JOURNALS-DRIVERS. 8" DIA x 10" LONG
WT. ON DRIVERS __ 103300 ".	" " CYL. VOL. __ 20837.	" " - FIREBOX __ 157.5 " .	" -ENG. TRUCK 5¼ " x 11"
" .OF ENGINE __ 135700 ".	TUBES- DIAMETER __ 2¼".	" " . TOTAL __ 1821.1 " .	" -TENDER __ 4¼ " x 8".
" . TENDER-EMPTY __ 41680 ".	" - LENGTH __ 14'-0".	FIREBOX- LENGTH __ 120⅜ IN.	" * 5 " x 0".
" -LOADED __ 91000 ".	" - NUMBER __ 203.	GRATE AREA __ 28.01 ".	
TOTAL WT. OF ENG. & TENDER. 226700 ".	T.P. 85% WORKING PRESS. __ 18920.	" - WIDTH __ 32 ⅞".	*ENG. 999.

*GN 600 was built by Baldwin as a Vauclain Compound, but was later simpled by GN shops.
It ultimately became a member of Class E-9. Railroad Museum of Pennsylvania (PHMC).*

*While this photograph of the 999 is a bit murky, it is one of the few known photographs of an E-9 Class Ten-Wheeler. It is believed to have been taken at Minot in 1917. It is no longer a compound and it has the standard GN headlight. It also now has a steel pilot and standard cab.
The engine was retired in 1929. From an old print given to R. V. Nixon*

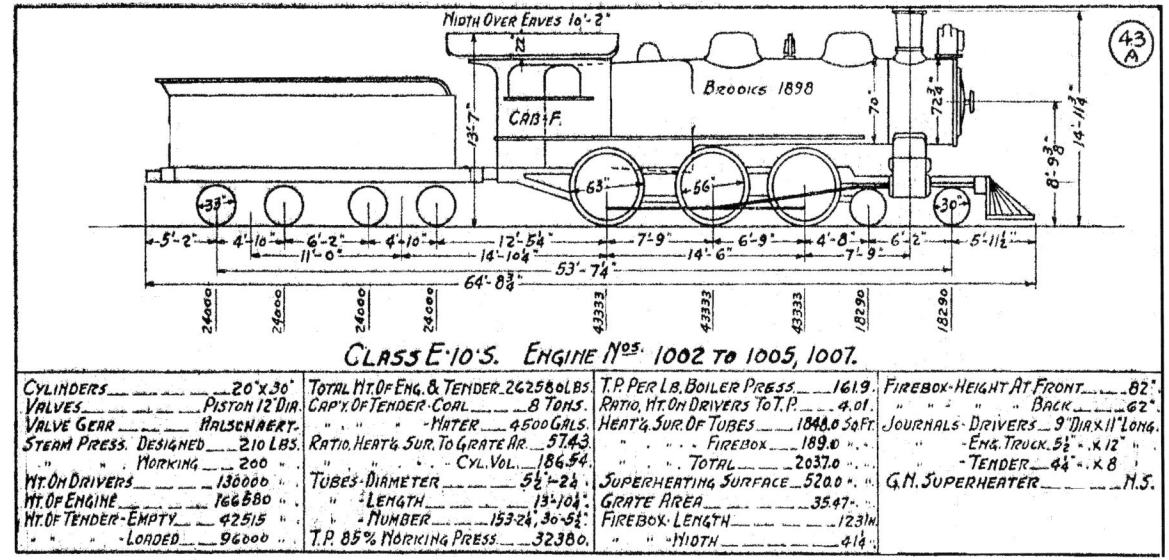

CLASS E-10'S. Engine Nos. 1002 to 1005, 1007.

CYLINDERS	20"x30"
VALVES	PISTON 12"DIA.
VALVE GEAR	WALSCHAERT.
STEAM PRESS. DESIGNED	210 LBS.
" WORKING	200 "
WT. ON DRIVERS	130000
WT. OF ENGINE	166680 "
WT. OF TENDER-EMPTY	42515 "
" " -LOADED	96000 "

TOTAL WT. OF ENG. & TENDER	262580 LBS.
CAP'Y OF TENDER-COAL	8 TONS.
" " -WATER	4500 GALS.
RATIO, HEAT'G SUR. TO GRATE AR.	57.43
" CYL. VOL.	186.54
TUBES-DIAMETER	5½"-2¼
" LENGTH	13'-10¼
" NUMBER	153-2¼, 30-5½
T.P. 85% WORKING PRESS.	32380.

T.P. PER LB. BOILER PRESS.	161.9
RATIO, WT. ON DRIVERS TO T.P.	4.01
HEAT'G SUR. OF TUBES	1848.0 SQ.FT.
" " FIREBOX	189.0 "
" TOTAL	2037.0 "
SUPERHEATING SURFACE	520.0 "
GRATE AREA	35.47 "
FIREBOX-LENGTH	123 IN.
" WIDTH	41¼ "

FIREBOX-HEIGHT AT FRONT	82
" BACK	62
JOURNALS-DRIVERS	9"DIA.X11"LONG.
-ENG. TRUCK	5½"-X12"
-TENDER	4¾"-X8
G.N. SUPERHEATER	N.S.

Class E-10

Eight locomotives built by the Brooks Locomotive Works in 1898, with 20-inch by 30-inch cylinders, 63-inch driving wheels and total engine weights of 166,580 pounds became the members of Class E-10. These were among the heaviest Ten-Wheelers in service at the time they were built.[5] They were actually purchased by the Eastern of Minnesota as its Nos. 150-157, and were placed in Class 46. They had Walschaert valve gear and piston valves, the first Ten-Wheelers on the GN to be so equipped. Upon their receipt, the engines were tested in both freight and passenger service on the Montana Central.[6] About 1900 they became Nos. 1000-1007. Five of the locomotives were superheated between 1913 and 1918, but they retained their inside steam pipes. The last was retired in 1936.

Class E-11

The one member of Class E-11, the 957, was rebuilt from a Class E-7 locomotive and was later returned to Class E-7 (see above). The 63-inch drivers increased the tractive effort to 20,260 pounds compared with the original 17,480 pounds with 73-inch drivers, assuming the same working pressure of 160 psi.

Classes E-12 and E-13

Classes E-12 (970 and 971) and E-13 (948 and 949) were all locomotives that were acquired when GN took over the Spokane Falls and Northern (SF&N) in 1907. The members of E-12 were 1897 products of Baldwin, with 19-inch by 24-inch cylinders, 55-inch drivers and engine weights of 122,300 pounds. They had been built as SF&N 11 and 12. The members of Class E-13 (948 and 949) had similar dimensions to the E-12's, but engine weights of only 110,000 pounds. They had been built in 1893 (as Nelson & Fort Sheppard 8) and 1896 (as SF&N 10). The engines all had wagontop boilers with radial stay fireboxes. Despite their small size, one of each class survived into the 1940's. No. 970 was used on the Spokane Division until 1940, and No. 948 was used on the Kalispell Division until 1947.

Eastern of Minnesota No. 150 was built by Brooks Locomotive Works in 1898. The cylinder and valve heads were highly polished for the occasion. Collection of William Bissinger.

Great Northern No. 1000 is the same E-10 locomotive that appears in the previous photograph. It is shown at East Cascade, WA about 1900, prior to receiving an electric headlight. It does have a stack blast hood. Great Northern Railway photograph from the collection of Wolfgang Weber.

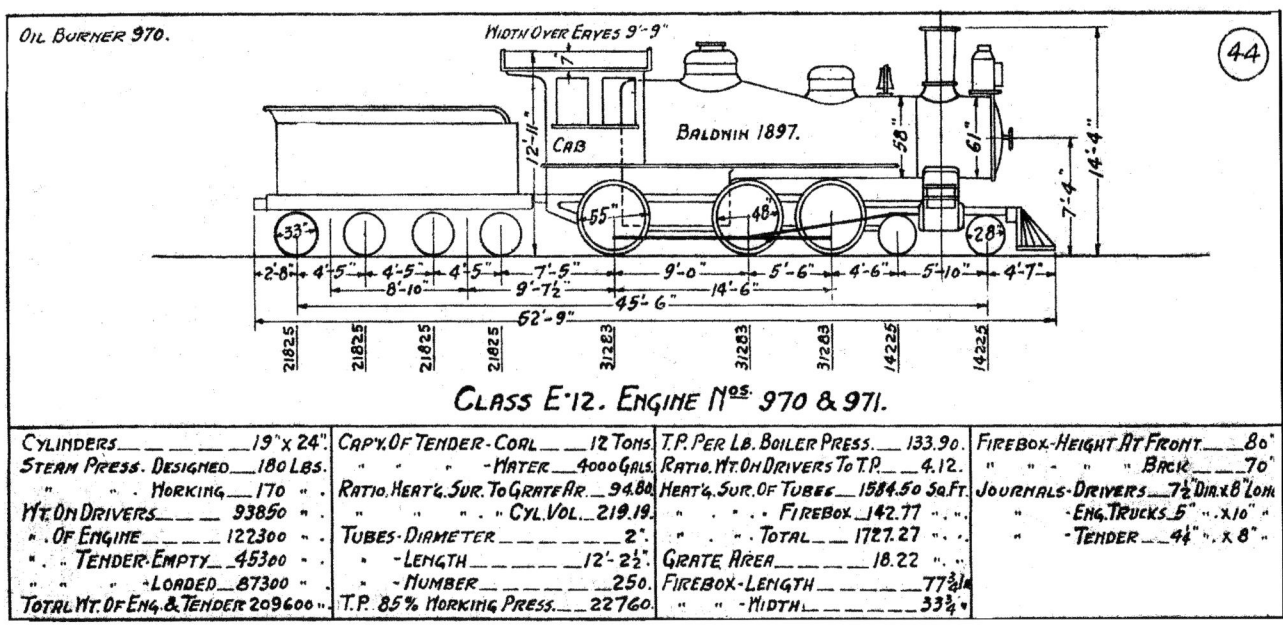

CLASS E-12. ENGINE Nᵒˢ 970 & 971.

CYLINDERS _ _ _ _ _ 19"x 24".	CAP'Y. OF TENDER-COAL _ _ 12 TONS.	T.P. PER LB. BOILER PRESS. _ 133.90.	FIREBOX-HEIGHT AT FRONT _ 80"
STEAM PRESS. DESIGNED _ 180 LBS.	" " " -WATER_4000 GALS.	RATIO. WT. ON DRIVERS TO T.P._ 4.12.	" " " BACK_ 70"
" " . WORKING _ 170 "	RATIO. HEAT'G. SUR. TO GRATE AR. _ 94.80.	HEAT'G. SUR. OF TUBES _ 1584.50 Sq. FT.	JOURNALS-DRIVERS _ 7½" DIA. x 8" LONG.
WT. ON DRIVERS _ _ _ 93850 "	" " " " CYL. VOL. 219.19.	" " . " FIREBOX_142.77 " .	" -ENG. TRUCKS 5" " . x10"
" . OF ENGINE _ _ _ 122300 " .	TUBES-DIAMETER _ _ _ _ _ _ 2".	" . " . TOTAL _ 1727.27 " .	" -TENDER _ 4¼" . x 8"
" . " TENDER-EMPTY _45300 . .	" -LENGTH _ _ _ _ _12'-2½"	GRATE AREA_ _ _ _ _ 18.22 " .	
" . " " -LOADED_87300 " .	" -NUMBER _ _ _ _ _ _250.	FIREBOX-LENGTH _ _ _ _ _77¾"	
TOTAL WT. OF ENG. & TENDER 209600 " .	T.P. 85% WORKING PRESS. _ 22760.	" " -WIDTH _ _ _ _ _33¾"	

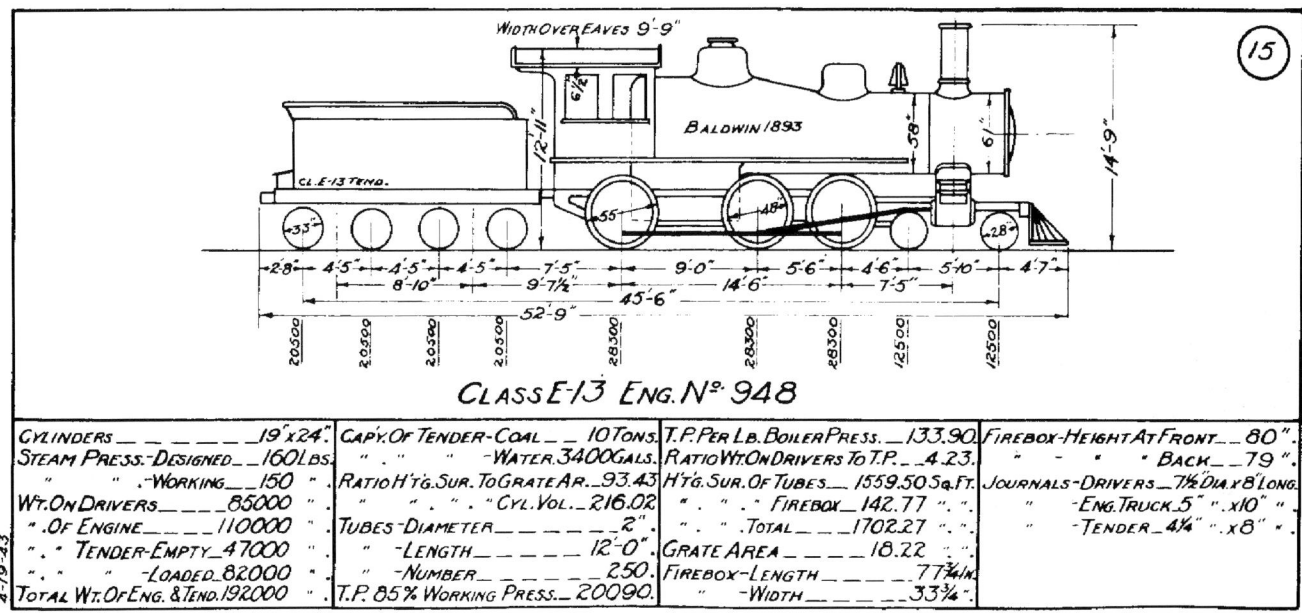

CLASS E-13 ENG. Nᵒ 948.

CYLINDERS _ _ _ _ _ 19"x24".	CAP'Y. OF TENDER-COAL _ _ 10 TONS.	T.P. PER LB. BOILER PRESS. _ 133.90.	FIREBOX-HEIGHT AT FRONT _ 80".
STEAM PRESS.-DESIGNED _ _160 LBS.	" " " -WATER.3400 GALS.	RATIO WT. ON DRIVERS TO T.P. _ 4.23.	" " " . BACK _ 79 ".
" " . -WORKING _ _150 "	RATIO H'T'G. SUR. TO GRATE AR. _ 93.43.	H'T'G. SUR. OF TUBES _ 1559.50 Sq. FT.	JOURNALS-DRIVERS _ 7½" DIA. x 8" LONG.
WT. ON DRIVERS _ _ _ 85000 "	" " " " CYL. VOL. 216.02.	" . " . FIREBOX_ 142.77 " . " .	" -ENG. TRUCK 5" " . x10" "
" . OF ENGINE _ _ _ _ 110000 "	TUBES-DIAMETER _ _ _ _ _ _ 2".	" . " . TOTAL _ 1702.27 " .	" -TENDER 4¼" . x 8" ".
" . " TENDER-EMPTY _47000 " .	" -LENGTH _ _ _ _ _ 12'-0".	GRATE AREA _ _ _ _ 18.22 " . .	
" . " " -LOADED_82000 " .	" -NUMBER _ _ _ _ _250.	FIREBOX-LENGTH _ _ _ _ _ 77¾ IN.	
TOTAL WT. OF ENG. & TEND. 192000 "	T.P. 85% WORKING PRESS. _ 20090.	" -WIDTH _ _ _ _ 33¾" .	

The 948, a class E-13, worked out of Hillyard for many years. It appears to be out of service here, perhaps on a weekend, since it is in immaculate condition. It was photographed at Hillyard, WA, on June 1939. Collection of Robert W. Johnston.

In good condition following World War II, the 948 was still at Hillyard in October 1945, and would serve another two years before meeting the torch. Note that it was a coal burner. William J. Pontin (RPS) photograph from the collection of Norman F. Priebe.

The 970, the last remaining E-12, is at Wenatchee, WA, on May 14, 1939. Not in service, it either is having its headlight replaced or permanently removed prior to scrapping. Photograph by Wilbur C. Whittaker.

E-12 970 was originally built as Spokane Falls & Northern No. 11 in 1897. It was photographed in Vancouver, BC, in April 1936. Collection of Harold K. Vollrath.

Class E-14

Early experience with the H-4 Pacific locomotives indicated that, in view of the increased capacity per ton of weight obtained through the use of superheated steam, it would be practicable to build a 4-6-0 locomotive with the same weight on driving wheels as Class H-4, that would have ample steaming capacity and permit a greater proportion of the total weight to be utilized for adhesion, due to the omission of the rear truck. Such a locomotive, designated as Class E-14, was accordingly designed in 1909, and 25 were built by The Baldwin Locomotive Works during that year (Nos. 1008-1032). These locomotives had 73-inch drivers and 26-inch by 30-inch cylinders, the same as Class H-4. Like the H-4's they carried a steam pressure of 150 pounds, which was subsequently increased to 200 pounds with a reduction in cylinder diameter from 26 to 23½ inches.[7] The engine weight was 200,000 pounds. In 1910 twenty more E-14's, 10,000 pounds heavier than the first order, were received (Nos. 1033-1052). Ten of these were immediately sold to the SP&S. Some of these heavier locomotives (all but 1037 and 1038) were equipped with outside steam

pipes from 1919 through 1921. Some of them (1034, 1035, 1039, 1040 and 1041) also received GN New Style superheaters. The two for which dates are known received their new superheaters in 1923 and 1924.

In spite of the wide fireboxes, the E-14's lacked the boiler power needed for the heaviest work. While the engines were built as coal burners, most photographs show them as oil burners. January 1921 correspondence indicates that two of them were to be converted to coal burners. However, the shallow fireboxes necessary due to being over the drivers made them perform very poorly as coal burners since they did not steam well. It was thus proposed that two of them be converted to Pacific engines.[8] In 1921 and 1922 the GN converted seven of the lighter locomotives (1008-1032) to Class H-5 Pacifics by lengthening the boiler and applying a deep, wide firebox which was placed back of the drivers and over the trailing truck.[9] From 1924 through 1927, the remainder of the lighter E-14's were converted to H-5's. In 1926 and 1927, the ten heavier E-14's (1033-1042) were converted to H-7 Pacifics.

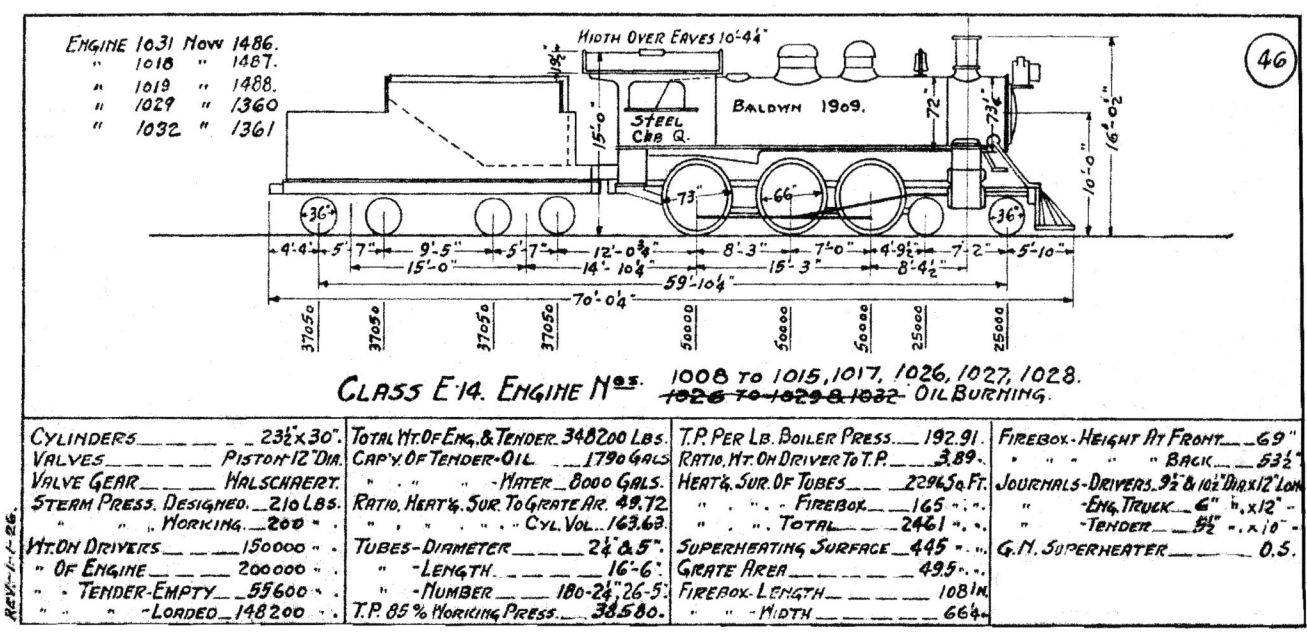

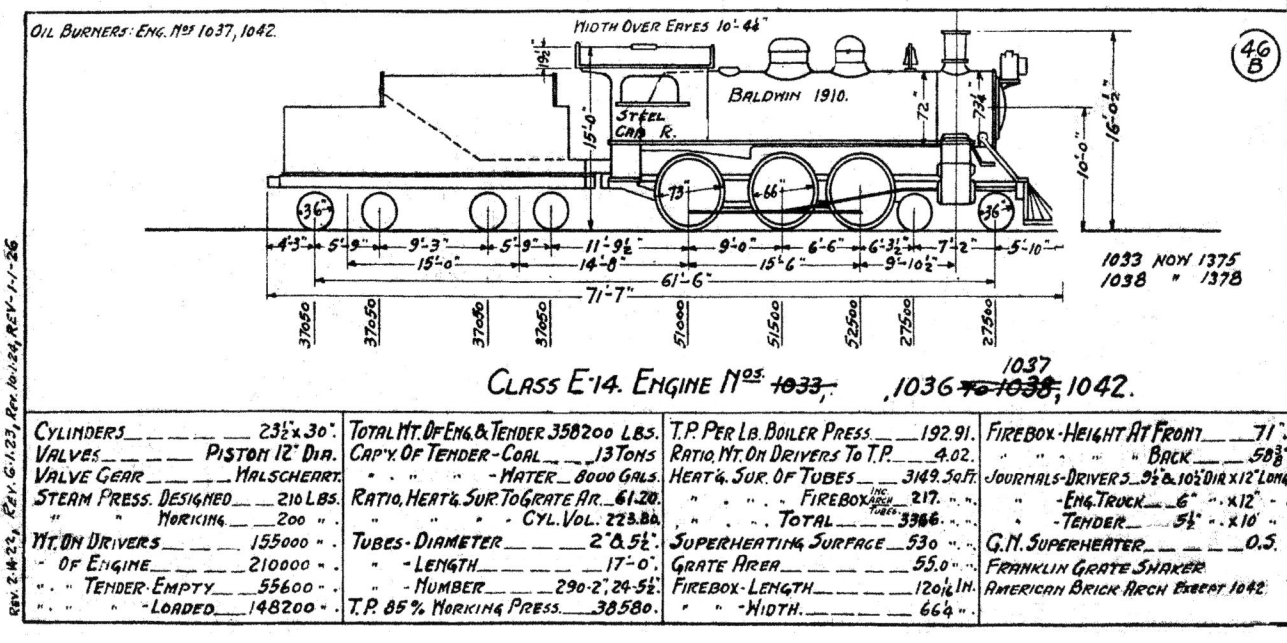

Great Northern officials believed that by constructing Ten-Wheelers with the same weight on drivers as the H-4 Pacific the locomotives would have better adhesion. Unfortunately, the small fireboxes made them poor steamers when burning coal. It's interesting that the photograph indicates that the E-14 locomotives were initially lettered as Class E-13's. These locomotives came with extended piston rods. Collection of H. L. Broadbelt.

Oil-burning E-14 No. 1010 was photographed at Tacoma, WA, in July 1923. Collection of Harold K. Vollrath.

The 1027 was in Portland service, shown here at Portland, OR. The photograph is undated, but the unlettered tender and the early headlight places the date prior to 1923. Collection of Jerrold F. Hilton.

E-14 1028 had flags painted on the cylinder jacket when it was used for President Harding's funeral train in 1923. By this time the engine had the standard GN cast headlight, a steel pilot and a lettered tender. International Newsreel – Courtesy of Minnesota Historical Society.

This transition scene of the 1032 shows a lettered tender, but the engine still has its old headlight. Location and date are unknown. The 1032 was in the second group of E-14's to be converted to class H-5, completed as the 1361 in March 1926. Jeffrey K. Winslow collection, courtesy of Eric Archer.

The engineer's side of No. 1032, the same engine as shown in the previous photograph, is shown at Tacoma, WA, in July 1923. By this time it had its standard GN cast headlight and a steel pilot. Collection of Harold K. Vollrath.

No. 1033 is one of the second heavier series of E-14. It is a coal burner, even though these engines performed poorly when fueled by coal. It was equipped with outside steam pipes in 1919. It is shown at Grand Forks, ND, on February 26, 1924. Railroad Museum of Pennsylvania (PHMC).

No. 1042 was the highest-numbered E-14 after ten engines from the same order were sold to the Spokane, Portland and Seattle. It was one of eight which received outside steam pipes prior to its conversion to an H-7 Pacific. It was photographed on June 8, 1924, at Auburn, WA. Railroad Museum of Pennsylvania (PHMC).

While built at nearly the same time as the second group of E-14's, the Class E-15 locomotives were substantially lighter. The rationale for this was the GN believed it needed a new, larger engine for heavy locals, yet smaller than the E-14 class, which had been intended for the same heavy, fast mainline trains as the H-4. Note the extended piston rod projecting through the front cylinder cover. This feature was also on the E-14. Collection of H. L. Broadbelt.

Class E-15

Also in 1910, GN purchased from Baldwin a group of twenty lighter ten-wheeled locomotives, Nos. 1073-1092, designated as Class E-15. These had 22-inch by 28-inch cylinders, 73-inch drivers, and weighed 177,000 pounds. These were apparently delivered with the GN Old Style superheater, and also had inside steam pipes. Four of them (1074-1076) were sold to the SP&S in 1925. Some of them later received outside steam pipes and GN New Style superheaters. Four of them received branch pipe heaters (Kelly feedwater heaters) in 1928. By 1935, only five of the locomotives were still in service, and these were all oil burners assigned to the Butte and Spokane Divisions. Three of these (1078, 1082 and 1090) lasted until the late 1940's on the Spokane Division.

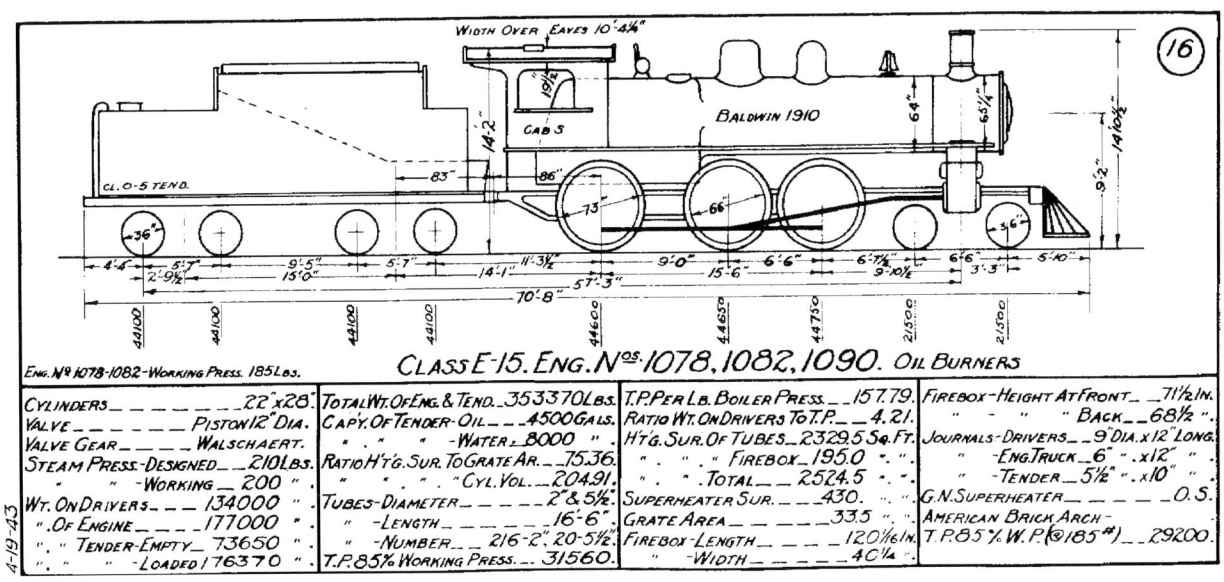

E-15 1078 was a Spokane Division oil burner, with extra bracing on the cylinders. It was photographed at Hillyard, WA, in August 1934. Collection of Harold K. Vollrath.

This photograph of the 1081 at Great Falls is so early that the engine still has the original Class E-15 tender. The date would be between 1910 and 1912. Note the extended piston rod, which did not stay on these engines very long. Jack Dykstra collection.

E-15 1082 is also at Great Falls. It was moved from the Butte Division to the Spokane Division about 1942, so this undated photograph was taken before then, believed to be about 1926. Note that it has a blowdown muffler and a speedometer connection to the front axle of the pilot truck. The extended piston rod has been removed. Photograph by Herman Rinke, courtesy of Eric Archer.

No. 1089, another Spokane Division oil-burning E-15, was photographed at Tacoma, WA, in July 1923. Collection of Harold K. Vollrath.

Notes:

1. Fr. Dale Peterka, "Early Steam Developments on the GN," Great Northern Railway Historical Society (GNRHS) Reference Sheet 224, December 1994.

2. Theodore F. Doyle, "The Great Northern Flyer," GNRHS Reference Sheet 290, December 2000..

3. "An Unusual Locomotive Performance," *Railway Review*, Vol. 78, No. 13, p. 598 (March 26, 1926).

4. Paul T. Warner, "The Great Northern Railway and Its Locomotives," *Baldwin Locomotives*, January 1925.

5. *Ibid.*

6. "Tests of the New 10-Wheel Locomotives of the Great Northern," *Railroad Gazette*, Vol. 30, No. 41, p. 735 (October 14, 1898).

7. Paul T. Warner, *op. cit.*

8. Great Northern Railway Company Authority for Expenditure 16530, approved January 28, 1921.

9. *Ibid.*

GN 450 was placed in Class 39 upon its arrival in 1892. It was later renumbered as 516 in 1899, and became a Class F-1 engine in 1903. ALCO Historic Photos.

Chapter 11

Class F 2-8-0 Consolidation

Class F-1

Great Northern received its first Consolidations in two different orders in 1892. The first fifty were from Brooks and were numbered 450-499 and were placed in Class 39, later F-1. Sixteen additional locomotives (numbered as 500-515) were received in late 1892. The first fifty were renumbered as 516-565 in the major renumbering of 1899. Like most of the Moguls previously ordered, these engines had 55-inch drivers. Most of these engines had 19-inch by 26-inch cylinders, with engine weights of 136,000 pounds. Two of the locomotives, Nos. 515 and 565, were delivered as tandem compounds,[1] with 13-inch and 22-inch diameter cylinders having strokes of 26 inches. The high-pressure cylinders had piston valves, and exhausted into the low-pressure cylinders immediately behind them.[2] The compounds were slightly heavier than the simple engines, with weights of 147,000 pounds. One of these engines, No. 515, was placed on exhibit at the Columbian Exposition, held in Chicago in 1893. About 1900 or 1901,[3] the compound locomotives were rebuilt to simple locomotives. Like all of the Consolidations ordered by the GN, the F-1's were delivered with Belpaire fireboxes.

Two of these engines were sold to the SP&S in 1908, but were returned in 1945. Six of the F-1's were superheated (two while on the SP&S), at that time receiving 10-inch piston valves and 22-inch by 26-inch cylinders. In the 1920's the wood pilots were replaced with steel, and a few received foot board switching pilots. Four of the engines (508, 511, 521 and 540) received low water alarms in the late 1940's, and one (508) received a Ragonnet power reverse gear in 1950. The majority of the F-1's were sold or scrapped in the 1920's, though a few held on until the late 1940's and early 1950's. Two of them were renumbered in 1947 to clear numbers for diesels. A few of the engines (those used on the Spokane Division) were converted to burn oil. The last F-1's were used primarily on the western divisions.

Class F-2

Contemporary with the Brooks engines which became Class F-1 were five Consolidations built by The Baldwin Locomotive Works in 1892. All had Belpaire boilers and Vauclain compound cylinders, with one high and one low-pressure, placed one above the other, on each side of the locomotive.[4] These were numbered 500-504 and had 13-inch and 22-inch by 26-inch cylinders, 55-inch drivers and engine weights of 142,000 pounds. They were placed in Class 40. Shortly after their receipt they were renumbered as 550-554, and in the 1899 renumbering they became 595-599. Between 1900 and 1918, they were changed to simple engines with 19-inch by 26-inch cylinders and were placed in Class F-2. All were retired in 1928 and 1929.

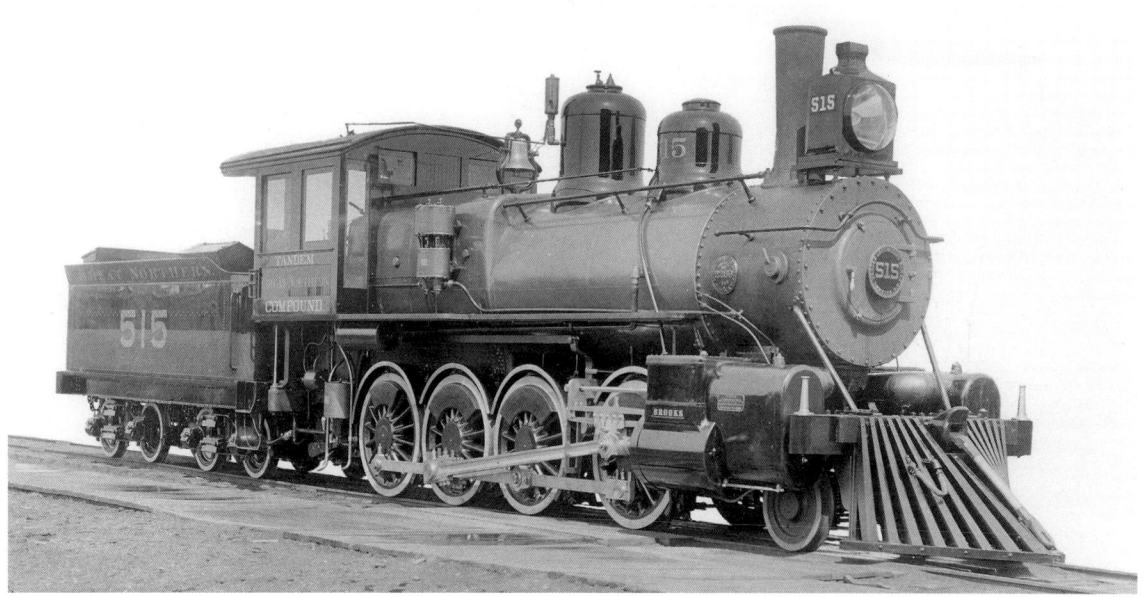

Engine 515, built (and labeled) as a tandem compound, shows the unusual cylinder arrangement in this photograph. This F-1 was placed on display at the Columbian Exposition in Chicago. ALCO Historic Photos, courtesy of Fr. Dale Peterka.

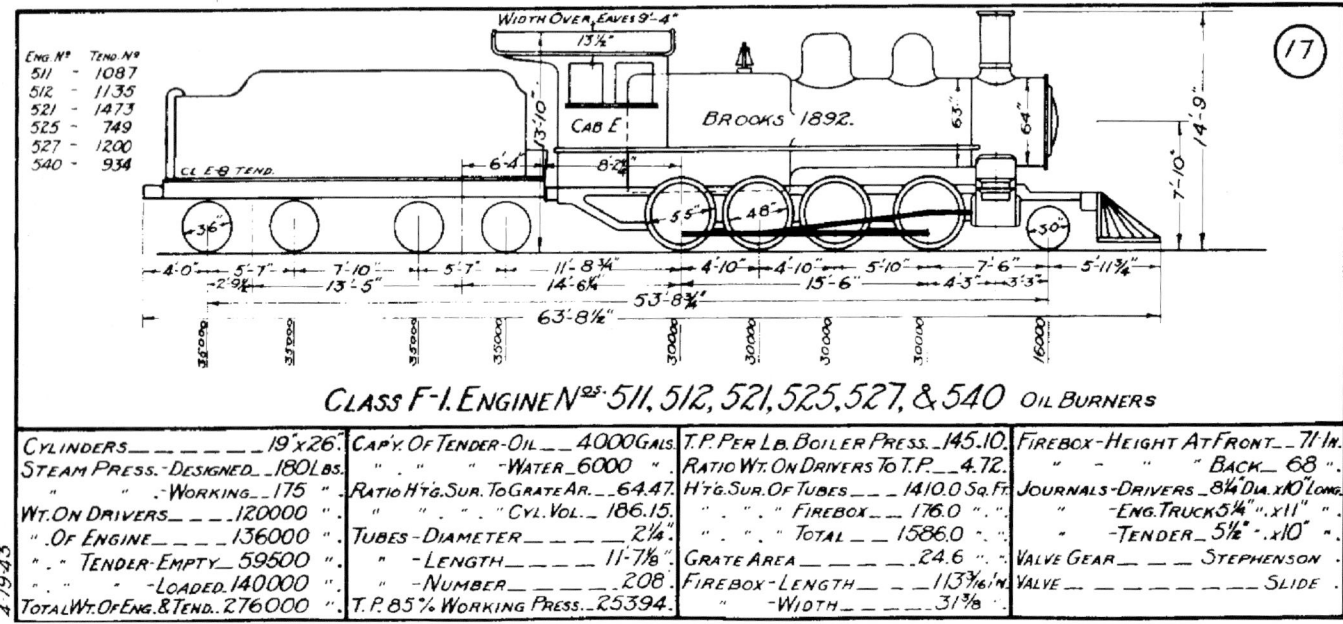

ENG.N°	TEND.N°
511	–	1087
512	–	1135
521	–	1473
525	–	749
527	–	1200
540	–	934

CLASS F-1. ENGINE N⁰ˢ. 511, 512, 521, 525, 527, & 540 OIL BURNERS

CYLINDERS _ _ _ _ _ _ 19"x 26".	CAP'Y. OF TENDER-OIL _ _ 4000 GALS.	T.P. PER LB. BOILER PRESS. _ 145.10.	FIREBOX-HEIGHT AT FRONT _ _ 71 IN.
STEAM PRESS.-DESIGNED _ 180 LBS.	" . " " -WATER _ 6000 "	RATIO WT. ON DRIVERS TO T.P. _ 4.72.	" . " " BACK _ 68 ".
" .-WORKING _ 175 "	RATIO HT'G. SUR. TO GRATE AR. _ 64.47.	HT'G. SUR. OF TUBES _ _ _ 1410.0 SQ.FT.	JOURNALS-DRIVERS _ 8¼" DIA. x 10" LONG.
WT. ON DRIVERS _ _ _ 120000 ".	" " . " CYL. VOL. _ 186.15.	" . " . " FIREBOX _ 176.0 " . "	" -ENG.TRUCK 5¼" . x 11 " .
" .OF ENGINE _ _ _ _ 136000 ".	TUBES-DIAMETER _ _ _ _ 2¼".	" . " . " TOTAL _ _ 1586.0 " . "	" -TENDER - 5½" -. x 10" .
" . " -TENDER-EMPTY 59500 ".	" -LENGTH _ _ _ _ 11'-7⅛".	GRATE AREA _ _ _ _ _ 24.6 " .	VALVE GEAR _ _ _ STEPHENSON .
" . " -LOADED. 140000 ".	" -NUMBER _ _ _ _ 208.	FIREBOX-LENGTH _ _ 113³/₁₆ IN.	VALVE _ _ _ _ _ _ _ _ SLIDE .
TOTAL WT. OF ENG. & TEND. 276000 ".	T.P. 85% WORKING PRESS. 25394.	" -WIDTH _ _ _ _ 31⅜".	

4-1-1943

F-1 No. 511, shown here with an E-15 tender (probably No. 1097), was photographed at an unknown location prior to World War II. The slide valves indicate that this was one of the non-superheated F-1's. Collection of William Raia.

Engine 521, with what is probably an H-4 class tender, was moved to the Spokane Division and equipped for oil burning relatively late in its career. The F-1 has also had a footboard pilot installed. The photograph was taken at Spokane, WA, in 1946. Wilbur C. Whittaker.

*No. 537 was sporting a rather unusual tender when photographed at Minneapolis in April 1932.
Cornwall-Martin collection (RPS) from the collection of Norman F. Priebe.*

Superheated F-1S No. 508 is shown here with one of the early wooden water cars (auxiliary tenders) that GN used until the last of them deteriorated beyond use in the 1930's. While the exact date of the photograph is unknown, water car 296039 only carried that number from June 1, 1914, through January 1927. Great Northern Railway, courtesy of Jerrold F. Hilton.

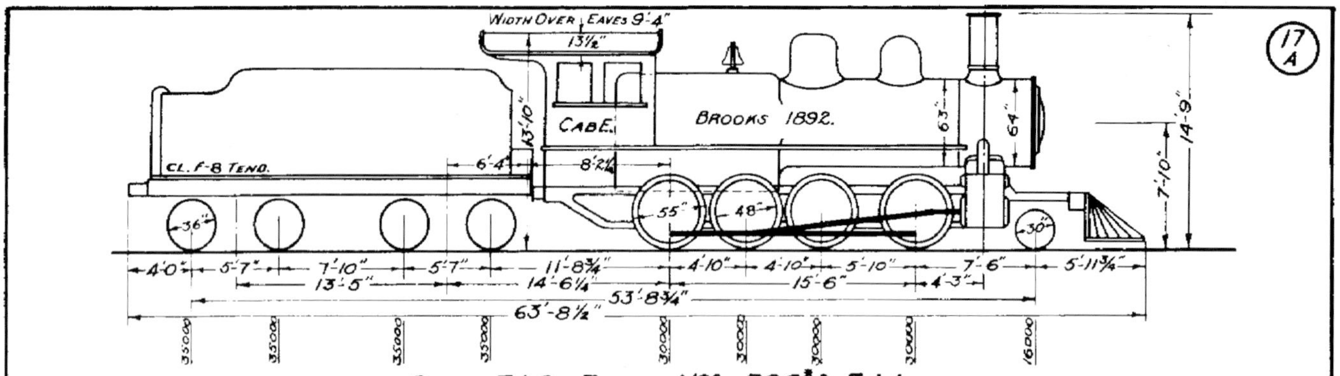

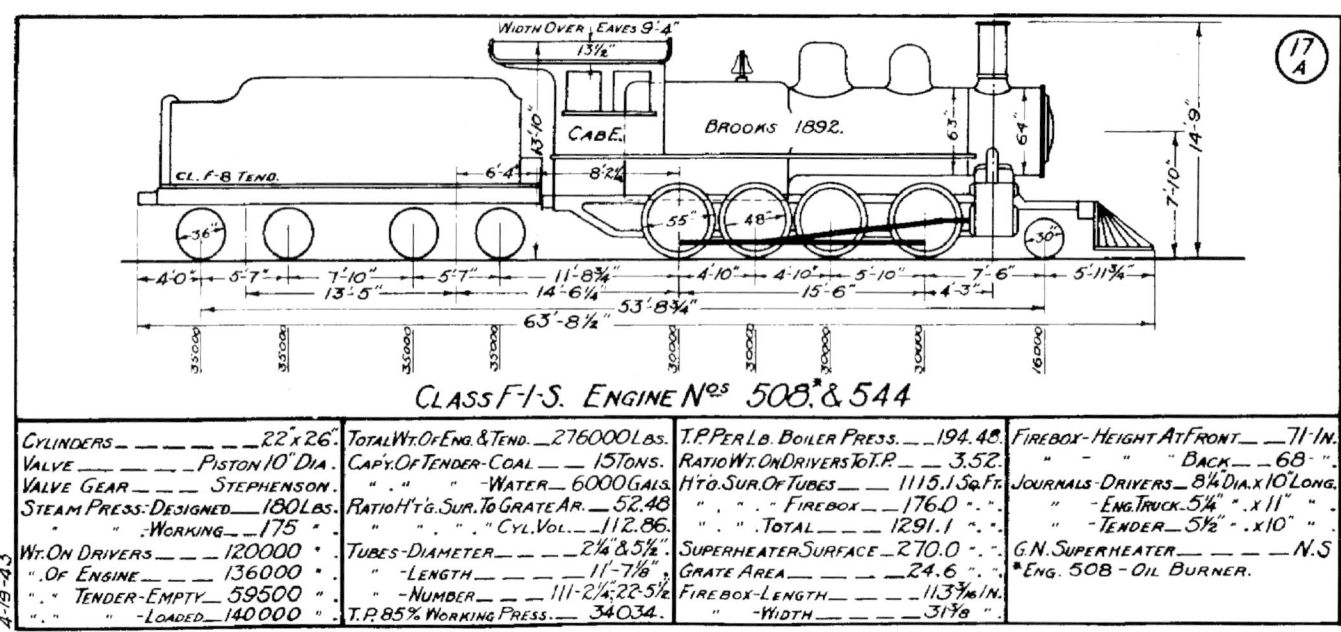

CLASS F-1-S. ENGINE NOS 508.* & 544

Cylinders ______ 22"x26".	Total Wt. Of Eng. & Tend. __ 276000 Lbs.	T.P. Per Lb. Boiler Press. __ 194.48.	Firebox-Height At Front __ 71-In.
Valve ______ Piston 10" Dia.	Cap'y. Of Tender-Coal __ 15 Tons.	Ratio Wt. On Drivers To T.P. __ 3.52.	" - " " Back __ 68 ".
Valve Gear ___ Stephenson.	" . " " -Water __ 6000 Gals.	H't'g. Sur. Of Tubes __ 1115.1 Sq. Ft.	Journals-Drivers __ 8¼" Dia. x 10" Long.
Steam Press:-Designed __ 180 Lbs.	Ratio H't'g. Sur. To Grate Ar. __ 52.48	" . " . " Firebox __ 176.0 " . ".	" -Eng. Truck 5¼" " . x 11" " .
" " :-Working __ 175 " .	" " . " . " Cyl. Vol. __ 112.86.	" . " . Total ___ 1291.1 " . ".	" -Tender __ 5½" " . x 10" " .
Wt. On Drivers ___ 120000 " .	Tubes-Diameter ____ 2¼" & 5½".	Superheater Surface __ 270.0 " . ".	G.N. Superheater ____ N.S
" . Of Engine ___ 136000 " .	" -Length ____ 11'-7⅛".	Grate Area ____ 24.6 " . ".	*Eng. 508 - Oil Burner.
" . " Tender-Empty __ 59500 " .	" -Number ___ 111-2¼"; 22-5½	Firebox-Length ____ 113 3/16 In.	
" . " " -Loaded __ 140000 " .	T.P. 85% Working Press. __ 34034.	" -Width ____ 31⅛ ".	

4-19-43

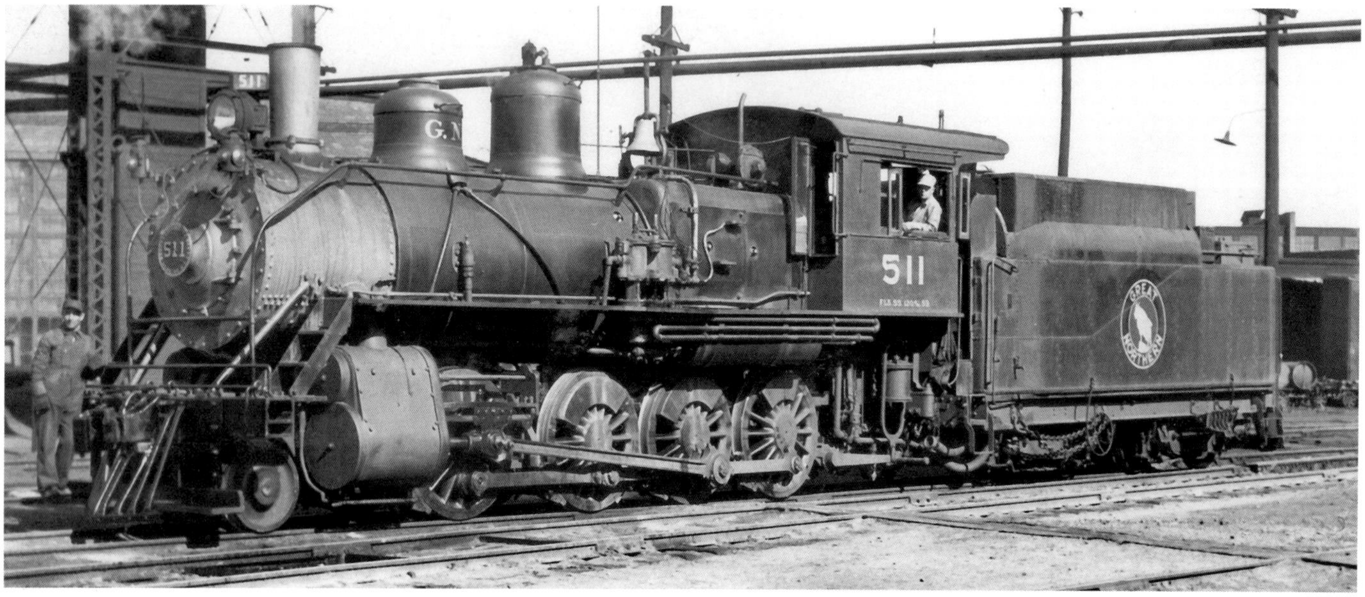

GN 511 was superheated in 1942, and appears here with its piston valves. This F-1 was photographed in October 1945 at Great Falls, MT. William J. Pontin (RPS) photograph from the collection of Norman F. Priebe.

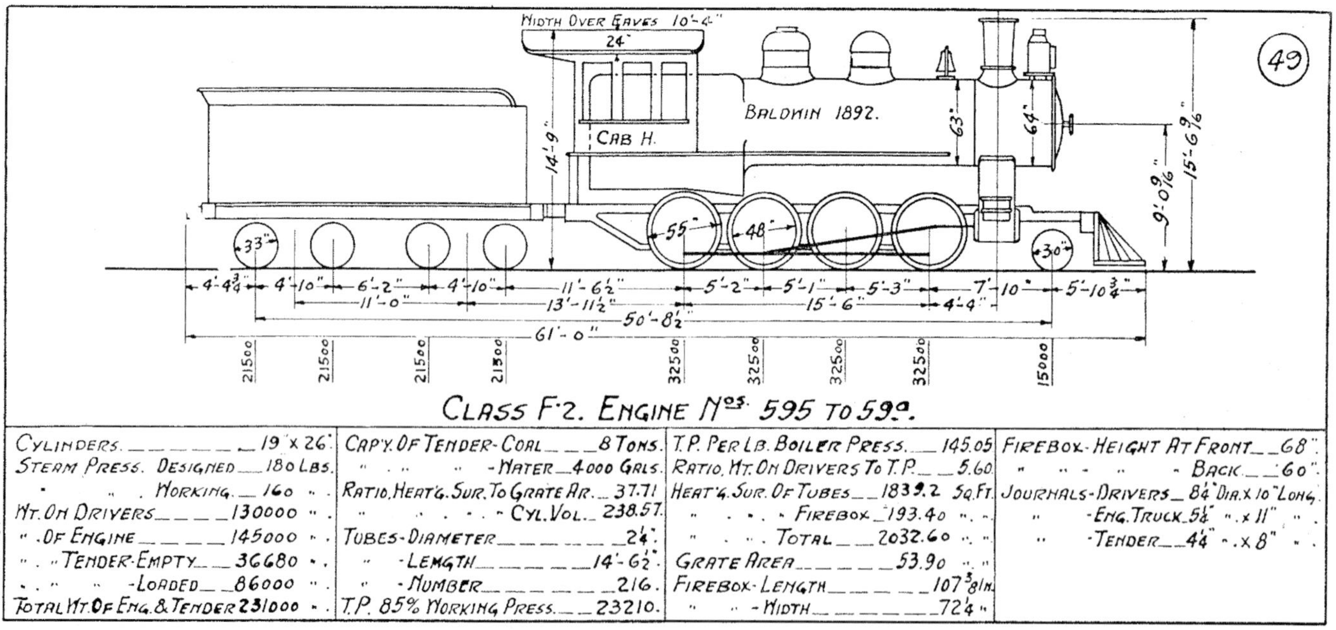

CLASS F-2. ENGINE NOS. 595 TO 599.

Cylinders ______ 19"x26".	Cap'y. Of Tender-Coal ___ 8 Tons.	T.P. Per Lb. Boiler Press. __ 145.05	Firebox-Height At Front __ 68".
Steam Press. Designed __ 180 Lbs.	" . " " -Water __ 4000 Gals.	Ratio. Wt. On Drivers To T.P. __ 5.60	" " - " " Back __ 60".
" " . Working __ 160 " .	Ratio. Heat'g. Sur. To Grate Ar. __ 37.71	Heat'g. Sur. Of Tubes __ 1839.2 Sq. Ft.	Journals-Drivers __ 8¼" Dia. x 10" Long.
Wt. On Drivers ____ 130000 " .	" " . " . " Cyl. Vol. __ 238.57.	" . " . " Firebox __ 193.40 " . ".	" -Eng. Truck 5½" " . x 11" " .
" . Of Engine ____ 145000 " .	Tubes-Diameter ______ 2¼".	" . " . Total ___ 2032.60 " . ".	" -Tender __ 4¼" " . x 8" " .
" . " Tender-Empty __ 36680 " .	" -Length ______ 14'-6½".	Grate Area ______ 53.90 " . ".	
" . " " -Loaded __ 86000 " .	" -Number ______ 216.	Firebox-Length ______ 107⅜ In.	
Total Wt. Of Eng. & Tender 231000 " .	T.P. 85% Working Press. ___ 23210.	" " -Width ______ 72¼ ".	

Rev. 5-1-28

Class F-3

In the 1890's Great Northern ordered a number of 4-8-0 Mastodon locomotives for freight service, but after 1900, that wheel arrangement was abandoned in new construction in favor of the 2-8-0 Consolidation. In fact, when one of the 4-8-0's was damaged in 1901, it was repaired as a Consolidation and was later assigned Class F-3. This locomotive was No. 701, a member of Class 45 (which would become Class G-2). The justification for the rebuild was to increase tractive power by placing more weight on the driving wheels, but an accompanying note provides a little more enlightenment: "This engine was badly wrecked on the Cascade Division by running into a push car loaded with dynamite; necessary repairs are heavy. Estimated cost of changing into consolidation type is the difference between repairing this engine as a Mastodon and repairing it as a Consolidation Engine."[5] As rebuilt, the engine retained its 19-inch by 32-inch cylinders, 55-inch drivers, and 176,000 pound engine weight. However, 18,000 additional pounds of its weight were now on the drivers.

This rare view shows F-2 598 in work train service. The wrecker is cleaning up the wreck of train No. 1 at Crary, ND in 1912. Collection of Norman F. Priebe.

Engine 701, the only member of Class F-3, was rebuilt from a wrecked 4-8-0. It was photographed at Grand Forks, ND, in 1936. Warren R. McGee.

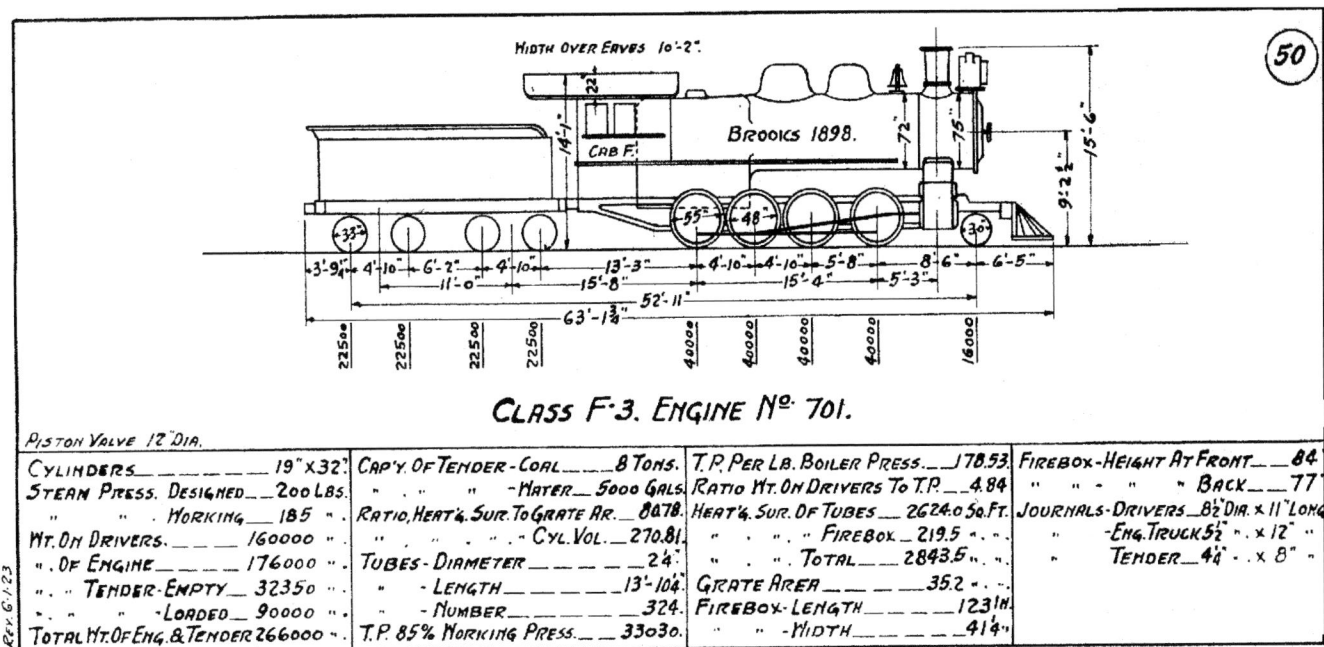

CLASS F-3. ENGINE Nº 701.

PISTON VALVE 12" DIA.

CYLINDERS _____ 19"x32"	CAP'Y. OF TENDER - COAL ___ 8 TONS.	T.P. PER LB. BOILER PRESS. ___ 178.53	FIREBOX - HEIGHT AT FRONT ___ 84
STEAM PRESS. DESIGNED __ 200 LBS.	" " " -WATER __ 5000 GALS	RATIO WT. ON DRIVERS TO T.P. __ 4.84	" " " BACK ___ 77
" " WORKING ___ 185 "	RATIO, HEAT'G SUR. TO GRATE AR. __ 80.78	HEAT'G. SUR. OF TUBES __ 2624.0 SQ.FT.	JOURNALS-DRIVERS __ 8½"DIA. x 11" LONG
WT. ON DRIVERS. ___ 160000 "	" " " -CYL. VOL. __ 270.81	" " " FIREBOX __ 219.5 " "	" -ENG.TRUCK 5½" " x 12"
" OF ENGINE ___ 176000 "	TUBES - DIAMETER _____ 2¼"	" " " TOTAL ___ 2843.5 " "	" TENDER__ 4¾" " x 8"
" TENDER-EMPTY __ 32350 "	" - LENGTH _____ 13'-10¾"	GRATE AREA _____ 35.2 " "	
" " -LOADED __ 90000 "	" - NUMBER _____ 324	FIREBOX-LENGTH _____ 123 IN.	
TOTAL WT.OF ENG.& TENDER 266000 "	T.P. 85% WORKING PRESS. __ 33030.	" -WIDTH _____ 41¼"	

Rev. 6-1-23

Class F-4 (1st)

In 1901, GN received five Consolidations from Rogers which were crossover compounds. They had 22-inch and 32-inch by 32-inch cylinders and 55-inch drivers. They were initially numbered as 1160-1164 and placed in Class 52, but less than a year after their receipt they were renumbered as 1195-1199. In 1903, they were again renumbered as 1095-1099. When the new class system was implemented they became Class F-4 engines. At some time prior to about 1915, they were converted to simple engines having 20-inch by 32-inch cylinders, and moved to Class F-5. Two were converted to C-5 switchers in 1930, and 1098 lasted until 1947.

Class F-4 (2nd)

Class F-4 was reused when the GN acquired the Spokane Falls & Northern (SF&N) engines. The single occupant of Class F-4(2nd) was GN 1094, which had originally been built by Baldwin as Red Mountain/Columbia & Red Mountain No. 9 (jointly owned by two

SF&N subsidiaries). It had 19-inch by 24-inch cylinders, 47-inch drivers, and weighed only 135,000 pounds. The engine had a wagontop boiler and a radial stay firebox. It was sold to a lumber company in 1925. No photographs of this engine are known to exist.

Class F-5

The original members of Class F-5 were received about the same time as the F-4's, also from Rogers. They were numbered as 1100-1109 and were originally placed in Class 50. These were simple engines with 20-inch by 32-inch cylinders and slide valves. They had 55-inch drivers and weighed 194,000 pounds. In 1921 and 1922 five of the engines (1100-1104) received GN New Style superheaters, outside steam pipes and piston valves and were classified as F-5S. By the mid-1920's all of the F-5's were oil burners, and they were assigned to the western divisions (Klamath, Spokane and Kalispell). In 1929 and 1930, four of them had the engine truck removed (1095, 1097, 1108 and 1109) and became Class C-5 0-8-0's. Many of these engines lasted well into

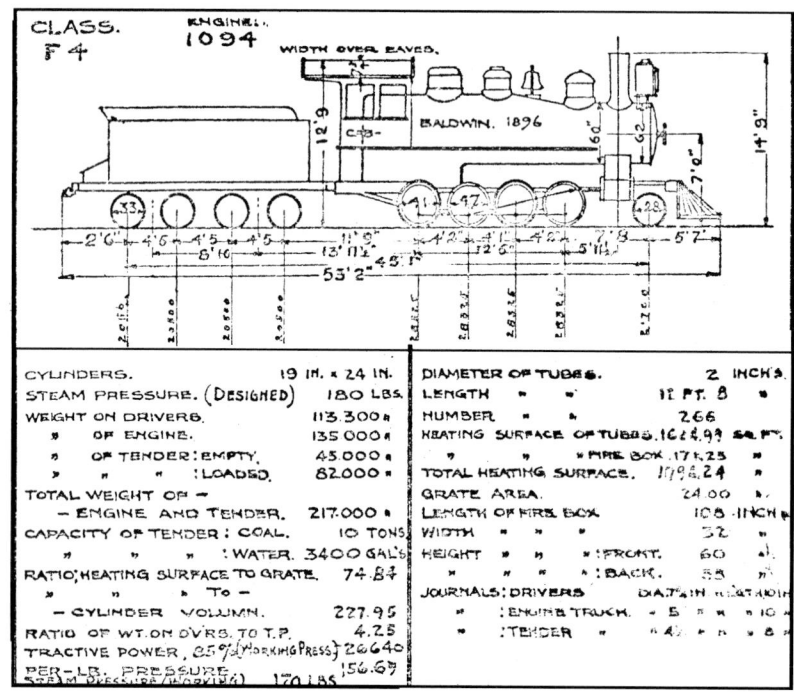

F-5 1103, with a smoke deflector and a wooden pilot, was photographed at Everett, WA, on June 9, 1920. J. Foster Adams photograph from the GNRHS collection.

the 1940's, and those that did received power reverses and low water alarms. Two of them (1098 and 1105) received electric train indicators. Two of the engines (1100 and 1107) were not scrapped until 1950

Class F-6

A third 1901 order, this one from Brooks, was comprised of engines 1110-1129, which were placed in Class 50B. Like the F-5's, they were simple locomotives with 20-inch by 32-inch cylinders, slide valves and 55-inch drivers. They were slightly heavier at 195,500 pounds. In 1903 they became Class F-6. Three of the engines (1124, 1127 and 1129) were equipped with branch pipe heaters. All but 1115, 1118, 1121, 1125 and 1126 received superheaters and 11-inch piston valves. Most received Great Northern Old Style superheaters, though 1119, 1124 and 1116 received Great Northern New Style. 1110, 1122, 1123, 1128 and 1129 received H&D superheaters. All of the superheated engines except 1116 received 23½-inch by 32-inch cylinders. Engine 1116

received 21-inch by 32-inch cylinders. It had a 200 psi working steam pressure, while the other superheated locomotives had only a 165 psi working pressure (all were designed for 210 psi). The superheated locomotives were reclassified as "F-6S". Beginning in 1925, the entire class was rebuilt to Class C-2 0-8-0's by removing the engine trucks. The final converted locomotive was completed in October 1928.

Class F-7

The fourth 1901 order for Consolidations, locomotives 1130-1139 from Cooke, were placed in Class 50A and later F-7. Dimensionally they were quite similar to the Class F-5 engines, with 20-inch by 32-inch cylinders, slide valves, 55-inch drivers and engine weights of 194,000 pounds. Six of these engines (1130-1133, 1136 and 1138) received Great Northern New Style superheaters in 1913 and 1914 (at least for the five for which dates are known). At the time they were superheated, they received 12-inch piston valves and 23½-inch by 30-

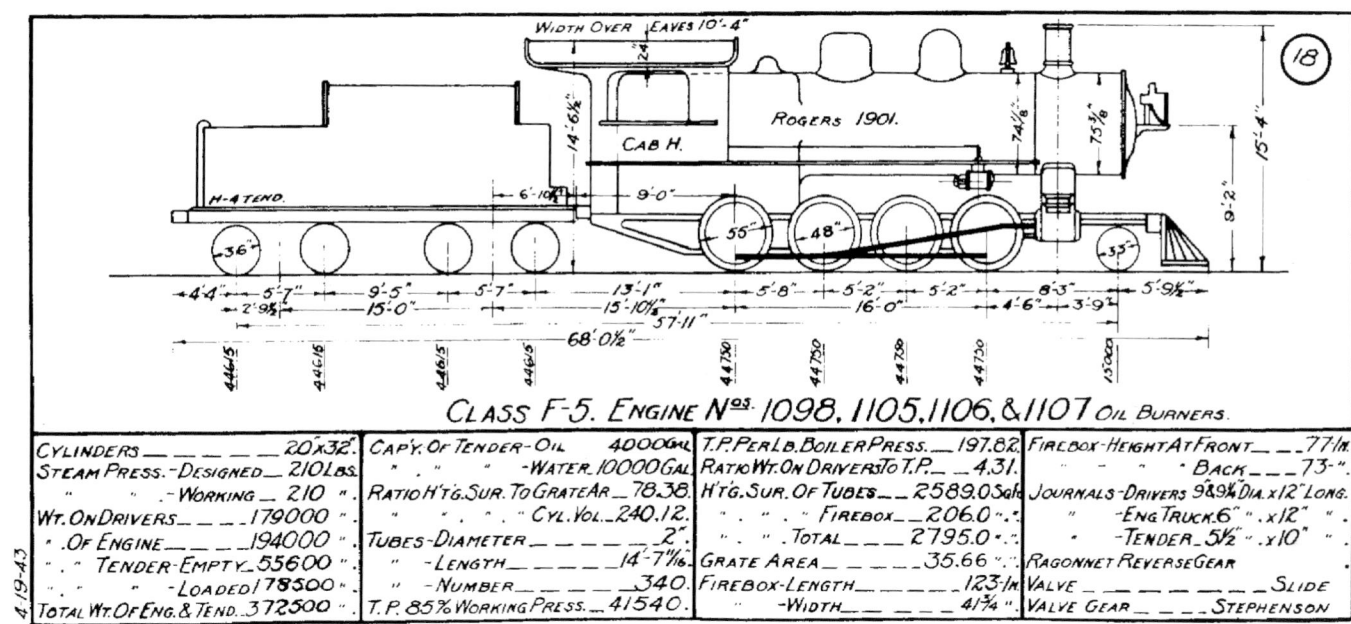

CLASS F-5. ENGINE Nos. 1098, 1105, 1106, & 1107 OIL BURNERS.

CYLINDERS _____ 20"x32".	CAP'Y. OF TENDER-OIL ___ 4000Gal	T.P. PER LB. BOILER PRESS. ___ 197.82.	FIREBOX-HEIGHT AT FRONT ___ 77 In.
STEAM PRESS.-DESIGNED ___ 210 Lbs.	" " " -WATER. 10000 Gal	RATIO WT. ON DRIVERS TO T.P. ___ 4.31.	" " " BACK ___ 73 "
" " .-WORKING ___ 210 "	RATIO H'TG. SUR. TO GRATE AR___ 78.38.	H'TG. SUR. OF TUBES ___ 2589.0 Sqft	JOURNALS-DRIVERS 9¾&9¾ DIA. x 12" LONG.
WT. ON DRIVERS ___ 179000 ".	" " " CYL. VOL. 240.12.	" " " FIREBOX ___ 206.0 ".	" -ENG TRUCK 6 " x 12 " "
" OF ENGINE ___ 194000 "	TUBES-DIAMETER ___ 2".	" " " TOTAL ___ 2795.0 ".	" -TENDER 5½ " x 10 " "
" TENDER-EMPTY 55600 "	" -LENGTH ___ 14'-7 7/16	GRATE AREA ___ 35.66 ".	RAGONNET REVERSE GEAR
" -LOADED 178500 "	" -NUMBER ___ 340.	FIREBOX-LENGTH ___ 123 In.	VALVE _____ SLIDE
TOTAL WT. OF ENG. & TEND. 372500 "	T.P. 85% WORKING PRESS. ___ 41540.	" -WIDTH ___ 41¾ "	VALVE GEAR ___ STEPHENSON

Huge smoke deflectors were installed on several engines. The long ones did double duty. The first objective was to minimize blast damage to tunnel and snowshed roofs. The second was to move the smoke past the engine crew. They failed because the extra length adversely affected the draft. Location was near the Cascade Tunnel in 1902. Collection of William Bissinger.

Engine 1107, with a sun visor over the cab window and footboard pilot, is at Hillyard in the 1930's and is probably engaged in switching duty. F-5's 1107 and 1108 both had non-typical capped stacks, which likely contained a spark arrestor. Unknown source.

No. 1098 was originally delivered as a crossover compound, and was a former member of Class F-4(1st), moved to F-5 when simpled. It was photographed on New Years Day in 1938 at Klamath Falls, OR. Collection of William Raia.

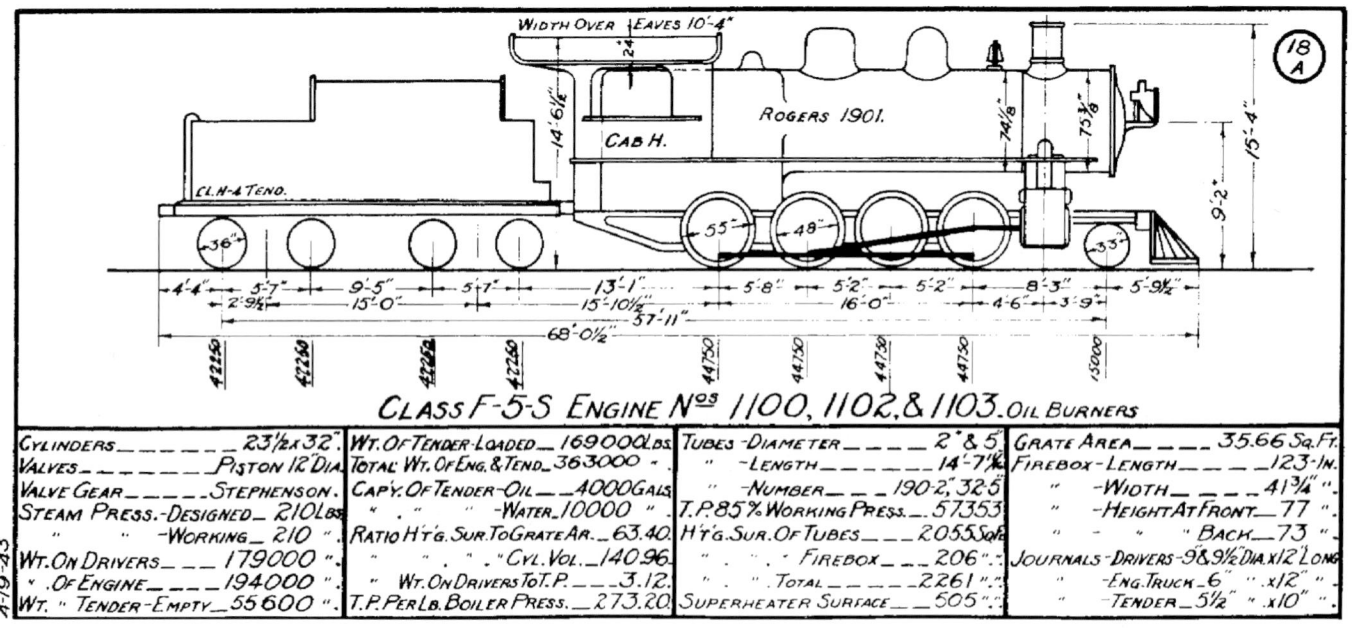

CLASS F-5-S ENGINE NOS 1100, 1102, & 1103. OIL BURNERS

CYLINDERS	23½x32"	WT. OF TENDER-LOADED	169000 LBS.	TUBES-DIAMETER	2"&5	GRATE AREA	35.66 SQ.FT.
VALVES	PISTON 12"DIA.	TOTAL WT. OF ENG.& TEND.	363000 "	" -LENGTH	14'-7½"	FIREBOX-LENGTH	123-IN.
VALVE GEAR	STEPHENSON.	CAP'Y. OF TENDER-OIL	4000 GALS	" -NUMBER	190-2, 325	" -WIDTH	41¾"
STEAM PRESS.-DESIGNED	210 LBS	" " -WATER	10000 "	T.P.85% WORKING PRESS.	57353	" -HEIGHT AT FRONT	77 "
" -WORKING	210 ".	RATIO HT'G. SUR. TO GRATE AR.	63.40	HT'G. SUR. OF TUBES	2055 SQF.	" " BACK	73 "
WT. ON DRIVERS	179000 ".	" CYL. VOL.	14096	" " FIREBOX	206 ".	JOURNALS-DRIVERS-9&9½ DIA.x12 LONG	
" " OF ENGINE	194000 ".	" WT. ON DRIVERS TO T. P.	3.12.	" " TOTAL	2261 ".	-ENG. TRUCK-6 " x12	
WT. " TENDER-EMPTY	55600 ".	T.P. PER LB. BOILER PRESS.	273.20.	SUPERHEATER SURFACE	505 ".	-TENDER- 5½ " x10"	

inch cylinders. They retained their Stephenson valve gear. From the mid-1930's on, the engines were assigned to the Mesabi Division. Six of the ten lasted into the 1950's.

Class F-8

The final order of Consolidations in 1901 was a group of five (1150-1154) received from Rogers. These were placed in Class 51. While these had the same 20-inch by 32-inch cylinders, slide valves, and 55-inch drivers like most of the rest of GN's 2-8-0's, they were remarkable in that they had wide (72¼-inch) fireboxes placed above the driving wheels. This improved steaming qualities and increased efficiency of the engines.[6] The previous F-5, F-6 and F-7 engines had narrow fireboxes with widths in the 41-inch to 42-inch range, which fit between the rear set of drivers. The F-8 engines weighed 195,000 pounds. GN was apparently satisfied with this design, as they acquired another

twenty-five in 1902 (1140-1149, 1155-1169) and another thirty (1170-1199) in 1903, all from Rogers. In 1905, fifteen more (1200-1214) were acquired from Rogers, which by this time was part of the Alco conglomerate. Class F-8 proved a highly satisfactory locomotive for heavy freight service on divisions having moderate grades.[7] All of the Rogers locomotives were equipped with Stephenson valve gear.

In 1907 and 1908, Baldwin built fifty additional F-8 locomotives. These differed from all previous 2-8-0's on the GN in that they had Walschaert valve gear rather than the older style Stephenson.[8] They also had 6,000 gallon tenders (Style 18) rather than the 4,000 gallon tenders (Style 17) of the Rogers engines. The last ten in the series (1255-1264) were sold to the SP&S in 1909, as were four others in 1936. The F-8's served as workhorses on the GN for many years, even though they were replaced in main line freight service by Prairies and Mikados. Most received steel pilot beams and steel pilots.

Superheated F-5S 1100 was photographed at Klamath Falls, OR, in June 1949. Collection of Harold K. Vollrath.

F-6 1122 was received in December 1901 from the Brooks Locomotive Works, and was originally placed in Class 50B. ALCO Historic Photos.

Thirty-four of them received superheaters by 1921. Nos. 1141, 1143, 1148, 1163, 1175, 1182,1183, 1189, 1190, 1195, 1196 received GN Old Style superheaters before June 1911 and had 26-inch by 32-inch cylinders. Nos. 1146, 1147, 1154, 1155, 1170, 1178, 1180, 1192 received GN New Style superheaters between 1912 and 1921. Nos. 1160, 1164-1166, 1168, 1171, 1174, 1176, 1177, 1179, 1186, 1187, 1193 received H&D superheaters in 1912 (at least those for which dates are known). It is interesting that only two of the Baldwin locomotives (1220 and 1223) were superheated. By 1926 all of the superheated locomotives had 12-inch piston valves and 23½-inch by 30-inch cylinders. Nos. 1181, 1185 and 1250 received 12-inch piston valves but no superheaters. Many of the engines received power

reverse gear, and a few received low water alarms in the late 1940's and early 1950's.

In 1910 one of these engines, the 1254, was rebuilt with a new front boiler section to a Class M-2(1st) 2-6-8-0. In 1926 it was rebuilt as first of its class to a C-4 0-8-0 (No. 780, later 870). In 1928, 1929 and 1937 ten more of the F-8's had the lead trucks removed to become C-4 switchers. A number of the F-8's operating on the western divisions (Butte, Kalispell and Spokane) were converted to oil burners. By the mid-1930's, all of the divisions had some F-8's assigned to them. The first F-8 to be retired left the roster in 1931, but many of these engines remained in service until the late 1940's and early 1950's. Only the oil burners survived beyond 1950.

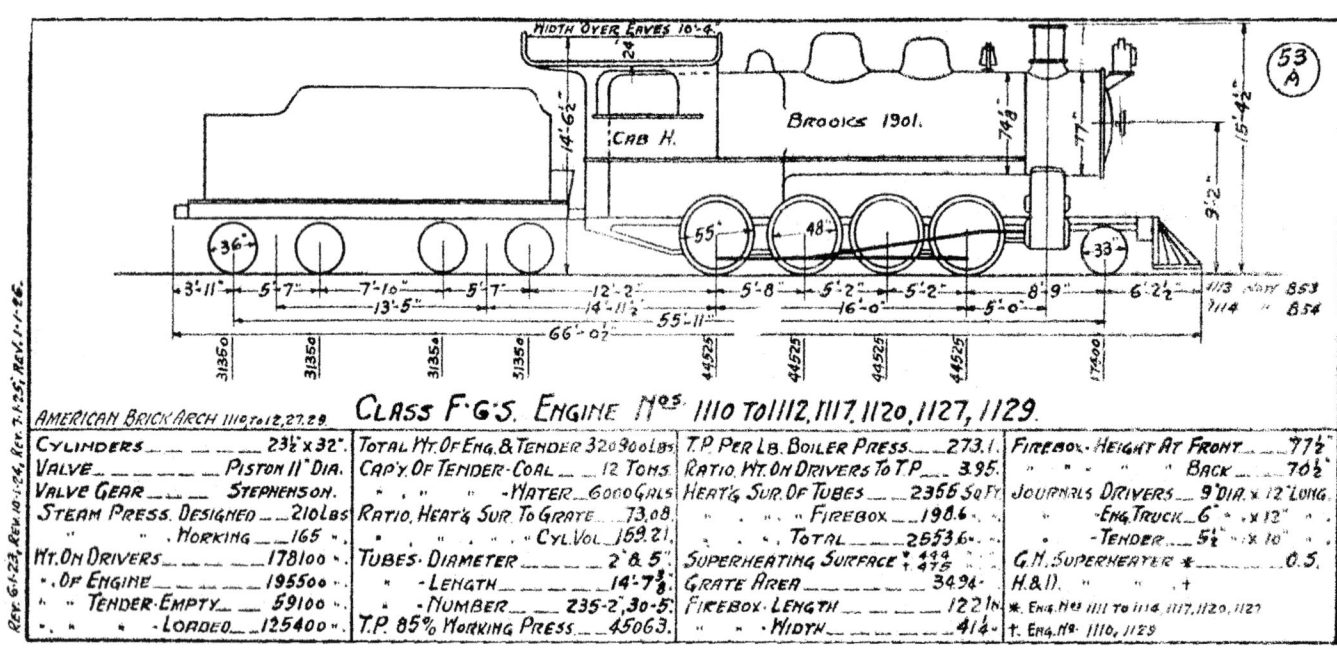

First of Class 1130 was one of the superheated F-7S engines. Most did not receive outside steam admission. This engine was sent to Korea in 1954, and in 1955 was seen working at Pusan. It was photographed at Kelly Lake, MN, on August 1, 1952. Charles E. Winters collection.

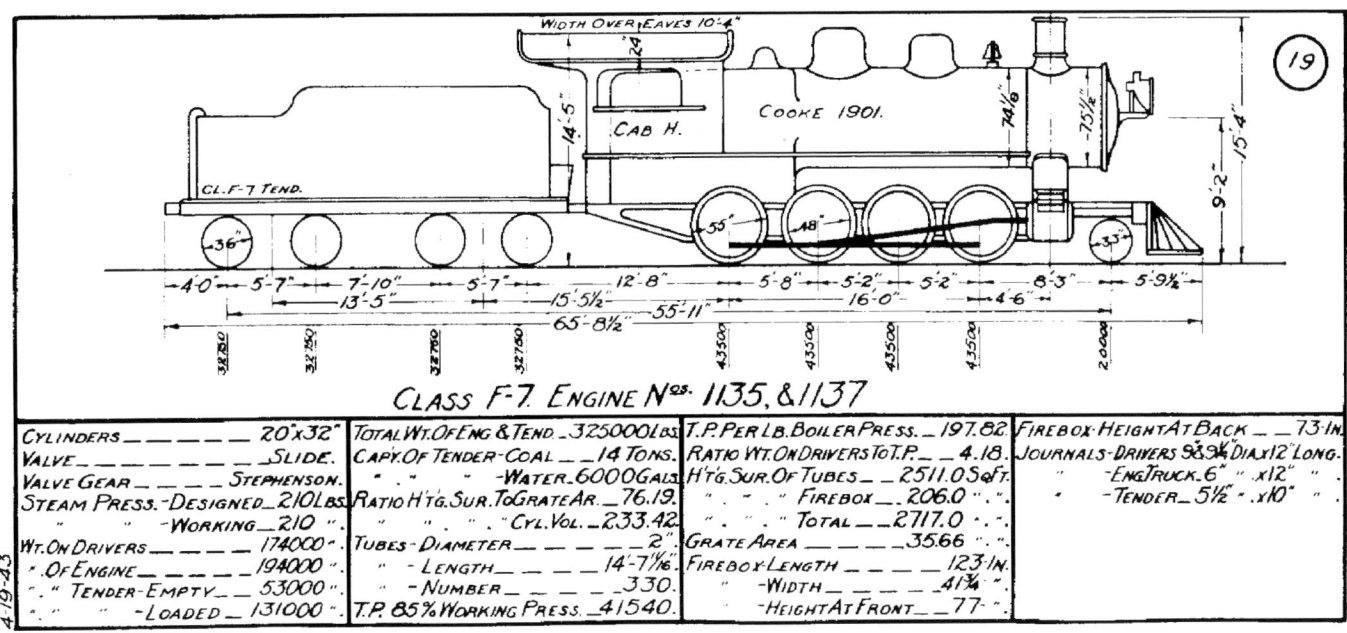

Class F-7. Engine Nos. 1135, & 1137

Cylinders _ _ _ _ _ _ _ _ 20"x32"	Total Wt. Of Eng & Tend. _ 325000 Lbs.	T.P. Per Lb. Boiler Press. _ 197.82.	Firebox-Height At Back _ _ 73-In.
Valve _ _ _ _ _ _ _ _ Slide.	Cap'y. Of Tender-Coal _ _ 14 Tons.	Ratio Wt. On Drivers To T.P. _ _ 4.18.	Journals-Drivers 9&9¼" Dia x 12" Long.
Valve Gear _ _ _ _ Stephenson.	" " " -Water 6000 Gals.	Htg. Sur. Of Tubes _ _ 2511.0 Sq.Ft.	" -Eng. Truck. 6" _ x 12" "
Steam Press.-Designed_ 210 Lbs.	Ratio H'tg. Sur. To Grate Ar. _ 76.19.	" " " Firebox _ 206.0 " "	" -Tender _ 5½" _ x 10" "
" " -Working _ 210 "	" " " " Cyl. Vol. 233.42	" " Total _ 2717.0 " "	
Wt. On Drivers _ _ _ 174000 "	Tubes-Diameter _ _ _ _ _ 2"	Grate Area _ _ _ _ 35.66 " "	
" . Of Engine _ _ _ _ 194000 "	" -Length_ _ _ _ 14-7 1/16 "	Firebox-Length _ _ _ _ 123-In.	
" . " Tender-Empty _ _ 53000 "	" -Number _ _ _ _ 330.	" -Width _ _ _ _ 41¾"	
" . " " -Loaded _ 131000 "	T.P. 85% Working Press. _ 41540.	" -Height At Front _ _ 77-"	

4-19-43

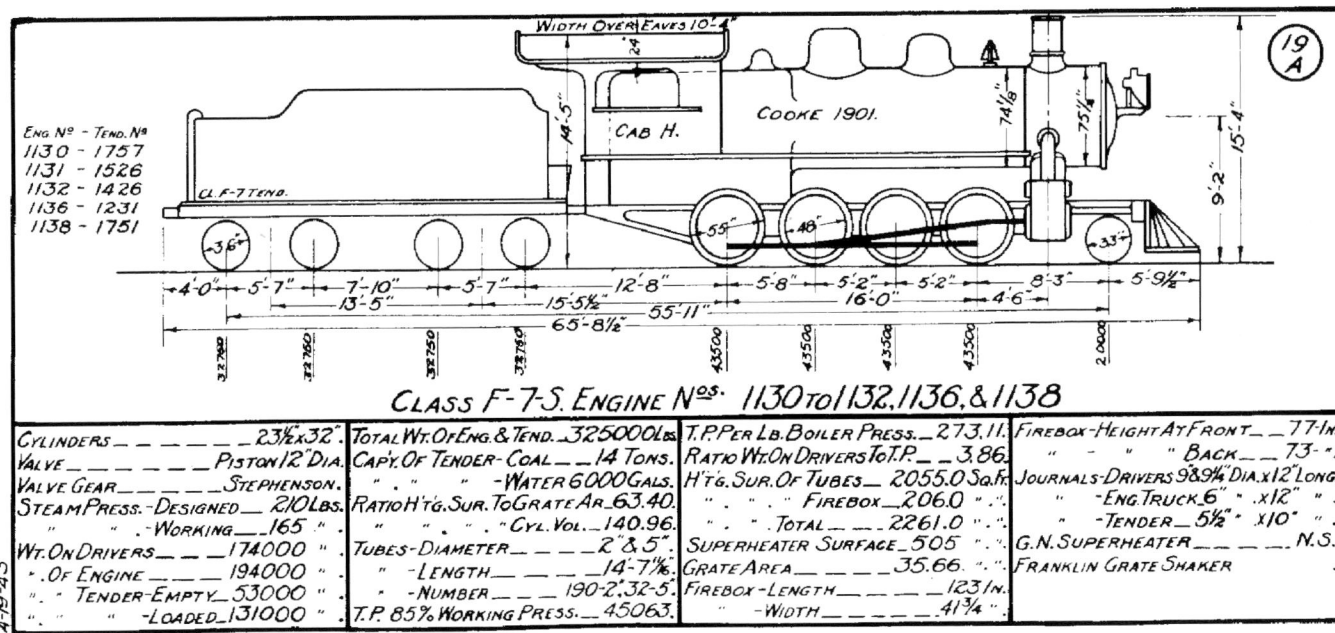

Eng N° - Tend. N°
1130 - 1757
1131 - 1526
1132 - 1426
1136 - 1231
1138 - 1751

Class F-7-S. Engine Nos. 1130 to 1132, 1136, & 1138

Cylinders _ _ _ _ _ _ 23½x32"	Total Wt. Of Eng & Tend. _ 325000 Lbs.	T.P. Per Lb. Boiler Press. _ 273.11.	Firebox-Height At Front _ _ 77-In.
Valve _ _ _ _ _ _ Piston 12" Dia.	Cap'y. Of Tender-Coal _ _ 14 Tons.	Ratio Wt. On Drivers To T.P. _ _ 3.86.	" " " Back _ _ 73-"
Valve Gear _ _ _ _ _ Stephenson.	" . " " -Water 6000 Gals.	Htg. Sur. Of Tubes _ _ 2055.0 Sq.Ft.	Journals-Drivers 9&9¼" Dia x 12" Long.
Steam Press.-Designed _ 210 Lbs.	Ratio H'tg. Sur. To Grate Ar. _ 63.40.	" " " Firebox _ 206.0 " "	" -Eng. Truck 6" . x 12" "
" " -Working _ 165 "	" " " " Cyl. Vol. 140.96.	" " Total _ 2261.0 " "	" -Tender _ 5½" . x 10" "
Wt. On Drivers _ _ _ 174000 "	Tubes-Diameter _ _ _ 2" & 5"	Superheater Surface _ 505 " "	G.N. Superheater _ _ _ _ N.S.
" . Of Engine _ _ _ _ 194000 "	" -Length_ _ _ _ 14-7 1/16 "	Grate Area _ _ _ _ 35.66. " "	Franklin Grate Shaker
" . " Tender-Empty _ 53000 "	" -Number _ _ _ 190-2", 32-5".	Firebox-Length _ _ _ 123 In.	
" . " " -Loaded _ 131000 "	T.P. 85% Working Press. _ 45063.	" -Width _ _ _ _ 41¾"	

4-19-43

Superheated No. 1136 was assigned to switching duty at Superior, WI, in 1948. Wilbur C. Whittaker.

Engine 1137, one of the non-superheated members of Class F-7 has a cab storm window commonly found on switchers.
It was photographed at Kelly Lake, MN, on April 28, 1949. P. Eilenberger photograph from the collection of William Raia.

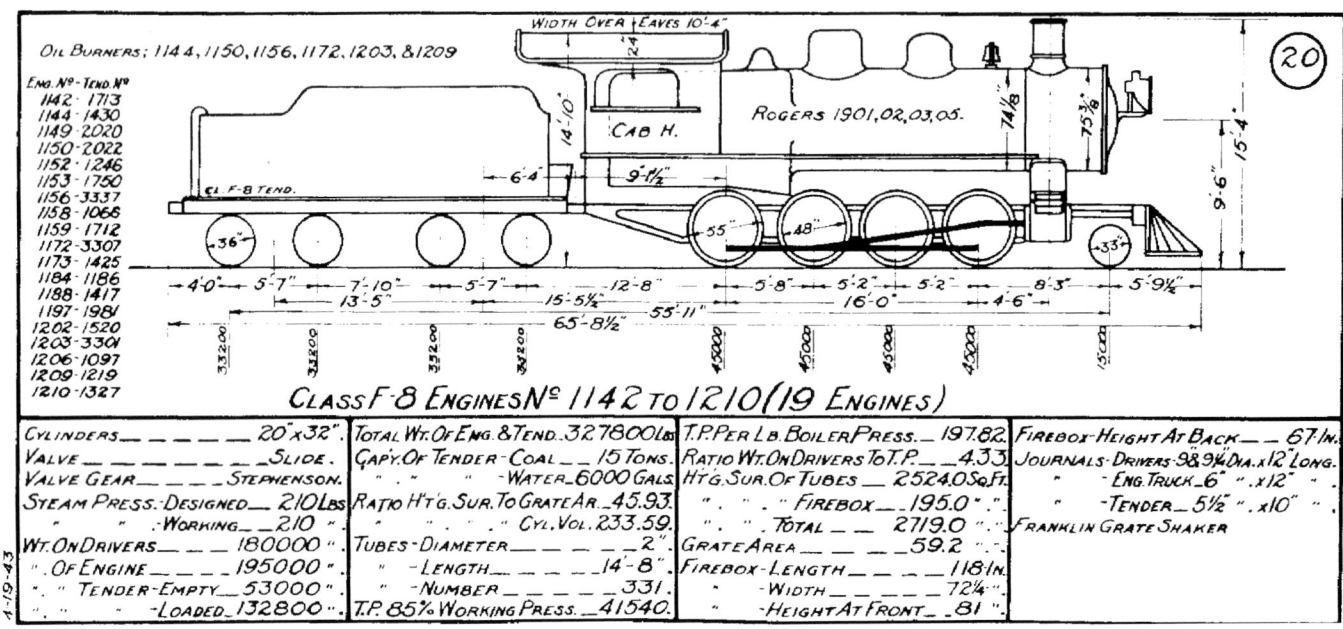

CLASS F-8 ENGINES Nº 1142 TO 1210 (19 ENGINES)

CYLINDERS ___ 20"x32".	TOTAL WT. OF ENG. & TEND. 327800 LBS	T.P. PER LB. BOILER PRESS. __ 197.82.	FIREBOX-HEIGHT AT BACK __ 67 IN.
VALVE ___ SLIDE.	CAP'Y. OF TENDER-COAL __ 15 TONS.	RATIO WT. ON DRIVERS TO T.P. __ 4.33.	JOURNALS-DRIVERS 9 & 9¼ DIA. x 12" LONG.
VALVE GEAR ___ STEPHENSON.	" __ " -WATER 6000 GALS.	H'T'G. SUR. OF TUBES __ 2524.0 SQ.FT.	" -ENG. TRUCK 6 " x 12"
STEAM PRESS.-DESIGNED __ 210 LBS	RATIO H'T'G. SUR. TO GRATE AR. 45.93.	" " FIREBOX __ 195.0 "	" -TENDER __ 5½ " x10"
" " -WORKING __ 210 "	" " " CYL. VOL. 233.59.	" " TOTAL __ 2719.0 "	FRANKLIN GRATE SHAKER
WT. ON DRIVERS ___ 180000 "	TUBES-DIAMETER ___ 2".	GRATE AREA ___ 59.2 "	
" -OF ENGINE ___ 195000 "	" -LENGTH ___ 14-8".	FIREBOX-LENGTH ___ 118 IN.	
" " TENDER-EMPTY __ 53000 "	" -NUMBER ___ 331.	" -WIDTH ___ 72¼ ".	
" " -LOADED 132800 ".	T.P. 85% WORKING PRESS. __ 41540.	" -HEIGHT AT FRONT __ 81 ".	

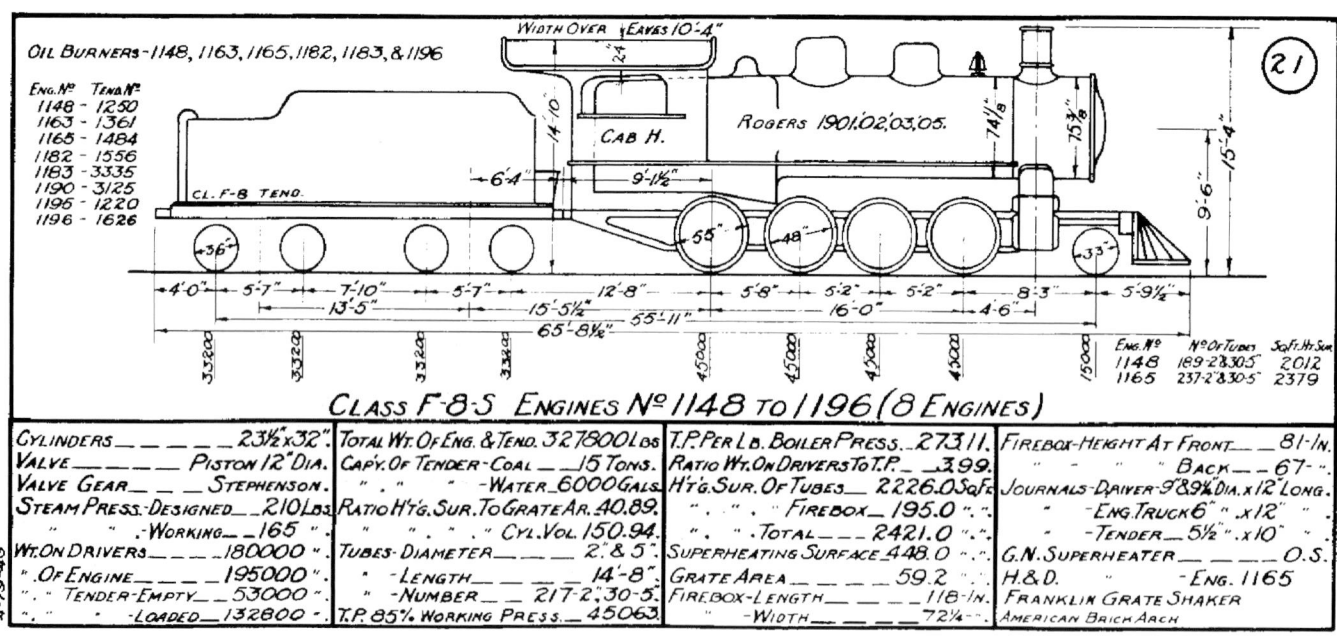

CLASS F-8-S ENGINES Nº 1148 TO 1196 (8 ENGINES)

CYLINDERS ___ 23½"x32".	TOTAL WT. OF ENG. & TEND. 327800 LBS	T.P. PER LB. BOILER PRESS. __ 273.11.	FIREBOX-HEIGHT AT FRONT __ 81 IN.
VALVE ___ PISTON 12"DIA.	CAP'Y. OF TENDER-COAL __ 15 TONS.	RATIO WT. ON DRIVERS TO T.P. __ 399.	" -BACK __ 67 "
VALVE GEAR ___ STEPHENSON.	" __ " -WATER 6000 GALS.	H'T'G. SUR. OF TUBES __ 2226.0 SQ.FT.	JOURNALS-DRIVER 9 & 9¼ DIA. x 12" LONG.
STEAM PRESS.-DESIGNED __ 210 LBS	RATIO H'T'G. SUR. TO GRATE AR. 40.89.	" " FIREBOX __ 195.0 "	" -ENG. TRUCK 6 " x 12"
" " -WORKING __ 165 "	" " " CYL. VOL. 150.94.	" " TOTAL __ 2421.0 "	" -TENDER __ 5½ " x10"
WT. ON DRIVERS ___ 180000 "	TUBES-DIAMETER ___ 2" & 5".	SUPERHEATING SURFACE 448.0 "	G.N. SUPERHEATER ___ O.S.
" -OF ENGINE ___ 195000 "	" -LENGTH ___ 14-8".	GRATE AREA ___ 59.2 "	H.& D. " -ENG. 1165
" " TENDER-EMPTY __ 53000 "	" -NUMBER ___ 217-2; 30-5.	FIREBOX-LENGTH ___ 118 IN.	FRANKLIN GRATE SHAKER
" " -LOADED 132800 "	T.P. 85% WORKING PRESS. __ 45063.	" -WIDTH ___ 72¼ ".	AMERICAN BRICK ARCH

F-8 1143, one of the Rogers engines that had been superheated, was photographed at St.Paul, MN, on May 14, 1934.
Robert Graham photograph from the collection of William Raia.

Engine 1178, another superheated Rogers F-8, was in fresh paint at Minot, ND, on November 1, 1941.
The black cylinder jacket seemed typical of Minot Division engines. Charles E. Winters collection.

Engine 1188, another Rogers F-8, has not been superheated as evidenced by the slide valves.
It was photographed at Minneapolis, MN, in August 1940. Collection of Harold K. Vollrath.

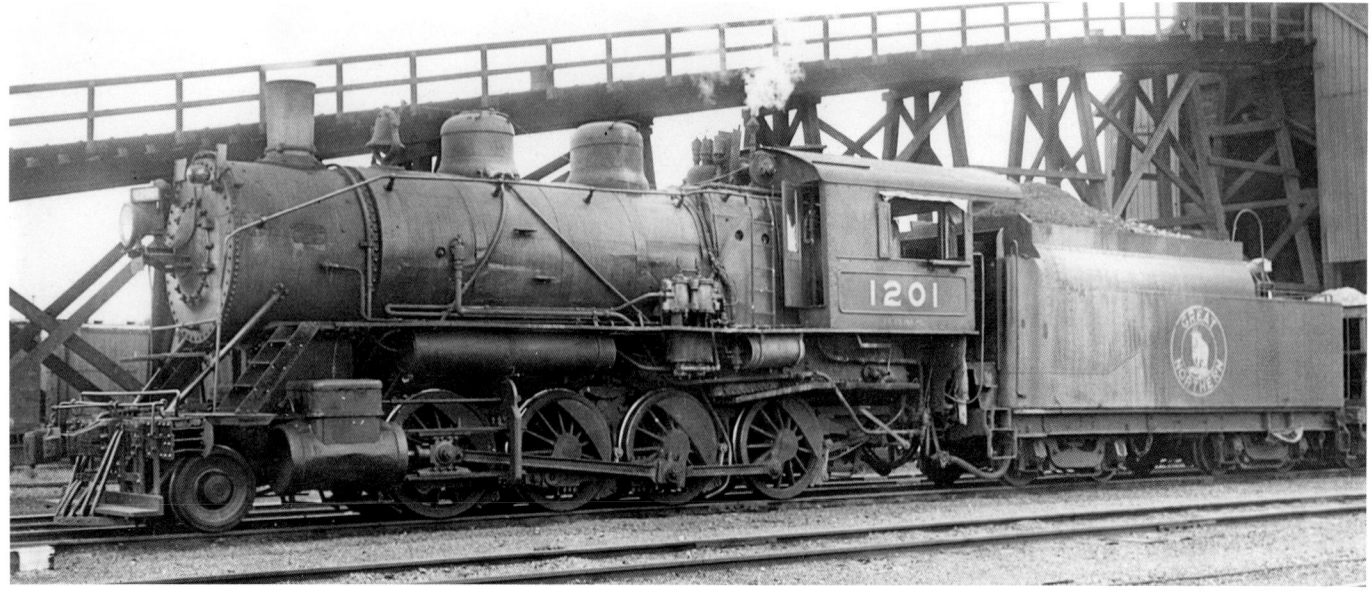

No. 1201, an Alco-Rogers engine received in 1905, has also not been superheated. This F-8 was photographed at Kelly Lake, MN, in July 1938, less than a year from its retirement. Collection of Harold K. Vollrath.

F-8S 1196 has a Style 49 J-2 Class tender (No. 1626) with a huge oil bunker. It was rebuilt to 10,000 gallon capacity by extending it 5 feet in 1926. The 1196 also had outside steam admission. This photograph was taken at Devils Lake, ND, in August 1949. R. Gray photograph from the collection of William Raia.

No. 1216 was one of the Baldwin F-8 engines with Walschaert valve gear. It is shown here with a Style 62 O-1 tender still having its original water capacity of 8,000 gallons. It is shown at Superior, WI, on October 7, 1947. J. Lawson photograph from the collection of Wilbur C. Whittaker.

F-8S 1220 was one of only two Baldwin engines which were superheated. It has piston valves, outside steam admission and is coupled here with a Style 55 Class M-2 tender. It is at Deer River, MN, in August 1949. Frank North collection.

This photo shows the fireman's side of No. 1220 and the Walschaert valve gear is very prominent. The locomotive is shown here in road service on the Butte Division in the 1930's. Nothing else is known about the view.

This unusual view shows the rear of the tender of engine 1221, another F-8 that was not superheated. The tender coal bunker sides have been cut down and new ones installed nearer the center to improve the view when switching. It was photographed at St. Cloud, MN, on June 16, 1949. Photograph by John Malven.

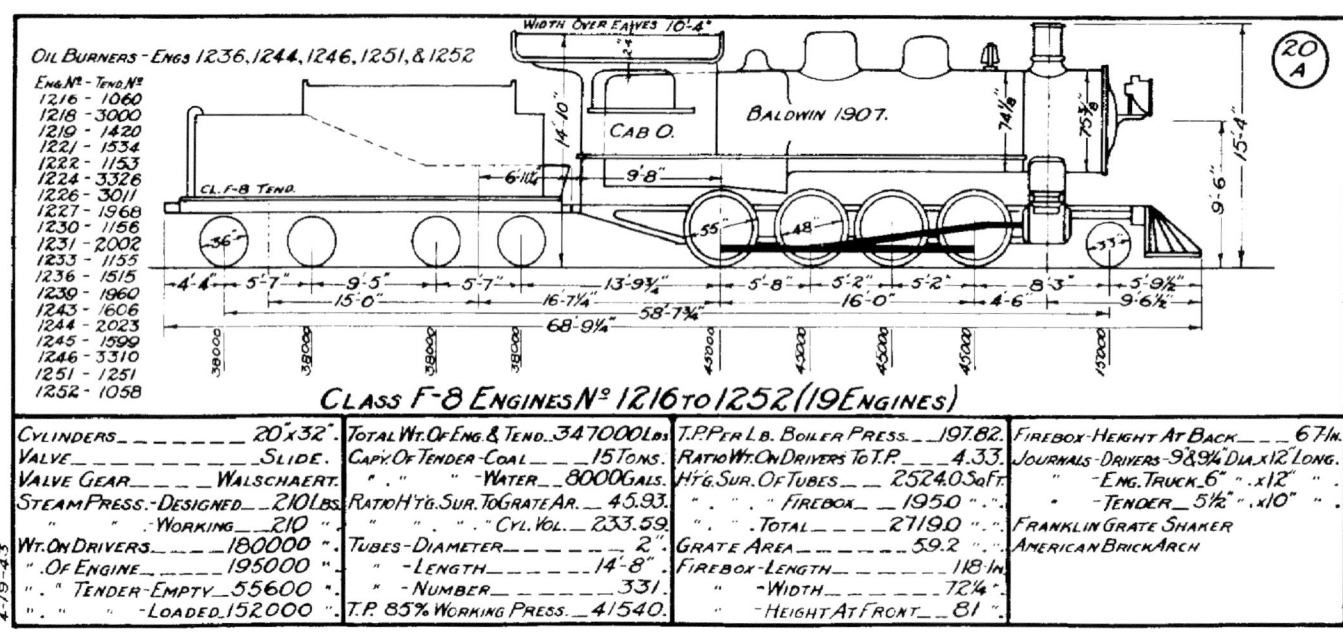

CLASS F-8 ENGINES Nº 1216 TO 1252 (19 ENGINES)

Oil Burners - Engs 1236, 1244, 1246, 1251, & 1252

ENG. Nº	- TEND. Nº
1216	- 1060
1218	- 3000
1219	- 1420
1221	- 1534
1222	- 1153
1224	- 3326
1226	- 3011
1227	- 1968
1230	- 1156
1231	- 2002
1233	- 1155
1236	- 1515
1239	- 1960
1243	- 1606
1244	- 2023
1245	- 1599
1246	- 3310
1251	- 1251
1252	- 1058

CYLINDERS _ _ _ _ _ 20"x32".	TOTAL WT. OF ENG. & TEND. 347000 LBS.	T.P. PER LB. BOILER PRESS. _ _ 197.82.	FIREBOX-HEIGHT AT BACK _ _ _ 67 IN.
VALVE _ _ _ _ _ _ SLIDE.	CAP'Y OF TENDER-COAL _ _ _ 15 TONS.	RATIO WT. ON DRIVERS TO T.P _ _ _ 4.33.	JOURNALS-DRIVERS 9 & 9¼ DIA x 12 LONG.
VALVE GEAR _ _ _ WALSCHAERT.	" . " -WATER _ 8000 GALS.	H'T'G. SUR. OF TUBES _ _ 2524.0 SQ.FT.	" -ENG. TRUCK 6" . x12" ".
STEAM PRESS.-DESIGNED _ _ 210 LBS.	RATIO H'T'G. SUR. TO GRATE AR. _ 45.93.	" . " . " FIREBOX _ _ 195.0 " .	" -TENDER _ 5½" . x10" ".
" . " -WORKING _ _ 210 ".	" . " . " CYL. VOL. 233.59.	" . " . TOTAL _ _ _ _ 2719.0 " .	FRANKLIN GRATE SHAKER
WT. ON DRIVERS _ _ _ 180000 ".	TUBES-DIAMETER _ _ _ _ _ 2".	GRATE AREA _ _ _ _ _ 59.2 ".	AMERICAN BRICK ARCH
" .OF ENGINE _ _ _ 195000 ".	" -LENGTH _ _ _ _ _ 14'-8".	FIREBOX-LENGTH _ _ _ _ 118 IN.	
" . " TENDER-EMPTY _ 55600 ".	" -NUMBER _ _ _ _ 331.	" -WIDTH _ _ _ _ 72¼".	
" . " -LOADED _ 152000 ".	T.P. 85% WORKING PRESS. _ 41540.	" -HEIGHT AT FRONT _ _ 81 ".	

4-19-43

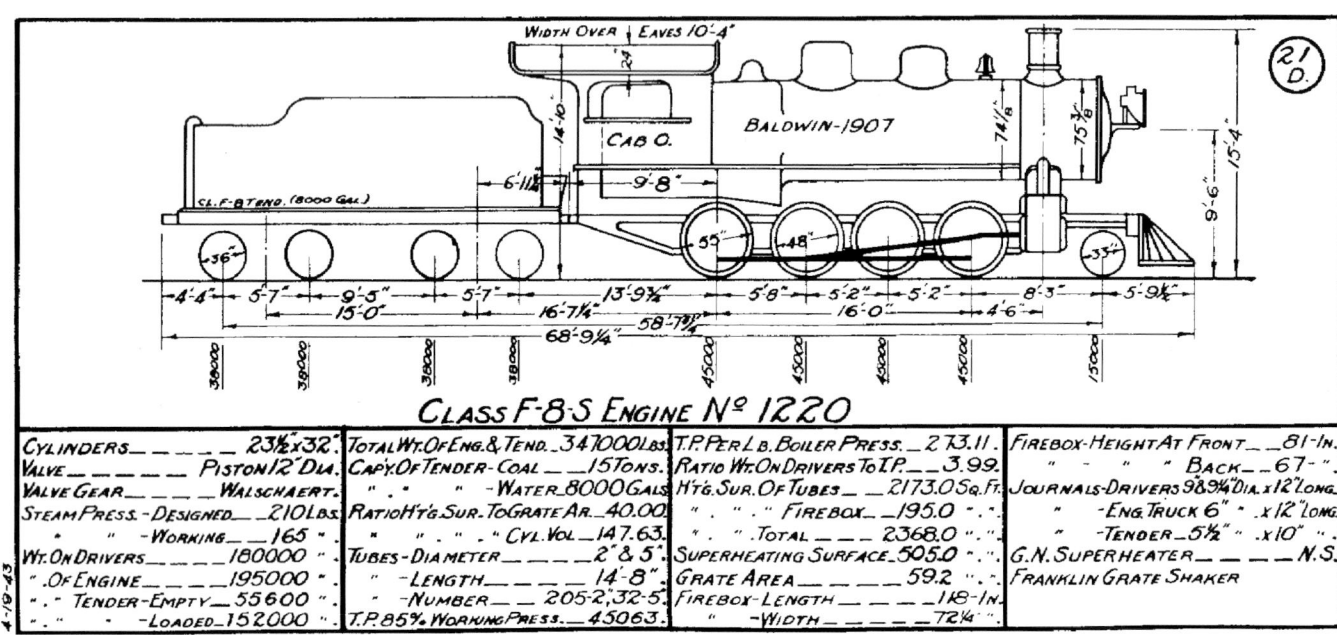

CLASS F-8-S ENGINE Nº 1220

CYLINDERS _ _ _ _ 23½"x32".	TOTAL WT. OF ENG. & TEND. 347000 LBS.	T.P. PER LB. BOILER PRESS. _ 273.11.	FIREBOX-HEIGHT AT FRONT _ _ 81 IN.
VALVE _ _ _ _ _ PISTON 12" DIA.	CAP'Y OF TENDER-COAL _ _ 15 TONS.	RATIO WT. ON DRIVERS TO T.P. _ _ 3.99.	" " . " _ _ BACK _ _ 67 ".
VALVE GEAR _ _ _ _ WALSCHAERT.	" . " -WATER 8000 GALS.	H'T'G. SUR. OF TUBES _ _ 2173.0 SQ.FT.	JOURNALS-DRIVERS 9 & 9¼ DIA x 12 LONG.
STEAM PRESS.-DESIGNED _ 210 LBS.	RATIO H'T'G. SUR. TO GRATE AR. _ 40.00.	" . " . " FIREBOX _ 195.0 " .	" -ENG. TRUCK 6" . x 12" LONG.
" . " -WORKING _ 165 ".	" . " . " CYL. VOL. 147.63.	" . " . TOTAL _ _ _ 2368.0 " .	" -TENDER _ 5½" . x10" ".
WT. ON DRIVERS _ _ 180000 ".	TUBES-DIAMETER _ _ _ 2" & 5".	SUPERHEATING SURFACE _ 505.0 " .	G.N. SUPERHEATER _ _ _ _ N.S.
" .OF ENGINE _ _ _ 195000 ".	" -LENGTH _ _ _ 14'-8".	GRATE AREA _ _ _ _ 59.2 ".	FRANKLIN GRATE SHAKER
" . " TENDER-EMPTY _ 55600 ".	" -NUMBER _ _ 205-2, 32-5.	FIREBOX-LENGTH _ _ _ 118 IN.	
" . " -LOADED _ 152000 ".	T.P. 85% WORKING PRESS. _ 45063.	" -WIDTH _ _ _ 72¼".	

4-19-43

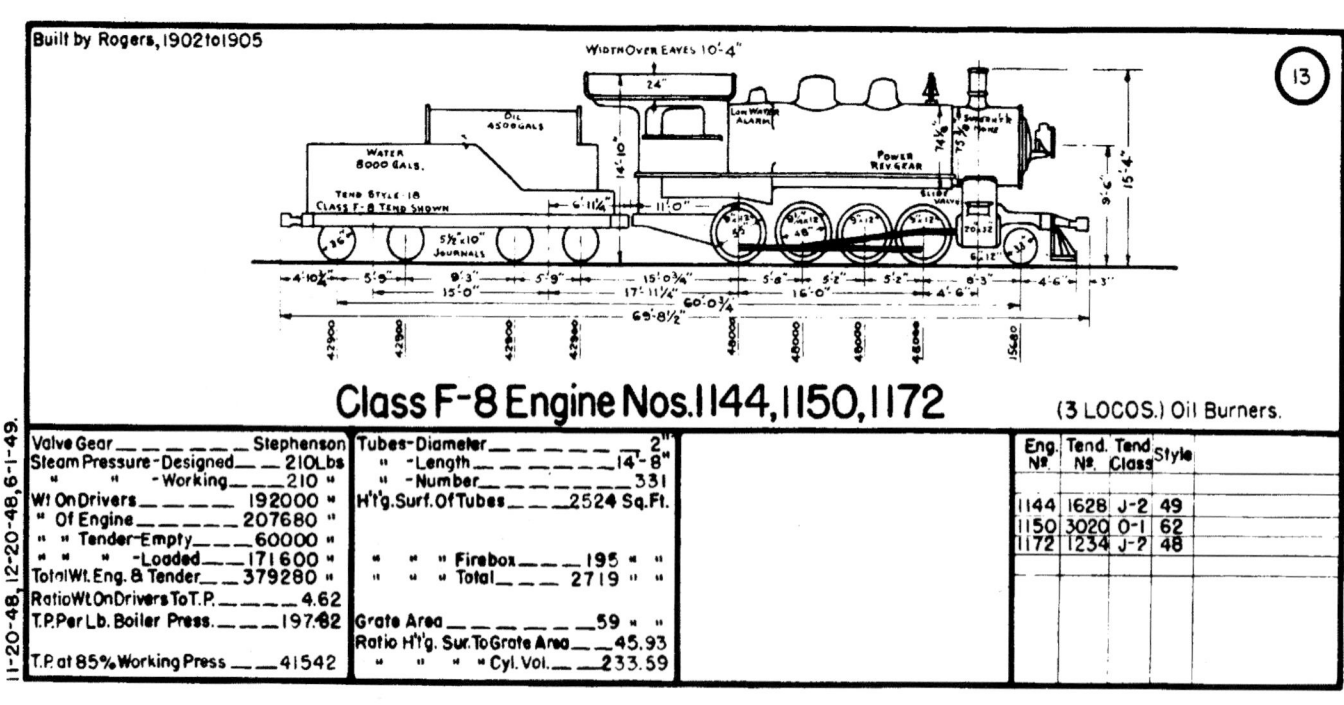

Built by Rogers, 1902 to 1905

Class F-8 Engine Nos. 1144, 1150, 1172

(3 LOCOS.) Oil Burners.

VALVE GEAR _ _ _ _ STEPHENSON	TUBES-DIAMETER _ _ _ _ 2"
STEAM PRESSURE -DESIGNED _ 210 LBS	" -LENGTH _ _ _ 14'-8"
" " -WORKING _ _ 210 "	" -NUMBER _ _ _ 331
WT ON DRIVERS _ _ _ 192000 "	H'T'G. SURF. OF TUBES _ _ 2524 SQ.FT.
" OF ENGINE _ _ _ 207680 "	
" " TENDER-EMPTY _ 60000 "	
" " -LOADED _ 171600 "	" " " FIREBOX _ _ _ 195 " "
TOTAL WT. ENG. & TENDER _ 379280 "	" " " TOTAL _ _ _ 2719 " "
RATIO WT. ON DRIVERS TO T.P. _ _ 4.62	
T.P. PER LB. BOILER PRESS. _ _ 197.82	GRATE AREA _ _ _ _ 59 " "
	RATIO H'T'G. SUR. TO GRATE AREA _ 45.93
T.P. AT 85% WORKING PRESS _ 41542	" " " " CYL. VOL. _ 233.59

11-20-48, 12-20-48, 6-1-49.

ENG. Nº	TEND. Nº	TEND. CLASS	STYLE
1144	1628	J-2	49
1150	3020	O-1	62
1172	1234	J-2	48

Class F-9

In mid-1903, twenty-five additional Consolidations were received, this order coming from Alco-Brooks. They were placed in Class 51B when they arrived, but a few months later became Class F-9. Like the F-8's these had wide fireboxes over the rear set of drivers. They had Stephenson valve gear. They had the typical 20-inch by 32-inch cylinders and 55-inch drivers and Belpaire fireboxes used on GN 2-8-0's. Engine weights were 196,000 pounds., slightly larger than any of the previous 2-8-0 orders. Twelve of the engines later received superheaters and were designated as Class "F-9S". Nos. 1307 and 1316 were superheated in 1915, while the others were completed from 1921 through 1924. Nos. 1300, 1302-1304, 1307, 1310, 1314, 1316, 1320 and 1323 received GN New Style superheaters, 11-inch piston valves and 23½-inch by 32-inch cylinders. Nos. 1311 and 1312 received the same superheaters and valves, but had their cylinder size changed to

21 inches by 32 inches. With the conversion of articulated engines to Mikados, the F-9's apparently became obsolete for road service and were placed in switching service. In order to increase the weight on drivers,[9] the entire class was converted to C-3 switchers in the mid to late 1920's.

Class F-10

The sole member of Class F-10 was a former G-5 4-8-0 (No. 806) that was converted to a Consolidation at Dale Street in 1905. It was not renumbered when rebuilt. It retained the same 21-inch by 34-inch cylinders and 55-inch drivers that it had as a Mastodon, but was slightly heavier at 216,600 pounds. The circumstances surrounding the conversion are unknown to the authors. The engine was retired in 1934.

This builders photograph is one of the few known photographs of an F-9, since they were rebuilt to 0-8-0's in the 1920's. ALCO Historic Photos.

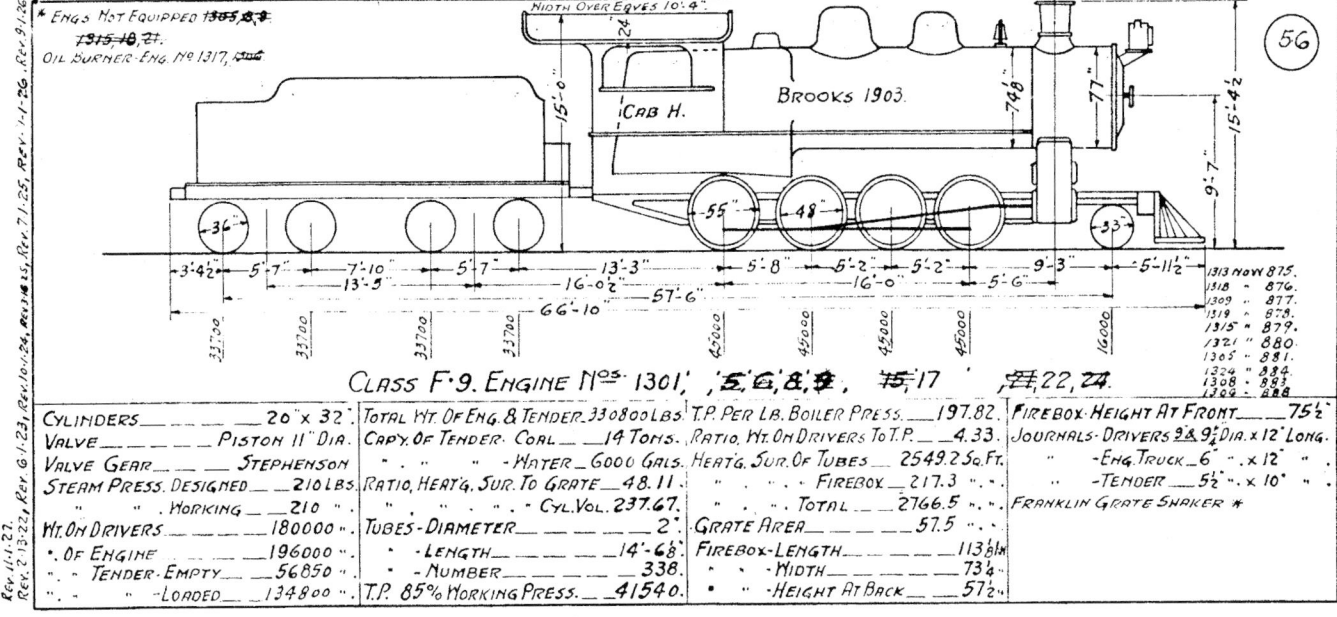

No. 806, the only member of Class F-10, was rebuilt from a G-5 4-8-0 in 1905. It was photographed at St.Paul, MN, in 1931. Collection of Harold K. Vollrath.

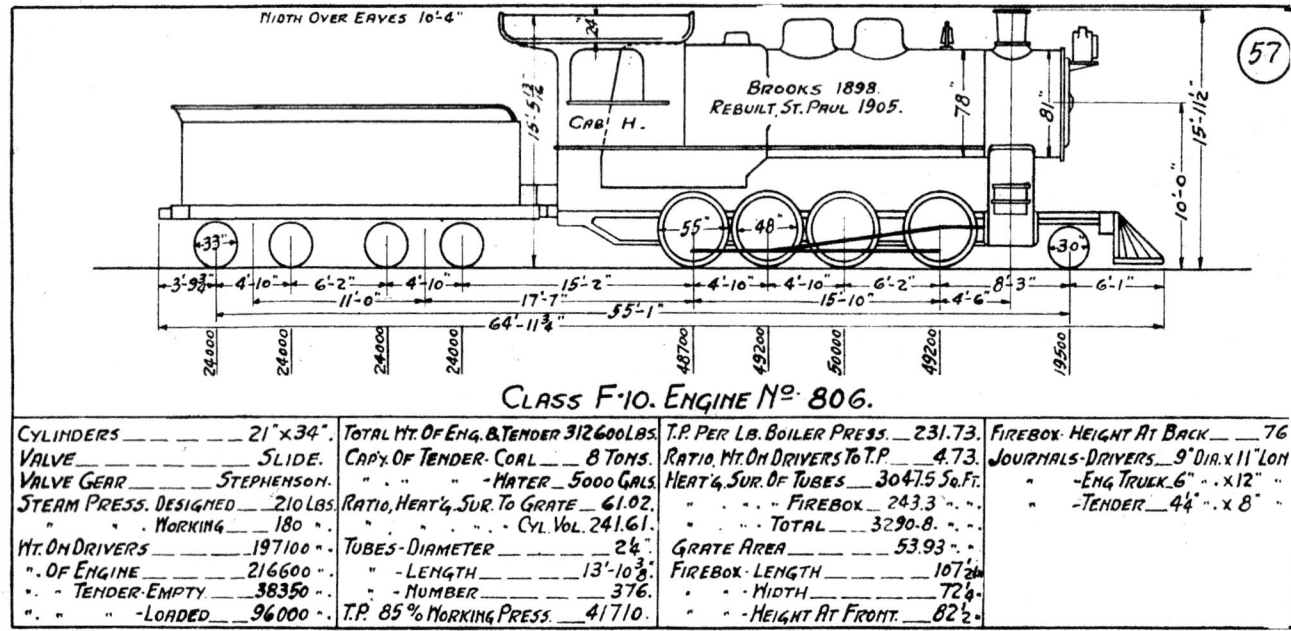

CLASS F·10. ENGINE Nº 806.

CYLINDERS _ _ _ _ 21"x34".	TOTAL HT. OF ENG. & TENDER 312600LBS.	T.P. PER LB. BOILER PRESS. _ 231.73.	FIREBOX· HEIGHT AT BACK _ _ 76
VALVE _ _ _ _ _ SLIDE.	CAP'Y. OF TENDER· COAL _ _ 8 TONS.	RATIO, WT. ON DRIVERS TO T.P. _ 4.73.	JOURNALS-DRIVERS__9"DIA. x 11"LONG
VALVE GEAR _ _ _ STEPHENSON.	" · " " -WATER _ 5000 GALS.	HEAT'G. SUR. OF TUBES _ 3047.5 SQ.FT.	" -ENG TRUCK 6" " X12" "
STEAM PRESS. DESIGNED _ 210 LBS.	RATIO, HEAT'G SUR. TO GRATE _ 61.02.	" " · " -FIREBOX _ 243.3 " · "	" -TENDER _ 4¼" " . x 8" "
" " · WORKING _ 180 " .	" " " · CYL. VOL. 241.61.	" · " · " -TOTAL _ 3290.8. " . "	
WT. ON DRIVERS _ _ _ 197100 " .	TUBES-DIAMETER _ _ _ 24."	GRATE AREA _ _ _ 53.93 " .	
" . OF ENGINE _ _ _ 216600 " .	" -LENGTH _ _ _ 13'-10⅜"	FIREBOX· LENGTH _ _ _ 107¼"	
" . " TENDER· EMPTY _ 38350 " .	" -NUMBER _ _ _ 376.	· " · WIDTH _ _ _ 72¼"	
" . " " -LOADED _ 96000 " .	T.P. 85% WORKING PRESS. _ 41710.	· " -HEIGHT AT FRONT. _ 82½"	

*South Dakota Central No. 15 eventually became GN 591, one of the two members of
Class F-11. It was scrapped after only a few years on the GN. ALCO Historic Photos.*

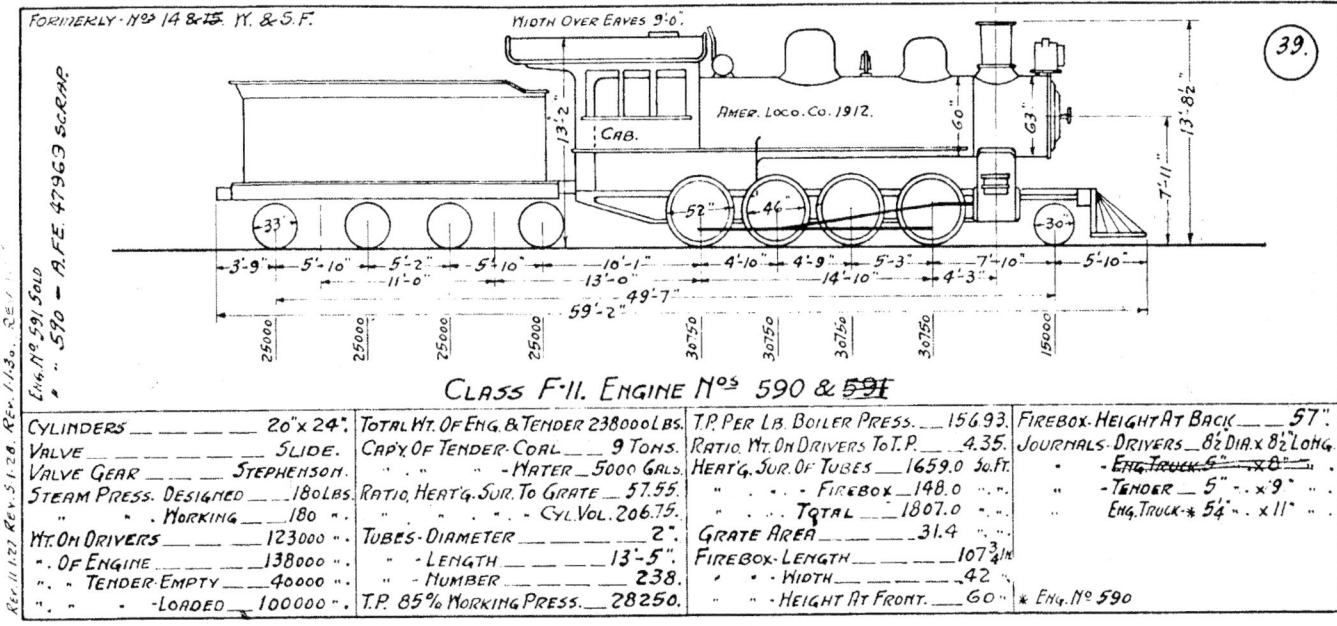

CLASS F-11. ENGINE Nos 590 & 591

CYLINDERS	20"x 24".	TOTAL WT. OF ENG. & TENDER	238000 LBS.	T.P. PER LB. BOILER PRESS.	156.93.	FIREBOX-HEIGHT AT BACK ____ 57".
VALVE	SLIDE.	CAP'Y. OF TENDER-COAL	9 TONS.	RATIO. WT. ON DRIVERS TO T.P.	4.35.	JOURNALS-DRIVERS 8½ DIA. x 8½ LONG.
VALVE GEAR	STEPHENSON.	" " " -WATER	5000 GALS.	HEAT'G. SUR. OF TUBES	1659.0 Sq.Ft.	~~" -ENG. TRUCK 5 x 8~~
STEAM PRESS. DESIGNED	180 LBS.	RATIO, HEAT'G. SUR. TO GRATE	57.55.	" " " FIREBOX	148.0 "	" -TENDER 5" -x 9"
" " WORKING	180 ".	" " " -CYL. VOL.	206.75.	" " TOTAL	1807.0 ".	ENG. TRUCK * 5¼" x 11"
WT. ON DRIVERS	123000 ".	TUBES-DIAMETER	2".	GRATE AREA	31.4 ".	
" - OF ENGINE	138000 ".	" -LENGTH	13'-5".	FIREBOX-LENGTH	107¾ IN.	
" - TENDER-EMPTY	40000 ".	" -NUMBER	238.	" " -WIDTH	42.	
" " -LOADED	100000 ".	T.P. 85% WORKING PRESS.	28250.	" " -HEIGHT AT FRONT.	60	* ENG. Nº 590

Class F-12 1326 was photographed at Butte, MT, on May 4, 1922, only about five years after its arrival on the GN. It still has its original arch-window cab and long, slope-backed tender. It is standing in front of a bucket-loader coal station. Railroad Museum of Pennsylvania (PHMC).

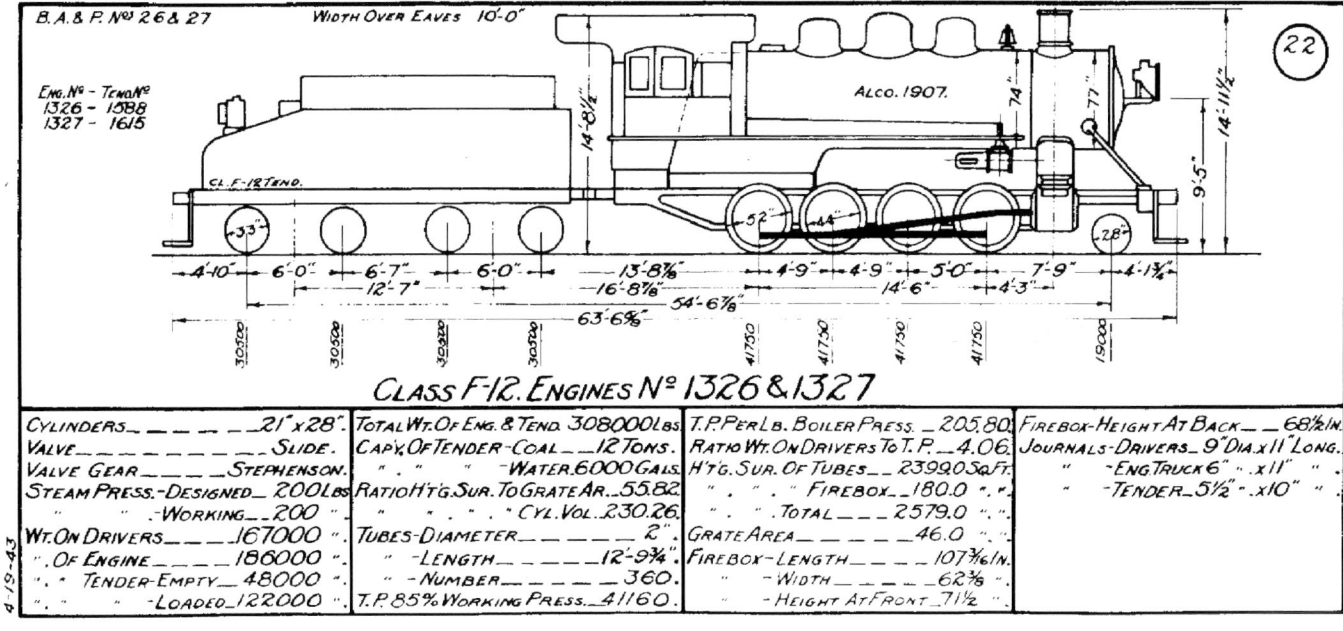

CLASS F-12. ENGINES Nº 1326 & 1327

CYLINDERS	21"x 28".	TOTAL WT. OF ENG. & TEND.	308000 LBS.	T.P. PER LB. BOILER PRESS.	205.80.	FIREBOX-HEIGHT AT BACK ____ 68½ IN.
VALVE	SLIDE.	CAP'Y. OF TENDER-COAL	12 TONS.	RATIO WT. ON DRIVERS TO T.P.	4.06.	JOURNALS-DRIVERS 9" DIA. x 11" LONG.
VALVE GEAR	STEPHENSON.	" " " -WATER	6000 GALS.	H'T'G. SUR. OF TUBES	2399.0 SQ.FT.	" -ENG. TRUCK 6" -x 11"
STEAM PRESS.-DESIGNED	200 LBS.	RATIO H'T'G. SUR. TO GRATE AR.	55.82.	" " " FIREBOX	180.0 ".	" -TENDER 5½" -x 10"
" " -WORKING	200 ".	" " " -CYL. VOL.	230.26.	" " TOTAL	2579.0 ".	
WT. ON DRIVERS	167000 ".	TUBES-DIAMETER	2".	GRATE AREA	46.0 ".	
" -OF ENGINE	186000 ".	" -LENGTH	12'-9¾".	FIREBOX-LENGTH	107³⁄₁₆ IN.	
" - TENDER-EMPTY	48000 ".	" -NUMBER	360.	" " -WIDTH	62⅜ ".	
" " -LOADED	122000 ".	T.P. 85% WORKING PRESS.	41160.	" " -HEIGHT AT FRONT	71½ ".	

Class F-11

Class F-11 was comprised of two locomotives acquired with the Watertown and Sioux Falls (W&SF). Both locomotives had been built by Alco-Brooks. W&SF 14 had originally been built as Tennessee, Alabama and Georgia 322 in April 1913. W&SF 15 was built as South Dakota Central 15 in September 1914.[10] Unlike the Consolidations ordered by GN, these had radial stay fireboxes. They had 20-inch by 24-inch cylinders with slide valves, 52-inch drivers and weighed only 138,000 pounds. They were renumbered as GN 590 and 591. Great Northern apparently did not find much use for these small low-drivered engines, as they were retired without spending much time on the GN.

Class F-12

Class F-12 also consisted of a pair of orphans. The two members, GN 1326 and 1327, had been built by Alco-Brooks in November 1907 for the Butte, Anaconda and Pacific as its 26 and 27. Great Northern acquired them in 1917. They had 21-inch by 28-inch cylinders with slide valves, 52-inch drivers and weighed 186,000 pounds. Like the F-11's, they had radial stay fireboxes. GN must have found these engines a little more useful than the F-11's, since they both lasted until the late 1940's. In the mid-1930's they had been assigned to the Butte Division, but by the early 1940's both had been moved to the Mesabi Division.

While the previous photo was taken early in its life, this view of 1326 was taken near the end of its life on April 14, 1947, at Superior. It was sold for scrap a year later. The engine has now received a Great Northern cab and a Class J-2 tender, but still has the spoked pilot wheels. Carl L. Ulrich Collection, courtesy of Jerrold F. Hilton.

F-12 1327 had also received a Great Northern cab, but still had its original tender when this photograph was taken at Butte, MT, on August 8, 1932. Collection of William Bissinger.

Notes:

1. Brooks Locomotive Works Order List.
2. Gordon Odegard, 1987. "Great Northern 1893 Tandem Compound Consolidation", *Model Railroader*, June 1987.
3. Great Northern Authority for Expenditure 3391 (November 10, 1900) and 4342 (June 12, 1901).
4. Paul T. Warner, 1925. "The Great Northern Railway and Its Locomotives", *Baldwin Locomotives*.
5. Great Northern Authority for Expenditure 4621 (August 1, 1901).
6. Paul T. Warner, op. cit.
7. *Ibid.*
8. *Ibid.*
9. W. Kelly, Memo to C.O. Jenks dated 1/12/1926.
10. Alco-Brooks Locomotive Works Order List.

Engine 400 was the first of what was to become GN's Class G-1 4-8-0, and one of five that were received with radial fireboxes and wagontop boilers. The engine was later numbered 600. ALCO Historic Photos.

Chapter 12
Class G 4-8-0 Mastodon

Class G-1

With the incorporation of the Great Northern Railway Company, and the approaching completion of the Puget Sound extension, a large amount of new motive power was required. During the years 1891 to 1893, over 100 locomotives were purchased from the Brooks Locomotive Works.[1] Sixteen of these locomotives were 4-8-0 Mastodons, a new wheel arrangement for the GN. The first five, StPM&M 400-404, had 20-inch by 24-inch cylinders, 55-inch drivers and engine weights of 156,000 pounds and were received in 1891. These five 4-8-0's were the only Mastodons on the GN that had radial stay rather than Belpaire fireboxes. The second five, StPM&M 405-409, had identical dimensions but did have Belpaire fireboxes – the first locomotives on the GN equipped with them. These were also received in 1891.[2] All ten of these locomotives were placed in Class 37 upon their receipt. Five additional 4-8-0's received in 1891 (StPM&M 410-414) were placed in Class 38. These engines were very similar to those in Class 37, but had 20-inch by 26-inch cylinders. In 1892, 410-414 were sold to the Montana Central. In 1893, a sixteenth engine of this group, with 20-inch by 26-inch cylinders,[3] numbered as 410, was received. This engine had been exhibited at the World's Columbian Exposition in Chicago prior to its delivery to GN. Probably about 1892 or 1893, all of the first ten locomotives except 409 were rebuilt with

20-inch by 26-inch cylinders, and all ten were moved to Class 38. During the 1899 renumbering, the first ten became GN 600-609, and the 1893 locomotive became 610. The Montana Central locomotives became 611-615 when they were incorporated into the GN numbering scheme about 1900. In 1903, all sixteen of these engines were placed in Class G-1.

It's somewhat surprising but five of these relatively small engines lasted until the 1940's with only minor modifications (e.g. foot board pilots on some). One of these, oil-burning 607, was assigned to the Spokane Division. The other four (603, 606, 612 and 613) were assigned to the Willmar Division.

Class G-2

The twenty members of Class G-2 were built by Brooks for the Eastern of Minnesota (EM) in 1893. They were received as EM 300-319 and were placed in Class 45. They had 19-inch by 32-inch cylinders with 12-inch piston valves, 55-inch drivers and engine weights of 176,000 pounds. These engines were intended for road service.[4] About 1901, one of these (No. 701) was rebuilt to a Class F-3 consolidation. Most had been converted to burn oil by the mid-1920's. Unlike the lighter G-1's, none of the G-2's lasted into the 1940's. The last two, 715 and 718, lasted until the late 1930's on the Dakota Division.

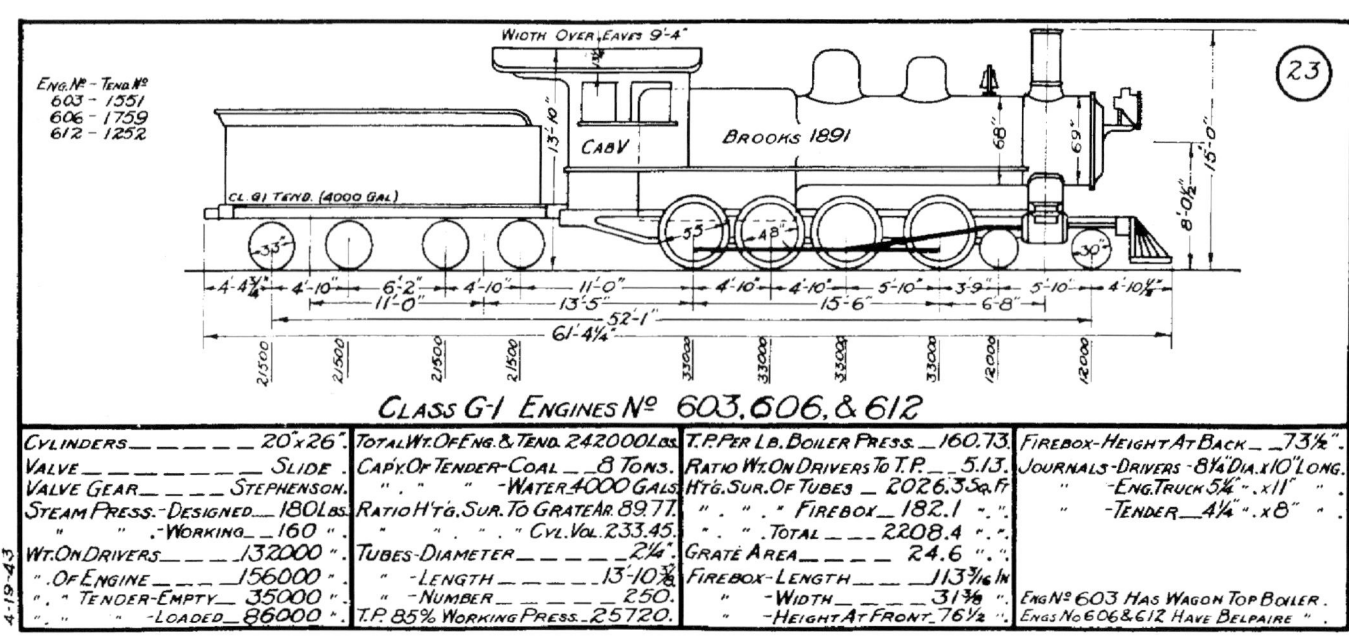

CLASS G-1 ENGINES Nº 603, 606, & 612

CYLINDERS _____ 20"x26".	TOTAL WT. OF ENG. & TEND. 242000 LBS.	T.P. PER LB. BOILER PRESS. __ 160.73.	FIREBOX-HEIGHT AT BACK __ 73½".
VALVE _____ SLIDE.	CAP'Y. OF TENDER-COAL __ 8 TONS.	RATIO WT. ON DRIVERS TO T.P. __ 5.13.	JOURNALS-DRIVERS 8¼"DIA. x 10"LONG.
VALVE GEAR __ STEPHENSON.	" " " -WATER 4000 GALS.	HT'G. SUR. OF TUBES _ 2026.3 SQ. FT	" -ENG. TRUCK 5¼" . x 11" .
STEAM PRESS.-DESIGNED __ 180 LBS.	RATIO H'T'G. SUR. TO GRATE AR. 89.77.	" . " . " FIREBOX __ 182.1 -. ".	" -TENDER __ 4¼" . x 8" .
" -WORKING __ 160 ".	" " " CYL. VOL. 233.45.	" . " . " TOTAL __ 2208.4 ". .	
WT. ON DRIVERS __ 132000 ".	TUBES-DIAMETER __ 2¼".	GRATE AREA __ 24.6 ". ".	
" . OF ENGINE __ 156000 ".	" -LENGTH __ 13-10⅞".	FIREBOX-LENGTH __ 113⅞₁₆ IN.	
" . " TENDER-EMPTY __ 35000 ".	" -NUMBER __ 250.	" -WIDTH __ 31⅜ ".	ENG. Nº 603 HAS WAGON TOP BOILER.
" . " -LOADED __ 86000 ".	T.P. 85% WORKING PRESS. 25720.	" -HEIGHT AT FRONT 76½ ".	ENGS. Nº 606 & 612 HAVE BELPAIRE ".

4-19-43

Engine 405 was the first engine on the GN to be equipped with a Belpaire firebox. Note that at this time the practice was to lag the front of the firebox as well as the boiler. The 405 became the 605 in 1899, and was placed in Class G-1 in 1903. ALCO Historic Photos.

No. 601 was one of the Class G-1 engines with a radial stay firebox. This photograph, taken at Sioux Falls, SD, in June 1927, shows the engine has been converted to burn oil. Collection of Harold K. Vollrath.

Class G-1 607 was a member of the first GN order for Belpaire-firebox equipped locomotives.
The engine is shown taking on water at Spokane, WA, in 1930. Bordertown Collection of GTC Collectibles.

Eastern of Minnesota No. 302 was part of an order of twenty locomotives which eventually became GN's Class G-2. ALCO Historic Photos.

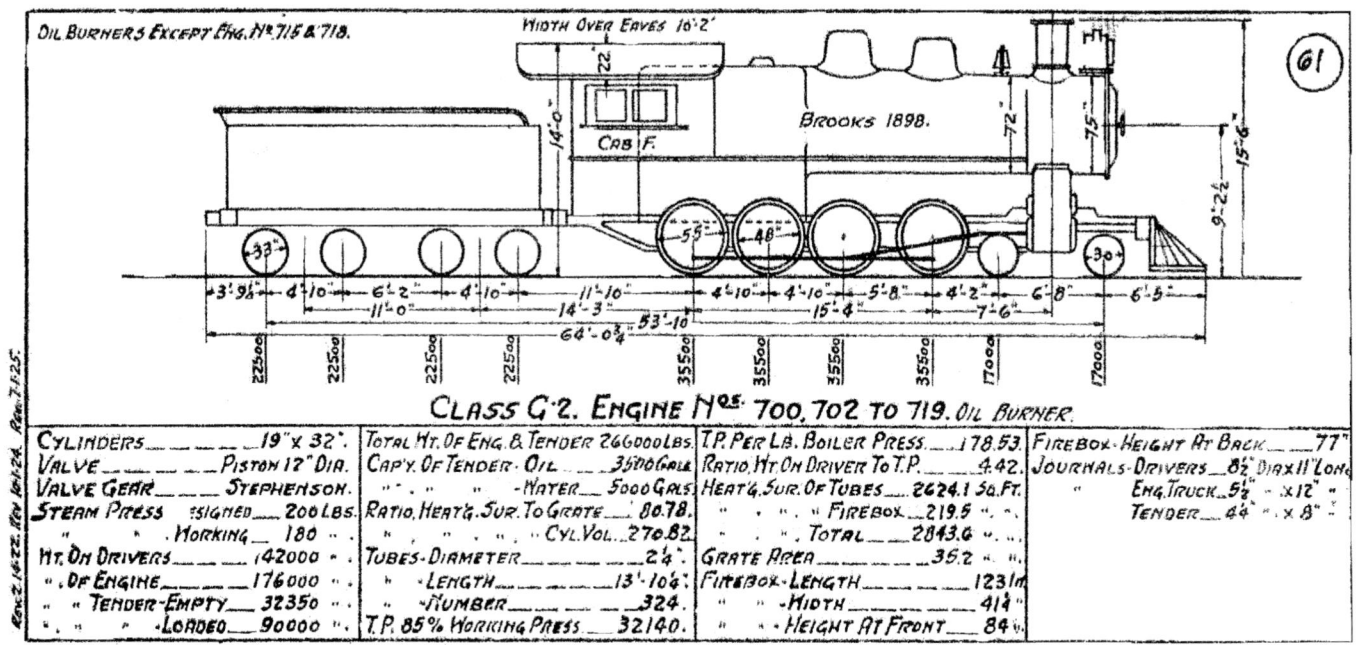

CLASS G-2. ENGINE Nos. 700, 702 TO 719. OIL BURNER.

CYLINDERS ___ 19"x 32".	TOTAL HT. OF ENG. & TENDER 266000 LBS.	T.P. PER LB. BOILER PRESS. ___ 178.53.	FIREBOX HEIGHT AT BACK ___ 77"
VALVE ___ PISTON 12" DIA.	CAP'Y. OF TENDER· OIL ___ 3500 GALS	RATIO, HT. ON DRIVER TO T.P. ___ 4.42.	JOURNALS-DRIVERS __ 8½" DIA x 11" LONG
VALVE GEAR ___ STEPHENSON.	" · " · " -WATER ___ 5000 GALS.	HEAT'G. SUR. OF TUBES ___ 2624.1 SQ. FT.	" ENG. TRUCK __ 5½" · x 12" "
STEAM PRESS ·ESIGNED ___ 200 LBS.	RATIO, HEAT'G. SUR. TO GRATE ___ 80.78.	" · " · " FIREBOX ___ 219.5 " ·".	" TENDER __ 44" · x 8" "
" · " · WORKING __ 180 " ·	" · " · " · " CYL. VOL. ___ 270.82.	" · " · " TOTAL ___ 2843.6 " ·".	
HT. ON DRIVERS ___ 142000 " ·	TUBES-DIAMETER ___ 2¼".	GRATE AREA ___ 35.2 " · "	
" · OF ENGINE ___ 176000 " ·	" · LENGTH ___ 13'·10⅝".	FIREBOX-LENGTH ___ 123¹ᵐ	
" · " TENDER-EMPTY ___ 32350 " ·	" · ·NUMBER ___ 324.	" · -WIDTH ___ 41¾"	
" · " · ·LOADED ___ 90000 " ·	T.P. 85% WORKING PRESS. ___ 32140.	" · -HEIGHT AT FRONT ___ 84 "	

Class G-3

An order of twenty-five 4-8-0's (720-744) was received from Rogers in 1899. These locomotives were slightly larger than the G-2's, with engine weights of 182,000 pounds. They had 19-inch by 32-inch cylinders (with slide valves) and the usual 55-inch drivers. These were placed in Class 48 upon receipt. An additional order of twenty-five (745-769) was received in 1900. In 1903 they became Class G-3 engines, the largest class of Mastodons on the GN. At some time prior to 1911, No. 734 received an H&D superheater and was moved to Class G-6 as its only member. In May 1911 it was returned to Class G-3. No. 722 also received an H&D superheater in 1913. Nos. 722 and

734 were then referred to as Class "G-3S" locomotives. As superheated engines, they had 23½-inch by 32-inch cylinders with 12-inch piston valves.

Unlike the other G-classes, most of the G-3's survived into the 1940's and some into the 1950's. Many received power reverses and low water alarms in the 1940's and early 1950's. They were assigned to all divisions, with those assigned to the Spokane Division (722, 748 and 764) being converted to oil. Despite the 723 being assigned to the Dakota Division, it lasted long enough to be converted to oil after 1951.

G-2 No. 713 was an oil burner, like most of its class except for 715 and 718. It was photographed at Hillyard, WA, in June 1924. Collection of Harold K. Vollrath.

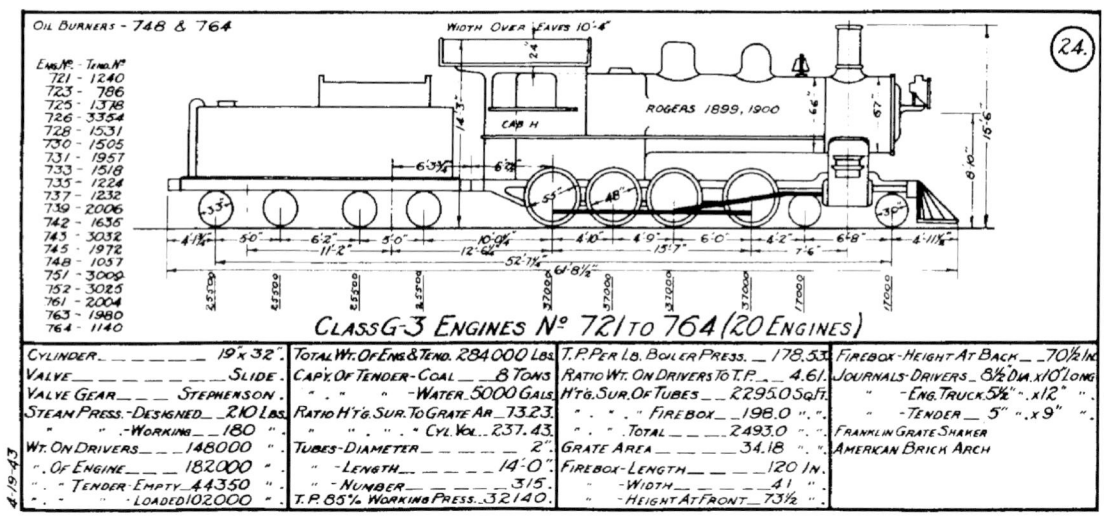

G-3 No. 726 is under steam at Minneapolis, MN, on June 19, 1948. Robert Graham photograph from the collection of William Raia.

GN 768, a Dakota Division G-3, was at Minot, ND, on July 16, 1947. Collection of William Raia.

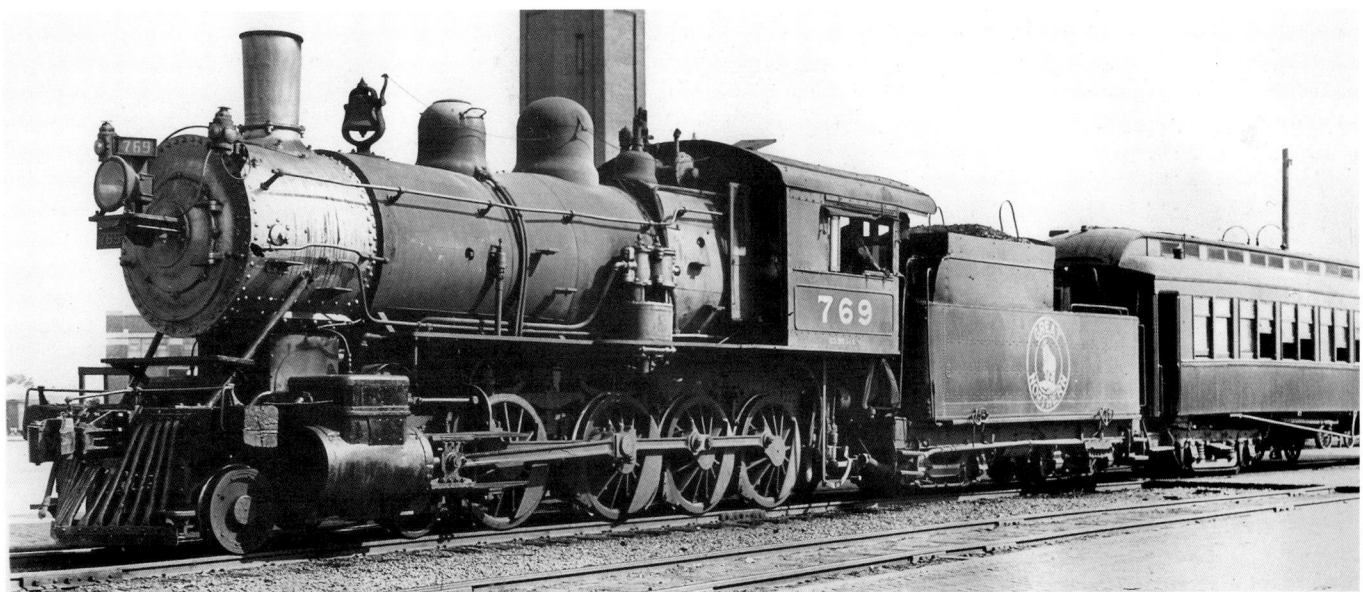

The 769 was in mixed train service in 1937, shown here at the Great Falls, MT, passenger station with the train's coach. Photograph by Herman Rinke, courtesy of Eric Archer.

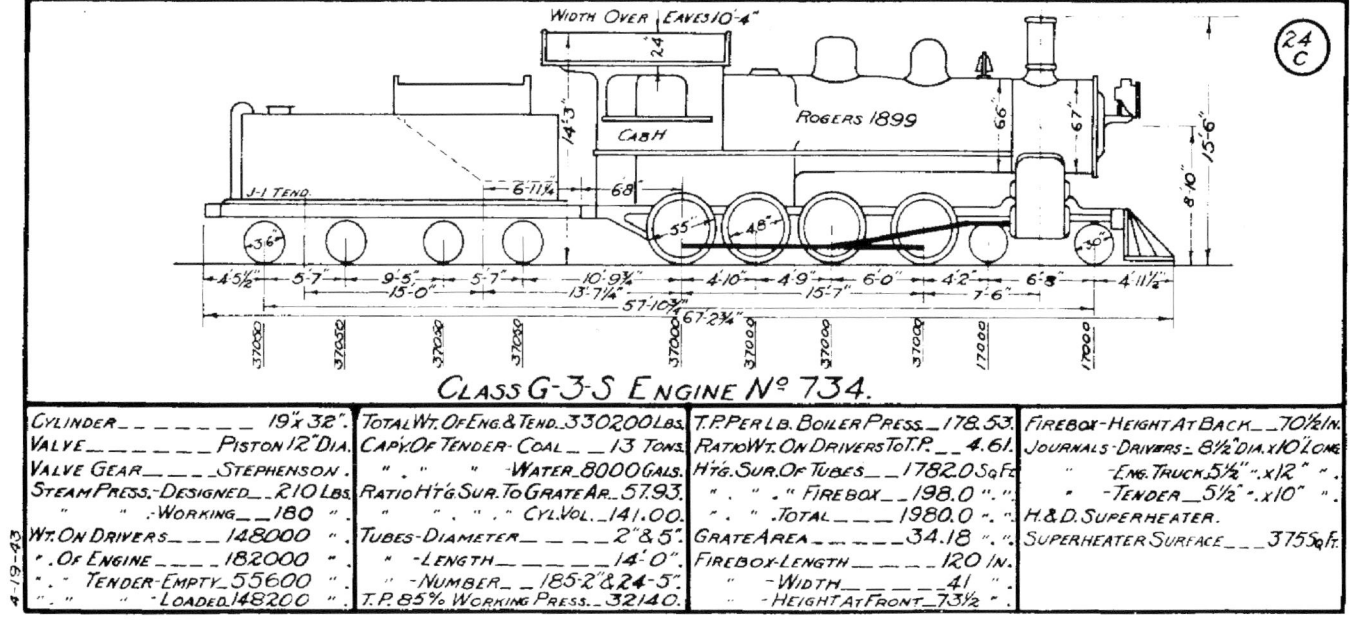

CLASS G-3-S ENGINE No 734.

CYLINDER _ _ _ _ _ _ 19"x 32".	TOTAL WT. OF ENG. & TEND. 330200 LBS.	T.P. PER LB. BOILER PRESS._178.53.	FIREBOX-HEIGHT AT BACK _ 70½ IN.
VALVE _ _ _ _ _ PISTON 12"DIA.	CAP'Y. OF TENDER - COAL _ 13 TONS.	RATIO WT. ON DRIVERS TO T.P. _ _ 4.61.	JOURNALS-DRIVERS = 8½"DIA. x 10" LONG
VALVE GEAR _ _ _ _ STEPHENSON.	" . " " WATER 8000 GALS.	HT'G. SUR. OF TUBES _ _ 1782.0 SQ FT.	" -ENG. TRUCK 5½" x 12" ".
STEAM PRESS.-DESIGNED _ 210 LBS.	RATIO HT'G SUR. TO GRATE AR. 57.93.	" . " FIREBOX _ _ 198.0 ". ".	" -TENDER _ 5½" -. x 10" ".
" -WORKING _ 180 " .	" . " " CYL. VOL. 141.00.	" . " TOTAL _ _ 1980.0 ". ".	H. & D. SUPERHEATER.
WT. ON DRIVERS _ _ 148000	TUBES-DIAMETER _ _ _ _ 2"& 5".	GRATE AREA _ _ _ 34.18 ". ".	SUPERHEATER SURFACE _ _ 375 SQ FT.
" -OF ENGINE _ _ _ 182000 " .	" -LENGTH _ _ _ _ _ 14'-0".	FIREBOX-LENGTH _ _ _ _ 120 IN.	
" - TENDER-EMPTY _ 55600 ".	" -NUMBER _ _ 185-2"& 24-5".	" -WIDTH _ _ _ _ _ 41 ".	
" " -LOADED _ 148200 ".	T.P. 85% WORKING PRESS. _ 32140.	" -HEIGHT AT FRONT _ 73½ ".	

No. 722 was an unusual G-3 for a couple reasons. It was one of the few oil burners in the class, and had also been superheated and received piston valves. It was photographed at Hillyard, WA, on September 13, 1946. Wilbur C. Whittaker photograph from the GNRHS Collection.

In what may be the latest view of an operational G-3 class locomotive, the 723 is shown in service at Fargo, ND, on March 17, 1953. It was removed from the roster by April 15, 1953. Photograph by Carl Ulrich, from the collection of Harold K. Vollrath.

Eastern of Minnesota No. 772 was built with piston valves and became a member of Class G-4 on the GN. ALCO Historic Photos.

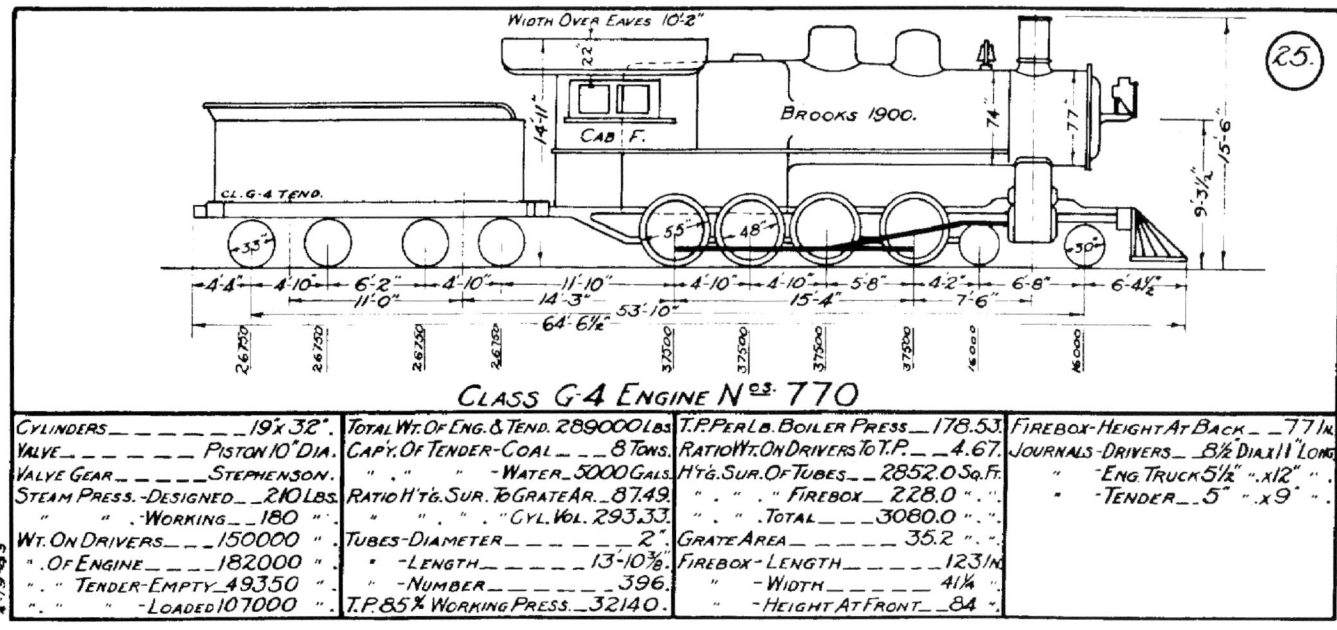

CLASS G-4 ENGINE Nº. 770

CYLINDERS _____ 19"x32".	TOTAL WT. OF ENG.& TEND. 289000 LBS	T.P. PER LB. BOILER PRESS. _ 178.53.	FIREBOX-HEIGHT AT BACK _ 77 IN.
VALVE _____ PISTON 10" DIA.	CAP'Y. OF TENDER-COAL __ 8 TONS.	RATIO WT. ON DRIVERS TO T.P. _ 4.67.	JOURNALS-DRIVERS _ 8½ DIA x 11"LONG.
VALVE GEAR _____ STEPHENSON.	" " -WATER 5000 GALS.	H'T'G. SUR. OF TUBES __ 2852.0 SQ. FT.	" -ENG. TRUCK 5½ ". x12 " .
STEAM PRESS.-DESIGNED _ 210 LBS.	RATIO H'T'G. SUR. TO GRATE AR. 87.49.	" . " FIREBOX 228.0 ".	" -TENDER__ 5" . x 9".
" " -WORKING__ 180	" " " CYL. VOL. 293.33.	" . TOTAL ___ 3080.0 ".	
WT. ON DRIVERS ___ 150000 "	TUBES-DIAMETER _____ 2"	GRATE AREA _____ 35.2 ".	
" .OF ENGINE ___ 182000 "	" -LENGTH _____ 13'-10⅜.	FIREBOX - LENGTH _____ 123 IN.	
" .TENDER-EMPTY 49350 "	" -NUMBER _____ 396.	" -WIDTH ___ 41¼ "	
" . -LOADED 107000 "	T.P. 85% WORKING PRESS. 32140.	" -HEIGHT AT FRONT __ 84 "	

4-19-43

G-4 locomotive 770 was photographed at Bemidji, MN, in 1946. It has an interesting snowplow pilot.
Photograph by Warren McGee. Montana Historical Society Research Center Photograph Archives, Helena, MT.

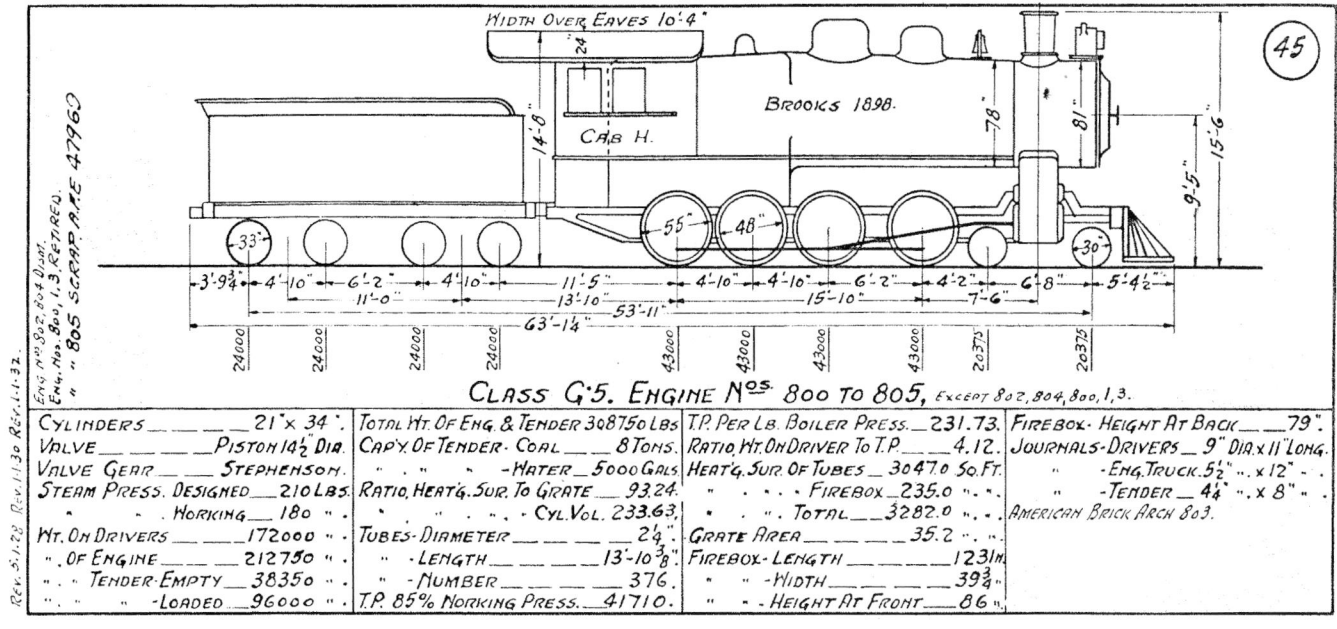

CLASS G-5. ENGINE Nºs. 800 TO 805, EXCEPT 802,804,800,1,3.

CYLINDERS _____ 21"x34".	TOTAL WT. OF ENG. & TENDER 308750 LBS	T.P. PER LB. BOILER PRESS. _ 231.73.	FIREBOX- HEIGHT AT BACK _ 79".
VALVE _____ PISTON 14½ DIA.	CAP'Y. OF TENDER- COAL __ 8 TONS.	RATIO, WT. ON DRIVER TO T.P. _ 4.12.	JOURNALS-DRIVERS _ 9" DIA. x 11" LONG.
VALVE GEAR ___ STEPHENSON.	" " -HATER 5000 GALS	HEAT'G. SUR. OF TUBES _ 3047.0 SQ. FT.	" -ENG. TRUCK 5½" . x 12 ".
STEAM PRESS. DESIGNED 210 LBS.	RATIO, HEAT'G. SUR. TO GRATE 93.24.	" . " FIREBOX 235.0 ".	" -TENDER- 4½" . x 8".
" . HORKING 180 ".	" " CYL. VOL. 233.63.	" . TOTAL ___ 3282.0 ".	AMERICAN BRICK ARCH 803.
WT. ON DRIVERS ___ 172000 ".	TUBES-DIAMETER _____ 2¼".	GRATE AREA _____ 35.2 ".	
" . OF ENGINE ___ 212750 ".	" -LENGTH _____ 13'-10⅜".	FIREBOX-LENGTH _____ 123 IN.	
" . TENDER-EMPTY 38350 ".	" -NUMBER _____ 376.	" -WIDTH ___ 39¾ ".	
" . -LOADED 96000 ".	T.P. 85% NORKING PRESS. 41710.	" - HEIGHT AT FRONT __ 86 ".	

Rev.5.1.28 Rev.11.30 Rev.4.4.32.
Eng. Nos.802,804 Dismt. Eng.Nos.800,1,3 Retired. 805 Scrap A.M.E 47960.

Class G-4

The final order for 4-8-0's on the GN system was built for the Eastern of Minnesota in 1900 as its 770-779. They were constructed by Brooks and had 19-inch by 32-inch cylinders with 10-inch piston valves, 55-inch drivers and weighed 182,000 pounds. They were originally placed in Class 45A. They kept the same numbers when taken over by the GN, and became Class G-4 engines. There are few records of any modifications of the locomotives. Only two lasted into the 1940's, one (770) on the Mesabi Division and one (776) on the Dakota Division.

Class G-5

The heaviest 4-8-0's on the GN had been purchased by the Montana Central (MC). They were built by Brooks in 1897 and 1898 as MC 100-107. They had 21-inch by 34-inch cylinders with 14½-inch piston valves and the usual 55-inch drivers. The engines weighed 212,750 pounds, and were believed to be the largest locomotives yet built at the time, with the longest piston stroke.[5] These engines were intended for heavy mountain and pusher service.[6] The boiler diameter, at 78 inches, seemed absolutely huge for the time. One of the engines received in 1898, MC 803, was the 3000th locomotive built by Brooks. In 1905 another of these engines, 806, was rebuilt as a Consolidation and placed in Class F-10. In 1928 engine 807 received a Schmidt superheater, and in an interesting twist had its piston valves replaced with Heron valves, making the steam chest look like it had slide valves. This superheated engine was the last of the class to be scrapped, but even it only lasted until 1936.

Class G-6

As mentioned above, G-3 734 occupied Class G-6 for a very short time prior to 1911.

Montana Central 100 was billed as the "Largest Locomotive in the World" when it was built by Brooks Locomotive Works in 1897. It became G-5 engine 800. ALCO Historic Photos.

G-5S 807 was a rather strange looking monster. It was the only member of the class that was superheated, but for some reason when the superheater was installed, the piston valves were removed and Heron valves installed. This produces the unusual image of having the outside steam pipes entering a square valve chest. It was the last of its class in operation, and is shown here at St.Paul in September 1933. Collection of Harold K. Vollrath.

Notes:

1. Paul T. Warner, "The Great Northern Railway and Its Locomotives," *Baldwin Locomotives*, January 1925.
2. Great Northern Railway 1880-1900 Historic Engine Record.
3. Brooks Locomotive Works Order List.
4. Paul T. Warner, *op. cit.*
5. "Heavy 12-Wheel Locomotives for the Great Northern," *Railroad Gazette*, Vol. 30, No. 1, p. 3 (January 7, 1898).
6. Paul T. Warner, *op. cit.*

No. 1458, a Class H-4, leads the advance section of the Puget Sounder, *a pre-International train for Vancouver, B. C., past Carkeek Park in Seattle on July 15, 1948. Frank Perrin, Great Northern Railway.*

Chapter 13
Early Class H 4-6-2 Pacific

Great Northern owned a total of 136 locomotives of the Pacific (4-6-2) type, comprised of seven different classes (H-1 through H-7). However, only locomotives in the first four of these classes (H-1 through H-4) were originally built as Pacifics. The last three classes were all rebuilt by GN from other locomotive types (4-6-0's or 2-6-2's). This chapter deals only with what will be called the "early" classes – those which were originally built as Pacifics and were received from 1905 through 1914.

Class H-1

The first six GN Pacifics were built in 1905 by Alco-Rogers as Class H-1 (Nos. 1400-1405). They were relatively light locomotives, weighing only 217,000 pounds, of which only 139,000 was on the 73-inch drivers. They had 21-inch by 28-inch cylinders with slide valves and Stephenson valve gear. The trailing truck was an inside frame type. The grate area of the Belpaire firebox was only 49 square feet, and the tractive effort produced only 28,760 pounds. Thus the grate area was actually smaller, and the tractive effort only slightly greater, than the K-1 4-4-2's which were delivered less than a year later. The tenders carried only 10 tons of coal and 7,000 gallons of water. No doubt the small size of these locomotives contributed to their early demise. They were retired in November of 1928 and November, 1930. All were stripped of their salvageable fittings at Superior in May, 1932, to be sold as scrap.

The basic appearance of the H-1's was very similar to the later H-2's. Few modifications were made over the relatively short service lives of the engines, but included steel pilots and pilot beams and GN style headlights.

Classes H-2 and H-3

The next Pacifics received were twenty H-2's (1406-1425), which were built by Baldwin in 1906. These were part of a huge order for eighty locomotives, including also the K-1 Atlantics and J-1 Prairies. These locomotives were designed with many parts in common. The H-2's had 69-inch drivers, but with an uneven spacing (like the J's and the later H-6's). They had Rushton inside-frame trailing trucks. They were equipped with slide valves and with Walschaert valve gear. They weighed 227,000 pounds when delivered, about 10,000 pounds more than the H-1. The cylinder dimensions were 22 inches by 30 inches, and the locomotives produced 33,090 pounds of tractive effort. The grate area of 54.15 square feet was slightly larger than that of the H-1's. The H-2 tenders had a coal capacity of 13 tons and a water capacity of 8,000 gallons, but still rode on arch bar trucks.

One of the locomotives was equipped with a Baldwin superheater.[1] This was apparently No. 1425, since a diagram dating from about 1915 shows this locomotive as "Class H.2.S" and indicates that it was changed from "H.3" on November 29, 1914. The contemporary diagram for the remainder of the class also has a note indicating that

This Rogers builders photo shows H-1 1402, a member of GN's first order of Pacifics, the only Pacific class equipped with Stephenson valve gear. ALCO Historic Photos.

The engineers side of H-1 1404 was photographed at Devils Lake, ND, on June 22, 1922, still eight years away from retirement. Note that the engine has now been assigned an 8,000 gallon tender with drop equalizer trucks. J. Foster Adams photograph from the collection of Kenneth R. Middleton.

The opposite side of No. 1404 is shown at St. Paul, MN, in August 1924. While it is in shadow, it appears that the tender now assigned has side boards on the coal bunker. Collection of Harold K. Vollrath.

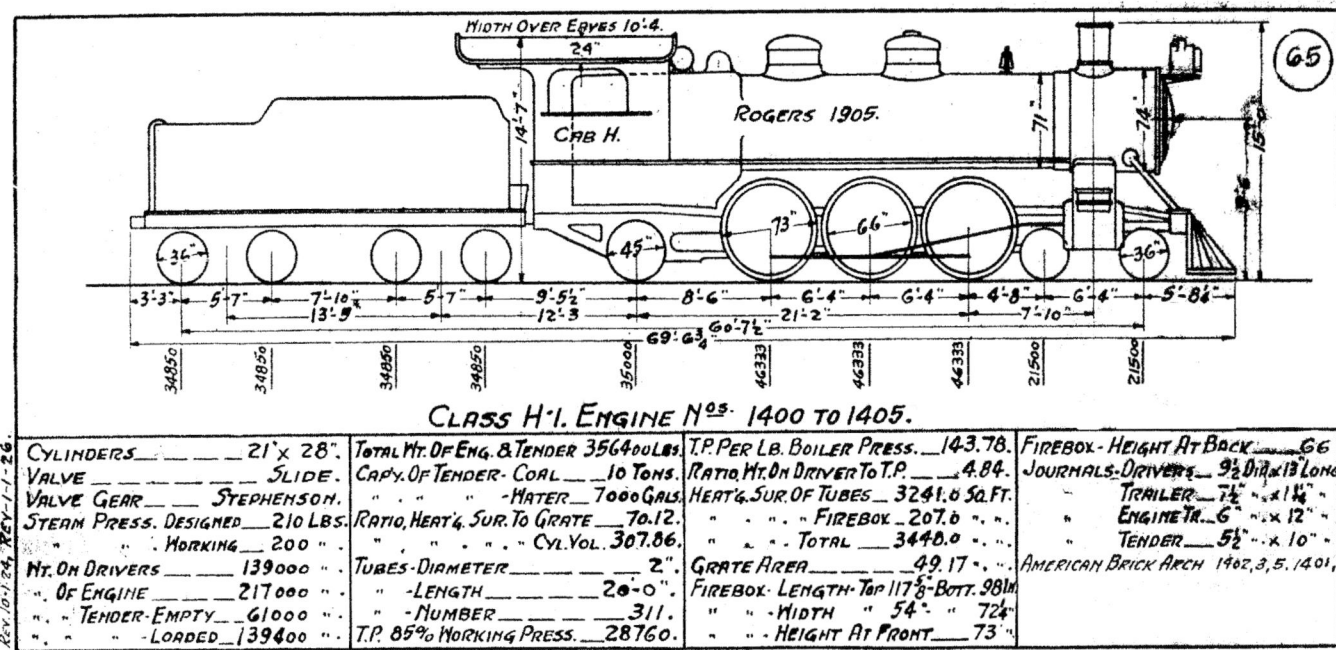

CLASS H·1. Engine Nos. 1400 to 1405.

Cylinders ___ 21" x 28".	Total Wt. Of Eng. & Tender 356400 Lbs	T.P. Per Lb. Boiler Press. ___ 143.78.
Valve ___ Slide.	Cap'y. Of Tender - Coal ___ 10 Tons.	Ratio, Wt. On Driver To T.P. ___ 4.84.
Valve Gear ___ Stephenson.	" " " - Water ___ 7000 Gals.	Heat'g. Sur. Of Tubes ___ 3241.0 Sq. Ft.
Steam Press. Designed ___ 210 Lbs.	Ratio, Heat'g. Sur. To Grate ___ 70.12.	" " " Firebox ___ 207.0 " ".
" " Working ___ 200 ".	" " " " Cyl. Vol. 307.86.	" " " Total ___ 3448.0 " ".
Wt. On Drivers ___ 139000 ".	Tubes - Diameter ___ 2".	Grate Area ___ 49.17 ". ".
" Of Engine ___ 217000 ".	" - Length ___ 20-0".	Firebox - Length - Top 117⅝ - Bott. 98 In.
" Tender - Empty ___ 61000 ".	" - Number ___ 311.	" " Width " 54" 72¼"
" " - Loaded ___ 139400 ".	T.P. 85% Working Press. ___ 28760.	" " Height At Front ___ 73 "

Firebox - Height At Back ___ 66
Journals - Drivers ___ 9½ Dia. x 13 Long
Trailer ___ 7½" x 14"
Engine Tr. 6 " x 12"
Tender ___ 5½" x 10"
American Brick Arch 1402,3,5, 1401

This builders photograph shows a member of the first order of H-2's received by Great Northern. Note the polished cylinder heads. Collection of H. L. Broadbelt.

The second order of H-2's had a different valve gear arrangement, but lacked the polished cylinder heads of the first. Collection of H. L. Broadbelt.

H-2 engine 1425 was moved to H-3 because of its superheater. By the time the diagram for 1425 was produced, the Baldwin superheater had been replaced with a Schmidt and 23½-inch by 30-inch cylinders.

A second order for fifteen additional H-2's (1426-1440) was received from Baldwin in 1907, bringing the total in the class to thirty-five. There were some subtle differences between the two orders. The valve gear hanger was different, and also the reverse lever of the second order is clearly visible in builder's photos above the right running board. The tenders with this order also had heavier drop equalizer trucks rather than the arch bars of the first order. Despite these minor differences, the basic dimensions and characteristics of these locomotives were the same as the first order.

Numerous modifications were made to these locomotives during their years of service on the GN. No. 1430 received a Halen superheater in 1912 (replaced by a Schmidt between 1926 and 1933). Twenty-three additional locomotives received G.N. New Style superheaters from 1913 through 1915. No. 1413 received a Schmidt superheater. No. 1438, the last of the H-2's to receive a superheater (a Schmidt), was not equipped until 1921, and No. 1425 kept its Schmidt superheater.

These locomotives were reclassified by GN as "H-2S". In 1918 and 1919 many of the H-2 and H-2S locomotives had their slide valves replaced with Heron valves. In the early 1920's, the wooden pilots were replaced with steel pilots. Different modifications at different times resulted in three different tractive efforts for these engines, 33,090; 37,760 and for No.1439 40,800 pounds.

About this time many of the locomotives began to be equipped with 12-inch piston valves and were reclassified as H-3 locomotives. A total of eleven locomotives were rebuilt in this manner by 1940. It is interesting to note that most of the locomotives receiving piston valves had a "canted" cylinder block much like the later H-6's, with the block being narrower across the piston valves than across the cylinders. However, one locomotive, No. 1423, received a different type of cylinder block with straight sides more like those of the H-4's. The locomotives which received piston valves apparently received outside steam pipes at the same time, but some of the H-2 locomotives were also equipped with outside steam pipes. The cylinders of the locomotives receiving piston valves were changed to dimensions of 23½ inches by 30 inches. The resulting tractive effort, 42,860 pounds, was higher than that of the H-4's.

H-2S 1417 was photographed at Hillyard, WA, on June 15, 1924. The locomotive retains much of its original appearance, though by this time it has received a superheater and Heron valves. Note that the locomotive has also received an outside-frame trailing truck, and now is pulling what is probably an O-1 class tender. Railroad Museum of Pennsylvania (PHMC).

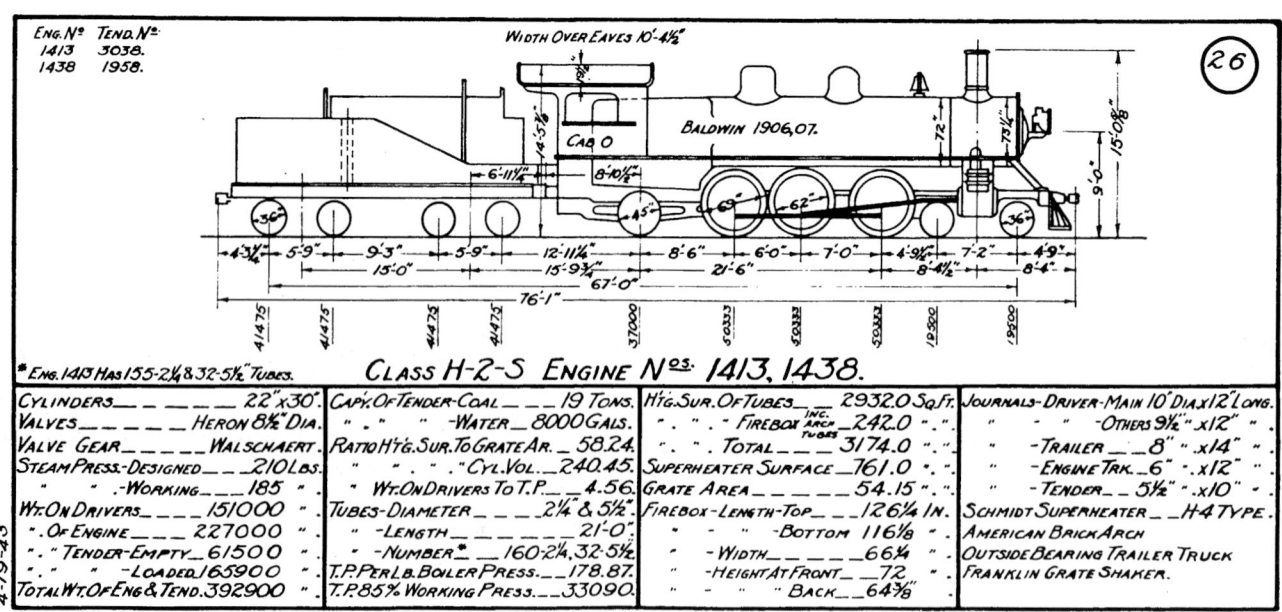

Class H-2-S Engine Nos. 1413, 1438.

* Eng.1413 Has 155-2¼ & 32-5½ Tubes.

CYLINDERS___ 22"x30"	CAP'Y.OF TENDER-COAL ___ 19 TONS.	HTG.SUR.OF TUBES ___ 2932.0 SQ.FT.	JOURNALS-DRIVER-MAIN 10"DIA.x12"LONG.
VALVES_____ HERON 8½ DIA.	" " " -WATER_ 8000 GALS.	" " - FIREBOX INC. TUBES 242.0 " "	" -OTHERS 9½"x12"
VALVE GEAR_____ WALSCHAERT.	RATIO HT'G. SUR. TO GRATE AR._ 58.24.	" " " . TOTAL___ 3174.0 " "	-TRAILER __ 8" x14"
STEAM PRESS.-DESIGNED__ 210 LBS.	" " " CYL. VOL.__240.45.	SUPERHEATER SURFACE_761.0 " "	-ENGINE TRK._ 6" x12"
" -WORKING___ 185 "	WT. ON DRIVERS TO T.P.__ 4.56.	GRATE AREA_____ 54.15 " "	-TENDER __ 5½" x10"
WT. ON DRIVERS____ 151000 "	TUBES-DIAMETER___ 2¼ & 5½	FIREBOX-LENGTH-TOP___ 126¼ IN.	SCHMIDT SUPERHEATER __ H-4 TYPE.
" -OF ENGINE___ 227000 "	" -LENGTH_____ 21'-0".	" " -BOTTOM 116⅛ "	AMERICAN BRICK ARCH.
" ." TENDER-EMPTY_ 61500 "	" -NUMBER.*___ 160-2¼, 32-5½	" -WIDTH___ 66¼ "	OUTSIDE BEARING TRAILER TRUCK
" -LOADED 165900 "	T.P. PER LB. BOILER PRESS.__178.87.	" -HEIGHT AT FRONT __ 72 "	FRANKLIN GRATE SHAKER.
TOTAL WT. OF ENG & TEND. 392900 "	T.P. 85% WORKING PRESS.__ 33090.	" " -BACK___ 64⅜ "	

4-19-43

No. 1413 is another H-2S locomotive from the 1906 order, shown here at Devils Lake, ND, on July 24, 1934. The locomotive has received outside steam pipes to the valve chest, a modern GN headlight, and an outside-frame trailing truck. The tender is probably an M-2 Class. Collection of Harold K. Vollrath.

Engine 1434 is a typical modernized version of the H-2 Pacific. Note the GN headlight, steel pilot and pilot beam, and outside trailing truck. Again, the tender has been replaced. Guy Thatcher Photo Collection, Siouxland Historical Railroad Association

H-3S 1425 is shown at Minneapolis, MN, prior to World War II. This locomotive shows the "canted" cylinder block typical of those used when the H-2's were rebuilt to H-3's and received piston valves. R. J. Foster photograph from the collection of William Raia.

Most of the H-2 and H-3 locomotives were assigned to the more level divisions of the GN including the Butte. Consequently, few of these locomotives were converted to burn oil rather than coal. Most if not all received outside frame trailing trucks of the Baldwin Hodges design in the early 1920's. The G.N. superheaters on some were replaced with Schmidt superheaters. At least one locomotive, No. 1423, was equipped with an Elesco exhaust steam injector. Those which remained on the roster long enough received power reverses in the late 1930's, and low water alarms in the 1940's.

In the 1920's GN began receiving and building large Vanderbilt tenders. While these were assigned to larger locomotives than the H-2's and H-3's, many of the tenders from locomotives receiving the Vanderbilt's found their way to the Pacifics. Many of the H-2's and H-3's received M-2 and N-2 tenders when those locomotives received their Vanderbilt tenders. In the mid-1920's GN rebuilt many of its 8,000-gallon tenders to 10,000-gallon capacity by lengthening the

tender frames and tanks by 5 feet. A number of the H-2 tenders were rebuilt in this manner, though they were not necessarily still with H-2/H-3 engines at the time. A number of the H-2/H-3 tenders also ended up as water cars (auxiliary tenders).

Most of the H-2 engines which had not been superheated were retired in the 1930's. Many of those which were superheated lasted until the 1940's, with a very few making it into the early 1950's.

Class H-4

In 1909 Great Northern took delivery of twenty more Pacific locomotives from the Baldwin Locomotive Works as Nos. 1441 through 1460. These were the largest passenger engines yet received by GN and were placed in Class H-4. The locomotives had 73-inch drivers and came equipped with outside-frame trailing trucks and Schmidt superheaters. The H-4's were delivered with 12-inch piston valves, 26-inch by 30-inch cylinders, and Walschaert valve gear and operated

Engine 1423 is somewhat atypical of the H-3S class in that it received a straight-sided cylinder block unlike the others of its class. It also has an Elesco exhaust steam injector and a power reverse. The tender is a Style 50 Class J-2 tender which has had its water capacity increased from 8,000 to 10,000 gallons by being lengthened five feet. The photograph was taken in August 1949 at Hutchinson, MN. Frank North Collection.

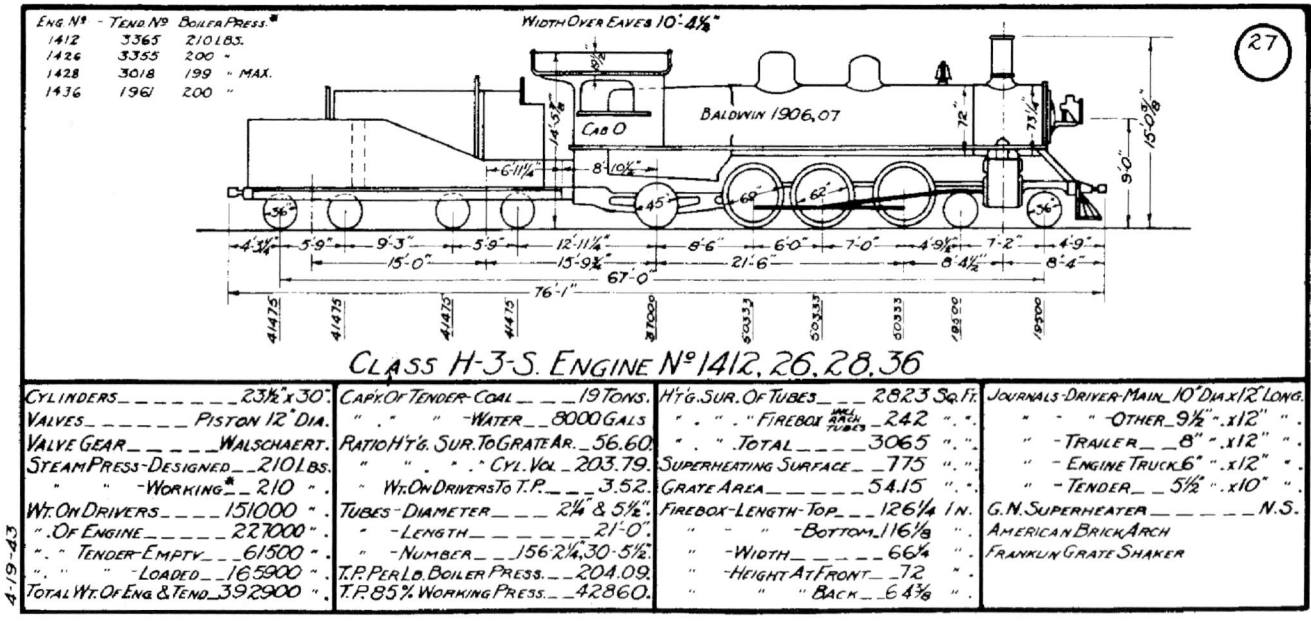

H-3S No. 1436 was photographed at Minneapolis, MN, in July 1934. The uneven driver spacing is very noticeable in this view. Collection of Harold K. Vollrath.

The H-4 engines were built with superheaters, but as can be seen in this photograph had inside steam pipes in the cylinder casting. This caused major maintenance problems with the engines because the cylinder castings would crack. Eventually, all of the engines were rebuilt with outside steam pipes. Collection of H. L. Broadbelt.

Baldwin H-4 1448 is shown at St.Paul, MN, on April 13, 1937, with what is probably M-2 tender 1960. The locomotive has received outside steam pipes and also has had a Delta trailing truck with booster engine installed. Robert Graham photograph from the collection of William Raia.

at a boiler pressure of 150 lb. Tractive effort was 35,420 pounds. The engines weighed 235,750 pounds, of which 152,000 was on the drivers. Shortly after delivery, though, the cylinders were bushed down to a diameter of 23½ inches and the working pressure was raised to 185 pounds, increasing tractive effort to 35,690 pounds. Experiments were conducted with cylinder size, since at first it was thought efficiency could be increased by lowering the boiler pressure and increasing the cylinder diameter to compensate for the tractive effort decrease. This was just backwards, but on June 9, 1909, J. M. Gruber wrote to Louis W. Hill on behalf of George H. Emerson with a favorable report of 1459 running with 27 by 30 cylinders at 120 psi.[2] GN was still experimenting with cylinder size in 1919-1920. Authority for Expenditure (AFE)

12264 covered shortening the stroke of one H-2 (1437) and one H-4 (1449) from 30 inches to 26 inches. AFE 12266 was written to shorten the stroke of one F-6 locomotive. The justification given was to reduce the piston speed, which was supposed to reduce wear of pistons, packings and crosshead shoes.[3] The AFE's were closed before the H-2 and F-6 were completed. However, engine 1449 was tested against 1448 on Train No. 3 between Breckenridge and Minot. The enginemen found that with the shorter stroke they had to use a longer cut-off to keep on schedule, which resulted in the use of more coal and water.[4] However, people still haven't changed – apparently the change was designed by a committee (the "Efficiency Committee").[5] There were also some comments that J.M. Gruber (general manager at the time)

Ten years later than the previous photograph, No. 1448 is shown at Minneapolis, MN, on May 30, 1947. The locomotive has lost its booster and Delta trailing truck, but now has a power reverse. The turbo generator has also been moved next to the stack from its normal position just forward from the cab. The locomotive is still accompanied by an M-2 tender, but records indicate that this is No. 1971. Charles T. Felstead photograph from the collection of William Raia.

Engine 1450, which spent most of its service life on the Spokane Division, is shown here at Kelly Lake, MN, on June 26, 1952. Over the course of years it has been converted to burn oil, and has received an Elesco exhaust steam injector and a power reverse as well as a slant front cab. The engine has also had electric train indicators installed next to the stack. The tender is an H-4 class, from sister 1453. It has had its length extended by five feet to increase water capacity and also has a large oil bunker installed. Charles T. Felstead photograph from the collection of William Raia.

made in a memo to A.C. Deverell (Supt. of Motive Power): "I'm afraid you have got the saving in fuel very much overestimated. We don't want to put anything on those AFEs that they can check us up on later and show that we are mistaken."[6]

By 1943 their boiler pressure had been increased to 200 psi with a resulting tractive effort of 38,545 pounds, except for three that were rated at 38,580 pounds. These three had the same pressure and cylinder dimensions as the others. The pressure for No. 1449 was raised to 210 psi, and it was given smaller cylinders of 23½ inches by 26 inches for a resultant tractive effort of 35,110 pounds. By 1949 the working boiler pressure had been raised to 210 psi, providing a tractive effort of 40,511 pounds. Note the H-4 class was reweighed for a final weight

of 176,500 pounds on drivers. Tender capacities were the same as the H-2 class: 8,000 gallons of water and 13 tons of coal.

In fact, except for the cylinders, valve gear and trailing trucks, the overall appearance of the H-4 was similar to the H-2/H-3 locomotives. The domes and bell were similarly positioned, and the cabs were nearly identical. The drivers, however, were spaced equally, with 6 feet, 6 inches, between axles. The tenders of the H-4's were virtually identical to those received with the second order of H-2's. Also like the earlier H-2's, the H-4's were modified by GN over the years. The locomotives were equipped with outside steam pipes, steel pilots, and modern GN headlights. Later years saw the addition of power reverses, low water alarms, and exhaust mufflers. One of the locomotives,

Another Spokane Division engine that has been exiled to the Minnesota Iron Range at the end, No. 1452 is shown here at Kelly Lake on September 16, 1951. The pilot has been rebuilt to a footboard style. While the electric train indicators next to the stack are absent the brackets remain. Charles T. Felstead photograph from the collection of William Raia.

No. 1459 is taking on water at Seattle, WA, on March 6, 1938. The engine still has a rather trim appearance, although it has received outside steam pipes and a modern headlight and has been equipped to burn oil. The tender is probably an H-class tender, but its short length indicates that it still has only an 8,000 gallon water capacity. Collection of William Raia.

No. 1443, was equipped with a Worthington feedwater heater. Nos. 1447, 1454, 1455, and 1456 were equipped with Sellers exhaust steam injectors. Nos. 1450, 1453, 1457, 1458 and 1459 were equipped with Elesco exhaust steam injectors. Of course there was the usual amount of tender swapping.

Unlike the earlier Pacifics, the H-4's were assigned to service more widely throughout the system, including the more mountainous divisions. As a result many of them, especially those assigned to the Butte and Spokane Divisions, were converted to burn oil rather than coal. Four of these locomotives (Nos. 1447, 1448, 1454 and 1456) were equipped with Delta trailing trucks with boosters during the late 1920's. The boosters added an additional 11,000 lb. of tractive effort. The Delta trailing trucks were removed from 1448 and 1456 during the 1930's. The booster was also removed from No. 1454, but it kept the Delta trailing truck.

Four of the Baldwin H-4's were scrapped in the early 1940's, but the others all survived into the 1950's.

Great Northern's final order of "new" Pacifics was received from Lima in 1914. These twenty-five engines were similar enough to the

1909 Baldwin order that they also were placed in Class H-4 as Nos. 1461-1485. The Lima H-4's were initially placed in service between St.Paul, Minnesota, and Cut Bank, Montana.[7] They weighed 251,200 pounds, slightly more than the Baldwin H-4's, but had less weight on the drivers, 150,700 pounds. Tractive effort was rated at 35,690 pounds using an operating boiler pressure of 185 pounds. The drivers had 73 inch diameters, like the Baldwin order. The cylinders were 23½ inches by 30 inches, the same dimensions to which the Baldwin engines had been changed. They had slightly different firebox dimensions. The locomotives were delivered with GN New Style superheaters (called Emerson superheaters by the trade press at the time). The engines had the usual Walschaert valve gear and Belpaire firebox. There were a few differences in appearance when compared with the Baldwin engines. The domes were positioned farther forward on the Lima engines, with the auxiliary dome being on the boiler rather than the firebox. The shape of the steam dome was also somewhat different. The valve gear hanger was much longer. The trailing truck also differed in design.

Experiments with pressure and cylinder dimensions, as was done with the Baldwin engines, resulted in tractive efforts from 38,580 to

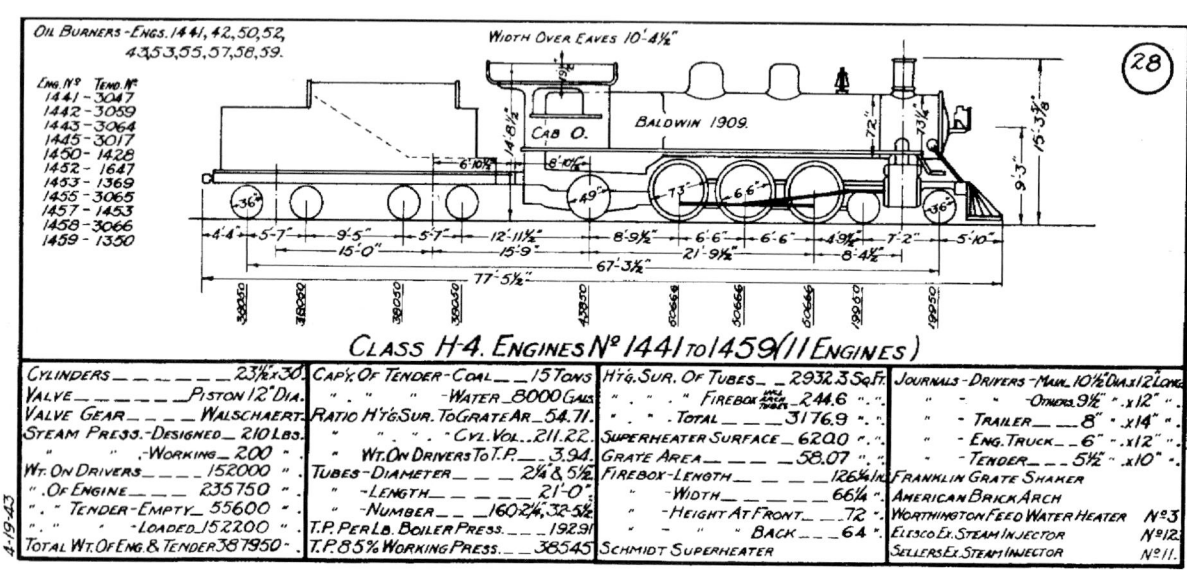

Engine 1462, one of the Lima engines, was photographed in St. Paul, MN, prior to World War II. The locomotive appears to have some sort of cylinder bracing and still has a manual reverse lever. Note the trailing truck, which differs from those used by Baldwin. The domes are farther forward on the Lima engines than the Baldwin's. The steam dome seems to have a more "squat" appearance and the auxiliary dome is mounted on the boiler rather than on the firebox as the Baldwin's. The authors believe that the wheel on the trailing truck and the box located above it on the firebox sides are part of a speed recording device. R. J. Foster photograph from the collection of William Raia.

In another prewar photograph, No. 1470 shows the type of outside steam pipes found on most of the Lima H-4's. This engine was one of the few H-4's with a Worthington feedwater heater, shown on the side just behind the air pump. The tender is probably from an M-2. R. J. Foster photograph from the collection of William Raia.

No. 1473 simmers at Minneapolis on May 22, 1948. The engine has acquired a power reverse with auxiliary reservoir and a low water alarm just below the auxiliary dome. The tender is a Style 60 O-1 tender, No. 3114. Robert Graham photograph from the collection of William Raia.

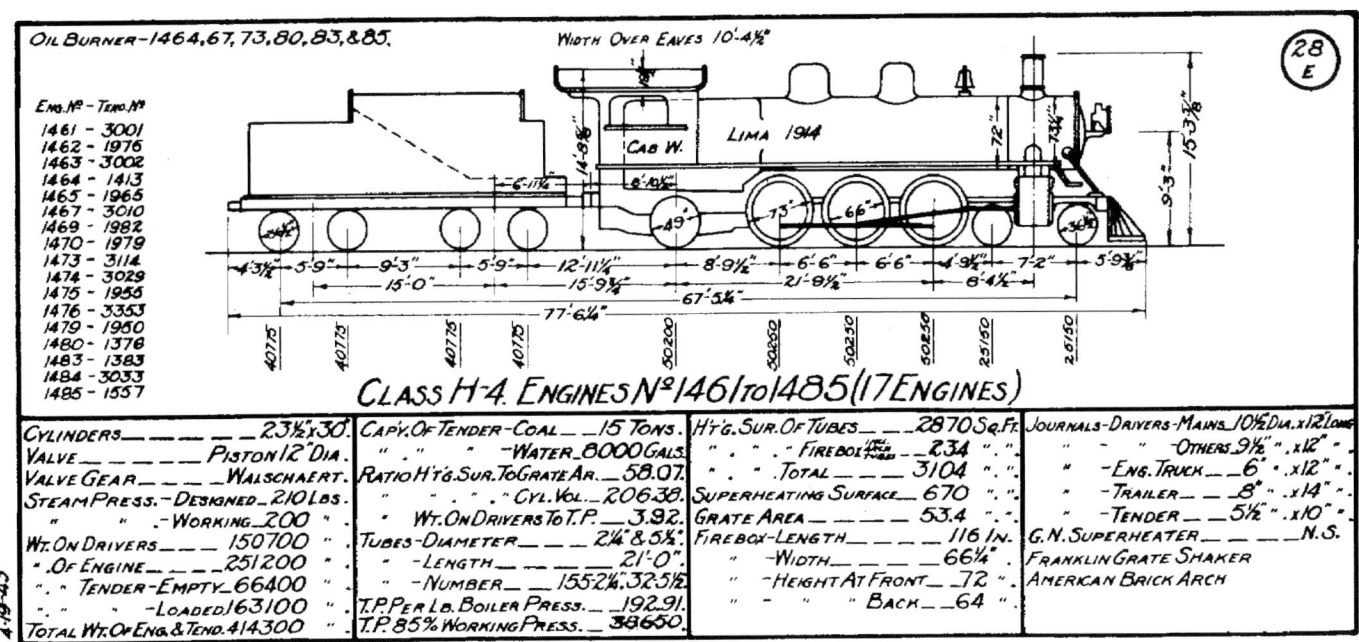

38,650 pounds by 1943. By 1949, the remaining engines had their boiler pressure raised to 210 psi and were rated at 40,511 pounds, the same as the Baldwin engines.

The Lima H-4's were assigned to the Willmar, Dakota, Minot and Spokane Divisions during the active years of steam power, and were modified accordingly. Most of those assigned to the Spokane Division were converted to oil burners. Like their Baldwin counterparts, the Lima engines received outside steam pipes, though the shape was markedly different on most of the Lima engines. There is no evidence that any of the Lima engines ever received boosters. Only two (1470 and 1472) received Worthington feedwater heaters, two (1471 and 1478) received Elesco exhaust steam injectors, and one (1477) received a Sellers exhaust steam injector.

Four of the Lima engines were scrapped in late 1941. Two of them,

Nos. 1466 and 1478, were sold to the Georgia Car & Locomotive Company in 1942 and 1941, respectively. They were then resold to the Atlanta, Birmingham & Coast Railway in 1942, where they became Nos. 153 and 175. When the AB&C became part of the Atlantic Coast Line, these engines became ACL Nos. 7153 and 7175. The other Lima engines remained on the roster until the late 1940's and early 1950's.

While Great Northern never purchased another Pacific locomotive from a commercial builder after 1914, it must have been deemed a successful design since all of the Class E-14 4-6-0's and a number of the Class J-1 and J-2 Prairies were rebuilt to the Pacific wheel arrangement in the 1920's. During their service lives the Pacifics pulled everything from the heavyweight *Oriental Limited* and *Empire Builder* trains to the lowly locals. The longest-lived of the early Pacifics, H-3's 1412 and 1425, worked on the Great Northern for 45 years.

Engine 1477 was photographed at St.Paul, MN, in July 1946. The engine has outside steam pipes more typical of the Baldwin engines and also has the cylinder jacket painted green. Clearly visible are the power reverse and the Sellers exhaust steam injector. The Style 8 C-4 tender No. 785 has a water capacity of only 6,000 gallons and seems dwarfed by the engine. Collection of Harold K. Vollrath.

Great Northern H-4 No. 1482 was photographed at an unknown date and location (possibly at Hillyard in 1936) before World War II. Note the bracing on the cylinder block and the manual reverse lever. The bracing on the tender has been cut off and an oil bunker installed. Collection of William Raia.

Notes:

1. "New Locomotives for the Great Northern", *Railroad Gazette*, Vol. 41, No. 17, p. 371 (October 26, 1906).
2. J. M. Gruber to Louis W. Hill, June 9, 1909. Minnesota Historical Society GN collection.
3. Great Northern Railway Authority for Expenditure (AFE) 12265, approved January 16, 1920.
4. G. E. Anderson to William Kelly, August 16, 1920 (in Great Northern Railway AFE 12265).
5. F. M. Fryburg to William Kelly, September 3, 1920 (in Great Northern Railway AFE 12265).
6. J. M. Gruber to William Kelly, September 27, 1919 (in Great Northern Railway AFE 12666, approved January 16, 1920).
7. "Passenger Locomotives for the Great Northern", *Railway Age Gazette*, Vol. 57, No. 23, p. 1047 (December 14, 1914).

Class H-5 4-6-2 No. 1360 is shown exiting the Ballard Bridge on a northbound
run in 1935. The train is No. 360 for Vancouver, BC. Photograph by Al Farrow.

Chapter 14

Class H 4-6-2 Pacific (Rebuilt Classes)

Class H-5

The E-14 4-6-0's proved speedy and satisfactory for certain classes of passenger service, but lacked the boiler power for heavier work.[1] The fireboxes of the E-14's were wide, mounted above the frames and driving wheels, but were very shallow with almost no slope to the grates.[2] The justification for building some of the first Pacifics from them stated that "These engines are being converted from oil to coal burners. They perform very poorly as coal burners and do not steam well. It is proposed to rebuild two of them as Pacific type engines, that is lengthen frame and add a trailer truck, lengthen boiler and add a combustion chamber, also deepen the fire box. In making this change an engine similar to, but somewhat heavier than the H-4S will be obtained. This engine will have greater tractive power with better steaming quality and will make a more efficient engine than the H-4S."[3] Apparently the GN considered having Baldwin perform the rebuilds, but decided that it would cost $40,000 to have the rebuilding done by Baldwin as opposed to $23,450 having it done in the railroad's own shop.[4] The first rebuild, designated as Class H-5, was completed at the Dale Street shops on July 8, 1921. During the rebuild the firebox was made deeper and was joined to the existing boiler by a semi-conical section. Flue length was increased from 17 feet to 21 feet. The frame was cut between the first two driver sets and a new rear frame section was installed. New cylinders with a lower smokebox saddle, allowing

the boiler to ride lower, were installed.[5] Schmidt superheaters replaced the GN New Style in the E-14's.

The new H-5 locomotives had engine weights varying from 260,800 pounds to 271,800 pounds (but see Chapter 4 on reweighing), compared to 200,000 pounds for the E-14's and 235,750 pounds for the Baldwin-built H-4's. The drivers remained at 73 inches, while the cylinders were 23½ inches by 30 inches, the same as the E-14's and the modified H-4's. The first ten engines rebuilt were numbered as 1486-1495. Apparently in 1926 the decision was made to rebuild all of the smaller E-14's into H-5's, and the existing H-5's were renumbered as 1350-1359 to avoid running into the J-1 1500-series numbers. In September 1926 approval was obtained to rebuild the remaining engines, and they were completed before the end of 1927, becoming engines 1360-1374.[6]

Initially the engines received two #11 Chicago non-lifting injectors, one on each side. However, in the mid and late 1920's, many of the engines received Sellers exhaust steam injectors (1352, 1354, 1355, 1357, 1367, 1368, 1372, 1373 and 1374) or Elesco exhaust steam injectors (1360, 1361, 1362, 1363, 1364, 1365, 1366, 1369, 1370 and 1371), and some also received Worthington No. 3 (BL) feedwater heaters (1350, 1351, 1353, 1356, 1358 and 1359). Photographs indicate that these appliances were removed near the end of steam operations. In the late 1930's, the engines received power reverses. In the 1940's they

Newly completed H-5 1486, the first of its class, posed for its builders photograph shortly after it was completed in July 1921. It is equipped with a Hodges trailing truck. In about five years this engine will become No. 1350. Great Northern Railway photograph from the collection of Wolfgang Weber.

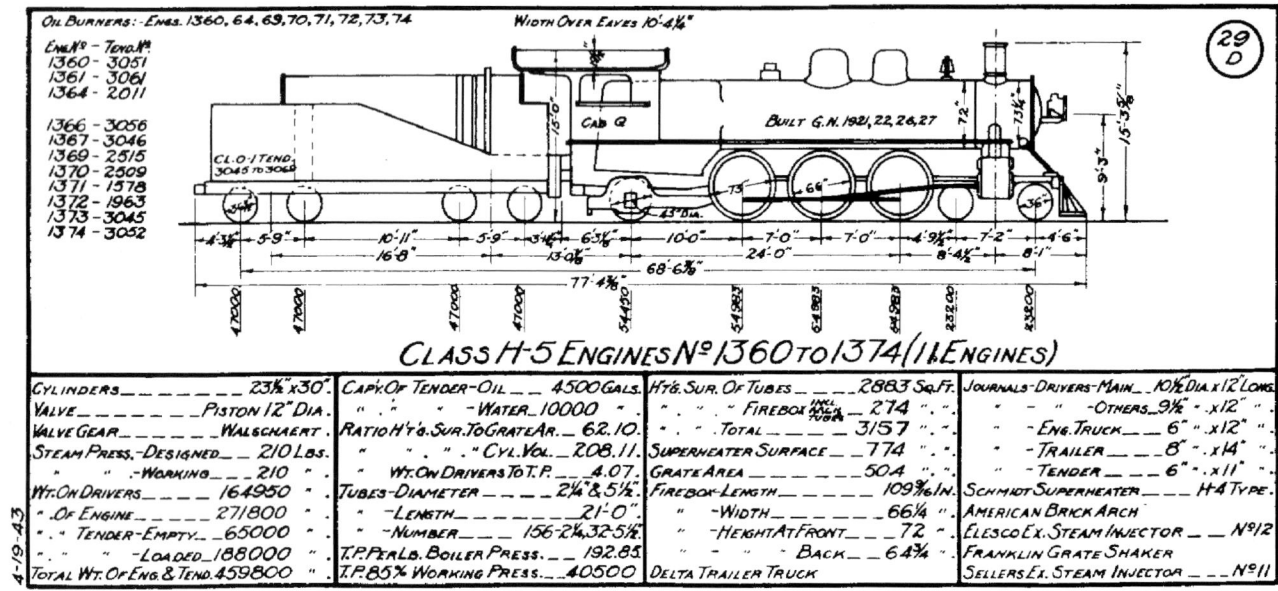

Engine 1357 was photographed at Winnipeg, MB, in May 1947. It is equipped with a Sellers exhaust steam injector, power reverse and has one set of spoked and one set of solid wheels on the engine truck. The tender is a Style 69 O-1 tender (No. 3015) which has been rebuilt to a 10,000 gallon water capacity. Stan F. Styles collection of GTC Collectibles.

H-5 1359 has received a streamlined cab and footboard pilot and also has been converted to burn oil. The tender is most likely a Style 50 J-1 tender (No. 1578). The footboard pilot was installed for mine run service on the iron range, and the oil tender was due to the large final switch to oil fuel that began in 1950. Kelly Lake, MN, September 30, 1950. Ted Gay photograph from the collection of Norman F. Priebe

No. 1361 was photographed at Portland, OR, in January 1950. It has a Delta trailing truck, even though the authors have found no evidence that it ever had a booster engine. Frank North Collection.

Engine 1363 did have a booster from 1926 to 1930, and retained the Delta truck after the booster was removed. The coal bunker bracing has been cut off of the O-1 tender so that an oil bunker could be put in place. This is either a Style 66 or Style 70 O-1 tender. These were rebuilt to 10,000 gallon capacity to be used with the N-1's, but did not follow GN's later pattern of just adding 5 feet in length for the conversion. The engine is shown here at Portland, OR in January 1950. Robert W. Johnston photograph from the Walter Ainsworth collection.

This engineer's side view of 1363 shows a brand new engine with the booster in place. Note the polished cylinder heads and manual reverse bar. The engine was photographed at Hillyard, WA, where it had been built, on May 30, 1926. Railroad Museum of Pennsylvania (PHMC).

Engine 1365 was photographed at Winnipeg, MB, in August 1946. It is still a coal burner (the tender is a Style 70 O-1 tender), but has been equipped with a slant-front cab, electronic train indicators and a power reverse. Stan F. Styles collection of GTC Collectibles.

No. 1369 is shown at Kelly Lake, MN, in July 1954. It still has a square cab, but has been fitted with cab storm windows. It is one of six H-5 engines known to have operated at times with a Style 115 "blank class" or Style 104 P-2 Class 12,000 gallon Vanderbilt tender. Carl Ulrich photograph from the collection of William Raia.

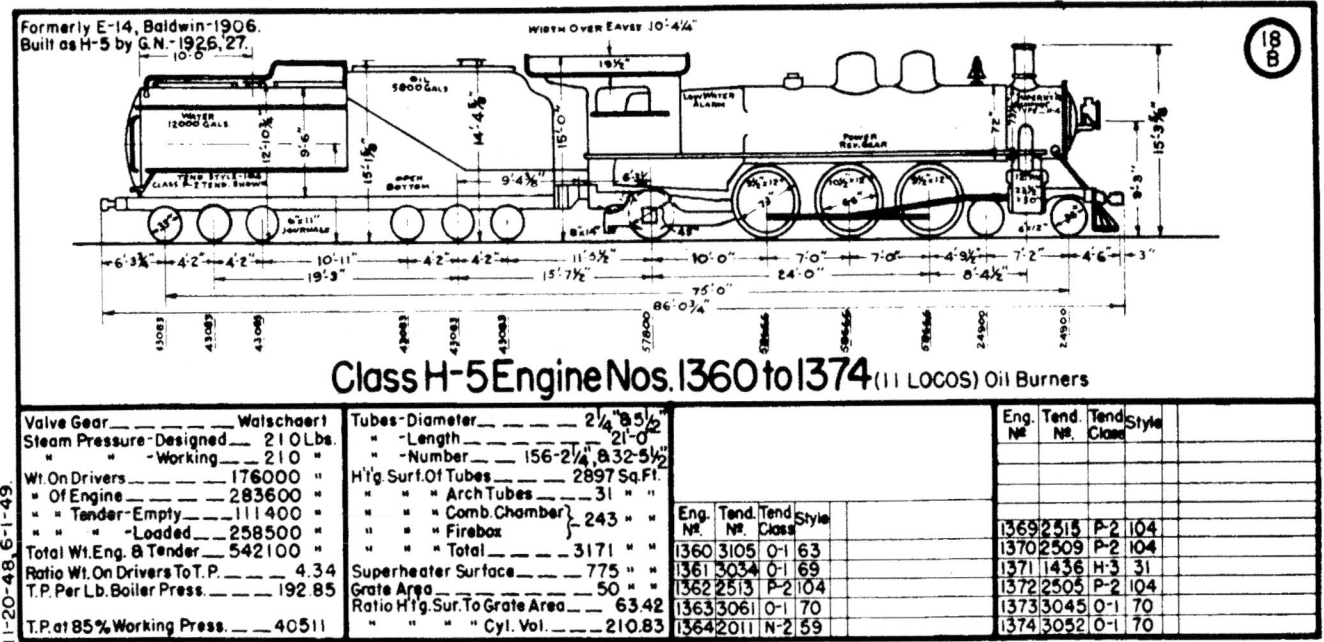

Class H-5 Engine Nos. 1360 to 1374 (11 LOCOS) Oil Burners

Valve Gear — Walschaert	Tubes-Diameter — 2¼"&5½"	
Steam Pressure-Designed — 210 Lbs.	" -Length — 21'-0"	
" -Working — 210 "	" -Number — 156-2¼", & 32-5½"	
Wt. On Drivers — 176000 "	H'tg. Surf. Of Tubes — 2897 Sq. Ft.	
" Of Engine — 283600 "	" " Arch Tubes — 31 "	
" " Tender-Empty — 111400 "	" " Comb. Chamber } — 243 "	
" " -Loaded — 258500 "	" " Firebox }	
Total Wt. Eng. & Tender — 542100 "	" " Total — 3171 "	
Ratio Wt. On Drivers To T.P. — 4.34	Superheater Surface — 775 "	
T.P. Per Lb. Boiler Press. — 192.85	Grate Area — 50 "	
	Ratio H'tg. Sur. To Grate Area — 63.42	
T.P. at 85% Working Press. — 40511	" " " Cyl. Vol. — 210.83	

Eng. Nº	Tend. Nº	Tend. Class	Style		Eng. Nº	Tend. Nº	Tend. Class	Style
1360	3105	O-1	63		1369	2515	P-2	104
1361	3034	O-1	69		1370	2509	P-2	104
1362	2513	P-2	104		1371	1436	H-3	31
1363	3061	O-1	70		1372	2505	P-2	104
1364	2011	N-2	59		1373	3045	O-1	70
					1374	3052	O-1	70

Oil-burning 1371 has been fitted with an Elesco exhaust steam injector and a power reverse. It is shown here at Interbay roundhouse, Seattle, in approximately 1948. R.W. Johnston photograph from the Walter Ainsworth collection.

H-5 1372 is shown at St. Paul, MN, in the mid-1930's. It has a Delta trailing truck and is pulling what is probably a Style 56 M-2 Class tender. Collection of Norman F. Priebe.

received mechanical lubricators, low water alarms, Nalco continuous blow down systems and electric train indicators. Several, including at least 1357, 1359, 1366, 1367 and 1372 received "back-slanted" semi-streamlined cabs.[7] Several engines also received boosters with Delta trailing trucks. Nos. 1352, 1353 and 1355 may have received their boosters at the time of rebuilding. Nos. 1362, 1363 and 1368 also received boosters. The boosters were removed in 1929 and the early 1930's, though most of the engines kept their Delta trailing trucks. Many were converted to burn oil at various times.

The H-5's were assigned to all divisions, and all but one lasted into the 1950's. Kelly Lake on the Mesabi Division became home to several between 1950 and 1953. Here they had the unlikely assignment of making iron range mine runs.

Class H-6

A second group of Pacifics (1710-1724) was rebuilt from Class J-1 and J-2 Prairies. The first of these, No. 1710, was completed on July 1, 1921, and was constructed from J-2 1634. The justification for rebuilding the second engine stated:

"There is an urgent and immediate need for additional passenger power between Seattle and Portland. This is mainly caused by conversion of the Class E-14 Engine from oil to coal burners. The Prairie Type (Class J-1) is gradually being replaced with a heavier Mikado type necessary to handle the heavy freight trains of recent years. By converting this type of engine to a Pacific type (Class H-2) [sic] this can be built for investment cost of less than $10,000.00. This work will be done in the course of making heavy repairs, and the engine will at the same time be fitted with superheater and other standard improvements."[8]

This later view of the same engine in the previous photograph shows it with a streamlined cab and a P-2 Vanderbilt tender. The photograph was taken on June 1, 1947, at St.Paul, MN. Charles T. Felstead photograph from the collection of William Raia.

Oil-burning H-6 1710 is equipped with a booster engine, Elesco exhaust steam injector, power reverse and electric train indicators. The tender is probably a Class P-1 Style 88 (No. 1758). D. H. Roberts photograph from the collection of William Raia.

The change of wheel arrangement also resulted in improved stability at high speeds.[9]

During the course of the rebuilding, the engines received GN New Style superheaters, piston valve cylinders and outside steam pipes. The last seven received Schmidt superheaters with a corresponding difference in flue arrangement. By 1938, three more, 1710, 1713 and 1714, had received the Schmidt type. Outside bearing trailing trucks replaced the inside bearing trucks on the J-class engines. The boilers were also lengthened (J-1 flues were 18 feet 6 inches long, while those of the H-6's were 21 feet 0 inches long).

The new Pacifics had the same 23½-inch by 30-inch cylinders and 69-inch drivers as carried by the superheated Prairies, but weighed 249,500 pounds compared with the 209,000 pounds for the Prairies. They also kept the uneven driver spacing of the Prairies. Nos. 1710,

1713, 1714, 1722, 1723 and 1724 received Delta trailing trucks and boosters, probably in the late 1920's. The boosters were removed in the early 1950's. Engines 1710 and 1722 received Elesco exhaust steam injectors, while 1711, 1720, 1723 and 1724 received Sellers exhaust steam injectors. A Worthington BL feedwater heater was applied to engine 1716 and 1717 received a branch pipe heater.

The H-6 Pacifics were assigned to the western divisions (Butte, Spokane and Klamath, with occasional assignments to the SP&S and Oregon Trunk). As a result, several were equipped as oil burners. All of them lasted into the 1950's. All but one ended up in freight service on the Dakota Division. The other, Spokane/Cascade Division veteran 1723, went to the Willmar Division. It even powered a railfan excursion before it ran its last.

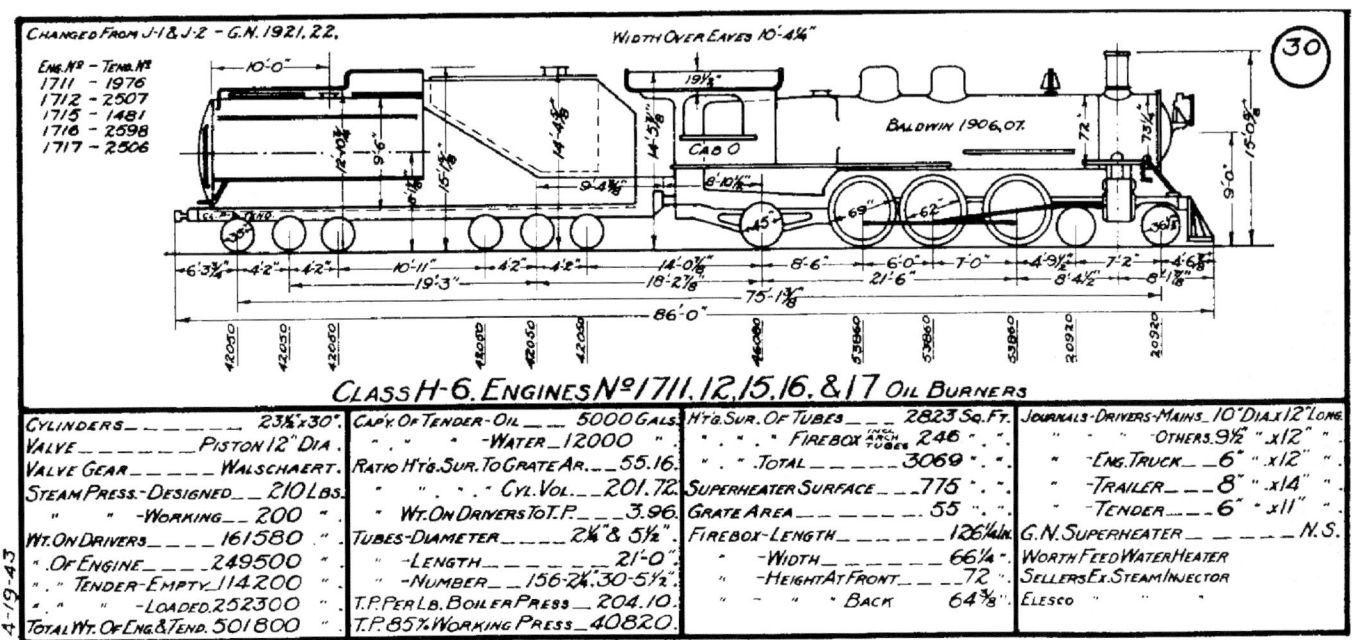

No. 1711 has received a Sellers exhaust steam injector and has a Hodges trailing truck. Note that the cylinder blocks are canted inward rather than being straight-sided like those of the H-5 and H-7 classes. The engine was at Bend, OR, on August 17, 1946. Wally Swanson photograph from the collection of Wilbur C. Whittaker.

Engine 1714 was equipped with a booster engine, as shown here, from 1937 to 1950 views. The engine is at Portland, OR on June 24, 1947. Photograph from the Westphal collection, courtesy of John Luecke.

This later view of the fireman's side of 1714 shows that the engine has received a slant front cab some time between the two views. Here the engine is at Interbay roundhouse, Seattle, in 1950. A Lewis photograph from the collection of Norman F. Priebe.

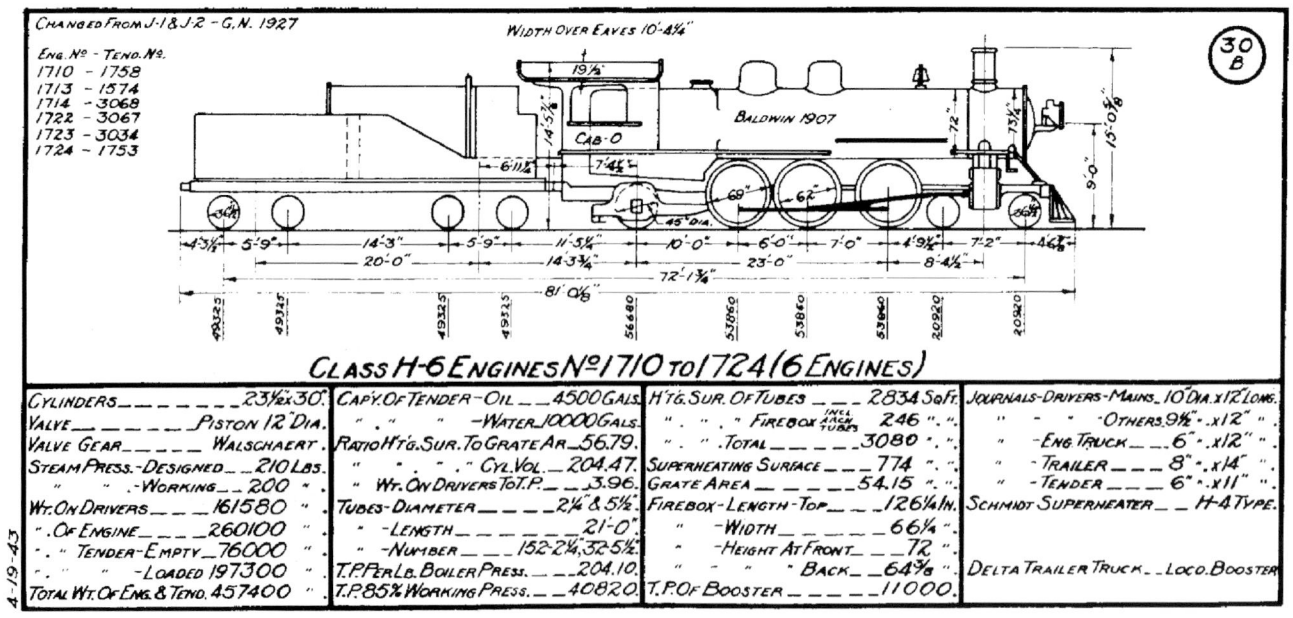

CLASS H-6 ENGINES Nº 1710 to 1724 (6 ENGINES)

CYLINDERS — 23½"x30"	CAP'Y.OF TENDER-OIL — 4500 GALS.	H'T'G. SUR. OF TUBES — 2834 SQ.FT.	JOURNALS-DRIVERS-MAINS 10"DIA.x12"LONG.
VALVE — PISTON 12" DIA.	" " " -WATER 10000 GALS.	" " " FIREBOX INCL. TUBES 246 " "	" " " -OTHERS 9½".x12"
VALVE GEAR — WALSCHAERT.	RATIO H'T'G.SUR.TO GRATE AR. 56.79.	" " " .TOTAL — 3080 " "	" -ENG.TRUCK — 6".x12"
STEAM PRESS.-DESIGNED — 210 LBS.	" " " CYL.VOL. — 204.47.	SUPERHEATING SURFACE — 774 "	" -TRAILER — 8".x14"
" -WORKING — 200 "	WT. ON DRIVERS TO T.P. — 3.96.	GRATE AREA — 54.15 "	" -TENDER — 6".x11"
WT. ON DRIVERS — 161580 "	TUBES-DIAMETER — 2¼ & 5½"	FIREBOX-LENGTH-TOP — 126¼ IN.	SCHMIDT SUPERHEATER — H-A TYPE.
" .OF ENGINE — 260100 "	" -LENGTH — 21'-0"	" -WIDTH — 66¼"	
" -TENDER-EMPTY 76000 "	" -NUMBER — 152-2¼,32-5½"	" -HEIGHT AT FRONT — 72"	
" -LOADED 197300 "	T.P. PER LB. BOILER PRESS. — 204.10.	" -BACK — 64⅝"	DELTA TRAILER TRUCK — LOCO. BOOSTER
TOTAL WT. OF ENG. & TEND. 457400 "	T.P. 85% WORKING PRESS. — 40820 "	T.P. OF BOOSTER — 11000 "	

CHANGED FROM J-1 & J-2 - G.N. 1927

ENG. Nº - TEND. Nº
1710 - 1758
1713 - 1574
1714 - 3068
1722 - 3067
1723 - 3034
1724 - 1753

WIDTH OVER EAVES 10'-4¼"

BALDWIN 1907

CAB-0

4-19-43

H-6 1716 is shown at Klamath Falls, OR, in October 1938. It has been equipped with electric train indicators for operation over the Southern Pacific. The engine also has a Worthington BL feedwater heater, and is accompanied by a Style 115 "blank class" 12,000 gallon Vanderbilt tender (No. 2598). E. Keilty photograph from the collection of William Raia.

The engineer's side of 1716 is shown as it switches at Vancouver, WA, on April 17, 1941. Photograph from R. W. Johnston, courtesy of Walter Ainsworth.

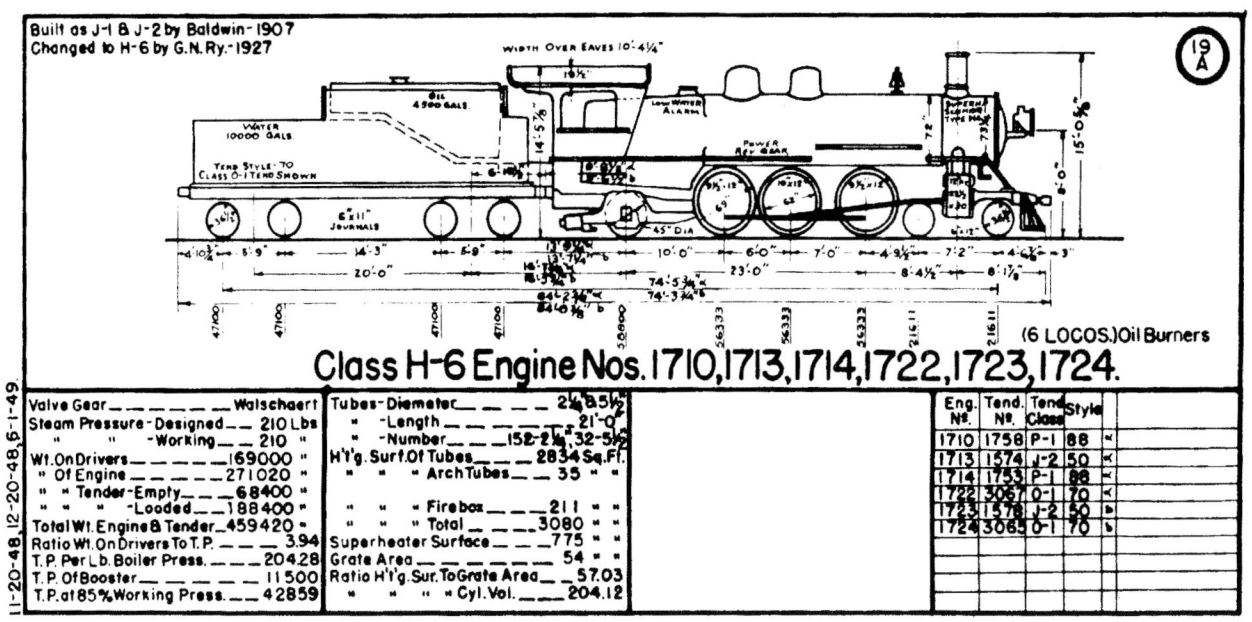

Built as J-1 & J-2 by Baldwin-1907
Changed to H-6 by G.N. Ry.-1927

WIDTH OVER EAVES 10'-4¼"

WATER 10000 GALS.

OIL 4900 GALS.

TEND. STYLE - 70 CLASS O-1 TEND. SHOWN

(6 LOCOS.) Oil Burners

Class H-6 Engine Nos. 1710, 1713, 1714, 1722, 1723, 1724.

Valve Gear	Walschaert	Tubes-Diameter	2¼ &5½"	
Steam Pressure-Designed	210 Lbs	" -Length	21'-0"	
" " -Working	210 "	" -Number	152-24, 32-5½	
Wt. On Drivers	169000 "	H't'g. Surf. Of Tubes	2834 Sq. Ft.	
" Of Engine	271020 "	" " Arch Tubes	35 "	
" Tender-Empty	68400 "			
" " -Loaded	188400 "	" " Firebox	211 "	
Total Wt. Engine & Tender	459420 "	" " Total	3080 "	
Ratio Wt. On Drivers To T.P.	3.94	Superheater Surface	775 "	
T.P. Per Lb. Boiler Press.	204.28	Grate Area	54 "	
T.P. Of Booster	11500 "	Ratio H't'g. Sur. To Grate Area	57.03	
T.P. at 85% Working Press.	42859 "	" " Cyl. Vol.	204.12	

Eng. Nº	Tend. Nº	Tend. Class	Style	
1710	1758	P-1	88	×
1713	1574	J-2	50	×
1714	1753	P-1	88	×
1722	3067	O-1	70	×
1723	1576	J-2	50	▷
1724	3065	O-1	70	▷

11-20-48, 12-20-48, 6-1-49

This interesting view from above shows GN 1722 crossing the Fraser River Bridge at New Westminster, BC. It's interesting to see the way the oil bunker was fitted into the tender with additional sheeting behind it. The date was June 6, 1948. Wilbur C. Whittaker.

H-7

In 1925 GN decided to rebuild the larger series of E-14's to Pacifics. It appears that the construction methods used were similar to those used in constructing the H-5's, but there were a few differences. The driver spacing of the H-7's was not even, being only 6 feet 6 inches between the front two sets (same as the E-14) and 7 feet 0 inches between the center and rear driver sets. The cabs of the H-7's were also placed farther back than on the H-5's. This design resulted in a larger combustion chamber than was applied to the H-5. (It appears there was no combustion chamber at all on the H-6.) The justification for the first five engines stated "Five Pacific type locomotives are required for service on trains 1 and 4 between Barnesville and Devils Lake, also on fast trains between Seattle and Portland. It is proposed to dismantle 5 class E-14 locomotives and use the boiler, wheels, axles, etc., in the construction of the Pacific type."[10] The H-7 engines (1375-1384) weighed 289,400 pounds as compared to the 210,000 pounds of the E-14's, and had the same 23½-inch by 30-inch cylinders.

All of the engines received Delta trailing trucks when rebuilt. Five of the engines (1375, 1376, 1382, 1383 and 1384) were equipped with boosters when they were rebuilt. The other five received boosters in 1930. All of the engines received Elesco exhaust steam injectors when

Recently completed H-7 1375 was posed outside the Dale Street Shops in January 1926 for its builders photograph. It is equipped with an Elesco exhaust steam injector and a Delta trailing truck with booster. Great Northern Railway photograph from Burlington Northern.

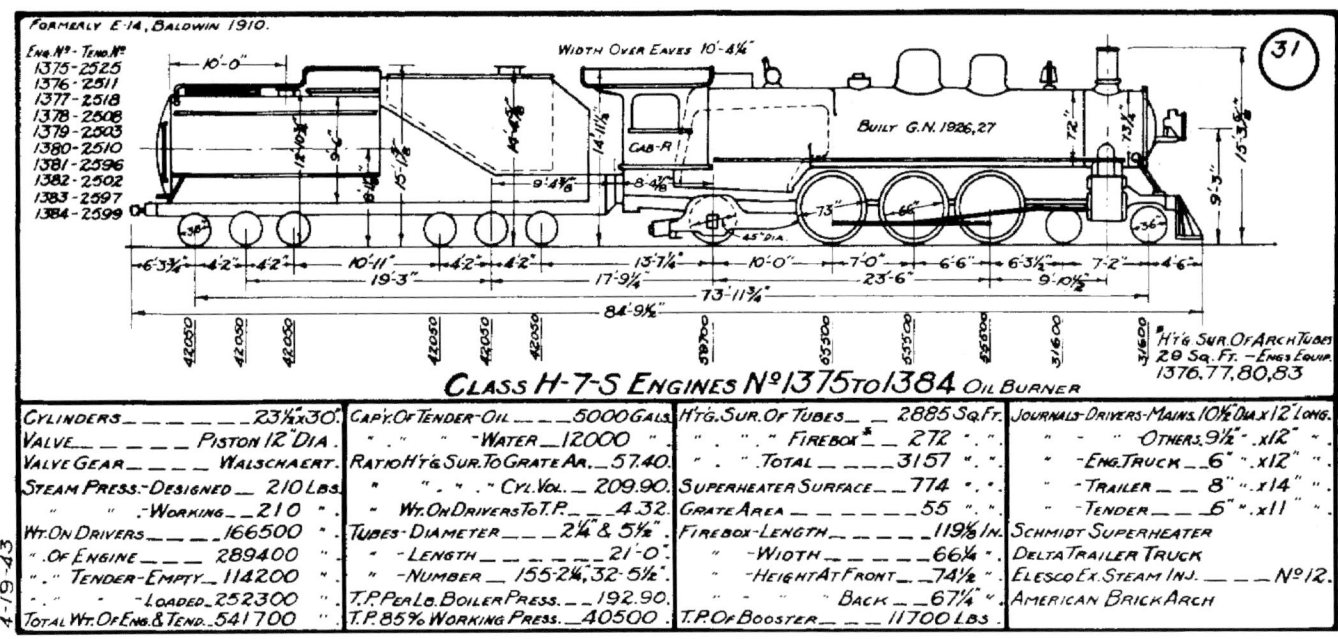

CLASS H-7-S ENGINES Nº 1375 to 1384 OIL BURNER

CYLINDERS _ _ _ _ _ 23½x30	CAP'Y. OF TENDER-OIL _ _ _ 5000 GALS	HT'G. SUR. OF TUBES _ _ 2885 SQ. FT.	JOURNALS-DRIVERS-MAINS 10½" DIA x 12" LONG
VALVE _ _ _ _ _ PISTON 12" DIA	" _ " _ " -WATER _ 12000 "	" _ " _ " FIREBOX* _ _ 272 " _ "	" _ - _ OTHERS 9½" _ x12"
VALVE GEAR _ _ _ _ WALSCHAERT	RATIO HT'G SUR. TO GRATE AR. _ 57.40	" _ " _ " TOTAL _ _ _ 3157 " _ "	" _ -ENG. TRUCK _ 6" _ x12"
STEAM PRESS.-DESIGNED _ 210 LBS	" _ " _ " CYL. VOL. _ 209.90	SUPERHEATER SURFACE _ _ 774 " _ "	" _ -TRAILER _ _ 8" _ x14"
" _ -WORKING _ _ 210 "	" WT. ON DRIVERS TO T.P. _ _ 4.32	GRATE AREA _ _ _ _ 55 " _ "	" _ -TENDER _ _ _ 6" _ x11"
WT. ON DRIVERS _ _ _ _ 166500	TUBES-DIAMETER _ _ 2¼ & 5½"	FIREBOX-LENGTH _ _ _ _ 119⅝ IN	SCHMIDT SUPERHEATER
" OF ENGINE _ _ _ 289400 "	" -LENGTH _ _ _ _ 21'-0"	" -WIDTH _ _ _ _ 66¼ "	DELTA TRAILER TRUCK
" TENDER-EMPTY 114200 "	" -NUMBER _ 155-2¼, 32-5½"	" -HEIGHT AT FRONT _ 74½ "	ELESCO EX. STEAM INJ. _ _ _ Nº 12
" -LOADED 252300 "	T.P. PER LB. BOILER PRESS. _ _ 192.90	" -BACK _ _ 67¼ "	AMERICAN BRICK ARCH
TOTAL WT. OF ENG. & TEND. 541700 "	T.P. 85% WORKING PRESS. _ 40500	T.P. OF BOOSTER _ _ _ 11700 LBS	

4-19-43

This view shows the fireman's side of recently completed H-7 1375. The tender appears to be a Style 66 or Style 70 O-1 tender but by 1933 all of the H-7's had been equipped with 12,000 gallon Vanderbilt tenders. Great Northern Railway, courtesy of Eric Archer.

By the time this photograph was taken in June 1947 at Winnipeg, MB, No. 1375 had received a slant-front raised cab. The large pipe going up alongside the stack is the booster exhaust, re-routed from its original location of exhausting into the smokebox. Stan F. Styles collection of GTC Collectibles.

This fireman's side view of No. 1375 was taken at St.Paul, MN, on July 2, 1948, while the engine was powering Train No. 8. Sid Davies photograph from the collection of William Raia.

Now in freight service, the 1380 is shown entering Union Yard in Minneapolis with an eastbound extra freight on April 28, 1951. Note its booster has been removed, and that it has an enlarged oil bunker. Photograph by John Malven.

This engineer's side view of H-7 1381 was taken at Superior, WI, in June 1947. The engine has a booster, power reverse, electric train indicators and a Nathan low-water alarm. Collection of Harold K. Vollrath.

The fireman's side of 1381 was photographed less than a year after the previous photograph.
It was in St.Paul, MN, in May 1948, when it was assigned to Trains 7 and 8. Collection of Harold K. Vollrath.

Engine 1383 is shown at St.Paul, MN, on May 12, 1946, arriving with Train 8. Robert Graham photograph from the collection of William Raia.

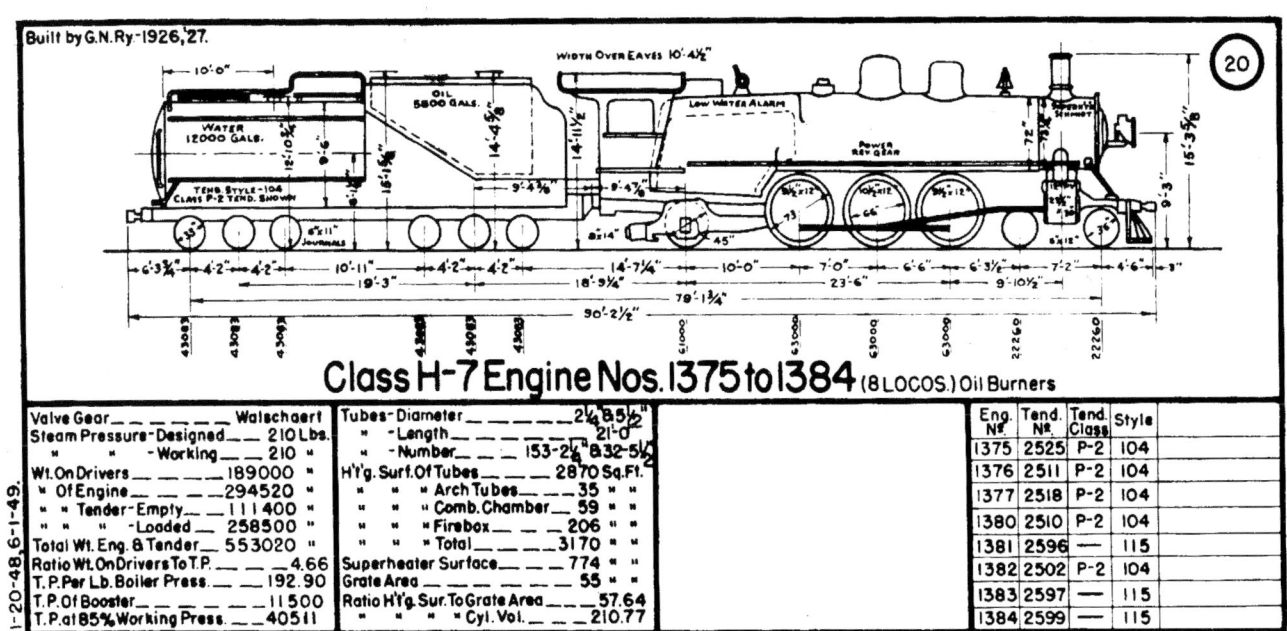

Class H-7 Engine Nos. 1375 to 1384 (8 LOCOS.) Oil Burners

Valve Gear	Walschaert
Steam Pressure-Designed	210 Lbs.
" -Working	210 "
Wt. On Drivers	189000 "
" Of Engine	294520 "
" Tender-Empty	111400 "
" " -Loaded	258500 "
Total Wt. Eng. & Tender	553020 "
Ratio Wt. On Drivers To T.P.	4.66
T.P. Per Lb. Boiler Press.	192.90
T.P. Of Booster	11500 "
T.P. at 85% Working Press.	40511 "

Tubes-Diameter	2¼" & 5½"
" -Length	21'-0"
" -Number	153-2¼" & 32-5½"
H'T'g. Surf. Of Tubes	2870 Sq. Ft.
" " Arch Tubes	35 " "
" " Comb. Chamber	59 " "
" " Firebox	206 " "
" " Total	3170 " "
Superheater Surface	774 " "
Grate Area	55 " "
Ratio H'T'g. Sur. To Grate Area	57.64
" " " Cyl. Vol.	210.77

Eng. Nº.	Tend. Nº.	Tend. Class	Style
1375	2525	P-2	104
1376	2511	P-2	104
1377	2518	P-2	104
1380	2510	P-2	104
1381	2596	—	115
1382	2502	P-2	104
1383	2597	—	115
1384	2599	—	115

Built by G.N.Ry-1926,'27.

11-20-48, 6-1-49.

No. 1384 is shown at Superior, WI, on May 30, 1952. The booster has been removed, but an auxiliary
reservoir for the power reverse has been added. Harold Olsen photograph from the collection of William Raia.

H-7 1376 was at Winnipeg, MB, when this engineer's side photograph was taken in May 1947. The engine still has its booster.
This was the only H-7 that didn't have its cab raised, giving it a rather ungainly appearance. Stan F. Styles collection of GTC Collectibles.

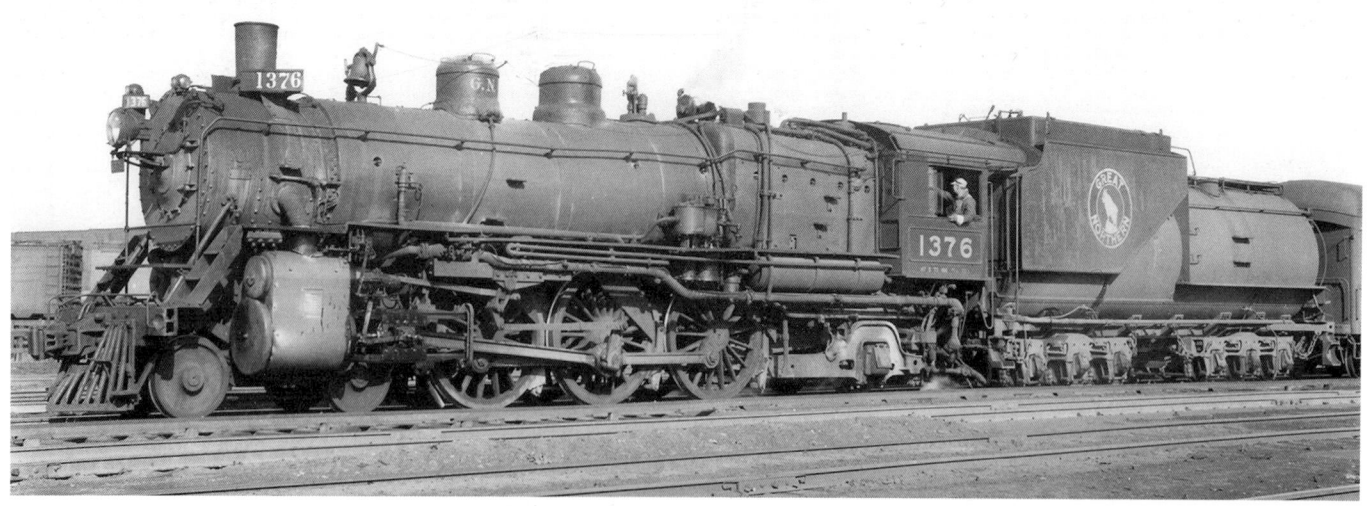

The 1376 is arriving at St. Paul with Train 8, the Winnipeg Limited. After returning to the Dakota Division about 1947, the engine held this
assignment until the arrival of diesels. Note the enlarged oil bunker, probably the last improvement made to this class. GNRHS Collection.

they were rebuilt, and Schmidt superheaters replaced the GN New Style of the E-14's. At first the engines were given rectangular tenders, but by 1933 all had been equipped with 12,000 gallon Vanderbilt tenders. When built the H-7's all had the cabs mounted low on the firebox, with the bottom of the cab being below the running boards. At some later time, all but 1376 had the cabs raised so that the floor was even with the running boards. This may have been done so that the cab floor was more on a level with the decks of the Vanderbilt tenders, but the reason why 1376 was not changed is unknown to the authors. Power reverses were applied from 1937 through 1940. In the early 1940's the engines received mechanical lubricators, and in the mid-1940's they received Nathan low water alarms and Nalco continuous blow down apparatus.

Some received electric train indicators in the mid-1940's. The engines were all oil burners, and most were assigned to either the Spokane or Kalispell divisions. One of the engines (1378) was sold to the SP&S in 1944, and 1379 was sold for scrap in 1947. All of the others lasted until 1955. Two were assigned to the Dakota Division after 1940, where their principal use was powering the *Winnipeg Limited*, trains 7 and 8. After World War II all but one were moved to the Dakota Division. The exception, 1384, went to the Mesabi division. The 1381 may have been the last H-7 in passenger service when it powered the last run of No. 32, St. Cloud to Sandstone, on March 14, 1951. All remaining engines were in freight service after 1951.

No. 1375 is rolling past Westminster Tower in St. Paul, with Train 8, the Winnipeg Limited, enroute to St. Paul Union Depot. This morning arrival view was taken in July 1948. Diesel replacements for trains 7 and 8 were already on the property, running on the Cascade Division. The 1375 kept its booster, of more utility while on the Spokane Division, until 1949. Photograph by Ben F. Cutler (RPS), collection of Norman F. Priebe.

Notes:

1. Paul T. Warner, 1925. "The Great Northern Railway and Its Locomotives", *Baldwin Locomotives*.
2. Douglas C. Bemrich, 1990. "Great Northern Steam Locomotives Class H-5", GNRHS Reference Sheet 170.
3. Great Northern Railway Company Authority for Expenditure (AFE) 16530, January 28, 1921.
4. William Kelly to C.O. Jenks, February 26, 1921 (in Great Northern Railway Company AFE 16530, January 28, 1921).
5. Douglas C. Bemrich, op. cit.
6. Great Northern Railway Company AFE 32751, September 29, 1926.
7. Douglas C. Bemrich, op. cit. See also Chapter 19.
8. Great Northern Railway Company AFE 16820, February 21, 1921.
9. Arthur D. Taylor, 1995. "Great Northern Class H-6 Pacific" GNRHS Reference Sheet 233.
10. Great Northern Railway Company AFE 29451, June 26, 1925.

In their heyday, the J class was a primary source of power on the Dakota Division between Fargo and St. Cloud.
Here a member of the class works an eastbound extra out of Melby, MN, in the 1920's. Courtesy of the Douglas County Historical Society.

Running at a good clip with bell ringing, class J-2 No. 1637 is enroute with a short extra, likely a local, north of Seattle. Many pictures of these engines carry no dates, and this one is no exception. However it can be dated to before 1923 by its old headlight and wooden pilot. Bordertown collection of GTC Collectibles.

Chapter 15
Class J 2-6-2 Prairie

Class J-1

In 1906, the Great Northern Railway placed its first order for Prairie type (2-6-2) locomotives with the Baldwin Locomotive Works. This order for fifty locomotives was part of a larger order which included twenty Pacific types (Class H-2), ten Atlantics (Class K-1) and five Mallet articulateds (Class L-1).

The Prairies had many parts in common with the Pacifics and Atlantics, greatly contributing to the "family appearance" among the locomotives. The boilers were nearly identical (the H-2's had slightly longer tubes – 21 feet vs. 18 feet 6 inches) with a boiler diameter of 72 inches for all three classes. All had Rushton trailing trucks with inside journal boxes and all had identical tenders with capacities of 8,000 gallons of water and 13 tons of coal and with arch-bar trucks. The J-1 Prairies had 22-inch diameter pistons with 30 inch strokes, slide valves and 69-inch drivers. Working steam pressure was given as 210 pounds, though later diagrams show it as 185 pounds. Tractive effort was 33,090 pounds. Weight on drivers was 151,000 pounds, with a total engine weight of 209,000 pounds. The engines were equipped with Walschaert valve motion and the usual Belpaire fireboxes.[1]

It should be noted that one of the Prairie locomotives (No. 1549) was equipped with a Baldwin smokebox superheater at the factory[2] and had an operating steam pressure of only 160 pounds. The cylinder diameter on this locomotive was 25¼ inches, which allowed it to produce 37,700 pounds of tractive force. Apparently this single superheated locomotive was placed in Class J-3 prior to 1910. On January 5, 1914, it was placed in Class J-1S, and by that time steam pressure was increased to 170 pounds though cylinder size remained the same. The increased boiler pressure increased the tractive effort to 40,060 pounds. At some time before it was sold to the Spokane, Portland & Seattle (SP&S) in 1925 it received the 23½-inch by 30-inch cylinders common to most of the J-1S engines.

Class J-2

In 1907, GN's second and final order for Prairie type locomotives was placed with Baldwin. This order was for one hundred additional locomotives having the same specifications as the first fifty. While the differences between the two groups were quite minor, this second order was placed in a new class, J-2. The main differences were apparently in the valve gear. On the J-1's, the combination lever and crosshead link were inside the crosshead guides. The J-2's had them on the outside of the crosshead guides, probably facilitating maintenance.

Modifications and Dispositions

During the course of time very few major changes in appearance were made to Great Northern's Prairies (unlike much of its motive power). This may have been in part because their service lives were relatively short. From about 1917 through 1924 they received steel pilot beams and pilots. J-1's 1506, 1514, 1524 and 1532 and J-2's 1573, 1613, 1624, 1637, 1641 and 1643 were modified to burn oil for at least parts of their service lives. They were delivered with acetylene headlights. These were converted to electric arc lamps and then to incandescent bulbs, housed in sheet metal cases, in 1921. The conversion to the standard cast iron headlight case happened at the same time as some of the J class were being rebuilt into class H-6 Pacifics, beginning in 1922.[3]

In June 1912 J-2 No. 1566 received a superheater, the first Prairie so modified. During the process it received 26-inch by 30-inch cylinders.[4] There is no evidence that No. 1566 received Heron valves before its sale to the SP&S in 1925, at which time it had an H&D superheater.

In 1914 and 1915, six additional J-1 locomotives were superheated and placed in Class J-1S. These included 1501, 1514, 1524, 1531, 1537 and 1539.[5] They received Great Northern New Style superheaters. Nos. 1514, 1524, 1531 and 1537 received 23-inch by 30-inch cylinders when superheated. Eight of the J-2's (1550, 1559, 1569,

J-1 1520 was received by GN on May 10, 1906, as part of a huge order for eighty-five locomotives. Collection of H. L. Broadbelt.

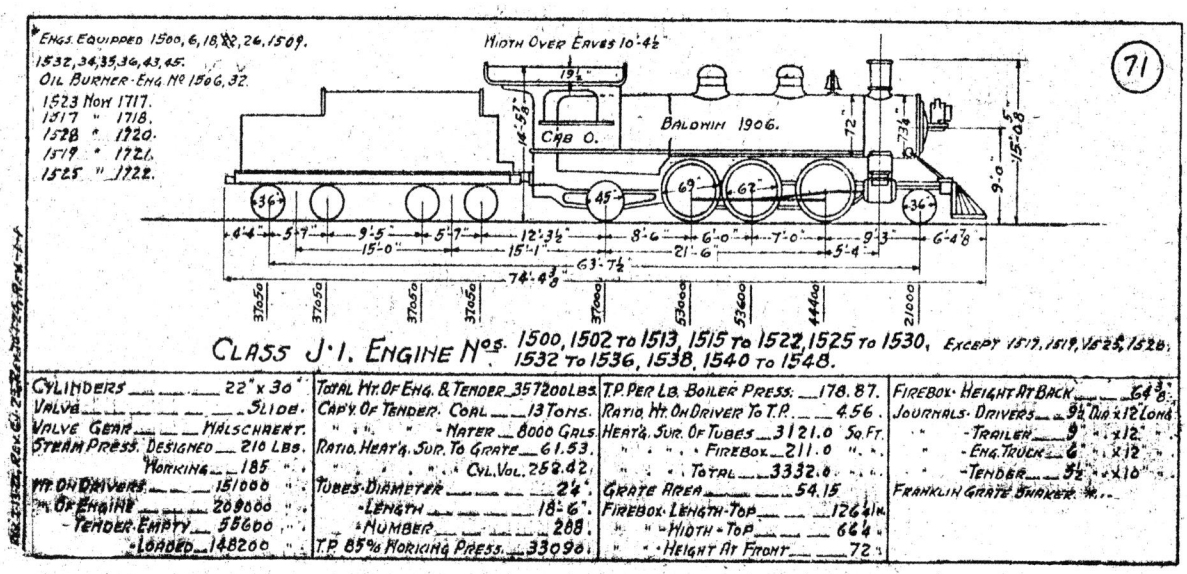

Oil-burning 1506 was photographed in Seattle no later than 1921. The style headlight shown here received handholds between 1919 and November 1921. This engine was one of the longest lasting J's, being retired in October 1936. Stan F. Styles collection of GTC Collectibles.

J-1 1532 had an oil bunker that looks too big for the tender. It was photographed at Argo, WA, in 1925. GNRHS Collection.

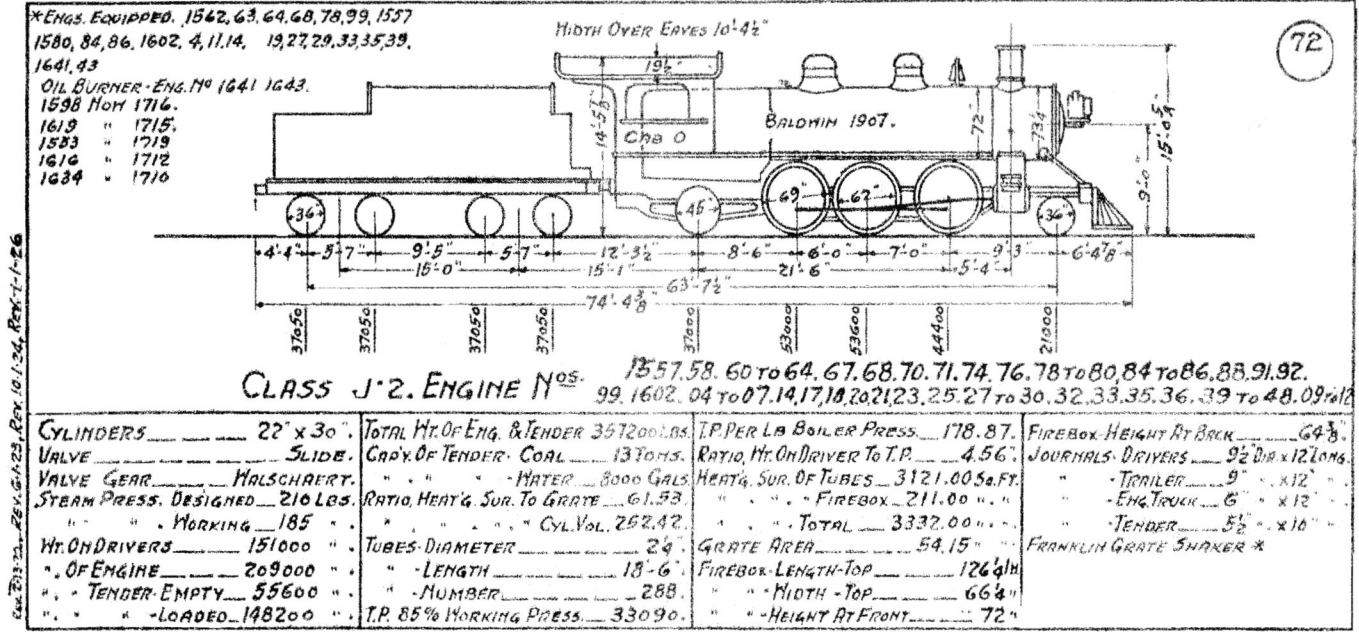

CLASS J·2. ENGINE Nº⁵· 1557.58. 60 to 64. 67.68.70.71.74.76.78 to 80.84 to 86.88.91.92. 99.1602.04 to 07.14.17.18.20.21.23.25.27 to 30.32.33.35.36.39 to 48.09 to 13

CYLINDERS	22" x 30"	TOTAL HT. OF ENG. & TENDER	357200 LBS.	T.P. PER LB BOILER PRESS.	178.87	FIREBOX-HEIGHT AT BACK	64⅜"
VALVE	SLIDE	CAP'Y. OF TENDER-COAL	13 TONS.	RATIO HT. ON DRIVER TO T.P.	4.56"	JOURNALS-DRIVERS	9½ DIA x 12 LONG
VALVE GEAR	WALSCHAERT.	" " -WATER	8000 GALS	HEAT'G. SUR. OF TUBES	3121.00 SQ.FT.	" -TRAILER	9" x 12"
STEAM PRESS. DESIGNED	210 LBS.	RATIO. HEAT'G SUR. TO GRATE	61.53	" " -FIREBOX	211.00 " "	" -ENG. TRUCK	6" x 12"
" " -WORKING	185 "	" -CYL. VOL.	252.42	" " -TOTAL	3332.00 " "	" -TENDER	5½" x 10"
WT. ON DRIVERS	151000 "	TUBES-DIAMETER	2¼"	GRATE AREA	54.15 "	FRANKLIN GRATE SHAKER *	
" -OF ENGINE	209000 "	" -LENGTH	18'-6"	FIREBOX-LENGTH-TOP	126 g/h		
" -TENDER-EMPTY	55600 "	" -NUMBER	288	" -WIDTH -TOP	66¼"		
" " -LOADED	148200 "	T.P. 85% WORKING PRESS.	33090	" -HEIGHT AT FRONT	72"		

Engine 1514 is one of the J-1S Class that has also been converted to burn oil. It was photographed at Seattle, WA, in July 1923. Collection of Harold K. Vollrath.

1573, 1615, 1624, 1631 and 1649) received the same modifications and were placed in Class J-2S.[6] In this configuration and operating at 185 pounds of steam pressure they produced 36,170 pounds of tractive effort.

At some time in 1915 (a clear date cannot be determined) GN began placing 23½-inch by 30-inch cylinders on the locomotives being superheated. Engines thus fitted out were J-2's 1554, 1556, 1582, 1594, 1596, 1613, 1622 and 1637.[7] It is likely that J-1's 1501 and 1539 and J-2's 1551, 1590, 1608 (not superheated until 1924) and 1626 also received the 23½-inch diameter cylinders when superheated. These engines were not superheated until after the Interstate Commerce Commission Valuation Engineering Report had been written. With the 23½-inch diameter cylinders, and again operating at 185 pounds of steam pressure, the engines produced 37,760 pounds of tractive effort. By 1926 (based on locomotive diagrams from that date) all of the superheated engines had been changed to have 23½-inch by 30-inch cylinders. A possible exception was J-2S 1569 which was converted to an H-6 Pacific in 1922. A known exception was J-2S 1566 which went to the SP&S in 1925 with its 26-inch by 30-inch cylinders. From 1918 through 1921 the J-1S and J-2S locomotives were equipped with Heron 8½-inch valves which held up to the superheated steam better than slide valves.[8] These valves fit into the square valve chests, so there was no change in appearance to the cylinder and valve chest assembly. There is no evidence that No. 1569 received Heron valves before it was converted to an H-6 4-6-2 beginning in 1921.

Perhaps because they disappeared from the GN locomotive roster fairly early (the last of the J-1's, Nos. 1524 and 1545, were retired in 1936 and the last of the J-2's, No. 1588, was scrapped in 1937) many of the J-Class locomotives retained tenders very similar to the originals until they were scrapped. While there are certainly exceptions, many of the photographs of J-Class locomotives show tenders very similar to the original tenders. Some of these even retained the arch-bar tender trucks, though some received drop equalizer trucks. Like the locomotives, the J-1 tenders received only slight modifications through the years. The Style 46 Class J-1 tenders remained virtually as delivered. Some of the J-1 tenders (Style 47) were increased in length by five feet, with a resultant increase in water capacity to 10,000 gallons. Style 47 tenders also had heavier truck journals added. The Style 48 Class J-1 tenders had increased coal capacities (fifteen tons) but were not lengthened and hence retained their 8,000 gallon water capacity.

As with the J-1's, many of the J-2 tenders received only slight modifications through the years. The Style 51 tenders remained nearly as delivered. Many of the J-2 tenders were also lengthened 5 feet to increase water capacity, but coal capacity for these J-2 tenders was also increased to fifteen tons (Styles 49 and 50). The Style 50 tenders also had heavier truck journals added. Once the J-Class locomotives began to be scrapped in large numbers, many of their tenders were transferred to maintenance service or assigned to other classes.

In the early to mid-1920's, fifteen of the Prairies were completely rebuilt at GN's Dale Street Shops to Class H-6 Pacifics (Nos. 1710-1724).

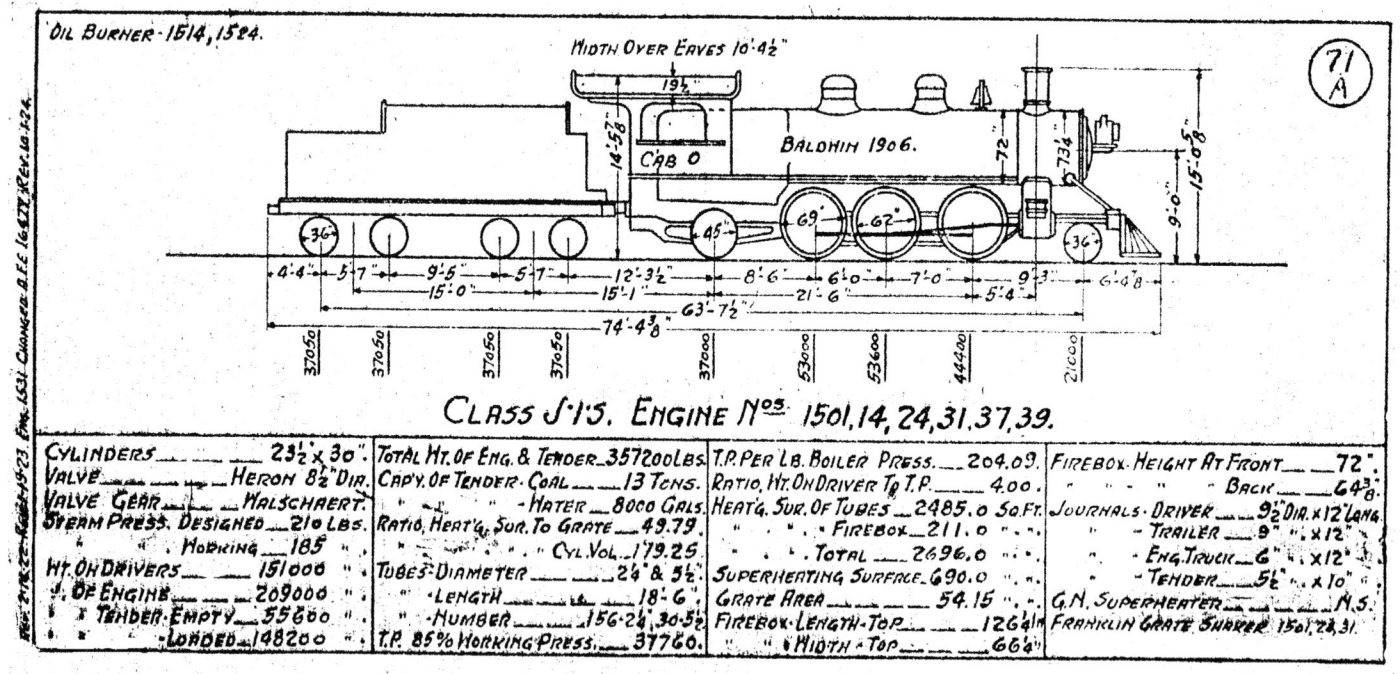

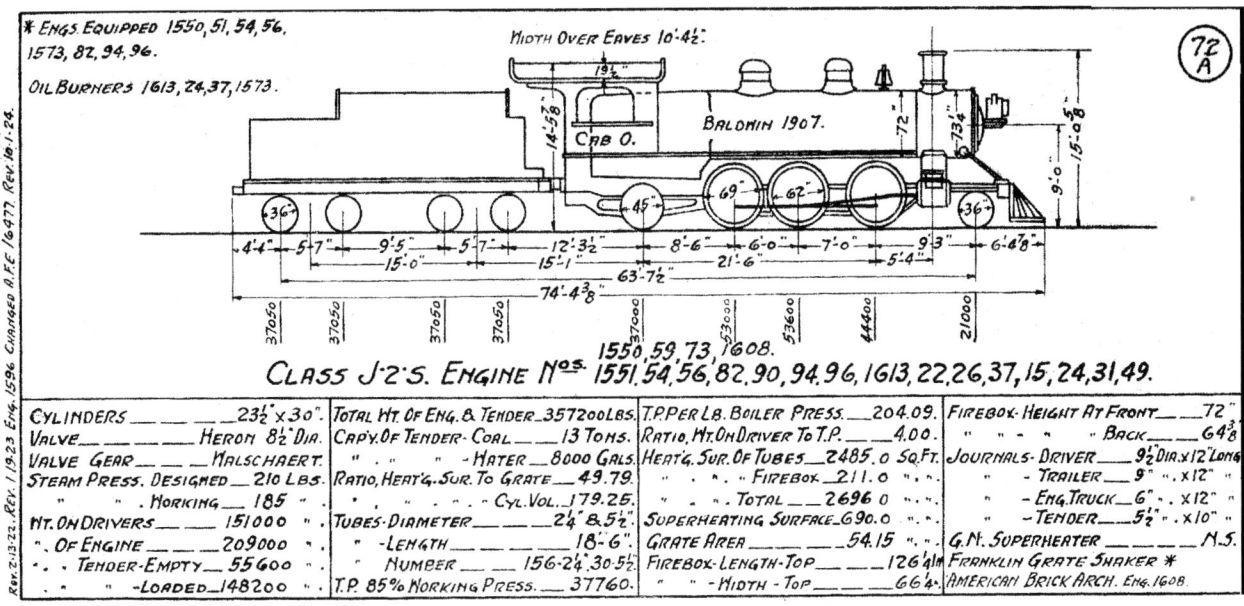

Rev. 2-13-23. Rev. 1 19-23. Eng. Changed A.F.E. 16477 Rev. 18-1-24. Eng. 16596

* ENGS. EQUIPPED 1550, 51, 54, 56, 1573, 82, 94, 96.

OIL BURNERS 1613, 24, 37, 1573.

WIDTH OVER EAVES 10'-4½"

BALDWIN 1907.

CAB O.

72/A

1550, 59, 73, 1608.

CLASS J-2-S. ENGINE Nos 1551, 54, 56, 82, 90, 94, 96, 1613, 22, 26, 37, 15, 24, 31, 49.

CYLINDERS ___ 23½" x 30".	TOTAL WT. OF ENG. & TENDER 357200LBS.	T.P. PER LB. BOILER PRESS. ___ 204.09.	FIREBOX- HEIGHT AT FRONT ___ 72"
VALVE ___ HERON 8½" DIA.	CAP'Y. OF TENDER- COAL ___ 13 TONS.	RATIO, WT. ON DRIVER TO T.P. ___ 4.00.	" " " BACK ___ 64⅜
VALVE GEAR ___ WALSCHAERT.	" " " -WATER ___ 8000 GALS.	HEAT'G. SUR. OF TUBES ___ 2485.0 SQ.FT.	JOURNALS- DRIVER ___ 9½"DIA.x12"LONG
STEAM PRESS. DESIGNED ___ 210 LBS.	RATIO, HEAT'G. SUR. TO GRATE ___ 49.79	" " " FIREBOX ___ 211.0 "	" - TRAILER ___ 9 ". x12"
" WORKING 185 "	" " " CYL. VOL. 179.25.	" " " TOTAL ___ 2696.0 "	" - ENG. TRUCK ___ 6 ". x12"
WT. ON DRIVERS ___ 151000 "	TUBES- DIAMETER ___ 2¼" & 5½".	SUPERHEATING SURFACE ___ 690.0 "	" - TENDER ___ 5½ ". x10".
" OF ENGINE ___ 209000 "	" -LENGTH ___ 18'-6".	GRATE AREA ___ 54.15 "	G.N. SUPERHEATER ___ N.S.
" TENDER-EMPTY ___ 55600 "	" NUMBER ___ 156-2¼, 30-5½.	FIREBOX- LENGTH-TOP ___ 126'4½	FRANKLIN GRATE SHAKER *
" " -LOADED ___ 148200 "	T.P. 85% WORKING PRESS. ___ 37760.	" " -WIDTH- TOP ___ 66'4"	AMERICAN BRICK ARCH. ENG.1608.

J-1S 1524 was another superheated oil burner, shown here in Seattle on an unknown date. This engine is known to have been in passenger service in 1929, as is shown here, entering King Street Station. GNRHS collection.

This view shows the engineer's side of the same engine in the previous photograph. No. 1524 was photographed in the GN yards at Vancouver, BC, in June 1929. Bordertown collection of GTC Collectibles.

J-1S 1531 is shown at St.Paul, MN, in 1922, only six years before it was scrapped. The tender is quite similar to the original, but has had sideboards added to the coal bunker. J. Foster Adams photograph from the GNRHS collection.

J-2S 1613 had been superheated in 1915, and has also been converted to burn oil. It was photographed at Interbay (Seattle), WA, in 1927. Bordertown collection of GTC Collectibles.

The fireman's side of GN 1613 is shown in the GN yards at Vancouver, BC, in 1929. Bordertown collection of GTC Collectibles.

While J-2S 1624 was not formally retired until October 1936, this photograph taken in Seattle, WA, in November 1935 shows that the engine has already lost its headlight. Collection of Harold K. Vollrath.

Class J-1 No. 1524 is shown running as the first section of a scheduled coast train, enroute to Vancouver, BC. This freight engine was likely pressed into passenger service because of high traffic volume due to a Shriners convention at Vancouver in June 1929. Bordertown collection of GTC Collectibles.

Another J-class in passenger service, this time J-2 No. 1647, is on train No. 14, the local, at Willmar, MN, in 1909. This seems to be a normal assignment. Martin A. Johnson collection.

The locomotives thus rebuilt were Nos. 1517, 1519, 1523, 1525, 1528, 1552, 1553, 1569, 1570, 1572, 1598, 1612, 1616, 1619 and 1634.

The Prairie locomotives were, of course, designed as freight engines for the more level portions of the Great Northern system. Throughout their service lives they were fairly light, though fast freight power (because of the 69-inch drivers). Apparently the nearly equal spacing of the drivers combined with the two-wheel pilot truck caused a stability problem when the engines were operated at higher speeds. The engine developed a tendency to rock back and forth, pivoting on the center driver.[9] Regardless, the large number of engines in these two classes is an indication of some success for its era.

The earliest assignment rosters known to the authors (1936) document only the assignments of the last remaining Prairies. These were assigned to the Dakota and Spokane Divisions. Photographs, however, indicate that the locomotives were probably assigned throughout the system for light freight and occasional passenger use. Number 1647 was used on passenger trains 9 and 10 (Willmar and Dakota Divisions) in 1909. The 1524 was in passenger service between Seattle and Vancouver, BC in 1929, although this may have been a temporary assignment.

While GN's Prairies left the roster early, one J-1 (No. 1549) and sixteen J-2's were sold to the Spokane, Portland & Seattle, where some of them remained in use until the late 1940's.

Class J-2 engine 1626 is shown at an unknown date and location, but with what is probably its original headlight.
Great Northern Railway photograph from the collection of Wolfgang F. Weber.

Notes:

1. "New Locomotives for the Great Northern," The Railroad Gazette, Volume 41, Number 17 (October 26, 1906).
2. Ibid.
3. Great Northern Railway Company Equipment Completion Report and Unit Record of Property Changes – Equipment. Examined in GN Valuation Department office.
4. Interstate Commerce Commission Valuation Engineering Report for the Great Northern Railway Company as of June 30, 1915.
5. Great Northern Railway New Equipment Registers 6 and 7 (Historic Car Records Volumes 41 and 42), Minnesota Historical Society.
6. Interstate Commerce Commission, op. cit.
7. Interstate Commerce Commission, op. cit.
8. Great Northern Railway Authorities for Expenditure (AFE) 12447 (Written February 3, 1920), 13522 (date unknown), 13638 (Approved May 6, 1920), 14017 (Approved May 27, 1920), 14335 (Approved June 24, 1920), 14700 (Approved July 15, 1920), 14701 (Approved July 15, 1920), 16132 (Approved November 21, 1920), 16282 (Approved January 1, 1921) and 16477 (Approved January 22, 1921).
9. Arthur D. Taylor, "Great Northern Class H-6 Pacific," Great Northern Railway Historical Society Reference Sheet No. 233, September 1995.

This builders view of 1700 shows the four-cylinder, balanced compound machinery, with its non-symmetrical counterbalancing. Collection of H. L. Broadbelt.

Chapter 16
Class K 4-4-2 Atlantic

The K-1 Atlantics were built by Baldwin in 1906 as part of an order which included 50 J-1 Prairies and 20 H-2 Pacifics. These three classes were all similar in design, and used many interchangeable parts. All had Belpaire fireboxes.

The Atlantics were built as Balanced Compounds, an improvement on the original Vauclain compound of 1889. They were provided with 15-inch and 25-inch by 26-inch cylinders. The high pressure cylinders were located between the frames and connected with the forward set of drivers, which had a crank axle. A Stephenson valve motion was used with the eccentrics on the front axle. The low pressure cylinders were outside the frames on a line with the high pressure cylinders and were connected to the rear drivers.[1] Each pair of high-pressure and low-pressure cylinders was controlled by a single piston valve with multiple packing rings. The rods from each pair were set 180 degrees from each other, giving a nearly perfect balance. The left side – right side setting was the normal 90 degrees. The result was a very smooth running engine. They were the state of the art at the time. With two cylinders inside the frame, two cranks (double-throw) had to be put on the front axle. This no doubt increased the stress on the axle and led to more frequent breakage. Not only was it hard to maintain the inside machinery, the design led to higher failure rates of the inside machinery (see below regarding replacement of the valve motion and simpling of the engines). The fact that these locomotives had four

cylinders accounts for the rather odd-appearing placement of driver counterweights in the builder's photos of these engines.

The locomotives were built with an inside-frame Rushton trailing truck, which carried an enormous (for 1906) weight of 50,000 pounds. One of the engines was equipped with a Baldwin smokebox superheater (see Chapter 3).[2] It was apparently removed before the locomotives had been in service very long. The total engine weight of the K-1's as built was 208,000 pounds, 105,000 of which were on the drivers. The boiler was designed to operate at a pressure of 210 psi, which resulted in a tractive effort of 23,000 pounds. The original Class K-1 tenders had a capacity of 8,000 gallons of water and 13 tons of coal. After delivery during the spring of 1906, these locomotives were put to work on the *Oriental Limited*.

GN began replacing the original Stephenson valve gear with Walschaerts valve gear in 1914, and apparently completed the changeover about 1917. One of the locomotives (1705) was simpled in 1915, while the remaining nine were not completed until 1920 and 1921. Quoting from AFE 16484:

They are constructed so that the high pressure engines are between the frames, connected to a special crank front axle. They are very troublesome in upkeep, costly in maintenance and difficult to properly inspect. The high pressure engines are not accessible under ordinary conditions and, therefore, do not get the attention they would otherwise. The benefit derived from compounding is doubtful, and is at any rate more than offset by the objectionable features in design. It is now proposed to disconnect the high pressure engines, change the front wheels and axle to ordinary design and bush down the outside or low pressure cylinders, thereby making a simple engine. This will eliminate the trouble mentioned and lessen the expense in keeping these engines in repair.

Engine 1702 was rebuilt to a simple type under AFE 15730. In making test runs, this engine was found to perform very efficiently. The engine is now assigned to train 27 on the Montana Division.[3]

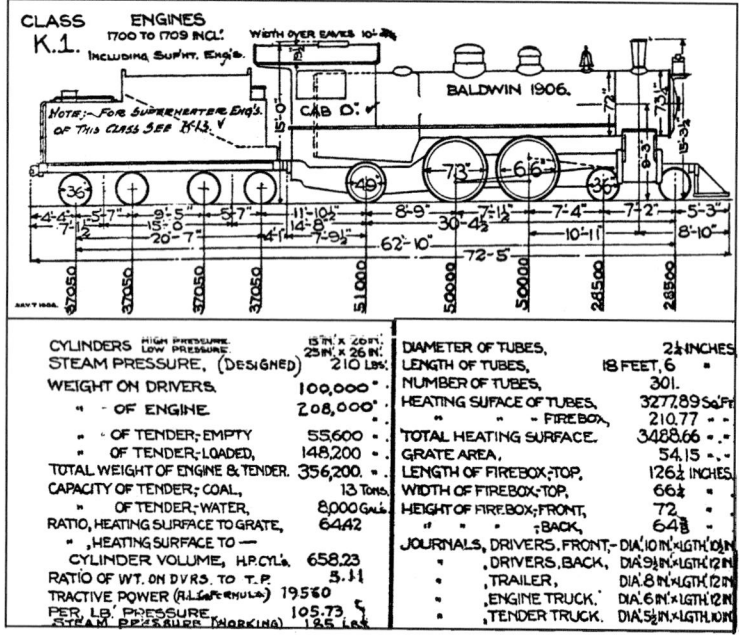

This diagram shows the K-1 in its original balanced-compound, four-cylinder configuration.

Cylinders on the simpled engines measured 21 inches by 26 inches. The new tractive effort was 26,700 pounds.

GN began to apply superheaters and outside steam pipes to the engines in 1914, work that continued until 1924. Most received GN New Style 30-element superheaters, but engines 1702 and 1704 received Schmidt 32-element superheaters, at least for a time. Between 1918 and 1920, all ten of the K-1's received outside bearing trailing trucks.

In addition, all members of the class had been converted to oil burners, their tenders having an oil capacity of 4,500 gallons. From 1923 to 1925, the entire class received Delta trailing trucks with boosters having 10,104 pounds of tractive effort. Total engine weight by this time had grown to 227,300 pounds, with 124,900 pounds on drivers. Tractive effort (without boosters) had increased to 26,700 pounds.

As late as 1925, the booster-equipped locomotives were still used on trains 1, 2, 27 and 28 between Havre and Wolf Point, Montana, though by then they had been considerably modified.[4] After being withdrawn from mainline service, two engines, 1701 and 1708, remained on the Butte Division. However it seems they never ran again, with photos showing them on a scrap line as early as 1934.

The boosters were removed in 1930 and 1931 from all but 1701 and 1708, which kept boosters until 1937. After the boosters were removed, four of engines (1701, 1702, 1705, and 1708) lost their Delta trailing trucks. Since the 1701 and 1708 boosters and Delta trucks were removed in 1937, and they were scrapped in January 1938, it is likely they sat without a replacement. Number 1702 received an O-1 Hodges trailing truck in 1931 and the 1705 in 1939. Two of the class (Nos. 1700 and 1707) were equipped with Elesco exhaust steam injectors in 1926 and 1927. Photographic evidence indicates that the exhaust steam injector was removed from 1700 about 1934 or 1935, but 1707 may well have kept the exhaust steam injector until it was sold for scrap in 1940.

Most of the engines were converted back to coal burners in the late 1920's and early 1930's, and most were moved to the eastern divisions.

The 1705 was the first to be converted to a simple engine, in 1915. It was selected by the GN for a publicity photo on the Oriental Limited after installation of its booster in March 1925. The photo was likely taken the same year in eastern Montana. Collection of William Bissinger.

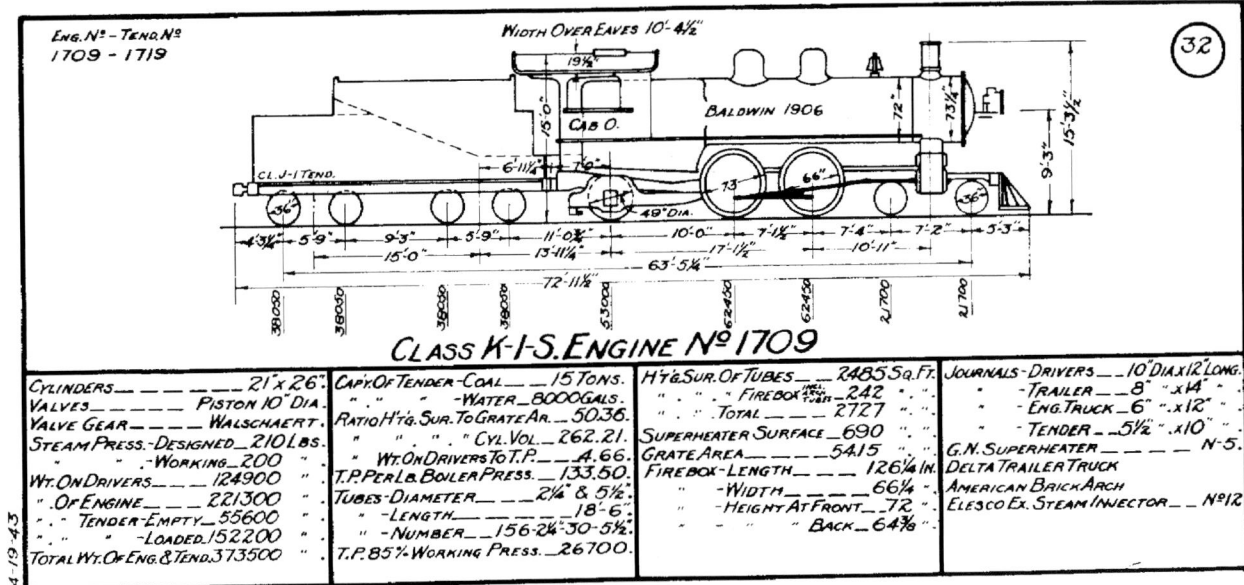

CYLINDERS — — — 21"x 26".	CAP.Y OF TENDER - COAL — 15 TONS.	H'T'G.SUR.OF TUBES — 2485 SQ.FT.	JOURNALS-DRIVERS — 10"DIA.x 12"LONG.
VALVES — — — — PISTON 10"DIA.	" " " -WATER 8000 GALS.	" " FIREBOX ⁵ᵗᵉᵉˡ — 242 " "	" -TRAILER — 8 " x14 "
VALVE GEAR — — — WALSCHAERT.	RATIO H'T'G. SUR.TO GRATE AR. — 50.36.	" " " .TOTAL — — 2727 " "	" -ENG.TRUCK — 6 " x12 "
STEAM PRESS.-DESIGNED — 210 LBS.	" " " " CYL.VOL. 262.21.	SUPERHEATER SURFACE — 690 " "	" -TENDER — 5½" .x10 "
" "-WORKING 200 "	" WT.ON DRIVERS TO T.P. — 4.66.	GRATE AREA — — — 54.15 " "	G.N.SUPERHEATER — — — N-5.
WT.ON DRIVERS — — 124900 "	T.P.PER LB. BOILER PRESS. — 133.50.	FIREBOX-LENGTH — — 126¼IN.	DELTA TRAILER TRUCK
" OF ENGINE — — 221300 "	TUBES-DIAMETER — — 2¼ & 5½.	" -WIDTH — — 66¼ "	AMERICAN BRICK ARCH
" " TENDER-EMPTY 55600 "	" -LENGTH — — 18'-6"	" -HEIGHT AT FRONT 72 "	ELESCO EX.STEAM INJECTOR — N°12
" " -LOADED 152200 "	" -NUMBER 156-2¼ 30-5½.	" " BACK 64⅜ "	
TOTAL WT.OF ENG.& TEND. 373500 "	T.P.85% WORKING PRESS. 26700.		

This diagram shows the K-1 as a simple, two-cylinder engine, with Walschaerts valve gear.

The 1702 was photographed at St. Paul, MN, in 1932 with a Hodges trailing truck after its booster was removed. A Chesney photograph (RPS) from the collection of Norman F. Priebe.

The 1704 is in service at Minneapolis on October 17, 1931, one month after the Badger began running from there. It shows an example of the Kelly feed water heater, or branch pipe heater. Robert Graham photograph from the GNRHS collection.

Here are two very similar views of the 1700 in passenger service from St. Paul. But look closely, they are not taken on the same day and the engine has been modified between the photos. This view of the 1700 was taken in July 1938. Collection of Harold K. Vollrath.

A year later the 1700 was again photographed with the Badger, train No. 24. This view is on July 9, 1939. The spoked pilot wheels have been moved from the front to the rear of the lead truck. F. Wesley Krambeck photograph, courtesy of Jack W. Farrell.

The 1703, 1704 and the 1709 were most frequently the power on the Alexandrian, Nos. 11 and 12, between St. Paul and Fargo during their last years of service. Here the 1704 is awaiting departure at St. Paul. Robert Graham photograph from the collection of William Raia.

The 1703 is on train No. 11, the Alexandrian, at Moorhead, MN, during 1934. Collection of William Bissinger.

The 1700, 1702, 1705, 1706 and the 1707 were in the power pool for the Badger, Nos. 23 and 24, between St. Paul and Duluth, during the 1930's. The 1706 is shown here outbound on August 22, 1935, at St. Paul. Robert Graham photograph from the collection of William Raia.

The 1706 had just been shopped at Superior prior to this photograph, indicating it would have continued use in this service. October 5, 1936. R. M. Hanft photograph from the collection of Norman F. Priebe.

Only 1701 and 1708 finished their service lives on Lines West (on the Butte Division), probably still as oil burners. The others were transferred east to the Willmar, Dakota and Mesabi Divisions, bumped from transcontinental service when the S-2 Northerns arrived.

K-class engines were used on the *Badger* and on the Dakota Division's *Alexandrian* in the 1930's. Otherwise, the engines were used, apparently, for work train service. A Willmar Division engineman mentioned the 1704 as "a good snowplowing engine". Only one of the engines, No. 1709, received a power reverse gear, in 1937. In 1947, it was retired as the last of its class. Most of the engines were scrapped between 1938 and 1941.

The *Badger* trains were cut back to terminate in Minneapolis instead of St. Paul from September 1931 through the summer of 1937. (Passengers for No. 24 at St. Paul were ferried via No. 11.) During this time, the use of the K-1 on the *Badger* was suspended for a period during the depth of the Depression. Beginning in June 1932, and ending in October 1934, motor cars were assigned to the *Badger*.[5]

Since the 1704 was stored at Superior during part of this time, it is likely this is when it was put into work train service. This also explains why there are photos of K-1's at the Minneapolis Junction roundhouse during the time frame. In addition, this extends the possibility that the train assignments stated in several of the photo captions are valid only from 1936 to 1940.

During their service lives, the coal capacity of K-1 tenders was increased to 15 tons. The 8,000 gallon K-1 tenders were classified as Style 52 by the GN. One of these tenders was lengthened by five feet to provide a water capacity of 10,000 gallons, and was classified as Style 53 (though it was no longer assigned to a K-1 locomotive). As usual on the GN, many of the K-1's lost their original tenders and had them replaced with tenders from other classes. However, the authors have found no evidence that any of the K-1's ever had anything but 8,000 gallon tenders assigned to them.

The new diesels 5700 A&B and 5701 A&B definitely closed the era on the K class upon their arrival in mid-1941.

The 1707 is between runs at Jackson Street Roundhouse in St. Paul. The Elesco exhaust steam injector shows clearly in this view. At the time of the photo, 1940, it was power for the Badger. *The engine was scrapped shortly after, in October 1940. Wilbur C. Whittaker.*

Notes:

1. Paul T. Warner, 1925. "The Great Northern Railway and Its Locomotives", *Baldwin Locomotives*.

2. "New Locomotives for the Great Northern". *The Railroad Gazette*, Vol. 41, No. 17, p. 372 (October 26, 1906).

3. Great Northern Railway Authority for Expenditure 16484 (Approved December 31, 1920).

4. Paul T. Warner, *op. cit.*

5. Great Northern Railway Passenger timetables, September 1931 through Autumn 1937, Table No. 13.

The engines of the L-1 class were first numbered in the 1800 series. Before arrival of the second order of L-2's, they were renumbered to the 1900 series. The engines were impressively large, and the boiler was sufficiently large to serve beyond the life of the Mallet articulated as a class O-6 Mikado. Note the lack of sand boxes on the pilot deck in the as-built configuration. Collection of H. L. Broadbelt.

Chapter 17

Class L 2-6-6-2 Articulated

Class L-1

Along with the Prairie, Pacific and Atlantic locomotives ordered in 1906, Great Northern ordered its first articulated locomotives from Baldwin. These were five 2-6-6-2 Mallet compounds and were the heaviest engines yet completed by Baldwin. The engines were designed to operate on 10-degree curves. All four cylinders had slide valves and Walschaert valve gear.[1] The locomotives attracted considerable interest at the time, and drawings were even published in *The Railroad Gazette*.[2] They were numbered 1800-1804 and were placed in Class L-1. They had 21½-inch by 32-inch high-pressure (rear) cylinders, and 33-inch by 32-inch low-pressure (front) cylinders and the 55-inch drivers typical of GN freight engines of the time. They were the first of several engine classes (L-1, M-1, N-1, O-1, O-4 and P-1) to have the large 78 square foot grate. Despite this large grate, they did not receive stokers and were converted to burn oil between 1914 and 1916. Quoting from Warner:

> The Mallet articulated locomotives were specially built for pushing service on the 2.2 per cent grades of the Cascade Division. At that time, freight traffic on this division was being handled by Consolidation type locomotives … and two such locomotives were capable of taking 1050 tons over the mountain. The only Mallet locomotive then in service

in the United States was one which had been built by the American Locomotive Company for the Baltimore and Ohio in 1904, and which had proved a success. Mr. Hill saw in this type a means of increasing the tonnage per train on the Cascade Division without increasing the number of motive power units, and he accordingly ordered the five Baldwin Mallets. These locomotives were so large that they could not enter the roundhouses nor be turned on the turntables then in use, and hence had to be so designed that they could safely back down the grades after helping trains up. To facilitate this, the 2-6-6-2 wheel arrangement was adopted, with a two-wheeled radial truck at each end; so that, while the total wheel base was 44 feet 10 inches, the rigid wheel base was only ten feet. The locomotives were the heaviest in use at that time, weighing, without tender, 355,000 pounds, and developing a tractive force of 69,900 pounds….

These locomotives were at once placed in service on the Cascade Mountain grades, and although most novel in design, did excellent work. The tonnage per train was increased from 1050 tons, handled by two Consolidation type locomotives, to 1300 tons handled by one Consolidation and one Mallet, the latter pushing 800 tons with no increase in fuel consumption as compared with the Consolidation, which handled the remainder. The new locomotives proved thoroughly reliable in operation, and in consideration of their capacity their maintenance charges were moderate. [3]

In December 1907 and January 1908 the five L-1's were renumbered from the 1800 series to the 1900 series to clear numbers for the second order of L-2's. Beginning in March 1908 a second order of twenty L-1's began being delivered. Three of these were retained by the CB&Q in Chicago, so the net receipt by GN was only seventeen. The last three were renumbered to replace the engines kept by the Burlington so the L-1 number series ended up as 1900-1921. With this additional motive power, the heavier L-1's were placed in road service as well as pusher service on the Cascade Division.

The two orders of L-1's had quite different tenders. The first order had tenders very similar to the early H-2 tenders with arch bar trucks

and "rolled" sides on the coal bunker. The second order had straight sides with bracing over the top and pedestal trucks.

Class L-2

The success of the heavy Mallets in pusher service led Great Northern to order 25 more 2-6-6-2's from Baldwin in 1907, but these were smaller engines than the first five. The boiler had the same dimensions as the H-2 Pacifics. They weighed much less than the first order, 288,000 pounds. They had 20-inch by 30-inch high-pressure cylinders and 31-inch by 30-inch low-pressure cylinders, 55-inch drivers and a grate area of 53.4 square feet, similar to the Pacifics.[4] These engines, numbered as 1805-1829 and classified as L-2's, were assigned as road engines between Leavenworth and Spokane, where they were rated at 1450 tons, replacing Consolidations rated at 1100 tons.[5]

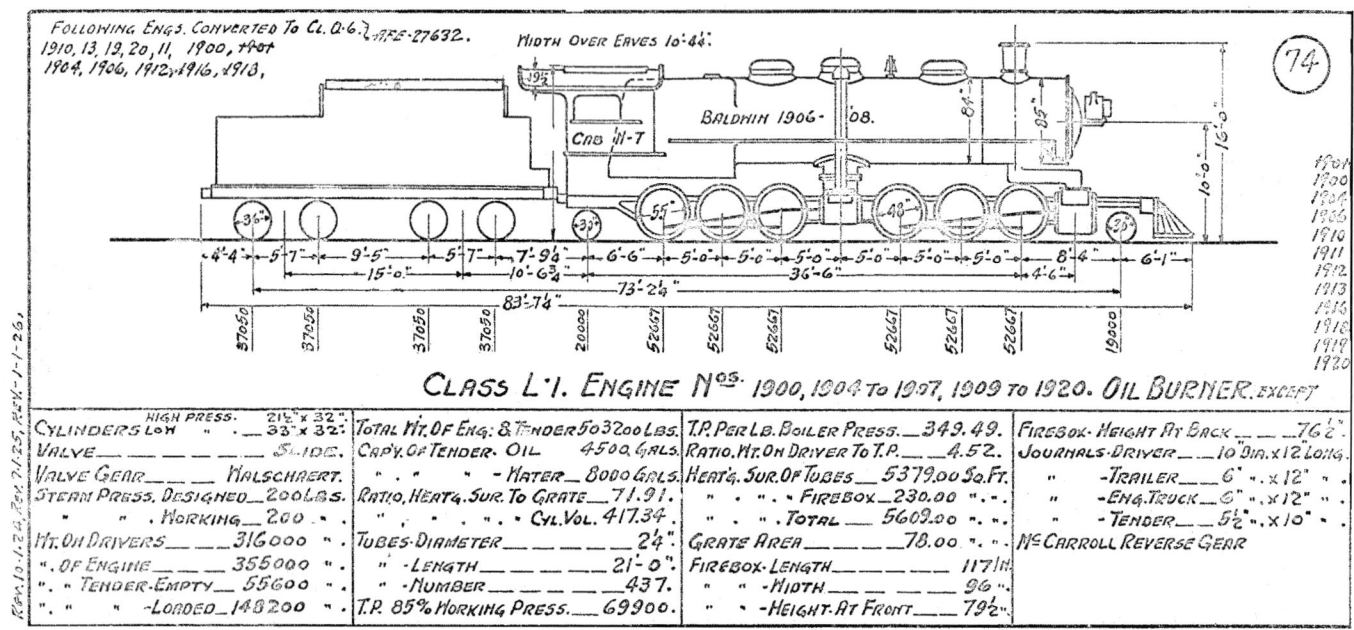

A renumbered L-1, the 1907 is at Leavenworth in September 1909. The engine had been delivered as No. 1924, but was renumbered because the Burlington retained three L-1's (1905-1907) at Chicago. Photograph by Wheeler Studio, courtesy of George Fischer.

In March 1908 the GN began receiving a second order of twenty L-2's (numbered as 1800-1804 and 1830-1844). While the L-1's remained on the Cascade Division, the lighter L-2's were distributed on more eastern divisions. "On the Kalispell Division, between Whitefish and Cut Bank, one of these [L-2] locomotives handled 1700 tons over grades of 0.8 per cent, being assisted up the 1.8 per cent grade from Essex to Summit by one of the heavy Mallet pushers. As compared with the single expansion Consolidation type locomotives, both classes of Mallets showed a very material saving in fuel." [6]

Like the L-1 class, the L-2's were delivered with two different style tenders, though neither was like the L-1 tenders. The first (1907) order had tenders resembling the H-4 tenders with rolled sides on the coal bunkers and pedestal trucks. The second (1908) order had straight sides but lacked the exterior bracing.

Modifications and Dispositions

Only a few of the 2-6-6-2's received superheaters. Among the L-1's, only 1902, 1903, 1908 and 1921 were superheated (from 1916 through 1919) with GN New Style superheaters. In 1916 Nos. 1901 and 1903 (at least) received piston valves on the high-pressure cylinders. At the time they were superheated, the high pressure cylinders were changed to 24 x 32 inches, and tractive effort increased to 73,460 lb.

Eight of the L-2's (1814, 1815, 1816, 1822, 1824, 1825, 1826 and 1842) were superheated, all in 1915. Nos. 1803, 1813, 1816, 1826 and 1842 received piston valves on their high-pressure cylinders. From 1916 through 1920 the engines all received steel pilot beams, and shortly thereafter steel pilots.

While all of the 2-6-6-2's were built to burn coal many of them were converted to burn oil. The L-1 tenders carried 13 tons of coal, while the

The 1907 is at Skykomish in a later view. By this time it is without its front boiler sand dome. Courtesy Burlington Northern.

The L-2 class was distinctly smaller than the L-1's, intended for road service on flatter ground, and to be an upgrade from the F-Class Consolidations. The small boiler however was not much larger than that of a Consolidation. This photograph shows the style tender delivered with the 1907 order. Collection of Harold K. Vollrath.

In 1908, several of the L-2 class are lined up at Baldwin Locomotive Works prior to delivery. The tender style is distinctly different from that shown with 1810. Collection of H. L. Broadbelt.

The 1805 is shown as it appeared during set-up at Dale Street shops. The date is 1907, and the well-dressed gentleman may very well be a GN officer. William H. Fowler photograph from the collection of Jerrold F. Hilton.

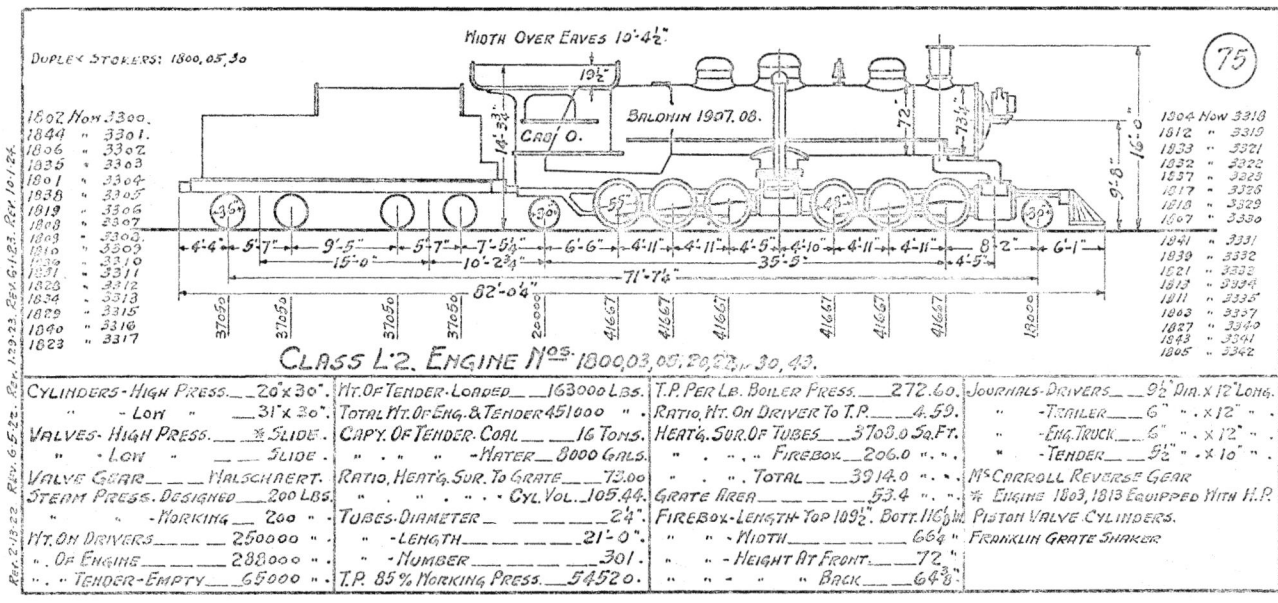

CLASS L 2 ENGINE Nos. 1800, 03, 05, 20, 22 30, 43.

CYLINDERS - HIGH PRESS.__20"x 30".	WT. OF TENDER-LOADED____163000 LBS.	T.P. PER LB. BOILER PRESS.___272.60.	JOURNALS-DRIVERS___9½ DIA. x 12"LONG.
" - LOW "___31"x 30".	TOTAL WT. OF ENG.& TENDER 451000 ".	RATIO, WT. ON DRIVER TO T.P.___4.59.	" -TRAILER___6 " . x 12 ".
VALVES- HIGH PRESS.___ % SLIDE .	CAPY. OF TENDER. COAL___16 TONS.	HEAT'G. SUR. OF TUBES___3708.0 SQ.FT.	" -ENG. TRUCK___6 " . x 12 ".
" - LOW " ___ SLIDE .	" . " . -WATER___8000 GALS.	" . " . FIREBOX___206.0 ". ".	" -TENDER___9½ ". x 10 ".
VALVE GEAR___WALSCHAERT.	RATIO, HEAT'G. SUR. TO GRATE___73.00	" . " . TOTAL___3914.0 ". ".	McCARROLL REVERSE GEAR
STEAM PRESS. DESIGNED___200 LBS.	" . " . " . CYL. VOL.___105.44	GRATE AREA___53.4 ". ".	% ENGINE 1803, 1813 EQUIPPED WITH H.P.
" " -WORKING ___ 200 "	TUBES-DIAMETER___2¼".	FIREBOX-LENGTH TOP 109½". BOTT. 116¾"	PISTON VALVE CYLINDERS.
WT. ON DRIVERS___250000 "	" -LENGTH___21'-0".	" " - WIDTH___66¾ "	FRANKLIN GRATE SHAKER
" " OF ENGINE___288000 "	" -NUMBER___301.	" " - HEIGHT AT FRONT___72 "	
" " TENDER-EMPTY___65000 "	T.P. 85% WORKING PRESS.___54520.	" " - " " BACK___64⅜ "	

No. 1903 is an example of an L-1 in service after renumbering from the 1800 series. Note the smoke deflector, something received by all steam engines working on the west slope of the Cascade Range. The photograph was taken at Skykomish, WA. GNRHS collection.

The engineers side of the 1903 is shown at Delta shops on June 9, 1920. Over the passage of time it has lost its forward boiler sand dome in favor of additional sand capacity on the pilot deck. Note that it is also an oil burner now, and it appears that the coal bunker has been extended rearward to accommodate a larger oil bunker. This was one of the few superheated L-1's, and had received piston valves on its high-pressure cylinders. J. Foster Adams photograph from the GNRHS collection.

The 1912 is in road service at Cascade Tunnel yard, eastbound, in 1908. Collection of H. L. Broadbelt.

*Perhaps the largest sand box ever to be mounted on a pilot deck graced the 1900 at Skykomish, in 1908 or shortly after.
It had both of its boiler sand domes too, in contrast to the 1903. Lee Pickett photograph from the collection of Jerrold F. Hilton.*

Another version of many different pilot sand boxes on the L-1 class is this one on the 1901 at Skykomish. Lee Pickett photograph from the collection of Jerrold F. Hilton.

The large L-1's were always a favorite of their crews and it was difficult to find a photo where they were not posing alongside. The same is true here with the 1916, believed to be at Skykomish. This engine carries the most common configuration of pilot deck sand box, two medium diameter cylinders. Unknown source.

L-2 tenders carried 12. Both carried 8,000 gallons of water. The L-2's received stokers between 1918 and 1921, when such devices began to come into common use.

As of 1908, the Great Northern apparently considered the 2-6-6-2 design to be quite successful. However, in 1911, GN began taking delivery of 2-8-2 Mikados, which was the first step in making the 2-6-6-2's obsolete. The Mikados had larger 63-inch drivers, which of course made them faster than the low-drivered 2-6-6-2's. Additional Mikados were received in 1913, 1916, 1917, 1918, 1919 and 1920. As a result, from 1921 through 1925, all of the smaller L-2's were rebuilt in company shops to O-5 2-8-2's. At this time thick tires were put on the 55-inch drivers to bring them up to a 63-inch diameter. In 1925 and 1926, the larger L-1's were rebuilt to Class O-6 2-8-2's, again with thick tires to increase the driver diameter.

The 1818 is shown at Everett, WA, on June 9, 1920 after shopping at Delta. The engine had lost its front sand dome, and prominently displayed a dimple in the air tank to clear the valve motion. Not present when delivered, the dimple must have allowed the engines considerably more tolerance on tight curves, likely on industrial sidings. It also was now an oil burner. J. Foster Adams photograph from the collection of Kenneth R. Middleton.

By 1915 the L-2's were on the Dakota Division. This view of 1804 and another at Minot, ND, show a different type of coal pusher on the 1908 L-2 tenders. This coal pusher design did not require the common GN "grape arbor". By 1921, these engines were being rebuilt to class O-5. Courtesy U.S. Library of Congress.

Notes:

1. "Mallet Compound Locomotive for the Great Northern". *The Railroad Gazette*, Volume 41, Number 7, p. 148 (August 17, 1906).

2. "Mallet Compound Locomotive for the Great Northern". *The Railroad Gazette*, Volume 41, Number 15, p. 315 (October 12, 1906).

3. Paul T. Warner, 1925. "The Great Northern Railway and Its Locomotives", *Baldwin Locomotives*.

4. *Ibid.*

5. Fr. Dale Peterka, 2005. "The GN L-Class Mallets", Great Northern Historical Society Reference Sheet 332.

6. Paul T. Warner, *op. cit.*

The builders photo of the 1959 clearly shows the piston valves and water delivery routed through the boiler fire tube type feedwater heater. Note the larger front cylinders, the obvious sign that the class was a compound locomotive. The cab lettering called the engine an L-3 at the time. Collection of H. L. Broadbelt.

Chapter 18
Class M 2-6-8-0 Articulated

In early 1910, Great Northern received ten articulated locomotives from Baldwin having a wheel arrangement new to the road: the 2-6-8-0. The engines, numbered as 1950-1959, had straight-topped boilers with GN's typical Belpaire firebox and became Class M-1. The design of the boiler was somewhat unusual in that the boiler tubes were only 15 feet long (the L-class engines had 21-foot boiler tubes), with a short combustion chamber just ahead of the tube sheet. The forward portion of the boiler had a feedwater heater which was comprised of 582 2¼-inch tubes 5 feet 2 inches long. The feedwater in the tubes was heated by the hot exhaust gases.[1] This particular boiler style, called a "Vauclain separable boiler", had distinctive features including a collar separating the feedwater heater/smokebox unit from the main portion of the boiler. It also had a distinctive feedwater pipe running from the top of the front unit to check valves on the rear (main) boiler.[2]

The engines were Mallet compounds, with the high pressure (rear) cylinders having a 23-inch diameter and 32-inch stroke, while the low pressure (front) cylinders had 35-inch diameter cylinders with a 32-inch stroke. Unlike previous orders of articulateds, the M-1's had piston valves and superheaters. While the trade press of the time indicated that the engines were equipped with Emerson superheaters[3], the earliest diagrams found indicate the they had Great Northern Old Style superheaters (as indicated in Chapter 3 these terms were apparently synonymous). The engines had 55-inch drivers and were equipped

with Ragonnet power reverse gears and Walschaert valve gear. The engines operated at a boiler pressure of 200 psi, which produced a tractive effort of 78,360 lb. Even though the engines had a grate area of 78 square feet, the engines were not equipped with stokers when received. These were applied by GN in the 1917-1919 time frame. It is interesting to note that the builder's photo of GN 1959, from the first order, shows the cab side of the locomotive with the class lettered as "L-3" rather than "M-1", but this apparently didn't last long. Later in 1910, twenty-five additional locomotives (Nos. 1960-1984) of the same design were received.

The 1950 was tested on the Pennsylvania Railroad from December 23, 1909 through February 11, 1910. This may have been at the initiative of the Baldwin Company and was prior to the delivery to the Great Northern. The engine was given a good workout in all types of service: road, helper and hump pusher. The testing included the use of a dynamometer car. A brief summary of the test follows.

The boiler was adequate, and never taxed to capacity during the testing. Only once was there trouble with steaming, and that likely was due to "too heavy a fire". On the other hand, the engine did very poorly in pulling tests. The tests were run to see if the GN mallet could do the work of two Consolidations. Tractive power fell off significantly as speed increased, faster than that of a Pennsylvania class H6 Consolidation used for comparison. By the time the 1950 reached 29 mph it could

The M-2's were the principal freight engines on the Great Falls to Butte line in 1936 but their numbers declined throughout World War II.
Immediately after the war, the 1973 was photographed between Sieben and Wolf Creek, MT, in October 1945. The timetable direction
is eastbound. Ben Cutler (RPS) photograph from the collection of Norman F. Priebe.

This rare view of an M-1 shows GN 1953 at an unknown location some time before October 1921 when it received a steel pilot. Unknown source.

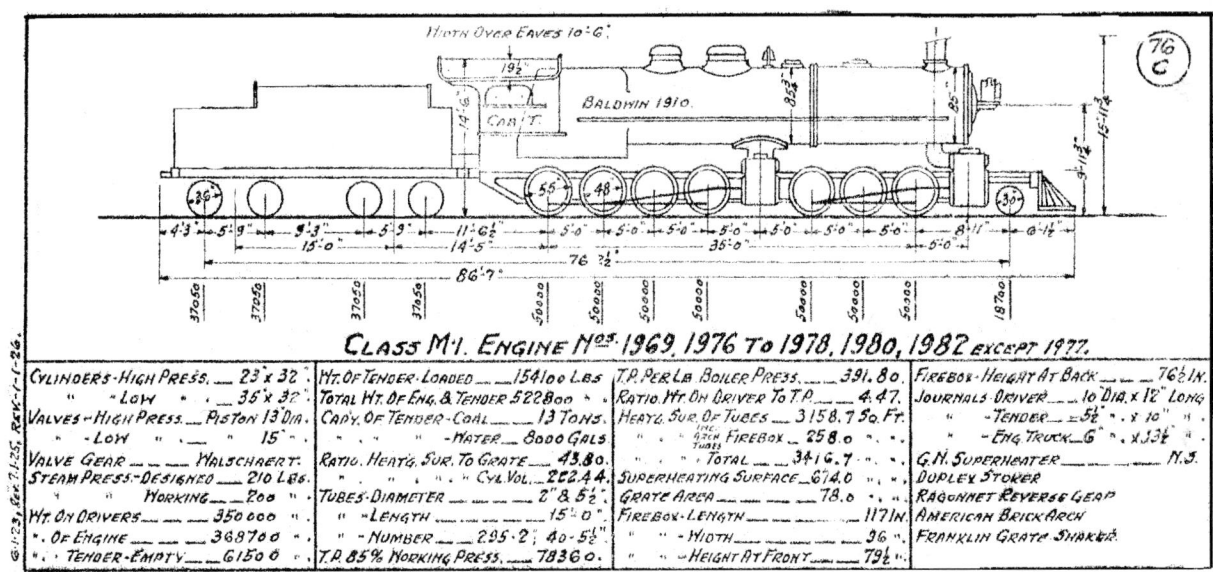

CLASS M-1. ENGINE Nos. 1969, 1976 TO 1978, 1980, 1982 EXCEPT 1977.

CYLINDERS-HIGH PRESS.___ 23 x 32	WT. OF TENDER-LOADED ___154100 LBS	T.P. PER LB. BOILER PRESS.___391.80	FIREBOX-HEIGHT AT BACK ___ 76½ IN.
" -LOW " ___ 35 x 32	TOTAL WT. OF ENG. & TENDER 522800 "	RATIO. WT. ON DRIVER TO T.P. ___ 4.47	JOURNALS-DRIVER___ 10 DIA. x 12" LONG
VALVES-HIGH PRESS.___PISTON 13 DIA.	CAP'Y. OF TENDER-COAL ___ 13 TONS.	HEAT'G. SUR. OF TUBES ___ 3158.7 SQ.FT.	" -TENDER ___5½ " .x 10 " "
" -LOW " ___ 15 "	" " -WATER___ 8000 GALS	" " INC. ARCH TUBES FIREBOX ___ 258.0 " "	" -ENG.TRUCK-6 " .x 13½ "
VALVE GEAR ___ ___ WALSCHAERT.	RATIO. HEAT'G. SUR. TO GRATE ___ 43.80	" " Total ___ 3416.7 " "	G.N. SUPERHEATER___ ___ N.S.
STEAM PRESS-DESIGNED ___ 210 LBS.	" " " CYL.VOL. 252.44	SUPERHEATING SURFACE___674.0 " "	DUPLEX STOKER
" " WORKING___ 200 "	TUBES-DIAMETER ___ 2"& 5½"	GRATE AREA ___ ___ 78.0 " "	RAGONNET REVERSE GEAR
WT. ON DRIVERS ___ ___ 350 000 "	" -LENGTH ___ ___15'-0"	FIREBOX-LENGTH ___ ___ 117 IN.	AMERICAN BRICK ARCH
" . OF ENGINE ___ ___368700 "	" -NUMBER ___ 295·2; 40-5½"	" -WIDTH ___ ___ 96 "	FRANKLIN GRATE SHAKER.
" . TENDER-EMPTY ___ 61500 "	T.P. 85% WORKING PRESS.___ 78360 "	" -HEIGHT AT FRONT ___ 79½ "	

The majority of the M-1 class conformed to these specifications and appearance.

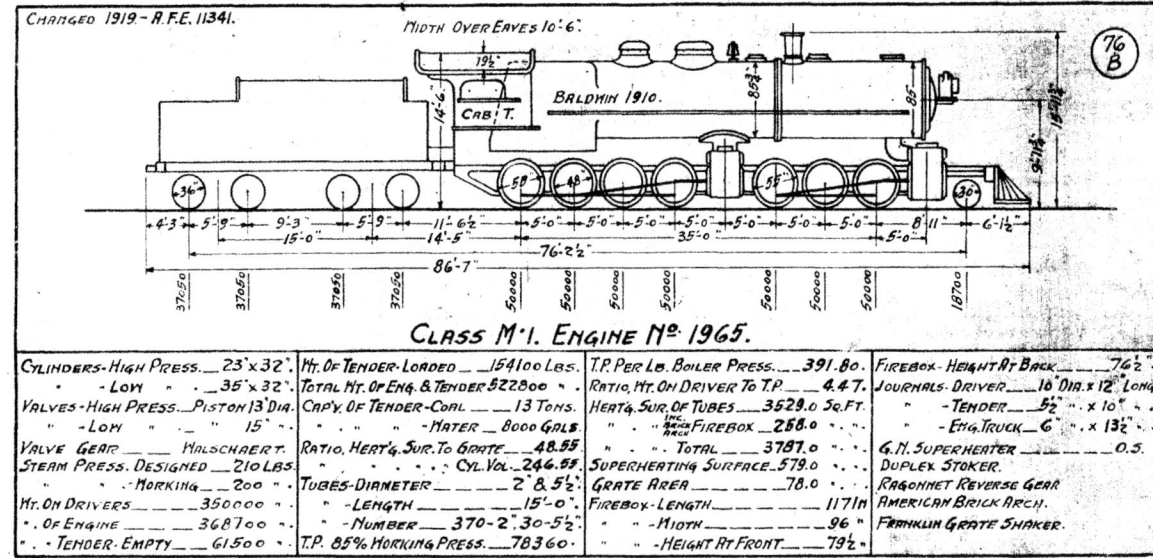

CLASS M-1. ENGINE Nº 1965.

CYLINDERS-HIGH PRESS.___ 23 x 32	WT. OF TENDER-LOADED ___ 154100 LBS.	T.P. PER LB. BOILER PRESS.___391.80	FIREBOX- HEIGHT AT BACK ___ 76½
" -LOW " ___ 35 x 32	TOTAL WT. OF ENG.& TENDER 522800 "	RATIO. WT. ON DRIVER TO T.P. ___ 4.47	JOURNALS-DRIVER___ 10 DIA. x 12" LONG
VALVES-HIGH PRESS.___PISTON 13 DIA.	CAP'Y. OF TENDER-COAL ___ 13 TONS.	HEAT'G. SUR. OF TUBES ___ 3529.0 SQ.FT.	" -TENDER___ 5½ " .x 10 " "
" -LOW " ___ 15 "	" " -WATER___ 8000 GALS.	" " INC. ARCH FIREBOX ___ 258.0 " "	" -ENG.TRUCK-6 " .x 13½ "
VALVE GEAR ___ ___ WALSCHAERT.	RATIO. HEAT'G. SUR. TO GRATE ___ 48.55	" " Total ___ 3787.0 " "	G.N. SUPERHEATER ___ ___ O.S.
STEAM PRESS. DESIGNED ___ 210 LBS.	" " " CYL.VOL. 246.55	SUPERHEATING SURFACE ___ 579.0 " "	DUPLEX STOKER.
" " WORKING ___ 200 "	TUBES-DIAMETER ___ 2" & 5½"	GRATE AREA ___ ___ 78.0 " "	RAGONNET REVERSE GEAR
WT. ON DRIVERS ___ ___ 350000 "	" -LENGTH ___ ___ 15'-0"	FIREBOX-LENGTH ___ ___ 117 IN.	AMERICAN BRICK ARCH.
" . OF ENGINE ___ ___ 368700 "	" -NUMBER ___ 370-2" 30-5½"	" -WIDTH ___ ___ 96 "	FRANKLIN GRATE SHAKER.
" . TENDER-EMPTY ___ 61500 "	T.P. 85% WORKING PRESS.___ 78360 "	" -HEIGHT AT FRONT ___ 79½ "	

One engine, the 1965, was arranged with the stack on the opposite end of the smokebox in an attempt to improve the performance of the exhaust-gas feedwater heater.

This is the special part delivered by Baldwin for the front unit of the original M-2. It consisted of the front articulated frame with low pressure cylinders driving three axles. It supported the front half of a Vauclain separable boiler that housed the fire tube type feedwater heater. This was the same type feedwater heater used on the M-1 class. Collection of H. L. Broadbelt.

This is the finished home built M-2, a Consolidation turned Mallet Compound. It is shown in 1910 at Minneapolis.
The engine lasted a surprisingly long time, sixteen years. Collection of Harold K. Vollrath.

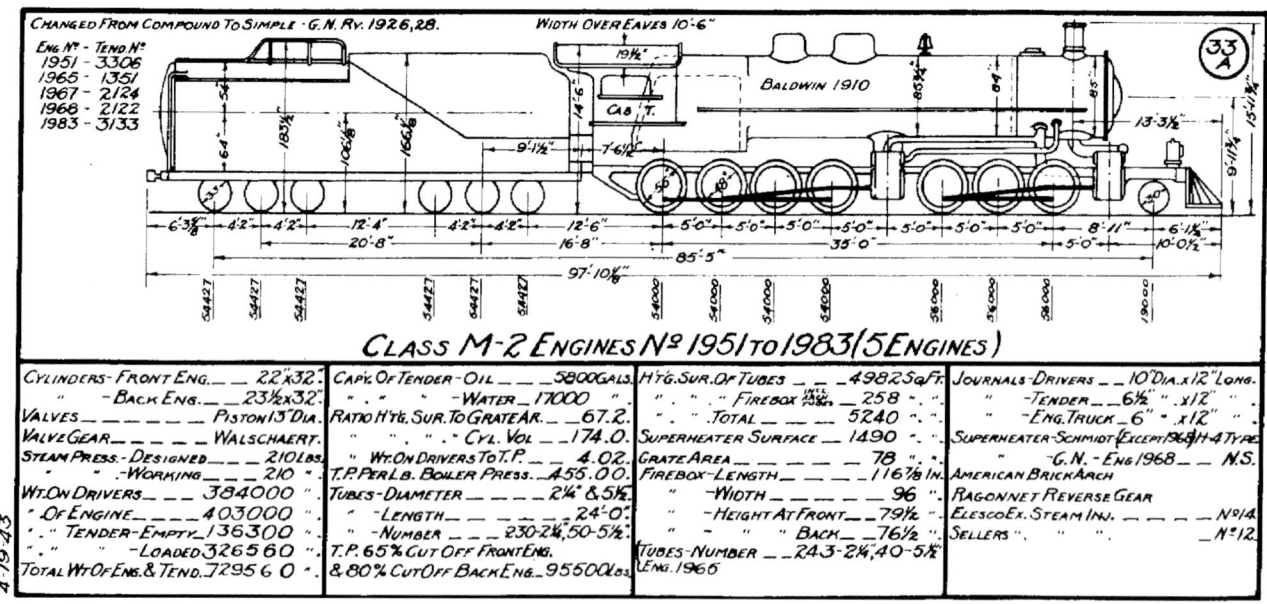

CHANGED FROM COMPOUND TO SIMPLE · G.N. RY. 1926,28.

ENG Nº - TEND Nº
1951 - 3306
1965 - 1351
1967 - 2124
1968 - 2122
1983 - 3133

WIDTH OVER EAVES 10'-6"

BALDWIN 1910

CLASS M-2 ENGINES Nº 1951 to 1983 (5 ENGINES)

CYLINDERS-FRONT ENG.	22"x32"	CAP'Y. OF TENDER-OIL	5800 GALS.	HT'G. SUR. OF TUBES	4982 SQ.FT.	JOURNALS-DRIVERS	10"DIA.x12"LONG.
" -BACK ENG.	23½x32"	" " -WATER	17000 "	" " " FIREBOX	258 "	" -TENDER	6½ " x12 "
VALVES	PISTON 13"DIA.	RATIO HT'G. SUR. TO GRATE AR.	67.2	" " TOTAL	5240 "	" -ENG. TRUCK	6 " x12 "
VALVE GEAR	WALSCHAERT.	" " CYL. VOL.	174.0	SUPERHEATER SURFACE	1490 "	SUPERHEATER-SCHMIDT (EXCEPT 1968) H-4 TYPE
STEAM PRESS.-DESIGNED	210 LBS.	" WT. ON DRIVERS TO T.P.	4.02	GRATE AREA	78 "	-G.N.-ENG 1968	N.S.
" " -WORKING	210 "	T.P. PER LB. BOILER PRESS.	455.00	FIREBOX-LENGTH	116⅞ IN.	AMERICAN BRICK ARCH
WT. ON DRIVERS	384000 "	TUBES-DIAMETER	2¼" & 5½"	" -WIDTH	96 "	RAGONNET REVERSE GEAR
" OF ENGINE	403000 "	" -LENGTH	24'-0"	" -HEIGHT AT FRONT	79½ "	ELESCO EX. STEAM INJ.	Nº 14
" -TENDER-EMPTY	136300 "	" -NUMBER	230-2¼, 50-5½	" " " BACK	76½ "	SELLERS " "	Nº 12
" " -LOADED	326560 "	T.P. 65% CUT OFF FRONT ENG.		TUBES-NUMBER	243-2¼, 40-5½	
TOTAL WT. OF ENG. & TEND.	729560 "	& 80% CUT OFF BACK ENG.	95500 LBS.	ENG. 1966		

The M-2 class was a simple Mallet articulated rebuilt from the compound M-1 class.

only move itself. Indications were the GN engine would not do useful work above 10 mph, which was too slow by Pennsylvania standards. The Pennsylvania test department blamed the superheater for having insufficient cross-sectional area through the tubes or other passages, that is, the superheater and high pressure delivery pipes acted like a choke, restricting the steam.[4]

Additionally, the feedwater heater design was not considered a complete success. In 1919, the 1965 had the smoke stack moved to the back of the feedwater section in an effort to improve the heating.[5] It ran in this configuration for several years, but eventually this style of feedwater heater was removed from the entire class.[6] In the early 1920's the engines received steel pilots. In the 1920's some of them were converted to burn oil. At least two of them (1951 and 1959) received Worthington No. 4 feedwater heaters in 1925. In the mid-1920's GN began replacing the Old Style superheaters with New Style superheaters.

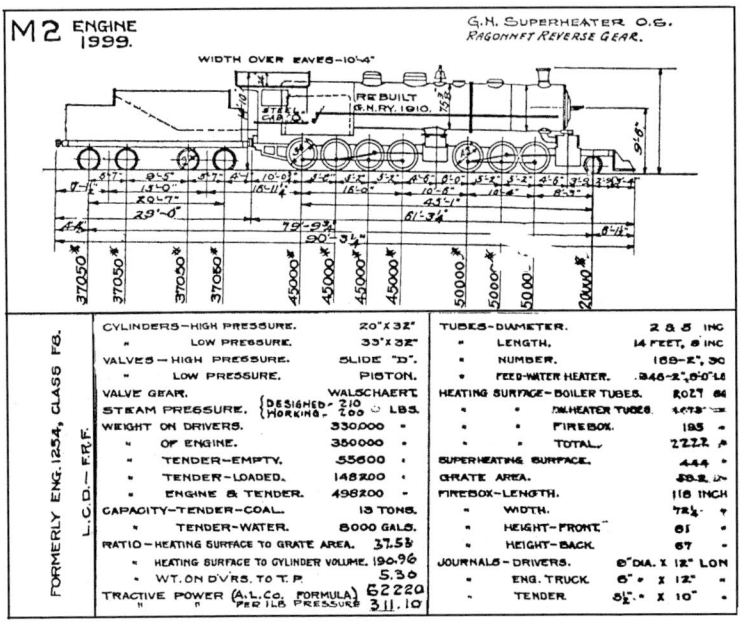

The 1915 specifications for the original M-2,
a single home-built 2-6-8-0, are shown here.

At about the same time that the first M-1's were being received, GN embarked upon its own experiment with the 2-6-8-0 wheel arrangement. A decision was made to convert one of GN's F-8 Consolidations to a 2-6-8-0. To accomplish this, a new front engine with a 6-wheel frame and low-pressure cylinders was ordered from the Baldwin Locomotive Works. Much like the M-1's, the converted engine had a boiler tube feedwater heater located in the new front section of the boiler (the flues were not lengthened – the original F-8 flues were kept). Again, the trade press indicated that the engine would use an Emerson superheater, but a GN Old Style is shown on diagrams. The feedwater heater in the front unit consisted of 346 tubes 2 inches in diameter and 8 feet long.[7]

F-8 Consolidation No. 1254 was brought into the Dale Street shops, and the conversion to a Mallet compound was completed on January, 15, 1910. The engine retained the 20-inch by 32-inch high-pressure cylinders of the F-8, and the new front unit provided 33-inch by 32-inch low-pressure cylinders. The high-pressure cylinders retained the slide valves of the F-8, while the low-pressure cylinders had 12-inch piston valves. The engine had considerably less power than the M-1's, with a tractive effort of only 62,220 lb. The new engine was classified as an M-2, and on January 18, 1910, three days after completion, the number was changed from 1254 to 2000. In 1912, when the order for the N-1 2-8-8-0's was placed, the engine was renumbered as 1999. The engine spent most if not all of its service life on Lines East.[8] In 1926, as many of the M-1's were being simpled, engine 1999 reentered the Dale Street shops, where the front engine and boiler extension were removed. The engine emerged as No. 870, the first of GN's C-4 0-8-0 switchers.

The GN was never truly satisfied with the performance of the M-1's as compounds. After the N-1's had been converted to simple engines as N-2's, GN management was favorably impressed with their improved performance. Consequently, on November 2, 1925, approval was obtained to simple three of the M-1's.[9] Nos. 1983 and 1984 entered the Dale Street shops before the end of the year to begin the conversion. The conversion of the first three locomotives was a success, demonstrating "the superiority of the simple type in design, performance and general efficiency." These engines became the first of the new, second M-2 class. The expenditure to simple the engines

The 1965 is shown at Hillyard (Spokane) on May 6, 1947. It's equipped with a Sellers exhaust steam injector.
A Bruce Black photograph from the John Westphal collection of John Luecke.

The 1967, at Klamath Falls on September 1, 1949, had been used on the Oregon, California and Eastern Railway about this time. It is one of the class with an Elesco exhaust steam injector and is assigned Style 70 O-1 tender 3051. It is the only one shown here that had a slant cab while serving in the west. Collection of Stan Kistler.

The 1973 is the power on an eastbound extra nearing Wolf Creek, between Butte and Great Falls, MT, in October 1945. It was equipped with a stack blast shield at the time. Note the Elesco exhaust steam injector. W. J. Pontin (RPS) photograph from the collection of Walter Ainsworth.

Oil-burning 1973 was at Kettle Falls, WA, in September 1948. This was after a post-war reassignment to the Spokane Division. The engine still has the stack blast shield, and is pulling a Style 104 P-2 tender. Stan F. Styles collection of GTC Collectibles.

Engine 1974 is shown arriving at Butte, MT, about 1943 with a circus train. Don Vang Collection.

Another Butte Division M-2, the 1981 was at Great Falls, MT, in October 1945. It had a stack blast shield to protect the many tunnels on the Butte to Great Falls route. H. W. Pontin (RPS) photograph from the collection of Norman F. Priebe.

The 1963 is at Kelly Lake in April 1949. It is among the majority of the class in having an Elesco exhaust steam injector. It also is one of two with O-4 class tenders. At this time it still burned coal. After 1950 generally, all surviving engines were converted to burn oil. Collection of Harold K Vollrath.

was only about $7,500 more than a normal shopping for the M-1's, and management apparently considered this well worthwhile.[10]

During the conversion, the rear cylinders were bored out to 23½ inches in diameter, while new front cylinders having 22-inch bores and 32-inch strokes were applied. The weights increased from 368,700 lb. to 403,000 lb., and the tractive effort increased to 95,500 lb.

In addition to simpling the engines, a number of other changes were made to the boilers while the engines were in the shops. New flues 24 feet in length were installed. Those engines which had not yet received Great Northern New Style superheaters had either those or Schmidt H-4 superheaters installed. This work must have made a significant improvement in performance, since no boiler changes were made when they were placed on the O-7. While the O-7 was not up to the designers expectations, it certainly did not suffer from the problems described earlier by the Pennsylvania test department.

The Worthington feedwater heaters which had been installed on a few engines were removed and replaced with either Elesco No. 14 or Sellers No. 12 exhaust steam injectors.[11] The engines known to have Elesco injectors were 1950-1952, 1955-1959, 1963, 1967, 1968, 1972-1974, 1977, 1980, 1983 and 1984. Those known to have Sellers injectors were 1953, 1954, 1965 and 1981.

With only 55-inch drivers, though, the engines were still limited by their speed. In 1929, the decision was made to rebuild most of them as Mikados with 69-inch drivers. On May 29, 1929, only about two years after conversion to a simple engine, GN 1969 entered the Great Falls shops for conversion. Ultimately, twenty-two of the M-2's were converted to O-7 Mikados, leaving thirteen in their articulated configuration. They were assigned primarily to the Butte and Kalispell Divisions. A few spent time on the Spokane Division, and ultimately as dieselization progressed most were moved to the Mesabi Division. In the 1940's many were equipped with mechanical lubricators, low water alarms and Nalco continuous blow down systems.

The M-2's were assigned a hodge-podge of tenders, and tender assignments were changed with some frequency (see Chapter 34).

The 1968 is at Kelly Lake on September 16, 1951. Another engine equipped with an Elesco exhaust steam injector, it is notable that it still had a square cab at this late date. Collection of Stan Kistler.

The 1972 is taking on water after having filled its coal bunker at Kelly Lake in June 1949. Note the slant cab and Elesco exhaust steam injector. Collection of Cordell R. Newby.

At Kelly Lake on June 26, 1952, the 1973, now with a slant cab, has retained its P-2 Vanderbilt tender, the only one assigned to an M-2. Collection of Stan Kistler.

Mesabi Division engines on the Iron Range were still burning coal in June 1949. The 1977 was in mine run service at Kelly Lake, MN. The "blockhouse" tender is J-2 tender 1611, which has had its water capacity increased to 10,000 gallons and had its coal bunker greatly enlarged. Collection of Cordell R. Newby.

The 1977 was at Kelly Lake in September 6, 1953, four years later than the previous photograph. It now had a slant cab and burned oil.
This was one of the very last M-2's in service, which was very near the end at the time of this photo. Collection of Stan Kistler.

Some were equipped with 17,000-gallon Vanderbilt tenders at times, but most had rectangular tenders of various classes which had been rebuilt to 10,000-gallon capacities.

All of the remaining M-2's except 1984 (which was sold in 1949) lasted into the 1950's. This group of 12 engines saw their last service on the Iron Range. The 1967, 1968 and 1981, which were on the Oregon, California and Eastern Railway in 1949, were transferred to the Mesabi Division when that assignment was finished, and became part of the last seven, the 1965, 1967, 1968, 1973, 1977, 1981 and 1983. They were all converted to oil and were on the Mesabi Division as of January 1, 1953, but only three saw service that year. The final three, 1973, 1977 and 1983, were sold in January and February 1955.

The 1981 is shown working at Kelly Lake on September 16, 1951. It was one of four in the class to have a Sellers exhaust steam injector. Sometime between 1945 and 1949 it lost its Vanderbilt tender and received Style 70 O-1 tender 3069. GNRHS Collection.

Another one of three shown here at Kelly Lake on September 16, 1951, the 1983 was one of the final three to serve in 1953. Collection of Stan Kistler.

Notes:

1. "Mallet Articulated Locomotives for the Great Northern Ry." *The Railway and Engineering Review*, Vol. 50, No. 13 (March 26, 1910), p. 306

2. Fr. Dale Peterka, 2001. "Great Northern's Home-Brew Mallet". Great Northern Railway Historical Society Reference Sheet No. 297.

3. "Mallet Articulated Locomotives for the Great Northern Ry.", *op. cit.*

4. Pennsylvania Railroad "Report of Great Northern No. 1950", February 16, 1910. Harrisburg PA   Archives, Dick Adams to Russ Wilcox, February 20, 2000

5. Great Northern Railway Authority for Expenditure (AFE) 11341 (from a reference on the 1922 diagram, page 76B)

6. Paul T. Warner, 1925. "The Great Northern Railway and Its Locomotives", *Baldwin Locomotives*. January 1925.

7. "Converted Mallet Locomotive for the Great Northern." *Railroad Age Gazette*, Vol. 47, No. 25 (December 17, 1909), p. 1185.

8. Fr. Dale Peterka, op. cit.

9. Great Northern Railway AFE 30185 (Approved November 2, 1925)

10. Great Northern Railway AFE 32629 (Approved September 14, 1926).

11. Great Northern Railway Unit Record of Property Changes – Equipment, Account No. 51.

In 1945 N-3 No. 2002 was on the Kalispell Division. Here it is ascending the west side 1.8% grade of Marias Pass with an eastbound scheduled freight, entering the horseshoe curve near Blacktail. William J. Pontin (RPS) photograph from the collection of Norman F. Priebe.

Chapter 19

Class N 2-8-8-0 Articulated and
Class R 2-8-8-2 Glacier Park

Class N and R Co-development History

As time went on the quest for ever-larger power continued. The logical follow-on to the 2-6-8-0 was the 2-8-8-0, and such a wheel arrangement would still obey the Hill dictum that the number of driving axles be maximized. In 1912, a contract was signed with Baldwin to build such a locomotive, the N-1 design, a Mallet compound with 63-inch drivers. This was the last compound locomotive built for the GN.

Once in operation, the N's were upgraded twice as ways to modernize them became apparent. The various N classes never existed simultaneously with each other except during the conversion periods. The upgrading was mixed with the acquisition and upgrading of the R classes in a constant quest for the optimum high-power and efficient freight engine.

The upgrading evolution went like this. In 1912 the N-1 type came from Baldwin as a compound with 93,250 pounds of tractive force. Starting in 1924 the GN began to rebuild the N-1's to Class N-2, a change marked primarily by their conversion to simple engines, with a tractive effort of 100,000 pounds. Before this project was completed, Baldwin delivered, in 1925, the first R-1 2-8-8-2's. These engines were larger than the N in all respects, with the new larger firebox forcing a break with the old Hill requirement, and requiring a trailing truck under the firebox. The R-1's came with a tractive effort of 127,500 pounds. The GN thought they could do better, and as soon as the N-2's were finished, began construction of the upgraded R-1 class, called the R-1b in this book. (The Baldwin R-1's will be referred to as the R-1a.)

These improved R-1's were almost what GN wanted, but not quite. They had a higher boiler pressure that resulted in a tractive force of

133,180 pounds, but kept the same size firebox as the originals, a fact that ultimately would be shown to limit the power of these behemoths.

The GN pressed on, immediately designing the R-2. Now, instead of upgrading the R-1's as they did with the N class, they continued the building marathon in 1929 with a new engine that could truly be classed in the superpower category, and one that boasted an original tractive power of 146,000 pounds. By the end of 1930 they had 25 N-2's, 14 R-1's and 16 R-2's, all simple articulated, but with only the R-2 considered superpower.

Here the GN rested the articulated program temporarily, but continued to build Mikados until 1934. After that, the poor economy dictated no new construction until the prospect of another World War loomed. In 1939 design started on yet another N upgrade, this time with a highly modified boiler that approached the superpower category.

Construction of the new N-3 class began in 1940 and continued through 1941. These engines had the largest firebox that could be accommodated within the design limits imposed, and yielded 118,400 pounds of tractive force. Later during 1943 and 1944, cast steel front engine beds with cylinders cast integral were added to the R-2's and the GN-built R-1's.

Even though the GN bought only diesels during World War II, they were not yet finished with their articulateds. In 1947 and 1948, at Hillyard, the R-2 class received new boilers. These were not only an in-kind replacement due to wear and embrittlement, but were improved by the addition of Security circulators. At the same time, the N-3's were also having major boiler work done at the other shops, primarily for replacement of all or large parts of the shell, because of cracking caused by steel failure due to embrittlement. This work also included

New N-1 No. 2004 was photographed at Breckenridge, MN, while in shipment. Note the many scratches on the extra-large low pressure cylinders due to clearance problems encountered on the way. Ottertail County Historical Society.

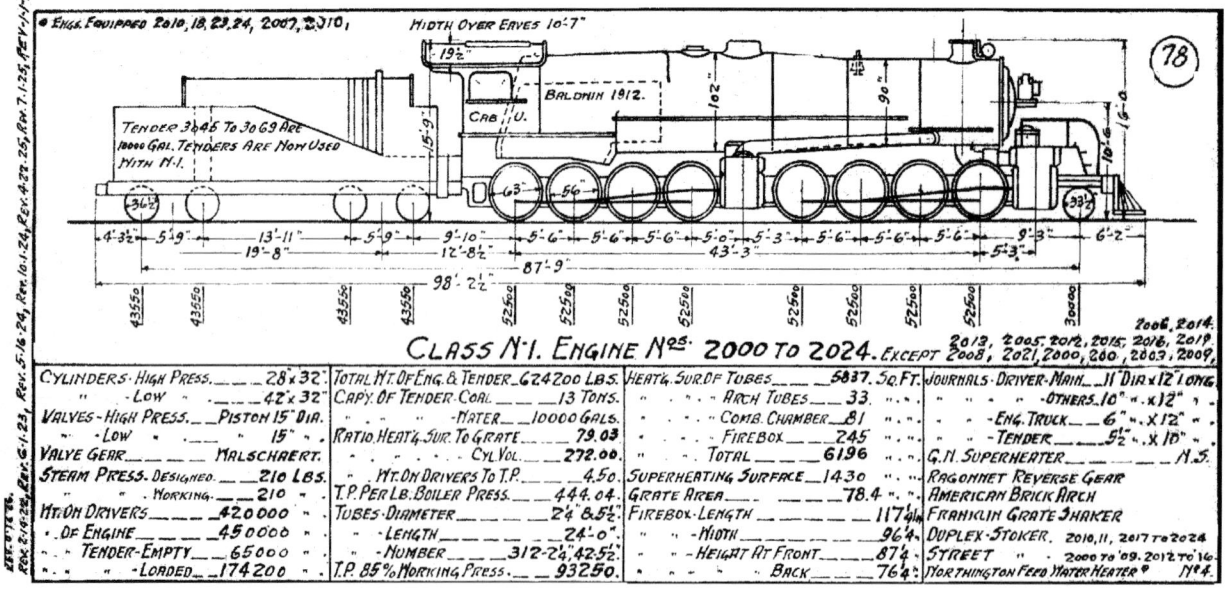

the addition of Security circulators. The embrittlement problem is discussed later in this chapter.

The completion of these projects ended the development of big steam power on the GN, and also marked the end of GN's long history of steam construction in its own shops. Unfortunately, the rebuilt locomotives would have an additional active life of only six or seven years.

Class N-1

The original N-1 class arrived from Baldwin in 1912. There were 25 total. Two improvements in these articulateds over any that came before were the 63-inch driver diameter, and the addition of a large combustion chamber. They were built as compounds, as were all of the GN articulateds at the time. But these engines were exceptional. They

had record sized (for the GN) low pressure pistons of 42-inch diameter. (In fact only later designs of the Virginian 2-8-8-0 and 2-8-8-2 ever exceeded it, at 44 inches.) Such size resulted in a width over the low-pressure cylinders of 11 feet 3 inches, also a first, which presented a clearance problem at the time. Seventeen of the new engines (2000-2016) were delivered as coal burners and the remaining eight (2017-2024) were delivered as oil burners.[1]

The switch to 63-inch drivers was an important innovation, since it allowed faster train speeds, something learned from the O-1 Mikados. This was countered, however, by the weight of the low-pressure machinery, which was more than could be completely accounted for in the counterbalances. This restricted the speed. The N-1 was significantly larger than the M-1, yet it suffered from a serious drawback. While the N-1 had approximately double the heating surface

Looking past the three gentlemen in the foreground, one can see N-1 2020 with an original factory-supplied oil tender.
Only eight of the class came equipped as oil burners. The engine was photographed at Hillyard, WA, on an unknown date. GNRHS Collection.

The builders photo of 2009 shows the original coal tender supplied with the coal burning N-1's.
One of the first "grape-arbor" types, it was distinctly different from the oil tenders shipped with the oil burners. Collection of H. L. Broadbelt.

and superheater surface of the M-1, the firebox had the same grate area. To heat the additional surface at the same rate as in the M-1, the N-1 had to be fired at twice the rate, with lower efficiency. However, the combustion chamber was a significant help in countering the situation, enabling the locomotive to get more heat out the fuel. It is not known if its effectiveness was ever tested, but combustion chambers became a standard feature on GN locomotives after this.

The boiler was the largest yet applied to a GN locomotive. Coupled to this was the fact that with the wide firebox mounted above the driving axles, the boiler stood high, making the locomotive the tallest owned by the GN, at 16 feet over the stack. Appliances had to be carefully positioned to fit within the clearance diagram, and initially there was no sand box at all on the boiler. Early in the N history, a low profile box was added to the boiler top, of a shape that would fit

TABLE 1. SIGNIFICANT FEATURES OF M-1 AND N-1 COMPARED

Class	B.P.	Heating Surface	Superheater Surface	Grate Area	Tractive Effort
M-1	200 psi.	3,295 sq. ft.	600 sq. ft.	78 sq. ft.	78,360 lb.
N-1	210 psi.	6,196 sq. ft.	1,430 sq. ft.	78 sq. ft.	93,250 lb.

This 1926 view of No. 2020 as an N-1 at Allouez, WI, shows the addition of the boiler-top sandbox, the enlargement of the front engine sandboxes, the new cast headlight, a larger tender (from the series 3045 to 3069) and the use of an auxiliary water car. The front cylinder jackets seem to have some dents, and outside bracing has been placed on the rear cylinders. Wayne Olsen Collection.

On June 23, 1923, N-1 No. 2022 departed the iron range for Allouez with a record 150 cars in a 13,221 ton train. This amounted to 10,186 short tons of ore. It is shown near State Line Tower. Great Northern Railway.

the reduced clearance. In typical articulated fashion there were two sandboxes on the pilot deck. The sand from these boxes was applied to the front engine, and once a boiler sand box was applied, sand from it was delivered to the rear engine.

The new locomotives came equipped with arch tubes, which stayed with the engines into the N-3 era. An Emerson superheater with 1,368 square feet of superheating surface was provided. With this arrangement the fire-tube heating surface was 6,120 square feet.[2] As mentioned in Chapter 3, the Great Northern "new style" superheater found on the 1915 and later diagrams is believed to be a different name for the same design. There was a slight change in area given in the diagrams, to 1,430 square feet. The boiler sandbox was likely applied by 1915, but an exact date was not found. The pilot deck sandboxes appear to have been lengthened at various times while still N-1's.

Additional information on the original engines was provided in Baldwin Locomotives Magazine.[3] The length of the combustion chamber was 58 inches, and the valves for all four cylinders were 15 inches in diameter. The low-pressure cylinder valves were double ported.

Refer to the N-1 diagram page reproduced here for the remaining technical specifications.

The oil burning engines went to the Spokane division, and perhaps also to the Cascade division as they were separate entities at the time. The coal burning N-1's were initially assigned to the Kalispell division, and nine of them were confirmed to be there in 1913. These were the 2000, 2001, 2002, 2004, 2005, 2006, 2007, 2008, and 2009. There were none on the Butte division at this time.[4] Shift of some engines to the Mesabi Division began in the spring of 1923. On June 4th, Mr. A.H. Hogeland began the description of the route to be taken to C. O. Jenks as follows: "Referring to the routing of N-1 engines, now on its [sic] way from the Kalispell division to the Mesabi division."[5] The transferred engines included the oil burners. The 2017 through 2024 were converted to coal between December 1923 and July 1924.[6]

Soon after their arrival on the iron range, the GN put together a test train to determine the load these engines were capable of hauling. On June 23, 1923, engine 2022 with Engineer Arten and Conductor Bradley brought in 150 cars of ore with a train weight of 13,221 tons, carrying 10,186 short tons of ore. This was a record haul at the time, but the road immediately increased the ore train length to 150 cars

based on this performance.

The remaining N's on the Kalispell division stayed for a short time until replaced by the Q-1 class in November 1923. At this time they were moved to the Minot division, running between Minot and Williston. Here they were rated at 4,000 tons on the 0.7% ruling grade.[7]

The Great Northern began modifying the N's almost immediately after their arrival. Already mentioned was the addition of the boiler top sand box. Other details included a change of headlight style in 1919, and the equipping with steel pilots between 1920 and 1923. An important change not often noted was the construction of heavier back frame sections for 2000, 2002, 2012 and 2013 between February 1920 and February 1921. A late change was the replacement of the superheaters. This began independently of the conversion to N-2 in 1924. This time the Schmidt superheater replaced the GN new style superheater. Where the GN design had 42 elements, the new Schmidt had 60 elements.[8]

The N-1's were delivered with two different tender styles, one for the coal burners and another for the oil burners. Refer to the photographs to note the difference. Replacement of the small original tenders with newly enlarged class O-1 tenders 3045 to 3069 took place about 1915. The new tenders provided 10,000 gallons of water instead of 8,000 gallons, and were the result of a new GN tender rebuilding program. That these large engines came with small tenders originally was due to the restricting lengths of the small turntables in place at the time. As the turntables were lengthened, larger more useful-sized tenders could be provided. At the time the N-2 rebuilding started, all N-1's were coal burners. The Mesabi division engines stayed as coal burners until approximately 1950, but the locomotives on the western divisions began to be changed to oil for good in 1926 and 1927.

Class N-2

Simple articulateds were developed as early as 1919, when the Pennsylvania Railroad built a big one. The Pennsy HC-1 2-8-8-0 simple articulated was the first successful engine of this type, and one of the largest 2-8-8-0's ever. It had an extraordinary combustion chamber 139 inches long, a grate area of 112 square feet, 62-inch diameter drivers, 30-inch diameter pistons, used the new Type E superheater and had a tractive effort of 135,000 pounds. After the Pennsylvania and the

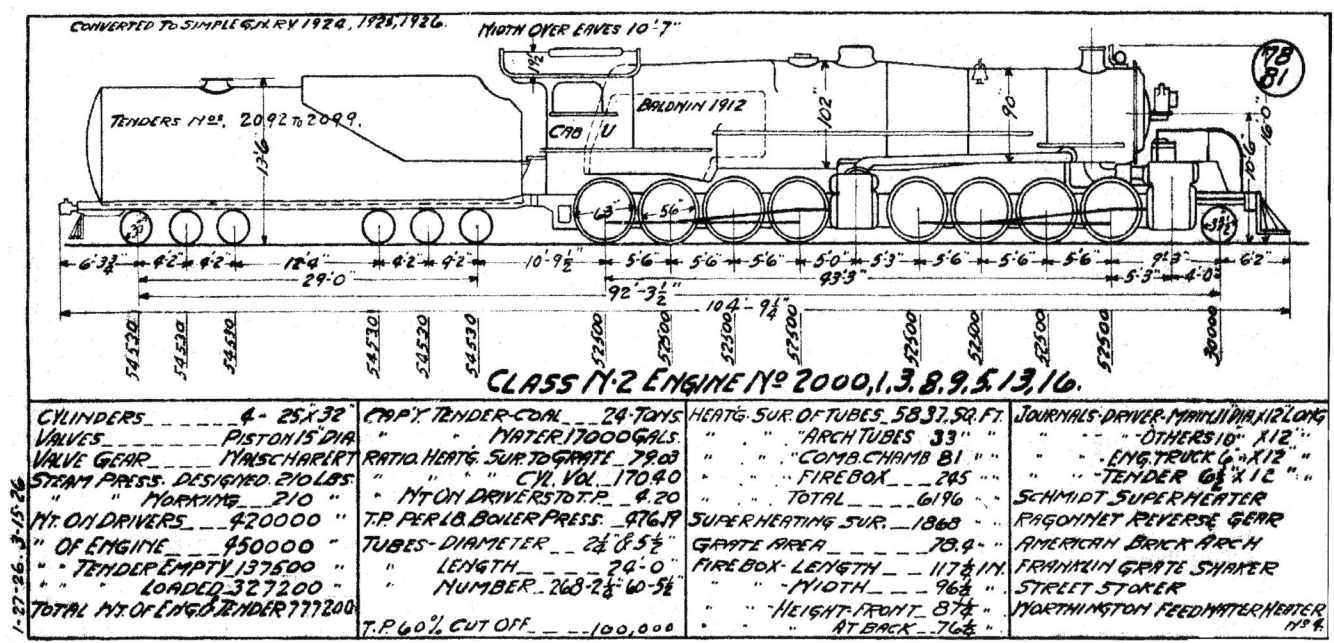

rest of the industry had a chance to study the results, the Chesapeake & Ohio Railway introduced an Alco-built simple articulated 2-8-8-2 with 23-inch diameter pistons in 1923,[9] and the GN started building a 25-inch diameter piston simple 2-8-8-0, the first N-2, in February 1924. Although the new concept of limited cutoff became a feature of the N-2, this pioneer unit likely did not receive it until later. The GN was still debating the concept in June as related below. Then Baldwin proposed two new simple articulated engines to the GN in June 1924: one a 2-8-8-0, and the other a 2-8-8-2.[10]

The proposed 2-8-8-0 was about 8% larger than the N-1, and offered a tractive effort of 121,000 pounds. A key feature was the use of limited cutoff in the valves: the introduction of fresh steam into the cylinders would be stopped after 60% of the valve travel, allowing the rest of the piston motion to result from the expanding steam already in the cylinder. This went a long way to conserve steam and offset the absence of a second expansion in the low-pressure cylinders of a compound engine.

The Great Northern looked at these proposals and within four days had proposed a trial modification to a 2-8-8-0 compound, changing it into a simple engine with limited cutoff for tests.[11] The proposal was to take an engine with a Schmidt superheater, (the 2021 received one in June 1924, nearly six months before it's conversion to N-2 began) arrange the valve motion for 50% cutoff and bush the present low-pressure cylinder diameter from 42 inches down to 28 inches, the same size as the N-1 high-pressure cylinders. (Note that one would not be able tell from the outside that this rebuild was a simple because the road bushed down the low pressure cylinders instead of replacing them.) The 50% cutoff was even less than proposed by Baldwin, and the 28-inch cylinders were larger by 3 inches than the GN had specified for their simple engine. The GN was determined to find out if locomotives of this type would run out of steam. No results of this test have been found, nor is it known if it was even performed, but limited cutoff of 60% was incorporated in the GN's new engines.

One can see from Table 2 that GN did not strive for a large boiler

TABLE 2. N-1 COMPOUND 2-8-8-0 COMPARED TO TWO SIMPLE DESIGNS

Class	B.P.	Heating Surface	Superheater Surface	Grate Area	Tractive Effort
N-1	210 psi.	6,196 sq. ft.	1,430 sq. ft.	78.4 sq. ft.	93,250 lb.
Baldwin*	210 psi.	6,510 sq. ft.	1,810 sq. ft.	103.5 sq. ft.	121,000 lb.
N-2	210 psi.	6,163 sq. ft.	1,868 sq. ft.	78.4 sq. ft.	100,000 lb

* proposed

The N-2 was easily identified by the Worthington feedwater heater (here a model BL-2) placed on the engineer's side and the trio of air pumps on the fireman's side. The 2006 was photographed by Robert Graham at Minneapolis in May 1938, and the 2017 is at Superior in September 1938. The line of rivets along the side of the tender with 2006 indicates that it is a Style 114. Both photographs from the collection of William Raia.

No. 2000 when first rebuilt to N-2 had a Worthington model BL feedwater heater and retained its enlarged O-1 class rectangular tender. The photo was taken shortly after completion in 1925. On June 20, 1925, The Railway Review trade magazine ran this photo and remarked that placing the Worthington feedwater heater on the engineers side was unusual. Great Northern Railway photograph from the collection of Wolfgang Weber.

The Worthington Type S feedwater heater was installed on No. 2018 during 1930. It was removed, as were the others, when it was converted to an N-3. In this view, the engine is at Minneapolis before World War II. Robert Graham photograph from the collection of William Raia.

Another engine with the type S Worthington was the 2024, shown at Minneapolis, MN, on October 17, 1935. Robert Graham photograph from the collection of William Raia.

increase with the rebuilding plan. Primarily, they opted for a single-expansion machine, coupled with an improved superheater. The superheater change was started before the conversion to simple. The other internal changes were a reduction of all pistons to 25 inches in diameter, and the introduction of limited cutoff.

The external changes were interesting. They added an air pump, for a total of three. This was the only time the GN did that. The need was based on the desire to reduce the time it took to pump up the air in the long trains these engines were capable of pulling. The line of three pumps on the fireman's side made a distinctive identifying mark for them. On the opposite side was located a Worthington No. 4½ BL feedwater heater. The pilot sand boxes were redesigned from the cylindrical shape to rectangular. Other ongoing changes in the life of these engines include a change to Duplex type II stokers from the Street type between 1920 and 1926, and replacement of the headlight with the new distinctive GN cast iron headlight between 1923 and 1925.

The conversion to N-2 was considered complete for all engines in 1927. Following that, heavier front engine frames were installed between August 1927 and April 1930. GN records indicate specifically all the former oil-burning engines had this work done between March 1928 and May 1929.[12] During 1930 Worthington No. 5 Type S feedwater heaters replaced the BL-type units on 2007, 2018, 2023 and 2024. From 1933 through 1935, five locomotives received new boilers (see roster). Also about this time some of them received vestibule cabs in place of the original square cabs (2001, 2003, 2008 and 2016.) There also was a change in the style of the pilot deck sandboxes on the N-2's but the exact time this was done has not been determined.

The first N-2's finished did not immediately get the new blank-class Vanderbilt tenders, but kept the O-1 tenders they had been assigned as N-1's. However, between 1925 and 1928 members of the 2034-2060 (Style 114) and 2092-2099 (Style 112) series of tenders were completed and assigned to these engines.

The conversion of the N-1 class to simple marked the end of

On May 12, 1940, N-2 No. 2022 arrived at Allouez with a typical ore train of the period, 175 loads, 15,750 tons of iron ore. Photographer Warren McGee says it was the "heaviest train I ever saw". Warren R. McGee.

No. 2003 is representative of the N-2 class engines with vestibule cabs. It also shows its distinctive Worthington BL feedwater heater and oil separator on the engineers side. The photograph was taken at Spokane on October 30, 1938. H. Miller photograph from the collection of William Raia.

compound locomotives on the Great Northern. In a memo to J.A. Lengby on January 26, 1927, D.A. Kerr wrote "…the reason for the discontinuance of the compound locomotives…was a desire to obtain a greater tractive effort than it was found possible to develop with the compound engines."[13] An unanticipated benefit was that the smaller diameter pistons permitted higher speed operation, due to their lighter weight.

The N-2's were assigned as follows in 1936:

Mesabi Division: 2002, 2004, 2006, 2007, 2010, 2011, 2012, 2014, 2015, 2017, 2018, 2019, 2020, 2021, 2022, 2023, 2024.

Butte Division: 2000, 2001, 2003, 2009, 2013, 2016.

Kalispell Division: 2005, 2008.

It is obvious the majority of the engines were in iron ore service. After the conversion to N-2 was complete, the GN raised the typical ore train load to 175 cars and 15,750 tons of ore. The reduced numbers of the class on the Kalispell division reflected the appearance of the

R-class engines by 1936. Within a short time the 2000, 2001, 2003 and 2016 were assigned to operate from Bend, OR, to Bieber, CA, on the Klamath division. The engines were routed via the SP as they could not negotiate the sharp curves on the Oregon Trunk between Wishram, WA, and Bend. The N-2's remained at these assignments until 1940.

Class R-1

The Baldwin proposal of June 1924 included a 2-8-8-2. The GN first decided to go with three engines very similar to this proposal, then added one more to the order in January 1925. The GN modified the specifications of the Baldwin proposal before ordering. There is no known reason for the reduction in boiler pressure, but the reduced grate and heating surface area may be attributed to a slightly larger combustion chamber on the GN-designed engines. The Baldwin proposal specified 118 square feet of combustion chamber heating surface, whereas the locomotive the GN ordered had 155 square feet with a length of 72 inches. Also, the wheelbase the GN specified was

The fireman's side of the 2003 with vestibule cab, also taken at Spokane in October 1938, shows the trio of air pumps installed on the class. Collection of Harold K. Vollrath.

This is the first R-1, a Baldwin product received in August 1925 and photographed in St. Paul for promotional purposes before regular service. At this time it was the most powerful single expansion engine built by Baldwin. The slant front cab and the smokebox-mounted air pumps are new features on the GN. The R-1 was also the largest GN engine to use the steam dome throttle. Great Northern Railway.

11 inches shorter than the Baldwin proposal. After ordering a smaller version of the Baldwin engine, the GN spent four years developing a locomotive to surpass it.

The four Baldwin engines were completed in August, and set up at Dale Street in October, 1925.[14] They were numbered 2030 to 2033 and were designated class R-1. At the time they were the most powerful single expansion engines completed by Baldwin.[15] They also were the first GN engines to come from the builder with the slant-front cab. After set up they were sent to the Kalispell Division, to run between Cut Bank and Whitefish, MT. Here they would replace the Q-1's that had replaced the N-1's earlier.

At this time the GN was still converting their older compound engines to simple. Impressed by the performance of the R-1, when the conversion work was completed, the GN set out to build a complete simple articulated engine in their own shops. This was the largest project attempted up to this time. The GN designers believed a few small changes to the Baldwin engine would give them an optimum locomotive, so the resulting design remained classed as an R-1.

Authority for Expenditure (AFE) 33319 explained "The success of this class of power in handling trains over the Rocky Mountains has been very pronounced from the point of operation as well as economy...."[16] Four of the modified locomotives were to be built under this AFE. The AFE went on to state the new engines would have higher boiler pressure, more tubes for an increase in heating surface area and larger 22,000 gallon tenders. By the time they were finished, they had tenders with 17,000 gallons water capacity. A second series of six followed in 1928, built under AFE 35658.[17] Both orders were assembled at Hillyard Shops, with wheel centers, driving boxes and tender parts made at Dale Street Shops. The boilers were made by Puget Sound Machinery Depot of Seattle.[18] All of the R class engines were built as oil burners.[19] The Great Northern saved twenty eight thousand dollars per unit by building the engines themselves.

Since the design of the new engines increased the boiler pressure to 225 psi, the tractive effort also increased to 133,180 pounds. To separate the differences the home-built engines will be referred to in the text as Class R-1b. These engines were numbered 2034 to 2043.

The official Baldwin builders photo of the R-1 was of the 2031. At the time this was the GN's most powerful and heaviest locomotive. Collection of H. L. Broadbelt.

Soon after going into service the 2031 was photographed on Marias Pass with a long eastbound. Collection of William Bissinger.

The 2031 eventually went to the Spokane Division where it is shown near Interbay. Bordertown collection of GTC collectibles.

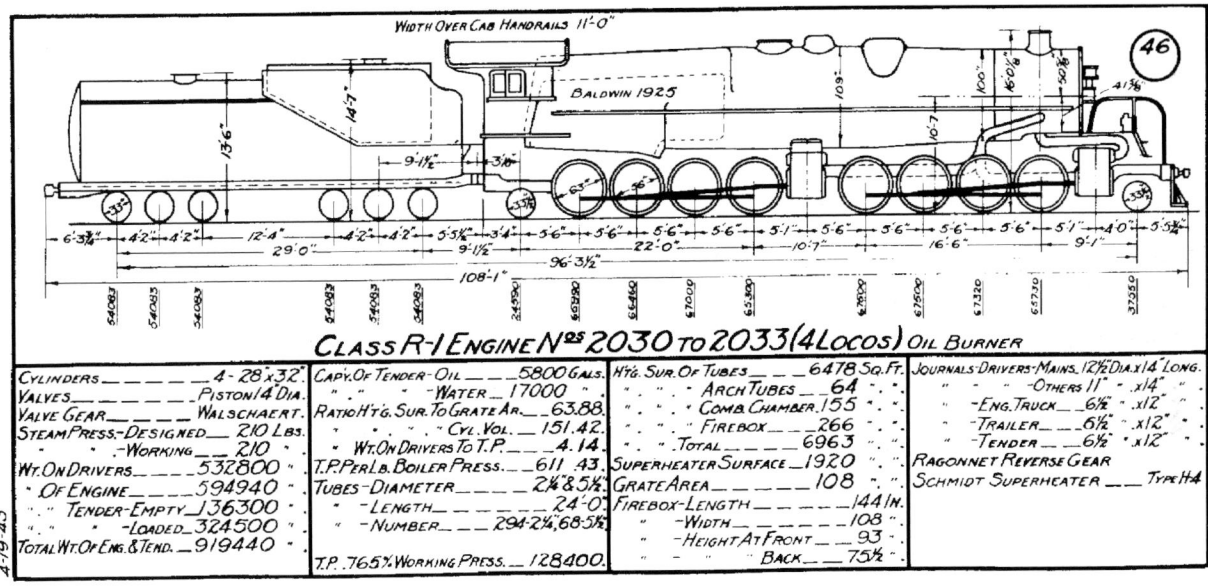

CLASS R-1 ENGINE Nos 2030 TO 2033 (4 LOCOS) OIL BURNER

CYLINDERS ___ 4-28"x32"	CAPY. OF TENDER-OIL ___ 5800 GALS.	HT'G. SUR. OF TUBES ___ 6478 Sq. Ft.	JOURNALS-DRIVERS-MAINS 12½ DIA. x14 LONG.
VALVES ___ PISTON 14" DIA.	" " -WATER ___ 17000 "	" " ARCH TUBES ___ 64 "	" -OTHERS 11" x14"
VALVE GEAR ___ WALSCHAERT.	RATIO HT'G. SUR. TO GRATE AR. ___ 63.88	" " COMB. CHAMBER ___ 155 "	" -ENG. TRUCK ___ 6½" x12"
STEAM PRESS-DESIGNED ___ 210 Lbs.	" " " CYL. VOL. ___ 151.42	" " FIREBOX ___ 266 "	" -TRAILER ___ 6½" x12"
" " -WORKING ___ 210	" " WT. ON DRIVERS TO T.P. ___ 4.14	" TOTAL ___ 6963	" -TENDER ___ 6½" x12"
WT. ON DRIVERS ___ 532800 "	T.P. PER LB. BOILER PRESS. ___ 611.43	SUPERHEATER SURFACE ___ 1920 "	RAGONNET REVERSE GEAR
" OF ENGINE ___ 594940 "	TUBES-DIAMETER ___ 2¼ & 5½	GRATE AREA ___ 108 "	SCHMIDT SUPERHEATER ___ TYPE H4
" " TENDER-EMPTY ___ 136300 "	" -LENGTH ___ 24-0"	FIREBOX-LENGTH ___ 144 IN.	
" " -LOADED ___ 324500 "	" -NUMBER ___ 294-2¼, 68-5½	" -WIDTH ___ 108 "	
TOTAL WT. OF ENG. & TEND. ___ 919440 "		" -HEIGHT AT FRONT ___ 93 "	
4-19-43	T.P. .765% WORKING PRESS. ___ 128400	" - BACK ___ 75½ "	

This diagram is of the Baldwin-built R-1 class.

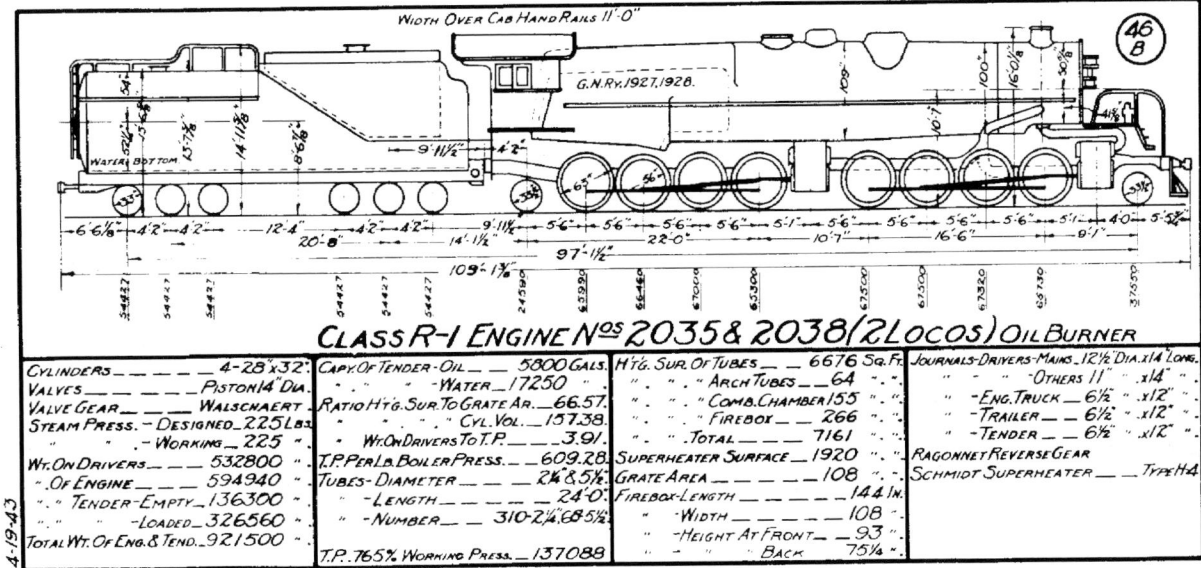

CLASS R-1 ENGINE Nos 2035 & 2038 (2 LOCOS) OIL BURNER

CYLINDERS ___ 4-28"x32"	CAPY. OF TENDER-OIL ___ 5800 GALS.	HT'G. SUR. OF TUBES ___ 6676 Sq. Ft.	JOURNALS-DRIVERS-MAINS 12½ DIA. x14 LONG.
VALVES ___ PISTON 14" DIA.	" " -WATER ___ 17250 "	" " ARCH TUBES ___ 64 "	" -OTHERS 11" x14"
VALVE GEAR ___ WALSCHAERT	RATIO HT'G. SUR. TO GRATE AR. ___ 66.57	" " COMB. CHAMBER ___ 155 "	" -ENG. TRUCK ___ 6½" x12"
STEAM PRESS.-DESIGNED ___ 225 Lbs.	" " " CYL. VOL. ___ 157.38	" " FIREBOX ___ 266 "	" -TRAILER ___ 6½" x12"
" " -WORKING ___ 225	" " WT. ON DRIVERS TO T.P. ___ 3.91	" TOTAL ___ 7161	" -TENDER ___ 6½" x12"
WT. ON DRIVERS ___ 532800 "	T.P. PER LB. BOILER PRESS. ___ 609.28	SUPERHEATER SURFACE ___ 1920 "	RAGONNET REVERSE GEAR
" OF ENGINE ___ 594940 "	TUBES-DIAMETER ___ 2¼ & 5½	GRATE AREA ___ 108 "	SCHMIDT SUPERHEATER ___ TYPE H4
" " TENDER-EMPTY ___ 136300 "	" -LENGTH ___ 24-0"	FIREBOX-LENGTH ___ 144 IN.	
" " -LOADED ___ 326560 "	" -NUMBER ___ 310-2¼, 68-5½	" -WIDTH ___ 108 "	
TOTAL WT. OF ENG. & TEND. ___ 921500 "		" -HEIGHT AT FRONT ___ 93 "	
4-19-43	T.P. .765% WORKING PRESS. ___ 137088	" - BACK ___ 75½ "	

This diagram is of the GN-built R-1 class.

The locomotives employed the Ragonnet power reverse gear, a No. 16 Elesco exhaust steam injector and a Schmidt type H4 superheater. Nathan low water alarms came in 1934. Brick arches and arch tubes were added to the firebox between 1940 and 1942. A Nalco continuous blow-down system came in 1943-1949. Those that got new boilers in 1947 and 1948 (2034, 2040, 2042 and 2043) received Security circulators as part of that project.[20] Both types of R-1's had steam dome throttles, the last articulated type to use them. They could negotiate a 16 degree curve, something the N-2 could not.[21]

Photographs show a curious placement of the classification lamps on some R-1's and R-2's. These engines have the fireman's side class lamp raised higher and closer to the boiler than the lamp on the engineer's side. This is illustrated by the action photo of 2043. The reason for this is not known for certain, but it may be to clear the air pump when it was swung over to open the smokebox.

The R class comparison table (Table 3) shows the tractive effort as built. During the 1930's the diagram sheet showed an alternate calculation for the tractive effort, where a different pressure was used at the auxiliary steam admission ports. This calculation resulted in a tractive effort of 134,200 pounds for the R-1a and 143,500 pounds for the R-1b. The same formula was used to give an alternative tractive effort rating to the R-2 as well. The diagrams reported both numbers until redrawn in 1943.

There were subsequent tractive effort changes. Since there were no known concurrent machinery changes, the differing numbers seen on diagram sheets from 1932 until 1945 may represent efforts by the motive power department to modify the calculations to better correspond with performance as seen on the road. Otherwise it is possible the road made undocumented changes to the valve cut-off settings. The R-1a's were changed to 128,400 pounds tractive effort by 1945, then 129,622 pounds, without a reduction in the diameter of the front cylinders. The R-1b's were changed to 136,600, then 137,088

There was little external evidence to discern a GN-built R-1 from the Baldwin-built units. However, there was a difference in the superheater damper counterweight visible on the outside of the smokebox, and most of the GN-built engines had fewer washout plugs on the firebox side than did the Baldwin-built units. No. 2035 is at Superior in April, 1948. Photograph by Bruce Black.

Note the headlight visor used during World War II to limit visibility from the air at night. R-1 2037 was photographed at Vancouver, WA, in October 1942. Collection of Harold K. Vollrath.

The freshly shopped and painted 2041 is shown at Hillyard shops on June 10, 1947. John Westphal collection, courtesy John Luecke.

No. 2039 with a vestibule cab is at Minot in October, 1952. Collection of Harold K. Vollrath.

This engineers side view of 2039 is at Spokane on August 2, 1949. Charles E. Winters Collection.

No. 2043, another R-1 equipped with a vestibule cab, is shown at Hillyard in 1946. Photograph by Wilbur C. Whittaker.

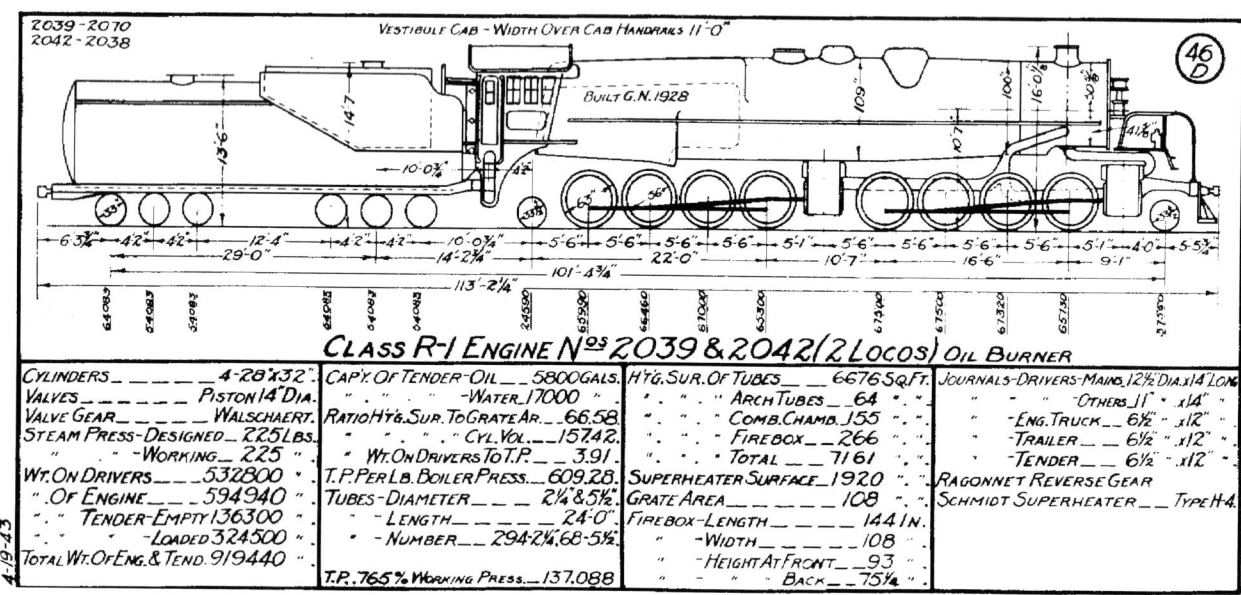

This diagram defined the R-1's equipped with vestibule cabs.

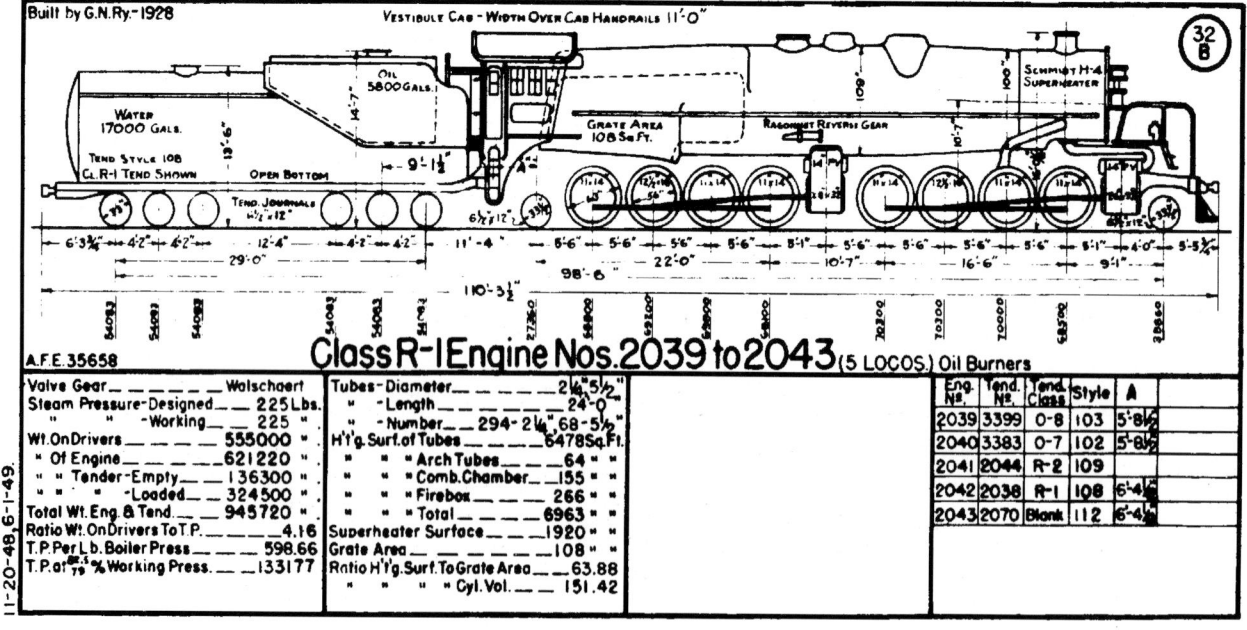

This diagram shows the GN-built R-1 in its final configuration and gives the correct last weights.

pounds, and after a true machinery change about 1945, to 133,177 pounds. The last change was a reduction due to reduced diameter front cylinders. This was done undoubtedly to reduce slipping of the front engine, and was accomplished by making the cast-integral cylinders on the new cast frames 2 inches smaller in diameter. The last change essentially brought the engine rating back to what it was when built. Similar changes were made to the R-2's.

The need for R-1 cast front engine frames was discussed during June 1943. It was necessary to convince the War Production Board and the Office of Defense Transportation that the necessary work was a repair and not a conversion. Mr. Pool stated that the engines are continually out of service "due to broken frames, loose cylinders, [with] loose and broken binders on the No. 1 engine."[22] The integral cast frames

and cylinders were installed in 1944 and 1945 under AFE 65179 and 65758.

AFE 70293, dated February 19, 1945, was written to obtain new boilers for the R classes, because of boiler shell cracking. At the time, the railroad believed the cracking was due to running "double their normal mileage over the past several years," on account of the exceptional traffic demands of World War II. But in retrospect, what was happening was the appearance of the embrittlement problem. The problem as quoted from the AFE demonstrates the classic symptoms of embrittlement. "It has recently been observed that the cracks beneath some of the circumferential patches are starting to work out beyond the patches which means removing the present patches and applying new ones...."

The AFE was written to equip both R-1a and R-2 classes.

R-1 No. 2043 is working upgrade in the Cascades near Baring, WA, during World War II. Note the asymmetrical class lamp locations. Photograph by Stuart B. Hertz.

The proposal included the intention to give the R-1a's new boilers at 225 psi, to bring them up to the same performance as the R-1b's.[23] This never materialized. Instead, one of the engines was scrapped and the remainder were assigned to ore steaming. These engines remained in ore steaming service until 1956.[24] The new boilers were applied instead to four R-1b's. See the roster, Chapter 31, for details.

The R-1's had been delivered with smaller Vanderbilt tenders of 17,000 gallon water capacity. New 22,000 gallon tenders were ordered for three of them. The three displaced 17,000 gallon tenders were to go to the Q-1's, to begin a tender swap that would eventually see the majority of the original Q-1 tenders going to the P-2's in order to extend their range.[25] However, the available records show that very few 22,000 gallon tenders were assigned to R-1's. By 1949 only the 2041 had one. A detailed record of tender assignments will be found in Chapter 34.

Class R-2

After acquiring 14 of the Class R-1, the GN decided to build a simple articulated with an even larger firebox. A new AFE, 37379, using the same justification as was used for AFE 33319, was written to begin the construction.[26] Beginning in March 1929, and running through November 1930, the Great Northern built 16 units at Hillyard Shops. The engines were numbered 2044 to 2059.

These were the largest steam locomotives the Great Northern ever owned, likewise, the largest locomotives built in their shops. Their construction was a great accomplishment for Hillyard. An idea of their great size can be gained by referring to the comparative table. As with the R-1's, the boilers were manufactured by the Puget Sound Machinery Depot. The new engines boasted a grate area of 126 square feet, and a boiler pressure of 240 psi. This was enough for them to enter the "superpower" league.

TABLE 3. R CLASS COMPARISONS AS BUILT

Class	B.P. psi	Heating Surface sq. ft.	Superheater Surface sq. ft.	Grate Area sq. ft.	Tractive Effort lbs.
Baldwin*	225	7,503	2,034	113	130,000
R-1a	210	6,963	1,920	108	127,500
R-1b	225	7,161	1,920	108	133,180
R-2	240	7,947	3,515	126	146,000

* proposal

Excellent views of both sides of R-2 2047 were obtained at Hillyard in October 1945. The fireman's side view clearly shows the Delta trailing truck. H. W. Pontin photograph from the collection of Norman F. Priebe.

The companion engineer's side view from October 1945 shows the vestibule cab, front end throttle with extended linkage and an otherwise similar appearance to the R-1. H. W. Pontin (RPS) photograph from the collection of Norman F. Priebe.

The 2049 is shown at Hillyard when new in 1929. Great Northern Railway.

This late fireman's side view of 2049 at Minot, ND, on August 28, 1949, shows the final piping arrangement for the latest appliances added. John Westphal collection, courtesy of John Luecke.

The 2055 was in frequent use between Williston and Minot in 1952. Here it is at Williston,
preparing to take an eastbound to Minot on September 30, 1952. Collection of Stan Kistler.

No. 2056 was still working on the Spokane/Cascade Division in 1948. (The Cascade Division was reinstated between 1947 and 1949.)
Here it is at Interbay, Seattle, departing eastbound on July 17, 1948. John Westphal collection, courtesy of John Luecke.

The 2058 is shown outside of the Hillyard shops after receiving its first major shopping in 1935. Photograph by Maynard Rikerd.

Locomotive accessories used included Ragonnet power reverse gear, a No. 16 Elesco exhaust steam injector and a Type E superheater. Only the superheater differed from R-1, with the R-2's using the Type E to achieve greater superheater surface. The engines also used a Delta trailing truck for the heavier firebox. An American multiple-valve front-end throttle was installed on these engines, as it would be on the N-3's later. They also had Nathan low water alarms. Vestibule cabs were applied after completion, and eventually all of the R-2's and a few of the R-1's acquired them. Modern appliances added after completion included an Electromatic foam collapsing system, a Nalco continuous blow-down system, and mechanical force-feed and Edna lubricators. Brick arches and arch tubes were added to the firebox between 1941 and 1943. Franklin radial buffers were installed on the R-2's, but no record of radial buffers applied to the R-1 class has been found.

All R-2's and 4 R-1's received new boilers in 1947 and 1948. The first AFE covered the four R-1's and six of the R-2's.[27] The last boiler AFE, 73626, covered the remainder of the R-2's.[28] Details may be found in the roster. The new boilers included Security circulators and Elesco steam dryers. Also installed under this AFE were new cast steel one piece frames and cylinders for the front engines. The work was completed in late 1948.

As with the R-1's, the GN carried an alternative tractive effort calculation on the diagrams for the R-2's from 1932 until 1943. The rating of 153,000 pounds, without booster, is believed to be a record for North American steam. Yet the GN did not continue to use this number after 1943, and instead even reduced the tractive effort somewhat. The normally used tractive effort rating of 146,000 pounds was reduced to 142,055 pounds after the diameter of the front cylinders was reduced in 1945. As with the R-1b, it is believed that a desire to reduce slipping was responsible for the reduction of tractive effort from the front engine. Refer to the diagrams for weights and other specifications. Note that weight on drivers and total weight differences after 1948 are the result both of the rebuilding program and the reweigh program. See Chapter 4.

The GN kept tonnage ratings for all of its steam locomotives. These were re-calculated from time to time as changes were made to the locomotives. The ratings for the N-3, R-1 and R-2 in approximately 1940 are given in Table 2 of Chapter 26. The R-2 ratings are before the front cylinders were reduced, when its tractive effort was 146,000 pounds.

The Great Northern did not incorporate all of the improvements that went into the R-class engines at one time. Many features beyond those of the basic engine were installed only after a strongly defined need arose. This also happened to the N-3 class. As it turned out, the N-3 class had been designed and built before the last of the R class modifications were completed.

When dealing with the R-2, one can get into the "Biggest" or "Most Powerful" discussion. To aid the comparison, Table 4 lists key specifications, including calculated boiler horsepower comparing the R-2 and large engines from other roads. Final weight and tractive effort figures (from 1948) are used for the R-2. Recall the tractive effort had been rated at 153,000 pounds between

TABLE 4. THE R-2 COMPARED TO OTHER LARGE SIMPLE ARTICULATEDS

Road	GN	WP	DM&IR	UP	C&O
Engine class	R-2	M-137-151	M-3	4000	H-8
Engine type	2-8-8-2	2-8-8-2	2-8-8-4	4-8-8-4	2-6-6-6
Weight of engine	686,440	665,100	695,040	762,000	724,500
Weight on drivers	592,000	552,700	560,257	540,000	471,000
Tractive effort, no booster	142,000	137,000	140,000	135,375	110,200
Grate Area, sq. ft.	126	145	125	150	135.2
Boiler horsepower, calculated	6,820	6,590	7,140	6,520	7,330
Driver Dia., inches	63	63	63	68	67

The potential boiler horsepower figure is used here as a figure of merit and size comparison, everything else being equal. It assumes identical BTU value fuel and a firebox that can deliver equal BTU's in each case. Johnson's method[29] is used, but with all locomotives calculated using a heat transfer factor of 80 instead of 55 and use of 300 degree superheat temperature.

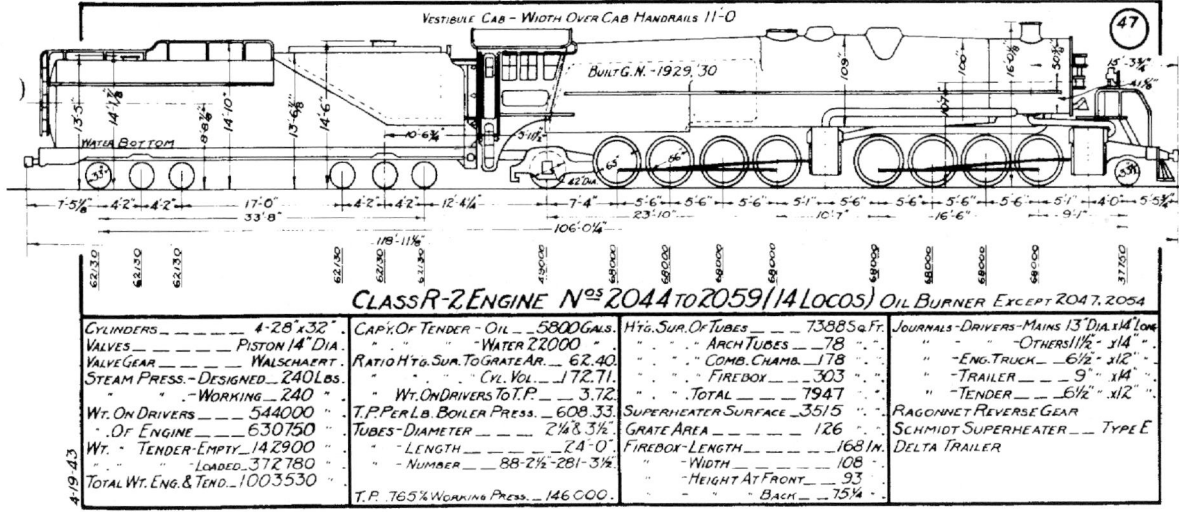

1932 and 1943.

In 1934, consideration was given to creating a new, even larger class by converting the R-1's into 2-8-8-4 type locomotives. A large new coal-burning firebox was to be put on, and the engines assigned to Minot to Williston runs. Mr. Kelly did not like the idea.[30] By December, more thought had been given to this matter, and both a GN design and a Baldwin proposal for a new 2-8-8-4 were drawn.[31] The GN designed engine was to have a grate area of 180 square feet. Neither engine was constructed. Mr. C. O. Jenks instead suggested putting a coal-burning R-2 on the Minot to Williston run and envisioned buying a superior new engine for the Kalispell Division.[32]

Eventually R-2's were put on the Minot to Williston run, but they remained oil-burners. Meanwhile, Mr. Jenks had to wait until 1939 for his new engine. It was in 1939 that Electro Motive Corporation (later the Electro Motive Division of General Motors, EMD) demonstrated the first FT, No. 103, a diesel.

The R's were assigned as follows in 1936. Both classes are shown. At this time they were "King of the Hill" so to speak, and had all of the heavy assignments.

Minot Division: 2030, 2031, 2032.
Kalispell Division: 2042, 2043, 2044, 2045, 2046, 2047, 2048, 2049, 2050, 2051, 2052, 2053, 2054, 2055, 2056, 2057, 2058, 2059.
Spokane Division: 2033, 2034, 2035, 2036, 2037, 2038, 2039, 2040, 2041.

Class N-3

During the 1930's, the Great Northern received several Baldwin and Alco proposals for modern superpower articulated locomotives, including 4-4-4-6, 2-6-6-4 and 4-6-6-4 arrangements. After studying them, the GN decided that the cost of new locomotives would be too much, given the economic conditions of the time. However with the

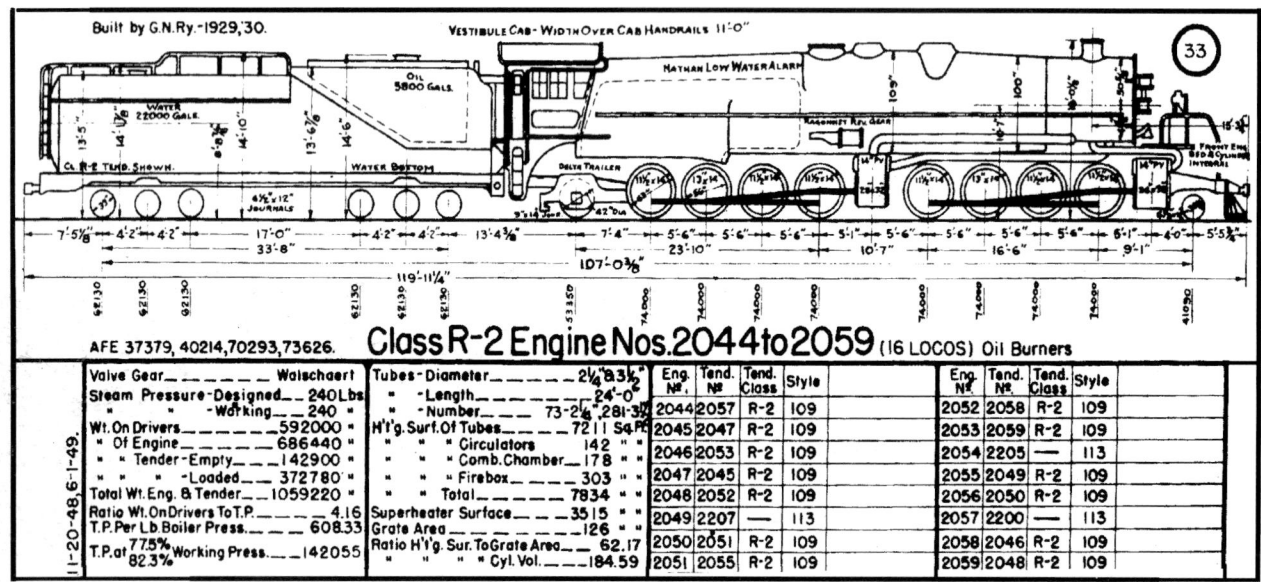

This revision of the locomotive diagram documents the last improvements made to the class as well as the correct weights and reduced tractive effort.

No. 2048 is ascending the east slope of Marias Pass with a westbound on September 19, 1940. Photograph by Henry R. Griffiths.

No. 2050 is eastbound at Essex (Walton) on the west slope of Marias Pass in approximately 1948 to 1950.
The train will stop to pick up a helper here. Frank McKinlay (RPS) photograph from the collection of Norman F. Priebe.

In the later days of service on the Cascade Division, 2050 is shown westbound along Puget Sound on
July 8, 1949. James A. Turner photograph from the Warren Wing collection, courtesy of Walter Ainsworth.

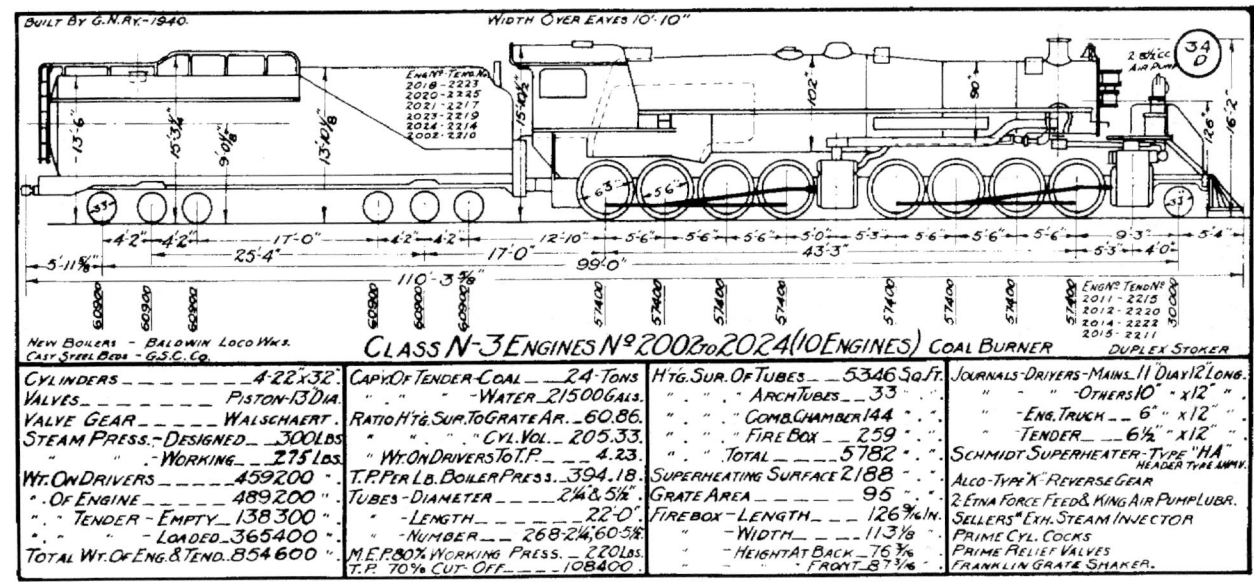

All of the coal-burning N-3 class engines assigned to the iron range initially had streamlined cabs and Sellers exhaust steam injectors.

clouds of war looming on the horizon, it was necessary that something be done to modernize their locomotive fleet. The result was the decision to design and build a modern replacement for the N-2 locomotive, to achieve a performance level as close to that of the R-classes as possible. This would be an entirely new locomotive, using an insignificant amount of material from the N-2. There were constraints, however. The new locomotive was to retain the identical wheelbase of the N-2 to be able to use existing turntables. It also was to keep the same external dimensions of the boiler. It was to be able to run at 50 mph, and it would have to negotiate a 16-degree curve. The other requirement was to give the engine the highest boiler horsepower possible within the size constrains, by using the latest state of the art. This meant high pressure, so the boiler was designed for 300 psi. A high degree of superheat was also an objective. Nickel steel had been used in the industry for several years by this time and had been used on the S-2's in 1930. It was selected for the N-3 boiler shell to take advantage of its high strength and lightweight characteristics.

The N-3 was considered an entirely new engine and received a new group number (Group 55) in the Unit Record of Property Changes. Very few N-2 parts were reused in the N-3. Those that were used included the original journals and axles, driving wheel centers, sandboxes, turbo generators and while not stated, probably the whistle, bell and headlight. The boiler incorporated the same number and size of flues and the same flue pattern used in the N-2. This resulted in the same superheater flue diameter of 5½ inches as was used with the Type A. To improve the superheater under these constraints required the design of a new type of superheater steam element to obtain the increased superheating surface area needed.

Howard S. (Sam) Silver was the design engineer, working under H. W. (Herb) Miller. Design work started in the summer of 1939. Commonwealth cast steel one-piece frames with integral cylinders were part of the design from the start. The flexible live steam lines to the front engine received 7-labyrinth seals as opposed to the usual 4 or 5-labyrinth design. The arch tubes of the N-2 were retained. The

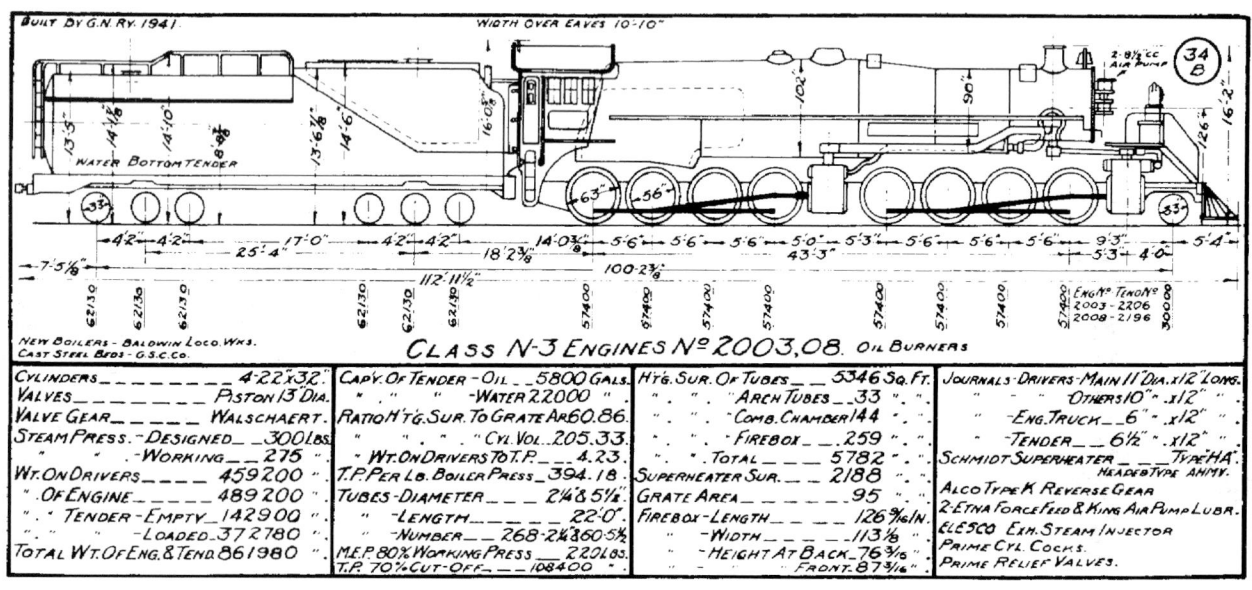

Although there are many diagrams of the N-3 class with a vestibule cab, the vestibules lasted only a very short while, and no photographs of them were found by the authors.

No. 2018, shown eastbound at State Line tower, was a typical iron range coal burning N-3.
This early view shows the streamlined cab and the Sellers exhaust steam injector. Great Northern Railway.

firebox was enlarged from a grate area of 78 square feet to 95 square feet, and the combustion chamber was enlarged from 81 square feet of heating surface to 144 square feet. The resulting N-3 combustion chamber was 70 inches long. Consequently, the flues were shortened from 24 feet to 22 feet. The design resulted in a 15-inch rear frame extension that lengthened the total wheelbase by a like amount.

Mr. Silver designed a unique superheater to fit in the 5½ inch flue which would give greater surface area than the classic Type A. Designated the HA type, it consisted of an inflow tube with the return flow tube wrapped helically around it. The element assembly was 4 inches in diameter.[33] The design was very effective. The superheater surface was increased from 1,868 square feet to 2,188 square feet in the new engines, despite a shorter flue and the use of only two passes instead of the four of a Type A. The result was a locomotive with an old drag service wheel arrangement that was the equal in every respect except top speed to the 4-6-6-4 type. A detailed comparison of the N-3 to the NP designed Z-6 class 4-6-6-4 is in chapter 26. Yet even

in the area of speed, they were undoubtedly the fastest 2-8-8-0 type ever built.

In keeping with the 50 mph speed requirement, a careful spring design was executed. For the best ride, the springs were designed to be at half deflection at operating weight. Improved counterbalancing methods also helped to increase the top speed of these engines.

Unusual for a steam engine was the use of finned radiator air aftercoolers. On most of the engines they were mounted over the top of the boiler behind the stack. A few had them under the running boards in the usual location. Others had them on the engineer's side of the tender. All engines were equipped with a Barco low water alarm. The Alco type K power reverse was used on these engines. The 2002 and 2009 received Security circulators when new, probably as a trial. The others had to wait several years for theirs. All locomotives received Franklin radial buffers between the engine frame and tender. Fourteen had Sellers exhaust steam injectors and eleven had Elesco.

Streamlining was a hot subject in the late 1930's. Mr. Silver had

Freshly painted into an all-black scheme, No. 2001 was one of the last N-3's still operating when photographed at Minneapolis, MN, on September 5, 1953. This engine had its finned air after-coolers mounted under the fireman's side running board. Frequently seen running between Minneapolis and Superior, at this time the N's also ran to Minot from Minneapolis. Bruce Black photograph from the collection of Norman F. Priebe.

Shown late in life on June 26, 1952, at Kelly Lake, MN, No. 2022 had the finned air after-coolers mounted behind the stack. Collection of Stan Kistler.

been asked to design a shroud for the H-5, with a streamlined slanted cab that directed the air up over the top of the cab. Earlier, Mr. Kelly and C. O. Jenks had decided a shroud would impair inspection and maintenance, so the shroud never came to be.[34] But the streamlined cab stayed, and was applied to several of the H-5's and some of the N-3's as well. These cabs were eventually replaced on the N-3's.

The N-3 regained the position of tallest of them all by going up to 16 feet, 2 inches over the smokestack. The R classes had exceeded the N-2 height by one-eighth inch! All received new blank class Vanderbilt tenders with 21,500 or 22,000-gallon water capacity with either 5,700 or 5,800 gallons of fuel oil capacity or 24 tons of coal. (Tender Style 113 had 22,000 gallons water and 5,800 gallons oil, Style 114 "only" 21,500 gallons and 5,700 gallons oil.)

Construction started immediately after the design was completed. The engines were built both at Superior and Hillyard shops. The first one finished was the 2024, on February 10, 1940. The rollout was accompanied by some bad luck. On the first try, a nut left in one of the cylinders blew out the cylinder head. On the second try, a rail rolled over under the engine and derailed it while on the way to the turntable. Things went better after that. On its first shakedown run, the locomotive pulled 97 cars from Superior to Minneapolis. The GN built 10 units first.[35] After trying them, a second AFE said "all N-2 engines to be disposed of and replaced with Class N-3, assuring more economical and dependable service on the iron range and elsewhere on the system."[36]

After the rebuilding, assignment of the N-3's put ten coal-burners on the Mesabi Division. They were 2010, 2011, 2012, 2014, 2015, 2018, 2020, 2021, 2023, and 2024. Two coal burners were on the Butte Division: 2001 and 2002, and thirteen, all but one oil burners, were on the Kalispell Division: 2000, 2003-2009, 2013 (the remaining coal burner), 2016, 2017, 2019 and 2022. Except for a six-month stint for the 2019, ending in April 1941, no N-3's were on the Klamath Division until after World War II.

Operation uncovered a problem with the journals of the driving

This spectacular view of the 2023 at Superior in July 1953 shows the late black boiler jacket, finned aftercoolers on the tender, and generator located forward, the normal location on the N-3 due to clearance restrictions. The view also shows the Sellers exhaust steam injector to good advantage. W. Krawiec photograph from the collection of William Raia.

Stopped in the siding at Stonehill, MT, No. 2013 was the lone coal-burning N-3 on the Kalispell Division for many years. This trip may have been its first with new roller bearings. In this view taken on May 13, 1944, it still had the lower front engine sandbox, but it had received its electric train indicators. Photograph by R. E. Johnson.

During World War II, the Kalispell Division was home to 13 N-3's, running primarily west of Whitefish. Here in October 1945 the 2005 is shown beginning a light run to Spokane to pick up an eastbound troop train of returning servicemen. This view by H. W. Pontin received wide distribution by the GN Public Relations department. Collection of Norman F. Priebe.

The next day, 2005 was turned and coupled to 16 cars of returning troops. Running as Second No. 28, it is shown storming up the 1% grade past Hillyard. Note the superheater is doing its job, as oil residue on the external steam pipes to the front engine is smoking profusely from the heat. H. W. Pontin (RPS) photograph from the collection of Norman F. Priebe.

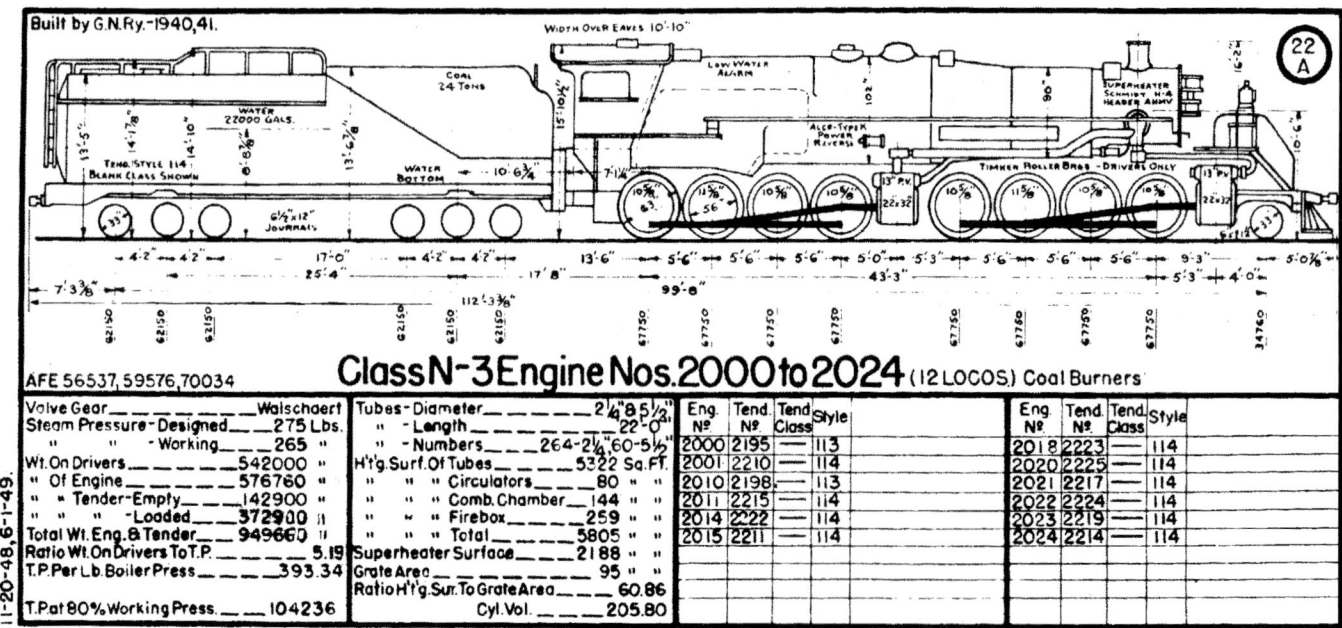

Built by G.N.Ry.-1940,41. — WIDTH OVER EAVES 10'-10" — 22 A

AFE 56537, 59576, 70034

Class N-3 Engine Nos. 2000 to 2024 (12 LOCOS) Coal Burners

Valve Gear	Walschaert			
Steam Pressure-Designed	275 Lbs.			
" " -Working	265 "			
Wt. On Drivers	542000 "			
" Of Engine	576760 "			
" " Tender-Empty	142900 "			
" " " -Loaded	372900 "			
Total Wt. Eng. & Tender	949660 "			
Ratio Wt. On Drivers To T.P.	5.19			
T.P. Per Lb. Boiler Press	393.34			
T.P. at 80% Working Press.	104236			

Tubes - Diameter	2¼"& 5½"	
" - Length	22'-0"	
" - Numbers	264-2¼"60-5½"	
H't'g. Surf. Of Tubes	5322 Sq. Ft.	
" " " Circulators	80 "	
" " " Comb. Chamber	144 "	
" " " Firebox	259 "	
" " " Total	5805 "	
Superheater Surface	2188 "	
Grate Area	95 " "	
Ratio H't'g. Sur. To Grate Area	60.86	
Cyl. Vol.	205.80	

Eng. Nº	Tend. Nº	Tend. Class	Style		Eng. Nº	Tend. Nº	Tend. Class	Style
2000	2195	—	113		2018	2223	—	114
2001	2210	—	114		2020	2225	—	114
2010	2198	—	113		2021	2217	—	114
2011	2215	—	114		2022	2224	—	114
2014	2222	—	114		2023	2219	—	114
2015	2211	—	114		2024	2214	—	114

11-20-48, 6-1-49.

Use this diagram for the correct weights and final configuration of the N-3.

R-2's continued to hold center stage between Minot and Williston after World War II. Here the 2045 is westbound at Gassman Coulee bridge out of Minot, ND, photographed from the north side in September 1945. W. J. Pontin (RPS) photograph from the collection of Norman F. Priebe.

wheels. The reused old journals and axles proved to be undersized for the weight of the new engine, and they always ran hot. It would frequently be necessary to run water over them to cool them when on the road. Cut boxes and journals were often found. The main driver journals were 11 inches by 12 inches and the other drivers were 10 inches by 12 inches, and had not been changed since the N-1 days. For comparison, the R-1 had 12½ by 14-inch journals on the main axle with 11 by 14 inches on the remainder. Even larger were the 13 by 14-inch main journals on the R-2, which had 11½ by 14-inch journals on the remainder of the driving axles. The problem was solved for the N-3 with the installation of roller bearings on the driving axles in 1944 and 1945. The first N-3 to receive the new bearings was the 2013 in May 1944. Roller bearings also eliminated a pounding problem with these engines. The electric train indicators were also installed in the 1944 and 1945 time frame. Another later change was the increased size of the front deck sand boxes.

Operation proved the high performance that was designed into these engines. On Rexford Hill, between Hillyard and Whitefish, they could haul approximately 4,000 tons on the 0.7 percent grade. Engineers reported they rode better than either of the R classes. Running up Rexford Hill, with the firing valve wide open and with a clear stack, the pyrometer indicated 750 degrees F steam heat. The effect of the high superheat achieved was noticed in a way not expected; grease and oil that had collected on the external steam pipes would burst into flame when the engine was working hard. To assist with the moving of troops during the war, nine engines were equipped with steam heat and air signal connections. In troop train service an N-3 could take any size train handed over from a level district, haul it over the Kalispell Division grades without a helper, and push the speed limits all the way. The engines assigned to the Mesabi Division set new tonnage records for the iron ore traffic during the war, hauling 180 cars and 16,740 tons per train. The downward grade to the docks with the loads contributed to the high tonnage capability.

There were 10 coal burners originally which were assigned to the Mesabi Division for use on the iron range. Most of the original coal burners stayed that way, but there were a few that had been changed to oil at some time. Others took their place until in 1949 there were 12 coal burners on the range. Good eastern bituminous coal was plentiful at Duluth-Superior, since it was a common back-haul for the lake ore boats. After 1950, all Great Northern steam locomotives were switched to oil fuel, including the range engines, and they ran the rest of their days on oil.

By 1948, the embrittlement problem had grown to such an extent that the design of boiler patches was a major task for the motive power department. Consequently the N-3's, along with the R's as mentioned earlier, and the S-2's underwent major boiler renewal work. For the N, this did not mean 100% boiler replacement, but some had to have all new boilers. All engines that did not have Security circulators received them at the time of the boiler work. Also at this time, the flues were reduced by four, which reduced the evaporative surface from 5,346 to 5,322 square feet. The arch tubes were removed, losing an additional 33 square feet. The circulators on the other hand added 80 square feet to the evaporative surface area for a net gain. The circulators, it was said, prolonged the life of the firebox side sheets.[37]

Embrittlement

The N-3 suffered an extreme case of the embrittlement problem because of its nickel steel boilers. This alloy and silico-manganese steel were more susceptible than boilers made with ordinary carbon steel. Nevertheless, all steel is sensitive to this problem to some degree. The R-1's, R-2's, N-3's and S-2's all had the problem, and research at the time did not fully explain the cause. By 1942, after all of the engines had been completed, the cause was beginning to be understood. The steel was reacting with high concentrations of sodium hydroxide in the water. High concentrations built up at the seam edges and rivet holes of the boilerplate where slow leakage and evaporation occurred. The preferred cure required welded boilers to eliminate the edges from which the cracking started. This was not possible because the ICC did not allow welded boilers at the time. The next best thing was to chemically treat the water to reduce the chemical reaction with the boiler surface. The easy way to treat the water was by adding acid, but that method had its own problems, so other chemicals have been used, especially sodium nitrate, with varying success.[38] The problem was still under study by the boiler industry in 1989, mainly in respect to stationary boilers.[39]

GN long had a water treatment program for the usual scale, or

R-2 No. 2049 is shown arriving at Minot, ND, in September 1949 with an eastbound extra with a large livestock shipment on the head end. Bruce Fales photograph from the Cornelius Hauck collection, courtesy of Jack W. Farrell.

No. 2055 gets a heavy westbound underway with a second R as a helper at Minot, ND, on October 3, 1952. The R-2's had about one year left of full-time assignments before they would be bounced by diesels. P. Slager photograph from the collection of William Raia.

*One of the last regular assignments for the N-3 class was on the Klamath Division.
Here No. 2008 is entering Bieber, CA, in 1951. W. A. Edgecomb (RPS) photograph from the collection of Norman F. Priebe.*

In May 1953 the 2014 was one of several N-3's running between Minot and Minneapolis. By this time diesels had already displaced most of the iron range engines, so this represented the last stand of the class. George Harris photograph from the collection of Norman F. Priebe.

encrustation, problem due to ordinary hard water. Their water treatment program employed both line-side and on-board treatment methods.[40] A program to add embrittlement treatment was added to this, but the success was marginal. It is not known whether the GN used different steel in the replacement boilers.

Final Service

All three classes were reweighed in 1948. The N-3 oil-burners were found to weigh 537,880 pounds on drivers with an engine weight of 572,375 pounds, the N-3 coal-burners were at 542,000 pounds on drivers and 576,760 pounds engine weight. The R-1's were found to be 555,000 pounds on drivers with an engine weight of 621,220 pounds and the R-2's came in at 592,000 pounds on drivers and an engine weight of 686,440 pounds.

By 1949, diesels had displaced many of the big articulateds from their original haunts. The 1949 assignment list for both the N and R classes shows a large buildup on the Klamath and Minot Divisions.

Mesabi Division: 2000, 2001, 2010, 2011, 2014, 2015, 2018, 2020, 2121, 2022, 2023, 2024.

Minot Division: 2003, 2004, 2009, 2016, 2044, 2045, 2046, 2047, 2049, 2051, 2052, 2053, 2055, 2056, 2059.

Kalispell Division: 2058.

Spokane Division: 2030, 2031, 2032, 2033, 2034, 2035, 2036, 2037, 2038, 2039, 2040, 2041, 2042, 2043.

Cascade Division: 2048, 2050, 2054, 2057.

Klamath Division: 2002, 2005, 2006, 2007, 2008, 2012, 2013, 2017, 2019.

R-2 No. 2053 is eastbound near Emerado, ND, on September 11, 1956, with 101 cars, as many loads as the Minot yardmaster could find. In a few weeks this magnificent locomotive would be permanently retired. Joe Collias photograph from the collection of Norman F. Priebe.

In September of 1952, two R-1's were requested for mine run service on the Mesabi Division. A strike had reduced production in the face of high demand and greater capacity was needed. They joined the smaller M-2 class articulateds in this service. The R-1's could haul more ore from a mine, were flexible enough for the sharp curves, and the axle loading was not too heavy for the branch line nature of the mine trackage. They stayed in this service for no longer than three months, until replaced by SD7 diesels early in 1953. One of the engines was 2040; the other number is not known.[41] The final service assignment for the R-1's was ore steaming. The first set, 2030, 2031 and 2033, served from 1951 until the spring of 1956. They were replaced by 2040, 2042 and 2043 in time for the winter of 1956. The second set served until 1958.

All classes remained available for active assignment in 1953 but the iron range N-3's had been displaced from their regular runs by F7 diesels in mid-1952. However, the record demand for ore in 1953 kept some in service through the summer, specifically the 2022 and 2023. A number of R-2's were still working out of Minot. The end came abruptly in 1954. None of these engines ran after September that year. No record of them running in 1955 can be found and only four R-2's returned in 1956. They were the 2047, 2053, 2054 and 2055, used between Minot and Grand Forks, ND on the Dakota Division.[42] High grain volumes required the R-2's that autumn, on the opposite side of Minot from their historical assignment. Afterwards, they dumped their fires for the last time. So ends the story of the largest and most powerful steam locomotives the Great Northern ever owned, displaced by an even better technology.

Notes:

1. "Mallet Locomotives for the Great Northern," *Railway Age Gazette*, Vol. 53, No. 13, p.572, September 27, 1912.
2. Baldwin Locomotive Company Builders card.
3. Paul T. Warner, "The Great Northern Railway and its Locomotives," *Baldwin Locomotives Magazine*, January 1925 (Also reprinted in *Pacific Railway Journal*, Summer 1956; and by the Fraternal Order of Empire Builders, February 1978.).
4. Engine Hours and Mileage, attached to a memo from J. F. Pratt to G. H. Emerson, May 7, 1913.
5. A.H. Hogeland, memo to C.O. Jenks, June 4, 1923. GN papers MHS.
6. Unit Record of Property Changes - Equipment (URPC), groups 1849-4, 1849-5. The books were studied at the GN offices in St. Paul. Partial copies are now in the possession of the authors.
7. Warner, *op. cit.*
8. URPC, *op. cit.* Great Northern Railway Authority for Expenditure (AFE) 40216, which was written to cover all 25 locomotives, was referenced.
9. Neil L. Carlson, "Simple Articulateds", *Trains Magazine*, January 2002.
10. Henry Blanchard, Manager, The Baldwin Locomotive Works, letter to C. O. Jenks, June 26, 1924. GN papers, MHS.
11. William Kelly, memo to C. O. Jenks, June 30, 1924. GN papers MHS.
12. URPC, *op. cit.*
13. D. A. Kerr, memo to J. A. Lengby, January 26, 1927. GN papers MHS.
14. Great Northern Railway AFE 27138, September 22, 1924.
15. "2-8-8-2 Type Locomotives for the Great Northern Railway", *Railway and Locomotive Engineering*, p. 223, August 1925.
16. Great Northern Railway AFE 33319, December 15, 1926. Mr. J. M. Hurley was Superintendent and A. B. Colville General Foreman at Hillyard at this time.
17. Great Northern Railway AFE 35658, December 5, 1927.
18. The Puget Sound Machinery Depot had been located in the Edmonds area since the turn of the century. They were in the boiler making and steam machinery business. Likely a large portion of their work was for ships. They overhauled locomotives for the GN in 1922 but it is not known if this was an ongoing practice. They built the large boilers for the GN R classes from 1927 through 1930, and during World War II they built boilers for Liberty ships. They went out of business in 1948.
19. No. 2042 was converted to coal in July 1929 per URPC, but changed back by 1938.
20. URPC Group No. 40.
21. Reference 15, *op. cit.* has 20 degrees, but A. B. Colville's personal notes have 16 degrees.
22. I. G. Pool to A. N. Cranshaw, Purchasing Agent, June 22, 1943. GN collection, MHS.
23. Great Northern Railway AFE 70293, February 19, 1945.
24. Great Northern Railway AFE 89838, December 6, 1957. The first ore steamers were the 2030, 2031 and 2033. A second series of R-1's, the 2040, 2042 and 2043, served until 1958. From the record, it looks like there was no ore steaming done in 1959.
25. Great Northern Railway AFE 39539, March 21,1929.
26. Great Northern Railway AFE 37379, June 20, 1928.
27. AFE 70293, *op. cit.*
28. Great Northern Railway AFE 73626, October 5, 1946.
29. Ralph P. Johnson, *The Steam Locomotive*, Simmons-Boardman Publishing Corporation, New York, NY 1942. Page 167 and Appendix C.
30. William Kelly, memo to C.O. Jenks, May 1 1934. GN papers, MHS.
31. C. Riddell, memo to C.O Jenks, December 18, 1934, C.O. Jenks, memo to W. Kelly, December 20, 1934. GN papers, MHS.
32. C. O. Jenks to W. Kelly, December 20, 1934. GN papers, MHS.
33. A problem with this description, related to the author by the designer, is that the 1941 Locomotive Cyclopedia says the inflow and outflow tubes of the type HA were concentric with each other (not helically wound) and that the inflow went through the outer tube. It is possible the design was changed before construction.
34. C. O. Jenks to Ralph Budd, June 12, 1931. GN papers, MHS. Mr. Jenks had received a correspondence from Wm. Kelly regarding his opposition a few days earlier. Wm. Kelly to C. O. Jenks, April 27, 1931. GN papers, MHS. See Chapter 28.
35. Great Northern Railway AFE 56537, October 14, 1938.
36. Great Northern Railway AFE 59575, July 1, 1940.
37. Great Northern Railway AFE 59576, July 1, 1940, and Great Northern Railway AFE 70034, November 8, 1944.
38. Johnson, page 65 ff., *op. cit.*
39. NISTIR 88-3099, National Technical Information Service, Springfield, VA 22161.
40. Colville, *op. cit.*
41. Robert Downing, GN, BN, Vice Chairman and Chief Operating Officer, retired, in a speech before the GNRHS at the Grand Forks Convention July 12, 1999. Mr. Downing was Trainmaster at Kelly Lake in 1952 and was responsible for obtaining the engines.
42. Dakota Division Dispatcher Logs, 1956. GNRHS.

The builders photograph depicts the tall stack, square cab, large ash hoppers and inside admission to the cylinders of the original first version of O-1's. Note also the long cylindrical and short conical portions of the boiler, and minimum amount of air aftercooling piping. The tenders from this order were later designated as Style 62. Collection of H. L. Broadbelt.

Chapter 20
Early Class O 2-8-2 Mikado

As with Chapter 13 on the Pacific classes, the term "Early 2-8-2" here means those locomotives which were originally built as Mikados, as opposed to those which were constructed in Great Northern's own shops from other wheel arrangements. These encompass Classes O-1 through O-4.

Class O-1

In late 1911, Baldwin produced the first locomotives of 2-8-2 wheel arrangement to be built for the Great Northern Railway. Each of these 20 locomotives (3000-3019) weighed 287,000 pounds, and had 220,000 pounds on the driving wheels. Cylinders were 28 inches in diameter with a 32-inch stroke, and were equipped with 13-inch piston valves. Drivers were 63 inches in diameter, and tractive effort was rated at 60,930 pounds, which exceeded that of the L-2 articulated locomotives already on the road. Valve gear was of Walschaert design. The main frame was cast in one piece, while the rear frames were separate and were arranged to accommodate the Hodges trailing truck. The lateral play between rails and flanges was sufficient to enable the locomotives to easily negotiate ten degree curves.

The boilers used on the O-1's had Belpaire fireboxes and were similar to those used on the L-1 2-6-6-2's previously received by the GN. The boiler shell was 82 inches in diameter at the front end, and increased to 89 inches at the dome ring. The boilers had a designed steam pressure of 210 psi, and an operating pressure of 180 psi. The trade press at the time indicated that Emerson superheaters were used on these locomotives, which markedly increased the total equivalent

heating surface.[1] Early diagrams, though, indicate that the engines had Great Northern Old Style superheaters. As indicated in Chapter 3, these terms were apparently synonymous.

The firebox had a grate area of 78 square feet, but there is no evidence that these engines were equipped with stokers when delivered. One rather unusual feature on the O-1's was the ash pan, which was equipped with six drop-bottom hoppers. These hoppers were placed outside the rail line for ready access, and are very prominent (two in front and one behind the trailing truck on each side) in the builder's photos of the O-1. The locomotives of this order were equipped with inside steam pipes. They were large engines for their time. The GN's neighboring roads either never received Mikados this large, or did not receive any of this size until at least five years later. Among those of the C&NW, NP and SOO Line, there were none with as large a boiler, although the original tractive effort was met or slightly exceeded by some of these later engines.

The success of these first Mikados led to the purchase of others, and fifty additional Class O-1 locomotives were constructed in 1913.[2] These engines were numbered as 3020-3069. The earliest diagrams for this group known to the authors indicate that like the previous order, this order had inside steam pipes. The diagrams also indicate that these engines were equipped with Great Northern New Style superheaters. The only major differences between this order and the first was in the number and size of boiler tubes (which may have been related to superheater differences), and that locomotives 3020 and 3021 were apparently built as oil burners.

This 1913 view of 3001 at Alcott, MN, on the iron range, emphasizes the non-electric headlight. This photograph also gives a good view of the long reverse lever or "Johnson Bar" used before power assisted reverse mechanisms. Courtesy of George Fischer.

Until approximately 1919, there were just minor changes to the appearance to the engines. An example is the 3000, which had been booster-equipped, but retained the tall stack and square cab. The locomotive has also been equipped with a 17,000-gallon Style 112 tender as evidenced by the tank anchor lugs along the frame. This view is at Minneapolis on an unknown date in the 1930's. Collection of John R. Quinn.

The 3009 as shown here at Minneapolis, MN, is representative of the 1930-era appearance of the O-1 class. Typical are the square cab, original tall stack, the 1923 cast headlight and coal-fuel rectangular tender. The main difference is that is it one of ten that received an Elesco feed water heater. Photograph from the F. G. Zahn collection, courtesy of Eric Archer.

Another tall stack, square cab view shows the 3004 with a Sellers exhaust steam injector and booster at Minneapolis before World War II. R. J. Foster photograph from the collection of William Raia.

This is a good example of the transition period with square cabs and short stacks. No. 3006 is shown at Minneapolis, MN, on March 26, 1938. Collection of William Raia.

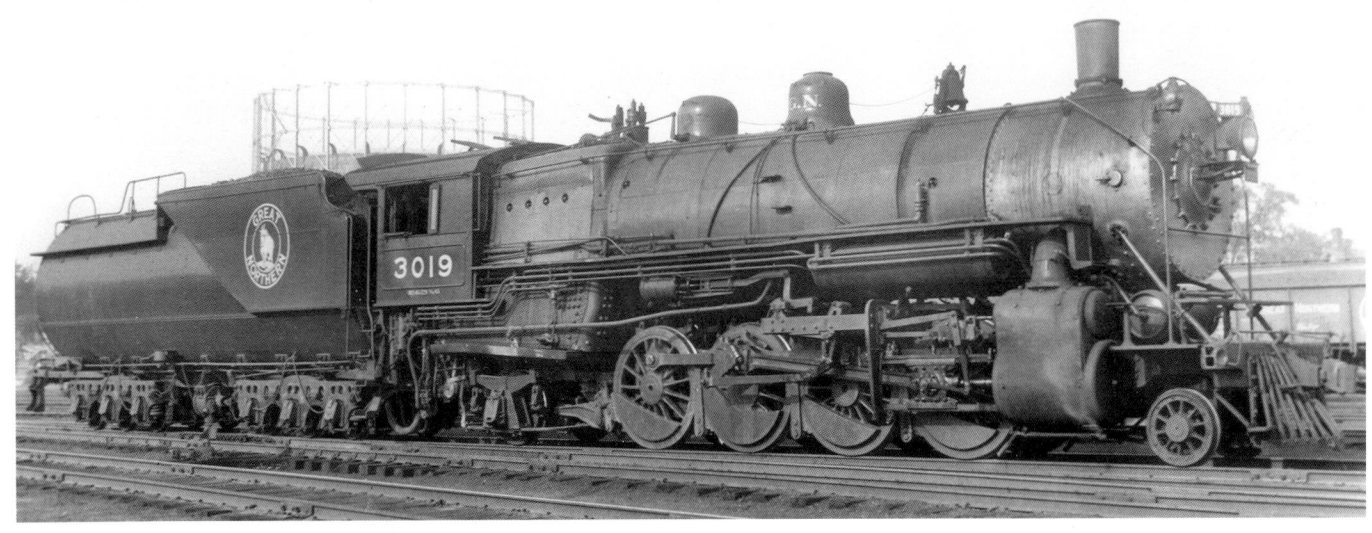

While it still has both a square cab and long stack, the 3019 has been upgraded to a large Style 112 Vanderbilt tender in this pre-World War II view at Minneapolis. R. J. Foster photograph from the collection of William Raia.

In September 1949, coal burner No. 3002 was at Kelly Lake, MN. The engine came to the Mesabi Division during World War II. It is doubtful it went through the universal conversion to oil, as it was scrapped in 1952. The engine is equipped with Prime cylinder protection bypass valves, something only a few O-1's possessed. The engine was equipped with a Nalco continuous blowdown system in 1947. Photograph from the John Allen collection.

The 3002 is shown here at Minneapolis in May 1946. The locomotive had electric train indicators earlier, but they had been removed by this time. The tender is Style 68 O-1 tender No. 3102. Stan F. Styles collection of GTC Collectibles.

A coal burner shown at Minneapolis on October 9, 1946, the 3010 was one of the eastern coal burners replaced by a western oil burner as part of the 1950 universal switch to oil. By this time it is in its final configuration. The original smokebox front has been replaced with a plain flat steel front. Robert Graham photograph from the collection of William Raia.

The 3013 may never have been converted to burn oil. Here at Superior on June 21, 1951, it still is burning coal, a very late date for coal burners. It is accompanied by tender No. 1614, a J-2 Style 49. It was scrapped in 1953. John Westphal, collection of John Luecke.

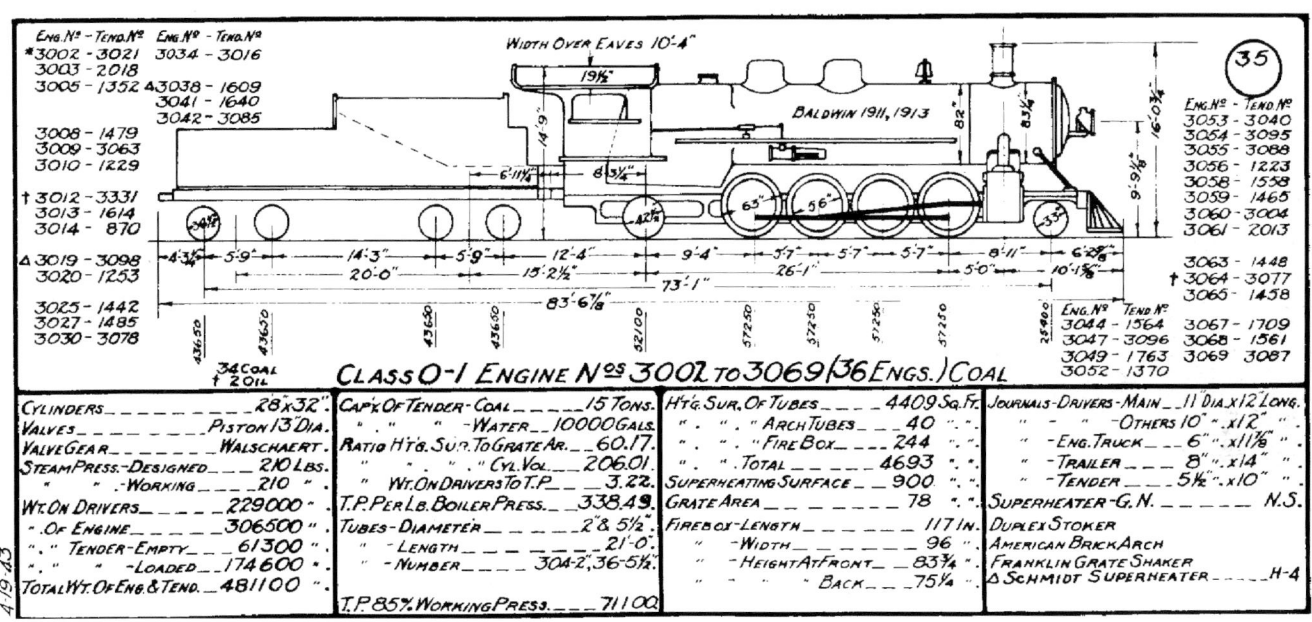

CLASS O-1 ENGINE Nos 3002 to 3069 (36 ENGS.) COAL

CYLINDERS — 28 x 32"	CAP'Y OF TENDER - COAL — 15 TONS.	HT'G. SUR. OF TUBES — 4409 Sq.Ft.	JOURNALS-DRIVERS-MAIN — 11" DIA x 12" LONG.
VALVES — PISTON 13 DIA.	" " —WATER — 10000 GALS.	" " "ARCH TUBES — 40 " "	" " -OTHERS 10" x 12" "
VALVE GEAR — WALSCHAERT.	RATIO HT'G. SUR. TO GRATE AR. — 60.17.	" " "FIRE BOX — 244 " "	" -ENG. TRUCK — 6" x 11⅞" "
STEAM PRESS.-DESIGNED — 210 LBS.	" " " CYL. VOL. — 206.01.	" " "TOTAL — 4693 " "	" -TRAILER — 8" x 14" "
" " -WORKING — 210 "	WT. ON DRIVERS TO T.P. — 3.22.	SUPERHEATING SURFACE — 900 " "	" -TENDER — 5½" x 10" "
WT. ON DRIVERS — 229000	T.P. PER LB. BOILER PRESS. — 338.49.	GRATE AREA — 78 " "	SUPERHEATER-G.N. — N.S.
" OF ENGINE — 306500	TUBES-DIAMETER — 2 & 5½"	FIREBOX-LENGTH — 117 IN.	DUPLEX STOKER
" " TENDER-EMPTY — 61300	" -LENGTH — 21'-0".	" -WIDTH — 96 "	AMERICAN BRICK ARCH
" " -LOADED — 174600	" -NUMBER — 304-2, 36-5½.	" -HEIGHT AT FRONT — 83¾ "	FRANKLIN GRATE SHAKER
TOTAL WT. OF ENG. & TEND. — 481100 "		" -BACK — 75¼ "	△ SCHMIDT SUPERHEATER — H-4
4-19-43	T.P. 85% WORKING PRESS. — 71100		

Eng.Nº - Tend.Nº
*3002 - 3021 3034 - 3016
3003 - 2018
3005 - 1352 △3038 - 1609
　　　　　　3041 - 1640
　　　　　　3042 - 3085
3008 - 1479
3009 - 3063
3010 - 1229
†3012 - 3331
3013 - 1614
3014 - 870
△3019 - 3098
3020 - 1253
3025 - 1442
3027 - 1485
3030 - 3078

Eng.Nº - Tend.Nº
3053 - 3040
3054 - 3095
3055 - 3088
3056 - 1223
3058 - 1558
3059 - 1465
3060 - 3004
3061 - 2013

3063 - 1448
†3064 - 3077
3065 - 1458

3044 - 1564 3067 - 1709
3047 - 3096 3068 - 1561
3049 - 1763 3069 3087
3052 - 1370

34 COAL
† 2 OIL

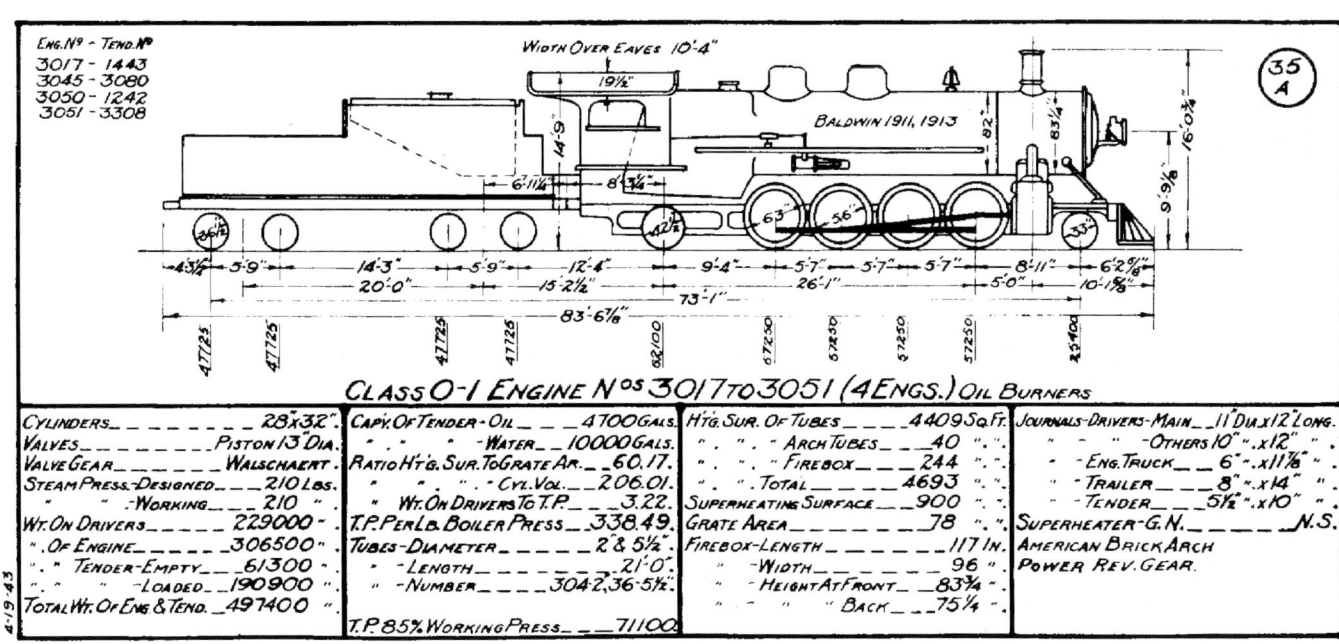

CLASS O-1 ENGINE Nos 3017 to 3051 (4 ENGS.) OIL BURNERS

CYLINDERS — 28 x 32"	CAP'Y OF TENDER - OIL — 4700 GALS.	HT'G. SUR. OF TUBES — 4409 Sq.Ft.	JOURNALS-DRIVERS-MAIN — 11" DIA x 12" LONG.
VALVES — PISTON 13 DIA.	" " —WATER — 10000 GALS.	" " "ARCH TUBES — 40 " "	" " -OTHERS 10" x 12" "
VALVE GEAR — WALSCHAERT.	RATIO HT'G. SUR. TO GRATE AR. — 60.17.	" " "FIRE BOX — 244 " "	" -ENG. TRUCK — 6" x 11⅞" "
STEAM PRESS.-DESIGNED — 210 LBS.	" " " CYL. VOL. — 206.01.	" " "TOTAL — 4693 " "	" -TRAILER — 8" x 14" "
" " -WORKING — 210 "	WT. ON DRIVERS TO T.P. — 3.22.	SUPERHEATING SURFACE — 900 " "	" -TENDER — 5½" x 10" "
WT. ON DRIVERS — 229000 -	T.P. PER LB. BOILER PRESS. — 338.49.	GRATE AREA — 78 " "	SUPERHEATER-G.N. — N.S.
" OF ENGINE — 306500	TUBES-DIAMETER — 2 & 5½"	FIREBOX-LENGTH — 117 IN.	AMERICAN BRICK ARCH
" " TENDER-EMPTY — 61300	" -LENGTH — 21'-0".	" -WIDTH — 96 "	POWER REV. GEAR.
" " -LOADED — 190900	" -NUMBER — 304-2, 36-5½.	" -HEIGHT AT FRONT — 83¾ "	
TOTAL WT. OF ENG. & TEND. — 497400 "		" -BACK — 75¼ "	
4-19-43	T.P. 85% WORKING PRESS. — 71100		

Eng.Nº - Tend.Nº
3017 - 1443
3045 - 3080
3050 - 1242
3051 - 3308

Twenty-five more O-1's (3070-3094) were received in 1916, this time with a few more apparent differences. The rear section of the boiler (the dome ring) was slightly longer, while the conical portion was shortened. The size and number of boiler tubes was the same as the 1913 order. The sandbox, however, had been shifted forward noticeably. Engine weight was increased to 306,500 pounds, and weight on drivers increased to 229,000 pounds. These locomotives were also equipped with Street Stokers and Franklin grate shakers, and were the first to be received with outside steam pipes. An article released at the time this order was built states that they also had Emerson superheaters,[3] though diagrams show them with Great Northern New Style superheaters, indicating that Mr. Emerson had a hand in the New Style design as well.

The last group of O-1's (3095-3144) were received by the Great Northern from 1917 through 1919. These were quite similar to the 1916 order, but were equipped with larger sandboxes than previous O-1's, also located in a position forward of that in the original order. Locomotives 3140 through 3144 were equipped with Southern rather than Walschaert valve gear. The railroads at this time were under control of the United States Railroad Administration (USRA), and there is some evidence that engines 3103-3106 and 3110 were diverted to the Wheeling & Lake Erie Railroad by the USRA for a time. Engines 3107-3109 and 3111-3114 were all received in June 1918, while 3103-3106 and 3110 were not received until December 1918. A note found in New Equipment Register 8 states that "F.A. Bushnell on 5/13/18 advises Bills of lading show shipment consigned to A.H. Smith Regional Director of Eastern Railroads c/o Wheeling & Lake Erie RR at Canton O."[4]

Great Northern began modifying the engines before too long. Apparently among the first of these was the removal of the ash hoppers from the firebox. Stokers were added to those not built with them from about 1917 to 1920.[5] During the 1920's, those not originally equipped received outside steam pipes, and many of the Great Northern style superheaters were replaced with Schmidt superheaters. It is interesting to note that the tenders of 3045 to 3069 were rebuilt, possibly before

3021 was a second order O-1. In the middle of the transition period, at Minneapolis MN, July 1938, it has the short stack and a square cab. The large Vanderbilt tenders were put on a few O-1's in the 1930's and remained into World War II. Eventually they were put on class O-4's. Collection of Harold K. Vollrath.

The 3030 is a second order engine with a third order tender (Style 64, having had capacity increased to 10,000 gallons water, probably No. 3078). The curved lower edge of the coal bunker on the tender is evident here. The engine has the new short stack, but the square cab has not been changed at the time of the photograph at Devils Lake, ND, on February 26, 1943. Photograph by Don Vang, GNRHS collection.

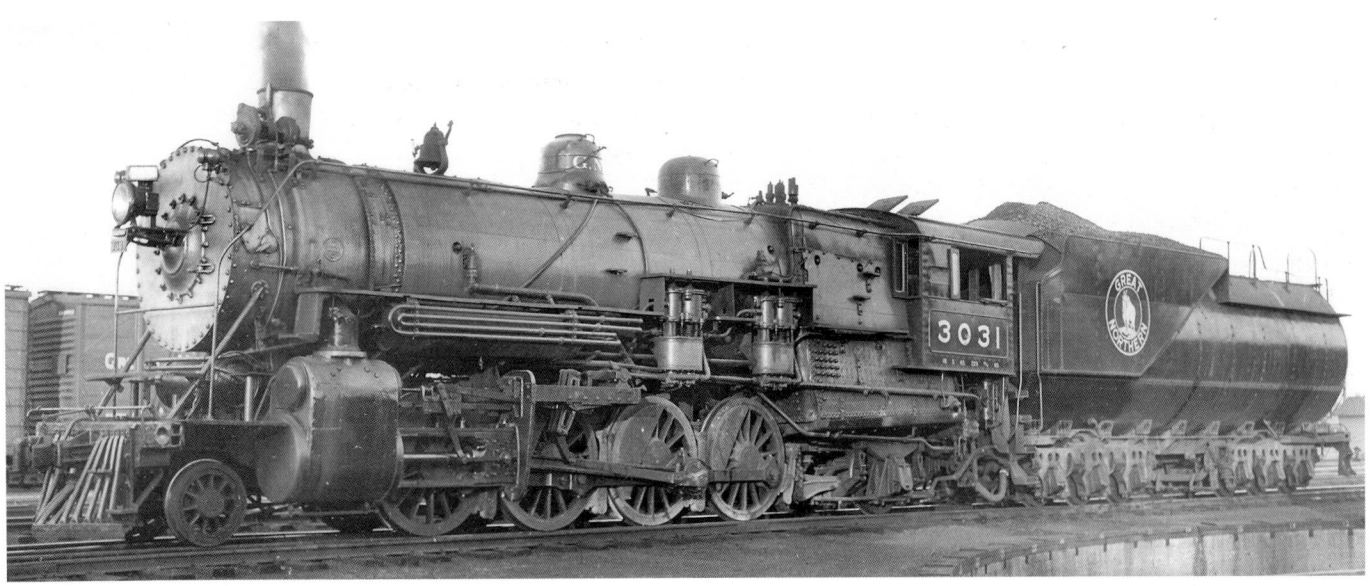

The second order O-1's had the same boiler style and dome position as the first order. The ash hoppers were the first feature to be removed. Conversion to outside steam admission began in 1924. When photographed at Minneapolis, MN, on July 2, 1938, the 3031 had both a square cab and tall stack. Robert Graham photograph from the collection of William Raia.

The 3046 had a square cab, tall stack, booster and was a coal burner in this October 10, 1937, view at Minneapolis, MN. The tender is No. 2008, a Style 59 N-2 tender. Robert Graham photograph from the collection of William Raia.

No. 3025 came to the Mesabi Division before World War II and remained until it was retired. Here it is at Kelly Lake on April 28, 1949. The most obvious late era changes are the slant-front cab and foot board pilot. This engine was not converted to oil before its retirement. The tender is 1442, a Style 32 H-4 class. P. Eilenberger photograph from the collection of William Raia.

*The 3042 went from the Dakota Division to the Spokane Division and then to the Mesabi Division.
It is in its final configuration at Spokane, WA, in 1947. Wilbur C. Whittaker photograph.*

*No. 3034 is shown at Minot, ND, on August 27, 1949, accompanied by Style 62 O-1 tender 3016 from the first order. The engine is one
of the few O-1's to have Prime automatic cylinder protection valves. John Westphal photograph from the collection of John Luecke.*

*After being transferred east from the Spokane Division, the 3051 worked at Minot, ND, as seen here, before going on to the Willmar division.
The 3051 was one of several O-1's that received large sand domes. October 1949. Photograph from the John Allen collection.*

The 3065 is at Superior, WI, on July 7, 1948. This engine was converted to burn oil between 1949 and 1952.
It was scrapped in 1953. Photograph from the John Westphal collection of John Luecke.

This view clearly shows the change in boiler contour for the third order, continued use of the ash hoppers and the factory
installed outside admission steam pipes. Baldwin photograph, courtesy of Jerrold F. Hilton.

The 3073, at Devils lake, ND, on January 1, 1944, has a short stack, a square cab and is trailing a later design rectangular auxiliary tender.
The rectangular auxiliary cars were made from older small tenders. They carried only water. Photograph by Don Vang, GNRHS collection.

An earlier water-only auxiliary tender was adapted from tank cars. Here one is with the 3077 at Bieber, CA, on May 30, 1941. The engine has its short stack but the original square cab. Photograph by Frank Guernsey, from the John Westphal collection of John Luecke.

On November 11, 1939, the 3080 still had both a tall stack and a square cab, but had otherwise been modernized with power reverse gear. Photograph by Don Vang, GNRHS collection.

Another transition variation was the change from coal to oil on the eastern divisions. Here is 3081, an early oil-burner at Devils Lake, ND, March 20, 1943. Photograph by Don Vang, GNRHS collection.

No. 3082, here at Devils Lake, ND, is another example of the transition period with square cab and short stack. It has a Sellers exhaust steam injector. Note the boxcar of coal in the background being winched into the coal dock in August 1943. Photograph by Don Vang, GNRHS collection.

The 3071 is shown at Minneapolis in June 1947, with slant cab and short stack. It also has a booster, which would last for two more years before removal. On the other side is a Worthington feed water heater. Photograph by Larry Stuckey, from the John Westphal collection of John Luecke.

Although an earlier view of the fireman's side of 3071 was used in Chapter 3 to illustrate the Worthington feed water heater, this view more closely matches the date of the engineer's side view shown above. In the four intervening years since the Portland view was taken the only visible changes were a changed smokebox front and the repainted cylinder jackets. The engine was at Minneapolis on June 29, 1947. K. L. Zurn photograph from the collection of William Raia.

the ICC valuation in 1915, to a 10,000 gallon water capacity, the first 8,000 gallon tenders thus modified by the GN. After rebuilding these tenders were transferred to the N-1 2-8-8-0 locomotives.

Numerous other modifications and rebuilds were completed on the engines during their nearly fifty years of service. During the early 1920's they received steel pilots. Beginning in the mid-1920's, most of the engines received power reverse gear. Many of the O-1's were eventually fitted for burning oil. A number were also fitted with feedwater heaters or exhaust steam injectors during the late 1920's and early 1930's. Locomotives 3003, 3009, 3037, 3052, 3079, 3085, 3103, 3104, 3105 and 3106 are known to have been equipped with Elesco feedwater heater systems during at least a portion of their service lives. Numbers 3005, 3014, 3022, 3042, 3054, 3071, 3072, 3098, 3117, 3121, 3132, 3133 and 3135 were equipped with Worthington BL or BL2 feedwater heaters. Engine 3033 was equipped with a Worthington SA feedwater heater, and engine 3046 was equipped with a Worthington S feedwater heater. Number 3143 had either a Worthington Type S or SA feedwater

heater, but it was removed in 1942.[6] Many engines were equipped with exhaust steam injectors (either Elesco No. 14 or Sellers No. 11). Engines known to have been equipped with Elesco devices were 3007, 3010, 3011, 3031, 3032, 3045, 3053, 3064, 3069 and 3129. Those known to have been equipped with Sellers exhaust steam injectors were 3004, 3013, 3015, 3016, 3018, 3019, 3021, 3031, 3032, 3048, 3057, 3066, 3082, 3094, 3095, 3100, 3101 and 3111. Engines 3011 and 3035 were equipped with Elesco exhaust steam injectors, which diagrams indicate were later replaced with Sellers. The 3122 and 3140 received the GN's Kelly branch pipe heater. Photographs indicate that many of these feedwater heating devices were removed or replaced during the later years of steam operation.

Illuminated number boards, referred to as electric train indicators in GN records, were installed on top of the smokebox adjacent to the stack on most of the locomotives, with the first installations done in 1932 for operation over the Southern Pacific joint trackage in Oregon. This was necessary to comply with the SP operating rules. Many others

On February 16, 1947 the 3078 was on the Cascade Division at Portland, OR. A western oil burner, it was another of the Lines West engines moved east to displace veteran coal burners. Ultimately it was scrapped the same year as the engines it displaced, 1953. Photograph by Frank Guernsey from the John Westphal collection of John Luecke.

In July 1951 the 3078 was at Willmar, MN, still with a green boiler but with all black cylinders. In the four intervening years since the Portland view was taken the only visible changes were a changed smokebox front and the repainted cylinder jackets. Photograph by Bruce Black.

This early fireman's side view is close to the delivered state of the fourth order. The locomotive still has ash hoppers, tall stack and old headlight. Date, location and photographer are unknown. GNRHS collection.

The 3108 was photographed during shipment at Eddystone, PA, in 1918. Do not confuse the air line going over the boiler top with boiler-top water feed. By the time of this order, electric headlights were being put on at the factory. Collection of Harold K. Vollrath.

This view of 3098 shows the larger sand dome of this order, and by the date this view was taken, it already had its short stack and a Worthington BL-2 feedwater heater, installed backwards. It had a square cab and Style 112 Vanderbilt tender. These tenders were moved to class O-4 engines during World War II. Photographed at Minneapolis by Robert Graham, courtesy of Eric Archer.

CYLINDERS	28"x32".	CAPY. OF TENDER - COAL	15 TONS	H'T'G. SUR. OF TUBES	4233 SQ. FT.	JOURNALS - DRIVERS - MAINS	11" DIA. x 12" LONG.
VALVES	PISTON 13" DIA.	" . " - WATER	10000 GALS.	" . " . " ARCH TUBES	40 " . ".	" - " OTHERS	10" " . x 12" " .
VALVE GEAR	WALSCHAERT	RATIO H'T'G. SUR. TO GRATE AR.	58.16.	" . " . " FIREBOX	244 " . ".	" - ENG. TRUCK	6" " . x 12" " .
STEAM PRESS. - DESIGNED	210 LBS.	" " . " . " CYL. VOL.	198.30.	" . " . TOTAL	4517 " . ".	" - TRAILER	8" " . x 14" " .
" " . - WORKING	210 " .	" WT. ON DRIVERS TO T.P.	3.22	SUPERHEATING SURFACE	1043 " . ".	" - TENDER	6" " . x 11" " .
WT. ON DRIVERS	229000 " .	T.P. PER LB. BOILER PRESS.	338.49	GRATE AREA	78 " . ".	SUPERHEATER	SCHMIDT H-A TYPE
" . OF ENGINE	317100 " .	TUBES - DIAMETER	2¼" & 5½".	FIREBOX - LENGTH	117 IN.	DUPLEX STOKER	
" . " TENDER - EMPTY	67200 " .	" - LENGTH	21'-0" .	" - WIDTH	96 " .	DELTA TRAILER	LOCO BOOSTER.
" . " " - LOADED	180600 " .	" - NUMBER	234-2¼. 45-5½".	" - HEIGHT AT FRONT	83¾ " .	FRANKLIN GRATE SHAKER	
TOTAL WT. OF ENG. & TEND.	497700 " .	T.P. OF BOOSTER	12200.	" - " BACK	75¼ " .	RAGONNET REVERSE GEAR	
		T.P. 85% WORKING PRESS	71100.			AMERICAN BRICK ARCH	

4-19-43

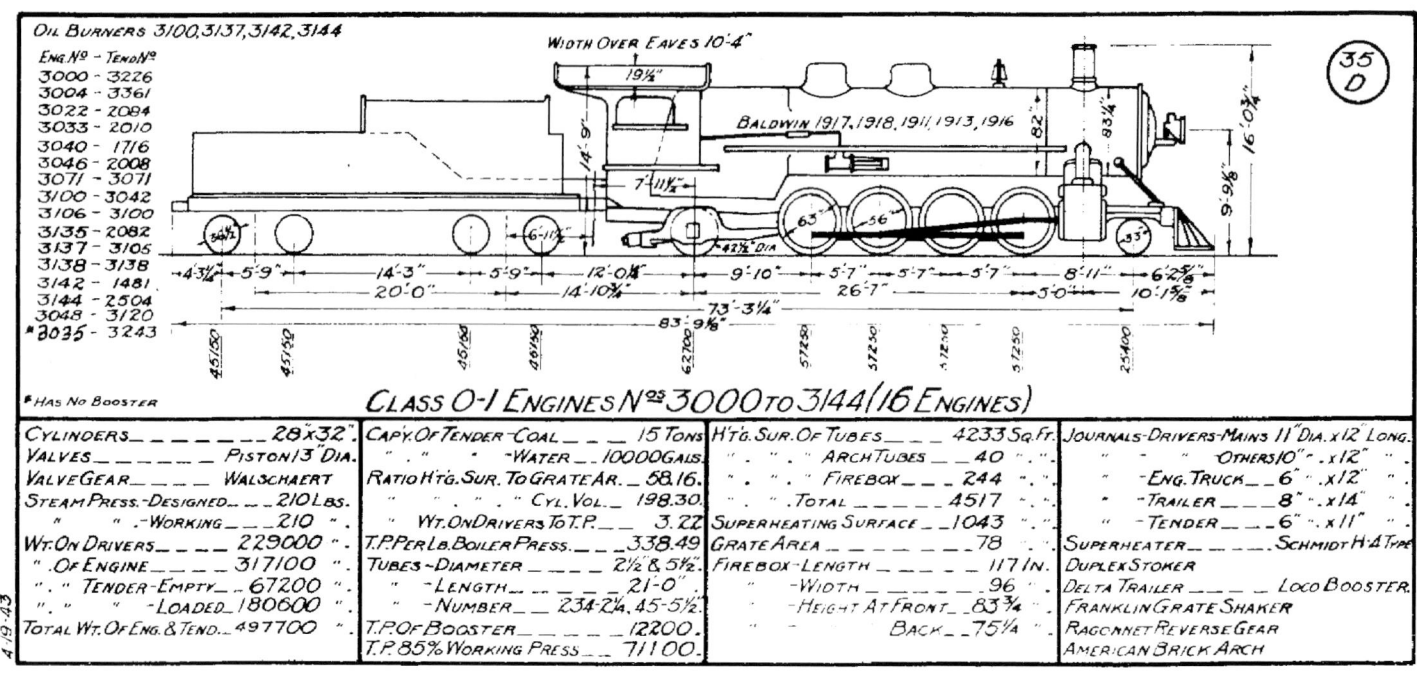

Despite the span in acquisition dates and the varied changes made to the class over the years, the entire class was considered as one with no sub classes, as demonstrated by this diagram of booster-equipped engines.

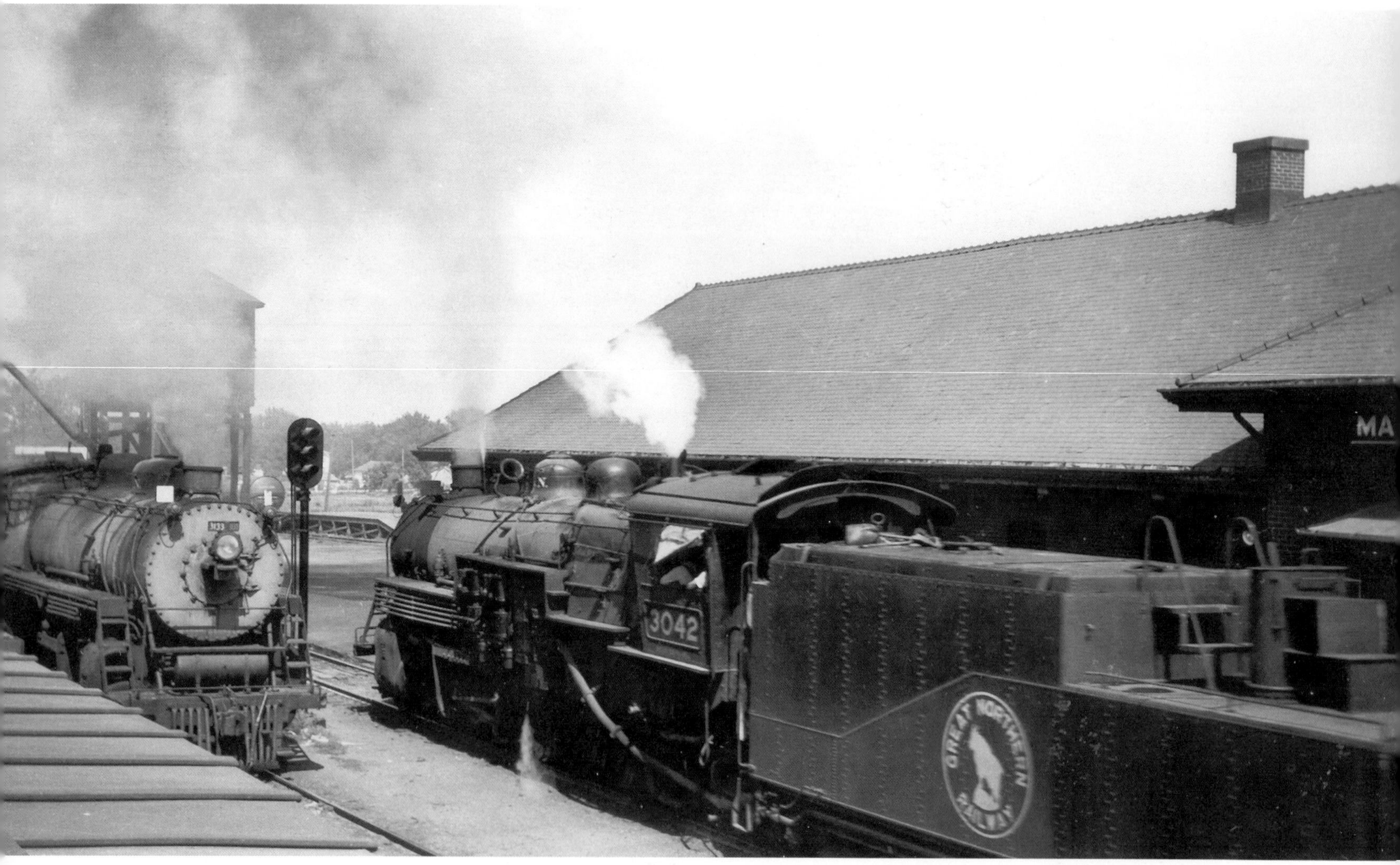

By July 1950, these former Lines West engines were hard at work on the Willmar Division. The 3042 had been stationed at Hillyard and the 3133 at Tacoma, WA. Both engines have Worthington feedwater heaters but only the 3042 had electric train Indicators. By this late date they also have short stacks and slant front cabs. The 3042 is running a seasonal "Willmar Box" with a myriad of empties from the Burlington picked up at Sioux City, IA. The 3133 is on the westbound local, Willmar Division Train No. 575. The meet is at Marshall, MN. The local is running as an extra, the box train appears to have green flags, indicating it is running as First 418. Photograph by Norman F. Priebe.

had them installed in 1944, in a large-scale effort to equip the entire fleet. Also, the Southern valve gear arrangement of 3140-3144 was replaced with a Walschaert in the 1941 to 1943 time period. In the 1940's most were equipped with low water alarms, Nalco continuous blow down equipment and mechanical lubricators. In the late 1940's auxiliary reservoirs for the power reverse gear were added. Most of the 145 locomotives (if not all) received shorter stacks during their service lives. This modification probably began in the late 1930's, and in advance of the installation of slant front cabs. A few of the engines (including at least 3021, 3022, 3037, 3041, 3051, and 3129) were equipped with larger sand boxes as well. As with a number of other classes, the standard cast Baldwin Smokebox fronts eventually cracked. They were replaced with fronts cut from slab steel plates. As the Baldwin-supplied smokestacks began to wear, they were replaced with the GN standard design, also seen on many other GN engines. Most of these changes occurred after 1945.

The O-1's were delivered from Baldwin with square cabs. Examination of photographs reveals that the railway began replacing these cabs during the early 1940's with slant-front cabs. (The authors are fairly certain the installation of slant front cabs also resulted in the set-back of the cab with a resultant longer superstructure.) Certain of the O-1's were equipped with boosters for some time (see roster), and others were modified by the addition of a Delta type trailing truck (some of these were also apparently removed as well). Locomotives 3004, 3022, 3071, 3100, 3135, 3137, 3140 and 3142 were among those with Delta trucks. Between 1938 and 1943, the GN raised the working pressure of the O-1 to 210 psi with a corresponding increase in tractive effort to 71,100 pounds. Due to the reweigh case of 1948, a new weight on drivers for the O-1 was determined to be 236,000 pounds for the oil-burners and 242,000 pounds for the coal-burners.

While the first O-1's as delivered clearly showed their 1911 era origins, by the end of their life all in the class resembled a late 1920's design. However, each one was unique. It is unlikely any two can be found exactly the same.

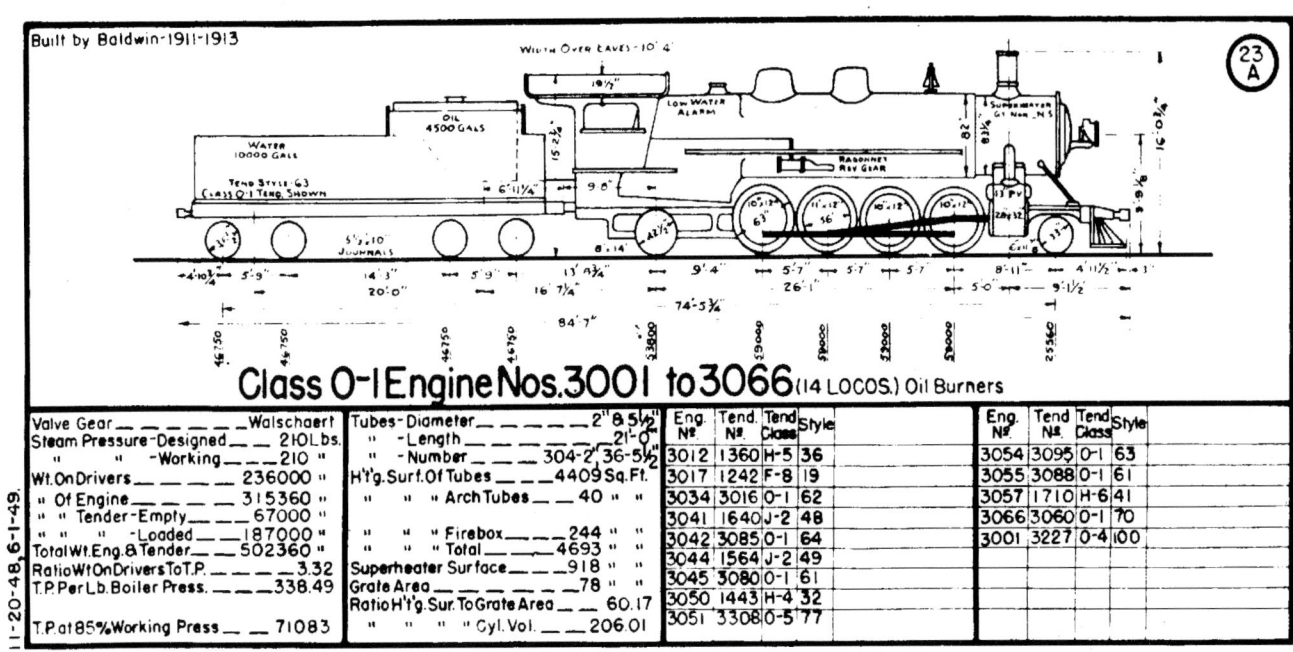

These diagrams show the later increased weights of the O-1's.

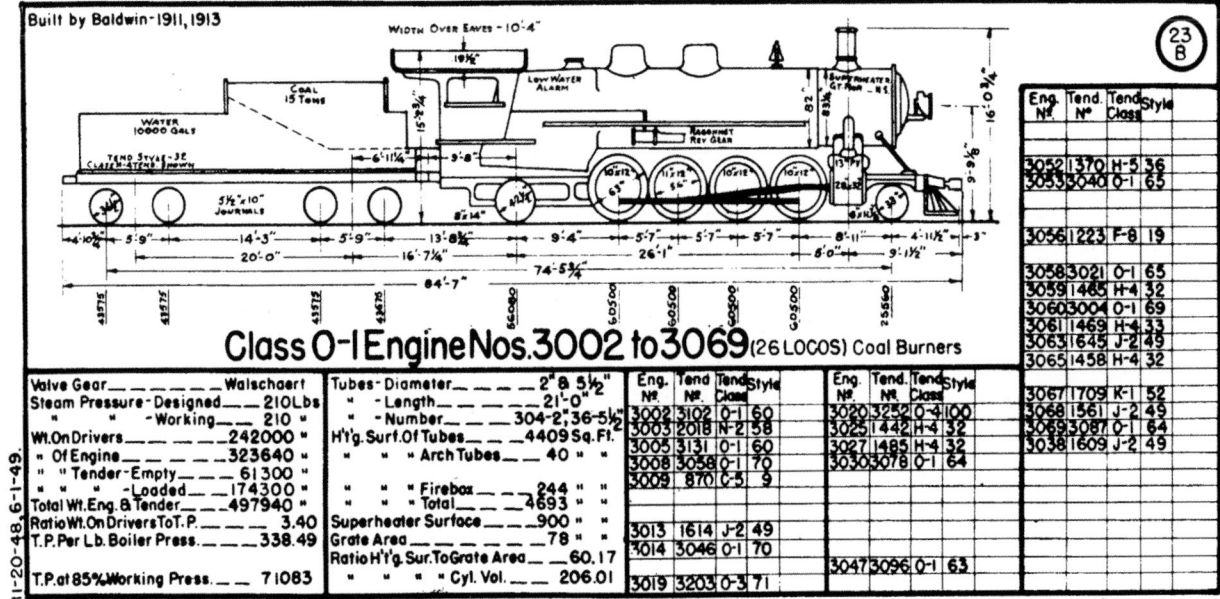

Tender assignments on the O-1's varied greatly, with each locomotive often having carried, at different times, up to two or three different tenders (in addition to the one with which it was delivered). Great Northern company diagrams did not begin listing locomotive-tender assignments until the late 1930's, so up until that time one can only use photographs to determine which tender types were assigned to which locomotives. The O-1's were one of the prime classes subjected to GN's tender-swapping policy, which definitely contributed to a variety of appearances within the class.

Even the tenders delivered with the O-1's differed from order to order, though they were all originally delivered with tender capacities of 13 tons coal and 8,000 gallons of water. Locomotives 3000 to 3044 were delivered with tenders having exterior bracing (the "grape arbor" appearance) on the coal bunkers. Tenders 3045 to 3069 were probably quite similar in appearance, but were rebuilt to 10,000 gallon capacities very early (see above). Locomotives 3070 to 3094 were delivered with a rather different style tender, the lower rear portion of

the coal bunker having a curved contour The final major type of O-1 tender was delivered with locomotives 3094 to 3144. These lacked the coal bunker bracing of the previous O-1 tenders, resulting in a rather clean-lined, squarish-looking style.

With 145 engines in the class, the O-1's were the most numerous of any GN class. They were assigned to all operating divisions of the GN. Locomotives 3023, 3024, 3026, 3028, 3029, 3039, 3043 and 3099 were early departures from the GN roster, being sold to the Spokane, Portland & Seattle in the 1920's. These were followed by 3064, 3108, 3121, 3122 and 3134, which also went to the SP&S during World War II.

Additionally, a few O-1's were leased to the Santa Fe, and operated out of Kansas City for two months during World War II. The Santa Fe had a severe motive power shortage at the time and the GN engines did not return home until after the Santa Fe purchased three Pennsylvania engines and seven Boston and Maine engines to replace them. The GN engines were the 3003, 3011, 3019, 3021, 3022, 3035, 3052 and 3105, all from the Willmar Division at the time. They left the GN on

The 3107 is at Great Falls, MT, in October 1945. Note that it has a black boiler jacket but green cylinder jacket. H. W. Pontin (RPS) photograph from the collection of Norman F. Priebe.

The 3125 is shown at Hillyard on August 18, 1949. It had received a Nathan low water alarm and an automatic lubricator since 1946. It is accompanied by Style 50 J-2 tender 1617. Wilbur C. Whittaker collection.

The 3125 finished its years at Kelly Lake, MN, after coming from the Kalispell Division. It was photographed on June 13, 1951. Paul Eilenberger collection.

There were two coal-burners on the Cascade Division. Both were stationed on the NP. The 3131, shown here in April 1946, was at Auburn, WA, and the 3133 was at Tacoma. Collection of Harold K. Vollrath.

The 3137, with P-2 tender 2520, is at Winlock, WA, on the Northern Pacific coast line in July 1950. Hoff-Nelson collection.

Another engine with a P-2 tender (No. 2504) was the 3142, shown here in its last assignment at Kelly Lake on the Mesabi Division in September 1949. John Allen collection.

A GN class O-1 No. 3022 is on the AT&SF at Kansas City, KS, on June 25, 1945. Photograph by Charles E. Winters.

No. 3135 was one of the very last class O-1's in service. Here it is at Cold Spring, MN, between St. Cloud and Willmar in 1956. The engine remained in local service on this line into 1957. Note that it once had a Worthington feedwater heater but that it had been removed by this time. Photograph by Ted Cornwell, courtesy Bill Cornwell.

June 13, 1945, and returned during the last few days of August.[7]

In 1946, the first GN O-1 was scrapped, beginning the demise of the class. The majority of the class was scrapped during the mid-1950's. Fourteen O-1's survived into the 1960's, all but one, however, only as hulks in a deadline. By 1963, all but one had been scrapped, leaving locomotive 3059 as the last surviving representative of its class. It was put on display at Williston, North Dakota and dedicated on August 2. 1958. The O-1 class has been lauded by GN employees as the engines that "built the railroad".

Class O-2

The only member of Great Northern's Class O-2 was something of an orphan. It had been built by Alco-Brooks in 1915 for the South Dakota Central (SDC), as that road's No. 18. It had 20-inch by 28-inch cylinders, small 52-inch drivers, and a total engine weight of only 128,000 pounds.[8] Being an Alco engine, it had the Cole trailing truck. It became Watertown & Sioux Falls No. 18 when the SDC was taken over by that road in 1916. In 1922 it was renumbered as GN 3149, even though the GN did not formally acquire the Watertown & Sioux Falls until December 31, 1928. The tiny Mikado had two sand domes. In 1926 it received a standard Great Northern steel cab, and was assigned an H-4 tender. Even with those modifications, its radial stay boiler left it with a non-standard appearance. The engine received a GN New Style superheater and a brick arch with three arch tubes in 1926.[9] A second No. 5 air compressor was added in 1943, placed on the engineer's side.[10] It never strayed far from its original territory, being assigned to the Willmar Division and operated out of Sioux Falls, SD. Sioux Falls crews affectionately called it "Rosie" due to its diminutive size. It was scrapped in 1947.

This pair of pictures illustrate the appearance of GN's singular O-2 class locomotive as it left the Alco plant in 1915.
ALCO Historic Photos (engineer's side). Collection of George M. Sittig (fireman's side).

At some point between 1922 and the end of 1926, the 3149 was photographed at Sioux Falls, SD, with what is probably its original tender. Technically this was still a Watertown and Sioux Falls engine at the time, since the road was not formally merged into the GN until 1928. Collection of George M. Sittig.

These two photos taken on May 11, 1946, illustrate the final appearance of the locomotive as it awaited scrapping at St. Paul, MN. Note that some time after 1926 the top-feed check valves were replaced, to follow the usual GN practice of using two side-feed check valves. There is a single air compressor on each side of the locomotive. The original tender has been replaced with H-4 Style 34 No. 1457. Photographs by Robert Graham, with the fireman's side view from the collection of William Raia.

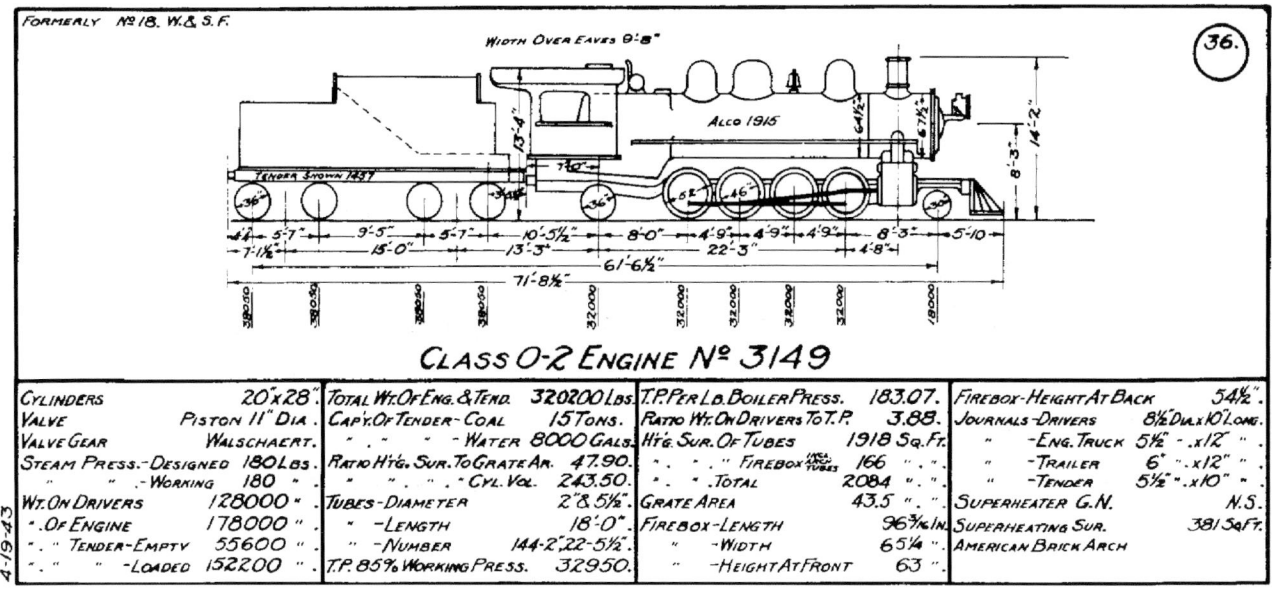

FORMERLY N2 18. W.&S.F.

WIDTH OVER EAVES 9'-8"

ALCO 1915

36.

CLASS O-2 ENGINE N₂ 3149

CYLINDERS	20"x28"	TOTAL WT.OF ENG.&TEND.	320200 LBS.	T.P. PER LB. BOILER PRESS.	183.07.	FIREBOX-HEIGHT AT BACK	54½".
VALVE	PISTON 11" DIA.	CAP'Y. OF TENDER - COAL	15 TONS.	RATIO WT. ON DRIVERS TO T.P.	3.88.	JOURNALS -DRIVERS	8½ DIA x 10 LONG.
VALVE GEAR	WALSCHAERT.	" . " . " - WATER	8000 GALS.	HT'G. SUR. OF TUBES	1918 SQ. FT.	" -ENG. TRUCK	5½ " .x12 " .
STEAM PRESS.-DESIGNED	180 LBS.	RATIO HT'G. SUR. TO GRATE AR.	47.90.	" . " . " FIREBOX (TUBES)	166 " ."	" -TRAILER	6" .x12" .
" " .-WORKING	180 " .	" " . " . " - CYL. VOL.	243.50.	" . " . TOTAL	2084 " . ".	" -TENDER	5½ " .x10" .
WT. ON DRIVERS	128000 "	TUBES - DIAMETER	2" & 5½"	GRATE AREA	43.5 " . " .	SUPERHEATER G.N.	N.S.
" .- OF ENGINE	178000 "	" - LENGTH	18'-0".	FIREBOX-LENGTH	96 ³/₁₆ IN.	SUPERHEATING SUR.	381 SQ FT.
" . " TENDER-EMPTY	55600 "	" - NUMBER	144-2",22-5½"	" - WIDTH	65¼ " .	AMERICAN BRICK ARCH	
" . " " -LOADED	152200 " .	T.P. 85% WORKING PRESS.	32950.	" - HEIGHT AT FRONT	63 " .		

4-19-43

Class O-3

Great Northern had nine locomotives in its Class O-3. These engines were all constructed in accordance with the USRA's Heavy Mikado design. The first four were built by Alco's Schenectady works, assigned to the GN by the USRA, and were received in April 1919 as GN 3145-3148. Apparently the office that assigned these numbers was not aware that the engines were of a different design than the O-1's. Once this was pointed out, the engines were renumbered as 3200-3203 within a few days of their receipt.[11] It is also interesting to note that AFE 12186, under which the engines were purchased, was not completed until December 27, 1919, months after the locomotives were received. The AFE was approved by the federal manager on January 9, 1920. The engines were initially assigned to the Minot Division.[12]

A second group of five USRA heavy 2-8-2's was received in January 1920 and numbered as 3204-3208. These had been built in November 1918 by Alco's Brooks works.[13] They had been allocated to the El Paso & Southwestern Railway Company by the USRA, but that road found

them too heavy. GN had been pleased with the first four such engines, and felt that these five could be put to good use. They apparently had been used very little, and were obtained for a price considerably below that being asked by manufacturers for new locomotives.[14]

The O-3's had 27-inch by 32-inch cylinders, 63-inch drivers, and engine weights of 320,000 pounds They were clean-lined, and being of USRA design had radial stay fireboxes rather than GN's usual Belpaire. As purchased, they were all coal burners and were equipped with stokers, Schmidt superheaters, Walschaert valve gear, Lewis reverse gear and Cole trailing trucks, an Alco design of 1903. The GN cast iron headlight was applied in 1923. The Lewis reverse gear was replaced by the Ragonnet type in 1927 and 1928. In the late 1920's, 3200, 3205 and 3206 were equipped with Sellers exhaust steam injectors and 3204 was equipped with an Elesco exhaust steam injector. Coal board extensions were also added to the tenders, but aside from these changes the appearance of the locomotives remained fairly similar to as-built until 1943. By 1936 the engines had been moved to the Mesabi

The 3200 was photographed at Minneapolis after the transfer of the O-3 class to the Mesabi Division. The Standard stoker engine, located under the cab and behind the injector, was easy to access. This photograph and those of the 3205 most closely represent the appearance of the USRA O-3s when delivered, the principal exception being the headlight. Robert Graham photograph, date unknown, from the collection of Norman F. Priebe.

The 3205 is at Minneapolis in this early view. The date is unknown, but it is after the application of the Sellers exhaust steam injector. Collection of Jerrold F. Hilton.

In one of the best early views ever of an O-3, the 3205 is at Minneapolis on September 2, 1939. Charles E. Winters collection.

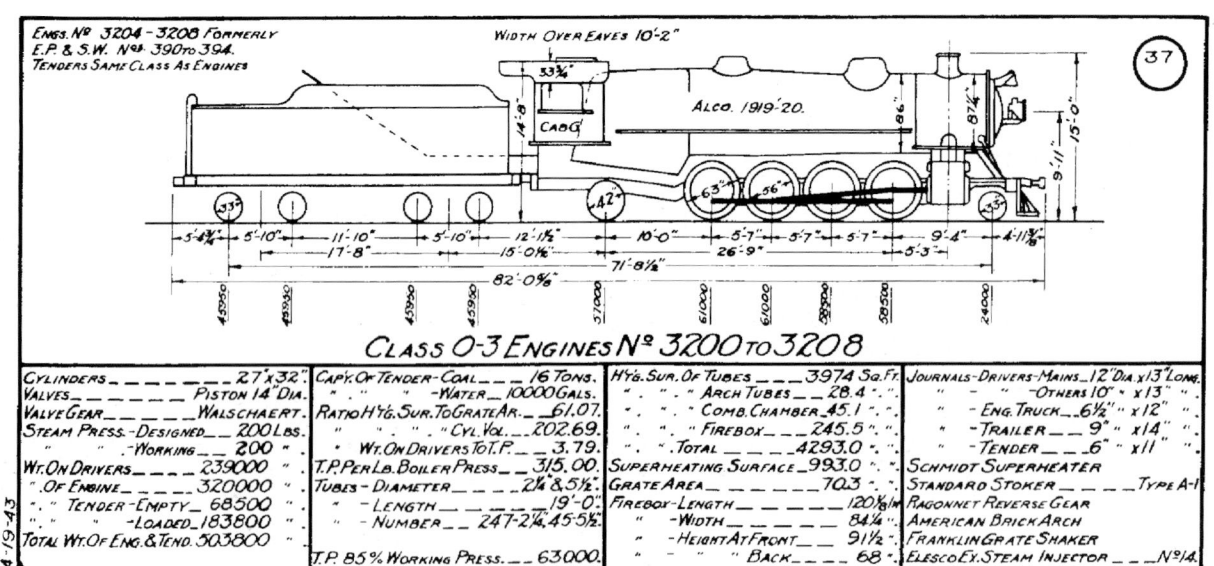

ENGS. Nº 3204-3208 FORMERLY E.P.& S.W. Nº5. 390 TO 394. TENDERS SAME CLASS AS ENGINES

WIDTH OVER EAVES 10'-2"

ALCO. 1919-'20.

37

CLASS O-3 ENGINES Nº 3200 TO 3208

CYLINDERS	27"x32"	CAP'Y. OF TENDER-COAL	16 TONS.	HT'G. SUR. OF TUBES	3974 SQ.FT.	JOURNALS-DRIVERS-MAINS 12"DIA. x13"LONG.
VALVES	PISTON 14"DIA.	" " -WATER	10000 GALS.	" " " ARCH TUBES	28.4 "	" " -OTHERS 10" x 13"
VALVE GEAR	WALSCHAERT.	RATIO HT'G. SUR. TO GRATE AR.	61.07.	" " " COMB. CHAMBER	45.1 "	" - ENG. TRUCK 6½" x 12"
STEAM PRESS.-DESIGNED	200 LBS.	" " " CYL. VOL.	202.69.	" " " FIREBOX	245.5 "	" -TRAILER 9" x14"
" " -WORKING	200 "	" WT. ON DRIVERS TO T.P.	3.79.	" " " TOTAL	4293.0 "	" -TENDER 6" x11"
WT. ON DRIVERS	239000 "	T.P. PER LB. BOILER PRESS.	315.00.	SUPERHEATING SURFACE	993.0 "	SCHMIDT SUPERHEATER
" OF ENGINE	320000 "	TUBES - DIAMETER	2¼ & 5½"	GRATE AREA	70.3 "	STANDARD STOKER TYPE A-1
" TENDER-EMPTY	68500 "	" - LENGTH	19'-0"	FIREBOX-LENGTH	120⅛"	RAGONNET REVERSE GEAR
" " -LOADED	183800 "	" - NUMBER	247-2¼, 45-5½"	" -WIDTH	84¼"	AMERICAN BRICK ARCH
TOTAL WT. OF ENG. & TEND.	503800 "			" -HEIGHT AT FRONT	91½"	FRANKLIN GRATE SHAKER
		T.P. 85% WORKING PRESS.	63000.	" " BACK	68 "	ELESCO EX. STEAM INJECTOR Nº 14.

4-19-43

All O-3's spent eighteen years in mine run or local service at Kelly Lake, MN. Clearly in its last days, well-maintained 3200 shows off its slant-front cab and Sellers exhaust steam injector during an idle moment. The oil burning O-3's received huge oil bunkers that gave their tenders a "blockhouse" appearance. Carl Ulrich photograph from the collection of William Raia.

Photographed on the same day as the 3200, the 3201 displays a slightly different appearance with a conventional non-lifting injector and smokebox-mounted bell. Slant-front cabs were a late addition to the O-3 class. W. Krawiec photograph from the collection of William Raia.

In later years the Standard stoker was replaced by the GN, but the engines continued to burn coal until 1951. No. 3202 is at Superior, WI, on September 4, 1946. Wilbur C. Whittaker collection, courtesy of Eric Archer.

Division, where they all remained until retirement.

In 1943 the engines went through a major (from a cosmetic point of view, at least) rebuilding program. They all received standard GN cabs, dual air pumps were placed on the smokebox front, and the tender sides were rebuilt to give more of a "blockhouse" look to the tender.[15] The engines also received footboard pilots. During the 1948 reweigh the original weight on drivers of 239,000 pounds was found to be now 246,000 pounds. By 1951, those remaining on the roster had been converted to oil burners. All were scrapped by 1955.

Class O-4

Great Northern's final commercial order for Mikados was built by Baldwin in 1920. These engines had a larger boiler than the O-1's, and a higher working steam pressure of 190 psi.[16] GN went back to Belpaire fireboxes for this order. Numbered as 3210-3254, they were classified as O-4's. They had the same 28-inch by 32-inch cylinders and 63-inch drivers as the O-1's, but were heavier, with engine weights of 319,700 pounds. There was an issue with the weight distribution of these

locomotives during their design at Baldwin. The original specification called for a limit of 60,000 pounds weight per driving axle, about that of the O-3. This was the weight the motive power department believed was all the track structure could accommodate. Once the design had been worked out and reviewed by Mr. C. O. Jenks, there was trouble. Mr. Jenks noticed that certain Northern Pacific Mikados were heavier on drivers and lighter on the trailing axle than the GN design. This did not sit well. Of course the reason was the GN's use of a larger and heavier Belpaire firebox, coupled with the self-imposed axle weight limit. The matter went to the top, and the 60,000 pound axle weight limit was scrapped. In mid year (undated) Baldwin wrote Mr. Ralph Budd, President, that the weight was being redistributed as much as possible to yield approximately 245,000 pounds on drivers and 320,000 total engine weight. Baldwin lamented that had they known at the start, they could have arranged to exceed that figure.[17]

A subtle fact that points out that the USRA was still in control of the railroads when the O-4's were built is that they had the same USRA pilot and headlight as the O-3's. The locomotives were equipped with

Coal was still the fuel of choice on the Mesabi Division when 3203 was viewed at Kelly Lake on April 30, 1949. From the Paul Eilenberger collection.

The 3204 was still burning coal when it was photographed in Minneapolis on October 9, 1946, but the stoker had been changed. Records of what type the GN used to replace the Standard have not been found. Robert Graham photograph from the collection of William Raia.

The 3207 was looking good between runs at Kelly Lake in this view taken September 10, 1952. In the spring of 1953, a record year for ore, diesels began to arrive. By 1954 Kelly Lake had a long deadline of steam power that had been dedicated to the iron ore business. Collection of Harold K. Vollrath.

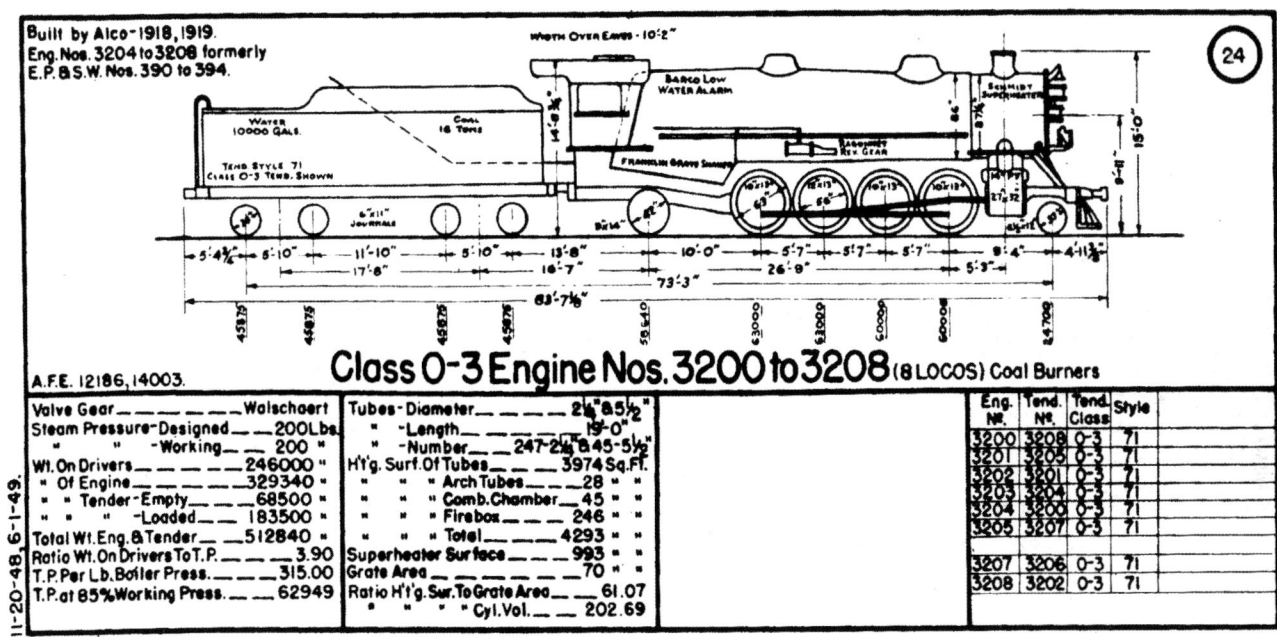

Built by Alco-1918, 1919.
Eng. Nos. 3204 to 3208 formerly
E.P. & S.W. Nos. 390 to 394.

WIDTH OVER EAVES - 10'-2"

24

WATER 10000 GALS.   COAL 16 TONS

BARCO LOW WATER ALARM

SCHMIDT SUPERHEATER

TEND. STYLE 71 CLASS O-3 TEND. SHOWN

FRANKLIN GROSS SHAKER

BAKER VALVE GEAR

A.F.E. 12186, 14003.

Class O-3 Engine Nos. 3200 to 3208 (8 LOCOS) Coal Burners

11-20-48, 6-1-49.

Valve Gear — — — — — — Walschaert	Tubes - Diameter — — — 2¼" & 5½"
Steam Pressure - Designed — — 200 Lbs.	" -Length — — — — 19'-0"
" " -Working — — 200 "	" -Number — — 247-2¼ & 45-5½
Wt. On Drivers — — — — 246000 "	H't'g. Surf. Of Tubes — — 3974 Sq. Ft.
" " Of Engine — — — — 329340 "	" " " Arch Tubes — — 28 "
" " Tender - Empty — — 68500 "	" " " Comb. Chamber — 45 "
" " -Loaded — — 183500 "	" " " Firebox — — 246 "
Total Wt. Eng. & Tender — 512840 "	" " " Total — — 4293 "
Ratio Wt. On Drivers To T.P. — — 3.90	Superheater Surface — — — 993 "
T.P. Per Lb. Boiler Press. — — 315.00	Grate Area — — — — 70 "
T.P. at 85% Working Press. — — 62949	Ratio H't'g. Sur. To Grate Area — 61.07
	" " " Cyl. Vol. — — 202.69

Eng. Nr.	Tend. Nr.	Tend. Class	Style
3200	3208	O-3	71
3201	3205	O-3	71
3202	3201	O-3	71
3203	3204	O-3	71
3204	3200	O-3	71
3205	3207	O-3	71
3207	3206	O-3	71
3208	3202	O-3	71

The as-delivered appearance of the O-4 showed a modified ash hopper and minor changes from the O-1.
The GN cast headlight was not yet being used. Collection of H. L. Broadbelt.

No. 3228 had a square cab, tall stack, spoked pilot wheels and a Worthington BL feed water heater in this view at Minneapolis on September 9, 1939. However it had lost its original O-4 class tender in exchange for a 17,000-gallon Style 112 tender. Robert Graham photograph from the collection of William Raia.

No. 3239, at Havre on August 4, 1934, had very little modification since its arrival on the GN. C. W. Jernstrom collection.

Smoky and dirty, the 3253 had retained most of its original appearance for fourteen years. It was at Minot, ND, in September, 1934. Photograph by Ron Nixon from the collection of Norman F. Priebe.

Duplex stokers and the Locomotive Superheater Company's Type A superheater.[18] They also had Ragonnet power reverse gear. These were the first locomotives on the GN to have Vanderbilt tenders, and the only Vanderbilt tenders on the GN with four-wheel trucks. The tender capacity was rated at 10,000 gallons of water.

As with the O-1's, a number of the O-4's received feedwater heating equipment. Numbers 3214, 3215, 3230, 3238, 3239, 3245, 3249 and 3250 received Elesco exhaust steam injectors. Numbers 3236 and 3247 received Sellers exhaust steam injectors. Numbers 3220, 3221, 3222, 3224, 3226, 3227, 3228, 3229, 3232, 3240, and 3254 received Worthington BL or BL2 feedwater heaters, mounted on the fireman's side. Number 3234 had a Worthington Type S feedwater heater. Many of these engines were later converted to oil burners, and most, if not all, received slant-front cabs. Many also received train number boards and low water alarms. Some of the engines had their four-wheel Vanderbilt tenders replaced with six-wheel versions. Only one of this class, 3224, received a booster engine. However, it had the distinction of being the last engine on the GN to have its booster removed. This was done in August 1953 because the booster was in need of repairs, but GN was no longer carrying a stock of booster repair parts.[19]

The GN raised the boiler pressure of the O-4's, as they did with the O-1's, to 210 psi between 1938 and 1943. This yielded a higher tractive effort of 71,100 pounds, same as the new value for the O-1. Because of the reweigh case in 1948, a new weight on drivers for the O-4 was determined to be 262,000 pounds for the coal-burners, and 254,000 pounds for the oil-burners.

Most of the O-4's were assigned to various Lines West divisions, with the Butte and Spokane Divisions having the most. A few were assigned to the Minot, Willmar, and Kalispell Divisions, and on a couple occasions an engine was assigned to the Dakota Division. The authors have found no evidence that any O-4's were ever assigned to the Mesabi Division. Two of them (3211 and 3214) were sold to the Spokane, Portland & Seattle in 1950, but the others remained on the roster until the massive steam locomotive scrapping of the middle and late 1950's. One, the 3212, is credited with making the last mainline steam run on the Dakota Division in 1956, and another, the 3243, is credited with making the last steam run on the Willmar Division in 1957.[20]

The 3217 had a slant-front cab and solid pilot wheels in this July 16, 1947, view at Portland, OR. It also had a class O-4 Vanderbilt tender, which it kept for a longer time than most other O-4's. John Westphal collection of John Luecke.

The 3220 was in classic late form at Fargo, ND, on October 25, 1955. Photograph by Bruce Black.

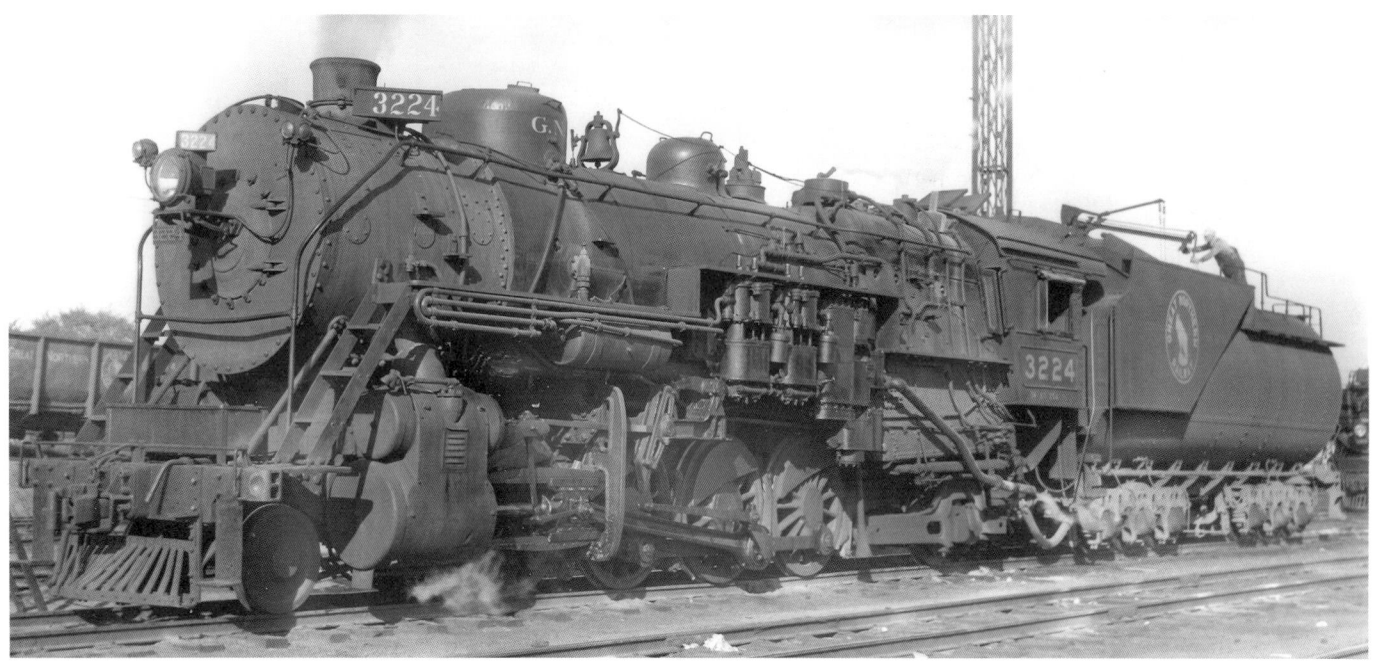

The 3224 was at Minneapolis in September 1953. Its booster is gone by now, having been removed in August 1953.
S. Davies photograph from the collection of William Raia.

The 3226 was at Sioux City, IA on August 20, 1950. The engine carried an auxiliary tender for both fuel and water on this assignment. Collection of Norman F. Priebe.

The 3226 was about to leave Minneapolis westbound in this view, August 31, 1955. The engine had a mysterious modification to a roof ventilator.
Bob Vierkant photograph from the collection of Norman F. Priebe.

The 3235 was an example of how an O-4 without a Worthington feed water heater appeared. It was at Minneapolis on October 10, 1950. From the Ted Gay collection.

The 3244 was one of a few O-4's that did not receive any feed water heating apparatus. Boiler water was supplied by conventional live steam non-lifting injectors on both sides of the engine. It was photographed at St.Paul, MN, in October 1946. Collection of Harold K. Vollrath.

The 3244 survived all the way to the end of steam. This view was taken on August 11, 1956, at Lyndale Junction in Minneapolis. It ran until the end of the seasonal autumn rush of 1956. Photograph by Norman F. Priebe.

The 3250 was at Minneapolis on July 12, 1947. Though parked near the coal dock, it had already been converted to burn oil. The spoked pilot wheel was replaced by 1950. F. Wesley Krambeck collection, courtesy of Jack W. Farrell.

The 3254 was at Minneapolis on July 4, 1953. It was one of eleven O-4's to receive a Worthington BL feed water heater. Collection of Harold K. Vollrath.

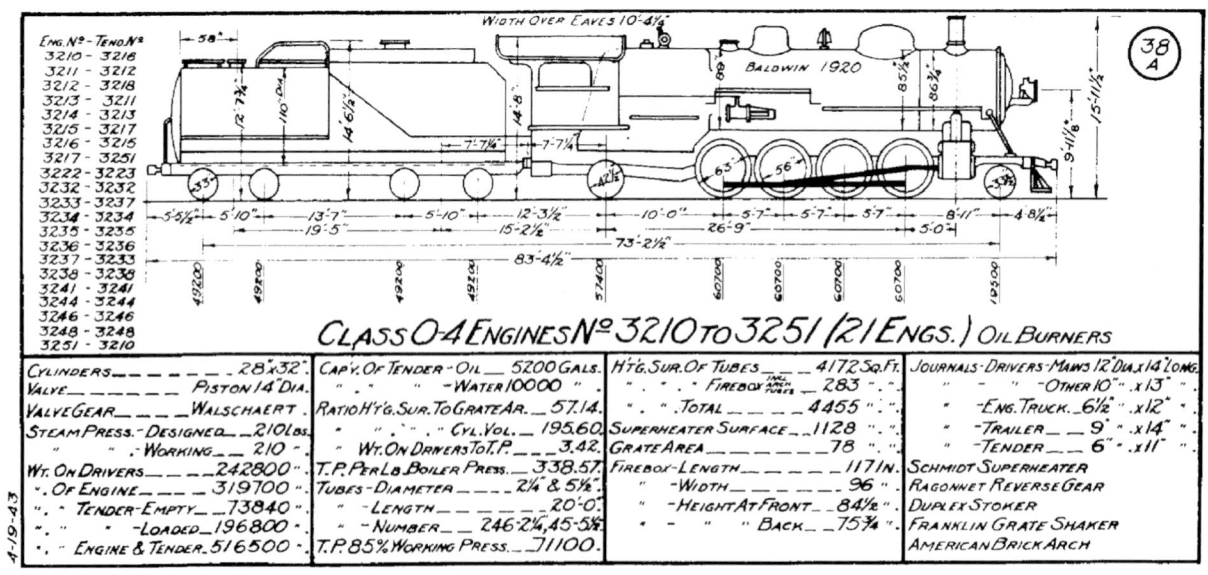

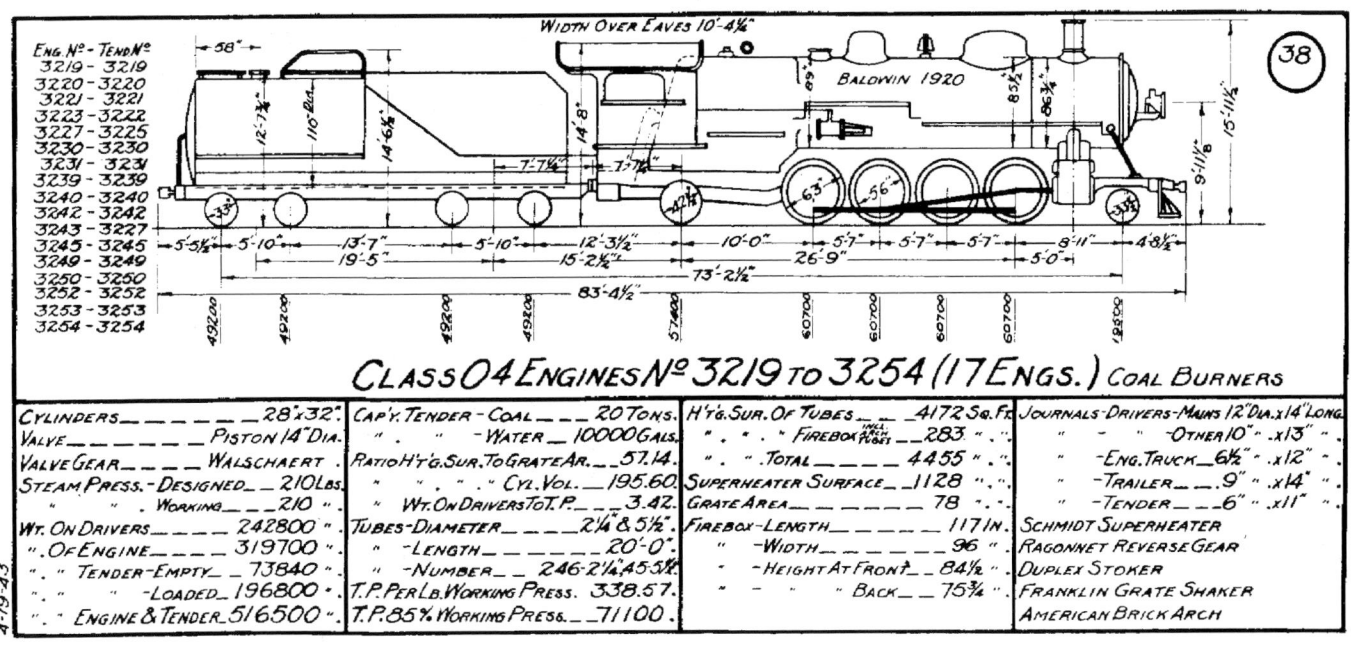

CLASS O4 ENGINES Nº 3219 TO 3254 (17 ENGS.) COAL BURNERS

CYLINDERS _ _ _ _ _ 28"x32"	CAP'Y. TENDER - COAL _ _ _ 20 TONS.	H'T'G. SUR. OF TUBES _ _ 4172 SQ.FT.	JOURNALS-DRIVERS-MAINS 12"DIA.x14"LONG
VALVE _ _ _ _ _ PISTON 14"DIA.	" " WATER _ 10000 GALS.	" " " FIREBOX(INCL.ARCH TUBES) _ 283 " "	" " -OTHER 10" .x13"
VALVE GEAR _ _ _ _ WALSCHAERT	RATIO H'T'G. SUR. TO GRATE AR._ 57.14	" " . Total _ _ _ _ 4455 " "	" -ENG. TRUCK _ 6½" .x12"
STEAM PRESS.-DESIGNED_ 210 LBS.	" " " CYL. VOL. _ 195.60	SUPERHEATER SURFACE _ 1128 " "	" -TRAILER _ _ _ 9" .x14"
" " . WORKING _ _ 210 "	" WT.ON DRIVERS TO T.P. _ _ 3.42	GRATE AREA _ _ _ _ _ 78 " "	" -TENDER _ _ _ 6" .x11"
WT. ON DRIVERS _ _ _ _ 242800 "	TUBES-DIAMETER _ _ _ _ 2¼ & 5½"	FIREBOX-LENGTH _ _ _ _ _ 117 IN.	SCHMIDT SUPERHEATER
" . OF ENGINE _ _ _ _ 319700 "	" -LENGTH _ _ _ _ 20'-0"	" -WIDTH _ _ _ _ 96 "	RAGONNET REVERSE GEAR
" " TENDER-EMPTY _ _ 73840 "	" -NUMBER _ _ 246-2¼,45-5½	" -HEIGHT AT FRONT_ 84½ "	DUPLEX STOKER
" -LOADED _ 196800 "	T.P. PER LB. WORKING PRESS. 338.57.	" " " BACK _ _ 75¾ "	FRANKLIN GRATE SHAKER
" . ENGINE & TENDER 516500 "	T.P. 85% WORKING PRESS. _ 71100.		AMERICAN BRICK ARCH

4-19-43

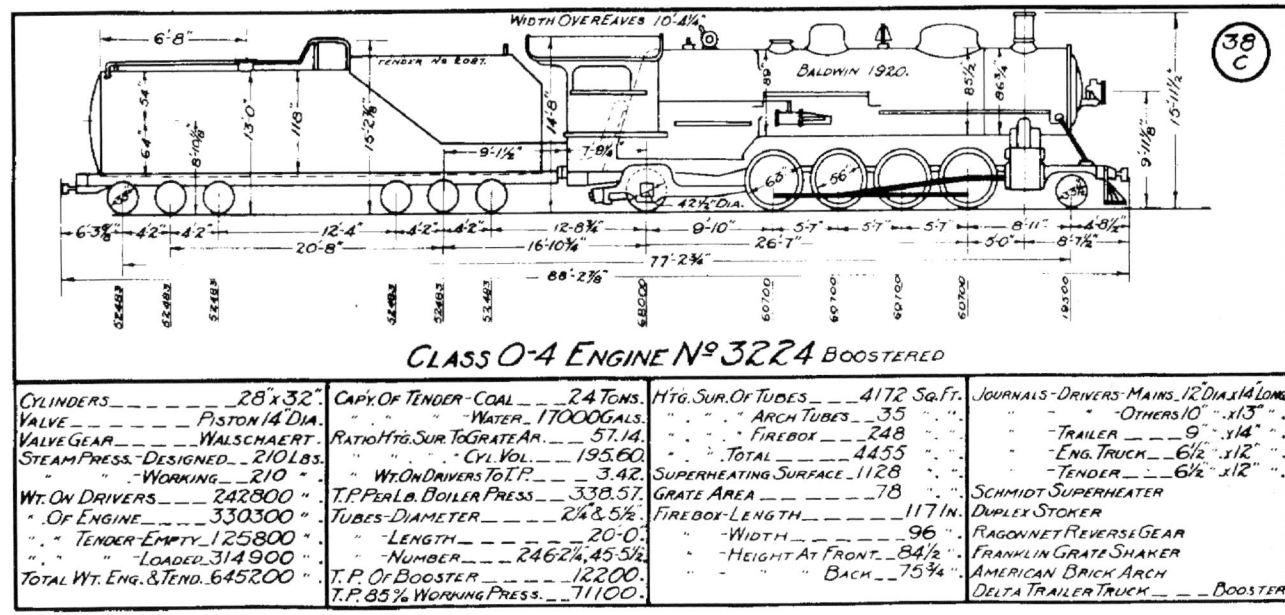

CLASS O-4 ENGINE Nº 3224 BOOSTERED

CYLINDERS _ _ _ _ _ 28"x32"	CAP'Y. OF TENDER-COAL _ _ 24 TONS.	H'T'G. SUR. OF TUBES_ _ _ 4172 SQ.FT.	JOURNALS-DRIVERS-MAINS 12"DIA.x14"LONG
VALVE _ _ _ _ _ PISTON 14"DIA.	" " WATER_ 17000 GALS.	" . " ARCH TUBES _ _ 35 " "	" -OTHERS 10" .x13"
VALVE GEAR _ _ _ WALSCHAERT	RATIO H'T'G. SUR. TO GRATE AR. _ _ 57.14	" . " FIREBOX _ _ _ 248 " "	" -TRAILER _ _ _ 9" .x14"
STEAM PRESS.-DESIGNED_ 210 LBS.	" " " CYL. VOL. _ 195.60	" . " Total _ _ _ 4455 " "	" -ENG. TRUCK _ 6½" .x12"
" " -WORKING _ 210 "	" WT. ON DRIVERS TO T.P. _ _ 3.42	SUPERHEATING SURFACE _ 1128 " "	" -TENDER _ _ 6½" .x12"
WT. ON DRIVERS _ _ _ 242800 "	T.P. PER LB. BOILER PRESS. _ 338.57	GRATE AREA _ _ _ _ _ 78 " "	SCHMIDT SUPERHEATER
" . OF ENGINE _ _ _ _ 330300 "	TUBES-DIAMETER _ _ _ _ 2¼ & 5½"	FIREBOX-LENGTH_ _ _ _ _ 117 IN.	DUPLEX STOKER
" . TENDER-EMPTY _ 125800 "	" -LENGTH _ _ _ _ 20'-0"	" -WIDTH _ _ _ _ 96 "	RAGONNET REVERSE GEAR
" -LOADED _ 314900 "	" -NUMBER _ _ 246-2¼, 45-5½	" -HEIGHT AT FRONT_ 84½ "	FRANKLIN GRATE SHAKER
TOTAL WT. ENG. & TEND. 645200 "	T.P. OF BOOSTER _ _ _ _ 12200	" " " BACK_ _ 75¾ "	AMERICAN BRICK ARCH
	T.P. 85% WORKING PRESS. _ 71100.		DELTA TRAILER TRUCK _ _ _ BOOSTER

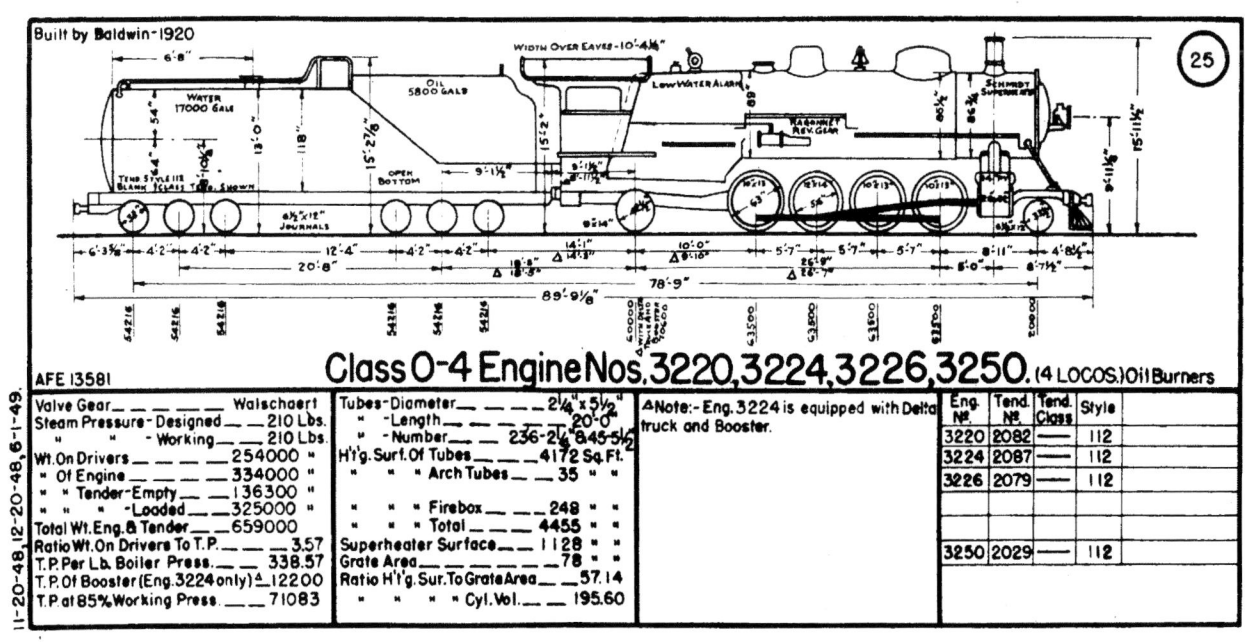

Built by Baldwin-1920

AFE 13581

CLASS O-4 Engine Nos. 3220, 3224, 3226, 3250. (4 LOCOS.) Oil Burners

Valve Gear _ _ _ _ _ _ Walschaert	Tubes-Diameter _ _ _ _ _ 2¼ x 5½"	△ Note:- Eng. 3224 is equipped with Delta truck and Booster.	
Steam Pressure - Designed _ _ 210 Lbs.	" -Length _ _ _ _ 20'-0"		
" - Working _ _ 210 Lbs.	" -Number _ _ _ 236-2¼ & 45-5½		
Wt. On Drivers _ _ _ _ _ 254000 "	H't'g. Surf. Of Tubes _ _ 4172 Sq. Ft.		
" Of Engine _ _ _ _ _ 334000 "	" " Arch Tubes _ _ 35 " "		
" Tender-Empty _ _ _ 136300 "			
" -Loaded _ _ _ 325000 "	" " Firebox _ _ 248 " "		
Total Wt. Eng. & Tender _ _ 659000 "	" " Total _ _ _ 4455 " "		
Ratio Wt. On Drivers To T.P. _ _ 3.57	Superheater Surface _ _ _ 1128 " "		
T.P. Per Lb. Boiler Press. _ _ 338.57	Grate Area _ _ _ _ _ 78 " "		
T.P. Of Booster (Eng. 3224 only)_ 12200	Ratio H't'g. Sur. To Grate Area _ _ 57.14		
T.P. at 85% Working Press. _ _ 71083	" " " Cyl. Vol. _ _ 195.60		

Eng. Nº.	Tend. Nº.	Tend. Class	Style
3220	2082	—	112
3224	2087	—	112
3226	2079	—	112
3250	2029	—	112

11-20-48,12-20-48,6-1-49

Steam on the Sioux City line was well on its way out by May 1951, when this picture was taken. The O-1 class engines were already scarce, and the O-4 shown had been given a large Vanderbilt tender. Here the 3252 is powering the eastbound local along the southern boundary of Minnesota's Camden State Park. The consist includes work equipment. In just a few days, new GP7's will be on this run. Photograph by Norman F. Priebe.

The 3220 was among the group that lasted until the end. This view of it on the Willmar Division west-end local at Benson, MN, was taken on September 1, 1956. Collection of Norman F. Priebe.

Notes:

1. "Mikado Locomotives for the Great Northern", Railway Age Gazette, Vol. 51, No. 24, p.1214 (December 15, 1911).

2. Paul T. Warner, 1925. "The Great Northern Railway and Its Locomotives", Baldwin Locomotives.

3. "Mikado Type Locomotives for the Great Northern", Railway Review, Vol. 60, No. 1, p. 3 (January 6, 1917).

4. Great Northern Railway New Equipment Register No. 8 (GN Historical Car Records Vol. 43, Minnesota Historical Society).

5. Great Northern Railway Unit Record of Property Changes – Equipment

6. Ibid.

7. Mark S. Wilkouski (Santa Fe Historical Society), personal communication to Norman F. Priebe, September 27, 2007.

8. The engine appears to have been somewhat of a standard design for Alco, for in 1914 the Cooke works built a similar engine for the Duluth, Winnipeg and Pacific. It differed only in having slide valves and 49-inch drivers. See Anthony Clegg and Ray Corley, Canadian National Steam Power, Railfare Enterprises (Trains and Trolleys), Montreal, 1969.

9. Great Northern Railway Authority for Expenditure (AFE) 30723, December 1, 1925, and AFE 33041, November 11, 1926.

10. Great Northern Railway AFE 66500, May 15, 1943.

11. Unsigned memo to A.C. Deverell. Minnesota Historical Society 21.F.5.7B GN File 40 Part 7.

12. Great Northern Railway AFE 14003, approved May 27, 1920.

13. George Sittig, personal communication to Norman C. Keyes, Jr.

14. AFE 14003, op. cit.

15. Cyril Durrenberger, 1983. "Great Northern's Class O-3 Mikados", Prototype Modeler July-August 1983, p. 32.

16. Warner, op. cit.

17. William Kelly to C. O. Jenks, May 27, 1920, A. H. Hogeland to C. O Jenks, June 18, 1920 and the Baldwin Locomotive Works to Ralph Budd, undated. GN papers, Minnesota Historical Society.

18. "Mikado Type Locomotives on The Great Northern", Railway Review, Vol. 68, No. 11, p. 405 (March 12, 1921).

19. Great Northern Railway AFE 84388, August 6, 1953.

20. Norman F. Priebe, "Steam's Last Days on the Great Northern" Reference Sheet No. 124, Great Northern Railway Historical Society, September 1987.

No. 3300 is shown in helper service on Second No. 2, the Empire Builder. *It is a misty day as the train, with road power 2506, prepares to get underway at Essex (Walton), MT, in October 1945. William J. Pontin (RPS) photograph from the collection of Norman F. Priebe.*

Chapter 21

Class O-5 and O-6 2-8-2 Mikado Rebuilds

Class O-5

The Great Northern Railway pioneered the use of the Mallet articulated in the Northwest with the introduction of the L-1 class in 1906, followed by the smaller L-2 in 1908. These low-drivered (55-inch) freight locomotives were ideal for the slow mountain drag service of the time. As locomotive design evolved, however, the GN's 2-6-6-2 fleet became outmoded.

In 1909, the GN began to use the O-1 class 2-8-2. As demonstrated in Chapter 20, the Great Northern had once again looked into the future for an improved freight locomotive design. These locomotives out-weighed the L-2 articulateds, (306,500 to 288,000 pounds, before the reweighing), had larger drivers (63-inch) and also a higher tractive effort (60,930 pounds for the O-1 vs. 54,520 for the L-2).

By the early 1920's, the Great Northern had received delivery of many newer and larger Mallet articulateds, 35 M-1's of 2-6-8-0 design in 1909-1910 and 25 N-1's of 2-8-8-0 design in 1912. Additionally, in testimony to the good performance of the first class O-1 Mikados, GN had acquired a vast fleet of Mikado types, 145 O-1's from 1911-1919, one O-2 after 1916,[1] nine O-3's in 1918 and 1919 (the USRA Heavy design), and 55 O-4's in 1920. The GN liked the 2-8-2 design for freight service. But as it turned out, the GN would buy no more complete Mikado locomotives from the commercial builders.

With the L-2 class rapidly becoming obsolete due to the large new

Mallets on the property, dissatisfaction with its high maintenance costs and the high regard for the performance of the Mikado type, the GN decided to rebuild the L-2 class into Mikados in its own shops. A year earlier, it had begun to convert ten-wheelers to Pacifics in its own shops, and the company was confident the Mikado program would be equally successful. It was, and the GN rebuild program would run for twenty-four more years.

In January 1922, the L-2's began entering the Dale Street (St. Paul), Hillyard (Spokane) and Delta (Everett) locomotive shops for rebuilding, and over a period of two years all of them were converted to class O-5 Mikados. The L-2 boilers, tenders, driver centers and parts of the running gear were salvaged and incorporated into the new engines. The outside diameter of the drive wheels was increased from 55 to 63 inches by shrinking steel bands, 4 inches thick, over the old wheel centers and applying new tires over these bands.[2]

The O-5's emerged from the shops with 25 by 30-inch cylinders, a weight on drivers of 220,000 pounds, a tractive effort of 50,600 pounds and a total engine weight of 283,420 pounds. Overall, they were slightly lighter than the L-2, nevertheless they had a higher weight per driving axle due to having four rather than six driving axles. The tractive effort was also slightly less than the 54,520 pounds of the L-2, due partly to the larger drivers and partly to less cylinder volume. The tractive effort ratio was a respectable 4.34. Roughly similar to the L-2 in capacity, they were faster and more efficient, but smaller than the O-1. Later the 3316 was modified in an experiment to raise the tractive effort. Its cylinders were bored out to 26 inches diameter, with a resulting increase of tractive effort to 54,700 pounds, slightly more than the L-2. The tractive effort ratio fell to 4.02, which was very acceptable. However, this was still a long way from the tractive effort of the O-1. The experiment was not repeated, and the 3316 was one of the first to be scrapped.

The boiler was modified in the process of its application to the O-5. The pressure remained the same, at 200 psi. The GN added a superheater, the GN New Style with 805 square feet, which in turn reduced the tube heating surface from 3,708 square feet to 2,834 square feet. Grate and firebox dimensions remained the same as they had been on the L-2, but the majority of the class were improved with a brick arch and arch tubes.

The installation of arch tubes on engine 3300 was tested with a dynamometer car from Willmar to Clearwater Junction (later known as Lyndale Junction, in western Minneapolis). The engine handled 4,200 tons without difficulty.[3]

Alternatively, two engines, the 3315 and 3316, were each given two Nicholson syphons in place of the arch tubes. The Nicholson syphon was a proprietary watertube system that increased water circulation in the firebox region and provided increased evaporation surface inside the firebox.[4] The syphons resembled large flattened funnels. They were effective but had the drawback of suffering erosion from cinders. Because of their location, they were difficult to repair. The Nicholson company claimed that based on tests of the new Union Pacific Mountains, the syphons improved the boiler horsepower from 97% of the cylinder horsepower to 111.5% of the cylinder horsepower. This of course depended on the specific design to which they were applied. Other claims were increased flue life and reduced fuel consumption.[5]

On the O-5, arch tubes increased the total evaporation surface by 31 square feet. But with the syphons the evaporation surface was increased by 57 square feet. Installed during the construction of the locomotives in the autumn of 1923, these O-5's were the first GN locomotives to

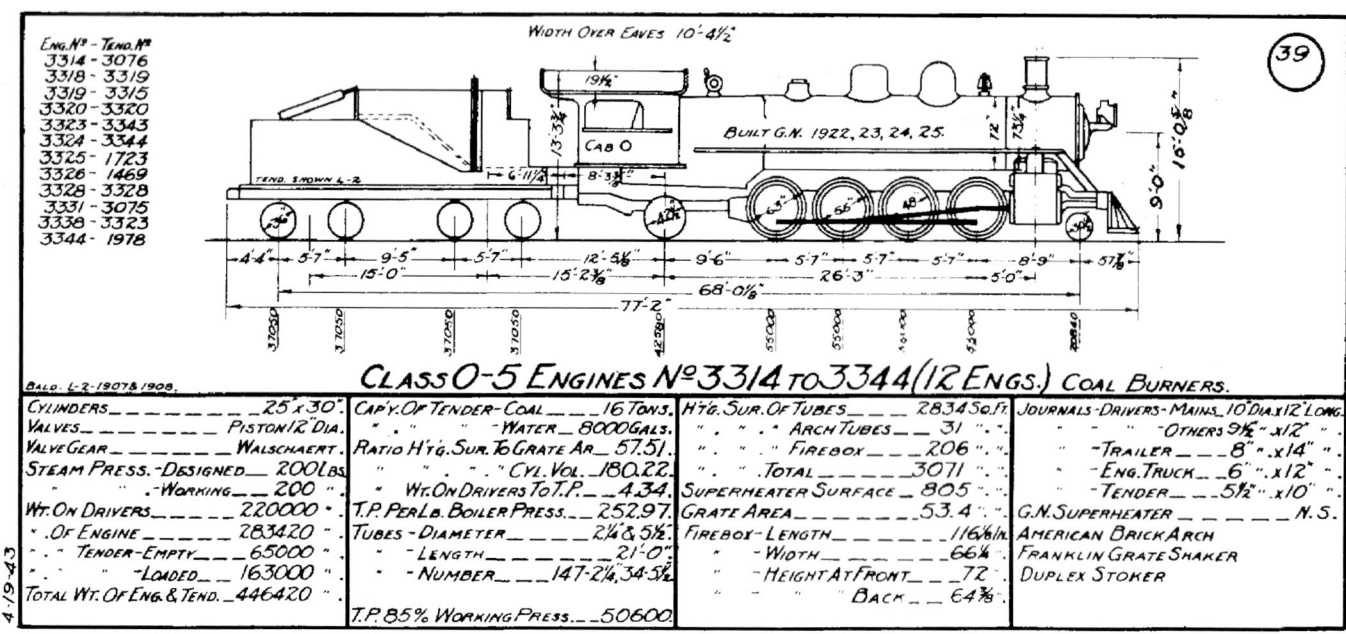

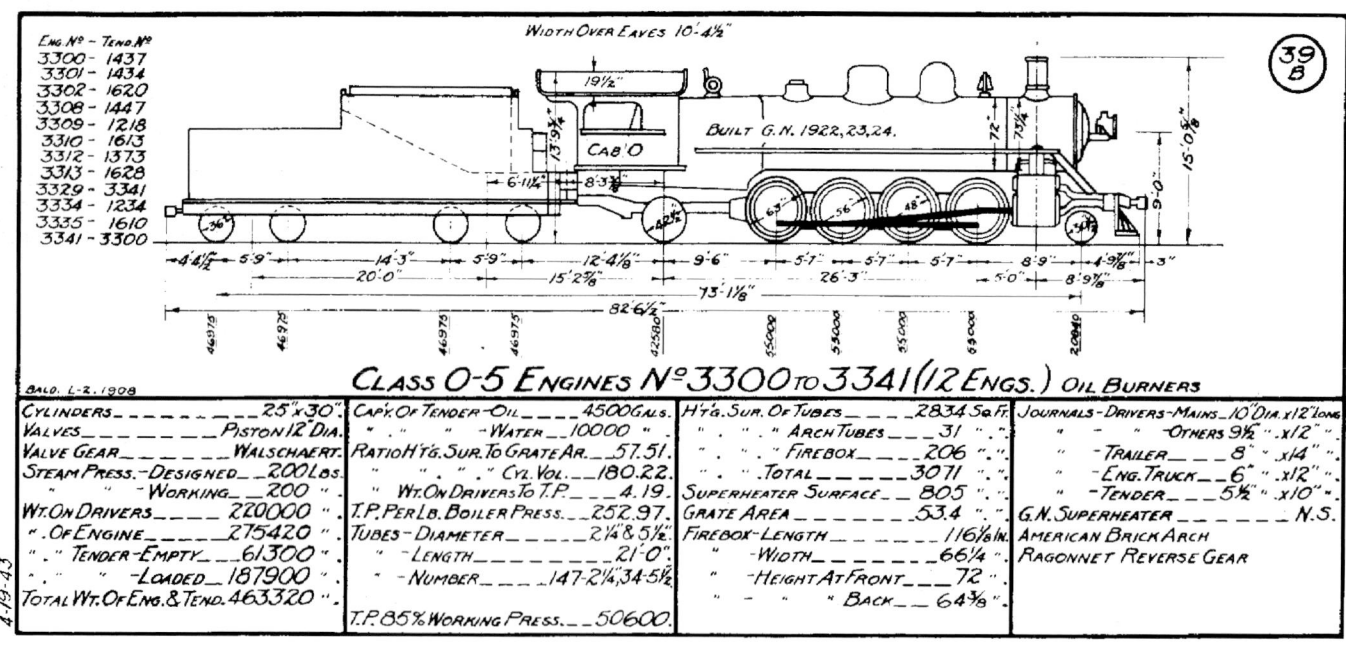

use the devices. The GN took delivery of ten class P-2's equipped with syphons only a few days later.

All 45 O-5's were equipped with 12-inch piston valves (the L-2's had slide valves) and Walschaert valve gear. The coal-burning locomotives (3314 to 3328, 3330 to 3333, 3338, 3340 and 3342 to 3344) carried 16 tons of coal, while the oil burners carried 4,500 gallons of oil. All tenders originally carried 8,000 gallons of water. These capacities changed as tenders were swapped and rebuilt. Tender assignments are presented in Chapter 34. The coal-burners were equipped with Duplex

stokers and Franklin grate shakers. The O-5's had two New York No. 5 duplex air pumps mounted on the fireman's side.

In only a few years, locomotives 3330, 3331, 3333 to 3336 and 3339 to 3344 were equipped with the Schmidt superheater. That the Schmidt superheaters do not show in the 1943 diagrams is believed to be an oversight. No. 3334 was converted to burn coal. Engines 3339, 3342 and 3344 were equipped with Worthington feedwater heaters, while Elesco No. 14 exhaust steam injectors were added to Nos. 3300 and 3333. The uniquely GN feedwater heating device, the branch pipe

This stunning early view of 3306 taken at Vancouver, BC, in 1931, shows a platform next to the stack. This engine did not get power reverse gear. Bordertown collection of GTC Collectibles.

The 3306 steams softly awaiting its next run. There was no branch pipe heater on the engine at the time of the photograph, taken at Vancouver, BC, in 1937. The tender is probably one of the tenders delivered with an oil-burning N-1. Tender 2022 is known to have been assigned to this engine by July 1938. Collection of George Harris.

The 3309 is shown at Vancouver, BC, in a 1927 view with a smoke hood. These devices are believed to have been removed by 1929. Bordertown collection of GTC Collectibles.

The 3309 is at Hillyard in July 1937. This view provides a companion to the engineer's side view of the engine. Photograph by Ron Nixon.

Stopped on the prairie in September 1939, along an unidentified North Dakota "picket fence" line, the engine crew is attending to a main rod bearing problem. This engine has a Ragonnet power reverse gear. The tender was one of the L-2 tenders delivered with the 1908 order, and has been reclassified as an O-5 tender. Collection of Norman F. Priebe.

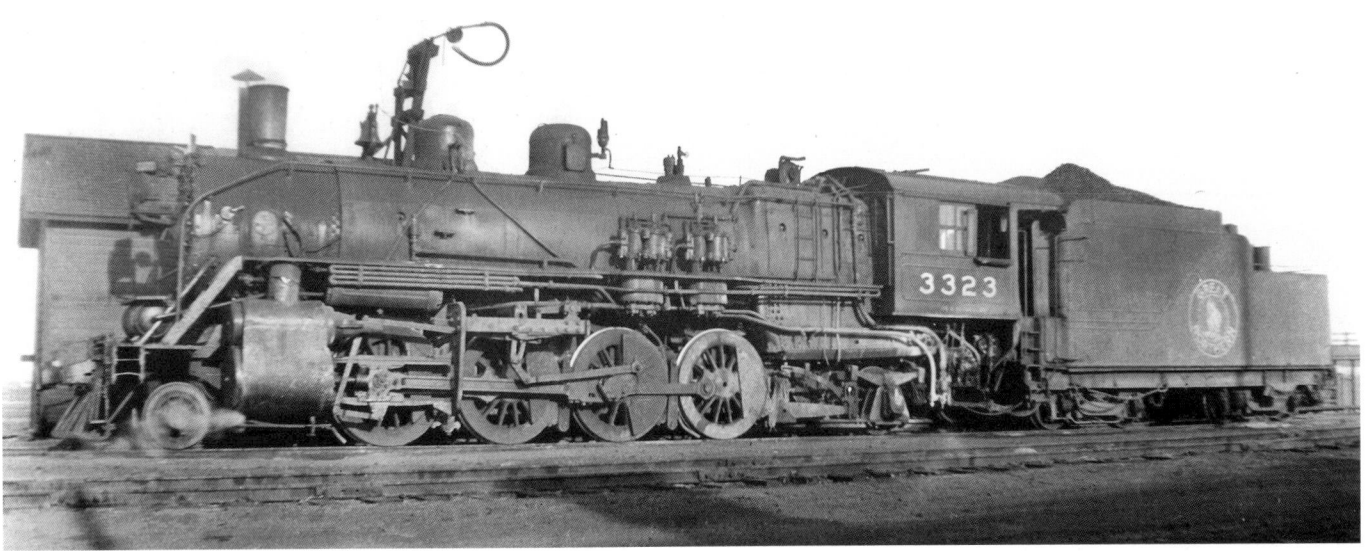

The 3323 fireman's side is the same as all O-5's without the Worthington feedwater heater. No photographs of an O-5 with a Worthington feedwater heater have been found. This photograph was taken at Fargo, ND, in October 1939. Collection of Harold K. Vollrath.

The Elesco exhaust steam injector is visible on this view of 3300 at Whitefish in 1945. Records show only two of the O-5 class received this water delivery system. The 3300 also received a Ragonnet power reverse and a Nathan low water alarm. William J. Pontin (RPS) photograph from the collection of Norman F. Priebe.

The well-maintained 3300 awaits its next helper assignment at Essex, MT, in October 1945. A sharp-eyed viewer may be able to detect the Nathan low water alarm on the boiler top. Ben Cutler (RPS) photograph.

During the winter the Whitefish O-5's were fitted with large wedge plows and dedicated to keeping Marias Pass open.
This is 3300 on August 18, 1940. Winter will be here soon. Cordell Newby collection, courtesy of Eric Archer.

This August 7, 1934, view of 3300, also at Whitefish, shows the appearance of the conversion from the
engineer's side. The practice continued for as long as there were O-5's available. C. W. Jernstrom collection.

In the summer of 1943, the 3338 is at Fergus Falls, MN, awaiting departure for Pelican Rapids, up the branch line.
Only the installation of the power reverse gear marks the progress of time for this locomotive. Photograph by Don Vang.

heater, was added to 3304, 3306, 3308-3310, 3312-3314, 3316, 3318, 3325, 3326 and 3328. Ultimately, fifteen of these locomotives were equipped with Ragonnet power reverse gear. These were Nos. 3300, 3301, 3302, 3304, 3308, 3309, 3310, 3312, 3313, 3329, 3331, 3334, 3335, 3338 and 3341. Only the 3335 is recorded to have received a low water alarm, but photographs of the 3300 show it having one.

Modernization of the O-5's stopped at this point in the early 1940's. In fact, scrapping of the class had already begun in 1938 and was carried into 1941. At this point scrapping was halted due to the war effort, and the remaining engines enjoyed an extended life. But modern devices such as cylinder protection valves, lubricators and blow-down mufflers were never seen on these engines. All engines retained their square cabs.

The O-5's were used on all divisions, and individual locomotives tended for the most part to remain on the same division from the 1930's until retirement. They were frequently used on branch lines due to their lower weight on drivers. Their lighter weight was required on the coast line of the Cascade Division, due to the bridge restrictions at Vancouver, BC.

On the Kalispell Division, they were used as helper engines over Marias Pass from Whitefish and in work service. A particularly interesting variant on the Kalispell Division was the installation of large snowplows directly on the locomotive in winter. Engines so equipped had their headlights relocated to the top of the smokebox to protect them from damage. The 3300, 3302, 3312 and 3313 are known to have had these plows attached. In October 1946 there were reportedly five such plows mounted on 2-8-2 type engines at Whitefish.[6]

On the Dakota Division, O-5's were regular power, along with H-3's, on passenger trains 199 and 200, locals running between Fargo and Minot via New Rockford. An O-5 also ran the Pelican Rapids branch from Fergus Falls.

Scrapping resumed in 1947, and the last one, the 3335, was retired in December 1949. Overall, the O-5 was a significant improvement over the L-2. The relatively low tractive effort for a 2-8-2 was no disadvantage on the flat territory and branches where it was used, as compared with the L-2 attempting to haul main line tonnage over mountain grades with a similar rating. The fact remains however, that as time went on, the GN had a surplus of branch line power. The road needed more powerful Mikados, capable of hauling main line tonnage. That need was met by the next conversion project.

Class O-6

In 1925, Great Northern began another of its major locomotive rebuilding programs – this time involving the twenty-two L-1 Class 2-6-6-2 articulated engines. These locomotives had been rendered obsolete by changing operational requirements and the delivery of newer articulated locomotives. No doubt the success of the L-2 to O-5 rebuilding also contributed to the decision to rebuild the L-1's. This rebuilding began in January 1925, when L-1's 1910 and 1919 entered the Hillyard and Delta locomotive shops, respectively, for dismantling. They emerged from the shops some seven months later as Nos. 3350 and 3352, the first O-6 2-8-2 locomotives. Like the O-5's, the O-6 engines re-used the boilers, tenders and driver centers of the articulateds. Again, the driver diameter was increased from 55 to 63 inches by shrinking four-inch steel bands over the old wheel centers and applying new tires.

The new O-6's were all constructed as oil burners and remained so throughout their service lives. As originally rebuilt, the tenders carried 4,500 gallons of oil and 8,000 gallons of water. By 1933, however, tender water capacities had been increased to 10,000 gallons in the rectangular tenders still assigned to O-6's, and several of the locomotives had received large Vanderbilt tenders. By 1943, most of the O-6 locomotives had received 17,000-gallon Style 112 Vanderbilt tenders. The first Style 112 tenders had been purchased separately (i.e., without accompanying locomotives) in November 1925 (Nos. 2092-2099) and the others were built in 1927 and 1928 (Nos. 2029 and 2061-2091). Specific tender assignments can be found in Chapter 34.

The O-6's had 28-inch by 32-inch cylinders equipped with 14-inch piston valves. The total engine weight was 320,100 pounds, of which 244,000 pounds was on the drivers (compared to the 355,000 pounds and 316,000 pounds, respectively, for the L-1's). By the O-6 Class's last years of service, total weight had been increased to 334,000

The 3359 appears to be just completed, and carries a rectangular tender. The photograph was taken at Delta shops in April 1926. GNRHS Collection.

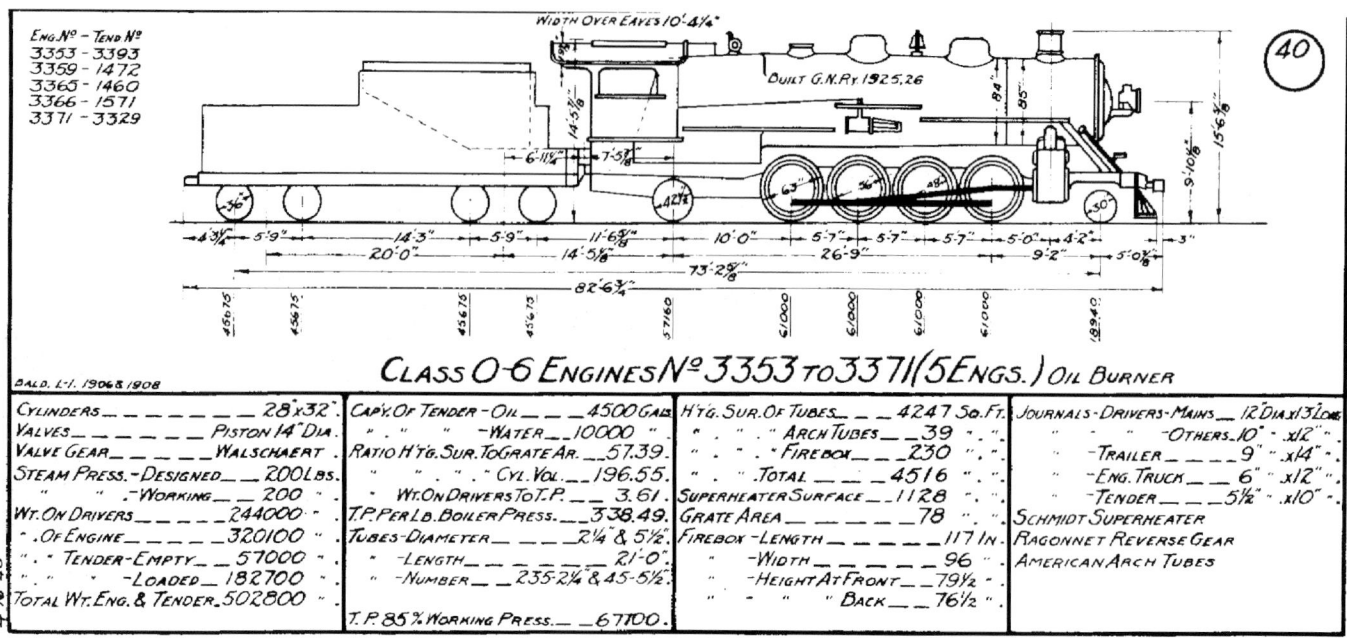

CLASS O-6 ENGINES № 3353 TO 3371 (5 ENGS.) OIL BURNER

CYLINDERS	28 x 32"	CAP'Y. OF TENDER - OIL	4500 Gals	H'TG. SUR. OF TUBES	4247 Sq. Ft.	JOURNALS - DRIVERS - MAINS — 12" Dia x 13" Long
VALVES	PISTON 14" DIA.	" - WATER	10000 "	" " " ARCH TUBES	39 "	" " - OTHERS 10" x 12"
VALVE GEAR	WALSCHAERT	RATIO H'TG. SUR. TO GRATE AR.	57.39	" " " FIREBOX	230 "	" - TRAILER 9" x 14"
STEAM PRESS. - DESIGNED	200 Lbs.	" " " CYL. VOL.	196.55	" " " TOTAL	4516 "	" - ENG. TRUCK 6" x 12"
" " - WORKING	200 "	WT. ON DRIVERS TO T.P.	3.61	SUPERHEATER SURFACE	1128 "	" - TENDER 5½" x 10"
WT. ON DRIVERS	244000 "	T.P. PER LB. BOILER PRESS.	338.49	GRATE AREA	78 "	SCHMIDT SUPERHEATER
" - OF ENGINE	320100 "	TUBES - DIAMETER	2¼ & 5½	FIREBOX - LENGTH	117 In.	RAGONNET REVERSE GEAR
" - TENDER - EMPTY	57000 "	" - LENGTH	21'-0"	" - WIDTH	96 "	AMERICAN ARCH TUBES
" " - LOADED	182700 "	" - NUMBER	235-2¼ & 45-5½	" - HEIGHT AT FRONT	79½ "	
TOTAL WT. ENG. & TENDER	502800 "			" - " " BACK	76½ "	
		T.P. 85% WORKING PRESS.	67700			

This view of 3357 at Hillyard shows the engine in August 1934 shortly after receiving a Vanderbilt tender. Collection of R. W. Johnston.

It appears the 3369 and one other engine have just received new Vanderbilt tenders in this view at Klamath Falls, OR, in 1938. GNRHS collection.

With eight years of life ahead, the 3350 is in its final configuration. Noteworthy is the normal main driver. It no longer has the original 55-inch banded wheel center. The normal wheel allowed more counterbalance weight to be applied, for higher speed operation. The engine has a Worthington BL-2 feedwater heater. At one time it carried electric train indicators, but they have been removed. The engine is shown at Minneapolis, MN, on September 21, 1946. Photograph by K. L. Zurn from the collection of William Raia.

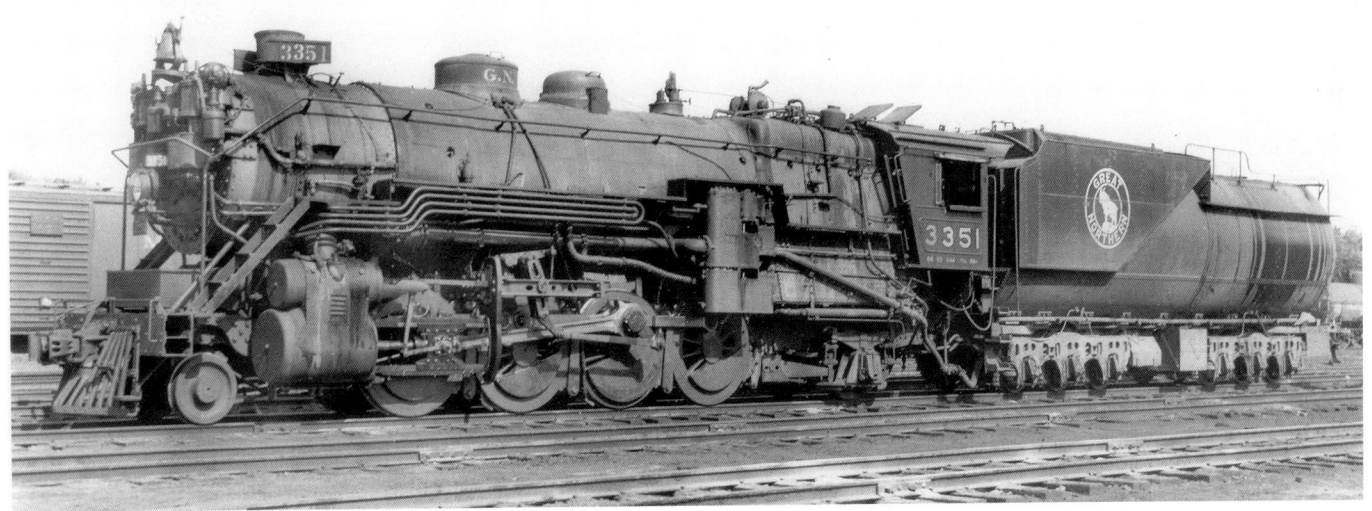

In another 1946 view, the 3351 differs from the 3350 only in a few details, most noticeably the type BL Worthington feedwater heater, and that it retained its electric train indicators. Most O-6's had had their main drivers replaced with a standard wheel by this time. The engine was at Minneapolis, MN, on August 12, 1946. Photograph by F. Wesley Krambeck from the collection of William Raia.

Still with its square cab, the 3353 is at Minneapolis, MN, on September 21, 1946. The conversion to slant-front cabs was underway, since both 3350 and 3351 had them on this date. Photograph from the Hoff-Nelson Collection.

*The 3353 must have been one of the last to receive a slant-front cab, as it still
carried its square cab here in July 1948 at Minneapolis, MN. Photograph by Robert Graham.*

*The 3363 has not had its main drive wheels replaced and it is likely it never did, since it was scrapped
two years after this photograph was taken at Minot, ND, in October 1952. Collection of Norman F. Priebe.*

*At Minneapolis in August 1946, the 3364 carries the signs of further attempts to improve the counterbalancing of these engines. Its last driver counterweight
has had a small amount of weight removed by having holes drilled into it. Photograph by Robert Graham from the collection of Harold K. Vollrath.*

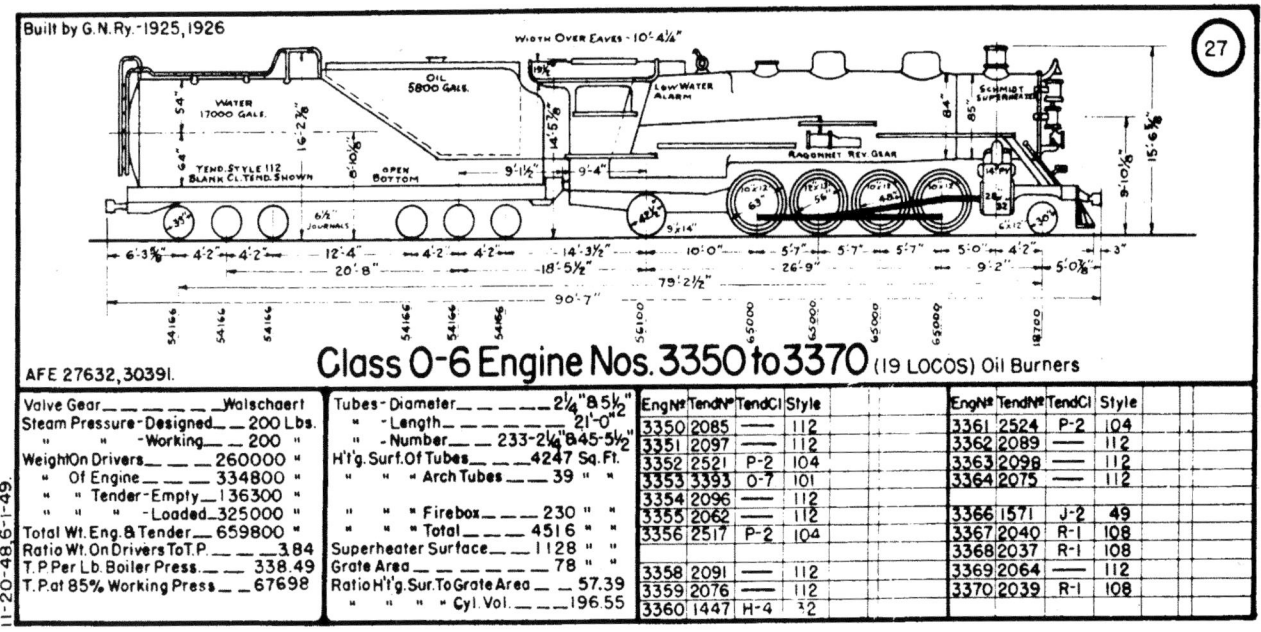

Built by G.N.Ry.-1925, 1926

AFE 27632, 30391.

Class O-6 Engine Nos. 3350 to 3370 (19 LOCOS) Oil Burners

Valve Gear	Walschaert
Steam Pressure-Designed	200 Lbs.
" " -Working	200 "
Weight On Drivers	260000 "
" Of Engine	334800 "
" " Tender-Empty	136300 "
" " " -Loaded	325000 "
Total Wt. Eng. & Tender	659800 "
Ratio Wt. On Drivers To T.P.	.384
T.P. Per Lb. Boiler Press.	338.49
T.P. at 85% Working Press	67698

Tubes-Diameter	2¼"&5½"
" -Length	21'-0"
" -Number	233-2¼"&45-5½"
H't'g. Surf. Of Tubes	4247 Sq. Ft.
" " " Arch Tubes	39 " "
" " " Firebox	230 " "
" " " Total	4516 " "
Superheater Surface	1128 " "
Grate Area	78 " "
Ratio H't'g. Sur. To Grate Area	57.39
" " " " Cyl. Vol.	196.55

Eng№	Tend№	TendCl	Style		Eng№	Tend№	TendCl	Style
3350	2085	—	112		3361	2524	P-2	104
3351	2097	—	112		3362	2089	—	112
3352	2521	P-2	104		3363	2098	—	112
3353	3393	O-7	101		3364	2075	—	112
3354	2096	—	112					
3355	2062	—	112		3366	1571	J-2	49
3356	2517	P-2	104		3367	2040	R-1	108
					3368	2037	R-1	108
3358	2091	—	112		3369	2064	—	112
3359	2076	—	112		3370	2039	R-1	108
3360	1447	H-4	12					

Working south of Bend toward Chemult, OR, the 3369 attacks the 1.3% grade to Lava with a helper. The date is the early 1940's and the engine wears an extended visor over the headlight to minimize its visibility to potential Japanese attackers. The train is the first section of No. 387, as displayed by the train indicators. Collection of Jerrold F. Hilton.

pounds and weight-on-drivers to 260,000 pounds. As they were being built, all of the engines received Schmidt superheaters (only four of the L-1's had been superheated). The diagram books do not indicate the type of the superheater used, but by this time the Type A was in use, and it is likely the type applied. All of the O-6's were equipped with Ragonnet reverse gear (the L-1's had utilized McCarroll reverse gear) and Walschaert valve gear. Design boiler pressure was 200 psi and this became the "working" boiler pressure soon after the locomotives began operation. Tractive effort was approximately 66,000 pounds - depending upon how it was calculated.

The first 14 locomotives (Nos. 3350-3363) were fitted with Worthington No. 4 feedwater heaters, while the last eight (Nos. 3364-3371) were equipped with Elesco No. 14 exhaust steam injectors. It is interesting to note that the O-6's were apparently among the first Great Northern steamers (along with the R-1's delivered from Baldwin at about the same time) to have their air pumps mounted on the smoke box front.

Except for the assignment of Vanderbilt tenders, the overall appearance of the O-6's changed relatively little during their service lives. In the late 1940's the cabs were rebuilt from the original square type to "slant-front" cabs. Most of the engines also received low water alarms and the turret covers were removed in later years to facilitate maintenance.

Some of the locomotives were in the pioneer group that received illuminated number boards next to their stacks in 1932. They were called electric train indicators by the Great Northern, and are referred to by that name elsewhere in the book. The locomotives that received them were those operating between Bend and Bieber, CA. A portion of the route used trackage rights over the Southern Pacific and the indicators were necessary to comply with SP operating rules.[7]

The O-6's were used primarily on the western portions of the Great Northern prior to World War II, with none being assigned further east than the Minot Division. A significant addition to the GN roster, they were considered the equivalent of the O-4. Many were assigned to the Kalispell and Butte Divisions, but, notably, none to the Cascade Division. Engines 3351, 3368, 3369 and 3371 spent most of their careers on the Klamath Division. Engines 3353 and 3357 were assigned to the Oregon Trunk for a time, while 3355 was assigned to the Spokane, Portland and Seattle for a time. After the War, the O-6's began to find a place farther east as the western divisions of the road were dieselized.

The first O-6 to leave the roster, No. 3365, was damaged in a boiler explosion at the Shelby, Montana, roundhouse. It was sold for scrap in March 1947 and was followed to the scrap yard by No. 3371 the next month and by No. 3357 in 1949. The remaining locomotives lasted well into the 1950's where they were very active on the Willmar Division. They ran from Minneapolis to Breckenridge and Willmar to St. Cloud. Nos. 3354, 3361, 3364 and 3370, the last survivors of the class, sat on the Superior dead line until 1963.

Assigned to troop train service during World War II, the 3356 was another example of an engine with its Worthington feedwater heater installed backwards. Here it is at Whitefish, MT, during October 1945, having just brought a troop train over the Rockies from Havre. An H-7 will take the train to Spokane. H.W. Pontin (RPS) photograph from the collection of Norman F. Priebe.

The 3371 had been transferred to the Kalispell Division for the war effort. In October 1945 it was at Browning, MT, with the eastbound local. A member of the group that received Elesco exhaust steam injectors, it was one of the few to retain a rectangular tender so late. B. F. Cutler (RPS) photograph.

The 3370 is shown here ready to leave the Minneapolis Junction engine terminal on August 22, 1952. The cab contains the hostler and the engine crew. Note the green classification flags. Given that this is a very late afternoon photograph, the locomotive will be coupling up to first 437, the advance Fargo Fast. The 3370 continued working, for autumn rushes at least, through September 2, 1956. Bruce Black photograph from the collection of Jerrold F. Hilton.

Notes:

1. Acquired with the purchase of the South Dakota Central in 1916, and operated under the name of the Watertown and Sioux Falls Railway until 1928.

2. Great Northern Railway Authority for Expenditure (AFE) 21009, June 26, 1922

3. *Ibid.* From supporting material found in the file.

4. *Locomotive Cyclopedia of American Practice*, Simmons-Boardman Publishing Company, New York. Any edition from 1931 to 1950.

5. AFE 21009, *op cit.*

6. S. Kip Farrington, *Railroading Coast to Coast*, page 182. Hastings House, New York, 1976.

7. AFE 44242, May 11, 1931, and AFE 45908, June 15, 1932. The first O-6 class engines to receive the train indicators were the 3350, 3351, 3355 and 3356. No more were installed until 1944.

Late in the steam era, the O-8 remained the core of the GN's steam fleet. Here 3390 begins yet another westbound run, accelerating through Lyndale Junction in Minneapolis during the autumn of 1956. Photograph by John Malven.

*Number 3390 is shown as a coal burning O-7 at Havre, MT, on May 2, 1940. This engine
has a vestibule cab and large ash pan with access ladder. GNRHS collection.*

Chapter 22

Class O-7 and O-8 2-8-2 Mikado Rebuilds

An Historical Overview

After the successful rebuilding of the L classes into Mikados, the Great Northern took the next logical step and began to transform the obsolescent M-2 class into Mikados as well. The M-2's were the result of a conversion into simple engines just a few years before, but their usefulness was limited by their slow speed. Since the railroad had more of them than needed, it was decided to convert 25 of them into the Class O-7.[1] Work started in 1929, and by 1930 three of the GN's largest locomotive shops, Hillyard, Superior and Great Falls, were busy with the project. Twenty-one units were finished by January 1932. At that time it was decided to try a larger boiler than those of the former M-2's, in keeping with the new superpower designs being developed elsewhere. It had been found that the old Mallet boilers did not have sufficient horsepower to run at the speeds permitted by the 69-inch drivers.[2]

Three new boilers were obtained from Baldwin, which created the first of the Class O-8. After building these three, the GN went back and finished one more O-7. This resulted in 22 Mallet boilers and 3 new superpower boilers applied to Mikado frames by the end of the project in 1934. The new locomotives were numbered consecutively: 3375 to 3396 being Class O-7, and 3397 through 3399 being Class O-8. No more Mikado work was done until 1944, when all of the 69-inch drivered Mikados, O-7 and O-8, were reworked into a common, improved O-8.

Class O-7

The choice of a 2-8-2 wheel arrangement to put under the Mallet boiler was made only after first considering other arrangements, including 2-10-0 and 2-10-2 types.[3] Once a Mikado had been decided upon, the use of 69-inch drivers for the new engine demonstrated that high speed was an important factor of the new design.

Drivers of this size were last seen on the Great Northern J-class Prairie type freight engines. Putting 69-inch drivers on a Mikado was a logical, if unprecedented next step. New Berkshire designs of the era were using 69-inch drivers, but no one had put drivers that large on a Mikado before. This was a first for the industry.[4]

The cylinder dimensions chosen for the new Mikes were 31 inches diameter by 32 inches stroke. There were no changes made to the boiler in the transfer from the Mallets to the Mikados. In fact, the same Elesco and Sellers exhaust steam injectors used with the M-2's were used on the O-7's. A consequence of this was the retention of the old Schmidt type H4 superheater. Other accessories also remained the same. Refer to the diagram for details.

Exhaust steam injectors used were split between No. 14 Elesco and No. 12 Sellers. The Sellers were used on the 3378, 3380, 3381, 3382, 3383, 3391 and 3393. However by 1938, diagrams indicated a larger No. 14 Sellers was installed on all of these engines. Nathan low water alarms were added during the life of the engines.

One O-7, the 3375, was equipped with a booster when new. This added 12,000 pounds of tractive power to the engine. However, the application was misguided, since with the booster, the engine could start a far heavier train than it could get up to speed using the available boiler. This attempt to increase tonnage resulted in the engine becoming a drag engine. As a result, the booster was removed at Havre in May 1930.[5] Tractive effort of the class without a booster, calculated by the standard formula, was 79,600 pounds. This was more than adequate. Early diagrams showed lesser amounts of 72,000 pounds or with limited cutoff of 68%, 76,200 pounds.

Many of the class received vestibule cabs. In 1938 they were to be found on engines 3375, 3380, and 3382 to 3396. By 1943 one had been applied to 3377 as well. All members of the class received large Vanderbilt tenders of 17,250 gallons water capacity built new at the time, except the 3375, which received tender 2072 with 17,000 gallons water capacity. Oil burners had a fuel capacity of 5,800 gallons, and the coal burners had a 24-ton capacity. See Chapters 32 and 34 for additional tender details. All of the O-7's except 3375 were arranged

to burn coal when new, and had stokers and grate shakers. Both Duplex and BK stokers were used. Unfortunately, with their assignment to the flat regions of Montana and to western North Dakota, they were given Montana Sand Coulee coal for fuel. The coal had a high mineral content that swelled as it burned, much like popcorn, into a clinker larger than the unburned fuel. This quickly clogged the grates, and to control it, an ash conveyor was built into 3387 for testing. In 1933 ash conveyors were found on 3388 through 3390. That the coal problem was an issue with the Mikes and not one (apparently) with the Mallets points to a higher firing rate with the Mikes in an attempt to get the most horsepower possible from them at higher speeds. In spite of this, by 1943 only four, Numbers 3376, 3379, 3380, and 3394, were burning oil. These four were all on the Minot Division, and close to the oil fields. Numbers 3375 and 3391 had been changed to burn coal. By the time the class began to be converted to O-8's they were back to burning oil and 3390 was also burning oil.

The assignment of these engines in 1936 found seven on the Minot

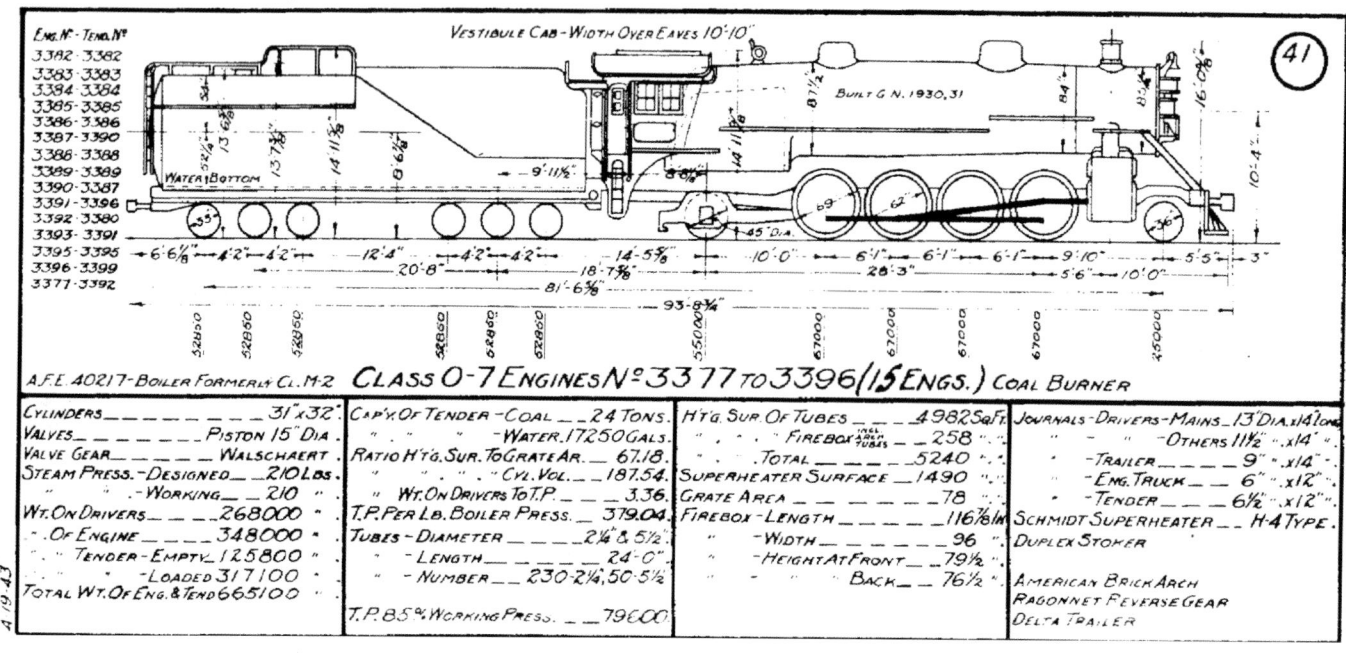

CYLINDERS _ _ _ _ _ _ _ _ 31"x32"	CAP'Y. OF TENDER -COAL _ _ 24 TONS.	H'T'G. SUR. OF TUBES _ _ _ 4,982 Sq.Ft.	JOURNALS-DRIVERS-MAINS _ 13"DIA.x14"LONG
VALVES_ _ _ _ _ PISTON 15" DIA.	" " " _WATER.17250 GALS.	" . " _FIREBOX AND TUBES _ _ 258 "	" " -OTHERS 11½ ".x14" .
VALVE GEAR _ _ _ _ WALSCHAERT .	RATIO H'T'G. SUR. TO GRATE AR._ 67.18 .	" . " _TOTAL _ _ _5240 "	" -TRAILER _ _ _ _ 9 " .x14" .
STEAM PRESS.-DESIGNED_ _ 210 LBS.	" . " . " . " _CYL. VOL. _ _ 187.54.	SUPERHEATER SURFACE _1490 " .	" -ENG. TRUCK _ _ 6 " .x12" .
" . " -WORKING_ _ 210 "	" WT. ON DRIVERS TO T.P. _ _ _ 3.36 .	GRATE AREA _ _ _ _ _ _ _78 " .	" -TENDER _ _ _ _ 6½ ".x12" .
WT. ON DRIVERS _ _ _ 268000 "	T.P. PER LB. BOILER PRESS._ _ 379.04.	FIREBOX -LENGTH _ _ _ _ 116⅞ IN.	SCHMIDT SUPERHEATER _ H-4 TYPE .
" . " OF ENGINE _ _ _ 348000 "	TUBES - DIAMETER _ _ _ _ 2¼ & 5½ "	" -WIDTH _ _ _ _ _ 96 "	DUPLEX STOKER
" . " TENDER -EMPTY _125800 "	" - LENGTH_ _ _ _ _ 24'-0" .	" -HEIGHT AT FRONT_ _79½ "	
" . " -LOADED 317100 "	" - NUMBER _ _ 230-2¼, 50-5½ "	" - BACK_ _ 76½ "	AMERICAN BRICK ARCH
TOTAL WT. OF ENG. & TEND 665100 "			RAGONNET REVERSE GEAR
	T.P. 85% WORKING PRESS. _ _79600 "		DELTA TRAILER

The first O-7 completed, the 3375, had a booster and burned oil. The GN builders photograph taken at Great Falls, MT, in November 1929, shows the booster and oil tank. While the oil preheater is obscured, the absence of an ash pan is obvious. Great Northern Railway.

Engine 3391 was another early oil burner that was changed to burn coal by 1943, and then back to oil by 1946.
This view is at Hillyard, WA, in April 1932. It has a vestibule cab and a Sellers exhaust steam injector. Richard Bartholow collection.

Number 3379 appears as a coal burning O-7 at Devils Lake, ND, on September 19, 1932. The engine does not
have a vestibule cab nor does it have a ladder on the ash pan. Robert Graham photograph from the GNRHS collection.

A clean O-7 was hard to find, but one is shown here. While it does not have a vestibule cab, the 3378 does have the large ash
pan with ladder. It is shown at Minneapolis on July 18, 1938. Robert Graham photograph from the GNRHS collection.

Division and fifteen on the Butte. By 1940, Minot had lost its coal burners. The 3378 went instead to the Willmar Division, and the 3375 and 3377 were moved to the Dakota Division. But they did not stay long. With the start of World War II, Butte Division received all of the class except the oil burners, which stayed on the Minot Division. Butte always had the majority of the O-7's, namely 3381 through 3393, 3395 and 3396.

The Remarkable Great Northern Berkshire

The performance of the Mallet boilers on the O-7's did not meet expectations. In addition, the 31-inch diameter cylinder bore was too large for several reasons. Consequently, design of a new high-power locomotive began while the O-7's were still in production. On January 24, 1931, the Motive Power Office released the design of an amazing Berkshire, one heavier on drivers and with a larger grate area than

any other built up to that time. Design drawing UF1517 and the specifications of Table 1 define the Berkshire.

TABLE 1. PROPOSED 2-8-4 TYPE LOCOMOTIVE

Weight on each Driver (axle)	70,000 pounds
Total weight on Drivers	280,000 pounds
Cylinders	29-inch by 32-inch
Boiler Pressure	250 pounds (psi)
Cutoff	60% with auxiliary starting ports
Drivers	69-inch diameter
Tractive Power	75,500 pounds
Ratio of Adhesion	3.71
Grate Area	126 square feet
Tube Length	20 feet

As an O-7, the 3387 was assigned to the Butte Division, and is shown at Williston in 1934. These engines were assigned to Williston-Glasgow and Glasgow-Havre runs. H. W. Pontin (RPS) photograph.

Another Butte Division O-7 was the 3386, which ran between Havre, MT, and Williston, ND. Here at Williston it is shown ready for another trip on May 3, 1940. Collection of Norman F. Priebe.

This is a late in life view of first O-7 No. 3375 at Minneapolis, MN, on September 1, 1946. Robert Graham photograph from the collection of William Raia.

Engine 3390 was at Minneapolis on September 14, 1946, in the waning days of the O-7 class. Robert Graham photograph from collection of William Raia.

The 3395 is at Harlem, MT, on the Butte Division on April 4, 1944. Note that while it is still a coal burner, it no longer has the ladder on the ash pan. R. E. Johnson photograph.

The design included a combustion chamber of 28-inch length, with the external features of vestibule cab and Vanderbilt tender. The weight on each trailing truck axle was 56,000 pounds, and total engine weight was 432,000 pounds. The ratio of adhesion and the driver diameter of the O-7 had been combined with a firebox equal to that on the R-2!

Class O-8

After more consideration, the designers, William Kelly, General Superintendent of Motive Power; Henry Yoerg, Superintendent of Motive Power, Lines East; William H. Elsner, Mechanical Engineer; and Herbert W. Miller, Design Engineer, decided to forego the R-2 sized firebox. Instead they revised the boiler so that it would fit on the O-7 frame, of which there were still four on the shop floor.[6] The firebox was cut back to have a grate area of 98.5 square feet which was still larger than that of many Berkshires and definitely "superpower." Incredibly, it was squeezed over a single axle Delta trailing truck at 60,000 pounds axle weight. This trailing truck axle weight was similar

to that of several other large GN engines and was no cause for concern at the time. The spring rigging and equalizers were designed so that some of the excess trailer weight was transferred onto the driving wheels.[7] At this point it was believed the weight on drivers was fairly normal.

Despite the reduction in firebox size, the result was still an extraordinary engine, since the firebox was large enough to qualify as the largest ever applied to a Mikado. Most of the other Berkshire specifications were applied to this new design unchanged. Comparing the 1932 O-8 specifications, found on the diagram, with those of the proposed Berkshire, one will see the cutoff was changed to 65%, resulting in an increased tractive effort and reduced factor of adhesion. The tube length was reduced to 19 feet to allow room for a larger combustion chamber of 45 inches, and there was less weight on the leading truck axle. These were the only changes. An American multiple-port, front-end throttle replaced the dome throttle that was used on the O-7. The exhaust steam injector was an Elesco No. 16

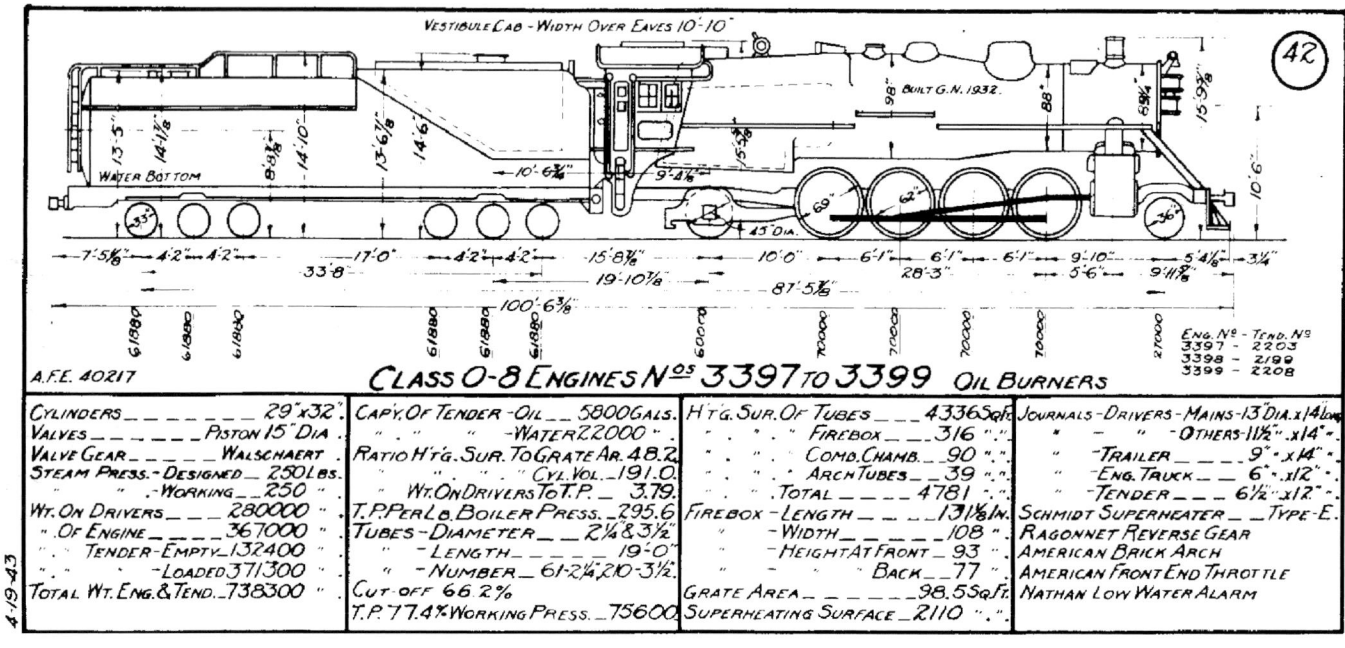

This diagram depicts the O-8 class as first built. There were only three of them from 1932 until 1944.

This is the official GN builder's photograph of the O-8 taken at Hillyard in August 1932. Great Northern Railway.

and there was a Sellers No. 13.8 non-lifting injector on the fireman's side. Other features included Ragonnet power reverse gear, a Nathan low water alarm, mechanical lubricators and blow-down mufflers. Note that a Type E superheater was used. This boiler was physically 15% smaller than that of the S-1 4-8-4 yet had only 2% less potential horsepower than the S-1 and 15% greater horsepower than the S-2. For increased stability, Franklin radial buffers were used between engine frame and tender. Lateral-motion driving boxes were not used. Without the lateral-motion devices, the engine was stiffer, which helped reduce nosing.

It was determined the road could afford to build three of the new engines, and the boilers were ordered from Baldwin.[8] The frame that was to have been used for O-7 No. 3395 was selected to receive the first new boiler. Three 22,000-gallon water capacity Vanderbilt tenders were found for them. The engines were built at Hillyard, under the supervision of Mr. J. M. Hurley, Superintendent of Hillyard shops, and Alex B. Colville, General Foreman of the shops. All three O-8's were

oil-burners. The first one was finished in August 1932 and the final one in October. The depression prevented the construction of more O-8's and the last engine of the order was completed as an O-7 in May 1934. The three O-8 engines were assigned to the Kalispell Division, running between Spokane (Hillyard) and Whitefish, over Rexford Hill. Here they were dubbed the "Spokaners". Together with the S-1's and a few O-6's they managed all mainline freight traffic on this stretch until replaced by the new N-3's. They then went to the Minot Division and joined the four oil-burning O-7's until the end of World War II. Normal practice on the Minot Division was to use the Mikados east of Minot and Q-1's and the R classes west of Minot.

While still on the Kalispell Division, tests were run at the request of the Baldwin Locomotive Company comparing them to the GN's other new high-drivered locomotives, the S-1 and S-2, in freight service. Mr. Samuel Vauclain of Baldwin then wrote an article describing the results with the idea of promoting larger diameter drivers for fast freight service.[9] While the results clearly showed larger drivers resulted in

An easy way to identify the original O-8's before later rebuilding is they have the sander pipes covered by the jacket.
The 3398 is at Hillyard in this view on July 16, 1939. L. T. Haug photograph from the Gerald M. Best collection, courtesy of Jack W. Farrell.

The three original O-8's had ladder access to the top of the valve gear hanger as did the
S-2 class originally. The 3399 is eastbound at Libby, MT, on April 16, 1940. Collection of Norman F. Priebe.

In August 1946 the 3375 paused in Dassel, MN, with the first section of a 402 time freight. This was one of its last trips as an O-7. On September 9 it was at Superior shops beginning the conversion to an O-8. Photograph by Milton Drefke.

The O-8 cast bed section is shown as it appeared at the General Steel Castings Corporation. Cylinders, front frame, valve gear hanger and pilot beam were all one piece. Courtesy of the General Steel Castings Corporation.

less time spent on the road, it was the O-8 that showed up with the best efficiency, using less fuel and water per ton-mile than either the S-1 or the S-2. When questioned by Mr. C. O. Jenks, Operating Vice President, about the speed assertions made by Mr. Vauclain, Mr. Kelly replied "the O-8 is as fast as we require".[10]

The 1944 Conversions

By 1943, it was obvious the GN needed more locomotives for the war effort. The GN was buying four-unit FT's now as fast as the War Production Board allowed, and they were not enough. The only recourse was to improve availability of the present fleet, and to convince the War Production Authority and the Office of Defense Transportation that the work was "not a conversion job." Mr. I. G. Pool included the O-7's in the same memo that addressed the need for new frames for the R-1's.[11] The road wanted to place "new boilers and new cylinders cast integral" on 12 O-7's. This would be a "maintenance repair job" to avoid time out of service due to "broken cylinders, cylinders working

loose, shearing and loosening of frame bolts, and working guides." He went on to state that in May 1943, "the O-7 class engines averaged only 4930 miles per month, whereas the three O-8's averaged 8000 miles per month." Approval was granted, and AFE 66250 was issued to convert the first 12 engines.

Superintendent Kelly and Design Engineer Miller had left the company's service by this time and Mr. Silver was in the Armed Forces, so design of the new O-8 was started by R. T. Meyers and L. M. (Bert) Baker until relieved by A. J. Trowbridge.[12] The three major improvements represented by this design were the reduction in cylinder bore, the change to cast-steel front bed sections with integral cylinders, and the boiler additions.

The new locomotive had a cylinder bore of 28 inches, one less than the original O-8. This allowed improved counterbalancing. It also cut the tractive effort to 75,900 pounds. But this in turn achieved a better factor of adhesion. Because the true weight of the engine was still unknown, the factor of adhesion was calculated at 3.68, better than the

A late view in the life of 3380 as an O-7 is shown at Minneapolis on September 2, 1946. Robert Graham photograph from the GNRHS Collection.

The 3380 presented a radically different appearance as an O-8, with its modern Alco boiler. Counterweight rework on the last axle dated from the O-7 days. There was no longer a vestibule cab. The engine is shown here at Breckenridge, MN, on October 25, 1955. Bruce Black photograph from the collection of Norman F. Priebe.

first O-8, but still low.[13] The counterbalancing was further improved by cross-balancing the main driver. The cutoff was changed to allow 77% at full stroke.

The cast bed section with integral cylinders extended back to the second pedestal opening where it was welded to the remainder of the original frame. It included the valve gear hanger bracket and extended forward to include the pilot beam. The General Steel Castings Corporation made the castings.

The design of the new boilers was improved by the addition of five Security circulators and Nalco foam-collapsing blowdown systems. There also was a reduction in the number of 2¼-inch flues from 61 to 50. Type E superheaters were installed. Elesco steam driers were installed on ten. Feedwater was provides by a Sellers, GN or Chicago injector on the fireman's side, and an Elesco No. 15 exhaust steam injector on the engineer's side. Prime cylinder protection valves of 3-inch diameter and larger mechanical lubricators were installed. Pyrometers were added. Steam-heat and air-signal lines were added to the entire class, to allow them to handle passenger trains. As before, all engines had power reverse gear, Nathan low water alarms and Franklin radial buffers.

Construction began in 1944 and continued through 1946. All but two of the new O-8's were built at the Superior, WI, shops. The exceptions, 3388 and 3394, were constructed at the Great Falls shops. Boilers were again fabricated outside the company, with Baldwin supplying 12 and Alco providing 10. The three original O-8 boilers were reworked to match the new specifications.

Four O-8's were equipped to burn coal and were given BK stokers. They were 3378, 3383, 3386 and 3392. However, because of the same problem with Sand Coulee coal mentioned earlier, the firing difficulties were insurmountable and all engines were converted to burn oil within 3 months. Mr. R. E. (Dick) Johnson was the traveling engineer who rode with the 3386 on its first trip from Glasgow to Havre. He related how several unscheduled stops had to be made to remove the clinkers and clean the ash pan.[14]

Construction ended in December 1946. In the interim, additional AFE's had been approved to rebuild the remainder of the engines, and add appliances and roller bearings.[15] The O-8 had larger journals than the N-3's but its weight per axle was considerably higher, though this was not yet recognized. As operation began to show a problem, a change to roller bearings was made midway in the program, in 1945. The first engines finished received the new bearings at the next major shopping.[16] The entire class was eventually equipped. Unlike the N-3's, the O-8's received roller bearings on all axles, including the tender.

After 1945 most if not all engines had the larger 8½-inch air compressors. All but two had vestibule cabs at the beginning, but they were gradually removed over the remaining life of the engines. By end of life, only 3377 and 3396 still had them. The reason was they required increased maintenance. The Great Northern was still painting its steam locomotives with the classic green boiler jackets when these engines were finished, but the order to paint them black was issued soon after, on October 6, 1950.[17]

Table 2 adequately demonstrates the progression of capability of the engines as their design improved. Readily apparent is the step backward with the use of the old M-2 boiler for the O-7.

The majority of the O-8's kept the tenders they received as O-7's.

O-8 No. 3386 as a coal-burner stopped at Savoy, MT, on its first trip in 1944. Coal burning was unsuccessful due to composition of the coal and all O-8's became oil-burners. Photograph by R.E. Johnson.

TABLE 2. O-8 COMPARED WITH ITS PREDECESSORS

Class	S-1	O-7	O-8 early	O-8
Year first built	1929	1929	1932	1944
Type	4-8-4	2-8-2	2-8-2	2-8-2
Boiler Pressure (psi)	250	210	250	250
Cylinders (inches)	28x30	31x32	29x32	28x32
Driver Dia. (inches)	73	69	69	69
Tractive Effort (pounds)	68,466	72,000	78,000	75,900
Factor of Adhesion	4.13	3.72	3.59	4.28
Grate area (sq. ft.)	102	78	98.5	98.5
Heating surface, direct* (sq. ft.)	491	258	445	506
Heating surface, tubes (sq. ft.)	4,960	4,982	4,336	4,220
Superheater surface (sq. ft.)	2,444 (E)	1,490 (H4)	2,110 (E)	2,110 (E)
Boiler max. outside diameter (inches)	98	87.5	98	98
Weight on drivers, last (pounds)	283,000	268,000	280,000	325,000
Weight of engine, last (pounds)	493,780	348,000	367,000	425,540

* Sum of firebox, combustion chamber and either circulators or arch tubes.

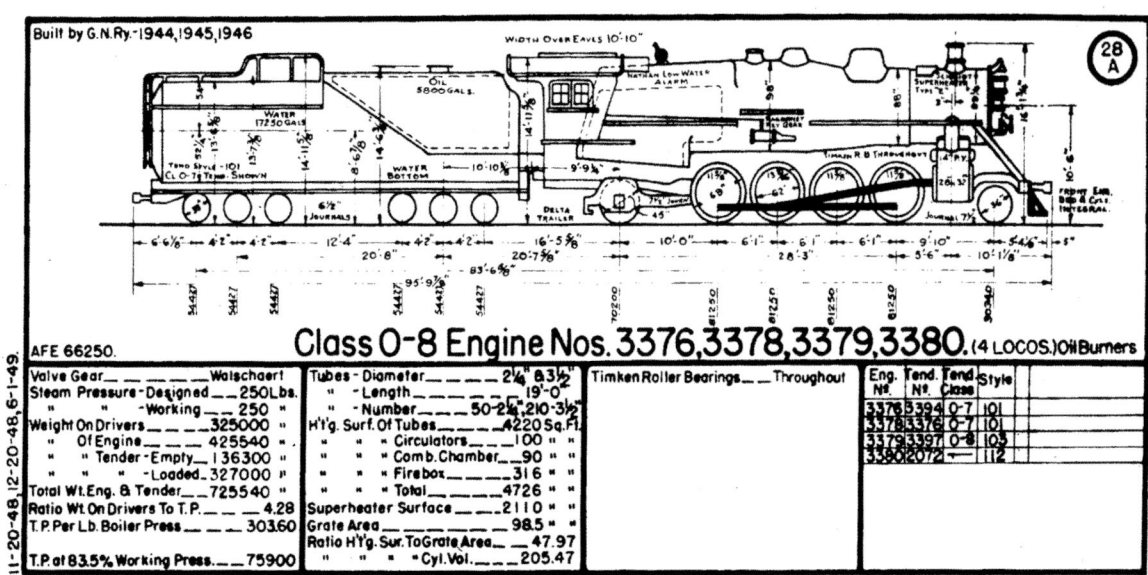

This diagram illustrates the standard cab version of the rebuilt O-8 class. This diagram and the following also give the corrected weight for the O-8's.

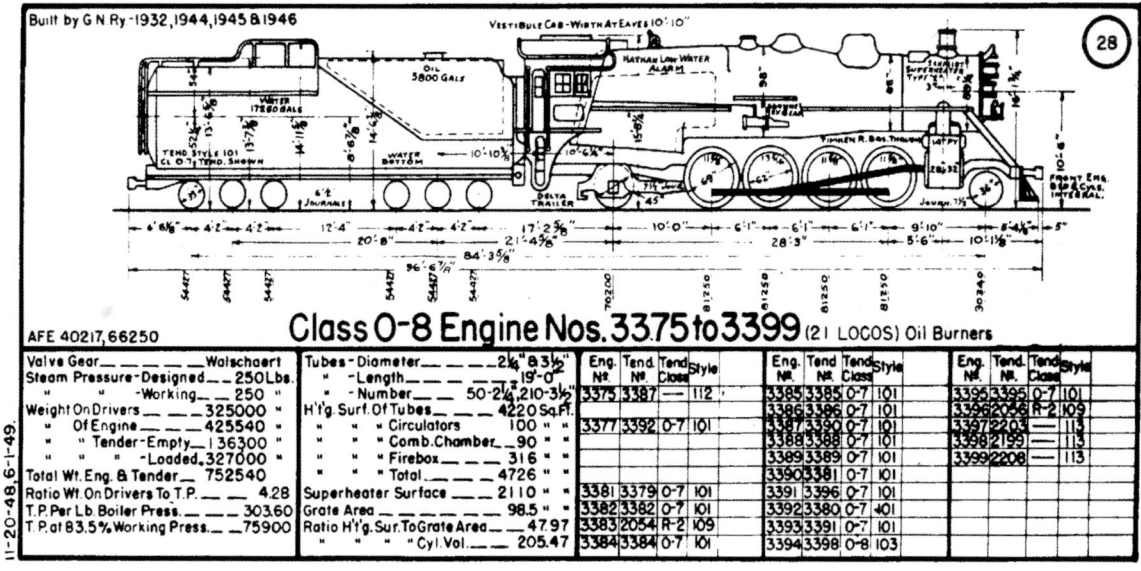

This diagram illustrates the vestibule cab version of the rebuilt O-8 class. By 1951, only two O-8's remained equipped with the vestibule cab.

However, 3383 and 3396 received 22,000-gallon tanks to join 3397 through 3399, and 3380 joined 3375 with a 17,000-gallon tank. Details are in Chapter 34.

The new engines were not on the road long before enginemen began to suspect they were considerably heavier than their design weight. By late 1945 enginemen had brought the issue up to their Brotherhood of Locomotive Engineers representative in St. Paul. The enginemen filed a grievance that caused the reweighing of 19 classes, some in various configurations. Rumors that the enginemen weighed an O-8 themselves, on the sly, to make their point leads one to believe that it was the O-8 that precipitated the weight issue. See Chapter 4 for the complete story. The results pertaining to the O-8 and the N-3 were significant. The O-8 was found to be 16% overweight and the N-3 17%. As related in Chapter 4, this had a considerable impact throughout the railroad. Of most interest to this discussion, the O-8 weight on drivers was found to be an unprecedented 325,000 pounds, 81,250 pounds per axle. Because of the high weight on drivers, even with the high tractive effort the true factor of adhesion was an impressive 4.28. The weight on the trailing truck was 70,200 pounds. Only booster-equipped engines had previously equaled or exceeded this trailing truck weight. Note that this is heavier than what had been stated for a single driving axle originally. The actual total weight of these engines, 425,540 pounds, was a record for Mikados, exceeded that of many Northerns, and in per-axle weight was exceeded by only the 2-6-6-6 Allegheny type. The C&O version had a per-axle weight of 84,000 pounds and the Virginian version had 82,500 pounds per axle. Their weight restricted the engines to the main lines, and required the GN to check all bridges wherever the locomotives were assigned.[18]

Yet, the weight was an advantage when it came to operation since it permitted a high starting tractive effort without a booster. Add to that the 69-inch drivers, roller bearings and a high output boiler that could move the extra tonnage at speed, the O-8 could outperform a Berkshire. Outside of the need for some care in the assignment of the class, they were everything one could wish for in a fast level-district steam engine.

Table 3, comparing O-8's to Berkshires is meant to demonstrate that the O-8, even though a Mikado, was the equal of the Berkshire type. Revised from earlier versions,[19] the table includes potential boiler

TABLE 3. O-8 COMPARED TO WELL-KNOWN LARGE BERKSHIRES

Road and Class	GN O-8	NKP S-3	Erie S-2	C&O K-4	L&N M-1
Wheel Arrangement	2-8-2	2-8-4	2-8-4	2-8-4	2-8-4
Total Engine Weight	425,540	444,290	457,500	489,680	448,100
Weight on Drivers	325,000	266,030	274,000	293,100	268,000
Tractive effort, no booster	75,900	64,100	72,000	69,350	65,290
Factor of Adhesion	4.28	4.15	3.81	4.23	4.10
Grate Area, square feet	98.5	90.3	100	90.3	90.2
Boiler horsepower, calculated	5,090	4,860	5,240	4,860	4,930
Driver size, inches	69	69	70	69	69

* The potential boiler horsepower figure is used here as a figure of merit and size comparison, everything else being equal. It assumes identical BTU value fuel and a firebox that can deliver equal BTU's in each case. Johnson's method[20] is used, but with all locomotives calculated using a heat transfer factor of 80 instead of 55 and use of 300 degree superheat temperature.

The 3397, on July 20, 1947, is in spectacular condition after shopping at Superior. Note it did not receive train indicator boards. The vestibule cab was later removed. Photograph from the Jack W. Farrell collection.

The 3377, in a decidedly dirty condition here, kept its vestibule cab. The engine is on a circus train at Superior, WI, on September 24, 1953. Bruce Black photograph from the collection of Norman F. Priebe.

The 3378 is an O-8 that was built with a standard cab. It still had the No. 5 New York air pumps at Minneapolis on a chilly winter day in 1950. From the John Westphal collection, courtesy of John Luecke.

The 3394 had a vestibule cab when built, but is one of the many engines that lost it to a standard cab during its lifetime. Here it is without it at Minneapolis in June 1953. It also has had new Westinghouse-type 8½ inch air pumps installed. Collection of Harold K. Vollrath.

The 3396 is rushing eastward with the first section of a scheduled freight near Harlem, MT, in August 1948. An S-2 was following with the second section. Frank McKinlay (RPS) photograph from the collection of Norman F. Priebe.

horsepower. The post-1948 weights are used for the O-8.

After the rebuilding, the O-8's were assigned to the Butte and Willmar Divisions. They ran over the main lines of the entire system east of Havre except from Williston to Minot. Performance was exemplary. They would out-perform a three-unit FT at speeds above 20 mph. It was told that on occasion they had been run at speeds in excess of 70 mph, but the enginemen refused to tell exactly how fast that was.

On the Willmar Division, where the ruling grade was 0.3 percent, speeds of 60 mph with 4,500 tons (about 75 cars, typical time freight tonnage) were common. If called for a drag, they would roll 6,500 tons or 125 loads at 45 mph. Enginemen considered its acceleration its best feature. It was able to get a train out of town faster than any other type on the system. An engineer told of a trip with the 3398 on No. 401 from Willmar to Breckenridge. The 113-mile trip took 2 hours, 45 minutes, including a water stop at Morris that could have taken anywhere from 15 to 30 minutes. The average speed, *including the standing time*, was 41 mph. On the Minot Division, the engines were rated at 5,000 tons

on the 0.3 % grade between New Rockford and Minot. Those that were finished in 1944 and 1945 saw troop train service as the war was not yet over. On one occasion at Minneapolis an O-8 was called for Second No. 3 with 22 heavyweight Pullmans. This train of 1800 tons easily averaged 45 mph to stay on No. 3's schedule.

As the GN dieselized from west to east, the engines were moved eastward. By 1954 the majority were on the Willmar Division, with 3376, 3377 and 3383 on the Minot Division. The O-8's formed the backbone of the remaining steam fleet and all 25 remained active until late in 1956. These engines were capable of any assignment given them and were the only Great Northern steam road-engine class to remain intact that late. It is known that the 3385 ran in 1957, but there was a downturn in business that year and by August there were enough diesels on the property to permanently end all use of steam. An era had ended. There was one last flicker of life when six were chosen for ore-steaming service beginning in the summer of 1960.[21]

The 3396 kept its vestibule cab until the end. It is shown here at Minot, ND, prior to coupling up for an eastbound run on October 16, 1954. H. Stirton photograph from the collection of William Raia.

The 3397 is coupled with the 3051 at Breckenridge, MN, on September 5, 1952, for a westbound double-headed time freight run via the cut-off to Minot. Bruce Black photograph from the GNRHS collection.

Another double-headed run, this time eastbound, is shown on August 1, 1955 at Minot, ND. The 3390 and the 3375 team up to get an extra-heavy scheduled freight rolling – quickly. Photographer Larry Stuckey wrote " those engineers really meant business." Photograph by Larry Stuckey.

The 3399, shown here near the end of use at Minneapolis in 1956, was the only O-8 to have the sanding pipes remain under the jacket. Photograph by Robert Graham.

Notes:

1. Great Northern Railway Authority for Expenditure (AFE) 40217. The first O-7 was built under AFE 39892 at Great Falls. The Great Falls shop was closed due to the depression before these engines were finished.

2. The Mallet boiler had approximately 3,000 h.p. and the O-8 boiler had approximately 5,000 h.p.

3. Drawings UF 584, dated 12-22-1922; UF 917, dated 4-1-1925; UF 948, dated 5-12-1926; and UF 1201, dated 9-10-1926. GN Collection, MHS. The O-7 apparently grew out of the latter, although there were two earlier Mikado designs. See also GNRHS Reference Sheet 50.

4. The Baltimore & Ohio added 70-inch drivers to four Mikados during World War II. Raymond W. Brown, *Locomotive Quarterly*, Vol. 4, Number 4, Summer 1981.

5. Great Northern Railway AFE 39892, approved May 18, 1929.

6. No record of this decision has yet been found, but it was likely made in the interest of economy.

7. L. M. Baker, quoted in correspondence from Frank Perrin to Norman F. Priebe, July 13, 1967.

8. This cost was also charged against AFE 40217.

9. *Baldwin Locomotives*, April-July 1934.

10. W. Kelly to C. O. Jenks, August 8, 1934. GN collection MHS.

11. I. G. Pool to A. N. Cranshaw, Purchasing Agent, June 22, 1943. GN collection MHS.

12. Mr. Trowbridge later became Mechanical Engineer for the Soo Line Railroad, stationed in Minneapolis.

13. The apparently better than usual traction at this low factor of adhesion should have been noticed.

14. From verbal communication with Mr. Johnson. A handwritten note on AFE 66250 says the application of the BK Stoker to 4 engines was not carried out. However, at least one received the stoker and was given tests per information given by and photograph taken by R. E. Johnson. Mr. Johnson was along on the test of 3386. The Great Northern Unit Record of Property Changes (URPC) states the 4 engines had the stokers for about a month in conflict with this note on the AFE. If one was installed and then removed in short order it is possible for the note writer to say none were installed, but the accountants didn't think so.

15. Great Northern Railway AFE 70800, Equip 10 engines with engine beds, high-pressure boilers, Elesco steam driers and roller bearings. Great Northern Railway AFE 69714 and AFE 73623, Equip with roller bearings. (Multiple classes).

16. Valuation Department Correspondence File No. 202, Roller Bearings Applied to Locomotives.

17. Alex Colville, Hillyard shop notes.

18. The GN maintained a Cooper E-72 rating on mainline bridges at that time. Thomas J. Lamphier, personal communication to Norman F. Priebe, February 22, 1982

19. Norman F. Priebe, GNRHS Reference Sheet No. 98, June 1985. See also "The World's Greatest Mikado", *Trains Magazine*, January 1969.

20. Ralph P. Johnson, *The Steam Locomotive*, Simmons-Boardman Publishing Corporation, New York, NY, 1942. Page 167 and Appendix C.

21. Great Northern Railway AFE 89838. The engines were the 3375, 3376, 3385, 3391, 3392 and 3394. A photograph also exists of 3386 steaming ore in 1953. There may have been other undocumented locomotives used in this service, perhaps bridging the 1959 gap indicated by the records.

The P-2 class was seen predominately on the Empire Builder *and* Fast Mail *during World War II. Here is the 2508 with an advance section of*
No. 1 in the tunnel region of Marias Pass just east of Belton, MT, in October 1945. Ben Cutler (RPS) photograph from the collection of Norman F. Priebe.

This 1915 view of 1752 shows the P-1 in a typical passenger service scene. At Columbia Falls, MT, it is on Train No. 1, the Oriental Limited, and is met by the Kalispell connection powered by the 291, a class B-8 4-4-0. GNRHS collection.

Chapter 23
Class P 4-8-2 Mountain

Class P-1

By 1913 the GN needed larger power to handle the increasing passenger traffic. Longer trains and steel cars had forced doubleheading on mountain grades for some time. The road even had begun to use the O-1 Mikado type in passenger service between Whitefish and Cut Bank, MT. The O-1's were reported as "giving good service in this assignment", and Mr. C. O. Jenks suggested that "more be used in this service".[1] Instead, a new wheel arrangement, the 4-8-2 Mountain type, was developed, and 15 units (1750 to 1764) were received from Lima in 1914. The 1760 to 1764 came as oil-burners, the remainder burned coal. The Great Northern put them in Class P-1.

Apparently derived from the successful O-1, the P-1 reflected many features of freight engine origin. The GN had had the O-1 class Mikado on the system since 1911, and found it to be a very successful locomotive. Therefore the P-1 took on many of the characteristics of the Mikado, but this was not all GN's doing. The pioneer 4-8-2's that preceded those of the GN shared similar characteristics: low drivers, a long stroke of 32 inches and a long main rod driving on the third axle. About the only concession to speed was the four-wheel engine truck.

The Great Northern was the fourth railroad to use this wheel arrangement. The first Mountain type, on the Chesapeake and Ohio, and the second, found on the Missouri Pacific had the same characteristics as the GN's. The Rock Island engines that followed in 1913 were the first to use a main rod driving on the second axle, as well as drivers

larger than 63 inches. The GN engines came next, and were the last to have the main rod driving on the third axle until construction of the Norfolk and Western's 200 series (K-3 class) in 1926. Obtaining high tractive effort was the primary concern for the C&O and the GN, with the GN's design achieving the highest rating among all roads until the construction of the Rio Grande's engines of 1922.[2]

How closely did the P-1 resemble the O-1? A comparison shows they had identical driver diameter, cylinder dimensions, boiler pressure, tractive effort and grate area. They both drove on the third axle. Due to the different weight distribution due to the four-wheel engine truck, the weight on drivers for the P-1 was slightly less than that of the O-1, which led to a lower Tractive Effort Ratio (Factor of Adhesion). The P-1 had the improved GN New Style superheater, and a tender with two tons greater coal capacity. The P-1 clearly was a modified, slightly faster Class O-1. There was one almost cosmetic difference. The Lima-designed Belpaire firebox top sloped down more steeply toward the cab than other Belpaire designs on the Great Northern. This is noticeable on both the P-1 and its derivative the Q-2.

The engines were put into service on the grades of the Rockies and Cascades, where they handled trains No. 1 and 2, the Oriental Limited, as well as other trains as needed. An insight into their assignment in 1915 is gained from a response to a request of the ICC District Engineer for a classification of locomotive assignments by "engine performing the largest amount of service" on the various lines of the railroad. The response, in the form of engine classes penciled in on a map of the system, shows the P-1 in service between Havre and Cut Bank, MT, and between Everett and Seattle, WA.[3] Even though this confirms only half of each expected assignment, it does not rule out the engines having operated over the entire route between Seattle and Leavenworth in the Cascades, and between Whitefish and Havre in the Rockies.

The P-1 class served in passenger service for six years, much of the time under USRA management. Then in 1920, the class was placed in freight service from Whitefish to Troy, MT.[4,5] They had proved to be too slow for passenger service, and may have been withdrawn sooner if it hadn't been for World War I. They ran in freight service for eight more years, and then were converted to 2-10-2's.

The Unit Record of Property Changes shows modest improvements were made while in service as a Mountain type.[6] The first significant change came in the period between November 1917 and November 1920, when the coal-burning engines were equipped with Duplex stokers and Franklin power grate shakers. The engines had been hand-fired until this time. Steel pilots replaced the original wooden pilots in the 1920 to 1925 period, followed by the changing of the pilot beam from wood to steel from 1923 to 1927. Outside steam pipes replaced

inside steam pipes in the 1919 to 1923 period. This was accompanied by a change to the superheater headers. In 1919 and 1920 the arc-type electric headlights were replaced by incandescent bulbs in a different sheet iron enclosure.

In 1920, in keeping with the re-assignment of the engines to freight service, their speed recorders and steam heat connections were removed. The oil-burning engines, 1760 to 1764, were converted to burn coal at this time. Once in freight service, between 1922 and 1924, to improve steaming, all of the class received a brick firebox arch supported by four arch tubes. Okadee blow-off cocks were installed on all in 1926. The entire class was converted to burn oil in 1926. Then in 1927, No. 14 Elesco exhaust steam injectors replaced one of the Chicago non-lifting injectors on some engines. The remainder were applied during conversion to Class Q-2. Two of them, the 1753 and 1759, received the Sellers model. Three, the 1751, 1755 and 1762, received the standard GN cast headlight before conversion to 2-10-2's. The final improvement made before the conversion to 2-10-2 was the addition of Ragonnet power reverse gear to all but five of the engines in 1927. The rest of the history of these engines is told in Chapter 24, the Q class.

The builder's photo of 1755 taken in 1914 is the only engineer's side view of the P-1 found. Note the hopper-style ash pans are nearly identical to those of the O-1. GNRHS collection.

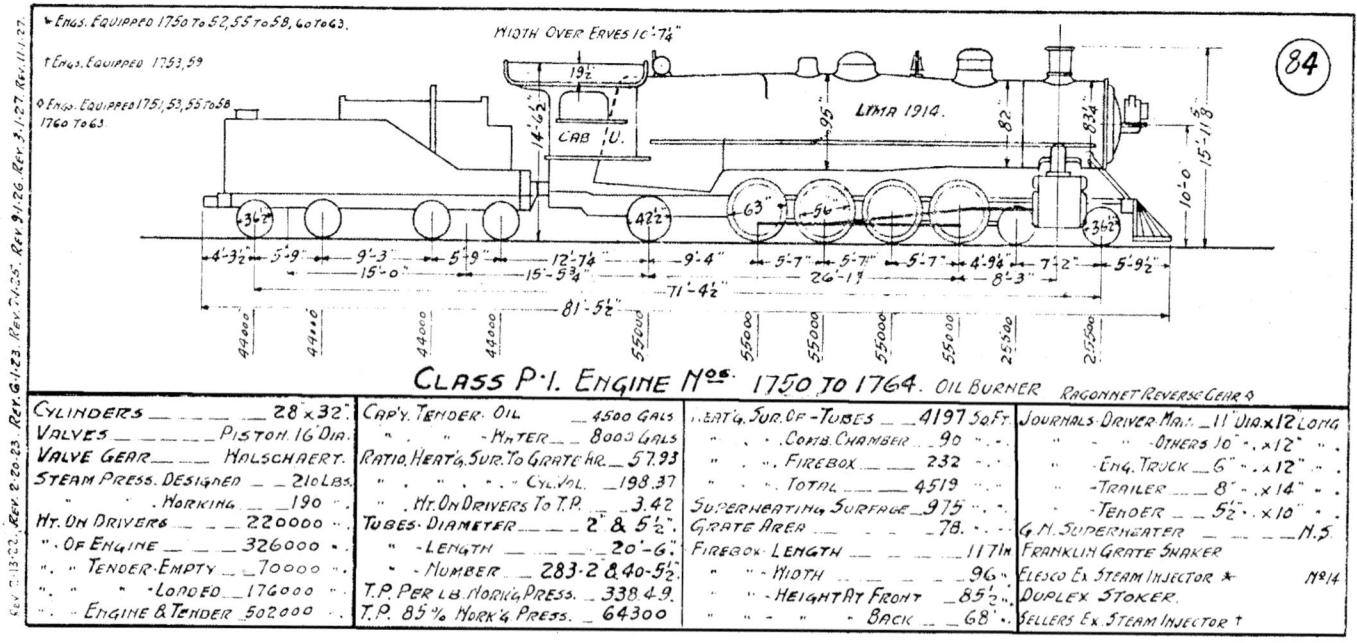

The 1754 is shown at Whitefish, MT, in 1916, while in passenger service. Note the wooden pilot and that it has inside steam admission to the cylinders. GNRHS collection.

Well into its freight hauling era, the 1757 displays its new outside steam pipes, steel pilot and modified tender.
The engine now has a stoker and has no need for the tender coal-lifting mechanism. Collection of James R. Vyverberg.

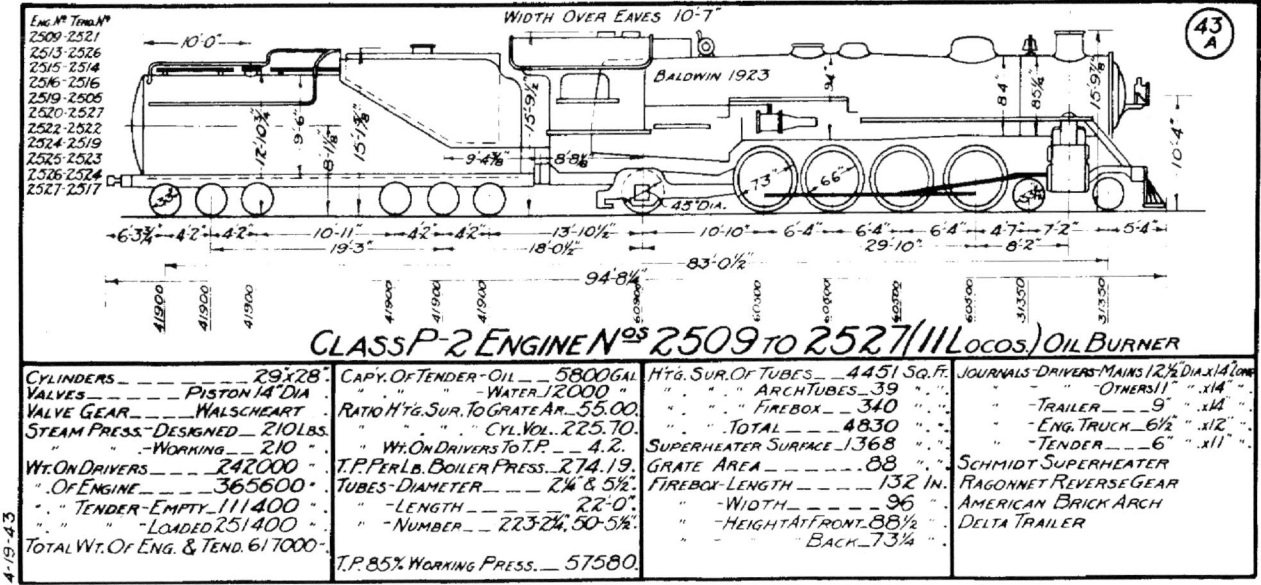

This diagram shows the P-2 tender with the P-2 locomotives.

Class P-2

The Great Northern made do without a high-powered passenger engine for three years after moving the P-1's to freight service. Then in 1923, a banner year for locomotive purchases on the Great Northern, two new classes were received from Baldwin. This order consisted of an entirely redesigned Mountain, and a class new to the road, the Santa Fe 2-10-2. The need for a high-powered passenger engine at this time was precipitated by the impending inauguration of a new *Oriental Limited*, a train to be equipped with all-steel cars and one that would run on a faster schedule. Twenty-eight locomotives of the type, designated class P-2, were received from Baldwin in 1923 from October through December. They were immediately followed by the Q-1 class 2-10-2's. The first eighteen P-2's were oil-burners and were assigned west of Cut Bank, MT. The last ten P-2s (from 2518 on) were coal-burners initially and were assigned to the eastern divisions.

This 4-8-2, designed in cooperation by the Great Northern and Baldwin[7], was partially based on the USRA heavy 4-8-2 of 1919. The Union Pacific MT-73 class of 1922 apparently influenced the design of the driving machinery, since the 73-inch driver diameter, the unusual "over-square" cylinder dimensions of 29 inches by 28 inches and the tractive effort are the same.[8] Perhaps the most visible difference with the USRA locomotive was the GN's use of the Walschaert valve gear, whereas the USRA used the Baker type. The P-2 had larger drivers than the USRA version, which resulted in less tractive effort. While the new design had a higher designed boiler pressure, the GN did not take advantage of it until about 1940, having run the engines at 200 psi until then. When the pressure was raised to the design level of 210 psi, the resulting tractive effort came within 1,000 pounds of the USRA design. Otherwise, the P-2 had a larger superheater, greater evaporation surface and a larger grate area with a resulting higher boiler horsepower. It also was heavier than either the USRA design or the UP design. In an effort to keep the weight down, the usual GN Belpaire firebox was abandoned in favor of the more conventional radial stay type used on the USRA design. This feature helped make

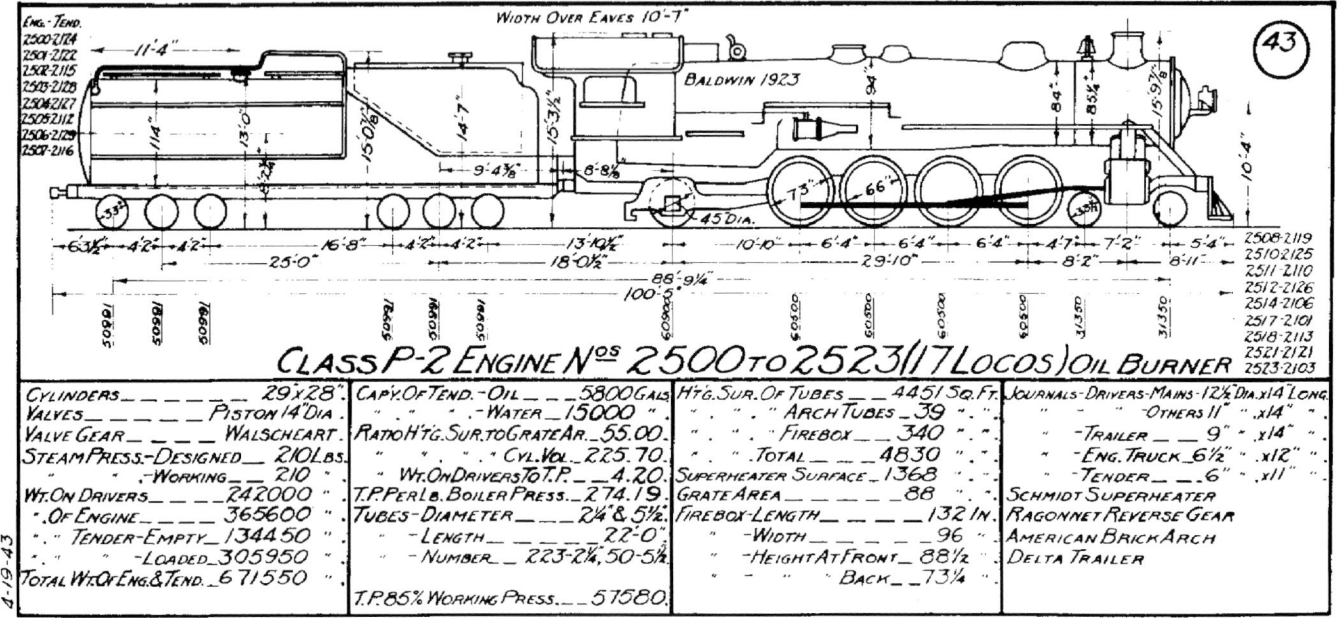

This diagram shows the higher capacity Q-1 tender with the P-2 locomotives.

No. 2505 is eastbound at Summit, Marias Pass, MT, in 1924. This view and that of the 2527 builders photo give a good impression of the old-style heavy main rod with its large bearing retainer. It also is a reminder of the single crew days. Shown here are engineer Bert Weller, on the ground, and fireman Jimmy Joy, in the cab. Courtesy of Francis June.

the P-2 the best-proportioned locomotive on the railroad.

Some of the class came with Nicholson syphons in the firebox. Records show that the coal–burners had the syphons and the oil-burners had arch tubes. The road was beginning a study to determine if the syphon device was something that would improve steam production, since they also equipped two class O-5 engines with them at this time.[9] On the P-2, the syphons provided 126 square feet of evaporation surface, while the arch tubes provided 39 square feet. The road experimented extensively with the use of water-tube devices in the firebox of the P-2's. Starting with the division between arch tubes and syphons in the initial delivery, beginning in 1925 they began to replace syphons so that by 1938, there were engines that had only arch tubes, others had only syphons, combinations of two syphons and one arch tube, or neither arch tubes nor syphons. By 1943 they all had arch tubes.[10]

The P-2's had a combustion chamber from the beginning. It can be seen on the erecting drawing and was approximately 47 inches long.[11] For some reason, it was not shown separately on the locomotive class

diagrams until 1948, where we learn it had a heating surface area of 95 square feet. However, there still is a minor mystery surrounding the situation, since the sum of the firebox and combustion chamber surface area was now 20 square feet larger than the combined figure that had been quoted since 1923.

The locomotives also came with the improved Schmidt superheater, which was in general use by then. They had a superheating surface area of 1,368 square feet, largest up to that time for the Great Northern. The type of superheater is not noted on the diagrams, but since the Q-1's came with the Type A, it is likely that is the type used on the P-2.

Tenders used on these engines originally were the second style of the Vanderbilt type used on the road, the Style 104. Soon, the P-2's began receiving the larger Santa Fe tenders, Style 105, with the P-2 type going to smaller power: Pacifics and Mikados. After 1943, seventeen locos had Q-1 tenders and eleven had P-2 tenders. This grew to nineteen Q-1 tenders by 1949. Eventually two P-2's received S-2 tenders, Style

P-2 2510 is westbound, downgrade on the upper Martin Creek Trestle, in the Cascades, in 1925. It does not have a booster, but does have the retractable smoke deflector. James A. Turner photograph from the Warren Wing collection.

111. The first, No. 2519, received one made surplus after the boiler explosion of No. 2581. Much later, the 2510 also received one, which may have been the same one, removed from the 2519. See also Chapter 34, Tender Assignments.

When new, the engines were single-crewed (each crew had their own engine), and made about 4800 miles per month under those conditions.[12] During the life span of these engines they moved from old to modern work practices, increasing utilization significantly.

Initial P-2 assignments covered the entire main line from St. Paul to Seattle, with heavy use on the west slope of the Cascades. They were the largest steam passenger power GN used into Seattle's King St. Station, because the later S classes had clearance problems there. The engines remained in use system-wide until bumped from passenger service by the diesels. The first redistribution occurred in 1929, when six were moved from the Cascades and sent east, as described later in this chapter. In 1936 Willmar Division had ten, the 2513, 2514, 2515, 2516, 2517, 2519, 2523, 2524, 2525 and 2526. The Dakota division had the 2527, Minot had 2505, 2509, 2518, 2520, 2521, 2522, Kalispell had 2506, 2507, 2408, 2510, 2511, 2512, and Spokane had 2500, 2501, 2502, 2503, and 2504. In 1953 the 2521 was the last steam engine out of Seattle.[13]

Boosters were installed on the engines working between Seattle and Wenatchee, the new eastern terminus of engines working over the Cascades, during 1924, 1925 and 1926. These engines were hauled through the first Cascade Tunnel by electric locomotives, but during 1924 and 1925 they were also equipped with air-operated retractable smoke deflectors (hoods) over the stack for the protection of the roofs of the other tunnels and the snowsheds.

Silk had been carried in special trains on the Great Northern since 1909, using the smaller engines then available. In August 1924, in response to a Northern Pacific challenge, the GN began to speed up the runs. By this time the P-2's were there to carry some of the load. By September 1925, the GN was ready to try another innovation. A large silk shipment was due on September 25, one that would require a longer than usual train of 18 cars. It was decided to assign the 2517 to the train, and to have it run through, without change, from Seattle to St. Paul. This would save much time. Then, if possible, the engine was to turn at St. Paul and return on the next No. 27, the *Fast Mail*. The 2517 did just that, running from Seattle to St. Paul in 52 hours and 35 minutes, and then on the morning of September 28 departed for Seattle on GN's fastest scheduled train, No. 27. The *Fast Mail's* schedule required just 47 hours and 30 minutes. The 2517's silk run was not the fastest. That was set back in August 1924, with a time of 38 hours and 50 minutes.[14] While the publicity of 2517's achievement was used to promote the speed capability of the Great Northern for hauling silk, the more important fact was that the 2517 had been released from its assigned crew and division for the marathon round trip and proved to be capable of the better utilization possible in pool service. The Great Northern named the 2517 the "Marathon" in honor of this achievement, and had the name attached to the tender for many years.

The P-2 was a very powerful locomotive for the time, and there was practically no comparison to the earlier smaller Pacifics and Ten-wheelers then in use on the GN. In fact, when built it ranked among the heaviest and most powerful passenger locomotives in use anywhere. Its

The 2517 is shown here at Breckenridge, MN, while on the marathon silk train run. It returned to Seattle powering the Fast Mail. *Photograph from the Minnesota Historical Society.*

This builder's photo of the last P-2 shows it to be equipped with a Standard stoker. Collection of H. L. Broadbelt.

The 2505 was one of two P-2's given boosters for the Seattle-Portland service in December 1947. It and the 2506 were assigned to passenger trains 401 and 402 at the time. Here it is at Portland in August 1949, about a year and a half later. This engine ran in passenger service on the Minot Division during World War II without a booster. Collection of Harold K. Vollrath.

The first Great Northern steam engine to receive an air horn was the 2517. This first installation was a single chime Leslie Tyfon. It was installed on October 26, 1936, and this photo was taken on June 19, 1938. By then the GN had switched to a dual-chime Leslie Tyfon for the other six engines that were equipped. The 2517 ultimately received a dual-chime unit as well. Robert Graham photograph from the collection of William Raia.

service on the west slope of the Cascades was nothing short of amazing to old railroad men. Early in 1924, Mr. C. W. Werst of the Baldwin Locomotive Company received permission to ride the cab of a P-2 in the Cascades. The following quote is excerpted from his report.[15]

We…left (Skykomish) at 11:40 A. M. on train Number 4, to make the trip up the west slope of the Cascade Mountains. Train Number 4 was comprised of eight cars, consisting of 1 baggage, 2 mail and express cars, 2 day coaches, diner, tourist and standard sleepers. The grade from Skykomish to Tye is 2.2 percent, and the distance 21 miles, the train making two stops, at Alpine and at Scenic, (both of these stops are on the 2.2 percent grade). Engine 2517, Engineer Grant. We rode the engine up the hill. I have ridden many engines on many grades before, but have never experienced the remarkable performance…this locomotive developed on this run. The rail that morning was particularly bad, there being a sort of mist all morning and a greasy substance (that comes from the fir trees) had settled on the rail, causing a slippery condition. In sizing up the situation before leaving Skykomish, Mr. Clark [this was the GN man accompanying Mr. Werst] stated to me that he had some doubt that the engine would be able to take the eight cars over the hill, on account of the miserable condition of the weather and the rail. However, we had gone but a short distance, when Mr. Clark realized we were to have a successful run. We went to the first stop, Alpine, a distance of eleven miles, exactly on the dot, and moved out of the station without any difficulty whatever, and stopped at Scenic, exactly on the dot, a distance of seven miles. Passing Scenic there is an exceedingly bad section of railroad, consisting of reverse curves and bridges. The utmost care must be taken by the engineer in manipulating the reverse lever to make the grade. This morning the rail being in such bad condition, the engine slipped on her drivers several times, but with the expert handling of the engine by Engineer Grant, the engine…proceeded with very little loss of speed…. We arrived at the summit about three minutes ahead of time, making a remarkably good run.

The route of the westbound *Oriental Limited* differed from that of the eastbound on the lines east of Minot. Consequently, P-2's handled only the eastbound train on the Willmar Division, from Breckenridge to St. Paul. Westbound, the job was assigned to the H-5 class, running via St. Cloud. By 1928, road officials had decided they wanted both the new eastbound and westbound *Empire Builder* trains to run via St. Cloud. With the inauguration of the *Empire Builder* on June 11, 1929, P-2's powered the trains both ways over the St. Cloud route.

The completion of the new Cascade Tunnel, arrival of new electric locomotives and the accompanying change of electric locomotive terminals brought new operating practices in 1929. This permitted the release of six locomotives, the 2512 through the 2517, from mountain duty and allowed them to be moved east. Their boosters and smoke deflectors were removed and they were converted to burn coal. The 2510 also had its booster removed but it remained in the west as an oil-burner. Much later, in December 1947, two others, the 2505 and 2506, were given boosters for Seattle-Portland passenger service.[16]

Beginning in 1926, feedwater heaters and exhaust steam injectors replaced one of the live steam injectors. Most engines received the Elesco No. 14 exhaust steam injector, these being the 2500, 2501, 2503, 2504, 2505, 2507, 2508, 2510, 2511, 2513, 2517, 2518, 2519, 2520, 2522, 2524, 2526 and 2527. The first Worthington No. 4 BL type feedwater heater went to 2511 in 1925, but was replaced by the Elesco exhaust steam injector a year later. The remaining units with the Worthington feedwater heater were the 2502, 2506, 2509, 2512, 2514, 2515, 2516, 2523 and 2525. A Sellers exhaust steam injector went to No. 2521, ending the program in December 1927. This Sellers was replaced with an Elesco later, perhaps about 1947. A record of this change has not been found.

On October 26, 1936, an air horn was applied to 2517 as a test. This was said to be a Leslie Tyfon Pneumatic Whistle, and the work seems to have been done at Dale Street without an Authority for Expenditure (AFE). An early photo shows this first one to be a single-chime horn. In May 1937 an AFE was written to equip 4 engines with the devices.[17] In October 1937, the GN installed dual-chime Leslie Tyfons on three P-2's and one S-2. These were the 2515, 2516 and 2517, the work being done at Jackson Street and 2587 at Whitefish.[18] Three others, the

The 2525 was one of seven locomotives to receive the dual-chime Leslie Tyfon air horn. Installed on the smokebox near the stack, one chime pointed forward and the other aft. By June 1940, when this photograph was taken at St.Paul, MN, the 2525 already had its lightweight main rods, but still had a square cab. Harold Van Horn photograph from the collection of William Raia.

This view of 2501 on the Portland pool train at Auburn, WA, on May 2, 1937, gives a very good view of an old style main rod. In the mid-1930's the P-2's along with several other classes received new lightweight main rods. The difference is clearly visible on the P-2. Charles E. Winters collection.

Much later in its life, the 2501 has the lightweight main rod and numerous other changes that were made along the way. It is shown in Minneapolis, MN, in freight service on October 21, 1948. Robert Graham photograph from the collection of William Raia.

This 1930's view of 2513 shows it backing in to the St. Paul Union Depot for the Empire Builder on August 14, 1938. The old heavy main rod is clearly shown. The engine still has its square cab as well. Robert Graham photograph from the collection of William Raia.

2523, 2525 and S-2 2586 ultimately received them. There is a photo of 2517 dated June 19, 1938 with the single chime horn. By 1939 a photo of 2517 shows the same dual chime Leslie seen on the other engines. It is likely the first air horn installation on the 2517 was not replaced until some time after the date of the later AFE. The reason for air horns was to improve visibility. Whistle steam frequently condensed on the cab window glass and obscured the crew's vision in the winter. While reports indicated the change was successful, the horns had been removed without comment by 1947.

As part of the on-going modernization program, there was a gradual reduction of number of 2¼ inch flues during the life span of these engines, from 232 to 217. This reduced the heating surface from 4,566 to 4,451 square feet, but gained better heat transfer around the superheaters. Lightweight main rods were put on the engines in the 1930's. The old main rod and piston weighed 976 pounds, and the lightweight piston and rod weighed 854 pounds, for a reduction of 122 pounds. Similarly, the old valve piston weighed 259 pounds,

while the lightweight version weighed 191 pounds, for a reduction of 68 pounds.[19] This permitted improved counterbalancing. Upgraded lubricating devices were installed from 1940 through 1942. Disc main drivers were put on the 2510 in December 1938. They were of the Baldwin type. Still on in 1941, they were removed by 1947, but the fact is not documented in records, only photos. The original speed limit for these engines was 50 mph.[20] The limit was eventually increased, likely after the lightweight rods were installed. Several unofficial references to a top speed of 90 mph have been made.[21]

All coal-burners were converted to oil during 1939 and 1941. These engines were a significant asset during World War II, doing a great job with the many extra sections of the *Empire Builder* and with troop trains. The distribution of the engines in 1942 was nearly identical to that of 1936, only the 2527 had been moved, from the Dakota Division to the Minot Division.

Improvements and changes continued during the war years and beyond. The change to a slant-front cab, first seen in 1938 on the

This much later view of the 2513 at the St. Paul Jackson Street roundhouse on June 14, 1947, shows the lightweight main rod and a slant-front cab. Air pumps on the pilot deck were to come later. John Westphal collection courtesy of John Luecke.

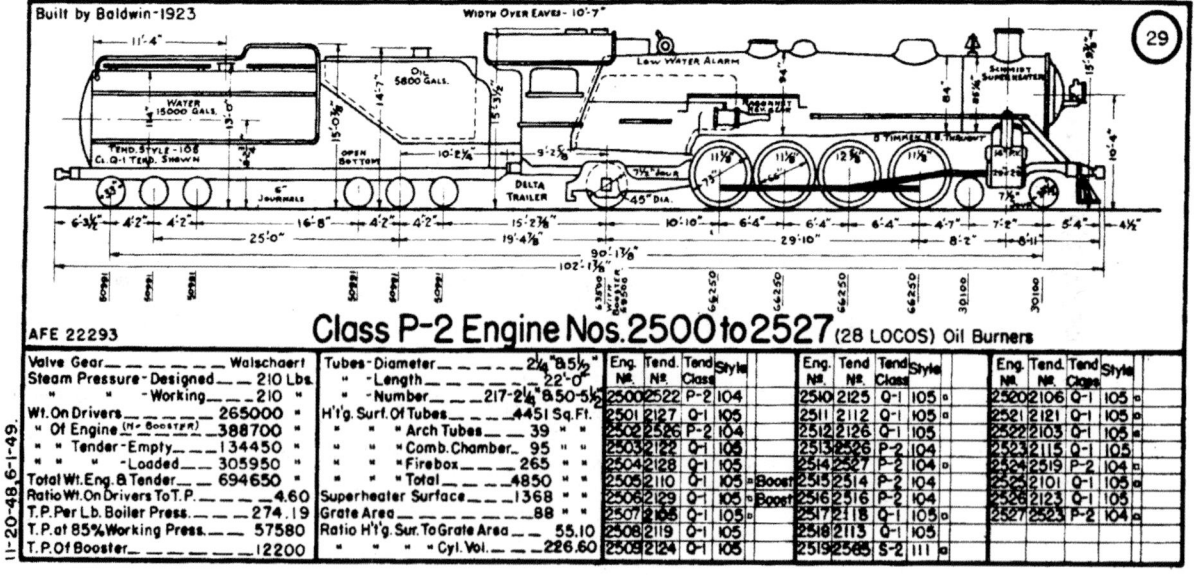

The P-2 in its final configuration is illustrated by this 1949 diagram.

The GN selected the 2510 to try out disk main drivers. This view at Hillyard, WA, shows the appearance of the main driver with extra counterweights and the heavy main rods before they were replaced with the disk wheel. Warren R. McGee.

The GN tried the Baldwin type of disk driver for the 2510. This view shows the driver and the lightweight main rod. The engine is on No. 1 at Whitefish, MT, on April 14, 1940. Warren R. McGee.

Between 1941 and 1947 the disk main driver was replaced with a conventional wheel. No record of the change was found. Here the 2510 is entering St. Paul, MN, on July 3, 1948. No record of any other installation was found. Sid Davies photograph from the collection of William Raia.

2506 and 2510, saw more installations during 1943 and continued through 1950. The slant cab was installed farther back on the engine than the original cab. Low water alarms, Nalco continuous blowdown systems, and electric train indicators were installed in 1943 and 1944. All engines received the low water alarms. The majority received the Nathan and the 2513, 2514, 2516, 2523, 2524 and 2525 received the Barco type.

Another burst of new work began in 1946 and continued through 1950. During this period all engines received auxiliary air reservoirs for the power reverse, and two No. 5 New York air pumps on the pilot deck, which replaced the single 8½ inch pump on the fireman's side. The new Elesco device, the steam dryer, was to be installed on all engines but due to delays two, the 2515 and 2525 never received one. This is also when the 2505 and 2506 received their boosters.

The 2521, shown here at Portland, OR, in April 1950 was in its final configuration. It remained in Seattle-Portland service until March 1953, when on the 24th, it became the last steam locomotive to operate out of Seattle and the Cascade Division. It then served intermittently on the Willmar Division until 1956. R. Gray photograph from the collection of William Raia.

The 2525 is shown in freight service, taking water at Hillsboro, ND. This is a good close-up of the dual New York No. 5 air pumps on the pilot deck. This feature helped speed up train line charging with long freight trains. Note the sacks of Nalco boiler water treatment between the pumps. The engine also has a steam heat connection at the pilot. It is not easily visible, but there is a dual beam Pyle headlight in the GN casing. The train is No. 438 and the date is October 24, 1955. Bruce Black photograph from collection of Norman F. Priebe.

The 2502 was one of many P-2's that were put into freight service after October 1945. Here it is at Minneapolis in 1948, before it received the two deck-mounted air pumps. From the Glen Monhart collection, courtesy of Ed Kanak.

This pair of photographs gives an excellent representation of the P-2 class in their final configuration and in freight service. The freshly painted (in black) 2511 is at Breckenridge, MN, about to start an eastbound extra for Willmar on November 14, 1955. Note the Q-1 tender, Nathan low water alarm, Elesco exhaust steam injector, lightweight main rod and twin air pumps on the pilot deck. Bruce Black photograph from the collection of Norman F. Priebe.

The next day, November 15, 1955, the 2511 had returned from Willmar and the fireman's side is visible. Here we see the blowdown muffler, the Nalco continuous blow down system, the steam lines to the deck mounted air pumps and the automatic lubricators. The engine also has the replacement stack and flat smokebox front. Not visible are the roller bearings and the Elesco steam dryer. Bruce Black photograph from the collection of Norman F. Priebe.

The GN began to install Timken roller bearings on the P-2's at this time. However the job was never finished. The new bearings were applied to the 2505, 2506, 2507, 2510, 2511, 2514, 2517, 2519, 2520, 2521, 2522, 2524, 2525 and 2527.[22]

The P-2's were reweighed in 1948, as part of the comprehensive locomotive reweigh program. See Chapter 4. The reweigh put the P-2 at 265,000 pounds on drivers, up from 242,000 pounds, placing it among the heaviest Mountain types built. This was good news for the engine crews, and explained the excellent performance of the class in freight service.

As the standard cast Baldwin smokebox fronts eventually cracked, they were replaced with fronts cut from slab steel plates. Also, as the Baldwin-supplied smokestacks began to wear, they were replaced with the GN standard design, also seen on many other GN engines.[23] Most of these changes occurred after 1945.

By October 25, 1945, there was no longer a need for all of the P-2's in passenger service. On that date, Mr. I. G. Pool, Superintendent of Motive Power at the time, issued a proposal for reassignment of many of the GN's largest roller-bearing equipped locomotives to fast freight service between Minneapolis and Minot, and Minneapolis and Grand Forks.[24] The area covered parts of the Willmar, Minot and Dakota divisions. Included in the plan were ten P-2's to serve between Minneapolis and Grand Forks. Much of the plan went into effect as stated, with more P-2's entering freight service in 1951, after the *Oriental Limited* and *Fast Mail* were dieselized. Thus in 1949 we find the 2500, 2501, 2502, 2503, 2513, 2515, 2516, 2518, 2523 and 2526 assigned to the Willmar Division, principally for freight service. By 1954 the 2507, 2511, 2520, 2522, 2524 and 2527, assigned to the Minot Division, were also in freight service. In addition, the 2508, 2510, 2512, 2514, 2519 and 2525 had come from Lines West and were assigned to the Dakota Division. Later the 2517 and 2521 were added to the Willmar engines and the 2505, 2506 and 2515 were added to the Minot engines, followed by some later minor shuffling between divisions. By now there were more than needed for freight service and

The 2514 is ready to depart for Fargo on October 9, 1956, with an eastbound extra from Grand Forks, ND. It differs from the 2511 in the type and location of appliances. This view shows a Barco low water alarm and automatic lubricators placed on the engineer's side. This engine also had a toolbox on the pilot deck, a Worthington BL-2 feedwater heater and the smaller class P-2 tender. See the photo in chapter 3. Bruce Black photograph from the collection of Norman F. Priebe.

It has been claimed the 2519 received the racy trim on the wheel tires and running board edge for a railroad fair at Grand Forks, ND. By the time of the photo, 1952, it was carrying an S-2 class tender and was the dedicated Grand Forks passenger protection engine. W. Krawiec photograph from the collection of William Raia.

On the morning of July 21, 1947, the 2524 is shown backing into St. Paul Union Depot in this view to pick up a westbound passenger train, which could be either No. 3 or No. 27. M. Nafus photograph from the collection of William Raia.

The 2524 is shown arriving at St. Paul, MN, with the Fast Mail, on June 1, 1947. This engine had an Elesco exhaust steam injector, and is now an oil-burner. Charles T. Felstead photograph from the collection of William Raia.

scrapping began. 2501, 2503, 2504, 2518 and 2526, engines without roller bearings, were the first to be found on the scrap line. There were so many engines available that they were rotated to use all of those with time left on flues. When time on flues ran out, the engine was moved to the scrap line.

The P-2's were rated for 5,000 tons on the 0.3% eastward ruling grade between Breckenridge and Willmar. This was pretty good considering the O-8's were rated at 6,500 tons. But the dispatchers were aware that if they started a P-2 east from Breckenridge with this load, they could not stop it until it reached Willmar, because it could not restart such a load on the grade. On the St. Cloud line, even with its 0.6% grades, the P-2's were seen clipping along at 50 mph, but with lighter loads.

It is likely the P-2's made their last runs in 1956. Available records for 1957 show no use of any steam except C-1's through April, and the known road service runs made later in 1957 involved only Mikados.

Two P-2's were saved and put on display. The 2507 went to the SP&S. In 1962 it was seen at Vancouver WA, painted in a SP&S scheme. It was then put on display at Maryhill, WA, and dedicated September 3, 1966. Later the engine was removed to Pasco in an attempt to restore this engine and run it, but this effort failed. The engine did get an exterior rehabilitation, was repainted back into its GN colors, and was again put on display at Maryhill. The 2523 was given an exterior rehabilitation and placed on display at Willmar, MN on October 7, 1965.

A classic view of a classic engine midway through its development is this of the 2523 at Minneapolis, MN. Taken on June 11, 1938, it displays such modern features as lightweight main rods, air horns and a Worthington feedwater heater, yet still has at least one spoked wheel in the engine truck and a square-front cab. Robert Graham photograph from the collection of William Raia.

Notes:

1. C.O. Jenks to G. H. Emerson, several, June 6, 1913, through June 29, 1913. MHS, GN papers, V. P. Operating, File 40-1.
2. Jack W. Farrell, *The Mountains*, Pacific Fast Mail, Edmunds, WA 1976.
3. Valuation Department Correspondence File No. 81, *Map showing Locomotives Operating on Various Branch and Main Lines – Year 1915*. Author's collection.
4. Great Northern Railway Unit Record of Property Changes (URPC), Account 51, page 1848, groups 7 and 8.
5. Paul T. Warner, *The Great Northern Railway and its Locomotives*, Baldwin Locomotives, January 1925.
6. URPC, *op. cit.*
7. Warner, *op. cit.*
8. Farrell, *op. cit.* See also William Kratville and Harold E. Ranks, *Motive Power of the Union Pacific*, Barnhart Press, Omaha, NE, 1959.
9. Great Northern Railway Locomotive Diagrams, 1926.
10. The URPC shows removal of three syphons from 2525 in 1925 and one from 2523 in 1926, replaced with a like number of arch tubes. Then the center syphon was removed from 2518 through 2527 from late 1926 into 1927. The problem with syphons was they were "sandblasted" by cinders and eroded until they leaked. Repairs were difficult due to their location.
11. Fr. Dale Peterka, "Classes P-1 and P-2," GNRHS Reference Sheet 174, March 1991. Much of this reference sheet has been incorporated into this chapter.
12. Warner, *op. cit.*
13. Norman F. Priebe, "Steam's Last Days on the Great Northern,"

GNRHS Reference Sheet 124, September 1987.
14. Robert H. Shober, "Silk Trains and Other Commerce on Hill's Road," GNRHS Reference Sheet 264, September 1998.
15. C. W. Werst, Baldwin Locomotive Co., to George H. Emerson, Baltimore and Ohio Railroad, March 15, 1924. Mr. Emerson was Chief of Motive Power on the B&O, and had been Superintendent of Motive Power and later General Manager on the Great Northern. Mr. Emerson left the GN in 1917. Mr. Werst related this experience to Mr. Emerson in an effort to sell him a Mountain type locomotive. GN Collection, MHS
16. URPC, *op. cit.*
17. Great Northern Railway Authority for Expenditure (AFE) 53155, May 4, 1937.
18. *Ibid.*, URPC, *op. cit.*
19. Alex Colville, Shop Notebook, Hillyard.
20. Warner, *op. cit.* Great Northern Railway AFE 54877 (May 10, 1932) authorized the installation of the disk drivers.
21. The most authoritative as well as the most descriptive account is found in David Plowden, *A Time of Trains*, W. W. Norton, New York, 1987. See pages 14 through 25.
22. URPC, op. cit.
23. Classes O-1, O-4, O-6, O-7, O-8, N-3, Q-1 and Q-2.
24. I. G. Pool, October 25, 1945, in the file of Great Northern Railway AFE 73623.

The 2103 is in its first winter at work on Marias Pass. It was photographed at Summit in early 1924 by J. R. Buhmiller. National Park Service collection.

Chapter 24

Class Q 2-10-2 Santa Fe

Class Q-1

The new Q-1 locomotives began to arrive immediately after the delivery of the P-2 class locomotives. The first arrived in late December of 1923, and the rest were delivered through February, 1924. There were 30 in the class, numbered from 2100 through 2129. The P-2 and Q-1 locomotives were designed as a pair, intended to bring the Great Northern into the booming economy of the 1920's. The P-2 was to handle the longer, heavier and faster passenger trains becoming common at the time, and the Q-1 was to do the same for freight traffic. With the arrival of the Q-1, the GN replaced older class N-1 Mallet compounds on the 1.8% mountain grades of Marias Pass with a powerful, rigid-frame locomotive.

The Santa Fe type had been around for 20 years, so there was a good basis for the design. In fact, the GN borrowed two Atchison, Topeka and Santa Fe 2-10-2's for testing in 1921. These were the older 915, built in 1903, and the large 3849, a brand new engine in 1921. They were compared to O-4 No. 3210 on 0.8% and 1.0% grades. It was found the O-4 was as good as the smaller 2-10-2, but the 3849 showed a significant increase in tonnage hauled.[1] This result was the start of the Santa Fe type on the GN. The choice of a 2-10-2 wheel arrangement was a logical extension of the O-4 Mikado, and many design features show they were sized up from the O-4. The grate area of 88 square feet, shared with the P-2, was the largest on the Great Northern up to that

time and likely was determined by a look at the USRA heavy 2-10-2. Otherwise, the Q-1 boiler outsized that of the P-2 and everything else on the railroad. It truly was a formidable giant of a locomotive.

It is clear the GN and Baldwin intended the design to be the new record holder for "largest" of the time, as it bested the USRA heavy, the Pennsy N1-s and the previously tested Santa Fe 3800 class. It was heavier than any of its contemporaries, had a larger boiler and a higher tractive effort. As delivered, the Q-1 possessed a tractive effort of 87,129 pounds and the largest cylinder dimensions of any GN engine except those of the low-pressure compound mallets, 31 inches by 32 inches. The GN also operated them at the designed boiler pressure of 210 psi, not often done on the GN at that time.

Other details of the large boiler may be obtained from the diagram. Note that like the P-2, the combustion chamber is missing from the firebox dimensions. Also like the P-2, when the combustion chamber does show up on the diagrams, the total of 399 square feet of combined surface area is larger by 29 square feet than the old figure. All of them were delivered as oil-burners, a good indication that the GN intended to run them exclusively on the western mountain grades. In 1927, the engines were converted to burn coal, indicating a change in operating location.[2]

After 1929, the assignment of these engines was split between the Minot, Butte and Spokane Divisions, having been bumped from their original assignment on Marias Pass of the Kalispell Division by the R-1's and R-2's. In 1936, the distribution was as follows: Minot, 2100, 2102, 2103, 2105, 2108, 2109, 2117, 2118, 2120, 2121, 2122, 2124, 2125, 2127 and 2128. Butte, 2101, 2104, 2106, 2107, 2110, 2111, 2113, 2114, 2116 and 2123. Spokane, 2112, 2115, 2119, 2126 and 2129.

By 1938, the majority still burned coal, with the 2102, 2103, 2108, 2116, 2117, 2119, 2123, 2127 and 2128 back as oil-burners. Changes continued so that by 1949 only three locomotives, 2109, 2113 and 2114, were coal-burners.

The high piston thrust necessary to obtain the remarkable tractive effort of these engines had a detrimental side effect that yielded frame difficulties and speed restrictions. This was due to the inability to fully counterbalance so much force in a 63-inch diameter wheel and was a common problem with ten-coupled engines.[3] A study was made toward revising the counterbalancing. A copy of the report has not come to light, but evidence of counterbalance changes can be seen on photographs of some of the engines. It is not known if these changes

were a result of the study or other factors. In the late 1940's, the piston thrust was decreased to reduce the dynamic counterbalancing needed. This was done by reducing the cylinder diameter from 31 inches to 29 inches. This in turn reduced the tractive effort to 76,251 pounds, equal to that of the Q-2, but only slightly more than the 75,900 pounds of the much faster O-8 Mikado. This was not a good sign for the future of the Q-1. All but two of the engines, 2113 and 2118, received this modification.

Some of the engines, including at least 2127 through 2129, were equipped with boosters by the builder. These were applied to engines designated as helpers on the 1.8% eastward grade of Marias Pass. At least four, and perhaps more, booster-equipped engines were in operation by the end of 1924.[4] Nearly all of the class had a booster applied at one time or another from 1925 through 1946, with likely exceptions being 2112 through 2116.

Drifting valves were applied during the Marias Pass years, 1924 and 1925. It did not take long before feedwater heaters were introduced. During 1925 and 1926, Worthington No. 4 BL type feedwater heaters

Builders photographs of the first Q-1 display its large size. Collection of H. L. Broadbelt.

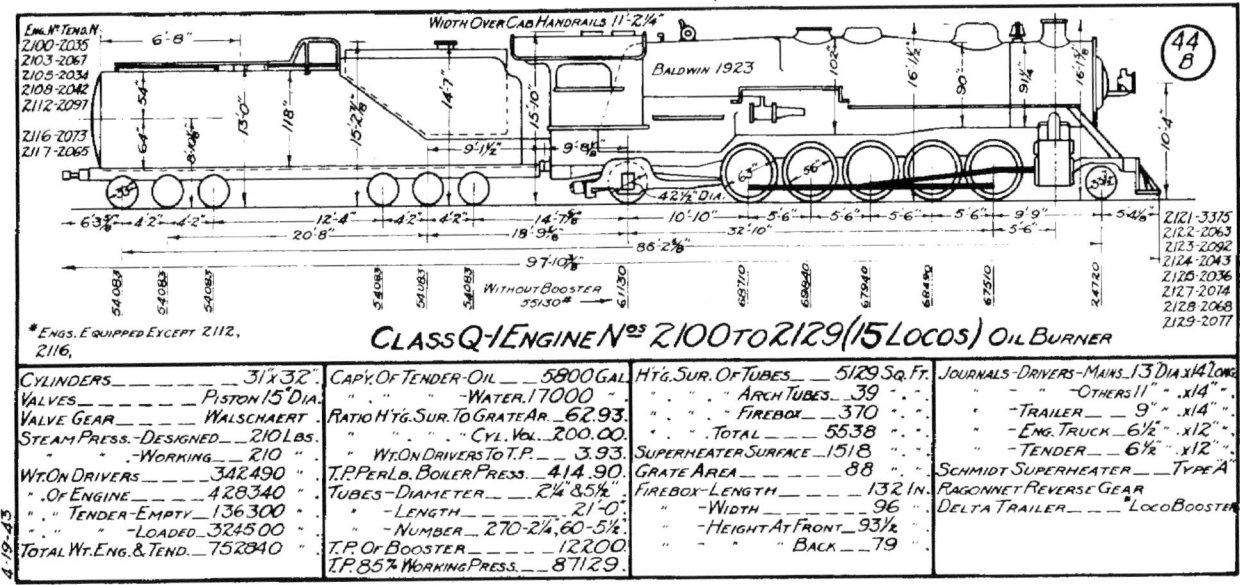

CLASS Q-1 ENGINE Nos 2100 to 2129 (15 LOCOS) OIL BURNER

Baldwin 1923

Width Over Cab Handrails 11'-2¼"

Eng. Nos Tend. N.
2100-2035
2103-2067
2105-2034
2108-2042
2112-2097
2116-2073
2117-2065

2121-3375
2122-2063
2123-2092
2124-2043
2126-2036
2127-2074
2128-2068
2129-2077

*Engs. Equipped Except 2112, 2116,

CYLINDERS _____ 31"x 32"	CAP'Y. OF TENDER-OIL __ 5800 GAL	H'T'G. SUR. OF TUBES __ 5129 SQ. FT.
VALVES _____ PISTON 15" DIA.	" " " -WATER. 17000 "	" " " ARCH TUBES. 39 " "
VALVE GEAR ____ WALSCHAERT	RATIO H'T'G. SUR. TO GRATE AR. 62.93	" " " FIREBOX __ 370 " "
STEAM PRESS.-DESIGNED __ 210 LBS.	" " " CYL. VOL. 200.00	" " " . TOTAL ___ 5538 " "
" " -WORKING __ 210 "	" WT. ON DRIVERS TO T.P. __ 3.93	SUPERHEATER SURFACE 1518 " "
WT. ON DRIVERS _____ 342490 "	T.P. PER LB. BOILER PRESS. 414.90 "	GRATE AREA ____ 88 "
" . OF ENGINE ___ 428340 "	TUBES-DIAMETER __ 2¼ & 5½"	FIREBOX-LENGTH ____ 132 IN.
" . " TENDER-EMPTY 136300 "	" -LENGTH ___ 21'-0"	" -WIDTH __ 96 "
" . " -LOADED 324500 "	" -NUMBER _ 270-2¼, 60-5½"	" -HEIGHT AT FRONT 93½ "
TOTAL WT. ENG. & TEND. 752840 "	T.P. OF BOOSTER ____ 12200 "	" " BACK __ 79 "
	T.P. 85% WORKING PRESS. __ 87129 "	

JOURNALS-DRIVERS-MAINS 13 DIA. x 14 LONG
" " " -OTHERS 11 " x 14"
" " -TRAILER __ 9 " x 14"
" " -ENG. TRUCK 6½" x 12"
" " -TENDER __ 6½ " x 12"
SCHMIDT SUPERHEATER __ TYPE A
RAGONNET REVERSE GEAR
DELTA TRAILER ____ LOCO BOOSTER

WITHOUT BOOSTER 55130# →

4-19-43

By 1943 the GN had split the Q-1 class into five sub-categories. This diagram represents the largest group. Note all of this group have larger tenders than the original Q-1 class tender. All locomotives on this diagram have boosters except 2112 and 2116. These are all oil burners. There were 5 coal burners on two different sheets in 1943.

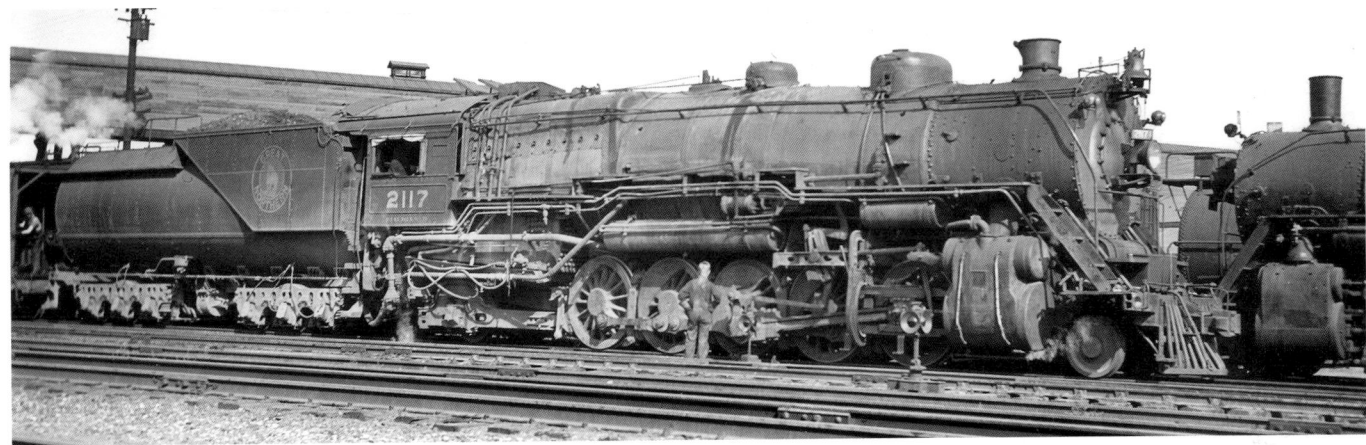

This view of the 2117 is interesting in two respects. The first is that the 2117 is a coal burner, the other is that it is shown having its tires turned by the Lidgerwood method. The Lidgerwood unloader is shown at the far left of the photograph. Its cable is attached to the tender coupler. The locomotive is run ahead, away from the unloader and a cutting tool is attached to the frame to work the tire to be turned. The Lidgerwood machine then slowly draws the locomotive toward itself, and the tire is turned as the wheel rotates. The process is repeated as necessary. The method avoids having to remove the drive wheels and set them up in a lathe. In the photograph, the machinist is keeping a careful eye on the wheel being turned. It appears he may have hung his caliper over the valve gear hanger. The photograph was taken at Minot, ND, in July 1938. George Harris photograph from the collection of Norman F. Priebe.

This view taken at Superior, WI, in August 1949 is an example of an externally visible counterbalancing change to the Q-1 class. Holes have been bored into the counterbalance weights of all except the main drivers. This example shows the 2106, although the procedure was applied to the majority of engines. It is likely this was done to reduce the overbalance that resulted from the reduction of piston thrust when the piston diameter was reduced. Collection of Ben Cutler.

The 2127 came from the builder with a booster, and retained it for much of its life. Collection of H. L. Broadbelt.

Most of the Q-1's retained their boosters until the end. Here is the 2122 at Portland on May 3, 1947. John Westphal collection of John Luecke.

According to the records, only five Q-1's had the Elesco exhaust steam injector applied. An example is the 2114, shown here near end of life, in June 1952 at Allouez, WI. At the time, the engine had recently been removed from service on the Allouez hump yard. Collection of Harold K. Vollrath.

The 2119 was one of six of the Q-1 class to receive the Worthington 5S2 SA type feedwater heater. This view of 2119 at Portland shows the engineer's side. The Q-1's had boosters while in the Portland service. The photograph was likely taken in 1947. Cordell Newby collection.

This fireman's side view of 2119 shows the opposite side of the Worthington 5S2 SA type feedwater heater. For another view of this device on the fireman's side, see 2105 in Chapter 3. The engine was photographed at Portland, OR, in August 1950. Collection of Don Gruber.

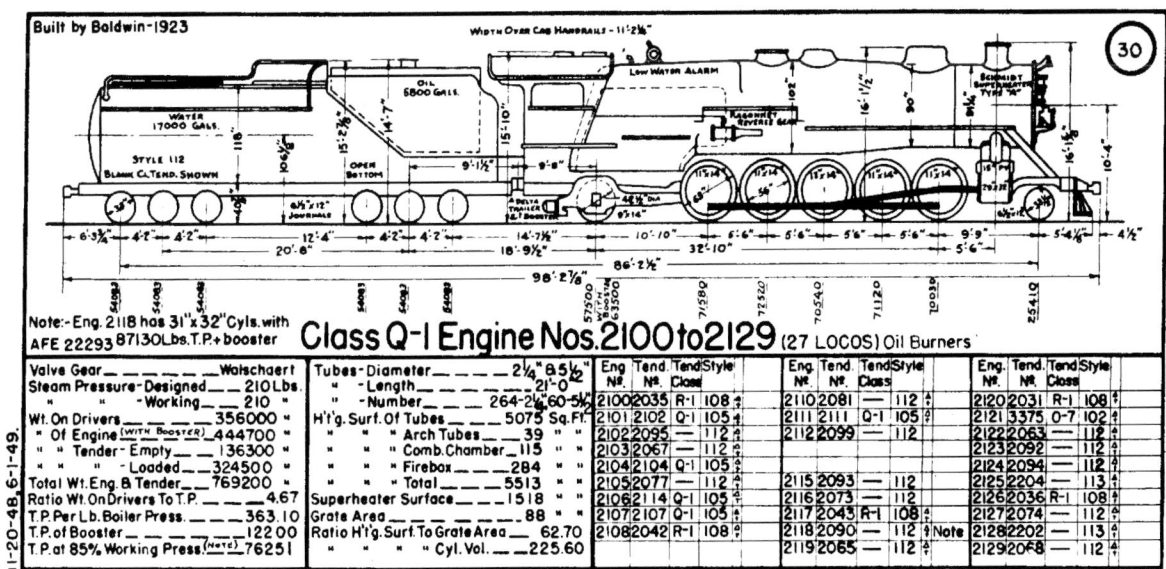

Class Q-1 Engine Nos. 2100 to 2129 (27 LOCOS) Oil Burners

Valve Gear	Walschaert	Tubes - Diameter	2¼ & 5½"
Steam Pressure-Designed	210 Lbs.	" - Length	21'-0"
" " -Working	210 "	" - Number	264-2¼,60-5½
Wt. On Drivers	356000 "	H't'g. Surf. Of Tubes	5075 Sq. Ft.
" Of Engine (WITH BOOSTER)	444700 "	" Arch Tubes	39 "
" Tender - Empty	136300 "	" Comb. Chamber	115 "
" " -Loaded	324500 "	" Firebox	284 "
Total Wt. Eng. & Tender	769200 "	" Total	5513 "
Ratio Wt. On Drivers To T.P.	4.67	Superheater Surface	1518 "
T.P. Per Lb. Boiler Press.	363.10	Grate Area	88 "
T.P. of Booster	12200 "	Ratio H't'g. Surf. To Grate Area	62.70
T.P. at 85% Working Press (NOTE)	76251	" " " Cyl. Vol.	225.60

Eng. Nº.	Tend. Nº.	Tend Class	Style	Eng. Nº.	Tend. Nº.	Tend Class	Style	Eng. Nº.	Tend. Nº.	Tend Class	Style
2100	2035	R-1	108	2110	2081	—	112	2120	2031	R-1	108
2101	2102	Q-1	105	2111	2111	Q-1	105	2121	3375	O-7	102
2102	2095	—	112	2112	2099	—	112	2122	2063	—	112
2103	2067	—	112					2123	2092	—	112
2104	2104	Q-1	105					2124	2094	—	112
2105	2077	—	112	2115	2093	—	112	2125	2204	—	113
2106	2114	Q-1	105	2116	2073	—	112	2126	2036	R-1	108
2107	2107	Q-1	105	2117	2043	R-1	108	2127	2074	—	112
2108	2042	R-1	108	2118	2090	—	112	Note	2128	2202	—	113
2109	2065	—	112	2119	2065	—	112	2129	2068	—	112

Built by Baldwin-1923

Note:- Eng. 2118 has 31"x32" Cyls. with AFE 22293 87130 Lbs. T.P.+ booster

By 1949 all but three Q-1's were on this diagram, drawn for the oil burners. Note the key for which engines had boosters.
A few Q-1 tenders were still in the mix. This diagram shows the combustion chamber and final weights.

were applied to the majority of the class. Exceptions were 2108, 2110, 2111, 2114 and 2123, which received Elesco No. 14 exhaust steam injectors, and 2104 and 2119, which were given Sellers exhaust steam injectors. For unknown reasons the units on the 2119 and 2123 were replaced with the Kelly feedwater heater in 1928. The 2123 was again given an Elesco exhaust steam injector by 1938. In 1943, Worthington 5S2 SA feedwater heaters replaced the units on six engines; 2105, 2109, 2115, 2118, 2119 and 2125, apparently due to failure of their earlier units.[5]

World War II saw a number of improvements made. First was improved mechanical lubrication, applied in 1941 and 1942, with Detroit, King, Chicago and Edna types installed. Cylinder protection valves from Prime and Whelan were next from 1942 to 1947.

Nalco Continuous Blow-down devices were installed from 1943 to 1947. Steam heat and air-signal lines were put on three engines in 1943. It is believed these were in helper service and the addition

allowed them to serve as helpers on the heavy passenger trains of the war era. Finally, electric train indicators and low water alarms went on during 1944 and 1945. Both Barco and Nathan alarms were used.[6] The movement of air pumps to the smokebox front of some engines also happened during the wartime period. Of course these heavy engines were reweighed during the 1948 reweigh case. The result was 356,000 pounds on drivers for the oil-burners and 367,000 pounds on drivers for the coal-burners. The total engine weight was 444,700 pounds for the oil-burners and 457,800 pounds for the coal burners. This weight included boosters. As with other classes, many of the original cast smokebox fronts cracked and were replaced with a flat steel front.

The Q-1's arrived from the builder with Vanderbilt tenders (GN Style 105) of 15,000-gallon water and 5,000 gallon oil capacity. As coal-burners they carried 25 tons of coal. Over the years many of these tenders migrated to the P-2 class, replaced by blank class and R-1 class types mostly. Refer to Chapters 32 and 34 for more information.

The 2129 was still an impressive machine in 1939. At this point in time it retained its square cab, but has recently had its Q-1 tender replaced with the larger blank class Style 112. This engine came from the builder equipped with a booster. It is at Hillyard on September 3, 1939. Photograph by Robert F. Collins, from the Eric Archer

By May 7, 1947, the 2129 was working the Seattle-Portland run on the Cascade Division, and has had some changes made. It now has a slant-front cab and a Nathan low water alarm. In two more years it will have had its air pumps moved to the smokebox front and have undergone counterbalance changes to reach its final configuration. The engine is at Portland, OR. From the John Westphal collection, courtesy of John Luecke.

OK, numerologists, this Portland, OR, photograph is for you. The 2102 stated its wheel arrangement in its number. At the time of the photograph, August 13, 1949, all its improvements have been made, and it will continue in this assignment for about one more year. Photograph by R.V. Nixon.

Also taken at Portland, this view of 2102 shows the Worthington BL feedwater heater. Compatriots 2117, 2122 and 2129 had the model BL-2. The engine was nearing the end of its life when photographed in 1950. Photograph from the Hoff-Nelson collection.

For a short time Q-1's were used in Minneapolis-Breckenridge service. Here the 2113 is enroute to pick up its train at Union Yard, Minneapolis, for a westbound run. A coal burner in 1949, by this date of August 22, 1952, the engine had been converted to burn oil. Bruce Black photograph from the collection of R. W. Johnston.

The final years of the Q-1 found them in heavy use on the Klamath, Cascade and Minot divisions. The Klamath Division had 2101, 2107, 2115 and 2127. The Cascade had 2102, 2105, 2117, 2118, 2119, 2120, 2122, 2124, 2128 and 2129, in Seattle-Portland service. Minot Division had 2100, 2103, 2104, 2106, 2108, 2110, 2111, 2112, 2116, 2121, 2123, and 2125. The Mesabi Division had 2109, 2113 and 2114. Here they operated on grades from 0.65% to 1.3%, where a slower speed was not a detriment. The last year of service for the class is not exactly known, but they were photographed on the Minot and Kalispell divisions in 1949, and between Portland and Seattle on the Cascade Division until 1950. The three Mesabi Division engines were the last to burn coal. The 2113 and 2114 were assigned to hump service at the Allouez ore yard. By 1950 the 2113 had been converted to burn oil and was running on the Willmar Division. The 2109 also ran on the Willmar Division after it was finished on the Mesabi Division. However, sixteen locomotives had been transferred to, and remained on the Mesabi and Dakota divisions by 1952. These saw very little service. The authors believe this to be due to the slower speed at which the Q-1 was required to operate, compared to the Mikados with the same sized drivers. Compared to the O-8's that had 69-inch drivers, an equivalent boiler and similar tractive effort, there was no contest.

Scrapping began in 1950. The last significant new service began in 1951 when three units, 2101, 2107 and 2120 were converted to stationary boilers for ore steaming at Allouez, WI. Here they served with a succession of R-1's until 1958. Authority for Expenditure (AFE) 89838 said the engines were to be replaced in the summer of 1960.[7] AFE 90251, under which these locomotives were retired and scrapped, shows them retired in 1958.[8] This may indicate no ore steaming took place in 1959. However, they could have continued in ore steaming service even after they had been retired. Also other locomotives are known to have been used, as seen in many photographs. See chapter 22, Note 21.

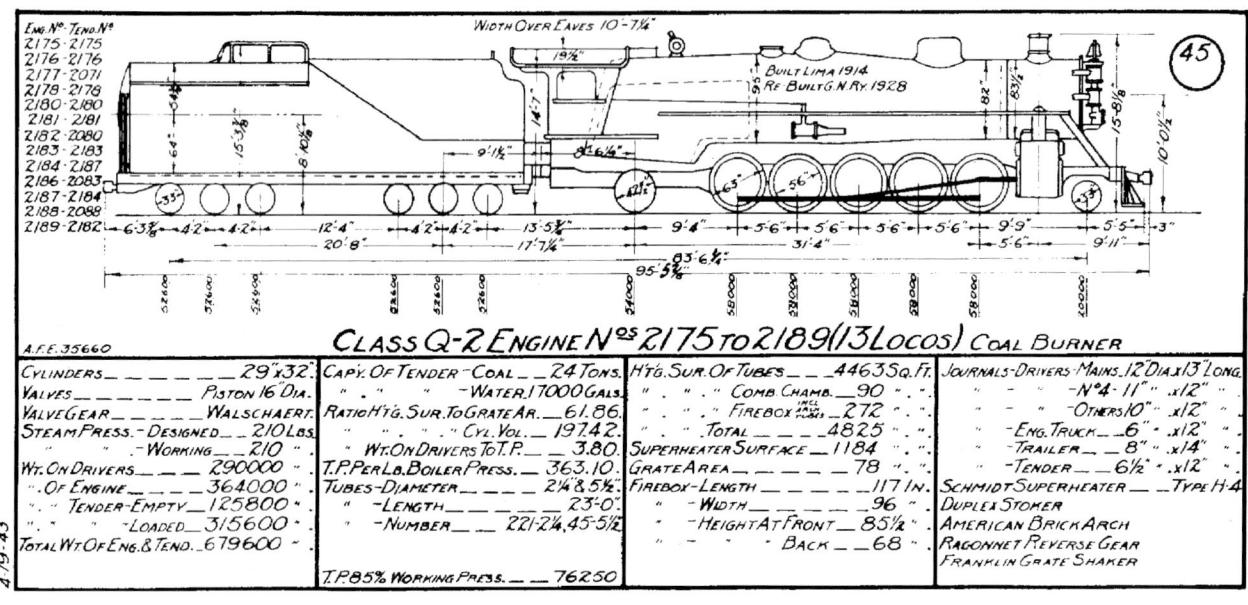

The majority of Q-2's were coal burners until late in life.

This early view of the 2177 at Superior shows it with a longer stack, which may have been the original P-1 stack. As time went on the stack was replaced and late in life the engine was converted to burn oil. This undated photograph was likely taken in 1928, immediately after its rebuilding was completed. Great Northern Railway.

Class Q-2

The conversion of the P-1 Mountains to Santa Fes was an unprecedented event in the history of the North American steam locomotive. However, it made good sense for the Great Northern to do so.

By 1927 the Great Northern had enough experience with the Q-1 to consider the acquisition of more of the Santa Fe type. They had 15 older Mountains in freight service, approximately equal to the O-1 Mikado type in capacity. By rebuilding them into 2-10-2's, a considerable gain in tractive effort could be obtained. The GN did not try to equal the Q-1 with these engines, but proportioned the tractive effort to the available boiler size. Consequently, AFE 35660 was written to authorize the construction of 15 Santa Fes from a like number of Mountains. Key points in the reason for the conversion were to install an improved superheater, to increase the tractive effort suitable for handling grain trains from Minot to Crookston, and generally be able to handle trains

out of Minot (eastbound) as large as those brought into Minot from the west. They would also be able to avoid the use of extra trains for coal traffic west on the 0.6% grade from Grand Forks to Minot.[9] The new engines would be converted from oil to coal and moved from the Whitefish and Spokane Divisions to the Dakota and Minot Divisions.

Consequently Hillyard, Great Falls and Superior shops were set up to make the conversion, with each shop taking on five engines. The detailed assignment may be found in the roster, Chapter 31. The job began in June and was completed by November 1928.

The tractive effort of the finished product went from 60,930 pounds to 76,250 pounds. During the rebuild, the boiler was lengthened 30 inches with a subsequent increase in tube length from 20 feet 6 inches to 23 feet. The new superheater was a Schmidt type and the size increased from 975 square feet to 1184 square feet. Arch tubes were added. The grate area and other firebox dimensions remained the same. New larger turrets and sandboxes were also applied during

By September 10, 1943, the 2177 had a standard GN cast stack, but was still a coal burner. It is shown here at Fergus Falls, MN, enroute from Fargo to St. Cloud. The train has stopped either for a set out or pick up; the engine is in reverse. Photograph by Don Vang.

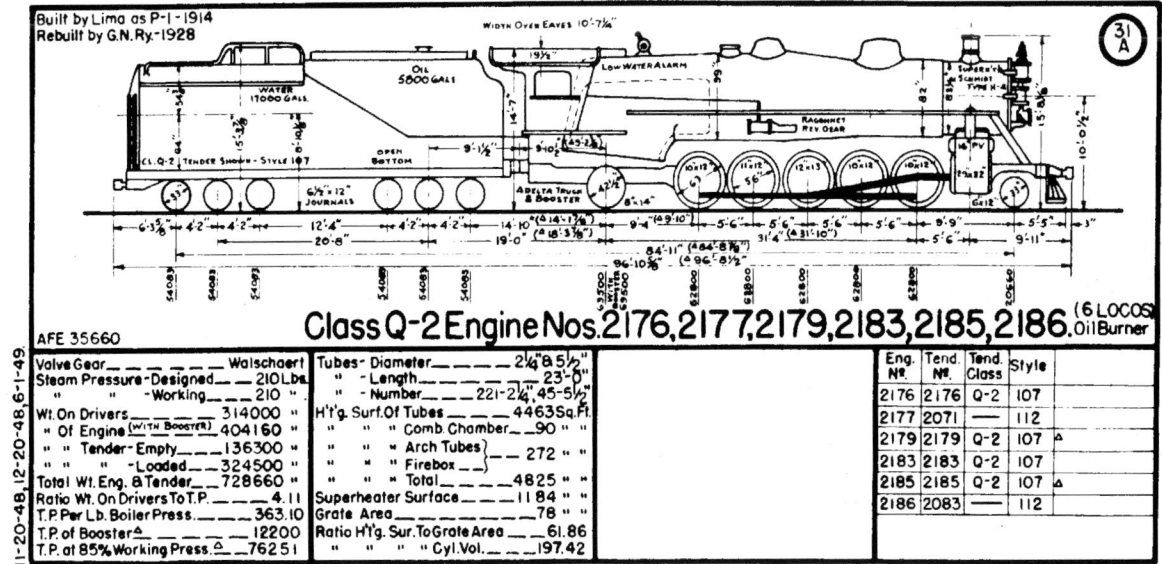

This diagram shows six oil-burners in 1949. By the end of 1951 all 15 locomotives were burning oil. Note the weight changes.

*The 2189 is beginning an eastbound run at Grand Forks, ND, in August of 1949,
and is still a coal burner. The train may be a section of No. 414. Collection of William Raia.*

*Running as a westbound extra, 2186 stopped for water at Niagara, ND, between Grand Forks and Devils Lake.
The date is October 24, 1955. Bruce Black photograph from the collection of Norman F. Priebe.*

The 2182 is an oil burner at Minneapolis, MN, in September 1953. The 2182, along with the 2188, ran for most of 1956. Collection of Harold K. Vollrath.

Oil burning 2181 is shown at Minneapolis on August 14, 1950. It is likely it did not last until 1956. John Westphal collection of John Luecke.

Clean No. 2180 was an oil burner already by 1947 at Superior, WI. Collection of Stan Kistler.

The 2178 was a coal burner when at Minneapolis on June 19, 1948. Robert Graham photograph from the collection of William Raia.

the rebuilding.

Those locomotives that did not have the new standard GN cast headlight received them during the rebuild. Likewise, they all had Elesco No. 14 exhaust steam injectors and Ragonnet power reverse gear when completed, except the 2175 which was given a Kelly branch pipe heater and 2176, which received a Sellers exhaust steam injector during rebuilding. The 2181 and 2186 had received Sellers units while still class P-1 (as engines No. 1759 and 1753, respectively). The five engines that received their power reverse gear during the rebuilding were the 2175, 2176, 2179, 2181 and 2188. Subsequently, in 1939 the 2179 and 2185 received boosters that were kept until 1950. These engines also were converted back to oil-burners in 1939.

New Vanderbilt tenders were provided for the entire class. They were designated Style 106 for the coal burners with 24 tons capacity and Style 107 for the oil burners with 5,000 gallons capacity. Both styles were of open bottom construction and had a water capacity of 17,000 gallons. Assignments may be found in Chapter 34.

Advancements that were made during the life of the engines included adding Whelan and Prime automatic cylinder protection devices in the 1941 to 1945 period, mechanical lubricators of Detroit and Edna manufacture in the 1941 to 1943 period, steam operated cylinder cocks instead of air-operated cocks in 1941 and 1942, with Barco low-water alarms applied in 1943, 1944 and 1945 (the 2185 was the only one to get a Nathan type). Nalco continuous blow-down systems were installed from 1943 through 1947, auxiliary air reservoirs for the power reverse gear from 1946 to 1948 and electric train indicators beginning in 1944. This feature was not applied to all in the class. The oil-burning Q-2's with boosters, No. 2179 and 2185, were equipped with steam heat and air signal connections for passenger (helper) service in 1943. Stokers were removed from 1939 to 1951 as the locomotives were converted to burn oil. One engine, the 2181, had a Security Circulator added for an increase in heating surface of 62.3 square feet.

The 2175 worked from St. Cloud to Minneapolis and Superior. Here it is a coal burner at Minneapolis on May 30, 1948. Charles Felstead photograph from the collection of William Raia.

Experimental increases in tractive effort were made during the late 1930's. The designed 29-inch by 32 inch cylinders were increased to 30 inch by 32 inch on the 2181, 2184, 2187, and 2189 to yield a tractive effort of 81,600 pounds. Changes in the cut-off reduced this to 79,200 pounds on the 2184, 2187 and 2189. The 2176 and 2186, which did not receive larger cylinders, had the same cut-off changes made, which reduced the tractive effort to 74,000 pounds. By 1943 they all had been returned to 76,250 pounds.[10, 11] The engines were reweighed during the 1948 reweigh case, resulting in an ultimate weight of 321,000 pounds on drivers and a total engine weight of 403,000 pounds for the coal-burners. The booster-equipped oil-burners had 314,000 pounds on drivers and a slightly higher total weight of 404,106 due to the booster.

The original locomotive assignment placed ten on the Mesabi Division and five on the Dakota Division. The Mesabi Division had the 2175, 2176, 2177, 2180, 2181, 2184, 2185, 2187, 2188 and 2189.

The Dakota division had the 2178, 2179, 2182, 2183 and 2186. In 1939 each division gave up one, the 2179 from the Dakota Division and the 2185 from the Minot Division, to go to the Spokane Division for what appeared to be helper service. After the war, they were both back on the Dakota Division, bringing the Dakota Division count to six. In the meantime, there were some swaps between Mesabi and Dakota, but the final distribution remained with nine on the Mesabi and six on the Dakota until scrapping began.

Unlike the Q-1's, the Q-2's saw considerable activity during the final days of steam operations. In addition to the original route from Minot to Crookston, their range was extended from Minot to Breckenridge, Crookston to Superior, St. Cloud to Superior, St. Cloud to Fargo, Fargo to Grand Forks and from Minneapolis to Willmar. It was a common event to see the Mesabi engines running on the Willmar Division. Scrapping began in 1953, but at least six were still in service in 1956.

Oil burning 2177 is at Minot, ND, on October 2, 1952. Cordell Newby collection.

Notes:

1. *Comparison Tonnage That Santa Fe and O-4 Class Engines Can Handle over Same Ruling Grades…*, Office General Superintendent Motive Power, 2-21-21. GN papers MHS.
2. Great Northern Railway Unit Record of Property Changes – Equipment (URPC).
3. Don Leach, "Counterbalancing 10-Coupled Power," *R&LHS Newsletter*, Vol.24, No.3 (Summer 2004).
4. Paul T. Warner, "The Great Northern Railway and its Locomotives," *Baldwin Locomotives*, January 1925.
5. URPC, *op. cit.*
6. *Ibid.*
7. Great Northern Railway Authority for Expenditure (AFE) 89838, approved January 3, 1958.
8. AFE 90251, approved April 29, 1958.
9. AFE 35660, approved December 10, 1927.
10. URPC, *op. cit.*
11. Great Northern Railway Steam Locomotive Diagrams, 1943.

The S-2 class was amazingly resilient and proved to be a good freight locomotive after it was no longer needed for passenger service. Here 2580 is rolling through Barnesville, MN, at 40 mph, and about to pick up orders on the fly. The date is October 10, 1956, and this is the last season for the S-2. Photograph by Stan Mailer.

The class S-1 builders photo was of the 2552, taken in April 1929. Note the large class S-1 tender, the Elesco exhaust steam injector, the Nathan low-water alarm and the linkage to the American front-end throttle. The ladder to the valve gear hanger is present too, but nearly invisible. Collection of H. L. Broadbelt.

Chapter 25
Class S 4-8-4 Empire Builder

The increasing prosperity of the 1920's kept the Great Northern Motive Power Department busy with designs for new, more powerful locomotives. By 1927 they had caught up, so to speak, with the freight needs and turned their attention to passenger power. The GN was planning a second all-steel, luxury transcontinental train, and new locomotives were needed to power it.

The P-2's were doing a great job on the *Oriental Limited* and the *Fast Mail*, but there were not enough of them to cover another train. In addition, it was necessary, if the new train was to keep up with the competition, for it to both carry more cars and to be faster. Therefore, the new locomotives needed to be larger. The Authority for Expenditure (AFE) for the S-2 had this to say: "The cars on the *Empire Builder* are even heavier than the *Oriental Limited* cars and we have had many *Empire Builders* of 13 or 14 cars…we must be prepared for still faster time, particularly between Spokane and Seattle where our line is somewhat longer than the Milwaukee. In addition, mail and express trains are becoming heavier…."[1] Note that the AFE was not prepared until after the *Empire Builder* had been placed in service.

With increased high-speed ability as the apparent primary design factor, the GN designed two different locomotives for the new train. One was to take the train over the 1.8% grades of the Rocky Mountains, the other was to be the ultimate speedster for use everywhere else. (A larger steam engine was not needed for the Cascade Mountains since the new electrification was in service in time for the introduction of the new train.) Even though the road required two completely different engines, the GN turned to the new 4-8-4 type for both of these new designs.

In an obvious attempt to promote the new train, the GN stated they wished to refer to this new design as the *Empire Builder* type.[2]

Class S-1

The S-1 designers had little to go on for acceptable sizing of a heavy-duty passenger 4-8-4 for the mountain grades, since all of the passenger 4-8-4's built up to then were lighter and had less tractive effort than the GN desired. This was despite the fact that most of them were designed for mountain service. The only predecessor engines with higher tractive power than the S-1 were the Delaware Lackawanna and Western Q-2 class, built early in 1929, designed for freight-only service and provided with 70-inch drivers.

In order to guarantee the new heavy hauler would have adequate power, the S-1 had more than a little freight engine philosophy built in. If one were to take the Q-1 boiler, the largest rigid frame boiler on the GN up until then, and revise it to include the latest developments of the era, such as a grate area of at least 100 square feet, a type E superheater and boiler pressure of 250 psi, one would come very close to the S-1 boiler. This boiler very adequately compared to other 4-8-4's of the period. A tractive effort comparable to large 2-8-2's completed the design. At 68,466 pounds, the S-1 tractive effort exceeded all preceding passenger-only 4-8-4 designs, and all preceding GN passenger power.

Once again, the S-1 was the heaviest of its type up to the time it was delivered, but it was immediately eclipsed by the C&NW H class, a freight design that followed a few months later. That design aside, it would be nine years before another 4-8-4 as heavy as the S-1 would appear. The ultimate success of the S-1 is indicated by the fact that it did what it was designed to do, and then when displaced from its original assignment, it very capably shouldered the role of dual-service. No more were built because no more were needed until World War II, and by then diesels were available.

Six units, the 2550 through 2555, were delivered between April and May of 1929. Immediately problems showed up. The journal brasses put on by Baldwin were too soft, and the bearings overheated. During delivery, the Pennsylvania had to set out the last four in Ohio for the journals to cool. The main rod for 2550 seized in the cross head which had to be jacked out before it could leave Minneapolis on its maiden trip (on a freight break-in run).[3] The superheater for 2553 developed a leak on September 2 and journal brass problems occurred until July 1930. It had been a difficult breaking in period. As soon as possible they were assigned to passenger traffic between Whitefish and Havre on the Montana (soon to be the Kalispell) Division.

Immediately after delivery, the original S-1 tenders were replaced with Q-1 class tenders of 15,000 gallons water capacity during set-up.[4] The reason for this has not been found, since the record for this move is incomplete. These tenders were used while the engines were in their original passenger assignment. However, after a delay to No. 2 out of Whitefish in May 1930, C. O. Jenks telegraphed Mr. Kelly "We made a mistake when we put the 15,000 gallon tanks on the S-1 engines."[5]

By 1929 slant front cabs were standard on new engines. This started in 1925 with the R-1. It continued with the R-2, Q-2 and the O-7, and was followed by the S classes.

All of the S-1 class were oil burners. The use of outside bearings on pilot truck axles was a new feature. All of the locomotives were equipped with an Elesco exhaust steam injector at the factory. As with other GN locomotives, it was mounted on the engineer's side, with a conventional live-steam injector mounted on the fireman's side. They also were equipped with the American multiple-port front end throttle.

The original factory-provided 22,000 gallon tanks were returned to the engines when they went into freight service. This happened in September 1931.[6] Once the S-1's got their original tenders back, they

kept them for the rest of their service lives. The S-1 tender, Style 110, was of 22,000 gallon water capacity, 5,800 gallon fuel oil capacity and of Vanderbilt water bottom construction. They weighed 142,900 pounds empty.

A vestibule cab was installed on the 2552, the only engine of the class to receive one. Records are incomplete, with the date of installation unable to be determined. The 2552 did lose its cab after hitting a rock slide near Milan, WA, December 3, 1933. The vestibule cab was likely put on during the repair. If not then, many S-1's, including the 2552 had back-end boiler and firebox renewal done in 1940.[7] This would have been another good time to change cabs, if it had not been done by then. However, the change did not get into the diagram book until 1948.

A series of upgrades progressed during the World War II years. Improved mechanical lubricators were installed during 1941 and 1942. Brick arches went in between 1940 and 1943. This included the addition of arch tubes, which added 48 square feet of evaporative surface. Nalco automatic blowdown devices were next in 1943 and 1944. Electric train indicators and Timken roller bearings were installed during 1945 and 1946. Prime cylinder protection devices were applied to all engines except the 2555. The records show the 2552, 2553 and 2554 received them in the 1945 to 1946 period.

The original intent for the S-1, according to the AFE, was to use it on the new heavier and faster *Empire Builder* as well as the other transcontinental passenger trains between Havre and Whitefish, MT.[8] They were delivered in time for use on the first run of the *Empire Builder* on June 29, 1929. The S-1 could handle 13, sometimes 14 *Empire Builder* cars on the 1.8% grade of the Montana/Kalispell Division without a helper. After the delivery of the S-2 class, it was a natural question to ask if S-2's could handle the *Empire Builder* on the same grade. The road found the S-2 could handle 11 *Empire Builder* cars on the 1.8% without a helper. That was close enough to the S-1 to permit its reassignment to freight service.

After September 1931 all six S-1's were assigned to freight service between Hillyard, WA, and Whitefish, MT. For ten years, they and the three oil-burning O-8's powered all of the time freights over this

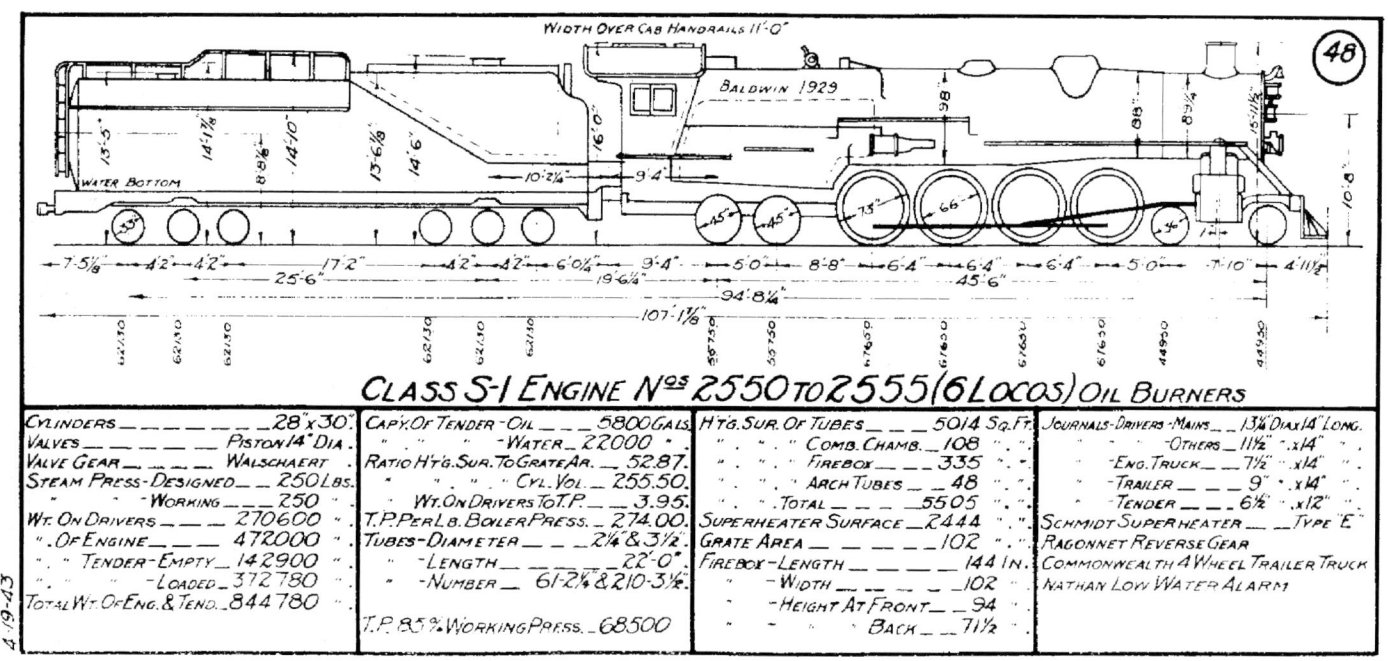

CLASS S-1 ENGINE Nos 2550 TO 2555 (6 LOCOS) OIL BURNERS			
CYLINDERS _ _ _ _ _ _ _ 28"x30"	CAP'Y. OF TENDER - OIL _ _ _ 5800 GALS.	HTG. SUR. OF TUBES _ _ _ 5014 SQ.FT.	JOURNALS-DRIVERS-MAINS _ _ 13¼ DIA x 14" LONG.
VALVES _ _ _ _ _ _ PISTON 14" DIA.	" " " -WATER _ 22000 "	" " " COMB. CHAMB. _ 108 " "	" " -OTHERS _ _ 11½ " x 14" "
VALVE GEAR _ _ _ _ WALSCHAERT .	RATIO HT'G.SUR.TO GRATE AR. _ 52.87	" " " FIREBOX _ _ 335 " "	" -ENG. TRUCK _ _ 7½ " x 14" "
STEAM PRESS-DESIGNED _ _ 250 LBS.	" " " CYL. VOL. _ 255.50	" " " ARCH TUBES _ _ 48 " "	" -TRAILER _ _ _ 9 " x 14" "
" -WORKING _ _ _ 250 "	WT. ON DRIVERS TO T.P. _ 3.95 .	" " " TOTAL _ _ _ 5505 " "	" -TENDER _ _ _ 6½ " x 12" "
WT. ON DRIVERS _ _ _ 270600 "	T.P. PER LB. BOILER PRESS. _ 274.00 .	SUPERHEATER SURFACE _ 2444 " "	SCHMIDT SUPERHEATER _ _ TYPE E
" .OF ENGINE _ _ _ _ 472000 "	TUBES-DIAMETER _ _ _ _ 2¼ & 3½ .	GRATE AREA _ _ _ _ _ 102 " "	RAGONNET REVERSE GEAR
" . " TENDER-EMPTY _ 142900 "	" -LENGTH _ _ _ _ _ 22'-0" .	FIREBOX-LENGTH _ _ _ 144 IN.	COMMONWEALTH 4 WHEEL TRAILER TRUCK
" . " -LOADED _ 372780 "	" -NUMBER _ _ 61-2¼ & 210-3½ .	" -WIDTH _ _ _ _ _ 102 "	NATHAN LOW WATER ALARM
TOTAL WT. OF ENG. & TEND. _ 844780 "		" -HEIGHT AT FRONT_ 94 "	
	T.P. 85% WORKING PRESS. _ 68500	" " " BACK _ _ 71½ "	

4-19-43

As soon as they arrived on GN property, the S-1 tenders were swapped for Q-1 tenders. The GN then took another "builders photo" of the 2550 so equipped. The ladder to the valve gear shows clearly on this view. Great Northern Railway.

The GN took several publicity photos of the new 2551 on the Empire Builder *in Marias Pass. The Q-1 tenders remained on the engines until September 1931. William Bissinger collection.*

The photographer focused on the tender in this view of the 2552 at Browning, MT, in 1930. The train is westbound. Large as they were, the Q-1 tenders were not adequate for the S-1, and were replaced with the originals when they went into freight service. That happened approximately a year after this photo was taken. Harold Davidson photograph from the collection of Norman F. Priebe.

The S-1's turned out to be tremendous freight engines, holding the assignment between Hillyard and Whitefish for ten years. Here the 2551 is rushing west with the first section of a time freight, with many reefers on the head end. The grade follows the Kootenai River here, and the location is near Libby, MT, on April 28, 1941. The 2551 was transferred to the Minot Division soon after. Photograph by Warren McGee from the GN Public Relations Department.

A 1946 view of the 2552 with its vestibule cab shows either the Oriental Limited or the Fast Mail departing St. Paul. The S-1's had returned to passenger service after 15 years in freight service. Photograph by Charles Ost from the collection of William Raia.

A summer 1947 view is at St. Paul, this time of the 2553 with the Oriental Limited Pullman section. *Ben Cutler (RPS) photograph from the collection of Norman F. Priebe.*

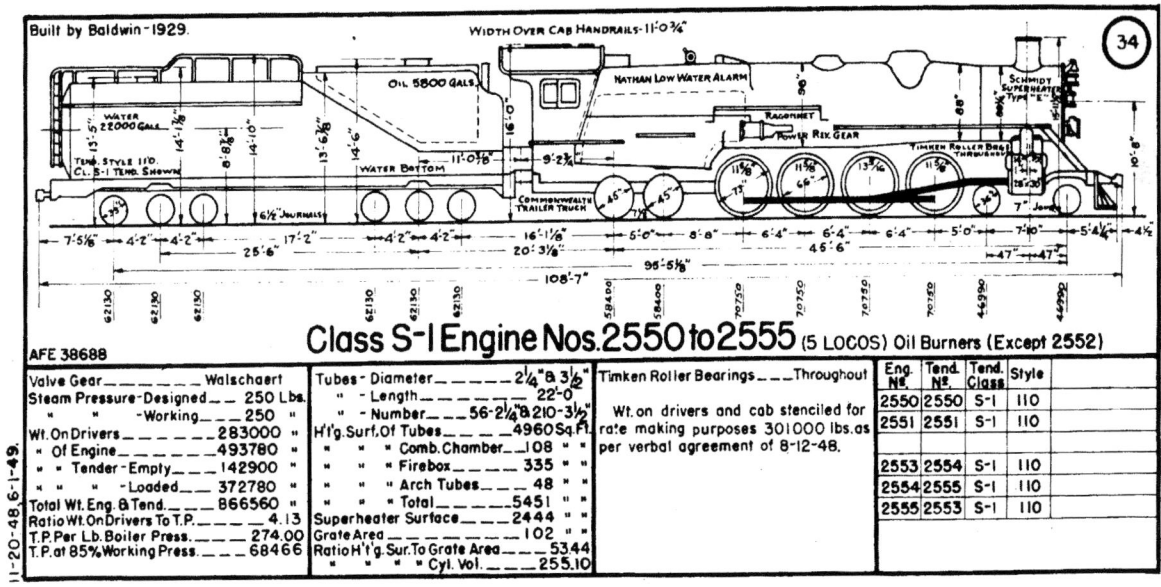

The 2552 is missing from this diagram due to its vestibule cab. It was now on its own page. Note the final official weights and the rate notice.

The 2555 was still in freight service in this late 1945 view at Minot. This mostly freshly painted high angle view gives a good idea of how the green and black was distributed. The view also strongly suggests a red cab roof. W. J. Pontin (RPS) photograph from the collection of Norman F. Priebe.

stretch. In 1941, they were replaced by the new N-3 class 2-8-8-0's, and three of them were sent with the O-8's to the Minot Division for freight service until the end of World War II. The other three, 2550, 2553 and 2555, went to the Willmar Division for freight service. All were assigned to the Minot Division in early 1947 for a return to passenger service on trains 3 and 4, the reinstated *Oriental Limited*. They ran between Minot and St. Paul with this train until 1948, when there were enough F3 passenger diesels available to cover both the *Fast Mail* and the *Oriental Limited*. After that, they saw limited passenger service, usually on extra sections of No's. 3 and 4, until 1951 when the streamlined *Western Star* replaced the *Oriental Limited*. Then they went back to mostly full-time freight service. During shopping at Hillyard between these assignments in 1951, the 2555 may have been the last GN steamer to have been painted with the deep green boiler jacket paint.

The S-1 was involved in the 1948 reweigh program with a curious result. Its weight on drivers came in under that of several other large rigid frame locomotives, which would have meant less pay for the enginemen manning it, in spite of the fact it was handling similar size trains. So the GN compromised with the unions and stenciled the cab at 301,000 pounds on drivers, for pay rate purposes, while the actual weight on drivers was 283,000 pounds. This act put it in the same pay category as the Q-2 and O-8.

The six engines remained on the Minot Division until the end of 1954, where they usually ran eastward from Minot to either Dakota Division or Willmar Division destinations. They were used less and less as time went on. The last frequent use of the S-1 was in 1954. Earlier that year they had seen 3,215 miles of passenger service. By the end of October they had accumulated 39,878 miles in freight service.[9] About 1955 the 2550, 2552, 2554 and the 2555 were assigned to the Dakota Division, and the 2551 went to the Mesabi Division. From late 1955 through late 1956, these five were back in freight service for the last time, between Minneapolis, Breckenridge, St. Cloud, Fargo, Grand Forks and Minot. The 2553 was the first to be retired, officially

The 2554 is shown arriving at St. Paul on July 14, 1947, while in passenger service. S. Davies photograph from the collection of William Raia.

The 2555 is waiting to back on to its train prior to departure from St. Paul Union Depot on August 9, 1947. R. J. Foster photograph from the collection of William Raia.

Back in freight service at Minot, ND, on August 24, 1949, the 2550 sports an unusual steam dome with a shallow conical top. This was a likely repair to dome damage. Photograph from Charles E. Winters collection.

In freight service at Willmar, MN, in August, 1949, the 2550 steam dome appears to have a totally flat top here, but it may be the angle of view. There is little else to differentiate it from the other S-1's, except for 2552. Collection of Harold K. Vollrath.

Still in service on October 9, 1956, the 2552 is between runs at Grand Forks, MN. The 2552 and 2555 ran until snowfall in 1956. Bruce Black photograph from the collection of Norman F. Priebe.

in April 1956, but it cannot be traced after November 1955. The others were retired in December 1957, with the 2555 held for service until April 1958.

Class S-2

The S-2 design proposal was basically complete by July 1, 1929, as shown in drawing UF1269. The purchase of 12 locomotives was covered in the first writing of AFE 40213, approved July 19, 1929. Two more were added to the order December 2, 1929, on an "Excess Permit". The bookkeeping followed the action, for on September 27, 1929, during final negotiations with Baldwin, C. O. Jenks turned down plans to have cast-steel frames on the engines. He telegraphed William Kelly, who was in Spokane, "have changed specifications from Commonwealth frame to ordinary frame and bought the 14 passenger locomotives. Please arrange quickly to complete details with Baldwin so there may be no delay."[10] It is likely the return to "ordinary frame" was a concession to reduce the cost of the increased order. Thus the

final order was for 14 S-2's in all, from the 2575 to the 2588, and it was placed three months before the Excess Permit was approved.

Before construction started in November 1929 the GN motive power people were forced to defend their S-2 design against comparisons with the 4-6-4 designs of the Burlington and the New York Central,[11] and in January 1930, against the C&NW H-class.[12] (The C&NW took delivery of their H class during the period October through December, 1929.) The GN consensus was that the 4-8-4 type was superior to a 4-6-4, and to not incorporate any ideas from the C&NW H for the S-2. (The H was designed to be a freight engine.)

Despite the lost opportunity to have cast steel frames, the locomotives did have Commonwealth one-piece cast steel cylinders. Weight was kept down by using the same radial-stay firebox design as on the P-2, as well as the use of the new nickel-steel alloy for the boiler shell.[13] Even the choice of Sellers exhaust steam injectors was based in part on weight.

The respect shown by the GN toward its very successful P-2 class

There were a number of builders photos taken of the 2577, the two used here are probably the best. Collection of H. L. Broadbelt.

This ¾ view from the engineer's side gives a good view of the front end. Collection of H. L. Broadbelt.

became evident when the new high speed 4-8-4 for the *Empire Builder* turned out to be a larger version of the P-2. While there may have been some resemblance between the Q-1 and S-1 boiler, in this case there was no doubt that the S-2 boiler was an enlarged version of that on the P-2. The P-2 boiler was taken as-is, and changed only by using a larger firebox of just under 100 square feet grate area and replacing the older type A superheater with a type E. The boiler length and various diameters remained the same. The flue length also remained the same, but the number of flues changed because of the type E superheater. The flue surface area was reduced somewhat as a result. There also was a reduction in arch tube area. But with a larger combustion chamber and firebox surface, the total heating surface came in just under that of the P-2, at 4,803 square feet. The superheater area, on the other hand, increased significantly from 1,368 to 2,265 square feet. The exciting innovation of the S-2 was the inclusion of 80-inch diameter drivers. By making this engine the first 4-8-4 with drivers of this size, the GN showed it was serious about creating a racehorse for its relatively level

regions. A slight increase in boiler pressure and an increase of one inch in the piston stroke compensated for the large wheel and brought the S-2 tractive effort up to just over that of the P-2 at 58,305 pounds.

The S-2 was no more slippery than the P-2, contrary to some commentary. The cylinder stroke to driver diameter ratio was the lowest of any GN engine, and the weight to tractive power ratio was high, at 4.40, which was higher than that of the S-1. Crews denied slipperiness. All crewmen interviewed considered the S-2 their favorite engine.

The S-2's were delivered between March 11 and April 10, 1930. All members of the class came from the builder with a Sellers exhaust steam injector located on the engineer's side. A conventional live-steam injector was located on the fireman's side. Many of the modern accessories were present on the S-2's when delivered from the factory. These features included Barco power reverse gear, Nathan low water alarms and American multiple-port throttles. Both leading and trailing trucks were of cast steel construction. The trailing truck was the standard Commonwealth design. The leading truck had the outside

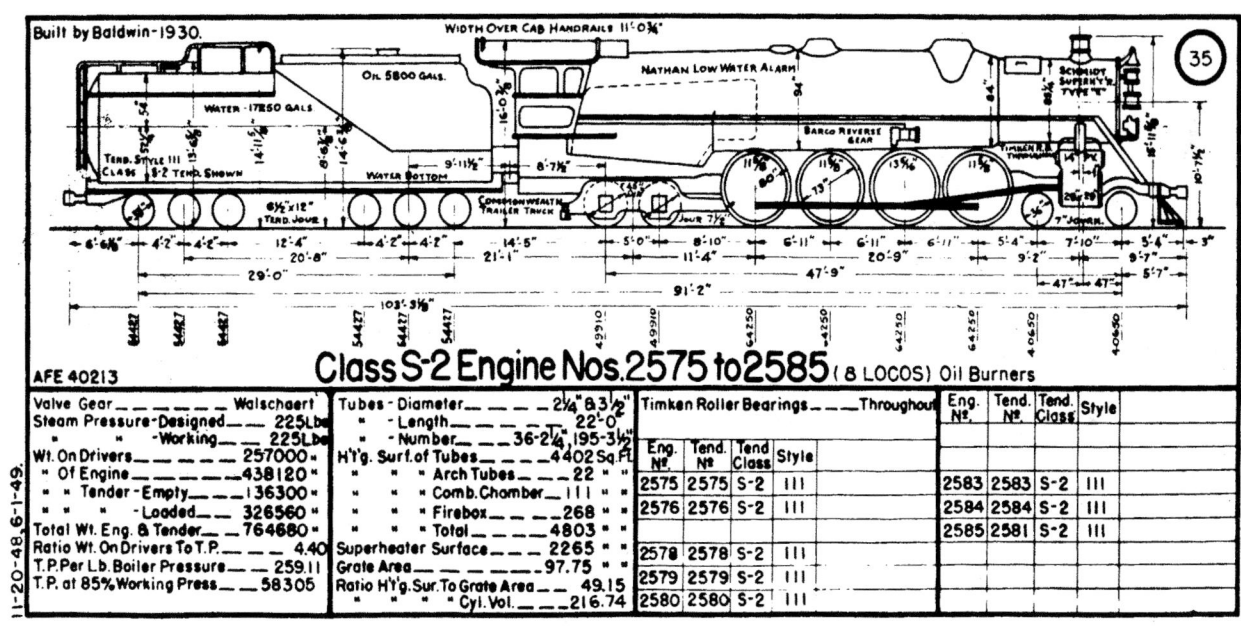

Both diagrams are shown to include both cab styles. These also have the later correct weights.

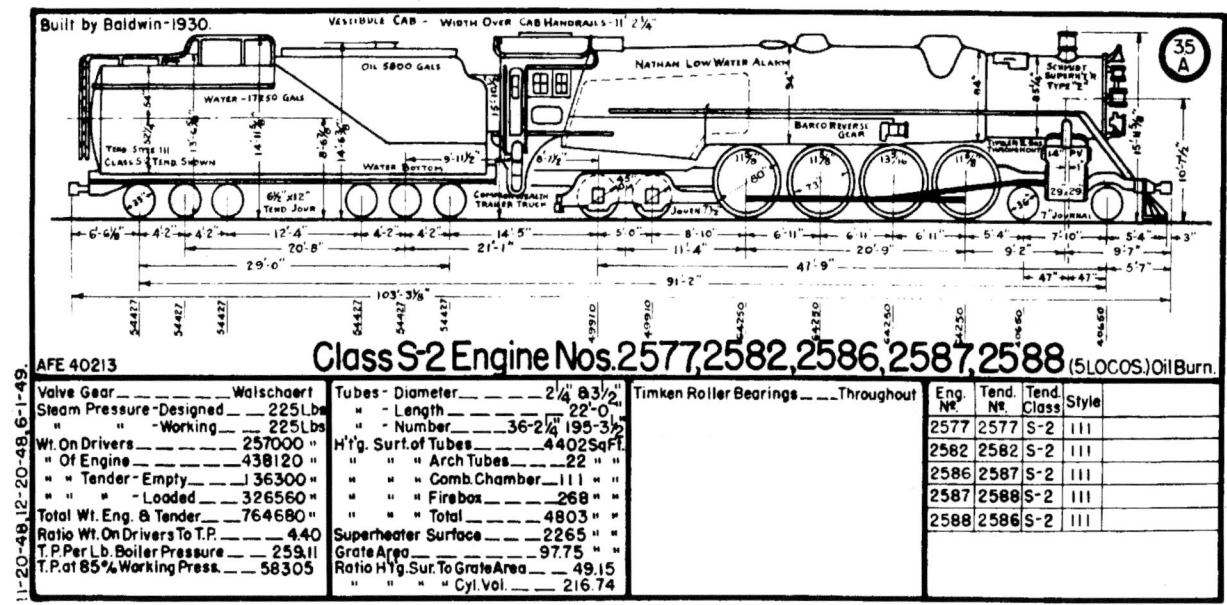

journal boxes cast integral to the truck.

Several engines were converted to burn coal at various times. The 2579 was converted to burn coal on the Montana Division in 1931 at a time when fuel oil rose to $1.06 a barrel. Costs were compared with the costs of running an oil-burning engine, in this case the 2584.[14] Four more were also converted to burn coal in 1931, the 2577, 2578, 2580 and 2581.[15] All five were returned to burn oil in 1933.[16] Later the 2578 was again converted to burn coal, and was photographed as a coal-burner at Minneapolis in 1939. It was returned to burn oil before 1943.

Vestibule cabs began to be installed as early as the late 1930's, with the 2577 apparently the first one to receive the upgrade. By 1936, the diagrams show such cabs on the 2577, 2582, 2586 and 2588. For some unknown reason, the 1943 diagrams do not show vestibule cabs on any S-2. However, by 1948, No. 2577, 2582, 2586, 2587 and 2588 had them. No more were changed.

Like a few P-2's, two S-2's had air horns installed in 1937. The engines were the 2586 and 2587. The model was the two chime Leslie Tyfon "pneumatic whistle."[17]

Electric train indicators were installed during 1944 and 1945. There was an installation of an Elesco exhaust steam injector on 2588 in April of 1944. This was considered an "unauthorized" replacement of the Sellers since no AFE was requested. The ICC Accident report for engine 2581 records it also had an Elesco exhaust steam injector. Elesco steam driers were installed between 1946 and 1950. The 2588 was the first to receive roller bearings, during October, 1945. The others were installed as engines were shopped, with the program completed in December 1947.[18]

The location of the injectors was changed on the engines as they underwent successive shoppings. Beginning during the last years of World War II, there was a systematic effort to move the injectors on both sides of the S-2 from their original location in front of the firebox to beneath the cab. No records were found for this move but a study of photographs show the earliest move had been made by 1944 (see the

The 2575 is at Hillyard on September 3, 1939. Only a blow-down muffler seems to have been added since it was new, although the cover for the Nathan low-water alarm is missing. Robert F. Collins photograph from the collection of John Krause.

By July 2, 1938, the 2586 had received its vestibule cab and a silver smokebox. It still retained the ladder to the valve gear hanger. It is shown at Belton MT, the western entrance to Glacier National Park. J. Riley photograph from the collection of William Raia.

photo of 2578 at Ft. Buford, page 353) and the latest move had not yet been made in 1946. It is believed the reason for the change was to place them in a cooler location. A hot injector will not operate reliably.

The S-2 tenders, Style 111, were of the Vanderbilt design, with water bottom Commonwealth cast-steel frames, and all-welded tank construction. They had a capacity of 17,250 gallons of water and 5,800 gallons of oil, and were the only all-welded tenders on the Great Northern. It was unusual, given the GN practice of wholesale tender swapping, that all of the S-2 locomotives were able to retain S-2 tenders until their retirement.

The S-2 class was reweighed during the 1948 reweigh case, and the correct weights are shown on the published diagrams from 1948 onward.

The *Empire Builder* had been inaugurated on June 10, 1929. Because the members of the new S-2 class were not delivered until early 1930, the P-2 class was given the responsibility of handling the new train on the level districts for nearly a year. It was the 2517 that was given the honor of pulling the first run from St. Paul. Note that the S classes did not handle the *Empire Builder* over its entire route, but they made it possible for the P-2's to replace the H-7 on several districts.

The initial assignment for the class was between Spokane and Wenatchee, WA, and between Williston, ND, and Havre, MT. Here they would cover the *Empire Builder*, the *Fast Mail* and the *Oriental Limited*, except that the *Oriental Limited* was taken out of service almost immediately afterward. However, there still was a No. 3 and 4, now a long distance local. Once it was established the S-2 could handle 11 *Empire Builder* cars on the 1.8% grade without a helper, their assignment was expanded to cover Whitefish to Havre, MT, as well.

In December 1938, the locomotive assignment for the *Empire Builder* was as follows:[19]

St. Paul to Breckenridge	P-2
Breckenridge to Minot	S-2
Minot to Williston	S-2
Williston to Havre	S-2
Havre to Whitefish	S-2
Whitefish to Spokane	P-2
Spokane to Wenatchee	S-2
Wenatchee to Skykomish	Electric
Skykomish to Seattle	P-2

Note the S-2 class did not run into Seattle. This was due to a train-shed canopy clearance problem at King Street Station.[20] However, despite this official assignment list, the H-7 class remained active on the Spokane to Whitefish segment throughout the 1930's and 1940's, along with the P-2's, hauling all of the mainline first class trains, including the *Empire Builder*.

In 1936, S-2's were assigned to the Minot, Butte, Kalispell and Spokane Divisions. Minot had 2577 through 2581, Butte had 2582 through 2585, Kalispell had 2586 through 2588, and Spokane had 2575 and 2576. This arrangement stayed through the World War II years, except that Butte gained the 2581 and, due to the heavy traffic, many times the western engines would run through to St. Paul. The result was that all of the engines were seen at St. Paul at one time or another. Many times during this period the *Empire Builder* ran in three sections. The practice turned deadly on August 9, 1945, when

Minot was an excellent location to photograph the locomotives of train No. 2, and many photographers have done so. One of the earliest is this view of 2580 during the station stop taken by Herb Arey on September 28, 1933. Mr. Arey was riding the train. This view shows the ladder over the valve gear that was ultimately removed. From the Hoff-Nelson collection.

No. 2578 was a coal-burner when shown here at Minneapolis, MN, on June 11, 1939. The location is strange since St. Paul handled the passenger engines. However, Minneapolis frequently took any overflow work. C. W. Jernstrom collection.

GN No. 1, the Empire Builder, with ten cars was near Browning, MT, on April 24, 1941. Power is a well-maintained S-2, No. 2588. Photograph by Warren R. McGee.

An S-2 is powering the eastbound Empire Builder with diesel helper on Marias Pass at Fielding Curve in April 1942. The helper is a new EMD FT type, the three-unit 5900, assigned to Marias Pass helper service. The train is twelve cars long, one more than the S-2 could reliably handle alone on the hill. Photograph by T. J. Hielman, courtesy U. S. National Park Service.

This is an example of an S-2 handling a freight train while still in passenger service. In such cases the locomotive would be on a break-in run after shopping. Here 2578 is westbound at Fort Buford, ND, in 1944. The ladders that were attached to the valve gear hanger have been removed by this time. Ben Cutler (RPS) photograph from the collection of Norman F. Priebe.

Engine 2588 is shown waiting for the highball at St. Paul, MN, on August 4, 1946. The train was likely the Empire Builder. *R. J. Foster photograph from the collection of William Raia.*

The 2579 is backing down to its train, likely No. 3, at St. Paul Union Depot on May 26, 1948. C. T. Felstead photograph from the collection of William Raia.

the 2588, on a second section, ran into a stopped first section around a curve at Michigan, ND. The accident precipitated the installation of automatic block signals on the Dakota Division. The 2588 was repaired to run again.[21]

Assignments began to change in 1945 when the new diesel E7's came on the scene. These engines were intended for use on the new streamlined *Empire Builder*. Since the new cars would not arrive for two more years, the E7s were used to power No. 27, the westbound *Fast Mail*, from St. Paul as far as Wenatchee. Turning there, the diesels would return with No. 2, the eastbound *Empire Builder*. This freed up some S-2's for extra sections, reducing the use of Pacifics in this service. S-2's were still seen on No. 28 during this period.

Near the end of its *Empire Builder* duty, the 2581 suffered a catastrophic boiler explosion while running with First No. 1 just west of Crary, ND, on January 9, 1947. All in the cab were killed, and the locomotive was scrapped.[22]

Once the new streamlined *Empire Builder* went into service in early 1947, the S-2's were relieved of all *Empire Builder* duty. The *Oriental Limited* was reinstated, using the heavyweight *Empire Builder*'s cars. This train required the S-2's, S-1's and many of the P-2's for the first year, but more diesels were coming. In November of 1947, the first of the F3 diesels, 3-unit 4,500 horsepower units, arrived. The transfer of all mainline transcontinental passenger trains to F3 or F7 diesel power was completed by the end of 1950, causing steam to be bumped down another tier. By 1948, S-2's saw only occasional service on extra sections of the *Oriental Limited*. By 1949, several S-2's (2575, 2578, 2579, 2582 and 2584) had been transferred to the Willmar Division, where they were put on trains 9 and 10, the *Dakotan*, a long and heavy local running between St. Paul and Williston, ND. Here they put in good service as primary power until 1951. Again diesel power arrived and was able to completely bump the S-2's by 1952.

After 1947, the Butte Division began using their S-2's in freight service, the first division to regularly do so. Butte was able to do this because the main line there was essentially level. S-2's had been seen

Arriving at St. Paul, MN, on July 2, 1948, No. 2575 is likely the power for No. 10. Photograph by Sid Davies from the collection of William Raia.

The 2582 is on No. 4, the eastbound Oriental Limited, *at Devils Lake, ND, in August 1949. Frank North Collection.*

At the time this photo was taken in August 1948, the 2583 was in full-time freight service. Here it is eastbound near Harlem, MT, with a scheduled freight. Frank McKinlay (RPS) photograph from the collection of Norman F. Priebe.

When Ron Nixon was running the telegraphy school in Minneapolis, at the end of the course he would set up a field trip to show the students railroading up close. In 1949 the trip went to St. Cloud on the Great Northern. The 2582 got the call, since it was no longer on a regular run. At St. Cloud on April 18, Ron managed to get several shots of the train before heading back. The S-2's also powered Shriner and Scout specials during this period. Photograph by Ron Nixon, from the J. R. Quinn collection.

in freight service before, but only while breaking in after shopping. In 1949 the Butte Division engines were the 2576, 2580 and 2583. The Kalispell Division no longer had any assigned. The Spokane Division put theirs (2585, 2586, 2587 and 2588) on trains 5 and 6, the *Cascadian*, for a short period.

From 1951 until 1956, S-2's remained as protection power for passenger trains, although this happened with less and less frequency as time went on. The last instance of this known to the authors was during December 1955, when both a P-2 and an S-2 were pressed into service on two sections of No. 28.[23] Otherwise, the engines were put to work in freight service. This was not as strange as it might seem. While they did not have the tractive effort of a Mikado, they did exceed that of the P-2, and they were fast. Fast freight was a GN byword, and the S-2's could deliver if not overloaded. This had been demonstrated

as early as 1934, when the Baldwin Locomotive Company sponsored a test comparing the S-2, the S-1 and the O-8 on the 0.7 percent grade between Troy and Whitefish, MT. While the O-8 ultimately demonstrated the greatest efficiency per 1,000 Gross Ton Miles in the test, the S-2 was consistently faster with its train.[24]

The use of nickel-steel in the S-2 boilers added to their maintenance problems in later years, due to embrittlement. However, unlike the large freight engines, they did not receive new boilers, but were patched as necessary.

The last S-2's in freight service were the 2577, 2580 and 2584, in 1956, on the Dakota Division between St. Cloud and Fargo, and on the Willmar Division between Minneapolis and St. Cloud. It is unlikely an S-2 ran in 1957. The 2584 ultimately survived the scrapper's torch and was preserved for display at Havre, MT, where it is today.

Engine 2577 had been in freight service for some time when it was photographed in October 1955 at Fargo, ND. Carl Ulrich photograph from the collection of William Raia.

This photo of 2578 shows the unusual use of Railroad Roman style lettering for the cab number after being repainted into black. The engine is in freight service at Grand Forks, ND, in October 1952. W. Krawiec photograph from the collection of William Raia.

No. 2579 was photographed at Minneapolis, MN, in September 1953. Collection of Harold K. Vollrath.

Taking water at Rothsay, MN, the 2580 was on an eastbound extra freight on October 10, 1956. The fading black boiler paint is beginning to let through glimpses of the former green. Despite this, it still presented an elegant image. Making good time, the crew would eat lunch here. Bruce Black photograph from the collection of Norman F. Priebe.

The 2577, 2580 and 2584 ended up as the last S-2's in service, running freight in 1955 and 1956. The 2584 is shown here at Fargo in September 1955. Note the all-welded tender, unique to the S-2. This is the best view the authors have of that style tender, the Class S-2 Style 111. It is of the water-bottom type. Bruce Black photograph from the collection of William Raia.

While the records found to date do not show the 2576 as having air horns, here is evidence to the contrary. They are located in the shadow of the electric train indicator. Contrary to photos of other horn installations, both chimes point forward. Also, the engine has had its injectors moved back by this date. This view was taken at St. Paul, MN, September 14, 1946. A Stan Styles photograph from GTC Collectibles.

Notes:

1. Great Northern Railway Authority for Expenditure (AFE) 40213. Approved July 19, 1929, amended December 2, 1929.
2. William Kelly to F. J. Gavin and J. H. O'Neill, March 1, 1930. GN Papers, MHS.
3. J. B. Smith to C. O. Jenks, May 23, 1929. GN papers, V.P. Operating, MHS Box 132.B.16.5B.
4. William Kelly to J. B. Smith, May 1, 1929. GN Papers, V.P. Operating, MHS Box 132.B.16.5B.
5. Copy of Telegram from C. O. Jenks to William Kelly, May 24, 1930. GN Papers, V.P. Operating, MHS Box 132.B.16.5B.
6. J. H. O'Neill to C. O. Jenks, August 28, 1931. GN Papers, V. P. Operating, MHS Box 132.B.16.5B.
7. Great Northern Railway Historic Engine Record Vol. 7, MHS Microfilm No. M 462.
8. Great Northern Railway AFE 38688, approved Nov. 7, 1928.
9. Performance of Locomotives and Motor Cars, Ten Months Ending October 1954. GN Statement No. AD–7.1. Authors collection.
10. Copy of telegram attached to Great Northern Railway AFE 40213.
11. Sequence of correspondence initiated by Ralph Budd with resultant assertions by F. E. Williamson, President of the CB&Q, October 23, 1929. GN Papers, MHS box 132.B.16.5B.
12. William Kelly to C. O. Jenks, January 24, 1930. GN Papers, MHS box 132.B.16.5B.
13. *Baldwin Locomotives* on the *Great Northern Railway*, Baldwin Locomotives, February 1939.
14. C. O. Jenks to William Kelly, April 24, 1931.
15. Great Northern Railway AFE 44004, approved April 9, 1931.
16. Great Northern Railway AFE 47092, approved July 1, 1933, and completed July 19, 1933.
17. Great Northern Railway AFE 53155 for 2587, photograph for 2586.
18. Great Northern Railway Unit Record of Property Changes, Account 51.
19. Loose table, December 15, 1938. GN Ry, GN papers, V. P. Operating, MHS.
20. Discussion with R. E. Johnson, September 8, 1971.
21. Robert Bye and James Larson, "Rear-end Collision – Two Passenger Trains, Michigan, North Dakota – August 9, 1945," GNRHS Reference Sheet No. 152, September 1989.
22. Brian Lerohl, "Crown Sheet Failure – Locomotive 2581, Crary, North Dakota – January 9, 1947," GNRHS Reference sheet No. 161, March 1990.
23. David Plowden, *A Time of Trains*, W. W. Norton, New York, 1987. See pages 14 through 25.
24. Samuel Vauclain, *What Size Drivers*, Baldwin Locomotives, April-July 1934.

Another trainload of wartime traffic for the SP&S has just left Hillyard and is entering the Fort Wright interlocking. The train, powered by Z-6 No. 4001, is crossing the Fort Wright bridge west of Spokane, WA. At Fort Wright, the train turned south to join the SP&S. The year was 1944. G.C. Corey (RPS) photograph from the collection of Norman F. Priebe.

Chapter 26
Class Z-6 4-6-6-4 Challenger

Introduction

The Z-6 was an unintended exception to the GN's locomotive development and procurement program. This class was acquired by the GN at the insistence of the Northern Pacific, to support the equalization of GN freight traffic on the SP&S in a manner deemed suitable by the NP.

The GN was required by contract to use locomotives of equal capacity as those used by the NP for the SP&S equalization service. Therefore, when the SP&S and NP obtained the NP Z-6 class locomotive, the GN felt it necessary to furnish a larger locomotive than they had been using up to that time, which were of the GN Class O 2-8-2 type. Mr. C. O. Jenks suggested the use of the GN Class N-2 2-8-8-0.[1]

The NP was not pleased with this offer and insisted on the use of their Z-6 class. The two roads argued this point for nearly two years, after which the GN capitulated and bought two locomotives from the SP&S.[2,3] At least a partial reason for the decision was the discovery that the N-2 could not negotiate the tight curves on the Oregon Trunk, the SP&S subsidiary that was one of the routes the engines would have to travel. There were three such curves: one of 15 degrees, one of 12 degrees 30 minutes, and one of 11 degrees. This shortcoming was later corrected in the design of the N-3 class. GN's R-1 class needed only a minor change to negotiate a 16-degree curve.

The condition that the Z-6 engines be used for traffic equalization limited them to running on the SP&S and the Oregon Trunk. When in the extremely rare instances the GN ran them on its own lines, the SP&S reacted vigorously in opposition.[4]

The Z-6 design on the NP and SP&S

The American Locomotive Company (Alco) Schenectady Works built the Z-6 in 1936 for the Northern Pacific. It was of the 4-6-6-4 type, commonly called the Challenger, after the name given by the first user, the Union Pacific. There were 21 locomotives, received in October 1936 and May 1937. Later in 1937, six more were built for the SP&S. These differed from those of the NP only in that they were oil-burners.

Intended for fast freight service, they had 69-inch drivers and a very large firebox. The firebox was larger than most so the NP could burn Rosebud semi-bituminous coal. The SP&S oil burners did not need as large a grate area as provided. The engines received most of the appliances expected of a "superpower" locomotive of the era, except that not all of those belonging to the NP had roller bearings, nor did any have cast frames. An important point in the context of the GN usage was that the Z-6 could negotiate 20-degree curves.

Locomotive accessories used included three Nicholson syphons in the firebox. This device was not used much by the GN. The GN motive power department preferred the Security circulator. The GN had previously tried syphons on the O-5 and P-2 classes, but they remained on only one O-5 by 1943. Other devices used were a Worthington Type SA feedwater heater, Hancock type W injectors and Alco type G reverse gear. The principal specifications are shown on the locomotive diagram. The diagram does not indicate the presence of a low water alarm, something all of the GN's other large engines had. However, photos show what looks to be a Barco alarm installed on both engines.[5]

The Z-6 on the GN

The GN purchased SP&S units 903 and 904, which were renumbered to 4000 and 4001. They arrived on the GN in January 1940. Electric train indicator boards were installed on the engines while operating under Great Northern ownership. Little else was done to modify the engines until the major frame replacement project.

The GN did not re-classify the Z-6's into its own class system when they were obtained. This was due to the specialized assignment of the engines. Had they done so, the engines would have become GN class T-1. Since the GN was already well into their dieselization program by that time, the road had no interest in widespread use of this newer steam power. In fact, the GN had evaluated both 2-6-6-4 and 4-6-6-4 designs in the late 1930's and declined to purchase any. Because of this it is interesting to compare the Z-6 with the GN's own large steam power.

As it turned out, heavy wartime traffic required quite a few additional GN locomotives in the equalization service, so it was possible to compare the Z-6 to both the N-3 and R-1 under the same operating conditions.

Despite GN ownership, the SP&S operated the GN Z-6's as if they were their own, using the SP&S terminals and shops. Only at Bend, OR were the Z-6's on GN rails for the entire time they were owned by the GN. Because the SP&S shifted terminal facilities at Spokane between the NP and the GN every ten years, the GN Z's did not touch GN rails at Spokane until May 15, 1942. At that time the SP&S moved from NP's Parkwater to GN's Hillyard terminal. Parkwater had been home to all of the Z-6's, NP, SP&S and GN alike, for two years. Once at Hillyard, the SP&S and GN locos moved in with the GN's N-3, R-1 and R-2 classes.

Operating Environment

Normal operations had one Z-6 running between Hillyard and Wishram, and the other on the Oregon Trunk between Wishram and Bend, Oregon. The SP&S was a very well engineered railroad, but the Oregon Trunk had a ruling grade of 1.5 % (on the portion owned by the UP) and many tight curves, as mentioned earlier. Many commentators considered the Z-6 running over the SP&S line as operating in territory suitable to its design, while the Z-6 running on the curvy and hilly Oregon Trunk was not. However, the Z-6 performed as well on the Oregon Trunk as any locomotive of comparable tractive effort.

It was on the Oregon Trunk that additional large GN locomotives eventually showed up. Charles Wood[6] tells of four tests conducted

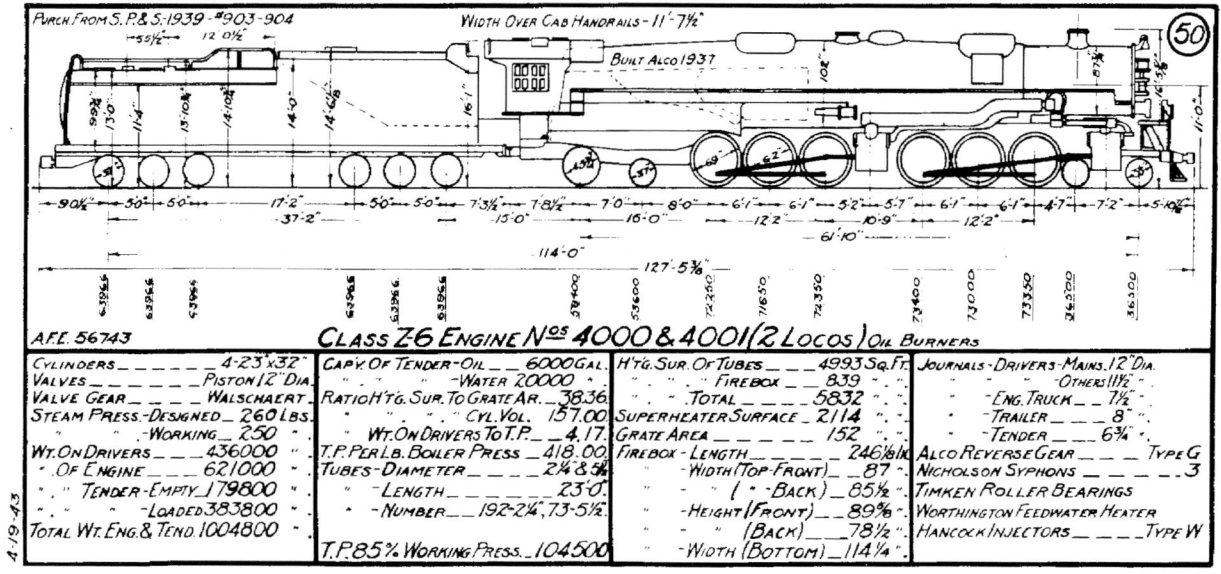

The engineer's side of No. 4000 is shown at Pasco, WA, on April 30, 1945. Built at Schenectady in 1937, it came to the Great Northern in January 1940. Photograph by Albert Farrow.

On the same day as the engineer's side view was taken (April 30, 1945), the photographer also recorded the fireman's side at Pasco. The electric train indicators had already been installed by this time. Photograph by Albert Farrow.

GN No. 4001 had been SP&S No. 904. Shown here at Wishram, WA, on the SP&S in July 1941, it shows the effects of operating in a very dusty environment. Collection of Harold K. Vollrath.

The 4000 is shown leaving Pasco, WA, on April 30, 1945, with a 73-car westbound train. Photograph by Albert Farrow.

by Assistant Superintendent of Motive Power, Mr. J. S. Miller, on the Oregon Trunk. These tests were run in September 1945. They were the first to compare the Z-6 with the R-1. Tonnage ratings and running time were similar, except that the R-1 required more water stops due to a smaller tender, therefore making it slower overall. The R-1 also could have benefited from roller bearings. The first N-3 to run in the equalization service, 2019, was assigned from November 1940 until April, 1941.[7] No other N-3's arrived until after the war, when several were assigned.

Table 1 compares the capabilities of the GN's articulated locomotives in this service.. Table 2 is a performance summary of all of the GN's large simple articulateds, including the R-2. The parameters found in Table 2 are from the shop notes of Mr. Alex Colville, Superintendent of Motive Power, Steam, from 1942 until 1953. Mr. Colville was stationed at Hillyard.

TABLE 1.
MAJOR SPECIFICATIONS OF ARTICULATEDS OPERATED ON THE OREGON TRUNK AND THE SP&S

Class	T.E. (lbs)	Wt. on Dr. (lbs)	Cyls. (in)	B.P. (psi)	Gt. Area (sq ft)	Htg. Surf. (sq ft)	Superhtr. (sq ft)
Z-6	104,266	436,000	23 x 32	250	152	5,832	2,114
N-3	104,236	542,000	22 x 32	265	95	5,805	2,188
R-1a	129,622	555,000	28 x 32	210	108	6,963	1,920
R-1b	133,177	555,000	26 x 32 F 28 x 32 R	225	108	6,963	1,920

TABLE 2.
PERFORMANCE COMPARISON OF LARGEST GREAT NORTHERN SIMPLE ARTICULATEDS

Class	HP	Tonnage Rating vs. % Grade					
		0.2%	0.4%	0.8%	1.0%	1.8%	2.2%
Z-6	4,050	10,500	7,000	4,260	3,530	1,990	1,595
N-3	4,200	11,413	7,856	4,850	4,032	2,332	1,890
R-1a	4,224	13,500	8,710	4,950	4,020	2,200	1,742
R-1b	4,370	14,470	9,310	5,310	4,320	2,370	1,900
R-2	5,193	15,540	10,000	5,720	4,660	2,570	2,060

R-1a: boiler pressure of 210 psi. (2030 to 2033)
R-1b: boiler pressure of 225 psi. (2034 to 2043)
Note: The locomotive horsepower ratings shown above were determined by the Great Northern and were found in the Alex Colville shop notebook.[8] They are likely cylinder horsepower, and differ from horsepower calculations used elsewhere.

The Z-6 class had built up frames throughout. This was their most serious weakness, and by 1945, frame breakage on the engines of all three roads had become such a problem that they agreed to cooperate in replacing the front engine frames with new one-piece cast frames, with integrally cast cylinders. Great Northern Authority for Expenditure (AFE) 72142 was issued December 1, 1945, for the purpose of replacing the front engine frames on both 4000 and 4001.

This order was combined with an order for six for the NP and two for the SP&S. The work on the GN and SP&S engines was done at Vancouver, WA. At the same time, the GN engines had mechanical lubricators and automatic bearing box compensators installed per AFE 72913. The lubricators may have been replacements, since mechanical lubricators show on photographs taken before this date.

The repair of the 4000 was completed during August 1947. The 4001 was sold back to the SP&S while in the shops and the work on it was completed under SP&S ownership. The new frames were a significant improvement and resulted in the engines being able to operate at higher speed where track conditions permitted.

It is unlikely the GN Z-6's were ever given a green boiler jacket. Most evidence found points to them remaining in the SP&S black they came in, because the engines were maintained by the SP&S at Vancouver. Several GN and NP operating men were surveyed, and they agreed that they remained in SP&S colors.[9] This may have included the use of graphite gray on the firebox jacket below the running board, something the SP&S did at times. The only evidence that suggests anything different are photographs of No. 4000, including those used in this chapter. And that could be nothing more than dirt, since the photographer himself did not recall the engine being green.[10] Likewise, cab roofs were not normally painted red by either the SP&S or GN's Hillyard shop.

As the volume of equalization traffic declined after World War II, the 4001 was sold back to the SP&S on July 1, 1946. As the GN increased its ownership of diesels, diesels began to be provided for equalization. The GN actually bought two diesel locomotives specifically for the equalization service, Alco FA-1, FB-1 4-unit sets 440 and 442.[11] Eventually all parties agreed to account for the equalization traffic in a different manner, and the equalization agreement was terminated as of January 1, 1950. As a result, the 4000 was sold back to the SP&S on January 5, along with the GN diesels 440 and 442, and two Mikados. After this, SP&S engines ran on the Oregon Trunk until a conventional power pool was set up in 1958. This permitted GN diesels to run through, often with SP&S units in the same consist.

Notes:

1. C. O. Jenks to H. E. Stevens, October 27, 1937. NP Presidents files, MHS.
2. C. O. Jenks to J. R. W. Davis, regarding revisions to Great Northern Railway Authority for Expenditure (AFE) 56743 giving the economic justification. GN Operating Vice President files, MHS.
3. Norman F. Priebe, "The Z-6 Challenger on the Great Northern," GNRHS Reference Sheet No. 262, June 1998.
4. Robert W. Downing, "The SP&S, the GN and the NP," GNRHS Reference Sheet No. 240, March 1996.
5. More information on the Z-6 can be found in Fry and Schrenk, *Northern Pacific Supersteam Era*, Golden West Books, San Marino, CA, 1985.
6. Charles R. Wood, *Lines West*, first edition, Superior Publishing Co. Seattle, 1967, page 110.
7. Alex Colville, Hillyard Shop Notebook.

8. *Ibid.*
9. Correspondence from Robert Downing to Norman F. Priebe, January 14, 1998. Mr. Downing contacted John Robson, who was GN Master Mechanic at Klamath Falls at the time, Dick Johnson, who was firing GN locomotives into Vancouver, WA, at the time, and Elmer Smoak, who held various NP Mechanical Supervisor positions at South Tacoma, WA, Missoula, MT. and Livingston, MT. Elmer said, "The SP&S treated them as their own even though for financial reasons, they bore the GN name."
10. Albert Farrow, in a telephone conversation with Norman F. Priebe, November 1997. Mr. Farrow had first-hand experience as a fireman on the Northern Pacific Z-6's, as well as having taken the photographs used here.
11. Great Northern Railway AFE 76682.

GN made its first tests of the Steam Motor Car when it was numbered No. 1. Here it is at Minneapolis in 1908, displaying white flags as an extra train. From the Martin Johnson collection.

Chapter 27
Miscellaneous Steam Locomotives

In addition to the locomotives described in previous chapters, Great Northern and one of its subsidiaries, the Somers Lumber Company, operated several locomotives which did not fit into the classification systems. These included a steam motor car, two Shays, two fireless locomotives and two narrow gauge tank engines.

The Steam Motor

Immediately after the beginning of the 20th Century, a rather different locomotive was designed by the Great Northern's chief engineer at the time, Mr. Max Toltz. Mr. Toltz, who was educated as a civil engineer, came to the Great Northern in 1882 from Montreal while it was still the St. Paul, Minneapolis and Manitoba. He began as a draftsman and eventually became chief engineer. After leaving the GN for a year from 1904 to 1905, he returned as chief engineer to take charge of the GN's first Cascade Tunnel electrification. He then resigned to start the Toltz Engineering Company in 1908, which has survived to this day as TKDA.[1]

This machine was a steam motor, quite commonly used as propulsion for street railways before electricity became widely used for this purpose. What made this effort unusual is that steam motors were already on the way out by the time this one was built, the machine was considerably smaller than the average 4-4-0 being used at the time, and that it was built by the Burlington.

A complete rationale for this design has not been found. The engine was constructed at the Burlington's Aurora Shops in 1906, as an 0-4-0T. The Burlington had experience with tank engines because of their suburban traffic requirements, and had built five, their class I-1 0-6-2T, between 1889 and 1893. The Burlington was testing motor cars at the time, and may have solicited the GN's involvement. When the car was finished, the Burlington had two other experimental cars on the property.[2] Great Northern officials stated the motor car was built for "experimental purposes" and "designed with the objective that if successful, cars of this type could be used to replace locomotives on short branch line runs." They continued, "After many trial trips and changes made by the CB&Q Railway, it was found that the car was not successful. It was then taken over by the Great Northern with the hopes that certain changes would make it satisfactory."[3] It can be seen from this that the Great Northern was already looking for ways to solve the "branch line problem."

The car, known at this time as the "Max Toltz Car No. 1," was jointly owned by the CB&Q, NP and GN Railways, with each road having a one third interest. After the GN took over the car in 1908, it paid the other two lines their respective share of its value. Upon receipt, the Great Northern began a reconstruction program. It was sent to Dale Street shops in St. Paul in 1908 for a new larger boiler and conversion from coal to oil. The original boiler had been of vertical design.[4] The NP bought the old boiler.[5]

The motor car was first run out of Minneapolis, likely on a commuter

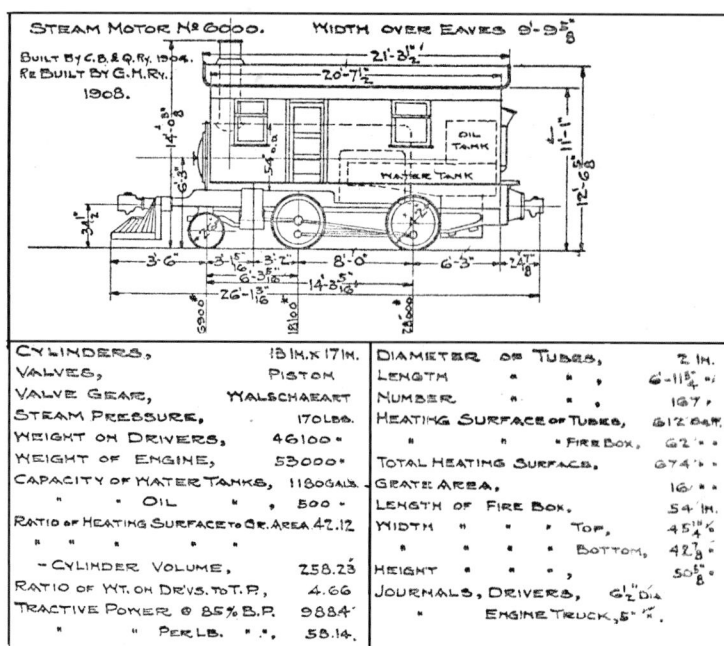

CYLINDERS,	13 IN. X 17 IN.	DIAMETER OF TUBES,	2 IN.
VALVES,	PISTON	LENGTH " " ,	6'-11⅝" ;
VALVE GEAR,	WALSCHAERT	NUMBER " " ,	187 ;
STEAM PRESSURE,	170 LBS.	HEATING SURFACE OF TUBES,	612 SQ.FT.
WEIGHT ON DRIVERS,	46100 #	" " FIRE BOX,	62 " "
WEIGHT OF ENGINE,	53000 #	TOTAL HEATING SURFACE,	674 " "
CAPACITY OF WATER TANKS,	1180 GALS.	GRATE AREA,	16 " "
" OIL " ,	500 "	LENGTH OF FIRE BOX,	54 IN.
RATIO OF HEATING SURFACE TO GR. AREA 42.12		WIDTH " " " TOP,	45⅛" %
" " " " "		" " " " BOTTOM,	42⅞" "
" CYLINDER VOLUME,	258.23	HEIGHT " " " ,	50⅝" "
RATIO OF WT. ON DRVS. TO T.P.,	4.66	JOURNALS, DRIVERS,	6½" DIA
TRACTIVE POWER @ 85% B.P.	9884 #	" ENGINE TRUCK, 5" " .	
" " PER LB. " " ,	58.14		

The amazing thing about this diagram is that we have it at all. It was drawn at the insistence of the ICC Valuation Engineer in 1915, after he found the car stored in a back stall at Delta Shops. This was five years after it had seen its last service.

train to Wayzata, as No. 1. When it was renumbered to No. 6000 is not known. It was then decided at St. Paul to assign the car to the Skagit Line covering trains between Anacortes, Burlington, and Rockport, WA. Before it could attempt this assignment, additional rework was performed at Delta shops. The first thing done was to expand the fuel oil capacity. Along with this a steam pump, to pump oil into the tanks, was added. This work was completed July 12, 1909,[6] with a test run having been made on June 26.[7]

The car, as an 0-4-0, was very rough riding. After a period of operation, it was decided to install a pony truck (engine, or leading

truck). The need for this was already established by November 1909, but it did not get done until May 20, 1910.[8] The AFE had been authorized February 14.[9] A need for a locomotive saddle between boiler and frame to stabilize the boiler was determined while in the shops. The saddle was installed, according to a penciled-in note on a completion report.[10] The car was now a 2-4-0T. After it was put back in service, an electric headlight was installed.[11] The engine was taken off the run on or after September 29, 1910,[12] perhaps as late as November, at which time it had accumulated 4109 miles of service.[13] It was then stored until authorized for scrapping during June 1918.[14]

The Somers Engines

The only two Shays known to have been owned and operated by Great Northern or its subsidiaries belonged to the Somers (MT) Lumber Company, a wholly owned subsidiary acquired by GN in 1906. In its earlier days, Somers operated both a sawmill and a tie-treating plant. Within the lumberyard itself a number of small narrow-gauge electric locomotives were used for switching. However, Great Northern power was used on the line from Kalispell to Somers. In fact, GN engine 215 once went for a swim in Flathead Lake, which was adjacent to the lumber company property. On the morning of October 27, 1908, No. 215 was parked in Kalispell with a full head of steam. The fireman accidentally opened the throttle while he was swinging down from the cab. The locomotive began moving too fast for him to catch it, and it continued unmanned to Somers. There it crashed through a small tool shed and continued off the end of the dock and into the lake.[15]

By 1914, though, the lumber business was good enough that Somers purchased its own locomotive, a two-truck wood-burning standard gauge Shay with three 10-inch by 12-inch cylinders and 29½-inch driving wheels. The locomotive was actually ordered by parent company Great Northern. However, the engine served only five years before being sold to P. L. Howe Lumber Mills of Eureka, MT. After passing through the hands of several other lumber companies, it was eventually placed on

The Motor Car was sent west and operated as No. 6000 out of Anacortes, WA. It was used for about a year before being withdrawn from service. With an oil headlight and no pony truck, the scene can be dated no later than the winter of 1909-1910. Dillinger photograph from the Warren Wing collection of Walter Ainsworth.

display at Columbia Falls, MT.[16]

In the 1920's, the trackage in the tie plant was rebuilt to standard gauge, and in 1926 Somers purchased a small 0-4-0 fireless switcher for use around the tie plant. It was built by the H. K. Porter Company and numbered S-1. The engine weighed 37,000 pounds and operated with steam from the mill's boiler.[17] It had 15-inch by 14-inch cylinders and 27-inch drivers.[18] The engine survived the Burlington Northern merger, and was used until the tie plant closed in July 1986.[19] After retirement, the engine was moved to the Miracle of America Museum in Polson, MT, where it is still on display.[20]

A second fireless 0-4-0, the S-2, was built by Porter for Somers in 1929. It had the same size cylinders and drivers as the S-1.[21] It too lasted until the tie plant closure, but was then moved to the Flathead County Museum in Kalispell, MT. However, it was returned to Somers on March 28, 2008, to be put on display there.[22]

The final new locomotive acquisition by the Somers Lumber Company was a Shay of the "Pacific Coast" type, given the number 2. It had three 13-inch by 15-inch cylinders with 6-inch piston valves and shifting link valve gear. It had 36-inch driving wheels, weighed 181,000 pounds and operated with a boiler pressure of 200 psi. The

Fireless S-1 is working the tie treatment retort at the tie plant. Northwest Montana Historical Society, Kalispell Museum, courtesy of Tiebucker's Pub, Bruce Ruby, Tom Sliter and John Coy.

The S-2 is shown in a late view, working at the Somers tie plant in July 1979. Photograph by Jack Porzig.

Somers Shay No. 1 in service. Date and location are unknown. Collection of Kenneth R. Middleton.

This builders photo shows Somers No. 2 as a typical Pacific Coast Shay constructed by Lima. While lettered for Somers, it does not yet have its number. Reproduced with permission of the Allen County Historical Society, Lima, Ohio.

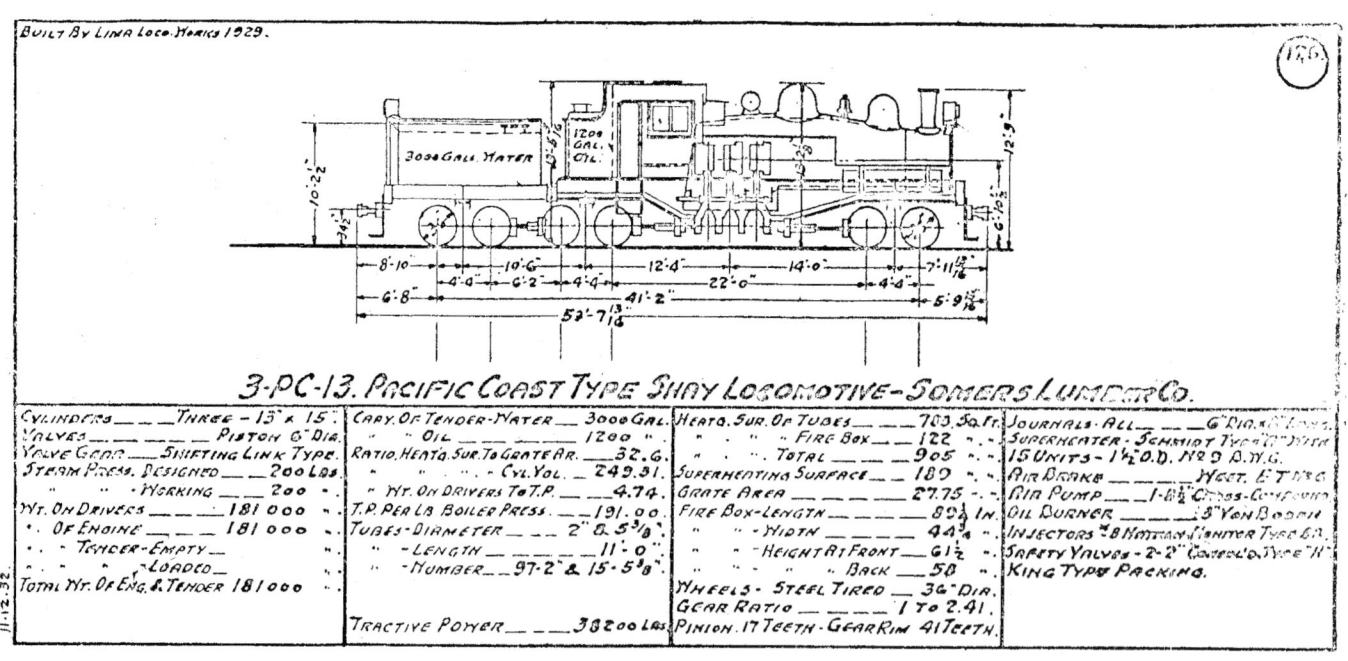

BUILT BY LIMA LOCO. WORKS 1929.

3-PC-13. PACIFIC COAST TYPE SHAY LOCOMOTIVE - SOMERS LUMBER CO.

CYLINDERS — THREE - 13" x 15".	CAP'Y. OF TENDER-WATER — 3000 GAL.	HEAT'G. SUR. OF TUBES — 783 SQ.FT.	JOURNALS-ALL — 6" DIA.
VALVES — PISTON 6" DIA.	" OIL — 1200 "	" " FIRE BOX — 122 " "	SUPERHEATER - SCHMIDT TYPE "D" WITH
VALVE GEAR — SHIFTING LINK TYPE.	RATIO, HEAT'G. SUR. TO GRATE AR. — 32.6.	" " TOTAL — 905 " "	15 UNITS - 1½" O.D. N° 9 B.W.G.
STEAM PRESS. DESIGNED — 200 LBS.	" " CYL. VOL. — 249.51.	SUPERHEATING SURFACE — 189 " "	AIR BRAKE — WEST. E.T. N° 6
" WORKING — 200 "	" WT. ON DRIVERS TO T.P. — 4.74.	GRATE AREA — 27.75 " "	AIR PUMP — 1-8½" CROSS-COMPOUND
WT. ON DRIVERS — 181000 "	T.P. PER LB. BOILER PRESS. — 191.00.	FIRE BOX-LENGTH — 80¾ IN.	OIL BURNER — 5" VON BOGGIE
" OF ENGINE — 181000 "	TUBES-DIAMETER — 2" & 5⅜".	" " WIDTH — 44¾ "	INJECTORS-B NATHAN'L IGNITOR TYPE 60.
" TENDER-EMPTY —	" -LENGTH — 11'-0"	" " HEIGHT AT FRONT — 61½ "	SAFETY VALVES- 2-2" CONTROL'D TYPE "H"
" " -LOADED —	" -NUMBER — 97-2" & 15-5⅜".	" " " BACK — 58 "	KING TYPE PACKING.
TOTAL WT. OF ENG. & TENDER 181000 "		WHEELS- STEEL TIRED — 36" DIA.	
		GEAR RATIO — 1 TO 2.41.	
	TRACTIVE POWER — 38200 LBS.	PINION. 17 TEETH - GEAR RIM 41 TEETH.	

"Pacific Coast Shay" was a particular Lima design. They were large three-truck machines with all-weather cabs. The first was built in October 1927. There were a total of 24 built. Somers bought theirs in November, 1929.

The first model of this Shay of 'radical' new design, called the Pacific Coast Shay, was completed at Lima in October of 1927 (C/N 3312) and shipped immediately to the Hofius Steel & Equipment Company, of Seattle, Washington, who were the Lima agents for the Pacific Northwest. Hofius got this new model Shay to Tacoma just in time for the Pacific Logging Congress held there in November of that year.

The Pacific Coast Shay…had built into it every desirable improvement that Lima engineers could bring together. It featured the girder frame, now with a single large opening for inspecting the staybolts, cast steel trucks, newly designed steam and exhaust manifolds, and improved cylinder supports which were attached to the girder frame and not the boiler….

The Pacific Coast Shay created an immediate sensation at the 1927 logging congress – in fact, Bloedel, Steward & Welch, Ltd., an important Canadian logging firm, were so taken by the new Shay that a company representative purchased the exhibit model right off the floor, and it was given road number 11.[23]

Somers No. 2 was used until 1942, when it was sold to the J. Neils Lumber Company of Klickitat, WA. The engine was eventually sent to the "Camp 6" Logging Museum in Point Defiance Park, Tacoma, WA., where it still may be found.[24]

Somers also operated at least four former GN engines. The first two, GN F-1 No. 525 and GN D-2 No. 342, were obtained in 1924 and 1925, respectively. The Somers numbers for these engines are unknown. The latter two, Somers No. S4 and No. S5 were the former GN A-7 No. 60(2), and GN F-8 No. 1244. The 60 was transferred to Somers in 1930, and the 1244 was transferred in 1935. See chapter 5 for a photo of the S4.

Other engines, especially those of narrow gauge, are known to have been used by Somers but have left a broken trail regarding their history. They are therefore omitted.

6715 H.K. Porter Co.[25]	
Builders Number	4175
Year Built	1908
Weight	14.5 tons
Driver Diameter	27 inches
Cylinders	9 x 14 inches
Gauge	3 feet

6927 Davenport Locomotive Works	
Builders Number	450
Year Built	unknown
Weight	14 tons
Driver Diameter	unknown
Cylinders	9 x 14 inches
Gauge	3 feet

The earliest view found of the engines at Hillyard, is this of the Davenport, from October 1931. Photograph by Ron Nixon from the collection of N. F. Priebe.

The engineer's side of 6927 was most often photographed. This view is dated August 10, 1932. Collection of William Bissinger.

Here the engine number is chalked on the cab side of the Porter. This view is also dated August 10, 1932. Collection of William Bissinger.

This later view of the 6715 on October 25, 1937, has its builders number, 4175, stenciled on the cab. The view confirms it lost its headlight, but why the number reverted to the builder's number is a mystery. Harold Buckley collection.

The Narrow Gauge Tank Engines

There were two tank-type narrow gauge locomotives in GN service. Called "dinkeys" by the GN, they were classified as work equipment rather than as locomotives. The engines were the 6715 and the 6927. The 6715 was a Porter with a wooden cab. The 6927 was a Davenport. A brief summary of the engines follows since there are no diagrams for them.

Both engines were first owned by A. Guthrie & Company, the prime contractor for the new Cascade Tunnel. The engines came from the tunnel site, where they had been used for tunnel construction. When ownership was transferred to the Great Northern is not known. The 6715 was sent to the Warland gravel washing plant in December 1929.[26] The Warland pit was located 95 miles west of Whitefish, MT, between Volcour and Yarnell, in Lincoln County. This area is now under Lake Koocanusa. The 6927 was sent to the ballast quarry at Walton, (Essex), MT, in January 1930.[27] The headlight of the 6715 was removed in December 1932 for use on ditcher X1789.[28] According to the records, the locomotive was in service at Warland at the time. The 6927 also

lost its headlight, according to photographs, but records for this have not been found. By the early 1930's, both were retired and set up on old telegraph pole crossarms used as rails, somewhere in the Hillyard facility. (The photograph dates and the dates found in the records do not agree. The photographs suggest the engines were completely retired by October 1931 and never again moved, once placed at Hillyard.) It is very likely they were not moved after December 1932, and sat at Hillyard for several more years until scrapped. The scrapping date is not known, but is considered to be between 1937 and 1940.

All of the tank engine scenes were taken at Hillyard, WA.

Leased Locomotives

During World War II the Great Northern used locomotives from other roads to help overcome locomotive shortages. At least one Southern Pacific locomotive was used on the Klamath Division for a time, and at least two DM&IR Class M3 locomotives were used during the winter of 1943. Other cases were likely.

DM&IR class M3 locomotives 223 and 222 are shown arriving at Devils Lake, ND, for work on the GN during the winter of 1943. The date is December 28, 1942. Their ultimate destination is believed to be the Williston-Minot line. Specifications for the DM&IR class M3 are given in Chapter 19. Photograph by Don Vang.

Notes:

1. Extracted from a biography on the web page of the Special Library, University of Minnesota. http://special.lib.umn.edu/findaid/html/mss/nwaa0107.html
2. Joseph R. Douda. Personal communication to Kenneth R. Middleton, February 18, 2008, CB&Q Annual Report of June 30, 1904, and clippings from Aurora, IL, newspapers, September 1904 through January 1905.
3. Great Northern Railway Authority for Expenditure (AFE) 6935.
4. Great Northern Railway Valuation Department Correspondence File No.7, New boilers for Locomotives.
5. Great Northern Railway AFE 6935, *op. cit.*
6. Great Northern Railway AFE 16196, July 2, 1909.
7. J. G. Drew. Memo to J. M. Gruber, July 7, 1909. GN Vice President, Operating, File 42-11. Minnesota Historical Society Box 132.B.16.10 F.
8. R. D. Hawkins. Memo to G. H. Emerson, May 13, 1910. GN Vice President, Operating, File 42-11.Minnesota Historical Society, Box 132. B.16.10 F
9. Great Northern Railway AFE 16980, February 14, 1910.
10. Reference 4, *op. cit.*
11. Great Northern Railway AFE 17439 (old series), as referenced in memos from P.W. Harvie, Delta Shop Superintendent, to W. R Wood, Valuation Engineering, found in Reference 4.
12. Great Northern Railway Historical Engine Record, Volume 5.
13. Reference 4, *op. cit.*

14. Reference 4, *op. cit.*
15. Henry Elwood (Ed.). *Somers, Montana, The Company Town*. Thomas Printing, Inc., Kalispell, MT, 1976.
16. Michael Koch. *The Shay Locomotive, Titan of the Timber*, World Press, Denver, CO, 1971.
17. Jerrold F. Hilton. "Somers Lumber Company," *Pacific News*, May 1971.
18. Paul Allen Copeland. Personal Communication to Robert C. Post, January 14, 1981.
19. Henry Elwood. *Somers, Montana*, Thomas Printing, Inc., Kalispell, MT, 1990.
20. Ty Williams. Personal Communication to Kenneth R. Middleton, April 24, 2008.
21. Paul Allen Copeland, *op. cit.*
22. Michael Richeson. Kalispell, MT, *Daily Interlake*, March 29, 2008.
23. Michael Koch, *op. cit.*
24. *Ibid.*
25. Lawrence Hargis (Porter historian). Personal communication to Norman F. Priebe, October 17, 2008.
26. Great Northern Railway AFE 41920, approved January 20, 1930.
27. Great Northern Railway AFE 41812, approved January 10, 1930.
28. Great Northern Railway AFE's 46756 and 46757, approved March 4, 1933.

Unlike later multi-unit single-locomotive gas turbines, GE steam turbines No. 1 and 2 were identical independent units. They tested on the GN between Hillyard and Wenatchee in 1943. Here they ascend Ft. Wright Hill westbound on April 6th. Photograph by R. E. Johnson.

Chapter 28

Experimental and Proposed Locomotive Designs on the Great Northern

While the Great Northern Railway operated a fleet of well-maintained steam locomotives, the road could hardly be considered a major innovator in steam locomotive design. The real forte of GN's Motive Power Department was the design of new motive power using parts scavenged from older members of the roster. This led to Class H-5, H-6 and H-7 4-6-2's, Class Q-2 2-10-2's. and Class O-5, O-6 and O-7 2-8-2's.

Before any of these were built, Baldwin worked with the GN on a proposal for a large new Pacific, larger than the H-4. A number of drawings were exchanged. The only one with a date came from the GN and was dated February 17, 1913. This drawing and Baldwin No. 23210 showed 28 by 28-inch cylinders, a boiler pressure of 200 psi, 73-inch diameter drivers, 176,000 pounds on drivers, 278,000 pounds total engine weight, a total heating surface of 4,330 square feet, a grate area of 66.5 square feet and a superheater of 1,050 square feet. Another undated Baldwin concept had run the grate area up to 78 square feet.[1] The GN did not order or build any Pacifics this large. Instead, in 1914 they ordered 25 copies of the H-4 from Lima. The later H-class rebuilds that followed were only slightly heavier than the H-4 class.

Among the earliest examples of an experimental locomotive (and

one of the few actually built) was GN's first No. 2000, a 2-6-8-0 rebuilt from F-8 consolidation No. 1254. See Chapter 18 for more information on this engine.

The next evidence of experimental locomotive design on the Great Northern surfaces as part of a diagram book dating from about 1915. In this diagram set are two tractor-trailer affairs, similar to those used on the Southern Railway. One, called a 2-6-2+0-6-2 is based on two J-Class 2-6-2's. The other is based on an O-1 2-8-2 with an F-1 2-8-0 running gear beneath the tender. There have been reports of yet a third such diagram based on an M-1 2-6-8-0 with a six-coupled engine beneath the tender (a 2-6-8-0+0-6-2).

The first design, based upon two Prairie locomotives, was actually approved by the president for construction. The estimated cost of completion was $8,895.43.[2] The number 1998 was assigned to the engine,[3] and it was to be placed in Class Q-1.[4] The castings required for the construction were ordered, and as of January 1917 were all on hand except for one cylinder head casting, which was expected late in the month.[5] However, by June 1917 it still had not arrived,[6] but time for No. 1998 was running out. J. M. Gruber, a Vice-President at the time, wrote to George Emerson, General Manager, "I suppose we will never now want to couple up two 'J's' and make a mallet, as with the large number of 'Os' now in service and on order, we are getting an engine that will be much better than a mallet 'J' and the 'J's' can be used on lighter density territories or the low grade lines to good advantage."[7] On July 24, 1917, Mr. Gruber asked that the AFE be cancelled.[8]

Approximately contemporary with the other tractor-trailer designs is a Baldwin drawing for a 2-6-6-6-2, a hypothetical rebuild from GN's Class L-1 2-6-6-2's. GN estimated the tractive effort of this early monster at 100,000 pounds and presumed that such a rebuild would cost approximately $15,000.[9]

In 1926 the Baldwin Locomotive Company completed No. 60000, a 4-10-2 three-cylinder compound with a high-pressure boiler operating at 350 psi. After testing on the Pennsylvania Railroad's Altoona test plant, it was sent on a barnstorming trip around the United States. Early in 1928 it tested on the Great Northern. In January it made nine measured runs while crossing the country from Delta (Everett) to Minot, and early in February it made four measured runs running between Minneapolis and Superior.[10] While it showed some improved

performance, it is sufficient to say that no one bought this locomotive. Today it is on display at the Franklin Museum in Philadelphia.

Another interesting example of locomotive development on the GN can be seen in the rebuilding of the Class M 2-6-8-0's. While these eventually (beginning in 1929) became Class O-7 Mikados, considerable energy was expended before arriving at this end. Among the earliest (1925) candidates for rebuild from the 2-6-8-0's was a "Class P-3" 4-8-2 with 28-inch by 28-inch cylinders.[11] By 1926, two Mikado designs had been developed, as well as a Santa Fe (Drawing UF-917) and a Decapod (Drawing UF-948).[12] The Mikado did, however, win out.

The 1930's brought a flourish of steam locomotive development work to the Great Northern. Some of this, no doubt, was due to pressure from locomotive manufacturers seeking orders during a depression economy. Some of the more interesting designs emerged from this period. A 2-8-4 design of 1931 is described in Chapter 22. In July of 1930, the Motive Power Department prepared drawings (Drawing UF-1505) of

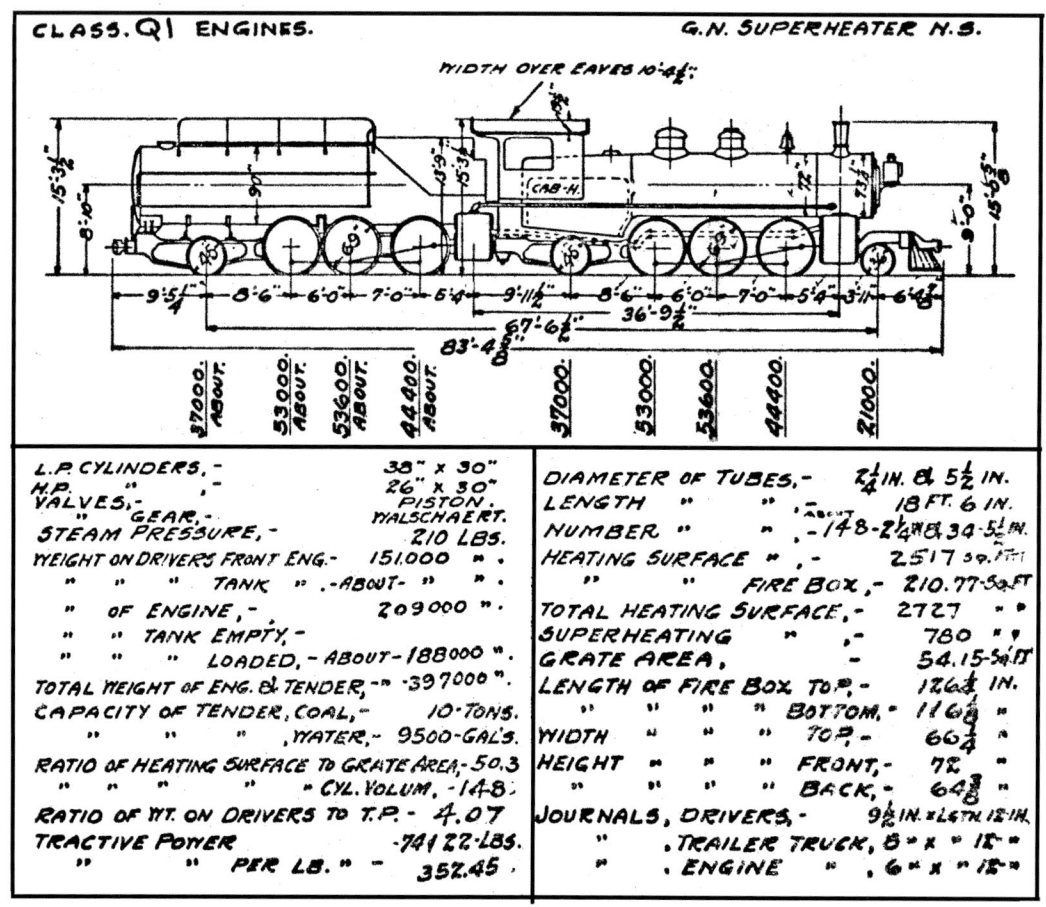

The first "Q-1" on the GN was intended to be this composite Mallet numbered 1998. Reproduced from the 1915 Diagram Book.

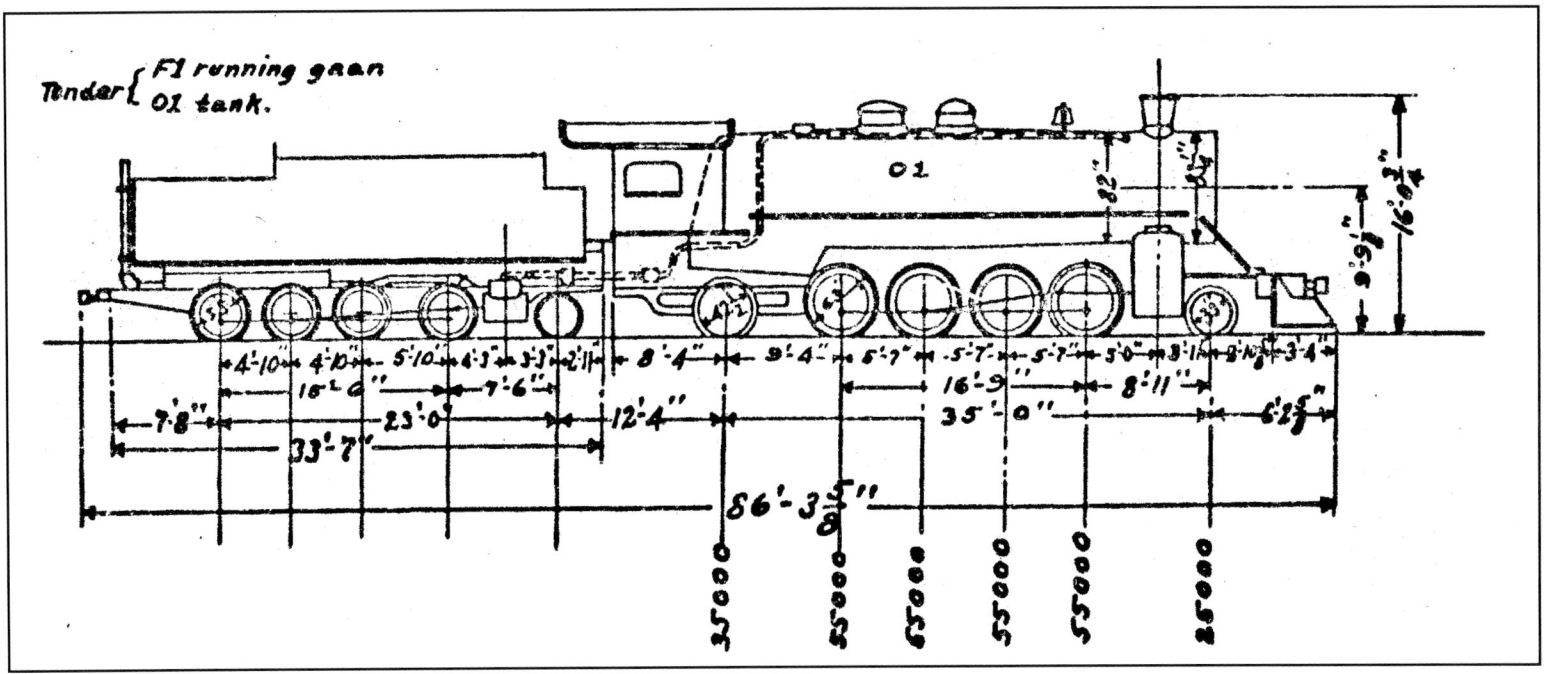

Cylinders   28"x 32"   &   23½"x26.7
Steam pressure   180#
Weight on drivers, Front Eng.   220,000#
    "   Total   ,   " " .   280,000#
    " of Tender Loaded .   235,000# App.
    "   "   " with ⅓ Load,   161,000# App.
Wgt. on Tender Drivers, Full Load, 206,000# App.
  "   "   "   , ⅓ Load,   140,000# App.
Ratio Heating Surf. to Grate Area, 60.8
  "   "   "   " Cyl. Vol. (4 Cyls.) 138.5
  " Wt. on Drivers to Tr. Power (Mikado) 3.61
  " Max. Wt. on Dr. " " " (Tender) 5.15
  " Wt. on Dr. to T.P. with ⅓ load (Tender) 3.50
Tractive Power @ 85% B.P.   60,900.#
    "   "   "   "   Tender 40,000.#
    "   "   "   "   Total 100,900.#
Ten   r. Coal Cap. 13 Tons, Water Cap. 10,000 gal.

The second tractor-trailer Mallet never received a class designation. It was to be a combination of O-1 and F-1 locomotives, a 2-8-2+2-8-0 type.

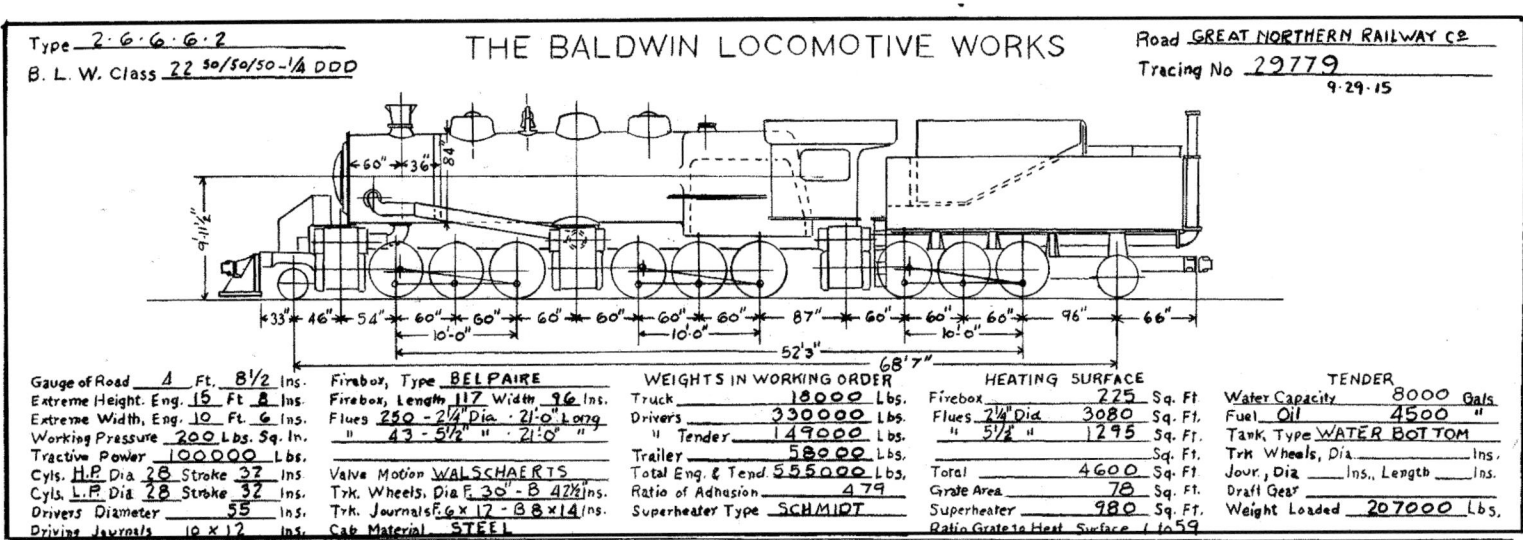

Baldwin proposed this tractor-trailer rebuild of a Class L-1 2-6-6-2 to GN in 1915.

what would have been a new wheel arrangement on the Great Northern – the 2-6-6-4. This locomotive had a typical GN Belpaire firebox, front-mounted air pumps and a Vanderbilt tender. It was to be equipped with 69-inch drivers and four 25-inch by 32-inch cylinders. No action was taken toward building such a locomotive. In 1934, Baldwin built the first of seven similar engines for the Pittsburgh & West Virginia that looked as if they had been built for the GN. However the specifications differed somewhat from those proposed by the GN.[13]

Other Company correspondence[14] indicates that industrial designer Otto Kuhler approached the Great Northern about streamlining a locomotive and an observation car. Unfortunately, drawings have not been found. The GN felt that the idea was impractical,[15] and Mr. Kuhler was apparently turned down. Later, the Milwaukee Road used Kuhler's talents in streamlining their famed Atlantics and beaver-tailed observation cars.

While 1930 saw the last major order from an outside manufacturer for steam motive power, 1934 saw another flurry of activity in GN's drafting department. One of the locomotives considered was a rebuild of a Class Q-1 2-10-2 into a 4-8-2 with 69-inch drivers (Drawing UF-1560). GN officers also considered converting R-1 2-8-8-2's into coal-burning 2-8-8-4's (Drawing UF-1559), but this was not deemed a satisfactory conversion.[16] Baldwin also contributed to the 1934 activity by designing a 2-8-8-4 (No. 71647) with 69-inch drivers for use between Williston and Minot, North Dakota.[17] GN management, however, felt that they would be better off to transfer Class R-2 2-8-8-2's to this area and purchase larger locomotives for the Kalispell Division.[18] The last major steam locomotive design activity on the Great Northern before the design and construction of the N-3 class occurred in 1937. By this time, the Great Northern's interests were fairly directed toward articulated locomotives. Two different

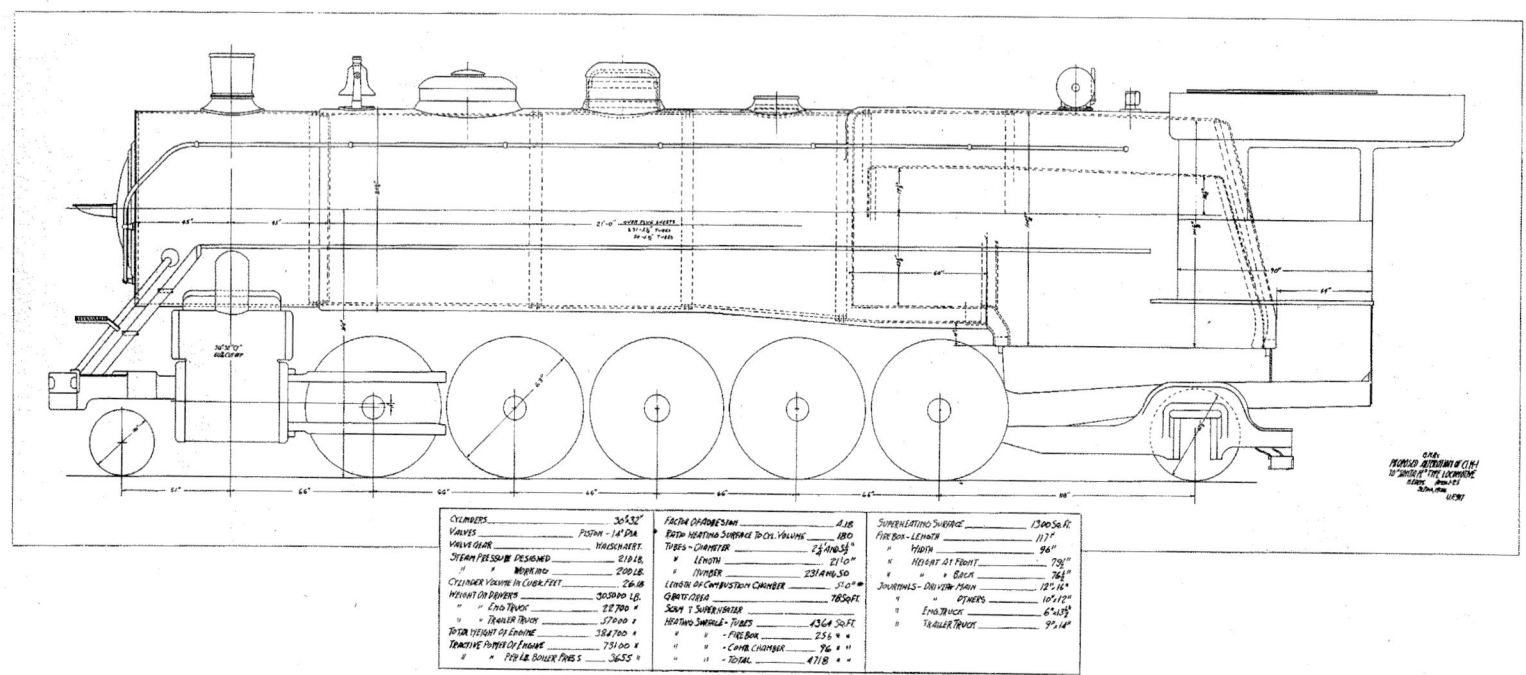

Drawing UF-917 shows a 2-10-2 design that was considered as a possible rebuild from a 2-6-8-0.

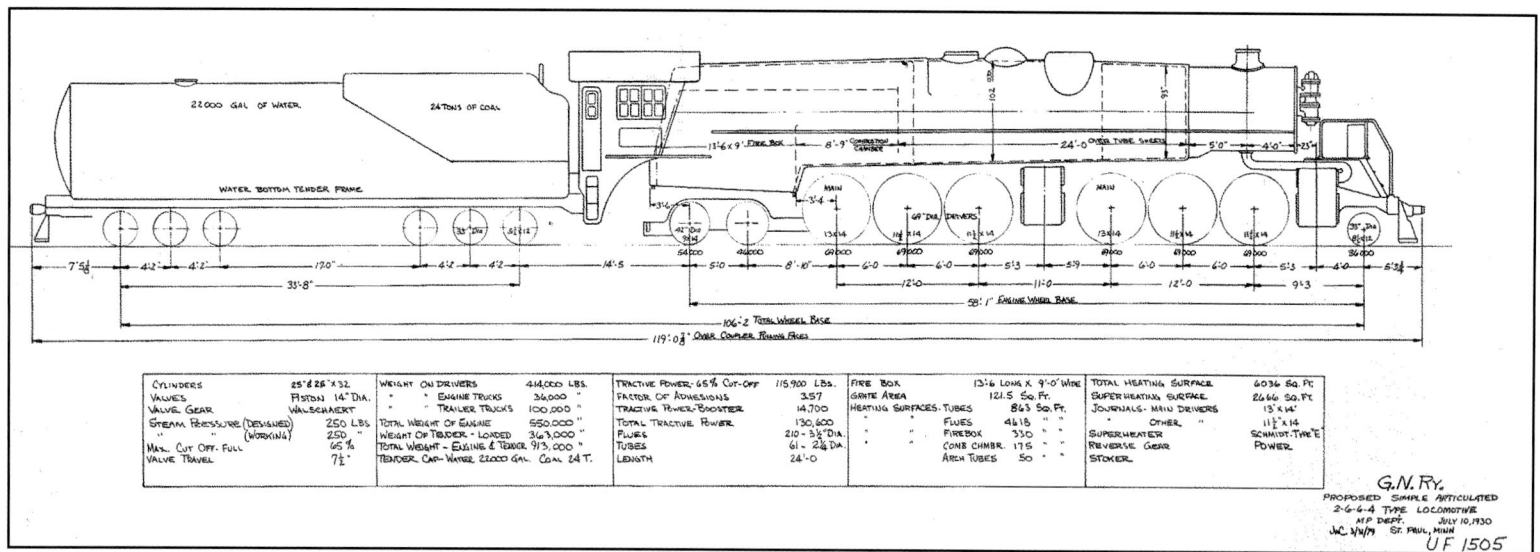

GN Drawing UF-1505 shows a proposed 2-6-6-4 that had many typical GN features, including a Vanderbilt tender, vestibule cab, Belpaire firebox and air pumps mounted on the smokebox front.

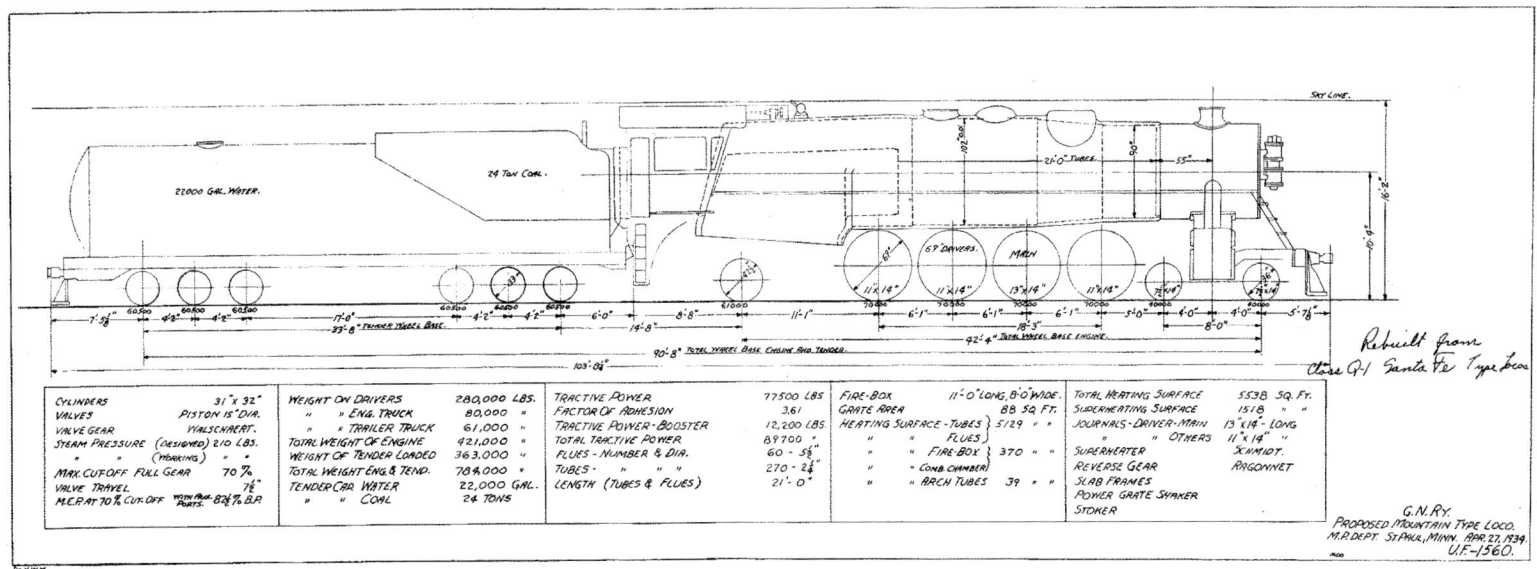

Drawing UF-1560 shows a 4-8-2 that GN considered rebuilding from a Q-1 2-10-2.

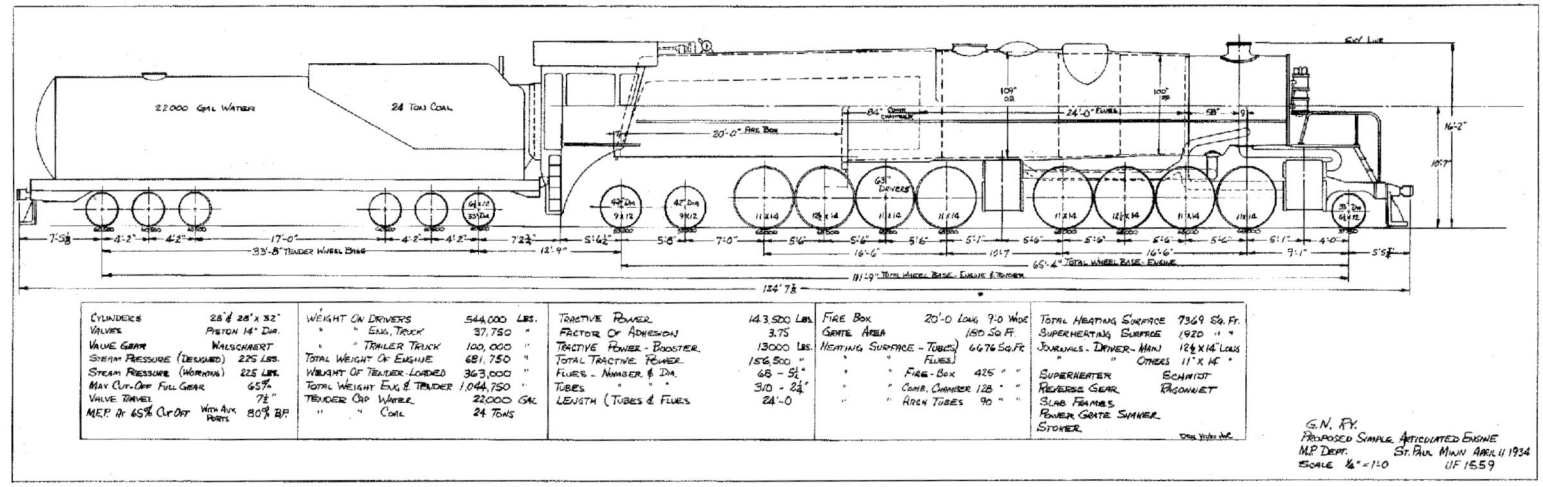

It was proposed to convert R-1 2-8-8-2's into this coal-burning 2-8-8-4, but this was not deemed satisfactory by GN management.

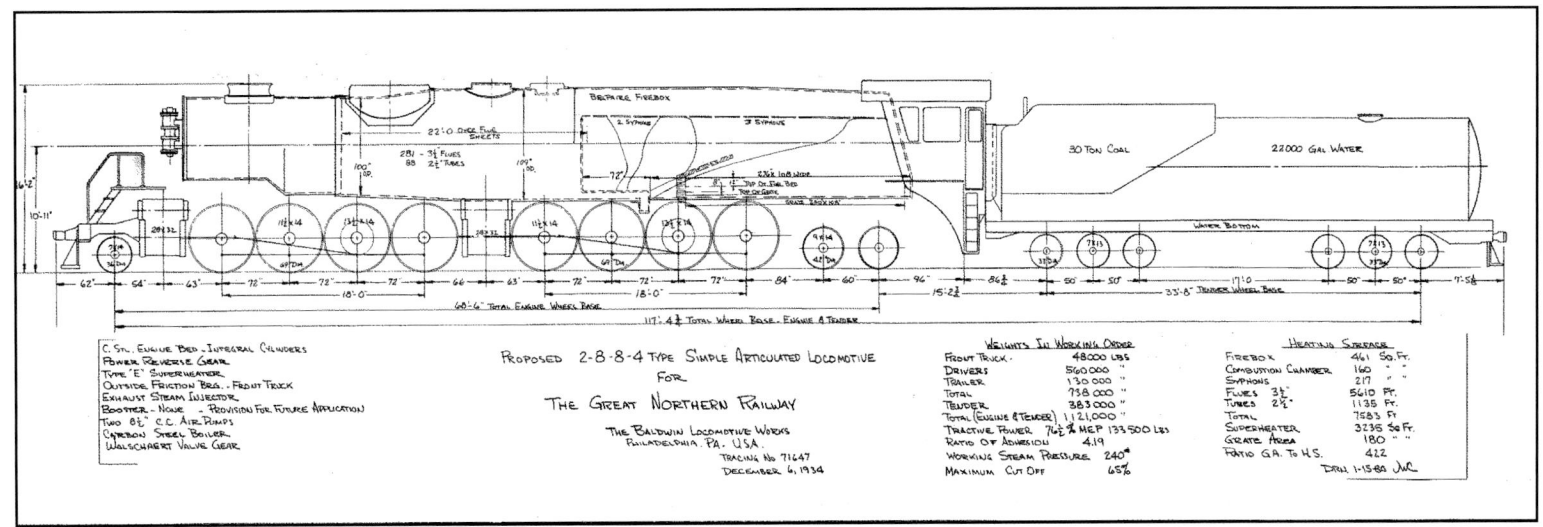

Baldwin proposed this 2-8-8-4 design with 69-inch drivers to GN in 1934.

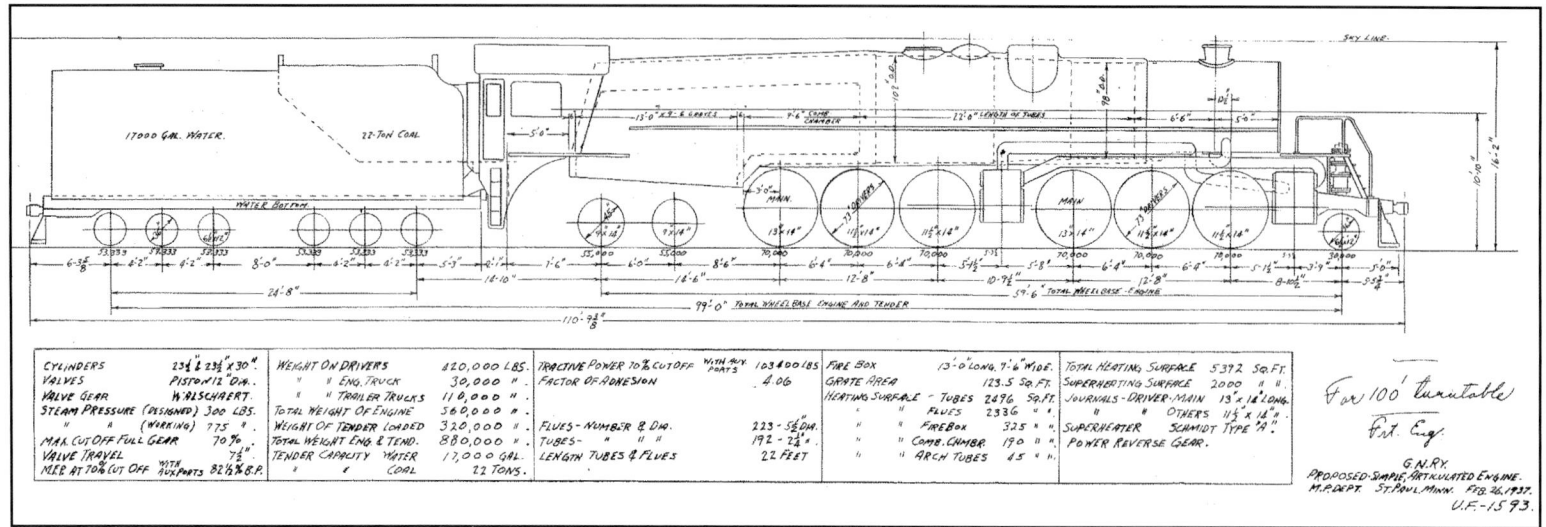

Great Northern designed this 2-6-6-4 with 73-inch drivers to fit on a 100-foot turntable.

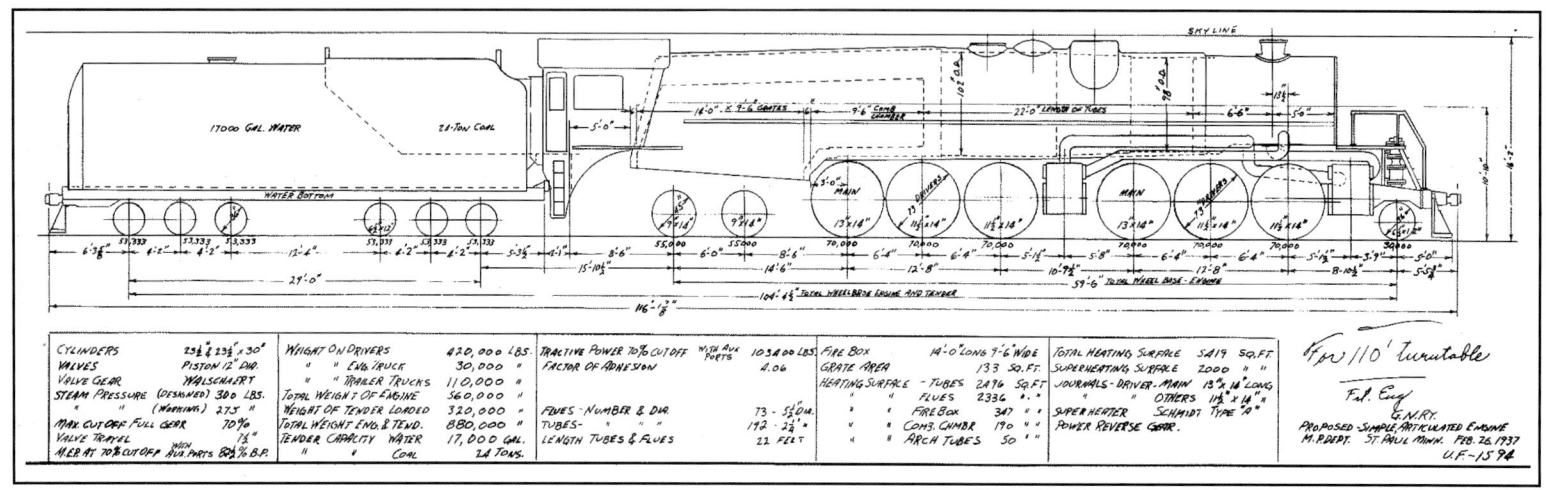

This 2-6-6-4 with 73-inch drivers is very similar to that shown in Drawing UF-1593 above, but would have required a 110-foot turntable.

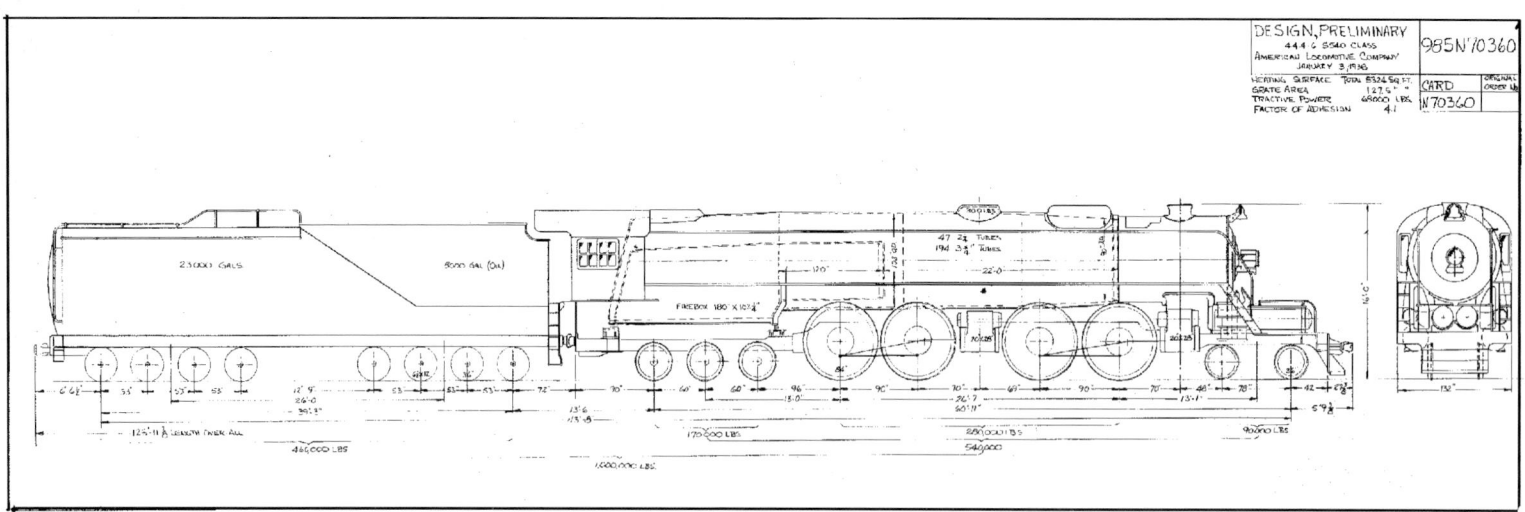

Alco submitted this design of a 4-4-4-6 which seems to have an appearance somewhat reminiscent of the Union Pacific's Challengers.

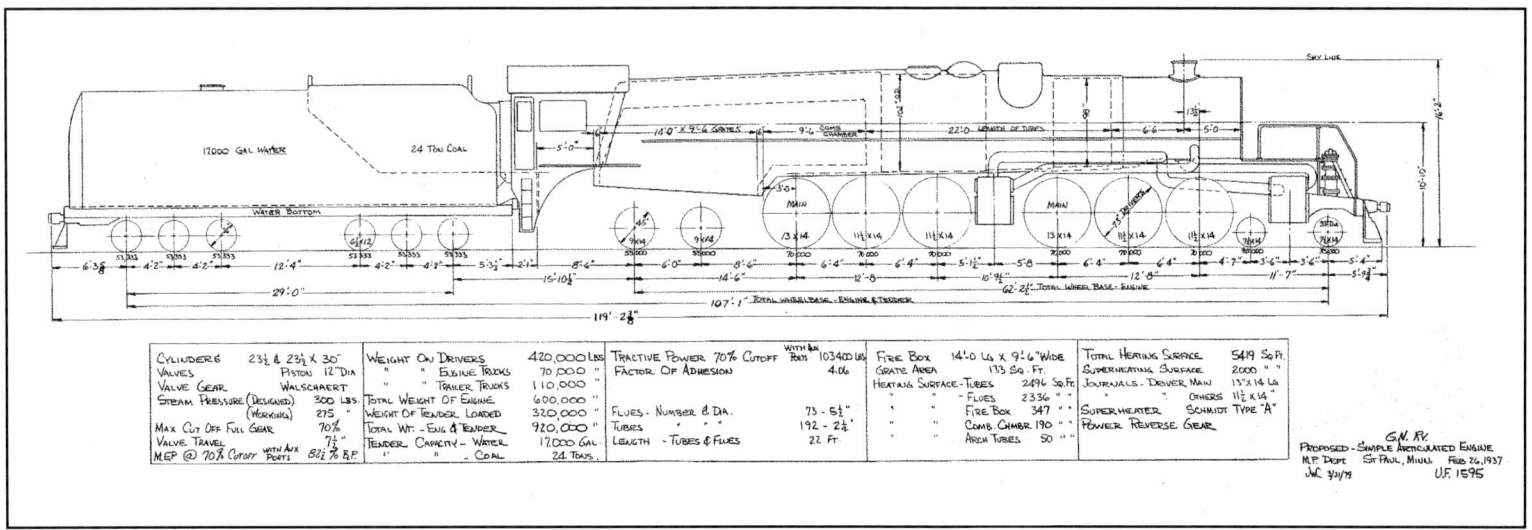

17000 GAL WATER
24 TON COAL
WATER BOTTOM
MAIN
MAIN
107'-1" TOTAL WHEELBASE - ENGINE & TENDER
62'-2½" TOTAL WHEEL BASE - ENGINE
119'-2⅜"
CYLINDERS 23½ & 23½ X 30"
VALVES PISTON 12" DIA
VALVE GEAR WALSCHAERT
STEAM PRESSURE (DESIGNED) 300 LBS.
(WORKING) 275 "
MAX CUT OFF FULL GEAR 70%
VALVE TRAVEL 7½"
M.E.P. @ 70% CUTOFF WITH AUX PORTS 82½ % B.P.
WEIGHT ON DRIVERS 420,000 LBS
" " ENGINE TRUCKS 70,000 "
" " TRAILER TRUCKS 110,000 "
TOTAL WEIGHT OF ENGINE 600,000 "
WEIGHT OF TENDER LOADED 320,000 "
TOTAL WT. - ENG & TENDER 920,000 "
TENDER CAPACITY - WATER 17,000 GAL.
" " - COAL 24 TONS.
TRACTIVE POWER 70% CUTOFF WITH AUX PORTS 103400 LBS
FACTOR OF ADHESION 4.06
FLUES - NUMBER & DIA. 73 - 5½"
TUBES " " 192 - 2¼"
LENGTH - TUBES & FLUES 22 FT.
FIRE BOX 14'-0 LG X 9'-6" WIDE
GRATE AREA 133 SQ. FT.
HEATING SURFACE - TUBES 2496 SQ. FT.
" " - FLUES 2336 " "
" " FIRE BOX 347 " "
" " COMB. CHMBR 190 " "
" " ARCH TUBES 50 " "
TOTAL HEATING SURFACE 5419 SQ. FT.
SUPERHEATING SURFACE 2000 " "
JOURNALS - DRIVER MAIN 13" X 14 LG
" " OTHERS 11½ X 14 "
SUPERHEATER SCHMIDT TYPE "A"
POWER REVERSE GEAR
G.N. RY.
PROPOSED - SIMPLE ARTICULATED ENGINE
M.P. DEPT ST PAUL, MINN. FEB 26, 1937
JWC 3/31/79 U.F. 1595

This 4-6-6-4 design with 73-inch drivers is somewhat surprising in that it has only a 17,000 gallon tender.

2

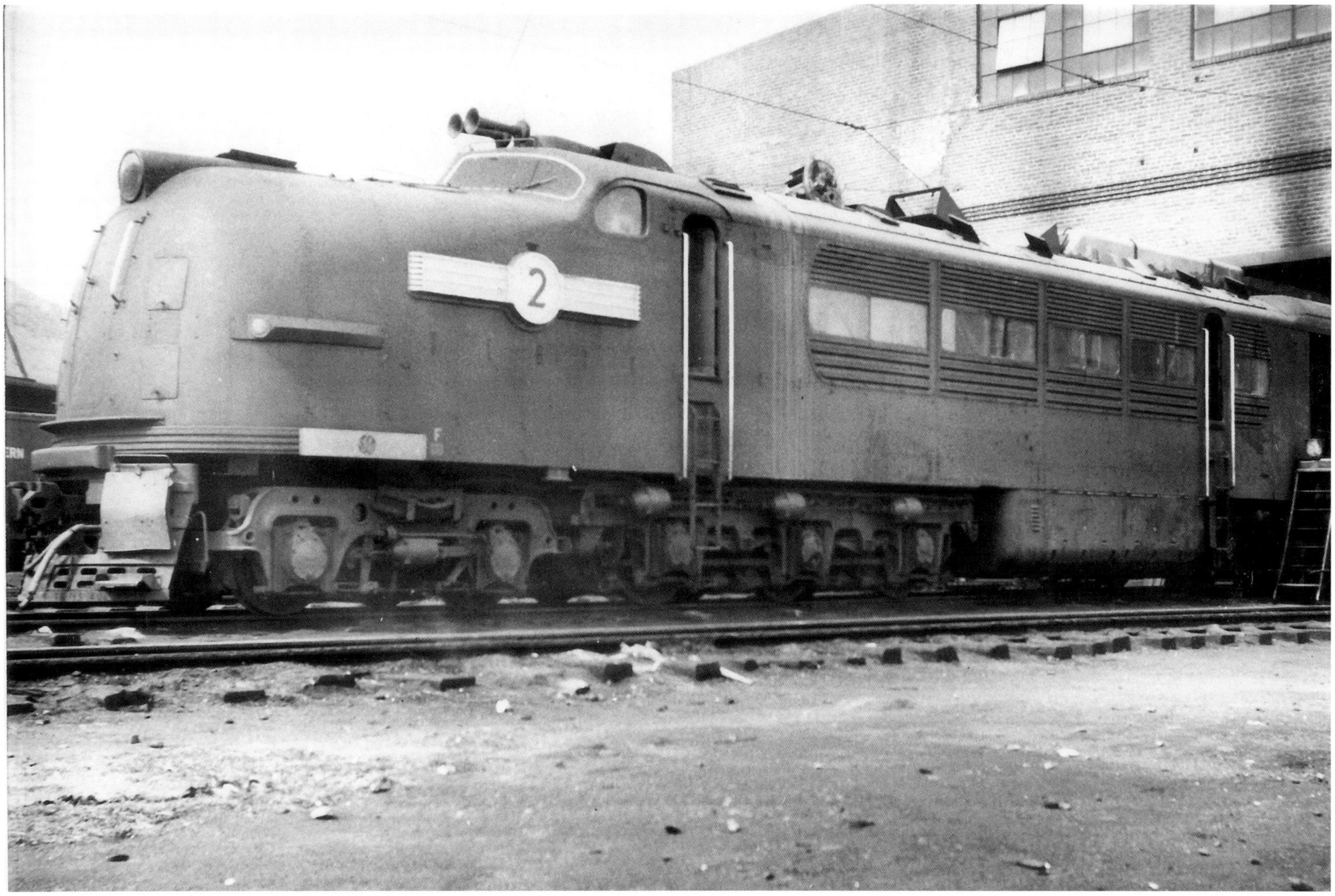

GE steam turbine No. 2 is in the electric shop at Wenatchee in April 1943, undoubtedly receiving attention to equipment problems. Photograph by R. E. Johnson.

2-6-6-4's (Drawings UF-1593 and UF-1594) for use with different length turntables were designed. Also, a 73-inch drivered 2-8-8-4 was drawn up.

The American Locomotive Company, in trying to drum up business, submitted drawings for a 4-4-4-6 (Drawing 985N70360). The Railway prepared a drawing for a 4-6-6-4 challenger (Drawing UF-1595). The depression economy prevailed, however, and resulted in a policy of "making do," so no new locomotives were ordered. Only two short years later, General Motors' demonstrator No. 103 began its historic tour, and Great Northern chose to make its new locomotive acquisitions diesel-powered.

In April 1943, the GN tested the General Electric steam turbine pair No. 1 and 2. Each unit was rated at 2500 horsepower. If they were found to be satisfactory, the intent was to use them to alleviate the serious locomotive shortage then being experienced by the GN. These units had been extensively tested by the Union Pacific in 1939 and rejected. They made 14 round trips on the GN between Hillyard (Spokane) and Appleyard (Wenatchee) during the testing period.[19] Testing ended when the units suffered electrical failure, and they were returned to GE.[20] There may have been mechanical problems as well.[21]

Notes:

1. Drawings at GNRHS Jackson Street, from BNSF, GN Vice President Operating, File 40 part 7, (F2).
2. Great Northern Railway Authority for Expenditure (AFE) 1661, Approved March 9, 1916.
3. J. H. Boyd. Memo to A. C. Deverell, September 12, 1916 (AFE 1661).
4. J. C. Heron. Memo to A. C. Deverell, May 25, 1917 (AFE 1661).
5. F. A. Bushnell. Memo to A. C. Deverell, January 19, 1917 (AFE 1661).
6. Superintendent of Motive Power (probably A. C. Deverell). Memo to J. C. Heron, June 15, 1917 (AFE 1661).
7. J. M. Gruber. Memo to George H. Emerson, July 17, 1917 (AFE 1661).
8. R. Budd. Memo to J. M. Gruber, July 28, 1917 (AFE 1661).
9. R. D. Hawkins. Memo to G. H. Emerson, October 5, 1915 (Minnesota Historical Society, General File – Engines).
10. Extract of test taken from Baldwin Magazine, undated, provided by Robert LeMassena. The complete history of this engine is now available on the Internet at: www.cwrr.com/Lounge/Reference/baldwin/baldwin.html.
11. W. Kelly. Memo to C. O. Jenks, June 19, 1925 (Great Northern File 40-1, Part 4, Minnesota Historical Society).
12. W. Kelly Memo to C. O. Jenks, May 13, 1926 (Great Northern File 40-1, Part 4, Minnesota Historical Society).
13. Robert LeMassena, Articulated Steam Locomotives of North America, Vol. 1 and 2, Sundance Books, 1979 and 1991.
14. R. Budd. Memo to C. O. Jenks, April 21, 1931 (Great Northern File 40-1, Part 5, Minnesota Historical Society).
15. W. Kelly. Memo to C. O. Jenks, April 27, 1931 (Great Northern File 40-1, Part 5, Minnesota Historical Society).
16. W. Kelly. Memo to C. O. Jenks, May 1,1934 (Great Northern File 40-1, Part 5, Minnesota Historical Society).
17. C. Riddell. Letter to C. O. Jenks, December 18, 1934 (Great Northern File 40-161, Minnesota Historical Society.
18. C. O. Jenks. Memo to W. Kelly, December 20, 1934 (Great Northern File 40-161, Minnesota Historical Society).
19. Alex Colville Shop Notebook
20. Walter Thayer, Wenatchee, correspondence with Norman F. Priebe
21. Thomas R. Lee, Turbines Westward, Lee Publications, 1975, as quoted in Wikipedia.

The drawings used to illustrate this chapter were found in the Great Northern Vice President Operating, General Manager Subject Files: 40, 40-01 and 50-161 (Minnesota Historical Society).

This interesting postcard view shows N-1 2008 with an interesting group of sand cars, apparently in ash service, in the foreground. Note the planking to allow the cars to be loaded with wheel barrows. These sand cars were numbered in the 195000-195736 series, and had been built in 1900, 1906 and 1907. In 1923 they were transferred to revenue service, and within a couple years were renumbered to the 79000-79621 series. Most were retired in 1927, but a few lasted until the mid-1930's. This photograph was probably taken between about 1915, when the N-1's received rebuilt O-1 tenders, and about 1917 when the engines received mechanical stokers. Collection of Ben Ringnalda.

Chapter 29

Great Northern Steam Locomotive Roster Preface and Abbreviations

The Great Northern numbering system had as its origin the St.Paul, Minneapolis and Manitoba Railway numbering system. As other railroads were acquired, their locomotives were incorporated into the numbering system of the StPM&M. For some time after 1890, at which time the StPM&M, along with several other Hill-controlled roads, was leased to the Great Northern, each of these roads retained its own numbering system. About 1892, however, the engines belonging to the StPM&M began to be considered "Great Northern" locomotives, with the appropriate letters ("G.N. Ry.") on their tenders, while the other GN-controlled roads' engines continued to be lettered as such. In 1899 and 1900, the locomotives of all these roads were incorporated into one numbering system, that of the Great Northern.

This roster is intended to include all steam locomotives owned by the Great Northern Railway Company and its predecessor lines. The time span extends from 1861 to 1970, when the Great Northern became part of the Burlington Northern. Locomotives are listed by road number in as sequential an order as possible while keeping the individual classes grouped together. This was done primarily to facilitate photographic identification, where a number may be obvious but the class unknown. Different sections in Chapter 30 are provided for each of the predecessor roads and subsidiary companies known to have owned locomotives. A roster of Great Northern locomotives is in Chapter 31. The locomotives

are sub-grouped by class. A cross-reference is included to enable one to find a locomotive knowing only its class rather than its number.

In the roster which follows all locomotives are standard gauge unless otherwise noted. If the locomotive carried more than one number during its service life, it is listed under each number, in hopes that this might aid in identification of photographs. Specifications are presented in the following order: cylinder diameter and stroke; driver diameter over tires; designed boiler pressure (working boiler pressure in parentheses if different from designed); engine weight excluding tender; weight on drivers; and tractive effort.

No major renumberings of steam locomotives occurred after 1899, though a few were renumbered in the 1940's to clear numbers for diesels.

Following the data of engine classes, roster information for the tenders is presented in Chapter 32. This was derived from Great Northern and Burlington Northern records. The information was obtained primarily from Great Northern/Burlington Northern "Change Number Record Accounts", from "Unit Records of Property Changes– Equipment", and from the "Authority for Expenditure" (AFE) files now held by GNRHS. Great Northern did keep track of the engines and tenders separately, and in official correspondence it was a common practice to refer to engine 1245 as "E1245" and tender 1245 as "T1245".

No attempt is made in the tender rosters to address tenders prior to the ICC valuation in 1915. It appears likely that most tenders which were retired prior to that time were retired with the locomotives bearing the same number. The few earlier records which are included are those which affected dispositions later (i.e. specific tender renumberings) or instances in which part of a class was gone by the valuation and part remained.

Great Northern was perhaps unusual in the degree to which it "swapped tenders", assigning various tenders to locomotives of different classes. The earliest record found of Great Northern's "tender swapping" is from New Equipment Register 5 (Historic Car Register Volume 40). A number of tenders were renumbered in 1908 and 1909, apparently to fill the numbers of tenders which had been sold to the Spokane, Portland and Seattle with J-2 locomotives. Prior to this instance, it appears that the tenders were normally renumbered at the same time (or within days) of the locomotives bearing the same number. Refer to the locomotive rosters for information prior to the valuation.

In later years, tender designs were assigned "Style" numbers. Where known, these are given in the roster. However, various Great Northern records sometimes conflict as to the style. Also, changes in coal or oil capacity were apparently not considered significant enough to justify issuance of an AFE. Consequently, when the water capacity was changed or new trucks added, the fuel capacity at the time may have been mentioned, but no evidence of the dates of such changes has been found.

Class-to-Number Cross Index

Class	Wheel Arrangement	Numbers
1	4-4-0	[M&P 1]; [StP&P 1]; StPM&M 1; GN 1(1)
2(1)	4-4-0	[M&P 2]; [StP&P 2]; StPM&M 2
2(2)	0-6-0	StPM&M 232,233; S&M 232; GN 30(2),31(2),233(1)
2A	0-6-0	SC&N 7,9; WSF 47,48; GN 47(2),48(2)
3	0-4-0	StPM&M 3,51(1); GN 3(1)
4	0-4-0	MW 1(1); StPM&M 87-89,187-193; GN14(2)-16(2),21(2)-26(2),87(1)-89(1),187(1)-193(1)
5(1)	4-4-0	[StP&P 6,7]; StPM&M 6,7
5(2)	4-4-0	StPM&M 16; GN 16(1),240
6	4-4-0	[StP&P 5]; StPM&M 5,15,16; GN 4(1)-7(1),5(2),8(2)-11(2),10(1)-15(1),17(1)
7(1)	4-4-0	[StP&P 12-14]; StPM&M 12-14
7(2)	0-6-0	EM 5-8,66-69; MC 25,26; GN 60(2)-69(2),250(1)-252(1),253,254,255(1)-258(1)
7A	0-6-0	GN 70(2)-82(2)
8(1)	4-4-0	[StP&P 15]; StPM&M 15
8(2)	4-4-0	StPM&M 12,13
8(3)	0-6-0	MC 9(2),27,28; GN 85(2)-87(2)
8A	0-6-0	EM 88,89; GN 88(2),89(2),98,99(2)
9(1)	4-4-0	[StP&P 16]; StPM&M 16
9(2)	4-4-0	StPM&M 9; GN 9(1)
9(3)	0-6-0	DS&WT 1,2; EM 58,59; GN 56(2)-59(2),378(2),379(2)
10(1)	4-4-0	[StP&P 8]; StPM&M 8; GN 8(1)
10(2)	4-6-0	F&S 1,2; S&M 298,299; GN 298,299
11(1)	4-4-0	[StP&P 9,11];StPM&M 9,11; GN 9(1)
11(2)	4-4-0	[PSL 13]; SC&N 1-4,8,10; SC&W 13; [SCO&W 13]; WSF 232-238; GN 232,233(2),234-238
12(1)	4-4-0	[StP&P 10]; StPM&M 10
12(2)	4-4-0	S&N 1,2; S&M 139; GN 139(2)
13	4-4-0	[StP&P 17-19,24-26]; StPM&M 17-19,24-26; GN 18(1),19(1),24(1)-26(1),241,242,247,248
14	4-4-0	StPM&M 68-77; GN 68(1)-77(1),284-293
15	4-4-0	StPM&M 67(2),78-86; GN 67(1),78(1)-86(1),187(2)-194(2),195,196(2)
16	4-4-0	[StP&P (47-50)]; StPM&M 22,47-50; GN 22(1),47(1)-50(1),245,249,250(2)-252(2)
17	4-4-0	[StP&P 20-23]; StPM&M 20-23; GN 20(1),21(1),23(1),243,244(1),246
18	4-4-0	StPM&M 51(2),52-66,67(1); GN 51(1),53(1)-61(1),63(1)-66(1),117(1),119(1),268-283
19	4-4-0	[StP&P 27-42]; StPM&M 27-42; FG&S 1; GN 27(1)-42(1),255(2)-258(2),259-267
20	4-4-0	[StP&P 43,44]; StPM&M 43,44; GN 43(1),44(1),294,295
21	2-6-0/0-6-0	[StP&P 45,46]; StPM&M 45,46; GN 12(2),13(2),45(1),46(1)
22	0-4-0	StPM&M 90-93; GN 17(2)-20(2),90(1)-93(1)
23	4-4-0	StPM&M 94(1),95(1),143(2),144(2); GN 143,144
24	4-4-0	StPM&M 100-124; MC 10(1),11(1); GN 100-116
24A	4-4-0	GN 52(1),62(1),117(2),118,119(2),120-124
25	4-4-0	StPM&M 125-133; GN 125-133
26	4-4-0	StPM&M 134-139; GN 134-138,139(1)
27(1)	4-4-0	StPM&M 96(1),97(1),140-142,143(1),144(1)
27(2)	4-6-0	SC&N 5,6; WSF 992-993; GN 992-993
27A	4-6-0	[PSL 15]; SC&W 15; [SCO&W 15]; WSF 997; GN 997
27B	4-6-0	[DMR&N 9]; EM 231,991; GN 991
27C	4-6-0	[PSL 10-12]; SC&W 16-18; [SCO&W 16-18]; WSF 994-996; GN 994-996
28	4-4-0	[DS&W 105,106]; EM 147; StPM&M 145-149; GN 145-149
29	4-4-0	StPM&M 150,151; GN 150,151
30	4-4-0	StPM&M 152-186; GN 152-186
31(1)	0-4-0	StPM&M 187-193
31(2)	0-6-0	EM 1-4,40-42; MW 1(2); MC 14,15; StPM&M 94(2)-97(2),98,99,226-231; GN 32(2)-46(2),94(1)-99(1),228(1)-231(1)
32	0-6-0	MW 2; StPM&M 194-196; GN 27(2)-29(2),194(1),196(1)
33	4-4-0	StPM&M 197-206; S&M 199,202; GN 197-206
34	4-4-0	MC 1-3,12,13; StPM&M 207-225; GN 207-218,219(1),220(1),221-225
34A	4-4-0	EM 101-105,226-230; GN 226,227,228(2)-230(2)
35	2-6-0	MC 4-8,10(2),11(2); StPM&M 300-321,322(1)-324(1),322(2),323(2),325; GN 300-325,327,328
36	2-6-0	EM 201-210,350-359; MC 9(1),16-18; StPM&M 324(2),326-347; S&M 329; GN 326,329-340,341(1),342-350,351(2)-359(2)
36A	2-6-0	[PSL 14]; SC&W 14; [SCO&W 14]; WSF 360; GN 360(2)
36B	2-6-0	EM 297; GN 297
37(1)	2-8-0	StPM&M 400-409; MC 54(1); GN 400(1)-409(1)
37(2)	2-8-0	EM 250-255,421-426; MC 30; GN 351(1)-361(1),361(2),362,363(1)-365(1),363(2)-365(2),366-370,400(2)-409(2),410(3),411(2)-414(2),415-426
38	4-8-0	MC 50-53,54(2); StPM&M 410-414; GN 400(1)-410(1),410(2),411(1)-414(1),600-615
39	2-8-0	GN 450(1)-480(1),481-499,500(2)-504(2),505-521,522(1),522(2),523(1),523(2),524,525(1),525(2),526-544,545(1),545(2),546(1),546(2),547-549,550(2)-554(2),555-565
40	2-8-0	GN 500(1)-504(1),550(1)-554(1),595-599
41	4-6-0	EM 600,601,998,999; GN 998,999
42	4-6-0	GN 650-669,950-969
43	2-6-0	EM 256-260,472-476; GN 371-377,378(1)-392(1),450(2)-476(2)
44	4-8-0	MC 100-107; GN 800-807
45	4-8-0	EM 300-319,700-719; GN 700-719
45A	4-8-0	EM 770-779; GN 770-779
46	4-6-0	EM 150-157,1000-1007; GN 1000-1007
47	4-6-0	GN 900-909
48	4-8-0	GN 720-769
49	4-6-0	GN 1050(1)-1052(1),1053-1069

Class	Wheel Arrangement	Numbers
50	2-8-0	GN 1100-1109
50A	2-8-0	GN 1130-1139
50B	2-8-0	GN 1110-1129
51, 51A	2-8-0	GN 1140-1159,1160(2)-1164(2),1165-1194,1195(2)-1199(2)
51B	2-8-0	GN 1300-1324
52	2-8-0	GN 1160(1)-1164(1),1095-1099,1195(1)-1199(1)
53	4-6-0	GN 925-939
A-1	0-6-0	GN 12(2),13(2)
A-2	0-6-0	GN 30(2),31(2)
A-3	0-6-0	GN 47(2),48(2)
A-4	0-6-0	GN 27(2)-29(2)
A-5(1)	0-6-0	GN 32(2)-46(2)
A-5(2)	0-6-0	GN 32(3)-34(3)
A-6	0-6-0	ABD 1,2; GN 56(2)-59(2),378(2),379(2)
A-7	0-6-0	SL S4; GN 60(2)-69(2)
A-8	0-6-0	GN 70(2)-72(2)
A-9	0-6-0	GN 1(2),2,3(2),4(2),5(3),6(2),7(2),8(3)-12(3),14(3)-26(3), 27(3)-29(3),49(2)-55(2),56(3),57(3),73(2)-84(2), 85(3)-89(3), 90(2)-94(2),380(2)-391(2), 391(3),392(2), 392(3),393(1), 393(2),394-396, 397(1)-399(1),397(2)-399(2)
A-10	0-6-0	GN 95(2)-97(2),98,99(2)
A-11	0-6-0	GN 30(3),31(3)
B-1	4-4-0	GN 240
B-2	4-4-0	GN 11(2),243,244(1),244(2)
B-3	4-4-0	GN 241,242,247,248
B-4	4-4-0	GN 245,249,250(2)-252(2)
B-5	4-4-0	GN 255(2)-258(2),259-267
B-6	4-4-0	GN 232,233(2),234-238
B-7	4-4-0	GN 139(2)
B-8	4-4-0	VTR&F 4; GN 284-293
B-9	4-4-0	GN 187(2)-194(2),195,196(2)
B-10	4-4-0	FG&S 2; GN 268-283
B-11(1)	4-4-0	GN 294,295
B-11(2)	4-4-0	[SF&N 5,6]; V&S 4; GN 141,142
B-12	4-4-0	GN 143,144
B-13	4-4-0	VW&Y 2; GN 100-116,219(2)
B-14	4-4-0	GN 117(2),118,119(2),120-124
B-15	4-4-0	GN 125-133
B-16	4-4-0	GN 134-138,139(1)
B-17	4-4-0	GN 145-149
B-18	4-4-0	GN 150,151
B-19	4-4-0	GN 152-186,220(2)
B-20	4-4-0	GN 197-206
B-21	4-4-0	GN 207-218,219(1),220(1),221-225
B-22	4-4-0	GN 226-227,228(2)-230(2)
B-23	4-4-0	[N&FS 7]; [SF&N 7]; GN 231(2)
C-1	0-8-0	GN 810-849
C-2	0-8-0	GN 850-869
C-3	0-8-0	GN 875-882,883(1),883(2),884-898
C-4	0-8-0	GN 780-790,870(1)
C-5	0-8-0	GN 870(2),871(2),872,873
D-1(1)	2-6-0	GN 360(2)
D-1(2)	2-6-0	[SF&N 1-4]; VW&Y 1(2); GN 477(2)-480(2)
D-2	2-6-0	BDL&S 4; GN 300-340,341(1),342-350,351(2)-359(2)
D-3(1)	2-6-0	FG&S 3; GN 297
D-3(2)	2-6-0	[SDC 13]; W&SF 13; GN 432
D-4	2-6-0	MTW 10; GN 400(2)-409(2),410(3),411(2)-414(2),415-426
D-5	2-6-0	GN 450(2)-476(2)
D-6	2-6-0	[SDC 11,12]; W&SF 11,12; GN 430(1),431
D-7	2-6-0	GN 430(2)
D-8	2-6-0	GN 341(2)
E-1	4-6-0	GN 992,993
E-2(1)	4-6-0	GN 994-996
E-2(2)	4-6-0	[SDC 16,17]; W&SF 16,17; GN 910-911
E-3	4-6-0	GN 900-909
E-4	4-6-0	GN 298,299
E-5	4-6-0	GN 997
E-6	4-6-0	GN 925-939
E-7	4-6-0	GN 950-969
E-8	4-6-0	GN 1050(1)-1052(1),1053-1072
E-9	4-6-0	GN 998,999
E-10	4-6-0	GN 1000-1007
E-11	4-6-0	GN 959
E-12	4-6-0	[SF&N 11,12]; GN 970,971
E-13	4-6-0	[N&FS 8]; [SF&N 8,10]; GN 948,949
E-14	4-6-0	GN 1008-1049,1050(2)-1052(2)
E-15	4-6-0	GN 1073-1092
F-1	2-8-0	GN 500(2)-504(2),505-521,522(1),522(2),523(1),523(2), 524-544,545(1),545(2),546(1),546(2),547-549, 550(2)-554(2),555-565; MTW 5
F-2	2-8-0	GN 595-599
F-3	2-8-0	GN 701
F-4(1)	2-8-0	GN 1095-1099
F-4(2)	2-8-0	[C&RM 9]; [RM 9]; [SF&N 9]; GN 1094
F-5	2-8-0	GN 1095-1109
F-6	2-8-0	GN 1110-1129
F-7	2-8-0	GN 1130-1139
F-8	2-8-0	SL S-5; GN 1140-1264
F-9	2-8-0	GN 1300-1324
F-10	2-8-0	GN 806
F-11	2-8-0	[SDC 14,15]; W&SF 14,15; GN 590,591
F-12	2-8-0	GN 1326,1327
G-1	4-8-0	GN 600-615
G-2	4-8-0	GN 700-719
G-3	4-8-0	GN 720-769
G-4	4-8-0	GN 770-779
G-5	4-8-0	GN 800-807
H-1	4-6-2	GN 1400-1405
H-2	4-6-2	GN 1406-1440
H-3(1)	4-6-2	GN 1425
H-3(2)	4-6-2	GN 1412,1421,1423,1425-1428,1430,1431,1433,1436
H-4	4-6-2	GN 1441-1485
H-5	4-6-2	GN 1350-1374,1486-1495
H-6	4-6-2	GN 1710-1724
H-7	4-6-2	GN 1375-1384
J-1	2-6-2	GN 1500-1549
J-2	2-6-2	GN 1550-1649
J-3	2-6-2	GN 1549
K-1	4-4-2	GN 1700-1709
L-1	2-6-6-2	GN 1800(1)-1804(1),1900-1904,1905(1)-1907(1),1905(2)- 1907(2),1908-1924
L-2	2-6-6-2	GN 1800(2)-1804(2),1805-1844
L-3	2-6-8-0	GN 1950-1959
M-1	2-6-8-0	GN 1950-1984
M-2(1)	2-6-8-0	GN 1254,1999,2000(1)
M-2(2)	2-6-8-0	GN 1950-1984
N-1	2-8-8-0	GN 2000(2),2001-2024
N-2	2-8-8-0	GN 2000(2),2001-2024
N-3	2-8-8-0	GN 2000(2),2001-2024
O-1	2-8-2	GN 3000-3144
O-2	2-8-2	[SDC 18]; W&SF 18; GN 3149
O-3	2-8-2	GN 3145-3148,3200-3208
O-4	2-8-2	GN 3210-3254
O-5	2-8-2	GN 3300-3344
O-6	2-8-2	GN 3350-3371
O-7	2-8-2	GN 3375-3396
O-8	2-8-2	GN 3375-3399
P-1	4-8-2	GN 1750-1764
P-2	4-8-2	GN 2500-2527
Q-1	2-10-2	GN 2100-2129
Q-2	2-10-2	GN 2175-2189
R-1	2-8-8-2	GN 2030-2043
R-2	2-8-8-2	GN 2044-2059
S-1	4-8-4	GN 2550-2555
S-2	4-8-4	GN 2575-2588
Z-6	4-6-6-4	GN 4000,4001

Abbreviations

Builders

Alco	American Locomotive Company		New York	New York Locomotive Works (Rome)
Baldwin	Baldwin Locomotive Works		Norris	Norris Locomotive Works
Brooks	Brooks Locomotive Works		Pittsburgh	Pittsburgh Locomotive and Car Works
Canadian	Canadian Locomotive Company		Porter	H.K. Porter
Cooke	Cooke Locomotive & Machine Works		PSMD	Puget Sound Machinery Depot
Danforth	Danforth Locomotive and Machine Company		Rhode Island	Rhode Island Locomotive Works
Dickson	Dickson Manufacturing Company		Rogers	Rogers Locomotive Works
GAC	General American Car Company		Schenectady	Schenectady Locomotive Works
Grant	Grant Locomotive Works		Smith & Jackson	New Jersey Locomotive & Machine Co. (Smith & Jackson)
Hinkley	Hinkley Locomotive Works		Souther	John Souther
Lima	Lima Locomotive Works		Taunton	Taunton Locomotive Manufacturing Company
Mason	Mason Machine Works			

Railroads

ABD	Allouez Bay Dock Company		PSL	Pacific Short Line
BA&P	Butte, Anaconda and Pacific		PV&Y	Portland, Vancouver and Yakima
BDL&S	Brandon, Devils Lake and Southern Railway Company		RM	Red Mountain Railway
BN	Burlington Northern, Inc.		S&M RR	Seattle and Montana Railroad Company
B&O	Baltimore & Ohio		S&M Ry	Seattle and Montana Railway Company
CB&Q	Chicago, Burlington & Quincy Railroad Company		S&N	Seattle and Northern Railroad Company
CStPM&O	Chicago, St.Paul, Minneapolis and Omaha		StP&D	St.Paul and Duluth
C&NW	Chicago and North Western		StP&P	St.Paul and Pacific Railroad Company
C&RM	Columbia and Red Mountain Railway Company		StP&SC	St.Paul and Sioux City
DMR&N	Duluth, Mississippi River and Northern Railroad Company		StPM&M	St.Paul, Minneapolis and Manitoba Railway Company
DSS&A	Duluth, South Shore & Atlantic		SC&N	Sioux City and Northern Railway Company
DS&W	Duluth, Superior and Western Railway Company		SC&StP	Sioux City and St.Paul
DS&WT	Duluth, Superior and Western Terminal Company		SC&W	Sioux City and Western Railway Company
D&W	Duluth and Winnipeg Railroad Company		SCO&W	Sioux City, O'Neill and Western Railway Company
EM	Eastern Railway Company of Minnesota		SDC	South Dakota Central Railway Company
EP&SW	El Paso and South Western		SF&N	Spokane Falls and Northern Railway Company
F&S	Fairhaven and Southern Railroad Company		SL	Somers Lumber Company
FG&S	Farmer's Grain and Shipping Company		SL-SF	St.Louis-San Francisco Railway
GN	Great Northern Railway Company		SOO	Soo Line Railway
GNIOP	Great Northern Iron Ore Properties		SP&S	Spokane, Portland and Seattle Railway Company
K&M	Kanawha and Michigan		TA&G	Tennessee, Alabama and Georgia Railway
LST&T	Lake Superior Terminal and Transfer Company		V&S	Victoria and Sidney Railway Company
M&P	Minnesota and Pacific Railroad Company		VL&M	Victoria Lumber and Manufacturing Company
MC	Montana Central Railway Company		VTR&F	Victoria Terminal Railway and Ferry Company
MCCo	Macon Construction Company		VW&Y	Vancouver, Westminster and Yukon Railway
MH&O	Marquette, Houghton and Ontonagon		WPI	Wyoming Pacific Improvement Company
MTW	Montana Western Railway Company		WSF	Willmar and Sioux Falls Railway Company
MW	Minneapolis Western			Note:This company was also sometimes referred to as "W&SF" in Great Northern company records, which could create some confusion with the Watertown and Sioux Falls Railway Company.
NP	Northern Pacific Railroad Company			
N&FS	The Nelson & Fort Sheppard Railway Company			
N&W	Nebraska and Western Railway Company			
OWR&N	Oregon-Washington Railway and Navigation Company		W&SF	Watertown and Sioux Falls Railway Company

Miscellaneous

36FWC	36'6" Flat Car with Water Cistern		PC	Paper Calmenson and Company
40FWC	40'6" Flat Car with Water Cistern		Rblt.	Rebuilt
40FFC	40'6" Flat Car with Fuel Oil Cistern		Reno.	Renumbered
40HFWC	40'6" Hart Flat Car with Water Cistern		Ret.	Retired
1880 HER	Great Northern 1880-1900 Historic Engine Record		Rtnd.	Returned
AFE	Authority for Expenditure		RT	Rotary Tender
ARMD	Great Northern Railway Annual Report, Machinery Department		SST	Steam Shovel Tender
CNRA	Change Number Record Accounts		St.	Tender Style
CHEM	Chemical Tank Car		T	Tender
DI&M	Duluth Iron and Metal Company		T.E.	Tractive Effort
E	Engine		URPC	Unit Record of Property Changes -- Equipment
FC	Fire Car		USRA	United States Railroad Administration
FO	Fuel Oil Car		WC	Water Car
HCR	Great Northern Historical Car Records		WEI&M	West End Iron and Metal Company
HER	Great Northern Historic Engine Records		WP	Wedge Plow
NE	Great Northern New Equipment Register		Wt.	Weight
NSRM	Northwest Steel Rolling Mills, Inc.			

Class B-13 219(2nd) was originally St. Paul, Minneapolis & Manitoba No. 103, received from Baldwin in 1882. It kept the number 103 until 1944, when it was renumbered to clear a number for a diesel-electric switcher being renumbered from the 5300 series. Shown here at Hillyard, WA, in October 1945, it was the next to last 4-4-0 to be active in revenue service on the Great Northern. William J. Pontin (RPS) photograph from the collection of Norman Priebe.

Chapter 30

Predecessor & Subsidiary Steam Locomotive Roster

ALLOUEZ BAY DOCK COMPANY

Class A-6 0-6-0: 18x26-49-180(160)-109,400-109,400-23,380

No.	Builder	Date Built	C/N	Original No.	Renumbered From	Date	Disposition	Notes
1	Brooks	9/1899	3301	DS&WT 1	GN 56(2)	3/24/1909	Sold to GN [No. 378(2)], 4/22/1913.	1
2	Brooks	9/1899	3302	DS&WT 2	GN 57(2)	2/16/1909	Sold to GN [No. 379(2)], 4/22/1913.	1

BRANDON, DEVILS LAKE & SOUTHERN RAILWAY COMPANY

Class D-2 2-6-0: 19x24-55-150(140)-105,040-97,290-18,745

No.	Builder	Date Rcvd.	C/N	Original No.	Renumbered From	Date	Disposition
4	Rogers	11/14/1888	4056	StPM&M 341	GN 341(1)	1906	Considered to be FG&S No. 4 some time prior to 1927.

COLUMBIA AND RED MOUNTAIN RAILWAY COMPANY

Class F-4(2) 2-8-0: 19x24-47-180(170)-135,000-113,300-26,640

No.	Builder	Date Built	C/N	Disposition	Notes
9	Baldwin	8/1896	15013	Sold to GN 7/1/1907. Renumbered GN 1094 at Hillyard 6/9/1908.	2

DULUTH AND WINNIPEG RAILROAD COMPANY

Class – 4-4-0: 17x24-61?- ? -67,000?- ?- ?

No.	Builder	Date Built	C/N	Original No.	Renumbered From	Date	Disposition	Notes
1	Dickson	8/1873	130?	MH&O 26?	DSS&A ?	c.1890	Sold to DS&W (No. 101), 12/1/1896.	3
2	Dickson	8/1873	131?	MH&O 27?	DSS&A ?	c.1890	Sold to DS&W (No. 2), 12/1/1896.	3
3	Dickson	8/1873	132?	MH&O 28?	DSS&A ?	c.1890	Sold to DS&W (No. 3), 12/1/1896.	3
4	Dickson	8/1873	133?	MH&O 29?	DSS&A ?	c.1890	Sold to DS&W (No. 104), 12/1/1896.	3
5	Dickson	8/1873	134?	MH&O 30?	DSS&A ?	c.1890	Off roster c.1894.	3

DULUTH AND WINNIPEG RAILROAD COMPANY - continued

Class – 2-6-0: 18x24-57-140-107,000-90,000-20,290

No.	Builder	Date Built	C/N	Disposition
6	Baldwin	7/1892	12854	Sold to DS&W (No. 200), 12/1/1896.
7	Baldwin	7/1892	12855	Traded to DSS&A (No. 500), 1894. Renumbered to DSS&A No. 415 in 1907. Dismantled at Marquette, MI, 10/1928.

DULUTH, MISSISSIPPI RIVER AND NORTHERN RAILROAD COMPANY

Class – 2-6-0: 12x18-40- ? -51,000- ? - ?

No.	Builder	Date Built	C/N	Original No.	Renumbered From	Date	Disposition	Notes
1	Porter	1892	1346	?	?	?	Unknown	4

Class – 2-6-0: 14x24-48- ? -64,000- ? - ?

No.	Builder	Date Built	C/N	Original No.	Renumbered From	Date	Disposition	Notes
2	Porter	1892	1353	?	?	?	Unknown	4

Class – 2-6-0: 14x22-43½- ? -63,000- ? - ?

No.	Builder	Date Built	C/N	Disposition
3	Brooks	12/1892	2205	Sold to Swan River Logging Co. (No. 3), 1893. Then sold to Birmingham Rail & Locomotive Co., date unknown, and rebuilt. Sold to Big Sandy Lumber Co., 1919.

Class – 2-6-0: 16x24-50- ? -85,000- ? - ?

No.	Builder	Date Built	C/N	Disposition
4	Brooks	4/1893	2273	Sold to Swan River Logging Co., 1894. Then sold to Birmingham Rail & Locomotive Co., date unknown, and rebuilt. Sold to Hemphill Lumber Co. (No. 4), 1920.
5	Brooks	4/1893	2274	Sold to Swan River Logging Co., 1894.

Class – 2-6-0: 14x22-44- ? -63,000- ? - ?

No.	Builder	Date Built	C/N	Disposition
6	Brooks	5/1894	2430	Unknown.

Class – 2-6-0: 18x24-51- ? -96,000- ? - ?

No.	Builder	Date Built	C/N	Disposition
7	Brooks	7/1895	2535	Sold to Swan River Logging Co., date unknown.

Class – 2-6-0: 18x24-51- ? -110,500- ? - ?

No.	Builder	Date Built	C/N	Disposition
8	Brooks	5/1898	2967	Sold to A. Guthrie & Co., date unknown.

Class – 4-6-0: 18x24-63-180-127,800-97,800-18,880

No.	Builder	Date Built	C/N	Disposition
9	Brooks	6/1898	2968	Sold to Eastern of Minnesota, 5/1/1899. Renumbered EM 231 at West Superior 10/23/1899.

Class – 2-8-0: 20x24- ?- ? - ? - ? - ?

No.	Builder	Date Built	C/N	Disposition
10	Baldwin	?	?	Sold, date unknown.

DULUTH, SUPERIOR AND WESTERN RAILWAY COMPANY

Class – 4-4-0: 17x24-61?- ? -67,000- ? - ?

No.	Builder	Date Built	C/N	Original No.	Renumbered From	Date	Disposition	Notes
2	Dickson	8/1873	131?	MH&O 27?	D&W 2	c.1896	Sold to EM (not renumbered) 6/22/1898.	3, 5
3	Dickson	8/1873	132?	MH&O 28?	D&W 3	c.1896	Sold to EM (not renumbered) 6/22/1898.	3, 5
101	Dickson	8/1873	130?	MH&O 26?	D&W 1	c.1896	Sold to EM (not renumbered) 6/22/1898.	3, 5
104	Dickson	8/1873	133?	MH&O 29?	D&W 4	c.1896	Sold to EM (not renumbered) 6/22/1898.	3, 5

Class 28 4-4-0: 17x24-63-140-70,000-43,650-13,100

No.	Builder	Date Built	C/N	Original No.	Renumbered From	Date	Disposition
105	Grant	7/6/1882	1524	StPM&M 147	StPM&M 147	9/15/1897	Renumbered DS&W 106 7/8/1898.
106	Grant	7/6/1882	1524	StPM&M 147	DS&W 105	7/8/1898	Sold to EM 6/22/1898. Renumbered EM 147 4/3/1899.

Class 36B 2-6-0: 18x24-57-140-107,000-90,000-20,290

No.	Builder	Date Built	C/N	Original No.	Renumbered From	Date	Disposition
200	Baldwin	7/1892	12854	D&W 6	D&W 6	c.1896	Sold to EM (No. 297) 6/22/1898.

DULUTH, SUPERIOR AND WESTERN TERMINAL COMPANY

Class 9(3) 0-6-0: 18x26-49-180(160)-109,400-109,400-23,380

No.	Builder	Date Built	C/N	Disposition	Notes
1	Brooks	9/1899	3301	Reno. GN 56(2) 1903. Sold GN 8/1/1908.	1
2	Brooks	9/1899	3302	Reno. GN 57(2) 1903. Sold GN 8/1/1908.	1

EASTERN RAILWAY COMPANY OF MINNESOTA (See Note 6)

Class 31(2) 0-6-0: 18x24-49-150(140)-86,450-86,450-18,880

No.	Builder	Date Built	C/N	Original No.	Renumbered From	Date	Disposition
1	Rogers	7/1888	3975	–	–	–	Reno. EM 40 c.1899.
2	Rogers	7/1888	3976	–	–	–	Reno. EM 41 c.1899.
3	Rogers	7/1888	3978	–	–	–	Reno. EM 42 c.1899.
4	Rogers	4/1887	3741	StPM&M 99	StPM&M 99	5/21/1894	Reno. EM 37 c.1899.

Class 7(2) 0-6-0: 19x26-49-180(160)-114,700-114,700-26,050

No.	Builder	Date Built	C/N	Disposition
5	Brooks	8/1895	2552	Reno. EM 66 c.1899.
6	Brooks	8/1895	2553	Reno. EM 67 c.1899.
7	Brooks	6/1898	2971	Reno. EM 68 c.1899.
8	Brooks	6/1898	2972	Reno. EM 69 c.1899.

Class 31(2) 0-6-0: 18x24-49-150(140)-86,450-86,450-18,880

No.	Builder	Date Built	C/N	Original No.	Renumbered From	Date	Disposition	Notes
37	Rogers	4/1887	3741	StPM&M 99	EM 4	c.1899	Leased to GN [as its No. 37(2)] 5/1/1902.	
40	Rogers	7/1888	3975	EM 1	EM 1	c.1899	Leased to GN [as its No. 40(2)] 5/1/1902.	
41	Rogers	7/1888	3976	EM 2	EM 2	c.1899	Leased to GN [as its No. 41(2)] 5/1/1902.	
42	Rogers	7/1888	3978	EM 3	EM 3	c.1899	Leased to GN [as its No. 42(2)] 5/1/1902.	

Class 9(3) 0-6-0: 18x26-49-180(160)-109,400-109,400-23,380

No.	Builder	Date Built	C/N	Disposition
58	Brooks	9/1899	3299	Leased to GN [as its No. 58(2)] 5/1/1902.
59	Brooks	9/1899	3300	Leased to GN [as its No. 59(2)] 5/1/1902.

Class 7(2) 0-6-0: 19x26-49-180(160)-114,700-114,700-26,050

No.	Builder	Date Built	C/N	Original No.	Renumbered From	Date	Disposition
66	Brooks	8/1895	2552	EM 5	EM 5	1900	Leased to GN [as its No. 66(2)] 5/1/1902.
67	Brooks	8/1895	2553	EM 6	EM 6	1900	Leased to GN [as its No. 67(2)] 5/1/1902.
68	Brooks	6/1898	2971	EM 7	EM 7	1900	Leased to GN [as its No. 68(2)] 5/1/1902.
69	Brooks	6/1898	2972	EM 8	EM 8	1900	Leased to GN [as its No. 69(2)] 5/1/1902.

Class 8A 0-6-0: 19x28-49-200(160)-137,000-137,000-28,060

No.	Builder	Date Built	C/N	Disposition
88	Brooks	7/1900	3573	Leased to GN [as its No. 88(2)] 5/1/1902.
89	Brooks	7/1900	3574	Leased to GN [as its No. 89(2)] 5/1/1902.

Class 34A 4-4-0: 18x24-63-150(140)-94,100-60,300-14,690

No.	Builder	Date Rcvd.	C/N	Disposition
101	Rogers	11/29/1888	4063	Reno. EM 226 c.1899.
102	Rogers	4/7/1889	4120	Reno. EM 227 c.1899.
103	Rogers	4/29/1889	4121	Reno. EM 228 c.1899.
104	Rogers	4/2/1889	4122	Reno. EM 229 c.1899.
105	Rogers	4/4/1889	4123	Reno. EM 230 c.1899.

Class – 4-4-0: 17x24-61?- ? - 67,000 - ?- ?

No.	Builder	Date Built	C/N	Original No.	Previous No.	Disposition	Notes
(101)	Dickson	8/1873	130?	MH&O 26?	DS&W 101	Sold prior to receiving EM number, date unknown.	3, 5
(102)	Dickson	8/1873	131?	MH&O 27?	DS&W 2	Sold prior to receiving EM number, date unknown.	3, 5
(103)	Dickson	8/1873	132?	MH&O 28?	DS&W 3	Sold prior to receiving EM number, date unknown.	3, 5
(104)	Dickson	8/1873	133?	MH&O 29?	DS&W 104	Sold prior to receiving EM number, date unknown.	3, 5

Class 28 4-4-0: 17x24-63-140-70,000-43,650-13,100

No.	Builder	Date Built	C/N	Original No.	Renumbered From	Date	Disposition
147	Grant	7/6/1882	1524	StPM&M 147	DS&W 106	4/3/1899	Leased to GN (as its No. 147) 5/1/1902.

EASTERN RAILWAY COMPANY OF MINNESOTA - continued

Class 46 4-6-0: 20x30-63-210(200)-166,580-130,000-32,380

No.	Builder	Date Built	C/N	Disposition
150	Brooks	5/1898	2954	Reno. EM 1000 c.1899.
151	Brooks	5/1898	2955	Reno. EM 1001 c.1899.
152	Brooks	5/1898	2956	Reno. EM 1002 c.1899.
153	Brooks	5/1898	2957	Reno. EM 1003 c.1899.
154	Brooks	5/1898	2958	Reno. EM 1004 c.1899.
155	Brooks	5/1898	2959	Reno. EM 1005 c.1899.
156	Brooks	5/1898	2960	Reno. EM 1006 c.1899.
157	Brooks	5/1898	2961	Reno. EM 1007 c.1899.

Class 36 2-6-0: 19x24-55-150(140)-105,040-87,290-18,750

No.	Builder	Date Built	C/N	Disposition
201	Rogers	8/1888	3985	Reno. EM 350 c.1899.
202	Rogers	8/1888	3986	Reno. EM 351 c.1899.
203	Rogers	8/1888	3995	Reno. EM 352 c.1899.
204	Rogers	8/1888	3996	Reno. EM 353 c.1899.
205	Rogers	8/1888	3997	Reno. EM 354 c.1899.
206	Rogers	9/1888	4021	Reno. EM 355 c.1899.
207	Rogers	9/1888	4022	Reno. EM 356 c.1899.
208	Rogers	9/1888	4023	Reno. EM 357 c.1899.
209	Rogers	9/1888	4026	Reno. EM 358 c.1899.
210	Rogers	9/1888	4027	Reno. EM 359 c.1899.

Class 34A 4-4-0: 18x24-63-150(140)-94,100-60,300-14,690

No.	Builder	Date Rcvd.	C/N	Original No.	Renumbered From	Date	Disposition
226	Rogers	11/29/1888	4063	EM 101	EM 101	c.1899	Leased to GN (as its No. 226) 5/1/1902.
227	Rogers	4/7/1889	4120	EM 102	EM 102	c.1899	Leased to GN (as its No. 227) 5/1/1902.
228	Rogers	4/29/1889	4121	EM 103	EM 103	c.1899	Leased to GN [as its No. 228(2)] 5/1/1902.
229	Rogers	4/2/1889	4122	EM 104	EM 104	c.1899	Leased to GN [as its No. 229(2)] 5/1/1902.
230	Rogers	4/4/1889	4123	EM 105	EM 105	c.1899	Leased to GN [as its No. 230(2)] 5/1/1902.

Class 27B 4-6-0: 18x24-63-180-127,800-97,800-18,880

No.	Builder	Date Built	C/N	Original No.	Renumbered From	Date	Disposition
231	Brooks	6/1898	2968	DMR&N 9	DMR&N 9	10/23/1899	Reno. EM 991 at West Superior 4/4/1900.

Class 37(2) 2-6-0: 19x24-55-180(160)-118,000-102,000-21,420

No.	Builder	Date Rcvd.	C/N	Disposition
250	Brooks	8/6/1895	2546	Reno. EM 421 c.1899.
251	Brooks	8/6/1895	2547	Reno. EM 422 c.1899.
252	Brooks	8/11/1895	2548	Reno. EM 423 c.1899.
253	Brooks	8/15/1895	2549	Reno. EM 424 c.1899.
254	Brooks	8/15/1895	2550	Reno. EM 425 c.1899.
255	Brooks	8/15/1895	2551	Reno. EM 426 c.1899.

Class 43 2-6-0: 19x26-55-180(170)-130,000-114,000-24,660

No.	Builder	Date Rcvd.	C/N	Disposition
256	Brooks	8/31/1897	2798	Reno. EM 472 1900.
257	Brooks	8/31/1897	2799	Reno. EM 473 1900.
258	Brooks	9/2/1897	2800	Reno. EM 474 1900.
259	Brooks	9/4/1897	2801	Reno. EM 475 1900.
260	Brooks	9/5/1897	2802	Reno. EM 476 1900.

Class 36B 2-6-0: 18x24-57-175-107,000-90,000-20,290

No.	Builder	Date Built	C/N	Original No.	Renumbered From	Date	Disposition
297	Baldwin	7/1892	12854	D&W 6	DS&W 200	c.1898	Leased to GN (as its No. 297) 5/1/1902. Sold FG&S (No. 3) 5/10/1905.

Class 45 4-8-0: 19x32-55-200(180)-176,000-142,000-32,140

No.	Builder	Date Built	C/N	Disposition
300	Brooks	6/1898	2973	Reno. EM 700 4/1899
301	Brooks	6/1898	2974	Reno. EM 701 4/1899
302	Brooks	6/1898	2975	Reno. EM 702 4/1899
303	Brooks	6/1898	2982	Reno. EM 703 c.1899.
304	Brooks	6/1898	2983	Reno. EM 704 c.1899.
305	Brooks	6/1898	2984	Reno. EM 705 c.1899.
306	Brooks	6/1898	2985	Reno. EM 706 c.1899.
307	Brooks	7/1898	2986	Reno. EM 707 c.1899.
308	Brooks	7/1898	2987	Reno. EM 708 c.1899.
309	Brooks	7/1898	2988	Reno. EM 709 c.1899.
310	Brooks	7/1898	2989	Reno. EM 710 c.1899.
311	Brooks	7/1898	2990	Reno. EM 711 c.1899.
312	Brooks	9/1898	3045	Reno. EM 712 c.1899.
313	Brooks	9/1898	3046	Reno. EM 713 c.1899.
314	Brooks	9/1898	3047	Reno. EM 714 c.1899.
315	Brooks	9/1898	3048	Reno. EM 715 c.1899.
316	Brooks	10/1898	3049	Reno. EM 716 c.1899.
317	Brooks	10/1898	3050	Reno. EM 717 c.1899.
318	Brooks	10/1898	3051	Reno. EM 718 c.1899.
319	Brooks	10/1898	3052	Reno. EM 719 c.1899.

Class 36 2-6-0: 19x24-55-150(140)-105,040-87,290-18,750

No.	Builder	Date Built	C/N	Original No.	Renumbered From	Date	Disposition
350	Rogers	8/1888	3985	EM 201	EM 201	c.1899	Leased to GN (as its No. 350) 5/1/1902.
351	Rogers	8/1888	3986	EM 202	EM 202	c.1899	Leased to GN [as its No. 351(2)] 5/1/1902.
352	Rogers	8/1888	3995	EM 203	EM 203	c.1899	Leased to GN [as its No. 352(2)] 5/1/1902.
353	Rogers	8/1888	3996	EM 204	EM 204	c.1899	Leased to GN [as its No. 353(2)] 5/1/1902.
354	Rogers	8/1888	3997	EM 205	EM 205	c.1899	Leased to GN [as its No. 354(2)] 5/1/1902.
355	Rogers	9/1888	4021	EM 206	EM 206	c.1899	Leased to GN [as its No. 355(2)] 5/1/1902.
356	Rogers	9/1888	4022	EM 207	EM 207	c.1899	Leased to GN [as its No. 356(2)] 5/1/1902.
357	Rogers	9/1888	4023	EM 208	EM 208	c.1899	Leased to GN [as its No. 357(2)] 5/1/1902.
358	Rogers	9/1888	4026	EM 209	EM 209	c.1899	Leased to GN [as its No. 358(2)] 5/1/1902.
359	Rogers	9/1888	4027	EM 210	EM 210	c.1899	Leased to GN [as its No. 359(2)] 5/1/1902.

Class 37(2) 2-6-0: 19x24-55-180(160)-118,000-102,000-21,420

No.	Builder	Date Rcvd.	C/N	Original No.	Renumbered From	Date	Disposition
421	Brooks	8/6/1895	2546	EM 250	EM 250	c.1899	Leased to GN (as its No. 421) 5/1/1902.
422	Brooks	8/6/1895	2547	EM 251	EM 251	c.1899	Leased to GN (as its No. 422) 5/1/1902.
423	Brooks	8/11/1895	2548	EM 252	EM 252	c.1899	Leased to GN (as its No. 423) 5/1/1902.
424	Brooks	8/15/1895	2549	EM 253	EM 253	c.1899	Leased to GN (as its No. 424) 5/1/1902.
425	Brooks	8/15/1895	2550	EM 254	EM 254	c.1899	Leased to GN (as its No. 425) 5/1/1902.
426	Brooks	8/15/1895	2551	EM 255	EM 255	c.1899	Leased to GN (as its No. 426) 5/1/1902.

Class 43 2-6-0: 19x26-55-180(170)-130,000-114,000-24,660

No.	Builder	Date Rcvd.	C/N	Original No.	Renumbered From	Date	Disposition
472	Brooks	8/31/1897	2798	EM 256	EM 256	c.1899	Leased to GN [as its No. 472(2)] 5/1/1902.
473	Brooks	8/31/1897	2799	EM 257	EM 257	c.1899	Leased to GN [as its No. 473(2)] 5/1/1902.
474	Brooks	9/2/1897	2800	EM 258	EM 258	c.1899	Leased to GN [as its No. 474(2)] 5/1/1902.
475	Brooks	9/4/1897	2801	EM 259	EM 259	c.1899	Leased to GN [as its No. 475(2)] 5/1/1902.
476	Brooks	9/5/1897	2802	EM 260	EM 260	c.1899	Leased to GN [as its No. 476(2)] 5/1/1902.

EASTERN RAILWAY COMPANY OF MINNESOTA - continued

Class 45 4-8-0: 19x32-55-200(180)-176,000-142,000-32,140

No.	Builder	Date Built	C/N	Original No.	Renumbered From	Date	Disposition
700	Brooks	6/1898	2973	EM 300	EM 300	c.1899	Leased to GN (as its No. 700) 5/1/1902.
701	Brooks	6/1898	2974	EM 301	EM 301	c.1899	Leased to GN (as its No. 701) 5/1/1902.
702	Brooks	6/1898	2975	EM 302	EM 302	c.1899	Leased to GN (as its No. 702) 5/1/1902.
703	Brooks	6/1898	2982	EM 303	EM 303	c.1899	Leased to GN (as its No. 703) 5/1/1902.
704	Brooks	6/1898	2983	EM 304	EM 304	c.1899	Leased to GN (as its No. 704) 5/1/1902.
705	Brooks	6/1898	2984	EM 305	EM 305	c.1899	Leased to GN (as its No. 705) 5/1/1902.
706	Brooks	6/1898	2985	EM 306	EM 306	c.1899	Leased to GN (as its No. 706) 5/1/1902.
707	Brooks	7/1898	2986	EM 307	EM 307	c.1899	Leased to GN (as its No. 707) 5/1/1902.
708	Brooks	7/1898	2987	EM 308	EM 308	c.1899	Leased to GN (as its No. 708) 5/1/1902.
709	Brooks	7/1898	2988	EM 309	EM 309	c.1899	Leased to GN (as its No. 709) 5/1/1902.
710	Brooks	7/1898	2989	EM 310	EM 310	c.1899	Leased to GN (as its No. 710) 5/1/1902.
711	Brooks	7/1898	2990	EM 311	EM 311	c.1899	Leased to GN (as its No. 711) 5/1/1902.
712	Brooks	9/1898	3045	EM 312	EM 312	c.1899	Leased to GN (as its No. 712) 5/1/1902.
713	Brooks	9/1898	3046	EM 313	EM 313	c.1899	Leased to GN (as its No. 713) 5/1/1902.
714	Brooks	9/1898	3047	EM 314	EM 314	c.1899	Leased to GN (as its No. 714) 5/1/1902.
715	Brooks	9/1898	3048	EM 315	EM 315	c.1899	Leased to GN (as its No. 715) 5/1/1902.
716	Brooks	10/1898	3049	EM 316	EM 316	c.1899	Leased to GN (as its No. 716) 5/1/1902.
717	Brooks	10/1898	3050	EM 317	EM 317	c.1899	Leased to GN (as its No. 717) 5/1/1902.
718	Brooks	10/1898	3051	EM 318	EM 318	c.1899	Leased to GN (as its No. 718) 5/1/1902.
719	Brooks	10/1898	3052	EM 319	EM 319	c.1899	Leased to GN (as its No. 719) 5/1/1902.

Class 45A 4-8-0: 19x32-55-210(180)-182,000-150,000-32,140

No.	Builder	Date Built	C/N	Disposition
770	Brooks	7/1900	3563	Leased to GN (as its No. 770) 5/1/1902.
771	Brooks	7/1900	3564	Leased to GN (as its No. 771) 5/1/1902.
772	Brooks	7/1900	3565	Leased to GN (as its No. 772) 5/1/1902.
773	Brooks	7/1900	3566	Leased to GN (as its No. 773) 5/1/1902.
774	Brooks	7/1900	3567	Leased to GN (as its No. 774) 5/1/1902.
775	Brooks	7/1900	3568	Leased to GN (as its No. 775) 5/1/1902.
776	Brooks	7/1900	3569	Leased to GN (as its No. 776) 5/1/1902.
777	Brooks	7/1900	3570	Leased to GN (as its No. 777) 5/1/1902.
778	Brooks	7/1900	3571	Leased to GN (as its No. 778) 5/1/1902.
779	Brooks	7/1900	3572	Leased to GN (as its No. 779) 5/1/1902.

Class 27B 4-6-0: 18x24-63-180-127,800-97,800-18,880

No.	Builder	Date Built	C/N	Original No.	Renumbered From	Date	Disposition
991	Brooks	6/1898	2968	DMR&N 9	EM 231	4/4/1900	Leased to GN (as its 991) 5/1/1902. Sold to Isaac Joseph Iron Company 11/28/1902. Then apparently sold to the St.Louis, Memphis & Southeastern, which was acquired by the St.Louis-San Francisco Railway while the locomotive was en route. Received SL-SF No. 698. Renumbered SL-SF 2698 c.1903.

Class 46 4-6-0: 20x30-63-210(200)-166,580-130,000-32,380

No.	Builder	Date Built	C/N	Original No.	Renumbered From	Date	Disposition
1000	Brooks	5/1898	2954	EM 150	EM 150	c.1899	Leased to GN (as its No. 1000) 5/1/1902.
1001	Brooks	5/1898	2955	EM 151	EM 151	c.1899	Leased to GN (as its No. 1001) 5/1/1902.
1002	Brooks	5/1898	2956	EM 152	EM 152	c.1899	Leased to GN (as its No. 1002) 5/1/1902.
1003	Brooks	5/1898	2957	EM 153	EM 153	c.1899	Leased to GN (as its No. 1003) 5/1/1902.
1004	Brooks	5/1898	2958	EM 154	EM 154	c.1899	Leased to GN (as its No. 1004) 5/1/1902.
1005	Brooks	5/1898	2959	EM 155	EM 155	c.1899	Leased to GN (as its No. 1005) 5/1/1902.
1006	Brooks	5/1898	2960	EM 156	EM 156	c.1899	Leased to GN (as its No. 1006) 5/1/1902.
1007	Brooks	5/1898	2961	EM 157	EM 157	c.1899	Leased to GN (as its No. 1007) 5/1/1902.

FAIRHAVEN AND SOUTHERN RAILROAD COMPANY

Class 10(2) 4-6-0: 18x24-55-150(140)-100,800-77,000-16,820

No.	Builder	Date Built	C/N	Disposition
1	Schenectady	5/1889	2860	Sold to S&M RR (No. 298) 3/30/1898.
2	Schenectady	5/1889	2861	Sold to S&M RR (No. 299) 3/30/1898.

FARMERS' GRAIN & SHIPPING COMPANY

Class B-5 (Old Class 19) 4-4-0: 16x24-55-140-66,170-41,600-13,290

No.	Builder	Date Rcvd.	C/N	Original No.	Renumbered From	Date	Disposition	Note
1	Rogers	6/5/1878	2478	StP&P 28	GN 256(2)	1902	Sold A. Guthrie & Co. 6/1913.	7

Class B-10 4-4-0: 17x24-55-140-72,650-45,400-15,006

No.	Builder	Date Rcvd.	C/N	Original No.	Renumbered From	Date	Disposition
2	Baldwin	5/21/1882	6190	StPM&M 117	GN 269	1905	Unknown.

Class D-3(1) 2-6-0: 18x24-57-175-107,000-90,000-20,292

No.	Builder	Date Built	C/N	Original No.	Renumbered From	Date	Disposition
3	Baldwin	7/1892	12854	D&W 6	GN 297	1905	Return to GN as No. 430(2) proposed in 1927, but sold for scrap DI&M in 1927 prior to return

Class D-2 2-6-0: 19x24-55-150(140)-105,040-97,290-18,745

No.	Builder	Date Rcvd.	C/N	Original No.	Renumbered From	Date	Disposition
4	Rogers	11/14/1888	4056	StPM&M 341	BDL&S 4	?	Return to GN as No. 341(2) proposed in 1927, but sold for scrap DI&M in 1927 prior to return.

KOOTENAI VALLEY RAILWAY COMPANY

Class 15 4-4-0: 17x24-63-140-74,800-49,200-13,100

No.	Builder	Date Rcvd.	C/N	Original No.	Renumbered From	Date	Disposition
187	Pittsburgh	3/23/1881	478	StPM&M 67(2)	GN 187(2)	8/30/1899	Relettered GN 187(2) 6/4/1901 at East Spokane.

Class 14 4-4-0: 17x24-55-140-73,400-48,000-15,010

No.	Builder	Date Rcvd.	C/N	Original No.	Renumbered From	Date	Disposition
290	Pittsburgh	9/25/1880	443	StPM&M 74	GN 290	8/30/1899	Relettered GN 290 7/20/1901 at East Spokane.

MINNEAPOLIS WESTERN RAILWAY COMPANY

Class 4 0-4-0: 15x24-49-140-53,900-53,900-15,430

No.	Builder	Date Rcvd.	C/N	Original No.	Renumbered From	Date	Disposition
1(1)	Brooks	8/16/1882	757	StPM&M 187	StPM&M 187	11/27/1891	Returned to StPM&M (as No. 187) 1/26/1892.

Class 31(2) 0-6-0: 18x24-49-150(140)-86,450-86,450-18,880

No.	Builder	Date Rcvd.	C/N	Original No.	Renumbered From	Date	Disposition
1(2)	Brooks	5/12/1887	3740	StPM&M 98	StPM&M 98	1/28/1892	Renumbered GN 36(2) c.1899. Sold GN after 1915.

Class 32 0-6-0: 17x24-49-140-67,050-67,050-16,840

No.	Builder	Date Rcvd.	C/N	Original No.	Renumbered From	Date	Disposition
2	Brooks	8/31/1882	765	StPM&M 195	StPM&M 195	11/27/1891	Renumbered GN 28(2) c.1899. Sold GN after 1915.

MINNESOTA AND PACIFIC RAILROAD COMPANY

Class – 4-4-0: 14x22-60?- ? -48,000- ? - ?

No.	Name	Builder	Date Rcvd.	C/N	Disposition		Notes
1	"William Crooks"	Smith & Jackson	9/9/1861	?	Sold StP&P (No. 1) 3/10/1862.		8
2	"Edmund Rice"	Smith & Jackson	9/28/1861	?	Sold StP&P (No. 2) 3/10/1862.		

THE MONTANA CENTRAL RAILWAY COMPANY (See Note 6)

Class 34 4-4-0: 18x24-63-140-94,100-60,300-14,690

No.	Builder	Date Rcvd.	C/N	Original No.	Renumbered From	Date	Disposition
1	Rogers	5/25/1887	3750	StPM&M 208	StPM&M 208	3/22/1888	Renumbered GN 208 c.1900.
2	Rogers	5/25/1887	3751	StPM&M 209	StPM&M 209	4/13/1888	Renumbered GN 209 c.1900.
3	Rogers	5/30/1887	3752	StPM&M 210	StPM&M 210	3/26/1888	Renumbered GN 210 c.1900.

Class 35 2-6-0: 19x24-55-150(140)-105,040-87,290-18,750

No.	Builder	Date Rcvd.	C/N	Original No.	Renumbered From	Date	Disposition
4	Rogers	8/27/1887	3802	StPM&M 322(1)	StPM&M 322(1)	3/22/1888	Renumbered GN 322 c.1900..
5	Rogers	8/31/1887	3804	StPM&M 323(1)	StPM&M 323(1)	4/2/1888	Renumbered GN 323 c.1900.
6	Rogers	9/11/1887	3807	StPM&M 324(1)	StPM&M 324(1)	2/25/1888	Renumbered GN 324 c.1900.
7	Rogers	7/27/1887	3783	StPM&M 306	StPM&M 306	10/13/1888	Renumbered StPM&M 306 5/25/1892 at Great Falls.
8	Rogers	9/9/1888	4004	StPM&M 325	StPM&M 325	11/16/1888	Renumbered GN 325 c.1900.

Class 36 2-6-0: 19x24-55-150(140)-105,040-87,290-18,750

No.	Builder	Date Rcvd.	C/N	Original No.	Renumbered From	Date	Disposition
9(1)	Rogers	9/9/1888	4007	StPM&M 326	StPM&M 326	11/17/1888	Renumbered StPM&M 326 6/20/1892 at Great Falls.

THE MONTANA CENTRAL RAILWAY COMPANY - continued

Class 8(3) 0-6-0: 19x28-49-200(160)-137,000-137,000-28,060

No.	Builder	Date Built	C/N	Disposition
9(2)	Brooks	10/1898	3055	Renumbered GN 85(2) c.1900.

Class 24 4-4-0: 17x24-63-140-76,650-49,159-13,100

No.	Builder	Date Rcvd.	C/N	Original No.	Renumbered From	Date	Disposition
10(1)	Baldwin	5/19/1882	6182	StPM&M 108	StPM&M 108	6/18/1888	Returned to StPM&M (as No. 108) in place of StPM&M No. 322(2) 1/14/1889. Renumbered StPM&M 108 at Minot 2/3/1889.
11(1)	Baldwin	5/18/1882	6181	StPM&M 109	StPM&M 109	11/18/1888	Returned to StPM&M (as No. 109) in place of StPM&M No. 323(2) 1/18/1889. Renumbered StPM&M 109 at Minot 2/3/1889.

Class 35 2-6-0: 19x24-55-150(140)-105,040-87,290-18,750

No.	Builder	Date Rcvd.	C/N	Original No.	Renumbered From	Date	Disposition
10(2)	Rogers	9/3/1888	4001	StPM&M 322(2)	StPM&M 322(2)	1/7/1889	Renumbered GN 327 c.1900.
11(2)	Rogers	9/3/1888	4002	StPM&M 323(2)	StPM&M 323(2)	1/7/1889	Renumbered GN 328 c.1900.

Class 34 4-4-0: 18x24-63-140-94,100-60,300-14,690

No.	Builder	Date Rcvd.	C/N	Original No.	Renumbered From	Date	Disposition
12	Rogers	5/30/1887	3753	StPM&M 211	StPM&M 211	11/20/1888	Renumbered GN 211 c.1900.
13	Rogers	6/3/1887	3754	StPM&M 212	StPM&M 212	11/11/1888	Renumbered GN 212 c.1900.

Class 31(2) 0-6-0: 18x26-49-150(140)-86,450-86,450-20,460

No.	Builder	Date Rcvd.	C/N	Original No.	Renumbered From	Date	Disposition
14	Rogers	9/17/1888	4010	StPM&M 226	StPM&M 226	12/14/1888	Renumbered GN 38(2) c.1900
15	Rogers	9/20/1888	4011	StPM&M 227	StPM&M 227	12/14/1888	Renumbered GN 39(2) c.1900.

Class 36 2-6-0: 19x24-55-150(140)-105,040-87,290-18,750

No.	Builder	Date Rcvd.	C/N	Original No.	Renumbered From	Date	Disposition
16	Rogers	9/5/1888	4003	StPM&M 324(2)	StPM&M 324(2)	1/2/1889	Returned to StPM&M (as No. 347) 1892.
17	Rogers	9/11/1888	4008	StPM&M 327	StPM&M 327	1/2/1889	Renumbered GN 348 c.1900.
18	Rogers	9/16/1888	4009	StPM&M 328	StPM&M 328	4/7/1889	Renumbered GN 349 c.1900.

Class 7(2) 0-6-0: 19x26-49-180(160)-114,700-114,700-26,050

No.	Builder	Date Rcvd.	C/N	Disposition
25	Brooks	1/1/1893	2206	Renumbered GN 64(2) 1900.
26	Brooks	1/1/1893	2207	Renumbered GN 65(2) 1900.

Class 8(3) 0-6-0: 19x28-49-200(160)-137,000-137,000-28,060

No.	Builder	Date Built	C/N	Disposition
27	Brooks	10/1898	3056	Renumbered GN 86(2) c.1900.
28	Brooks	10/1898	3057	Renumbered GN 87(2) c.1900.

Class 37(2) 2-6-0: 19x24-55-180(160)-118,000-102,000-21,420

No.	Builder	Date Built	C/N	Original No.	Renumbered From	Date	Disposition
30	Brooks	8/28/1893	2371	GN 361(1)	GN 361(1)	9/24/1893	Renumbered GN 420 c.1900.

Class 38 4-8-0: 20x26-55-180(160)-156,000-132,000-25,720

No.	Builder	Date Rcvd.	C/N	Original No.	Renumbered From	Date	Disposition
50	Brooks	12/3/1891	1998	StPM&M 410(1)	GN 410(1)	2/7/1892	Sold GN 6/1900 (No. 611).
51	Brooks	12/8/1891	1999	StPM&M 411(1)	GN 411(1)	2/9/1892	Sold GN 6/1900 (No. 612).
52	Brooks	12/8/1891	2000	StPM&M 412(1)	GN 412(1)	2/20/1892	Sold GN 6/1900 (No. 613).
53	Brooks	12/14/1891	2001	StPM&M 413(1)	GN 413(1)	5/6/1892	Sold GN 6/1900 (No. 614).
54(1)	Brooks	10/17/1891	1973	StPM&M 401	StPM&M 401	c.1892	Returned to StPM&M and leased to GN (as GN No. 401) c.1893.
54(2)	Brooks	12/14/1891	2002	StPM&M 414(1)	GN 414(1)	9/2/1893	Sold GN 6/1900 (No. 615).

Class 44 4-8-0: 21x34-55-210(180)-212,750-172,000-41,710

No.	Builder	Date Built	C/N	Disposition
100	Brooks	12/1897	2866	Renumbered GN 800 1900.
101	Brooks	12/1897	2867	Renumbered GN 801 1900.
102	Brooks	8/1898	2999	Renumbered GN 802 1900.
103	Brooks	8/1898	3000	Renumbered GN 803 1900.
104	Brooks	8/1898	3001	Renumbered GN 804 1900.
105	Brooks	8/1898	3002	Renumbered GN 805 1900.
106	Brooks	8/1898	3003	Renumbered GN 806 1900.
107	Brooks	8/1898	3004	Renumbered GN 807 1900.

MONTANA WESTERN RAILWAY COMPANY

Class F-1S 2-8-0: 22x26-55-180-(150)-136,000-120,000-29,170

No.	Builder	Date Rcvd.	C/N	Original No.	Renumbered From	Date	Disposition
5	Brooks	8/22/1892	2137	GN 478(1)	GN 544	10/1950	Sold for scrap at Seattle, 1956, to Pacific Hide and Fur Company, Great Falls, MT

Class D-4 2-6-0: 19x24-55-180(160)-119,900-108,000-21,420

No.	Builder	Date Rcvd.	C/N	Original No.	Renumbered From	Date	Disposition	Notes
10	Brooks	11/27/1893	2409	GN 364(1)	OWR&N 10	5/1916	Out of service in 1947, disposition unknown.	9, 95

THE NELSON & FORT SHEPPARD RAILWAY COMPANY

NOTE: WHILE THERE IS NO EVIDENCE THAT THE NELSON & FORT SHEPPARD USED A CLASS SYSTEM, CLASSES OF THE GREAT NORTHERN ARE USED FOR CLARITY.

Class B-23 4-4-0: 18x24-63-160(140)-94,100-56,100-14,690

No.	Builder	Date Built	C/N	Disposition	Notes
7	Baldwin	10/1893	13803	Transferred to SF&N (No. 7) c.1898.	10

Class E-13 4-6-0: 19x24-55-160(150)-110,000-85,000-20,090

No.	Builder	Date Built	C/N	Disposition	Notes
8	Baldwin	10/1893	13807	Transferred to SF&N (No. 8) c.1898.	10

PACIFIC SHORT LINE

NOTE: WHILE THERE IS NO EVIDENCE THAT THE PACIFIC SHORT LINE USED A CLASS SYSTEM, GREAT NORTHERN CLASSES ARE USED HERE FOR CLARITY.

Class 27C 4-6-0: 18x24-56-150-102,800-84,000-17,700

No.	Builder	Date Built	C/N	Original No.	Renumbered From	Date	Disposition	Notes
10	Rhode Island	12/1889	2264	MCCo 131(1)	MCCo 131(1)	12/1889	Sold SCO&W (No. 16) 12/1/1891.	36
11	Rhode Island	12/1889	2265	MCCo 132(1)	MCCo 132(1)	12/1889	Sold SCO&W (No. 17) 12/1/1891.	36
12	Rhode Island	4/1890	2328	–	–	–	Sold SCO&W (No. 18) 12/1/1891.	

Class 11(2) 4-4-0: 17x24-63-145-80,000-51,000-12,770

No.	Builder	Date Built	C/N	Disposition
13	Rhode Island	4/1889	2202	Sold SCO&W (No. 13) 12/1/1891.

Class 36A 2-6-0: 19x24-55-150-104,800-89,300-20,080

No.	Builder	Date Built	C/N	Disposition
14	Rhode Island	7/1890	2406	Sold SCO&W (No. 14) 12/1/1891.

Class 27A 4-6-0: 19x24-55-150-105,600-86,650-20,080

No.	Builder	Date Built	C/N	Disposition
15	Rhode Island	8/1890	2440	Sold SCO&W (No. 15) 12/1/1891.

RED MOUNTAIN RAILWAY COMPANY

NOTE: WHILE THERE IS NO EVIDENCE THAT THE RED MOUNTAIN USED A CLASS SYSTEM, CLASSES OF THE GREAT NORTHERN ARE USED FOR CLARITY.

Class F-4(2) 2-8-0: 19x24-47-180(170)-135,000-113,300-26,640

No.	Builder	Date Built	C/N	Disposition	Notes
9	Baldwin	8/1896	15013	Sold to GN 7/1/1907. Renumbered GN 1094 at Hillyard 6/9/1908.	2

THE ST. PAUL AND PACIFIC RAILROAD COMPANY
FIRST DIVISION OF THE ST. PAUL AND PACIFIC RAILROAD

NOTE: CLASS NUMBERS OF THE StPM&M ARE USED FOR CLARITY, EVEN THOUGH THE StP&P APPARENTLY DID NOT USE A CLASS SYSTEM

Class 1 4-4-0: 12x22-60- ? - 44,000- ? - ? as earliest known (1867). Weight increased to 48,000 pounds after the rebuild completed on 5/22/1869 (See Note 8).

No.	Name	Builder	Date Rcvd.	C/N	Original No.	Renumbered From	Date	Disposition
1	"William Crooks"	Smith & Jackson	9/9/1861	?	M&P 1	M&P 1	c.3/1862	Sold StPM&M (No. 1) 6/14/1879.

THE ST. PAUL AND PACIFIC RAILROAD COMPANY

FIRST DIVISION OF THE ST.PAUL AND PACIFIC RAILROAD - continued

Class 2 4-4-0: 14x22-54- ? - 52,000- ? - ? as earliest known (apparently after a major repair in 1865). Driver diameter changed to 48" by 1880. (See Note 8).

No.	Name	Builder	Date Rcvd.	C/N	Original No.	Renumbered From	Date	Disposition
2	"Edmund Rice"	Smith & Jackson	9/28/1861	?	M&P 2	M&P 2	c.3/1862	Name changed to "Sarachet" date unknown. Sold StPM&M (No. 2) 6/14/1879.

Class – 4-4-0: 14x22-54- ? - 50,000- ? - ? as earliest known. Cylinders may have been later changed to 12x22.

No.	Name	Builder	Date Rcvd.	C/N	Disposition	Notes
3	"Minnesota"	Norris	9/14/1863	?	Name changed to "E.L.Drake" date unknown. Name then changed to "Pacific" date unknown. Scrapped due to accident (lost in quicksand near Cedar Lake, MN) 5/1867.	12

Class – 4-4-0: 14x20-54- ? - 48,000- ? - ? as earliest known. Driver diameter changed to 48" by 1880.

No.	Name	Builder	Date Rcvd.	C/N	Disposition	Notes
4	"Itasca"	Souther	1/31/1865	?	Sold StPM&M (No. 4) 6/14/1879.	11

Class 6 4-4-0: 16x22-60- ? - 76,000- ? - ? as earliest known. Cylinders changed to 16x24 by 1880.

No.	Name	Builder	Date Built	C/N	Disposition
5	"Anoka"	Danforth	1866	?	Name changed to or from "C.V.Culver" date unknown. Sold StPM&M (No. 5) 6/14/1879.

Class 5(1) 4-4-0: 16x22-60- ? -64,000- ? - ?

No.	Name	Builder	Date Built	C/N	Disposition	Notes
6	"St.Paul"	Norris	1865	?	Sold StPM&M (No. 6) 6/14/1879.	12, 20
7	"St.Cloud"	Norris	1865	?	Sold StPM&M (No. 7) 6/14/1879.	12, 20

Class 10(1) 4-4-0: 14x22-63- ? -57,600-35,000- ?

No.	Name	Builder	Date Built	C/N	Disposition	Notes
8	"George L. Becker"	Mason	9/1867	270	Sold StPM&M (No. 8) 6/14/1879.	13

Class 11(1) 4-4-0: 15x24-63- ? -62,750-40,350- ?

No.	Name	Builder	Date Rcvd.	C/N	Disposition	Notes
9	"F.R. Delano"	Mason	5/1868	279	Sold StPM&M (No. 9) 6/14/1879.	13

Class 12(1) 4-4-0: 15x22-63- ? -60,000-37,600- ?

No.	Name	Builder	Date Rcvd.	C/N	Disposition	Notes
10	"Jared Benson"	Mason	7/1868	283	Sold StPM&M (No. 10) 6/14/1879.	14

Class 11(1) 4-4-0: 15x24-63- ? -62,750-40,350- ?

No.	Name	Builder	Date Rcvd.	C/N	Disposition	Notes
11	"Jud Rice"	Mason	5/1869	310	Sold StPM&M (No. 11) 6/14/1879.	15

Class 7(1) 4-4-0: 15x22-63- ? -64,500-41,800- ?

No.	Name	Builder	Date Built	C/N	Disposition
12	"Wayzata"	Danforth	1868	?	Sold StPM&M (No. 12) 6/14/1879.
13	"Willmar"	Danforth	1868	?	Sold StPM&M (No. 13) 6/14/1879.
14	"Litchfield"	Danforth	1868	?	Sold StPM&M (No. 14) 6/14/1879.

Class 8(1) 4-4-0: 16x24-63- ? -66,000-41,850- ?

No.	Name	Builder	Date Built	C/N	Disposition
15	"H. Trott"	Danforth	1869	?	Sold StPM&M (No. 15) 6/14/1879.

Class 9(1) 4-4-0: 16x24-63-140-66,000-41,850-11,610

No.	Name	Builder	Date Built	C/N	Disposition
16	"Kerkhoven"	Danforth	1869	?	Sold StPM&M (No. 16) 6/14/1879.

Class 13 4-4-0: 16x24-61½ -140-66,100-43,700-11,600

No.	Name	Builder	Date Built	C/N	Disposition
17	"Chippewa"	Pittsburgh	7/1870	75	Sold StPM&M (No. 17) 6/14/1879.
18	"Hancock"	Pittsburgh	9/1870	76	Sold StPM&M (No. 18) 6/14/1879.
19	"C.N.Parker"	Pittsburgh	9/1870	77	Sold StPM&M (No. 19) 6/14/1879.

Class 17 4-4-0: 15x24-63- ? -68,800-43,000- ? originally. No. 22 was rebuilt prior to 1880 to 16x24-63- ?–70,000-44,550- ? and consequently was placed in Class 16 after its purchase by StPM&M. (See Note 16)

No.	Name	Builder	Date Rcvd.	C/N	Original No.	Renumbered From	Date	Disposition
20		Baldwin	12/1871	2619	NP 20(1)	NP 20(1)	12/1871	Sold StPM&M (No. 20) 6/14/1879.
21		Baldwin	12/1871	2621	NP 21(1)	NP 21(1)	12/1871	Sold StPM&M (No. 21) 6/14/1879.
22	"J. H. Randall"	Baldwin	12/1871	2638	NP 22(1)	NP 22(1)	12/1871	Sold StPM&M (No. 22) 6/14/1879.
23		Baldwin	12/1871	2639	NP 23(1)	NP 23(1)	12/1871	Sold StPM&M (No. 23) 6/14/1879.

Class 13 4-4-0: 16x24-63-140-72,700-46,000-11,600

No.	Builder	Date Rcvd.	C/N	Disposition
24	Pittsburgh	12/1875	320	Sold StPM&M (No. 24) 6/14/1879.
25	Pittsburgh	12/1875	322	Sold StPM&M (No. 25) 6/14/1879.
26	Pittsburgh	12/1875	323	Sold StPM&M (No. 26) 6/14/1879.

Class 19 4-4-0: 16x24-57 5/8-140-66,170-41,600-12,605

No.	Name	Builder	Date Rcvd.	C/N	Disposition
27		Rogers	6/5/1878	2477	Sold StPM&M (No. 27) 6/14/1879.
28		Rogers	6/5/1878	2478	Sold StPM&M (No. 28) 6/14/1879.
29		Rogers	6/17/1878	2480	Sold StPM&M (No. 29) 6/14/1879.
30		Rogers	6/26/1878	2481	Sold StPM&M (No. 30) 6/14/1879.
31		Rogers	6/26/1878	2483	Sold StPM&M (No. 31) 6/14/1879.
32		Rogers	6/29/1878	2484	Sold StPM&M (No. 32) 6/14/1879.
33		Rogers	6/29/1878	2485	Sold StPM&M (No. 33) 6/14/1879.
34		Rogers	7/12/1878	2486	Sold StPM&M (No. 34) 6/14/1879.
35		Rogers	7/26/1878	2488	Sold StPM&M (No. 35) 6/14/1879.
36		Rogers	7/31/1878	2490	Sold StPM&M (No. 36) 6/14/1879.
37		Rogers	8/15/1878	2491	Sold StPM&M (No. 37) 6/14/1879.
38	"G. W. Turner"	Rogers	9/19/1878	2492	Sold StPM&M (No. 38) 6/14/1879.
39		Rogers	10/7/1878	2495	Sold StPM&M (No. 39) 6/14/1879.
40		Rogers	10/8/1878	2496	Sold StPM&M (No. 40) 6/14/1879.
41		Rogers	10/30/1878	2498	Sold StPM&M (No. 41) 6/14/1879.
42		Rogers	10/30/1878	2500	Sold StPM&M (No. 42) 6/14/1879.

Class 20 4-4-0: 17x24-575/8-140-70,300-44,800-14,230

No.	Builder	Date Rcvd.	C/N	Disposition
43	Rogers	1/27/1879	2509	Sold StPM&M (No. 43) 6/14/1879.
44	Rogers	1/27/1879	2511	Sold StPM&M (No. 44) 6/14/1879.

Class 21 2-6-0: 16x20-46-140-6,250-62,000-13,245

No.	Builder	Date Rcvd.	C/N	Disposition
45	Rogers	4/12/1879	2519	Sold StPM&M (No. 45) 6/14/1879.
46	Rogers	4/22/1879	2521	Sold StPM&M (No. 46) 6/14/1879.

Class 16 4-4-0: 16x24-63-140-70,000-44,550-11,600

No.	Builder	Date Rcvd.	C/N	Disposition	Notes
(47)	Baldwin	11/1879	4848	Delivered as StPM&M 47.	17
(48)	Baldwin	11/1879	4849	Delivered as StPM&M 48.	17
(49)	Baldwin	11/1879	4852	Delivered as StPM&M 49.	17
(50)	Baldwin	11/1879	4853	Delivered as StPM&M 50.	17

THE ST. PAUL, MINNEAPOLIS AND MANITOBA RAILWAY COMPANY

All of the St.Paul, Minneapolis and Manitoba (StPM&M) locomotives still on the roster as of February 1, 1890, were leased to the Great Northern, retaining their StPM&M numbers. About 1892, those locomotives remaining on the roster were considered to be Great Northern locomotives (See Note 43). The locomotives remaining on the roster on November 1, 1907, were formally sold to the Great Northern with the remainder of the StPM&M property.

Class 1 4-4-0: 12x22-60- ? -48,000- ? - ?- as acquired from StP&P. Rebuilt in 1887 to 12x22-63-120(110)-55,400-35,950-4,700, at which time the old straight-topped boiler was apparently replaced with a wagon-top boiler.

No.	Builder	Date Rcvd.	C/N	Original No.	Renumbered From	Date	Disposition
1	Smith & Jackson	9/9/1861	?	M&P 1	StP&P 1	c.6/1879	To GN as GN 1(1).

Class 2(1) 4-4-0: 14x22-56- ? -52,000- ? - ?

No.	Builder	Date Rcvd.	C/N	Original No.	Renumbered From	Date	Disposition
2	Smith & Jackson	9/28/1861	?	M&P 2	StP&P 2	c.6/1879	Broken up at St.Paul shop 4/23/1887.

THE ST. PAUL, MINNEAPOLIS AND MANITOBA RAILWAY COMPANY - continued

Class 3 0-4-0: 14x22-49-125-49,000-49,000-9,350

No.	Builder	Date Rcvd.	C/N	Original No.	Renumbered From	Date	Disposition	Notes
3	Brooks	10/13/1879	354	StPM&M 51(1)	StPM&M 51(1)	1880	Scrapped 6/1901 as GN 3(1).	

Class – 4-4-0: 14x20-48- ? -48,000- ? - ?

No.	Builder	Date Rcvd.	C/N	Original No.	Renumbered From	Date	Disposition	Notes
4	Souther	1/31/1865	?	?	StP&P 4	c.6/1879	Sold Langdon Shepard & Co. 1882.	11

Class 6 4-4-0: 16x24-60- ? –76,000- ? - ? as acquired from StP&P. Driver diameter increased to 61½" on 11/14/1881. Rebuilt at some time prior to 6/30/1891 to 16x24-63- ? - 66,000-41,850 - ?. Rebuilt again (with smaller drivers for switching) on 8/29/1891 to 16x24-49-125-68,500-45,530-13,320.

No.	Builder	Date Built	C/N	Original No.	Renumbered From	Date	Disposition	Notes
5	Danforth	1866	?	StP&P 5	StP&P 5	c.6/1879	Renumbered GN 4(1) 4/13/1899. Sold to Fitzhugh Co. 12/27/1902.	

Class 5(1) 4-4-0: 16x22-60- ? -64,000- ? - ?

No.	Builder	Date Built	C/N	Original No.	Renumbered From	Date	Disposition	Notes
6	Norris	1865	?	StP&P 6	StP&P 6	c.6/1879	Scrapped 11/5/1888.	12, 20
7	Norris	1865	?	StP&P 7	StP&P 7	c.6/1879	Scrapped 11/5/1888.	12, 20

Class 10(1) 4-4-0: 14x22-63- ? -57,600-35,000- ?. (See Note 13)

No.	Builder	Date Built	C/N	Original No.	Renumbered From	Date	Disposition
8	Mason	9/1867	270	StP&P 8	StP&P 8	c.6/1879	Engine stripped, boiler fitted for steam heating and sent to Breckenridge 12/9/1893.

Class 11(1) 4-4-0: 15x24-63- ? -62,750-40,350- ? originally. Rebuilt 12/30/1891 (with smaller drivers for switching) to 15x24-49- ? -65,250-43,850- ? and moved to Class 9(2) at that time. (See Note 13)

No.	Builder	Date Rcvd.	C/N	Original No.	Renumbered From	Date	Disposition
9	Mason	5/1868	279	StP&P 9	StP&P 9	c.6/1879	Received new boiler 3/28/1888. Sold to British Columbia Mills, Timber and Trading Co. 2/16/1898.

Class 12(1) 4-4-0: 15x22-63- ? -60,000-37,600- ? originally. Rebuilt 11/16/1891 (with smaller drivers for switching) 15x22-49-125-62,500-41,100-10,730. Moved to Class 6 at some time after 6/30/1892. (See Note 14)

No.	Builder	Date Rcvd.	C/N	Original No.	Renumbered From	Date	Disposition
10	Mason	7/1868	283	StP&P 10	StP&P 10	c.6/1879	Renumbered GN 5(2) 4/4/1899. Scrapped 9/1901.

Class 11(1) 4-4-0: 15x24-63- ? -62,750-40,350- ? originally. Rebuilt 6/10/1892 (with smaller drivers for switching) to 15x24-49-125-65,250-43,850-11,710. Moved to Class 6 at some time after 6/30/1892. (See Note 15)

No.	Builder	Date Rcvd.	C/N	Original No.	Renumbered From	Date	Disposition
11	Mason	5/1869	310	StP&P 11	StP&P 11	c.6/1879	Renumbered GN No. 6(1) 3/30/1899. Sold PV&Y (No. 3) 2/18/1902. Then transferred via merger to Washington Railway & Navigation Co. (No. unknown). Sold to Northern Pacific (No. 1153) 12/10/1903. Sold to Blumauer Lumber Co. (No. unknown) 6/26/1905.

Class 7(1) 4-4-0: 15x22-63- ? -64,500-41,800- ? originally. Nos. 12 and 13 were rebuilt on 6/19/1891 and 1/19/1892, respectively, (with smaller drivers for switching) to 15x22-49-125-67,000-45,300-10,730 and were moved to Class 8(2) at that time. On 8/2/1892, No. 14 was rebuilt to these same dimensions. All three locomotives were moved to Class 6.

No.	Builder	Date Built	C/N	Original No.	Renumbered From	Date	Disposition
12	Danforth	1868	?	StP&P 12	StP&P 12	c.6/1879	Renumbered GN No. 7(1) 4/1/1899. Scrapped at St.Paul 9/22/1901.
13	Danforth	1868	?	StP&P 13	StP&P 13	c.6/1879	Renumbered GN No. 8(2) 4/5/1899. Scrapped at Delta 4/28/1903.
14	Danforth	1868	?	StP&P 14	StP&P 14	c.6/1879	Renumbered GN No. 9(2) 4/11/1899. Sold to Fitzhugh Co. 9/8/1902.

Class 8(1) 4-4-0: 16x24-63- ? -66,000-41,850- ? originally. Moved to Class 6. Rebuilt 12/14/1891 (with smaller drivers for switching) to 16x24-49-125-68,500-45,350-13,320.)

No.	Builder	Date Built	C/N	Original No.	Renumbered From	Date	Disposition
15	Danforth	1869	?	StP&P 15	StP&P 15	c.6/1879	Renumbered GN No. 10(2) 4/13/1899. Sold to Fitzhugh Co. 6/4/1902.

Class 9(1) 4-4-0: 16x24-63-140-66,000-41,850-11,610. Moved to Class 6 before 6/30/1891. Then moved to Class 5(2) between 6/30/1891 and 6/30/1892.

No.	Builder	Date Built	C/N	Original No.	Renumbered From	Date	Disposition
16	Danforth	1869	?	StP&P 16	StP&P 16	c.6/1879	Renumbered GN 240 3/29/1899.

Class 13 4-4-0: 16x24-63-140-66,100-43,700-11,600 originally. No. 17 rebuilt 3/7/1893 (with smaller drivers for switching) to 16x24-49-130-68,600-47,200-13,860 and moved to Class 6.

No.	Builder	Date Built	C/N	Original No.	Renumbered From	Date	Disposition
17	Pittsburgh	7/1870	75	StP&P 17	StP&P 17	c.6/1879	Renumbered GN 11(2) 4/8/1899. Then renumbered GN 244(2) 1907.
18	Pittsburgh	9/1870	76	StP&P 18	StP&P 18	c.6/1879	Renumbered GN 241 1899.
19	Pittsburgh	9/1870	77	StP&P 19	StP&P 19	c.6/1879	Renumbered GN 242 4/7/1899.

Class 17 4-4-0: 15x24-63- ? -68,800-43,000- ? originally. No. 22 was rebuilt prior to 1880 to 16x24-63-140-70,000-44,550-11,600 and moved to Class 16. (See Note 16)

No.	Builder	Date Rcvd.	C/N	Original No.	Renumbered From	Date	Disposition
20	Baldwin	12/1871	2619	NP 20(1)	StP&P 20	c.6/1879	Renumbered GN 243 3/1899.
21	Baldwin	12/1871	2621	NP 21(1)	StP&P 21	c.6/1879	Renumbered GN 244(1) 4/1/1899. Scrapped at St.Paul Shops 11/18/1902.
22	Baldwin	12/1871	2638	NP 22(1)	StP&P 22	c.6/1879	Renumbered GN 245 4/8/1899.
23	Baldwin	12/1871	2639	NP 23(1)	StP&P 23	c.6/1879	Renumbered GN 246 3/30/1899. Scrapped 11/12/1900.

Class 13 4-4-0: 16x24-63-140-72,700-46,000-11,600

No.	Builder	Date Rcvd.	C/N	Original No.	Renumbered From	Date	Disposition
24	Pittsburgh	12/1875	320	StP&P 24	StP&P 24	c.6/1879	Renumbered GN 247 3/31/1899. Retired 1901, changed to weed burner 3/18/1902.
25	Pittsburgh	12/1875	322	StP&P 25	StP&P 25	c.6/1879	Scrapped 11/1898.
26	Pittsburgh	12/1875	323	StP&P 26	StP&P 26	c.6/1879	Renumbered GN 248 3/25/1899.

Class 19 4-4-0: 16x24-58-140-66,170-41,600-12,605 originally. Later changed to 16x24-55-140-66,170-41,600-13,290 (dates are shown in parentheses if known).

No.	Builder	Date Rcvd.	C/N	Original No.	Renumbered From	Date	Disposition
27	Rogers	6/5/1878	2477	StP&P 27	StP&P 27	c.6/1879	Renumbered GN 255(2) 3/31/1899. (10/5/1897)
28	Rogers	6/5/1878	2478	StP&P 28	StP&P 28	c.6/1879	Renumbered GN 256(2) 4/6/1899. Sold to Devils Lake & Northern 9/14/1902, and renumbered FG&S 1.
29	Rogers	6/17/1878	2480	StP&P 29	StP&P 29	c.6/1879	Renumbered GN 257(2) 4/7/1899. Sold to R.A. Elzy 7/17/1902.
30	Rogers	6/26/1878	2481	StP&P 30	StP&P 30	c.6/1879	Renumbered GN 258(2) 4/5/1899. Converted to weed burner 3/18/1902. Scrapped 8/6/1903. (7/1895?)
31	Rogers	6/26/1878	2483	StP&P 31	StP&P 31	c.6/1879	Renumbered GN 259 4/5/1899. Converted to weed burner 5/20/1902. Sold to Oregon Southern Railway 3/20/1905.
32	Rogers	6/29/1878	2484	StP&P 32	StP&P 32	c.6/1879	Renumbered GN 260 4/13/1899. Sold to R.A. Elzy 7/17/1902. (9/13/1897)
33	Rogers	6/29/1878	2485	StP&P 33	StP&P 33	c.6/1879	Renumbered GN 261 4/6/1899. Scrapped 1901. (7/29/1897)
34	Rogers	7/12/1878	2486	StP&P 34	StP&P 34	c.6/1879	Renumbered GN 262 4/13/1899. (4/19/1898)
35	Rogers	7/26/1878	2488	StP&P 35	StP&P 35	c.6/1879	Renumbered GN 263 1899. Scrapped at St.Paul Shops 10/1902. (5/15/1897)
36	Rogers	7/31/1878	2490	StP&P 36	StP&P 36	c.6/1879	Renumbered GN 264 1899. Scrapped 1901. (7/30/1892)
37	Rogers	8/15/1878	2491	StP&P 37	StP&P 37	c.6/1879	Scrapped 11/1898.
38	Rogers	9/19/1878	2492	StP&P 38	StP&P 38	c.6/1879	Destroyed by fire at Bottineau, ND, roundhouse, 11/23/1896, and broken up at St.Paul shops. (8/19/1895)
39	Rogers	10/7/1878	2495	StP&P 39	StP&P 39	c.6/1879	Renumbered GN 265 4/24/1899.
40	Rogers	10/8/1878	2496	StP&P 40	StP&P 40	c.6/1879	Renumbered GN 266 3/31/1899. (9/26/1896)
41	Rogers	10/30/1878	2498	StP&P 41	StP&P 41	c.6/1879	Renumbered GN 267 4/7/1899. Sold A. Guthrie & Co. 8/19/1900. (10/2/1897)
42	Rogers	10/30/1878	2500	StP&P 42	StP&P 42	c.6/1879	Scrapped 11/1898. (11/6/1897)

Class 20 4-4-0: 17x24-58-140-70,300-44,800-14,230. Driver diameter changed from 58" to 55" on 1/14/1896 and 10/23/1897, respectively, changing dimensions to 17x24-55-140-70,300-44,800-15,010.

No.	Builder	Date Rcvd.	C/N	Original No.	Renumbered From	Date	Disposition
43	Rogers	1/27/1879	2509	StP&P 43	StP&P 43	c.6/1879	Renumbered GN 294 3/31/1899. Scrapped 10/20/1905.
44	Rogers	1/27/1879	2511	StP&P 44	StP&P 44	c.6/1879	Renumbered GN 295 4/13/1899. Scrapped 10/1902.

Class 21 2-6-0: 16x20-46-140-67,250-62,000-13,245 originally. Sometime between 6/30/1892 and 1900, the lead trucks were removed, converting these engines to 0-6-0's. The drivers of Nos. 45 and 46 were also changed (possibly at the same time as lead truck removal) to 49" diameter, on an unknown date and on 8/22/1896, respectively, leaving these locomotives with dimensions of 16x20-49-140-67,250-67,250-12,435.

No.	Builder	Date Rcvd.	C/N	Original No.	Renumbered From	Date	Disposition
45	Rogers	4/12/1879	2519	StP&P 45	StP&P 45	c.6/1879	Renumbered GN 12(2) 4/18/1899. Sold to W.D. Hofius Co. 7/1902.
46	Rogers	4/22/1879	2521	StP&P 46	StP&P 46	c.6/1879	Renumbered GN 13(2) 4/15/1899.

THE ST. PAUL, MINNEAPOLIS AND MANITOBA RAILWAY COMPANY - continued

Class 16 4-4-0: 16x24-63-140-70,000-44,550-11,600. (See Note 17)

No.	Builder	Date Rcvd.	C/N	Original No.	Disposition
47	Baldwin	11/1879	4848	(StP&P 47)	Renumbered GN 249 4/10/1899.
48	Baldwin	11/1879	4849	(StP&P 48)	Renumbered GN 250(2) 4/11/1899.
49	Baldwin	11/1879	4852	(StP&P 49)	Renumbered GN 251(2) 4/11/1899. Retired 1901(?).
50	Baldwin	11/1879	4853	(StP&P 50)	Renumbered GN 252(2) 3/31/1899.

Class 3 0-4-0: 14x22-49-125-49,000-49,000-9,350

No.	Builder	Date Rcvd.	C/N	Disposition
51(1)	Brooks	10/13/1879	354	Renumbered StPM&M 3 1880.

Class 18 4-4-0: 17x24-58-140-70,050-44,650-14,230 originally. Driver diameter on most decreased to 55" (date shown in parentheses if known), giving dimensions of 17x24-55-140-70,050-44,650-15,010. Those engines indicated by an asterisk (*) below had driver diameter increased to 63" (dates shown in parentheses if known), with dimensions of 17x24-63-140-72,700-45,450-13,100. Class of the engines with 63" drivers was later changed to 24A.

No.	Builder	Date Rcvd.	C/N	Original No.	Renumbered From	Date	Disposition
51(2)	Baldwin	5/10/1880	5083	StPM&M 67(1)	StPM&M 67(1)	c.1880	Renumbered GN 268 4/8/1899.
52*	Baldwin	3/18/1880	4996	–	–	–	Renumbered GN 117(2) 4/11/1899. Sold to F. Weyerhauser (Hawthorne, Negamon & West Superior Ry.) 7/20/1900. (c.5/1893?)
53	Baldwin	3/13/1880	4993	–	–	–	Renumbered GN 270 3/31/1899. (11/20/1897)
54	Baldwin	3/13/1880	4994	–	–	–	Renumbered GN 271 4/8/1899. (4/8/1897)
55	Baldwin	3/18/1880	4998	–	–	–	Renumbered GN 272 4/9/1899.
56	Baldwin	4/6/1880	5033	–	–	–	Renumbered GN 273 4/15/1899. Sold B&O 5/1900.
57	Baldwin	4/6/1880	5028	–	–	–	Renumbered GN 274 1899. (5/19/1897)
58	Baldwin	4/17/1880	5043	–	–	–	Renumbered GN 275 4/6/1899. Scrapped 1902. Boiler used in Havre roundhouse. (1/31/1900)
59	Baldwin	4/17/1880	5046	–	–	–	Renumbered GN 276 4/1/1899. Sold B&O 5/1900.
60	Baldwin	4/28/1880	5061	–	–	–	Renumbered GN 277 1899. Sold B&O 5/1900.
61	Baldwin	4/28/1880	5062	–	–	–	Renumbered GN 278 4/11/1899. Sold B&O 5/1900. (2/5/1897)
62*	Baldwin	5/7/1880	5079	–	–	–	Renumbered GN 119(2) 4/18/1899. (4/7/1888)
63	Baldwin	5/7/1880	5074	–	–	–	Renumbered GN 280 4/1/1899. Sold to Wisconsin Central (probably for a connecting logging company) 1/6/1900.
64	Baldwin	5/17/1880	5085	–	–	–	Renumbered GN 281 4/5/1899. (4/7/1897)
65	Baldwin	5/17/1880	5086	–	–	–	Renumbered GN 282 3/31/1899. (5/7/1898)
66	Baldwin	5/10/1880	5078	–	–	–	Renumbered GN 283 4/1/1899. Sold B&O 5/1900.
67(1)	Baldwin	5/10/1880	5083	–	–	–	Renumbered StPM&M 51(2) 1880.

Class 15 4-4-0: 17x24-63-140-73,400-48,000-13,100

No.	Builder	Date Rcvd.	C/N	Disposition
67(2)	Pittsburgh	3/23/1881	478	Renumbered GN 187(2) 4/22/1899. Turned over to Kootenai Valley Railroad 8/30/1899 and relettered for KVRR. Relettered GN 187 at East Spokane, WA, 6/4/1901.

Class 14 4-4-0: 17x24-58-140-73,400-48,000-14,230. Drivers changed from 58" to 55" (dates indicated in parentheses where known), with dimensions changing to 17x24-55-140-73,400-48,000-15,010.

No.	Builder	Date Rcvd.	C/N	Disposition	Notes
68	Pittsburgh	8/20/1880	437	Renumbered GN 284 4/7/1899. Sold B&O 5/1900. (8/9/1895)	
69	Pittsburgh	8/25/1880	438	Renumbered GN 285 4/13/1899. Sold B&O 5/1900. (7/30/1894)	18
70	Pittsburgh	8/31/1880	439	Renumbered GN 286 3/30/1899. Sold B&O 5/1900. (11/21/1893)	
71	Pittsburgh	9/6/1880	440	Renumbered GN 287 3/31/1899. Scrapped 9/19/1900. (7/31/1895)	
72	Pittsburgh	9/18/1880	441	Renumbered GN 288 4/10/1899.	
73	Pittsburgh	9/18/1880	442	Renumbered GN 289 4/6/1899. (6/15/1898)	
74	Pittsburgh	9/25/1880	443	Renumbered GN 290 4/17/1899. Turned over to Kootenai Valley Railroad 8/30/1899 and relettered for KVRR. Relettered GN 187 at East Spokane, WA, 7/20/1901. (6/17/1898)	
75	Pittsburgh	9/25/1880	444	Renumbered GN 291 3/24/1899. (7/2/1897)	
76	Pittsburgh	9/30/1880	445	Renumbered GN 292 3/21/1899. (10/8/1897)	
77	Pittsburgh	9/30/1880	446	Renumbered GN 293 3/20/1899. (10/7/1895)	

Class 15 4-4-0: 17x24-63-140-74,800-49,200-13,100

No.	Builder	Date Rcvd.	C/N	Disposition
78	Pittsburgh	3/25/1881	479	Renumbered GN 188(2) 5/2/1899.
79	Pittsburgh	3/30/1881	480	Renumbered GN 189(2) 4/25/1899.
80	Pittsburgh	4/1/1881	481	Renumbered GN 190(2) 4/19/1899. Sold B&O 5/1900.
81	Pittsburgh	4/9/1881	482	Renumbered GN 191(2) 4/13/1899.
82	Pittsburgh	5/16/1881	483	Renumbered GN 192(2) 5/4/1899.
83	Pittsburgh	5/19/1881	484	Renumbered GN 193(2) 3/25/1899.
84	Pittsburgh	5/23/1881	485	Renumbered GN 194(2) 3/25/1899.
85	Pittsburgh	5/27/1881	486	Renumbered GN 195(2) 4/7/1899.
86	Pittsburgh	5/29/1881	487	Renumbered GN 196(2) 4/20/1899. Sold B&O 5/1900.

Class 4 0-4-0: 15x24-49-140-53,900-53,900-13,110

No.	Builder	Date Rcvd.	C/N	Disposition	Notes
87	Brooks	3/29/1881	519	Renumbered GN 14(2) 4/15/1899. Scrapped 6/1902.	
88	Brooks	4/9/1881	521	Renumbered GN 15(2) 4/17/1899. Scrapped 9/1903.	19
89	Brooks	4/7/1881	523	Renumbered GN 16(2) 4/19/1899. Sold to Kettle River Quarries 5/1904.	

Class 22 0-4-0: 15x24-49-135-62,000-62,000-12,650

No.	Builder	Date Rcvd.	C/N	Disposition	Notes
90	Rogers	4/12/1882	2968	Renumbered GN 17(2) 4/14/1899. Scrapped 1902.	21
91	Rogers	4/12/1882	2969	Renumbered GN 18(2) 4/13/1899. Scrapped 7/1902.	
92	Rogers	4/13/1882	2970	Renumbered GN 19(2) 4/13/1899. Scrapped 6/1902.	
93	Rogers	4/15/1882	2971	Renumbered GN 20(2) 5/2/1899. Scrapped 12/22/1900.	

Class 23 4-4-0: 17x24-63-140-77,500-49,275-13,100

No.	Builder	Date Rcvd.	C/N	Original No.	Renumbered From	Date	Disposition	Notes
94(1)	Rogers	3/16/1882	2928	StP&D 16(2)	StP&D 16(2)	3/16/1882	Renumbered StPM&M 143(2) at Barnesville 5/1/1887.	22
95(1)	Rogers	3/18/1882	2929	StP&D 17(2)	StP&D 17(2)	3/18/1882	Renumbered StPM&M 144(2) at Barnesville 5/1/1887.	22

Class 27(1) 4-4-0: 17x24-63- ? -78,100-50,200- ?

No.	Builder	Date Rcvd.	C/N	Disposition
96(1)	Taunton	5/28/1882	844	Renumbered StPM&M 140 5/28/1882 (upon delivery).
97(1)	Taunton	5/28/1882	845	Renumbered StPM&M 141 5/28/1882 (upon delivery).

Class 31(2) 0-6-0: 18x24-49-150(140)-86,450-86,450-18,880

No.	Builder	Date Rcvd.	C/N	Disposition
94(2)	Rogers	4/26/1887	3736	Renumbered GN 32(2) 4/22/1899.
95(2)	Rogers	4/29/1887	3737	Renumbered GN 33(2) 4/10/1899.
96(2)	Rogers	4/29/1887	3738	Renumbered GN 34(2) 4/17/1899.
97(2)	Rogers	5/1/1887	3739	Renumbered GN 35(2) 4/13/1899.
98	Rogers	5/12/1887	3740	Sold to Minneapolis Western 1892. Renumbered MW 1(2) 1/28/1892. Renumbered GN 36(2) 1899.
99	Rogers	5/12/1887	3741	Sold to Eastern of Minnesota 6/1893 and renumbered EM 4 5/21/1894. Renumbered EM 37(2) c.1900.

Class 24 4-4-0: 17x24-63-140-76,650-49,150-13,100

No.	Builder	Date Rcvd.	C/N	Disposition
100	Baldwin	5/11/1882	6170	To GN as GN 100.
101	Baldwin	5/11/1882	6171	Reno. VW&Y 2 at Delta 12/15/1903. Returned to GN (as No. 101) 11/9/1908.
102	Baldwin	5/14/1882	6175	To GN as GN 102.
103	Baldwin	5/14/1882	6177	To GN as GN 103.
104	Baldwin	5/19/1882	6179	To GN as GN 104.
105	Baldwin	5/15/1882	6176	Sold B&O 5/1900.
106	Baldwin	5/15/1882	6178	To GN as GN 106.
107	Baldwin	5/19/1882	6180	To GN as GN 107.
108	Baldwin	5/19/1882	6182	Sold Montana Central 1888. Renumbered MC 10(1) 6/18/1888. Returned to StPM&M 1/14/1889, renumbered StPM&M 108 at Minot 2/3/1889. Sold B&O 5/1900.
109	Baldwin	5/18/1882	6181	Sold Montana Central 1888. Renumbered MC 11(1) 11/18/1888. Returned to StPM&M 1/18/1889, renumbered StPM&M 109 at Minot 2/3/1889. To GN as GN 109.
110	Baldwin	5/18/1882	6183	To GN as GN 110.
111	Baldwin	5/19/1882	6184	To GN as GN 111.
112	Baldwin	5/19/1882	6185	Scrapped 11/12/1900.
113	Baldwin	5/19/1882	6186	To GN as GN 113.
114	Baldwin	5/20/1882	6187	Sold B&O 5/1900.

THE ST. PAUL, MINNEAPOLIS AND MANITOBA RAILWAY COMPANY - continued

Class 24 4-4-0: 17x24-63-140-72,700-45,450-13,100 originally. Those locomotives indicated below by an asterisk (*) had wheel centers changed to 51⅝" (i.e. 58" drivers) (date shown in parentheses if known), giving them dimensions of 17x24-58-140-72,700-45,450-14,230. These two engines then had wheel centers changed to 48" (55" drivers) (second date shown in parentheses if known), giving them dimensions of 17x24-55-140-70,050-44,650-15,010, and were moved to Class 18, probably due to the smaller drivers, on unknown dates. The remaining locomotives that were still on the roster were moved to Class 24A c. 6/1900(?).

No.	Builder	Date Rcvd.	C/N	Disposition	Notes
115	Baldwin	5/20/1882	6188	Sold B&O 5/1900.	66
116	Baldwin	5/21/1882	6189	Sold B&O 5/1900.	66
117*	Baldwin	5/21/1882	6190	Renumbered GN 269 4/5/1899. Sold FG&S (No. 2) 9/12/1905.	66
118	Baldwin	5/21/1882	6191	To GN as GN 118.	
119*	Baldwin	5/22/1882	6192	Renumbered GN 279 4/18/1899. Sold B&O 4/24/1900. (6/15/1888) (8/23/1897)	
120	Baldwin	5/21/1882	6193	To GN as GN 120.	
121	Baldwin	5/22/1882	6194	Sold B&O 5/1900.	
122	Baldwin	5/25/1882	6195	To GN as GN 122.	
123	Baldwin	5/25/1882	6196	To GN as GN 123.	
124	Baldwin	5/25/1882	6197	To GN as GN 124.	

Class 25 4-4-0: 17x24-63-140-75,150-49,450-13,100 originally. Those locomotives indicated below by an asterisk (*) had driver diameters changed to 64" (dates unknown), thus decreasing tractive effort to 12,900 lb.

No.	Builder	Date Rcvd.	C/N	Disposition
125	Schenectady	2/15/1882	1595	To GN as GN 125.
126	Schenectady	2/15/1882	1596	To GN as GN 126.
127*	Schenectady	3/21/1882	1573	To GN as GN 127.
128	Schenectady	4/6/1882	1574	To GN as GN 128.
129*	Schenectady	1/20/1882	1492	To GN as GN 129.
130*	Schenectady	1/20/1882	1493	To GN as GN 130.
131*	Schenectady	4/21/1882	1575	To GN as GN 131.
132	Schenectady	4/21/1882	1576	To GN as GN 132.
133	Schenectady	4/21/1882	1577	To GN as GN 133.

Class 26 4-4-0: 17x24-64-140-86,500-55,650-12,330

No.	Builder	Date Rcvd.	C/N	Disposition
134	Rhode Island	5/8/1882	1195	Sold Butte, Anaconda & Pacific 1894. Renumbered BA&P 51 1/31/1894.
135	Rhode Island	5/8/1882	1196	To GN as GN 135.
136	Rhode Island	5/13/1882	1197	To GN as GN 136.
137	Rhode Island	5/13/1882	1198	To GN as GN 137.
138	Rhode Island	5/17/1882	1199	To GN as GN 138.
139	Rhode Island	5/17/1882	1200	Sold Butte, Anaconda & Pacific 1893. Renumbered BA&P 50 11/27/1893.

Class 27(1) 4-4-0: 17x24-63- ? -78,100-50,200- ?

No.	Builder	Date Rcvd.	C/N	Original No.	Renumbered From	Date	Disposition	Notes
140	Taunton	5/28/1882	844	StPM&M 96(1)	StPM&M 96(1)	5/28/1882	Sold Mason City & Fort Dodge 11/1886.	23
141	Taunton	5/28/1882	845	StPM&M 97(1)	StPM&M 97(1)	5/28/1882	Sold Mason City & Fort Dodge (No. 6) 4/21/1892.	23
142	Taunton	7/8/1882	856	–	–	–	Sold Mason City & Fort Dodge 1892.	
143(1)	Taunton	7/21/1882	857	–	–	–	Sold Mason City & Fort Dodge 1886.	
144(1)	Taunton	7/21/1882	858	–	–	–	Sold Mason City & Fort Dodge 1886.	

Class 23 4-4-0: 17x24-63-140-77,500-49,275-13,100

No.	Builder	Date Rcvd.	C/N	Original No.	Renumbered From	Date	Disposition	Notes
143(2)	Rogers	3/16/1882	2928	StP&D 16(2)	StPM&M 94(1)	5/1/1887	To GN as GN 143	22
144(2)	Rogers	3/18/1882	2929	StP&D 17(2)	StPM&M 95(1)	5/1/1887	To GN as GN 144	22

Class 28 4-4-0: 17x24-63-140-70,000-43,650-13,100 (1880 HER indicates original driver diameter was 60⅞")

No.	Builder	Date Rcvd.	C/N	Disposition
145	Grant	7/1/1882	1522	To GN as GN 145.
146	Grant	7/2/1882	1523	Sold to Wisconsin Central Railway (probably for a connecting logging company) 1/7/1900.
147	Grant	7/6/1882	1524	Sold Duluth, Superior & Western 1897. Renumbered DS&W 105 9/15/1897.
148	Grant	7/7/1882	1525	Sold B&O 5/1900.
149	Grant	7/9/1882	1526	To GN as GN 149.

Class 29 4-4-0: 17x24-62-140-71,400-46,500-13,100 (1880 HER indicates original driver size may have been 60½")

No.	Builder	Date Rcvd.	C/N	Disposition
150	Brooks	7/6/1882	716	To GN as GN 150.
151	Brooks	7/6/1882	715	To GN as GN 151.

Class 30 4-4-0: 17x24-63-140(130)-83,200-52,500-12,170

No.	Builder	Date Rcvd.	C/N	Disposition	Notes
152	Brooks	7/27/1882	745	To GN as GN 152.	
153	Brooks	7/27/1882	746	To GN as GN 153.	
154	Brooks	7/30/1882	747	To GN as GN 154.	
155	Brooks	7/31/1882	748	To GN as GN 155.	
156	Brooks	8/2/1882	749	To GN as GN 156.	
157	Brooks	8/3/1882	750	To GN as GN 157.	
158	Brooks	8/7/1882	751	To GN as GN 158.	
159	Brooks	8/7/1882	752	To GN as GN 159.	
160	Brooks	8/10/1882	753	To GN as GN 160.	
161	Brooks	8/12/1882	754	To GN as GN 161.	
162	Brooks	10/19/1882	791	To GN as GN 162.	
163	Brooks	10/21/1882	792	To GN as GN 163.	
164	Brooks	10/19/1882	793	To GN as GN 164.	
165	Brooks	10/24/1882	794	To GN as GN 165.	
166	Brooks	10/24/1882	795	To GN as GN 166.	
167	Brooks	12/23/1882	829	To GN as GN 167.	
168	Brooks	12/27/1882	830	To GN as GN 168.	
169	Brooks	12/27/1882	831	To GN as GN 169.	
170	Brooks	12/27/1882	832	To GN as GN 170.	
171	Brooks	12/27/1882	833	To GN as GN 171.	
172	Brooks	3/19/1883	872	To GN as GN 172.	
173	Brooks	3/19/1883	873	To GN as GN 173.	
174	Brooks	3/19/1883	874	To GN as GN 174.	
175	Brooks	3/19/1883	875	To GN as GN 175.	
176	Brooks	3/23/1883	876	To GN as GN 176.	
177	Brooks	3/23/1883	877	To GN as GN 177.	
178	Brooks	3/23/1883	878	To GN as GN 178.	
179	Brooks	3/23/1883	879	To GN as GN 179.	
180	Brooks	3/31/1883	880	To GN as GN 180.	
181	Brooks	3/31/1883	881	To GN as GN 181.	
182	Brooks	3/31/1883	882	To GN as GN 182.	
183	Brooks	3/31/1883	885	To GN as GN 183.	
184	Brooks	4/7/1883	886	To GN as GN 184.	24
185	Brooks	4/7/1883	887	To GN as GN 185.	24
186	Brooks	4/7/1883	888	To GN as GN 186.	24

GN 208, a Class B-21 engine, was received in 1887 as St. Paul, Minneapolis & Manitoba 208. When less than a year old it was sold to the Montana Central and operated there as No. 1 until about the turn of the century. It is shown here at Fergus Falls, MN, on September 5, 1934. The stack-top spark netting was used on just a few locomotives. Robert Hanft photograph from the collection of Harold K. Vollrath.

THE ST. PAUL, MINNEAPOLIS AND MANITOBA RAILWAY COMPANY - continued

Class 31(1) 0-4-0: 15x24-49-140-53,900-53,900-13,110. Moved to Class 4 prior to 1887.

No.	Builder	Date Rcvd.	C/N	Disposition
187	Brooks	8/16/1882	757	Sold to Minneapolis Western 1891. Renumbered MW 1(1) 11/27/1891. Returned to StPM&M (as 187) 1/26/1892. Renumbered GN 21(2) 4/14/1899. Scrapped 1903.
188	Brooks	8/17/1882	758	Renumbered GN 22(2) 4/29/1899. Scrapped 1903.
189	Brooks	8/22/1882	759	Wrecked at Barnesville, MN, 12/2/1897. Scrapped 11/1898.
190	Brooks	8/22/1882	760	Renumbered GN 23(2) 4/10/1899. Scrapped 10/13/1900.
191	Brooks	8/25/1882	761	Renumbered GN 24(2) 4/13/1899. Scrapped 6/30/1901.
192	Brooks	8/25/1882	762	Renumbered GN 25(2) 4/17/1899. Scrapped at St.Paul 1901.
193	Brooks	8/28/1882	763	Renumbered GN 26(2) 3/21/1899. Scrapped 11/1902.

Class 32 0-6-0: 17x24-49-140-67,050-67,050-16,840

No.	Builder	Date Rcvd.	C/N	Disposition
194	Brooks	8/30/1882	764	Renumbered GN 27(2) 4/1/1899.
195	Brooks	8/31/1882	765	Sold to Minneapolis Western 1891. Renumbered MW 2 11/27/1891. Renumbered GN 28(2) 1899.
196	Brooks	9/4/1882	766	Renumbered GN 29(2) 4/10/1899.

Class 33 4-4-0: 18x24-63-145(140)-90,900-59,000-14,690

No.	Builder	Date Rcvd.	C/N	Disposition	Notes
197	Rhode Island	1/31/1883	1294	To GN as GN 197.	
198	Rhode Island	1/30/1883	1295	To GN as GN 198.	25
199	Rhode Island	2/5/1883	1296	Sold Seattle & Montana Ry. (No. 199) 6/30/1891.	26
200	Rhode Island	12/28/1882	1297	To GN as GN 200.	27
201	Rhode Island	2/5/1883	1298	To GN as GN 201.	27
202	Rhode Island	2/5/1883	1299	Sold Seattle & Montana Ry. (No. 202) 6/30/1891.	27
203	Rhode Island	12/28/1882	1300	To GN as GN 203.	28
204	Rhode Island	1/2/1883	1301	To GN as GN 204.	
205	Rhode Island	1/2/1883	1302	To GN as GN 205.	
206	Rhode Island	1/2/1883	1303	To GN as GN 206.	

Class 34 4-4-0: 18x24-63-140-94,100-60,300-14,690

No.	Builder	Date Rcvd.	C/N	Disposition
207	Rogers	5/28/1887	3749	To GN as GN 207.
208	Rogers	5/25/1887	3750	Sold Montana Central 1888. Renumbered MC 1 3/22/1888.
209	Rogers	5/25/1887	3751	Sold Montana Central 1888. Renumbered MC 2 4/13/1888.
210	Rogers	5/30/1887	3752	Sold Montana Central 1888. Renumbered MC 3 3/26/1888.
211	Rogers	5/30/1887	3753	Sold Montana Central 1888. Renumbered MC 12 11/20/1888.
212	Rogers	6/3/1887	3754	Sold Montana Central 1888. Renumbered MC 13 11/11/1888.
213	Rogers	6/3/1887	3755	To GN as GN 213.
214	Rogers	6/5/1887	3756	To GN as GN 214.
215	Rogers	6/8/1887	3757	To GN as GN 215.
216	Rogers	6/8/1887	3758	To GN as GN 216.
217	Rogers	6/19/1887	3759	To GN as GN 217.
218	Rogers	6/21/1887	3760	To GN as GN 218.
219	Rogers	6/28/1887	3764	Sold Seattle & Montana Ry. (No. 219) 9/28/1894. Returned to GN [as No. 219(1)] 5/10/1895. To GN as GN 219(1).
220	Rogers	6/28/1887	3765	To GN as GN 220(1).
221	Rogers	7/3/1887	3769	To GN as GN 221.
222	Rogers	7/7/1887	3770	To GN as GN 222.
223	Rogers	7/7/1887	3772	To GN as GN 223.
224	Rogers	7/7/1887	3773	To GN as GN 224.
225	Rogers	7/12/1887	3774	To GN as GN 225.

Class 31(2) 0-6-0: 18x24-49-150(140)-86,450-86,450-18,880

No.	Builder	Date Rcvd.	C/N	Disposition
226	Rogers	9/17/1888	4010	Sold Montana Central 1888. Renumbered MC 14 12/14/1888.
227	Rogers	9/20/1888	4011	Sold Montana Central 1888. Renumbered MC 15 12/14/1888.
228	Rogers	10/9/1888	4028	Renumbered GN 43(2) 4/6/1899.
229	Rogers	10/9/1888	4029	Renumbered GN 44(2) 4/17/1899.
230	Rogers	10/10/1888	4030	Renumbered GN 45(2) 4/28/1899.
231	Rogers	10/11/1888	4031	Renumbered GN 46(2) 4/23/1899.

Class 2(2) 0-6-0: 17x24-51-140-83,000-83,000-16,180 originally. Driver size decreased to 49" (with tractive effort change to 16,840 lb.) c. 1895 (date in parentheses if known). (See Note 237).

No.	Builder	Date Rcvd.	C/N	Disposition
232	Hinkley	8/1/1888	1765	Sold Seattle & Montana Ry. (No. 232) 4/3/1893. Reno. GN 30(2) 4/6/1899.
233	Hinkley	8/1/1888	1766	Renumbered GN 31(2) 3/29/1899. (2/16/1895)

Class 35 2-6-0: 19x24-55-150(140)-105,040-87,290-18,750

No.	Builder	Date Rcvd.	C/N	Disposition
300	Rogers	7/7/1887	3771	To GN as GN 300.
301	Rogers	7/12/1887	3775	To GN as GN 301.
302	Rogers	7/13/1887	3776	To GN as GN 302.
303	Rogers	7/19/1887	3777	To GN as GN 303.
304	Rogers	7/28/1887	3778	To GN as GN 304.
305	Rogers	7/26/1887	3781	To GN as GN 305.
306	Rogers	7/27/1887	3783	Sold Montana Central 1888. Renumbered MC 7 10/13/1888. Returned to StPM&M (as No. 306) 5/25/1892. To GN as GN 306.
307	Rogers	7/27/1887	3784	To GN as GN 307.
308	Rogers	7/31/1887	3785	To GN as GN 308.
309	Rogers	7/31/1887	3786	To GN as GN 309.
310	Rogers	8/1/1887	3787	To GN as GN 310.
311	Rogers	8/2/1887	3788	To GN as GN 311.
312	Rogers	8/7/1887	3789	To GN as GN 312.
313	Rogers	8/7/1887	3790	To GN as GN 313.
314	Rogers	8/7/1887	3791	To GN as GN 314.
315	Rogers	8/7/1887	3792	To GN as GN 315.
316	Rogers	8/12/1887	3793	To GN as GN 316.
317	Rogers	8/13/1887	3795	To GN as GN 317.
318	Rogers	8/15/1887	3796	To GN as GN 318.
319	Rogers	8/20/1887	3797	To GN as GN 319.
320	Rogers	8/21/1887	3799	To GN as GN 320.
321	Rogers	9/2/1887	3800	To GN as GN 321.
322(1)	Rogers	8/27/1887	3802	Sold Montana Central 1888. Renumbered MC 4 3/22/1888.
322(2)	Rogers	9/3/1888	4001	Sold Montana Central 1888. Renumbered MC 10(2) 1/7/1889.
323(1)	Rogers	8/31/1887	3804	Sold Montana Central 1888. Renumbered MC 5 4/2/1888.
323(2)	Rogers	9/3/1888	4002	Sold Montana Central 1888. Renumbered MC 11(2) 1/7/1889.
324(1)	Rogers	9/11/1887	3807	Sold Montana Central 1888. Renumbered MC 6 2/25/1888.

Class 36 2-6-0: 19x24-55-150(140)-105,040-87,290-18,750

No.	Builder	Date Rcvd.	C/N	Disposition
324(2)	Rogers	9/5/1888	4003	Sold Montana Central 1888. Renumbered MC 16 1/2/1889. Returned to StPM&M (as No. 347) 1892. To GN as GN 347.

Class 35 2-6-0: 19x24-55-150(140)-105,040-87,290-18,750

No.	Builder	Date Rcvd.	C/N	Disposition
325	Rogers	9/9/1888	4004	Sold Montana Central 1888. Renumbered MC 8 11/16/1888.

Class 36 2-6-0: 19x24-55-150(140)-105,040-87,290-18,750

No.	Builder	Date Rcvd.	C/N	Disposition
326	Rogers	9/9/1888	4007	Sold Montana Central 1888. Renumbered MC 9(1) 11/16/1888. Returned to StPM&M (as No. 326) 6/20/1892. To GN as GN 326.
327	Rogers	9/11/1888	4008	Sold Montana Central 1888. Renumbered MC 17 1/2/1889.
328	Rogers	9/16/1888	4009	Sold Montana Central 1888. Renumbered MC 18 4/7/1889.
329	Rogers	9/17/1888	4012	Sold Seattle & Montana Ry. (No. 329) 6/30/1891. Returned to GN (as No. 329) 9/28/1894. Returned back to S&M Ry. (No. 329) 5/10/1895.
330	Rogers	9/17/1888	4013	To GN as GN 330.
331	Rogers	9/20/1888	4014	To GN as GN 331.
332	Rogers	9/20/1888	4015	To GN as GN 332.
333	Rogers	9/24/1888	4016	To GN as GN 333.
334	Rogers	9/25/1888	4017	To GN as GN 334.
335	Rogers	10/21/1888	4041	To GN as GN 335.
336	Rogers	10/26/1888	4042	To GN as GN 336.
337	Rogers	10/28/1888	4043	To GN as GN 337.
338	Rogers	10/31/1888	4048	To GN as GN 338.
339	Rogers	10/31/1888	4049	To GN as GN 339.
340	Rogers	11/12/1888	4050	To GN as GN 340.
341	Rogers	11/14/1888	4056	To GN as GN 341(1). Sold Brandon, Devils Lake & Southern (No. 4) 1906.
342	Rogers	11/19/1888	4057	To GN as GN 342.
343	Rogers	11/19/1888	4058	To GN as GN 343.
344	Rogers	9/10/1889	4125	To GN as GN 344.
345	Rogers	9/14/1889	4126	To GN as GN 345.
346	Rogers	9/1889	4129	To GN as GN 346.

THE ST. PAUL, MINNEAPOLIS AND MANITOBA RAILWAY COMPANY - continued

Class 36 2-6-0: 19x24-55-150(140)-105,040-87,290-18,750

No.	Builder	Date Rcvd.	C/N	Original No.	Renumbered From	Date	Disposition
347	Rogers	9/5/1888	4003	StPM&M 324(2)	MC 16	1892	To GN as GN 347.

Class 43 2-6-0: See Note 29 and GN section of roster.

Class 37(1) 4-8-0: 20x24-55-180(160)-156,000-132,000-23,740 originally. Rebuilt (probably c. 1892 or 1893) with 20"x26" cylinders (raising tractive effort to 25,720 lb.) and moved at that time to Class 38. (See Note 238)

No.	Builder	Date Rcvd.	C/N	Disposition
400	Brooks	10/15/1891	1972	Renumbered GN 600 4/1899.
401	Brooks	10/17/1891	1973	Sold Montana Central [No. 54(1)] c.1892. Returned (as No. 401) c.1893. Renumbered GN 601 4/1899.
402	Brooks	10/17/1891	1974	Renumbered GN 602 4/1899.
403	Brooks	10/21/1891	1975	Renumbered GN 603 4/1899.
404	Brooks	10/21/1891	1976	Renumbered GN 604 4/1899.
405	Brooks	10/26/1891	1977	Renumbered GN 605 4/1899.
406	Brooks	10/26/1891	1978	Renumbered GN 606 4/1899.
407	Brooks	10/30/1891	1979	Renumbered GN 607 4/1899.
408	Brooks	10/29/1891	1980	Renumbered GN 608 4/1899.
409	Brooks	11/2/1891	1981	Renumbered GN 609 4/1899.

Class 38 4-8-0: 20x26-55-180(160)-156,000-132,000-25,720

No.	Builder	Date Rcvd.	C/N	Disposition
410	Brooks	12/3/1891	1998	Sold Montana Central 1892. Renumbered MC 50 2/7/1892.
411	Brooks	12/8/1891	1999	Sold Montana Central 1892. Renumbered MC 51 2/9/1892.
412	Brooks	12/8/1891	2000	Sold Montana Central 1892. Renumbered MC 52 2/20/1892.
413	Brooks	12/14/1891	2001	Sold Montana Central 1892. Renumbered MC 53 5/6/1892.
414	Brooks	12/14/1891	2002	Sold Montana Central 1892. Renumbered MC 54(2) 9/23/1893.

Class 39 2-8-0: See Note 30 and GN section of roster.

SEATTLE AND MONTANA RAILROAD COMPANY

Class A-2 [Old Class 2(2)] 0-6-0: 17x24-49-140-83,000-83,000-15,580

No.	Builder	Date Rcvd.	C/N	Original No.	Renumbered From	Date	Disposition
30	Hinkley	8/1/1888	1765	StPM&M 232	S&M RR 232	4/6/1899	Sold GN [No. 30(2)] 7/1/1907.

Class B-7 [Old Class 12(2)] 4-4-0: 17x24-63-140-78,000-49,000-13,100

No.	Builder	Date Built	C/N	Original No.	Renumbered From	Date	Disposition	Notes
139	New York	7/1890	627	S&N 2	S&N 2	10/11/1902	Sold GN [No. 139(2)] 7/1/1907.	31

Class B-20 (Old Class 33) 4-4-0: 18x24-63-145(140)-90,900-59,000-14,690

No.	Builder	Date Rcvd.	C/N	Original No.	Renumbered From	Date	Disposition
199	Rhode Island	2/5/1883	1296	StPM&M 199	S&M Ry 199	3/30/1898	Sold GN (No. 199) 7/1/1907.
202	Rhode Island	2/5/1883	1299	StPM&M 202	S&M Ry 202	3/30/1898	Sold GN (No. 202) 7/1/1907.

Class A-2 [Old Class 2(2)]: 17x24-49-140-83,000-83,000-16,840

No.	Builder	Date Rcvd.	C/N	Original No.	Renumbered From	Date	Disposition
232	Hinkley	8/1/1888	1765	StPM&M 232	S&M Ry 232	3/30/1898	Renumbered S&M RR 30(2) 4/6/1899. Sold GN 7/1/1907.

Class E-4 [Old Class 10(2)] 4-6-0: 18x24-55-150(140)-100,800-77,000-16,820

No.	Builder	Date Built	C/N	Original No.	Renumbered From	Date	Disposition
298	Schenectady	5/1889	2860	F&S 1	F&S 1	3/30/1898	Sold GN (No. 298) 7/1/1907.
299	Schenectady	5/1889	2861	F&S 2	F&S 2	3/30/1898	Sold GN (No. 299) 7/1/1907.

Class D-2 (Old Class 36) 2-6-0: 19x24-55-150(140)-105,040-87,090-18,745

No.	Builder	Date Rcvd.	C/N	Original No.	Renumbered From	Date	Disposition
329	Rogers	9/17/1888	4012	StPM&M 329	S&M Ry 329	3/30/1898	Sold GN (No. 329) 7/1/1907.

SEATTLE AND MONTANA RAILWAY COMPANY

Class 33 4-4-0: 18x24-63-145(140)-90,900-59,000-14,690

No.	Builder	Date Rcvd.	C/N	Original No.	Renumbered From	Date	Disposition
199	Rhode Island	2/5/1883	1296	StPM&M 199	StPM&M 199	6/30/1891	Sold S&M RR (No. 199) 3/30/1898.
202	Rhode Island	2/5/1883	1299	StPM&M 202	StPM&M 202	6/30/1891	Sold S&M RR (No. 202) 3/30/1898.

Class 34 4-4-0: 18x24-63-140-94,100-60,300-14,690

No.	Builder	Date Rcvd.	C/N	Original No.	Renumbered From	Date	Disposition
219	Rogers	6/28/1887	3764	StPM&M 219	GN 219(1)	9/28/1894	Returned to GN [as No. 219(1)] 5/10/1895.

Class 2(2) 0-6-0: 17x24-51-140-83,000-83,000-16,180 originally. Driver size decreased to 49" (with tractive effort change to 16,840 lb.) c.1895.

No.	Builder	Date Rcvd.	C/N	Original No.	Renumbered From	Date	Disposition
232	Hinkley	8/1/1888	1765	StPM&M 232	GN 232(1)	4/3/1893	Sold S&M RR (No. 232) 3/30/1898.

Class 36 2-6-0: 19x24-55-150(140)-105,040-87,090-18,745

No.	Builder	Date Rcvd.	C/N	Original No.	Renumbered From	Date	Disposition
329	Rogers	9/17/1888	4012	StPM&M 329	StPM&M 329	6/30/1891	Returned to GN (No. 329) 9/28/94. Returned to S&M Ry (No. 329) 5/10/1895. Sold S&M RR (No. 329) 3/30/1898.

SEATTLE AND NORTHERN RAILWAY COMPANY

Class – 4-4-0:

No.	Builder	Date Built	C/N	Disposition
1(1)	R. Norris	1866	?	Traded to Columbia & Puget Sound Railroad Co. [No. 5(2)] 1897 for C&PS No. 5(1). Sold for scrap to W.J.Hofius 1900.

Class 12(2) 4-4-0: 17x24-63-140-78,000-49,000-13,100

No.	Builder	Date Built	C/N	Original No.	Renumbered From	Date	Disposition	Notes
1(2)	New York	7/1890	628	PTS 1	C&PS 5(1)	1897	Transferred to Columbia & Puget Sound Railroad Co. [No. 5(3)] 1902. Sold to Neider J. Marcus 1923. Scrapped 3/1943.	32
2	New York	7/1890	627	–	–	–	Transferred to Columbia & Puget Sound Railroad Co. (No. 2) c.1897. Returned to Seattle & Northern (as No. 2) prior to1902. Sold to Seattle & Montana RR 2/1/1902. Reno. S&M 139 at Everett 10/11/1902.	31

THE SIOUX CITY AND NORTHERN RAILROAD COMPANY

NOTE: WHILE THERE IS NO EVIDENCE THAT THE SIOUX CITY & NORTHERN USED A CLASS SYSTEM, CLASSES OF THE GREAT NORTHERN ARE USED FOR CLARITY.

Class 11(2) 4-4-0: 17X24-63-145(140)-89,000-56,000-13,100

No.	Builder	Date Rcvd.	C/N	Disposition
1	Rogers	1/14/1890	4182	Sold WSF 1/15/1900. Renumbered WSF 232 c.1900.
2	Rogers	1/15/1890	4194	Sold WSF 1/15/1900. Renumbered WSF 233 at St.Paul 2/19/1901.
3	Rogers	1/18/1890	4205	Sold WSF 1/15/1900. Renumbered WSF 234 c.1900
4	Rogers	1/25/1890	4226	Sold WSF 1/15/1900. Renumbered WSF 235 at Willmar 1/25/1901.

Class 27(2) 4-6-0: 18x24-55-150-100,000-74,000-16,820

No.	Builder	Date Rcvd.	C/N	Disposition
5	Rogers	2/11/1890	4236	Sold WSF 1/15/1900. Renumbered WSF 992 at St.Paul 8/24/1900.
6	Rogers	2/8/1890	4237	Sold WSF 1/15/1900. Renumbered WSF 993 at St.Paul 3/24/1900.

Class 2A 0-6-0: 17x24-56-145-85,000-85,000-15,550 originally. Weights later increased to 90,000 lb.

No.	Builder	Date Rcvd.	C/N	Disposition
7	Rogers	8/16/1890	4350	Sold WSF 1/15/1900. Renumbered WSF 47 at Willmar 7/25/1900.

Class 11(2) 4-4-0: 17x24-63-145(140)-89,000-56,000-13,100

No.	Builder	Date Rcvd.	C/N	Disposition
8	Rogers	6/1/1890	4303	Sold WSF 1/15/1900. Renumbered WSF 236 at St.Paul 9/8/1900.

Class 2A 0-6-0: 17x24-56-145-85,000-85,000-15,550 originally. Weights later increased to 90,000 lb.

No.	Builder	Date Built	C/N	Disposition	Notes
9	Rogers	3/1891	4494	Sold WSF 1/15/1900. Renumbered WSF 48 at St.Paul 12/6/1900.	33

Class 11(2) 4-4-0: 17x24-63-145(140)-89,000-56,000-13,100

No.	Builder	Date Rcvd.	C/N	Disposition
10	Rogers	12/19/1890	4420	Sold WSF 1/15/1900. Renumbered WSF 237 at St.Paul 12/1/1900.

Class – 4-4-0: 15x22-56- ? - ? - ? - ?

No.	Builder	Date Rcvd.	C/N	Original No.	Renumbered From	Date	Disposition	Notes
11	Pittsburgh	10/29/1890	168	SC&StP 4(1)	CStPM&O 220	1890	Possibly purchased as source of parts. Sold or scrapped prior to 1900.	34

THE SIOUX CITY AND NORTHERN RAILROAD COMPANY - continued

Class – 4-4-0: 14x22-63- ? -56,600-36,480- ?

No.	Builder	Date Rcvd.	C/N	Original No.	Renumbered From	Date	Disposition	Notes
12	Taunton	11/13/1890	529	SC&StP 1	CStPM&O 221	1890	Sold WSF 1/15/1900. Apparently being held for sale as scrap at time of sale, and never renumbered. Scrapped at St.Paul 5/10/1902.	35

THE SIOUX CITY AND WESTERN RAILWAY COMPANY

NOTE: WHILE THERE IS NO EVIDENCE THAT THE SIOUX CITY AND WESTERN USED A CLASS SYSTEM, GREAT NORTHERN CLASSES ARE USED HERE FOR CLARITY.

Class 11(2) 4-4-0: 17x24-63-145-80,000-51,000-12,770

No.	Builder	Date Built	C/N	Original No.	Renumbered From	Date	Disposition
13	Rhode Island	4/1889	2202	PSL 13	SCO&W 13	c.1899	Leased WSF 1/1/1900. Renumbered WSF 238 at Sioux City 1/1/1901.

Class 36A 2-6-0: 19x24-55-150-104,800-89,300-20,080

No.	Builder	Date Built	C/N	Original No.	Renumbered From	Date	Disposition
14	Rhode Island	7/1890	2406	PSL 14	SCO&W 14	c.1899	Leased WSF 1/1/1900. Renumbered WSF 360 at St.Paul 7/3/1900.

Class 27A 4-6-0: 19x24-55-150-105,600-86,650-20,080

No.	Builder	Date Built	C/N	Original No.	Renumbered From	Date	Disposition
15	Rhode Island	8/1890	2440	PSL 15	SCO&W 15	c.1899	Leased WSF 1/1/1900. Renumbered WSF 997 at St.Paul 5/9/1900.

Class 27C 4-6-0: 18x24-56-150-102,800-84,000-17,700

No.	Builder	Date Built	C/N	Original No.	Renumbered From	Date	Disposition	Notes
16	Rhode Island	12/1889	2264	MCCo 131(1)	SCO&W 16	c.1899	Leased WSF 1/1/1900. Renumbered WSF 994 at St.Paul 7/3/1900.	36
17	Rhode Island	12/1889	2265	MCCo 132(1)	SCO&W 17	c.1899	Leased WSF 1/1/1900. Renumbered WSF 995 at St.Paul 3/24/1900.	36
18	Rhode Island	4/1890	2328	PSL 12	SCO&W 18	c.1899	Leased WSF 1/1/1900. Renumbered WSF 996 at St.Paul 5/10/1900.	

THE SIOUX CITY, O'NEILL AND WESTERN RAILWAY COMPANY

NOTE: WHILE THERE IS NO EVIDENCE THAT THE SIOUX CITY, O'NEILL AND WESTERN USED A CLASS SYSTEM, GREAT NORTHERN CLASSES ARE USED HERE FOR CLARITY.

Class – 0-6-0: 12x16- ? - ? -44,000-44,000- ?

No.	Builder	Date Built	C/N	Disposition	Notes
9	?	?	?	Sold c.1894.	37

Class 11(2) 4-4-0: 17x24-63-145-80,000-51,000-12,770

No.	Builder	Date Built	C/N	Original No.	Renumbered From	Date	Disposition
13	Rhode Island	4/1889	2202	PSL 13	PSL 13	c.1892	Sold SC&W (No. 13) 6/28/1899.

Class 36A 2-6-0: 19x24-55-150-104,800-89,300-20,080

No.	Builder	Date Built	C/N	Original No.	Renumbered From	Date	Disposition
14	Rhode Island	7/1890	2406	PSL 14	PSL 14	c.1892	Sold SC&W (No. 14) 6/28/1899.

Class 27A 4-6-0: 19x24-55-150-105,600-86,650-20,080

No.	Builder	Date Built	C/N	Original No.	Renumbered From	Date	Disposition
15	Rhode Island	8/1890	2440	PSL 15	PSL 15	c.1892	Sold SC&W (No. 15) 6/28/1899.

Class 27C 4-6-0: 18x24-56-150-102,800-84,000-17,700

No.	Builder	Date Built	C/N	Original No.	Renumbered From	Date	Disposition	Notes
16	Rhode Island	12/1889	2264	MCCo 131(1)	PSL 10	c.1892	Sold SC&W (No. 16) 6/28/1899.	36
17	Rhode Island	12/1889	2265	MCCo 132(1)	PSL 11	c.1892	Sold SC&W (No. 17) 6/28/1899.	36
18	Rhode Island	4/1890	2328	PSL 12	PSL 12	c.1892	Sold SC&W (No. 18) 6/28/1899.	

SOMERS LUMBER COMPANY
Class 42-2 2-truck Shay: 10x12-29½- ? - ? - ? - ?

No.	Builder	Date Built	C/N	Disposition
1	Lima	9/19/1914	2769	Sold to P.L.Howe Lumber Mills, Eureka, MT (No. unknown), 1919. Sold to Brooks Scanlon Lumber Co., Eureka, MT (No. unknown), 1923. Sold to State Lumber Co., Columbia Falls, MT (No. unknown), date unknown. Sold to F.H. Stoltze Land and Lumber Co., Columbia Falls and Half Moon, MT (No. unknown), date unknown. Placed on display at Columbia Falls, MT, date unknown.

Class 3-PC-13 Pacific Coast 3-truck Shay: 13x15-36-200-181,000-181,000-38,200

No.	Builder	Date Built	C/N	Disposition
2	Lima	11/29/1929	3346	Sold to J.Neils Lumber Co., Klickitat, WA (No. 7) 5/1942. Sold to Klickitat Logging & Lumber Co., subsidiary of St. Regis Paper Co., Klickitat, WA (No. 7), 1957. To "Camp 6" Logging Museum, Point Defiance Park, Tacoma, WA, 1964.

Class F-1 2-8-0: 19x26-55-180(160)-136,000-120,000-23,210

No.	Builder	Date Built	C/N	Original No.	Renumbered From	Date	Disposition
?	Brooks	6/27/1892	2102	GN 459(1)	GN 525	12/1924	Sold GN (No. 525) 10/1925.

Class D-2 2-6-0: 19x24-55-150(140)-99,800-78,200-18,750

No.	Builder	Date Built	C/N	Original No.	Renumbered From	Date	Disposition
?	Rogers	11/19/1888	4057	StPM&M 342	GN 342	10/1925	Dismantled c.2/1930.

Class – 0-4-0 (Fireless): Cylinders 15"x14", Drivers 27", Weight 37,000 lb.

No.	Builder	Date Built	C/N	Disposition
S1	H.K. Porter	6/1926	7016	Transferred to BN 1970. After tie plant closure in July 1986, engine was moved to the Miracle of America Museum, Polson, MT.

Class – 0-4-0 (Fireless): Cylinders 15"x14", Drivers 27", Weight 32,000 lb.

No.	Builder	Date Built	C/N	Disposition
S2	H.K. Porter	11/1929	7156	Transferred to BN 1970. After tie plant closure in July 1986, engine was moved to the Flathead County Museum, Kalispell, MT. Returned to Somers, MT, 3/28/2008.

Class A-7 0-6-0: 19x26-49-180(160)-114,700-114,700-26,050

No.	Builder	Date Rcvd.	C/N	Original No.	Renumbered From	Date	Disposition	Notes
S4	Brooks	1/1/1893	2208	GN 250(1)	GN 60(2)	3/1930	Sold GN, then resold U.S. Government 4/1939.	43

Class F-8 2-8-0: 20x32-55-210-195,000-180,000-41,540

No.	Builder	Date Rcvd.	C/N	Original No.	Renumbered From	Date	Disposition
S5	Baldwin	12/21/1907	32291	GN 1244	GN 1244	1935	Sold for scrap PC 5/4/1951.

SOUTH DAKOTA CENTRAL RAILWAY COMPANY

NOTE: WHILE THERE IS NO EVIDENCE THAT THE SOUTH DAKOTA CENTRAL USED A CLASS SYSTEM, CLASSES OF THE GREAT NORTHERN ARE USED FOR CLARITY.

Class D-6 2-6-0: 19x24-55-160-114,500-101,800-21,420

No.	Builder	Date Built	C/N	Original No.	Renumbered From	Date	Disposition	Notes
11	Alco-Schenectady	1902	?	?	?	?	Sold W&SF (No. 11) 6/30/1916.	39

Class D-6 2-6-0: 19x24-55-160(155)-126,900-113,800-20,750

No.	Builder	Date Built	C/N	Original No.	Renumbered From	Date	Disposition	Notes
12	Alco-Schenectady	1906	?	?	?	?	Sold W&SF (No. 12) 6/30/1916.	40

Class D-3(2) 2-6-0: 18x24-55-180(170)-119,000-106,500-20,430

No.	Builder	Date Built	C/N	Original No.	Renumbered From	Date	Disposition	Notes
13	Baldwin	5/1901	18999	K&M 279	K&M 540	1908-1911	Sold W&SF (No. 13) 6/30/1916.	41

Class F-11 2-8-0: 20x24-52-180-138,000-123,000-28,250

No.	Builder	Date Built	C/N	Original No.	Renumbered From	Date	Disposition	Notes
14	Alco-Brooks	4/1913	52834	TA&G 322	TA&G 322	8/1914	Sold W&SF (No. 14) 6/30/1916.	42
15	Alco-Brooks	9/1914	54970	–	–	–	Sold W&SF (No. 15) 6/30/1916.	

Class E-2(2) 4-6-0: 18x24-60-200-130,000-96,000-22,030

No.	Builder	Date Built	C/N	Disposition
16	Alco-Brooks	5/1915	55132	Sold W&SF (No. 16) 6/30/1916.

SOUTH DAKOTA CENTRAL RAILWAY COMPANY - continued

Class E-2(2) 4-6-0: 18x24-60-200-135,500-97,500-22,030

No.	Builder	Date Built	C/N	Disposition
17	Alco-Brooks	11/1915	55443	Sold W&SF (No. 17) 6/30/1916.

Class O-2 2-8-2: 20x28-52-180-178,000-128,000-32,950

No.	Builder	Date Built	C/N	Disposition
18	Alco-Brooks	10/1915	55444	Sold W&SF (No. 18) 6/30/1916.

SPOKANE FALLS AND NORTHERN RAILWAY

NOTE: WHILE THERE IS NO EVIDENCE THAT THE SPOKANE FALLS & NORTHERN USED A CLASS SYSTEM, CLASSES OF THE GREAT NORTHERN ARE USED FOR CLARITY.

Class D-1(2) 2-6-0: 18x24-55-145(140)-90,000-77,000-16,820

No.	Builder	Date Built	C/N	Disposition	Notes
1	Baldwin	4/1889	9968	Sold GN 7/1/1907. Reno. GN 478(2) at Hillyard 6/26/1908.	44
2	Baldwin	5/1889	9972	Sold GN 7/1/1907. Reno. GN 479(2) at Delta 5/21/1908.	44
3	Baldwin	6/1889	10036	Sold GN 7/1/1907. Reno. GN 480(2) at Hillyard 3/3/1908.	
4	Baldwin	6/1889	10037	Sold VW&Y [No. 1(2)] c.1904(?). Reno. GN 477(2) at Delta 11/4/1908.	

Class B-11(2) 4-4-0: 17x24-63-145(140)-85,000-52,000-13,100

No.	Builder	Date Built	C/N	Disposition
5	Baldwin	4/1890	10833	Sold GN 7/1/1907. Reno. GN 142 at Hillyard 7/6/1908.
6	Baldwin	4/1890	10830	Sold GN 7/1/1907. Reno. GN 141 at Hillyard 7/6/1908.

Class B-23 4-4-0: 18x24-63-160(140)-94,100-56,100-14,690

No.	Builder	Date Built	C/N	Original No.	Renumbered From	Date	Disposition	Notes
7	Baldwin	10/1893	13803	N&FS 7	N&FS 7	c.1898	Sold GN 7/1/1907. Reno. GN 231(2) at Hillyard 3/5/1908.	10

Class E-13 4-6-0: 19x24-55-160(150)-110,000-85,000-20,090

No.	Builder	Date Built	C/N	Original No.	Renumbered From	Date	Disposition	Notes
8	Baldwin	10/1893	13807	N&FS 8	N&FS 8	c.1898	Sold GN 7/1/1907. Reno. GN 948 at Hillyard 4/2/1908.	10

Class F-4(2) 2-8-0: 19x24-47-180(170)-135,000-113,300-26,640

No.	Builder	Date Built	C/N	Original No.	Renumbered From	Date	Disposition	Notes
9	Baldwin	8/1896	15013	RM 9	RM 9	?	Sold GN 7/1/1907. Reno. GN 1094 at Hillyard 6/9/1908.	2

Class E-13 4-6-0: 19x24-55-160(150)-110,000-85,000-20,090

No.	Builder	Date Built	C/N	Disposition
10	Baldwin	9/1896	15059	Sold GN 7/1/1907. Reno. GN 949 at Hillyard 6/26/1908.

Class E-12 4-6-0: 19x24-55-180(170)-122,300-93,850-22,760

No.	Builder	Date Built	C/N	Disposition
11	Baldwin	3/1897	15248	Sold GN 7/1/1907. Reno. GN 970 at Hillyard 3/13/1908.
12	Baldwin	3/1897	15249	Sold GN 7/1/1907. Reno. GN 971 at Hillyard 6/26/1908.

VANCOUVER, WESTMINSTER AND YUKON RAILWAY

Class – 4-4-0: ? -57- ? - ? - ? - ?

No.	Builder	Date Built	C/N	Original No.	Renumbered From	Date	Disposition	Notes
1(1)	Baldwin	4/1882	?	NP ?	V&S 3	1903	Returned V&S (No. 3) 1904.	45

Class D-1(2) 2-6-0: 18x24-55-145(140)-90,000-77,000-16,820

No.	Builder	Date Built	C/N	Original No.	Renumbered From	Date	Disposition
1(2)	Baldwin	6/1889	10037	SF&N 4	SF&N 4	c.1904	Reno. GN 477(2) at Delta 11/4/1908.

Class B-13 4-4-0: 17x24-63-140-76,650-49,150-13,100

No.	Builder	Date Rcvd.	C/N	Original No.	Renumbered From	Date	Disposition
2	Baldwin	5/11/1882	6171	StPM&M 101	GN 101	12/15/1903	Reno. GN 101 at Delta 11/9/1908.

VICTORIA & SIDNEY RAILWAY COMPANY

Class – 2-6-0: 16x24-50-150-80,000- ? - ?

No.	Builder	Date Built	C/N	Disposition
1	Canadian	1893	445	Received new boiler 1914. Sold to United Engineers c.1920. Resold Bloedel, Stewart and Welch, date unknown.

Class – 4-4-0: 16x24-62- ? - ? - ? -?

No.	Builder	Date Built	C/N	Original No.	Renumbered From	Date	Disposition	Notes
2	Canadian	1875	196?	?	?	?	Retired before 1910. Scrapped at Victoria 1918.	46

Class – 4-4-0: ? -57- ? - ? - ? -?

No.	Builder	Date Built	C/N	Original No.	Renumbered From	Date	Disposition	Notes
3	Baldwin	4/1882	?	NP ?	VL&M 1	6/1902	Reno. VW&Y 1(1) 1903. Returned V&S (No. 3) 1904. Abandoned at Bazan Bay, 1919. Scrapped at Sidney 1923.	45

Class B-11(2) 4-4-0: 17x24-63-145(140)-85,000-52,000-13,100

No.	Builder	Date Built	C/N	Original No.	Renumbered From	Date	Disposition
4	Baldwin	4/1890	10830	SF&N 6	GN 141	1908	Returned to GN (No. 141) 1908.

VICTORIA TERMINAL RAILWAY AND FERRY COMPANY

Class B-8 4-4-0: 17x24-55-140-73,400-48,000-15,010

No.	Builder	Date Rcvd.	C/N	Original No.	Renumbered From	Date	Disposition
4	Pittsburgh	9/25/1880	443	StPM&M 74	GN 290	9/19/1903	Reno. GN 290 at Delta 10/5/1908.

WATERTOWN AND SIOUX FALLS RAILWAY COMPANY

Class D-6 2-6-0: 19x24-55-160-114,500-101,800-21,420

No.	Builder	Date Built	C/N	Original No.	Renumbered From	Date	Disposition	Notes
11	Alco-Schenectady	1902	?	?	SDC 11	6/30/1916	Reno. GN 430 9/19/1921. Sold GN 12/31/1928.	39

Class D-6 2-6-0: 19x24-55-160(155)-126,900-113,800-20,750

No.	Builder	Date Built	C/N	Original No.	Renumbered From	Date	Disposition	Notes
12	Alco-Schenectady	1906	?	?	SDC 12	6/30/1916	Reno. GN 431 8/1/1921. Sold GN 12/31/1928.	40

Class D-3(2) 2-6-0: 18x24-55-180(170)-119,000-106,500-20,430

No.	Builder	Date Built	C/N	Original No.	Renumbered From	Date	Disposition	Notes
13	Baldwin	5/1901	18999	K&M 279	SDC 13	6/30/1916	Reno. GN 432 7/11/1921. Sold GN 12/31/1928.	41

Class F-11 2-8-0: 20x24-52-180-138,000-123,000-28,250

No.	Builder	Date Built	C/N	Original No.	Renumbered From	Date	Disposition	Notes
14	Alco-Brooks	4/1913	52834	TA&G 322	SDC 14	6/30/1916	Reno. GN 590 4/15/1922. Sold GN 12/31/1928.	42
15	Alco-Brooks	9/1914	54970	SDC 15	SDC 15	6/30/1916	Reno. GN 591 5/22/1922. Sold GN 12/31/1928.	

Class E-2(2) 4-6-0: 18x24-60-200-130,000-96,000-22,030

No.	Builder	Date Built	C/N	Original No.	Renumbered From	Date	Disposition	Notes
16	Alco-Brooks	5/1915	55132	SDC 16	SDC 16	6/30/1916	Reno. GN 910 at Sioux City 8/11/1921. Sold GN 12/31/1928.	138

Class E-2(2) 4-6-0: 18x24-60-200-135,500-97,500-22,030

No.	Builder	Date Built	C/N	Original No.	Renumbered From	Date	Disposition	Notes
17	Alco-Brooks	11/1915	55443	SDC 17	SDC 17	6/30/1916	Reno. GN 911 7/14/1921. Sold GN 12/31/1928.	139

Class O-2 2-8-2: 20x28-52-180-178,000-128,000-32,950

No.	Builder	Date Built	C/N	Original No.	Renumbered From	Date	Disposition
18	Alco-Brooks	10/1915	55444	SDC 18	SDC 18	6/30/1916	Reno. GN 3149 4/10/1922. Sold GN 12/31/1928.

THE WILLMAR AND SIOUX FALLS RAILWAY COMPANY

Class 2A 0-6-0: 17x24-56-145-90,000-90,000-15,550

No.	Builder	Date Rcvd.	C/N	Original No.	Renumbered From	Date	Disposition	Notes
47	Rogers	8/16/1890	4350	SC&N 7	SC&N 7	7/25/1900	Sold GN [No. 47(2)] 7/1/1907.	
48	Rogers	3/1891	4494	SC&N 9	SC&N 9	12/6/1900	Sold GN [No. 48(2)] 7/1/1907.	33

Class 11(2) 4-4-0: 17X24-63-145(140)-89,000-56,000-13,100

No.	Builder	Date Rcvd.	C/N	Original No.	Renumbered From	Date	Disposition
232	Rogers	1/14/1890	4182	SC&N 1	SC&N 1	c.1900	Sold GN [No. 232(2)] 7/1/1907.
233	Rogers	1/15/1890	4194	SC&N 2	SC&N 2	2/19/1901	Sold GN [No. 233(2)] 7/1/1907.
234	Rogers	1/18/1890	4205	SC&N 3	SC&N 3	c.1900	Sold GN (No. 234) 7/1/1907.
235	Rogers	1/25/1890	4226	SC&N 4	SC&N 4	1/25/1901	Sold GN (No. 235) 7/1/1907.
236	Rogers	6/1/1890	4303	SC&N 8	SC&N 8	9/8/1900	Sold GN (No. 236) 7/1/1907.
237	Rogers	12/19/1890	4420	SC&N 10	SC&N 10	12/1/1900	Sold GN (No. 237) 7/1/1907.

Class 11(2) 4-4-0: 17x24-63-145-80,000-51,000-12,770

No.	Builder	Date Built	C/N	Original No.	Renumbered From	Date	Disposition
238	Rhode Island	4/1889	2202	PSL 13	SC&W 13	1/1/1901	Leased GN (No. 238) 7/1/1907.

Class 36A 2-6-0: 19x24-55-150-104,800-89,300-20,080

No.	Builder	Date Built	C/N	Original No.	Renumbered From	Date	Disposition
360	Rhode Island	7/1890	2406	PSL 14	SC&W 14	7/3/1900	Leased GN [No. 360(2)] 7/1/1907.

Class 27(2) 4-6-0: 18x24-55-150-100,000-74,000-16,820

No.	Builder	Date Rcvd.	C/N	Original No.	Renumbered From	Date	Disposition
992	Rogers	2/11/1890	4236	SC&N 5	SC&N 5	8/24/1900	Sold GN (No. 992) 7/1/1907.
993	Rogers	2/8/1890	4237	SC&N 6	SC&N 6	3/24/1900	Sold GN (No. 993) 7/1/1907.

Class 27C 4-6-0: 18x24-56-150-102,800-84,000-17,700

No.	Builder	Date Built	C/N	Original No.	Renumbered From	Date	Disposition	Notes
994	Rhode Island	12/1889	2264	MCCo 131(1)	SC&W 16	7/3/1900	Leased GN (No. 994) 7/1/1907.	36
995	Rhode Island	12/1889	2265	MCCo 132(1)	SC&W 17	3/24/1900	Leased GN (No. 995) 7/1/1907.	36
996	Rhode Island	4/1890	2328	PSL 12	SC&W 18	5/10/1900	Leased GN (No. 996) 7/1/1907.	

Class 27A 4-6-0: 19x24-55-150-105,600-86,650-20,080

No.	Builder	Date Built	C/N	Original No.	Renumbered From	Date	Disposition
997	Rhode Island	8/1890	2440	PSL 15	SC&W 15	5/9/1900	Leased GN (No. 997) 7/1/1907.

Engine 186 was the last in the B-19 class, received by the StPM&M in 1883. In 1944 it was renumbered as GN 220(2nd) and lasted until 1947. It was photographed at Yankton, SD, in August 1940. Collection of Harold K. Vollrath.

Shown switching near the passenger depot at Great Falls, MT, on an unknown date, Class A-9 No. 14 was still active after World War II, but scrapped in 1947. This was the third No. 14 on the Great Northern. Photographer unknown, from the Jack Dykstra collection.

Chapter 31

Great Northern Steam Locomotive Roster

GREAT NORTHERN RAILWAY COMPANY

"WILLIAM CROOKS" (Old Class 1) 4-4-0: 12x22-63-120(110)-55,400-35,950-4,700

No.	Builder	Date Rcvd.	C/N	Original No.	Renumbered From	Date	Disposition
1(1)	Smith & Jackson	9/9/1861	?	M&P 1	StPM&M 1	c.1892	Retired 9/1897, stored at Jackson Street Shops. Refurbished at Jackson Street Shops in 1908 for exhibition purposes. Placed on exhibit at St.Paul, MN, Union Depot 1954. Donated to Minnesota Historical Society 6/28/1962. On indefinite custodial loan at the Lake Superior Railroad Museum since 1975.

Class A-9 0-6-0: 19x26-49-200(175)-135,000-135,000-28,490 originally. Those locomotives indicated by an asterisk (*) were rebuilt with 52" drivers (decreasing T.E. to 26,850 lb.), dates unknown. Total weights of those locomotives with 49" and 52" drivers were later increased to 142,800 lb. and 147,000 lb., respectively.

No.	Builder	Date Rcvd.	C/N	Disposition	Notes
1(2)*	GN (Dale Street)	7/30/1909	1	Sold for scrap DI&M 1/31/1947.	
2	Baldwin	11/4/1907	31906	Retired 1/1934. Sold for scrap PC 6/11/1934.	47
3(2)*	Baldwin	11/4/1907	31907	Dismantled at Great Falls 9/5/1931.	
4(2)	Baldwin	11/8/1907	31941	Sold for scrap Bethlehem Steel 9/1939.	
5(3)*	Baldwin	11/8/1907	31942	Reno. GN 391(3) 10/1949.	
6(2)*	Baldwin	11/22/1907	32056	Sold for scrap PC 1/25/1947.	
7(2)*	Baldwin	11/22/1907	32057	Scrapped 10/1940.	
8(3)*	Baldwin	11/22/1907	32080	Sold for scrap DI&M 1/25/1947.	
9(3)*	Baldwin	11/22/1907	32081	Sold to Becker County-Shiely Company 9/24/1934. Returned on unknown date. Reno. GN 392(3) 9/22/1949.	
10(3)*	Baldwin	11/30/1907	32114	Reno. GN 393(2) 10/1949.	
11(3)*	Baldwin	11/30/1907	32115	Sold for scrap PC 6/1947.	
12(3)*	GN (Dale Street)	8/6/1909	12	Sold for scrap DI&M 12/1949.	

Old Class 3 0-4-0: 14x22-49-125-49,000-49,000-9,350

No.	Builder	Date Rcvd.	C/N	Original No.	Renumbered From	Date	Disposition
3(1)	Brooks	10/13/1879	354	StPM&M 51(1)	StPM&M 3	c.1892	Scrapped 6/1901.

Class B-2 (Old Class 6) 4-4-0: 15x22-49-125-67,000-45,300-10,730. Those locomotives indicated by an asterisk (*) had dimensions of 16x24-49-125-68,500-45,350-13,320. Locomotive indicated by a plus (+) had dimensions of 15x22-49-125-62,500-41,100-10,730. Locomotive indicated by an equal sign (=) had dimensions of 15x24-49-125-65,250-43,850-11,710. Locomotive indicated by a per cent sign (%) had dimensions of 16x24-49-130-68,600-47,200-13,860. Dates with an asterisk (*) under "Date Rcvd." are dates built.

No.	Builder	Date Rcvd.	C/N	Original No.	Renumbered From	Date	Disposition	Notes
4(1)*	Danforth	1866*	?	StP&P 5	GN 5(1)	4/13/1899	Sold Fitzhugh Co. 12/27/1902.	
5(1)*	Danforth	1866*	?	StP&P 5	StPM&M 5	c.1892	Renumbered GN 4(1) 4/13/1899.	
5(2)+	Mason	7/1868	283	StP&P 10	GN 10(1)	4/4/1899	Scrapped 9/1901.	
6(1)=	Mason	5/1869	310	StP&P 11	GN 11(1)	3/30/1899	Sold PV&Y (No. 3) 2/18/1902. Then transferred via merger to Washington Railway & Navigation Co. (No. unknown). Sold to Northern Pacific (No. 1153) 12/10/1903. Sold to Blumauer Lumber Co. (No. unknown) 6/26/1905.	
7(1)	Danforth	1868*	?	StP&P 12	GN 12(1)	4/1/1899	Scrapped at St.Paul 9/22/1901.	
8(2)	Danforth	1868*	?	StP&P 13	GN 13(1)	4/5/1899	Scrapped at Delta 4/28/1903.	
9(2)	Danforth	1868*	?	StP&P 14	GN 14(1)	4/11/1899	Received major repairs and new paint 4/5/1900. Then sold Fitzhugh Co. 9/8/1902.	
10(2)*	Danforth	1869*	?	StP&P 15	GN 15(1)	4/13/1899	Received major repairs and new paint 9/23/1901, then sold Fitzhugh Co. 6/4/1902.	
11(2)%	Pittsburgh	7/1870*	75	StP&P 17	GN 17(1)	4/8/1899	Renumbered GN 244(2) 1907.	219
12(1)	Danforth	1868*	?	StP&P 12	StPM&M 12	c.1892	Reno. GN 7(1) 4/1/1899.	
13(1)	Danforth	1868*	?	StP&P 13	StPM&M 13	c.1892	Reno. GN 8(2) 4/5/1899.	

Old Class 10(1) 4-4-0: 14x22-63- ? -57,600-35,000- ?

No.	Builder	Date Built	C/N	Original No.	Renumbered From	Date	Disposition	Notes
8(1)	Mason	9/1867	270	StP&P 8	StPM&M 8	c.1892	Engine stripped and boiler fitted for steam heating and sent to Breckenridge 12/9/1893.	13

Old Class 9(2) 4-4-0: 15x24-49- ? -65,250-43,850- ?

No.	Builder	Date Built	C/N	Original No.	Renumbered From	Date	Disposition	Notes
9(1)	Mason	5/1868	279	StP&P 9	StPM&M 9	c.1892	Sold to British Columbia Mills, Timber and Trading Co. 2/16/1898.	13

Old Class 12(1) 4-4-0: 15x22-49-125-62,500-41,100-10,730. Moved to Class 6 at some time after 6/30/1892.

No.	Builder	Date Built	C/N	Original No.	Renumbered From	Date	Disposition	Notes
10(1)	Mason	7/1868	283	StP&P 10	StPM&M 10	c.1892	Renumbered GN 5(2) 4/4/1899.	

Old Class 11(1) 4-4-0: 15x24-63- ? -62,750-40,350- ? originally. Rebuilt 6/10/1892 (with smaller drivers for switching) to 15x24-49-125-65,250-43,850-11,710. Moved to Class 6 at some time after 6/30/1892.

No.	Builder	Date Built	C/N	Original No.	Renumbered From	Date	Disposition	Notes
11(1)	Mason	5/1869	310	StP&P 11	StPM&M 11	c.1892	Renumbered GN 6(1) 3/30/1899.	

Class A-1 (Old Class 21) 0-6-0: 16x20-49-140-67,250-67,250-12,430. Weight of No. 13 (at least) later increased to 69,950 lb. These locomotives were originally 2-6-0's.

No.	Builder	Date Rcvd.	C/N	Original No.	Renumbered From	Date	Disposition	Notes
12(2)	Rogers	4/12/1879	2519	StP&P 45	GN 45	4/18/1899	Sold W.D. Hofius Co. 7/1902.	
13(2)	Rogers	4/22/1879	2521	StP&P 46	GN 46	4/15/1899	Sold Kettle River Quarries 5/1917.	48

Old Class 7(1) 4-4-0: 15x22-63- ? -64,500-41,800- ? originally. Rebuilt on 8/2/1892 (with smaller drivers for switching) to 15x22-49-125-67,000-45,300-10,730 and moved to Class 6.

No.	Builder	Date Built	C/N	Original No.	Renumbered From	Date	Disposition	Notes
14(1)	Danforth	1868	?	StP&P 14	StPM&M 14	c.1892	Reno. GN 9(2) 4/11/1899.	

Old Class 4 0-4-0: 15x24-49-140-53,900-53,900-13,110

No.	Builder	Date Rcvd.	C/N	Original No.	Renumbered From	Date	Disposition	Notes
14(2)	Brooks	3/29/1881	519	StPM&M 87	GN 87(1)	4/15/1899	Scrapped 6/1902.	
15(2)	Brooks	4/9/1881	521	StPM&M 88	GN 88(1)	4/17/1899	Scrapped 9/1903.	19
16(2)	Brooks	4/7/1881	523	StPM&M 89	GN 89(1)	4/19/1899	Sold Kettle River Quarries 5/1904.	

Class A-9 0-6-0: 19x26-49-200(175)-135,000-135,000-28,490 originally. Those locomotives indicated by an asterisk (*) were rebuilt with 52" drivers (decreasing T.E. to 26,850 lb.), dates unknown. Total weights of those locomotives with 49" and 52" drivers were later increased to 142,800 lb. and 147,000 lb., respectively.

No.	Builder	Date Rcvd.	C/N	Disposition	Notes
14(3)	GN (Dale Street)	9/8/1906	14	Sold for scrap PC 6/1947.	
15(3)*	GN (Dale Street)	9/22/1906	15	Reno. GN 398(2) 4/1950.	
16(3)	GN (Dale Street)	9/27/1906	16	Reno. GN 397(2) 4/1950.	
17(3)	GN (Dale Street)	10/6/1906	17	Sold U.S. Army, Fort Peck Dam, MT, 9/22/1938.	49
18(3)	GN (Dale Street)	10/23/1906	18	Retired 12/1949. Sold for scrap PC 1/1950.	
19(3)	GN (Dale Street)	10/23/1906	19	Reno. GN 399(2) 4/1951.	
20(3)	GN (Dale Street)	10/25/1906	20	Sold for scrap Bethlehem Steel 9/1939.	
21(3)*	GN (Dale Street)	10/31/1906	21	Sold for scrap PC 2/1949.	
22(3)*	GN (Dale Street)	11/7/1906	22	Sold for scrap PC 1/31/1947.	
23(3)	GN (Dale Street)	11/14/1906	23	Retired 12/1949. Sold for scrap DI&M 1/1950.	
24(3)	GN (Dale Street)	8/16/1909	24	Ret. 5/1939.	
25(3)*	GN (Dale Street)	8/24/1909	25	Sold for scrap DI&M 6/4/1947.	
26(3)	GN (Dale Street)	8/31/1909	26	Ret. 1939.	

Old Class 6 4-4-0: 16x24-49-125-68,500-45,350-13,320

No.	Builder	Date Built	C/N	Original No.	Renumbered From	Date	Disposition
15(1)	Danforth	1869	?	StP&P 15	StPM&M 15	c.1892	Reno. GN 10(2) 4/13/1899.

Old Class 5(2) 4-4-0: 16x24-63-140-66,000-41,850-11,610

No.	Builder	Date Built	C/N	Original No.	Renumbered From	Date	Disposition
16(1)	Danforth	1869	?	StP&P 16	StPM&M 16	c.1892	Reno. GN 240 3/29/1899.

Old Class 13 4-4-0: 16x24-63-140-66,100-43,700-11,600 originally. Rebuilt 3/7/1893 (with smaller drivers for switching) to 16x24-49-130-68,600-47,200-13,860 and moved to Class 6.

No.	Builder	Date Built	C/N	Original No.	Renumbered From	Date	Disposition
17(1)	Pittsburgh	7/1870	75	StP&P 17	StPM&M 17	c.1892	Reno. GN 11(2) 4/8/1899.

Old Class 22 0-4-0: 15x24-49-135-62,000-62,000-12,650

No.	Builder	Date Rcvd.	C/N	Original No.	Renumbered From	Date	Disposition	Notes
17(2)	Rogers	4/12/1882	2968	StPM&M 90	GN 90(1)	4/14/1899	Scrapped 1902.	21
18(2)	Rogers	4/12/1882	2969	StPM&M 91	GN 91(1)	4/13/1899	Scrapped 7/1902.	
19(2)	Rogers	4/13/1882	2970	StPM&M 92	GN 92(1)	4/13/1899	Scrapped 6/1902.	
20(2)	Rogers	4/15/1882	2971	StPM&M 93	GN 93(1)	5/2/1899	Scrapped 12/22/1900.	

Old Class 13 4-4-0: 16x24-63-140-66,100-43,700-11,600

No.	Builder	Date Built	C/N	Original No.	Renumbered From	Date	Disposition
18(1)	Pittsburgh	8/1870	76	StP&P 18	StPM&M 18	c.1892	Reno. GN 241 1899.
19(1)	Pittsburgh	9/1870	77	StP&P 19	StPM&M 19	c.1892	Reno. GN 242 4/7/1899.

Old Class 17 4-4-0: 15x24-63- ? -68,800-43,000- ?

No.	Builder	Date Built	C/N	Original No.	Renumbered From	Date	Disposition	Notes
20(1)	Baldwin	12/1871	2619	NP 20(1)	StPM&M 20	c.1892	Reno. GN 243 3/1899.	16
21(1)	Baldwin	12/1871	2621	NP 21(1)	StPM&M 21	c.1892	Reno. GN 244(1) 4/1/1899.	16

Old Class 4 0-4-0: 15x24-49-140-53,900-53,900-13,110

No.	Builder	Date Rcvd.	C/N	Original No.	Renumbered From	Date	Disposition
21(2)	Brooks	8/16/1882	757	StPM&M 187	GN 187	4/14/1899	Scrapped 1903.
22(2)	Brooks	8/17/1882	758	StPM&M 188	GN 188	4/29/1899	Scrapped 1903.
23(2)	Brooks	8/22/1882	760	StPM&M 190	GN 190	4/10/1899	Scrapped 10/13/1900.
24(2)	Brooks	8/25/1882	761	StPM&M 191	GN 191	4/13/1899	Scrapped 6/30/1901.
25(2)	Brooks	8/25/1882	762	StPM&M 192	GN 192	4/17/1899	Scrapped at St.Paul 1901.
26(2)	Brooks	8/28/1882	763	StPM&M 193	GN 193	3/21/1899	Scrapped 1902.

Old Class 16 4-4-0: 16x24-63-140-70,000-44,550-11,600

No.	Builder	Date Built	C/N	Original No.	Renumbered From	Date	Disposition	Notes
22(1)	Baldwin	12/1871	2638	NP 22(1)	StPM&M 22	c.1892	Converted to weedburner 1898. Reno. GN 245 4/8/1899.	16

Old Class 17 4-4-0: 15x24-63- ? -68,800-43,000- ?

No.	Builder	Date Built	C/N	Original No.	Renumbered From	Date	Disposition	Notes
23(1)	Baldwin	12/1871	2639	NP 23(1)	StPM&M 23	c.1892	Reno. GN 246 3/30/1899.	16

Old Class 13 4-4-0: 16x24-63-140-72,700-46,000-11,600

No.	Builder	Date Built	C/N	Original No.	Renumbered From	Date	Disposition
24(1)	Pittsburgh	12/1875	320	StP&P 24	StPM&M 24	c.1892	Reno. GN 247 3/31/1899.
25(1)	Pittsburgh	12/1875	322	StP&P 25	StPM&M 25	c.1892	Scrapped 11/1898.
26(1)	Pittsburgh	12/1875	323	StP&P 26	StPM&M 26	c.1892	Reno. GN 248 3/25/1899.

Class A-9 0-6-0: 19x26-49-200(175)-142,800-142,800-26,850

No.	Builder	Date Rcvd.	C/N	Original No.	Renumbered From	Date	Disposition
26(4)	Rogers	8/27/1903	6015	GN 74(2)	GN 74(2)	2/28/1944	Sold for scrap PC 5/21/1947.
27(3)	Rogers	8/31/1903	6018	GN 77(2)	GN 77(2)	3/1/1944	Sold for scrap DI&M 7/1947.
28(3)	Rogers	8/31/1903	6019	GN 78(2)	GN 78(2)	3/1/1944	Sold for scrap PC 3/1/1949.
29(3)	Rogers	9/3/1903	6021	GN 80(2)	GN 80(2)	3/27/1944	Sold for scrap PC 10/10/1952.

Old Class 19 4-4-0: 16x24-55-140-66,170-41,600-13,290

No.	Builder	Date Rcvd.	C/N	Original No.	Renumbered From	Date	Disposition
27(1)	Rogers	6/5/1878	2477	StP&P 27	StPM&M 27	c.1892	Reno. GN 255(2) 3/31/1899.
28(1)	Rogers	6/5/1878	2478	StP&P 28	StPM&M 28	c.1892	Reno. GN 256(2) 4/6/1899.
29(1)	Rogers	6/17/1878	2480	StP&P 29	StPM&M 29	c.1892	Reno. GN 257(2) 4/7/1899.
30(1)	Rogers	6/26/1878	2481	StP&P 30	StPM&M 30	c.1892	Reno. GN 258(2) 4/5/1899.
31(1)	Rogers	6/26/1878	2483	StP&P 31	StPM&M 31	c.1892	Reno. GN 259 4/5/1899.
32(1)	Rogers	6/29/1878	2484	StP&P 32	StPM&M 32	c.1892	Reno. GN 260 4/13/1899.
33(1)	Rogers	6/29/1878	2485	StP&P 33	StPM&M 33	c.1892	Reno. GN 261 4/6/1899.
34(1)	Rogers	7/12/1878	2486	StP&P 34	StPM&M 34	c.1892	Reno. GN 262 4/13/1899.
35(1)	Rogers	7/26/1878	2488	StP&P 35	StPM&M 35	c.1892	Reno. GN 263 1899.
36(1)	Rogers	7/31/1878	2490	StP&P 36	StPM&M 36	c.1892	Reno. GN 264 1899.
37(1)	Rogers	8/15/1878	2491	StP&P 37	StPM&M 37	c.1892	Scrapped 11/1898.
38(1)	Rogers	9/19/1878	2492	StP&P 38	StPM&M 38	c.1892	Destroyed by fire at Bottineau, ND, roundhouse 11/23/1896.
39(1)	Rogers	10/7/1878	2495	StP&P 39	StPM&M 39	c.1892	Reno. GN 265 4/24/1899.
40(1)	Rogers	10/8/1878	2496	StP&P 40	StPM&M 40	c.1892	Reno. GN 266 3/31/1899.
41(1)	Rogers	10/30/1878	2498	StP&P 41	StPM&M 41	c.1892	Reno. GN 267 4/7/1899.
42(1)	Rogers	10/30/1878	2500	StP&P 42	StPM&M 42	c.1892	Scrapped 11/1898.

Class A-4 (Old Class 32) 0-6-0: 17x24-49-140-67,050-67,050-16,840

No.	Builder	Date Rcvd.	C/N	Original No.	Renumbered From	Date	Disposition
27(2)	Brooks	8/30/1882	764	StPM&M 194	GN 194(1)	4/1/1899	Scrapped at Dale Street 9/1916.
28(2)	Brooks	8/31/1882	765	StPM&M 195	MW 2	1899	Scrapped at Dale Street 9/1916.
29(2)	Brooks	9/4/1882	766	StPM&M 196	GN 196(1)	4/10/1899	Sold A. Guthrie (No. 150) 4/30/1918.

Class A-2 [Old Class 2(2)] 0-6-0: 17x24-49-140-83,000-83,000-15,850

No.	Builder	Date Rcvd.	C/N	Original No.	Renumbered From	Date	Disposition
30(2)	Hinkley	8/1/1888	1765	StPM&M 232	S&M RR 232	4/6/1899	Sold McCoy Logging Co. 3/1915.
31(2)	Hinkley	8/1/1888	1766	StPM&M 233	GN 233(1)	3/29/1899	Scrapped 3/10/1915 at St.Paul.

Class A-11 0-6-0: 20x24-49-200(180)-130,000-130,000-29,980

No.	Builder	Date Built	C/N	Original No.	Renumbered From	Date	Disposition	Notes
30(3)	Lima	4/1916	5135	GNIOP 203	GNIOP 203	10/25/1917	Ret. 5/1939. Sold for scrap DI&M 10/15/1939.	50
31(3)	Lima	4/1916	5136	GNIOP 204	GNIOP 204	10/28/1917	Sold Midland Railway Company of Manitoba (No. 5) 7/1946.	50

Class A-5(1) [Old Class 31(2)] 0-6-0: 18x24-49-150(140)-86,450-86,450-18,880 originally. Weights later increased to 87,300 lb. Dates with an asterisk (*) below are dates built.

No.	Builder	Date Rcvd.	C/N	Original No.	Renumbered From	Date	Disposition	Notes
32(2)	Rogers	4/26/1887	3736	StPM&M 94(2)	GN 94(1)	4/22/1899	Sold John Cox 2/1923.	
33(2)	Rogers	4/29/1887	3737	StPM&M 95(2)	GN 95(1)	4/10/1899	Sold John Cox 2/1923.	
34(2)	Rogers	4/29/1887	3738	StPM&M 96(2)	GN 96(1)	4/17/1899	Sold Great Lakes Coal & Dock Co. 11/21/1921.	51
35(2)	Rogers	5/1/1887	3739	StPM&M 97(2)	GN 97(1)	4/13/1899	Scrapped 9/1920.	
36(2)	Rogers	5/12/1887	3740	StPM&M 98	MW 1(2)	1899	Scrapped at Dale Street 9/30/1920.	
37(2)	Rogers	5/12/1887	3741	StPM&M 99	EM 37	5/1/1902	Sold John Cox 3/1923.	52
38(2)	Rogers	9/17/1888	4010	StPM&M 226	MC 14	c.1900	Sold for scrap DI&M 2/2/1922.	
39(2)	Rogers	9/20/1888	4011	StPM&M 227	MC 15	c.1900	Sold John Cox 3/1923.	52
40(2)	Rogers	7/1888*	3975	EM 1	EM 40	5/1/1902	Sold John Cox 3/1923.	52
41(2)	Rogers	7/1888*	3976	EM 2	EM 41	5/1/1902	Sold John Cox 12/1922.	
42(2)	Rogers	7/1888*	3978	EM 3	EM 42	5/1/1902	Sold John Cox 12/1922.	
43(2)	Rogers	10/9/1888	4028	StPM&M 228	GN 228(1)	4/6/1899	Sold for scrap DI&M 2/2/1922.	
44(2)	Rogers	10/9/1888	4029	StPM&M 229	GN 229(1)	4/17/1899	Sold John Cox 2/1923.	
45(2)	Rogers	10/10/1888	4030	StPM&M 230	GN 230(1)	4/28/1899	Sold for scrap DI&M 2/10/1922.	
46(2)	Rogers	10/11/1888	4031	StPM&M 231	GN 231(1)	4/23/1899	Sold for scrap DI&M 2/10/1922.	

Class A-5(2) 0-6-0 (rebuilt from D-5 2-6-0): 19x26-55-180(170)-126,000-126,000-24,660. See Note 54.

No.	Builder	Date Finish A-5	C/N	Original No.	Rebuilt From	Disposition	Notes
32(3)	GN (Jackson Street)	2/16/1925	2706	GN 379(1)	GN 458(2)	Sold Midland of Manitoba [No. 3(2)] 9/24/1929.	53, 220
33(3)	GN (Jackson Street)	2/19/1926	2703	GN 376	GN 455(2)	Retired 11/1929. Scrapped 1931.	53

Old Class 20 4-4-0: 17x24-58-140-70,300-44,800-14,230. Driver diameter changed from 58" to 55" on 1/14/1896 and 10/23/1897, respectively, changing dimensions to 17x24-55-140-70,300-44,800-15,010.

No.	Builder	Date Rcvd.	C/N	Original No.	Renumbered From	Date	Disposition
43(1)	Rogers	1/27/1879	2509	StP&P 43	StPM&M 43	c.1892	Reno. GN 294 3/31/1899.
44(1)	Rogers	1/27/1879	2511	StP&P 44	StPM&M 44	c.1892	Reno. GN 295 4/13/1899.

Old Class 21 2-6-0: 16x20-46-140-67,250-62,000-13,245 originally. Sometime after 6/30/1892, the lead trucks were removed, converting these engines to 0-6-0's. The drivers of Nos. 45(1) and 46(1) were also changed (possibly at the same time as lead truck removal) to 49" diameter, on an unknown date and on 8/22/1896, respectively. This left these locomotives with dimensions of 16x20-49-140-67,250-67,250-12,430.

No.	Builder	Date Rcvd.	C/N	Original No.	Renumbered From	Date	Disposition
45(1)	Rogers	4/12/1879	2519	StP&P 45	StPM&M 45	c.1892	Reno. GN 12(2) 4/18/1899.
46(1)	Rogers	4/22/1879	2521	StP&P 46	StPM&M 46	c.1892	Reno. GN 13(2) 4/15/1899.

Old Class 16 4-4-0: 16x24-63-140-70,000-44,550-11,600

No.	Builder	Date Built	C/N	Original No.	Renumbered From	Date	Disposition	Notes
47(1)	Baldwin	11/1879	4848	(StP&P 47)	StPM&M 47	c.1892	Converted to weedburner 1898. Reno. GN 249 4/10/1899.	17
48(1)	Baldwin	11/1879	4849	(StP&P 48)	StPM&M 48	c.1892	Converted to weedburner 5/30/1898. Reno. GN 250(2)4/11/1899.	17
49(1)	Baldwin	11/1879	4852	(StP&P 49)	StPM&M 49	c.1892	Reno. GN 251(2) 4/11/1899.	17
50(1)	Baldwin	11/1879	4853	(StP&P 50)	StPM&M 50	c.1892	Converted to weedburner 1898. Reno. GN 252(2) 3/31/1899.	17

Class A-3 (Old Class 2A) 0-6-0: 17x24-56-145-90,000-90,000-15,550. Date with asterisk (*) is date built.

No.	Builder	Date Rcvd.	C/N	Original No.	Renumbered From	Date	Disposition	Notes
47(2)	Rogers	8/16/1890	4350	SC&N 7	WSF 47	7/1/1907	Sold National Surface Guard Co. 1/1918.	55
48(2)	Rogers	3/1891*	4494	SC&N 9	WSF 58	7/1/1907	Scrapped 5/1918.	33, 56

Class A-9 0-6-0: 19x26-49-200(175)-135,000-135,000-28,490 originally. Those locomotives indicated by an asterisk (*) were rebuilt with 52" drivers (decreasing T.E. to 26,850 lb.), dates unknown. Total weights of those locomotives with 49" and 52" drivers were later increased to 142,800 lb. and 147,000 lb., respectively.

No.	Builder	Date Rcvd.	C/N	Disposition	Notes
49(2)	GN (Dale Street)	9/7/1909	49	Sold for scrap DI&M 3/24/1947.	
50(2)	GN (Dale Street)	9/15/1909	50	Ret. 5/1939.	
51(2)	GN (Dale Street)	9/18/1909	51	Ret. 4/1937, sold for scrap.	
52(2)*	Baldwin	9/5/1907	31382	Scrapped 1/1938.	57
53(2)*	Baldwin	9/5/1907	31383	Sold for scrap Dulien Steel Products 1/15/1953.	
54(2)	Baldwin	9/5/1907	31384	Sold for scrap DI&M 10/16/1951.	
55(2)*	Baldwin	9/5/1907	31412	Sold for scrap PC 12/1941.	
56(3)	GN (Dale Street)	9/25/1909	56	Sold for scrap PC 8/22/1941.	
57(3)	GN (Dale Street)	9/30/1909	57	Ret. 12/1949. Sold for scrap PC.	

Old Class 18 4-4-0: 17x24-58-140-70,050-44,650-14,230 originally. Driver diameter on most decreased to 55" (date shown in parentheses if known), giving dimensions of 17x24-55-140-70,050-44,650-15,010. Those engines indicated by an asterisk (*) below had driver diameter increased to 63" (dates shown in parentheses if known), with dimensions of 17x24-63-140-72,700-45,450-13,100. Class of the engines with 63" drivers was later changed to 24A.

No.	Builder	Date Rcvd.	C/N	Original No.	Renumbered From	Date	Disposition
51(1)	Baldwin	5/10/1880	5083	StPM&M 67(1)	StPM&M 51(2)	c.1892	Reno. GN 268 4/8/1899.
52(1)*	Baldwin	3/18/1880	4996	StPM&M 52	StPM&M 52	c.1892	Reno. GN 117(2) 4/11/1899.
53(1)	Baldwin	3/13/1880	4993	StPM&M 53	StPM&M 53	c.1892	(11/20/1897) Reno. GN 270 3/31/1899.
54(1)	Baldwin	3/13/1880	4994	StPM&M 54	StPM&M 54	c.1892	(4/8/1897) Reno. GN 271 4/8/1899.
55(1)	Baldwin	3/18/1880	4998	StPM&M 55	StPM&M 55	c.1892	Reno. GN 272 4/9/1899.
56(1)	Baldwin	4/6/1880	5033	StPM&M 56	StPM&M 56	c.1892	Reno. GN 273 4/15/1899.
57(1)	Baldwin	4/6/1880	5028	StPM&M 57	StPM&M 57	c.1892	(5/19/1897) Reno. GN 274 1899.
58(1)	Baldwin	4/17/1880	5043	StPM&M 58	StPM&M 58	c.1892	(1/31/1900) Reno. GN 275 4/6/1899.
59(1)	Baldwin	4/17/1880	5046	StPM&M 59	StPM&M 59	c.1892	Reno. GN 276 4/1/1899.
60(1)	Baldwin	4/28/1880	5061	StPM&M 60	StPM&M 60	c.1892	Reno. GN 277 1899.
61(1)	Baldwin	4/28/1880	5062	StPM&M 61	StPM&M 61	c.1892	(2/5/1897) Reno. GN 278 4/11/1899.
62(1)*	Baldwin	5/7/1880	5079	StPM&M 62	StPM&M 62	c.1892	(4/7/1888) Reno. GN 119(2) 4/18/1899.
63(1)	Baldwin	5/7/1880	5074	StPM&M 63	StPM&M 63	c.1892	Reno. GN 280 4/1/1899.
64(1)	Baldwin	5/17/1880	5085	StPM&M 64	StPM&M 64	c.1892	(4/7/1897) Reno. GN 281 4/5/1899.
65(1)	Baldwin	5/17/1880	5086	StPM&M 65	StPM&M 65	c.1892	(5/7/1898) Reno. GN 282 3/31/1899.
66(1)	Baldwin	5/10/1880	5078	StPM&M 66	StPM&M 66	c.1892	Reno. GN 283 4/1/1899.

Class A-6 [Old Class 9(3)] 0-6-0: 18x26-49-180(160)-109,400-109,400-23,380

No.	Builder	Date Built	C/N	Original No.	Renumbered From	Date	Disposition	Notes
56(2)	Brooks	9/1899	3301	DS&WT 1	DS&WT 1	1903	Sold Allouez Bay Dock Co. 1909. Reno. ABD 1 at Superior 3/24/1909. Resold GN [No. 378(2)] 4/22/1913.	1
57(2)	Brooks	9/1899	3302	DS&WT 2	DS&WT 2	1903	Sold Allouez Bay Dock Co. 1909. Reno. ABD 2 at Superior 2/16/1909. Resold GN [No. 379(2)] 4/22/1913.	1
58(2)	Brooks	9/1899	3299	EM 58	EM 58	5/1/1902	Sold for scrap DI&M 12/1926.	58
59(2)	Brooks	9/1899	3300	EM 59	EM 59	5/1/1902	Sold McCree & Co. 7/1926.	

Class A-7 [Old Class 7(2)] 0-6-0: 19x26-49-180(160)-114,700-114,700-26,050. Dates with asterisk (*) are dates received.

No.	Builder	Date Built	C/N	Original No.	Renumbered From	Date	Disposition	Notes
60(2)	Brooks	1/1/1893*	2208	GN 250(1)	GN 250(1)	4/13/1899	Sold Somers Lumber Co. (S4) 2/1930. Repurchased by GN and sold U.S. Government 4/1939.	
61(2)	Brooks	1/1/1893*	2209	GN 251(1)	GN 251(1)	4/15/1899	Sold Landers, Morrison, Christianson Co. 3/31/1931.	
62(2)	Brooks	1/10/1893*	2215	GN 257(1)	GN 257(1)	4/12/1899	Sold for scrap DI&M 10/1929.	59
63(2)	Brooks	11/16/1893*	2262	GN 258(1)	GN 258(1)	4/11/1899	Sold for scrap DI&M 5/1926.	60
64(2)	Brooks	1/1/1893*	2206	MC 25	MC 25	1900	Ret. 5/1937, sold for scrap.	
65(2)	Brooks	1/1/1893*	2207	MC 26	MC 26	1900	Sold Great Lakes Coal & Dock Co. 9/1927.	61
66(2)	Brooks	8/1895	2552	EM 5	EM 66	5/1/1902	Ret. 7/2/1930. Sold for scrap DI&M 8/1932.	
67(2)	Brooks	8/1895	2553	EM 6	EM 67	5/1/1902	Ret. 1/1934. Sold for scrap PC 3/18/1934.	
68(2)	Brooks	6/1898	2971	EM 7	EM 68	5/1/1902	Ret. 3/1934. Sold for scrap DI&M 3/12/1934.	
69(2)	Brooks	6/1898	2972	EM 8	EM 69	5/1/1902	Ret. 3/1934. Sold for scrap DI&M 3/18/1934.	62

Old Class 15 4-4-0: 17x24-63-140-74,800-49,200-13,100

No.	Builder	Date Rcvd.	C/N	Original No.	Renumbered From	Date	Disposition
67(1)	Pittsburgh	3/23/1881	478	StPM&M 67(2)	StPM&M 67(2)	c.1892	Reno. GN 187(2) 4/22/1899.

The engineer's side of B-19 No. 185 was photographed at Minot, ND, on June 23, 1922. This engine has a different style boiler than sister engine 162 shown on page 71. No. 185 had received a new boiler in 1911. J. Foster Adams photograph, courtesy of Jerrold F. Hilton.

Old Class 14 4-4-0: 17x24-58-140-73,400-48,000-14,230 originally. Drivers changed from 58" to 55" (dates indicated in parentheses where known), with dimensions changing to 17x24-55-140-73,400-48,000-15,010

No.	Builder	Date Rcvd.	C/N	Original No.	Renumbered From	Date	Disposition	Notes
68(1)	Pittsburgh	8/20/1880	437	StPM&M 68	StPM&M 68	c.1892	(8/9/1895) Reno. GN 284 4/7/1899.	
69(1)	Pittsburgh	8/25/1880	438	StPM&M 69	StPM&M 69	c.1892	(7/30/1894) Reno. GN 285 4/13/1899.	18
70(1)	Pittsburgh	8/31/1880	439	StPM&M 70	StPM&M 70	c.1892	(11/21/1893) Reno. GN 286 3/30/1899.	
71(1)	Pittsburgh	9/6/1880	440	StPM&M 71	StPM&M 71	c.1892	(7/31/1895) Reno. GN 287 3/31/1899.	
72(1)	Pittsburgh	9/18/1880	441	StPM&M 72	StPM&M 72	c.1892	Reno. GN 288 4/10/1899.	
73(1)	Pittsburgh	9/18/1880	442	StPM&M 73	StPM&M 73	c.1892	(6/15/1898) Reno. GN 289 4/6/1899.	
74(1)	Pittsburgh	9/25/1880	443	StPM&M 74	StPM&M 74	c.1892	(6/17/1898) Reno. GN 290 4/17/1899.	
75(1)	Pittsburgh	9/25/1880	444	StPM&M 75	StPM&M 75	c.1892	(7/2/1897) Reno. GN 291 3/24/1899.	
76(1)	Pittsburgh	9/30/1880	445	StPM&M 76	StPM&M 76	c.1892	(10/8/1897) Reno. GN 292 3/21/1899.	
77(1)	Pittsburgh	9/30/1880	446	StPM&M 77	StPM&M 77	c.1892	(10/7/1895) Reno. GN 293 3/20/1899.	

Class A-8 (Old Class 7A) 0-6-0: 19x26-49-200(160)-137,000-137,000-26,050

No.	Builder	Date Built	C/N	Disposition
70(2)	Rogers	5/1900	5555	Ret. 6/1928. Dismantled at Superior 9/22/1928.
71(2)	Rogers	6/1900	5560	Ret. 5/1939, scrapped.
72(2)	Rogers	6/1900	5563	Scrapped 12/1938.

Class A-9 0-6-0: 19x26-49-200(175)-135,000-135,000-28,490 originally. Those locomotives indicated by an asterisk (*) were rebuilt with 52" drivers (decreasing T.E. to 26,850 lb.), dates unknown. Total weights of those locomotives with 49" and 52" drivers were later increased to 142,800 lb. and 147,000 lb., respectively.

No.	Builder	Date Rcvd.	C/N	Disposition	Notes
73(2)*	Rogers	8/27/1903	6014	Scrapped 1931.	63
74(2)	Rogers	8/27/1903	6015	Reno. GN 26(4) 2/28/1944.	63
75(2)*	Rogers	8/30/1903	6016	Ret. 5/1939.	63
76(2)*	Rogers	8/30/1903	6017	Sold J.L.Shiely Co. 3/1930.	63
77(2)*	Rogers	8/31/1903	6018	Reno. GN 27(3) 3/1/1944.	63
78(2)	Rogers	8/31/1903	6019	Reno. GN 28(3) 3/1/1944.	63
79(2)	Rogers	9/3/1903	6020	Ret. 1/1934. Sold for scrap DI&M 3/18/1934.	63
80(2)	Rogers	9/3/1903	6021	Reno. GN 29(3) 3/27/1944.	63
81(2)	Rogers	9/9/1903	6022	Sold Addison Miller, Inc., and Fielding & Shepley, Inc., 5/31/1935.	63
82(2)	Rogers	9/9/1903	6023	Ret. 4/1937, sold for scrap.	63
83(2)	Alco-Rogers	9/4/1905	38017	Sold for scrap DI&M 8/26/1941.	
84(2)*	Alco-Rogers	9/4/1905	38018	Sold for scrap PC 9/1/1941.	
85(3)*	Alco-Rogers	9/7/1905	38019	Sold for scrap DI&M 8/26/1941.	
86(3)	Alco-Rogers	9/7/1905	38020	Sold for scrap DI&M 4/25/1952.	
87(3)*	Alco-Rogers	9/7/1905	38021	Ret. 7/1930. Stripped at Dale Street 6/28/1932.	
88(3)	Alco-Rogers	9/7/1905	38022	Ret. 4/1937, sold for scrap.	
89(3)	Baldwin	9/8/1907	31413	Sold for scrap DI&M 10/16/1951.	
90(2)	Baldwin	9/8/1907	31414	Sold for scrap PC 9/1/1941.	
91(2)*	Baldwin	9/5/1907	31440	Sold for scrap DI&M 3/11/1949.	
92(2)	Baldwin	9/5/1907	31451	Sold for scrap PC 9/1949.	
93(2)*	Baldwin	9/11/1907	31512	Ret. 12/1938.	
94(2)	Baldwin	9/11/1907	31513	Ret. 8/19/1931. Sold for scrap DI&M 1932.	

Old Class 15 4-4-0: 17x24-63-140-74,800-49,200-13,100

No.	Builder	Date Rcvd.	C/N	Original No.	Renumbered From	Date	Disposition
78(1)	Pittsburgh	3/25/1881	479	StPM&M 78	StPM&M 78	c.1892	Reno. GN 188(2) 5/2/1899.
79(1)	Pittsburgh	3/30/1881	480	StPM&M 79	StPM&M 79	c.1892	Reno. GN 189(2) 4/25/1899.
80(1)	Pittsburgh	4/1/1881	481	StPM&M 80	StPM&M 80	c.1892	Reno. GN 190(2) 4/19/1899.
81(1)	Pittsburgh	4/9/1881	482	StPM&M 81	StPM&M 81	c.1892	Reno. GN 191(2) 4/13/1899.
82(1)	Pittsburgh	5/16/1881	483	StPM&M 82	StPM&M 82	c.1892	Reno. GN 192(2) 5/4/1899.
83(1)	Pittsburgh	5/19/1881	484	StPM&M 83	StPM&M 83	c.1892	Reno. GN 193(2) 3/25/1899.
84(1)	Pittsburgh	5/23/1881	485	StPM&M 84	StPM&M 84	c.1892	Reno. GN 194(2) 3/25/1899.
85(1)	Pittsburgh	5/27/1881	486	StPM&M 85	StPM&M 85	c.1892	Reno. GN 195(2) 4/7/1899.
86(1)	Pittsburgh	5/29/1881	487	StPM&M 86	StPM&M 86	c.1892	Reno. GN 196(2) 4/20/1899.

Class A-10 [Old Class 8(3)] 0-6-0: 19x28-49-200(160)-137,000-137,000-28,060

No.	Builder	Date Built	C/N	Original No.	Renumbered From	Date	Disposition
85(2)	Brooks	10/1898	3055	MC 9(2)	MC 9(2)	c.1900	Reno. GN 95(2) 1905.
86(2)	Brooks	10/1898	3056	MC 27	MC 27	c.1900	Reno. GN 96(2) 1905.
87(2)	Brooks	10/1898	3057	MC 28	MC 28	c.1900	Reno. GN 97(2) 1905.

Old Class 4 0-4-0: 15x24-49-140-53,900-53,900-13,110

No.	Builder	Date Rcvd.	C/N	Original No.	Renumbered From	Date	Disposition	Notes
87(1)	Brooks	3/29/1881	519	StPM&M 87	StPM&M 87	c.1892	Reno. GN 14(2) 4/15/1899.	
88(1)	Brooks	4/9/1881	521	StPM&M 88	StPM&M 88	c.1892	Reno. GN 15(2) 4/17/1899.	19
89(1)	Brooks	4/7/1881	523	StPM&M 89	StPM&M 89	c.1892	Reno. GN 16(2) 4/19/1899.	

Class A-10 (Old Class 8A) 0-6-0: 19x28-49-200(160)-137,000-137,000-28,060

No.	Builder	Date Built	C/N	Original No.	Renumbered From	Date	Disposition	Notes
88(2)	Brooks	7/1900	3573	EM 88	EM 88	5/1/1902	Reno. GN 98 1905.	221
89(2)	Brooks	7/1900	3574	EM 89	EM 89	5/1/1902	Reno. GN 99(2) 1905.	221

Old Class 22 0-4-0: 15x24-49-135-62,000-62,000-12,650

No.	Builder	Date Rcvd.	C/N	Original No.	Renumbered From	Date	Disposition	Notes
90(1)	Rogers	4/12/1882	2968	StPM&M 90	StPM&M 90	c.1892	Reno. GN 17(2) 4/14/1899.	21
91(1)	Rogers	4/12/1882	2969	StPM&M 91	StPM&M 91	c.1892	Reno. GN 18(2) 4/13/1899.	
92(1)	Rogers	4/13/1882	2970	StPM&M 92	StPM&M 92	c.1892	Reno. GN 19(2) 4/13/1899.	
93(1)	Rogers	4/15/1882	2971	StPM&M 93	StPM&M 93	c.1892	Reno. GN 20(2) 5/2/1899.	

Old Class 31(2) 0-6-0: 18x24-49-150(140)-86,450-86,450-18,880

No.	Builder	Date Rcvd.	C/N	Original No.	Renumbered From	Date	Disposition
94(1)	Rogers	4/26/1887	3736	StPM&M 94(2)	StPM&M 94(2)	c.1892	Reno. GN 32(2) 4/22/1899.
95(1)	Rogers	4/29/1887	3737	StPM&M 95(2)	StPM&M 95(2)	c.1892	Reno. GN 33(2) 4/10/1899.
96(1)	Rogers	4/29/1887	3738	StPM&M 96(2)	StPM&M 96(2)	c.1892	Reno. GN 34(2) 4/17/1899.
97(1)	Rogers	5/1/1887	3739	StPM&M 97(2)	StPM&M 97(2)	c.1892	Reno. GN 35(2) 4/13/1899.
–	–	–	–	–	–	–	–
99(1)	Rogers	5/12/1887	3741	StPM&M 99	StPM&M 99	c.1892	Sold EM 6/1893 and reno. EM 4 5/21/1894. Reno. EM 37(2) 1899.

Class A-10 0-6-0: 19x28-49-200(160)-137,000-137,000-28,060 originally. Weights later increased to 145,000 lb.

No.	Builder	Date Built	C/N	Original No.	Renumbered From	Date	Disposition	Notes
95(2)	Brooks	10/1898	3055	MC 9(2)	GN 85(2)	1905	Ret. 1939, scrapped.	
96(2)	Brooks	10/1898	3056	MC 27	GN 86(2)	1905	Scrapped 1937.	64
97(2)	Brooks	10/1898	3057	MC 28	GN 87(2)	1905	Scrapped 1937.	64
98	Brooks	7/1900	3573	EM 88	GN 88(2)	1905	Scrapped 1937.	64, 221
99(2)	Brooks	7/1900	3574	EM 89	GN 89(2)	1905	Scrapped 1937.	64, 221

Class B-13 (Old Class 24) 4-4-0: 17x24-63-140-76,650-49,150-13,100

No.	Builder	Date Rcvd.	C/N	Original No.	Renumbered From	Date	Disposition	Notes
100	Baldwin	5/11/1882	6170	StPM&M 100	StPM&M 100	c.1892	Scrapped at Dale Street 1916.	
101	Baldwin	5/11/1882	6171	StPM&M 101	StPM&M 101	c.1892	Reno. VW&Y (No. 2) at Delta 12/15/1903. Returned to GN (as No. 101) 11/9/1908. Scrapped 1916.	
102	Baldwin	5/14/1882	6175	StPM&M 102	StPM&M 102	c.1892	Scrapped at Dale Street 1916.	
103	Baldwin	5/14/1882	6177	StPM&M 103	StPM&M 103	c.1892	Received new boiler (Baldwin No. 7960) 1/1910. Reno. 219(2) at Hillyard 3/4/1944.	65
104	Baldwin	5/19/1882	6179	StPM&M 104	StPM&M 104	c.1892	Scrapped at Dale Street 1916.	
105	Baldwin	5/15/1882	6176	StPM&M 105	StPM&M 105	c.1892	Sold B&O 5/1900.	
106	Baldwin	5/15/1882	6178	StPM&M 106	StPM&M 106	c.1892	Scrapped at Dale Street 1916.	
107	Baldwin	5/19/1882	6180	StPM&M 107	StPM&M 107	c.1892	Scrapped at Dale Street 1916.	
108	Baldwin	5/19/1882	6182	StPM&M 108	StPM&M 108	c.1892	Sold B&O 5/1900.	
109	Baldwin	5/18/1882	6181	StPM&M 109	StPM&M 109	c.1892	Scrapped at Dale Street 1916.	
110	Baldwin	5/18/1882	6183	StPM&M 110	StPM&M 110	c.1892	Scrapped at Dale Street 1916.	
111	Baldwin	5/19/1882	6184	StPM&M 111	StPM&M 111	c.1892	Scrapped at Dale Street 1916.	
112	Baldwin	5/19/1882	6185	StPM&M 112	StPM&M 112	c.1892	Scrapped 11/12/1900.	
113	Baldwin	5/19/1882	6186	StPM&M 113	StPM&M 113	c.1892	Scrapped at Dale Street 1916.	
114	Baldwin	5/20/1882	6187	StPM&M 114	StPM&M 114	c.1892	Sold B&O 5/1900.	

Class B-14 (Old Class 24) 4-4-0: 17x24-63-140-72,700-45,450-13,100. Those locomotives still on the roster moved to Class 24A c.6/1900(?).

No.	Builder	Date Rcvd.	C/N	Original No.	Renumbered From	Date	Disposition	Notes
115	Baldwin	5/20/1882	6188	StPM&M 115	StPM&M 115	c.1892	Sold B&O 5/1900.	66
116	Baldwin	5/21/1882	6189	StPM&M 116	StPM&M 116	c.1892	Sold B&O 5/1900.	66
117(2)	Baldwin	3/18/1880	4996	StPM&M 52	GN 52(1)	4/11/1899	Sold F. Weyerhauser (Hawthorne, Negamon & West Superior Ry.) 7/20/1900.	
118	Baldwin	5/21/1882	6191	StPM&M 118	StPM&M 118	c.1892	Scrapped at Dale Street 1916.	
119(2)	Baldwin	5/7/1880	5079	StPM&M 62	GN 62(1)	4/18/1899	Scrapped at Dale Street 1916.	
120	Baldwin	5/21/1882	6193	StPM&M 120	StPM&M 120	c.1892	Scrapped at Dale Street 1916.	
121	Baldwin	5/22/1882	6194	StPM&M 121	StPM&M 121	c.1892	Sold B&O 5/1900.	
122	Baldwin	5/25/1882	6195	StPM&M 122	StPM&M 122	c.1892	Received new boiler 1908. Ret. at Minot 2/10/1930. Delivered to DI&M 8/4/1932.	
123	Baldwin	5/25/1882	6196	StPM&M 123	StPM&M 123	c.1892	Scrapped at Dale Street 1916.	
124	Baldwin	5/25/1882	6197	StPM&M 124	StPM&M 124	c.1892	Scrapped at Dale Street 1916.	

Old Class 24 4-4-0: 17x24-58-140-72,700-45,450-14,230 when acquired from StPM&M. These two engines then had wheel centers changed to 48" (55" drivers) on an unknown date and 8/23/1897, respectively. This gave them dimensions of 17x24-55-140-70,050-44,650-15,010. These locomotives were moved to Old Class 18 on an unknown date between 1892 and 1900.

No.	Builder	Date Rcvd.	C/N	Original No.	Renumbered From	Date	Disposition	Notes
117(1)	Baldwin	5/21/1882	6190	StPM&M 117	StPM&M 117	c.1892	Reno. GN 269 4/5/1899.	66
–	–	–	–	–	–	–	–	
119(1)	Baldwin	5/22/1882	6192	StPM&M 119	StPM&M 119	c.1892	Reno. GN 279 4/18/1899.	

Class B-15 (Old Class 25) 4-4-0: 17x24-63-140-75,150-49,450-13,100. Locomotives indicated below with an asterisk (*) had 64" drivers and 12,900 lb. tractive effort.

No.	Builder	Date Rcvd.	C/N	Original No.	Renumbered From	Date	Disposition	Notes
125	Schenectady	2/15/1882	1595	StPM&M 125	StPM&M 125	c.1892	Received new GN-built boiler (No. 125) 9/1907. Sold for scrap DI&M 10/1929.	
126	Schenectady	2/15/1882	1596	StPM&M 126	StPM&M 126	c.1892	Received new GN-built boiler (No. 126) 9/1907. Sold for scrap DI&M 10/9/1929.	
127*	Schenectady	3/21/1882	1573	StPM&M 127	StPM&M 127	c.1892	Scrapped at Dale Street 4/26/1916.	
128	Schenectady	4/6/1882	1574	StPM&M 128	StPM&M 128	c.1892	Scrapped at Dale Street 1916.	
129*	Schenectady	1/20/1882	1492	StPM&M 129	StPM&M 129	c.1892	Scrapped at Dale Street 1916.	
130*	Schenectady	1/20/1882	1493	StPM&M 130	StPM&M 130	c.1892	Received new GN-built boiler (No. 130) 12/1910. Ret. 1937.	67
131*	Schenectady	4/21/1882	1575	StPM&M 131	StPM&M 131	c.1892	Received new GN-built boiler (No. 131) 12/1910. Ret. 1937.	67
132	Schenectady	4/21/1882	1576	StPM&M 132	StPM&M 132	c.1892	Received new GN-built boiler (No. 132) 6/1911. Ret. 1937.	67
133	Schenectady	4/21/1882	1577	StPM&M 133	StPM&M 133	c.1892	Received new GN-built boiler (No. 133) 1907. Scrapped at Dale Street 1916.	

Class B-16 (Old Class 26) 4-4-0: 17x24-64-140-86,500-55,650-12,330. Locomotives indicated by an asterisk (*) below later had dimensions changed to 17x24-63-130-86,500-55,650-12,170.

No.	Builder	Date Rcvd.	C/N	Original No.	Renumbered From	Date	Disposition	Notes
134	Rhode Island	5/8/1882	1195	StPM&M 134	StPM&M 134	c.1892	Sold Butte, Anaconda & Pacific 1894. Reno. BA&P 51 1/31/1894.	
135*	Rhode Island	5/8/1882	1196	StPM&M 135	StPM&M 135	c.1892	Dismantled at Hillyard 7/11/1925.	
136*	Rhode Island	5/13/1882	1197	StPM&M 136	StPM&M 136	c.1892	Scrapped at Dale Street 10/26/1918.	68
137*	Rhode Island	5/13/1882	1198	StPM&M 137	StPM&M 137	c.1892	Scrapped at Hillyard 8/31/1920.	
138*	Rhode Island	5/17/1882	1199	StPM&M 138	StPM&M 138	c.1892	Scrapped at Great Falls 8/12/1920.	
139(1)	Rhode Island	5/17/1882	1200	StPM&M 139	StPM&M 139	c.1892	Sold Butte, Anaconda & Pacific 1893 Reno. BA&P 50 11/27/1893.	

Class B-7 [Old Class 12(2)] 4-4-0: 17x24-63-140-78,000-49,000-13,100

No.	Builder	Date Built	C/N	Original No.	Renumbered From	Date	Disposition	Notes
139(2)	New York	7/1890	627	S&N 2	S&M RR 139	7/1/1907	Received new Baldwin boiler 11/1908. Boiler exploded at Mulkiteo, WA, and retired at Delta 1/1930. Sold for scrap DI&M 10/1933.	31

Class B-11 (2) 4-4-0: 17x24-63-145(140)-85,000-52,000-13,100

No.	Builder	Date Built	C/N	Original No.	Renumbered From	Date	Disposition	Notes
141	Baldwin	4/1890	10830	SF&N 6	SF&N 6	7/6/1908	Transferred to V&S (No. 4) in 1908 for a short time, then returned to GN (No. 141). Sold for scrap NSRM 3/1926.	69
142	Baldwin	4/1890	10833	SF&N 5	SF&N 5	7/6/1908	Sold for scrap NSRM 5/1926.	38

Class B-12 (Old Class 23) 4-4-0: 17x24-63-140-77,500-49,275-13,100

No.	Builder	Date Rcvd.	C/N	Original No.	Renumbered From	Date	Disposition	Notes
143	Rogers	3/16/1882	2928	StP&D 16(2)	StPM&M 143(2)	c.1892	Rebuilt to GN X368 (Weed Burner) at Minot 8/21/1912.	
144	Rogers	3/18/1882	2929	StP&D 17(2)	StPM&M 144(2)	c.1892	Scrapped at Dale Street 1916.	

Class B-17 (Old Class 28) 4-4-0: 17x24-63-140-70,000-43,650-13,100

No.	Builder	Date Rcvd.	C/N	Original No.	Renumbered From	Date	Disposition	Notes
145	Grant	7/1/1882	1522	StPM&M 145	StPM&M 145	c.1892	Scrapped at Dale Street 12/2/1918.	
146	Grant	7/2/1882	1523	StPM&M 146	StPM&M 146	c.1892	Sold Wisconsin Central Railway (probably for a connecting logging company) 1/7/1900.	
147	Grant	7/6/1882	1524	StPM&M 147	StPM&M 147	c.1892	Sold DS&W 1897. Reno. DS&W 105 9/15/1897. Reno. DS&W 106 7/8/1898. Sold to EM (with DS&W) 6/22/1898. Reno. EM 147 4/3/1899. Leased to GN 5/1/1902. Received new boiler 9/1907. Ret. 11/1930. Sold for scrap DI&M 7/5/1932.	70
148	Grant	7/7/1882	1525	StPM&M 148	StPM&M 148	c.1892	Sold B&O 5/1900.	
149	Grant	7/9/1882	1526	StPM&M 149	StPM&M 149	c.1892	Scrapped at Dale Street 1916.	

Class B-18 (Old Class 29) 4-4-0: 17x24-62-140-71,400-46,500-13,100

No.	Builder	Date Rcvd.	C/N	Original No.	Renumbered From	Date	Disposition	Notes
150	Brooks	7/6/1882	716	StPM&M 150	StPM&M 150	c.1892	Scrapped at Dale Street 1916.	76
151	Brooks	7/6/1882	715	StPM&M 151	StPM&M 151	c.1892	Scrapped at Dale Street 1916.	

Class B-19 (Old Class 30) 4-4-0: 17x24-63-140(130)-83,200-52,500-12,170 originally. Working pressure later increased to 140 psi, increasing T.E. to 13,100 lb.

No.	Builder	Date Rcvd.	C/N	Original No.	Renumbered From	Date	Disposition	Notes
152	Brooks	7/27/1882	745	StPM&M 152	StPM&M 152	c.1892	Converted to weedburner at Willmar 6/11/1920. Sold for scrap DI&M 2/1926.	
153	Brooks	7/27/1882	746	StPM&M 153	StPM&M 153	c.1892	Scrapped at Dale Street 12/11/1918.	
154	Brooks	7/3/1882	747	StPM&M 154	StPM&M 154	c.1892	Scrapped at Dale Street 9/18/1920.	
155	Brooks	7/31/1882	748	StPM&M 155	StPM&M 155	c.1892	Scrapped at Dale Street 12/17/1918.	
156	Brooks	8/2/1882	749	StPM&M 156	StPM&M 156	c.1892	Received new GN-built boiler (No. 156) 11/1910. Ret. 1939. Sold for scrap DI&M 9/24/1940.	
157	Brooks	8/3/1882	750	StPM&M 157	StPM&M 157	c.1892	Sold for scrap DI&M 12/1926.	
158	Brooks	8/7/1882	751	StPM&M 158	StPM&M 158	c.1892	Scrapped at Dale Street 11/1/1918.	
159	Brooks	8/7/1882	752	StPM&M 159	StPM&M 159	c.1892	Received new Baldwin-built boiler 9/1908. Scrapped 12/1938.	222
160	Brooks	8/10/1882	753	StPM&M 160	StPM&M 160	c.1892	Sold for scrap DI&M 11/1927.	
161	Brooks	8/12/1882	754	StPM&M 161	StPM&M 161	c.1892	Scrapped at Hillyard 7/11/1925.	
162	Brooks	10/19/1882	791	StPM&M 162	StPM&M 162	c.1892	Sold for scrap DI&M 10/1927.	
163	Brooks	10/21/1882	792	StPM&M 163	StPM&M 163	c.1892	Received new Baldwin-built boiler 8/1908. Ret. 5/5/1931. Sold for scrap DI&M 8/20/1932.	222
164	Brooks	10/19/1882	793	StPM&M 164	StPM&M 164	c.1892	Received new GN-built boiler, date unknown. Sold for scrap DI&M 10/1927.	
165	Brooks	10/24/1882	794	StPM&M 165	StPM&M 165	c.1892	Scrapped at Dale Street 11/23/1918.	
166	Brooks	10/24/1882	795	StPM&M 166	StPM&M 166	c.1892	Scrapped at Dale Street 9/17/1920.	
167	Brooks	12/23/1882	829	StPM&M 167	StPM&M 167	c.1892	Scrapped at Dale Street 8/31/1920.	
168	Brooks	12/27/1882	830	StPM&M 168	StPM&M 168	c.1892	Received new GN-built boiler 11/1911. Sold for scrap DI&M 3/1926 (delivered 8/19/1927).	
169	Brooks	12/27/1882	831	StPM&M 169	StPM&M 169	c.1892	Sold for scrap DI&M 10/1927.	
170	Brooks	12/27/1882	832	StPM&M 170	StPM&M 170	c.1892	Scrapped at Dale Street 12/26/1918.	
171	Brooks	12/27/1882	833	StPM&M 171	StPM&M 171	c.1892	Received new GN-built boiler 1923. Scrapped 12/1938.	
172	Brooks	3/19/1883	872	StPM&M 172	StPM&M 172	c.1892	Scrapped at Dale Street 11/6/1918.	71
173	Brooks	3/19/1883	873	StPM&M 173	StPM&M 173	c.1892	Sold for scrap Pacific Coast Steel Co. 12/1926.	72
174	Brooks	3/19/1883	874	StPM&M 174	StPM&M 174	c.1892	Scrapped at Dale Street 8/31/1920.	
175	Brooks	3/19/1883	875	StPM&M 175	StPM&M 175	c.1892	Ret. 6/1926. Sold for scrap DI&M 7/1927.	73
176	Brooks	3/23/1883	876	StPM&M 176	StPM&M 176	c.1892	Scrapped at Dale Street 12/2/1918.	
177	Brooks	3/23/1883	877	StPM&M 177	StPM&M 177	c.1892	Scrapped at Dale Street 11/18/1918.	71
178	Brooks	3/23/1883	878	StPM&M 178	StPM&M 178	c.1892	Sold for scrap DI&M 12/1926.	74
179	Brooks	3/23/1883	879	StPM&M 179	StPM&M 179	c.1892	Scrapped at Dale Street 11/23/1918.	
180	Brooks	3/31/1883	880	StPM&M 180	StPM&M 180	c.1892	Scrapped at Havre 2/19/1925 to 3/27/1925.	
181	Brooks	3/31/1883	881	StPM&M 181	StPM&M 181	c.1892	Scrapped at Dale Street 11/30/1918.	
182	Brooks	3/31/1883	882	StPM&M 182	StPM&M 182	c.1892	Scrapped at Dale Street 11/18/1918.	71
183	Brooks	3/31/1883	885	StPM&M 183	StPM&M 183	c.1892	Received new GN-built boiler 11/1914. Ret. 1939.	
184	Brooks	4/7/1883	886	StPM&M 184	StPM&M 184	c.1892	Received new GN-built boiler, date unknown. Scrapped at Dale Street 9/4/1920.	24
185	Brooks	4/7/1883	887	StPM&M 185	StPM&M 185	c.1892	Received new GN-built boiler 1911. Scrapped 1937.	24, 75
186	Brooks	4/7/1883	888	StPM&M 186	StPM&M 186	c.1892	Received new GN-built boiler 1908 Reno. GN 220(2) at Willmar 3/21/1944.	24

Old Class 4 0-4-0: 15x24-49-140-53,900-53,900-13,110

No.	Builder	Date Rcvd.	C/N	Original No.	Renumbered From	Date	Disposition
187(1)	Brooks	8/16/1882	757	StPM&M 187	StPM&M 187	c.1892	Reno. GN 21(2) 4/14/1899.
188(1)	Brooks	8/17/1882	758	StPM&M 188	StPM&M 188	c.1892	Reno. GN 22(2) 4/29/1899.
189(1)	Brooks	8/22/1882	759	StPM&M 189	StPM&M 189	c.1892	Wrecked at Barnesville, MN, 12/2/1897. Scrapped 11/1898.
190(1)	Brooks	8/22/1882	760	StPM&M 190	StPM&M 190	c.1892	Reno. GN 23(2) 4/10/1899.
191(1)	Brooks	8/25/1882	761	StPM&M 191	StPM&M 191	c.1892	Reno. GN 24(2) 4/13/1899.
192(1)	Brooks	8/25/1882	762	StPM&M 192	StPM&M 192	c.1892	Reno. GN 25(2) 4/17/1899.
193(1)	Brooks	8/28/1882	763	StPM&M 193	StPM&M 193	c.1892	Reno. GN 26(2) 3/21/1899.

Class B-9 (Old Class 15) 4-4-0: 17x24-63-140-74,800-49,200-13,100

No.	Builder	Date Rcvd.	C/N	Original No.	Renumbered From	Date	Disposition
187(2)	Pittsburgh	3/23/1881	478	StPM&M 67(2)	GN 67(1)	4/22/1899	Turned over to Kootenai Valley Railroad 8/30/1899 and relettered for KVRR. Relettered GN 187 at East Spokane, WA, 6/4/1901. Received new GN-built boiler 6/16/1905. Sold for scrap DI&M 9/15/1941.
188(2)	Pittsburgh	3/25/1881	479	StPM&M 78	GN 78(1)	5/22/1899	Received new GN-built boiler 6/30/1905. Sold for scrap DI&M 10/1929.
189(2)	Pittsburgh	3/30/1881	480	StPM&M 79	GN 79(1)	4/25/1899	Received new GN-built boiler 7/19/1905. Received second new GN-built boiler 1/1910. Sold for scrap PC 12/1941.
190(2)	Pittsburgh	4/1/1881	481	StPM&M 80	GN 80(1)	4/19/1899	Sold B&O 5/1900.
191(2)	Pittsburgh	4/9/1881	482	StPM&M 81	GN 81(1)	4/13/1899	Received new GN-built boiler 8/9/1905. Wrecked 5/24/1907 and received second new GN-built boiler 5/1907. Ret. 1/1938, scrapped.
192(2)	Pittsburgh	5/16/1881	483	StPM&M 82	GN 82(1)	5/4/1899	Received new GN-built boiler 8/22/1905. Sold for scrap Bethlehem Steel 9/1939.
193(2)	Pittsburgh	5/19/1881	484	StPM&M 83	GN 83(1)	3/25/1899	Received new Alco-built boiler 11/17/1905. Ret. 12/1938, scrapped.
194(2)	Pittsburgh	5/23/1881	485	StPM&M 84	GN 84(1)	3/25/1899	Received new Alco-built boiler 11/17/1905. Sold for scrap PC 9/8/1941.
195	Pittsburgh	5/27/1881	486	StPM&M 85	GN 85(1)	4/7/1899	Received new GN-built boiler 11/17/1905. Ret. 8/1925. Sold Hyman-Michaels Co. 9/2/1925.
196(2)	Pittsburgh	5/29/1881	487	StPM&M 86	GN 86(1)	4/20/1899	Sold B&O 5/1900.

Old Class 32 0-6-0: 17x24-49-140-67,050-67,050-16,840

No.	Builder	Date Rcvd.	C/N	Original No.	Renumbered From	Date	Disposition
194(1)	Brooks	8/30/1882	764	StPM&M 194	StPM&M 194	c.1892	Reno. GN 27(2) 4/1/1899.
–	–	–	–	–	–	–	–
196(1)	Brooks	9/4/1882	766	StPM&M 196	StPM&M 196	c.1892	Reno. GN 29(2) 4/10/1899.

Class B-20 (Old Class 33) 4-4-0: 18x24-63-145(140)-90,900-59,000-14,690

No.	Builder	Date Rcvd.	C/N	Original No.	Renumbered From	Date	Disposition	Notes
197	Rhode Island	1/31/1883	1294	StPM&M 197	StPM&M 197	c.1892	Received new boiler (GN 197A) 1917. Ret. 1/1938, scrapped.	
198	Rhode Island	1/30/1883	1295	StPM&M 198	StPM&M 198	c.1892	Sold for scrap DI&M 10/1927.	25
199	Rhode Island	2/5/1883	1296	StPM&M 199	S&M RR 199	7/1/1907	Received new boiler (GN 199A) 1917. Sold for scrap DI&M 12/1941.	26
200	Rhode Island	12/28/1882	1297	StPM&M 200	StPM&M 200	c.1892	Ret. 9/1923, dismantled at Havre 12/21/1923.	27
201	Rhode Island	2/5/1883	1298	StPM&M 201	StPM&M 201	c.1892	Sold for scrap DI&M 9/1927.	27
202	Rhode Island	2/5/1883	1299	StPM&M 202	S&M RR 202	7/1/1907	Dismantled Hillyard 9/19/1925.	27
203	Rhode Island	12/28/1882	1300	StPM&M 203	StPM&M 203	c.1892	Dismantled Hillyard 9/19/1925.	28
204	Rhode Island	1/2/1883	1301	StPM&M 204	StPM&M 204	c.1892	Received new boiler (GN 204A) 1917. Ret. 1/1938, scrapped.	
205	Rhode Island	1/2/1883	1302	StPM&M 205	StPM&M 205	c.1892	Sold for scrap Pacific Coast Steel Co. 1/1927.	77
206	Rhode Island	1/2/1883	1303	StPM&M 206	StPM&M 206	c.1892	Received new boiler 1916. Ret. 8/1931, sold for scrap DI&M 6/18/1932.	

Class B-21 (Old Class 34) 4-4-0: 18x24-63-140-94,100-60,300-14,690

No.	Builder	Date Rcvd.	C/N	Original No.	Renumbered From	Date	Disposition	Notes
207	Rogers	5/28/1887	3749	StPM&M 207	StPM&M 207	c.1892	Ret. 1939. Sold for scrap DI&M 9/24/1940.	
208	Rogers	5/25/1887	3750	StPM&M 208	MC 1	c.1900	Sold for scrap PC 1/21/1947.	
209	Rogers	5/25/1887	3751	StPM&M 209	MC 2	c.1900	Ret. 5/1939, scrapped.	
210	Rogers	5/30/1887	3752	StPM&M 210	MC 3	c.1900	Ret. 1/1934. Sold for scrap PC 6/11/1934.	
211	Rogers	5/30/1887	3753	StPM&M 211	MC 12	c.1900	Dismantled Hillyard 11/14/1928. Sold Abe Goldberg Co.	
212	Rogers	6/3/1887	3754	StPM&M 212	MC 13	c.1900	Usable parts removed at Delta 11/23/1928. Sold Abe Goldberg Co.	
213	Rogers	6/3/1887	3755	StPM&M 213	StPM&M 213	c.1892	Sold for scrap PC 11/1928.	78
214	Rogers	6/5/1887	3756	StPM&M 214	StPM&M 214	c.1892	Sold for scrap PC 2/22/1949.	
215	Rogers	6/8/1887	3757	StPM&M 215	StPM&M 215	c.1892	Retired 11/1928, sold for scrap DI&M 12/12/1928.	
216	Rogers	6/8/1887	3758	StPM&M 216	StPM&M 216	c.1892	Sold for scrap DI&M 1/25/1947.	
217	Rogers	6/19/1887	3759	StPM&M 217	StPM&M 217	c.1892	Retired 1927, sold for scrap DI&M 3/23/1928.	79
218	Rogers	6/21/1887	3760	StPM&M 218	StPM&M 218	c.1892	Sold for scrap PC 1/21/1947.	
219(1)	Rogers	6/28/1887	3764	StPM&M 219	StPM&M 219	c.1892	Sold Seattle & Montana Ry. (No. 219) 9/28/1894. Returned to GN [as No. 219(1)] 5/10/1895. Scrapped 12/1938.	
220(1)	Rogers	6/28/1887	3765	StPM&M 220	StPM&M 220	c.1892	Scrapped 12/1938.	
221	Rogers	7/3/1887	3769	StPM&M 221	StPM&M 221	c.1892	Scrapped 12/1938.	
222	Rogers	7/7/1887	3770	StPM&M 222	StPM&M 222	c.1892	Sold for scrap DI&M 10/9/1929.	80
223	Rogers	7/7/1887	3772	StPM&M 223	StPM&M 223	c.1892	Sold for scrap DI&M 5/1926.	
224	Rogers	7/7/1887	3773	StPM&M 224	StPM&M 224	c.1892	Sold for scrap DI&M 10/9/1929.	80
225	Rogers	7/12/1887	3774	StPM&M 225	StPM&M 225	c.1892	Retired 6/1928, sold for scrap DI&M 8/28/1928.	81

Class B-13 4-4-0: 17x24-63-140-76,650-49,150-13,100

No.	Builder	Date Rcvd.	C/N	Original No.	Renumbered From	Date	Disposition
219(2)	Baldwin	5/14/1882	6177	StPM&M 103	GN 103	3/4/1944	Ret. 7/1947, sold for scrap PC 7/6/1947.

Class B-19 4-4-0: 17x24-63-140-83,200-52,500-13,100

No.	Builder	Date Rcvd.	C/N	Original No.	Renumbered From	Date	Disposition
220(2)	Brooks	4/7/1883	888	StPM&M 186	GN 186	3/21/1944	Sold for scrap PC 1/25/1947.

Class B-22 (Old Class 34A) 4-4-0: 18x24-63-150(140)-94,100-60,300-14,690

No.	Builder	Date Rcvd.	C/N	Original No.	Renumbered From	Date	Disposition	Notes
226	Rogers	11/29/1888	4063	EM 101	EM 226	5/1/1902	Sold for scrap DI&M 10/9/1929.	
227	Rogers	4/7/1889	4120	EM 102	EM 227	5/1/1902	Sold for scrap DI&M 11/25/1925.	82
228(2)	Rogers	4/29/1889	4121	EM 103	EM 228	5/1/1902	Ret. 1/1938, scrapped.	83
229(2)	Rogers	4/2/1889	4122	EM 104	EM 229	5/1/1902	Sold for scrap DI&M 10/1929.	
230(2)	Rogers	4/4/1889	4123	EM 105	EM 230	5/1/1902	Sold for scrap DI&M 2/1926.	

Class 31(2) 0-6-0: 18x24-49-150(140)-86,450-86,450-18,880

No.	Builder	Date Rcvd.	C/N	Original No.	Renumbered From	Date	Disposition
228(1)	Rogers	10/9/1888	4028	StPM&M 228	StPM&M 228	c.1892	Reno. GN 43(2) 4/6/1899.
229(1)	Rogers	10/9/1888	4029	StPM&M 229	StPM&M 229	c.1892	Reno. GN 44(2) 4/17/1899.
230(1)	Rogers	10/10/1888	4030	StPM&M 230	StPM&M 230	c.1892	Reno. GN 45(2) 4/28/1899.
231(1)	Rogers	10/11/1888	4031	StPM&M 231	StPM&M 231	c.1892	Reno. GN 46(2) 4/23/1899.

Class B-23 4-4-0: 18x24-63-160(140)-94,100-56,100-14,690

No.	Builder	Date Built	C/N	Original No.	Renumbered From	Date	Disposition	Notes
231(2)	Baldwin	10/1893	13803	N&FS 7	SF&N 7	3/5/1908	Sold for scrap Ike Statman 3/1926.	10, 84

Old Class 2(2) 0-6-0: 17x24-49-140-83,000-83,000-16,840

No.	Builder	Date Rcvd.	C/N	Original No.	Renumbered From	Date	Disposition
232(1)	Hinkley	8/1/1888	1765	StPM&M 232	StPM&M 232	c.1892	Sold Seattle & Montana RR (No. 232) 4/3/1893.
233(1)	Hinkley	8/1/1888	1766	StPM&M 233	StPM&M 233	c.1892	Reno. GN 31(2) 3/29/1899.

Class B-6 [Old Class 11(2)] 4-4-0: 17x24-63-145(140)-89,000-56,000-13,100. Locomotive indicated by an asterisk (*) had dimensions 17x24-63-145-80,000-51,000-12,770. Date indicated below with an asterisk (*) is date built.

No.	Builder	Date Rcvd.	C/N	Original No.	Renumbered From	Date	Disposition
232(2)	Rogers	1/14/1890	4182	SC&N 1	WSF 232	7/1/1907	Ret. 6/1928. Dismantled at Dale Street 8/31/1928.
233(2)	Rogers	1/15/1890	4194	SC&N 2	WSF 233	7/1/1907	Sold for scrap Hyman-Michaels Co. 8/1925.
234	Rogers	1/18/1890	4205	SC&N 3	WSF 234	7/1/1907	Ret. 6/1928. Dismantled at Superior 10/16/1928.
235	Rogers	1/25/1890	4226	SC&N 4	WSF 235	7/1/1907	Ret. 6/1928. Dismantled at Superior 9/22/1928.
236	Rogers	6/1/1890	4303	SC&N 8	WSF 236	7/1/1907	Ret. 6/1928. Dismantled at Dale Street 8/31/1928.
237	Rogers	12/19/1890	4420	SC&N 10	WSF 237	7/1/1907	Ret. 8/1925. Dismantled 1925.
238*	Rhode Island	4/1889*	2202	PSL 13	WSF 238	7/1/1907	Assigned CB&Q as part of SC&W by lease on 11/1/1907. Delivered CB&Q 1/29/1908, and sold CB&Q (No. 373) 12/1/1908. Operated on CB&Q as Class A-2, ret. 7/1918.

Class B-1 [Old Class 5(2)] 4-4-0: 16x24-63-140-66,000-41,850-11,610

No.	Builder	Date Built	C/N	Original No.	Renumbered From	Date	Disposition
240	Danforth	1869	?	StP&P 16	GN 16(1)	3/29/1899	Scrapped at Dale Street 1916.

Class B-3 (Old Class 13) 4-4-0: 16x24-63-140-66,100-43,700-11,600

No.	Builder	Date Built	C/N	Original No.	Renumbered From	Date	Disposition
241	Pittsburgh	8/1870	76	StP&P 18	GN 18(1)	1899	Received new Baldwin-built boiler 10/1907. Sold for scrap PC 3/1926.
242	Pittsburgh	9/1870	77	StP&P 19	GN 19(1)	4/7/1899	Received new Baldwin-built boiler 11/1906. Dismantled at Devils Lake 7/12/1923.

Class B-2 (Old Class 17) 4-4-0: 15x24-63- ? -68,000-43,000- ?

No.	Builder	Date Rcvd.	C/N	Original No.	Renumbered From	Date	Disposition
243	Baldwin	12/1871	2619	NP 20(1)	GN 20(1)	3/1899	Rebuilt X367 (Weed Burner) 10/28/1910.
244(1)	Baldwin	12/1871	2621	NP 21(1)	GN 21(1)	4/1/1899	Scrapped at St.Paul Shops 11/18/1902.

Class B-2 (Old Class 6) 4-4-0: 16x24-49-130-68,600-47,200-13,040

No.	Builder	Date Built	C/N	Original No.	Renumbered From	Date	Disposition	Notes
244(2)	Pittsburgh	7/1870	75	StP&P 17	GN 11(2)	1907	Sold Northern Dakota Railway 10/10/1908.	219

Class B-4 (Old Class 16) 4-4-0: 16x24-63-140-70,000-44,550-11,600

No.	Builder	Date Rcvd.	C/N	Original No.	Renumbered From	Date	Disposition
245	Baldwin	12/1871	2638	NP 22(1)	GN 22(1)	4/8/1899	Received new Baldwin-built boiler at St.Paul 11/13/1906. Sold Minnesota State Fair Association 8/17/1921 and destroyed in staged head-on collision at the Minnesota State Fair.

Old Class 17 4-4-0: 15x24-63- ? -68,800-43,000- ?

No.	Builder	Date Rcvd.	C/N	Original No.	Renumbered From	Date	Disposition
246	Baldwin	12/1871	2639	NP 23(1)	GN 23(1)	3/30/1899	Scrapped 11/12/1900.

Class B-3 (Old Class 13) 4-4-0: 16x24-63-140-72,700-46,000-11,600

No.	Builder	Date Rcvd.	C/N	Original No.	Renumbered From	Date	Disposition
247	Pittsburgh	12/1875	320	StP&P 24	GN 24(1)	3/31/1899	Retired 1901, changed to weed burner 3/18/1902.
248	Pittsburgh	12/1875	323	StP&P 26	GN 26(1)	3/25/1899	Received new Baldwin-built boiler 1906. Dismantled at Dale Street 7/7/1923.

Class B-4 (Old Class 16) 4-4-0: 16x24-63-140-70,000-44,550-11,600

No.	Builder	Date Rcvd.	C/N	Original No.	Renumbered From	Date	Disposition	
249	Baldwin	11/1879	4848	(StP&P 47)	GN 47(1)	4/10/1899	Received new Baldwin-built boiler at St.Paul 7/10/1906. Sold for scrap DI&M 6/1926.	17
250(2)	Baldwin	11/1879	4849	(StP&P 48)	GN 48(1)	4/11/1899	Received new Baldwin-built boiler at St.Paul 8/30/1906. Sold for scrap DI&M 2/1926.	17
251(2)	Baldwin	11/1879	4852	(StP&P 49)	GN 49(1)	4/11/1899	Sold 5/16/1901(?)	17, 85
252(2)	Baldwin	11/1879	4853	(StP&P 50)	GN 50(1)	3/31/1899	Received new Baldwin-built boiler at St.Paul 11/30/1906. Sold for scrap PC 3/1926.	17

Old Class 7(2) 0-6-0: 19x24-49-180(160)-114,700-114,700-26,050

No.	Builder	Date Rcvd.	C/N	Disposition	Notes
250(1)	Brooks	1/1/1893	2208	Reno. GN 60(2) 4/13/1899.	
251(1)	Brooks	1/1/1893	2209	Reno. GN 61(2) 4/15/1899.	
252(1)	Brooks	1/1/1893	2210	Sold Butte, Anaconda & Pacific. Reno. BA&P 3 8/27/1893.	
253	Brooks	1/7/1893	2211	Sold Butte, Anaconda & Pacific. Reno. BA&P 4 8/7/1893.	86
254	Brooks	1/7/1893	2212	Sold Butte, Anaconda & Pacific. Reno. BA&P 5 9/28/1893.	86
255(1)	Brooks	1/7/1893	2213	Sold Butte, Anaconda & Pacific. Reno. BA&P 1 7/12/1893.	
256(1)	Brooks	1/7/1893	2214	Sold Butte, Anaconda & Pacific. Reno. BA&P 2 7/10/1893.	
257(1)	Brooks	1/10/1893	2215	Reno. GN 62(2) 4/12/1899.	
258(1)	Brooks	11/16/1893	2262	Reno. GN 63(2) 4/11/1899.	60

Class B-5 (Old Class 19) 4-4-0: 16x24-58-140-66,170-41,600-12,605 originally. Changed to 16x24-55-140-66,170-41,600-13,290 (dates are shown in parentheses if known).

No.	Builder	Date Rcvd.	C/N	Original No.	Renumbered From	Date	Disposition	Notes
255(2)	Rogers	6/5/1878	2477	StP&P 27	GN 27(1)	3/31/1899	(10/5/1897) Sold A. Guthrie & Co. (No. 202) 6/1913.	
256(2)	Rogers	6/5/1878	2478	StP&P 28	GN 28(1)	4/6/1899	Sold Devils Lake & Northern 9/14/1902 and renumbered FG&S 1. Later sold A. Guthrie & Co.	7
257(2)	Rogers	6/17/1878	2480	StP&P 29	GN 29(1)	4/7/1899	Sold R.A. Elzy 7/17/1902.	
258(2)	Rogers	6/26/1878	2481	StP&P 30	GN 30(1)	4/5/1899	(7/1895?) Equipped with weed burner 3/18/1902. Scrapped 8/6/1903.	
259	Rogers	6/26/1878	2483	StP&P 31	GN 31(1)	4/5/1899	Equipped with weed burner 5/20/1902. Sold Oregon Southern Railway (No. 259) 3/20/1905. Later sold A. Guthrie & Co.	
260	Rogers	6/29/1878	2484	StP&P 32	GN 32(1)	4/13/1899	(9/13/1897) Sold R.A. Elzy 7/17/1902.	
261	Rogers	6/29/1878	2485	StP&P 33	GN 33(1)	4/6/1899	(7/29/1897) Scrapped 1901(?).	223
262	Rogers	7/12/1878	2486	StP&P 34	GN 34(1)	4/13/1899	(4/19/1898) Equipped with weed burner 6/18/1902. Sold A. Guthrie & Co. (No. 203) 6/1913.	
263	Rogers	7/26/1878	2488	StP&P 35	GN 35(1)	1899	(5/15/1897) Scrapped at St.Paul Shops 10/1902.	
264	Rogers	7/31/1878	2490	StP&P 36	GN 36(1)	1899	(7/30/1892) Scrapped 1901.	
265	Rogers	10/7/1878	2495	StP&P 39	GN 39(1)	4/24/1899	Received new Baldwin-built boiler 11/26/1906. Scrapped at Havre Shops 9/17/1920.	
266	Rogers	10/8/1878	2496	StP&P 40	GN 40(1)	3/31/1899	(9/26/1896) Received new Baldwin-built boiler 12/13/1906. Sold Minnesota State Fair Association 8/17/1921 and destroyed in staged head-on collision at the Minnesota State Fair.	
267	Rogers	10/30/1878	2498	StP&P 41	GN 41(1)	4/7/1899	(10/2/1897) Sold A. Guthrie & Co. 8/19/1900.	

Class B-10 (Old Class 18) 4-4-0: 17x24-55-140-70,050-44,650-15,010. Locomotive indicated by an asterisk (*) had drivers changed to 63" on 12/13/1918, decreasing T.E. to 13,100 lb.

No.	Builder	Date Rcvd.	C/N	Original No.	Renumbered From	Date	Disposition
268	Baldwin	5/10/1880	5083	StPM&M 67(1)	GN 51(1)	4/8/1899	Scrapped at Hillyard 3/15/1915.
269	Baldwin	5/21/1882	6190	StPM&M 117	GN 117(1)	4/5/1899	Sold FG&S (No. 2) 9/12/1905.
270	Baldwin	3/13/1880	4993	StPM&M 53	GN 53(1)	3/31/1899	Scrapped at Dale Street 1916.
271	Baldwin	3/13/1880	4994	StPM&M 54	GN 54(1)	4/8/1899	Scrapped at Dale Street 1916.
272	Baldwin	3/18/1880	4998	StPM&M 55	GN 55(1)	4/9/1899	Scrapped at Dale Street 6/1916.
273	Baldwin	4/6/1880	5033	StPM&M 56	GN 56(1)	4/15/1899	Sold B&O 5/1900.
274	Baldwin	4/6/1880	5028	StPM&M 57	GN 57(1)	1899	Scrapped at Delta 1916.
275	Baldwin	4/17/1880	5043	StPM&M 58	GN 58(1)	4/6/1899	Scrapped 1902. Boiler used in Havre, MT, roundhouse.
276	Baldwin	4/17/1880	5046	StPM&M 59	GN 59(1)	4/1/1899	Sold B&O 5/1900.
277	Baldwin	4/28/1880	5061	StPM&M 60	GN 60(1)	1899	Sold B&O 5/1900.
278	Baldwin	4/28/1880	5062	StPM&M 61	GN 61(1)	4/11/1899	Sold B&O 5/1900.
279	Baldwin	5/22/1882	6192	StPM&M 119	GN 119(1)	4/18/1899	Sold B&O 4/24/1900.
280	Baldwin	5/7/1880	5074	StPM&M 63	GN 63(1)	4/1/1899	Sold Wisconsin Central Railway (probably for a connecting logging company) 1/6/1900.
281	Baldwin	5/17/1880	5085	StPM&M 64	GN 64(1)	4/5/1899	Scrapped at Dale Street 1916.
282*	Baldwin	5/17/1880	5086	StPM&M 65	GN 65(1)	3/31/1899	Received new GN-built boiler 7/1907. Ret. 9/1923. Dismantled at Hillyard 8/4/1924.
283	Baldwin	5/10/1880	5078	StPM&M 66	GN 66(1)	4/1/1899	Sold B&O 5/1900.

Class B-8 (Old Class 14) 4-4-0: 17x24-55-140-73,400-48,000-15,010. Locomotive indicated by an asterisk (*) rebuilt (between 1900 and 1918) with dimensions 17x24-63-140-73,400-48,000-13,100.

No.	Builder	Date Rcvd.	C/N	Original No.	Renumbered From	Date	Disposition	Notes
284	Pittsburgh	8/20/1880	437	StPM&M 68	GN 68(1)	4/7/1899	Sold B&O 5/1900.	
285	Pittsburgh	8/25/1880	438	StPM&M 69	GN 69(1)	4/13/1899	Sold B&O 5/1900.	
286	Pittsburgh	8/31/1880	439	StPM&M 70	GN 70(1)	3/30/1899	Sold B&O 5/1900.	
287	Pittsburgh	9/6/1880	440	StPM&M 71	GN 71(1)	3/31/1899	Scrapped 9/19/1900.	
288	Pittsburgh	9/18/1880	441	StPM&M 72	GN 72(1)	4/10/1899	Received new boiler 1905. Scrapped at Havre 3/27/1925.	
289	Pittsburgh	9/18/1880	442	StPM&M 73	GN 73(1)	4/6/1899	Received new boiler 1906. Sold for scrap PC 10/1929.	87
290*	Pittsburgh	9/25/1880	443	StPM&M 74	GN 74(1)	4/17/1899	Turned over to Kootenai Valley Railroad 8/1899, later returned to GN and relettered back at East Spokane c.7/1901. Sold VTR&F (No. 4) 9/19/1903. Received new boiler at Delta 2/1906. Reno. GN 290 Delta 10/5/1908. Used for a time on Victoria & Sidney. Sold NSRM 5/1926.	
291	Pittsburgh	9/25/1880	444	StPM&M 75	GN 75(1)	3/24/1899	Received new boiler 1906. Ret. 9/1923. Dismantled at Hillyard 5/14/1924.	
292	Pittsburgh	9/30/1880	445	StPM&M 76	GN 76(1)	3/21/1899	Turned over to Kootenai Valley Railroad 8/24/1899 (relettered for KVRR). Later returned to GN and relettered back at East Spokane 7/20/1901. Received New boiler 1905. Sold for scrap DI&M 8/3/1927.	88, 89
293	Pittsburgh	9/30/1880	446	StPM&M 77	GN 77(1)	3/20/1899	Received new boiler 1905. Sold for scrap DI&M 8/3/1927.	89

Class B-11(1) (Old Class 20) 4-4-0: 17x24-55-140-70,300-44,800-15,010

No.	Builder	Date Rcvd.	C/N	Original No.	Renumbered From	Date	Disposition	Notes
294	Rogers	1/27/1879	2509	StP&P 43	GN 43(1)	3/31/1899	Scrapped 10/20/1905.	
295	Rogers	1/27/1879	2511	StP&P 44	GN 44(1)	4/13/1899	Scrapped 10/1902.	90

Class D-3(1) (Old Class 36B) 2-6-0: 18x24-57-175-107,000-90,000-20,290

No.	Builder	Date Built	C/N	Original No.	Renumbered From	Date	Disposition
297	Baldwin	7/1892	12584	D&W 6	EM 297	5/1/1902	Sold FG&S (No. 3) 5/10/1905, while still actually owned by EM. Return to GN c.1927 was proposed [as GN 430(2), Class D-7]. Locomotive was apparently scrapped prior to actually being returned to GN.

Class E-4 [Old Class 10(2)] 4-6-0: 18x24-55-150(140)-100,800-77,000-16,820

No.	Builder	Date Built	C/N	Original No.	Renumbered From	Date	Disposition
298	Schenectady	5/1889	2860	F&S 1	S&M RR 298	7/1/1907	Scrapped 6/1923.
299	Schenectady	5/1889	2861	F&S 2	S&M RR 299	7/1/1907	Sold Waterville Railway (No. 299) 2/28/1911. Ret. 5/1934, scrapped 1/1935.

Class D-2 (Old Class 35) 2-6-0: 19x24-55-150(140)-105,040-87,290-18,745 originally. Total weight and weight on drivers later decreased to 99,800 lb. and 78,200 lb., respectively.

No.	Builder	Date Rcvd.	C/N	Original No.	Renumbered From	Date	Disposition
300	Rogers	7/7/1887	3771	StPM&M 300	StPM&M 300	c.1892	Sold for scrap DI&M 6/1924.
301	Rogers	7/12/1887	3775	StPM&M 301	StPM&M 301	c.1892	Sold for scrap DI&M 1/25/1922.
302	Rogers	7/13/1887	3776	StPM&M 302	StPM&M 302	c.1892	Ret. 9/1923, sold for scrap.
303	Rogers	7/19/1887	3777	StPM&M 303	StPM&M 303	c.1892	Sold Truax, Whittier, Truax Co. 10/1923.
304	Rogers	7/28/1887	3778	StPM&M 304	StPM&M 304	c.1892	Ret. 9/1923, sold for scrap.
305	Rogers	7/26/1887	3781	StPM&M 305	StPM&M 305	c.1892	Scrapped 1/1924.
306	Rogers	7/27/1887	3783	StPM&M 306	MC 7	5/25/1892	Sold for scrap NSRM 12/1926.
307	Rogers	7/27/1887	3784	StPM&M 307	StPM&M 307	c.1892	Ret. 9/1923, sold for scrap.
308	Rogers	7/31/1887	3785	StPM&M 308	StPM&M 308	c.1892	Sold for scrap NSRM 12/1926.
309	Rogers	7/31/1887	3786	StPM&M 309	StPM&M 309	c.1892	Sold for scrap DI&M 12/1924.
310	Rogers	8/1/1887	3787	StPM&M 310	StPM&M 310	c.1892	Ret. 9/1923, sold for scrap.
311	Rogers	8/2/1887	3788	StPM&M 311	StPM&M 311	c.1892	Sold for scrap Hyman-Michaels Co. 10/1925.
312	Rogers	8/7/1887	3789	StPM&M 312	StPM&M 312	c.1892	Ret. 9/1923, sold for scrap DI&M.
313	Rogers	8/7/1887	3790	StPM&M 313	StPM&M 313	c.1892	Ret. 9/1923, sold for scrap DI&M 12/1924.
314	Rogers	8/7/1887	3791	StPM&M 314	StPM&M 314	c.1892	Sold for scrap DI&M 12/1925.
315	Rogers	8/7/1887	3792	StPM&M 315	StPM&M 315	c.1892	Scrapped 9/1920.
316	Rogers	8/12/1887	3793	StPM&M 316	StPM&M 316	c.1892	Ret. 9/1923, sold for scrap DI&M.
317	Rogers	8/13/1887	3795	StPM&M 317	StPM&M 317	c.1892	Ret. 9/1923, scrapped.
318	Rogers	8/15/1887	3796	StPM&M 318	StPM&M 318	c.1892	Sold for scrap DI&M 1/25/1922.
319	Rogers	8/20/1887	3797	StPM&M 319	StPM&M 319	c.1892	Ret. 9/1923, sold for scrap DI&M 12/1924.
320	Rogers	8/21/1887	3799	StPM&M 320	StPM&M 320	c.1892	Sold for scrap Hyman-Michaels Co. 10/1925.
321	Rogers	9/2/1887	3800	StPM&M 321	StPM&M 321	c.1892	Sold Midland of Manitoba (No. 1) 11/1911.
322	Rogers	8/27/1887	3802	StPM&M 322(1)	MC 4	c.1900	Sold for scrap PC 3/1926.
323	Rogers	8/31/1887	3804	StPM&M 323(1)	MC 5	c.1900	Sold for scrap Hyman-Michaels Co. 10/1925.
324	Rogers	9/11/1887	3807	StPM&M 324(1)	MC 6	c.1900	Sold for scrap DI&M 12/1924.
325	Rogers	9/9/1888	4004	StPM&M 325	MC 8	c.1900	Ret. 9/1923, sold for scrap DI&M c.12/1923.

Class D-2 (Old Class 36) 2-6-0: 19x24-55-150(140)-105,040-87,290-18,745 originally. Total weight and weight on drivers later decreased to 99,800 lb. and 78,200 lb., respectively.

No.	Builder	Date Rcvd.	C/N	Original No.	Renumbered From	Date	Disposition
326	Rogers	9/9/1888	4007	StPM&M 326	StPM&M 326	c.1892	Sold for scrap 7/1925.

Great Northern Class B-22 226 was built by Rogers as Eastern of Minnesota 101 in 1888. The engine is shown here fitted with a snow plow in February 1922 at St. Paul, MN. It powered passenger trains 815 and 816 to and from Hutchinson, MN, at this time. Collection of Harold K. Vollrath.

Class D-2 (Old Class 35) 2-6-0: 19x24-55-150(140)-105,040-87,290-18,745 originally. Total weight and weight on drivers later decreased to 99,800 lb. and 78,200 lb., respectively.

No.	Builder	Date Rcvd.	C/N	Original No.	Renumbered From	Date	Disposition
327	Rogers	9/3/1888	4001	StPM&M 322(2)	MC 10(2)	1900	Sold for scrap DI&M 1/25/1922.
328	Rogers	9/3/1888	4002	StPM&M 323(2)	MC 11(2)	1900	Sold for scrap DI&M 12/1924.

Class D-2 (Old Class 36) 2-6-0: 19x24-55-150(140)-105,040-87,290-18,745 originally. Total weight and weight on drivers later decreased to 99,800 lb. and 78,200 lb., respectively. Dates indicated with an asterisk (*) are dates built.

No.	Builder	Date Rcvd.	C/N	Original No.	Renumbered From	Date	Disposition
329	Rogers	9/17/1888	4012	StPM&M 329	S&M RR 329	7/1/1907	Sold for scrap DI&M 12/1926.
330	Rogers	9/17/1888	4013	StPM&M 330	StPM&M 330	c.1892	Sold for scrap DI&M 12/1925.
331	Rogers	9/20/1888	4014	StPM&M 331	StPM&M 331	c.1892	Sold for scrap DI&M 12/1925.
332	Rogers	9/20/1888	4015	StPM&M 332	StPM&M 332	c.1892	Ret. 9/1923, sold for scrap DI&M.
333	Rogers	9/24/1888	4016	StPM&M 333	StPM&M 333	c.1892	Ret. 9/1923, sold for scrap DI&M.
334	Rogers	9/25/1888	4017	StPM&M 334	StPM&M 334	c.1892	Scrapped 9/1920.
335	Rogers	10/21/1888	4041	StPM&M 335	StPM&M 335	c.1892	Ret. 9/1923, sold for scrap DI&M.
336	Rogers	10/26/1888	4042	StPM&M 336	StPM&M 336	c.1892	Sold for scrap PC 3/1926.
337	Rogers	10/28/1888	4043	StPM&M 337	StPM&M 337	c.1892	Ret. 9/1923, sold for scrap DI&M.
338	Rogers	10/31/1888	4048	StPM&M 338	StPM&M 338	c.1892	Sold for scrap PC 3/1926.
339	Rogers	10/31/1888	4049	StPM&M 339	StPM&M 339	c.1892	Sold for scrap DI&M 12/1926.
340	Rogers	11/12/1888	4050	StPM&M 340	StPM&M 340	c.1892	Sold for scrap DI&M 12/1925.
341(1)	Rogers	11/14/1888	4056	StPM&M 341	StPM&M 341	c.1892	Sold Brandon, Devils Lake & Southern (No. 4) 1906, while still actually owned by StPM&M. Reno. FG&S 4, date unknown. Return to GN as No. 341(2), Class D-8, in 1927 was proposed, but locomotive scrapped prior to actual return to GN.
342	Rogers	11/19/1888	4057	StPM&M 342	StPM&M 342	c.1892	Sold Somers Lumber Co. 10/1925.
343	Rogers	11/19/1888	4058	StPM&M 343	StPM&M 343	c.1892	Sold for scrap DI&M 10/1926.
344	Rogers	9/10/1889	4125	StPM&M 344	StPM&M 344	c.1892	Sold for scrap NSRM 3/1926.
345	Rogers	9/14/1889	4126	StPM&M 345	StPM&M 345	c.1892	Sold for scrap PC 3/1926.
346	Rogers	c.9/1889	4129	StPM&M 346	StPM&M 346	c.1892	Ret. 9/1923, scrapped.
347	Rogers	9/5/1888	4003	StPM&M 324(2)	StPM&M 347	c.1892	Ret. 9/1923, sold for scrap DI&M.
348	Rogers	9/11/1888	4008	StPM&M 327	MC 17	c.1900	Sold for scrap DI&M 2/2/1922.
349	Rogers	9/16/1888	4009	StPM&M 328	MC 18	c.1900	Ret. 9/1923, sold for scrap DI&M.
350	Rogers	8/1888*	3985	EM 201	EM 350	5/1/1902	Ret. 9/1923, sold Truax Coal Co.
351(2)	Rogers	8/1888*	3986	EM 202	EM 351	5/1/1902	Sold for scrap DI&M 12/1925.
352(2)	Rogers	8/1888*	3995	EM 203	EM 352	5/1/1902	Ret. 9/1923, sold for scrap DI&M.
353(2)	Rogers	8/1888*	3996	EM 204	EM 353	5/1/1902	Sold for scrap NSRM 12/1926.
354(2)	Rogers	8/1888*	3997	EM 205	EM 354	5/1/1902	Sold for scrap DI&M 5/1926.
355(2)	Rogers	9/1888*	4021	EM 206	EM 355	5/1/1902	Sold for scrap DI&M 6/1924.
356(2)	Rogers	9/1888*	4022	EM 207	EM 356	5/1/1902	Sold for scrap PC 5/1925.
357(2)	Rogers	9/1888*	4023	EM 208	EM 357	5/1/1902	Sold for scrap NSRM 3/1926.
358(2)	Rogers	9/1888*	4026	EM 209	EM 358	5/1/1902	Sold for scrap DI&M 3/1926.
359(2)	Rogers	9/1888*	4027	EM 210	EM 359	5/1/1902	Sold for scrap DI&M 2/3/1922.

Class D-8 2-6-0: 19x24-55-150(140)-105,040-87,090-18,750

No.	Builder	Date Rcvd.	C/N	Original No.	Renumbered From	Notes
341(2)	Rogers	11/14/1888	4056	StPM&M 341	FG&S 4	91

Old Class 37(2) 2-6-0: 19x24-55-180(160)-118,000-102,000-21,420

No.	Builder	Date Rcvd.	C/N	Disposition	Notes
351(1)	Brooks	11/16/1893	2266	Reno. GN 400(2) 4/18/1899.	60, 92
352(1)	Brooks	8/15/1893	2362	Reno. GN 401(2) 4/11/1899.	
353(1)	Brooks	8/15/1893	2363	Reno. GN 402(2) 4/13/1899.	
354(1)	Brooks	8/17/1893	2364	Reno. GN 403(2) 4/9/1899.	
355(1)	Brooks	8/17/1893	2365	Reno. GN 404(2) 4/13/1899.	
356(1)	Brooks	8/22/1893	2366	Reno. GN 405(2) 4/15/1899.	
357(1)	Brooks	8/22/1893	2367	Reno. GN 406(2) 5/4/1899.	
358(1)	Brooks	8/28/1893	2368	Reno. GN 407(2) 5/4/1899.	
359(1)	Brooks	8/26/1893	2369	Reno. GN 408(2) 1899.	93
360(1)	Brooks	8/28/1893	2370	Reno. GN 409(2) 4/8/1899.	
361(1)	Brooks	8/28/1893	2371	Sold Montana Central (No. 30) 9/24/1893. Returned to GN (No. 420) c.1899.	
361(2)	Brooks	7/29/1895	2537	Reno. GN 410(3) 3/31/1899.	
362	Brooks	11/22/1893	2407	Reno. GN 411(2) 3/28/1899.	94
363(1)	Brooks	11/22/1893	2408	Sold Butte, Anaconda & Pacific. Reno. BA&P 30 at St.Paul 11/30/1893.	94
363(2)	Brooks	7/29/1895	2538	Reno. GN 412(2) 4/15/1899.	
364(1)	Brooks	11/28/1893	2409	Sold Butte, Anaconda & Pacific. Reno. BA&P 31(1) at St.Paul 11/30/1893. Reno. BA&P 10(1) 1898. Sold Columbia Southern (No. 10) before 1906. Sold Oregon Railway & Navigation (No. 10) 7/1/1906. Sold Oregon-Washington Railway & Navigation Co. (No. 10) 12/23/1910. Assigned Union Pacific No. 4209 9/1/1915, but sold Montana Western (No. 10) 5/1916, before renumbering. Retired 1947.	95

364(2)	Brooks	7/30/1895	2539	Reno. GN 413(2) 4/1/1899.
365(1)	Brooks	11/28/1893	2410	Sold Butte, Anaconda & Pacific. Reno. BA&P 32 at St.Paul 11/30/1893.
365(2)	Brooks	7/30/1895	2540	Reno. GN 414(2) 4/6/1899.
366	Brooks	8/1/1895	2541	Reno. GN 415 3/30/1899.
367	Brooks	8/1/1895	2542	Reno. GN 416 4/14/1899.
368	Brooks	8/4/1895	2543	Reno. GN 417 4/18/1899.
369	Brooks	8/4/1895	2544	Reno. GN 418 4/5/1899.
370	Brooks	8/6/1895	2545	Reno. GN 419 4/22/1899.

95

Class D-1(1) (Old Class 36A) 2-6-0: 19x24-55-150-104,800-89,300-20,080

No.	Builder	Date Built	C/N	Original No.	Renumbered From	Date	Disposition
360(2)	Rhode Island	7/1890	2406	PSL 14	WSF 360	7/1/1907	Assigned CB&Q as part of SC&W by lease on 11/1/1907. Delivered to CB&Q c.1908, and sold CB&Q [No. 1115(2)] 12/1/1908. Rebuilt [possibly with spare parts from CB&Q 1115(1)] to compound (Class H-1C). Ret. 11/1916.

Old Class 43 2-6-0: 19x26-55-180(170)-130,000-114,000-24,660. See Note 29

No.	Builder	Date Rcvd.	C/N	Disposition
371	Brooks	9/16/1896	2698	Reno. GN 450(2) 4/4/1899.
372	Brooks	9/16/1896	2699	Reno. GN 451(2) 4/6/1899.
373	Brooks	9/18/1896	2700	Reno. GN 452(2) 4/18/1899.
374	Brooks	9/18/1896	2701	Reno. GN 453(2) 4/13/1899.
375	Brooks	9/21/1896	2702	Reno. GN 454(2) 4/27/1899.
376	Brooks	9/21/1896	2703	Reno. GN 455(2) 4/19/1899.
377	Brooks	9/22/1896	2704	Reno. GN 456(2) 5/2/1899.
378(1)	Brooks	9/22/1896	2705	Reno. GN 457(2) 4/10/1899.
379(1)	Brooks	9/25/1896	2706	Reno. GN 458(2) 3/30/1899.
380(1)	Brooks	9/25/1896	2707	Reno. GN 459(2) 4/10/1899.
381(1)	Brooks	9/28/1896	2708	Reno. GN 460(2) 4/18/1899.
382(1)	Brooks	9/28/1896	2709	Reno. GN 461(2) 5/10/1899.
383(1)	Brooks	8/13/1897	2788	Reno. GN 462(2) 4/22/1899.
384(1)	Brooks	8/16/1897	2789	Reno. GN 463(2) 4/22/1899.
385(1)	Brooks	8/16/1897	2790	Reno. GN 464(2) 4/13/1899.
386(1)	Brooks	8/19/1897	2791	Reno. GN 465(2) 4/28/1899.
387(1)	Brooks	8/19/1897	2792	Reno. GN 466(2) 4/10/1899.
388(1)	Brooks	8/20/1897	2793	Reno. GN 467(2) 4/28/1899.
389(1)	Brooks	8/20/1897	2794	Reno. GN 468(2) 6/18/1899.
390(1)	Brooks	8/24/1897	2795	Reno. GN 469(2) 5/19/1899.
391(1)	Brooks	8/24/1897	2796	Reno. GN 470(2) 3/30/1899.
392(1)	Brooks	8/24/1897	2797	Reno. GN 471(2) 4/17/1899.

Class A-6 [Old Class 9(3)] 0-6-0: 18x26-49-180(160)-109,400-109,400-23,380

No.	Builder	Date Built	C/N	Original No.	Renumbered From	Date	Disposition	Notes
378(2)	Brooks	9/1899	3301	DS&WT 1	ABD 1	4/22/1913	Sold McCree & Co., St.Paul, 7/1926.	1
379(2)	Brooks	9/1899	3302	DS&WT 2	ABD 2	4/22/1913	Sold McCree & Co., St.Paul, 7/1926.	1

Class A-9 0-6-0: 19x26-49-200(175)-135,000-135,000-28,490 originally. Those locomotives indicated by an asterisk (*) were rebuilt with 52" drivers (decreasing T.E. to 26,850 lb.), dates unknown. Total weights of those locomotives with 49" and 52" drivers were later increased to 142,800 lb. and 147,000 lb., respectively.

No.	Builder	Date Rcvd.	C/N	Original No.	Renumbered From	Date	Disposition
380(2)*	Baldwin	11/6/1912	38460	–	–	–	Sold for scrap PC 1/25/1947.
381(2)*	Baldwin	11/6/1912	38461	–	–	–	Sold for scrap DI&M 2/25/1947.
382(2)	Baldwin	11/6/1912	38462	–	–	–	Sold for scrap PC 1/20/1947.
383(2)*	Baldwin	11/6/1912	38463	–	–	–	Sold for scrap DI&M 9/1949.
384(2)	Baldwin	11/2/1912	38464	–	–	–	Sold for scrap PC 8/30/1952.
385(2)	Baldwin	11/2/1912	38465	–	–	–	Sold for scrap PC 10/1950.
386(2)*	Baldwin	11/6/1912	38466	–	–	–	Sold for scrap WEI&M 10/16/1951.
387(2)*	Baldwin	11/6/1912	38467	–	–	–	Ret. 5/1939.
388(2)*	Baldwin	11/13/1912	38468	–	–	–	Sold for scrap PC 1/14/1955.
389(2)*	Baldwin	11/13/1912	38469	–	–	–	Sold for scrap DI&M 1/15/1955
390(2)	Baldwin	9/23/1912	38256	–	–	–	Sold for scrap PC 10/18/1951.
391(2)	Baldwin	9/23/1912	38257	–	–	–	Sold for scrap PC 9/21/1940.
391(3)*	Baldwin	11/8/1907	31942	GN 5(3)	GN 5(3)	10/1949	Sold for scrap Dulien Steel Products 1/13/1953.
392(2)	Baldwin	9/23/1912	38258	–	–	–	Ret. 5/1939.
392(3)*	Baldwin	11/22/1907	32081	GN 9(3)	GN 9(3)	9/22/1949	Sold for scrap WEI&M 1/12/1955.
393(1)	Baldwin	9/23/1912	38259	–	–	–	Sold for scrap PC 9/27/1941.
393(2)*	Baldwin	11/30/1907	32114	GN 10(3)	GN 10(3)	10/1949	Sold for scrap Dulien Steel Products 7/1953.
394	Baldwin	10/2/1912	38260	–	–	–	Sold for scrap DI&M 10/16/1951.
395	Baldwin	10/2/1912	38261	–	–	–	Sold for scrap PC 10/10/1952.

Class A-9 0-6-0: Continued

No.	Builder	Date Rcvd.	C/N	Original No.	Renumbered From	Date	Disposition
396*	Baldwin	9/25/1912	38262	–	–	–	Sold for scrap DI&M 11/10/1951.
397(1)	Baldwin	9/25/1912	38263	–	–	–	Sold for scrap PC 12/1949.
397(2)	GN (Dale Street)	9/27/1906	16	GN 16(3)	GN 16(3)	4/1950	Sold for scrap PC 4/20/1952.
398(1)*	Baldwin	9/30/1912	38264	–	–	–	Sold for scrap PC 12/1949.
398(2)*	GN (Dale Street)	9/22/1906	15	GN 15(3)	GN 15(3)	4/1950	Sold for scrap Dulien Steel Products 1/13/1953.
399(1)	Baldwin	9/30/1912	38265	–	–	–	Sold for scrap PC 6/4/1947.
399(2)	GN (Dale Street)	10/23/1906	19	GN 19(3)	GN 19(3)	4/1951	Sold for scrap WEI&M 4/26/1952.

Old Class 37(1) 4-8-0: 20x24-55-180(160)-156,000-132,000-23,740 originally. Rebuilt (apparently prior to 1900) with 20"x26" cylinders (raising T.E. to 25,750 lb.) and at that time moved to Old Class 38.

No.	Builder	Date Rcvd.	C/N	Original No.	Renumbered From	Date	Disposition
400(1)	Brooks	10/15/1891	1972	StPM&M 400	StPM&M 400	c.1892	Reno. GN 600(2) 4/1899.
401(1)	Brooks	10/17/1891	1973	StPM&M 401	StPM&M 401	c.1892	Sold Montana Central [No. 54(1)] c.1892. Rtnd. GN [No. 401(1)] c.1893. Reno. GN 601(2) 4/1899.
402(1)	Brooks	10/17/1891	1974	StPM&M 402	StPM&M 402	c.1892	Reno. GN 602 4/1899.
403(1)	Brooks	10/21/1891	1975	StPM&M 403	StPM&M 403	c.1892	Reno. GN 603 4/1899.
404(1)	Brooks	10/21/1891	1976	StPM&M 404	StPM&M 404	c.1892	Reno. GN 604 4/1899.
405(1)	Brooks	10/26/1891	1977	StPM&M 405	StPM&M 405	c.1892	Reno. GN 605 4/1899.
406(1)	Brooks	10/26/1891	1978	StPM&M 406	StPM&M 406	c.1892	Reno. GN 606 4/1899.
407(1)	Brooks	10/30/1891	1979	StPM&M 407	StPM&M 407	c.1892	Reno. GN 607 4/1899.
408(1)	Brooks	10/29/1891	1980	StPM&M 408	StPM&M 408	c.1892	Reno. GN 608 4/1899.
409(1)	Brooks	11/2/1891	1981	StPM&M 409	StPM&M 409	c.1892	Reno. GN 609 4/1899.

Old Class 38 4-8-0: 20x26-55-180(160)-156,000-132,000-25,720

No.	Builder	Date Rcvd.	C/N	Original No.	Renumbered From	Date	Disposition	Notes
410(1)	Brooks	12/3/1891	1998	StPM&M 410	StPM&M 410	c.1892	Sold Montana Central. Reno. MC 50 2/7/1892.	
410(2)	Brooks	11/15/1893	2261	–	–	–	Reno. GN 610 4/1899.	60
411(1)	Brooks	12/8/1891	1999	StPM&M 411	StPM&M 411	c.1892	Sold Montana Central. Reno. MC 51 2/9/1892.	
412(1)	Brooks	12/8/1891	2000	StPM&M 412	StPM&M 412	c.1892	Sold Montana Central. Reno. MC 52 2/20/1892.	
413(1)	Brooks	12/14/1891	2001	StPM&M 413	StPM&M 413	c.1892	Sold Montana Central. Reno. MC 53 5/6/1892.	
414(1)	Brooks	12/14/1891	2002	StPM&M 414	StPM&M 414	c.1892	Sold Montana Central. Reno. MC 54(2) 9/23/1893.	

Class D-4 [Old Class 37(2)] 2-6-0: 19x24-55-180(160)-118,000-102,000-21,420 originally. Total weight later increased to 119,900 lb., weight on drivers to 108,000 lb.

No.	Builder	Date Rcvd.	C/N	Original No.	Renumbered From	Date	Disposition	Notes
400(2)	Brooks	11/16/1893	2266	GN 351(1)	GN 351(1)	4/18/1899	Sold for scrap Pacific Coast Steel Co. 2/1926.	60, 92
401(2)	Brooks	8/15/1893	2362	GN 352(1)	GN 352(1)	4/11/1899	Sold for scrap DI&M 4/1926.	101
402(2)	Brooks	8/15/1893	2363	GN 353(1)	GN 353(1)	4/13/1899	Sold for scrap NSRM 12/1926.	96, 102
403(2)	Brooks	8/17/1893	2364	GN 354(1)	GN 354(1)	4/9/1899	Sold for scrap NSRM 4/1926.	103
404(2)	Brooks	8/17/1893	2365	GN 355(1)	GN 355(1)	4/13/1899	Sold for scrap NSRM 4/1926.	103
405(2)	Brooks	8/22/1893	2366	GN 356(1)	GN 356(1)	4/15/1899	Sold for scrap DI&M 3/1926.	101
406(2)	Brooks	8/22/1893	2367	GN 357(1)	GN 357(1)	5/4/1899	Sold for scrap DI&M 6/1926.	
407(2)	Brooks	8/28/1893	2368	GN 358(1)	GN 358(1)	5/4/1899	Sold for scrap DI&M 11/1927 (delivered 9/2/1927).	
408(2)	Brooks	8/26/1893	2369	GN 359(1)	GN 359(1)	1899	Sold for scrap DI&M 3/1926.	93, 101
409(2)	Brooks	8/28/1893	2370	GN 360(1)	GN 360(1)	4/8/1899	Sold for scrap NSRM 3/1926.	101
410(3)	Brooks	7/29/1895	2537	GN 361(2)	GN 361(2)	3/31/1899	Sold for scrap DI&M 3/1926.	101
411(2)	Brooks	11/22/1893	2407	GN 362	GN 362	3/28/1899	Sold for scrap DI&M 4/1926.	94, 103
412(2)	Brooks	7/29/1895	2538	GN 363(2)	GN 363(2)	4/15/1899	Sold for scrap DI&M 3/1926.	101
413(2)	Brooks	7/30/1895	2539	GN 364(2)	GN 364(2)	4/1/1899	Sold for scrap DI&M 9/1927.	97, 105
414(2)	Brooks	7/30/1895	2540	GN 365(2)	GN 365(2)	4/6/1899	Sold for scrap DI&M 3/1926.	101
415	Brooks	8/1/1895	2541	GN 366	GN 366	3/30/1899	Sold for scrap DI&M 3/1926.	101
416	Brooks	8/1/1895	2542	GN 367	GN 367	4/14/1899	Ret. 9/1923. Sold for scrap DI&M 12/1923.	
417	Brooks	8/4/1895	2543	GN 368	GN 368	4/18/1899	Dismantled at Delta 3/24/1925.	98
418	Brooks	8/4/1895	2544	GN 369	GN 369	4/5/1899	Sold for scrap DI&M 3/1926.	101
419	Brooks	8/6/1895	2545	GN 370	GN 370	4/22/1899	Sold for scrap DI&M 4/1926.	103
420	Brooks	8/28/1893	2371	GN 361(1)	MC 30	c.1900	Sold SP&S (No. 201) 10/1924. Ret. 3/26/1944.	99
421	Brooks	8/6/1895	2546	EM 250	EM 421	5/1/1902	Sold for scrap DI&M 3/1926.	101
422	Brooks	8/6/1895	2547	EM 251	EM 422	5/1/1902	Dismantled at Delta 11/12/1925.	
423	Brooks	8/11/1895	2548	EM 252	EM 423	5/1/1902	Sold for scrap PC 4/1926.	103
424	Brooks	8/15/1895	2549	EM 253	EM 424	5/1/1902	Sold for scrap DI&M 5/1926.	104
425	Brooks	8/15/1895	2550	EM 254	EM 425	5/1/1902	Sold for scrap DI&M 12/1926.	100
426	Brooks	8/15/1895	2551	EM 255	EM 426	5/1/1902	Sold for scrap DI&M 12/1926.	100

Class D-6 2-6-0: 19x24-55-160-114,500-101,800-21,420

No.	Builder	Date Built	C/N	Original No.	Renumbered From	Date	Disposition	Notes
430(1)	Alco-Schenectady	1902	?	?	W&SF 11	9/19/1921	Sold for scrap DI&M 6/1926.	39

Class D-7 2-6-0: 18x24-57-140-107,000-90,000-16,230

No.	Builder	Date Built	C/N	Original No.	Renumbered From			Notes
430(2)	Baldwin	7/1892	12854	D&W 6	FG&S 3			106

Class D-6 2-6-0: 19x24-55-160(155)-126,900-113,800-20,750

No.	Builder	Date Built	C/N	Original No.	Renumbered From	Date	Disposition	Notes
431	Alco-Schenectady	1906	?	?	W&SF 12	8/1/1921	Sold for scrap PC 1/18/1929.	40

Class D-3(2) 2-6-0: 18x24-55-180(170)-119,000-106,500-20,430

No.	Builder	Date Built	C/N	Original No.	Renumbered From	Date	Disposition	Notes
432	Baldwin	5/1901	18999	K&M 279	W&SF 13	7/11/1921	Sold for scrap DI&M 6/1926.	41

Old Class 39 2-8-0: 19x26-55-180(160)-136,000-120,000-23,210. See Note 30.

No.	Builder	Date Rcvd.	C/N	Disposition	Notes
450(1)	Brooks	6/16/1892	2093	Renumbered GN 516 4/1899.	
451(1)	Brooks	6/16/1892	2094	Renumbered GN 517 4/1899.	
452(1)	Brooks	6/19/1892	2095	Renumbered GN 518 4/1899.	108
453(1)	Brooks	6/19/1892	2096	Renumbered GN 519 4/1899.	108
454(1)	Brooks	6/21/1892	2097	Renumbered GN 520 4/1899.	
455(1)	Brooks	6/21/1892	2098	Renumbered GN 521 4/1899.	
456(1)	Brooks	6/28/1892	2099	Renumbered GN 522(1) 4/1899.	109
457(1)	Brooks	6/28/1892	2100	Renumbered GN 523(1) 4/1899.	109
458(1)	Brooks	6/28/1892	2101	Renumbered GN 524 4/1899.	109
459(1)	Brooks	6/28/1892	2102	Renumbered GN 525 4/1899.	109
460(1)	Brooks	6/30/1892	2103	Renumbered GN 526 4/1899.	
461(1)	Brooks	6/30/1892	2104	Renumbered GN 527 4/1899.	
462(1)	Brooks	7/2/1892	2105	Renumbered GN 528 4/1899.	
463(1)	Brooks	7/2/1892	2106	Renumbered GN 529 4/1899.	
464(1)	Brooks	7/7/1892	2107	Renumbered GN 530 4/1899.	
465(1)	Brooks	7/7/1892	2108	Renumbered GN 531 4/1899.	
466(1)	Brooks	7/8/1892	2109	Renumbered GN 532 4/1899.	
467(1)	Brooks	7/8/1892	2110	Renumbered GN 533 4/1899.	
468(1)	Brooks	7/15/1892	2111	Renumbered GN 534 4/1899.	
469(1)	Brooks	7/15/1892	2112	Renumbered GN 535 4/1899.	
470(1)	Brooks	7/19/1892	2113	Renumbered GN 536 4/1899.	
471(1)	Brooks	7/19/1892	2114	Renumbered GN 537 4/1899.	
472(1)	Brooks	7/22/1892	2115	Renumbered GN 538 4/1899.	
473(1)	Brooks	7/22/1892	2116	Renumbered GN 539 4/1899.	
474(1)	Brooks	8/15/1892	2133	Renumbered GN 540 4/1899.	
475(1)	Brooks	8/15/1892	2134	Renumbered GN 541 4/1899.	
476(1)	Brooks	8/20/1892	2135	Renumbered GN 542 4/1899.	
477(1)	Brooks	8/20/1892	2136	Renumbered GN 543 4/1899.	
478(1)	Brooks	8/22/1892	2137	Renumbered GN 544 4/1899.	
479(1)	Brooks	8/22/1892	2138	Renumbered GN 545(1) 4/1899.	
480(1)	Brooks	8/28/1892	2139	Renumbered GN 546(1) 4/1899.	
481	Brooks	8/28/1892	2140	Renumbered GN 547 4/1899.	
482	Brooks	8/28/1892	2141	Renumbered GN 548 4/1899.	
483	Brooks	8/28/1892	2142	Renumbered GN 549 4/1899.	
484	Brooks	8/31/1892	2143	Renumbered GN 550(2) 4/1899.	
485	Brooks	8/31/1892	2144	Renumbered GN 551(2) 4/1899.	
486	Brooks	9/1/1892	2145	Renumbered GN 552(2) 4/1899.	
487	Brooks	9/1/1892	2146	Renumbered GN 553(2) 4/1899.	
488	Brooks	9/4/1892	2147	Renumbered GN 554(2) 4/1899.	
489	Brooks	9/4/1892	2148	Renumbered GN 555 4/1899.	
490	Brooks	9/6/1892	2149	Renumbered GN 556 4/1899.	
491	Brooks	9/6/1892	2150	Renumbered GN 557 4/1899.	
492	Brooks	9/9/1892	2151	Renumbered GN 558 4/1899.	
493	Brooks	9/9/1892	2152	Renumbered GN 559 4/1899.	
494	Brooks	9/10/1892	2153	Renumbered GN 560 4/1899.	
495	Brooks	9/16/1892	2154	Renumbered GN 561 4/1899.	
496	Brooks	9/16/1892	2155	Renumbered GN 562 4/1899.	
497	Brooks	9/18/1892	2156	Renumbered GN 563 4/1899.	
498	Brooks	9/18/1892	2157	Renumbered GN 564 4/1899.	
499	Brooks	10/26/1892	2117	Renumbered GN 565 4/1899.	107

Class D-5 (Old Class 43) 2-6-0: 19x26-55-180(170)-130,000-114,000-24,660. See Note 29.

No.	Builder	Date Rcvd.	C/N	Original No.	Renumbered From	Date	Disposition	Notes
450(2)	Brooks	9/16/1896	2698	GN 371	GN 371	4/4/1899	Ret. 4/1937. Sold for scrap Dulien Steel Products Co. 5/1937.	
451(2)	Brooks	9/16/1896	2699	GN 372	GN 372	4/6/1899	Sold for scrap DI&M 4/1926.	103
452(2)	Brooks	9/18/1896	2700	GN 373	GN 373	4/18/1899	Ret. 6/1928. Dismantled at Superior 9/24/1928.	
453(2)	Brooks	9/18/1896	2701	GN 374	GN 374	4/13/1899	Sold for scrap Dulien Steel Products Co. 8/1940.	
454(2)	Brooks	9/21/1896	2702	GN 375	GN 375	4/27/1899	Dismantled at Hillyard, sold for scrap to Abe Goldberg & Co. 5/1929.	
455(2)	Brooks	9/21/1896	2703	GN 376	GN 376	4/19/1899	Rblt. A-5 33(3) at Jackson Street 2/19/1926.	
456(2)	Brooks	9/22/1896	2704	GN 377	GN 377	5/2/1899	Dismantled at Delta 6/2/1928.	
457(2)	Brooks	9/22/1896	2705	GN 378(1)	GN 378(1)	4/10/1899	Possibly rebuilt A-5 34(3) at Delta 1/1926, but if so apparently converted back to D-5 457(2). Ret. 9/1939, sold for scrap Bethlehem Steel.	54
458(2)	Brooks	9/25/1896	2706	GN 379(1)	GN 379(1)	3/30/1899	Rblt. A-5 32(3) at Jackson Street 2/16/1925.	
459(2)	Brooks	9/25/1896	2707	GN 380(1)	GN 380(1)	4/10/1899	Ret. at Watertown 1/11/1931. Delivered DI&M 8/29/1932.	
460(2)	Brooks	9/28/1896	2708	GN 381(1)	GN 381(1)	4/18/1899	Sold for scrap DI&M 6/1926.	
461(2)	Brooks	9/28/1896	2709	GN 382(1)	GN 382(1)	5/10/1899	Sold for scrap Dulien Steel Products Co. 10/1940.	
462(2)	Brooks	8/13/1897	2788	GN 383(1)	GN 383(1)	4/22/1899	Sold for scrap DI&M 7/1927 (delivered 8/6/1927).	
463(2)	Brooks	8/16/1897	2789	GN 384(1)	GN 384(1)	4/22/1899	Dismantled at Hillyard, sold for scrap to Abe Goldberg & Co. 5/1929.	
464(2)	Brooks	8/16/1897	2790	GN 385(1)	GN 385(1)	4/13/1899	Sold for scrap DI&M 8/1927 (delivered 9/2/1927).	
465(2)	Brooks	8/19/1897	2791	GN 386(1)	GN 386(1)	4/28/1899	Ret. 3/1930. Delivered to DI&M 7/16/1932.	
466(2)	Brooks	8/19/1897	2792	GN 387(1)	GN 387(1)	4/10/1899	Ret. 10/1929. Scrapped at Superior 2/1930.	
467(2)	Brooks	8/20/1897	2793	GN 388(1)	GN 388(1)	4/28/1899	Sold for scrap DI&M 11/1927 (delivered 8/3/1927).	
468(2)	Brooks	8/20/1897	2794	GN 389(1)	GN 389(1)	6/18/1899	Sold for scrap NSRM 12/1926.	102, 110
469(2)	Brooks	8/24/1897	2795	GN 390(1)	GN 390(1)	5/19/1899	Sold for scrap DI&M 4/1926.	103
470(2)	Brooks	8/24/1897	2796	GN 391(1)	GN 391(1)	3/30/1899	Sold for scrap DI&M 11/1927 (delivered 9/1/1927).	
471(2)	Brooks	8/24/1897	2797	GN 392(1)	GN 392(1)	4/17/1899	Sold for scrap NSRM 12/1926.	102, 110
472(2)	Brooks	8/31/1897	2798	EM 256	EM 472	5/1/1902	Sold for scrap PC 3/21/1929.	
473(2)	Brooks	8/31/1897	2799	EM 257	EM 473	5/1/1902	Ret. 6/1928. Dismantled at Superior 9/29/1928.	
474(2)	Brooks	9/2/1897	2800	EM 258	EM 474	5/1/1902	Ret. 6/1928. Dismantled at Dale Street 8/27/1928.	
475(2)	Brooks	9/4/1897	2801	EM 259	EM 475	5/1/1902	Sold for scrap DI&M 9/1927.	
476(2)	Brooks	9/5/1897	2802	EM 260	EM 476	5/1/1902	Sold for scrap DI&M 5/1926.	

Class D-1(2) 2-6-0: 18x24-55-145(140)-90,000-77,000-16,820

No.	Builder	Date Built	C/N	Original No.	Renumbered From	Date	Disposition
477(2)	Baldwin	6/1889	10037	SF&N 4	VW&Y 1(2)	11/4/1908	Sold for scrap NSRM 4/1926.
478(2)	Baldwin	4/1889	9968	SF&N 1	SF&N 1	6/26/1908	Sold for scrap NSRM 4/1926.
479(2)	Baldwin	5/1889	9972	SF&N 2	SF&N 2	5/21/1908	Sold for scrap NSRM 4/1926.
480(2)	Baldwin	6/1889	10036	SF&N 3	SF&N 3	3/3/1908	Sold for scrap NSRM 4/1926.

Old Class 40 2-8-0: 13 and 22x26-55-180(160)-142,000-127,600-17,690 (Vauclain Compound)

No.	Builder	Date Rcvd.	C/N	Disposition
500(1)	Baldwin	8/9/1892	12817	Reno. GN 550(1) 9/2/1892.
501(1)	Baldwin	8/9/1892	12818	Reno. GN 551(1) 8/31/1892.
502(1)	Baldwin	8/14/1892	12819	Reno. GN 552(1) 8/31/1892.
503(1)	Baldwin	8/14/1892	12820	Reno. GN 553(1) 9/2/1892.
504(1)	Baldwin	8/15/1892	12823	Reno. GN 554(1) 9/17/1892.

Old Class 40 2-8-0: 13 and 22x26-55-180(160)-142,000-127,600-17,690 (Vauclain Compound)

No.	Builder	Date Rcvd.	C/N	Original No.	Renumbered From	Date	Disposition
550(1)	Baldwin	8/9/1892	12817	GN 500(1)	GN 500(1)	9/2/1892	Reno. GN 595 1899.
551(1)	Baldwin	8/9/1892	12818	GN 501(1)	GN 501(1)	8/31/1892	Reno. GN 596 1899.
552(1)	Baldwin	8/14/1892	12819	GN 502(1)	GN 502(1)	8/31/1892	Reno. GN 597 1899.
553(1)	Baldwin	8/14/1892	12820	GN 503(1)	GN 503(1)	9/2/1892	Reno. GN 598 1899.
554(1)	Baldwin	8/15/1892	12823	GN 504(1)	GN 504(1)	9/17/1892	Reno. GN 599 1899.

Class F-1 (Old Class 39) 2-8-0: 19x26-55-180(160)-136,000-120,000-23,210 originally (except Nos. 515 and 565, which were built as tandem compounds with dimensions 13 and 22x26-55-180-147,000-130,000-18,120 but were rebuilt to standard dimensions). Those engines indicated by an asterisk (*) below were later rebuilt to 22x26-55-180(150)-136,000-120,000-29,170, had piston valves and superheaters added (dates given below if known), and were classed as "F-1S" by GN.

No.	Builder	Date Rcvd.	C/N	Original No.	Renumbered From	Date	Disposition	Notes
500(2)	Brooks	11/29/1892	2187	–	–	–	Ret. 6/1928. Dismantled at Superior 8/14/1928.	
501(2)	Brooks	12/5/1892	2188	–	–	–	Sold for scrap NSRM 6/1926.	
502(2)	Brooks	12/5/1892	2189	–	–	–	Ret. 11/9/1929 at Hillyard, scrapped 1932.	
503(2)	Brooks	12/7/1892	2190	–	–	–	Sold for scrap DI&M 7/1927 (delivered 8/30/1927).	
504(2)	Brooks	12/7/1892	2191	–	–	–	Ret. 12/1930 at Great Falls, sold for scrap DI&M c.8/1932.	
505	Brooks	12/9/1892	2192	–	–	–	Ret. 10/1936, sold for scrap Bethlehem Steel.	
506	Brooks	12/9/1892	2193	–	–	–	Ret. 7/1925, sold for scrap.	
507	Brooks	12/12/1892	2194	–	–	–	Sold for scrap DI&M 7/1927 (delivered 8/6/1927).	
508*	Brooks	12/12/1892	2195	–	–	–	Superheated at Dale Street 2/1922. Reno. 522(2) 2/26/1947.	
509	Brooks	12/15/1892	2196	–	–	–	Sold for scrap NSRM 6/1926.	
510	Brooks	12/15/1892	2197	–	–	–	Ret. 1/1928. Sold for scrap DI&M 6/1928.	
511*	Brooks	12/17/1892	2198	–	–	–	Superheated 10/1942 at Great Falls. Reno. GN 523(2) 2/13/1947.	
512	Brooks	12/17/1892	2199	–	–	–	Sold for scrap DI&M 1/1947.	
513	Brooks	12/19/1892	2200	–	–	–	Ret. 5/1930 at Great Falls. Usable parts removed at Great Falls 5/19/1931.	
514	Brooks	12/19/1892	2201	–	–	–	Ret. 12/1938, scrapped.	
515	Brooks	11/15/1893	2269	–	–	–	Simpled c.1900. Sold for scrap NSRM 6/1926.	60, 224
516	Brooks	6/16/1892	2093	GN 450(1)	GN 450(1)	4/1899	Ret. 6/1928. Dismantled at Delta 10/20/1928.	
517	Brooks	6/16/1892	2094	GN 451(1)	GN 451(1)	4/1899	Sold for scrap DI&M 1/1928.	
518	Brooks	6/19/1892	2095	GN 452(1)	GN 452(1)	4/1899	Sold for scrap DI&M 3/18/1929.	108
519	Brooks	6/19/1892	2096	GN 453(1)	GN 453(1)	4/1899	Sold for scrap Dulien Steel Products 8/1940.	108
520	Brooks	6/21/1892	2097	GN 454(1)	GN 454(1)	4/1899	Sold for scrap DI&M 1/1928.	
521	Brooks	6/21/1892	2098	GN 455(1)	GN 455(1)	4/1899	Sold for scrap PC 10/1950.	
522(1)	Brooks	6/28/1892	2099	GN 456(1)	GN 456(1)	4/1899	Scrapped 10/1940.	109
522(2)*	Brooks	12/12/1892	2195	GN 508	GN 508	2/26/1947	Sold for scrap PC 11/13/1951.	
523(1)	Brooks	6/28/1892	2100	GN 457(1)	GN 457(1)	4/1899	Sold for scrap PC 9/8/1941.	109
523(2)*	Brooks	12/17/1892	2198	GN 511	GN 511	2/13/1947	Ret. 12/1949, sold for scrap PC.	
524	Brooks	6/28/1892	2101	GN 458(1)	GN 458(1)	4/1899	Sold for scrap DI&M 1/1928.	109
525	Brooks	6/28/1892	2102	GN 459(1)	GN 459(1)	4/1899	Sold Somers Lumber Co. 12/1924. Repurchased 10/1925. Sold for scrap DI&M 11/24/1951.	109, 112
526	Brooks	6/30/1892	2103	GN 460(1)	GN 460(1)	4/1899	Sold for scrap DI&M 2/1928.	
527	Brooks	6/30/1892	2104	GN 461(1)	GN 461(1)	4/1899	Sold for scrap PC 1/21/1947.	
528	Brooks	7/2/1892	2105	GN 462(1)	GN 462(1)	4/1899	Ret. 12/28/1929. Sold for scrap PC 10/1933.	
529	Brooks	7/2/1892	2106	GN 463(1)	GN 463(1)	4/1899	Ret. 6/1928. Dismantled at Dale Street 8/20/1928.	
530	Brooks	7/7/1892	2107	GN 464(1)	GN 464(1)	4/1899	Sold SP&S (No. 350) 4/15/1908. Returned 3/25/1945 and renumbered GN 545(2) 4/5/1945.	
531	Brooks	7/7/1892	2108	GN 465(1)	GN 465(1)	4/1899	Sold for scrap DI&M 1/1927.	
532	Brooks	7/8/1892	2109	GN 466(1)	GN 466(1)	4/1899	Dismantled 4/1924.	
533	Brooks	7/8/1892	2110	GN 467(1)	GN 467(1)	4/1899	Sold for scrap DI&M 6/1926.	
534	Brooks	7/15/1892	2111	GN 468(1)	GN 468(1)	4/1899	Sold for scrap 12/1928.	
535	Brooks	7/15/1892	2112	GN 469(1)	GN 469(1)	4/1899	Ret. 1/1934. Sold for scrap PC 4/10/1934.	
536	Brooks	7/19/1892	2113	GN 470(1)	GN 470(1)	4/1899	Sold for scrap PC 6/1926.	
537	Brooks	7/19/1892	2114	GN 471(1)	GN 471(1)	4/1899	Ret. 1/1934. Sold for scrap DI&M 3/18/1934.	
538	Brooks	7/22/1892	2115	GN 472(1)	GN 472(1)	4/1899	Ret. 6/1928. Dismantled at Superior 9/24/1928.	
539	Brooks	7/22/1892	2116	GN 473(1)	GN 473(1)	4/1899	Sold SP&S (No. 351) 3/27/1908. Scrapped 9/1946.	
540	Brooks	8/15/1892	2133	GN 474(1)	GN 474(1)	4/1899	Sold for scrap WEI&M 5/1948.	
541	Brooks	8/15/1892	2134	GN 475(1)	GN 475(1)	4/1899	Ret. 5/1929. Sold for scrap DI&M 8/1932.	
542	Brooks	8/20/1892	2135	GN 476(1)	GN 476(1)	4/1899	Sold for scrap NSRM 6/1926.	
543	Brooks	8/20/1892	2136	GN 477(1)	GN 477(1)	4/1899	Sold for scrap DI&M 1/1928.	
544*	Brooks	8/22/1892	2137	GN 478(1)	GN 478(1)	4/1899	Superheated at Dale Street 4/1923. Sold Montana Western (No. 5) 10/1950. Sold for scrap 1956.	
545(1)	Brooks	8/22/1892	2138	GN 479(1)	GN 479(1)	4/1899	Ret. 9/30/1928 at Grand Forks. Usable parts removed at Superior 11/17/1931.	
545(2)*	Brooks	7/7/1892	2107	GN 464(1)	SP&S 350	4/5/1945	Sold for scrap WEI&M 10/18/1951.	
546(1)	Brooks	8/28/1892	2139	GN 480(1)	GN 480(1)	4/1899	Scrapped 12/1938.	
546(2)*	Brooks	9/16/1892	2154	GN 495	SP&S 352	4/5/1945	Sold for scrap DI&M 11/1951.	
547	Brooks	8/28/1892	2140	GN 481	GN 481	4/1899	Dismantled 10/1925.	
548	Brooks	8/28/1892	2141	GN 482	GN 482	4/1899	Ret. 6/1928. Dismantled at Superior 9/24/1928.	
549	Brooks	8/28/1892	2142	GN 483	GN 483	4/1899	Sold Morissey, Fernie & Michel 1904.	
550(2)	Brooks	8/31/1892	2143	GN 484	GN 484	4/1899	Sold for scrap DI&M 7/1927 (delivered 8/6/1927).	
551(2)	Brooks	8/31/1892	2144	GN 485	GN 485	4/1899	Sold for scrap DI&M 11/1927 (delivered 8/31/1927).	

Class F-1 (Old Class 39) 2-8-0: Continued

No.	Builder	Date Rcvd.	C/N	Original No.	Renumbered From	Date	Disposition	Notes
552(2)	Brooks	9/1/1892	2145	GN 486	GN 486	4/1899	Sold for scrap DI&M 12/1927.	
553(2)	Brooks	9/1/1892	2146	GN 487	GN 487	4/1899	Ret. 2/8/1930 at Hillyard. Dismantled at Dale Street 6/30/1932.	
554(2)	Brooks	9/4/1892	2147	GN 488	GN 488	4/1899	Sold Truax Traer Lignite Coal Co., Kincaid, ND, 9/27/1936.	
555	Brooks	9/4/1892	2148	GN 489	GN 489	4/1899	Sold for scrap NSRM 5/1926.	
556	Brooks	9/6/1892	2149	GN 490	GN 490	4/1899	Sold for scrap DI&M 11/1927.	
557	Brooks	9/6/1892	2150	GN 491	GN 491	4/1899	Sold for scrap DI&M 5/1926.	
558	Brooks	9/9/1892	2151	GN 492	GN 492	4/1899	Ret. 9/5/1931. Sold for scrap DI&M 1932.	
559	Brooks	9/9/1892	2152	GN 493	GN 493	4/1899	Sold for scrap DI&M 5/1926.	
560	Brooks	9/10/1892	2153	GN 494	GN 494	4/1899	Sold for scrap NSRM 5/1926.	
561	Brooks	9/16/1892	2154	GN 495	GN 495	4/1899	Sold SP&S (No. 352) 3/27/1908. Returned 3/25/1945 and Renumbered GN 546(2) 4/5/1945.	
562	Brooks	9/16/1892	2155	GN 496	GN 496	4/1899	Dismantled 3/1925.	
563	Brooks	9/18/1892	2156	GN 497	GN 497	4/1899	Ret. 3/4/1931. Sold for scrap DI&M 1932.	
564*	Brooks	9/18/1892	2157	GN 498	GN 498	4/1899	Superheated 1908. Sold Deer Park Lumber Co. 8/1928.	
565	Brooks	10/26/1892	2117	GN 499	GN 499	4/1899	Simpled c.1901. Ret. 6/1928. Dismantled at Dale Street 8/20/1928.	107

Class F-11 2-8-0: 20x24-52-180-138,000-123,000-28,250

No.	Builder	Date Built	C/N	Original No.	Renumbered From	Date	Disposition	Notes
590	Alco-Brooks	4/1913	52834	TA&G 322	W&SF 14	4/15/1922	Ret. 1/1934. Sold for scrap DI&M 4/15/1934.	42
591	Alco-Brooks	9/1914	54970	SDC 15	W&SF 15	5/22/1922	Scrapped 12/1927.	

Class F-2 (Old Class 40) 2-8-0: 13 and 22x26-55-180-134,220-115,270-19,900 (Vauclain Compound) originally. Later (between 1900 and 1918) changed to simple with dimensions of 19x26-55-180(160)-145,000-130,000-23,210.

No.	Builder	Date Rcvd.	C/N	Original No.	Renumbered From	Date	Disposition
595	Baldwin	8/9/1892	12817	GN 500(1)	GN 550(1)	1899	Ret. 6/1928.
596	Baldwin	8/9/1892	12818	GN 501(1)	GN 551(1)	1899	Sold for scrap PC 10/1929.
597	Baldwin	8/14/1892	12819	GN 502(1)	GN 552(1)	1899	Ret. 6/1928. Dismantled at Superior 8/17/1928.
598	Baldwin	8/14/1892	12820	GN 503(1)	GN 553(1)	1899	Ret. 6/1928. Dismantled at Dale Street 8/20/1928.
599	Baldwin	8/15/1892	12823	GN 504(1)	GN 554(1)	1899	Ret. 6/1928.

Old Class 41 4-6-0: 14 and 24x24-68-180-134,600-102,800-17,450 (Vauclain Compound) originally. Rebuilt to simple before 1900 with dimensions of 20x24-69-180(160)-135,700-103,300-18,920.

No.	Builder	Date Rcvd.	C/N	Disposition	Notes
600(1)	Baldwin	8/7/1892	12779	Reno. GN 998 1899.	113
601(1)	Baldwin	8/7/1892	12780	Reno. GN 999 1899.	113

Class G-1 (Old Class 38) 4-8-0: 20x26-55-180(160)-156,000-132,000-25,720 when renumbered to this series. No. 609 was either rebuilt to or retained the original 20" x 24" cylinders, thus having a T.E. of 23,740 lb. (NOTE: Nos. 600-604 had radial stay fireboxes)

No.	Builder	Date Rcvd.	C/N	Original No.	Renumbered From	Date	Disposition	Notes
600(2)	Brooks	10/15/1891	1972	StPM&M 400	GN 400(1)	4/1899	Sold for scrap PC 10/1929.	
601(2)	Brooks	10/17/1891	1973	StPM&M 401	GN 401(1)	4/1899	Sold for scrap PC 11/1928.	114
602	Brooks	10/17/1891	1974	StPM&M 402	GN 402(1)	4/1899	Sold for scrap DI&M 9/1927.	
603	Brooks	10/21/1891	1975	StPM&M 403	GN 403(1)	4/1899	Sold for scrap PC 1/25/1947.	
604	Brooks	10/21/1891	1976	StPM&M 404	GN 404(1)	4/1899	Sold for scrap PC 10/1929.	
605	Brooks	10/26/1891	1977	StPM&M 405	GN 405(1)	4/1899	Sold for scrap DI&M 11/29/1928.	115
606	Brooks	10/26/1891	1978	StPM&M 406	GN 406(1)	4/1899	Sold for scrap PC 6/30/1947.	
607	Brooks	10/30/1891	1979	StPM&M 407	GN 407(1)	4/1899	Sold for scrap PC 10/1941.	116
608	Brooks	10/29/1891	1980	StPM&M 408	GN 408(1)	4/1899	Sold for scrap DI&M 10/1927.	
609	Brooks	11/2/1891	1981	StPM&M 409	GN 409(1)	4/1899	Ret. 3/29/1930. Sold for scrap DI&M 9/16/1932.	
610	Brooks	11/15/1893	2261	GN 410(2)	GN 410(2)	4/1899	Ret. 5/1929. Sold for scrap PC 10/1929.	60
611	Brooks	12/3/1891	1998	StPM&M 410	MC 50	6/1900	Sold for scrap DI&M 6/1926.	
612	Brooks	12/8/1891	1999	StPM&M 411	MC 51	6/1900	Sold for scrap PC 6/4/1947.	
613	Brooks	12/8/1891	2000	StPM&M 412	MC 52	6/1900	Sold for scrap DI&M 12/1941.	
614	Brooks	12/14/1891	2001	StPM&M 413	MC 53	6/1900	Sold for scrap DI&M 5/1926.	
615	Brooks	12/14/1891	2002	StPM&M 414	MC 54(2)	6/1900	Sold for scrap DI&M 4/28/1926.	

Old Class 42 4-6-0: 19x26-72-180-138,000-110,000-21,588

No.	Builder	Date Rcvd.	C/N	Disposition	Notes
650	Brooks	10/16/1893	2267	Renumbered GN 950 1899.	60
651	Brooks	4/30/1893	2275	Renumbered GN 951 1899.	
652	Brooks	4/30/1893	2276	Renumbered GN 952 1899.	
653	Brooks	5/2/1893	2277	Renumbered GN 953 1899.	
654	Brooks	5/2/1893	2278	Renumbered GN 954 1899.	
655	Brooks	5/4/1893	2279	Renumbered GN 955 1899.	
656	Brooks	5/4/1893	2280	Renumbered GN 956 1899.	
657	Brooks	5/7/1893	2281	Renumbered GN 957 1899.	
658	Brooks	5/7/1893	2282	Renumbered GN 958 1899.	
659	Brooks	5/9/1893	2283	Renumbered GN 959 1899.	
660	Brooks	5/9/1893	2284	Renumbered GN 960 1899.	
661	Brooks	5/12/1893	2286	Renumbered GN 961 1899.	
662	Brooks	5/12/1893	2287	Renumbered GN 962 1899.	
663	Brooks	5/15/1893	2288	Renumbered GN 963 1899.	
664	Brooks	5/15/1893	2289	Renumbered GN 964 1899.	
665	Brooks	5/17/1893	2290	Renumbered GN 965 1899.	
666	Brooks	5/17/1893	2291	Renumbered GN 966 1899.	
667	Brooks	5/19/1893	2292	Renumbered GN 967 1899.	
668	Brooks	5/19/1893	2293	Renumbered GN 968 1899.	
669	Brooks	5/20/1893	2294	Renumbered GN 969 1899.	

Class G-2 (Old Class 45) 4-8-0: 19x32-55-200(180)-176,000-142,000-32,140

No.	Builder	Date Built	C/N	Original No.	Renumbered From	Date	Disposition	Notes
700	Brooks	6/1898	2973	EM 300	EM 700	5/1/1902	Ret. 10/1931. Sold for scrap DI&M 10/22/1932.	
701	Brooks	6/1898	2974	EM 301	EM 701	5/1/1902	Rblt. F-3 2-8-0 (No. 701 retained) 1902.	225
702	Brooks	6/1898	2975	EM 302	EM 702	5/1/1902	Ret. 6/1928. Dismantled at Delta 8/18/1928.	
703	Brooks	6/1898	2982	EM 303	EM 703	5/1/1902	Ret. 8/1928.	
704	Brooks	6/1898	2983	EM 304	EM 704	5/1/1902	Ret. 12/27/1927. Scrapped at Delta 4/30/1928.	
705	Brooks	6/1898	2984	EM 305	EM 705	5/1/1902	Ret. 2/17/1932. Sold for scrap DI&M 1932.	
706	Brooks	6/1898	2985	EM 306	EM 706	5/1/1902	Ret. 12/31/1930 at Appleyard, scrapped 1932.	
707	Brooks	7/1898	2986	EM 307	EM 707	5/1/1902	Ret. 10/1931. Sold for scrap DI&M 10/1933.	
708	Brooks	7/1898	2987	EM 308	EM 708	5/1/1902	Ret. 6/30/1932. Sold for scrap DI&M 1932.	
709	Brooks	7/1898	2988	EM 309	EM 709	5/1/1902	Ret. 12/1927. Scrapped at Delta 4/30/1928.	
710	Brooks	7/1898	2989	EM 310	EM 710	5/1/1902	Ret. 11/21/1930 at Appleyard, scrapped 1932.	
711	Brooks	7/1898	2990	EM 311	EM 711	5/1/1902	Ret. 7/23/1932. Sold for scrap DI&M 1932.	
712	Brooks	9/1898	3045	EM 312	EM 712	5/1/1902	Ret. 12/20/1930 at Appleyard. Sold for scrap 9/29/1932.	
713	Brooks	9/1898	3046	EM 313	EM 713	5/1/1902	Ret. 11/1930 at Appleyard, scrapped 1932.	
714	Brooks	9/1898	3047	EM 314	EM 714	5/1/1902	Scrapped at Delta 5/16/1928.	
715	Brooks	9/1898	3048	EM 315	EM 715	5/1/1902	Ret. 5/1939.	
716	Brooks	10/1898	3049	EM 316	EM 716	5/1/1902	Ret. 11/13/1929 at Delta, scrapped 1932.	
717	Brooks	10/1898	3050	EM 317	EM 717	5/1/1902	Ret. 12/1930 at Delta, scrapped 1932.	
718	Brooks	10/1898	3051	EM 318	EM 718	5/1/1902	Ret. 12/1938.	
719	Brooks	10/1898	3052	EM 319	EM 719	5/1/1902	Ret. 6/1930 at Whitefish, scrapped 1932.	

Class F-3 2-8-0: 19x32-55-200(185)-176,000-160,000-33,030 (Rebuilt from Class G-2 4-8-0)

No.	Builder	Date Start F-3	Date Finish F-3	C/N	Original No.	Rblt. From G-2 No.	Disposition	Notes
701	GN		c.1901	2974	EM 301	GN 701	Sold for scrap PC 5/1939.	225

Class G-3 (Old Class 48) 4-8-0: 19x32-55-210(180)-182,000-148,000-32,140 originally. Those engines indicated below by an asterisk (*) later rebuilt to 23½x32-55-210(150)-182,000-148,000-40,970 (with addition of piston valves and superheaters) and classified as "G-3S" by GN.

No.	Builder	Date Rcvd.	C/N	Disposition	Notes
720	Rogers	5/17/1899	5370	Ret. 9/1939. Sold for scrap Bethlehem Steel c.10/1939.	
721	Rogers	5/17/1899	5371	Ret. 2/1947. Sold for scrap DI&M 3/4/1947.	
722*	Rogers	5/19/1899	5372	Superheated at Hillyard 10/31/1913. Sold for scrap PC 9/29/1949.	
723	Rogers	5/19/1899	5373	Sold for scrap PC 5/20/1953.	
724	Rogers	5/19/1899	5379	Sold for scrap PC 10/18/1951.	
725	Rogers	5/26/1899	5380	Ret. 12/1949. Sold for scrap PC 1/31/1950.	
726	Rogers	5/28/1899	5381	Ret. 12/1949. Sold for scrap PC 1/31/1950.	
727	Rogers	6/7/1899	5382	Ret. 1/1938.	
728	Rogers	6/7/1899	5383	Received boiler from GN 746 at Dale Street 8/26/1909. Ret. 12/1949. Sold for scrap DI&M 1/31/1950.	
729	Rogers	6/15/1899	5384	Received boiler from GN 762 at Dale Street 3/28/1912. Sold for scrap DI&M 9/30/1949.	
730	Rogers	6/20/1899	5385	Ret. 2/1947. Sold for scrap DI&M 3/4/1947.	
731	Rogers	7/11/1899	5399	Sold for scrap PC 2/25/1947.	
732	Rogers	7/11/1899	5400	Ret. 12/1949. Sold for scrap PC 1/31/1950.	
733	Rogers	7/15/1899	5401	Wrecked c.9/1914, and received boiler from GN 729 at Dale Street 12/30/1914. Sold for scrap DI&M 9/30/1949.	
734*	Rogers	7/20/1899	5402	Moved to Class G-6 (with addition of superheater) prior to 1911. Returned to Class G-3 5/17/1911. Sold for scrap DI&M 2/25/1947.	

Class G-3 (Old Class 48) 4-8-0: Continued

No.	Builder	Date Rcvd.	C/N	Disposition	Notes
735	Rogers	8/1/1899	5403	Sold for scrap PC 1/20/1947.	
736	Rogers	8/28/1899	5404	Sold Pacific & Eastern Ry. (No. 101) 3/5/1910.	
737	Rogers	8/23/1899	5405	Sold for scrap PC 7/6/1947.	
738	Rogers	8/1899	5407	Ret. 10/1932. Sold for scrap PC 10/1933.	
739	Rogers	8/21/1899	5408	Sold for scrap DI&M 10/16/1951.	
740	Rogers	8/26/1899	5409	Ret. 12/1938.	
741	Rogers	8/27/1899	5416	Ret. 1/1938.	
742	Rogers	8/28/1899	5417	Received boiler from GN 755 at Dale Street 1/1911. Sold for scrap PC 3/26/1948.	117, 118
743	Rogers	9/2/1899	5418	Sold for scrap PC 9/21/1952.	
744	Rogers	9/4/1899	5419	Sold for scrap PC 5/1/1948.	
745	Rogers	5/18/1900	5542	Sold for scrap PC 5/23/1951.	
746	Rogers	5/19/1900	5543	Received new GN-built boiler at Dale Street 9/30/1908. Sold for scrap PC 5/16/1947.	
747	Rogers	5/20/1900	5546	Sold for scrap DI&M 4/30/1947.	119
748	Rogers	5/24/1900	5548	Sold for scrap PC 5/16/1953.	120
749	Rogers	5/27/1900	5549	Sold for scrap DI&M 8/5/1949.	121
750	Rogers	6/2/1900	5551	Sold for scrap DI&M 9/1/1941.	
751	Rogers	6/2/1900	5553	Sold for scrap PC 6/4/1947.	
752	Rogers	6/2/1900	5554	Ret. 12/1949. Sold for scrap DI&M 1/31/1950.	
753	Rogers	6/3/1900	5556	Ret. 12/1949. Sold for scrap WEI&M 1/31/1950.	
754	Rogers	6/8/1900	5557	Sold for scrap PC 4/15/1947.	
755	Rogers	6/10/1900	5558	Received boiler from GN 767 at Dale Street 8/1910. Scrapped at Great Falls 8/28/1928.	122
756	Rogers	6/12/1900	5559	Sold for scrap WEI&M 3/20/1948.	123
757	Rogers	6/16/1900	5561	Sold Truax-Traer Coal Co. 9/17/1944.	124
758	Rogers	6/19/1900	5562	Sold for scrap PC 2/1941.	125
759	Rogers	6/18/1900	5564	Sold for scrap DI&M 3/26/1948.	123
760	Rogers	6/22/1900	5565	Sold for scrap PC 10/18/1951.	
761	Rogers	6/24/1900	5566	Sold for scrap PC 6/20/1947.	
762	Rogers	6/25/1900	5567	Received boiler from GN 742 at Dale Street 7/28/1911. Ret. 1/1934. Sold for scrap PC 4/10/1934.	
763	Rogers	6/25/1900	5568	Sold for scrap DI&M 4/16/1948.	126
764	Rogers	6/29/1900	5569	Sold for scrap PC 8/28/1950.	127
765	Rogers	6/30/1900	5570	Sold for scrap DI&M 2/25/1947.	
766	Rogers	6/30/1900	5571	Sold for scrap DI&M 3/1941.	
767	Rogers	7/1/1900	5572	Received boiler from GN 728 at Dale Street 3/31/1910. Sold for scrap PC 6/4/1947.	
768	Rogers	7/7/1900	5573	Sold for scrap PC 9/30/1949.	
769	Rogers	7/7/1900	5574	Ret. 12/1949. Sold for scrap PC 1/31/1950.	

Number 781 was one of the superheated C-4's. Robert Graham photographed it at Minneapolis, MN, on August 12, 1946. The locomotive, a coal burner, likely never became an oil burner, yet Minneapolis, where it spent its entire life, was home to oil burners by this date, as evidenced by the oil-filler column behind the tender. Collection of William Raia.

Class G-6 4-8-0: 25¼x32-55-145-182,000-148,000-45,720 (Rebuilt from Class G-3 4-8-0)

No.	Builder	Date Rblt. F-3	C/N	Rblt. From G-2 No.	Disposition
734	GN	?	5402	GN 734	Returned to Class G-3 5/17/1911.

Class G-4 (Old Class 45A) 4-8-0: 19x32-55-210(180)-182,000-150,000-32,140

No.	Builder	Date Built	C/N	Original No.	Renumbered From	Date	Disposition
770	Brooks	7/1900	3563	EM 770	EM 770	5/1/1902	Sold for scrap PC 1/31/1947.
771	Brooks	7/1900	3564	EM 771	EM 771	5/1/1902	Ret. 4/1931 at Dale Street. Stripped at Dale Street 6/30/1932.
772	Brooks	7/1900	3565	EM 772	EM 772	5/1/1902	Ret. 10/1936, sold for scrap PC.
773	Brooks	7/1900	3566	EM 773	EM 773	5/1/1902	Ret. 1939. Sold for scrap DI&M 9/29/1940.
774	Brooks	7/1900	3567	EM 774	EM 774	5/1/1902	Ret. 12/1928, sold for scrap.
775	Brooks	7/1900	3568	EM 775	EM 775	5/1/1902	Wrecked at Willmar and scrapped at Dale Street 3/27/1930.
776	Brooks	7/1900	3569	EM 776	EM 776	5/1/1902	Sold for scrap PC 9/1/1941.
777	Brooks	7/1900	3570	EM 777	EM 777	5/1/1902	Ret. 1/1934. Sold for scrap DI&M 4/15/1934.
778	Brooks	7/1900	3571	EM 778	EM 778	5/1/1902	Ret. 5/12/1932. Sold for scrap DI&M 9/1932.
779	Brooks	7/1900	3572	EM 779	EM 779	5/1/1902	Ret. 1/1934. Sold for scrap DI&M 4/15/1934.

Class C-4S 0-8-0: 20x32-55-210-209,300-209,300-41,540 [Rebuilt from M-2(1) 2-6-8-0]

No.	Builder	Date Finish Rebuild	C/N	Original No.	Rblt. From M-2(1) No.	Renumbered From	Date	Disposition
780	GN (Dale Street)	2/13/1926	32363	GN 1254	GN 1999	GN 870(1)	10/21/1929	Sold for scrap PC 1/20/1947.

Class C-4 0-8-0: 20x32-55-210-209,300-209,300-41,540 (Rebuilt from Class F-8 2-8-0). Those engines indicated by an asterisk (*) below were rebuilt from superheated F-8 locomotives, had dimensions of 23½x32-55-210(165)-209,300-209,300-45,060 originally and were classified as "C-4S" (working boiler pressure later increased to 180 psi, increasing T.E. to 49,160 lb.). Locomotive indicated by a plus sign (+), also rebuilt from a superheated F-8, had these dimensions but with the 180 psi working pressure at time of rebuild. Locomotive indicated by an equal sign (=) received superheater and Heron valves at time of rebuilding, had dimensions of 21x32-55-210(200)-209,300-209,300-43,620, and was also classified as "C-4S".

No.	Builder	Date Finish Rebuild	C/N	Rblt. From F-8 No.	Renumbered From	Date	Disposition
781*	GN	11/16/1928	5832	GN 1166	GN 871(1)	10/25/1929	Sold for scrap DI&M 3/1/1949.
782*	GN (Dale Street)	3/7/1930	6032	GN 1174	–	–	Sold for scrap DI&M 7/1947.
783+	GN (Dale Street)	10/25/1929	6033	GN 1175	–	–	Sold for scrap WEI&M 5/1951.
784	GN (Superior)	10/26/1929	6059	GN 1191	–	–	Ret. 12/1949. Sold for scrap PC c.1/1950.
785=	GN (Hillyard)	12/31/1929	5801	GN 1157	–	–	Sold for scrap DI&M 6/1951.
786	GN (Dale Street)	2/19/1930	5806	GN 1162(2)	–	–	Ret. 12/1949. Sold for scrap DI&M c.1/1950.
787	GN (Dale Street)	3/4/1937	32134	GN 1215	–	–	Sold for scrap PC 2/7/1947.
788	GN (Dale Street)	6/30/1937	6062	GN 1194	–	–	Sold for scrap DI&M 1/25/1947.
789	GN (Dale Street)	8/11/1937	6066	GN 1198	–	–	Sold for scrap PC 12/1941.
790	GN (Dale Street)	9/30/1937	32215	GN 1234	–	–	Sold for scrap DI&M 12/1941.

Class G-5 (Old Class 44) 4-8-0: 21x34-55-210(180)-212,750-172,000-41,710. Locomotive indicated by an asterisk (*) was superheated and received Heron valves.

No.	Builder	Date Built	C/N	Original No.	Renumbered From	Date	Disposition
800	Brooks	12/1897	2866	MC 100	MC 100	1900	Ret. 2/1931, scrapped 10/1932.
801	Brooks	12/1897	2867	MC 101	MC 101	1900	Ret. 6/1929. Sold for scrap DI&M 8/1932.
802	Brooks	8/1898	2999	MC 102	MC 102	1900	Sold for scrap DI&M 3/21/1929.
803	Brooks	8/1898	3000	MC 103	MC 103	1900	Ret. 1/1930, scrapped 9/1932.
804	Brooks	8/1898	3001	MC 104	MC 104	1900	Sold for scrap PC 3/21/1929.
805	Brooks	8/1898	3002	MC 105	MC 105	1900	Ret. 1/1934. Sold for scrap DI&M 3/29/1934.
806	Brooks	8/1898	3003	MC 106	MC 106	1900	Rebuilt to Class F-10 (No. 806 retained) 1905.
807*	Brooks	8/1898	3004	MC 107	MC 107	1900	Superheated 10/1928. Ret. 10/1936, sold for scrap DI&M.

Class F-10 2-8-0: 21x34-55-210(180)-216,600-197,100-41,710 originally. Weights later increased to 233,200 lb. and 213,700 lb., respectively. (Rebuilt from Class G-5 4-8-0)

No.	Builder	Date Finish Rebuild	C/N	Original No.	Rblt. From G-5 No.	Disposition
806	GN (Dale Street)	1905	3003	MC 106	GN 806	Ret. 1/1934. Sold for scrap PC 4/10/1934.

Class C-1 0-8-0: 26x28-55-210(200)-232,600-232,600-58,500 originally. Those locomotives indicated below with an asterisk (*) later changed to 26x28-55-210-253,200-253,200-61,430, while the remainder were changed to 26x28-55-210-245,640-245,640-61,430 as a result of engine reweighing.

No.	Builder	Date Rcvd.	C/N	Disposition
810*	Baldwin	7/4/1918	48890	Ret. 3/1958. Sold for scrap DI&M 4/1962.
811*	Baldwin	7/20/1918	48891	Ret. 5/1958. Sold for scrap DI&M 3/1962.
812*	Baldwin	7/20/1918	48951	Ret. 8/1956. Sold for scrap PC 9/16/1956.
813	Baldwin	7/23/1918	48999	Ret. 5/1958. Sold for scrap PC 7/1963.
814	Baldwin	7/25/1918	49077	Ret. 12/1957. Sold for scrap WEI&M 6/1962.
815	Baldwin	7/23/1918	49078	Ret. 5/1958. Sold for scrap PC 7/1963.
816*	Baldwin	8/4/1918	49155	Ret. 12/1957. Sold for scrap c.1962.
817*	Baldwin	8/8/1918	49242	Ret. 5/1958. Sold for scrap DI&M 3/1962.
818*	Baldwin	8/8/1918	49243	Ret. 3/1958. Sold for scrap DI&M 4/1962.
819*	Baldwin	9/1/1918	49297	Ret. 5/1958. Sold for scrap DI&M 3/1962.

Class C-1 0-8-0: Continued

No.	Builder	Date Rcvd.	C/N	Disposition
820	Baldwin	9/1/1918	49298	Ret. 3/1958. Sold for scrap DI&M 3/1963.
821	Baldwin	9/4/1918	49354	Ret. 5/1958. Sold for scrap 5/1963.
822*	Baldwin	9/20/1918	49405	Ret. 3/1958. Sold for scrap DI&M 4/1962.
823	Baldwin	9/20/1918	49406	Ret. 5/1958. Sold for scrap WEI&M 3/1963.
824	Baldwin	9/14/1918	49477	Ret. 5/1958. Sold for scrap WEI&M 3/1963.
825	Baldwin	10/2/1918	49478	Ret. 3/1958. Sold for scrap PC 2/1963.
826	Baldwin	10/2/1918	49541	Ret. 12/1957. Sold for scrap WEI&M 6/1962.
827	Baldwin	10/20/1918	49637	Ret. 12/1957. Sold for scrap DI&M 4/1962.
828	Baldwin	10/20/1918	49658	Ret. 12/1957. Sold for scrap DI&M 5/1963.
829*	Baldwin	10/22/1918	49732	Ret. 12/1957. Sold for scrap DI&M 5/1963.
830*	Baldwin	10/23/1918	49826	Ret. 3/1958. Sold for scrap DI&M 4/1962.
831*	Baldwin	11/1/1918	50134	Ret. 5/1958. Sold for scrap DI&M 3/1962.
832	Baldwin	3/18/1919	51262	Ret. 5/1958. Sold for scrap PC 12/1962.
833	Baldwin	3/18/1919	51263	Ret. 5/1958. Sold for scrap PC 12/1962.
834	Baldwin	3/24/1919	51348	Ret. 12/1957. Sold for scrap c.1962.
835	Baldwin	3/24/1919	51389	Ret. 12/1957. Sold for scrap DI&M 4/1962.
836*	Baldwin	4/7/1919	51443	Ret. 3/1958. Sold for scrap DI&M 3/1962.
837*	Baldwin	4/7/1919	51444	Ret. 5/1958. Sold for scrap DI&M 3/1962.
838*	Baldwin	4/12/1919	51486	Ret. 3/1958. Sold for scrap DI&M 5/1963.
839*	Baldwin	4/12/1919	51523	Ret. 12/1957. Sold for scrap c.1962.
840*	Baldwin	4/14/1919	51536	Ret. 3/1958. Sold for scrap DI&M 3/1962.
841*	Baldwin	4/14/1919	51537	Ret. 5/1958. Sold for scrap DI&M 3/1962.
842	Baldwin	4/28/1919	51538	Ret. 5/1958. Sold for scrap DI&M 5/1963.
843*	Baldwin	4/28/1919	51567	Ret. 5/1958. Sold for scrap DI&M 3/1962.
844	Baldwin	4/29/1919	51568	Ret. 4/1955. Sold for scrap DI&M 5/28/1955.
845*	Baldwin	4/29/1919	51596	Ret. 3/1958. Sold for scrap PC 12/10/1962.
846	Baldwin	5/19/1919	51634	Ret. 12/1957. Sold for scrap c.1962.
847	Baldwin	5/19/1919	51635	Ret. 5/1958. Sold for scrap WEI&M 6/1963.
848	Baldwin	6/26/1919	51636	Ret. 12/1957. Sold for scrap DI&M 4/1962.
849*	Baldwin	6/26/1919	51671	Ret. 12/1957. Sold for scrap WEI&M 6/1962.

Class C-2 0-8-0: 21x32-55-210(190)-190,500-190,500-41,440 originally (Rebuilt from Class F-6 2-8-0). Later changed to 21x32-55-210-204,000-204,000-45,780. Those locomotives indicated below by an asterisk (*) were rebuilt from superheated F-6 engines, had dimensions of 23½x32-55-210(185)-204,000-204,000-50,250, and were classified by GN as "C-2S". Locomotive indicated below by a plus sign (+) was also rebuilt from a superheated F-6, had dimensions of 21x32-55-210-204,000-204,000-45,780, and was classified as "C-2S".

No.	Builder	Date Finish Rebuild	C/N	Original No.	Rblt. From F-6 No.	Disposition	Notes
850	GN (Dale Street)	5/29/1925	4047	GN 1115	GN 1115	Ret. 9/1941. Sold for scrap DI&M 10/14/1941.	
851	GN (Dale Street)	5/8/1925	4050	GN 1118	GN 1118	Sold for scrap DI&M 12/1941.	
852	GN (Dale Street)	10/30/1925	4058	GN 1126	GN 1126	Sold for scrap PC 4/14/1948.	128
853*	GN (Dale Street)	10/19/1925	4045	GN 1113	GN 1113	Sold for scrap DI&M 1/31/1947.	129
854*	GN (Dale Street)	10/9/1925	4046	GN 1114	GN 1114	Sold for scrap WEI&M 3/29/1952.	
855*	GN (Dale Street)	3/9/1926	4054	GN 1122	GN 1122	Sold for scrap PC 10/18/1951.	
856*	GN (Dale Street)	6/26/1926	4056	GN 1124	GN 1124	Ret. 12/1949. Sold for scrap DI&M 1/31/1950.	
857	GN (Dale Street)	9/30/1926	4053	GN 1121	GN 1121	Sold for scrap DI&M 1/19/1947.	
858	GN (Dale Street)	7/28/1926	4057	GN 1125	GN 1125	Ret. 5/1939.	130
859+	GN (Dale Street)	9/10/1926	4048	GN 1116	GN 1116	Sold for scrap DI&M 10/16/1951.	
860*	GN (Dale Street)	11/24/1926	4060	GN 1128	GN 1128	Sold for scrap PC 1/25/1947.	
861*	GN (Dale Street)	2/14/1927	4051	GN 1119	GN 1119	Sold for scrap WEI&M 5/7/1953.	131
862*	GN (Dale Street)	5/6/1927	4042	GN 1110	GN 1110	Ret. 5/1939.	
863*	GN (Dale Street)	6/30/1927	4055	GN 1123	GN 1123	Sold for scrap PC 3/29/1952.	
864*	GN (Dale Street)	11/5/1927	4043	GN 1111	GN 1111	Ret. 12/1949. Sold for scrap PC 1/31/1950.	
865*	GN (Dale Street)	12/23/1927	4044	GN 1112	GN 1112	Ret. 5/1939.	
866*	GN (Dale Street)	3/15/1928	4052	GN 1120	GN 1120	Sold for scrap DI&M 4/28/1947.	132
867*	GN (Dale Street)	6/8/1928	4049	GN 1117	GN 1117	Ret. 5/1939. Sold for scrap DI&M 10/15/1939.	
868*	GN (Dale Street)	7/31/1928	4061	GN 1129	GN 1129	Sold for scrap PC 3/14/1947.	
869*	GN (Dale Street)	10/20/1928	4059	GN 1127	GN 1127	Sold for scrap PC 3/26/1948.	133

Class C-4S 0-8-0: 20x32-55-210(200)-190,000-190,000-39,560 [Rebuilt from Class M-2(1) 2-6-8-0]

No.	Builder	Date Finish Rebuild	C/N	Original No.	Rblt. From M-2(1) No.	Disposition
870(1)	GN (Dale Street)	2/13/1926	32363	GN 1254	GN 1999	Reno. GN 780 at St.Cloud 10/21/1929.

Class C-4S 0-8-0: 23½x32-55-210(165)-209,300-209,300-45,060 (Rebuilt from Class F-8 2-8-0)

No.	Builder	Date Finish Rebuild	C/N	Rblt. From F-8 No.	Disposition
871(1)	GN (Dale Street)	11/16/1928	5832	GN 1166	Reno. GN 781 at St.Paul 10/25/1929.

Class C-5 0-8-0: 20x32-55-210-195,600-195,600-41,540 (Rebuilt from Class F-5 2-8-0). Locomotive indicated by asterisk had dimensions of 20x32-55-210-200,900-200,900-41,540.

No.	Builder	Date Start Rebuild	Date Finish Rebuild	C/N	Rblt. From F-5 No.	Disposition	Notes
870(2)*	GN (Hillyard)		11/16/1929	5664	GN 1109	Ret. 12/1938.	
871(2)	GN (Hillyard)		12/4/1930	5670	GN 1095	Sold for scrap PC 7/22/1947.	
872	GN (Hillyard)	10/23/1930	12/19/1930	5672	GN 1097	Sold for scrap PC 9/29/1949.	
873	GN (Delta)	10/31/1930	12/31/1930	5663	GN 1108	Ret. 9/1939. Sold for scrap Bethlehem Steel c.10/1939.	134

Class C-3 0-8-0: 21x32-55-210(190)-195,000-195,000-41,440 originally (Rebuilt from Class F-9 2-8-0). Those engines indicated below by an asterisk (*) were equipped with superheaters while still in Class F-9, had dimensions of 23½x32-55-210-210,000-210,000-57,350, and were classified as "C-3S" by GN. Those engines indicated by a plus (+) were also equipped with superheaters while still in Class F-9, had dimensions of 21x32-210(165)-196,000-196,000-35,985, and were also classified as "C-3S". The non-superheated locomotives were later changed to 21x32-55-210-210,000-210,000-45,780.

No.	Builder	Date Finish Rebuild	C/N	Rblt. From F-9 No.	Disposition	Notes
875	GN	3/1925	27909	GN 1313	Sold for scrap DI&M 9/15/1941.	
876	GN (Great Falls)	4/1925	27914	GN 1318	Sold for scrap DI&M 9/21/1952.	
877	GN (Hillyard)	4/25/1925	27905	GN 1309	Ret. 9/1939. Sold for scrap Bethlehem Steel c.10/1939.	
878	GN (Hillyard)	9/12/1925	27915	GN 1319	Sold for scrap PC 5/5/1953.	135
879	GN (Hillyard)	2/17/1926	27911	GN 1315	Sold for scrap DI&M 5/5/1953.	135
880	GN (Hillyard)	10/30/1925	27917	GN 1321	Ret. 12/1949. Sold for scrap DI&M 1/31/1950.	
881	GN (Hillyard)	4/20/1926	27901	GN 1305	Ret. 12/1949. Sold for scrap DI&M 1/31/1950.	
882+	GN (Great Falls)	4/22/1926	27907	GN 1311	Ret. 9/1939. Sold for scrap Bethlehem Steel c.10/1939.	
883(1)+	GN (Hillyard)	7/31/1926	27908	GN 1312	Sold Minnesota Transfer (No. 21) 10/29/1926.	
883(2)	GN (Hillyard)	12/7/1926	27904	GN 1308	Sold for scrap PC 10/2/1952.	136, 137
884	GN (Hillyard)	9/15/1926	27920	GN 1324	Sold for scrap DI&M 9/21/1952.	
885*	GN (Hillyard)	6/28/1927	27903	GN 1307	Sold for scrap Dulien Steel Products 10/1940.	
886*	GN (Hillyard)	7/8/1927	27912	GN 1316	Sold for scrap DI&M 11/13/1951.	
887*	GN (Hillyard)	8/5/1927	27899	GN 1303	Sold for scrap DI&M 5/23/1951.	
888	GN (Hillyard)	8/4/1927	27902	GN 1306	Ret. 12/1949. Sold for scrap PC 1/31/1950.	
889*	GN (Hillyard)	9/24/1927	27898	GN 1302	Ret. 2/1940. Scrapped 10/1940.	
890*	GN (Hillyard)	10/28/1927	27916	GN 1320	Sold for scrap DI&M 10/2/1952.	137
891*	GN (Great Falls)	11/21/1927	27896	GN 1300	Sold for scrap WEI&M 6/14/1951.	
892*	GN (Hillyard)	12/23/1927	27906	GN 1310	Sold for scrap DI&M 1/21/1947.	
893*	GN (Great Falls)	1/13/1928	27919	GN 1323	Sold for scrap DI&M 10/22/1951.	
894*	GN (Hillyard)	2/27/1928	27910	GN 1314	Ret. 12/1949. Sold for scrap PC 1/31/1950.	
895*	GN (Great Falls)	2/25/1928	27900	GN 1304	Sold for scrap PC 2/25/1947.	
896	GN (Hillyard)	6/25/1928	27897	GN 1301	Sold for scrap PC 10/22/1951.	
897	GN (Hillyard)	3/26/1928	27913	GN 1317	Sold for scrap DI&M 6/4/1947.	
898	GN (Hillyard)	8/31/1928	27918	GN 1322	Sold for scrap WEI&M 5/6/1948.	
899	GN (Hillyard)	12/7/1926	27904	GN 1308	Reno. GN 883(2) 12/1926.	136

Class E-3 (Old Class 47) 4-6-0: 18x26-73-210(185)-146,000-112,000-18,150

No.	Builder	Date Built	C/N	Disposition
900	Rogers	3/1899	5359	Sold for scrap DI&M 1/1928.
901	Rogers	3/1899	5360	Ret. 3/16/1932. Sold for scrap DI&M 1932.
902	Rogers	3/1899	5361	Ret. 3/1930, scrapped 1931.
903	Rogers	3/1899	5362	Ret. 1/1938.
904	Rogers	3/1899	5363	Ret. 7/1929. Stripped at Superior 5/23/1932.
905	Rogers	3/1899	5364	Ret. 1/1934. Sold for scrap PC 6/11/1934.
906	Rogers	3/1899	5365	Ret. 10/1931. Stripped at Grand Forks 1/16/1932.
907	Rogers	4/1899	5367	Ret. 1939.
908	Rogers	4/1899	5368	Ret. 1/1938.
909	Rogers	4/1899	5369	Ret. 1/1934. Sold for scrap DI&M 4/15/1934.

Class E-2(2) 4-6-0: 18x24-60-200-130,000-96,000-22,030 originally. Driver diameter later changed to 63", decreasing T.E. to 20,980 lb.

No.	Builder	Date Built	C/N	Original No.	Renumbered From	Date	Disposition	Notes
910	Alco-Brooks	5/1915	55132	SDC 16	W&SF 16	8/11/1921	Sold for scrap PC 3/8/1949.	138

Class E-2(2) 4-6-0: 18x24-60-200-135,500-97,500-22,030 originally. Driver diameter later changed to 61", decreasing T.E. to 21,670 lb.

No.	Builder	Date Built	C/N	Original No.	Renumbered From	Date	Disposition	Notes
911	Alco-Brooks	11/1915	55443	SDC 17	W&SF 17	7/14/1921	Sold for scrap PC 3/8/1949.	139

Class E-6 (Old Class 53) 4-6-0: 19x26-63-210(200)-152,000-120,000-25,330

No.	Builder	Date Rcvd.	C/N	Disposition	Notes
925	Rogers	6/18/1902	5754	Sold for scrap PC 6/20/1947.	
926	Rogers	6/22/1902	5755	Sold for scrap PC 5/6/1948.	
927	Rogers	6/22/1902	5756	Sold for scrap DI&M 10/10/1950.	140
928	Rogers	6/26/1902	5757	Sold for scrap PC 8/8/1941.	141
929	Rogers	6/26/1902	5758	Ret. 12/1949. Sold for scrap WEI&M 1/31/1950.	
930	Rogers	7/8/1902	5764	Sold for scrap PC 6/20/1947.	
931	Rogers	7/8/1902	5765	Sold for scrap PC 4/14/1948.	142
932	Rogers	7/10/1902	5766	Sold for scrap PC 3/28/1947.	143
933	Rogers	7/18/1902	5767	Dismantled at Minneapolis Junction 11/1948. Sold for scrap PC (without boiler) 1/19/1949.	
934	Rogers	7/21/1902	5768	Dismantled at Hillyard 3/25/1932.	
935	Rogers	7/21/1902	5769	Sold for scrap PC 7/6/1947.	
936	Rogers	7/21/1902	5770	Sold for scrap PC 7/6/1948.	
937	Rogers	7/21/1902	5771	Sold for scrap WEI&M 4/16/1948.	144
938	Rogers	7/26/1902	5772	Sold Pacific & Eastern (No. 3) 3/5/1910. Sold SP&S (No. 159) 12/1912. Ret. 12/1940.	
939	Rogers	7/26/1902	5773	Sold for scrap DI&M 4/16/1948.	144

Class E-13 4-6-0: 19x24-55-160(150)-110,000-85,000-20,090

No.	Builder	Date Built	C/N	Original No.	Renumbered From	Date	Disposition	Notes
948	Baldwin	10/1893	13807	N&FS 8	SF&N 8	4/2/1908	Sold for scrap DI&M 1/21/1947.	10
949	Baldwin	9/1896	15059	SF&N 10	SF&N 10	6/26/1908	Sold Waterville Railway (No. 949) 4/1934.	

Class E-7 (Old Class 42) 4-6-0: 19x26-72-180-138,000-110,000-17,730 originally. Dimensions changed to 19x26-73-180(160)-138,000-110,000-17,480 between 1900 and 1918.

No.	Builder	Date Rcvd.	C/N	Original No.	Renumbered From	Date	Disposition	Notes
950	Brooks	10/16/1893	2267	GN 650	GN 650	1899	Sold for scrap DI&M 10/1926.	60
951	Brooks	4/30/1893	2275	GN 651	GN 651	1899	Sold for scrap DI&M 12/1926.	
952	Brooks	4/30/1893	2276	GN 652	GN 652	1899	Sold for scrap DI&M 1/1927.	
953	Brooks	5/2/1893	2277	GN 653	GN 653	1899	Sold for scrap DI&M 6/1926.	
954	Brooks	5/2/1893	2278	GN 654	GN 654	1899	Sold for scrap Pacific Coast Steel 2/1926.	226
955	Brooks	5/4/1893	2279	GN 655	GN 655	1899	Scrapped 5/1924.	
956	Brooks	5/4/1893	2280	GN 656	GN 656	1899	Sold for scrap DI&M 3/1926.	
957	Brooks	5/7/1893	2281	GN 657	GN 657	1899	Sold for scrap DI&M 1/1927.	
958	Brooks	5/7/1893	2282	GN 658	GN 658	1899	Sold for scrap Ike Statman 6/1926.	
959	Brooks	5/9/1893	2283	GN 659	GN 659	1899	Rblt. Class E-11 (retaining No. 959) at some time between 1900 and 1912. Returned to Class E-7 9/1912. Sold for scrap NSRM 4/3/1926.	
960	Brooks	5/9/1893	2284	GN 660	GN 660	1899	Sold for scrap NSRM 6/1926.	
961	Brooks	5/12/1893	2286	GN 661	GN 661	1899	Sold for scrap PC 3/1926.	
962	Brooks	5/12/1893	2287	GN 662	GN 662	1899	Sold for scrap DI&M 1/1927.	
963	Brooks	5/15/1893	2288	GN 663	GN 663	1899	Sold for scrap DI&M 9/1926.	
964	Brooks	5/15/1893	2289	GN 664	GN 664	1899	Sold for scrap DI&M 9/1926.	
965	Brooks	5/17/1893	2290	GN 665	GN 665	1899	Scrapped 8/1925.	
966	Brooks	5/17/1893	2291	GN 666	GN 666	1899	Scrapped 9/1925.	
967	Brooks	5/19/1893	2292	GN 667	GN 667	1899	Sold for scrap Pacific Coast Steel 2/1926.	226
968	Brooks	5/19/1893	2293	GN 668	GN 668	1899	Sold for scrap DI&M 5/10/1926.	
969	Brooks	5/20/1893	2294	GN 669	GN 669	1899	Sold for scrap DI&M 6/1926.	

Class E-11 4-6-0: 19x26-63-180(160)-138,000-110,000-20,260

No.	Builder	Date Finish Rebuild	C/N	Original No.	Rblt. From E-7 No.	Disposition
959	GN	?	2283	GN 659	GN 959	Returned to Class E-7 (retaining No. 959) 9/1912.

Class E-12 4-6-0: 19x24-55-180(170)-122,300-93,850-22,760

No.	Builder	Date Built	C/N	Original No.	Renumbered From	Date	Disposition
970	Baldwin	3/1897	15248	SF&N 11	SF&N 11	3/13/1908	Ret. 2/1940. Scrapped 10/1940.
971	Baldwin	3/1897	15249	SF&N 12	SF&N 12	6/26/1908	Ret. 7/4/1932. Sold for scrap DI&M 7/29/1932.

Old Class 27B 4-6-0: 18x24-63-180-127,800-97,800-18,880

No.	Builder	Date Built	C/N	Original No.	Renumbered From	Date	Disposition
991	Brooks	6/1898	2968	DMR&N 9	EM 991	5/1/1902	Sold Isaac Joseph Iron Company 11/28/1902. Then apparently sold to the St.Louis, Memphis & Southeastern, which was acquired by the St.Louis-San Francisco Railway while the locomotive was en route. Received SL-SF No. 698. Reno. SL-SF 2698 c.1903.

Class E-1 [Old Class 27(2)] 4-6-0: 18x24-55-150(140)-100,000-74,000-16,280

No.	Builder	Date Rcvd.	C/N	Original No.	Renumbered From	Date	Disposition
992	Rogers	2/11/1890	4236	SC&N 5	WSF 992	7/1/1907	Sold for scrap Hyman-Michaels Co. 10/1925.
993	Rogers	2/8/1890	4237	SC&N 6	WSF 993	7/1/1907	Sold for scrap PC 3/1926.

Class E-2(1) (Old Class 27C) 4-6-0: 18x24-56-150-102,800-84,000-17,700

No.	Builder	Date Built	C/N	Original No.	Renumbered From	Date	Disposition	Notes
994	Rhode Island	12/1889	2264	MCCo 131(1)	WSF 994	7/1/1907	Assigned CB&Q as part of SC&W by lease on 11/1/1907. Delivered to CB&Q 11/11/1907, and sold CB&Q (No. 942?) 12/1/1908. Operated on CB&Q as Class K-9. Ret. 10/1912.	36
995	Rhode Island	12/1889	2265	MCCo 132(1)	WSF 995	7/1/1907	Assigned CB&Q as part of SC&W by lease on 11/1/1907. Delivered to CB&Q 12/10/1907, and sold CB&Q (No. 943?) 12/1/1908. Operated on CB&Q as Class K-9. Ret. 10/1913.	36
996	Rhode Island	4/1890	2328	PSL 12	WSF 996	7/1/1907	Assigned CB&Q as part of SC&W by lease on 11/1/1907. Delivered to CB&Q 11/20/1907, and sold CB&Q (No. 944?) 12/1/1908. Operated on CB&Q as Class K-9. Ret. 11/1913.	

Class E-5 (Old Class 27A) 4-6-0: 19x24-55-150-105,600-86,650-18,900

No.	Builder	Date Built	C/N	Original No.	Renumbered From	Date	Disposition
997	Rhode Island	8/1890	2440	PSL 15	WSF 997	7/1/1907	Assigned CB&Q as part of SC&W by lease on 11/1/1907. Delivered to CB&Q 11/16/1907, and sold CB&Q (No. 945?) 12/1/1908. Operated on CB&Q as Class K-9. Disposition unknown.

Class E-9 (Old Class 41) 4-6-0: 20x24-69-180(160)-135,700-103,300-18,920

No.	Builder	Date Rcvd.	C/N	Original No.	Renumbered From	Date	Disposition	Notes
998	Baldwin	8/7/1892	12779	GN 600(1)	GN 600(1)	1899	Ret. 6/1929. Sold for scrap DI&M 7/18/1932.	113
999	Baldwin	8/7/1892	12780	GN 601(1)	GN 601(1)	1899	Ret. 12/1929. Stripped at Dale Street 6/27/1932.	113

Class E-10 (Old Class 46) 4-6-0: 20x30-63-210(200)-166,580-130,000-32,380. Those engines indicated below by an asterisk (*) had superheaters installed (dates shown below) and were classified by GN as "E-10S".

No.	Builder	Date Built	C/N	Original No.	Renumbered From	Date	Disposition	Notes
1000	Brooks	5/1898	2954	EM 150	EM 1000	5/1/1902	Dismantled at Great Falls 4/17/1929.	
1001	Brooks	5/1898	2955	EM 151	EM 1001	5/1/1902	Scrapped 11/1928.	
1002*	Brooks	5/1898	2956	EM 152	EM 1002	5/1/1902	Superheated at Dale Street 12/31/1913. Scrapped at Great Falls 5/16/1929	
1003*	Brooks	5/1898	2957	EM 153	EM 1003	5/1/1902	Superheated at Dale Street 7/7/1914. Ret. 10/1936, sold for scrap DI&M.	
1004*	Brooks	5/1898	2958	EM 154	EM 1004	5/1/1902	Superheated at Dale Street 2/20/1914. Stripped at Superior 8/20/1931 and sold for scrap DI&M 1932.	
1005*	Brooks	5/1898	2959	EM 155	EM 1005	5/1/1902	Superheated at Dale Street 6/11/1914. Ret. 12/15/1929 at St.Cloud. Scrapped 1932.	
1006	Brooks	5/1898	2960	EM 156	EM 1006	5/1/1902	Ret. 10/1930. Stripped at Fargo 6/10/1932.	
1007*	Brooks	5/1898	2961	EM 157	EM 1007	5/1/1902	Superheated 10/1918 at Dale Street. Sold for scrap DI&M 2/1928.	145

Class E-14 4-6-0: 26x30-73-150-200,000-150,000-35,420 originally. Changed to 23½x30-73-210(200)-200,000-150,000-38,580 by 1915. See Note 146

No.	Builder	Date Rcvd.	C/N	Disposition
1008	Baldwin	10/27/1909	33840	Rblt. H-5 1364 at Delta 4/24/1926 to 6/15/1926.
1009	Baldwin	10/27/1909	33841	Rblt. H-5 1373 at Hillyard 6/4/1927 to 8/9/1927.
1010	Baldwin	10/31/1909	33842	Rblt. H-5 1362 at Hillyard 3/13/1926 to 5/8/1926.
1011	Baldwin	10/31/1909	33843	Rblt. H-5 1370 at Delta 1/26/1927 to 4/29/1927.
1012	Baldwin	10/31/1909	33844	Rblt. H-5 1365 at Dale Street, completed 12/23/1926.
1013	Baldwin	10/31/1909	33845	Rblt. H-5 1368 at Dale Street, completed 6/17/1927.
1014	Baldwin	11/4/1909	33883	Rblt. H-5 1369 at Delta 11/12/1926 to 1/24/1927.
1015	Baldwin	11/4/1909	33884	Rblt. H-5 1371 at Hillyard 2/19/1927 to 5/27/1927.
1016	Baldwin	11/5/1909	33885	Rblt. H-5 1492 at Dale Street 4/25/1922 to 3/26/1923.
1017	Baldwin	11/5/1909	33886	Rblt. H-5 1372 at Delta 4/8/1927 to 7/9/1927.
1018	Baldwin	11/7/1909	33887	Rblt. H-5 1487 at Dale Street 8/25/1921 to 1/11/1922.
1019	Baldwin	11/7/1909	33907	Rblt. H-5 1488 at Dale Street 7/5/1921 to 10/6/1921.
1020	Baldwin	11/13/1909	33908	Rblt. H-5 1494 at Dale Street 2/19/1924 to 5/29/1924.
1021	Baldwin	11/13/1909	33909	Rblt. H-5 1366 at Dale Street 10/28/1926 to 2/9/1927.
1022	Baldwin	11/13/1909	33910	Rblt. H-5 1490 at Dale Street 12/5/1921 to 3/20/1922.
1023	Baldwin	11/13/1909	33911	Rblt. H-5 1491 at Dale Street, completed 12/30/1922.
1024	Baldwin	11/18/1909	33912	Rblt. H-5 1493 at Dale Street 12/6/1924 to 1/26/1925.
1025	Baldwin	11/28/1909	33913	Rblt. H-5 1489 at Dale Street 8/3/1921 to 11/14/1921.

Class E-14 4-6-0: Continued

No.	Builder	Date Rcvd.	C/N	Disposition
1026	Baldwin	11/18/1909	33914	Rblt. H-5 1374 at Delta 7/27/1927 to 11/18/1927.
1027	Baldwin	11/28/1909	33940	Rblt. H-5 1363 at Hillyard 4/3/1926 to 5/28/1926.
1028	Baldwin	11/28/1909	33941	Rblt. H-5 1367 at Dale Street 11/16/1926 to 4/11/1927.
1029	Baldwin	11/28/1909	33942	Rblt. H-5 1360 at Delta 12/10/1925 to 4/16/1926.
1030	Baldwin	11/30/1909	33943	Rblt. H-5 1495 at Dale Street 4/4/1924 to 6/4/1924.
1031	Baldwin	10/27/1909	33948	Rblt. H-5 1486 at Dale Street, completed 7/8/1921.
1032	Baldwin	10/27/1909	33989	Rblt. H-5 1361 at Hillyard 1/23/1926 to 3/22/1926.

Class E-14 4-6-0: 23½x30-73-210(200)-210,000-155,000-38,580

No.	Builder	Date Rcvd.	C/N	Disposition
1033	Baldwin	8/29/1910	34988	Rblt. H-7 1375 at Dale Street, completed 1/25/1926.
1034	Baldwin	8/29/1910	34989	Rblt. H-7 1379 at Dale Street, completed 7/13/1926.
1035	Baldwin	9/1/1910	34990	Rblt. H-7 1377 at Dale Street, completed 6/12/1926.
1036	Baldwin	9/2/1910	35008	Rblt. H-7 1380 at Dale Street, completed 8/31/1926.
1037	Baldwin	9/2/1910	35009	Rblt. H-7 1383 at Hillyard 9/30/1926 to 1/21/1927.
1038	Baldwin	9/4/1910	35010	Rblt. H-7 1378 at Dale Street, completed 5/14/1926.
1039	Baldwin	9/4/1910	35011	Rblt. H-7 1381 at Dale Street, completed 11/17/1926.
1040	Baldwin	9/4/1910	35012	Rblt. H-7 1376 at Dale Street, completed 3/6/1926.
1041	Baldwin	9/8/1910	35013	Rblt. H-7 1382 at Dale Street, completed 10/23/1926.
1042	Baldwin	9/8/1910	35014	Rblt. H-7 1384 at Hillyard 1/15/1927 to 4/20/1927.
1043	Baldwin	9/11/1910	35055	Sold SP&S (No. 100) 1910. Scrapped 5/1937.
1044	Baldwin	9/11/1910	35056	Sold SP&S (No. 101) 1910. Scrapped 5/1937.
1045	Baldwin	9/14/1910	35057	Sold SP&S (No. 102) 1910. Rblt. 4-6-2 No. 622 at Hillyard 12/1928. Scrapped 6/1953.
1046	Baldwin	9/14/1910	35058	Sold SP&S (No. 103) 1910. Rblt. 4-6-2 No. 620 at Hillyard 11/1927. Scrapped 4/1944.
1047	Baldwin	9/14/1910	35059	Sold SP&S (No. 104) 1910. Rblt. 4-6-2 No. 624 at Hillyard 4/1930. Scrapped 1/1952.
1048	Baldwin	9/14/1910	35096	Sold SP&S (No. 105) 1910. Rblt. 4-6-2 No. 623 at Hillyard 10/1928. Scrapped 7/1953.
1049	Baldwin	9/26/1910	35097	Sold SP&S (No. 106) 1910. Scrapped 5/1937.
1050(2)	Baldwin	10/1/1910	35098	Sold SP&S (No. 107) 1910. Rblt. 4-6-2 No. 621 at Hillyard 12/1927. Scrapped 6/1953.
1051(2)	Baldwin	9/26/1910	35099	Sold SP&S (No. 108) 1910. Scrapped 5/1937.
1052(2)	Baldwin	10/1/1910	35100	Sold SP&S (No. 109) 1910. Rblt. 4-6-2 No. 625 at Hillyard 1/1930. Scrapped 8/1953.

Class E-8 (Old Class 49) 4-6-0: 19x28-73-210(200)-164,000-134,000-23,540

No.	Builder	Date Rcvd.	C/N	Original No.	Renumbered From	Date	Disposition	Notes
1050(1)	Rogers	12/4/1901	5675	–	–	–	Reno. GN 1070 at Great Falls 4/7/1910.	
1051(1)	Rogers	12/9/1901	5676	–	–	–	Reno. GN 1071 at Superior 3/1/1910.	
1052(1)	Rogers	12/9/1901	5677	–	–	–	Reno. GN 1072 at Great Falls 4/1/1910.	
1053	Rogers	12/10/1901	5678	–	–	–	Sold for scrap DI&M 6/4/1947.	
1054	Rogers	12/10/1901	5679	–	–	–	Ret. 3/1930, scrapped 1931.	
1055	Rogers	12/16/1901	5680	–	–	–	Ret. 1/1930. Stripped at Superior 5/27/1932.	
1056	Rogers	12/16/1901	5681	–	–	–	Ret. 5/1928. Stripped at Dale Street 8/15/1932.	
1057	Rogers	12/18/1901	5682	–	–	–	Ret. 5/1928. Stripped at Superior 5/27/1932.	
1058	Rogers	12/22/1901	5683	–	–	–	Ret. 10/1929. Dismantled at Hillyard 11/9/1929.	
1059	Rogers	1/9/1902	5684	–	–	–	Ret. 1/1934. Sold for scrap PC 6/11/1934.	
1060	Rogers	2/28/1904	6068	–	–	–	Ret. 10/15/1930. Sold for scrap DI&M 1932.	
1061	Rogers	2/28/1904	6069	–	–	–	Ret. 4/1931. Stripped at Hillyard 7/6/1932.	
1062	Rogers	3/2/1904	6070	–	–	–	Ret. 1/1934. Sold for scrap PC 6/11/1934.	
1063	Rogers	3/2/1904	6071	–	–	–	Sold for scrap DI&M 8/27/1941.	
1064	Rogers	3/3/1904	6072	–	–	–	Ret. 5/1928. Stripped at Dale Street 7/25/1932. Sold for scrap DI&M 10/1933.	
1065	Rogers	3/4/1904	6073	–	–	–	Ret. 12/16/1929. Sold for scrap DI&M 1932.	
1066	Rogers	3/6/1904	6074	–	–	–	Ret. 1/1934. Sold for scrap PC 4/10/1934.	
1067	Rogers	3/9/1904	6075	–	–	–	Dismantled at Great Falls 5/6/1930.	
1068	Rogers	3/19/1904	6076	–	–	–	Ret. 1/1934. Sold for scrap PC 3/12/1934.	
1069	Rogers	3/31/1905	6077	–	–	–	Ret. 7/1930. Stripped at Superior 5/27/1932.	147
1070	Rogers	12/4/1901	5675	GN 1050(1)	GN 1050(1)	4/7/1910	Ret. 9/20/1929. Sold for scrap DI&M 8/1932.	
1071	Rogers	12/9/1901	5676	GN 1051(1)	GN 1051(1)	3/1/1910	Ret. 5/1928. Stripped at Dale Street 7/16/1932.	
1072	Rogers	12/9/1901	5677	GN 1052(1)	GN 1052(1)	4/1/1910	Ret. 5/1928. Stripped at Superior 5/24/1932.	

Class E-15 4-6-0: 22x28-73-210(185)-177,000-134,000-29,190 originally. Working boiler pressure later increased to 200 psi, increasing T.E. to 31,560 lb.

No.	Builder	Date Rcvd.	C/N	Disposition	Notes
1073	Baldwin	8/1/1910	34898	Ret. 6/1930. Sold for scrap DI&M c.8/1932.	227
1074	Baldwin	8/1/1910	34899	Sold SP&S (No. 160) 6/1925. Ret. 4/1944.	228
1075	Baldwin	8/7/1910	34900	Sold SP&S (No. 161) 6/1925. Ret. 4/1944.	228
1076	Baldwin	8/7/1910	34901	Sold SP&S (No. 162) 6/1925. Ret. 4/1944.	228
1077	Baldwin	8/4/1910	34902	Sold for scrap DI&M 3/18/1929.	
1078	Baldwin	8/4/1910	34904	Sold for scrap PC 8/1947.	229
1079	Baldwin	8/5/1910	34936	Ret. 1/1934. Sold for scrap DI&M 3/12/1934.	
1080	Baldwin	8/5/1910	34937	Ret. 1/1934. Sold for scrap DI&M 5/3/1934.	
1081	Baldwin	8/7/1910	34938	Dismantled at Great Falls 11/30/1927.	

1082	Baldwin	8/7/1910	34939	Sold for scrap DI&M 3/11/1949.
1083	Baldwin	8/13/1910	34940	Ret. 12/1928.
1084	Baldwin	8/13/1910	34959	Ret. 9/1939. Sold for scrap Bethlehem Steel c.10/1939.
1085	Baldwin	8/16/1910	34960	Ret. 8/1/1930. Sold for scrap DI&M 1932.
1086	Baldwin	8/16/1910	34961	Ret. 12/1928.
1087	Baldwin	8/24/1910	34962	Ret. 12/31/1929 at Superior. Dismantled at Superior 8/19/1932.
1088	Baldwin	8/24/1910	34963	Ret. 12/1928.
1089	Baldwin	8/24/1910	34979	Ret. 9/1941. Sold for scrap DI&M 10/14/1941.
1090	Baldwin	8/24/1910	34980	Sold for scrap DI&M 11/1949.
1091	Baldwin	9/1/1910	34981	Ret. 3/31/1930 at Great Falls. Usable parts removed at Great Falls 5/19/1931.
1092	Baldwin	9/4/1910	35023	Ret. 11/2/1929. Sold for scrap DI&M 1932.

Class F-4(2) 2-8-0: 19x24-47-180(170)-135,000-113,300-26,640

No.	Builder	Date Built	C/N	Original No.	Renumbered From	Date	Disposition	Notes
1094	Baldwin	8/1896	15013	RM 9	SF&N 9	6/9/1908	Sold McGoldrick Lumber Co. 7/1925.	2

Class F-4(1) (Old Class 52) 2-8-0: 22 and 33x32-55-210-194,000-179,000-69,599 (Crossover Compound) originally. Converted to 20x32-55-210-194,000-179,000-41,540 and moved to Class F-5.

No.	Builder	Date Rcvd.	C/N	Original No.	Renumbered From	Date	Disposition	Notes
1095	Rogers	11/26/1901	5670	GN 1160(1)	GN 1195(1)	1903	Rblt. C-5 871(2), completed 12/4/1930.	148
1096	Rogers	11/26/1901	5671	GN 1161(1)	GN 1196(1)	1903	Ret. 12/1930. Sold for scrap DI&M 10/7/1932.	148
1097	Rogers	11/27/1901	5672	GN 1162(1)	GN 1197(1)	3/16/1903	Rblt. C-5 872 10/23/1930 to 12/19/1930.	148
1098	Rogers	12/1/1901	5673	GN 1163(1)	GN 1198(1)	3/16/1903	Sold for scrap DI&M 1/31/1947.	148
1099	Rogers	12/4/1901	5674	GN 1164(1)	GN 1199(1)	3/26/1903	Ret. 1/1938.	148, 149

Class F-5 (Old Class 50) 2-8-0: 20x32-55-210-194,000-179,000-41,540 originally. Those locomotives indicated below by an asterisk (*) were later equipped with superheaters and piston valves (dates shown below), had dimensions changed to 23½x32-55-210(175)-194,000-179,000-47,790, and were classified by GN as "F-5S". Working boiler pressure of F-5S engines later increased to 210 psi, increasing T.E. to 57,350 lb.

No.	Builder	Date Rcvd.	C/N	Disposition	Notes
1100*	Rogers	10/2/1901	5655	Superheated at Delta 5/1922. Ret. 12/1949. Sold for scrap PC 1/31/1950.	
1101*	Rogers	9/30/1901	5656	Superheated at Delta 2/1922. Ret. 12/1938.	
1102*	Rogers	10/2/1901	5657	Superheated at Delta 8/12/1921. Sold City of Prineville Railway (No. 6), delivered at Bend, OR, 7/7/1945. Scrapped by California Bag & Metal Company 10/1955.	
1103*	Rogers	10/2/1901	5658	Superheated at Delta 9/23/1921. Badly damaged in wreck at Grand Forks, BC, 6/2/1948. Sold for scrap PC 10/4/1948.	150
1104*	Rogers	10/8/1901	5659	Superheated at Delta 11/30/1921. Sold for scrap DI&M 5/1937.	
1105	Rogers	10/14/1901	5660	Sold for scrap PC 3/14/1947.	
1106	Rogers	10/15/1901	5661	Sold for scrap DI&M 5/6/1948.	
1107	Rogers	10/17/1901	5662	Ret. 12/1949. Sold for scrap PC 1/31/1950.	
1108	Rogers	10/20/1901	5663	Rblt. C-5 873 10/31/1930 to 12/31/1930.	
1109	Rogers	10/20/1901	5664	Rblt. C-5 870(2), completed 11/16/1929.	

Class F-6 (Old Class 50B) 2-8-0: 20x32-55-210-195,500-178,100-41,540 originally. Those locomotives indicated below by an asterisk (*) received superheaters (dates shown below if known) and were classified by GN as "F-6S". When the locomotives were superheated, No. 1116 had dimensions changed to 21x32-55-210(200)-195,500-178,100-43,620, while the other superheated locomotives had dimensions changed to 23½x32-55-210(165)-195,500-178,100-45,060.

No.	Builder	Date Rcvd.	C/N	Disposition	Notes
1110*	Brooks	12/6/1901	4042	Superheated at Dale Street 4/30/1912. Rblt. C-2 862 at Dale Street, completed 5/6/1927.	
1111*	Brooks	12/6/1901	4043	Rblt. C-2 864 at Dale Street, completed 11/5/1927.	
1112*	Brooks	12/7/1901	4044	Rblt. C-2 865 at Dale Street, completed 12/23/1927.	
1113*	Brooks	12/7/1901	4045	Rblt. C-2 853 at Dale Street, completed 10/19/1925.	129
1114*	Brooks	12/9/1901	4046	Rblt. C-2 854 at Dale Street, completed 10/9/1925.	
1115	Brooks	12/9/1901	4047	Rblt. C-2 850 at Dale Street, completed 5/29/1925.	
1116*	Brooks	12/10/1901	4048	Superheated at Dale Street 2/1922. Rblt. C-2 859 at Dale Street, completed 9/10/1926.	
1117*	Brooks	12/10/1901	4049	Rblt. C-2 867 at Dale Street, completed 6/8/1928.	
1118	Brooks	12/13/1901	4050	Rblt. C-2 851 at Dale Street, completed 5/8/1925.	
1119*	Brooks	12/13/1901	4051	Superheated at Dale Street 4/23/1915. Rblt. C-2 861 at Dale Street, completed 2/14/1927.	
1120*	Brooks	12/15/1901	4052	Rblt. C-2 866 at Dale Street, completed 3/15/1928.	
1121	Brooks	12/15/1901	4053	Rblt. C-2 857 at Dale Street, completed 9/30/1926.	
1122*	Brooks	12/15/1901	4054	Superheated at Dale Street 4/30/1912. Rblt. C-2 855 at Dale Street, completed 3/9/1926.	
1123*	Brooks	12/15/1901	4055	Superheated at Dale Street 5/7/1911. Rblt. C-2 863 at Dale Street, completed 6/30/1927.	
1124*	Brooks	12/22/1901	4056	Superheated at Dale Street 6/29/1914. Rblt. C-2 856 at Dale Street, completed 6/26/1926.	
1125	Brooks	12/22/1901	4057	Rblt. C-2 858 at Dale Street, completed 7/28/1926.	130
1126	Brooks	12/24/1901	4058	Rblt. C-2 852 at Dale Street, completed 10/30/1925.	128
1127*	Brooks	12/24/1901	4059	Rblt. C-2 869 at Dale Street, completed 10/20/1928.	
1128*	Brooks	12/24/1901	4060	Superheated at Dale Street 4/17/1912. Rblt. C-2 860 at Dale Street, completed 11/24/1926.	
1129*	Brooks	12/24/1901	4061	Superheated at Dale Street 9/11/1912. Rblt. C-2 868 at Dale Street, completed 7/31/1928.	

Class F-7 (Old Class 50A) 2-8-0: 20x32-55-210-194,000-174,000-41,540 originally. Those locomotives indicated below by an asterisk (*) were equipped with superheaters and piston valves (dates shown if known), had dimensions changed to 23½x32-55-210(165)-194,000-174,000-45,063 and were classified by GN as "F-7S".

No.	Builder	Date Rcvd.	C/N	Disposition
1130*	Cooke	12/6/1901	2736	Superheated at Dale Street 1/31/1914. Donated to American Korean Foundation for Korean National Railways 10/1954.
1131*	Cooke	12/6/1901	2737	Superheated at Dale Street 7/13/1914. Sold for scrap PC 9/14/1952.
1132*	Cooke	12/15/1901	2738	Superheated at Dale Street 1/9/1914. Sold for scrap DI&M 5/16/1947.
1133*	Cooke	12/15/1901	2739	Ret. 5/1939.
1134	Cooke	12/22/1901	2740	Ret. 5/1939.
1135	Cooke	12/22/1901	2741	Sold for scrap DI&M 10/22/1951.
1136*	Cooke	12/22/1901	2742	Superheated at Dale Street 11/30/1913. Sold for scrap PC 9/3/1952.
1137	Cooke	12/22/1901	2743	Sold for scrap PC 10/22/1951.
1138*	Cooke	12/31/1901	2744	Superheated at Dale Street 11/8/1913. Sold for scrap PC 8/1953.
1139	Cooke	12/31/1901	2745	Sold for scrap PC 12/1941.

Class F-8 (Old Classes 51, 51A) 2-8-0: 20x32-55-210-195,000-180,000-41,540 originally. A diagram found with the original ordering information for GN 1150-1154 indicates that these locomotives were in Old Class 51. It is likely that the locomotives received in 1902 comprised Old Class 51A. Those locomotives indicated below by an asterisk (*) received superheaters and piston valves (dates shown below if known) and were classified by GN as "F-8S". Superheated locomotives Nos. 1141, 1143, 1148, 1163, 1175, 1182, 1183, 1189, 1190, 1195, and 1196 (which were apparently superheated before 6/1911) had dimensions changed to 26x32-55-210(165)-195,000-180,000-45,060. By 1926, all superheated locomotives then had dimensions changed to 23½x32-55-210(165)-195,000-180,000-45,060 (it is quite possible that locomotives superheated after 6/1911 were rebuilt directly to these dimensions). As a result of engine reweighing, weights of oil burners changed to 207,680 lb. (192,000 on drivers); weights of coal burners changed to 211,460 lb. (195,000 on drivers).

No.	Builder	Date Rcvd.	C/N	Disposition	Notes
1140	Rogers	8/24/1902	5789	Ret. 2/16/1932. Sold for scrap DI&M 1932.	
1141*	Rogers	8/24/1902	5790	Sold for scrap DI&M 6/1951.	
1142	Rogers	8/27/1902	5791	Ret. 7/1952. Sold for scrap DI&M 8/28/1952.	
1143*	Rogers	8/27/1902	5792	Ret. 5/1939.	
1144	Rogers	8/31/1902	5793	Ret. 7/1952. Sold for scrap DI&M 8/28/1952.	
1145	Rogers	9/1/1902	5794	Ret. 1/1938.	151
1146*	Rogers	9/4/1902	5795	Superheated at Dale Street 1/7/1913. Sold for scrap DI&M 8/28/1952.	
1147*	Rogers	9/9/1902	5796	Superheated at Dale Street 12/31/1912. Donated Wenatchee Park Board 5/19/1956, and placed on exhibition in City Park, Wenatchee, WA 6/2/1956.	
1148*	Rogers	9/9/1902	5797	Sold for scrap DI&M 10/10/1952.	
1149	Rogers	9/10/1902	5798	Sold for scrap PC 3/22/1948.	
1150	Rogers	10/29/1901	5665	Ret. 12/1949. Sold for scrap PC c.1/1950.	
1151	Rogers	10/29/1901	5666	Ret. 10/1936, sold for scrap PC.	
1152	Rogers	11/1/1901	5667	Sold for scrap WEI&M 9/10/1952.	
1153	Rogers	11/16/1901	5668	Ret. 12/1949. Sold for scrap DI&M c.1/1950.	
1154*	Rogers	11/9/1901	5669	Superheated at Delta 10/1921. Sold for scrap DI&M 2/10/1947.	
1155*	Rogers	9/16/1902	5799	Superheated at Dale Street 4/21/1913. Ret. 4/1937, sold for scrap.	
1156	Rogers	9/16/1902	5800	Sold for scrap DI&M 3/20/1948.	
1157	Rogers	9/16/1902	5801	Rebuilt to C-4 785 at Hillyard, completed 12/31/1929.	
1158	Rogers	9/20/1902	5802	Sold for scrap PC 2/7/1947.	
1159	Rogers	9/23/1902	5803	Sold for scrap WEI&M 9/1949.	
1160(2)	Rogers	9/25/1902	5804	Ret. 1939.	
1161(2)	Rogers	9/26/1902	5805	Ret. 9/1941. Sold for scrap PC 10/14/1941.	
1162(2)	Rogers	9/28/1902	5806	Rebuilt to C-4 786 at Dale Street, completed 2/19/1930.	
1163(2)*	Rogers	10/2/1902	5807	Sold for scrap PC 1/15/1955.	
1164(2)*	Rogers	10/4/1902	5808	Superheated at Dale Street 9/16/1912. Ret. 5/1939.	
1165*	Rogers	11/7/1902	5831	Superheated at Dale Street 2/19/1912. Sold for scrap DI&M 5/3/1952.	
1166*	Rogers	11/10/1902	5832	Rebuilt to C-4 871(1), completed at Dale Street 11/16/1928.	
1167	Rogers	12/10/1902	5849	Ret. 6/1931. Stripped at Hillyard 7/6/1932.	
1168*	Rogers	12/12/1902	5850	Superheated at Dale Street 5/25/1912. Sold for scrap WEI&M 10/16/1952.	
1169	Rogers	12/19/1902	5851	Scrapped 10/1940.	
1170*	Rogers	9/27/1903	6028	Superheated at Dale Street 5/28/1915. Sold for scrap PC 9/8/1952.	
1171*	Rogers	9/27/1903	6029	Superheated at Dale Street 7/26/1912. Sold for scrap WEI&M 3/29/1952.	
1172	Rogers	9/28/1903	6030	Sold for scrap DI&M 12/7/1951.	
1173	Rogers	9/28/1903	6031	Sold for scrap PC 4/30/1953.	
1174*	Rogers	9/20/1903	6032	Superheated 6/19/1912. Rebuilt to C-4 782 at Dale Street, completed 3/7/1930.	
1175*	Rogers	10/1/1903	6033	Rebuilt to C-4 783 at Dale Street, completed 10/25/1929.	
1176*	Rogers	10/1/1903	6034	Superheated at Dale Street 3/29/1912. Sold for scrap DI&M 4/15/1947.	
1177*	Rogers	10/6/1903	6035	Superheated at Dale Street 6/21/1912. Sold for scrap DI&M 5/16/1953.	
1178*	Rogers	10/6/1903	6036	Superheated at Hillyard 10/20/1913. Sold for scrap PC 4/15/1947.	
1179*	Rogers	10/13/1903	6037	Superheated at Dale Street 5/9/1912. Sold for scrap PC 2/22/1949.	
1180*	Rogers	10/10/1903	6038	Superheated at Dale Street 6/24/1915. Sold for scrap DI&M 2/11/1947.	
1181	Rogers	10/13/1903	6039	Received piston valves prior to 1926. Sold for scrap PC 1/31/1947.	
1182*	Rogers	10/15/1903	6040	Sold SP&S (No. 369) 10/1944. Scrapped 2/1950.	
1183*	Rogers	10/15/1903	6041	Sold for scrap PC 1/21/1955.	
1184	Rogers	11/2/1903	6042	Sold for scrap PC 5/16/1947.	
1185	Rogers	11/3/1903	6043	Received piston valves at Dale Street 7/1917. Ret. 10/1936. Sold for scrap DI&M 1/30/1937.	
1186*	Rogers	11/3/1903	6044	Superheated 3/8/1912. Sold for scrap DI&M 2/10/1947.	
1187*	Rogers	11/6/1903	6045	Superheated at Dale Street 4/23/1912. Sold for scrap WEI&M 3/17/1949.	
1188	Rogers	11/8/1903	6046	Sold for scrap DI&M 3/25/1949.	
1189*	Rogers	11/8/1903	6047	Sold for scrap DI&M 6/1951.	

No.	Builder	Date Rcvd.	C/N	Disposition	
1190*	Rogers	11/13/1903	6058	Sold for scrap PC 1/15/1955.	
1191	Rogers	11/20/1903	6059	Rebuilt to C-4 784 at Superior, completed 10/26/1929.	
1192*	Rogers	11/20/1903	6060	Superheated at Dale Street 3/15/1915. Sold for scrap DI&M 1/8/1955.	
1193*	Rogers	11/29/1903	6061	Superheated at Dale Street 3/11/1912. Sold for scrap PC 1/21/1955.	
1194	Rogers	11/29/1903	6062	Rebuilt to C-4 788, completed at Dale Street 6/30/1937.	
1195(2)*	Rogers	12/14/1903	6063	Sold for scrap DI&M 7/31/1953.	
1196(2)*	Rogers	12/18/1903	6064	Sold for scrap DI&M 1/15/1955.	
1197(2)	Rogers	12/25/1903	6065	Sold for scrap PC 9/21/1952.	
1198(2)	Rogers	12/25/1903	6066	Rebuilt to C-4 789, completed at Dale Street 8/11/1937.	
1199(2)	Rogers	12/31/1903	6067	Ret. 10/1936, sold for scrap PC.	
1200	Alco-Rogers	9/13/1905	38879	Ret. 1/1938.	151
1201	Alco-Rogers	9/13/1905	38880	Ret. 5/1939.	
1202	Alco-Rogers	9/17/1905	38881	Sold for scrap WEI&M 5/13/1953.	
1203	Alco-Rogers	9/24/1905	38882	Sold for scrap PC 5/5/1947.	
1204	Alco-Rogers	9/24/1905	38883	Sold for scrap PC 3/1941.	
1205	Alco-Rogers	9/21/1905	38884	Ret. 1/1938.	151
1206	Alco-Rogers	9/21/1905	38885	Ret. 12/1949. Sold for scrap PC c.1/1950.	
1207	Alco-Rogers	9/21/1905	38886	Ret. 12/1938.	152
1208	Alco-Rogers	10/6/1905	38887	Sold to SP&S (No. 365) 6/1925. Scrapped 3/1952.	
1209	Alco-Rogers	10/6/1905	38888	Sold for scrap PC 11/1949.	
1210	Alco-Rogers	10/6/1905	38889	Ret. 12/1949. Sold for scrap WEI&M c.1/1950.	
1211	Alco-Rogers	10/6/1905	38890	Stripped at Dale Street 3/10/1932.	151
1212	Alco-Rogers	10/7/1905	38891	Sold for scrap PC 12/1941.	
1213	Alco-Rogers	10/19/1905	38892	Sold to Lake Superior Terminal and Transfer Co. 6/1930. Converted to 0-8-0 at Superior 8/23/1930 and reno. LST&T 19.	
1214	Alco-Rogers	10/8/1905	38893	Ret. 1/1938.	151

Class F-8 2-8-0: 20x32-55-210-195,000-180,000-41,540 originally. Those locomotives indicated below by an asterisk (*) later received piston valves and superheaters and were classified by GN as "F-8S". Superheated locomotives' dimensions were 23½x32-55-210(165)-195,000-180,000-45,060. As a result of engine reweighing, weights of oil burners changed to 207,680 lb. (192,000 on drivers); weights of coal burners changed to 211,460 lb. (195,000 on drivers).

No.	Builder	Date Rcvd.	C/N	Disposition
1215	Baldwin	11/23/1907	32134	Rebuilt to C-4 787, completed at Dale Street 3/4/1937.
1216	Baldwin	11/23/1907	32135	Sold for scrap DI&M 10/22/1951.
1217	Baldwin	12/3/1907	32136	Scrapped 1937.
1218	Baldwin	12/3/1907	32137	Ret. 1949. Sold for scrap WEI&M c.1/1950.
1219	Baldwin	12/3/1907	32148	Sold for scrap DI&M 2/25/1947.
1220*	Baldwin	12/3/1907	32149	Superheated at Superior 10/17/1921. Sold for scrap PC 10/26/1951.
1221	Baldwin	12/3/1907	32155	Sold for scrap PC 3/29/1952.
1222	Baldwin	12/3/1907	32156	Sold for scrap DI&M 9/1/1952.
1223*	Baldwin	12/3/1907	32157	Ret. 9/1939. Sold for scrap Bethlehem Steel c.10/1939.
1224	Baldwin	12/3/1907	32158	Sold for scrap DI&M 6/1947.
1225	Baldwin	12/3/1907	32159	Ret. 9/1939. Sold for scrap Bethlehem Steel c.10/1939.
1226	Baldwin	12/3/1907	32183	Sold for scrap PC 1/25/1947.
1227	Baldwin	12/6/1907	32184	Sold for scrap WEI&M 1949.
1228	Baldwin	12/6/1907	32191	Sold to SP&S (No. 366) 10/1936. Scrapped 3/1953.
1229	Baldwin	12/6/1907	32192	Ret. 9/1939. Sold for scrap Bethlehem Steel c.10/1939.
1230	Baldwin	12/6/1907	32193	Sold for scrap WEI&M 1/22/1955.
1231	Baldwin	12/9/1907	32212	Sold for scrap PC 1/8/1955.
1232	Baldwin	12/9/1907	32213	Sold for scrap DI&M 12/1941.
1233	Baldwin	12/20/1907	32214	Sold for scrap WEI&M 1/15/1955.
1234	Baldwin	12/20/1907	32215	Rebuilt to C-4 790, completed at Dale Street 9/30/1937.
1235	Baldwin	12/10/1907	32238	Sold for scrap DI&M c.2/1941.
1236	Baldwin	12/10/1907	32239	Sold for scrap PC 5/1951.
1237	Baldwin	12/17/1907	32240	Sold for scrap PC c.2/1941.
1238	Baldwin	12/17/1907	32241	Sold for scrap DI&M c.2/1941.
1239	Baldwin	12/17/1907	32242	Sold for scrap DI&M 1/25/1947.
1240	Baldwin	12/17/1907	32243	Sold SP&S (No. 367) 10/1936. Scrapped 3/1954.
1241	Baldwin	12/18/1907	32244	Sold for scrap DI&M 10/14/1941.
1242	Baldwin	12/18/1907	32245	Ret. 10/1936. Sold for scrap DI&M 1/30/1937.
1243	Baldwin	12/21/1907	32266	Sold for scrap DI&M 8/27/1952.
1244	Baldwin	12/21/1907	32291	Reno. Somers Lumber Co. No. S5 1934. Sold for scrap PC 5/4/1951.
1245	Baldwin	12/21/1907	32295	Sold for scrap WEI&M 9/14/1952.
1246	Baldwin	12/21/1907	32297	Donated to Seattle Board of Park Commissioners 7/1953. Placed on exhibition in Woodland Park, Seattle, WA, 7/18/1953. Removed to Merrill, OR, date unknown, status uncertain.
1247	Baldwin	12/21/1907	32299	Sold for scrap DI&M 9/29/1940.
1248	Baldwin	12/21/1907	32302	Sold for scrap Dulien Steel Products 9/1940.
1249	Baldwin	12/27/1907	32314	Sold for scrap Dulien Steel Products 9/1940.
1250	Baldwin	12/27/1907	32332	Ret. 1949. Sold for scrap PC c.1/1950.
1251	Baldwin	1/1/1908	32333	Ret. 12/1949. Sold for scrap Union Scrap Iron & Metal Co. 1/31/1950.
1252	Baldwin	1/1/1908	32353	Sold for scrap PC 1/31/1947.
1253	Baldwin	1/3/1908	32362	Sold SP&S (No. 368) 10/1936. Scrapped 3/1954.

Class F-8 2-8-0: Continued

No.	Builder	Date Rcvd.	C/N	Disposition
1254	Baldwin	1/3/1908	32363	Rebuilt to M-2(1) 1254 at Dale Street, completed 1/15/1910. Renumbered GN 2000(1) 1/18/1910 at Dale Street Shops(?). Renumbered GN 1999 at Superior Roundhouse 4/12/1912. Rebuilt to C-4 870(1) at Dale Street, completed 2/13/1926.
1255	Baldwin	1/5/1908	32391	Sold SP&S (No. 362) 1909. Scrapped 2/1953.
1256	Baldwin	1/5/1908	32392	Sold SP&S (No. 355) 1909. Scrapped 9/1952.
1257	Baldwin	1/11/1908	32413	Sold SP&S (No. 360) 1909. Scrapped 11/1952.
1258	Baldwin	1/11/1908	32425	Sold SP&S (No. 358) 1909. Scrapped 9/1953.
1259	Baldwin	1/17/1908	32426	Sold SP&S (No. 359) 1909. Scrapped 5/1952.
1260	Baldwin	1/17/1908	32464	Sold SP&S (No. 356) 1909. Scrapped 3/1954.
1261	Baldwin	1/17/1908	32478	Sold SP&S (No. 357) 1909. Scrapped 8/1951.
1262	Baldwin	1/17/1908	32479	Sold SP&S (No. 361) 1909. Scrapped 8/1952
1263	Baldwin	1/30/1908	32485	Sold SP&S (No. 364) 1909. Scrapped 10/1952.
1264	Baldwin	1/30/1908	32519	Sold SP&S (No. 363) 1909. Scrapped 4/1953.

Old Class 52 2-8-0: 22 and 33x32(Crossover Compound)-55-210-194,000-179,000-69,599

No.	Builder	Date Rcvd.	C/N	Original No.	Renumbered From	Date	Disposition	Notes
1160(1)	Rogers	11/26/1901	5670	–	–	–	Reno. GN 1195(1) 4/30/1902.	148
1161(1)	Rogers	11/26/1901	5671	–	–	–	Reno. GN 1196(1) 4/22/1902.	148
1162(1)	Rogers	11/27/1901	5672	–	–	–	Reno. GN 1197(1) 4/23/1902.	148
1163(1)	Rogers	12/1/1901	5673	–	–	–	Reno. GN 1198(1) 4/22/1902.	148
1164(1)	Rogers	12/4/1901	5674	–	–	–	Reno. GN 1199(1) 4/22/1902.	148
–								
1195(1)	Rogers	11/26/1901	5670	GN 1160(1)	GN 1160(1)	4/30/1902	Reno. GN 1095 1903.	148
1196(1)	Rogers	11/26/1901	5671	GN 1161(1)	GN 1161(1)	4/22/1902	Reno. GN 1096 1903.	148
1197(1)	Rogers	11/27/1901	5672	GN 1162(1)	GN 1162(1)	4/23/1902	Reno. GN 1097 at Hillyard 3/16/1903.	148
1198(1)	Rogers	12/1/1901	5673	GN 1163(1)	GN 1163(1)	4/22/1902	Reno. GN 1098 at Hillyard 3/16/1903.	148
1199(1)	Rogers	12/4/1901	5674	GN 1164(1)	GN 1164(1)	4/22/1902	Reno. GN 1099 at Hillyard 3/26/1903.	148

Class M-2(1) 2-6-8-0: 20x32-33x32-55-210(200)-350,000-330,000-62,220 (Rebuilt from Class F-8 2-8-0)

No.	Builder	Date Completed	C/N	Original No.	Rblt. From F-8 No.	Disposition
1254	GN (Dale Street)	1/15/1910	32363	GN 1254	GN 1254	Reno. GN 2000(1) at Dale Street Shops(?) 1/18/1910.

Class F-9 (Old Class 51B) 2-8-0: 20x32-55-210-196,000-180,000-41,540 originally. Those locomotives indicated below by an asterisk (*) received superheaters and were classified by GN as "F-9S". Nos. 1311 and 1312 had dimensions changed to 21x32-55-210(165)-196,000-180,000-35,985. Other superheated engines had dimensions changed to 23½x32-55-210(165)-196,000-180,000-45,060.

No.	Builder	Date Rcvd.	C/N	Disposition	Notes
1300*	Alco-Brooks	7/14/1903	27896	Superheated at Hillyard 3/1923. Rblt. C-3S 891 at Great Falls, completed 11/21/1927.	
1301	Alco-Brooks	7/14/1903	27897	Rblt. C-3 896 at Hillyard, completed 6/25/1928.	
1302*	Alco-Brooks	7/16/1903	27898	Superheated at Hillyard 6/1923. Rblt. C-3S 889 at Hillyard, completed 9/24/1927.	
1303*	Alco-Brooks	7/16/1903	27899	Superheated 11/1923. Rblt. C-3S 887 at Hillyard, completed 8/5/1927.	
1304*	Alco-Brooks	7/16/1903	27900	Superheated at Hillyard 1/1923. Rblt. C-3S 895 at Great Falls, completed 2/25/1928.	
1305	Alco-Brooks	7/16/1903	27901	Rblt. C-3 881 at Hillyard, completed 4/20/1926.	
1306	Alco-Brooks	7/20/1903	27902	Rblt. C-3 888 at Hillyard, completed 8/4/1927.	
1307*	Alco-Brooks	7/20/1903	27903	Superheated at Hillyard 5/24/1915. Rblt. C-3S 885 at Hillyard, completed 6/28/1927.	
1308	Alco-Brooks	7/20/1903	27904	Rblt. C-3 899 at Hillyard, completed 12/7/1926.	136
1309	Alco-Brooks	7/20/1903	27905	Rblt. C-3 877 at Hillyard, completed 4/25/1925.	
1310*	Alco-Brooks	7/22/1903	27906	Superheated at Hillyard 4/1923. Rblt. C-3S 892 at Hillyard, completed 12/23/1927.	
1311*	Alco-Brooks	7/22/1903	27907	Superheated 4/1922. Rblt. C-3S 882 at Great Falls, completed 4/22/1926.	
1312*	Alco-Brooks	7/22/1903	27908	Superheated at Hillyard 2/1922. Rblt. C-3S 883(1) at Hillyard, completed 7/31/1926.	
1313	Alco-Brooks	7/22/1903	27909	Rblt. C-3 875, completed 3/1925.	
1314*	Alco-Brooks	7/24/1903	27910	Superheated 8/1921. Rblt. C-3S 894 at Hillyard, completed 2/27/1928.	
1315	Alco-Brooks	7/24/1903	27911	Rblt. C-3 879 at Hillyard, completed 2/17/1926.	
1316*	Alco-Brooks	7/26/1903	27912	Superheated at Hillyard 6/30/1915. Rblt. C-3S 886 at Hillyard, completed 7/8/1927.	
1317	Alco-Brooks	7/26/1903	27913	Rblt. C-3 897 at Hillyard, completed 3/26/1928.	
1318	Alco-Brooks	7/26/1903	27914	Rblt. C-3 876 at Hillyard, completed 4/1925.	
1319	Alco-Brooks	7/26/1903	27915	Rblt. C-3 878 at Hillyard, completed 9/12/1925.	
1320*	Alco-Brooks	7/26/1903	27916	Superheated at Hillyard 9/1923. Rblt. C-3S 890 at Hillyard, completed 10/28/1927.	
1321	Alco-Brooks	7/27/1903	27917	Rblt. C-3 880 at Hillyard, completed 10/30/1925.	
1322	Alco-Brooks	7/27/1903	27918	Rblt. C-3 898 at Hillyard, completed 8/31/1928.	
1323*	Alco-Brooks	7/27/1903	27919	Superheated 2/1924. Rblt. C-3S 893 at Great Falls, completed 1/13/1928.	
1324	Alco-Brooks	7/27/1903	27920	Rblt. C-3 884 at Hillyard, completed 9/15/1926.	

Class F-12 2-8-0: 21x28-52-200-186,000-167,000-41,160

No.	Builder	Date Built	C/N	Original No.	Renumbered From	Date	Disposition	Notes
1326	Alco-Brooks	11/1907	44334	BA&P 26	BA&P 26	5/24/1917	Sold for scrap PC 7/1948.	153
1327	Alco-Brooks	11/1907	44335	BA&P 27	BA&P 27	3/17/1917	Sold for scrap DI&M 4/30/1947.	153

Class H-5 4-6-2: 23½x30-73-210(200)-271,800-164,000 (weights varied)-38,580 originally. Working boiler pressure later increased to 210 psi, increasing T.E. to 40,510 lb. Locomotive Nos. 1352, 1353, 1355, 1362, 1363, and 1368 had boosters (11,000 lb. T.E.) mounted on trailing trucks. As a result of reweighing, oil burner weights increased to 279,000 lb. (176,000 on drivers) and coal burners increased to 289,840 lb. (180,000 on drivers). (Rebuilt from Class E-14 4-6-0)

No.	Builder	Date Start Rbld.	Date Finish Rbld	C/N	Rblt. From E-14 No.	Renumbered From	Date	Disposition
1350	GN (Dale Street)		7/8/1921	33948	GN 1031	GN 1486	2/10/1926	Sold for scrap WEI&M 7/28/1953.
1351	GN (Dale Street)	8/25/1921	1/11/1922	33887	GN 1018	GN 1487	2/24/1926	Wrecked at New Westminster, BC, 7/24/1941, dismantled 10/1941.
1352	GN (Dale Street)	7/5/1921	10/6/1921	33907	GN 1019	GN 1488	3/3/1926	Booster removed at Dale Street 5/31/1929. Sold for scrap PC 8/29/1953.
1353	GN (Dale Street)	8/3/1921	11/14/1921	33913	GN 1025	GN 1489	2/12/1926	Booster removed at Dale Street 6/1/1929. Sold for scrap DI&M 8/29/1953.
1354	GN (Dale Street)	12/5/1921	3/20/1922	33910	GN 1022	GN 1490	2/8/1926	Sold for scrap PC 4/26/1952.
1355	GN (Dale Street)	2/19/1924	5/29/1924	33908	GN 1020	GN 1494	4/10/1926	Booster removed at Dale Street 5/29/1929. Donated Sioux City, IA, 6/6/1955. Placed on public exhibition, Municipal Auditorium, Sioux City, IA, 7/14/1955.
1356	GN (Dale Street)	4/25/1922	3/26/1923	33885	GN 1016	GN 1492	2/8/1926	Sold for scrap DI&M 4/26/1952.
1357	GN (Dale Street)	12/6/1924	1/26/1925	33912	GN 1024	GN 1493	2/10/1926	Sold for scrap PC 5/2/1952.
1358	GN (Dale Street)		12/30/1922	33911	GN 1023	GN 1491	2/24/1926	Ret. 11/1949. Sold for scrap PC 10/1950.
1359	GN (Dale Street)	4/4/1924	6/4/1924	33943	GN 1030	GN 1495	2/10/1926	Sold for scrap WEI&M 8/25/1955.
1360	GN (Delta)	12/10/1925	4/16/1926	33942	GN 1029	–	–	Sold for scrap PC 8/1953.
1361	GN (Hillyard)	1/23/1926	3/22/1926	33989	GN 1032	–	–	Sold for scrap PC 6/6/1953.
1362	GN (Hillyard)	3/13/1926	5/8/1926	33842	GN 1010	–	–	Booster applied at Hillyard 5/6/1926, removed 11/1932. Sold for scrap DI&M 11/13/1951.
1363	GN (Hillyard)	4/3/1926	5/28/1926	33940	GN 1027	–	–	Booster applied at Hillyard 5/31/1926, removed 7/1930. Sold for scrap DI&M 8/1953.
1364	GN (Delta)	4/24/1926	6/15/1926	33840	GN 1008	–	–	Sold for scrap PC 10/23/1952.
1365	GN (Dale Street)		12/23/1926	33844	GN 1012	–	–	Sold for scrap DI&M 5/1/1952.
1366	GN (Dale Street)	10/28/1926	2/9/1927	33909	GN 1021	–	–	Sold for scrap DI&M 1/21/1955.
1367	GN (Dale Street)	11/16/1926	4/11/1927	33941	GN 1028	–	–	Sold for scrap DI&M 6/8/1951.
1368	GN (Dale Street)	3/31/1927	6/17/1927	33845	GN 1013	–	–	Booster applied at Dale Street 4/7/1928, removed 4/1931. Sold for scrap PC 4/22/1952.
1369	GN (Delta)	11/12/1926	1/24/1927	33883	GN 1014	–	–	Sold for scrap WEI&M 5/17/1955.
1370	GN (Delta)	1/26/1927	4/29/1927	33843	GN 1011	–	–	Sold for scrap DI&M 9/27/1952.
1371	GN (Hillyard)	2/19/1927	5/31/1927	33884	GN 1015	–	–	Sold for scrap WEI&M 9/1955.
1372	GN (Delta)	4/8/1927	7/9/1927	33886	GN 1017	–	–	Sold for scrap DI&M 5/13/1953.
1373	GN (Hillyard)	6/4/1927	8/9/1927	33841	GN 1009	–	–	Sold for scrap DI&M 1/15/1955.
1374	GN (Delta)	7/27/1927	11/18/1927	33914	GN 1026	–	–	Sold for scrap PC 10/10/1952.

Class H-7 4-6-2: 23½x30-73-210(200)-289,400-166,500 (weights varied)-38,580 originally. Nos. 1375, 1376, 1382, 1383, and 1384 equipped with boosters which had 11,000 lb. T.E. when built. Other locomotives equipped with boosters on dates indicated. Working boiler pressure later increased to 210 psi, raising T.E. 40,510 lb. Boosters removed on dates shown below. As a result of reweighing, weight of engines with boosters increased to 294,520 lb., and those without boosters increased to 288,520 lb. Reweighing showed the weight on drivers to be 250,000 lb., but diagrams were changed to show 189,000 lb. (Rebuilt from Class E-14 4-6-0)

No.	Builder	Date Start Rbld.	Date Finish Rbld	C/N	Rblt. From E-14 No.	Disposition	Notes
1375	GN (Dale Street)		1/25/1926	34988	GN 1033	Booster removed at Jackson Street 8/1949. Ret. 8/1955. Sold for scrap PC 11/4/1955.	
1376	GN (Dale Street)		3/6/1926	35012	GN 1040	Booster removed at Grand Forks 12/30/1951. Ret. 8/1955. Sold for scrap DI&M 10/10/1955.	
1377	GN (Dale Street)		6/12/1926	34990	GN 1035	Booster applied 2/1930, removed at Grand Forks 11/1949. Sold for scrap PC 1/21/1955.	
1378	GN (Dale Street)		5/14/1926	35010	GN 1038	Booster applied 5/1930. Sold SP&S (No. 626) 10/1944. Scrapped 9/1953.	154
1379	GN (Dale Street)		7/13/1926	34989	GN 1034	Booster applied 6/1930, removed 12/1946. Sold for scrap 4/28/1947.	
1380	GN (Dale Street)		8/31/1926	35008	GN 1036	Booster applied 4/1930, removed at Jackson Street 8/1949. Ret. 4/1955. Sold for scrap WEI&M 6/4/1955.	
1381	GN (Dale Street)		11/17/1926	35011	GN 1039	Booster applied 6/1930, removed at Superior 8/1949. Sold for scrap DI&M 2/5/1955.	
1382	GN (Dale Street)		10/23/1926	35013	GN 1041	Booster removed at Grand Forks 8/1949. Ret. 4/1955. Sold for scrap DI&M 5/28/1955.	
1383	GN (Hillyard)	9/30/1926	1/21/1927	35009	GN 1037	Booster removed at Grand Forks 7/1949. Ret. 4/1955. Sold for scrap PC 5/28/1955.	
1384	GN (Hillyard)	1/15/1927	4/20/1927	35014	GN 1042	Booster removed at Jackson Street 9/17/1949. Ret. 8/1955. Sold for scrap PC 9/7/1955.	

Class H-1 4-6-2: 21x28-73-210(200)-217,000-139,000-28,760

No.	Builder	Date Rcvd.	C/N	Disposition
1400	Alco-Rogers	10/11/1905	38894	Ret. 11/1930. Stripped at Superior 5/27/1932.
1401	Alco-Rogers	10/11/1905	38895	Ret. 11/1928. Stripped at Superior 5/27/1932.
1402	Alco-Rogers	10/15/1905	38896	Ret. 11/1928. Stripped at Superior 5/24/1932.
1403	Alco-Rogers	10/15/1905	38897	Ret. 11/1928. Stripped at Superior 5/27/1932.
1404	Alco-Rogers	10/19/1905	38898	Ret. 11/1930. Stripped at Superior 5/27/1932.
1405	Alco-Rogers	10/19/1905	38899	Ret. 10/1930. Stripped at Superior 5/24/1932.

Class H-2 4-6-2: 22x30-69-210(185)-227,000-151,000-33,090 originally.

Those locomotives indicated below by an asterisk (*) received superheaters (dates shown if known) and were classified by GN as "H-2S". These engines also received 8½-inch Heron valves (dates shown if known). No. 1425 was delivered with a superheater, and therefore at some time prior to 1910 became the only locomotive of Class H-3(1). It was either delivered with or changed to dimensions of 23½x30-69-200-227,000-151,000-40,820. Nos. 1413, 1414, and 1438 retained the original dimensions. No. 1439 had dimensions changed to 23½x30-69-210(200)-227,000-151,000-40,800. All other H-2S engines had dimensions changed to 23½x30-69-210(185)-227,000-151,000-37,760. Several of these locomotives, as indicated below, received 12-inch piston valves, were classified as H-3(2) (or "H-3S" on diagrams), and were given dimensions of 23½x30-69-210-227,000-151,000-42,860 (working boiler pressure may have differed from designed on some locomotives).

No.	Builder	Date Rcvd.	C/N	Disposition	Notes
1406	Baldwin	6/8/1906	28136	Ret. 1931. Sold for scrap PC 10/1933.	155
1407*	Baldwin	6/8/1906	28146	Superheated at Hillyard 7/22/1915. Heron valves at Great Falls 10/28/1918. Sold for scrap PC 9/8/1941.	
1408*	Baldwin	6/10/1906	28157	Superheated at Dale Street 12/31/1913. Heron valves at Hillyard 4/24/1919. Ret. 12/1938.	
1409*	Baldwin	6/10/1906	28158	Heron valves at Dale Street 8/2/1919. Sold for scrap DI&M 9/3/1941.	230
1410	Baldwin	6/16/1906	28159	Ret. 8/6/1932. Sold for scrap DI&M 9/1932.	
1411	Baldwin	6/16/1906	28188	Ret. 8/6/1932. Sold for scrap DI&M 9/1932.	
1412*	Baldwin	6/17/1906	28189	Heron valves at Great Falls 1/30/1919. **Rblt. H-3(2)** at Dale Street c.5/1923. Sold for scrap PC 10/18/1951.	
1413*	Baldwin	6/17/1906	28203	Ret. 1949. Sold for scrap DI&M c.1/1950.	
1414*	Baldwin	6/16/1906	28207	Superheated at Hillyard 7/30/1914. Heron valves at Hillyard 3/6/1919. Ret. 1/1938.	156, 231
1415	Baldwin	6/16/1906	28229	Ret. 1931. Sold for scrap PC 10/1933.	
1416	Baldwin	6/24/1906	28239	Heron valves at Whitefish 12/22/1920. Scrapped 1937.	
1417*	Baldwin	6/24/1906	28240	Superheated at Dale Street 2/26/1914. Heron valves at Great Falls 11/20/1918. Ret. 9/1939. Sold for scrap Bethlehem Steel c.10/1939.	
1418*	Baldwin	7/1/1906	28309	Superheated at Dale Street 4/5/1913. Heron valves at Jackson Street 1/28/1919. Sold for scrap DI&M 5/1948.	
1419*	Baldwin	7/1/1906	28316	Superheated at Hillyard 8/28/1913. Heron valves at Dale Street 3/28/1919. Ret. 12/1938.	231
1420	Baldwin	7/4/1906	28317	Ret. 8/12/1932. Sold for scrap DI&M 10/1933.	
1421*	Baldwin	7/4/1906	28318	Heron valves at Dale Street 6/16/1919. **Rblt. to H-3(2)** at Dale Street c.1/1921. Sold for scrap PC c.2/1941.	157
1422	Baldwin	7/18/1906	28377	Heron valves at Hillyard 8/16/1920. Scrapped 1938.	
1423*	Baldwin	7/25/1906	28378	Superheated at Dale Street 5/25/1914. Heron valves at Dale Street. 9/25/1918. **Rblt. to H-3(2)** at Great Falls 7/12/1926. Sold for scrap PC 5/1951.	231
1424*	Baldwin	7/18/1906	28230	Superheated at Dale Street 6/22/1914. Heron valves at Dale Street 6/15/1918. Ret. 12/1938.	231
1425*	Baldwin	8/27/1906	28523	Placed in Class H-3(1) at some time between 8/1906 and 1910. Returned to Class H-2 11/29/1914. **Rblt. to H-3(2)** c.1/1921. Sold for scrap DI&M 10/16/1951.	157, 158
1426*	Baldwin	8/11/1907	31211	Superheated at Hillyard 12/19/1913. Heron valves at Hillyard 4/8/1919. **Rblt. to H-3(2)** c.1940(?). Sold for scrap PC 10/18/1951.	159
1427*	Baldwin	8/11/1907	31212	Superheated at Hillyard 10/23/1913. Heron valves at Hillyard 11/22/1919. **Rblt. to H-3(2)** between 1/1926 and 9/1939. Sold for scrap PC 9/15/1941.	
1428*	Baldwin	8/18/1907	31213	Heron valves at Dale Street 4/30/1919. **Rblt. to H-3(2)** at Dale Street c.1/1921. Ret. 1949. Sold for scrap PC c.1/1950.	157
1429*	Baldwin	8/18/1907	31214	Superheated at Dale Street 11/25/1913. Heron valves at Hillyard 12/27/1918. Ret. 1949. Sold for scrap DI&M c.1/1950.	
1430*	Baldwin	8/15/1907	31276	Superheated 7/31/1912. **Rblt. to H-3(2)** c.1/1921. Sold for scrap DI&M 5/1951.	157
1431*	Baldwin	8/15/1907	31277	Superheated at Dale Street 7/17/1914. Heron valves at Dale Street 9/18/1918. **Rblt. to H-3(2)** between 1/1926 and 7/1940. Sold for scrap PC 12/1941.	
1432	Baldwin	8/26/1907	31301	Scrapped 1937.	
1433*	Baldwin	8/26/1907	31302	Superheated at Hillyard 1/10/1914. Heron valves at Dale Street 5/1918. **Rblt. to H-3(2)** c.1/1921. Ret. 1949. Sold for scrap DI&M c.1/1950.	157
1434*	Baldwin	8/26/1907	31303	Superheated at Hillyard 1/14/1914. Heron valves at Great Falls 1/4/1919. Sold for scrap DI&M 9/15/1941.	
1435	Baldwin	8/26/1907	31332	Scrapped 1937.	
1436*	Baldwin	8/29/1907	31333	Heron valves at Dale Street 5/2/1919. **Rblt. to H-3(2)** between 3/1921 and 1/1922. Sold for scrap DI&M 10/22/1951.	
1437*	Baldwin	8/29/1907	31350	Superheated at Dale Street 5/25/1914. Scrapped at Dale Street 11/5/1935.	
1438*	Baldwin	9/6/1907	31351	Heron valves at Devils Lake 1/31/1919. Superheated at Dale Street c.3/1921. Retired 1949. Sold for scrap PC c.1/1950.	
1439*	Baldwin	9/6/1907	31415	Superheated 9/22/1913. Heron valves at Dale Street 11/14/1918. Sold for scrap PC 9/15/1941.	
1440*	Baldwin	9/7/1907	31448	Superheated at Hillyard 11/26/1913. Heron valves at Whitefish 5/1919. Sold for scrap DI&M 9/3/1941.	

Class H-3(1) 4-6-2: 23½x30-69-200-227,000-151,000-40,820

No.	Builder	Date Rcvd.	C/N	Disposition	Notes
1425	Baldwin	8/27/1906	28523	Returned to Class H-2 11/29/1914.	158

Class H-3(2) 4-6-2: 23½x30-69-210-227,000-151,000-42,860 (working boiler pressure may have differed from designed on some locomotives). Ten engines were moved to this class from Class H-2 as a result of having piston valves installed. Engines equipped with superheaters and commonly classified by GN as "H-3S". See Class H-2 for individual locomotive numbers and dispositions.

Class H-4 4-6-2: 26x30-73-210(150)-235,750-152,000-35,420 originally, but rebuilt (apparently shortly after delivery) to 23½x30-73-210(185)-235,750-152,000-35,690. Engine weights increased throughout the service lives of the locomotives. No. 1449 was rebuilt to 23½x30-73-210-235,750-152,000-35,110. Working boiler pressures on the others also increased by stages to 210 psi, with this and the reweighing resulting in final dimensions of 23½x 30-73-210-273,760-176,500-40,511. Nos. 1447, 1448, 1454, and 1456 received Delta trailing trucks with boosters (11,000 lb. T.E.) during the late 1920's. The Delta trucks and boosters were removed from Nos. 1448 and 1456 during 1939 for application to Class Q-2 engines. The booster was also removed from No. 1454, though it kept the Delta truck.

No.	Builder	Date Rcvd.	C/N	Disposition
1441	Baldwin	5/1/1909	33312	Sold for scrap WEI&M 8/10/1953.
1442	Baldwin	5/1/1909	33313	Sold for scrap PC 10/24/1951.
1443	Baldwin	4/30/1909	33314	Sold for scrap DI&M 9/13/1952.
1444	Baldwin	4/30/1909	33330	Sold for scrap PC 8/1953.
1445	Baldwin	5/5/1909	33331	Sold for scrap PC 5/13/1953.
1446	Baldwin	5/5/1909	33332	Sold for scrap DI&M 12/1941.
1447	Baldwin	5/5/1909	33343	Booster applied 3/1927. Sold for scrap PC 12/1941.
1448	Baldwin	5/5/1909	33344	Booster applied, date unknown. Booster removed 10/1939. Sold for scrap DI&M 10/16/1951.
1449	Baldwin	5/8/1909	33345	Sold for scrap DI&M 9/1953.
1450	Baldwin	5/8/1909	33346	Sold for scrap PC 8/1953.
1451	Baldwin	5/10/1909	33350	Sold for scrap DI&M 12/1941.
1452	Baldwin	5/10/1909	33351	Sold for scrap DI&M 4/26/1952.
1453	Baldwin	5/11/1909	33359	Sold for scrap PC 8/1953.
1454	Baldwin	5/11/1909	33360	Booster applied 7/1927. Booster removed by 5/1938. Sold for scrap WEI&M 1/31/1950.
1455	Baldwin	5/11/1909	33361	Sold for scrap DI&M 7/28/1953.
1456	Baldwin	5/11/1909	33362	Booster applied 5/1927. Booster removed 10/1939. Sold for scrap DI&M 1/31/1950.
1457	Baldwin	5/17/1909	33363	Sold for scrap WEI&M 10/18/1951.
1458	Baldwin	5/18/1909	33364	Sold for scrap DI&M 9/27/1952.
1459	Baldwin	5/17/1909	33380	Sold for scrap PC 9/27/1952.
1460	Baldwin	5/18/1909	33381	Dismantled at Great Falls 9/15/1940.

Class H-4 4-6-2: 23½x30-73-210(185)-251,200-150,700-35,690 originally. Engine weights were gradually increased throughout service lives of the locomotives. Working boiler pressures were also increased by stages to 210 psi, thus raising T.E. to 40,510 lb.

No.	Builder	Date Rcvd.	C/N	Disposition
1461	Lima	3/28/1914	1339	Sold for scrap WEI&M 1/31/1950.
1462	Lima	3/28/1914	1340	Sold for scrap PC 1/31/1950.
1463	Lima	4/4/1914	1341	Sold for scrap DI&M 1/31/1950.
1464	Lima	4/4/1914	1342	Sold for scrap WEI&M 4/15/1952.
1465	Lima	4/4/1914	1343	Sold for scrap DI&M 3/8/1949.
1466	Lima	4/4/1914	1344	Sold Georgia Car & Locomotive Co. 1/1942. Resold Atlanta, Birmingham & Coast Ry (No. 153) 1/22/1942. Reno. Atlantic Coast Line No. 7153. Scrapped 4/4/1949.
1467	Lima	4/10/1914	1345	Sold for scrap PC 6/14/1951.
1468	Lima	4/10/1914	1346	Sold for scrap DI&M 10/11/1941.
1469	Lima	4/10/1914	1347	Sold for scrap PC 5/2/1952.
1470	Lima	4/10/1914	1348	Sold for scrap DI&M 1/31/1950.
1471	Lima	4/17/1914	1349	Sold for scrap DI&M 5/7/1953.
1472	Lima	4/17/1914	1350	Sold for scrap PC 12/1941.
1473	Lima	4/17/1914	1351	Sold for scrap PC 9/27/1952.
1474	Lima	4/17/1914	1352	Sold for scrap PC 11/10/1951.
1475	Lima	4/20/1914	1353	Sold for scrap PC 10/24/1951.
1476	Lima	4/20/1914	1354	Sold for scrap DI&M 1/31/1950.
1477	Lima	4/24/1914	1355	Sold for scrap DI&M 10/22/1951.
1478	Lima	4/24/1914	1356	Sold Georgia Car & Locomotive Co. 1/1942. Resold Atlanta, Birmingham & Coast Ry. (No. 175) 1/22/1942. Reno. Atlantic Coast Line No. 7175. Scrapped 1/31/1950.
1479	Lima	4/24/1914	1357	Sold for scrap DI&M 4/20/1952.
1480	Lima	4/24/1914	1358	Sold for scrap PC 4/14/1948.
1481	Lima	5/1/1914	1359	Sold for scrap PC 9/29/1941.
1482	Lima	5/1/1914	1360	Sold for scrap DI&M 9/29/1941.
1483	Lima	5/2/1914	1361	Sold for scrap DI&M 3/20/1948.
1484	Lima	5/2/1914	1362	Sold for scrap PC 1/31/1950.
1485	Lima	5/7/1914	1363	Sold for scrap DI&M 4/16/1948.

Class H-5 4-6-2: 23½x30-73-210(200)-260,800-164,600-38,582. Locomotive Nos. 1488, 1489, and 1494 had boosters (11,000 lb. T.E.) mounted on trailing trucks.

No.	Builder	Date Start Rbld.	Date Finish Rbld	C/N	Rblt. From E-14 No.	Disposition
1486	GN (Dale Street)		7/8/1921	33948	GN 1031	Reno. GN 1350 2/10/1926.
1487	GN (Dale Street)	8/25/1921	1/11/1922	33887	GN 1018	Reno. GN 1351 2/24/1926.
1488	GN (Dale Street)	7/5/1921	10/6/1921	33907	GN 1019	Booster applied 4/1925. Reno. GN 1352 3/3/1926.
1489	GN (Dale Street)	8/3/1921	11/14/1921	33913	GN 1025	Booster applied 6/1925. Reno. GN 1353 2/12/1926.
1490	GN (Dale Street)	12/5/1921	3/20/1922	33910	GN 1022	Reno. GN 1354 2/8/1926.
1491	GN (Dale Street)		12/30/1922	33911	GN 1023	Reno. GN 1358 2/24/1926.
1492	GN (Dale Street)	4/25/1922	3/26/1923	33885	GN 1016	Reno. GN 1356 2/8/1926.
1493	GN (Dale Street)	12/6/1924	1/26/1925	33912	GN 1024	Reno. GN 1357 2/10/1926.
1494	GN (Dale Street)	2/19/1924	5/29/1924	33908	GN 1020	Booster applied 1/1925. Reno. GN 1355 4/10/1926.
1495	GN (Dale Street)	4/4/1924	6/4/1924	33943	GN 1030	Reno. GN 1359 2/10/1926.

Class J-1 2-6-2: 22x30-69-210(185)-209,000-151,000-33,090 originally. No. 1549 was delivered with a Baldwin superheater installed and had dimensions of 25¼x30-69-170-209,000-151,000-40,060. For a time it was placed in Class J-3. Those engines indicated below by an asterisk (*) had superheaters installed (dates given below if known) and were classified by GN as "J-1S". Nos. 1514 and 1537 had dimensions of 23x30-69-185-209,000-151,000-36,170. All the J-1S engines eventually had dimensions changed to 23½x30-69-210(185)-209,000-151,000-37,760.

No.	Builder	Date Rcvd.	C/N	Disposition	Notes
1500	Baldwin	4/19/1906	27792	Scrapped 1931.	
1501*	Baldwin	4/19/1906	27793	Superheated at Dale Street 9/17/1915. Heron valves at Devils Lake 1/31/1919. Ret. 5/9/1930. Sold for scrap PC 10/1933.	
1502	Baldwin	4/19/1906	27808	Sold for scrap DI&M 2/1928.	
1503	Baldwin	4/19/1906	27809	Sold for scrap DI&M 11/1927.	
1504	Baldwin	4/22/1906	27816	Sold for scrap PC 4/23/1929.	
1505	Baldwin	4/22/1906	27817	Ret. 9/27/1928 at Grand Forks. Dismantled at Superior 8/27/1932.	
1506	Baldwin	4/24/1906	27818	Sold SP&S 9/1923, but not accepted. Ret. 10/1936, sold for scrap Bethlehem Steel.	
1507	Baldwin	4/24/1906	27829	Ret. 11/2/1928. Sold for scrap DI&M 10/1933.	
1508	Baldwin	4/30/1906	27867	Sold for scrap DI&M 10/1928.	
1509	Baldwin	4/30/1906	27868	Retired and sold for scrap 12/1928.	
1510	Baldwin	4/29/1906	27869	Ret. 6/1928. Dismantled at Dale Street 8/27/1928.	
1511	Baldwin	4/29/1906	27870	Ret. 6/1928. Dismantled at Superior 10/17/1928.	
1512	Baldwin	5/1/1906	27871	Sold for scrap DI&M 2/1928.	
1513	Baldwin	5/1/1906	27872	Sold for scrap DI&M 4/1928.	
1514*	Baldwin	5/4/1906	27878	Superheated at Dale Street 9/21/1914. Heron valves at Havre 12/19/1918. Ret. 6/1928. Dismantled at Delta 6/16/1928.	
1515	Baldwin	5/4/1906	27879	Sold for scrap PC 11/1928.	
1516	Baldwin	5/4/1906	27919	Ret. 6/1928. Dismantled at Superior 9/27/1928.	
1517	Baldwin	5/4/1906	27920	Rblt. H-6 1718 at Dale Street 4/3/1922 to 7/31/1923.	
1518	Baldwin	5/9/1906	27921	Sold for scrap DI&M 10/1929.	
1519	Baldwin	5/9/1906	27945	Rblt. H-6 1721 at Dale Street 10/1/1925 to 2/12/1926.	
1520	Baldwin	5/10/1906	27946	Sold for scrap DI&M 11/29/1928.	
1521	Baldwin	5/10/1906	27947	Ret. 10/1936, sold for scrap PC.	
1522	Baldwin	5/15/1906	27955	Sold for scrap DI&M 1/1928.	
1523	Baldwin	5/15/1906	27956	Rblt. H-6 1717 at Dale Street 11/9/1921 to 3/30/1922.	
1524*	Baldwin	5/15/1906	27973	Superheated at Havre 7/9/1915. Heron valves at Hillyard 10/13/1919. Ret. 10/1936, sold for scrap Bethlehem Steel.	
1525	Baldwin	5/15/1906	27974	Rblt. H-6 1722 at Dale Street 10/22/1925 to 7/9/1926.	
1526	Baldwin	5/24/1906	27975	Ret. 1/27/1928. Sold for scrap DI&M 10/1932.	
1527	Baldwin	7/13/1906	28418	Scrapped 1931.	
1528	Baldwin	7/13/1906	28419	Rblt. H-6 1720 at Dale Street 9/21/1925 to 4/7/1926.	
1529	Baldwin	7/25/1906	28428	Ret. 6/1928. Dismantled at Dale Street 8/27/1928.	
1530	Baldwin	7/25/1906	28429	Ret. 5/25/1931. Sold for scrap DI&M 1932.	
1531*	Baldwin	7/25/1906	28430	Superheated at Havre 9/30/1915. Heron valves at Superior 11/30/1921. Sold for scrap DI&M 3/1928.	
1532	Baldwin	7/25/1906	28452	Sold SP&S 9/1923, but not accepted. Ret. 5/15/1930 at Delta.	
1533	Baldwin	7/28/1906	28496	Ret. 11/15/1928 at Superior. Sold for scrap DI&M 7/22/1932.	
1534	Baldwin	7/28/1906	28522	Ret. 6/1928. Dismantled at Superior 9/11/1928.	
1535	Baldwin	8/3/1906	28527	Ret. 6/1928. Dismantled at Superior 9/11/1928.	
1536	Baldwin	8/3/1906	28528	Sold for scrap PC 3/23/1929.	
1537*	Baldwin	8/10/1906	28548	Superheated at Dale Street 7/23/1914. Heron valves at Dale Street 6/30/1920. Ret. 10/24/1930. Sold for scrap DI&M c.10/1932.	
1538	Baldwin	8/10/1906	28637	Sold for scrap DI&M 10/1929.	
1539*	Baldwin	8/17/1906	28638	Superheated at Dale Street 9/30/1915. Heron valves at Dale Street 7/25/1919. Sold for scrap DI&M 1/1928.	
1540	Baldwin	8/17/1906	28648	Sold for scrap DI&M 10/1929.	
1541	Baldwin	10/7/1906	28654	Sold for scrap PC 12/1929.	
1542	Baldwin	10/7/1906	28671	Sold for scrap DI&M 2/1928.	
1543	Baldwin	8/27/1906	28687	Ret. 11/5/1928. Sold for scrap DI&M 1932.	
1544	Baldwin	8/27/1906	28704	Ret. at Grand Forks 11/6/1930. Sold for scrap DI&M 7/14/1932.	
1545	Baldwin	9/12/1906	28756	Ret. 10/1936, sold for scrap DI&M.	
1546	Baldwin	9/12/1906	28757	Ret. 1/11/1930 at Superior. Sold for scrap DI&M 7/22/1932.	
1547	Baldwin	9/30/1906	28782	Ret. 1/18/1929 at Grand Forks. Dismantled at Superior 8/19/1932.	
1548	Baldwin	9/30/1906	28783	Sold for scrap PC 11/1928.	
1549*	Baldwin	10/4/1906	28851	Sold SP&S (No. 466) 7/14/1925. Scrapped 5/1948.	160

Class J-3 2-6-2: 25¼x30-69-170-209,000-151,000-40,060

No.	Builder	Date Rcvd.	C/N	Disposition	Notes
1549	Baldwin	10/4/1906	28851	Returned to Class J-1S, with installation of Schmidt superheater, 1/5/1914.	160

Class J-2 2-6-2: 22x30-69-210(185)-209,000-151,000-33,090 originally. Those engines indicated below by an asterisk (*) had superheaters installed (dates given where known) and were classified by GN as "J-2S". Nos. 1550, 1559, 1569, 1615, 1624, 1631, and 1649 had dimensions of 23x30-69-185-209,000-151,000-36,170. All the J-2S engines except No. 1566 and possibly No. 1569 eventually had dimensions changed to 23½x30-69-210(185)-209,000-151,000-37,760. No. 1566 had dimensions of 26x30-69-210(185)-209,000-151,000-46,220.

No.	Builder	Date Rcvd.	C/N	Disposition	Notes
1550*	Baldwin	3/5/1907	30080	Superheated at Dale Street 1/8/1915. Heron valves at Wolf Point 4/29/1922. Ret. 12/15/1928. Sold for scrap PC 10/1933.	
1551*	Baldwin	3/5/1907	30093	Superheated at Dale Street 9/30/1915. Heron valves at Dale Street 3/31/1920. Ret. and sold for scrap 12/1928.	
1552	Baldwin	3/13/1907	30094	Rblt. H-6 1713 at Dale Street 5/4/1921 to 11/7/1921.	
1553	Baldwin	3/13/1907	30095	Rblt. H-6 1719 at Dale Street, completed 9/29/1923.	
1554*	Baldwin	3/4/1907	30126	Superheated at Havre 6/28/1915. Heron valves at Havre 11/1918. Ret. 11/11/1928. Sold for scrap DI&M 10/1933.	
1555	Baldwin	3/4/1907	30134	Sold SP&S (No. 450) 1908. Scrapped 5/1937.	

1556*	Baldwin	3/18/1907	30135	Superheated at Dale Street 6/16/1915. Heron valves 5/1920. Ret. 11/1929, scrapped 1931(?).	
1557	Baldwin	3/18/1907	30136	Scrapped 1931.	
1558	Baldwin	3/17/1907	30137	Ret. 10/1936. Sold for scrap PC 1/20/1937.	
1559*	Baldwin	3/17/1907	30138	Superheated at Dale Street 6/30/1914. Heron valves at Dale Street 10/26/1918. Ret. 1927. Sold for scrap DI&M 3/1928.	
1560	Baldwin	3/17/1907	30171	Ret. 11/8/1928. Sold for scrap PC 10/1933.	
1561	Baldwin	3/17/1907	30172	Sold for scrap DI&M 3/1928.	
1562	Baldwin	3/15/1907	30173	Sold for scrap DI&M 5/1928.	
1563	Baldwin	3/15/1907	30174	Ret. 2/10/1929. Sold for scrap DI&M 1932.	
1564	Baldwin	3/14/1907	30175	Ret. 8/12/1931. Sold for scrap DI&M 1932.	
1565	Baldwin	3/14/1907	30201	Sold SP&S (No. 451) 1908. Scrapped 6/1945.	
1566*	Baldwin	3/16/1907	30202	Superheated at Dale Street 6/28/1912. Sold SP&S (No. 465) 6/1925. Scrapped 5/1948.	
1567	Baldwin	3/16/1907	30236	Ret. 12/24/1931. Sold for scrap DI&M c.10/1932.	
1568	Baldwin	3/14/1907	30237	Ret. and sold for scrap 12/1928.	
1569*	Baldwin	3/14/1907	30238	Superheated at Dale Street 2/9/1915. Rblt. H-6 1714 at Dale Street 8/24/1921 to 1/25/1922.	
1570	Baldwin	3/23/1907	30239	Rblt. H-6 1724 at Dale Street 10/25/1926 to 10/28/1927.	
1571	Baldwin	3/23/1907	30287	Sold for scrap DI&M 2/1928.	
1572	Baldwin	3/20/1907	30293	Rblt. H-6 1711 at Dale Street, completed 8/24/1921.	
1573*	Baldwin	3/20/1907	30312	Superheated at Havre 6/30/1915. Heron valves at Havre 1/19/1922. Ret. 10/1936, sold for scrap Bethlehem Steel.	
1574	Baldwin	3/26/1907	30332	Sold for scrap DI&M 2/1928.	
1575	Baldwin	3/26/1907	30333	Sold SP&S (No. 452) 1908. Scrapped 9/1944.	
1576	Baldwin	3/28/1907	30334	Ret. 8/9/1929 at Superior. Sold for scrap DI&M 7/18/1932.	
1577	Baldwin	3/28/1907	30335	Sold SP&S (No. 453) 1908. Scrapped 1948.	
1578	Baldwin	4/2/1907	30393	Ret. 6/1928. Dismantled at Great Falls 8/10/1928.	
1579	Baldwin	4/2/1907	30394	Sold for scrap DI&M 3/1928.	
1580	Baldwin	4/13/1907	30395	Scrapped 1931.	
1581	Baldwin	4/13/1907	30396	Sold SP&S (No. 454) 1908. Scrapped 5/1938.	
1582*	Baldwin	4/15/1907	30397	Superheated at Havre 10/15/1915. Heron valves at Dale Street 8/10/1918. Ret. 10/1936. Sold for scrap DI&M 1/20/1937.	
1583	Baldwin	4/15/1907	30440	Sold SP&S (No. 455) 1908. Scrapped 9/1945.	
1584	Baldwin	4/13/1907	30467	Sold for scrap DI&M 4/1928.	
1585	Baldwin	4/13/1907	30468	Sold for scrap DI&M 3/1928.	
1586	Baldwin	4/19/1907	30489	Ret. 6/1928. Dismantled at Willmar 8/1928.	
1587	Baldwin	4/19/1907	30502	Sold SP&S (No. 456) 1908. Scrapped 2/1949.	
1588	Baldwin	4/30/1907	30513	Ret. 10/28/1928 at Grand Forks.	
1589	Baldwin	4/30/1907	30527	Sold SP&S (No. 460) 1908. Scrapped 5/1937.	
1590*	Baldwin	5/4/1907	30528	Superheated at Dale Street 10/13/1915. Heron valves at Superior 8/14/1920. Ret. 10/29/1928.	
1591	Baldwin	4/28/1907	30560	Sold for scrap DI&M 5/1928.	
1592	Baldwin	4/28/1907	30561	Heron valves at Melrose 12/31/1920. Ret. 2/9/1928. Sold for scrap DI&M 1932.	
1593	Baldwin	4/28/1907	30568	Sold SP&S (No. 457) 1908. Scrapped 3/1949.	
1594*	Baldwin	4/28/1907	30569	Superheated at Dale Street 7/23/1915. Heron valves at Dale Street c.3/1921. Ret. and sold for scrap 12/1928.	
1595	Baldwin	5/4/1907	30580	Sold SP&S (No. 461) 1908. Scrapped 5/1948.	
1596*	Baldwin	5/4/1907	30600	Superheated at Havre 8/19/1915. Heron valves at Havre 11/30/1921. Ret. 3/11/1928. Sold for scrap DI&M 10/1933.	
1597	Baldwin	5/4/1907	30601	Sold SP&S (No. 462) 1908. Scrapped 5/1938.	
1598	Baldwin	5/15/1907	30654	Rblt. H-6 1716 at Dale Street 8/30/1921 to 5/26/1922.	
1599	Baldwin	5/15/1907	30655	Sold for scrap DI&M 4/1928.	
1600	Baldwin	5/19/1907	30656	Sold SP&S (No. 463) 11/14/1908. Scrapped 5/1937.	
1601	Baldwin	5/19/1907	30657	Sold SP&S (No. 464) 11/14/1908. Scrapped 5/1937.	
1602	Baldwin	5/19/1907	30658	Sold for scrap DI&M 3/1928.	
1603	Baldwin	5/19/1907	30672	Sold SP&S (No. 459) 8/28/1908. Scrapped 5/1937.	
1604	Baldwin	5/21/1907	30717	Ret. 10/26/1930. Sold for scrap DI&M 1932.	
1605	Baldwin	5/21/1907	30718	Sold for scrap DI&M 1/1928.	
1606	Baldwin	5/27/1907	30733	Ret. 8/12/1932. Sold for scrap PC 10/1933.	
1607	Baldwin	5/27/1907	30735	Ret. 10/1936. Sold for scrap PC 1/20/1937.	
1608*	Baldwin	5/28/1907	30736	Superheated at Superior 8/8/1924. Ret. 10/26/1930. Sold for scrap DI&M 1932.	161
1609	Baldwin	5/28/1907	30737	Sold for scrap PC 12/1929.	161
1610	Baldwin	5/26/1907	30738	Sold for scrap DI&M 5/1928.	
1611	Baldwin	5/26/1907	30756	Sold for scrap PC 11/1928.	
1612	Baldwin	5/26/1907	30757	Rblt. H-6 1723 at Dale Street 10/7/1926 to 9/30/1927.	
1613*	Baldwin	5/26/1907	30758	Superheated at Havre 9/25/1915. Heron valves at Delta 9/15/1920. Ret. 10/1936, sold for scrap Bethlehem Steel.	
1614	Baldwin	6/2/1907	30759	Stripped at Superior 7/22/1932. Sold for scrap DI&M 9/1932.	
1615*	Baldwin	6/2/1907	30778	Superheated at Dale Street 1/13/1915. Heron valves at Dale Street 10/31/1918. Ret. 6/1928. Dismantled at St.Cloud 8/1928.	
1616	Baldwin	6/6/1907	30779	Rblt. H-6 1712 at Dale Street 3/17/1921 to 10/6/1921.	
1617	Baldwin	6/6/1907	30780	Sold for scrap PC 5/1929.	
1618	Baldwin	6/8/1907	30796	Ret. 10/1936. Sold for scrap DI&M 1/20/1937.	
1619	Baldwin	6/8/1907	30812	Rblt. H-6 1715 at Dale Street 10/7/1921 to 3/30/1922.	
1620	Baldwin	6/9/1907	30813	Sold for scrap DI&M 10/1929.	
1621	Baldwin	6/10/1907	30849	Sold for scrap PC 12/1929.	
1622*	Baldwin	6/13/1907	30838	Superheated at Havre 6/26/1915. Heron valves at Devils Lake 7/29/1920. Ret. 10/1936, sold for scrap PC.	
1623	Baldwin	6/13/1907	30839	Sold for scrap DI&M 10/1929.	
1624*	Baldwin	6/14/1907	30840	Superheated at Dale Street 2/26/1915. Heron valves at Delta 12/31/1920. Ret. 10/1936, sold for scrap Bethlehem Steel.	
1625	Baldwin	6/14/1907	30861	Ret. 1931. Stripped at Dale Street 4/7/1932. Sold for scrap DI&M 10/1933.	

Class J-2 2-6-2: continued

No.	Builder	Date Rcvd.	C/N	Disposition	Notes
1626*	Baldwin	6/12/1907	30862	Superheated at Dale Street 10/30/1915. Heron valves at Dale Street 12/17/1920. Ret. 11/15/1928. Sold for scrap DI&M 8/1932.	
1627	Baldwin	6/12/1907	30879	Ret. 1931.	
1628	Baldwin	6/16/1907	30880	Ret. 1931.	162
1629	Baldwin	6/16/1907	30881	Sold for scrap PC 12/1929.	162
1630	Baldwin	6/18/1907	30882	Ret. 6/2/1931. Sold for scrap DI&M 1932.	
1631*	Baldwin	6/18/1907	30898	Superheated at Dale Street 12/11/1914. Heron valves at Dale Street 2/10/1920. Ret. 8/1930. Stripped at Dale Street 8/15/1932. Sold for scrap PC 10/1933.	
1632	Baldwin	6/29/1907	30899	Sold for scrap DI&M 11/17/1928.	
1633	Baldwin	6/29/1907	30900	Ret. 1931. Stripped at Dale Street 9/10/1932.	
1634	Baldwin	6/29/1907	30937	Rblt. H-6 1710 at Dale Street 12/28/1920 to 7/1/1921.	
1635	Baldwin	6/29/1907	30957	Ret. 1931.	
1636	Baldwin	6/30/1907	30967	Sold for scrap DI&M 11/17/1928.	
1637*	Baldwin	6/30/1907	30968	Superheated at Havre 7/31/1915. Heron valves at Dale Street 11/7/1918. Retired at Delta 7/1/1930.	
1638	Baldwin	7/2/1907	30999	Sold to SP&S (No. 458) 8/19/1908. Scrapped 6/1945.	163
1639	Baldwin	7/2/1907	31000	Stripped at Superior 5/23/1932.	
1640	Baldwin	7/8/1907	31005	Sold for scrap PC 1929.	
1641	Baldwin	7/8/1907	31006	Sold SP&S 9/1923, but not accepted. Ret. 6/1928. Dismantled at Delta 9/17/1928 to 10/6/1928.	
1642	Baldwin	7/9/1907	31007	Sold for scrap DI&M 12/23/1928.	
1643	Baldwin	7/9/1907	31035	Ret. 10/31/1930. Sold for scrap DI&M 1932.	
1644	Baldwin	7/13/1907	31082	Ret. 1931.	
1645	Baldwin	7/13/1907	31100	Ret. 11/13/1930 at Superior. Dismantled at Superior 8/27/1932.	
1646	Baldwin	7/28/1907	31117	Sold for scrap DI&M 11/29/1928.	
1647	Baldwin	7/28/1907	31118	Sold for scrap DI&M 5/1928.	
1648	Baldwin	7/28/1907	31119	Sold for scrap DI&M 10/1929.	
1649*	Baldwin	7/28/1907	31120	Superheated at Dale Street 10/12/1914. Heron valves at Dale Street 1/24/1922. Ret. 11/8/1928. Sold for scrap DI&M 8/1932.	

Class K-1 4-4-2: 15 and 25x26-73-210(185)-208,000-100,000-19,560 (Balanced Compound) originally. All engines were simpled and also received superheaters (dates given below where known) and were classified by GN as "K-1S". This changed the dimensions of the class to 21x26-73-210(200)-221,300-124,900-26,700. The engines received Delta trailing trucks with boosters (10,100 lb. T.E.). The boosters were then removed from 1930 to 1937.

No.	Builder	Date Rcvd.	C/N	Disposition	Notes
1700	Baldwin	5/29/1906	28037	Simpled at Havre 7/15/1921. Superheated at Havre 10/31/1923. Booster applied at Dale Street 12/5/1925, removed at Superior 2/6/1931. Sold for scrap DI&M 12/1941.	
1701	Baldwin	5/29/1906	28038	Simpled and superheated at Dale Street 9/30/1921. Booster applied at Dale Street 11/13/1924, removed 2/1937. Ret. 1/1938. Boiler sold for scrap WEI&M 6/21/1938.	
1702	Baldwin	5/29/1906	28078	Simpled at Dale Street 11/13/1920. Superheated and booster applied at Dale Street 7/21/1924, booster removed 3/1930. Sold for scrap PC 10/1940.	
1703	Baldwin	5/29/1906	28092	Simpled and superheated at Havre 11/30/1921. Booster applied at Dale Street 1/26/1925, removed at Superior 5/14/1931. Sold for scrap PC 12/1941.	
1704	Baldwin	6/6/1906	28107	Simpled at Dale Street 5/27/1921 (may have been superheated at same time). Booster applied at Dale Street 6/27/1925, removed at Superior 3/17/1931. Sold for scrap PC 9/1/1941.	164
1705	Baldwin	6/6/1906	28108	Simpled 10/20/1915. Superheated at Dale Street 2/6/1922. Booster applied at Dale Street 3/30/1925, removed at Superior 3/19/1931. Sold for scrap DI&M 12/1941.	164
1706	Baldwin	6/6/1906	28148	Superheated at Dale Street 6/23/1914. Simpled at Dale Street 1/31/1921. Booster applied at Dale Street 10/31/1923, removed 3/1930. Sold for scrap DI&M 9/9/1941.	164, 165
1707	Baldwin	6/6/1906	28162	Superheated at Dale Street 9/25/1914. Simpled at Havre 5/11/1921. Booster applied at Dale Street 3/15/1924, removed at Superior 5/18/1931. Sold for scrap PC 10/1940.	164
1708	Baldwin	6/26/1906	28198	Simpled and superheated at Havre 3/31/1921. Booster applied at Dale Street 8/31/1923, removed 3/1937. Ret. 1937. Boiler sold for scrap WEI&M 6/21/1938.	166
1709	Baldwin	6/26/1906	28270	Superheated at Dale Street 6/26/1919. Simpled at Dale Street 3/24/1921. Booster applied at Dale Street 6/15/1923, removed 5/1930. Sold for scrap PC 6/30/1947.	166

Class H-6 4-6-2: 23½x30-69-210(200)-249,500-161,580-40,820 originally. Nos. 1710, 1713, 1714, and 1722-1724 later equipped with Delta trailing trucks and boosters (11,000 lb. T.E.), which increased weights to 260,100 lb. and 161,580 lb., respectively. Boosters were then removed and working boiler pressure on all locomotives increased to 210 psi (increasing T.E. to 42,859 lb.). Reweighing resulted in weight of 271,020 lb. (169,000 lb. on drivers). (Rebuilt from Class J-1 and J-2 2-6-2)

No.	Builder	Date Start Rbld.	Date Finish Rbld	C/N	Rblt. From J No.	Disposition	
1710	GN (Dale Street)	12/28/1920	7/1/1921	30937	GN 1634	Booster removed at Hillyard 4/17/1951. Sold for scrap DI&M 7/1/1956.	167
1711	GN (Dale Street)		8/24/1921	30293	GN 1572	Sold for scrap WEI&M 5/7/1953.	168
1712	GN (Dale Street)	3/17/1921	10/6/1921	30779	GN 1616	Sold for scrap PC 5/13/1953.	168
1713	GN (Dale Street)	5/4/1921	11/7/1921	30094	GN 1552	Booster removed at Minot 11/1950. Sold for scrap PC 4/22/1956.	167
1714	GN (Dale Street)	8/24/1921	1/25/1922	30238	GN 1569	Booster applied at Great Falls 2/16/1937, removed at Interbay 12/7/1950. Sold for scrap DI&M 5/15/1953.	168
1715	GN (Dale Street)	10/7/1921	3/30/1922	30812	GN 1619	Sold for scrap DI&M 2/5/1955.	169
1716	GN (Dale Street)	8/30/1921	5/26/1922	30654	GN 1598	Sold for scrap PC 5/28/1953.	168
1717	GN (Dale Street)	11/9/1921	3/30/1922	27956	GN 1523	Sold for scrap DI&M 5/5/1953.	168
1718	GN (Dale Street)	4/3/1922	7/31/1923	27920	GN 1517	Sold for scrap WEI&M 5/28/1953.	168

1719	GN (Dale Street)		9/29/1923	30095	GN 1553	Sold for scrap DI&M 9/23/1956.	170
1720	GN (Dale Street)	9/21/1925	4/7/1926	28419	GN 1528	Sold for scrap WEI&M 6/4/1955.	232
1721	GN (Dale Street)	10/1/1925	2/12/1926	27945	GN 1519	Sold for scrap DI&M 8/19/1950.	
1722	GN (Dale Street)	10/22/1925	7/9/1926	27974	GN 1525	Booster removed at Grand Forks 12/13/1950. Sold for scrap DI&M 4/30/1953.	168
1723	GN (Dale Street)	10/7/1926	9/30/1927	30757	GN 1612	Booster removed at Breckenridge 11/21/1950. Sold for scrap PC 8/16/1956.	
1724	GN (Dale Street)	10/25/1926	10/28/1927	30239	GN 1570	Booster applied 10/1927, removed at Breckenridge 11/29/1950. Sold for scrap PC 8/1953.	171

Class P-1 4-8-2: 28x32-63-210(180)-326,000-220,000-60,930 originally. Working boiler pressure later increased to 190 psi, with resultant T.E. increase to 64,300 lb.

No.	Builder	Date Rcvd.	C/N	Disposition	Notes
1750	Lima	5/21/1914	1364	Rblt. Q-2 2188 at Superior beginning 8/2/1928.	
1751	Lima	5/28/1914	1365	Rblt. Q-2 2183 at Great Falls beginning 5/31/1928.	
1752	Lima	5/24/1914	1366	Rblt. Q-2 2179 at Hillyard beginning 2/27/1928.	
1753	Lima	5/28/1914	1367	Rblt. Q-2 2186 at Superior beginning 6/29/1928.	
1754	Lima	5/29/1914	1368	Rblt. Q-2 2175 at Hillyard beginning 1/24/1928.	
1755	Lima	6/1/1914	1369	Rblt. Q-2 2180 at Great Falls beginning 2/28/1928.	
1756	Lima	6/4/1914	1370	Rblt. Q-2 2187 at Hillyard beginning 7/31/1928.	218
1757	Lima	6/4/1914	1371	Rblt. Q-2 2177 at Superior beginning 2/18/1928.	
1758	Lima	6/4/1914	1372	Rblt. Q-2 2182 at Superior beginning 4/2/1928.	
1759	Lima	6/4/1914	1373	Rblt. Q-2 2181 at Great Falls beginning 2/29/1928.	
1760	Lima	6/14/1914	1374	Rblt. Q-2 2185 at Hillyard beginning 7/12/1928.	
1761	Lima	6/14/1914	1375	Rblt. Q-2 2178 at Hillyard beginning 2/11/1928.	
1762	Lima	6/18/1914	1376	Rblt. Q-2 2184 at Great Falls beginning 7/2/1928.	
1763	Lima	6/22/1914	1377	Rblt. Q-2 2189 at Superior beginning 8/21/1928.	
1764	Lima	6/18/1914	1378	Rblt. Q-2 2176 at Great Falls beginning 1/23/1928.	

Class L-1 2-6-6-2: 21½x32/33x32-55-200-355,000-316,000-69,900

No.	Builder	Date Rcvd.	C/N	Disposition	Notes
1800(1)	Baldwin	9/6/1906	28601	Reno. GN 1900 at Delta 12/27/1907.	172
1801(1)	Baldwin	9/11/1906	28641	Reno. GN 1901 at Delta 1/13/1908.	172
1802(1)	Baldwin	9/22/1906	28739	Reno. GN 1902 at Delta 1/6/1908.	
1803(1)	Baldwin	9/30/1906	28854	Reno. GN 1903 at Delta 12/30/1907.	172
1804(1)	Baldwin	10/22/1906	28933	Reno. GN 1904 at Delta 1/18/1908.	

As enginemen attend to the 1721, express and baggage is being loaded onto train 235, the Havre to Butte passenger train, during the stop at Great Falls on an unknown date. The 1721, a Class H-6 Pacific, is a rebuilt engine converted from a Prairie in 1926. It was assigned to the Butte Division for most of its life. Photographer unknown, from the Jack Dykstra collection.

Class L-2 2-6-6-2: 20x30/31x30-55-200-288,000-250,000-54,520 originally. Those engines indicated below by an asterisk (*) received superheaters (dates shown below), were classified by GN as "L-2S", and may have had dimensions changed.

No.	Builder	Date Rcvd.	C/N	Disposition	Notes
1800(2)	Baldwin	3/25/1908	32688	Dismantled at Dale Street beginning 1/30/1925, parts to O-5 3344.	173
1801(2)	Baldwin	3/25/1908	32689	Dismantled at Hillyard 1/25/1922 to 4/10/1922, parts to O-5 3304.	173
1802(2)	Baldwin	3/25/1908	32690	Dismantled at Dale Street 11/17/1921 to 1/10/1922, parts to O-5 3300.	173
1803(2)	Baldwin	3/27/1908	32691	Dismantled at Delta beginning 7/18/1924, parts to O-5 3337.	
1804(2)	Baldwin	3/25/1908	32696	Dismantled at Hillyard 9/27/1923 to 1/24/1924, parts to O-5 3318.	174
1805	Baldwin	5/17/1907	30400	Dismantled at Hillyard beginning 11/7/1924, parts to O-5 3342.	
1806	Baldwin	5/17/1907	30422	Dismantled at Dale Street 12/22/1921 to 2/3/1922, parts to O-5 3302.	175
1807	Baldwin	5/17/1907	30445	Dismantled at Dale Street beginning 3/13/1924, parts to O-5 3330.	175
1808	Baldwin	5/20/1907	30446	Dismantled at Delta 1/8/1923 to 3/20/1923, parts to O-5 3307.	176
1809	Baldwin	5/20/1907	30563	Dismantled at Delta 6/21/1922 to 1/30/1923, parts to O-5 3308.	176
1810	Baldwin	5/22/1907	30564	Dismantled at Delta 4/17/1923 to 5/4/1923, parts to O-5 3309.	
1811	Baldwin	5/22/1907	30565	Dismantled at Hillyard beginning 7/10/1924, parts to O-5 3335.	
1812	Baldwin	6/2/1907	30588	Dismantled at Hillyard beginning 10/6/1923, parts to O-5 3319.	177
1813	Baldwin	5/28/1907	30800	Dismantled at Delta beginning 10/13/1924, parts to O-5 3334.	177
1814*	Baldwin	9/24/1907	30801	Superheated at Hillyard 9/7/1915. Dismantled at Hillyard beginning 10/16/1924, parts to O-5 3338.	177
1815*	Baldwin	5/28/1907	30802	Superheated at Dale Street 7/13/1915. Dismantled at Hillyard beginning 8/6/1924, parts to O-5 3336.	177
1816*	Baldwin	6/6/1907	30803	Superheated at Hillyard 8/27/1915. Dismantled at Delta 11/8/1923 to 3/29/1924, parts to O-5 3324.	178
1817	Baldwin	6/5/1907	30846	Dismantled at Hillyard beginning 3/12/1924, parts to O-5 3328.	178
1818	Baldwin	6/5/1907	30847	Dismantled at Hillyard beginning 5/14/1924, parts to O-5 3329.	178
1819	Baldwin	6/9/1907	30848	Dismantled at Delta 1/19/1922 to 5/19/1922, parts to O-5 3306.	178
1820	Baldwin	6/26/1907	30918	Dismantled at Delta beginning 5/14/1924, parts to O-5 3339.	179
1821	Baldwin	6/25/1907	30919	Dismantled at Dale Street beginning 4/21/1924, parts to O-5 3333.	180
1822*	Baldwin	6/30 1907	30943	Superheated at Hillyard 2/26/1915. Dismantled at Delta 3/1/1923 to 10/13/1923, parts to O-5 3314.	181
1823	Baldwin	6/30/1907	31002	Dismantled at Hillyard 1/26/1923 to 11/14/1923, parts to O-5 3317.	181
1824*	Baldwin	8/11/1907	31003	Superheated at Hillyard 7/16/1915. Dismantled at Hillyard 1/25/1924 to 5/20/1924, parts to O-5 3320.	
1825*	Baldwin	7/6/1907	31004	Superheated at Hillyard 3/17/1915. Dismantled at Dale Street beginning 11/27/1923, parts to O-5 3325.	182
1826*	Baldwin	7/21/1907	31065	Superheated at Dale Street 8/30/1915. Dismantled at Delta 4/24/1924 to 7/17/1924, parts to O-5 3327.	183
1827	Baldwin	7/28/1907	31105	Dismantled at Dale Street beginning 9/15/1924, parts to O-5 3340.	184
1828	Baldwin	7/30/1907	31183	Dismantled at Dale Street 5/29/1922 to 12/30/1922, parts to O-5 3312.	
1829	Baldwin	8/6/1907	31184	Dismantled at Dale Street 3/1/1923 to 8/31/1923, parts to O-5 3315.	185
1830	Baldwin	3/25/1908	32697	Dismantled at Hillyard beginning 12/11/1924, parts to O-5 3343.	186
1831	Baldwin	3/25/1908	32698	Dismantled at Hillyard 1/17/1923 to 2/24/1923, parts to O-5 3311.	186
1832	Baldwin	3/31/1908	32699	Dismantled at Dale Street beginning 6/4/1923, parts to O-5 3322.	
1833	Baldwin	3/27/1908	32700	Dismantled at Delta 8/30/1923 to 1/30/1924, parts to O-5 3321.	
1834	Baldwin	3/27/1908	32701	Dismantled at Dale Street 1/3/1923 to 2/28/1923, parts to O-5 3313.	
1835	Baldwin	3/31/1908	32702	Dismantled at Dale Street 12/23/1921 to 2/14/1922, parts to O-5 3303.	
1836	Baldwin	3/31/1908	32703	Dismantled at Hillyard 4/13/1923 to 6/3/1923, parts to O-5 3310.	
1837	Baldwin	4/3/1908	32704	Dismantled at Dale Street 9/4/1923 to 5/28/1924, parts to O-5 3323.	
1838	Baldwin	4/3/1908	32705	Dismantled at Hillyard 1/25/1922 to 4/10/1922, parts to O-5 3305.	
1839	Baldwin	4/3/1908	32706	Dismantled at Delta beginning 5/13/1924, parts to O-5 3332.	187
1840	Baldwin	4/7/1908	32707	Dismantled at Dale Street 4/23/1923 to 11/9/1923, parts to O-5 3316.	
1841	Baldwin	4/7/1908	32708	Dismantled at Dale Street beginning 6/2/1924, parts to O-5 3331.	188
1842*	Baldwin	4/7/1908	32709	Superheated at Hillyard 8/12/1915. Dismantled at Delta 2/13/1924 to 5/14/1924, parts to O-5 3326.	
1843	Baldwin	4/7/1908	32710	Dismantled at Delta beginning 9/11/1924, parts to O-5 3341.	188
1844	Baldwin	4/14/1908	32711	Dismantled at Dale Street 11/25/1921 to 12/23/1921, parts to O-5 3301.	188

Class L-1 2-6-6-2: 21½x32/33x32-55-200-355,000-316,000-69,900 originally. Those engines indicated below by an asterisk (*) received superheaters (dates shown below), had dimensions changed to 24x32/33x32-55-200-355,000-316,000-73,460, and were classified by GN as "L-1S". Dates listed below with an asterisk (*) are dates built.

No.	Builder	Date Rcvd.	C/N	Original No.	Renumbered From	Date	Disposition	Notes
1900	Baldwin	9/6/1906	28601	GN 1800(1)	GN 1800(1)	12/27/1907	Dismantled at Hillyard 8/19/1925 to 8/28/1925, parts to O-6 3357.	172
1901	Baldwin	9/11/1906	28641	GN 1801(1)	GN 1801(1)	1/13/1908	Dismantled at Hillyard 5/7/1925 to 11/7/1925, parts to O-6 3354.	172
1902*	Baldwin	9/22/1906	28739	GN 1802(1)	GN 1802(1)	1/6/1908	Superheated at Delta 12/29/1916. Dismantled at Delta beginning 10/5/1925, parts to O-6 3359.	
1903*	Baldwin	9/30/1906	28854	GN 1803(1)	GN 1803(1)	12/30/1907	Superheated at Delta 3/15/1918. Dismantled at Delta beginning 8/13/1925, parts to O-6 3358.	172
1904	Baldwin	10/22/1906	28933	GN 1804(1)	GN 1804(1)	1/18/1908	Dismantled at Hillyard beginning 12/3/1925, parts to O-6 3362.	
1905(1)	Baldwin	3/30/1908*	32722	–	–	–	Retained at Chicago by CB&Q (No. 4000).	
1905(2)	Baldwin	5/12/1908	32759	GN 1922	GN 1922	6/10/1908	Dismantled at Delta 5/19/1926 to 6/30/1926, parts to O-6 3369.	189
1906(1)	Baldwin	3/31/1908*	32723	–	–	–	Retained at Chicago by CB&Q (No. 4001).	
1906(2)	Baldwin	5/16/1908	32760	GN 1923	GN 1923	6/10/1908	Dismantled at Delta 11/24/1925 to 1/27/1926, parts to O-6 3363.	189
1907(1)	Baldwin	4/1/1908*	32724	–	–	–	Retained at Chicago by CB&Q (No. 4002).	
1907(2)	Baldwin	5/25/1908	32761	GN 1924	GN 1924	6/10/1908	Dismantled at Delta 2/13/1926 to 3/31/1926, parts to O-6 3366.	189
1908*	Baldwin	4/17/1908	32725	–	–	–	Superheated at Delta 4/30/1919. Dismantled at Delta beginning 6/20/1925, parts to O-6 3356.	190
1909	Baldwin	4/17/1908	32732	–	–	–	Dismantled at Hillyard 6/17/1926 to 7/17/1926, parts to O-6 3370.	190
1910	Baldwin	4/27/1908	32734	–	–	–	Dismantled at Hillyard 1/28/1925 to 8/25/1925, parts to O-6 3350.	191
1911	Baldwin	4/27/1908	32735	–	–	–	Dismantled at Hillyard beginning 7/16/1925, parts to O-6 3355.	191

									Notes
1912	Baldwin	4/27/1908	32740	–	–	–	Dismantled at Hillyard beginning 1/25/1926, parts to O-6 3364.		191
1913	Baldwin	4/27/1908	32741	–	–	–	Dismantled at Hillyard 3/2/1925 to 9/14/1925, parts to O-6 3351.		191
1914	Baldwin	5/1/1908	32742	–	–	–	Dismantled at Delta 4/21/1926 to 5/26/1926, parts to O-6 3368.		
1915	Baldwin	5/1/1908	32743	–	–	–	Dismantled at Hillyard 4/23/1926 to 5/22/1926, parts to O-6 3367.		
1916	Baldwin	5/4/1908	32746	–	–	–	Dismantled at Hillyard beginning 11/5/1925, parts to O-6 3361.		192
1917	Baldwin	5/4/1908	32747	–	–	–	Dismantled at Hillyard beginning 2/16/1926, parts to O-6 3365.		192
1918	Baldwin	5/9/1908	32748	–	–	–	Dismantled at Hillyard beginning 10/14/1925, parts to O-6 3360.		
1919	Baldwin	5/9/1908	32749	–	–	–	Dismantled at Delta 1/20/1925 to 8/29/1925, parts to O-6 3352.		
1920	Baldwin	5/12/1908	32755	–	–	–	Dismantled at Delta 3/30/1925 to 9/29/1925, parts to O-6 3353.		189
1921*	Baldwin	5/16/1908	32758	–	–	–	Superheated at Delta 4/23/1917. Dismantled at Hillyard 8/17/1926 to 9/17/1926, parts to O-6 3371.		189
1922	Baldwin	5/12/1908	32759	–	–	–	Renumbered GN 1905(2) at St.Paul 6/10/1908.		189
1923	Baldwin	5/16/1908	32760	–	–	–	Renumbered GN 1906(2) at St.Paul 6/10/1908.		189
1924	Baldwin	5/25/1908	32761	–	–	–	Renumbered GN 1907(2) at St.Paul 6/10/1908.		189

Class M-1 2-6-8-0: 23x32/35x32-55-210(200)-368,700-350,000-78,360. See Note 193.

No.	Builder	Date Rcvd.	C/N	Disposition	Notes
1950	Baldwin	3/7/1910	34024	Rblt. M-2(2) (same number) at Delta 11/17/1926 to 3/31/1927.	194
1951	Baldwin	1/19/1910	34025	Rblt. M-2(2) (same number) at Delta 1/7/1927 to 6/22/1927.	194
1952	Baldwin	1/17/1910	34026	Rblt. M-2(2) (same number) at Hillyard 3/23/1926 to 7/7/1926.	194
1953	Baldwin	1/19/1910	34027	Rblt. M-2(2) (same number) at Great Falls 5/6/1927 to 8/27/1927.	194
1954	Baldwin	1/23/1910	34028	Rblt. M-2(2) (same number) at Hillyard 6/6/1927 to 9/2/1927.	194
1955	Baldwin	2/5/1910	34074	Rblt. M-2(2) (same number) at Great Falls 1/3/1927 to 5/5/1927.	194
1956	Baldwin	2/5/1910	34075	Rblt. M-2(2) (same number) at Hillyard 7/14/1926 to 10/4/1926.	
1957	Baldwin	2/5/1910	34076	Rblt. M-2(2) (same number) at Great Falls 3/1/1927 to 6/30/1927.	
1958	Baldwin	2/15/1910	34104	Rblt. M-2(2) (same number) at Great Falls 1/3/1927 to 4/26/1927.	
1959	Baldwin	3/7/1910	34105	Rblt. M-2(2) (same number) at Hillyard 2/24/1927 to 7/19/1927.	195
1960	Baldwin	7/13/1910	34824	Rblt. M-2(2) (same number) at Great Falls 6/28/1926 to 10/27/1926.	
1961	Baldwin	7/13/1910	34825	Rblt. M-2(2) (same number) at Great Falls 11/6/1926 to 2/28/1927.	
1962	Baldwin	7/23/1910	34826	Rblt. M-2(2) (same number) at Delta 6/23/1927 to 10/28/1927.	196
1963	Baldwin	7/26/1910	34827	Rblt. M-2(2) (same number) at Great Falls 9/30/1926 to 12/23/1926.	
1964	Baldwin	7/14/1910	34828	Rblt. M-2(2) (same number) at Delta 7/29/1926 to 12/29/1926.	
1965	Baldwin	7/11/1910	34829	Rblt. M-2(2) (same number) at Great Falls 11/5/1927 to 2/18/1928.	
1966	Baldwin	7/23/1910	34830	Rblt. M-2(2) (same number) at Delta 4/1/1927 to 8/24/1927.	196
1967	Baldwin	7/27/1910	34831	Rblt. M-2(2) (same number) at Great Falls 7/9/1927 to 10/28/1927.	
1968	Baldwin	7/30/1910	34832	Rblt. M-2(2) (same number) at Great Falls 2/9/1926 to 6/19/1926.	
1969	Baldwin	8/13/1910	34833	Rblt. M-2(2) (same number) at Hillyard 10/23/1926 to 2/23/1927.	
1970	Baldwin	8/22/1910	34965	Rblt. M-2(2) (same number) at Dale Street 11/14/1927 to 2/29/1928.	
1971	Baldwin	8/22/1910	34967	Rblt. M-2(2) (same number) at Superior 10/27/1927 to 1/21/1928.	
1972	Baldwin	8/22/1910	34968	Rblt. M-2(2) (same number) at Dale Street 12/7/1926 to 5/11/1927.	
1973	Baldwin	9/1/1910	34997	Rblt. M-2(2) (same number) at Superior 10/13/1926 to 1/31/1927.	
1974	Baldwin	8/28/1910	34998	Rblt. M-2(2) (same number) at Dale Street 8/23/1926 to 12/21/1926.	
1975	Baldwin	9/2/1910	34999	Rblt. M-2(2) (same number) at Superior 6/8/1927 to 10/11/1927.	
1976	Baldwin	9/8/1910	35046	Rblt. M-2(2) (same number) at Dale Street 1/3/1927 to 7/28/1927.	
1977	Baldwin	9/5/1910	35047	Rblt. M-2(2) (same number) at Dale Street 2/18/1926 to 10/14/1926.	197
1978	Baldwin	9/1/1910	35048	Rblt. M-2(2) (same number) at Dale Street 11/8/1926 to 3/29/1927.	
1979	Baldwin	9/9/1910	35049	Rblt. M-2(2) (same number) at Dale Street 5/26/1927 to 11/16/1927.	
1980	Baldwin	9/15/1910	35050	Rblt. M-2(2) (same number) at Superior 10/22/1926 to 2/12/1927.	
1981	Baldwin	9/18/1910	35051	Rblt. M-2(2) (same number) at Superior 5/10/1927 to 8/24/1927.	
1982	Baldwin	9/18/1910	35052	Rblt. M-2(2) (same number) at Superior 10/11/1927 to 11/30/1927.	
1983	Baldwin	9/15/1910	35088	Rblt. M-2(2) (same number) at Dale Street 11/23/1925 to 6/30/1926.	
1984	Baldwin	10/10/1910	35089	Rblt. M-2(2) (same number) at Dale Street 12/11/1925 to 8/31/1926.	198

Class M-2(2) 2-6-8-0: 23½x32/22x32-55-210-403,000-384,000-95,500 as rebuilt to M-2(2). Those still on the roster as M-2's by the late 1940's had weight increased to 413,440 lb., weight on drivers to 394,000 lb., and T.E. increased to 102,592 lb. (Rebuilt from M-1 2-6-8-0, same numbers)

No.	Builder	Date Start Rbld.	Date Finish Rbld	C/N	Disposition	Notes
1950	GN (Delta)	11/17/1926	3/31/1927	34024	Dismantled at Hillyard 11/14/1930 to 12/20/1930. Parts to O-7 3388.	
1951	GN (Delta)	1/7/1927	6/22/1927	34025	Sold for scrap PC 8/29/1950.	
1952	GN (Hillyard)	3/23/1926	7/7/1926	34026	Dismantled at Hillyard 5/4/1931 to 6/1/1931. Parts to O-7 3394.	
1953	GN (Great Falls)	5/6/1927	8/27/1927	34027	Dismantled at Great Falls beginning 11/14/1929. Parts to O-7 3380.	
1954	GN (Hillyard)	6/6/1927	9/2/1927	34028	Dismantled at Hillyard 11/26/1929 to 12/28/1929. Parts to O-7 3381.	
1955	GN (Great Falls)	1/3/1927	5/5/1927	34074	Dismantled at Hillyard 2/4/1931 to 3/12/1931. Parts to O-7 3392.	
1956	GN (Hillyard)	7/14/1926	10/4/1926	34075	Dismantled at Great Falls beginning 7/29/1931. Parts to O-7 3395.	
1957	GN (Great Falls)	3/1/1927	6/30/1927	34076	Dismantled at Great Falls beginning 4/30/1930. Parts to O-7 3385.	
1958	GN (Great Falls)	1/3/1927	4/26/1927	34104	Dismantled at Hillyard 10/7/1930 to 10/25/1930. Parts to O-7 3387.	
1959	GN (Hillyard)	2/24/1927	7/19/1927	34105	Dismantled at Great Falls beginning 12/5/1930. Parts to O-7 3390.	
1960	GN (Great Falls)	6/28/1926	10/27/1926	34824	Dismantled at Hillyard beginning 7/23/1931. Parts to O-7 3396.	
1961	GN (Great Falls)	11/6/1926	2/28/1927	34825	Dismantled at Great Falls beginning 11/2/1929. Parts to O-7 3379.	
1962	GN (Delta)	6/23/1927	10/28/1927	34826	Dismantled at Great Falls beginning 8/6/1930. Parts to O-7 3386.	
1963	GN (Great Falls)	9/30/1926	12/23/1926	34827	Sold for scrap DI&M 1/31/1950.	
1964	GN (Delta)	7/29/1926	12/29/1926	34828	Dismantled at Hillyard 4/22/1930 to 5/7/1930. Parts to O-7 3384.	

Class M-2(2) 2-6-8-0: Continued

No.	Builder	Date Start Rbld.	Date Finish Rbld	C/N	Disposition	Notes
1965	GN (Great Falls)	11/5/1927	2/18/1928	34829	Sold for scrap PC 5/16/1953.	168
1966	GN (Delta)	4/1/1927	8/24/1927	34830	Dismantled at Hillyard 8/16/1929 to 9/21/1929. Parts to O-7 3376.	
1967	GN (Great Falls)	7/9/1927	10/28/1927	34831	Sold for scrap DI&M 5/16/1953.	168
1968	GN (Great Falls)	2/9/1926	6/19/1926	34832	Sold for scrap PC 5/15/1953.	168
1969	GN (Hillyard)	10/23/1926	2/23/1927	34833	Dismantled at Great Falls beginning 5/29/1929. Parts to O-7 3375.	
1970	GN (Dale Street)	11/14/1927	2/29/1928	34965	Dismantled at Great Falls beginning 4/29/1931. Parts to O-7 3393.	
1971	GN (Superior)	10/27/1927	1/21/1928	34967	Dismantled at Superior beginning 11/2/1929. Parts to O-7 3378.	
1972	GN (Dale Street)	12/7/1926	5/11/1927	34968	Sold for scrap DI&M 11/7/1951.	
1973	GN (Superior)	10/13/1926	1/31/1927	34997	Sold for scrap PC 1/29/1955.	169
1974	GN (Dale Street)	8/23/1926	12/21/1926	34998	Sold for scrap DI&M 5/25/1951.	
1975	GN (Superior)	6/8/1927	10/11/1927	34999	Dismantled at Hillyard 3/12/1930 to 3/31/1930. Parts to O-7 3382.	
1976	GN (Dale Street)	1/3/1927	7/28/1927	35046	Dismantled at Superior beginning 11/21/1930. Parts to O-7 3389.	
1977	GN (Dale Street)	2/18/1926	10/14/1926	35047	Sold for scrap DI&M 2/5/1955.	169
1978	GN (Dale Street)	11/8/1926	3/29/1927	35048	Dismantled at Great Falls beginning 8/22/1929. Parts to O-7 3377.	
1979	GN (Dale Street)	5/26/1927	11/16/1927	35049	Dismantled at Great Falls beginning 2/19/1931. Parts to O-7 3391.	
1980	GN (Superior)	10/22/1926	2/12/1927	35050	Sold for scrap DI&M 11/7/1951.	
1981	GN (Superior)	5/10/1927	8/24/1927	35051	Sold for scrap DI&M 6/24/1953.	168
1982	GN (Superior)	10/11/1927	11/30/1927	35052	Dismantled at Superior beginning 4/4/1930. Parts to O-7 3383.	
1983	GN (Dale Street)	11/23/1925	6/30/1926	35088	Sold for scrap PC 1/14/1955.	169
1984	GN (Dale Street)	12/11/1925	8/31/1926	35089	Sold for scrap DI&M 9/29/1949.	

Class M-2(1) 2-6-8-0: 20x32/33x32-55-210(200)-350,000-330,000-62,220 (Rebuilt from F-8 2-8-0)

No.	Builder	Date	C/N	Original No.	Renumbered From	Date	Disposition
1999	GN (Dale Street)	1/15/1910	32363	GN 1254	GN 2000(1)	4/12/1912	Rblt. C-4 870(1) at Dale Street 2/13/1926.
2000(1)	GN (Dale Street)	1/15/1910	32363	GN 1254	GN 1254	1/18/1910	Reno. GN 1999 at Superior Roundhouse 4/12/1912.

Class N-1 2-8-8-0: 28x32/42x32-63-210-450,000-420,000-93,250

No.	Builder	Date Rcvd.	C/N	Disposition	Notes
2000(2)	Baldwin	9/13/1912	38074	Rblt. N-2 (same number) at Superior 9/9/1924 to 3/31/1925.	
2001	Baldwin	9/13/1912	38130	Rblt. N-2 (same number) at Superior 2/2/1925 to 6/30/1925.	
2002	Baldwin	9/13/1912	38131	Rblt. N-2 (same number) at Superior 12/21/1925 to 4/28/1926.	
2003	Baldwin	9/18/1912	38132	Rblt. N-2 (same number) at Superior 7/1/1925 to 10/6/1925.	
2004	Baldwin	9/13/1912	38167	Rblt. N-2 (same number) at Superior 1/4/1926 to 4/5/1926.	
2005	Baldwin	9/18/1912	38186	Rblt. N-2 (same number) at Superior 8/18/1925 to 10/29/1925.	
2006	Baldwin	9/23/1912	38187	Rblt. N-2 (same number) at Superior 2/12/1926 to 5/28/1926.	
2007	Baldwin	9/26/1912	38188	Rblt. N-2 (same number) at Superior 11/5/1926 to 3/5/1927.	
2008	Baldwin	9/27/1912	38189	Rblt. N-2 (same number) at Dale Street 2/15/1924 to 5/6/1924.	
2009	Baldwin	10/2/1912	38225	Rblt. N-2 (same number) at Superior 4/22/1925 to 8/22/1925.	
2010	Baldwin	10/12/1912	38226	Rblt. N-2 (same number) at Superior 5/14/1926 to 8/12/1926.	
2011	Baldwin	10/12/1912	38227	Rblt. N-2 (same number) at Superior 8/3/1926 to 10/6/1926.	
2012	Baldwin	10/7/1912	38228	Rblt. N-2 (same number) at Superior 10/29/1925 to 2/26/1926.	
2013	Baldwin	10/10/1912	38281	Rblt. N-2 (same number) at Superior 9/24/1925 to 11/25/1925.	
2014	Baldwin	10/13/1912	38282	Rblt. N-2 (same number) at Superior 2/8/1926 to 5/2/1926.	
2015	Baldwin	10/17/1912	38283	Rblt. N-2 (same number) at Superior 11/6/1925 to 2/11/1926.	
2016	Baldwin	10/17/1912	38284	Rblt. N-2 (same number) at Superior 10/20/1925 to 2/6/1926.	
2017	Baldwin	11/2/1912	38371	Rblt. N-2 (same number) at Superior 6/14/1926 to 8/28/1926.	
2018	Baldwin	10/23/1912	38372	Rblt. N-2 (same number) at Superior 11/15/1926 to 3/31/1927.	
2019	Baldwin	11/6/1912	38373	Rblt. N-2 (same number) at Superior 11/18/1925 to 3/6/1926.	
2020	Baldwin	10/25/1912	38382	Rblt. N-2 (same number) at Superior 3/3/1926 to 6/10/1926.	
2021	Baldwin	10/27/1912	38383	Rblt. N-2 (same number) at Superior 12/11/1925 to 3/31/1926.	
2022	Baldwin	11/3/1912	38384	Rblt. N-2 (same number) at Superior 1/20/1926 to 4/28/1926.	199
2023	Baldwin	10/27/1912	38415	Rblt. N-2 (same number) at Superior 11/5/1926 to 2/24/1927.	
2024	Baldwin	11/3/1912	38416	Rblt. N-2 (same number) at Superior 10/4/1926 to 11/23/1926.	

Class N-2 2-8-8-0: 25x32/25x32-63-210-450,000-420,000-100,000 (Rebuilt from Class N-1 2-8-8-0 with same numbers)

No.	Builder	Date Start Rbld.	Date Finish Rbld	C/N	Disposition	Notes
2000(2)	GN (Superior)	9/9/1924	3/31/1925	38074	Rblt. N-3 (same number) at Hillyard 2/11/1941 to 6/27/1941.	
2001	GN (Superior)	2/2/1925	6/30/1925	38130	Rblt. N-3 (same number) at Hillyard 7/15/1941 to 9/26/1941.	
2002	GN (Superior)	12/21/1925	4/28/1926	38131	Rblt. N-3 (same number) at Superior 8/2/1941 to 10/16/1941.	
2003	GN (Superior)	7/1/1925	10/6/1925	38132	Rblt. N-3 (same number) at Hillyard 5/13/1941 to 7/18/1941.	
2004	GN (Superior)	1/4/1926	4/5/1926	38167	Received new Baldwin-built boiler EX7412-1 at Superior 11/15/1933 to 5/11/1934. Rblt. N-3 (same number) at Superior 4/22/1941 to 6/30/1941.	
2005	GN (Superior)	8/18/1925	10/29/1925	38186	Rblt. N-3 (same number) at Hillyard 8/28/1941 to 10/22/1941.	
2006	GN (Superior)	2/12/1926	5/28/1926	38187	Rblt. N-3 (same number) at Superior 3/13/1941 to 5/31/1941.	
2007	GN (Superior)	11/5/1926	3/5/1927	38188	Received new Baldwin-built boiler EX7412-5 at Superior 10/15/1934 to 1/31/1935. Rblt. N-3 (same number) at Superior 9/1/1941 to 9/12/1941.	
2008	GN (Dale Street)	2/15/1924	5/6/1924	38189	Rblt. N-3 (same number) at Hillyard 10/11/1941 to 11/25/1941.	
2009	GN (Superior)	4/22/1925	8/22/1925	38225	Rblt. N-3 (same number) at Hillyard 10/15/1941 to 2/13/1942.	

2010	GN (Superior)	5/14/1926	8/12/1926	38226	Received new Baldwin-built boiler EX7412-3 at Superior 8/6/1934 to 10/31/1934. Rblt. N-3 (same number) at Superior 12/5/1940 to 3/13/1941.	
2011	GN (Superior)	8/3/1926	10/6/1926	38227	Rblt. N-3 (same number) at Superior 6/4/1940 to 9/30/1940.	
2012	GN (Superior)	10/29/1925	2/26/1926	38228	Rblt. N-3 (same number) at Superior 1/16/1941 to 4/19/1941.	
2013	GN (Superior)	9/24/1925	11/25/1925	38281	Rblt. N-3 (same number) at Hillyard 12/11/1940 to 5/17/1941.	
2014	GN (Superior)	2/8/1926	5/2/1926	38282	Rblt. N-3 (same number) at Superior 1/24/1940 to 4/29/1940.	
2015	GN (Superior)	11/6/1925	2/11/1926	38283	Rblt. N-3 (same number) at Superior 8/28/1940 to 11/30/1940.	
2016	GN (Superior)	10/20/1925	2/6/1926	38284	Rblt. N-3 (same number) at Hillyard 7/14/1941 to 8/25/1941.	
2017	GN (Superior)	6/14/1926	8/28/1926	38371	Rblt. N-3 (same number) at Superior 10/1/1940 to 12/21/1940.	
2018	GN (Superior)	11/15/1926	3/31/1927	38372	Rblt. N-3 (same number) at Superior 11/24/1939 to 3/29/1940.	
2019	GN (Superior)	11/18/1925	3/6/1926	38373	Rblt. N-3 (same number) at Superior 4/29/1940 to 8/16/1940.	
2020	GN (Superior)	3/3/1926	6/10/1926	38382	Received new Baldwin-built boiler EX7412-4 at Superior 5/29/1934 to 9/29/1934. Rblt. N-3 (same number) at Superior 10/16/1940 to 1/15/1941.	
2021	GN (Superior)	12/11/1925	3/31/1926	38383	Rblt. N-3 (same number) at Superior 3/29/1940 to 7/19/1940.	199
2022	GN (Superior)	1/20/1926	4/28/1926	38384	Received new Baldwin-built boiler EX7412-2 at Superior 12/13/1933 to 7/20/1934. Rblt. N-3 (same number) at Superior 6/3/1941 to 7/31/1941.	
2023	GN (Superior)	11/5/1926	2/24/1927	38415	Rblt. N-3 (same number) at Superior 2/13/1940 to 5/31/1940.	
2024	GN (Superior)	10/4/1926	11/23/1926	38416	Rblt. N-3 (same number) at Superior 10/6/1939 to 2/10/1940.	

Class N-3 2-8-8-0: 22x32/22x32-63-300-489,200-459,200-118,400 as rebuilt. Designed boiler pressure later decreased to 275 psi, working boiler pressure to 265 psi, with resultant decrease in T.E. to 104,236 lb. As result of reweighing, engine weights of coal burners increased to 576,780 lb. (542,000 lb. on drivers). Engine weights of oil burners increased to 572,375 lb. (537,880 lb. on drivers). (Rebuilt using parts from Class N-2 2-8-8-0 with same numbers)

No.	Builder	Date Start Rbld.	Date Finish Rbld.	C/N	Disposition	Notes
2000(2)	GN (Hillyard)	2/11/1941	6/27/1941	X6808-5	Ret. 4/1955. Sold for scrap DI&M 7/20/1955.	232
2001	GN (Hillyard)	7/15/1941	9/26/1941	X6808-11	Ret. 12/1957. Sold for scrap c.1962.	
2002	GN (Superior)	8/2/1941	10/16/1941	X6808-10	Ret. 12/1957. Sold for scrap c.1962.	
2003	GN (Hillyard)	5/13/1941	7/18/1941	X6808-8	Ret. 4/1955. Sold for scrap DI&M 8/1/1955.	
2004	GN (Superior)	4/22/1941	6/30/1941	X6808-6	Ret. 4/1955. Sold for scrap DI&M 7/8/1955.	232
2005	GN (Hillyard)	8/28/1941	10/22/1941	X6808-14	Ret. 12/1957. Sold for scrap DI&M 2/1963.	
2006	GN (Superior)	3/13/1941	5/31/1941	X6808-3	Ret. 8/1956. Sold for scrap PC 9/12/1956.	200
2007	GN (Superior)	9/1/1941	9/12/1941	X6808-12	Ret. 4/1955. Sold for scrap DI&M 8/13/1955.	232
2008	GN (Hillyard)	10/11/1941	11/25/1941	X6808-15	Ret. 9/1955. Sold for scrap PC 1/15/1956.	233
2009	GN (Hillyard)	10/15/1941	2/13/1942	X6808-13	Ret. 4/1955. Sold for scrap PC 8/9/1955.	201
2010	GN (Superior)	12/5/1940	3/13/1941	X6808-1	Ret. 8/1956. Sold for scrap PC 8/16/1956.	
2011	GN (Superior)	6/4/1940	9/30/1940	X5880-7	Ret. 8/1956. Sold for scrap PC 9/6/1956.	200
2012	GN (Superior)	1/16/1941	4/19/1941	X6808-2	Ret. 12/1957. Sold for scrap c.1962.	
2013	GN (Hillyard)	12/11/1940	5/17/1941	X6808-4	Ret. 12/1957. Sold for scrap c.1962.	
2014	GN (Superior)	1/24/1940	4/29/1940	X5880-3	Ret. 8/1956. Sold for scrap DI&M 10/7/1956.	200
2015	GN (Superior)	8/28/1940	11/30/1940	X5880-8	Ret. 9/1955. Sold for scrap PC 10/27/1955.	233
2016	GN (Hillyard)	7/14/1941	8/25/1941	X6808-9	Ret. 12/1957. Sold for scrap c.1962.	
2017	GN (Superior)	10/1/1940	12/21/1940	X5880-9	Ret. 8/1956. Sold for scrap DI&M 10/7/1956.	200
2018	GN (Superior)	11/24/1939	3/29/1940	X5880-2	Ret. 12/1957. Sold for scrap c.1962.	
2019	GN (Superior)	4/29/1940	8/16/1940	X5880-6	Ret. 9/1955. Sold for scrap DI&M 10/24/1955.	233
2020	GN (Superior)	10/16/1940	1/15/1941	X5880-10	Ret. 8/1956. Sold for scrap DI&M 10/7/1956.	200
2021	GN (Superior)	3/29/1940	7/19/1940	X5880-5	Ret. 12/1957. Sold for scrap WEI&M 7/1963.	
2022	GN (Superior)	6/3/1941	7/31/1941	X6808-7	Ret. 9/1955. Sold for scrap DI&M 10/27/1955.	233
2023	GN (Superior)	2/13/1940	5/31/1940	X5880-4	Ret. 12/1957. Sold for scrap c.1962.	
2024	GN (Superior)	10/16/1939	2/10/1940	X5880-1	Ret. 9/1955. Sold for scrap DI&M 10/24/1955.	233

Class R-1 2-8-8-2: 28x32/28x32-63-210-594,940-532,800-127,500 originally. Weights later increased as result of reweighing to 621,220-555,000-129,622.

No.	Builder	Date Rcvd.	C/N	Disposition	Notes
2030	Baldwin	8/5/1925	58480	Assigned ore steaming 8/20/1951. Sold for scrap PC 9/6/1956.	200
2031	Baldwin	8/22/1925	58481	Assigned ore steaming 8/20/1951. Sold for scrap DI&M 9/9/1956.	200
2032	Baldwin	8/24/1925	58528	Sold for scrap PC 6/9/1952.	
2033	Baldwin	8/31/1925	58542	Assigned ore steaming 8/20/1951. Sold for scrap PC 9/6/1956.	200

Class R-1 2-8-8-2: 28x32/28x32-63-225-594,940-532,800-136,600 originally. Rebuilt and reweighed in the 1940's to 26x32/28x32-63-225-621,220-555,000-133,177.

No.	Builder	Date Started	Date Completed	C/N	Disposition	Notes
2034	GN (Hillyard)	10/14/1927	11/21/1927	PSMD 501	Received new Alco boiler No. 46207-2 at Hillyard, 10/2/1947 to 11/28/1947. Sold for scrap 9/16/1956.	200, 202
2035	GN (Hillyard)	10/24/1927	12/12/1927	PSMD 502	Ret. 9/1955. Sold for scrap DI&M 12/25/1955.	202, 233
2036	GN (Hillyard)	11/21/1927	1/16/1928	PSMD 503	Ret. 9/1955. Sold for scrap DI&M 11/20/1955.	202, 233
2037	GN (Hillyard)	12/19/1927	2/6/1928	PSMD 504	Ret. 9/1955. Sold for scrap PC 11/20/1955.	202, 233
2038	GN (Hillyard)	6/19/1928	7/19/1928	PSMD 505	Ret. 9/1955. Sold for scrap PC 1/29/1956.	202, 233
2039	GN (Hillyard)	7/5/1928	8/9/1928	PSMD 506	Ret. 9/1955. Sold for scrap PC 12/12/1955.	202, 233
2040	GN (Hillyard)	7/26/1928	9/4/1928	PSMD 507	Received new Alco boiler No. 46207-3 at Hillyard, 1/27/1948 to 3/24/1948. Assigned ore steaming, ret. 5/1958. Setout for scrap 8/15/1960, sold PC 3/1962.	202
2041	GN (Hillyard)	8/14/1928	9/24/1928	PSMD 508	Sold for scrap DI&M 6/10/1956.	167, 202
2042	GN (Hillyard)	9/17/1928	10/26/1928	PSMD 509	Received new Alco boiler No. 46207-4 at Hillyard, 3/26/1948 to 5/4/1948. Assigned ore steaming, ret. 5/1958. Setout for scrap 8/15/1960, sold PC 3/1962.	202
2043	GN (Hillyard)	10/14/1928	11/21/1928	PSMD 510	Received new Alco boiler No. 46207-1 at Hillyard, 5/19/1948 to 7/22/1948. Assigned ore steaming, ret. 5/1958. Setout for scrap 8/15/1960, sold PC 3/1962.	202

Class R-2 2-8-8-2: 28x32/28x32-63-240-630,750-544,000-146,000 originally. Weights later increased as a result of reweighing to 686,440-592,000 and T.E. decreased to 142,055.

No.	Builder	Date Started	Date Completed	C/N	Disposition	Notes
2044	GN (Hillyard)	3/22/1929	5/14/1929	PSMD 511	Received new Alco boiler No. 52715-1 at Hillyard 11/18/1947 to 1/17/1948. Retired 12/1957. Sold for scrap PC 3/1962.	202
2045	GN (Hillyard)	4/9/1929	6/1/1929	PSMD 512	Received new Alco boiler No. 52715-2 at Hillyard 1/20/1948 to 3/12/1948. Sold for scrap PC 6/1953.	168, 202
2046	GN (Hillyard)	4/19/1929	6/19/1929	PSMD 513	Received new Alco boiler No. 46208-5 at Hillyard 8/13/1947 to 9/30/1947. Retired 12/1957. Sold for scrap c.1962.	202
2047	GN (Hillyard)	5/2/1929	7/9/1929	PSMD 514	Received new Alco boiler No. 46208-2 at Hillyard 1/18/1947 to 3/21/1947. Retired 12/1957. Sold for scrap c.1962.	202, 203
2048	GN (Hillyard)	5/17/1929	7/23/1929	PSMD 515	Received new Alco boiler No. 52715-3 at Hillyard 10/2/1948 to 11/20/1948. Sold for scrap DI&M 11/18/1956.	200, 202
2049	GN (Hillyard)	6/2/1929	8/6/1929	PSMD 516	Received new Alco boiler No. 52715-10 at Hillyard 5/4/1948 to 6/30/1948. Sold for scrap PC 11/25/1956.	200, 202
2050	GN (Hillyard)	6/18/1929	8/21/1929	PSMD 517	Received new Alco boiler No. 52715-8 at Hillyard 11/1/1948 to 12/15/1948. Sold for scrap DI&M 11/11/1956.	200, 202
2051	GN (Hillyard)	7/2/1929	9/4/1929	PSMD 518	Received new Alco boiler No. 52715-9 at Hillyard 3/13/1948 to 4/28/1948. Ret. 4/1958. Sold for scrap 4/1963.	202
2052	GN (Hillyard)	7/17/1929	9/16/1929	PSMD 519	Received new Alco boiler No. 52715-6 at Hillyard 5/24/1948 to 7/30/1948. Sold for scrap PC 11/4/1956.	200, 202
2053	GN (Hillyard)	8/6/1929	9/27/1929	PSMD 520	Received new Alco boiler No. 52715-4 at Hillyard 7/2/1948 to 8/31/1948. Ret. 4/1958. Sold for scrap 4/1963.	202
2054	GN (Hillyard)	2/27/1930	3/31/1930	PSMD 521	Received new Alco boiler No. 46208-1 at Hillyard 9/14/1946 to 1/17/1947. Retired 12/1957. Sold for scrap c.1962.	202
2055	GN (Hillyard)	3/19/1930	5/21/1930	PSMD 522	Received new Alco boiler No. 46208-3 at Hillyard 3/22/1947 to 5/28/1947. Retired 12/1957. Sold for scrap c.1962.	202
2056	GN (Hillyard)	4/19/1930	6/23/1930	PSMD 523	Received new Alco boiler No. 46208-4 at Hillyard 8/26/1947 to 10/29/1947. Retired 12/1957. Sold for scrap PC 7/1962.	202
2057	GN (Hillyard)	5/12/1930	7/28/1930	PSMD 524	Received new Alco boiler No. 52715-7 at Hillyard 9/7/1948 to 10/29/1948. Sold for scrap PC 2/12/1955.	202, 232
2058	GN (Hillyard)	6/17/1930	9/6/1930	PSMD 525	Received new Alco boiler No. 52715-5 at Hillyard 7/29/1948 to 9/25/1948. Sold for scrap WEI&M 8/16/1956.	202
2059	GN (Hillyard)	8/1/1930	11/3/1930	PSMD 526	Received new Alco boiler No. 46208-6 at Hillyard 5/31/1947 to 8/9/1947. Retired 12/1957. Sold for scrap PC 7/1962.	202

Class Q-1 2-10-2: 31x32-63-210-422,340-342,490-87,127 originally. Some of these locomotives were equipped with boosters having a T.E. of 12,200 lb. when new, and most others were later equipped with them (probable exceptions are Nos. 2113, 2114, 2115, and 2116). This changed total weight to 428,340 lb. During the late 1940's, all except Nos. 2113 and 2118 had dimensions changed to 29x32-63-210-444,700-356,000-76,251.

No.	Builder	Date Rcvd.	C/N	Disposition	Notes
2100	Baldwin	12/26/1923	57410	Booster applied and removed, dates unknown. Ret. 12/1949. Sold for scrap PC 1/31/1950.	
2101	Baldwin	12/28/1923	57442	Booster applied at Great Falls 12/30/1945, removed at Klamath Falls 8/1949. Changed to steam ore for Mesabi Division, 8/20/1951. Ret. 5/1958. Sold for scrap PC 3/1962.	
2102	Baldwin	12/28/1923	57517	Booster removed at Superior 10/1951. Ret. 4/1955. Sold for scrap WEI&M 8/1/1955.	232, 236
2103	Baldwin	12/28/1923	57518	Booster removed at Superior 8/11/1950. Ret. 9/1955. Sold for scrap WEI&M 11/4/1955.	233
2104	Baldwin	12/28/1923	57519	Booster applied at Great Falls 3/31/1947, removed at Superior 12/30/1949. Sold for scrap DI&M 8/10/1953.	171
2105	Baldwin	12/28/1923	57520	Booster removed 12/1951. Ret. 9/1955. Sold for scrap PC 11/12/1955.	233
2106	Baldwin	2/6/1924	57521	Booster applied at Great Falls 11/21/1946, removed at Superior 11/10/1949. Sold for scrap DI&M 8/25/1955.	
2107	Baldwin	1/9/1924	57522	Booster removed at Klamath Falls 8/1949. Changed to steam ore for Mesabi Division 8/20/1951. Ret. 5/1958. Sold for scrap PC 3/1962.	
2108	Baldwin	1/9/1924	57523	Booster removed at Superior 12/15/1949. Sold for scrap DI&M 10/3/1950.	
2109	Baldwin	1/9/1924	57524	Booster removed at Superior 8/1949. Sold for scrap PC 5/3/1952.	
2110	Baldwin	1/9/1924	57525	Booster applied at Great Falls 6/21/1947, removed at Superior 11/23/1949. Ret. 9/1955. Sold for scrap PC 11/12/1955.	233
2111	Baldwin	1/11/1924	57526	Booster applied at Great Falls 6/22/1945, removed at Superior 1/12/1950. Sold for scrap DI&M 7/21/1951.	
2112	Baldwin	1/11/1924	57527	Booster applied c.1945 and removed, date unknown. Ret. 9/1955. Sold for scrap DI&M 11/12/1955.	233
2113	Baldwin	1/13/1924	57528	Sold for stationary boiler use to Erie Mining Co. 12/13/1954.	
2114	Baldwin	1/11/1924	57529	Sold for stationary boiler use to Erie Mining Co. 12/13/1954.	
2115	Baldwin	1/11/1924	57530	Sold for scrap DI&M 9/16/1956.	200
2116	Baldwin	1/16/1924	57531	Sold for scrap DI&M 9/7/1955.	234
2117	Baldwin	1/16/1924	57532	Booster removed at Hillyard 11/21/1950. Sold for scrap DI&M 10/7/1956.	200
2118	Baldwin	1/16/1924	57559	Booster applied and removed, dates unknown. Ret. 12/1949. Sold for scrap DI&M 1/31/1950.	
2119	Baldwin	1/16/1924	57560	Booster applied and removed, dates unknown. Sold for scrap PC 8/1953.	171
2120	Baldwin	1/16/1924	57561	Booster applied and removed, dates unknown. Changed to steam ore for Mesabi Division 8/20/1951. Ret. 5/1958. Sold for scrap PC 5/1962.	
2121	Baldwin	1/18/1924	57562	Booster removed at Superior 12/22/1949. Ret. 4/1956. Sold for scrap PC 5/13/1956.	167, 204
2122	Baldwin	1/18/1924	57563	Booster removed at Hillyard 11/27/1951. Ret. 12/1957. Sold for scrap c.1963.	204
2123	Baldwin	1/18/1924	57564	Booster removed at Grand Forks 12/27/1951. Ret. 4/1955. Sold for scrap WEI&M 6/10/1955.	232
2124	Baldwin	1/18/1924	57565	Booster removed 12/1951. Sold for scrap PC 1/15/1955.	169

2125	Baldwin	1/18/1924	57566	Booster removed at Superior 4/21/1950. Sold for scrap DI&M 5/6/1956.	167
2126	Baldwin	1/18/1924	57567	Booster removed at Superior 12/11/1949. Sold for scrap PC 9/6/1956.	200
2127	Baldwin	2/4/1924	57568	Booster removed at Klamath Falls 8/1949. Ret. 12/1957. Sold for scrap c.1963.	
2128	Baldwin	2/6/1924	57592	Booster removed at Hillyard 4/18/1951. Ret. 12/1957. Sold for scrap PC 6/1962.	
2129	Baldwin	2/6/1924	57593	Booster applied and removed, dates unknown. Ret. 12/1949. Sold for scrap Dulien Steel Products 11/19/1950.	

Class Q-2 2-10-2: 29x32-63-210-364,000-290,000-76,250 originally. As result of reweighing, weight increased to 404,660 lb. (314,000 lb. on drivers). Nos. 2179 and 2185 received boosters (12,200 lb. T.E.) which had been removed from H-4 locomotives (dates shown below). (Rebuilt from Class P-1 4-8-2)

No.	Builder	Date Start Rbld.	Date Finish Rbld	C/N	Reblt. From P-1 No.	Disposition	Notes
2175	GN (Hillyard)	1/24/1928	6/22/1928	1368	GN 1754	Sold for scrap DI&M 8/29/1953.	171
2176	GN (Great Falls)	1/23/1928	6/27/1928	1378	GN 1764	Sold for scrap PC 8/1953.	171
2177	GN (Superior)	2/18/1928	6/26/1928	1371	GN 1757	Ret. 4/1958. Sold for scrap 2/1963.	
2178	GN (Hillyard)	2/11/1928	7/23/1928	1375	GN 1761	Ret. 4/1958. Sold for scrap PC 12/3/1962.	
2179	GN (Hillyard)	2/27/1928	8/16/1928	1366	GN 1752	Booster applied at Superior 10/23/1939, removed 4/1950. Sold for scrap PC 10/25/1955.	234
2180	GN (Great Falls)	2/28/1928	7/27/1928	1369	GN 1755	Sold for scrap DI&M 11/4/1955.	233
2181	GN (Great Falls)	2/29/1928	8/24/1928	1373	GN 1759	Ret. 3/1958. Sold for scrap PC 3/1962.	
2182	GN (Superior)	4/2/1928	7/31/1928	1372	GN 1758	Ret. 4/1958. Scrapped at St.Cloud 12/1960.	
2183	GN (Great Falls)	5/31/1928	9/22/1928	1365	GN 1751	Sold for scrap DI&M 7/28/1953.	171
2184	GN (Great Falls)	7/2/1928	10/30/1928	1376	GN 1762	Sold for scrap DI&M 9/7/1955.	234
2185	GN (Hillyard)	7/12/1928	10/10/1928	1374	GN 1760	Booster applied at Superior 10/20/1939, removed at Grand Forks 12/27/1950. Sold for scrap PC 8/29/1953.	171
2186	GN (Superior)	6/29/1928	8/31/1928	1367	GN 1753	Ret. 12/1957. Sold for scrap PC 3/1962.	
2187	GN (Hillyard)	7/31/1928	11/13/1928	1370	GN 1756	Sold for scrap WEI&M 8/1953.	171, 218
2188	GN (Superior)	8/2/1928	9/29/1928	1364	GN 1750	Ret. 4/1958. Sold for scrap 3/1963.	
2189	GN (Superior)	8/21/1928	10/31/1928	1377	GN 1763	Ret. 4/1958. Sold for scrap PC 12/10/1962.	

Class P-2 4-8-2: 29x28-73-210(200)-365,600-242,000-54,838 originally. Dimensions later changed to 29x28-73-210-388,700-265,000-57,580. Locomotives indicated by an asterisk (*) below received boosters (12,200 lb. T.E.) (dates shown where known).

No.	Builder	Date Rcvd.	C/N	Disposition	Notes
2500	Baldwin	10/10/1923	57000	Sold for scrap PC 7/12/1955.	169
2501	Baldwin	10/10/1923	57001	Ret. 4/1955. Sold for scrap PC 8/1/1955.	
2502	Baldwin	10/15/1923	57002	Sold for scrap PC 4/23/1956.	167
2503	Baldwin	10/20/1923	57084	Ret. 4/1955. Sold for scrap PC 7/8/1955.	169
2504	Baldwin	10/20/1923	57085	Ret. 4/1955. Sold for scrap PC 8/9/1955.	169
2505*	Baldwin	10/24/1923	57182	Booster applied at Hillyard 12/24/1947, removed at Interbay 10/21/1952. Ret. 12/1957. Sold for scrap c.1962.	
2506*	Baldwin	10/24/1923	57183	Booster applied at Hillyard 1/6/1948, removed at Interbay 10/24/1952. Ret. 9/1955. Sold for scrap PC 10/31/1955.	233
2507	Baldwin	11/2/1923	57184	Ret. 12/1957. Sold SP&S for display at Maryhill, WA, dedicated 9/3/1966.	
2508	Baldwin	10/30/1923	57185	Ret. 9/1955. Sold for scrap PC 11/26/1955.	233
2509	Baldwin	10/31/1923	57186	Ret. 9/1955. Sold for scrap PC 10/31/1955.	233
2510*	Baldwin	11/5/1923	57187	Booster applied at Delta 2/8/1926, removed at Delta 5/29/1929. Ret. 12/1957. Sold for scrap DI&M 7/1963.	
2511	Baldwin	11/5/1923	57188	Ret. 12/1957. Sold for scrap WEI&M 7/1963.	
2512*	Baldwin	11/9/1923	57189	Booster applied at Delta 11/6/1924, removed at Hillyard 6/28/1929. Ret. 9/1955. Sold for scrap PC 11/26/1955.	233
2513*	Baldwin	11/14/1923	57190	Booster applied 3/1925, removed at Hillyard 6/6/1929. Ret. 4/1958. Sold for scrap 2/1963.	
2514*	Baldwin	11/17/1923	57256	Booster applied at Delta 12/24/1924, removed at Delta 2/14/1929. Ret. 3/1958. Sold for scrap PC 3/1963.	
2515*	Baldwin	11/18/1923	57257	Booster applied at Delta 5/31/1924, removed at Delta 4/10/1929. Ret. 9/1955. Sold for scrap DI&M 11/12/1955.	233
2516*	Baldwin	11/27/1923	57258	Booster applied at Delta 3/19/1925, removed at Delta 4/25/1929. Ret. 9/1955. Sold for scrap DI&M 11/12/1955.	233
2517*	Baldwin	11/27/1923	57339	Booster applied at Delta 9/12/1924, removed at Hillyard 3/11/1929. Ret. 4/1956. Sold for scrap DI&M 5/6/1956.	167
2518	Baldwin	11/9/1923	57012	Ret. 4/1955. Sold for scrap DI&M 8/13/1955.	169
2519	Baldwin	11/14/1923	57253	Ret. 4/1956. Sold for scrap PC 5/6/1956.	167
2520	Baldwin	11/27/1923	57340	Ret. 12/1957. Sold for scrap c.1962.	
2521	Baldwin	12/4/1923	57341	Ret. 12/1957. Sold for scrap c.1962.	
2522	Baldwin	12/7/1923	57342	Ret. 8/1956. Sold for scrap WEI&M 9/12/1956.	200
2523	Baldwin	12/7/1923	57343	Ret. 4/1958. Donated to the city of Willmar, MN, 10/7/1965. Placed on display at Kandiyohi County Historical Society, Willmar, MN.	
2524	Baldwin	12/17/1923	57344	Ret. 4/1958. Sold for scrap 5/1963.	
2525	Baldwin	12/17/1923	57345	Ret. 12/1957. Sold for scrap c.1962.	
2526	Baldwin	12/29/1923	57346	Ret. 4/1955. Sold for scrap PC 7/20/1955.	169
2527	Baldwin	12/29/1923	57347	Ret. 4/1956. Sold for scrap DI&M 5/27/1956.	167

Class S-1 4-8-4: 28x30-73-250-472,000-270,600-68,466 originally. Weights later increased to 493,780 lb. and 283,000 lb.

No.	Builder	Date Built	C/N	Disposition	Notes
2550	Baldwin	4/1929	60781	Ret. 12/1957. Sold for scrap WEI&M 6/1963.	206
2551	Baldwin	4/1929	60782	Ret. 12/1957. Sold for scrap c.1962.	206
2552	Baldwin	5/1929	60807	Ret. 12/1957. Sold for scrap PC 9/1963.	206
2553	Baldwin	5/1929	60808	Ret. 4/1956. Sold for scrap PC 5/13/1956.	167, 206
2554	Baldwin	5/1929	60809	Ret. 12/1957. Sold for scrap PC 7/1963.	206
2555	Baldwin	5/1929	60810	Ret. 4/1958. Sold for scrap 3/1963.	206

Class S-2 4-8-4: 29x29-80-225-420,900-247,300-58,305 originally. Weights later increased to 438,120 lb. and 257,000 lb.

No.	Builder	Date Rcvd.	C/N	Disposition	Notes
2575	Baldwin	3/11/1930	61211	Ret. 8/1955. Sold for scrap DI&M 9/7/1955.	234
2576	Baldwin	3/12/1930	61212	Ret. 4/1956. Sold for scrap DI&M 6/24/1956.	167
2577	Baldwin	3/17/1930	61213	Ret. 12/1957. Sold for scrap c.1962.	
2578	Baldwin	3/17/1930	61214	Sold for scrap PC 4/29/1956.	167
2579	Baldwin	3/18/1930	61215	Ret. 12/1957. Sold for scrap DI&M 6/1963.	
2580	Baldwin	3/18/1930	61216	Ret. 4/1958. Sold for scrap 9/1963.	
2581	Baldwin	3/21/1930	61224	Ret. after destroyed in boiler explosion at Crary, ND, on 1/9/1947. Remains sold for scrap PC 2/4/1947.	
2582	Baldwin	3/21/1930	61225	Ret. 8/1955. Sold for scrap PC 10/10/1955.	234
2583	Baldwin	3/25/1930	61237	Ret. 12/1957. Sold for scrap c.1962.	
2584	Baldwin	3/25/1930	61238	Ret. 12/1957. Held at Superior for historical purposes 3/21/1958. Placed on public exhibition at GN Depot, Havre, MT, 5/15/1964.	
2585	Baldwin	4/1/1930	61239	Ret. 9/1955. Sold for scrap DI&M 1/29/1956.	233
2586	Baldwin	4/1/1930	61240	Ret. 4/1958. Sold for scrap 9/1963.	
2587	Baldwin	4/10/1930	61241	Ret. 9/1955. Sold for scrap WEI&M 1/9/1956.	233
2588	Baldwin	4/10/1930	61242	Ret. 4/1956. Sold for scrap WEI&M 7/8/1956.	167

Class O-1 2-8-2: 28x32-63-210(180)-280,000-220,000-60,930 originally. Weights of engines increased as a result of reweighing, and working boiler pressure was later increased to 210 psi (increasing T.E. to 71,083 lb.). Those engines indicated by an asterisk (*) below received boosters (dates given where known) rated at between 11,000 lb. and 12,200 lb. T.E. Boosters were removed by the early 1950's.

No.	Builder	Date Rcvd.	C/N	Disposition
3000*	Baldwin	10/2/1911	36832	Booster applied at Dale Street 6/17/1930, removed at Willmar 6/15/1945. Ret. 12/1957. Sold for scrap c.1962.
3001	Baldwin	10/2/1911	36833	Sold for scrap PC 5/15/1953.
3002	Baldwin	10/4/1911	36910	Sold for scrap DI&M 4/18/1952.
3003	Baldwin	10/4/1911	36911	Sold for scrap DI&M 4/25/1952.
3004*	Baldwin	10/7/1911	36912	Booster applied 3/1931, removed at Willmar 7/15/1945. Sold for scrap PC 4/20/1952.
3005	Baldwin	10/4/1911	36913	Ret. 12/1949. Sold for scrap DI&M c.1/1950.
3006	Baldwin	10/4/1911	36914	Ret. 8/1955. Sold for scrap DI&M 10/20/1955.
3007	Baldwin	10/7/1911	36915	Sold for scrap WEI&M 3/29/1952.
3008	Baldwin	10/10/1911	36916	Sold for scrap PC 4/26/1952.

O-1 3042 was photographed on March 20, 1935. The location is unknown, but in 1935 the engine was probably assigned to either the Willmar or Dakota Division. The tender is believed to be a Style 68 tender, delivered with the 1917-1918 orders of O-1's. These engines were received with automatic stokers, so there is no bracing over the coal bunker. The tender has been stretched five feet to increase the water capacity to 10,000 gallons, and the coal bunker has been enlarged. Collection of William Raia.

3009	Baldwin	10/10/1911	36917	Sold for scrap DI&M 4/18/1952.
3010	Baldwin	10/9/1911	36937	Sold for scrap PC 2/22/1949.
3011	Baldwin	10/9/1911	36938	Sold for scrap DI&M 5/5/1952.
3012	Baldwin	10/18/1911	36939	Ret. 12/1957. Sold for scrap c.1962.
3013	Baldwin	10/18/1911	36940	Sold for scrap DI&M 5/28/1953.
3014	Baldwin	10/15/1911	36941	Ret. 12/1949. Sold for scrap DI&M c.1/1950.
3015	Baldwin	10/15/1911	36942	Sold for scrap PC 5/1951.
3016	Baldwin	10/24/1911	36969	Sold for scrap PC 5/1951.
3017	Baldwin	10/24/1911	36970	Sold for scrap WEI&M 5/16/1953.
3018	Baldwin	11/4/1911	36971	Sold for scrap PC 6/1951.
3019	Baldwin	11/4/1911	36972	Sold for scrap DI&M 9/8/1952.
3020	Baldwin	2/18/1913	39089	Sold for scrap PC 5/21/1953.
3021	Baldwin	2/18/1913	39090	Sold for scrap DI&M 5/5/1953.
3022*	Baldwin	1/30/1913	39091	Booster applied 3/1931, removed at Willmar 6/5/1945. Ret. 8/1952. Sold for scrap DI&M 9/1/1952.
3023	Baldwin	1/30/1913	39092	Sold SP&S (No. 506) 6/1929. Delivered 7/13/1929. Scrapped 11/1950.
3024	Baldwin	2/15/1913	39093	Sold SP&S (No. 507) 6/1929. Delivered 7/3/1929. Scrapped 4/1945.
3025	Baldwin	2/15/1913	39094	Sold for scrap PC 5/20/1953.
3026	Baldwin	2/11/1913	39095	Sold SP&S (No. 500) 6/1925. Scrapped 6/1949.
3027	Baldwin	2/11/1913	39096	Sold for scrap DI&M 9/8/1952.
3028	Baldwin	2/10/1913	39097	Sold SP&S (No. 501) 6/1925. Scrapped 6/1950.
3029	Baldwin	2/10/1913	39098	Sold SP&S (No. 502) 6/1925. Scrapped 7/1952.
3030	Baldwin	2/15/1913	39099	Ret. 8/1955. Sold for scrap DI&M 9/7/1955.
3031	Baldwin	2/15/1913	39100	Sold for scrap PC 4/11/1952.
3032	Baldwin	2/14/1913	39101	Sold for scrap PC 5/3/1952.
3033*	Baldwin	2/14/1913	39102	Booster applied 4/1931. Sold for scrap DI&M 5/15/1953.
3034	Baldwin	2/18/1913	39103	Sold for scrap PC 4/30/1953.
3035	Baldwin	2/18/1913	39104	Sold for scrap PC 5/16/1953.
3036	Baldwin	2/18/1913	39150	Sold for scrap DI&M 1/14/1955.
3037	Baldwin	2/18/1913	39151	Sold for scrap PC 1/12/1955.
3038	Baldwin	2/18/1913	39152	Sold for scrap DI&M 9/4/1952.
3039	Baldwin	2/18/1913	39153	Sold SP&S (No. 504) 4/1928. Delivered 4/6/1928. Scrapped 6/1949.
3040*	Baldwin	2/20/1913	39154	Booster applied at Dale Street 9/24/1929, removed at Willmar 6/10/1945. Sold for scrap DI&M 5/5/1953.
3041	Baldwin	2/20/1913	39155	Sold for scrap PC 9/10/1952.
3042	Baldwin	3/11/1913	39156	Sold for scrap PC 4/1955.
3043	Baldwin	3/11/1913	39157	Sold SP&S (No. 505) 4/1928. Scrapped 5/1950.
3044	Baldwin	3/11/1913	39158	Ret. 4/1958. Sold for scrap 2/1963.
3045	Baldwin	3/11/1913	39163	Ret. 12/1957. Sold for scrap c.1962.
3046*	Baldwin	2/26/1913	39164	Booster applied at Dale Street 2/28/1930, removed at Willmar 6/6/1945. Sold for scrap PC 6/1951.
3047	Baldwin	2/26/1913	39165	Sold for scrap DI&M 4/23/1952.
3048*	Baldwin	3/13/1913	39166	Booster applied at Dale Street 8/27/1930, removed at Grand Forks 7/1949. Ret. 12/1949. Sold for scrap PC c.1/1950.
3049	Baldwin	3/13/1913	39167	Sold for scrap PC 6/1948.
3050	Baldwin	2/27/1913	39168	Ret. 12/1957. Sold for scrap DI&M 5/1962.
3051	Baldwin	2/27/1913	39169	Sold for scrap PC 9/1953.
3052	Baldwin	3/7/1913	39170	Sold for scrap DI&M 1/21/1955.
3053	Baldwin	3/7/1913	39171	Sold for scrap DI&M 8/30/1952.
3054	Baldwin	3/8/1913	39172	Sold for scrap DI&M 1/14/1955.
3055	Baldwin	3/8/1913	39205	Sold for scrap PC 9/3/1952.
3056	Baldwin	3/8/1913	39206	Sold for scrap PC 6/24/1953.
3057	Baldwin	3/8/1913	39207	Sold for scrap PC 10/7/1952.
3058	Baldwin	3/13/1913	39208	Sold for scrap DI&M 6/24/1953.
3059	Baldwin	3/13/1913	39209	Ret. 12/1957. Placed on public exhibition at GN Depot, Williston, ND, 8/2/1958.
3060	Baldwin	3/7/1913	39210	Sold for scrap DI&M 4/26/1952.
3061	Baldwin	3/7/1913	39211	Sold for scrap DI&M 8/1953.
3062	Baldwin	3/21/1913	39212	Sold for scrap DI&M 2/12/1955.
3063	Baldwin	3/21/1913	39296	Sold for scrap PC 4/30/1953.
3064	Baldwin	3/7/1913	39297	Sold SP&S (No. 508) 6/12/1943. Scrapped 11/1949.
3065	Baldwin	3/7/1913	39298	Sold for scrap DI&M 6/24/1953.
3066	Baldwin	3/11/1913	39299	Ret. 8/1955. Sold for scrap DI&M 10/20/1955.
3067	Baldwin	3/11/1913	39300	Sold for scrap PC 1/8/1955.
3068	Baldwin	4/1/1913	39301	Sold for scrap DI&M 9/4/1952.
3069	Baldwin	4/1/1913	39302	Sold for scrap DI&M 7/31/1953.

Class O-1 2-8-2: 28x32-63-210(180)-306,500-229,000-60,930 originally. Weights of engines increased due to reweighing, and working boiler pressure was later increased to 210 psi (increasing T.E. to 71,083 lb.). Those engines indicated by an asterisk (*) below received boosters (dates given where known) rated at between 11,000 lb. and 12,200 lb. T.E. Boosters were removed by the early 1950's.

No.	Builder	Date Rcvd.	C/N	Disposition	Notes
3070	Baldwin	10/6/1916	43989	Sold for scrap PC 5/3/1952.	
3071*	Baldwin	10/6/1916	43990	Booster applied 7/1931, removed at Minneapolis 8/1949. Sold for scrap DI&M 1/15/1955.	
3072	Baldwin	9/29/1916	43991	Sold for scrap PC 5/1/1952.	
3073	Baldwin	9/29/1916	43992	Sold for scrap WEI&M 9/1953.	
3074	Baldwin	9/29/1916	43993	Sold for scrap DI&M 5/1951.	
3075	Baldwin	10/16/1916	44095	Ret. 4/1955. Sold for scrap DI&M 6/4/1955.	
3076	Baldwin	10/16/1916	44096	Ret. 4/1955. Sold for scrap DI&M 5/28/1955.	
3077	Baldwin	10/17/1916	44097	Ret. 4/1956. Sold for scrap DI&M 7/1/1956.	
3078	Baldwin	10/17/1916	44098	Sold for scrap DI&M 8/1953.	

Class O-1 2-8-2: Continued

No.	Builder	Date Rcvd.	C/N	Disposition	Notes
3079	Baldwin	10/16/1916	44099	Sold for scrap DI&M 4/24/1952.	
3080	Baldwin	11/4/1916	44144	Sold for scrap PC 5/20/1953.	
3081	Baldwin	11/4/1916	44145	Ret. 4/1955. Sold for scrap DI&M 6/10/1955.	
3082	Baldwin	11/2/1916	44146	Sold for scrap DI&M 8/30/1952.	
3083	Baldwin	11/2/1916	44197	Ret. 4/1955. Sold for scrap DI&M 5/14/1955.	
3084	Baldwin	11/4/1916	44198	Sold for scrap DI&M 4/15/1952.	
3085	Baldwin	11/4/1916	44199	Sold for scrap PC 8/1953.	
3086	Baldwin	11/9/1916	44200	Sold for scrap DI&M 5/1948.	
3087	Baldwin	11/25/1916	44201	Sold for scrap DI&M 8/10/1953.	
3088	Baldwin	11/25/1916	44202	Ret. 7/1952. Stripped at Great Falls 9/1952.	
3089	Baldwin	12/3/1916	44203	Sold for scrap PC 1/14/1955.	
3090	Baldwin	12/3/1916	44204	Ret. 8/1955. Sold for scrap PC 10/20/1955.	
3091	Baldwin	12/22/1916	44253	Sold for scrap DI&M 6/1951.	
3092	Baldwin	12/16/1916	44254	Sold for scrap PC 9/1949.	
3093	Baldwin	12/22/1916	44438	Sold for scrap PC 5/3/1952.	
3094	Baldwin	12/16/1916	44439	Ret. 12/1949. Sold for scrap PC c.1/1950.	
3095	Baldwin	9/11/1917	46066	Sold for scrap PC 8/1953.	
3096	Baldwin	9/11/1917	46067	Sold for scrap DI&M 4/30/1953.	
3097	Baldwin	9/14/1917	46068	Sold for scrap PC 5/20/1953.	
3098	Baldwin	9/14/1917	46110	Ret. 12/1949. Sold for scrap DI&M c.1/1950.	
3099	Baldwin	9/19/1917	46163	Sold SP&S (No. 503) 3/1926. Scrapped 8/1949.	
3100*	Baldwin	10/26/1917	46213	Booster applied at Great Falls 8/30/1929, removed 12/1947. Ret. 8/1955. Sold for scrap PC 10/3/1955.	
3101	Baldwin	10/26/1917	46277	Ret. 3/1958. Sold for scrap DI&M 12/1962.	
3102	Baldwin	12/10/1917	46891	Sold for scrap PC 9/21/1952.	
3103	Baldwin	12/20/1918	48150	Ret. 4/1955. Sold for scrap DI&M 6/10/1955.	207
3104	Baldwin	12/1/1918	48257	Sold for scrap PC 3/29/1952.	207
3105	Baldwin	12/20/1918	48258	Sold for scrap PC 9/4/1952.	207
3106*	Baldwin	12/7/1918	48259	Booster applied at Dale Street 9/21/1929, removed at Superior 1/1950. Ret. 7/1953. Sold for scrap WEI&M 8/4/1953.	207
3107	Baldwin	6/5/1918	48260	Sold for scrap WEI&M 3/20/1948.	
3108	Baldwin	6/5/1918	48468	Sold SP&S (No. 511) 8/1944. Scrapped 11/1949.	
3109	Baldwin	6/1/1918	48524	Ret. 4/1955. Sold for scrap DI&M 5/14/1955.	
3110	Baldwin	12/3/1918	48573	Sold for scrap DI&M 5/13/1953.	207
3111	Baldwin	6/22/1918	48675	Ret. 12/1949. Sold for scrap DI&M c.1/1950.	
3112	Baldwin	6/22/1918	48676	Ret. 12/1957. Sold for scrap c.1962.	
3113	Baldwin	6/21/1918	48732	Wrecked near Kloan, OR (on Oregon Trunk Railway), 9/29/1945. Usable parts removed at Hillyard 10/24/1946.	
3114	Baldwin	6/21/1918	48733	Sold for scrap DI&M 2/12/1955.	
3115	Baldwin	7/4/1918	48775	Ret. 9/1955. Sold for scrap WEI&M 10/15/1955.	
3116	Baldwin	7/20/1918	48893	Ret. 4/1956. Sold for scrap PC 7/15/1956.	
3117	Baldwin	7/20/1918	48943	Ret. 12/1957. Sold for scrap c.1962.	
3118	Baldwin	7/22/1918	48995	Sold for scrap PC 9/1953.	
3119	Baldwin	7/25/1918	49079	Ret. 12/1957. Sold for scrap DI&M 6/1962.	
3120	Baldwin	7/23/1918	49080	Sold for scrap DI&M 7/31/1953.	
3121	Baldwin	8/4/1918	49158	Sold SP&S (No. 509) 6/12/1943. Scrapped 12/1945.	
3122	Baldwin	8/18/1918	49226	Sold SP&S (No. 510) 1/1944. Scrapped 11/1949.	
3123	Baldwin	8/18/1918	49299	Sold for scrap PC 5/7/1953.	
3124	Baldwin	9/3/1918	49300	Sold for scrap PC 8/1953.	
3125	Baldwin	8/26/1918	49356	Ret. 4/1955. Sold for scrap DI&M 5/28/1955.	
3126	Baldwin	8/26/1918	49357	Ret. 9/1955. Sold for scrap PC 10/22/1955.	
3127	Baldwin	9/20/1918	49408	Sold for scrap DI&M 5/13/1953.	
3128	Baldwin	9/20/1918	49481	Wrecked on Oregon Trunk near Oakbrook, OR, 9/22/1949, remains sold for scrap PC 12/1949.	
3129	Baldwin	10/1/1918	49482	Ret. 3/1958. Sold for scrap PC 6/1962.	
3130	Baldwin	10/1/1918	49639	Ret. 9/1955. Sold for scrap PC 12/12/1955.	
3131	Baldwin	10/27/1918	49659	Sold for scrap DI&M 4/24/1952.	
3132	Baldwin	10/4/1918	49660	Sold for scrap DI&M 5/15/1953.	
3133	Baldwin	10/13/1918	49661	Ret. 4/1955. Sold for scrap DI&M 6/4/1955.	
3134	Baldwin	10/17/1918	49731	Sold SP&S (No. 512) 8/1944. Scrapped 11/1949.	
3135*	Baldwin	10/17/1918	50051	Booster applied at Great Falls 10/21/1930, removed at Grand Forks 10/1949. Ret. 4/1958. Sold for scrap 12/1962.	
3136	Baldwin	12/7/1918	50359	Ret. 4/1955. Sold for scrap DI&M 8/1/1955.	
3137*	Baldwin	12/20/1918	50360	Booster applied at Great Falls 8/21/1929, removed at Interbay 10/1949. Ret. 9/1955. Sold for scrap WEI&M 10/7/1955.	
3138*	Baldwin	1/21/1919	51011	Booster applied at Great Falls 2/28/1930, removed at St.Cloud 3/1950. Ret. 4/1958. Sold for scrap DI&M 12/6/1962.	
3139	Baldwin	2/2/1919	51035	Ret. 12/1957. Sold for scrap c.1962.	
3140	Baldwin	2/14/1919	51083	Ret. 9/1955. Sold for scrap PC 11/4/1955.	
3141	Baldwin	2/21/1919	51156	Sold for scrap DI&M 7/31/1953.	
3142*	Baldwin	2/24/1919	51234	Booster applied 3/1942, removed 12/1947. Ret. 8/1955. Sold for scrap PC 10/3/1955.	
3143	Baldwin	3/11/1919	51235	Sold for scrap DI&M 3/11/1949.	
3144*	Baldwin	3/16/1919	51256	Booster applied 6/1942, removed at Minot 9/1949. Ret. 4/1958. Sold for scrap DI&M 12/1962.	

Class O-3 2-8-2: 27x32-63-200(190)-320,000-239,000-59,800

No.	Builder	Date Rcvd.	C/N	Disposition
3145	Alco-Schenectady	4/7/1919	61038	Reno. GN 3200 4/16/1919.
3146	Alco-Schenectady	4/7/1919	61039	Reno. GN 3201 4/17/1919.
3147	Alco-Schenectady	4/2/1919	61040	Reno. GN 3202 4/9/1919.
3148	Alco-Schenectady	4/2/1919	61041	Reno. GN 3203 4/22/1919.

Class O-2 2-8-2: 20x28-52-180-178,000-128,000-32,950. Superheater installed between 1926 and 1930 with no changes in dimensions.

No.	Builder	Date Built	C/N	Original No.	Renumbered From	Date	Disposition
3149	Alco-Brooks	10/1915	55444	SDC 18	W&SF 18	4/10/1922	Sold for scrap PC 3/28/1947.

Class O-3 2-8-2: 27x32-63-200(190)-320,000-239,000-59,800 originally. Working boiler pressure later increased to 200 psi, thus increasing T.E. to 62,949 lb. Weights increased to 320,900 lb. and 240,000 lb.

No.	Builder	Date Rcvd.	C/N	Original No.	Renumbered From	Date	Disposition	Notes
3200	Alco-Schenectady	4/7/1919	61038	GN 3145	GN 3145	4/16/1919	Ret. 8/1955. Sold for scrap PC 9/1955.	
3201	Alco-Schenectady	4/7/1919	61039	GN 3146	GN 3146	4/17/1919	Ret. 4/1955. Sold for scrap PC 6/10/1955.	
3202	Alco-Schenectady	4/2/1919	61040	GN 3147	GN 3147	4/9/1919	Sold for scrap PC 10/24/1951.	
3203	Alco-Schenectady	4/2/1919	61041	GN 3148	GN 3148	4/22/1919	Ret. 8/1955. Sold for scrap PC 10/3/1955.	
3204	Alco-Brooks	1/1920	60400	EP&SW 390	EP&SW 390	1/1920	Ret. 4/1955. Sold for scrap PC 6/27/1955.	208
3205	Alco-Brooks	1/1920	60401	EP&SW 391	EP&SW 391	1/1920	Ret. 12/1949. Sold for scrap PC c.1/1950.	208
3206	Alco-Brooks	1/1920	60402	EP&SW 392	EP&SW 392	1/1920	Sold for scrap PC 3/22/1948.	208
3207	Alco-Brooks	1/1920	60403	EP&SW 393	EP&SW 393	1/1920	Sold for scrap DI&M 5/28/1953.	208
3208	Alco-Brooks	1/1920	60404	EP&SW 394	EP&SW 394	1/1920	Ret. 4/1955. Sold for scrap DI&M 6/10/1955.	208

Class O-4 2-8-2: 28x32-63-210(190)-319,700-242,800-64,313 originally. Weights increased as a result of reweighing on oil burners to 334,000 lb. (254,000 lb. on drivers) and on coal burners to 344,820 lb. (262,000 lb. on drivers). Working boiler pressure changed to 210 psi (increasing T.E. to 71,083 lb.). No. 3224 had booster installed during dates indicated (this was the last locomotive on the GN to have a booster).

No.	Builder	Date Built	C/N	Disposition
3210	Baldwin	10/1920	53792	Sold for scrap DI&M 4/19/1956.
3211	Baldwin	10/1920	53793	Sold SP&S (No. 550) 4/1950. Scrapped 4/1953.
3212	Baldwin	10/1920	53794	Ret. 12/1957. Sold for scrap PC 6/1962.
3213	Baldwin	10/1920	53834	Ret. 12/1957. Scrapped c.1962.
3214	Baldwin	10/1920	53835	Sold SP&S (No. 551) 4/1950. Scrapped 5/1953.
3215	Baldwin	10/1920	53836	Ret. 4/1956. Sold for scrap WEI&M 5/27/1956.
3216	Baldwin	10/1920	53837	Ret. 12/1957. Sold for scrap PC 6/1962.
3217	Baldwin	10/1920	53838	Ret. 4/1956. Sold for scrap PC 5/27/1956.
3218	Baldwin	10/1920	53866	Ret. 12/1957. Sold for scrap DI&M 6/1962.
3219	Baldwin	10/1920	53911	Ret. 12/1957. Sold for scrap PC 12/1962.
3220	Baldwin	10/1920	53912	Ret. 12/1957. Sold for scrap PC 12/3/1962.
3221	Baldwin	11/1920	53940	Ret. 4/1955. Sold for scrap DI&M 7/5/1955.
3222	Baldwin	11/1920	53941	Ret. 12/1957. Sold for scrap 5/1962.
3223	Baldwin	11/1920	53942	Sold for scrap PC 1/8/1955.
3224	Baldwin	11/1920	53984	Booster installed 5/1923, removed at Dale Street 4/7/1928. Booster installed at Dale Street 1939, removed at St.Cloud 8/1953. Ret. 12/1957. Sold for scrap DI&M 12/10/1962.
3225	Baldwin	11/1920	53985	Received new boiler XO-305642 in 1943. Ret. 4/1955. Sold for scrap PC 6/10/1955.
3226	Baldwin	11/1920	53986	Ret. 4/1958. Sold for scrap DI&M 12/1962.
3227	Baldwin	11/1920	54027	Sold for scrap PC 1/15/1955.
3228	Baldwin	11/1920	54028	Ret. 4/1956. Sold for scrap DI&M 6/17/1956.
3229	Baldwin	11/1920	54029	Ret. 12/1957. Scrapped c.1962.
3230	Baldwin	11/1920	54030	Ret. 3/1958. Sold for scrap DI&M 12/1962.
3231	Baldwin	11/1920	54031	Ret. 4/1956. Sold for scrap PC 6/27/1956.
3232	Baldwin	11/1920	54032	Ret. 4/1955. Sold for scrap PC 6/10/1955.
3233	Baldwin	11/1920	54033	Ret. 4/1956. Sold for scrap DI&M 7/15/1956.
3234	Baldwin	11/1920	54034	Ret. 4/1955. Sold for scrap PC 5/18/1955.
3235	Baldwin	11/1920	54035	Ret. 4/1955. Sold for scrap PC 6/10/1955.
3236	Baldwin	11/1920	54091	Ret. 12/1957. Scrapped c.1962.
3237	Baldwin	11/1920	54092	Ret. 4/1956. Sold for scrap PC 5/27/1956.
3238	Baldwin	11/1920	54102	Ret. 4/1955. Sold for scrap PC 5/18/1955.
3239	Baldwin	11/1920	54123	Sold for scrap WEI&M 4/19/1956.
3240	Baldwin	11/1920	54124	Sold for scrap PC 1/21/1955.
3241	Baldwin	9/1920	53650	Sold for scrap PC 8/1956.
3242	Baldwin	9/1920	53681	Ret. 4/1955. Sold for scrap PC 6/4/1955.
3243	Baldwin	9/1920	53682	Ret. 3/1958. Sold for scrap DI&M 12/10/1962.
3244	Baldwin	9/1920	53683	Ret. 3/1958. Sold for scrap PC 12/4/1962.
3245	Baldwin	8/1920	53597	Ret. 4/1958. Sold for scrap PC 12/4/1962.
3246	Baldwin	8/1920	53598	Ret. 4/1956. Sold for scrap WEI&M 5/20/1956.
3247	Baldwin	9/1920	53622	Ret. 3/1958. Sold for scrap DI&M 12/1962.
3248	Baldwin	9/1920	53623	Ret. 4/1955. Sold for scrap PC 5/18/1955.
3249	Baldwin	9/1920	53649	Ret. 4/1955. Sold for scrap PC 5/28/1955.

Class O-4 2-8-2: Continued

No.	Builder	Date Built	C/N	Disposition
3250	Baldwin	9/1920	53707	Ret. 4/1958. Sold for scrap DI&M 12/1962.
3251	Baldwin	9/1920	53747	Ret. 3/1958. Sold for scrap DI&M 12/6/1962.
3252	Baldwin	9/1920	53748	Sold for scrap PC 8/1956.
3253	Baldwin	9/1920	53749	Ret. 4/1955. Sold for scrap PC 6/27/1955.
3254	Baldwin	9/1920	53750	Ret. 12/1957. Scrapped c.1962.

Class O-5 2-8-2: 25x30-63-200-283,420-220,000-50,600 (Rebuilt from Class L-2 2-6-6-2)

No.	Builder	Date Start Rbld.	Date Finish Rbld	C/N	Reblt. From L-2 No.	Disposition	Notes
3300	GN (Dale Street)	1/10/1922	5/11/1922	32690	GN 1802(2)	Ret. 6/1948. Sold for scrap PC 7/6/1948.	209
3301	GN (Dale Street)	12/23/1921	6/19/1922	32711	GN 1844	Sold for scrap PC 4/15/1947.	
3302	GN (Dale Street)	2/3/1922	12/21/1922	30422	GN 1806	Sold for scrap DI&M 5/6/1948.	
3303	GN (Dale Street)	2/14/1922	2/28/1923	32702	GN 1835	Sold for scrap PC 12/1941.	
3304	GN (Hillyard)	4/10/1922	2/28/1923	32689	GN 1801(2)	Sold for scrap PC 9/27/1941.	
3305	GN (Hillyard)	4/10/1922	2/27/1923	32705	GN 1838	Sold for scrap DI&M 9/15/1941.	
3306	GN (Delta)	5/19/1922	11/24/1922	30848	GN 1819	Sold for scrap DI&M 12/1941.	
3307	GN (Delta)	3/20/1923	4/18/1923	30446	GN 1808	Sold for scrap PC 9/27/1941.	
3308	GN (Delta)	1/30/1923	3/8/1923	30563	GN 1809	Sold for scrap PC 5/6/1948.	
3309	GN (Delta)	5/4/1923	8/18/1923	30564	GN 1810	Sold for scrap DI&M 4/15/1947.	
3310	GN (Hillyard)	6/3/1923	9/8/1923	32703	GN 1836	Sold for scrap PC 5/5/1947.	
3311	GN (Hillyard)	2/24/1923	5/29/1923	32698	GN 1831	Sold for scrap PC 12/1941.	210
3312	GN (Dale Street)	12/30/1922	4/30/1923	31183	GN 1828	Sold for scrap DI&M 4/2/1947.	
3313	GN (Dale Street)	2/28/1923	6/2/1923	32701	GN 1834	Sold for scrap PC 1/25/1947.	211
3314	GN (Delta)		10/13/1923	30943	GN 1822	Sold for scrap WEI&M 3/17/1949.	
3315	GN (Dale Street)		8/31/1923	31184	GN 1829	Sold for scrap DI&M 1/31/1947.	
3316	GN (Dale Street)		11/9/1923	32707	GN 1840	Ret. 12/1938.	
3317	GN (Hillyard)		11/14/1923	31002	GN 1823	Ret. 12/1938.	
3318	GN (Hillyard)		1/29/1924	32696	GN 1804(2)	Sold for scrap PC 6/12/1947.	
3319	GN (Hillyard)		3/12/1924	30588	GN 1812	Sold for scrap PC 5/1/1948.	
3320	GN (Hillyard)		5/20/1924	31003	GN 1824	Sold for scrap PC 6/20/1947.	
3321	GN (Delta)	1/30/1924	2/2/1924	32700	GN 1833	Sold for scrap DI&M 9/1/1941.	
3322	GN (Dale Street)		3/27/1924	32699	GN 1832	Sold for scrap DI&M 12/1941.	
3323	GN (Dale Street)		5/28/1924	32704	GN 1837	Sold for scrap PC 5/21/1947.	
3324	GN (Delta)		3/29/1924	30803	GN 1816	Sold for scrap DI&M 9/30/1949.	212
3325	GN (Dale Street)		8/6/1924	31004	GN 1825	Sold for scrap PC 2/17/1947.	
3326	GN (Delta)		5/14/1924	32709	GN 1842	Sold for scrap PC 9/30/1949.	
3327	GN (Delta)		7/17/1924	31065	GN 1826	Sold for scrap PC 9/8/1941.	213
3328	GN (Hillyard)		7/29/1924	30846	GN 1817	Sold to Otter Tail Power Co., Bemidji, MN, 4/29/1947.	
3329	GN (Hillyard)		9/3/1924	30847	GN 1818	Sold for scrap DI&M 4/16/1948.	
3330	GN (Dale Street)		10/20/1924	30445	GN 1807	Sold for scrap DI&M 9/15/1941.	
3331	GN (Dale Street)		2/2/1925	32708	GN 1841	Sold for scrap DI&M 2/17/1947.	214
3332	GN (Delta)		9/11/1924	32706	GN 1839	Sold for scrap PC 12/1941.	
3333	GN (Dale Street)	5/14/1924	11/26/1924	30919	GN 1821	Sold for scrap PC 9/1/1941.	
3334	GN (Delta)		3/18/1925	30800	GN 1813	Sold for scrap DI&M 5/6/1948.	
3335	GN (Hillyard)		12/11/1924	30565	GN 1811	Ret. 12/1949. Sold for scrap DI&M 1/31/1950.	
3336	GN (Hillyard)		12/16/1924	30802	GN 1815	Sold for scrap DI&M 2/1941.	
3337	GN (Delta)		12/3/1924	32691	GN 1803(2)	Sold for scrap PC 2/1941.	
3338	GN (Hillyard)		2/26/1925	30801	GN 1814	Sold for scrap PC 1/20/1947.	
3339	GN (Delta)		5/29/1925	30918	GN 1820	Sold for scrap DI&M 2/1941.	
3340	GN (Dale Street)	10/20/1924	5/16/1925	31105	GN 1827	Sold for scrap DI&M 9/29/1941.	
3341	GN (Delta)		1/22/1925	32710	GN 1843	Sold for scrap DI&M 2/10/1947.	
3342	GN (Hillyard)		4/30/1925	30400	GN 1805	Sold for scrap PC 10/14/1941.	215
3343	GN (Hillyard)		5/20/1925	32697	GN 1830	Sold for scrap DI&M 12/1941.	
3344	GN (Dale Street)	1/30/1925	10/3/1925	32688	GN 1800(2)	Sold for scrap DI&M 3/26/1948.	

Class O-6 2-8-2: 28x32-63-200(195)-320,100-244,000-66,000 originally. As a result of reweighing, engine weights increased to 334,800 lb. (260,000 lb. on drivers). Working boiler pressure later increased to 200 psi, raising T.E. to 67,700 lb. (Rebuilt from Class L-1 2-6-6-2)

No.	Builder	Date Start Rbld.	Date Finish Rbld.	C/N	Reblt. From L-1 No.	Disposition	Notes
3350	GN (Hillyard)	1/28/1925	8/25/1925	32734	GN 1910	Sold for scrap PC 2/20/1955.	169
3351	GN (Hillyard)	3/2/1925	9/14/1925	32741	GN 1913	Ret. 8/1955. Sold for scrap WEI&M 10/3/1955.	
3352	GN (Delta)	1/20/1925	8/29/1925	32749	GN 1919	Sold for scrap PC 1/29/1955.	169
3353	GN (Delta)	3/30/1925	9/29/1925	32755	GN 1920	Sold for scrap DI&M 1/22/1955.	169
3354	GN (Hillyard)	5/7/1925	11/7/1925	28641	GN 1901	Ret. 12/1957. Sold for scrap c.1962.	
3355	GN (Hillyard)	8/14/1925	11/23/1925	32735	GN 1911	Sold for scrap DI&M 1/22/1955.	169
3356	GN (Delta)	6/20/1925	11/21/1925	32725	GN 1908	Ret. 9/1955. Sold for scrap DI&M 11/12/1955.	
3357	GN (Hillyard)	9/12/1925	12/22/1925	28601	GN 1900	Sold for scrap PC 3/5/1949.	
3358	GN (Delta)	10/1/1925	1/29/1926	28854	GN 1903	Sold for scrap DI&M 2/5/1955.	169

3359	GN (Delta)	11/21/1925	4/13/1926	28739	GN 1902	Sold for scrap PC 2/5/1955.	169
3360	GN (Hillyard)	11/3/1925	2/26/1926	32748	GN 1918	Sold for scrap PC 5/20/1953.	168
3361	GN (Hillyard)	12/1/1925	5/1/1926	32746	GN 1916	Ret. 3/1958. Sold for scrap PC 2/1963.	
3362	GN (Hillyard)	1/9/1926	6/26/1926	28933	GN 1904	Sold for scrap PC 5/20/1956.	167
3363	GN (Delta)	1/27/1926	5/29/1926	32760	GN 1906(2)	Sold for scrap PC 1/29/1955.	169
3364	GN (Hillyard)	2/14/1926	7/28/1926	32740	GN 1912	Ret. 3/1958. Sold for scrap 2/1963.	
3365	GN (Hillyard)	3/13/1926	8/31/1926	32747	GN 1917	Damaged by boiler explosion at Shelby engine house. Boiler sold for scrap DI&M 3/31/1947.	
3366	GN (Delta)	3/31/1926	7/31/1926	32761	GN 1907(2)	Ret. 4/1955. Sold for scrap PC 6/27/1955.	
3367	GN (Hillyard)	5/22/1926	10/26/1926	32743	GN 1915	Sold for scrap PC 2/12/1955.	169
3368	GN (Delta)	5/26/1926	9/15/1926	32742	GN 1914	Sold for scrap PC 5/28/1953.	168
3369	GN (Delta)	6/30/1926	10/29/1926	32759	GN 1905(2)	Ret. 9/1955. Sold for scrap DI&M 11/12/1955.	
3370	GN (Hillyard)	7/17/1926	11/23/1926	32732	GN 1909	Ret. 3/1958. Sold for scrap DI&M 2/1963.	
3371	GN (Hillyard)	9/17/1926	12/21/1926	32758	GN 1921	Sold for scrap PC 4/15/1947.	

Class O-7 2-8-2: 31x32-69-210-348,000-268,000-79,600 [Rebuilt from Class M-2(2) 2-6-8-0]. No. 3375 was equipped with a booster having 12,200 lb. T.E. when it was built.

No.	Builder	Date Start Rbld.	Date Finish Rbld.	C/N	Reblt. From M-2 No.	Disposition
3375	GN (Great Falls)	5/29/1929	11/13/1929	34833	GN 1969	Booster removed at Havre 5/19/1930. Rblt. O-8 at Superior 9/9/1946 to 11/8/1946.
3376	GN (Hillyard)	9/21/1929	1/14/1930	34830	GN 1966	Rblt. O-8 at Superior 4/6/1945 to 5/26/1945.
3377	GN (Great Falls)		2/15/1930	35048	GN 1978	Rblt. O-8 at Superior 2/19/1945 to 3/31/1945.
3378	GN (Superior)		3/26/1930	34967	GN 1971	Rblt. O-8 at Superior 10/16/1944 to 12/7/1944.
3379	GN (Great Falls)		4/26/1930	34825	GN 1961	Rblt. O-8 at Superior 8/23/1946 to 10/24/1946.
3380	GN (Great Falls)		7/31/1930	34027	GN 1953	Rblt. O-8 at Superior 10/25/1946 to 12/26/1946.
3381	GN (Hillyard)	12/28/1929	4/21/1930	34028	GN 1954	Rblt. O-8 at Superior 10/11/1946 to 11/30/1946.
3382	GN (Hillyard)	3/31/1930	8/2/1930	34999	GN 1975	Rblt. O-8 at Superior 12/14/1944 to 2/9/1945.
3383	GN (Superior)		10/21/1930	35052	GN 1982	Rblt. O-8 at Superior 7/14/1944 to 10/24/1944.
3384	GN (Hillyard)	5/8/1930	10/14/1930	34828	GN 1964	Rblt. O-8 at Superior 5/1/1945 to 7/21/1945.
3385	GN (Great Falls)		11/22/1930	34076	GN 1957	Rblt. O-8 at Superior 5/28/1945 to 8/10/1945.
3386	GN (Great Falls)		12/20/1930	34826	GN 1962	Rblt. O-8 at Superior 7/10/1944 to 10/5/1944.
3387	GN (Hillyard)	10/25/1930	2/2/1931	34104	GN 1958	Rblt. O-8 at Superior 7/19/1946 to 9/18/1946.
3388	GN (Hillyard)	1/5/1931	4/30/1931	34024	GN 1950	Rblt. O-8 at Great Falls 8/2/1946 to 10/31/1946.
3389	GN (Superior)	11/21/1930	4/6/1931	35046	GN 1976	Rblt. O-8 at Superior 7/26/1946 to 10/10/1946.
3390	GN (Great Falls)	12/8/1930	4/30/1931	34105	GN 1959	Rblt. O-8 at Superior 9/17/1946 to 11/19/1946.
3391	GN (Great Falls)		7/18/1931	35049	GN 1979	Rblt. O-8 at Superior 7/5/1946 to 9/7/1946.
3392	GN (Hillyard)	3/12/1931	6/17/1931	34074	GN 1955	Rblt. O-8 at Superior 11/16/1944 to 1/11/1945.
3393	GN (Hillyard)	11/15/1931	2/12/1932	34965	GN 1970	Rblt. O-8 at Superior 1/12/1945 to 2/8/1945.
3394	GN (Hillyard)	6/1/1931	9/24/1931	34026	GN 1952	Rblt. O-8 at Great Falls 10/11/1946 to 12/20/1946.
3395	GN (Hillyard)		5/29/1934	34075	GN 1956	Rblt. O-8 at Superior 3/1/1945 to 4/21/1945.
3396	GN (Hillyard)	9/26/1931	1/16/1932	34824	GN 1960	Rblt. O-8 at Superior 4/14/1945 to 6/22/1945.

Class O-8 2-8-2: 28x32-69-250-425,540-325,000-75,900 (Rebuilt from Class O-7 2-8-2 with same numbers)

No.	Builder	New Boiler Bldr.	C/N	Date Start Rbld.	Date Finish Rbld.	Disposition
3375	GN (Superior)	Alco	46650-6	9/9/1946	11/8/1946	Ret. 3/1958. Sold for scrap c.1962.
3376	GN (Superior)	Baldwin	305741-9	4/6/1945	5/26/1945	Ret. 5/1958. Sold for scrap c.1962.
3377	GN (Superior)	Baldwin	305741-7	2/19/1945	3/31/1945	Ret. 5/1958. Sold for scrap DI&M 10/1963.
3378	GN (Superior)	Baldwin	305741-3	10/16/1944	12/7/1944	Ret. 3/1958. Sold for scrap PC 2/1963.
3379	GN (Superior)	Alco	46650-5	8/23/1946	10/24/1946	Ret. 3/1958. Sold for scrap PC 5/1962.
3380	GN (Superior)	Alco	46650-10	10/25/1946	12/26/1946	Ret. 12/1957. Sold for scrap c.1962.
3381	GN (Superior)	Alco	46650-9	10/11/1946	11/30/1946	Ret. 3/1958. Sold for scrap PC 2/1963.
3382	GN (Superior)	Baldwin	305741-5	12/14/1944	2/9/1945	Ret. 5/1958. Sold for scrap DI&M 5/1962.
3383	GN (Superior)	Baldwin	305741-2	7/14/1944	10/24/1944	Ret. 5/1958. Sold for scrap DI&M 6/1963.
3384	GN (Superior)	Baldwin	305741-11	5/1/1945	7/21/1945	Ret. 12/1957. Sold for scrap PC 10/1963.
3385	GN (Superior)	Baldwin	305741-12	5/28/1945	8/10/1945	Ret. 5/1958. Sold for scrap c.1962.
3386	GN (Superior)	Baldwin	305741-1	7/10/1944	10/5/1944	Ret. 5/1958. Sold for scrap PC 12/1963.
3387	GN (Superior)	Alco	46650-2	7/19/1946	9/18/1946	Ret. 5/1958. Sold for scrap PC 4/1963.
3388	GN (Great Falls)	Alco	46650-4	8/2/1946	10/31/1946	Ret. 12/1957. Sold for scrap PC 10/1963.
3389	GN (Superior)	Alco	46650-3	7/26/1946	10/10/1946	Ret. 5/1958. Sold for scrap DI&M 10/1963.
3390	GN (Superior)	Alco	46650-7	9/17/1946	11/19/1946	Ret. 5/1958. Sold for scrap WEI&M 10/1963.
3391	GN (Superior)	Alco	46650-1	7/5/1946	9/7/1946	Ret. 5/1958. Sold for scrap c.1962.
3392	GN (Superior)	Baldwin	305741-4	11/16/1944	1/11/1945	Ret. 5/1958. Sold for scrap c.1962.
3393	GN (Superior)	Baldwin	305741-6	1/12/1945	2/8/1945	Ret. 5/1958. Sold for scrap PC 10/1963.
3394	GN (Great Falls)	Alco	46650-8	10/11/1946	12/20/1946	Ret. 5/1958. Sold for scrap DI&M 12/1963.
3395	GN (Superior)	Baldwin	305741-8	3/1/1945	4/21/1945	Ret. 3/1958. Sold for scrap c.1962.
3396	GN (Superior)	Baldwin	305741-10	4/14/1945	6/22/1945	Ret. 5/1958. Sold for scrap DI&M 2/1963.

Class O-8 2-8-2: 29x32-69-250-367,000-280,000-78,000 originally. Rebuilt at Superior on dates indicated to 28x32-69-250-425,540-325,000-75,900

No.	Builder	New Boiler Bldr.	C/N	Date Start	Date Finish	Date Start Rbld.	Date Finish Rbld.	Disposition
3397	GN (Hillyard)	Baldwin	5890-1	1/23/1932	8/10/1932	1/30/1946	3/21/1946	Ret. 3/1958. Sold for scrap WEI&M 10/1963.
3398	GN (Hillyard)	Baldwin	5890-2	7/29/1932	9/8/1932	3/1/1946	4/30/1946	Ret. 3/1958. Sold for scrap DI&M 9/1963.
3399	GN (Hillyard)	Baldwin	5890-3	8/10/1932	10/6/1932	11/24/1945	1/28/1946	Ret. 3/1958. Sold for scrap DI&M 4/1963.

Class Z-6 4-6-6-4: 23x32/23x32-69-260(250)-621,000-436,000-104,266

No.	Builder	Date Built	C/N	Original No.	Renumbered From	Date	Disposition	Notes
4000	Alco-Schenectady	5/1937	68993	SP&S 903	SP&S 903	1/25/1940	Sold SP&S (No. 903) 4/27/1950.	216
4001	Alco-Schenectady	5/1937	68994	SP&S 904	SP&S 904	1/18/1940	Sold SP&S (No. 904) 7/1/1946 (delivered 10/21/1946).	216

Class – 2-4-0T Steam Motor Car: 13x17-42-170-53,000-46,100-9,884. Locomotive was received as an 0-4-0T, and lead truck was applied in GN shops during May, 1910.

No.	Builder	Date	C/N	Original No.	Renumbered From	Date	Disposition	Notes
6000	CB&Q	1904	?	1	1	?	Ret. 6/1918.	217

Class – 0-4-0T Narrow Gauge (3 feet): 9x14-27-?-29,000-29,000-?

No.	Builder	Date	C/N	Disposition
6715	Porter	1908	4175	?

Class – 0-4-0T Narrow Gauge (3 feet): 9x14-?-?-28,000-28,000-?

No.	Builder	Date	C/N	Disposition
6927	Davenport	?	450	?

Class H-4 engine 1441 was photographed at Great Falls, MT, in September 1945. It has been equipped with outside steam pipes, a blow-down muffler and electric train indicators. The tender is Style 70 O-1 tender 3047, one of the tenders rebuilt to 10,000 gallon water capacity about 1915 for use with the N-1's. Photograph by H. W. Pontin (RPS) from the collection of Norman F. Priebe.

F-8S 1192 was probably the last Great Northern 2-8-0 to operate in the U.S., at Sioux City, IA, in June 1953. Here it is in standby service at Sioux Falls, SD, on November 1, 1952. While the engine has been superheated and received piston valves, it appears to still have inside admission steam pipes, as did at least most of the superheated F-8 engines with Stephenson valve gear. Photograph by Norman F. Priebe.

Tank type auxiliary tender X929 in shown in locomotive service at Marshall, MN, in June 1950, the last month of this car in such service. Photograph by Norman F. Priebe.

Chapter 32

Great Northern Steam Locomotive Tender Roster

Tender Numbering

In general, tenders bore the same numbers as the locomotive with which they were received. Exceptions to this rule include tenders which were built or purchased without locomotives. The tender number was located on a brass plate fastened to the tender frame. When tender numbers changed brass plates with the new number were sent out from Mechanical Valuation Engineer's office in St. Paul to the appropriate shop by registered mail. The responsible personnel at the shop removed the old brass plates, applied the new, and then returned the old plates to the Mechanical Valuation Engineer's office, which had the old plates destroyed.[1] An example of this number plate is shown. Tender numbers were changed when tenders went into maintenance service or when the numbers of the engines with which they were received were changed. For example the E-14 tenders were renumbered (and reclassified) when the locomotives with which they were received were rebuilt to H-5 and H-7 Pacifics. Tenders retained their own numbers even when assigned to locomotives of a different number. This happened frequently.

Water Cars and Auxiliary Tenders

Great Northern commonly used water cars as auxiliary tenders to decrease the number of water stops or to operate over branches where there were few water towers. Originally they had a number of water cars used as auxiliary tenders that were not made from old tenders. These water cars had wooden water tanks mounted on a flatcar-like

This view shows the brass plate on the frame of the tender with H-5 1355 at Sioux City, IA. The plate indicates that this was H-4 tender No. 1451 (or at least the tender frame of 1451), the last tender known to have been assigned to No. 1355 before its retirement. Photograph by Douglas C. Bemrich.

frame. The first were received by the St.Paul, Minneapolis & Manitoba (StPM&M) from the Haskell & Barker Car Company in 1887. These were originally numbered in the StPM&M X45-X80 series. These became GN X501-X530 in 1891 and 1892. During the general renumbering of 1913 and 1914 those that remained became 296000-296017. In 1901 the St.Cloud shops began building similar cars. Some of these were used to fill in the numbers of Haskell & Barker cars that had been destroyed, and others were placed in the X531-X567 series. In the 1913-1914 renumbering these became 296020-296051. In 1913 a number of other shops got into the act and 296052-296073 were constructed. During the 1913-1926 time period a few of these cars were "duty paid" so they could operate into Canada, and these were in the 390150-390159 series. All of these cars were renumbered in another general renumbering in 1926, the remaining cars becoming X850-X907. Most of these cars were retired in the late 1920's and early 1930's, but a few lasted until the late 1930's. The last one to be retired was X883, in November 1939. One of these cars is shown in auxiliary tender service with F-1 508 in Chapter 11.

However, most water cars used by GN were steam locomotive tenders that had been renumbered and/or rebuilt for use as auxiliary engine tenders or for use in maintenance service. As early as 1925, Great Northern began to transfer its excess steam locomotive tenders to the water car fleet. In that year twenty-one tenders were given numbers in the 296075-296095 series. These were small older tenders with water capacities of approximately 2500 to 3500 gallons.[2] Those still on the roster were renumbered as X930-X946, with a few going to the X1900 series, in the 1926 renumbering. Within a year X930-X946 had been renumbered into the X1900 series as well. Ultimately the entire series of X1900-X1999, except for two well flat cars numbered as X1910 and X1911, was composed of steam locomotive tenders in water car service, and most of these numbers were used more than once. In 1927 GN also began renumbering extra tenders into the X2800 series, and eventually the numbers from X2817 through X2893 were occupied by water cars rebuilt from steam locomotive tenders. The X1900 and X2800 series tenders were apparently used primarily in maintenance service (e.g. with rotary snow plows, pile drivers or in outfit car service).

In 1928 Great Northern began to introduce steel tank cars to the water car fleet. They continued to be used as auxiliary tenders or for support of maintenance service. In 1928 Great Northern leased fifty tank cars (that had been built by American Car & Foundry) from the American Sugar Refining Company. These were numbered as X1450-X1499, and Great Northern's Lists of Equipment[3] designated them as steel water tanks (not called cars).

The first evidence of using extra locomotive tenders as auxiliary tenders found by the authors was in 1934. An Authority for Expenditure (AFE) was written to justify fitting up twelve 8,000-gallon tenders with permanent draw bars for use as water cars. The AFE stated "On the Dakota Division it is necessary to haul water cars on practically all of the branches. Nine of the large wooden water cars are in bad order and should be retired as it is a waste of money to repair them. To replace these cars and to provide three additional cars it is proposed to fit up twelve steel underframe 8,000 gallon capacity tenders, which are available from engines which have been retired. Retirement of wooden water cars to be included in monthly retirement AFE."[4]

After the wooden water cars were retired, many numbers in the X800 and X900 series were used again for water cars. However, most of the cars in these series were flat cars upon which water cisterns (commonly old tender tanks) had been placed. These cars were used in outfit car service rather than as auxiliary tenders.

In 1940 it was proposed to apply permanent draw bar, running boards and ladders and also enclose the coal pit in three tenders. "These tenders are required fitted up for service as extra tenders or water cars on the Skagit Branch, Mansfield Line and between Marcus and Republic on the Spokane Division." Tender 1446 was converted to an auxiliary water car and renumbered X1920 at the Hillyard Shop on March 30, 1940. This car was assigned to local freight service on the Skagit Branch between Burlington and Rockport. The original intent was to rebuild these cars and give them X-series numbers. However, there was a ruling from the Accounting Department that when tenders were converted to auxiliary water cars and remained in transportation service they were not to be transferred to Work Equipment, and brass number plates on the tenders were not to be changed. One of the tenders had already been renumbered, but was then renumbered again to its original number.[5] This apparently caused considerable consternation for mechanical personnel.[6] I. G. Pool (Master Mechanic) wrote "It is the intention to permanently assign these engine tenders as water cars and use them as such in train service or work service, whatever the occasions demand from time to time and I believe they

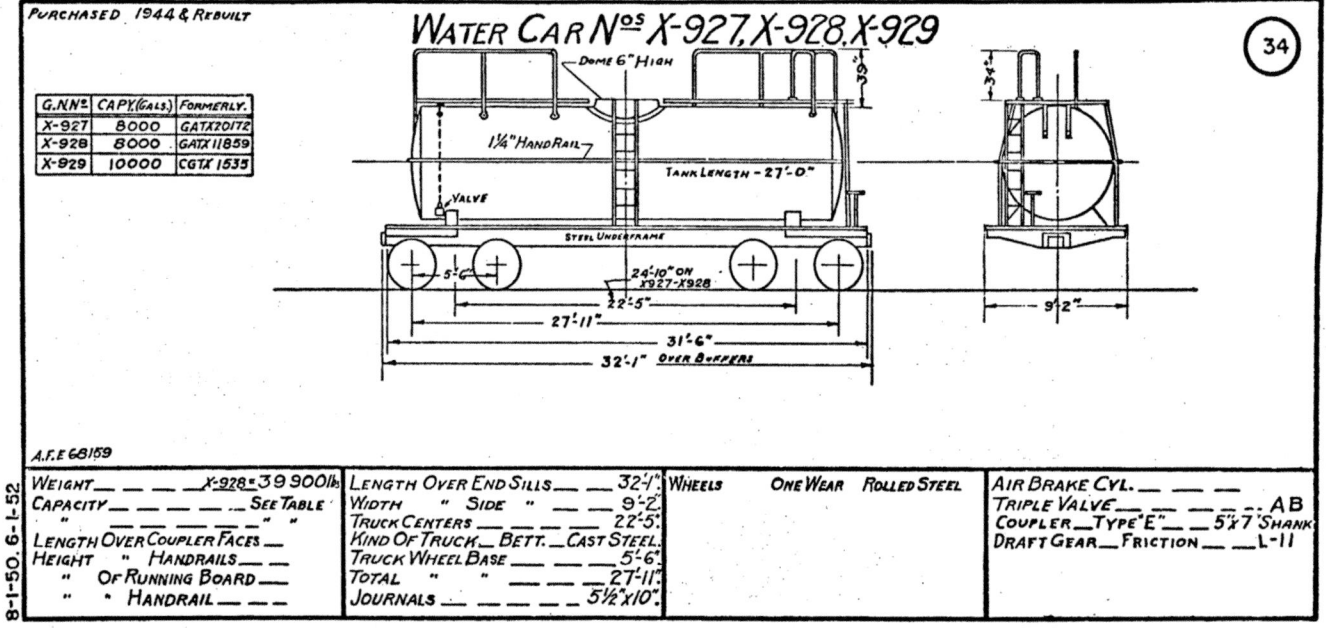

Tank cars X927-X929 were purchased used in 1944 and rebuilt as water cars for locomotive service.

Water car X928 was at Whitefish, MT, in 1945 and was being used to provide water for the new E7's. This required the use of an electric-powered pump mounted on the car. Note the power cord wrapped on hooks. Companion tank cars X1110 and X1117 handled the fueling duties. Photograph by Ben Cutler, Rail Photo Service.

should be re-numbered to work service numbers as shown in your letter of September 12th, same as the many other engine tender water cars we already have in this same service.... If we do not number these tenders in this service with "X" numbers we have one continual round of pleasure trying to keep track of them and keep records straight, as Conductors and others invariable get "X" numbers with them whether they are so numbered or not."[7]

Quite a number of auxiliary tenders were set up in the X3200 series during the first part of World War II. This included both water cars and full tenders with fuel oil space which were intended primarily for use as auxiliary engine tenders. The reason can be found in a common justification used for the AFE's to rebuild these cars: "Due to shortage of tank cars it was necessary to place in revenue service all available tank cars, including cars used for hauling water as extra tenders in train service. This caused a shortage of water cars and…it is proposed

that they be converted into water cars which can be used to very good advantage."[8] There is some doubt as to exactly what was meant by "revenue service," since a statement has also been found stating "All tubular tank cars in water service have been released for regular fuel oil service."[9] None of the tank cars were renumbered for this service.

Apparently a compromise between the accounting and mechanical organizations was reached with regard to numbering of auxiliary tenders. In November 1943 all cars in the X3200 series were removed from Valuation Account 57 (Work Equipment) and placed in Valuation Account 51 (Steam Locomotives).[10] Very few other tenders were converted to the X3200-series after 1943. The X3200 series did not show up in the List of Equipment until 1952, where they were called Extra Engine Tenders. In March 1958, with steam locomotives no longer in use, all of the X3200 series cars were transferred back to Valuation Account 57.

In 1943 and 1944 five additional tank cars were purchased second-hand and rebuilt for use as water cars. These were numbered as X925-X929. They were used both in maintenance and locomotive service. The X929 was still in locomotive service in 1950, but this appeared to be the end of such use.

In 1950, a new series of water cars was introduced, X3300-X3345, which consisted of 19 cars. Nos. X3300-X3306 and probably X3308 were flat cars fitted with water cisterns. No. X3307 was a former O-3 tender used with rotary snow plow X1505. Nos. X3336-X3345 were former locomotive tenders.

Vanderbilt Tenders

In Chapter 3 it was noted that after 1920 all tenders ordered or built new by the GN were of the Vanderbilt type. The first of these, of course, were the Style 100 O-4 tenders, the only four-wheel truck Vanderbilt tenders owned by GN. The Style 104 P-2 and Style 105 Q-1 tenders followed in 1923 and 1924. Then in 1924, GN received four Vanderbilt tenders from Baldwin,[11] the first that they had purchased without locomotives. These became the Style 115 "blank class" tenders, though the authors have been unable to discern any differences between these and the Style 104 P-2 tenders.

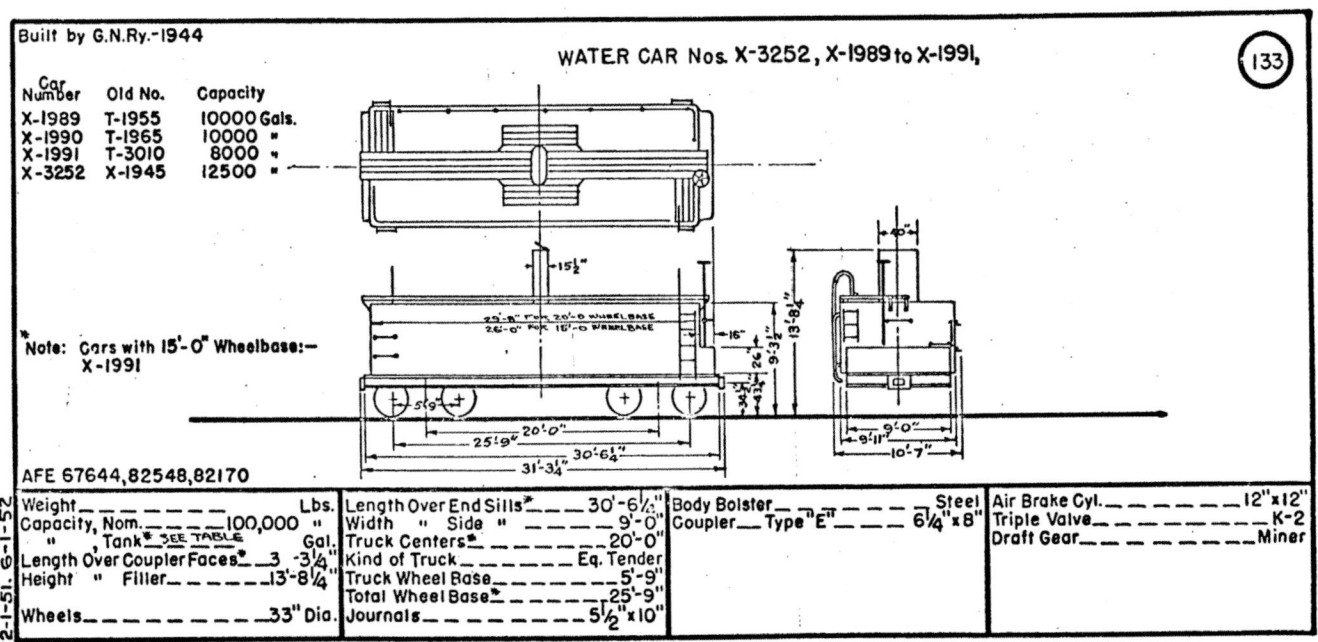

Very few of the former locomotive tenders had specific diagrams drawn of them. In the great majority of cases the diagram book indices simply referred to a Style Number on the general tender diagram pages which are reproduced in this chapter.

Converted tender X3201 replaced the X929 as the auxiliary tender for O-1 3052. It was rebuilt from F-8 tender No. 1236 in 1942, and is shown at Marshall, MN, in August 1950. Photograph by Norman F. Priebe.

In 1925 Baldwin again supplied Vanderbilt tenders without locomotives. These were numbered 2092-2099 and were the first of the 17,000 gallon Style 112 "blank class" tenders. Great Northern ultimately built 32 more of this style tender in its own shops. These were the only 17,000 or 17,250-gallon Vanderbilt tenders on the GN which were not water-bottom tenders, in which the frame forms the bottom of the tank. Consequently the Style 112 tenders had distinctive rivet plates along the frame, called "tank anchor lugs" on the tender drawings.

In 1926 GN received its final order of Vanderbilt tenders without locomotives from an outside supplier. These were purchased from General American Car Company and had water capacities of 21,500 gallons. These were water-bottom tenders, but are distinctive from the other 21,500-gallon and 22,000-gallon tenders on the GN in having a rivet line running from front to back along the side of the tank at about the same height as the bottom of the coal bunker. These became GN's

Style 114 "blank class" tenders.

The final group of tenders built without locomotives was called Style 113. These were again water-bottom tenders but with 22,000-gallon water capacities. They are quite similar in appearance to the R-2 tenders. All were built in the company shops in 1929 and 1930.

Rectangular Tender Modifications

While GN was busy buying and building Vanderbilt tenders, it was also engaged in upgrading and modifying many of its rectangular tenders. The first instance is believed to have occurred about 1915, when O-1 tenders 3045-3069 were rebuilt from an 8,000 gallon water capacity to 10,000 gallons. This was done so that they could be placed behind the N-1 engines. While most of GN's later conversions involved inserting a 5-foot long section into the tender frame and tender tank, the authors believe that these tenders were enlarged using an alternate construction method. These eventually were called the Style 66 and Style 70 tenders, and were later commonly assigned to Pacifics such as the H-5's.

In 1926, GN began the practice of rebuilding rectangular tenders from 8,000 gallons to 10,000 gallons by extending the length 5 feet.[12] In conjunction with this change it was a common, though not universal, practice to also increase the size of the axle journals from 5½ inches by 10 inches to 6 inches by 11 inches. These rebuilds continued until 1929, when the outstanding AFE's were cancelled by Ralph Budd, no doubt due to the economic times.[13] One additional tender requiring heavy repairs was completed in 1940,[14] and the program resumed again in 1941.[15] About this time the shops began to systematically go back and retrofit tenders that retained the 5½-inch by 10-inch journals to 6-inch by 11-inch.[16] The justification was normally given as "Several of the 10,000 gallon capacity tenders having 5½" x 10" axles in service with oil burning engines have failed due to broken axles, indicating fatigue of metal due to excessive load." The problem was apparently worse in tenders equipped for carrying oil.[17] Changing journal size continued until 1948, when the last AFE the authors have seen for this change was cancelled.[18]

Notes:

1. Great Northern Railway Authority for Expenditure (AFE) 30189, c.1925.
2. Great Northern Railway AFE 30189, c.1925.
3. List of Equipment, Great Northern Railway Co. years, 1923, 1926, 1930, 1940, 1942, 1947, 1950, 1952, 1954, and 1956. Note there are missing lists, between 1926 and 1930, 1930 and 1940.
4. Great Northern Railway AFE 48907, approved September 7, 1934.
5. Great Northern Railway AFE 58983, approved June 3, 1940.
6. Great Northern Railway AFE 63744, approved March 26, 1942.
7. I. G. Pool (Master Mechanic), letter to P. J. Coliton dated October 17, 1942 (in AFE 63744).

8. Great Northern Railway AFE 67645, approved November 3, 1943.
9. Great Northern Railway AFE 63974, approved April 28, 1942.
10. Great Northern Railway Change Number Record Account 57.
11. Great Northern Railway AFE 24854, approved 1/2/1924
12. Great Northern Railway AFE 32229, approved 7/1/1926.
13. Great Northern Railway AFE 41355, approved 11/1/1929.
14. Great Northern Railway AFE 53376, approved 6/17/1937.
15. Great Northern Railway AFE 66488, approved 5/21/1943.
16. Great Northern Railway AFE 61398, approved 5/6/1941.
17. Great Northern Railway AFE 61398, approved 5/6/1941.
18. Great Northern Railway AFE 71644, approved 10/1/1945.

GREAT NORTHERN TENDER ROSTER

Tender Class A-9, Style 1: 6 Tons Coal; 4,000 Gallons Water; 4¼" x 8" Axle Journals

No.	Builder	Date Rcvd.	Disposition	Notes
1(2)	GN (Dale Street)	7/30/1909	Sold for scrap DI&M 9/1949.	
2	Baldwin	11/4/1907	Sold for scrap DI&M 9/1932.	
3(2)	Baldwin	11/4/1907	Ret. 12/1949. Sold for scrap DI&M 1/1950.	
3(3)			Sold for scrap WEI&M 1/12/1955.	
4(2)	Baldwin	11/8/1907	Sold Becker County-Shiely Company (with E9) 9/24/1934.	
4(3)			Sold for scrap WEI&M 1/1955.	
5(3)	Baldwin	11/8/1907	Sold for scrap PC 2/17/1947.	
6(2)	Baldwin	11/22/1907	Sold for scrap DI&M 12/1949.	
7(2)	Baldwin	11/22/1907	Sold for scrap DI&M 2/25/1947.	239
8(3)	Baldwin	11/22/1907	Sold for scrap Pacific Coast Steel 2/1926.	240
9(3)	Baldwin	11/22/1907	Sold for scrap Dulien Steel Products 1/13/1953.	
10(3)	Baldwin	11/30/1907	Sold Addison Miller, Inc., and Fielding & Shepley, Inc., [with E81(2)] 5/31/1935.	
11(3)	Baldwin	11/30/1907	Ret. 11/1927. Reno. X1990(1) (WC) 1/1928. Ret. 11/1932.	
12(3)	GN (Dale Street)	8/6/1909	Sold for scrap PC 1/14/1955.	

Tender Class A-1, Style Unassigned: 4 Tons Coal; 1,750 Gallons Water; 3¾" x 7" Axle Journals

No.	Builder	Date Rcvd.	Original No.	Disposition
12(2)	Rogers	4/12/1879	StP&P 45	Probably sold W.D.Hofius Co. [with E12(2)] 7/1902.
13(2)	Rogers	4/22/1879	StP&P 46	Dismantled 11/1926.

Tender Old Class 4: Style Unassigned: 8 Tons Coal; 4,000 Gallons Water

No.	Builder	Date Rcvd.	Original No.	Renumbered From	Date	Disposition	Notes
15(2)	Brooks	4/9/1881	StPM&M 88	GN 88(1)	c.1899	Reno. T375 at Breckenridge 4/2/1909.	19

Tender Class A-9, Style 1: 6 Tons Coal; 4,000 Gallons Water; 4¼" x 8" Axle Journals

No.	Builder	Date Rcvd.	Disposition	Notes
14(3)	GN (Dale Street)	9/8/1906	Sold for scrap 8/1940.	
15(3)	GN (Dale Street)	9/22/1906	Sold for scrap Dulien Steel Products 1/13/1953.	
16(3)	GN (Dale Street)	9/27/1906	Sold for scrap PC 8/12/1936.	
17(3)	GN (Dale Street)	10/6/1906	Ret. 7/1942, tank placed on flat car.	
18(3)	GN (Dale Street)	10/23/1906	Dismantled at Great Falls 10/12/1928.	241
19(3)	GN (Dale Street)	10/23/1906	Dismantled at Superior 7/27/1937, cistern to flat car.	
20(3)	GN (Dale Street)	10/25/1906	Sold for scrap WEI&M 6/1948.	
21(3)	GN (Dale Street)	10/31/1906	Sold John Cox (with E37) 3/1923.	
22(3)	GN (Dale Street)	11/7/1906	Ret. 1/1929. Sold for scrap PC 2/21/1929.	
23(3)	GN (Dale Street)	11/14/1906	Dismantled at Dale Street 9/14/1929.	
24(3)	GN (Dale Street)	8/16/1909	Ret. 2/1931. Dismantled at Superior 8/27/1932.	
25(3)	GN (Dale Street)	8/24/1909	Sold for scrap PC 2/17/1947.	
26(3)	GN (Dale Street)	8/31/1909	Ret. 5/21/1937.	242

Tender Class A-4, Style Unassigned: 4 Tons Coal; 2,080 Gallons Water; 3¾" x 7" Axle Journals

No.	Builder	Date Rcvd.	Original No.	Disposition
27(2)	Brooks	8/30/1882	StPM&M 194	Scrapped 9/1916.
28(2)	Brooks	8/31/1882	StPM&M 195	Ret. 9/1916.
29(2)	Brooks	9/4/1882	StPM&M 196	Sold A. Guthrie (No. 150) 4/30/1918 [with E29(2)].

Tender Class A-2, Style Unassigned: 4 Tons Coal; 2,070 Gallons Water; 3¾" x 7" Axle Journals

No.	Builder	Date Rcvd.	Original No.	Disposition
30(2)	Hinkley	8/1/1888	StPM&M 232	Reno. 787(1), date unknown.
31(2)	Hinkley	8/1/1888	StPM&M 233	Reno. 788, date unknown.

Tender Class A-11, Style Unassigned: 6 Tons Coal; 4,000 Gallons Water; 4¼" x 8" Axle Journals

No.	Builder	Date Built	Original No.	Disposition
30(3)	Lima	4/1916	GNIOP 203	Sold for scrap 10/1940.
31(3)	Lima	4/1916	GNIOP 204	Sold Midland Railway Company of Manitoba (No. 5) [with E31(3)] 7/1946.

Tender Class A-5(1), Style Unassigned: 4 Tons Coal; 2,345 Gallons Water; 3¾" x 7" Axle Journals. Dates with an asterisk (*) are dates built.

No.	Builder	Date Rcvd.	Original No.	Disposition	Notes
32(2)	Rogers	4/26/1887	StPM&M 94(2)	Sold John Cox [with E32(2)] 2/1923.	
33(2)	Rogers	4/29/1887	StPM&M 95(2)	Dismantled 11/1925.	
34(2)	Rogers	4/29/1887	StPM&M 96(2)	Reno. X947(1) (WC) 3/1926. Reno. X1942(1) 6/1/1927. Ret. 4/1934. Sold for scrap DI&M 4/15/1934.	
35(2)	Rogers	5/1/1887	StPM&M 97(2)	Scrapped [with E35(2)] 9/1920.	
36(2)	Rogers	5/12/1887	StPM&M 98	Scrapped at Dale Street [with E36(2)] 9/30/1920.	
37(2)	Rogers	5/12/1887	StPM&M 99	Sold John Cox [with E40(2)] 3/1923.	243
38(2)	Rogers	9/17/1888	StPM&M 226	Sold for scrap [with E38(2)] DI&M 2/2/1922.	
39(2)	Rogers	9/20/1888	StPM&M 227	Sold Great Lakes Coal & Dock Co. [with E34(2)] 11/21/1921.	244
40(2)	Rogers	7/1888*	EM 1	Sold for scrap [with E46(2)] DI&M 2/10/1922.	
41(2)	Rogers	7/1888*	EM 2	Sold John Cox [with E41(2)] 12/1922.	
42(2)	Rogers	7/1888*	EM 3	Ret. 3/1918.	
43(2)	Rogers	10/9/1888	StPM&M 228	Sold for scrap [with E43(2)] DI&M 2/2/1922.	
44(2)	Rogers	10/9/1888	StPM&M 229	Sold John Cox [with E44(2)] 2/1923.	
45(2)	Rogers	10/10/1888	StPM&M 230	Sold for scrap [with E45(2)] DI&M 2/10/1922.	
46(2)	Rogers	10/11/1888	StPM&M 231	Sold John Cox [with E42(2)] 12/1922.	

Tender Class A-5(2), Style Unassigned: 8 Tons Coal; 4,000 Gallons Water; 4¼" x 8" Axle Journals

No.	Builder	Date Finish A-5	Original No.	Disposition	Notes
32(3)	GN (Jackson Street)	2/16/1925	GN 379(1)	Dismantled at Dale Street 8/4/1928.	53, 245
33(3)	GN (Jackson Street)	2/19/1926	GN 376	Sold for scrap DI&M 9/25/1928.	53

Tender Class A-3, Style Unassigned: 6 Tons Coal; 1,800 Gallons Water; 3¾" x 7" Axle Journals. Date with asterisk (*) is date built.

No.	Builder	Date Rcvd.	Original No.	Disposition	Notes
47(2)	Rogers	8/16/1890	SC&N 7	Ret. 4/1918.	246
48(2)	Rogers	3/1891*	SC&N 9	Sold John Cox [with E39(2)] 3/1923.	243

Tender Class A-9, Style 1: 6 Tons Coal; 4,000 Gallons Water; 4¼" x 8" Axle Journals

No.	Builder	Date Rcvd.	Disposition
49(2)	GN (Dale Street)	9/7/1909	Sold for scrap DI&M 6/1932.
50(2)	GN (Dale Street)	9/15/1909	Sold for scrap DI&M 7/1939.
51(2)	GN (Dale Street)	9/18/1909	Dismantled at Superior 7/19/1937, cistern to flat car.
52(2)	Baldwin	9/5/1907	Sold U.S. Army, Fort Peck Dam, MT, (with E17) 9/22/1938.
53(2)	Baldwin	9/5/1907	Sold for scrap Dulien Steel Products 1/13/1953.
54(2)	Baldwin	9/5/1907	Sold for scrap DI&M 9/1932.
55(2)	Baldwin	9/5/1907	Sold for scrap 5/1940.
56(3)	GN (Dale Street)	9/25/1909	Sold for scrap DI&M 2/1928.
57(3)	GN (Dale Street)	9/30/1909	Sold for scrap DI&M 9/4/1927.

Tender Class A-6, Style Unassigned: 12 Tons Coal; 4,000 Gallons Water; 3¾" x 7" Axle Journals

No.	Builder	Date Built	Original No.	Disposition	Notes
58(2)	Brooks	9/1899	EM 58	Sold for scrap PC 7/28/1936.	
59(2)	Brooks	9/1899	EM 59	Sold for scrap DI&M 8/27/1941.	247

Tender Class A-7, Style Unassigned: 5½ Tons Coal; 3,100 Gallons Water; 4¼" x 8" Axle Journals. Dates with asterisks (*) are dates built.

No.	Builder	Date Rcvd.	Original No.	Disposition
60(2)	Brooks	1/1/1893	GN 250(1)	Sold McCree & Co. [with E59(2)] 7/1926.
61(2)	Brooks	1/1/1893	GN 251(1)	Sold Landers, Morrison, Christianson Co. [with E61(2)] 3/31/1931.
62(2)	Brooks	1/10/1893	GN 257(1)	Sold for scrap DI&M 9/4/1927.
63(2)	Brooks	11/16/1893	GN 258(1)	Sold for scrap DI&M [with E63(2)] 5/1926.
64(2)	Brooks	1/1/1893	MC 25	Sold for scrap DI&M 8/1926.
65(2)	Brooks	1/1/1893	MC 26	Sold Somers Lumber Co. [with E60(2)] 2/1930. Returned to GN (Tender only) 7/1935. Resold Somers Lumber Co. 9/1935.
66(2)	Brooks	8/1895*	EM 5	Sold for scrap DI&M 8/8/1936.
67(2)	Brooks	8/1895*	EM 6	Sold for scrap DI&M 8/1932.
68(2)	Brooks	6/1898*	EM 7	Sold for scrap PC 8/1/1936.
69(2)	Brooks	6/1899*	EM 9	Sold for scrap DI&M 7/1932.

Tender Class A-8, Style Unassigned: 6 Tons Coal; 3,000 Gallons Water; 3¾" x 7" Axle Journals

No.	Builder	Date Built	Disposition
70(2)	Rogers	5/1900	Sold J.L.Shiely Co. [with E76(2)] 3/1930.
71(2)	Rogers	6/1900	Sold for scrap DI&M 5/1928.
72(2)	Rogers	6/1900	Sold for scrap 10/1940.

Tender Class A-9, Style 1: 6 Tons Coal; 4,000 Gallons Water; 4¼" x 8" Axle Journals

No.	Builder	Date Rcvd.	Disposition
73(2)	Rogers	8/27/1903	Sold for scrap PC 5/1948.
74(2)	Rogers	8/27/1903	Sold for scrap DI&M 8/6/1936.
75(2)	Rogers	8/30/1903	Ret. 10/1940.
76(2)	Rogers	8/30/1903	Ret. 1/1934. Sold for scrap DI&M 3/12/1934.
77(2)	Rogers	8/31/1903	Ret. 1/1947. Sold for scrap DI&M 3/24/1947.
78(2)	Rogers	8/31/1903	Sold for scrap PC 9/1939.
79(2)	Rogers	9/3/1903	Ret. 9/1940.
80(2)	Rogers	9/3/1903	Ret. 12/1949. Sold for scrap DI&M 1/1950.
81(2)	Rogers	9/9/1903	Sold for scrap DI&M 1/1942.
82(2)	Rogers	9/9/1903	Ret. 1/1939. Sold for scrap DI&M 8/1939.
83(2)	Alco-Rogers	9/4/1905	Sold for scrap DI&M 1/1942.
84(2)	Alco-Rogers	9/4/1905	Sold for scrap PC 7/1939.
85(3)	Alco-Rogers	9/7/1905	Sold for scrap DI&M 1/1942.
86(3)	Alco-Rogers	9/7/1905	Ret. 9/1939. Sold for scrap Bethlehem Steel 12/1939.
87(3)	Alco-Rogers	9/7/1905	Ret. 1/1934. Sold for scrap PC 6/11/1934.
88(3)	Alco-Rogers	9/7/1905	Dismantled at Superior 7/19/1937, cistern to flat car.
89(3)	Baldwin	9/8/1907	Sold for scrap PC 8/1/1936.
90(2)	Baldwin	9/8/1907	Sold for scrap DI&M 9/1939.
91(2)	Baldwin	9/5/1907	Sold for scrap PC 9/21/1940.
92(2)	Baldwin	9/5/1907	Sold for scrap PC 9/1949.
93(2)	Baldwin	9/11/1907	Ret. 1/1934. Sold for scrap DI&M 5/3/1934.
94(2)	Baldwin	9/11/1907	Sold for scrap PC 6/1947.

Tender Class A-10, Style 3: 8 Tons Coal; 4,000 Gallons Water; 4¼" x 8" Axle Journals

No.	Builder	Date Built	Original No.	Disposition
95(2)	Brooks	10/1898	MC 9(2)	Sold for scrap Bethlehem Steel Co. 1/1940.
96(2)	Brooks	10/1898	MC 27	Sold for scrap DI&M 7/1947.
97(2)	Brooks	10/1898	MC 28	Sold for scrap 12/1938.
98	Brooks	7/1900	EM 88	Sold for scrap DI&M 8/1939.
99(2)	Brooks	7/1900	EM 89	Sold for scrap 9/1940.

Tender Class B-13, Style Unassigned: 9 Tons Coal; 2,500 Gallons Water; 3¾" x 7" Axle Journals

No.	Builder	Date Rcvd.	Original No.	Disposition
100	Baldwin	5/11/1882	StPM&M 100	Ret. 11/1916.
101	Baldwin	5/11/1882	StPM&M 101	Ret. 4/1937.
102	Baldwin	5/14/1882	StPM&M 102	Reno. X1948(1) (WC) 6/1927. Stripped at Superior 8/8/1932. Ret. 8/1934.
103	Baldwin	5/14/1882	StPM&M 103	Reno. X946(2) (WC) 8/17/1938. Sold for scrap Dulien Steel Products 9/1939.
104	Baldwin	5/19/1882	StPM&M 104	Sold for scrap DI&M 10/1929.
105	Baldwin	5/15/1882	StPM&M 105	Probably sold B&O (with E105) 5/1900.
106	Baldwin	5/15/1882	StPM&M 106	Reno. X1908(1) (WC) 6/1927. Ret. 3/1928.
107	Baldwin	5/19/1882	StPM&M 107	Dismantled 12/1925.
108	Baldwin	5/19/1882	StPM&M 108	Probably sold B&O (with E108) 5/1900.
109	Baldwin	5/18/1882	StPM&M 109	Reno. 95001 (RT) 10/1925.
110	Baldwin	5/18/1882	StPM&M 110	(Engine scrapped 1916)
111	Baldwin	5/19/1882	StPM&M 111	Sold for scrap DI&M 6/1926.
112	Baldwin	5/19/1882	StPM&M 112	Probably scrapped with E112 11/20/1900.
113	Baldwin	5/19/1882	StPM&M 113	Reno. 296077 (WC) at Minot 11/25/1925. Reno. X932(1) 11/1926. Ret. 1/8/1927, sold for scrap DI&M.
114	Baldwin	5/20/1882	StPM&M 114	Probably sold B&O (with E114) 5/1900.

Tender Class B-14, Style Unassigned: 7 Tons Coal; 2,500 Gallons Water; 3¾" x 7 " Axle Journals

No.	Builder	Date Rcvd.	Original No.	Disposition
117(2)	Baldwin	3/18/1880	StPM&M 52	Probably sold F. Weyerhauser for Hawthorne, Negamon & West Superior Railway [with E117(2)] 6/19/1900.
118	Baldwin	5/21/1882	StPM&M 118	Reno. X1949(1) (WC) 6/1927. Ret. 3/1928.
119(2)	Baldwin	5/7/1880	StPM&M 62	Scrapped at Dale Street 3/24/1920.
120	Baldwin	5/21/1882	StPM&M 120	Sold for scrap PC 10/1929.
121	Baldwin	5/22/1882	StPM&M 121	Probably sold B&O (with E121) 5/1900.
122	Baldwin	5/25/1882	StPM&M 122	Sold for scrap DI&M 8/19/1927.
123	Baldwin	5/25/1882	StPM&M 123	Ret. 8/1918.
124	Baldwin	5/25/1882	StPM&M 124	Dismantled 9/1925.

Tender Class B-15, Style Unassigned: 6 Tons Coal; 2,750 Gallons Water; 3¾" x 7" Axle Journals

No.	Builder	Date Rcvd.	Original No.	Disposition	Notes
125	Schenectady	2/15/1882	StPM&M 125	Sold for scrap Pacific Coast Steel Co. 4/1927.	
126	Schenectady	2/15/1882	StPM&M 126	Reno. 296076 (WC) at Superior 11/24/1925. Reno. X931(1) 7/1926. Reno. X1931 6/1/1927. Ret. 9/1932.	
127	Schenectady	3/21/1882	StPM&M 127	Sold for scrap DI&M 1/1927.	
128	Schenectady	4/6/1882	StPM&M 128	Reno. X1915(1) (WC) 6/1927. Ret. 3/1937.	248
129	Schenectady	1/20/1882	StPM&M 129	Sold for scrap DI&M 6/1932.	249
130	Schenectady	1/20/1882	StPM&M 130	Ret. 2/1929. Dismantled at St.Cloud 3/29/1929.	
131	Schenectady	4/21/1882	StPM&M 131	Ret. to be scrapped 5/21/1937.	
132	Schenectady	4/21/1882	StPM&M 132	Off roster before 6/30/1915.	
133	Schenectady	4/21/1882	StPM&M 133	Reno. X1950(1) (WC) 6/1927. Ret. 3/1928.	

Tender Class B-16, Style Unassigned: 8 Tons Coal; 2,600 Gallons Water; 3¾" x 7" Axle Journals

No.	Builder	Date Rcvd.	Original No.	Disposition	Notes
134	Rhode Island	5/8/1882	StPM&M 134	Probably sold Butte, Anaconda & Pacific (with E134) 1894.	
135	Rhode Island	5/8/1882	StPM&M 135	Ret. 1/1934. Sold for scrap PC 4/10/1934.	
136	Rhode Island	5/13/1882	StPM&M 136	Dismantled 8/1925.	
137	Rhode Island	5/13/1882	StPM&M 137	Dismantled at Devils Lake 9/1923.	
138	Rhode Island	5/17/1882	StPM&M 138	Sold for scrap DI&M 2/1926.	250
139(1)	Rhode Island	5/17/1882	StPM&M 139	Probably sold Butte, Anaconda & Pacific [with E139(1)] 1894.	

Tender Class B-7, Style Unassigned: 5 Tons Coal; 2,800 Gallons Water; 3¾" x 7" Axle Journals

No.	Builder	Date Built	Original No.	Disposition
139(2)	New York	7/1890	S&N 2	Dismantled 5/1926.

Tender Class B-11(2), Style Unassigned: 9 Tons Coal; 2,700 Gallons Water; 4¼" x 8" Axle Journals

No.	Builder	Date Built	Original No.	Disposition	Notes
141	Baldwin	4/1890	SF&N 6	Sold for scrap Pacific Coast Steel Co. 12/1926.	
142	Baldwin	4/1890	SF&N 5	Sold for scrap DI&M 6/1927.	251

Tender Class B-12, Style Unassigned: 8 Tons Coal; 2,777 Gallons Water; 3¾" x 7" Axle Journals

No.	Builder	Date Rcvd.	Original No.	Renumbered From	Date	Disposition	Notes
143	Rogers	3/16/1882	StP&D 16(2)	StPM&M 143(2)	c.1892	Reno. X1909(1) (WC) 6/1927. Cistern to X900(2) at Superior 6/29/1946. Ret. 4/1961.	252
144	Rogers	3/18/1882	StP&D 17(2)	StPM&M 144(2)	c.1892	Reno. X951(1) (WC) 1/1927. Sold DI&M 3/1927.	253

Tender Class B-17, Style Unassigned: 6 Tons Coal; 2,550 Gallons Water; 3¾" x 7" Axle Journals

No.	Builder	Date Rcvd.	Original No.	Disposition
145	Grant	7/1/1882	StPM&M 145	Off roster before 6/30/1915.
146	Grant	7/2/1882	StPM&M 146	Probably sold Wisconsin Central (with E146) 1/7/1900.
147	Grant	7/6/1882	StPM&M 147	Reno. 296079 (WC) 10/1925. Reno. X934(1) 7/1926. Reno. X1933(1) 6/15/1927. Ret. 8/1928.
148	Grant	7/7/1882	StPM&M 148	Probably sold B&O (with E148) 5/1900.
149	Grant	7/9/1882	StPM&M 149	Reno. X1952(1) (WC) 6/1927. Ret. 10/1929.

Tender Class B-18, Style Unassigned: 9 Tons Coal; 2,850 Gallons Water; 4¼" x 8" Axle Journals

No.	Builder	Date Rcvd.	Original No.	Disposition	Notes
150	Brooks	7/6/1882	StPM&M 150	Dismantled at Dale Street 8/28/1926.	
151	Brooks	7/6/1882	StPM&M 151	Reno. X1916(1) (WC) 6/1927. Ret. 9/1934.	254

Tender Class B-19, Style Unassigned: 9 Tons Coal; 3,000 Gallons Water; 4¼" x 8" Axle Journals

No.	Builder	Date Rcvd.	Original No.	Disposition	Notes
152	Brooks	7/27/1882	StPM&M 152	Ret. 2/1928. Reno. X1946(2) (WC) 6/1928. Ret. 3/1934. Sold for scrap DI&M 3/29/1934.	255
153	Brooks	7/27/1882	StPM&M 153	Dismantled at Grand Forks 10/1929.	
154	Brooks	7/3/1882	StPM&M 154	Sold for scrap DI&M 3/1928.	
155	Brooks	7/31/1882	StPM&M 155	Dismantled 7/1926.	
156	Brooks	8/2/1882	StPM&M 156	Reno. X1997(1) (WC) 6/1927. Ret. 9/1941.	
157	Brooks	8/3/1882	StPM&M 157	Reno. X1953(1) (WC) 6/1927. Ret. 9/1932.	
158	Brooks	8/7/1882	StPM&M 158	Reno. X1954(1) (WC) 6/1927. Ret. 3/1928.	
159	Brooks	8/7/1882	StPM&M 159	Sold for scrap Pacific Coast Steel Co. 2/1926.	256
160	Brooks	8/10/1882	StPM&M 160	Dismantled at St.Cloud 7/1926.	
161	Brooks	8/12/1882	StPM&M 161	Dismantled 12/1924.	
162	Brooks	10/19/1882	StPM&M 162	Sold for scrap DI&M 6/1924.	
163	Brooks	10/21/1882	StPM&M 163	Dismantled 6/1925.	
164	Brooks	10/19/1882	StPM&M 164	Dismantled at Dale Street 8/31/1928.	257
165	Brooks	10/24/1882	StPM&M 165	Sold for scrap DI&M 1/25/1922.	
166	Brooks	10/24/1882	StPM&M 166	Dismantled at Grand Forks 8/3/1937, cistern to flat car.	
167	Brooks	12/23/1882	StPM&M 167	Off roster prior to 6/1915.	
168	Brooks	12/27/1882	StPM&M 168	Ret. 12/1930. Dismantled at Dale Street 3/3/1931.	258
169	Brooks	12/27/1882	StPM&M 169	Sold for scrap DI&M 9/4/1927.	
170	Brooks	12/27/1882	StPM&M 170	Scrapped at Dale Street (with E170) 1/17/1919.	
171	Brooks	12/27/1882	StPM&M 171	Reno. 95007 (RT) 10/1925. Reno. X1507 10/1926. Reno. X1982(1) 7/6/1927. Ret. 11/1938.	
172	Brooks	3/19/1883	StPM&M 172	Scrapped at Dale Street (with E172) 12/4/1918.	
173	Brooks	3/19/1883	StPM&M 173	Sold for scrap Pacific Coast Steel Co. 1/1927.	
174	Brooks	3/19/1883	StPM&M 174	Sold for scrap DI&M 11/1927.	
175	Brooks	3/19/1883	StPM&M 175	Dismantled 7/1942. Cistern to X897(2) (40FWC) 7/8/1942. Ret. 12/1947.	
176	Brooks	3/23/1883	StPM&M 176	Sold for scrap PC 8/1939.	
177	Brooks	3/23/1883	StPM&M 177	Sold for scrap 7/1940.	
178	Brooks	3/23/1883	StPM&M 178	Reno. X1918(2) (WC) 12/1928. Ret. 11/1941.	
179	Brooks	3/23/1883	StPM&M 179	Sold for scrap DI&M 12/1928.	259
180	Brooks	3/31/1883	StPM&M 180	Reno. 296086 (WC) at Seattle Docks 12/14/1925. Reno. X941(1) 7/1926. Reno. X1938(1) 7/11/1927. Ret. 8/1928. Sold for scrap DI&M 7/14/1932.	
181	Brooks	3/31/1883	StPM&M 181	Ret. 12/1918. Scrapped at Dale Street 1/17/1919.	
182	Brooks	3/31/1883	StPM&M 182	Sold for scrap DI&M 6/1928.	
183	Brooks	3/31/1883	StPM&M 183	Dismantled 1/1924.	
184	Brooks	4/7/1883	StPM&M 184	Sold for scrap DI&M 3/1927.	24, 260
185	Brooks	4/7/1883	StPM&M 185	Sold for scrap DI&M 7/1939.	24
186	Brooks	4/7/1883	StPM&M 186	Dismantled 6/1932.	24

Tender Class B-9, Style Unassigned: 8 Tons Coal; 2,600 Gallons Water; 3¾" x 7" Axle Journals

No.	Builder	Date Rcvd.	Original No.	Disposition	Notes
187(2)	Pittsburgh	3/23/1881	StPM&M 67(2)	Reno. X2825(1) (WC) 6/1934. Ret. 5/1937.	
188(2)	Pittsburgh	3/25/1881	StPM&M 78	Reno. 296082 (WC) 10/1925. Reno. X937(1) 10/1926. Reno. X1935(1) 11/23/1927. Ret. at Great Falls 8/12/1932. Sold for scrap DI&M 3/29/1934.	261
189(2)	Pittsburgh	3/30/1881	StPM&M 79	Reno. 296094 (WC) at Delta 9/29/1925. Reno. T95004 at Everett 12/16/1925. Reno. (T)X1504 10/1926. Reno. X1979 6/11/1927. Ret. 7/1930.	
190(2)	Pittsburgh	4/1/1881	StPM&M 80	Probably sold B&O [with E190(2)] 5/1900.	
191(2)	Pittsburgh	4/9/1881	StPM&M 81	Dismantled at Dale Street 6/30/1928.	
192(2)	Pittsburgh	5/16/1881	StPM&M 82	Sold for scrap DI&M 10/21/1928.	
193(2)	Pittsburgh	5/19/1881	StPM&M 83	Reno. X1955(1) (WC) 6/1927. Ret. 4/1928.	
194(2)	Pittsburgh	5/23/1881	StPM&M 84	Ret. 1/1934. Sold for scrap PC 3/18/1934.	
195	Pittsburgh	5/27/1881	StPM&M 85	Ret. 5/1929. Reno. X1940(2) (WC) 6/1929. Ret. 11/1929.	
196(2)	Pittsburgh	5/29/1881	StPM&M 86	Probably sold B&O [with E196(2)] 5/1900.	

Tender Class B-20, Style Unassigned: 8 Tons Coal; 3,000 Gallons Water; 4¼" x 8" Axle Journals

No.	Builder	Date Rcvd.	Original No.	Disposition	Notes
197	Rhode Island	1/31/1883	StPM&M 197	To work equipment (number unknown) 11/1927.	
198	Rhode Island	1/30/1883	StPM&M 198	Sold for scrap DI&M 2/1926.	25, 262
199	Rhode Island	2/5/1883	StPM&M 199	Reno. T96212 (Locomotive Crane Tender) 12/1924. Reno. (T)X1786 (with Locomotive Crane) 7/19/1926. Reno. X1987(1) 8/31/1927. Ret. 10/1928. Dismantled at Great Falls 10/21/1928.	
200	Rhode Island	12/28/1882	StPM&M 200	Ret. 1/1934. Sold for scrap PC 3/20/1934.	27
201	Rhode Island	2/5/1883	StPM&M 201	Reno. X1956(1) (WC) 6/1927. Ret. 3/1928.	27
202	Rhode Island	2/5/1883	StPM&M 202	Reno. X1995(1) (WC) 6/1927. Ret. 11/1932.	27
203	Rhode Island	12/28/1882	StPM&M 203	Sold for scrap DI&M 9/2/1927.	
204	Rhode Island	1/2/1883	StPM&M 204	Sold for scrap DI&M 7/1939.	
205	Rhode Island	1/2/1883	StPM&M 205	Reno. X1903 (WC) 1/1928. Reno. X1925(2) 11/23/1928. Reno. X821(2) (40FWC) 1/22/1946. Ret. 10/1957.	
206	Rhode Island	1/2/1883	StPM&M 206	Ret. 12/1918. Scrapped at Dale Street 1/17/1919.	

Tender Class B-21, Style 4: 5 Tons Coal; 3,000 Gallons Water; 4¼" x 8" Axle Journals

No.	Builder	Date Rcvd.	Original No.	Disposition	Notes
207	Rogers	5/28/1887	StPM&M 207	Reno. X1957(1) (WC) 6/1927. Ret. 9/1932.	
208	Rogers	5/25/1887	StPM&M 208	Reno. X947(2) (WC) 10/12/1938. Ret. 12/1938.	
209	Rogers	5/25/1887	StPM&M 209	Sold for scrap DI&M 10/1932.	
210	Rogers	5/30/1887	StPM&M 210	Sold for scrap DI&M 9/25/1928.	263
211	Rogers	5/30/1887	StPM&M 211	Reno. X2826(1) (WC) 6/1934. Ret. 11/1941.	
212	Rogers	6/3/1887	StPM&M 212	Reno. X1923(2) 10/1929. Ret. 10/1932.	
213	Rogers	6/3/1887	StPM&M 213	Reno. X1953(3) 4/27/1946. Ret. 2/1951.	
214	Rogers	6/5/1887	StPM&M 214	Ret. 12/1918. Scrapped at Dale Street 1/17/1919.	
215	Rogers	6/8/1887	StPM&M 215	Sold for scrap DI&M 10/1932.	
216	Rogers	6/8/1887	StPM&M 216	Sold for scrap DI&M 8/1932.	
217	Rogers	6/19/1887	StPM&M 217	Sold for scrap DI&M 6/1924.	
218	Rogers	6/21/1887	StPM&M 218	Sold for scrap DI&M 6/1924.	
219(1)	Rogers	6/28/1887	StPM&M 219	Dismantled at Hillyard 5/1926.	
220(1)	Rogers	6/28/1887	StPM&M 220	Ret. 1/1929. Sold for scrap PC 2/21/1929.	
221	Rogers	7/3/1887	StPM&M 221	To X1983(1) (probably just tank) 8/1928. Ret. 6/1934. Sold for scrap PC 6/11/1934.	264
222	Rogers	7/7/1887	StPM&M 222	Sold for scrap DI&M 8/1926.	
223	Rogers	7/7/1887	StPM&M 223	Sold for scrap DI&M 12/1928.	386
224	Rogers	7/7/1887	StPM&M 224	Reno. X1958(2) (WC) 8/26/1931. Ret. 11/1939.	
225	Rogers	7/12/1887	StPM&M 225	Sold for scrap DI&M 9/1932.	

Tender Class B-22, Style Unassigned: 5 Tons Coal; 3,000 Gallons Water; 4¼" x 8" Axle Journals

No.	Builder	Date Rcvd.	Original No.	Disposition
226	Rogers	11/29/1888	EM 101	Sold for scrap DI&M 10/1932.
227	Rogers	4/7/1889	EM 102	Sold for scrap DI&M 9/1927.
228(2)	Rogers	4/29/1889	EM 103	Dismantled 9/1925.
229(2)	Rogers	4/2/1889	EM 104	Sold for scrap DI&M 10/1927.
230(2)	Rogers	4/4/1889	EM 105	Sold for scrap DI&M 3/1927.

Tender Class B-23, Style Unassigned: 9 Tons Coal; 3,000 Gallons Water; 4¼" x 8" Axle Journals

No.	Builder	Date Built	Original No.	Disposition
231(2)	Baldwin	10/1893	SF&N 7	Reno. X2850(2) (WC) 9/1931. Ret. 3/1934. Sold for scrap DI&M 3/29/1934.

Tender Class B-6, Style Unassigned: 8 Tons Coal; 3,000 Gallons Water; 3¾" x 7" Axle Journals

No.	Builder	Date Rcvd.	Original No.	Disposition	Notes
232(2)	Rogers	1/14/1890	SC&N 1	Sold for scrap DI&M 8/31/1927.	
233(2)	Rogers	1/15/1890	SC&N 2	Dismantled at Dale Street 10/30/1920.	
234	Rogers	1/18/1890	SC&N 3	Reno. X1940(3) (WC) 5/1930. Ret. 3/1937.	
235	Rogers	1/25/1890	SC&N 4	Sold for scrap DI&M 10/1929.	
236	Rogers	6/1/1890	SC&N 8	Sold for scrap DI&M 6/1924.	
237	Rogers	12/19/1890	SC&N 10	Sold for scrap DI&M 12/18/1927.	265

Tender Class B-6, Style Unassigned: 8 Tons Coal; 2,800 Gallons Water; 3¾" x 7" Axle Journals

No.	Builder	Date Built	Original No.	Disposition
238	Rhode Island	4/1889	PSL 13	Ret. 5/1916.

Tender Class B-1, Style Unassigned: 8 Tons Coal; 3,000 Gallons Water; 3¾" x 7" Axle Journals

No.	Builder	Date Built	Original No.	Disposition
240	Danforth	1869	StP&P 16	Reno. X1919(1) (WC) 6/1927. Ret. 7/1934.

Tender Class B-3, Style Unassigned: 7 Tons Coal; 2,800 Gallons Water; 3¾" x 7" Axle Journals..

No.	Builder	Date Built	Original No.	Disposition	Notes
241	Pittsburgh	8/1870	StP&P 18	Dismantled 2/1921.	266
242	Pittsburgh	9/1870	StP&P 19	Sold for scrap DI&M 3/1927.	

Tender Class B-2, Style Unassigned: 6 Tons Coal; 2,400 Gallons Water; 3¾" x 7" Axle Journals.

No.	Builder	Date Rcvd.	Renumbered From	Date	Disposition
243	Baldwin	12/1871	GN 20(1)	3/1899	Reno. 296088 (WC) at Delta 1/27/1926. Reno. X943(1) 7/1926. Sold for scrap Pacific Coast Steel 1/8/1927.
244(1)	Baldwin	12/1871	GN 21(1)	4/1/1899	(Engine scrapped 11/19/1902)

Tender Class B-4, Style Unassigned: 8½ Tons Coal; 2,860 Gallons Water; 3¾" x 7" Axle Journals

No.	Builder	Date Rcvd.	Renumbered From	Date	Disposition
245	Baldwin	12/1871	GN 22(1)	4/8/1899	Dismantled 6/1925.

Tender Class Unassigned (Old Class 17), Style Unassigned: 6(?) Tons Coal; 2,600 Gallons Water

No.	Builder	Date Rcvd.	Renumbered From	Date	Disposition
246	Baldwin	12/1871	GN 23(1)	3/30/1899	Dismantled 9/1921.

Tender Class B-3, Style Unassigned: 7 Tons Coal; 2,800 Gallons Water; 3¾" x 7" Axle Journals

No.	Builder	Date Rcvd.	Original No.	Disposition
247	Pittsburgh	12/1875	StP&P 24	(Engine retired 1901)
248	Pittsburgh	12/1875	StP&P 26	Sold for scrap 12/1938.

Tender Class B-4, Style Unassigned: 8½ Tons Coal; 2,860 Gallons Water; 3¾" x 7" Axle Journals

No.	Builder	Date Rcvd.	Original No.	Disposition	Notes
249	Baldwin	11/1879	(StP&P 47)	Off roster before 6/30/1915.	17
250(2)	Baldwin	11/1879	(StP&P 48)	Sold for scrap DI&M 12/1927.	17
251(2)	Baldwin	11/1879	(StP&P 49)	(Engine sold 1901)	17
252(2)	Baldwin	11/1879	(StP&P 50)	Sold for scrap DI&M 10/1927.	17

Tender Class Unassigned [Old Style 7(2)], Style Unassigned: 5½ Tons Coal; 3,100 Gallons Water; 4¼" x 8" Axle Journals

No.	Builder	Date Rcvd.	Disposition	Notes
252(1)	Brooks	1/1/1893	Probably sold Butte, Anaconda & Pacific [with E252(1)] 1893.	
253	Brooks	1/7/1893	Probably sold Butte, Anaconda & Pacific (with E253) 1893.	86
254	Brooks	1/7/1893	Sold for scrap DI&M 10/1929.	86
255(1)	Brooks	1/7/1893	Probably sold Butte, Anaconda & Pacific [with E255(1)] 1893.	
256(1)	Brooks	1/7/1893	Probably sold Butte, Anaconda & Pacific [with E256(1)] 1893.	

Tender Class B-5, Style Unassigned: 6 Tons Coal; 2,500 Gallons Water; 3¾" x 7" Axle Journals

No.	Builder	Date Rcvd.	Original No.	Disposition	Notes
255(2)	Rogers	6/5/1878	StP&P 27	Reno. 296093 (WC) at Delta 9/26/1925. Reno. 95008 10/21/1925. Reno. (T)X1508 8/1926. Reno. X1983(1) 7/9/1927. Ret. 6/1934. Sold for scrap PC 6/11/1934.	264
256(2)	Rogers	6/5/1878	StP&P 28	Changed to Weed Burner Tank X380(2) at Breckenridge 12/19/1911. Reno. 99960 at Breckenridge 8/3/1915. Further disposition unknown.	
257(2)	Rogers	6/17/1878	StP&P 29	Probably sold R.A. Elzy [with E256(2)] 7/17/1902.	
258(2)	Rogers	6/26/1878	StP&P 30	Reno. X1907(1) (WC) 6/1927. Cistern to X898(2) at Klamath Falls 3/15/1945. Ret. 11/1962.	267
259	Rogers	6/26/1878	StP&P 31	Probably sold Oregon Southern Railway (with E259) 3/20/1905.	
260	Rogers	6/29/1878	StP&P 32	Probably sold R.A. Elzy (with E260) 7/17/1902.	
261	Rogers	6/29/1878	StP&P 33	Reno. 296087 (WC) at Delta 12/14/1925. Further disposition unknown.	
262	Rogers	7/12/1878	StP&P 34	Changed to Weed Burner Tank X381(2) at Willmar 1/4/1912. Reno. 99961 at Williston 6/25/1913. Further disposition unknown.	
263	Rogers	7/26/1878	StP&P 35	(Engine scrapped 10/1902)	
264	Rogers	7/31/1878	StP&P 36	(Engine scrapped 1901)	
265	Roger	10/7/1878	StP&P 39	Changed to Weed Burner Tank X382(2) at Garretson 2/8/1912. Reno. 99962 at St.Paul 6/11/1914. Further disposition unknown.	
266	Rogers	10/8/1878	StP&P 40	Reno. X1921(1) (WC) 6/1927. Ret. 9/1928.	
267	Rogers	10/30/1878	StP&P 41	Probably sold A. Guthrie & Co. (with E267) 8/19/1900.	

Tender Class B-10, Style Unassigned: 7½ Tons Coal; 2,550 Gallons Water; 3¾" x 7" Axle Journals

No.	Builder	Date Rcvd.	Original No.	Disposition	Notes
268	Baldwin	5/10/1880	StPM&M 67(1)	Sold for scrap DI&M 2/1928.	
269	Baldwin	5/21/1882	StPM&M 117	Probably sold FG&S (with E269) 9/12/1905.	
270	Baldwin	3/13/1880	StPM&M 53	Sold for scrap Hyman-Michaels Co. 10/1925.	
271	Baldwin	3/13/1880	StPM&M 54	Reno. X1985(2) (WC) 6/1928. Ret. 11/1928. Stripped at Superior 8/8/1932. Sold DI&M 10/1932.	268
272	Baldwin	3/18/1880	StPM&M 55	Scrapped at Dale Street 8/31/1920.	
273	Baldwin	4/6/1880	StPM&M 56	Probably sold B&O (with E273) 5/1900.	
274	Baldwin	4/6/1880	StPM&M 57	Dismantled 12/1926.	
275	Baldwin	4/17/1880	StPM&M 58	Reno. X1912(1) (WC) 6/19/1927. Ret. 9/1934.	
276	Baldwin	4/17/1880	StPM&M 59	Probably sold B&O (with E276) 5/1900.	
277	Baldwin	4/28/1880	StPM&M 60	Probably sold B&O (with E277) 5/1900.	
278	Baldwin	4/28/1880	StPM&M 61	Probably sold B&O (with E278) 5/1900.	
279	Baldwin	5/22/1882	StPM&M 119	Probably sold B&O (with E279) 4/24/1900.	
280	Baldwin	5/7/1880	StPM&M 63	Probably sold Wisconsin Central (with E280) 1/6/1900.	
281	Baldwin	5/17/1880	StPM&M 64	(Engine scrapped 1916)	
282	Baldwin	5/17/1880	StPM&M 65	Reno. X2827(1) (WC) 6/1934. Sold for scrap DI&M 9/1939.	
283	Baldwin	5/10/1880	StPM&M 66	Probably sold B&O (with E283) 5/1900.	

Tender Class B-8, Style Unassigned: 8 Tons Coal; 2,600 Gallons Water; 3¾" x 7" Axle Journals

No.	Builder	Date Rcvd.	Original No.	Disposition	Notes
284	Pittsburgh	8/20/1880	StPM&M 68	Probably sold B&O (with E284) 5/1900.	
285	Pittsburgh	8/25/1880	StPM&M 69	Probably sold B&O (with E285) 5/1900.	
286	Pittsburgh	8/31/1880	StPM&M 70	Probably sold B&O (with E286) 5/1900.	
287	Pittsburgh	9/6/1880	StPM&M 71	Sold for scrap Pacific Coast Steel Co. 1/1927.	269
288	Pittsburgh	9/18/1880	StPM&M 72	Reno. X1914(1) (WC) 6/1927. Ret. 3/1937.	
289	Pittsburgh	9/18/1880	StPM&M 73	Sold for scrap DI&M 12/1927.	
290	Pittsburgh	9/25/1880	StPM&M 74	To work equipment (number unknown) c.9/1931.	
291	Pittsburgh	9/25/1880	StPM&M 75	Dismantled 3/1924.	
292	Pittsburgh	9/30/1880	StPM&M 76	Dismantled at Hillyard 9/1926.	
293	Pittsburgh	9/30/1880	StPM&M 77	Dismantled at Dale Street 8/31/1928.	270

Tender Class B-11(1), Style Unassigned: Coal Capacity Unknown; 2,500 Gallons Water; Axle Journal Size Unknown

No.	Builder	Date Rcvd.	Original No.	Disposition
294	Rogers	1/27/1879	StP&P 43	Sold for scrap DI&M 5/1928.
295	Rogers	1/27/1879	StP&P 44	Ret. 12/1920.

Tender Class E-4, Style Unassigned: 10 Tons Coal; 3,500 Gallons Water; 3¾" x 7" Axle Journals

No.	Builder	Date Built	Original No.	Disposition
298	Schenectady	5/1889	F&S 1	Reno. 296089 (WC) at Delta 12/21/1925. Reno. X944(1) 7/1926. Reno. X1939(1) 7/18/1926. Ret. 10/1932.
299	Schenectady	5/1889	F&S 2	Probably sold Waterville Railway (with E299) 2/28/1911.

Tender Class D-2, Style Unassigned: 5 Tons Coal; 3,000 Gallons; 4¼" x 8" Axle Journals. Dates with asterisks (*) are dates built.

No.	Builder	Date Rcvd.	Original No.	Disposition	Notes
300	Rogers	7/7/1887	StPM&M 300	Dismantled 7/1925.	
301	Rogers	7/12/1887	StPM&M 301	Ret. 11/1923.	
302	Rogers	7/13/1887	StPM&M 302	Dismantled at Delta 1/14/1929.	
303	Rogers	7/19/1887	StPM&M 303	Sold for scrap Hyman-Michaels Co. 3/1926.	
304	Rogers	7/28/1887	StPM&M 304	Reno. X1958(1) (WC) 6/1927. Ret. 11/28/1928.	
305	Rogers	7/26/1887	StPM&M 305	Reno. X1959(1) (WC) 6/1927. Ret. 8/1928.	
306	Rogers	7/27/1887	StPM&M 306	Dismantled at Dale Street 8/20/1928.	271
307	Rogers	7/27/1887	StPM&M 307	Dismantled 9/1925.	
308	Rogers	7/31/1887	StPM&M 308	Reno. 296091 (WC) 10/1925. Reno. X1913(2) 2/2/1929. Retired at Great Falls 8/6/1932. Sold for scrap DI&M 9/1932.	272
309	Rogers	7/31/1887	StPM&M 309	Reno. X1960(1) (WC) 6/1927. Ret. 7/1934.	
310	Rogers	8/1/1887	StPM&M 310	To work equipment (number unknown) 11/1927.	
311	Rogers	8/2/1887	StPM&M 311	Reno. X1961(1) (WC) 6/1927. Ret. 5/1934.	
312	Rogers	8/7/1887	StPM&M 312	Sold for scrap 9/1940.	
313	Rogers	8/7/1887	StPM&M 313	Sold Truax Coal Co. 8/1924.	
314	Rogers	8/7/1887	StPM&M 314	Dismantled at Grand Forks 8/3/1937, cistern to flat car.	
315	Rogers	8/7/1887	StPM&M 315	Reno. 95002 (RT) 10/1925. Reno. (T)X1502 10/1926. Reno. X1977(1) 5/26/1927. Ret. 12/1941.	
316	Rogers	8/12/1887	StPM&M 316	Dismantled at Grand Forks 10/1929.	
317	Rogers	8/13/1887	StPM&M 317	Sold for scrap DI&M 1/25/1922.	
318	Rogers	8/15/1887	StPM&M 318	Sold for scrap DI&M 8/1928.	273
319	Rogers	8/20/1887	StPM&M 319	Sold for scrap DI&M 8/1926.	
320	Rogers	8/21/1887	StPM&M 320	Reno. 296083 (WC) 10/1925. Reno. X938(1) 8/1926. Reno. X1936(1) 5/26/1927. Ret. 10/1932.	387
321	Rogers	9/2/1887	StPM&M 321	3,000 gallon cistern replaced with 4,500 gallon cistern 4/1917. Reno. X1950(2) 10/1929. Ret. 3/1934. Sold for scrap DI&M 5/3/1934.	
322	Rogers	8/27/1887	StPM&M 322(1)	Sold for scrap DI&M 12/1924.	
323	Rogers	8/31/1887	StPM&M 323(1)	To work equipment (number unknown) 11/1927.	
324	Rogers	9/11/1887	StPM&M 324(1)	Reno. X1962(1) (WC) 6/1927. Ret. 12/1942.	
325	Rogers	9/9/1888	StPM&M 325	Sold for scrap DI&M 1/25/1922.	
326	Rogers	9/9/1888	StPM&M 326	Reno. T96211 (Locomotive Crane Tender) 12/1924. Reno. (T)X1785 (with Locomotive Crane) 11/12/1926. Reno. X1986(1) 8/21/1927. Ret. 7/1934, sold for scrap.	
327	Rogers	9/3/1888	StPM&M 322(2)	Reno. 296084 (WC) 10/1925. Reno. X939(1) 7/1926. Reno. X1937(1) 6/18/1927. Ret. 11/27/1928.	
328	Rogers	9/3/1888	StPM&M 323(2)	Dismantled at Dale Street 10/30/1920.	
329	Rogers	9/17/1888	StPM&M 329	Sold for scrap DI&M 1/1927.	
330	Rogers	9/17/1888	StPM&M 330	Reno. 296075 (WC) at Superior 12/16/1925. Reno. X930(1) 10/1926. Reno. X1930(1) 6/1/1927. Stripped at Superior 7/22/1932. Sold for scrap DI&M 9/1932.	
331	Rogers	9/20/1888	StPM&M 331	Ret. 12/1930. Sold for scrap DI&M 7/1932.	
332	Rogers	9/20/1888	StPM&M 332	Sold for scrap DI&M 8/1926.	
333	Rogers	9/24/1888	StPM&M 333	Sold Minnesota State Fair Association (with E245) 8/17/1921 and destroyed in staged head-on collision at the Minnesota State Fair.	
334	Rogers	9/25/1888	StPM&M 334	Scrapped 10/1937.	
335	Rogers	10/21/1888	StPM&M 335	Sold for scrap DI&M 10/1929.	
336	Rogers	10/26/1888	StPM&M 336	Sold for scrap DI&M 2/3/1922.	
337	Rogers	10/28/1888	StPM&M 337	Reno. X1963(1) (WC) 6/1927. Sold for scrap DI&M 8/25/1927.	
338	Rogers	10/31/1888	StPM&M 338	Reno. X2852(2) (WC) 9/1931. Ret. 8/1934.	
339	Rogers	10/31/1888	StPM&M 339	Reno. 296085 (WC) at Delta 1/15/1926. Reno. X940(1) 7/1926. Ret. 1/8/1927. Sold for scrap Pacific Coast Steel.	274

340	Rogers	11/12/1888	StPM&M 340	Sold for scrap DI&M 7/8/1927.
341(1)	Rogers	11/14/1888	StPM&M 341	Reno. X1922(1) (WC) 6/1927. Ret. 9/1928.
342	Rogers	11/19/1888	StPM&M 342	Dismantled 6/1925.
343	Rogers	11/19/1888	StPM&M 343	Dismantled at Hillyard 5/10/1926.
344	Rogers	9/10/1889	StPM&M 344	Ret. 10/1923.
345	Rogers	9/14/1889	StPM&M 345	Dismantled 8/1924.
346	Rogers	c.9/1889	StPM&M 346	Sold for scrap DI&M 1/1925.
347	Rogers	9/5/1888	StPM&M 324(2)	Sold for scrap DI&M 1/1927.
348	Rogers	9/11/1888	StPM&M 327	Sold for scrap DI&M 9/2/1927.
349	Rogers	9/16/1888	StPM&M 328	Reno. X1964(1) (WC) 6/1927. Ret. 7/1934.
350	Rogers	8/1888*	EM 201	Scrapped and frame sold to Midland Railway Company of Manitoba 7/1927.
351(2)	Rogers	8/1888*	EM 202	Sold for scrap DI&M 8/1932.
352(2)	Rogers	8/1888*	EM 203	Reno. X1965(1) (WC) 6/1927. Ret. 8/1937.
353(2)	Rogers	8/1888*	EM 204	Ret. 4/1924 to be used with Combination Locomotive Crane & Ditcher.
354(2)	Rogers	8/1888*	EM 205	To work equipment (number unknown) 11/1927.
355(2)	Rogers	9/1888*	EM 206	Sold Minnesota State Fair Association (With E266) 8/17/1921 and destroyed in staged head-on collision at the Minnesota State Fair.
356(2)	Rogers	9/1888*	EM 207	Reno. X1966(1) (WC) 6/1927. Ret. 9/1932.
357(2)	Rogers	9/1888*	EM 208	Reno. X1967(1) (WC) 6/1927. Ret. 3/1928.
358(2)	Rogers	9/1888*	EM 209	Dismantled at Superior 4/16/1930.
359(2)	Rogers	9/1888*	EM 210	Reno. X1968(1) (WC) 6/1927. Ret. 10/1932.

275

Tender Class — , Style Unassigned: 8 Tons Coal; 4,000 Gallons Water

No.	Builder	Date Rcvd.	Original No.	Renumbered From	Date	Disposition
371	?	?	?	?	?	Dismantled 9/1925.
372	?	?	?	?	?	Reno. X2839(2) 7/20/1946. Ret. 4/1951. Sold for scrap PC 6/24/1953.
373	?	?	?	?	?	Reno. 296090 (WC) at Delta 12/21/1925. Reno. X945(1) 10/20/1926. Reno. X1940(1) 6/15/1927. Dismantled at Delta 4/23/1928.
374	?	?	?	?	?	Disposition unknown.
375	Brooks	4/9/1881	StPM&M 88	T15(2)	4/2/1909	Reno. X1918(1) 6/1927. Ret. 3/1928.
376	?	?	?	?	?	Sold for scrap DI&M 8/1926.

Tender Class A-6, Style Unassigned: 12 Tons Coal; 4,000 Gallons Water; 3¾" x 7" Axle Journals

No.	Builder	Date Rcvd.	Original No.	Disposition
378(2)	Brooks	9/1899	DS&WT 1	Sold McCree & Co. [with E378(2)] 7/1926.
379(2)	Brooks	9/1899	DS&WT 2	Sold McCree & Co. [with E379(2)] 7/1926.

Tender Class A-9, Style 1: 6 Tons Coal; 4,000 Gallons Water; 4¼" x 8" Axle Journals

No.	Builder	Date Rcvd.	Disposition	Notes
380(2)	Baldwin	11/6/1912	Sold for scrap PC 3/22/1947.	
381(2)	Baldwin	11/6/1912	Sold for scrap DI&M 2/17/1947.	
382(2)	Baldwin	11/6/1912	Sold for scrap 6/1937.	
383(2)	Baldwin	11/6/1912	Sold for scrap PC 5/1951.	
384(2)	Baldwin	11/2/1912	Sold for scrap PC 10/14/1941.	
385(2)	Baldwin	11/2/1912	Sold for scrap 9/1940.	
386(2)	Baldwin	11/6/1912	Scrapped 9/1940.	
387(2)	Baldwin	11/6/1912	Ret. 7/1942, tank placed on flat car.	
388(2)	Baldwin	11/13/1912	Sold for scrap PC 3/10/1947.	
389(2)	Baldwin	11/13/1912	Retired 9/1931. Dismantled at Hillyard 11/6/1931.	
390(2)	Baldwin	9/23/1912	Ret. 6/1943.	
391(2)	Baldwin	9/23/1912	Sold for scrap 6/1937.	
392(2)	Baldwin	9/23/1912	Sold for scrap DI&M 3/11/1949.	
393(1)	Baldwin	9/23/1912	Scrapped at Superior 1/19/1937, cistern to flat car.	
394	Baldwin	10/2/1912	Sold for scrap PC 3/1/1949.	
395	Baldwin	10/2/1912	Sold for scrap PC 5/16/1947.	
396	Baldwin	9/25/1912	Scrapped 5/21/1937.	
397(1)	Baldwin	9/25/1912	Sold for scrap WEI&M 10/16/1951.	
398(1)	Baldwin	9/30/1912	Sold for scrap 12/1938.	
399(1)	Baldwin	9/30/1912	Sold for scrap PC 4/2/1949.	

276

Tender Class D-4, Style 10: 8 Tons Coal; 4,000 Gallons Water; 4¼" x 8" Axle Journals

No.	Builder	Date Rcvd.	Original No.	Disposition	Note
400(2)	Brooks	11/16/1893	GN 351(1)	Sold for scrap Dulien Steel Products 7/1953.	92
401(2)	Brooks	8/15/1893	GN 352(1)	Reno. X1908(3) (WC) at Sioux City 2/5/1940. Rblt. X840(2) (40FWC) (with Gondola 76458) 2/2/1945. Ret. 12/1971.	
402(2)	Brooks	8/15/1893	GN 353(1)	Sold for scrap DI&M 1/15/1955.	
403(2)	Brooks	8/17/1893	GN 354(1)	Cistern to X951(3) (40FWC) (with Boxcar 34744) at Hillyard 3/31/1947. Reno. X5154 6/1955. Ret. 6/1962.	277
404(2)	Brooks	8/17/1893	GN 355(1)	Ret. 11/1927. Reno. X1904 (WC) 1/1928. Reno. X1921(2) 10/1928. Ret. 5/1936.	
405(2)	Brooks	8/22/1893	GN 356(1)	Ret. 1/1934. Sold for scrap PC 3/12/1934.	
406(2)	Brooks	8/22/1893	GN 357(1)	Sold for scrap DI&M 7/1926.	
407(2)	Brooks	8/28/1893	GN 358(1)	Ret. 5/1926. Reno. X1999(1) (WC) 6/1927. Sold for scrap Dulien Steel Products 8/1939.	278
408(2)	Brooks	8/26/1893	GN 359(1)	Sold for scrap DI&M 9/1932.	93
409(2)	Brooks	8/28/1893	GN 360(1)	Sold Great Lakes Coal Co. [with E65(2)] 9/1927.	
410(3)	Brooks	7/29/1895	GN 361(2)	Sold for scrap DI&M 8/14/1936.	
411(2)	Brooks	11/22/1893	GN 362	Sold for scrap DI&M 7/1926.	94
412(2)	Brooks	7/29/1895	GN 363(2)	Reno. X1906(3) (WC) at Sioux City 5/16/1940. Rblt. X835(2) (40FWC?) (with Boxcar 36613) 7/1945. Tank apparently removed 5/1948.	279
413(2)	Brooks	7/30/1895	GN 364(2)	Sold for scrap PC 12/1949.	
414(2)	Brooks	7/30/1895	GN 365(2)	Sold for scrap DI&M 7/1926.	
415	Brooks	8/1/1895	GN 366	Sold for scrap DI&M 5/1928.	
416	Brooks	8/1/1895	GN 367	Sold for scrap DI&M 12/1923.	
417	Brooks	8/4/1895	GN 368		
418	Brooks	8/4/1895	GN 369	Sold for scrap Pacific Coast Steel Co. 1/1927.	
419	Brooks	8/6/1895	GN 370	Scrapped at Superior 1/19/1937, cistern to flat car.	
420	Brooks	8/28/1893	GN 361(1)	Sold SP&S (with E420) 10/1924.	280
421	Brooks	8/6/1895	EM 250	Sold for scrap DI&M 8/1926.	
422	Brooks	8/6/1895	EM 251	Sold for scrap Pacific Coast Steel Co. 2/1926.	281
423	Brooks	8/11/1895	EM 252	Sold for scrap 12/1938.	
424	Brooks	8/15/1895	EM 253	Sold for scrap DI&M 8/1926.	
425	Brooks	8/15/1895	EM 254	Ret. 5/1929. Reno. X1937(2) (WC) 6/1929. Ret. 3/1937.	
426	Brooks	8/15/1895	EM 255	Sold for scrap DI&M 12/1924.	

Tender Class D-6, Style Unassigned: 9 Tons Coal (No. 430)/5 Tons Coal (No. 431); 3,600 Gallons Water; 4¼" x 8" Axle Journals

No.	Builder	Date Built	Previous No.	Disposition
430(1)	Alco-Schenectady	1902	W&SF 11	Sold for scrap PC 1/18/1929.
431	Alco-Schenectady	1906	W&SF 12	Ret. 4/1937.

Tender Class D-3(2), Style Unassigned: 9 Tons Coal; 4,000 Gallons Water; 4¼" x 8" Axle Journals

No.	Builder	Date Built	Previous No.	Disposition
432	Baldwin	5/1901	W&SF 13	Sold for scrap DI&M 8/1926.

Tender Class D-5, Style Unassigned: 8 Tons Coal; 4,000 Gallons Water; 4¼" x 8" Axle Journals

No.	Builder	Date Rcvd.	Original No.	Disposition	Notes
450(2)	Brooks	9/16/1896	GN 371	Sold for scrap DI&M 10/1927.	
451(2)	Brooks	9/16/1896	GN 372	Sold for scrap DI&M 6/1924.	
452(2)	Brooks	9/18/1896	GN 373	Reno. X949(1) (WC) 6/1926. Reno. X1944(1) 10/31/1927. Ret. 9/1931.	
453(2)	Brooks	9/18/1896	GN 374	Cistern to X842(2) (40FWC) (with Boxcar 4659) at Hillyard 6/5/1945. Reno. X2657(2) (tank probably removed) 10/1953. Ret. 8/1958.	
454(2)	Brooks	9/21/1896	GN 375	Reno. 296095 (WC) 10/1925. Reno. 95003 (RT) at Skykomish 11/23/1925. Reno. (T)X1503 9/1926. Reno. X1978 5/1927. Reno. X834(1) (40FWC) (with Box 34731) 11/15/1945. Ret. 1/1953.	
455(2)	Brooks	9/21/1896	GN 376	Reno. T33(3) 2/1926.	
456(2)	Brooks	9/22/1896	GN 377	Dismantled at Hillyard 11/1945.	
457(2)	Brooks	9/22/1896	GN 378(1)	Reno. X1996(1) (WC) 6/1927. Ret. 10/1932.	
458(2)	Brooks	9/25/1896	GN 379(1)	Reno. T32(3) 2/1925.	
459(2)	Brooks	9/25/1896	GN 380(1)	Reno. X2853(2) (WC) 8/1931. Dismantled at Superior 8/19/1932.	282
460(2)	Brooks	9/28/1896	GN 381(1)	Dismantled at Dale Street 8/27/1928.	283
461(2)	Brooks	9/28/1896	GN 382(1)	Reno. X1994(1) (WC) 6/1927. Ret. 11/1939.	
462(2)	Brooks	8/13/1897	GN 383(1)	Reno. X2854(2) (WC) 9/1931. Ret. 5/1939. Sold for scrap PC 10/1939.	
463(2)	Brooks	8/16/1897	GN 384(1)	Sold for scrap DI&M 1/1929.	
464(2)	Brooks	8/16/1897	GN 385(1)	Sold for scrap DI&M 8/1926.	
465(2)	Brooks	8/19/1897	GN 386(1)	Reno. X1926(1) (WC) 1/1927. Ret. 3/1934. Sold for scrap DI&M 4/15/1934.	
466(2)	Brooks	8/19/1897	GN 387(1)	Reno. X2855(2) (WC) 9/1931. Rblt. X841 (40FWC) (with Flatcar 62797) 1/12/1945. Ret. 4/1952.	
467(2)	Brooks	8/20/1897	GN 388(1)	Reno. X1913(1) (WC) 6/1927. Ret. 1/1929.	
468(2)	Brooks	8/20/1897	GN 389(1)	Reno. X952(1) (WC) 11/1926. Reno. X1947(1) 5/6/1927. Ret. 3/1934. Sold for scrap DI&M 3/29/1934.	
469(2)	Brooks	8/24/1897	GN 390(1)	Sold for scrap DI&M 9/25/1928.	284
470(2)	Brooks	8/24/1897	GN 391(1)	Reno. X1969(1) (WC) 6/1927. Ret. 11/1929.	

471(2)	Brooks	8/24/1897	GN 392(1)	Ret. 1/1934. Sold for scrap PC 6/11/1934.	
472(2)	Brooks	8/31/1897	EM 256	Reno. X2856(2) (WC) 9/1931. Ret. 7/1941.	
473(2)	Brooks	8/31/1897	EM 257	Off roster before 6/30/1915.	
474(2)	Brooks	9/2/1897	EM 258	Sold for scrap DI&M 9/21/1928.	284
475(2)	Brooks	9/4/1897	EM 259	Sold for scrap DI&M 8/1932.	
476(2)	Brooks	9/5/1897	EM 260	Dismantled at Dale Street 8/4/1928.	283

Tender Class D-1(2), Style Unassigned: 9 Tons Coal; 3,000 Gallons Water; 4¼" x 8" Axle Journals

No.	Builder	Date Built	Original No.	Disposition	Notes
477(2)	Baldwin	6/1889	SF&N 4	Ret. c.6/1927.	285
478(2)	Baldwin	4/1889	SF&N 1	Reno. X2857(2) (WC) 9/1931. Ret. 3/1946.	
479(2)	Baldwin	5/1889	SF&N 2	Reno. X1994(2) (WC) at Everett 11/1939. Ret. 8/1946.	286
480(2)	Baldwin	6/1889	SF&N 3	Dismantled at Hillyard 9/1926.	

Tender Class F-1, Style 14: 8 Tons Coal; 4,000 Gallons Water; 4¼" x 8" Axle Journals

No.	Builder	Date Rcvd.	Original No.	Disposition	Notes
500(2)	Brooks	11/29/1892	–	Sold for scrap DI&M 12/1925.	
501(2)	Brooks	12/5/1892	–	Sold for scrap DI&M 9/1932.	
502(2)	Brooks	12/5/1892	–	Sold for scrap DI&M 9/25/1928.	284
503(2)	Brooks	12/7/1892	–	Sold for scrap 7/1940.	
504(2)	Brooks	12/7/1892	–	Sold for scrap PC 10/1929.	
505	Brooks	12/9/1892	–	Reno. X2823 (WC) at Spokane 11/11/1940. Sold for scrap PC 2/25/1947.	287
506	Brooks	12/9/1892	–	Reno. X2858(2) (WC) 9/1931. Ret. 3/1934. Sold for scrap DI&M 4/15/1934.	
507	Brooks	12/12/1892	–	Sold for scrap DI&M 10/1932.	
508	Brooks	12/12/1892	–	Sold for scrap PC 4/20/1952.	
509	Brooks	12/15/1892	–	Off roster before 6/30/1915.	
510	Brooks	12/15/1892	–	Dismantled at Delta 4/14/1932.	288
511	Brooks	12/17/1892	–	Sold for scrap DI&M 8/1932.	
512	Brooks	12/17/1892	–	Sold for scrap DI&M 5/1928.	
513	Brooks	12/19/1892	–	Sold for scrap DI&M 10/1932.	
514	Brooks	12/19/1892	–	Sold for scrap DI&M 6/1924.	
515	Brooks	11/15/1893	–	Reno. 296078 (WC) at Navajo, MT, 1/2/1926. Reno. X933(1) 10/1926. Reno. X1932(1) 7/21/1927. Ret. 3/1934. Sold for scrap DI&M 3/29/1934.	289
516	Brooks	6/16/1892	GN 450(1)	Sold for scrap DI&M 2/2/1922.	
517	Brooks	6/16/1892	GN 451(1)	Ret. 12/1930. Dismantled at Great Falls 2/16/1931.	
518	Brooks	6/19/1892	GN 452(1)	Sold for scrap 9/1939.	108
519	Brooks	6/19/1892	GN 453(1)	Reno. X1954(2) (WC) 11/22/1930. Dismantled at Superior 8/19/1932.	108, 290
520	Brooks	6/21/1892	GN 454(1)	Sold for scrap DI&M 1/1929.	
521	Brooks	6/21/1892	GN 455(1)	Ret. 12/1930. Sold for scrap PC 4/10/1934.	
522(1)	Brooks	6/28/1892	GN 456(1)	Sold for scrap DI&M 9/1932.	109
522(2)	Brooks			Scrapped 4/1952.	
523	Brooks	6/28/1892	GN 457(1)	Sold for scrap DI&M 8/1932.	109
524	Brooks	6/28/1892	GN 458(1)	Sold for scrap 3/1937.	109
525	Brooks	6/28/1892	GN 459(1)	Sold Somers Lumber Co. (with E525) 12/1924. Returned 10/1925. Reno. X1969(2) (WC) 12/15/1931. Ret. 11/1/1939.	109
526	Brooks	6/30/1892	GN 460(1)	Sold for scrap DI&M 10/1926.	
527	Brooks	6/30/1892	GN 461(1)	Sold Somers Lumber Co. (with E342) 10/1925.	
528	Brooks	7/2/1892	GN 462(1)	Sold for scrap DI&M 9/1932.	
529	Brooks	7/2/1892	GN 463(1)		
530	Brooks	7/7/1892	GN 464(1)	Reno. T603(2) at Breckenridge 3/10/1909.	
531	Brooks	7/7/1892	GN 465(1)	Reno. X3347 (FO) 10/26/1942. Sold Hyman-Michaels 10/1978.	291
532	Brooks	7/8/1892	GN 466(1)	Sold for scrap DI&M 1/1927.	
533	Brooks	7/8/1892	GN 467(1)	Sold for scrap DI&M 10/1929.	
534	Brooks	7/15/1892	GN 468(1)	Dismantled 8/1931 (with E206).	
535	Brooks	7/15/1892	GN 469(1)	Sold for scrap DI&M 10/1929.	
536	Brooks	7/19/1892	GN 470(1)	Sold for scrap DI&M 2/1928.	
537	Brooks	7/19/1892	GN 471(1)	Sold for scrap DI&M 2/1928.	
538	Brooks	7/22/1892	GN 472(1)	Reno. X948(2) (WC) 11/17/1938. Ret. 11/1939.	
539	Brooks	7/22/1892	GN 473(1)		
540	Brooks	8/15/1892	GN 474(1)	Sold for scrap DI&M 2/1928.	
541	Brooks	8/15/1892	GN 475(1)	Sold for scrap DI&M 11/1928.	292
542	Brooks	8/20/1892	GN 476(1)	Sold for scrap 10/1940.	
543	Brooks	8/20/1892	GN 477(1)	Dismantled 4/1925.	
544	Brooks	8/22/1892	GN 478(1)	Reno. X1927(2) (WC) 6/1927. Ret. 7/1935.	
545(1)	Brooks	8/22/1892	GN 479(1)	Reno. X1970(1) (WC) 6/1927. Ret. 7/1932.	
546(1)	Brooks	8/28/1892	GN 480(1)	Sold for scrap DI&M 9/4/1927.	
547	Brooks	8/28/1892	GN 481	Scrapped at Grand Forks 8/3/1937, cistern to flat car.	
548	Brooks	8/28/1892	GN 482	Scrapped 4/1931 (with E771)	
549	Brooks	8/28/1892	GN 483		

Tender Class F-1, Style 14: Continued

No.	Builder	Date Rcvd.	Original No.	Disposition	Notes
550(2)	Brooks	8/31/1892	GN 484	Reno. X950(1) (WC) 1/1927. Reno. X1945(1) 6/1/1927. Stripped at Superior 8/19/1932. Ret. 9/1932. Tank may have been salvaged and used to construct X906(2) (with Boxcar 14688) 10/1946. Ret. 9/1951.	293
551(2)	Brooks	8/31/1892	GN 485	Scrapped 9/1940.	
552(2)	Brooks	9/1/1892	GN 486	Reno. X948(1) (WC) 7/1926. Reno. X1943(1) 3/31/1927. Ret. 6/1934.	
553(2)	Brooks	9/1/1892	GN 487	Sold for scrap DI&M 6/1928.	
554(2)	Brooks	9/4/1892	GN 488	Sold for scrap DI&M 9/1932.	
555	Brooks	9/4/1892	GN 489	Sold for scrap DI&M 10/1929.	
556	Brooks	9/6/1892	GN 490	Ret. 1/1934. Sold for scrap DI&M 4/15/1934.	
557	Brooks	9/6/1892	GN 491	Reno. X1971(1) (WC) 6/1927. Ret. 3/1928.	
558	Brooks	9/9/1892	GN 492	Sold for scrap DI&M 12/1927.	
559	Brooks	9/9/1892	GN 493	Sold for scrap DI&M 5/1928.	
560	Brooks	9/10/1892	GN 494	Reno. TX1793 (Crane & Ditcher Tender) 4/1925. Reno. X1988(1) 6/7/1927. Ret. 7/1934.	
561	Brooks	9/16/1892	GN 495	Reno. T610(2) at Superior 2/24/1909.	
562	Brooks	9/16/1892	GN 496	Sold for scrap DI&M 2/17/1947.	
563	Brooks	9/18/1892	GN 497	Off roster prior to 6/30/1915.	
564	Brooks	9/18/1892	GN 498	Sold for scrap PC 10/1929.	
565	Brooks	10/26/1892	GN 499	Ret. 10/1928. Dismantled at St.Cloud 11/8/1928.	

Tender Class H-7, Style 44: 13 Tons Coal (later increased to 16 Tons); 8,000 Gallons Water; 5½" x 10" Axle Journals.

No.	Builder	Date	Original No.	Renumbered From	Date	Disposition
545(2)	Baldwin	10/1/1910	GN 1052(2)	SP&S 625	4/5/1945	Sold for scrap WEI&M 10/18/1951.
546(2)	Baldwin	10/1/1910	GN 1050(2)	SP&S 621	4/5/1945	Reno. X1944(3) c.6/1951. Ret. 8/1961.

Tender Class —, Style Unassigned: Dimensions Unknown

No.	Builder	Date	Original No.	Renumbered From	Date	Disposition
566	?	?	?	?	?	Ret. 1/1934. Sold for scrap PC 3/18/1934.

Tender Class F-11, Style Unassigned: 9 Tons Coal; 5,000 Gallons Water; 5" x 9" Axle Journals

No.	Builder	Date Built	Original No.	Disposition
590	Alco-Brooks	4/1913	TA&G 322	Ret. 7/1942, tank placed on flat car.
591	Alco-Brooks	9/1914	SDC 15	Scrapped at Dale Street 11/9/1927.

Tender Class F-2, Style Unassigned: 8 Tons Coal; 4,000 Gallons Water; 4¼" x 8" Axle Journals

No.	Builder	Date Rcvd.	Original No.	Disposition	Notes
595	Baldwin	8/9/1892	GN 500(1)	4,500 gallon water cistern replaced 4,000 gallon 4/1917. Cistern to X851(3) (40FWC) (with Boxcar 3188) at St.Cloud 2/3/1945. Further disposition unknown.	
596	Baldwin	8/9/1892	GN 501(1)	Reno. X2859(2) (WC) 9/1931. Sold for scrap DI&M 3/29/1934.	
597	Baldwin	8/14/1892	GN 502(1)	Cistern to X819(2) (40FWC) (with Boxcar 13029) at St.Cloud 3/6/1945. Ret. 6/1954.	
598	Baldwin	8/14/1892	GN 503(1)	Reno. X3348 (FO) 10/26/1942. Ret. 6/1956.	291
599	Baldwin	8/15/1892	GN 504(1)	Sold for scrap DI&M 9/1927.	

Tender Class G-1, Style Unassigned: 8 Tons Coal; 4,000 Gallons Water; 4¼" x 8" Axle Journals

No.	Builder	Date Rcvd.	Original No.	Renumbered From	Date	Disposition	Notes
600(2)	Brooks	10/15/1891	StPM&M 400	–	–	Sold for scrap PC 10/1929.	
601(2)	Brooks	10/17/1891	StPM&M 401	–	–	Reno. X2860(2) (WC) 9/1931. Ret. 9/1932.	
602	Brooks	10/17/1891	StPM&M 402	–	–	Sold for scrap NSRM 5/1926.	
603(1)	Brooks	10/21/1891	StPM&M 403	–	–		
603(2)	Brooks	7/7/1892	GN 464(1)	T530	3/10/1909	Reno. X1998(1) (WC) 6/1927. Ret. 6/1932.	
604	Brooks	10/21/1891	StPM&M 404	–	–	Sold for scrap DI&M 7/1932.	
605	Brooks	10/26/1891	StPM&M 405	–	–	Reno. X1924(2) (WC) 5/3/1928. Ret. 12/1930.	
606	Brooks	10/26/1891	StPM&M 406	–	–	Reno. 296081 (WC) 10/1925. Further disposition unknown.	
607	Brooks	10/30/1891	StPM&M 407	–	–	Reno. X1928(1) (WC) 6/1927. Ret. 11/1932.	
608	Brooks	10/29/1891	StPM&M 408	–	–	Reno. X1972(1) (WC) 6/1927. Ret. 2/1928.	
609	Brooks	11/2/1891	StPM&M 409	–	–	Sold for scrap DI&M 10/18/1928.	294
610(1)	Brooks	11/15/1893	GN 410(2)	–	–		
610(2)	Brooks	9/16/1892	GN 495	T561	2/24/1909	Ret. 1/1934. Sold for scrap DI&M 3/18/1934.	
611	Brooks	12/3/1891	StPM&M 410	–	–	Sold for scrap DI&M 2/1928.	
612	Brooks	12/8/1891	StPM&M 411	–	–	Cistern to X856(2) (40FWC) (with Boxcar 5190) at St.Cloud 2/28/1945. Ret. 1/1953.	
613	Brooks	12/8/1891	StPM&M 412	–	–	Sold for scrap DI&M 6/1926.	
614	Brooks	12/14/1891	StPM&M 413	–	–	Reno. 296080 (WC) at Great Falls 12/16/1925. Reno. X935(1) 9/1926. Reno. X1934(1) 6/12/1927. Ret. 10/1941.	
615	Brooks	12/14/1891	StPM&M 414	–	–	Sold Hyman-Michaels Co. 4/1926.	

Tender Class G-2, Style 21: 8 Tons Coal; 5,000 Gallons Water; 4¼" x 8" Axle Journals

No.	Builder	Date Built	Original No.	Disposition	Notes
700	Brooks	6/1898	EM 300	Cistern to X889(2) (40FWC) (with Boxcar 34959) at Hillyard 2/28/1946. Sold NSRM 5/1979.	
701	Brooks	6/1898	EM 301	[Reclassified as F-3 with locomotive] Sold for scrap DI&M 8/1928.	295
702	Brooks	6/1898	EM 302	Reno. X1973(1) (WC) 6/1927. Ret. 9/1941.	
703	Brooks	6/1898	EM 303	Ret. 1/1934. Sold for scrap PC 4/10/1934.	
704	Brooks	6/1898	EM 304	Sold for scrap PC 5/14/1947.	
705	Brooks	6/1898	EM 305	Sold for scrap DI&M 10/1932.	
706	Brooks	6/1898	EM 306	Sold for scrap DI&M 9/1932.	
707	Brooks	7/1898	EM 307	Sold for scrap DI&M 9/1932.	
708	Brooks	7/1898	EM 308	Scrapped at Grand Forks 8/3/1937, cistern to flat car.	
709	Brooks	7/1898	EM 309	Sold for scrap DI&M 10/1932.	
710	Brooks	7/1898	EM 310	Sold for scrap PC 7/1939.	
711	Brooks	7/1898	EM 311	Sold for scrap 12/1938.	
712	Brooks	9/1898	EM 312	Reno. X949(2) (WC) 11/26/1938. Ret. 11/1945.	
713	Brooks	9/1898	EM 313	Scrapped 6/1928.	
714	Brooks	9/1898	EM 314	Sold Deer Park Lumber Co. (with E564) 8/1928.	
715	Brooks	9/1898	EM 315	Sold for scrap DI&M 8/1932.	
716	Brooks	10/1898	EM 316	Reno. X2828(1) (WC) 6/1934. Ret. 9/1941.	
717	Brooks	10/1898	EM 317	Reno. X1955(2) (WC) 5/15/1930. Ret. 3/1944.	
718	Brooks	10/1898	EM 318	Sold for scrap DI&M 2/1928.	
719	Brooks	10/1898	EM 319	Sold for scrap DI&M 7/1932.	

Tender Class G-3, Style 22: 8 Tons Coal (some equipped with 4,000 Gallon Oil Cistern); 5,000 Gallons Water; 5" x 9" Axle Journals

No.	Builder	Date Rcvd.	Disposition	Notes
720	Rogers	5/17/1899	Sold for scrap 5/1940.	
721	Rogers	5/17/1899	Reno. X1933(2) (WC) 9/1928. Rblt. X862(3) (40FWC) (with Boxcar 32018) 4/1946. Ret. 5/1958.	
722	Rogers	5/19/1899	Reno. X2883(2) (WC) 11/1931. Rblt. X887(3) (40FWC) (with Boxcar 5186) 4/2/1945. Ret. 4/1956.	
723	Rogers	5/19/1899	Ret. 1/1934. Sold for scrap DI&M 3/12/1934.	
724	Rogers	5/19/1899	Sold for scrap PC 6/1951.	
725	Rogers	5/26/1899	Ret. 1/1934. Sold for scrap DI&M 3/29/1934.	
726	Rogers	5/28/1899	Sold for scrap DI&M 9/1932.	
727	Rogers	6/7/1899	Ret. 1/1934. Sold for scrap DI&M 4/5/1934.	
728	Rogers	6/7/1899	Ret. 3/1930. Dismantled at Dale Street 8/14/1930.	
729	Rogers	6/15/1899	Sold for scrap PC 12/1949.	
730	Rogers	6/20/1899	Sold for scrap 11/1932.	
731	Rogers	7/11/1899	Sold for scrap PC 5/1929.	
732	Rogers	7/11/1899	Scrapped PC 10/1929.	
733	Rogers	7/15/1899	Reno. X2861(2) (WC) 9/1931. Rblt. X880(1) (40FWC) (with Boxcar 27027) 4/26/1945. Ret. 1/1952.	
734	Rogers	7/20/1899	Sold for scrap DI&M 7/1932.	
735	Rogers	8/1/1899	Sold for scrap PC 7/1939.	
736	Rogers	8/28/1899	Reno. T749(2) at Great Falls 4/7/1910.	
737	Rogers	8/23/1899	Reno. X1963(2) (WC) 5/22/1928. Ret. 1/1942.	
738	Rogers	8/1899	Sold for scrap DI&M 8/1/1936.	
739	Rogers	8/21/1899	Sold for scrap PC 3/22/1947.	
740	Rogers	8/26/1899	Ret. 1/1934. Sold for scrap DI&M 3/18/1934.	
741	Rogers	8/27/1899	Ret. 1/1934. Sold for scrap PC 3/12/1934.	
742	Rogers	8/28/1899	Reno. X948(3) (WC) at Sioux Falls 5/23/1940. Rblt. X891(2) (40FWC) (with Boxcar 14195) 7/31/1945. Lost car 3/2/1989.	
743	Rogers	9/2/1899	Reno. X2862(2) (WC) 9/1931. Ret. 2/1948.	
744	Rogers	9/4/1899	Sold for scrap Bethlehem Steel Co. 11/1939.	
745	Rogers	5/18/1900	Ret. 1/1934. Sold for scrap DI&M 3/18/1934.	
746	Rogers	5/19/1900	Ret. 12/1930. Dismantled at Dale Street 3/3/1931.	
747	Rogers	5/20/1900	Ret. 1/1934. Sold for scrap DI&M 3/29/1934.	
748	Rogers	5/24/1900	Sold for scrap DI&M 10/1932.	
749(1)	Rogers	5/27/1900	Probably sold Pacific & Eastern Ry. (with E736) 3/5/1910.	
749(2)	Rogers	8/28/1899	Ret. 5/1947.	296
750	Rogers	6/2/1900	Ret. 5/21/1937.	
751	Rogers	6/2/1900	Reno. X2829(1) (WC) 6/1934. Sold for scrap 1937.	
752	Rogers	6/2/1900	Ret. 12/1930.	
753	Rogers	6/3/1900	Sold for scrap DI&M 7/1932.	
754	Rogers	6/8/1900	Sold for scrap PC 5/1929.	
755	Rogers	6/10/1900	Cistern to X952(3) (40FWC) (with Boxcar 36280) at Hillyard 3/31/1947. Ret. 11/1956.	297

Tender Class G-3, Style 22: Continued

No.	Builder	Date Rcvd.	Disposition	Notes
756	Rogers	6/12/1900	Dismantled at Superior 10/26/1929.	
757	Rogers	6/16/1900	Converted to water car 9/23/1941 at Hillyard. Reno. X3254 (WC) at Klamath Falls 5/27/1945. Reno. X1949(4) 2/1953. Ret. 9/1964.	298
758	Rogers	6/19/1900	Ret. 1/1934. Sold for scrap DI&M 3/29/1934.	
759	Rogers	6/18/1900	Reno. X2863(2) (WC) 9/1931. Ret. 6/1936.	
760	Rogers	6/22/1900	Sold for scrap DI&M 9/1932.	
761	Rogers	6/24/1900	Sold for scrap DI&M 5/5/1952.	
762	Rogers	6/25/1900	Sold for scrap DI&M 10/1932.	
763	Rogers	6/25/1900	Sold for scrap 9/1940.	
764	Rogers	6/29/1900	Ret. 12/1930.	
765	Rogers	6/30/1900	Ret. 1/1934. Sold for scrap PC 4/10/1934.	
766	Rogers	6/30/1900	Ret. 1/1934. Sold for scrap DI&M 4/5/1934.	
767	Rogers	7/1/1900	Sold for scrap DI&M 7/1939.	
768	Rogers	7/7/1900	Reno. X1956(2) (WC) 7/1931. Ret. 7/1934.	
769	Rogers	7/7/1900	Scrapped 12/1938.	

Tender Class G-4, Style 23: 8 Tons Coal; 5,000 Gallons Water; 5" x 9" Axle Journals

No.	Builder	Date Built	Original No.	Disposition
770	Brooks	7/1900	EM 770	Reno. X1952(2) (WC) 9/1929. Ret. 11/1959.
771	Brooks	7/1900	EM 771	Sold for scrap DI&M 9/1932.
772	Brooks	7/1900	EM 772	Reno. X3349 (FO) 10/26/1942. Ret. 9/1955.
773	Brooks	7/1900	EM 773	Sold Truax-Traer Coal Co., Kincaid, ND, [with E554(2)] 9/27/1936.
774	Brooks	7/1900	EM 774	Sold for scrap DI&M 8/1932.
775	Brooks	7/1900	EM 775	Sold for scrap DI&M 2/1928.
776	Brooks	7/1900	EM 776	Sold for scrap DI&M 9/15/1941.
777	Brooks	7/1900	EM 777	Sold for scrap PC 8/12/1936.
778	Brooks	7/1900	EM 778	Sold for scrap WEI&M 4/26/1952.
779	Brooks	7/1900	EM 779	Sold for scrap DI&M 1/1927.

Tender Class C-4, Style 8: 13 Tons Coal (Some equipped with 4,500 Gallon Oil Cistern); 8,000 Gallons Water; 5½" x 10" Axle Journals (6" x10" Axle Journals with Oil Cistern)

No.	Builder	Date Rcvd.	Original No.	Renumbered From	Date	Disposition	Notes
780	Rogers	7/26/1902	GN 938	GN 938	3/27/1910	Reno. X1979(2) (WC) 10/1932. Ret. 3/1958.	
781	Rogers	11/10/1902	GN 1166	GN 781	5/14/1932	Reno. X2864(2) (WC) 9/1931. Ret. 12/1939.	299

Tender Class —, Style —: Coal Capacity Unknown, 4,500 Gallons Water

No.	Builder	Date Built	Disposition
782	Dale Street	c.1916	Sold for scrap DI&M 10/1932.
783	Dale Street	5/1916	Reno. X2831 (WC) 6/1934. Ret. 1/1959.

Tender Class —, Style —: Coal Capacity Unknown, 8,000 Gallons Water

No.	Builder	Date Built	Disposition
784	Dale Street	1917	Sold for scrap DI&M 6/1948.
785	Dale Street	1917	Sold for scrap DI&M 10/22/1951.
786	Dale Street	1917	Sold for scrap PC 6/6/1953.

Tender Class —, Style —: Coal and water capacity unknown.

No.	Builder	Date Rcvd.	Original No.	Renumbered From	Date	Disposition	Notes
787(1)	Hinkley	8/1/1888	StPM&M 232	GN 30(2)	?	Ret. 2/1923.	
787(2)	Rogers	12/9/1901	GN 1052(1)	GN 1072	?	Reno. X947(3) (WC) 7/1947. Ret. 1/1956.	
788	Hinkley	8/1/1888	StPM&M 233	GN 31(2)	?	Reno. 296092 (WC) at Delta 2/19/1926. Reno. X946(1) 10/20/1926. Reno. X1941(1) 5/26/1927. Ret. 9/1932.	300

Tender Class G-5, Style 24: 8 Tons Coal; 5,000 Gallons Water; 4¼" x 8" Axle Journals

No.	Builder	Date Built	Original No.	Disposition	Notes
800	Brooks	12/1897	MC 100	Sold for scrap PC 10/1950.	
801	Brooks	12/1897	MC 101	Sold for scrap PC 10/1929.	
802	Brooks	8/1898	MC 102	Reno. X950(2) (WC) 6/1938. Rblt. X923 (40FWC) (with Boxcar 16728) 2/27/1945. Ret. 10/1983.	
803	Brooks	8/1898	MC 103	Sold for scrap DI&M 7/27/1936.	301
804	Brooks	8/1898	MC 104	Reno. X951(2) (WC) 6/1938. Ret. 4/1942.	
805	Brooks	8/1898	MC 105	Ret. 10/1928. Sold for scrap DI&M 11/1928.	
806	Brooks	8/1898	MC 106	Reclassified as F-10, 1905. Reno. X2865(2) (WC) 9/1931. Ret. 10/1932.	
807	Brooks	8/1898	MC 107	Sold for scrap DI&M 8/1928.	302

Tender Class C-1, Style 5: 12 Tons Coal (Some equipped with 3,000 Gallon Oil Cistern); 6,000 Gallons Water; 5½" x10" Axle Journals

No.	Builder	Date Rcvd.	Disposition
810	Baldwin	7/4/1918	Ret. 3/1958. Sold for scrap PC 12/1962.
811	Baldwin	7/20/1918	Ret. 3/1958. Sold for scrap DI&M 3/1962.
812	Baldwin	7/20/1918	Ret. 8/1956. Sold for scrap PC 9/16/1956.
813	Baldwin	7/23/1918	Ret. 5/1958. Sold for scrap PC 7/1963.
814	Baldwin	7/25/1918	Ret. 12/1957. Sold for scrap WEI&M 6/1962.

815	Baldwin	7/23/1918	Ret. 5/1958. Sold for scrap PC 7/1963.
816	Baldwin	8/4/1918	Ret. 12/1957. Sold for scrap c.1962.
817	Baldwin	8/8/1918	Ret. 5/1958. Sold for scrap DI&M 3/1962.
818	Baldwin	8/8/1918	Ret. 5/1958. Sold for scrap DI&M 3/1962.
819	Baldwin	9/1/1918	Ret. 5/1958. Sold for scrap DI&M 3/1962.
820	Baldwin	9/1/1918	Ret. 3/1958. Sold for scrap DI&M 3/1963.
821	Baldwin	9/4/1918	Ret. 5/1958. Sold for scrap 5/1963.
822	Baldwin	9/20/1918	Ret. 3/1958. Sold for scrap DI&M 4/1962.
823	Baldwin	9/20/1918	Ret. 4/1955. Sold for scrap WEI&M 5/28/1955.
824	Baldwin	9/14/1918	Ret. 5/1958. Sold for scrap WEI&M 3/1963.
825	Baldwin	10/2/1918	Ret. 5/1958. Sold for scrap PC 12/10/1962.
826	Baldwin	10/2/1918	Ret. 12/1957. Sold for scrap WEI&M 6/1962.
827	Baldwin	10/20/1918	Ret. 5/1958. Sold for scrap DI&M 3/1962.
828	Baldwin	10/20/1918	Ret. 12/1957. Sold for scrap DI&M 5/1963.
829	Baldwin	10/22/1918	Ret. 12/1957. Sold for scrap DI&M 4/1962.
830	Baldwin	10/23/1918	Ret. 5/1958. Sold for scrap DI&M 3/1962.
831	Baldwin	11/1/1918	Ret. 12/1957. Sold for scrap DI&M 5/1963.
832	Baldwin	3/18/1919	Ret. 5/1958. Sold for scrap PC 12/1962.
833	Baldwin	3/18/1919	Ret. 12/1957. Sold for scrap c.1962.
834	Baldwin	3/24/1919	Ret. 12/1957. Sold for scrap c.1962.
835	Baldwin	3/24/1919	Ret. 12/1957. Sold for scrap DI&M 4/1962.
836	Baldwin	4/7/1919	Ret. 3/1958. Sold for scrap DI&M 4/1962.
837	Baldwin	4/7/1919	Ret. 5/1958. Sold for scrap DI&M 3/1962.
838	Baldwin	4/12/1919	Ret. 3/1958. Sold for scrap DI&M 5/1963.
839	Baldwin	4/12/1919	Ret. 12/1957. Sold for scrap c.1962.
840	Baldwin	4/14/1919	Ret. 3/1958. Sold for scrap DI&M 3/1962.
841	Baldwin	4/14/1919	Ret. 3/1958. Sold for scrap DI&M 4/1962.
842	Baldwin	4/28/1919	Ret. 5/1958. Sold for scrap DI&M 5/1963.
843	Baldwin	4/28/1919	Ret. 3/1958. Sold for scrap DI&M 4/1962.
844	Baldwin	4/29/1919	Ret. 12/1957. Sold for scrap DI&M 4/1962.
845	Baldwin	4/29/1919	Ret. 5/1958. Sold for scrap DI&M 3/1962.
846	Baldwin	5/19/1919	Ret. 3/1958. Sold for scrap PC 2/1963.
847	Baldwin	5/19/1919	Ret. 5/1958. Sold for scrap WEI&M 6/1963.
848	Baldwin	6/26/1919	Ret. 5/1958. Sold for scrap WEI&M 3/1963.
849	Baldwin	6/26/1919	Ret. 12/1957. Sold for scrap WEI&M 6/1962.

Tender Class C-2, Style 6: 14 Tons Coal (Some equipped with 4,000 Gallon Oil Cistern); 6,000 Gallons Water; 5½" x10" Axle Journals

No.	Builder	Date Built	Original (F-6) No.	Disposition	Notes
850	Brooks	12/9/1901	GN 1115	Dismantled at Great Falls 5/31/1929.	
851	Brooks	12/13/1901	GN 1118	Sold for scrap DI&M 10/16/1951.	
852	Brooks	12/24/1901	GN 1126	Cistern to X914(3) at Great Falls 9/3/1946. Ret. 3/1953.	
853	Brooks	12/7/1901	GN 1113	Sold for scrap Bethlehem Steel Co. 11/1939.	
854	Brooks	12/9/1901	GN 1114	Reno. X2866(2) (WC) 9/1931. Sold DI&M 7/1939.	
855	Brooks	12/15/1901	GN 1122	Sold for scrap PC 8/8/1936.	
856	Brooks	12/22/1901	GN 1124	Sold for scrap DI&M 7/1947.	
857	Brooks	12/15/1901	GN 1121	Ret. 1/1947. Cistern to X822(2) (40FWC) (with Boxcar 23268) at Great Falls 5/8/1947. Ret. 1/1959.	303
858	Brooks	12/22/1901	GN 1125	Sold for scrap Bethlehem Steel Co. 11/1939.	
859	Brooks	12/10/1901	GN 1116	Sold for scrap PC 10/22/1951.	
860	Brooks	12/24/1901	GN 1128	Sold for scrap PC 3/29/1952.	
861	Brooks	12/13/1901	GN 1119	Reno. X2832(1) (WC) 6/1934. Rblt. X913(3) (with Flatcar 63057) 11/1944. Ret. 1/1955.	
862	Brooks	12/6/1901	GN 1110	Reno. X959(2) (WC) at South Cheney, WA, 5/27/1940. Cistern to X933(3) at Hillyard 10/25/1945. Reno. X4128 7/18/1956 (cistern probably removed).	304
863	Brooks	12/15/1901	GN 1123	Sold for scrap PC 10/18/1951.	
864	Brooks	12/6/1901	GN 1111	Reno. X2833(1) (WC) 6/1934. Ret. 11/1939.	
865	Brooks	12/7/1901	GN 1112	Reno. X2834(1) (WC) 6/1934. Ret. 6/1936. Sold PC 7/27/1936.	
866	Brooks	12/15/1901	GN 1120	Sold for scrap DI&M 10/1932.	
867	Brooks	12/10/1901	GN 1117	Sold for scrap DI&M 7/1932.	
868	Brooks	12/24/1901	GN 1129	Sold for scrap PC 9/1949.	
869	Brooks	12/24/1901	GN 1127	Reno. X2835(1) (WC) 6/1934. Sold Dulien Steel Products 8/14/1939.	

Tender Class C-4, Style 8: 13 Tons Coal (Some equipped with 4,500 Gallon Oil Cistern); 8,000 Gallons Water; 5½" x 10" Axle Journals (6" x10" Axle Journals with Oil Cistern)

No.	Builder	Date Built	Original (F-8) No.	Disposition
870(1)	Baldwin	1/3/1908	GN 1254	Rblt. to 10,000 Gallon capacity 8/3/1927 at Superior. Sold for scrap DI&M 4/18/1952.
871(1)	Rogers	11/10/1902	GN 1166	Reno. GN 781 5/14/1932.

Tender Class C-5, Style 9: 15 Tons Coal; 10,000 Gallons Water; 5½" x 10" Axle Journals (Origin of these tenders unknown -- only evidence of their existence is a reference in maintenance diagrams.)

Tender Class C-3, Style 7: 14 Tons Coal (Some equipped with 4,000 Gallon Oil Cisterns); 6,000 Gallons Water; 5½" x10" Axle Journals

No.	Builder	Date Built	Original (F-9) No.	Disposition	Notes
875	Alco-Brooks	7/22/1903	GN 1313	Sold for scrap DI&M 9/12/1928.	305
876	Alco-Brooks	7/26/1903	GN 1318	Reno. X2867(2) (WC) 9/1931. Rblt. X908(2) (40FWC) (with Boxcar 26671) 12/1946. Ret. 1/1961.	
877	Alco-Brooks	7/20/1903	GN 1309	Reno. X2836(1) (WC) 6/1934. Ret. 2/1943.	
878	Alco-Brooks	7/26/1903	GN 1319	Reno. X1934(3) (WC) 1/1949. Ret. 5/1958.	
879	Alco-Brooks	7/24/1903	GN 1315	Sold for scrap PC 10/1950.	
880	Alco-Brooks	7/27/1903	GN 1321	Reno. X1920(1) (WC) 6/1927. Sold DI&M 9/1939.	
881	Alco-Brooks	7/16/1903	GN 1305	Reno. X1967(2) (WC) 10/19/1931. Ret. 4/18/1945.	
882	Alco-Brooks	7/22/1903	GN 1311	Reno. X963(2) (WC) at Fort Browning, MT, 5/24/1940. Rblt. X936(2) (40FWC) (with Boxcar 27048) 8/16/1945. Ret. 10/1955.	
883(1)	Alco-Brooks	7/22/1903	GN 1312	Sold Minnesota Transfer Railway Co. [with E883(1)] 10/29/1926.	
883(2)	Alco-Brooks	7/20/1903	GN 1308	Sold for scrap DI&M 8/1932.	
884	Alco-Brooks	7/27/1903	GN 1324	Sold for scrap PC 12/1947.	
885	Alco-Brooks	7/20/1903	GN 1307	Sold for scrap DI&M 11/1949.	
886	Alco-Brooks	7/26/1903	GN 1316	Stripped at Fargo 6/10/1932. Sold for scrap DI&M 7/1932.	
887	Alco-Brooks	7/16/1903	GN 1303	Reno. X1922(3) (WC) 5/1948. Ret. 3/1953.	
888	Alco-Brooks	7/20/1903	GN 1306	Reno. X952(2) (WC) 9/1938. Rblt. X919(1) (40FWC) (with Boxcar 35728) 5/1945. Rblt. X3659 (Idler Car– cistern probably removed) 4/1948.	
889	Alco-Brooks	7/16/1903	GN 1302	Reno. X1960(3) (WC) at Great Falls 1/1945. Ret. 7/1957.	306
890	Alco-Brooks	7/26/1903	GN 1320	Reno. X1927(3) (WC) at Whitefish, MT, 5/16/1940. Rblt. X901(2) (40FWC) (with Boxcar 16009) 1/10/1946. Ret. 10/1957.	
891	Alco-Brooks	7/14/1903	GN 1300	Sold for scrap PC 3/20/1947.	
892	Alco-Brooks	7/22/1903	GN 1310	Cistern to X916(3) (40FWC) (with Boxcar 36020) at Great Falls 3/23/1946. Ret. 11/1955.	
893	Alco-Brooks	7/27/1903	GN 1323	Reno. X1922(2) (WC) 6/1928. Ret. 5/1936. Sold for scrap PC 9/1939.	
894	Alco-Brooks	7/24/1903	GN 1314	Reno. X2837(1) (WC) 6/1934. Ret. 7/1937.	
895	Alco-Brooks	7/16/1903	GN 1304	Sold Gray's Harbor Pacific Railroad 8/1930.	
896	Alco-Brooks	7/14/1903	GN 1301	Scrapped 12/1951.	
897	Alco-Brooks	7/26/1903	GN 1317	Dismantled at Great Falls 12/18/1947, cistern to X3301 (40FWC). Ret. 6/1958.	307
898	Alco-Brooks	7/27/1903	GN 1322	Reno. X2856(4) (WC) at Skykomish 4/10/1947. Ret. 7/1928.	
899	Alco-Brooks	7/20/1903	GN 1308	Reno. 883(2) 1926.	

Tender Class E-3, Style Unassigned: 8 Tons Coal; 4,500 Gallons Water; 5" x 9" Axle Journals

No.	Builder	Date Built	Disposition
900	Rogers	3/1899	Sold for scrap DI&M 8/1932.
901	Rogers	3/1899	Sold for scrap DI&M 7/1939.
902	Rogers	3/1899	Sold for scrap DI&M 7/1932.
903	Rogers	3/1899	Sold for scrap DI&M 10/1929.
904	Rogers	3/1899	Reno. X2868(2) (WC) 9/1931.Ret. 10/1932.
905	Rogers	3/1899	Sold for scrap DI&M 6/1932.
906	Rogers	3/1899	Reno. X959(1) (WC) 8/1938. Ret. 12/1938.
907	Rogers	4/1899	Sold for scrap PC 9/1939.
908	Rogers	4/1899	Sold for scrap DI&M 6/1932.
909	Rogers	4/1899	Ret. 12/1930. Sold for scrap DI&M 3/29/1934.

Tender Class E-2(2), Style Unassigned: 8 Tons Coal; 5,000 Gallons Water; 5" x 9" Axle Journals

No.	Builder	Date Built	Original No.	Disposition
910	Alco-Brooks	5/1915	SDC 16	Ret. 9/1939. Sold for scrap Bethlehem Steel 1/1940.
911	Alco-Brooks	11/1915	SDC 17	Sold for scrap DI&M 6/1932.

Tender Class E-6, Style 11: 11 Tons Coal (Capacity later increased to 15 Tons; some equipped with 4,000 Gallon Oil Cistern); 6,000 Gallons Water; 5½" x 10" Axle Journals

No.	Builder	Date Rcvd.	Disposition
925	Rogers	6/18/1902	Reno. X2838(1) (WC) 6/1934. Sold for scrap PC 7/1939.
926	Rogers	6/22/1902	Sold for scrap DI&M 8/1/1936.
927	Rogers	6/22/1902	Sold for scrap PC 8/8/1936.
928	Rogers	6/26/1902	Dismantled at Superior 12/1952.
929	Rogers	6/26/1902	Sold for scrap DI&M 6/1932.
930	Rogers	7/8/1902	Sold for scrap DI&M 5/5/1953.
931	Rogers	7/8/1902	Sold for scrap PC 10/10/1952.
932	Rogers	7/10/1902	Sold Somers Lumber Co. 7/1935.
933	Rogers	7/18/1902	Sold for scrap DI&M 6/1951.
934	Rogers	7/21/1902	Sold for scrap DI&M 10/1947.
935	Rogers	7/21/1902	Sold for scrap DI&M 7/1932.
936	Rogers	7/21/1902	Reno. X2839 (1) (WC) 6/1934. Ret. 6/1937, sold for scrap.
937	Rogers	7/21/1902	Cistern to X917(3) (40FWC) (with Boxcar 5612) at Hillyard 4/7/1945. Ret. 11/1949.
938	Rogers	7/26/1902	Reno. T780 at Weston 3/27/1910.
939	Rogers	7/26/1902	Sold for scrap DI&M 10/1932.

Tender Class E-13, Style Unassigned: 10 Tons Coal; 3,400 Gallons Water; 4¼" x 8" Axle Journals

No.	Builder	Date Built	Original No.	Disposition
948	Baldwin	10/1893	SF&N 8	Sold Waterville Railway (with E949) 4/1934.
949	Baldwin	9/1896	SF&N 10	Reno. X1936(3) (WC) 12/1945. Sold for scrap DI&M 4/4/1947.

Tender Class E-7, Style Unassigned: 8 Tons Coal; 4,000 Gallons Water; 5" x 9" Axle Journals

No.	Builder	Date Rcvd.	Original No.	Disposition	Notes
950	Brooks	10/16/1893	GN 650	Reno. X2869(2) (WC) 9/1931. Sold for scrap DI&M 4/5/1934.	
951	Brooks	4/30/1893	GN 651	Ret. to be scrapped 12/1940.	
952	Brooks	4/30/1893	GN 652	Sold for scrap DI&M 8/28/1928.	308
953	Brooks	5/2/1893	GN 653	Dismantled 9/1925.	
954	Brooks	5/2/1893	GN 654	Sold for scrap DI&M 8/14/1936.	
955	Brooks	5/4/1893	GN 655	Sold for scrap PC 10/1929.	
956	Brooks	5/4/1893	GN 656	Sold for scrap PC 5/1929.	
957	Brooks	5/7/1893	GN 657	Ret. 4/1937.	
958	Brooks	5/7/1893	GN 658	Reno. X1974(2) (WC) 5/3/1928. Stripped at Superior 8/18/1932. Ret. 9/1932.	
959	Brooks	5/9/1893	GN 659	Reno. X1929(1) (WC) 6/1927. Ret. at Great Falls 8/12/1932. Sold for scrap DI&M 9/1932.	309
960	Brooks	5/9/1893	GN 660	Sold for scrap PC 8/4/1936.	
961	Brooks	5/12/1893	GN 661	Reno. X1993(1) (WC) 6/1927.Ret. 10/1932.	
962	Brooks	5/12/1893	GN 662	Sold for scrap DI&M 11/30/1928.	310
963	Brooks	5/15/1893	GN 663	Sold for scrap DI&M 9/1932.	
964	Brooks	5/15/1893	GN 664	Sold for scrap DI&M 10/1932.	
965	Brooks	5/17/1893	GN 665	Ret. 5/1929. Reno. X1949(2) (WC) 6/1929. Ret. 9/1932.	
966	Brooks	5/17/1893	GN 666	Sold for scrap DI&M 8/1/1936.	
967	Brooks	5/19/1893	GN 667	Scrapped 10/1937.	
968	Brooks	5/19/1893	GN 668	Reno. X2870(2) (WC) 9/1931. Ret. 3/1934. Sold for scrap PC 6/11/1934.	311
969	Brooks	5/20/1893	GN 669	Reno. X1989(1) (WC) 6/1927. Ret. 7/1934.	

Tender Class E-12, Style Unassigned: 12 Tons Coal; 4,000 Gallons Water; 4¼" x 8" Axle Journals

No.	Builder	Date Built	Original No.	Disposition
970	Baldwin	3/1897	SF&N 11	Sold for scrap DI&M 8/6/1927.
971	Baldwin	3/1897	SF&N 12	Sold for scrap DI&M 10/1926.

Tender Class E-1, Style Unassigned: 8 Tons Coal; 3,500 Gallons Water; 3¾" x 7" Axle Journals

No.	Builder	Date Rcvd.	Original No.	Disposition	Notes
992	Rogers	2/11/1890	SC&N 5	Reno. X1974(1) (WC) 6/1927. Sold for scrap DI&M 8/25/1927.	312
993	Rogers	2/8/1890	SC&N 6	Sold for scrap DI&M 7/1926.	

Tender Class E-9, Style Unassigned: 8 Tons Coal; 4,000 Gallons Water; 5" x9" Axle Journals

No.	Builder	Date Rcvd.	Original No.	Disposition
998	Baldwin	8/7/1892	GN 600(1)	Sold for scrap DI&M 7/1932.
999	Baldwin	8/7/1892	GN 601(1)	Sold Midland Railway Company of Manitoba [with E32(3)] 9/24/1929.

Tender Class E-10, Style Unassigned: 8 Tons Coal; 4,500 Gallons Water; 4¼" x 8" Axle Journals

No.	Builder	Date Built	Original No.	Disposition	Notes
1000	Brooks	5/1898	EM 150	Sold for scrap PC 8/1/1936.	
1001	Brooks	5/1898	EM 151	Sold for scrap DI&M 10/1929.	
1002	Brooks	5/1898	EM 152	Reno. X1929(2) (WC) at Hopkins 5/18/1940. Ret. 9/1949.	
1003	Brooks	5/1898	EM 153	Scrapped 3/1937.	
1004	Brooks	5/1898	EM 154	Dismantled at Dale Street 8/20/1928.	313
1005	Brooks	5/1898	EM 155	Scrapped at Grand Forks 8/3/1937, cistern to flat car.	
1006	Brooks	5/1898	EM 156	Sold for scrap PC 9/1/1941.	
1007	Brooks	5/1898	EM 157	Off roster before 6/30/1915.	

Tender Class E-14, Style Unassigned: 13 Tons Coal; 8,000 Gallons Water; 5½" x 10" Axle Journals

No.	Builder	Date Rcvd.	Disposition	Notes
1008	Baldwin	10/27/1909	Reno. H-5 1364 c.6/1926.	
1009	Baldwin	10/27/1909	Rblt. to 10,000 Gallon capacity at Hillyard 7/28/1926. Reno. H-5 1373 at Spokane 6/15/1927.	
1010	Baldwin	10/31/1909	Reno. H-5 1362 c.5/1926.	
1011	Baldwin	10/31/1909	Reno. H-5 1370 at Havre 2/23/1927.	
1012	Baldwin	10/31/1909	Reno. H-5 1365 at Spokane 10/18/1926.	
1013	Baldwin	10/31/1909	Reno. H-5 1368 at Walton, MT, 2/11/1927.	
1014	Baldwin	11/4/1909	Reno. H-5 1369 at Havre 12/15/1926.	
1015	Baldwin	11/4/1909	Reno. H-5 1371 at Interbay 2/15/1927.	
1016	Baldwin	11/5/1909	Reno. H-5 1492 c.3/1923.	
1017	Baldwin	11/5/1909	Rblt. to 10,000 Gallon capacity at Havre 1/15/1927. Reno. H-5 1372 at Havre 2/23/1927.	314
1018	Baldwin	11/7/1909	Reno. H-5 1487 c.1/1922.	
1019	Baldwin	11/7/1909	Reno. H-5 1488 c.10/1921.	
1020	Baldwin	11/13/1909	Reno. H-5 1494 c.5/1924.	
1021	Baldwin	11/13/1909	Reno. H-5 1366 at Whitefish 11/24/1926.	
1022	Baldwin	11/13/1909	Reno. H-5 1490 at Minot 2/27/1922.	
1023	Baldwin	11/13/1909	Reno. H-5 1491 c.12/1922.	
1024	Baldwin	11/18/1909	Reno. H-5 1493 c.1/1925.	
1025	Baldwin	11/28/1909	Reno. H-5 1489 c.11/1921.	
1026	Baldwin	11/18/1909	Reno. H-5 1374 at Havre 6/14/1927.	
1027	Baldwin	11/28/1909	Reno. H-5 1363 c.5/1926.	
1028	Baldwin	11/28/1909	Reno. H-5 1367 at Delta 2/24/1927.	
1029	Baldwin	11/28/1909	Reno. H-5 1360 c.4/1926.	
1030	Baldwin	11/30/1909	Reno. H-5 1495 c.6/1924.	
1031	Baldwin	10/27/1909	Reno. H-5 1486 c.7/1921.	
1032	Baldwin	10/27/1909	Reno. H-5 1361 c.3/1926.	
1033	Baldwin	8/29/1910	Reno. H-7 1375 at Superior 12/3/1925.	
1034	Baldwin	8/29/1910	Reno. H-7 1379 c.7/1926.	
1035	Baldwin	9/1/1910	Reno. H-7 1377 c.6/1926.	
1036	Baldwin	9/2/1910	Reno. H-7 1380 c.8/1926.	
1037	Baldwin	9/2/1910	Reno. H-7 1383 c.1/1927.	
1038	Baldwin	9/4/1910	Reno. H-7 1378 c.5/1926.	
1039	Baldwin	9/4/1910	Reno. H-7 1381 c.11/1926.	
1040	Baldwin	9/4/1910	Reno. H-7 1376 at Hillyard 12/3/1925.	
1041	Baldwin	9/8/1910	Reno. H-7 1382 c.10/1926.	
1042	Baldwin	9/8/1910	Reno. H-7 1384 at Superior 2/16/1927.	
1043	Baldwin	9/11/1910	Sold SP&S (No. 100) 1910.	
1044	Baldwin	9/11/1910	Sold SP&S (No. 101) 1910.	
1045	Baldwin	9/14/1910	Sold SP&S (No. 102) 1910.	
1046	Baldwin	9/14/1910	Sold SP&S (No. 103) 1910.	
1047	Baldwin	9/14/1910	Sold SP&S (No. 104) 1910.	
1048	Baldwin	9/14/1910	Sold SP&S (No. 105) 1910.	
1049	Baldwin	9/26/1910	Sold SP&S (No. 106) 1910.	
1050(2)	Baldwin	10/1/1910	Sold SP&S (No. 107) 1910. Returned to GN as SP&S T621 and renumbered T546(2) 4/5/1945.	
1051(2)	Baldwin	9/26/1910	Sold SP&S (No. 108) 1910.	
1052(2)	Baldwin	10/1/1910	Sold SP&S (No. 109) 1910. Returned to GN as SP&S T625 and renumbered T545(2) 4/5/1945.	

Tender Class E-8, Style 12: 12 Tons Coal (Capacity later increased to 15 Tons; some equipped with 4,000 Gallon Oil Cistern); 6,000 Gallons Water; 5½" x 10" Axle Journals

No.	Builder	Date Rcvd.	Original No.	Disposition	Notes
1050(1)	Rogers	12/4/1901	–	Reno. GN 1070 4/1910.	
1051(1)	Rogers	12/9/1901	–	Reno. GN 1071 3/1910.	
1052(1)	Rogers	12/9/1901	–	Reno. GN 1072 4/1910.	
1053	Rogers	12/10/1901	–	Sold for scrap PC 10/1950.	
1054	Rogers	12/10/1901	–	Wrecked at St.Paul 7/17/1941. Ret. 9/1941.	
1055	Rogers	12/16/1901	–	Reno. X2840(1) (WC) 6/1934. Ret. 6/1936. Sold for scrap DI&M 7/27/1936.	
1056	Rogers	12/16/1901	–	Sold for scrap DI&M 9/1932.	
1057	Rogers	12/18/1901	–	Reno. X2822 (WC) 8/7/1946. Ret. 4/1958.	
1058	Rogers	12/22/1901	–	Sold for scrap DI&M 11/24/1951.	
1059	Rogers	1/9/1902	–	Reno. X1932(2) (WC) at Montrose 5/28/1940. Rblt. X902(2) (40FWC) (with Boxcar 32306) 6/1946. Ret. 11/1973.	
1060	Rogers	2/28/1904	–	Sold for scrap PC 10/1947.	
1061	Rogers	2/28/1904	–	Sold for scrap PC 11/13/1951.	
1062	Rogers	3/2/1904	–	Sold for scrap DI&M 10/2/1952.	
1063	Rogers	3/2/1904	–	Sold for scrap DI&M 9/1939.	
1064	Rogers	3/3/1904	–	Reno. X2871(2) (WC) 9/1931. Ret. 7/1934.	
1065	Rogers	3/4/1904	–	Reno. X2841(1) (WC) 6/1934. Ret. 6/1936. Sold for scrap PC 7/27/1936.	
1066	Rogers	3/6/1904	–	Reno. X946(3) (WC) 12/1946. Ret. 12/1954.	316
1067	Rogers	3/9/1904	–	Sold for scrap DI&M 10/1932.	
1068	Rogers	3/19/1904	–	Reno. X960(1) (WC) 9/26/1938. Rblt. X934(3) (40FWC) (with Boxcar 34428) 4/1946. Ret. 10/1955.	

No.	Builder	Date		Disposition	
1069	Rogers	3/31/1905	–	Reno. X1935(2) (WC) at Spokane 7/3/1940. Sold for scrap DI&M 5/27/1947.	147,315
1070	Rogers	12/4/1901	GN 1050(1)	Dismantled at Whitefish 12/1931.	317
1071	Rogers	12/9/1901	GN 1051(1)	Sold for scrap DI&M 7/28/1936.	
1072	Rogers	12/9/1901	GN 1052(1)	Reno. GN 787 (Class C-4), date unknown (footboards, handrails and backup light added 3/1937).	

Tender Class E-15, Style 13: 13 Tons Coal (later increased to 14 Tons; some equipped with 3,000 Gallon oil cistern); 6,000 Gallons Water; 5½" x 10" Axle Journals

No.	Builder	Date Rcvd.	Disposition	Notes
1073	Baldwin	8/1/1910	Cistern to X849 (40FWC) (with Boxcar 35597) at Great Falls 5/8/1947. Ret. 6/1953.	318
1074	Baldwin	8/1/1910	Cistern to X918(3) (40FWC) (with Boxcar 36712) at Hillyard 5/22/1945. Ret. 3/1959.	
1075	Baldwin	8/7/1910	Sold for scrap PC 6/1947.	
1076	Baldwin	8/7/1910	Reno. X2842 (WC) 6/1934. Rblt. X905(2) (40FWC) (with Boxcar 14167) 4/1947. Ret. 12/1956.	
1077	Baldwin	8/4/1910	Reno. X1927(4) (WC) 5/1949. Ret. 1/1959.	
1078	Baldwin	8/4/1910	Sold Montana Western (with E544) 10/1950.	
1079	Baldwin	8/5/1910	Sold for scrap PC 9/1939.	
1080	Baldwin	8/5/1910	Sold SP&S (with E-15 locomotive) 6/1925.	
1081	Baldwin	8/7/1910	Reno. X1967(3) (WC) 5/22/1945. Ret. 11/1959.	
1082	Baldwin	8/7/1910	Reno. X3249 (coal space enclosed) at St. Cloud 1/13/1944. Ret. 6/1963.	
1083	Baldwin	8/13/1910	Placed behind Montana Western E10 at Great Falls 3/8/1941, sold Montana Western 10/22/1941.	319
1084	Baldwin	8/13/1910	Reno. X2872(2) (WC) 9/1931. Ret. 10/1956.	
1085	Baldwin	8/16/1910	Sold SP&S (with E-15 locomotive) 6/1925.	
1086	Baldwin	8/16/1910	Reno. X1926(2) (WC) 6/1949. Ret. 2/1959.	
1087	Baldwin	8/24/1910	Sold for scrap DI&M 5/1951.	
1088	Baldwin	8/24/1910	Reno. X958 (RT) 1/1938. Ret. 9/1955.	
1089	Baldwin	8/24/1910	Sold SP&S (with E-15 locomotive) 6/1925.	
1090	Baldwin	8/24/1910	Reno. X1924(3) (WC) 10/15/1932. Ret. 3/1957.	
1091	Baldwin	9/1/1910	Reno. X1923(3) (WC) 2/1933. Ret. 6/1958.	
1092	Baldwin	9/4/1910	Reno. X1912(2) (WC) 2/1933. Ret. 4/1951.	388

Tender Class F-4(2), Style Unassigned: 10 Tons Coal; 3,400 Gallons Water; 4¼" x 8" Axle Journals

No.	Builder	Date Built	Original No.	Disposition
1094	Baldwin	8/1896	RM 9	Sold McGoldrick Lumber Co. (with E1094) 7/1925.

Tender Class F-5, Style 15: 12 Tons Coal (Capacity later increased to 14 Tons; some equipped with 4,000 Gallon oil cistern); 6,000 Gallons Water; 5½" x 10" Axle Journals

No.	Builder	Date Rcvd.	Original No.	Disposition	Notes
1095	Rogers	11/26/1901	GN 1160(1)	Sold for scrap DI&M 6/1932.	
1096	Rogers	11/26/1901	GN 1161(1)	Sold for scrap DI&M 10/16/1951.	
1097	Rogers	11/27/1901	GN 1162(1)	Sold for scrap DI&M 12/1949.	
1098	Rogers	12/1/1901	GN 1163(1)	Reno. X2843(1) (WC) 6/1934. Sold for scrap Dulien Steel Products 8/1939.	320
1099	Rogers	12/4/1901	GN 1164(1)	Sold for scrap DI&M 9/8/1941.	
1100	Rogers	10/2/1901	–	Ret. 2/1930.	
1101	Rogers	9/30/1901	–	Sold for scrap PC 5/5/1953.	
1102	Rogers	10/2/1901	–	Reno. X2844(1) (WC) 6/1934. Ret. 5/1942.	
1103	Rogers	10/2/1901	–	Ret. 10/1951. Sold for scrap DI&M 11/13/1951.	
1104	Rogers	10/8/1901	–	Reno. X961(1) (WC) 6/1938. Ret. 5/1943.	321
1105	Rogers	10/14/1901	–	Reno. X1987(2) (WC) 10/1932. Ret. 8/1934, sold for scrap PC.	
1106	Rogers	10/15/1901	–	Sold for scrap 8/1940.	
1107	Rogers	10/17/1901	–	Sold for scrap PC 12/1949.	
1108	Rogers	10/20/1901	–	Reno. X2873(2) (WC) 9/1931. Ret. 5/1947.	
1109	Rogers	10/20/1901	–	Sold for scrap DI&M 9/21/1952.	

Tender Class F-6, Style Unassigned: 12 Tons Coal (Later increased to 14 Tons; some equipped with 4,000 Gallon oil cistern); 6,000 Gallons Water; 5½" x 10" Axle Journals

No.	Builder	Date Rcvd.	Disposition
1110	Brooks	12/6/1901	Reno. C-2 862 5/1927.
1111	Brooks	12/6/1901	Reno. C-2 864 11/1927.
1112	Brooks	12/7/1901	Reno. C-2 865 at Kelly Lake, MN, 11/10/1927.
1113	Brooks	12/7/1901	Reno. C-2 853 11/1925.
1114	Brooks	12/9/1901	Reno. C-2 854 10/1925.
1115	Brooks	12/9/1901	Reno. C-2 850 5/1925.
1116	Brooks	12/10/1901	Reno. C-2 859 9/1926.
1117	Brooks	12/10/1901	Reno. C-2 867 6/1928.
1118	Brooks	12/13/1901	Reno. C-2 851 5/1925.
1119	Brooks	12/13/1901	Reno. C-2 861 2/1927.
1120	Brooks	12/15/1901	Reno. C-2 866 at Butte, MT, 1/3/1928.
1121	Brooks	12/15/1901	Reno. C-2 857 9/1926.
1122	Brooks	12/15/1901	Reno. C-2 855 3/1926.
1123	Brooks	12/15/1901	Reno. C-2 863 6/1927.
1124	Brooks	12/22/1901	Reno. C-2 856 6/1926.
1125	Brooks	12/22/1901	Reno. C-2 858 7/1926.
1126	Brooks	12/24/1901	Reno. C-2 852 5/1925.
1127	Brooks	12/24/1901	Reno. C-2 869 10/1928.
1128	Brooks	12/24/1901	Reno. C-2 860 11/1926.
1129	Brooks	12/24/1901	Reno. C-2 868 7/1928.

Tender Class F-7, Style 16: 12 Tons Coal (Later increased to 14 Tons; some equipped with 4,000 Gallon oil cistern); 6,000 Gallons Water; 5½" x 10" Axle Journals

No.	Builder	Date Rcvd.	Disposition	Notes
1130	Cooke	12/6/1901	Reno. X1961(3) (WC) 10/1934. Ret. 2/1957.	
1131	Cooke	12/6/1901	Sold for scrap DI&M 7/1932.	
1132	Cooke	12/15/1901	Sold for scrap DI&M 2/17/1947.	
1133	Cooke	12/15/1901	Sold for scrap DI&M 5/1951.	
1134	Cooke	12/22/1901	Cistern to X920(2) (40FWC) (with Boxcar 34526) at Hillyard 12/6/1945. Ret. 6/1954.	
1135	Cooke	12/22/1901	Reno. X1962(2) (WC) 11/1948. Tank transferred to X889(2) at Delta 6/15/1949. Remainder ret. 12/1949. X889(2) sold Northwest Steel Rolling Mills 5/1979.	
1136	Cooke	12/22/1901	Reno. X962(1) (WC) 8/1938. Rblt. X935(3) (40FWC) (with Boxcar 14051) 11/30/1945. Ret. 2/1955.	322
1137	Cooke	12/22/1901	Sold for scrap DI&M 6/1951.	
1138	Cooke	12/31/1901	Ret. 5/1958.	
1139	Cooke	12/31/1901	Reno. X1961(2) (WC) 9/1932. Ret. 5/1934.	

Tender Class F-8, Style 17: 12 Tons Coal (Later increased to 15 Tons; some equipped with 4,000 Gallon oil cistern); 6,000 Gallons Water; 5½" x 10" Axle Journals

No.	Builder	Date Rcvd.	Disposition	Notes
1140	Rogers	8/24/1902	Reno. X1941(3) (WC) 9/1950. Ret. 3/1963.	323
1141	Rogers	8/24/1902	Reno. X2850(3) (WC) 6/1934. Rblt. X907(2) (40FWC) (with Boxcar 37096) 1/26/1945. Ret. 6/1954.	
1142	Rogers	8/27/1902	Reno. X1937(3) (WC) at Milaca 5/30/1940. Rblt. X903(2) (40FWC) (with Boxcar 7333) 8/7/1945. Ret. 10/1955.	
1143	Rogers	8/27/1902	Sold for scrap PC 8/1/1936.	
1144	Rogers	8/31/1902	Sold for scrap 12/1938.	
1145	Rogers	9/1/1902	Sold for scrap DI&M 3/1/1949.	
1146	Rogers	9/4/1902	Reno. X2845 (WC) 6/1934. Ret. 10/1946.	
1147	Rogers	9/9/1902	Cistern to X921(2) (40FWC) (with Boxcar 33025) at Hillyard 7/8/1945. Ret. 3/1963.	
1148	Rogers	9/9/1902	Scrapped 9/1940.	
1149	Rogers	9/10/1902	Reno. X1940(4) (WC) at Whitefish, MT, 5/16/1940. Ret. 12/1949, sold for scrap PC.	
1150	Rogers	10/29/1901	Sold for scrap PC 12/1949.	
1151	Rogers	10/29/1901	Sold for scrap DI&M 8/1/1936.	
1152	Rogers	11/1/1901	Sold for scrap PC 10/10/1952.	
1153	Rogers	11/16/1901	Cistern to X922(2) (40FWC) (with Boxcar 6769) at Superior 7/27/1945. Reno. X2341(3) (Idler – cistern probably removed) 6/1951.	
1154	Rogers	11/9/1901	Reno. X1942(2) (WC) at Fort Browning, MT, 5/22/1940. Rblt. X904(2) (40FWC) (with Boxcar 15756) 7/1945. Ret. 8/1958.	
1155	Rogers	9/16/1902	Sold for scrap DI&M 10/1947.	
1156	Rogers	9/16/1902	Reno. X1901 (WC) at Superior 4/26/1954. Ret. 5/1956.	
1157	Rogers	9/16/1902	Reno. X1906(2) (WC) 6/1928. Sold for scrap PC 7/1939.	
1158	Rogers	9/20/1902	Sold for scrap 9/1940.	
1159	Rogers	9/23/1902	Sold for scrap DI&M 10/1950.	
1160(2)	Rogers	9/25/1902	Sold for scrap PC 12/1949.	
1161(2)	Rogers	9/26/1902	Sold for scrap DI&M 10/1932.	
1162(2)	Rogers	9/28/1902	Sold for scrap PC 10/1947.	
1163(2)	Rogers	10/2/1902	Sold SP&S 6/1925.	
1164(2)	Rogers	10/4/1902	Reno. X2874(2) (WC) 9/1931. Rblt. X911(3) (40FWC) (with Boxcar 6816) 4/1945. Ret. 8/1958.	
1165	Rogers	11/7/1902	Sold for scrap PC 8/30/1952.	
1166	Rogers	11/10/1902	Reno. 871(1) (C-4) 11/1928.	
1167	Rogers	12/10/1902	Cistern to X932(3) (40FWC) (with Boxcar 16453) at Superior 7/8/1946. Reno. X4141 (Idler – cistern probably removed) 4/1957.	
1168	Rogers	12/12/1902	Reno. X2846(1) (WC) 6/1934. Ret. 6/1937, sold for scrap.	
1169	Rogers	12/19/1902	Sold for scrap DI&M 12/1949.	
1170	Rogers	9/27/1903	Sold Lake Superior Terminal and Transfer Co. (with E1213) 8/1930.	
1171	Rogers	9/27/1903	Sold for scrap PC 8/1936.	
1172	Rogers	9/28/1903	Dismantled at Dale Street 8/27/1928.	324
1173	Rogers	9/28/1903	Dismantled at Dale Street 8/27/1928.	324
1174	Rogers	9/20/1903	Sold for scrap DI&M 8/27/1952.	
1175	Rogers	10/1/1903	Sold for scrap PC 6/1948.	
1176	Rogers	10/1/1903	Sold for scrap PC 5/14/1947.	
1177	Rogers	10/6/1903	Sold for scrap PC 10/18/1951.	
1178	Rogers	10/6/1903	Reno. X1970(2) (WC) 10/1932. Ret. 4/1933.	
1179	Rogers	10/13/1903	Sold for scrap PC 7/1947.	
1180	Rogers	10/10/1903	Reno. X1908(2) (WC) 6/1928. Ret. 6/1937, sold for scrap.	
1181	Rogers	10/13/1903	Sold for scrap DI&M 12/1949.	
1182	Rogers	10/15/1903	Wrecked at Willmar (with E775) and scrapped at Dale Street 3/27/1930.	
1183	Rogers	10/15/1903	Reno. X2875(2) (WC) 9/1931. Rblt. X912(3) (40FWC) (with Boxcar 3840) 2/8/1945. Ret. 1/1952.	
1184	Rogers	11/2/1903	Reno. X1998(2) (WC) 10/1932. Ret. 6/1937, sold for scrap.	
1185	Rogers	11/3/1903	Sold for scrap 5/1940.	
1186	Rogers	11/3/1903	Sold for scrap DI&M 10/1947.	
1187	Rogers	11/6/1903	Reno. X963(1) (WC) 10/1938. Ret. 11/1939.	325
1188	Rogers	11/8/1903	Sold for scrap PC 10/1941.	
1189	Rogers	11/8/1903	Reno. X2876(2) (WC) 9/1931. Ret. 12/1938.	
1190	Rogers	11/13/1903	Reno. X2847 (WC) 6/1934. Ret. 6/1958.	
1191	Rogers	11/20/1903	Sold for scrap PC 3/29/1952.	
1192	Rogers	11/20/1903	Sold for scrap PC 7/1939.	
1193	Rogers	11/29/1903	Reno. X2848(1) (WC) 6/1934. Ret. 12/1938.	
1194	Rogers	11/29/1903	Sold for scrap 6/1940.	

1195(2)	Rogers	12/14/1903	Reno. 95000 (RT) c.1925. Reno. X1500 10/1926. Reno. X1975 5/26/1927. Reno. T1195 7/24/1943. Reno. X3346 (FO) 10/26/1942. Ret. 1/1960.		326
1196(2)	Rogers	12/18/1903	Sold for scrap DI&M 10/16/1951.		
1197(2)	Rogers	12/25/1903	Reno. X1972(2) (WC) 6/1928. Ret. 6/1937, sold for scrap.		
1198(2)	Rogers	12/25/1903	Sold for scrap 12/1938.		
1199(2)	Rogers	12/31/1903	Sold for scrap DI&M 10/1932.		
1200	Alco-Rogers	9/13/1905	Cistern to X931(3) (40FWC) (with Boxcar 32583) at Hillyard 7/3/1946. Ret. 10/1955.		
1201	Alco-Rogers	9/13/1905	Sold for scrap DI&M 6/1932.		
1202	Alco-Rogers	9/17/1905	Reno. X964(1) (WC) 9/1938. Ret. 5/1943.		
1203	Alco-Rogers	9/24/1905	Sold for scrap DI&M 10/16/1951.		
1204	Alco-Rogers	9/24/1905	Reno. X948(4) (WC) 7/1947. Ret. 10/1955.		327
1205	Alco-Rogers	9/21/1905	Sold for scrap PC 2/17/1947.		
1206	Alco-Rogers	9/21/1905	Sold for scrap DI&M 8/8/1936.		
1207	Alco-Rogers	9/21/1905	Reno. X2849(1) (WC) 6/1934. Ret. 2/1943.		
1208	Alco-Rogers	10/6/1905	Sold for scrap DI&M 8/1932.		
1209	Alco-Rogers	10/6/1905	Sold for scrap WEI&M 5/1951.		
1210	Alco-Rogers	10/6/1905	Sold for scrap PC 7/1939.		
1211	Alco-Rogers	10/6/1905	Reno. X2877(2) (WC) 9/1931. Sold for scrap DI&M 7/1939.		
1212	Alco-Rogers	10/7/1905	Sold for scrap 12/1938.		
1213	Alco-Rogers	10/19/1905	Sold for scrap WEI&M 5/7/1953.		
1214	Alco-Rogers	10/8/1905	Sold for scrap PC 9/1939.		

Tender Class F-8, Style 18: 13 Tons Coal (Later increased to 15 Tons; some equipped with 4,500 Gallon oil cistern); 8,000 Gallons Water; 5½" x 10" Axle Journals. Some rebuilt to **Style 19** (10,000 Gallons Water). Some rebuilt to **Style 20** (10,000 Gallons Water, 6" x 11" Axle Journals).

No.	Builder	Date Rcvd.	Renumbered From	Date	Disposition	Notes
1215	Baldwin	11/23/1907	–	–	Reno. X1936(4) (WC) 1/1950. Ret. 11/1959.	
1216	Baldwin	11/23/1907	–	–	Rblt. Style 19 at Great Falls 3/19/1927. Rblt. Style 20 at Great Falls 4/13/1928. Rblt. back to Style 19 at Havre 5/15/1928. Ret. 12/1957. Sold for scrap c.1962.	
1217	Baldwin	12/3/1907	–	–	Sold for scrap PC 10/22/1951.	
1218	Baldwin	12/3/1907	–	–	Rblt. Style 19 (4,000 Gallons Oil) at Delta 9/9/1927. Rblt. Style 20 at Hillyard c.8/1946. Ret. 12/1957. Sold for scrap DI&M 6/1962.	
1219(1)	Baldwin	12/3/1907	–	–	Probably sold SP&S 1909.	
1219(2)	Baldwin	1/5/1908	GN 1255	8/16/1909	Sold for scrap PC 5/1951.	
1220	Baldwin	12/3/1907	–	–	Reno. X1920(3) (WC) 1/1949. Ret. 3/1958.	
1221	Baldwin	12/3/1907	–	–	Coal pit enclosed and reno. X3211 (WC) at St.Cloud 3/30/1942. Ret. 7/1971. (St. 18)	
1222	Baldwin	12/3/1907	–	–	Sold for scrap DI&M 3/29/1952.	
1223	Baldwin	12/3/1907	–	–	Rblt. Style 19 at Superior 1/27/1928. Sold for scrap PC 6/24/1953.	
1224	Baldwin	12/3/1907	–	–	Reno. X2819(2) (WC) 8/1948. Ret. 11/1973.	
1225	Baldwin	12/3/1907	–	–	Rblt. Style 19 at Delta 6/15/1927. Rblt. Style 20 at Havre 5/15/1928. Sold for scrap WEI&M 7/28/1953.	
1226	Baldwin	12/3/1907	–	–	Rblt. Style 19 at Superior 11/21/1927. Sold for scrap DI&M 1/14/1955.	
1227	Baldwin	12/6/1907	–	–	Sold for scrap PC 6/1948.	
1228	Baldwin	12/6/1907	–	–	Rblt. Style 20 at Delta 5/21/1929. Sold City of Prineville Railway (with E1102), delivered at Bend, OR, 7/7/1945.	
1229	Baldwin	12/6/1907	–	–	Rblt. Style 19 at Dale Street 9/26/1927. Wrecked at St.Cloud 9/8/1945, dismantled.	
1230(1)	Baldwin	12/6/1907	–	–	Probably Sold SP&S 1909.	
1230(2)	Baldwin	1/15/1908	GN 1256	6/21/1909	Sold for scrap PC 5/1951.	
1231	Baldwin	12/9/1907	–	–	Sold for scrap PC 6/1951.	
1232(1)	Baldwin	12/9/1907	–	–	Probably sold SP&S 1909.	
1232(2)	Baldwin	1/11/1908	GN 1258	6/7/1909	Sold for scrap PC 7/1947.	
1233(1)	Baldwin	12/20/1907	–	–	Probably sold SP&S 1909.	
1233(2)	Baldwin	1/17/1908	GN 1259	6/8/1909		328
1234(1)	Baldwin	12/20/1907	–	–	Probably sold SP&S 1909.	
1234(2)	Baldwin	1/17/1908	GN 1260	6/1/1909	Rblt. Style 19 (4,000 Gallons Oil) at Delta 8/26/1927. Sold for scrap DI&M 12/7/1951.	
1235(1)	Baldwin	12/10/1907	–	–	Probably sold SP&S 1909.	
1235(2)	Baldwin	1/17/1908	GN 1261	6/21/1909	Rblt. Style 19 3/23/1928. Sold SP&S (with E3039), delivered 4/6/1928.	
1236	Baldwin	12/10/1907	–	–	Reno. X3201 (WC) at St.Cloud 2/21/1942. Ret. 10/1972. (St. 18)	
1237	Baldwin	12/17/1907	–	–	Rblt. Style 19 (4,000 Gallons Oil) at Delta 11/16/1927. Rblt. X1576(3) (WP) 3/30/1953. Reno. BN 972802 10/1980. Lost car 11/11/1989.	
1238	Baldwin	12/17/1907	–	–	Rblt. Style 19 at Superior 8/24/1927. Rblt. X1577(2) (WP) 4/1953. Reno. BN 972801 9/1980. Ret. 9/22/1989. Sold Azcon Corp. 11/20/1989.	
1239	Baldwin	12/17/1907	–	–	Reno. X953(1) (WC) at St.Cloud 8/24/1937. Reno X3272 7/26/1943. Off roster between 6/1952 and 3/1958.	329
1240(1)	Baldwin	12/17/1907	–	–	Probably sold SP&S 1909.	
1240(2)	Baldwin	1/30/1908	GN 1263	8/16/1909	Reno. X949(3) (WC) 10/1947. Ret. 1/1956.	330
1241	Baldwin	12/18/1907	–	–	Sold for scrap DI&M 6/1932.	
1242	Baldwin	12/18/1907	–	–	Rblt. Style 19 at Dale Street 7/26/1927. Ret. 12/1957. Sold for scrap c.1962.	
1243	Baldwin	12/21/1907	–	–	Rblt. Style 19 at Delta 6/7/1928. Rblt. Style 20 at Hillyard 10/22/1943. Sold SP&S (with E3134) 8/1944.	
1244	Baldwin	12/21/1907	–	–	Reno. X1937(4) (WC) at Grand Forks 5/8/1951. Reno. X3262 at Grand Forks 8/1951. Further disposition unknown.	

Tender Class F-8, Style 18: Continued

No.	Builder	Date Rcvd.	Renumbered From	Date	Disposition	Notes
1245	Baldwin	12/21/1907	–	–	Fitted up as water car 10/3/1934 at St.Cloud. Reno. X954(1) (WC) at St.Cloud 8/13/1937. Reno. X3351 (FO) 5/7/1943. Ret. 12/1956.	
1246	Baldwin	12/21/1907	–	–	Sold for scrap WEI&M 9/10/1952.	
1247	Baldwin	12/21/1907	–	–	Reno. X1894(1) (WC) at St.Cloud 11/1/1941. Reno. X3204 1/25/1942.	
1248	Baldwin	12/21/1907	–	–	Rblt. Style 19 11/29/1926 at Delta. Reno. X2828(2) (WC) 11/21/1946. Ret. 11/1969.	
1249	Baldwin	12/27/1907	–	–	Reno. X6701 (WC) 9/1955. Sold Hyman-Michaels 3/1978.	
1250	Baldwin	12/27/1907	–	–	Rblt. Style 19 at Hillyard 4/4/1927.	328
1251	Baldwin	1/1/1908	–	–	Rblt. Style 19 at Delta 10/23/1928. Rblt. X1573(2) (WP) 3/3/1953. Reno. BN 972807 9/14/1981. Ret. 7/14/1993. Sold Paul Mardian Co., Inc., 9/21/1995.	
1252	Baldwin	1/1/1908	–	–	Sold for scrap DI&M 6/4/1947.	
1253(1)	Baldwin	1/3/1908	–	–	Probably sold SP&S 1909.	
1253(2)	Baldwin	1/30/1908	GN 1264	6/23/1909	Rblt. Style 19 at Dale Street 6/18/1927. Reno. X3336 (WC) 11/18/1948. Ret. 8/1962.	
1254	Baldwin	1/3/1908	–	–	Reno. T2000(1) 1/1910.	
1255	Baldwin	1/5/1908	–	–	Reno. T1219(2) at Superior 8/16/1909.	
1256	Baldwin	1/5/1908	–	–	Reno. T1230(2) at St.Paul 6/21/1909.	
1257	Baldwin	1/11/1908	–	–	Probably sold SP&S 1909.	
1258	Baldwin	1/11/1908	–	–	Reno. T1232(2) at Havre 6/7/1909.	
1259	Baldwin	1/17/1908	–	–	Reno. T1233(2) at Havre 6/8/1909.	
1260	Baldwin	1/17/1908	–	–	Reno. T1234(2) at Hillyard 6/1/1909.	
1261	Baldwin	1/17/1908	–	–	Reno. T1235(2) at St.Paul 6/21/1909.	
1262	Baldwin	1/17/1908	–	–	Probably sold SP&S 1909.	
1263	Baldwin	1/30/1908	–	–	Reno. T1240(2) at Superior 8/16/1909.	
1264	Baldwin	1/30/1908	–	–	Reno. T1253(2) at St.Paul 6/23/1909.	

Tender Class F-9, Style Unassigned: 12 Tons Coal (Later increased to 14 Tons; some equipped with 4,000 Gallon oil cistern); 6,000 Gallons Water; 5½" x 10" Axle Journals

No.	Builder	Date Rcvd.	Disposition	Notes
1300	Alco-Brooks	7/14/1903	Reno. C-3 891 11/1927.	
1301	Alco-Brooks	7/14/1903	Reno. C-3 896 6/1928.	
1302	Alco-Brooks	7/16/1903	Reno. C-3 889 9/1927.	
1303	Alco-Brooks	7/16/1903	Reno. C-3 887 8/1927.	
1304	Alco-Brooks	7/16/1903	Reno. C-3 895 2/1928.	331
1305	Alco-Brooks	7/16/1903	Reno. C-3 881 4/1926.	
1306	Alco-Brooks	7/20/1903	Reno. C-3 888 8/1927.	
1307	Alco-Brooks	7/20/1903	Reno. C-3 885 6/1927.	
1308	Alco-Brooks	7/20/1903	Reno. C-3 899 7/1926.	
1309	Alco-Brooks	7/20/1903	Reno. C-3 877 4/1925.	
1310	Alco-Brooks	7/22/1903	Reno. C-3 892 at Whitefish 12/28/1927.	
1311	Alco-Brooks	7/22/1903	Reno. C-3 882 at Whitefish 4/20/1926.	
1312	Alco-Brooks	7/22/1903	Reno. C-3 883(1) 8/17/1926.	
1313	Alco-Brooks	7/22/1903	Reno. C-3 875 3/1925.	
1314	Alco-Brooks	7/24/1903	Reno. C-3 894 2/1928.	
1315	Alco-Brooks	7/24/1903	Reno. C-3 879 2/1926.	
1316	Alco-Brooks	7/26/1903	Reno. C-3 886 7/1927.	
1317	Alco-Brooks	7/26/1903	Reno. C-3 897 4/1928.	
1318	Alco-Brooks	7/26/1903	Reno. C-3 876 4/1925.	
1319	Alco-Brooks	7/26/1903	Reno. C-3 878 9/1925.	
1320	Alco-Brooks	7/26/1903	Reno. C-3 890 11/1927.	
1321	Alco-Brooks	7/27/1903	Reno. C-3 880 10/1925.	
1322	Alco-Brooks	7/27/1903	Reno. C-3 898 8/1928.	
1323	Alco-Brooks	7/27/1903	Reno. C-3 893 at Grand Forks 2/14/1928.	
1324	Alco-Brooks	7/27/1903	Reno. C-3 884 7/1927.	

Tender Class F-12, Style Unassigned: 12 Tons Coal; 6,000 Gallons Water; 5½" x 10" Axle Journals

No.	Builder	Date Rcvd.	Renumbered From	Date	Disposition
1326	Alco-Brooks	11/1907	BA&P 26	5/24/1917	Sold for scrap DI&M 6/1948.
1327	Alco-Brooks	11/1907	BA&P 27	3/17/1917	Sold for scrap WEI&M c.1/1950.

Tender Class H-5, Style Unassigned: 13 Tons Coal (Later increased to 15 Tons; some equipped with 4,500 Gallon oil cistern); 8,000 Gallons Water; 5½" x 10" Axle Journals. Rebuilt to Style 36 (10,000 Gallons Water) or Style 37 (10,000 Gallons Water; 6" x 11" Axle Journals).

No.	Builder	Date Rcvd.	Former E-14 No.	Renumbered From	Disposition	Notes
1350	Baldwin	10/27/1909	GN 1031	GN 1486	Rblt. Style 37 at Hillyard 4/28/1943. Sold for scrap WEI&M 10/18/1951.	
1351	Baldwin	11/7/1909	GN 1018	GN 1487	Rblt. Style 36 at Dale Street 12/23/1926. Sold for scrap PC 5/16/1953.	
1352	Baldwin	11/7/1909	GN 1019	GN 1488	Rblt. Style 36 at Dale Street 9/26/1927. Rblt. X1574(2) (WP) 11/21/1951. Ret. 5/23/1983. Sold Pacific Hide & Fur 7/22/1985.	
1353	Baldwin	11/28/1909	GN 1025	GN 1489	Rblt. Style 36, date unknown. Reno. X3250 (WC) (coal space enclosed) at St.Cloud 1/18/1944. Ret. 11/1961.	
1354	Baldwin	11/13/1909	GN 1022	GN 1490	Rblt. Style 36, date unknown. Reno. X1945(2) (WC) 3/1933. Reno. X3252 1/1944. Ret. 12/1957.	293

No.	Builder	Date Rcvd.			Disposition	Notes
1355	Baldwin	11/13/1909	GN 1020	GN 1494	Rblt. Style 36, date unknown. Reno. X1895(1) (WC) at St.Cloud 11/5/1941. Reno. X3205 at Willmar 1/21/1942. Sold for scrap PC 12/1976.	
1356	Baldwin	11/5/1909	GN 1016	GN 1492	Rblt. Style 36 at Hillyard 2/11/1927. Scrapped at Hillyard 4/16/1942. [T1493 sold before renumbering to T1357]	
–	–	–	–	–	–	
1358	Baldwin	11/13/1909	GN 1023	GN 1491	Rblt. Style 36 at Hillyard 12/2/1927. Wrecked on Oregon Trunk near Oakbrook, OR, (with E3128) 9/22/1949. Remains sold for scrap PC 12/8/1949.	
1359	Baldwin	11/30/1909	GN 1030	GN 1495	Rblt. Style 36, date unknown. Reno. X1997(3) (WC) 12/1949. Ret. 4/1962.	332
1360	Baldwin	11/28/1909	GN 1029	–	Rblt. Style 36 at Delta 1/23/1928. Rblt. X1575(3) (WP) 2/25/1953. Reno. BN 972544 11/1979. Active 9/22/1995.	
1361	Baldwin	10/27/1909	GN 1032	–	Rblt. Style 36 at Delta 8/21/1928. Donated Wenatchee Park Board (with E1147) 5/19/1956.	
1362	Baldwin	10/31/1909	GN 1010	–	Rblt. Style 36 at Hillyard 3/14/1927. Rblt. Style 37 11/1940. Sold SP&S (with E3108) 8/1944.	
1363	Baldwin	11/28/1909	GN 1027	–	Reno. X3216 at St.Cloud 3/31/1942. Ret. 12/1966.	
1364	Baldwin	10/27/1909	GN 1008	–	Reno. X1928(2) (WC) 8/1933. Reno. X3278 8/6/1943. Further disposition unknown.	
1365	Baldwin	10/31/1909	GN 1012	–	Dismantled at St.Cloud 6/1954.	333
1366	Baldwin	11/13/1909	GN 1021	–	Rblt. Style 36, date unknown. Rblt. WC at Klamath Falls 9/15/1941. Reno. X1945(4) (WC) 7/1951. Ret. 5/1957.	334
1367	Baldwin	11/28/1909	GN 1028	–	Rblt. Style 36 at Delta 6/15/1927. Reno. X2821(2) (WC) 9/23/1946. Ret. 12/1964.	
1368	Baldwin	10/31/1909	GN 1013	–	Reno. X3253 (WC) (coal pit enclosed) at Great Falls 5/3/1944. Ret. 5/1959.	
1369	Baldwin	11/4/1909	GN 1014	–	Rblt. Style 37 at Hillyard 1/16/1946. Sold for scrap PC 8/1953.	
1370	Baldwin	10/31/1909	GN 1011	–	Rblt. Style 36 at Havre 3/24/1927. Rblt. Style 37 at Great Falls 7/31/1929. Reno. X2832(2) (WC) 5/1956. Sold Luria Brothers 7/1980.	335
1371	Baldwin	11/4/1909	GN 1015	–	Sold SP&S 10/1936 (with F-8 engine).	
1372	Baldwin	11/5/1909	GN 1017	–	Rblt. Style 36 at Havre 1/15/1927 (as E-14). Reno. X1982(3) (WC) 9/1942. Ret. 7/1962.	314
1373	Baldwin	10/27/1909	GN 1009	–	Rblt. Style 36 at Hillyard 7/28/1926 (as E-14). Rblt. Style 37 12/1937. Sold for scrap PC 6/6/1953.	
1374	Baldwin	11/18/1909	GN 1026	–	Reno. X965 (WC) 6/1938. Ret. 4/1958.	

Tender Class H-7, Style 44: 13 Tons Coal (Later increased to 16 Tons; some equipped with 4,500 Gallon oil cistern); 8,000 Gallons Water; 5½" x 10" Axle Journals. Some rebuilt to **Style 45** (10,000 Gallons Water).

No.	Builder	Date Rcvd.	Former E-14 No.	Disposition	Notes
1375	Baldwin	8/29/1910	GN 1033	Reno. X2830(3) (WC) 12/1946. Ret. 6/1953.	336
1376	Baldwin	9/4/1910	GN 1040	Sold for scrap PC 10/2/1952.	
1377	Baldwin	9/1/1910	GN 1035	Rblt. Style 45 12/20/1926 at Delta. Wrecked 7/1937, dismantled.	
1378	Baldwin	9/4/1910	GN 1038	Reno. X2820(2) (WC) 11/1947. Ret. 7/1959.	337
1379	Baldwin	8/29/1910	GN 1034	Rblt. WC 8/26/1941 at Great Falls. Reno. X3279 (WC) 8/13/1943 at Great Falls. Ret. 8/1971.	
1380	Baldwin	9/2/1910	GN 1036	Rblt. Style 45 10/24/1927 at Delta. 6" x 11" Axle journals at Delta 1/16/1929. Reno. X1900 (WC) 2/1954. Ret. 9/1962.	
1381	Baldwin	9/4/1910	GN 1039		
1382	Baldwin	9/8/1910	GN 1041	Rblt. Style 45 6/30/1927 at Dale Street. Reno. X1947(3) (WC) 10/1952. Ret. 12/1964.	338
1383	Baldwin	9/2/1910	GN 1037	Reno. X3342 (WC) 3/1948. Ret. 9/1960.	
1384	Baldwin	9/8/1910	GN 1042	Reno. X1913(3) (WC) 4/1933. Reno. X3276 9/21/1943. Further disposition unknown.	339

Tender Class H-1, Style Unassigned: 10 Tons Coal; 7,000 Gallons Water; 5½" x 10" Axle Journals

No.	Builder	Date Rcvd.	Disposition
1400	Alco-Rogers	10/11/1905	Sold for scrap PC 10/1929.
1401	Alco-Rogers	10/11/1905	To work equipment (number unknown) 6/1928.
1402	Alco-Rogers	10/15/1905	Rblt. to 10,500 Gallon capacity, fitted out as water car 11/1937. Reno. X1943(2) at St.Cloud 5/17/1940. Reno. X3213 8/1943. Further disposition unknown.
1403	Alco-Rogers	10/15/1905	Sold for scrap Dulien Steel Products 7/1939.
1404	Alco-Rogers	10/19/1905	Scrapped 12/1938.
1405	Alco-Rogers	10/19/1905	Reno. X966 (WC) 8/1938. Ret. 9/1953.

Tender Class H-2, Style 25: 13 Tons Coal (Some with 4,500 Gallon oil cisterns); 8,000 Gallons Water; 5½" x 10" Axle Journals. These became **Style 29** when engines were rebuilt to Class H-3. Some rebuilt to **Style 26** (15 Tons Coal). These became **Style 30** when locomotives were rebuilt to Class H-3. Some rebuilt to **Style 27** (15 Tons Coal; 10,000 Gallons Water). Some rebuilt to **Style 28** (15 Tons Coal; 10,000 Gallons Water; 6" x 11" Axle Journals). These became **Style 31** when locomotives were rebuilt to Class H-3. Note that 1406-1425 had arch bar trucks.

No.	Builder	Date Rcvd.	Renumbered From	Date	Disposition	Notes
1406	Baldwin	6/8/1906	–	–	Sold for scrap PC 1947.	
1407	Baldwin	6/8/1906	–	–	Reno. X967(1) (WC) 11/1937. Ret. 12/1951. (St. 25).	340
1408	Baldwin	6/10/1906	–	–	Sold for scrap WEI&M 12/1949.	
1409	Baldwin	6/10/1906	–	–	Ret. 4/1955. Sold for scrap PC 9/3/1955.	
1410	Baldwin	6/16/1906	–	–	Retired 5/1958. Sold for scrap c.1962.	
1411	Baldwin	6/16/1906	–	–	Rblt. WC 10/4/1934 at Dale Street. Reno. X1946(3) at Grand Forks 7/8/1940. Ret. 4/1958 (St. 25).	

Tender Class H-2, Style 25: Continued

No.	Builder	Date Rcvd.	Renumbered From	Date	Disposition	Notes
1412	Baldwin	6/17/1906	–	–	**[H-3]** Reno. X2878(2) (WC) 9/1931. Ret. 5/1958 (St. 25).	
1413(1)	Baldwin	6/17/1906	–	–	Sold SP&S (with J-2 engine) 1908.	
1413(2)	Baldwin	3/26/1907	1575	11/9/1908	Sold for scrap WEI&M 4/15/1952.	
1414	Baldwin	6/16/1906	–	–	Reno. X1914(2) (WC) 8/1940. Ret. 4/1958 (St. 25).	
1415	Baldwin	6/16/1906	–	–	Reno. X2852(3) (WC) 6/1934. Ret. 11/1949 (St. 25).	
1416	Baldwin	6/24/1906	–	–	Reno. X2853(3) (WC) 6/1934. Ret. 5/29/1940.	
1417	Baldwin	6/24/1906	–	–	Sold for scrap WEI&M 6/1951.	
1418	Baldwin	7/1/1906	–	–	Reno. X1947(2) (WC) at Irby, WA, 9/5/1940. Ret. 5/1951 (St. 25).	
1419	Baldwin	7/1/1906	–	–	Reno. X1944(2) (WC) 8/1932. Reno. X3280 8/19/1943. Ret. 10/1968. (St. 25).	
1420	Baldwin	7/4/1906	–	–	Sold for scrap DI&M 5/14/1947.	
1421	Baldwin	7/4/1906	–	–	**[H-3]** Reno. X2858(3) (WC) 6/1934. Rblt. X954(2) (40FWC) (with Boxcar 6813) 10/1947. Ret. 4/1958.	
1422	Baldwin	7/18/1906	–	–	Reno. X1950(3) (WC) at Delta 5/29/1940. Ret. 10/1955 (St. 25).	
1423	Baldwin	7/25/1906	–	–	**[H-3]** Reno. X2879(2) (WC) 9/1931. Ret. 5/1958 (St. 25).	
1424	Baldwin	7/18/1906	–	–	Reno. X2824 (WC) at Interbay 11/22/1940. Ret. 5/1951 (St. 25).	341
1425	Baldwin	8/27/1906	–	–	**[H-3]** Sold for scrap PC 4/30/1953 (St. 29).	
1426	Baldwin	8/11/1907	–	–	**[H-3]** Reno. X3255, date unknown. Sold Porter Bros. 5/1/1980 (St. 26).	357
1427	Baldwin	8/11/1907	–	–	**[H-3]** Rblt. Style 26, date unknown. Reno. X2859(3) (WC) 6/1934. Reno. X3284 9/1943. Off roster between 6/1952 and 11/1958 (St. 26).	
1428	Baldwin	8/18/1907	–	–	**[H-3]** Rblt. Style 31 4/18/1945 at Hillyard. Sold for scrap DI&M 7/28/1953.	
1429	Baldwin	8/18/1907	–	–	Rblt. Style 28 at Delta 3/12/1929. Reno. X1591 (CHEM) 4/1950. Ret. 7/1961.	
1430	Baldwin	8/15/1907	–	–	**[H-3]** Rblt. Style 30, date unknown. Reno. X943(3) (WC) 4/9/1947 at Hillyard. Ret. 3/1957.	
1431	Baldwin	8/15/1907	–	–	**[H-3]** Rblt. Style 26, date unknown. Reno. X2890(2) (WC) 6/10/1943. Ret. 4/1956.	
1432	Baldwin	8/26/1907	–	–	Rblt. Style 26, date unknown. Reno. X3217 (WC) 4/22/1942 at Hillyard. Ret. 9/1964.	342
1433	Baldwin	8/26/1907	–	–	**[H-3]** Rblt. Style 30, date unknown. Rblt. WC 10/3/1934 at St.Cloud. Reno. X968(1) (WC) 8/1938. Reno. X3358 8/17/1942. Ret. 9/1958.	
1434	Baldwin	8/26/1907	–	–	Rblt. Style 27 at Delta 10/27/1927. Sold for scrap DI&M 11/1949.	
1435	Baldwin	8/26/1907	–	–	Rblt. Style 27 at Delta 7/29/1926. Reno. X1909(2) (WC) 5/1948. Ret. 9/1960.	
1436	Baldwin	8/29/1907	–	–	**[H-3]** Rblt. Style 31 at Hillyard 4/1927. Sold for scrap PC 6/6/1953.	
1437	Baldwin	8/29/1907	–	–	Rblt. Style 27 at Hillyard 11/22/1926. Rblt. Style 28 at Whitefish 4/15/1945. Reno. X6700 6/1955. Ret. 10/1962.	
1438	Baldwin	9/6/1907	–	–	Rblt. Style 28 at Dale Street 3/20/1928. Reno. X1592 (CHEM) 4/1950. Ret. 6/1960.	
1439	Baldwin	9/6/1907	–	–	Rblt. Style 27 at Dale Street 7/22/1926. Rblt. Style 28 at Hillyard 2/24/1928. Sold for scrap DI&M 2/5/1955.	
1440	Baldwin	9/7/1907	–	–	Rblt. Style 27 9/10/1927 at Hillyard. Sold SP&S (with E3023), delivered 7/13/1929.	

Tender Class H-4, Style 34: 13 Tons Coal (Later increased to 15 Tons; some equipped with 4,500 Gallon oil cisterns); 8,000 Gallons Water; 5½" x 10" Axle Journals. Some rebuilt to Style 35 (6" x 11" Axle Journals). Some rebuilt to Style 32 (10,000 Gallons Water). Some rebuilt to Style 33 (10,000 Gallons Water; 6" x 11" Axle Journals).

No.	Builder	Date Rcvd.	Disposition	Notes
1441	Baldwin	5/1/1909	Rblt. Style 32 8/2/1927 at Havre. Rblt. Style 33 at Great Falls 4/12/1928. Rblt. back to Style 32 at Havre 5/15/1928. Ret. 4/1956. Reinstated 7/1956. Dismantled at St.Cloud 3/1957.	
1442	Baldwin	5/1/1909	Rblt. Style 32 3/23/1927 at Havre. Sold for scrap PC 5/20/1953.	
1443	Baldwin	4/30/1909	Rblt. Style 33 at Dale Street 5/29/1929.	
1444	Baldwin	4/30/1909	Ret. 12/1957. Sold for scrap DI&M 5/1962.	
1445	Baldwin	5/5/1909	Reno. X3260, date unknown. Ret. 9/1966.	343
1446	Baldwin	5/5/1909	Rblt. X1920(2) (WC) (coal pit enclosed) 3/30/1940 at Hillyard. Reno. T1446 at Concrete, WA, 6/4/1940. Reno. X3277 (WC) 7/26/1943. Ret. 12/1965. (St. 34)	
1447	Baldwin	5/5/1909	Rblt. Style 32 at Delta 9/29/1927. Rblt. Style 33 at Whitefish 6/30/1945.	
1448	Baldwin	5/5/1909	Rblt. Style 33 at Superior 4/29/1943. Sold for scrap DI&M 4/30/1953.	
1449	Baldwin	5/8/1909	Reno. X2880(2) (WC) 9/1931. Ret. 8/1958 (St. 34).	
1450	Baldwin	5/8/1909	Sold Truax-Traer Coal Co. (with E757) 9/17/1944.	
1451	Baldwin	5/10/1909	Rblt. Style 35 at Great Falls 6/30/1928. Rblt. Style 33 at Great Falls 7/7/1928. Donated Sioux City, IA, (with E1355) 6/6/1955.	
1452	Baldwin	5/10/1909	Reno. X1930(2) (WC) 3/1933. Ret. 1/1952 (St. 34).	
1453	Baldwin	5/11/1909	Rblt. Style 32 at Dale Street 1/31/1927. Rblt. Style 33 at Havre 5/15/1928. Sold for scrap PC 8/1953.	
1454	Baldwin	5/11/1909	Rblt. Style 32 at Superior 5/15/1928. Reno. X1593 (CHEM) 4/1950. Ret. 2/1960.	
1455	Baldwin	5/11/1909	Rblt. Style 32 at Great Falls 10/5/1928. Rblt. Style 33 5/14/1942. Sold for scrap DI&M 7/31/1953.	
1456	Baldwin	5/11/1909	Reno. X1966(2) (WC) 8/1933. Reno. X3215 7/26/1943. Ret. 1/1961 (St. 34).	
1457	Baldwin	5/17/1909	Reno. X3337 (WC) 10/1948. Ret. 8/1962 (St. 34).	
1458	Baldwin	5/18/1909	Rblt. Style 32 at Dale Street 5/21/1927. Sold for scrap DI&M 6/24/1953.	
1459	Baldwin	5/17/1909	Rblt. Style 32 at Havre 8/31/1927. Sold for scrap PC 8/1953.	

1460	Baldwin	5/18/1909	Rblt. Style 32 at Delta 2/29/1928. Rblt. Style 33 at Great Falls 7/15/1941. Reno. X1594 (CHEM) 3/1950. Ret. 9/1961.
1461	Lima	3/28/1914	Rblt. Style 32 at Hillyard 6/13/1929. Rblt. Style 33 1/2/1942. Sold for scrap PC 1/15/1955.
1462	Lima	3/28/1914	Rblt. Style 32 at Superior 2/12/1927. Rblt. X1589 (WP) 10/1951. Reno. BN 972805 11/1980. Ret. 2/23/1989. Sold Azcon Corp. 3/13/1989.
1463	Lima	4/4/1914	Rblt. Style 32 at Superior 10/4/1927. Sold for scrap DI&M 5/15/1953.
1464	Lima	4/4/1914	Reno. X1915(2) (WC) 5/11/1939. Ret. 12/1959 (St. 34).
1465	Lima	4/4/1914	Rblt. Style 32 at Dale Street 11/30/1927. Sold for scrap WEI&M 9/1953.
1466	Lima	4/4/1914	Rblt. Style 32 at Great Falls 7/24/1926. Wrecked at Great Falls, dismantled at Great Falls 12/31/1929.
1467	Lima	4/10/1914	Rblt. Style 32, date unknown. Reno. X2860(3) (WC) 6/1934. Reno. X3285 7/26/1943. Off roster between 6/1/1952 and 11/1958.
1468	Lima	4/10/1914	Rblt. Style 32 at Delta 10/21/1926. Rblt. Style 33 at Minot 8/31/1943. Sold for scrap PC 7/10/1953.
1469	Lima	4/10/1914	Rblt. Style 33 at Superior 7/22/1944. Sold for scrap PC 8/1953.
1470	Lima	4/10/1914	Reno. X1951(2) (WC) at Willmar, MN, 5/16/1940. Ret. 8/1958 (St. 34).
1471	Lima	4/17/1914	Rblt. Style 32 at Superior 1/27/1927. Rblt. Style 33 at Great Falls 7/7/1943. Sold for scrap PC 5/15/1953.
1472	Lima	4/17/1914	Rblt. Style 32 at Great Falls 10/17/1926. Sold for scrap PC 4/22/1952.
1473	Lima	4/17/1914	Sold for scrap PC 10/1950.
1474	Lima	4/17/1914	Rblt. Style 33 at Superior 9/30/1942. Ret. 4/1955. Sold for scrap DI&M 6/10/1955.
1475	Lima	4/20/1914	Rblt. Style 32 at Great Falls 12/24/1926. Rblt. Style 33 at Great Falls 6/2/1943. Sold for scrap PC 1/12/1955.
1476	Lima	4/20/1914	Reno. X1939(2) (WC) 3/1933. Reno. X3289 8/20/1943. Off roster between 6/1/1952 and 11/1958 (St. 34).
1477	Lima	4/24/1914	Rblt. Style 32 at Havre 8/2/1927. Rblt. Style 33 at Grand Forks 11/22/1941. Sold for scrap 2/1963.
1478	Lima	4/24/1914	Rblt. Style 32 at Dale Street 8/1926. Sold for scrap DI&M 12/25/1955.
1479	Lima	4/24/1914	Rblt. Style 32 at Dale Street 5/18/1927. Rblt. Style 33 at Dale Street 10/15/1929. Retired 4/1956, reinstated 7/1956. Dismantled at St.Cloud 3/1957.
1480	Lima	4/24/1914	Reno. X1928(3) (WC) 6/1949. Ret. 8/1962 (St. 34).
1481	Lima	5/1/1914	Rblt. Style 35 at Great Falls 3/19/1942. Ret. 4/1955. Sold for scrap DI&M 5/28/1955.
1482	Lima	5/1/1914	Reno. X1956(3) (WC) at Great Falls 7/22/1940. Ret. 4/1955 (St. 34).
1483	Lima	5/2/1914	Sold for scrap PC 9/3/1952.
1484	Lima	5/2/1914	Sold for scrap PC 5/20/1953.
1485	Lima	5/7/1914	Rblt. Style 32 at Dale Street 5/11/1927. Rblt. Style 33 at Dale Street 2/21/1942. Sold for scrap PC 6/6/1953.

Tender Class H-5, Style Unassigned: 13 Tons Coal (Later increased to 15 Tons; some equipped with 4,500 Gallon oil cistern); 8,000 Gallons Water; 5½" x 10" Axle Journals.

No.	Builder	Former E-14 No.	Disposition
1486	Baldwin	GN 1031	Reno. GN 1350 2/1926.
1487	Baldwin	GN 1018	Reno. GN 1351 2/1926.
1488	Baldwin	GN 1019	Reno. GN 1352 3/1926.
1489	Baldwin	GN 1025	Reno. GN 1353 2/1926.
1490	Baldwin	GN 1022	Reno. GN 1354 2/1926.
1491	Baldwin	GN 1023	Reno. GN 1358 2/1926.
1492	Baldwin	GN 1016	Reno. GN 1356 2/1926.
1493	Baldwin	GN 1024	Sold SP&S 6/1925.
1494	Baldwin	GN 1020	Reno. GN 1355 4/1926.
1495	Baldwin	GN 1030	Reno. GN 1359 2/1926.

Tender Class J-1, Style 46: 13 Tons Coal (Some equipped with 4,500 Gallon Oil Cistern); 8,000 Gallons Water; 5½" x 10" Axle Journals. Some rebuilt to **Style 47** (10,000 Gallons Water; 6" x 11" Axle Journals)

No.	Builder	Date Rcvd.	Renumbered From	Date	Disposition
1500	Baldwin	4/19/1906	–	–	Reno. X2881(2) (WC) 9/1931. Ret. 8/1955 (St. 46).
1501	Baldwin	4/19/1906	–	–	Reno. X2865(3) (WC) 6/1934. Reno. X3297 8/1/1943. Off roster between 6/1/1952 and 3/1958 (St. 46).
1502	Baldwin	4/19/1906	–	–	
1503	Baldwin	4/19/1906	–	–	Rblt. WC 10/3/1934 at St.Cloud. Reno. X1958(3) (WC) at Grand Forks 5/15/1940. Reno. X3355 7/27/1942. Ret. 8/1962 (St. 46).
1504	Baldwin	4/22/1906	–	–	Sold for scrap DI&M 1947.
1505	Baldwin	4/22/1906	–	–	Sold for scrap DI&M 5/14/1947.
1506	Baldwin	4/24/1906	–	–	Reno. X2868(3) (WC) 6/1934. Reno. X3286 7/24/1943. Off roster between 6/1/1952 and 11/1958 (St. 46).
1507	Baldwin	4/24/1906	–	–	Reno. X1959(2) (WC) 10/1932. Reno. X3292 8/23/1943. Sold Smith Brothers 10/1979 (St. 46).
1508	Baldwin	4/30/1906	–	–	Reno. X2869(3) (WC) 6/1934. Ret. 11/1953 (St. 46).
1509	Baldwin	4/30/1906	–	–	Reno. X2882(2) (WC) 9/1931. Reno. X3299 8/1/1943. Off roster between 6/1/1952 and 11/1958 (St. 46).
1510	Baldwin	4/29/1906	–	–	Reno. X2813(1) (WC) at St.Cloud 12/17/1941. Reno. X3221 at Grand Forks 5/9/1942. Ret. 7/1959 (St. 46).
1511	Baldwin	4/29/1906	–	–	Reno. X1960(2) (WC) at Appleyard 7/3/1940. Reno. X2868(2) 5/29/1945. Ret. 5/1953 (St. 46).
1512	Baldwin	5/1/1906	–	–	Rblt. WC at Grand Forks 11/13/1934. Reno. X1964(2) (WC) at Minot 5/16/1940. Ret. 1/1953 (St. 46).
1513	Baldwin	5/1/1906	–	–	Reno. X1941(2) (WC) 3/1933. Reno. X3271 8/1943. Off roster between 6/1/1952 and 11/1958 (St. 46).
1514	Baldwin	5/4/1906	–	–	Sold SP&S (with F-8) 10/1936.

Tender Class J-1, Style 46: Continued

No.	Builder	Date Rcvd.	Renumbered From	Date	Disposition	Notes
1515	Baldwin	5/4/1906	–	–	Reno. X1983(2) 7/1943. Sold for scrap DI&M 5/7/1947.	
1516	Baldwin	5/4/1906	–	–	Reno. X2884(2) (WC) 6/1934. Ret. 7/1958 (St. 46).	
1517	Baldwin	5/4/1906	–	–	Reno. H-6 1718 8/1923.	
1518	Baldwin	5/9/1906	–	–	Sold for scrap DI&M c.1/1950.	
1519	Baldwin	5/9/1906	–	–	Reno. H-6 1721 2/1926.	
1520	Baldwin	5/10/1906	–	–	Sold for scrap WEI&M 5/13/1953.	
1521	Baldwin	5/10/1906	–	–	Rblt. WC at Grand Forks 12/24/1934. Reno. X1965(2) (WC) at Grand Forks 8/2/1940. Ret. 12/1954 (St. 46).	
1522	Baldwin	5/15/1906	–	–	Reno. X2885(2) (WC) 6/1934. Reno. X3288 9/27/1943. Off roster between 6/1/1952 and 11/1958 (St. 46).	
1523	Baldwin	5/15/1906	–	–	Reno. H-6 1717 3/1922.	
1524	Baldwin	5/15/1906	–	–	Reno. X1925(3) (WC) 7/1949. Ret. 12/1954 (St. 46).	
1525	Baldwin	5/15/1906	–	–	Reno. H-6 1722 7/1926.	
1526	Baldwin	5/24/1906	–	–	Reno. X2837(3) (WC) 8/1948. Ret. 11/1968 (St. 46).	
1527	Baldwin	7/13/1906	–	–	Reno. X1954(3) (WC) 3/1933. Reno. X3282 8/27/1943. Ret. 12/1959 (St. 46).	
1528	Baldwin	7/13/1906	–	–	Reno. H-6 1720 4/1926.	
1529	Baldwin	7/25/1906	–	–	Reno. X2886(2) (WC) 6/1934. Ret. 6/1954 (St. 46).	
1530	Baldwin	7/25/1906	–	–	Rblt. WC at Grand Forks 12/18/1934. Reno. X1969(3) at Grand Forks 5/24/1940. Reno. X3294 8/6/1943. Off roster between 6/1/1952 and 11/1958 (St. 46).	
1531	Baldwin	7/25/1906	–	–	Sold for scrap DI&M 5/1948.	
1532	Baldwin	7/25/1906	–	–	Ret. 11/1927. Reno. X1992 (WC) 1/1928. Ret. 6/1956 (St. 46).	
1533	Baldwin	7/28/1906	–	–	Reno. X1957(2) (WC) 3/1933. Ret. 8/1954 (St. 46).	
1534	Baldwin	7/28/1906	–	–	Reno. X950(3) 12/1946. Ret. 1/1956 (St. 46).	
1535	Baldwin	8/3/1906	–	–	Sold for scrap DI&M 5/14/1947.	
1536	Baldwin	8/3/1906	–	–	Ret. 11/1927. Reno. X1991(1) (WC) 1/1928. Ret. 1/1944.	
1537(1)	Baldwin	8/10/1906	–	–	Reno. 1556 at Minot 1/28/1909.	
1537(2)	Baldwin	?	?	?	Reno. X2814(1) (WC) at Grand Forks 1/10/1942. Reno. X3222 at Minot 5/11/1942. Ret. 7/1959 (St. 46).	
1538(1)	Baldwin	8/10/1906	–	–	Sold to SP&S 1908 (with J-2 engine).	
1538(2)	Baldwin	4/30/1907	1589(1)	2/26/1909	Rblt. 10,000 Gallon Capacity without 6" x 11" journals at Delta 3/15/1927. Sold SP&S (with E3043) 4/1928.	
1539	Baldwin	8/17/1906	–	–	Reno. X2887(2) (WC) 6/1934. Ret. 12/1949 (St. 46).	
1540	Baldwin	8/17/1906	–	–	Sold for scrap 6/1940.	
1541(1)	Baldwin	10/7/1906	–	–	Sold to SP&S 1908 (with J-2 engine).	
1541(2)	Baldwin	5/19/1907	1601	2/25/1909	Rblt. 10,000 Gallon Capacity without 6" x 11" journals at Great Falls 8/30/1926. Dismantled c.4/1938.	
1542	Baldwin	10/7/1906	–	–	Reno. X937(3) (WC) at Havre 8/25/1941. Ret. 2/1957 (St. 46).	344
1543	Baldwin	8/27/1906	–	–	Rblt. WC 11/3/1934 at Grand Forks. Reno. X1972(3) at Grand Forks 8/16/1940. Reno. X3295 8/1943. Off roster between 6/1/1952 and 11/1958 (St. 46).	
1544	Baldwin	8/27/1906	–	–	Reno. X1997(2) (WC) 11/12/1941 at Superior. Reno. X3235 at Minot 5/4/1942. Ret. 10/1958 (St. 46).	
1545	Baldwin	9/12/1906	–	–	Reno. X2888(2) (WC) 6/1934. Ret. 11/1946.	
1546	Baldwin	9/12/1906	–	–	Reno. X1980(2) (WC) at Delta 5/28/1940. Ret. 6/1956 (St. 46).	
1547	Baldwin	9/30/1906	–	–	Reno. X2889 (WC) 6/1934. Rblt. X940(4) (40FWC) (with Boxcar 36697) 5/1947. Ret. 6/1954.	
1548	Baldwin	9/30/1906	–	–	Sold for scrap 6/1940.	
1549	Baldwin	10/4/1906	–	–	Reno. X2815(1) (WC) at Grand Forks 12/29/1941. Reno. X3223 at Minot 5/11/1942. Ret. 12/1957 (St. 46).	

Tender Class J-2, Style 51: 13 Tons Coal (Some equipped with 4,700 Gallon oil cistern); 8,000 Gallons Water; 5½" x 10" Axle Journals. Some rebuilt to **Style 48** (15 Tons Coal) Some rebuilt to **Style 49** (15 Tons Coal; 10,000 Gallons Water). Some rebuilt to **Style 50** (15 Tons Coal; 10,000 Gallons Water; 6" x 11" Axle Journals).

No.	Builder	Date Rcvd.	Renumbered From	Date	Disposition	Notes
1550	Baldwin	3/5/1907	–	–	Rblt. Style 48, date unknown. Reno. X1982(2) (WC) at Willmar 7/24/1940. Reno. X3357 8/14/1942. Ret. 5/1962.	345
1551	Baldwin	3/5/1907	–	–	Rblt. Style 48, date unknown. Reno. X1958(4) (WC) 10/12/1945. Ret. 6/1960.	
1552(1)	Baldwin	3/13/1907	–	–	Sold SP&S 1908 (with J-2 engine).	
1552(2)	Baldwin	5/4//1907	1595	2/26/1909	Reno. H-6 1713 11/1921.	
1553	Baldwin	3/13/1907	–	–	Reno. H-6 1719 9/1923.	
1554	Baldwin	3/4/1907	–	–	Reno. X3202 (WC) (coal pit enclosed) at St.Cloud 3/13/1942. Ret. 12/1964 (St. 48).	
1555	Baldwin	3/4/1907	–	–	Sold SP&S (No. 450) 1908.	
1556(1)	Baldwin	3/18/1907	–	–	Sold SP&S 1908 (with J-2 engine).	
1556(2)	Baldwin	5/4/1907	1597	4/28/1909	Rblt. to 10,000 Gallon capacity (4,500 Gallons Oil) (Style 49?) at Hillyard 10/26/1926. Sold SP&S (with E1182) 10/1944.	
1557	Baldwin	3/18/1907	–	–	Rblt. Style 48, date unknown. Sold for scrap DI&M 9/21/1952.	
1558(1)	Baldwin	3/17/1907	–	–	Sold SP&S 1908 (with J-2 engine).	
1558(2)	Baldwin	4/13/1907	1581	11/24/1908	Rblt. Style 49 at Dale Street 7/30/1927. Sold for scrap PC 9/21/1952.	
1559	Baldwin	3/17/1907	–	–	Sold for scrap DI&M 6/1932.	

No.	Builder	Date			Notes	
1560	Baldwin	3/17/1907	–	–	Rblt. Style 49 (but only 13 Ton coal capacity) at Great Falls 2/28/1927. Sold SP&S (with E3121) 9/1943.	
1561	Baldwin	3/17/1907	–	–	Rblt. Style 49 at Dale Street 8/29/1927. Sold for scrap DI&M 9/4/1952.	
1562	Baldwin	3/15/1907	–	–	Rblt. Style 48, date unknown. Reno. X2816(1) (WC) at Grand Forks 12/4/1941. Reno. X3224 at Grand Forks 4/20/1942. Off roster between 6/1/1952 and 11/1958.	
1563	Baldwin	3/15/1907	–	–	Rblt. Style 50 10/1927. Retired at Great Falls 2/1948.	
1564	Baldwin	3/14/1907	–	–	Rblt. Style 49 at Dale Street 1/31/1928. Rblt. Style 50 at Grand Forks 2/28/1944. Sold for scrap PC 5/20/1953.	
1565	Baldwin	3/14/1907	–	–	Sold SP&S (No. 451) 1908.	
1566	Baldwin	3/16/1907	–	–	Rblt. Style 48, date unknown. Reno. X969 (WC) 6/1938. Ret. 5/1957.	
1567	Baldwin	3/16/1907	–	–	Sold Somers Lumber Co. (with E1244) 1934. Returned to GN, date unknown. Rblt. WC (coal pit enclosed) at Hillyard 7/23/1940. Retired 5/1958. Rblt. X6300 (FO) 11/1958. Ret. 10/1959.	
1568	Baldwin	3/14/1907	–	–	Ret. 12/1930. Dismantled at Dale Street 3/3/1931.	
1569	Baldwin	3/14/1907	–	–	Reno. H-6 1714 c.1922.	
1570	Baldwin	3/23/1907	–	–	Reno. H-6 1724 10/1927.	
1571	Baldwin	3/23/1907	–	–	Rblt. Style 49 (but only 13 Ton coal capacity) 6/30/1927 at Great Falls.	
1572	Baldwin	3/20/1907	–	–	Reno. H-6 1711 8/1921.	
1573	Baldwin	3/20/1907	–	–	Rblt. Style 48, date unknown. Reno. X3247 (WC) at Great Falls 9/30/1941. Reno. X1968(3) 12/1950. Ret. 11/1961.	
1574	Baldwin	3/26/1907	–	–	Rblt. Style 50 6/1927. Ret. 4/1956. Reinstated 7/1956. Dismantled at St.Cloud 3/1957.	
1575	Baldwin	3/26/1907	–	–	Reno. 1413(2) at St.Paul 11/9/1908.	
1576	Baldwin	3/28/1907	–	–	Rblt. Style 49 at Dale Street 7/26/1927. Ret. 4/1955. Sold for scrap DI&M 6/4/1955.	
1577	Baldwin	3/28/1907	–	–	Sold SP&S (No. 453) 1908.	
1578	Baldwin	4/2/1907	–	–	Rblt. Style 50 at Great Falls 6/30/1928. Ret. 8/1955. Sold for scrap WEI&M 9/1955.	
1579	Baldwin	4/2/1907	–	–	Rblt. Style 48, date unknown. Rblt. WC at Dale Street 10/10/1934. Reno. X955(1) (WC) at St.Cloud 9/14/1937.Reno. X3273 7/26/1943. Off roster between 6/1/1952 and 11/1958.	
1580	Baldwin	4/13/1907	–	–	Sold for scrap DI&M c.1/1950.	
1581	Baldwin	4/13/1907	–	–	Reno. 1558(2) at Superior 11/24/1908.	
1582	Baldwin	4/15/1907	–	–	Rblt. Style 48, date unknown. Reno. 95009 (RT) 10/1925. Reno. (T)X1509 10/1926. Reno. X1984 5/24/1927. Ret. 2/1957.	
1583	Baldwin	4/15/1907	–	–	Reno. 1585 at Superior 11/24/1908.	
1584	Baldwin	4/13/1907	–	–	Rblt. Style 49 at Great Falls 8/27/1927. Rblt. Style 50 at Hillyard 3/1943. Ret. 3/1958. Sold for scrap PC 6/1962.	
1585(1)	Baldwin	4/13/1907	–	–	Sold to SP&S 1908 (with J-2 engine).	
1585(2)	Baldwin	4/15/1907	1583	11/24/1908	Rblt. Style 48, date unknown. Reno. X3208 (WC) (coal pit enclosed) at St.Cloud 3/9/1942. Ret. 9/1969.	
1586	Baldwin	4/19/1907	–	–	Rblt. Style 48, date unknown. Reno. X2825(3) (WC) 8/1948. Ret. 1/1961.	
1587	Baldwin	4/19/1907	–	–	Sold SP&S (No. 456) 1908.	
1588	Baldwin	4/30/1907	–	–	Retired 5/1958.	
1589	Baldwin	4/30/1907	–	–	Sold SP&S 1908 (with J-2 engine).	
1590	Baldwin	5/4/1907	–	–	Rblt. Style 48, date unknown. Reno. X1948(2) (WC) 3/1933. Reno. X3281 8/19/1943. Ret. 5/1959.	
1591	Baldwin	4/28/1907	–	–	Rblt. Style 48, date unknown. Reno. X2838(3) (WC) 8/1948. Ret. 11/1971.	
1592	Baldwin	4/28/1907	–	–	Rblt. Style 48, date unknown. Reno. X3237 (WC) at Great Falls 7/6/1942. Ret. 1/1961.	
1593	Baldwin	4/28/1907	–	–	Sold SP&S (No. 457) 1908.	
1594	Baldwin	4/28/1907	–	–	Rblt. Style 50 at Hillyard 4/1927. Ret. 4/1955. Sold for scrap DI&M 5/14/1955.	
1595	Baldwin	5/4/1907	–	–	Reno. 1552(2) at Willmar 2/26/1909.	
1596	Baldwin	5/4/1907	–	–	Rblt. Style 49 at Delta 1/18/1926. Sold for scrap DI&M 3/11/1949.	
1597	Baldwin	5/4/1907	–	–	Reno. 1556(2) at Minot 4/28/1909.	
1598	Baldwin	5/15/1907	–	–	Reno. H-6 1716 5/1922.	
1599	Baldwin	5/15/1907	–	–	Sold for scrap DI&M 10/22/1951.	
1600	Baldwin	5/19/1907	–	–	Sold SP&S (No. 463) 11/14/1908.	
1601	Baldwin	5/19/1907	–	–	Reno. 1541(2) at Superior 2/25/1909.	
1602	Baldwin	5/19/1907	–	–	Rblt. Style 48, date unknown. Reno. X2853(4) (WC) at Havre 3/1/1941. Reno. X3246 6/1/1943. Ret. 11/1962.	
1603	Baldwin	5/19/1907	–	–	Sold SP&S (No. 459) 8/28/1908.	
1604	Baldwin	5/21/1907	–	–	Rblt. Style 49 at Dale Street 5/18/1927. Sold for scrap PC 9/4/1952.	
1605	Baldwin	5/21/1907	–	–	Rblt. Style 48, date unknown. Reno. X1916(2) (WC) 2/1933. Reno. X335910/19/1942. Ret. 11/1960.	346
1606	Baldwin	5/27/1907	–	–	Rblt. Style 48, date unknown. Sold for scrap DI&M 9/1/1952.	
1607	Baldwin	5/27/1907	–	–	Scrapped at Hillyard 3/13/1928.	
1608	Baldwin	5/28/1907	–	–	Rblt. Style 49 at Hillyard 9/10/1927. Sold SP&S (with E3024) 6/1929, delivered 7/3/1929.	161
1609	Baldwin	5/28/1907	–	–	Rblt. Style 50 at Dale Street 10/23/1929. Sold for scrap DI&M 9/4/1952.	161
1610	Baldwin	5/26/1907	–	–	Rblt. Style 49 at Hillyard 12/23/1926. Ret. 4/1955. Sold for scrap DI&M 8/1/1955.	
1611	Baldwin	5/26/1907	–	–	Rblt. Style 49 at Superior 2/1/1928. Sold for scrap DI&M 2/5/1955.	
1612	Baldwin	5/26/1907	–	–	Rblt. Style 49 (but only 13 Ton coal capacity) 10/14/1926 at Dale Street. Reno. H-6 1723 9/1927.	
1613	Baldwin	5/26/1907	–	–	Rblt. Style 48, date unknown. Sold for scrap PC 9/21/1952.	

Tender Class J-2, Style 51: Continued

No.	Builder	Date Rcvd.	Renumbered From	Date	Disposition	Notes
1614	Baldwin	6/2/1907	–	–	Rblt. Style 49 (but only 13 Ton coal capacity) 4/26/1927 at Great Falls. Rblt. Style 50 at Dale Street 10/30/1944. Sold for scrap DI&M 5/28/1953.	
1615	Baldwin	6/2/1907	–	–	Sold for scrap PC 12/1949.	
1616	Baldwin	6/6/1907	–	–	Reno. H-6 1712 10/1921.	
1617	Baldwin	6/6/1907	–	–	Rblt. Style 50 at Great Falls 3/24/1928. Sold for scrap PC 12/20/1951.	
1618	Baldwin	6/8/1907	–	–	Rblt. Style 48, date unknown. Rblt. WC 10/3/1934 at St. Cloud. Reno. X1985(3) (WC) at Grand Forks 5/27/1940. Reno. X3283 8/21/1943. Off roster between 6/1/1952 and 11/1958.	
1619	Baldwin	6/8/1907	–	–	Reno. H-6 1715 3/1922.	
1620	Baldwin	6/9/1907	–	–	Rblt. Style 49 at Hillyard 9/25/1926.	
1621	Baldwin	6/10/1907	–	–	Reno. X3251 (coal space enclosed) (WC) at St.Cloud 1/21/1944. Ret. 11/1960.	
1622	Baldwin	6/13/1907	–	–	Rblt. Style 48, date unknown. Reno. X1917(2) (WC) 4/1933. Ret. 12/1959.	347
1623	Baldwin	6/13/1907	–	–		
1624	Baldwin	6/14/1907	–	–	Sold for scrap DI&M 7/1932.	
1625	Baldwin	6/14/1907	–	–	Reno. X938(3) (WC) at Great Falls 8/30/1941. Ret. 12/1960. (St. 51).	348
1626	Baldwin	6/12/1907	–	–	Rblt. Style 49 at Delta 9/18/1926. Sold for scrap DI&M 1/15/1955.	
1627	Baldwin	6/12/1907	–	–	Sold for scrap PC 3/5/1949.	
1628	Baldwin	6/16/1907	–	–	Rblt. Style 49 at Hillyard 8/30/1926. Sold for scrap DI&M 8/28/1952.	162
1629	Baldwin	6/16/1907	–	–	Reno. X2864(3) (WC) 10/4/1940. Ret. 9/1957 (St. 51).	162
1630	Baldwin	6/18/1907	–	–	Sold SP&S (with F-8) 10/1936.	
1631	Baldwin	6/18/1907	–	–	Rblt. Style 49 at Hillyard 7/2/1926. Rblt. Style 50 at Delta 5/21/1939. Sold for scrap DI&M 5/13/1953.	349
1632	Baldwin	6/29/1907	–	–	Rblt. Style 49 at Hillyard 8/9/1927. Sold for scrap PC 10/22/1955.	
1633	Baldwin	6/29/1907	–	–	Reno. X3200 (WC) at St.Cloud 2/17/1942. Ret. 10/1969 (St. 51).	
1634	Baldwin	6/29/1907	–	–	Reno. H-6 1710 7/1921.	
1635	Baldwin	6/29/1907	–	–		
1636	Baldwin	6/30/1907	–	–	Rblt. Style 48, date unknown. Reno. X2817 (WC) at St.Cloud 10/28/1941. Reno. X3225 at Grand Forks 4/20/1942. Ret. 5/1959.	
1637	Baldwin	6/30/1907	–	–	Rblt. Style 49 (but only 13 Ton coal capacity) at Dale Street 5/18/1927. Reno. X1959(3) (WC) 10/1952. Ret. 9/1957.	350
1638	Baldwin	7/2/1907	–	–	Reno. 1709(2) at Hillyard 11/23/1908.	163
1639	Baldwin	7/2/1907	–	–	Sold for scrap DI&M c.1/1950.	
1640	Baldwin	7/8/1907	–	–	Rblt. Style 50 at Great Falls 8/7/1943. Sold for scrap PC 10/10/1952.	
1641	Baldwin	7/8/1907	–	–	Rblt. Style 49, date unknown. Sold for scrap PC 5/15/1953.	
1642	Baldwin	7/9/1907	–	–	Ret. 12/1930. Dismantled at Superior 8/21/1931.	
1643	Baldwin	7/9/1907	–	–	Reno. X956(1) (WC) at St.Cloud 8/14/1937. Reno. X3274 7/24/1943. Off roster between 6/1/1952 and 11/1958 (St. 51).	
1644	Baldwin	7/13/1907	–	–	Reno. X3353 (FO) at St.Cloud 7/14/1942. Ret. 11/1970 (St. 51).	
1645	Baldwin	7/13/1907	–	–	Rblt. Style 49 at Havre 6/29/1927. Sold for scrap PC 4/30/1953.	
1646	Baldwin	7/28/1907	–	–	Reno. X957(1) (WC) at St.Cloud 8/14/1937. Reno. X3275 7/25/1943. Ret. 7/1959 (St. 51).	
1647	Baldwin	7/28/1907	–	–	Sold for scrap PC 6/6/1953.	
1648	Baldwin	7/28/1907	–	–	Reno. X1986(2) (WC) at Great Falls 7/22/1940 (St. 51). Ret. 3/1963.	351
1649	Baldwin	7/28/1907	–	–	Rblt. Style 48, date unknown. Reno. X2818(1) (WC) at St.Cloud 10/31/1941. Reno. X3226 at Grand Forks 4/22/1942. Reno. BN 973040 11/1971. Scrapped 12/1977.	

Tender Class K-1, Style 52: 13 Tons Coal; 8,000 Gallons Water; 5½" x 10" Axle Journals. Some rebuilt to Style 53 (10,000 Gallons Water; 6" x 11" Axle Journals)

No.	Builder	Date Rcvd.	Renumbered From	Date	Disposition	Notes
1700	Baldwin	5/29/1906	–	–	Equipped as water car at St.Cloud 10/20/1934. Reno. X1987(3) (WC) at Grand Forks 6/13/1940. Reno. X3213 4/13/1942. Reno. X3354 6/9/1942. Ret. 6/1968.	
1701	Baldwin	5/29/1906	–	–	Reno. X2890(1) (WC) 6/1934. Ret. 9/1943.	
1702	Baldwin	5/29/1906	–	–	Reno. X2891 (WC) 6/1934. Ret. 4/1947.	
1703	Baldwin	5/29/1906	–	–	Reno. X1988(2) (WC) at Klamath Falls, OR, 8/12/1940. Ret. 6/1948.	352
1704	Baldwin	6/6/1906	–	–	Reno. X1989(2) (WC) at Whitefish, MT, 7/12/1940. Reno. X3218 6/13/1942. Ret. 11/1958 (St. 52).	164, 353
1705	Baldwin	6/6/1906	–	–	Reno. X1990(2) (WC) at St.Cloud 5/16/1940. Reno. X3214 2/26/1942. Ret. 3/1964 (St. 52).	164
1706	Baldwin	6/6/1906	–	–	Reno. X1919(2) (WC) 2/28/1940. Ret. 12/1964.	164
1707	Baldwin	6/6/1906	–	–	Sold for scrap DI&M 6/1932.	164
1708	Baldwin	6/26/1906	–	–	Reno. X1971(2) (WC) 10/1932. Reno. X3356 7/31/1942. Ret. 4/1958 (St. 52).	166
1709(1)	Baldwin	6/26/1906	–	–	Sold SP&S 1908 (with J-2 engine).	166
1709(2)	Baldwin	7/2/1907	1638	11/23/1908	Rblt. Style 53 11/15/1941 at Superior. Reno. X1595 (CHEM) 4/1950. Ret. 4/1961.	163

Tender Class H-6, Multiple Styles: Dimensions indicate that those tenders which were renumbered from Class J-1 had coal capacity increased to 15 Tons and were placed in **Style 39** (15 Tons Coal; 8,000 Gallons Water; 5½" x 10" Axle Journals). Those tenders renumbered from Class J-2 were placed in **Style 38** (13 Tons Coal; 8,000 Gallons Water; 5½" x 10" Axle Journals). Some of the former J-2 tenders were rebuilt to **Style 40** (10,000 Gallons Water); **Style 41** (15 Tons Coal; 10,000 Gallons Water); or **Style 42** (15 Tons Coal); or **Style 43** (15 Tons Coal; 10,000 Gallons Water; 6" x 11" Axle Journals). Note that some GN records do not agree with this scheme, which was developed from dimensions of the various styles.

No.	Builder	Date Rcvd.	Renumbered From J No.	Disposition
1710	Baldwin	6/29/1907	GN 1634	Rblt. Style 41 at Dale Street 4/9/1928. Sold for scrap PC 6/6/1953.
1711	Baldwin	3/20/1907	GN 1572	Sold for scrap DI&M 6/1932.
1712	Baldwin	6/6/1907	GN 1616	[Diagrams show Style 39 despite fact this was former J-2] Sold for scrap PC 1/21/1955.
1713	Baldwin	4/28/1907	GN 1552(2)	Sold for scrap PC 6/1948.
1714	Baldwin	3/14/1907	GN 1569	[Diagrams show Style 39 despite fact this was former J-2] Ret. 11/1927. Reno. X1905 (RT) 1/1928. Ret. 9/1952.
1715	Baldwin	6/8/1907	GN 1619	Rblt. Style 42, date unknown. Reno. X1921(3) (WC) 2/24/1939. Ret. 3/1952.
1716	Baldwin	5/15/1907	GN 1598	Rblt. Style 40 (4,500 Gallons Oil) at Hillyard 10/20/1926. Sold for scrap PC 5/20/1953.
1717	Baldwin	5/15/1906	GN 1523	Reno. X1993(2) (WC) at Sioux Falls 5/23/1940. Reno. X3350 5/5/1942. Ret. 5/1952 (St. 39).
1718	Baldwin	5/4/1906	GN 1517	Reno. X1936(2) (WC) 3/1933. Reno. X3352 6/20/1942. Ret. 5/1959 (St. 39).
1719	Baldwin	3/13/1907	GN 1553	Sold for scrap PC 1947.
1720	Baldwin	7/13/1906	GN 1528	Reno. X1938(3) (WC) 3/1933. Reno. X3361 (FO) 10/19/1942. Ret. 2/1960.
1721	Baldwin	5/9/1906	GN 1519	Reno. X2892 (WC) 6/1934. Ret. 4/1956 (St. 39).
1722	Baldwin	5/15/1906	GN 1525	Reno. X2893(1) (WC) at Fargo 8/12/1934. Reno. X3241 7/28/1943. Ret. 12/1959 (St. 39).
1723	Baldwin	5/26/1907	GN 1612	Rblt. Style 41 (19 Tons Coal) at Great Falls 8/30/1928. Rblt. X1584 (WP) 1/11/1951. Sold Pacific Hide & Fur 12/1982.
1724	Baldwin	3/23/1907	GN 1570	Sold for scrap PC c.1/1950.

Tender Class P-1, Style 86: 15 Tons Coal (Some with 4,500 Gallon oil cisterns); 8,000 Gallons Water; 5½" x 10" Axle Journals. Some rebuilt to Style 87 (10,000 Gallons Water) and some rebuilt to Style 88 (10,000 Gallons Water; 6" x 11" Axle Journals).

No.	Builder	Date Rcvd.	Disposition	Notes
1750	Lima	5/21/1914	Retired 12/1949. Sold for scrap DI&M c.1/1950.	
1751	Lima	5/28/1914	Rblt. Style 88, date unknown. Sold for scrap PC 8/1953.	
1752	Lima	5/24/1914	Reno. X2805(3) (WC) at St.Cloud 12/20/1941. Reno. X3220 4/20/1942. Ret. 7/1959 (St. 86).	
1753	Lima	5/28/1914	Rblt. Style 88 at Dale Street 3/10/1928. Sold for scrap DI&M 5/15/1953.	
1754	Lima	5/29/1914	Scrapped at Great Falls 9/3/1941.	
1755	Lima	6/1/1914	Reno. X939(3) (WC) at Great Falls 9/3/1941. Reno. X3242 1/15/1943. Sold Luria Brothers 8/1978 (St. 86).	354
1756	Lima	6/4/1914	Reno. X3234 (WC) (coal pit enclosed) at Great Falls 4/24/1942. Ret. 5/1963 (St. 86)	
1757	Lima	6/4/1914	Rblt. Style 88, date unknown. Sold for scrap PC 9/21/1952.	
1758	Lima	6/4/1914	Rblt. Style 88 at Dale Street 10/18/1927. Ret. 4/1956, reinstated 7/1956. Sold for scrap 11/1956.	
1759	Lima	6/4/1914	Sold for scrap PC 10/18/1951 (St. 86).	
1760	Lima	6/14/1914	Rblt. Style 87 at Havre 5/28/1927. Rblt. X1582 (WP) 12/27/1950. Reno. BN 972538 7/1980. Ret. 6/1983. Sold Smith Brothers 8/29/1983.	
1761	Lima	6/14/1914	Rblt. Style 87 at Great Falls 6/20/1927. Rblt. Style 88 12/1940. Sold for scrap PC 5/7/1953.	
1762	Lima	6/18/1914	Rblt. Style 87 at Great Falls 4/23/1927. Rblt. Style 88 12/1938. Sold for scrap PC 12/12/1955.	
1763	Lima	6/22/1914	Rblt. Style 87 at Havre 6/27/1927. Retired 12/1949. Sold for scrap PC c.1/1950.	
1764	Lima	6/18/1914	Rblt. Style 87 at Great Falls 10/21/1927. Sold for scrap WEI&M 5/16/1953.	

Tender Class L-1, Style Unassigned: 13 Tons Coal; 8,000 Gallons Water; 5½" x 10" Axle Journals

No.	Builder	Date Rcvd.	Disposition	Notes
1800(1)	Baldwin	9/6/1906	Reno. GN 1900 12/1907.	172
1801(1)	Baldwin	9/11/1906	Reno. GN 1901 1/1908.	172
1802(1)	Baldwin	9/22/1906	Reno. GN 1902 1/1908.	
1803(1)	Baldwin	9/30/1906	Reno. GN 1903 12/1907.	172
1804(1)	Baldwin	10/22/1906	Reno. GN 1904 1/1908.	

Tender Class L-2, Style Unassigned: 12 Tons Coal; 8,000 Gallons Water; 5½" x 10" Axle Journals

No.	Builder	Date Rcvd.	Disposition	Notes
1800(2)	Baldwin	3/25/1908	Reno. O-5 3344 10/1925.	173
1801(2)	Baldwin	3/25/1908	Reno. O-5 3304 2/1923.	173
1802(2)	Baldwin	3/25/1908	Reno. O-5 3300 5/1922.	173
1803(2)	Baldwin	3/27/1908	Reno. O-5 3337 12/1924.	
1804(2)	Baldwin	3/25/1908	Reno. O-5 3318 1/1924.	174
1805	Baldwin	5/17/1907	Reno. O-5 3342 4/1925.	
1806	Baldwin	5/17/1907	Reno. O-5 3302 12/1922.	175
1807	Baldwin	5/17/1907	Reno. O-5 3330 10/1924.	175
1808	Baldwin	5/20/1907	Reno. O-5 3307 4/1923.	176
1809	Baldwin	5/20/1907	Reno. O-5 3308 3/1923.	176
1810	Baldwin	5/22/1907	Reno. O-5 3309 8/1923.	
1811	Baldwin	5/22/1907	Reno. O-5 3335 12/1924.	
1812	Baldwin	6/2/1907	Reno. O-5 3319 3/1924.	177
1813	Baldwin	5/28/1907	Reno. O-5 3334 3/1925.	177
1814	Baldwin	9/24/1907	Reno. O-5 3338 2/1925.	177
1815	Baldwin	5/28/1907	Reno. O-5 3336 12/1924.	177

Tender Class L-2, Style Unassigned: Continued

No.	Builder	Date Rcvd.	Disposition	Notes
1816	Baldwin	6/6/1907	Reno. O-5 3324 3/1924.	178
1817	Baldwin	6/5/1907	Reno. O-5 3328 7/1924.	178
1818	Baldwin	6/5/1907	Reno. O-5 3329 9/1924.	178
1819	Baldwin	6/9/1907	Reno. O-5 3306 11/1922.	178
1820	Baldwin	6/26/1907	Reno. O-5 3339 5/1925.	179
1821	Baldwin	6/25/1907	Reno. O-5 3333 11/1924.	180
1822	Baldwin	6/30/1907	Reno. O-5 3314 10/1923.	181
1823	Baldwin	6/30/1907	Reno. O-5 3317 11/1923.	181
1824	Baldwin	8/11/1907	Reno. O-5 3320 5/1924.	
1825	Baldwin	7/6/1907	Reno. O-5 3325 8/1924.	182
1826	Baldwin	7/21/1907	Reno. O-5 3327 7/1924.	183
1827	Baldwin	7/28/1907	Reno. O-5 3340 5/1925.	184
1828	Baldwin	7/30/1907	Reno. O-5 3312 4/1923.	
1829	Baldwin	8/6/1907	Reno. O-5 3315 8/1923.	185
1830	Baldwin	3/25/1908	Reno. O-5 3343 5/1925.	186
1831	Baldwin	3/25/1908	Reno. O-5 3311 5/1923.	186
1832	Baldwin	3/31/1908	Reno. O-5 3322 3/1924.	
1833	Baldwin	3/27/1908	Reno. O-5 3321 1/1924.	
1834	Baldwin	3/27/1908	Reno. O-5 3313 5/1923.	
1835	Baldwin	3/31/1908	Reno. O-5 3303 2/1923.	
1836	Baldwin	3/31/1908	Reno. O-5 3310 9/1923.	
1837	Baldwin	4/3/1908	Reno. O-5 3323 5/1924.	
1838	Baldwin	4/3/1908	Reno. O-5 3305 2/1923.	
1839	Baldwin	4/3/1908	Reno. O-5 3332 9/1924.	187
1840	Baldwin	4/7/1908	Reno. O-5 3316 11/1923.	
1841	Baldwin	4/7/1908	Reno. O-5 3331 2/1925.	188
1842	Baldwin	4/7/1908	Reno. O-5 3326 5/1924.	
1843	Baldwin	4/7/1908	Reno. O-5 3341 1/1925.	188
1844	Baldwin	4/14/1908	Reno. O-5 3301 12/1921.	188

Tender Class L-1, Style Unassigned: 13 Tons Coal; 8,000 Gallons Water; 5½" x 10" Axle Journals

No.	Builder	Date Rcvd.	Original No.	Disposition	Notes
1900	Baldwin	9/6/1906	GN 1800(1)	Reno. O-6 3357 12/1925.	172
1901	Baldwin	9/11/1906	GN 1801(1)	Reno. O-6 3354 11/1925.	172
1902	Baldwin	9/22/1906	GN 1802(1)	Reno. O-6 3359 4/1926.	
1903	Baldwin	9/30/1906	GN 1803(1)	Reno. O-6 3358 1/1926.	172
1904	Baldwin	10/22/1906	GN 1804(1)	Reno. O-6 3362 6/1926.	
1905(2)	Baldwin	5/12/1908	GN 1922	Reno. O-6 3369 10/1926.	189
1906(2)	Baldwin	5/16/1908	GN 1923	Reno. O-6 3363 5/1926.	189
1907(2)	Baldwin	5/25/1908	GN 1924	Reno. O-6 3366 7/1926.	189
1908	Baldwin	4/17/1908	–	Reno. O-6 3356 11/1925.	190
1909	Baldwin	4/17/1908	–	Reno. O-6 3370 11/1926.	190
1910	Baldwin	4/27/1908	–	Reno. O-6 3350 8/1925.	191
1911	Baldwin	4/27/1908	–	Reno. O-6 3355 11/1925.	191
1912	Baldwin	4/27/1908	–	Reno. O-6 3364 7/1926.	191
1913	Baldwin	4/27/1908	–	Reno. O-6 3351 9/1925.	191
1914	Baldwin	5/1/1908	–	Reno. O-6 3368 9/1926.	
1915	Baldwin	5/1/1908	–	Reno. O-6 3367 10/1926.	
1916	Baldwin	5/4/1908	–	Reno. O-6 3361 5/1926.	192
1917	Baldwin	5/4/1908	–	Reno. O-6 3365 8/1926.	192
1918	Baldwin	5/9/1908	–	Reno. O-6 3360 2/1926.	
1919	Baldwin	5/9/1908	–	Reno. O-6 3352 8/1925.	
1920	Baldwin	5/12/1908	–	Reno. O-6 3353 9/1925.	189
1921	Baldwin	5/16/1908	–	Reno. O-6 3371 12/1926.	189
1922	Baldwin	5/12/1908	–	Renumbered GN 1905(2) at St.Paul 6/10/1908.	189
1923	Baldwin	5/16/1908	–	Renumbered GN 1906(2) at St.Paul 6/10/1908.	189
1924	Baldwin	5/25/1908	–	Renumbered GN 1907(2) at St.Paul 6/10/1908.	189

Tender Class M-2(2), Style 54 (Originally Class M-1): 13 Tons Coal (Later increased to 19 Tons; some equipped with 4,500 Gallon oil cisterns); 8,000 Gallons Water; 5½" x 10" Axle Journals. Some rebuilt to **Style 55** (10,000 Gallons Water) and some rebuilt to **Style 56** (10,000 Gallons Water; 6" x 11" Axle Journals).

No.	Builder	Date Rcvd.	Disposition	Notes
1950	Baldwin	3/7/1910	Sold for scrap DI&M 1/8/1955 (St. 54).	194
1951	Baldwin	1/19/1910	Reno. X3340 (WC) 8/1948. Ret. 10/1958.	194, 355
1952	Baldwin	1/17/1910	Reno. X1912(3) (WC) 10/1952. Ret. 7/1969	194
1953	Baldwin	1/19/1910	Sold for scrap WEI&M 12/1949.	194
1954	Baldwin	1/23/1910	Rblt. Style 56 at Devils Lake 6/30/1927. Sold for scrap DI&M 8/1953.	194
1955	Baldwin	2/5/1910	Reno. X1989(3) (WC) 7/1952. Ret. 7/1974 (St. 54).	194, 356
1956	Baldwin	2/5/1910	Reno. X1995(2) (WC) at Great Falls 7/4/1940. Ret. 5/1957 (St. 54).	358
1957	Baldwin	2/5/1910	Sold for scrap PC 9/14/1952 (St. 54).	
1958	Baldwin	2/15/1910	Sold for scrap PC 12/1949.	
1959	Baldwin	3/7/1910	Reno. X1908(4) (WC) at Great Falls 10/15/1947. Ret. 1/1958 (St. 54).	195, 359
1960	Baldwin	7/13/1910	Sold for scrap WEI&M c.1/1950.	
1961	Baldwin	7/13/1910	Sold for scrap PC 3/5/1949.	
1962	Baldwin	7/23/1910	Sold for scrap DI&M 3/11/1949 (St. 54).	196
1963	Baldwin	7/26/1910	Rblt. Style 56 at Dale Street 7/1927.	
1964	Baldwin	7/14/1910	Reno. X2851(3) (WC) 12/1946. Ret. 12/1958 (St. 54).	
1965	Baldwin	7/11/1910	Reno. X1990(3) (WC) 6/1953. Ret. 10/1984.	
1966	Baldwin	7/23/1910	Sold for scrap PC c.1/1950.	196
1967	Baldwin	7/27/1910	Rblt. Style 55 at Superior 4/6/1928. Sold for scrap PC 10/26/1951.	
1968	Baldwin	7/30/1910	Reno. X1932(3) (WC) 8/1949. Ret. 4/1964 (St. 54).	
1969	Baldwin	8/13/1910	Sold for scrap DI&M 10/16/1951 (St. 54).	
1970	Baldwin	8/22/1910	Sold Georgia Car & Locomotive Co. 1/1942.	
1971	Baldwin	8/22/1910	Sold for scrap DI&M 10/16/1951.	
1972	Baldwin	8/22/1910	Reno. X1916(3) (WC) at Great Falls 3/4/1948. Ret. 12/1960 (St. 54).	360
1973	Baldwin	9/1/1910	Sold for scrap DI&M c.1/1950 (St. 54).	
1974	Baldwin	8/28/1910	Sold for scrap PC c.1/1950.	
1975	Baldwin	9/2/1910	Sold for scrap PC c.1/1950.	
1976	Baldwin	9/8/1910	Reno. X2840(3) (WC) 10/1948. Ret. 1/1959 (St. 54).	
1977	Baldwin	9/5/1910	Scrapped at Superior 10/5/1940.	197
1978	Baldwin	9/1/1910	Sold Otter Tail Power Company (with E3328) 4/29/1947.	
1979	Baldwin	9/9/1910	Sold for scrap PC c.1/1950.	
1980	Baldwin	9/15/1910	Dismantled 5/18/1948 (St. 54). Rblt. X864(3) (40FWC) 7/1949. Ret. 4/1958.	
1981	Baldwin	9/18/1910	Sold for scrap WEI&M 1/1955 (St. 54).	
1982	Baldwin	9/18/1910	Sold for scrap PC 10/18/1951 (St. 54).	
1983	Baldwin	9/15/1910	Rblt. Style 56 at Dale Street 11/19/1927. Sold for scrap DI&M 4/26/1952.	
1984	Baldwin	10/10/1910	Reno. X2849(2) (WC) 12/1949. Ret. 5/1966 (St. 54).	198, 332

Tender Class M-2(1), Style Unassigned: 13 Tons Coal; 8,000 Gallons Water; 5½" x 10" Axle Journals

No.	Builder	Original No.	Disposition
1999	Baldwin	GN 1254	Reno. 871 at Willmar 12/3/1925 in error. Reno. C-4 870(1) at Dale Street 12/22/1925.
2000(1)	Baldwin	GN 1254	Reno. GN 1999 at Great Falls 4/23/1912.

Tender Class N-2, Style 57 (Originally Class N-1): 13 Tons Coal (Later rebuilt to 19 Tons; some equipped with 4,500 Gallon oil cistern); 8,000 Gallons Water; 5½" x 10" Axle Journals. Some rebuilt to **Style 58** (10,000 Gallons Water) and to **Style 59** (10,000 Gallons Water; 6" x 11" Axle Journals).

No.	Builder	Date Rcvd.	Disposition	Notes
2000(2)	Baldwin	9/13/1912	Sold for scrap DI&M 1/29/1956.	
2001	Baldwin	9/13/1912	Reno. X1988(3), date unknown. Ret. 7/1959.	361
2002	Baldwin	9/13/1912	Donated American Korean Foundation (for Korean National Railways) (with E1130) 10/1954 (St. 57).	
2003	Baldwin	9/18/1912	Reno. X2836(2) (WC) 4/17/1945. Ret. 9/1967 (St. 57).	
2004	Baldwin	9/13/1912	Sold for scrap DI&M c.1/1950.	
2005	Baldwin	9/18/1912	Reno. X3209 (WC) at St.Cloud 3/27/1942. Ret. 11/1964 (St. 57).	
2006	Baldwin	9/23/1912	Sold for scrap DI&M 3/4/1947.	
2007	Baldwin	9/26/1912	Rblt. Style 58 at Dale Street 2/25/1927. Rblt. Style 59 at Dale Street 9/19/1929. Apparently rblt. back to Style 58 at some time, and then rblt. Style 59 again 7/25/1942. Sold for scrap DI&M 5/5/1953.	
2008	Baldwin	9/27/1912	Rblt. Style 59 at Dale Street 12/31/1929. Rblt. X1569(2) (WP) 3/10/1953. Reno. BN 972546 1/1980. Sold Smith Brothers 2/15/1989.	
2009	Baldwin	10/2/1912	Sold for scrap DI&M 5/7/1953 (St. 57).	
2010	Baldwin	10/12/1912	Rblt. Style 58 at Dale Street 5/20/1927. Sold for scrap PC 4/26/1952.	
2011	Baldwin	10/12/1912	Rblt. Style 59 at Dale Street 3/1927. Sold for scrap PC 6/6/1953.	
2012	Baldwin	10/7/1912	Sold for scrap DI&M c.1/1950.	
2013	Baldwin	10/10/1912	Rblt. Style 58 at Superior 8/6/1927. Ret. 8/1955. Sold for scrap DI&M 10/20/1955.	
2014	Baldwin	10/13/1912	Rblt. Style 58 at Dale Street 4/20/1929. Reno. X1596 (CHEM) 4/1950. Ret. 6/1960.	
2015	Baldwin	10/17/1912	Rblt. Style 58 (13 tons coal) at Dale Street 8/23/1927. Rblt. X1587 (WP) 10/4/1951. Sold PC 12/1976.	
2016	Baldwin	10/17/1912	Rblt. Style 59 at Dale Street 3/1927. Sold for scrap PC 4/26/1952.	
2017	Baldwin	11/2/1912	Rblt. Style 58 (13 tons coal) at Dale Street 5/25/1927. Rblt. Style 59 6/24/1942. Sold for scrap NSRM 11/1953.	
2018	Baldwin	10/23/1912	Rblt. Style 58 at Havre 1/31/1927. Reno. X1930(3) (WC) 10/1952. Ret. 5/1964.	376
2019	Baldwin	11/6/1912	Reno. X1996(2) (WC) at Havre 7/1/1940. Ret. 4/1947.	

Tender Class N-2, Style 57 (Originally Class N-1): Continued

No.	Builder	Date Rcvd.	Disposition
2020	Baldwin	10/25/1912	Sold for scrap PC 12/1949.
2021	Baldwin	10/27/1912	Reno. X940(3) (WC) 8/20/1941. Reno. X3239 12/1942. Ret. 7/1958 (St. 57).
2022	Baldwin	11/3/1912	Rblt. Style 58 at Delta 2/10/1927. Sold for scrap DI&M 5/3/1952.
2023	Baldwin	10/27/1912	Rblt. Style 59 at Great Falls 6/27/1929. Sold for scrap DI&M 8/28/1952.
2024	Baldwin	11/3/1912	Sold for scrap DI&M 10/1947.

Tender Class —, Style 112: 24 Tons Coal (May have had 5,800 Gallon oil cistern); 17,000 Gallons Water; 6½" x 12" Axle Journals

No.	Builder	Date Rcvd.	Disposition
2029	GN (Dale Street)	12/31/1928	Ret. 4/1958. Sold for scrap DI&M 12/1962.

Tender Class R-1, Style 108: 5,800 Gallons Oil; 17,000 Gallons Water; 6½" x 12" Axle Journals

No.	Builder	Date Rcvd.	Disposition	Notes
2030	Baldwin	8/5/1925	Ret. 8/1956. Sold for scrap DI&M 9/16/1956.	
2031	Baldwin	8/22/1925	Reno. X3343 (WC) at Hillyard 6/15/1950. Reno. X1940(5) (RT) at Essex 8/24/1950. Ret. 6/1960.	362
2032	Baldwin	8/24/1925	Sold for scrap PC 11/20/1955.	
2033	Baldwin	8/31/1925	Ret. 3/1958. Sold for scrap PC 2/1963.	
2034(2)	GN (Hillyard)	11/21/1927	Sold for scrap DI&M 11/20/1955.	
2035(2)	GN (Hillyard)	12/12/1927	Sold for scrap PC 12/10/1962.	
2036(2)	GN (Hillyard)	1/16/1928	Ret. 8/1956. Sold for scrap PC 9/6/1956.	
2037(2)	GN (Hillyard)	2/6/1928	Sold for scrap WEI&M 8/16/1956.	
2038(2)	GN (Hillyard)	7/19/1928	Ret. 8/1956. Sold for scrap DI&M 9/8/1956.	
2039(2)	GN (Hillyard)	8/9/1928	Ret. 3/1958. Sold for scrap DI&M 2/1963.	
2040(2)	GN (Hillyard)	9/4/1928	Sold for scrap PC 8/16/1956.	
2041(2)	GN (Hillyard)	9/24/1928	Ret. 8/1956. Sold for scrap PC 11/25/1956.	
2042(2)	GN (Hillyard)	10/26/1928	Sold for scrap DI&M 5/6/1956.	
2043(2)	GN (Hillyard)	11/21/1928	Sold for scrap PC 8/16/1956.	

Tender Class —, Style 114: 24 Tons Coal (Some equipped with 5,700 Gallon oil cistern); 21,500 Gallons Water; 6½" x 12" Axle Journals

No.	Builder	Date Built	Original No.	Renumbered From	Date	Disposition
2034(1)	GAC	6/1926	–	–	–	Reno. 2051(1) 11/14/1927.
2035(1)	GAC	7/1926	–	–	–	Reno. 2052(1) 11/22/1927.
2036(1)	GAC	7/1926	–	–	–	Reno. 2053(1) 11/2/1927.
2037(1)	GAC	7/1926	–	–	–	Reno. 2054(1) 11/2/1927.
2038(1)	GAC	7/1926	–	–	–	Reno. 2055(1) 11/2/1927.
2039(1)	GAC	8/1926	–	–	–	Reno. 2056(1) 11/2/1927.
2040(1)	GAC	8/1926	–	–	–	Reno. 2057(1) 11/2/1927.
2041(1)	GAC	8/1926	–	–	–	Reno. 2058(1) 10/31/1927.
2042(1)	GAC	8/1926	–	–	–	Reno. 2059(1) 11/2/1927.
2043(1)	GAC	8/1926	–	–	–	Reno. 2060 11/2/1927.
2044(1)	GAC	9/1926	–	–	–	Reno. 2210(2) 11/11/1930.
2045(1)	GAC	9/1926	–	–	–	Reno. 2211(2) 11/13/1930.
2046(1)	GAC	9/1926	–	–	–	Reno. 2212(2) 11/7/1930.
2047(1)	GAC	9/1926	–	–	–	Reno. 2213(2) 11/11/1930.
2048(1)	GAC	9/1926	–	–	–	Reno. 2214(2) 11/11/1930.
2049(1)	GAC	9/1926	–	–	–	Reno. 2215(2) 11/11/1930.
2050(1)	GAC	9/1926	–	–	–	Reno. 2216(2) 11/30/1930.
2051(1)	GAC	6/1926	2034(1)	2034(1)	11/14/1927	Reno. 2217(2) 11/11/1930.
2052(1)	GAC	7/1926	2035(1)	2035(1)	11/22/1927	Reno. 2218(2) 11/7/1930.
2053(1)	GAC	7/1926	2036(1)	2036(1)	11/2/1927	Reno. 2219(2) 12/9/1930.
2054(1)	GAC	7/1926	2037(1)	2037(1)	11/2/1927	Reno. 2220(2) 11/11/1930.
2055(1)	GAC	7/1926	2038(1)	2038(1)	11/2/1927	Reno. 2221(2) 11/11/1930.
2056(1)	GAC	8/1926	2039(1)	2039(1)	11/2/1927	Reno. 2222(2) 11/15/1930.
2057(1)	GAC	8/1926	2040(1)	2040(1)	11/2/1927	Reno. 2223(2) 11/15/1930.
2058(1)	GAC	8/1926	2041(1)	2041(1)	10/31/1927	Reno. 2224(2) 11/4/1930.
2059(1)	GAC	8/1926	2042(1)	2042(1)	11/2/1927	Reno. 2225(2) 11/15/1930.
2060	GAC	8/1926	2043(1)	2043(1)	11/2/1927	Reno. 2226 11/13/1930.

Tender Class R-2, Style 109: 5,800 Gallons Oil; 22,000 Gallons Water; 6½" x 12" Axle Journals

No.	Builder	Date Built	Original No.	Renumbered From	Date	Disposition
2044(2)	GN (Hillyard)	5/14/1929	2210(1)	2210(1)	11/21/1930	Ret. 4/1956. Sold for scrap DI&M 6/10/1956.
2045(2)	GN (Hillyard)	6/1/1929	2211(1)	2211(1)	11/22/1930	Ret. 12/1957. Sold for scrap c.1962.
2046(2)	GN (Hillyard)	6/19/1929	2212(1)	2212(1)	11/21/1930	Ret. 12/1957. Sold for scrap PC 3/1962.
2047(2)	GN (Hillyard)	7/9/1929	2213(1)	2213(1)	11/21/1930	Ret. 5/1958. Sold for scrap PC 3/1963.
2048(2)	GN (Hillyard)	7/23/1929	2214(1)	2214(1)	11/21/1930	Ret. 12/1957. Sold for scrap PC 7/1962.
2049(2)	GN (Hillyard)	8/6/1929	2215(1)	2215(1)	11/21/1930	Ret. 12/1957. Sold for scrap c.1962.
2050(2)	GN (Hillyard)	8/21/1929	2216(1)	2216(1)	10/30/1930	Ret. 12/1957. Sold for scrap PC 7/1962.

2051(2)	GN (Hillyard)	9/4/1929	2217(1)	2217(1)	11/21/1930	Ret. 12/1957. Sold for scrap DI&M 3/1963.
2052(2)	GN (Hillyard)	9/16/1929	2218(1)	2218(1)	11/22/1930	Ret. 12/1957. Sold for scrap DI&M 3/1963.
2053(2)	GN (Hillyard)	9/27/1929	2219(1)	2219(1)	11/22/1930	Ret. 12/1957. Sold for scrap c.1962.
2054(2)	GN (Hillyard)	3/31/1930	2220(1)	2220(1)	11/24/1930	Ret. 5/1958. Sold for scrap DI&M (with E3383) 6/1963.
2055(2)	GN (Hillyard)	5/21/1930	2221(1)	2221(1)	11/11/1930	Ret. 5/1958. Sold for scrap 4/1963.
2056(2)	GN (Hillyard)	6/23/1930	2222(1)	2222(1)	11/21/1930	Ret. 5/1958. Sold for scrap DI&M (with E3396) 2/1963.
2057(2)	GN (Hillyard)	7/28/1930	2223(1)	2223(1)	11/23/1930	Reno. X1969(4) (WC) 8/1953. Ret. 6/1960.
2058(2)	GN (Hillyard)	9/6/1930	2224(1)	2224(1)	11/23/1930	Ret. 5/1958. Sold for scrap WEI&M 3/1963.
2059(2)	GN (Hillyard)	11/3/1930	2225(1)	2225(1)	11/23/1930	Ret. 4/1958. Sold for scrap 3/1963.

Tender Class —, Style 112: 24 Tons Coal (Some equipped with 5,800 Gallon oil cistern); 17,000 Gallons Water; 6½" x 12" Axle Journals

No.	Builder	Date Rcvd.	Disposition	Notes
2061	GN (Dale Street)	9/3/1927	Ret. 12/1957. Sold for scrap c.1962.	
2062	GN (Dale Street)	10/10/1927	Ret. 8/1956. Sold for scrap PC 11/4/1956.	
2063	GN (Dale Street)	10/22/1927	Ret. 3/1958. Sold for scrap PC 12/4/1962.	
2064	GN (Dale Street)	11/3/1927	Ret. 9/1955. Sold for scrap DI&M 11/12/1955.	
2065	GN (Dale Street)	11/14/1927	Ret. 12/1957. Sold for scrap c.1962.	
2066	GN (Dale Street)	11/28/1927	Ret. 3/1958. Sold for scrap PC 12/1962.	
2067	GN (Dale Street)	12/13/1927	Ret. 9/1955. Sold for scrap WEI&M 11/4/1955.	
2068	GN (Dale Street)	12/24/1927	Ret. 8/1956. Sold for scrap DI&M 9/23/1956.	
2069	GN (Dale Street)	3/31/1928	Ret. 9/1955. Sold for scrap DI&M 11/12/1955.	
2070	GN (Dale Street)	4/17/1928	Ret. 8/1956. Sold for scrap PC 9/6/1956.	
2071	GN (Dale Street)	5/5/1928	Ret. 4/1958. Sold for scrap 2/1963.	
2072	GN (Great Falls)	6/25/1928	Reno. X6011 (Diesel Fuel Service Car) 3/7/1958. Ret. 7/1961.	
2073	GN (Hillyard)	5/22/1928	Ret. 8/1956. Sold for scrap DI&M 11/11/1956.	
2074	GN (Hillyard)	5/31/1928	Ret. 12/1957. Sold for scrap c.1962.	
2075	GN (Hillyard)	6/9/1928	Ret. 3/1958. Sold for scrap 2/1963.	
2076	GN (Great Falls)	3/16/1928	Ret. 5/1958. Sold for scrap PC 1/1964.	
2077	GN (Hillyard)	4/20/1928	Ret. 9/1955. Sold for scrap PC 11/12/1955.	
2078	GN (Hillyard)	5/11/1928	Ret. 8/1956. Sold for scrap PC 8/16/1956.	
2079	GN (Dale Street)	5/1928	Ret. 4/1958. Sold for scrap PC 12/1962.	
2080	GN (Dale Street)	5/1928	Ret. 4/1958. Dismantled at St.Cloud 12/1960.	
2081	GN (Dale Street)	6/1928	Ret. 9/1955. Sold for scrap PC 11/12/1955.	
2082	GN (Dale Street)	7/1928	Ret. 12/1957. Sold for scrap PC 12/3/1962.	363
2083	GN (Dale Street)	8/1928	Ret. 12/1957. Sold for scrap PC 3/1962.	
2084	GN (Dale Street)	8/1928	Ret. 12/1957. Sold for scrap PC 12/1962.	
2085	GN (Hillyard)	8/1928	Ret. 12/1957. Sold for scrap c.1962.	
2086	GN (Dale Street)	9/1928	Ret. 5/1958. Sold for scrap PC 11/16/1956.	
2087	GN (Dale Street)	9/1928	Ret. 12/1957. Sold for scrap DI&M 12/10/1962.	
2088	GN (Dale Street)	9/1928	Ret. 9/1955. Sold for scrap DI&M 11/4/1955.	
2089	GN (Great Falls)	11/24/1928	Ret. 4/1956. Sold for scrap PC 5/20/1956.	
2090	GN (Great Falls)	12/22/1928	Reno. X6010 4/1957. Ret. 7/1959.	
2091	GN (Great Falls)	12/26/1928	Ret. 5/1958.	
2092	Baldwin	11/1925	Ret. 8/16/1956. Sold for scrap DI&M 10/7/1956.	
2093	Baldwin	11/1925	Ret. 8/16/1956. Sold for scrap DI&M 9/16/1956.	
2094	Baldwin	11/1925	Reno. X1994(3) (WC) 7/1953. Ret. 10/1961.	
2095	Baldwin	11/1925	Ret. 8/16/1956. Sold for scrap DI&M 10/7/1956.	
2096	Baldwin	11/1925	Ret. 12/1957. Sold for scrap c.1962.	
2097	Baldwin	11/1925	Ret. 8/16/1956. Sold for scrap DI&M 11/18/1956.	
2098	Baldwin	11/1925	Ret. 4/1958. Sold for scrap DI&M 12/6/1962.	
2099	Baldwin	11/1925	Ret. 10/7/1955. Sold for scrap DI&M 11/12/1955.	

Tender Class Q-1, Style 105: 25 Tons Coal (Some equipped with 5,800 Gallon oil cisterns); 15,000 Gallons Water; 6" x 11" Axle Journals

No.	Builder	Date Rcvd.	Disposition	Notes
2100	Baldwin	12/26/1923	Donated to National Museum of Transportation, St.Louis, MO, 1964 (last assigned to E2513).	
2101	Baldwin	12/28/1923	Ret. 12/1957. Sold for scrap c.1962.	
2102	Baldwin	12/28/1923	Ret. 12/1957. Sold for scrap PC 6/1962.	
2103	Baldwin	12/28/1923	Ret. 8/1956. Sold for scrap WEI&M 9/12/1956.	
2104	Baldwin	12/28/1923	Reno. X1981(3) (WC) 8/1952. Ret. 4/1959.	
2105	Baldwin	12/28/1923	Sold SP&S (with E2507) for display at Maryhill, WA. Dedicated 9/3/1966.	
2106	Baldwin	2/6/1924	Ret. 12/1957. Sold for scrap c.1962.	
2107	Baldwin	1/9/1924	Sold for scrap PC 6/27/1956.	364
2108	Baldwin	1/9/1924	Sold Erie Mining Co. (with Q-1 locomotive) 12/13/1954.	
2109	Baldwin	1/9/1924	Ret. 12/1957. Sold for scrap c.1962.	
2110	Baldwin	1/9/1924	Ret. 12/1957. Sold for scrap c.1962.	
2111	Baldwin	1/11/1924	Ret. 4/1958. Sold for scrap 5/1963.	
2112	Baldwin	1/11/1924	Ret. 12/1957. Sold for scrap WEI&M 7/1963.	
2113	Baldwin	1/13/1924	Ret. 4/1956. Reno. X6900 10/1956. Ret. 7/1965.	
2114	Baldwin	1/11/1924	Ret. 8/1955. Sold for scrap DI&M 9/1955.	
2115	Baldwin	1/11/1924	Ret. 4/1958.	
2116	Baldwin	1/16/1924	Dismantled 6/10/1948.	
2117	Baldwin	1/16/1924	Sold Erie Mining Co. (with Q-1 locomotive) 12/13/1954.	
2118	Baldwin	1/16/1924	Ret. 4/1956. Sold for scrap DI&M 5/6/1956.	

Tender Class Q-1, Style 105: Continued

No.	Builder	Date Rcvd.	Disposition
2119	Baldwin	1/16/1924	Sold for scrap PC 11/26/1955.
2120	Baldwin	1/16/1924	Ret. 3/1958. Sold for scrap DI&M 12/1962.
2121	Baldwin	1/18/1924	Ret. 12/1957. Sold for scrap c.1962.
2122	Baldwin	1/18/1924	Ret. 4/1956. Sold for scrap DI&M 6/17/1956.
2123	Baldwin	1/18/1924	Ret. 4/1956. Sold for scrap DI&M 6/24/1956.
2124	Baldwin	1/18/1924	Ret. 4/1956. Sold for scrap PC 4/23/1956.
2125	Baldwin	1/18/1924	Ret. 4/1956. Sold for scrap PC 5/6/1956.
2126	Baldwin	1/18/1924	Sold for scrap PC 11/26/1955.
2127	Baldwin	2/4/1924	Reno. X1929(3) (WC) 10/1952. Ret. 10/1959.
2128	Baldwin	2/6/1924	Sold for scrap PC 1/29/1956.
2129	Baldwin	2/6/1924	Sold for scrap PC 10/31/1955.

Tender Class Q-2, Style 106 and Style 107: 24 Tons Coal (Style 106) or 5,800 Gallons Oil (Style 107); 17,000 Gallons Water; 6½" x 12" Axle Journals

No.	Builder	Date Built	Disposition
2175	GN (Hillyard)	6/22/1928	Reno. X6703 9/1955. Lost car 3/30/1889.
2176	GN (Great Falls)	6/27/1928	Ret. 5/1958. Sold for scrap DI&M 5/1962.
2177	GN (Dale Street)	6/26 1928	Ret. 12/1957. Sold for scrap 6/1962.
2178	GN (Hillyard)	7/23/1928	Ret. 4/1958. Sold for scrap PC 12/3/1962.
2179	GN (Hillyard)	8/16/1928	Ret. 5/1958. Sold for scrap 3/1963.
2180	GN (Great Falls)	7/27/1928	Ret. 12/1957. Sold for scrap DI&M (with E3382) 5/1962.
2181	GN (Great Falls)	8/24/1928	Sold for scrap 2/1963.
2182	GN (Dale Street)	7/31/1928	Ret. 4/1956. Sold for scrap PC 5/27/1956.
2183	GN (Great Falls)	9/22/1928	Ret. 4/1958. Sold for scrap 12/4/1962.
2184	GN (Great Falls)	10/30/1928	Reno. X1955(3) (RT) 10/3/1951. Lost car 10/25/1989.
2185	GN (Hillyard)	10/10/1928	Ret. 12/1957. Sold for scrap c.1962.
2186	GN (Dale Street)	8/31/1928	Ret. 4/1956. Sold for scrap PC 11/16/1956.
2187	GN (Hillyard)	11/13/1928	Ret. 4/1956. Sold for scrap DI&M 4/19/1956.
2188	GN (Dale Street)	9/29/1928	Ret. 3/1958. Sold for scrap DI&M 12/10/1962.
2189	GN (Dale Street)	10/31/1928	Ret. 12/1957. Sold for scrap PC 10/1963.
2190	GN (Hillyard)	2/21/1930	Reno. T3375 at Minot 10/27/1930.

Tender Class —, Style 113: 24 Tons Coal (Some equipped with 5,800 Gallon oil cisterns); 22,000 Gallons Water; 6½" x 12" Axle Journals

No.	Builder	Date Built	Disposition	Notes
2194	GN (Great Falls)	7/5/1930	Ret. 12/1957. Sold for scrap DI&M 2/1963.	
2195	GN (Great Falls)	9/13/1930	Ret. 12/1957. Sold for scrap c.1962.	
2196	GN (Great Falls)	11/8/1930	Ret. 12/1957. Sold for scrap c.1962.	
2197	GN (Great Falls)	10/16/1929	Ret. 3/1958. Sold for scrap WEI&M 9/1962.	
2198	GN (Great Falls)	12/1929	Ret. 12/1957. Sold for scrap c.1962.	
2199	GN (Great Falls)	12/1929	Ret. 3/1958. Sold for scrap DI&M 9/1963.	
2200	GN (Dale Street)	6/1929	Reno. X1823 (FC) 10/1954. Ret. 6/24/1883. Sold Schnitzer Steel Products 7/27/1883.	
2201	GN (Dale Street)	7/1929	Ret. 12/1957. Sold for scrap c.1962.	
2202	GN (Dale Street)	7/1929	Ret. 12/1957. Sold for scrap PC 6/1962.	
2203	GN (Dale Street)	7/1929	Ret. 3/1958. Sold for scrap WEI&M 10/1963.	
2204	GN (Great Falls)	6/1929	Ret. 2/1950. Reno. X1939(3) (WC) 4/1950. Ret. 5/1968.	365
2205	GN (Great Falls)	7/1929	Ret. 12/1957. Sold for scrap c.1962.	
2206	GN (Great Falls)	8/1929	Ret. 3/1958. Sold for scrap WEI&M 7/1963.	
2207	GN (Hillyard)	7/1929	Ret. 3/1958. Sold for scrap WEI&M 6/1963.	
2208	GN (Hillyard)	9/1929	Ret. 5/1958. Sold for scrap DI&M (with E3399) 4/1959.	
2209	GN (Hillyard)	9/1929	Ret. 3/1958. Sold for scrap PC 11/1963.	

Tender Class R-2, Style 109: 5,800 Gallons Oil; 22,000 Gallons Water; 6½" x 12" Axle Journals

No.	Builder	Date Built	Disposition
2210(1)	GN (Hillyard)	5/14/1929	Reno. 2044(2) 11/21/1930.
2211(1)	GN (Hillyard)	6/1/1929	Reno. 2045(2) 11/22/1930.
2212(1)	GN (Hillyard)	6/19/1929	Reno. 2046(2) 11/21/1930.
2213(1)	GN (Hillyard)	7/9/1929	Reno. 2047(2) 11/21/1930.
2214(1)	GN (Hillyard)	7/23/1929	Reno. 2048(2) 11/21/1930.
2215(1)	GN (Hillyard)	8/6/1929	Reno. 2049(2) 11/21/1930.
2216(1)	GN (Hillyard)	8/21/1929	Reno. 2050(2) 10/30/1930.
2217(1)	GN (Hillyard)	9/4/1929	Reno. 2051(2) 11/21/1930.
2218(1)	GN (Hillyard)	9/16/1929	Reno. 2052(2) 11/22/1930.
2219(1)	GN (Hillyard)	9/27/1929	Reno. 2053(2) 11/22/1930.
2220(1)	GN (Hillyard)	3/31/1930	Reno. 2054(2) 11/24/1930.
2221(1)	GN (Hillyard)	5/21/1930	Reno. 2055(2) 11/11/1930.
2222(1)	GN (Hillyard)	6/23/1930	Reno. 2056(2) 11/21/1930.
2223(1)	GN (Hillyard)	7/28/1930	Reno. 2057(2) 11/23/1930.
2224(1)	GN (Hillyard)	9/6/1930	Reno. 2058(2) 11/23/1930.
2225(1)	GN (Hillyard)	11/3/1930	Reno. 2059(2) 11/23/1930.

Tender Class —, Style 114: 24 Tons Coal (Some equipped with 5,700 Gallon oil cistern); 21,500 Gallons Water; 6½" x 12" Axle Journals

No.	Builder	Date Built	Original No.	Renumbered From	Date	Disposition
2210(2)	GAC	8/1926	2044(1)	2044(1)	11/11/1930	Ret. 12/1957. Sold for scrap c.1962.
2211(2)	GAC	9/1926	2045(1)	2045(1)	11/13/1930	Ret. 9/1955. Sold for scrap PC 10/27/1955.
2212(2)	GAC	9/1926	2046(1)	2046(1)	11/7/1930	Ret. 9/1955. Sold for scrap DI&M 10/24/1955.
2213(2)	GAC	9/1926	2047(1)	2047(1)	11/11/1930	Ret. 3/1958. Reno. X7601 (CHEM) 5/1962. Ret. 12/1969.
2214(2)	GAC	9/1926	2048(1)	2048(1)	11/11/1930	Ret. 9/1955. Sold for scrap DI&M 10/24/1955.
2215(2)	GAC	9/1926	2049(1)	2049(1)	11/11/1930	Ret. 8/1956. Sold for scrap PC 9/6/1956.
2216(2)	GAC	9/1926	2050(1)	2050(1)	11/30/1930	Ret. 12/1957. Reno. X1826 (FC) 9/1963. Ret. 11/28/1984. Sold J.B. Enterprises 5/1/1985.
2217(2)	GAC	6/1926	2034(1)	2051(1)	11/11/1930	Ret. 12/1957.
2218(2)	GAC	7/1926	2035(1)	2052(1)	11/7/1930	Ret. 8/1956. Sold for scrap PC 9/12/1956.
2219(2)	GAC	7/1926	2036(1)	2053(1)	12/9/1930	Ret. 3/1958. Sold for scrap DI&M 9/1963.
2220(2)	GAC	7/1926	2037(1)	2054(1)	11/11/1930	Ret. 12/1957. Sold for scrap c.1962.
2221(2)	GAC	7/1926	2038(1)	2055(1)	11/11/1930	Ret. 12/1957. Reno. X1827 (FC) 9/1963. Ret. 5/7/1990. Donated Province of Alberta 6/12/1990.
2222(2)	GAC	8/1926	2039(1)	2056(1)	11/15/1930	Ret. 8/1956. Sold for scrap DI&M 10/7/1956.
2223(2)	GAC	8/1926	2040(1)	2057(1)	11/15/1930	Ret. 12/1957. Sold for scrap c.1962.
2224(2)	GAC	8/1926	2041(1)	2058(1)	11/4/1930	Ret. 9/1955. Sold for scrap DI&M 10/27/1955.
2225(2)	GAC	8/1926	2042(1)	2059(1)	11/15/1930	Ret. 8/1956. Sold for scrap DI&M 10/7/1956.
2226	GAC	8/1926	2043(1)	2060	11/13/1930	Ret. 3/19/1958. Reno. X7602 (CHEM) 5/1962. Reno. X1830 (FC) 4/1969. Ret. 5/25/1983. Sold Schnitzer Steel Products 7/27/1983.

Tender Class P-2, Style 104: 5,800 Gallons Oil; 12,000 Gallons Water; 6" x 11" Axle Journals

No.	Builder	Date Rcvd.	Disposition	Notes
2500	Baldwin	10/10/1923	Sold for scrap PC 1/29/1955.	
2501	Baldwin	10/10/1923	Ret. 4/1958. Sold for scrap PC 12/1962.	
2502	Baldwin	10/15/1923	Ret. 4/1955. Sold for scrap DI&M 5/28/1955.	
2503	Baldwin	10/20/1923	Sold for scrap PC 3/7/1947.	
2504	Baldwin	10/20/1923	Ret. 8/1955. Sold for scrap PC 10/3/1955.	
2505	Baldwin	10/24/1923	Sold for scrap WEI&M 1/9/1956.	
2506	Baldwin	10/24/1923	Sold for scrap PC 10/16/1955.	
2507	Baldwin	11/2/1923	Ret. 8/1955. Sold for scrap PC 10/3/1955.	
2508	Baldwin	10/30/1923	Sold SP&S (with E1378) 10/1944.	366
2509	Baldwin	10/31/1923	Sold for scrap DI&M 1/21/1955.	
2510	Baldwin	11/5/1923	Ret. 4/1955. Sold for scrap WEI&M 6/4/1955.	
2511	Baldwin	11/5/1923	Ret. 8/1955. Sold for scrap DI&M 10/10/1955.	
2512	Baldwin	11/9/1923	Sold for scrap DI&M 1/21/1955.	
2513	Baldwin	11/14/1923	Sold for scrap PC 12/12/1955.	
2514	Baldwin	11/17/1923	Sold for scrap DI&M 11/12/1955.	
2515	Baldwin	11/18/1923	Ret. 4/1955. Sold for scrap WEI&M 5/17/1955.	
2516	Baldwin	11/27/1923	Sold for scrap DI&M 11/12/1955.	
2517	Baldwin	11/27/1923	Ret. 12/1957. Sold for scrap c.1962.	
2518	Baldwin	11/9/1923	Ret. 4/1955. Sold for scrap PC 11/4/1955.	
2519	Baldwin	11/14/1923	Ret. 8/1955. Sold for scrap PC 11/4/1955.	
2520	Baldwin	11/27/1923	Sold for scrap WEI&M 11/20/1955.	
2521	Baldwin	12/4/1923	Ret. 4/1956. Sold for scrap WEI&M 5/20/1956.	
2522	Baldwin	12/7/1923	Sold for scrap PC 7/12/1955.	
2523	Baldwin	12/7/1923	Ret. 4/1956. Sold for scrap DI&M 5/27/1956.	
2524	Baldwin	12/17/1923	Ret. 4/1955. Sold for scrap PC 6/10/1955.	
2525	Baldwin	12/17/1923	Sold for scrap PC 1/21/1955.	
2526	Baldwin	12/29/1923	Sold for scrap PC 10/31/1955.	
2527	Baldwin	12/29/1923	Ret. 3/1958. Sold for scrap PC 10/1963.	

Tender Class S-1, Style 110: 5,800 Gallons Oil; 22,000 Gallons Water; 6½" x 12" Axle Journals

No.	Builder	Date Built	Disposition	Notes
2550	Baldwin	4/1929	Ret. 12/1957. Sold for scrap DI&M 9/1963 or PC 10/1963.	206
2551	Baldwin	4/1929	Ret. 12/1957. Sold for scrap c.1962.	206
2552	Baldwin	5/1929	Ret. 12/1957. Sold for scrap PC 9/1963.	206
2553	Baldwin	5/1929	Ret. 4/1958. Sold for scrap 9/1963.	206
2554	Baldwin	5/1929	Ret. 5/1958. Sold for scrap WEI&M 9/1962.	206
2555	Baldwin	5/1929	Ret. 12/1957. Sold for scrap PC 7/1963.	206

Tender Class S-2, Style 111: 5,800 Gallons Oil; 17,250 Gallons Water; 6½" x 12" Axle Journals

No.	Builder	Date Rcvd.	Disposition
2575	Baldwin	3/11/1930	Reno. X1824 (FC) 9/1955. Reno. BN 973165 2/1982. Ret. 3/13/1984. Donated Pacific Railroad Preservation Association 2/24/1986 [used as auxiliary tender with SP&S 4-8-4].
2576	Baldwin	3/12/1930	Rblt. X6000 (Tank) (with T2586) 1/1957. Ret. 7/1959.
2577	Baldwin	3/17/1930	Rblt. X6001 (Tank) (with T2583) 2/1958. Ret. 6/1968.
2578	Baldwin	3/17/1930	Rblt. X6002 (Tank) (with T2581) 2/1958. Ret. 6/1968.
2579	Baldwin	3/18/1930	Ret. 5/1958. Sold for scrap DI&M 6/1963.
2580	Baldwin	3/18/1930	Ret. 4/1958. Sold for scrap 9/1963.
2581	Baldwin	3/21/1930	Rblt. X6002 (Tank) (With T2578) 2/1958. Ret. 6/1968.
2582	Baldwin	3/21/1930	Ret. 5/1958. Sold for scrap DI&M 10/1963.
2583	Baldwin	3/25/1930	Rblt. X6001 (Tank) (with T2577) 2/1958. Ret. 6/1968.
2584	Baldwin	3/25/1930	Ret. 5/1958. Sold for scrap c.1962.
2585	Baldwin	4/1/1930	Ret. 5/1958. Reno. X1825 (FC) 4/1962. Ret. 6/24/1983. Sold Schnitzer Steel Products 7/27/1983.
2586	Baldwin	4/1/1930	Rblt. X6000 (Tank) (with T2576) 1/1957. Ret. 7/1959.
2587	Baldwin	4/10/1930	Ret. 4/1958. Sold for scrap 9/1963.
2588	Baldwin	4/10/1930	Ret. 5/1958. Sold for scrap PC 11/1963.

Tender Class —, Style 115: 20 Tons Coal (5,800 Gallons Oil); 12,000 Gallons Water; 6" x 11" Axle Journals

No.	Builder	Date Built	Disposition
2596	Baldwin	3/1924	Sold for scrap DI&M 2/5/1955.
2597	Baldwin	3/1924	Ret. 4/1955. Sold for scrap PC 5/28/1955.
2598	Baldwin	3/1924	Reno. X1822 (FC) 2/1953. Sold T.T. Tuttle 9/1983.
2599	Baldwin	3/1924	Ret. 8/1955. Sold for scrap PC 9/7/1955.

Tender Class O-1, Style 62: 13 Tons Coal (Later increased to 19 Tons; some equipped with 4,500 Gallon oil cisterns); 8,000 Gallons Water; 5½" x 10" Axle Journals. Some rebuilt to **Style 65** (10,000 Gallons Water) and some rebuilt to **Style 69** (10,000 Gallons Water; 6" x 11" Axle Journals).

No.	Builder	Date Rcvd.	Disposition	Notes
3000	Baldwin	10/2/1911	Ret. 6/1948. Reno. X2826(2) (WC) 8/1948. Ret. 11/1958 (St. 62).	
3001	Baldwin	10/2/1911	Sold for scrap WEI&M c.1/1950.	
3002	Baldwin	10/4/1911	Sold for scrap DI&M c.1/1950.	
3003	Baldwin	10/4/1911	Reno. X2844(2) (WC) 8/1948. Ret. 11/1961 (St. 62).	
3004	Baldwin	10/7/1911	Rblt. Style 69 at Superior 6/24/1946. Sold for scrap DI&M 4/26/1952.	
3005	Baldwin	10/4/1911	Reno. X1934(2) (WC) at St.Cloud 12/31/1941. Reno. X3232 4/20/1942. Donated Minnesota Transportation Museum 2/1983 (St. 62).	
3006	Baldwin	10/4/1911	Sold for scrap DI&M 1/15/1955.	
3007	Baldwin	10/7/1911	Sold Georgia Car & Locomotive Co. 1/1942.	
3008	Baldwin	10/10/1911	Sold for scrap WEI&M c.1/1950.	
3009	Baldwin	10/10/1911	Reno. X3338 (WC) 7/1948. Ret. 3/1954 (St. 62).	
3010	Baldwin	10/9/1911	Reno. X1991(2) (WC) 6/1953. Lost car 3/2/1989 (St. 62).	367
3011	Baldwin	10/9/1911	Sold for scrap DI&M 10/16/1951.	
3012	Baldwin	10/18/1911	Reno. X1998(3) (WC) at Great Falls 4/13/1940. Ret. 5/1959 (St. 62).	368
3013	Baldwin	10/18/1911	Ret. 6/1948. Dismantled 7/15/1948. Rblt. to X3306 (40FWC) (with Boxcar 3380) 8/1948. Ret. 7/1958.	
3014	Baldwin	10/15/1911	Reno. X1999(2) (WC) at Bonners Ferry 7/25/1940. Ret. 2/1964 (St. 62).	
3015	Baldwin	10/15/1911	Rblt. Style 69 at Dale Street 4/28/1928. Sold for scrap PC 1/15/1955.	
3016	Baldwin	10/24/1911	Rblt. Style 69 at Dale Street 10/5/1940. Sold for scrap PC 4/30/1953.	
3017	Baldwin	10/24/1911	Rblt. Style 69 at Great Falls 2/29/1944. Sold for scrap PC 5/13/1953.	
3018	Baldwin	11/4/1911	Sold for scrap PC c.1/1950 (St. 62).	
3019	Baldwin	11/4/1911	Reno. X800(2) (WC) 11/1948. Ret. 2/1960.	369
3020	Baldwin	2/18/1913	Sold for scrap DI&M 5/16/1953 (St. 62).	
3021	Baldwin	2/18/1913	Rblt. Style 65 at Dale Street 3/12/1927. Sold for scrap DI&M 6/24/1953.	
3022	Baldwin	1/30/1913	Sold for scrap PC 10/18/1951 (St. 62).	
3023	Baldwin	1/30/1913	Reno. X941(3) (WC) at Great Falls 8/25/1941. Ret. 12/1957 (St. 62).	370
3024	Baldwin	2/15/1913	Reno. X1933(3) (WC) 12/22/1949. Sold Smith Brothers 2/1979 (St. 62).	371
3025	Baldwin	2/15/1913	Sold for scrap DI&M c.1/1950.	
3026	Baldwin	2/11/1913	Reno. X2825(2) (WC) at Great Falls 9/17/1940. Reno. X3244 4/28/1943. Ret. 3/2/1989 (St. 62).	372
3027	Baldwin	2/11/1913	Sold for scrap DI&M 10/22/1951 (St. 62).	
3028	Baldwin	2/10/1913	Sold for scrap PC 9/8/1952 (St. 62).	
3029	Baldwin	2/10/1913	Sold for scrap PC 11/10/1951 (St. 62).	
3030	Baldwin	2/15/1913	Reno. X2827(2) (WC) at Bonners Ferry 6/10/1940. Ret. 5/1959 (St. 62).	
3031	Baldwin	2/15/1913	Sold for scrap PC c.1/1950.	
3032	Baldwin	2/14/1913	Reno. X1918(3) (WC) at Great Falls 3/4/1948. Ret. 10/1964 (St. 62).	373
3033	Baldwin	2/14/1913	Sold for scrap DI&M 10/22/1951 (St. 62).	
3034	Baldwin	2/18/1913	Rblt. Style 69 at Dale Street 9/30/1927. Ret. 8/1955. Sold for scrap WEI&M 9/1955.	
3035	Baldwin	2/18/1913	Reno. X2812(2) (WC) at St.Cloud 12/11/1941. Reno. X3206 at Willmar 2/7/1942. Ret. 6/1968.	
3036	Baldwin	2/18/1913	Sold for scrap DI&M c.1/1950.	
3037	Baldwin	2/18/1913	Rblt. Style 65 at Dale Street 9/27/1927. Rblt. Style 69 at Dale Street 9/27/1929. Apparently rblt. back to Style 65,and then rblt. back to Style 69 at Superior 4/21/1942. Sold for scrap PC 5/16/1953.	
3038	Baldwin	2/18/1913	Sold for scrap DI&M c.1/1950.	

3039	Baldwin	2/18/1913	Sold for scrap DI&M 10/1950.
3040	Baldwin	2/20/1913	Rblt. Style 65 at Dale Street 7/26/1927. Sold for scrap DI&M 8/30/1952.
3041	Baldwin	2/20/1913	Reno. X2830(2) (WC) at St.Cloud 11/22/1941. Reno. X3230 at Willmar 4/21/1942. Ret. 9/1969 (St. 60).
3042	Baldwin	3/11/1913	Rblt. Style 65 (15 Tons Coal) at Delta 7/3/1928. Rblt. Style 69, date unknown. Sold for scrap PC 5/13/1953.
3043	Baldwin	3/11/1913	Rblt. Style 65 at Superior 6/28/1928. Reno. X2829(2) (WC) at Fort Benton, MT, 9/17/1940. Ret. 11/1962.
3044	Baldwin	3/11/1913	Dismantled at Great Falls 10/31/1930.

Tender Class O-1, Style Unassigned: 13 Tons Coal; 8,000 Gallons Water; 5½" x 10" Axle Journals. Rebuilt to 10,000 Gallon Water capacity c.1915 (?) for use with N-1 locomotives. Rebuilt to either **Style 66** (20 Tons Coal; 10,000 Gallons Water) or to **Style 70** (20 Tons Coal; 10,000 Gallons Water; 6" x 11" Axle Journals).

No.	Builder	Date Rcvd.	Disposition
3045	Baldwin	3/11/1913	Rblt. Style 70 at Hillyard 11/24/1926. Sold for scrap DI&M 8/1953.
3046	Baldwin	2/26/1913	Rblt. Style 66, date unknown. Rblt. Style 70 4/1927. Sold for scrap PC 1/8/1955.
3047	Baldwin	2/26/1913	Rblt. Style 70 at Dale Street 10/7/1926. Sold for scrap WEI&M 8/10/1953.
3048	Baldwin	3/13/1913	Rblt. Style 70 at Dale Street 5/14/1926. Sold for scrap DI&M 7/31/1953.
3049	Baldwin	3/13/1913	Rblt. Style 70 at Dale Street 7/12/1926. Sold for scrap DI&M 10/1950.
3050	Baldwin	2/27/1913	Rblt. Style 70 at Dale Street 11/2/1926. Sold for scrap DI&M 7/31/1953.
3051	Baldwin	2/27/1913	Rblt. Style 70 at Dale Street 3/11/1926. Sold for scrap DI&M 5/16/1953.
3052	Baldwin	3/7/1913	Rblt. Style 70 at Dale Street 2/5/1926. Sold for scrap PC 6/6/1953.
3053	Baldwin	3/7/1913	Rblt. Style 70 at Dale Street 7/1/1926. Sold for scrap DI&M 4/15/1952.
3054	Baldwin	3/8/1913	Rblt. Style 70 at Dale Street 10/30/1926. Sold for scrap PC 5/21/1953.
3055	Baldwin	3/8/1913	Rblt. Style 70 at Dale Street 12/16/1926. Sold for scrap DI&M 5/1/1952.
3056	Baldwin	3/8/1913	Rblt. Style 70 2/1927. Sold for scrap WEI&M 1/15/1955.
3057	Baldwin	3/8/1913	Rblt. Style 70 at Dale Street 4/3/1926. Sold for scrap PC 6/6/1953.
3058	Baldwin	3/13/1913	Rblt. Style 70 6/1927. Ret. 4/1955. Sold for scrap DI&M 6/4/1955.
3059	Baldwin	3/13/1913	Rblt. Style 70 at Dale Street 3/23/1926. Sold for scrap DI&M 5/13/1953.
3060	Baldwin	3/7/1913	Rblt. Style 70 at Dale Street 6/15/1927. Ret. 8/1955. Sold for scrap DI&M 10/20/1955.
3061	Baldwin	3/7/1913	Rblt. Style 70 at Dale Street 8/21/1926. Sold for scrap DI&M 1/15/1955.
3062	Baldwin	3/21/1913	Rblt. Style 70 at Delta 6/15/1927. Ret. 12/1956.
3063	Baldwin	3/21/1913	Rblt. Style 66, date unknown. Ret. 4/1955. Sold for scrap DI&M 6/10/1955.
3064	Baldwin	3/7/1913	Rblt. Style 70 at Dale Street 5/7/1926. Sold for scrap PC 6/6/1953.
3065	Baldwin	3/7/1913	Rblt. Style 70 at Delta 12/24/1926. Rblt. Style 66, date unknown. Rblt. Style 70 at Delta 1/18/1927. Sold for scrap DI&M 2/12/1955.
3066	Baldwin	3/11/1913	Rblt. Style 70 at Dale Street 3/8/1926. Sold for scrap PC 5/28/1953.
3067	Baldwin	3/11/1913	Rblt. Style 70 at Dale Street 7/1/1926. Sold for scrap DI&M 4/30/1953.
3068	Baldwin	4/1/1913	Rblt. Style 70 at Delta 3/1/1927. Ret. 12/1956.
3069	Baldwin	4/1/1913	Rblt. Style 70 at Hillyard 12/20/1926. Sold for scrap DI&M 6/24/1953.

Tender Class O-1, Style 61: 13 Tons Coal (Later increased to 17 Tons; Some equipped with 4,500 Gallon oil cistern); 8,000 Gallons Water; 5½" x 10" Axle Journals. Some rebuilt to **Style 64** (10,000 Gallons Water).

No.	Builder	Date Rcvd.	Disposition	Notes
3070	Baldwin	10/6/1916	Rblt. Style 64 at Dale Street 7/26/1927. Sold for scrap PC 1/8/1955.	
3071	Baldwin	10/6/1916	Rblt. Style 64 at Dale Street 3/22/1928. 6" x 11" axle journals at Dale Street 10/24/1944. Rblt. X1585 (WP) 1/1951. Sold Dakota Hide & Fur 3/8/1984.	
3072	Baldwin	9/29/1916	Sold for scrap DI&M c.1950.	
3073	Baldwin	9/29/1916	Rblt. WC at Hillyard 8/30/1941. Reno. X1996(3) (WC) 6/1953. Ret. 6/1960 (St. 61).	
3074	Baldwin	9/29/1916	Reno. X3339 (WC) 7/1948. Ret. 1/1955 (St. 61).	
3075	Baldwin	10/16/1916	Reno. X3344 (WC) 5/1948. Ret. 11/1962 (St. 61).	
3076	Baldwin	10/16/1916	Sold for scrap PC c.1/1950 (St. 61).	
3077	Baldwin	10/17/1916	Rblt. Style 64, date unknown. 6" x 11" Axle journals at Superior 10/31/1942. Sold SP&S (with E3064) 9/1943.	
3078	Baldwin	10/17/1916	Rblt. Style 64 8/19/1927 at Dale Street. Ret. 8/1955. Sold for scrap DI&M 9/7/1955.	
3079	Baldwin	10/16/1916	Rblt. Style 64 5/12/1927 at Dale Street. 6" x 11" axle journals at Dale Street 11/21/1929. Rblt. X1583 (WP) 1/4/1951. Ret. 8/1968.	
3080	Baldwin	11/4/1916	Rblt. Style 64 (with 6" x 11" axle journals) at Superior 8/13/1942. Ret. 12/1957. Sold for scrap c.1962.	
3081	Baldwin	11/4/1916	Reno. X2856(3) (WC) at St.Cloud 11/17/1941. Reno. X3231 at Willmar 4/21/1942. Off roster between 6/1/1952 and 3/1958 (St. 61).	
3082	Baldwin	11/2/1916	Rblt. Style 64 at Dale Street 6/30/1927. Sold for scrap DI&M 8/30/1952.	
3083	Baldwin	11/2/1916	Rblt. Style 64 at Dale Street 8/29/1927. 6" x 11" axle journals 11/11/1942. Damaged beyond repair in fire at Bend, OR, 12/7/1942. Dismantled at Hillyard 4/1943.	
3084	Baldwin	11/4/1916	Rblt. Style 64 at Dale Street 6/22/1927. 6" x 11" axle journals at Minot 1/1943. Rblt. X1586 (WP) 2/1951. Sold Purdy 2/1983.	374
3085	Baldwin	11/4/1916	Rblt. Style 64 at Dale Street 5/18/1927. 6" x 11" axle journals at Great Falls 9/23/1943. Ret. 4/1955, sold for scrap PC.	
3086	Baldwin	11/9/1916	Rblt. Style 64 (with 6" x 11" axle journals) at Devils Lake 8/9/1927. 6" x 11" Axle journals removed at Dale Street 4/1928.	
3087	Baldwin	11/25/1916	Rblt. Style 64 (with 6" x 11" axle journals) at Superior 4/6/1929. Sold for scrap DI&M 7/31/1953.	
3088	Baldwin	11/25/1916	Rblt. Style 64 (with 6" x 11" axle journals) at Superior 5/28/1943. Sold for scrap PC 9/3/1952.	
3089	Baldwin	12/3/1916	Rblt. Style 64 at Superior 7/26/1929. Sold for scrap PC 1/14/1955.	
3090	Baldwin	12/3/1916	Sold for scrap WEI&M 9/14/1952 (St. 61).	
3091	Baldwin	12/22/1916	Rblt. Style 64 at Superior 2/7/1929. 6" x 11" axle journals at Dale Street 10/11/1941. Rblt. X1590 (WP) 10/25/1951. Sold JMD Salvage 2/1983.	
3092	Baldwin	12/16/1916	Rblt. Style 64 at Dale Street 3/18/1927. Sold for scrap DI&M 1/8/1955.	
3093	Baldwin	12/22/1916	Rblt. Style 64 (with 6" x 11" axle journals) 6/1927. Sold for scrap PC 5/3/1952.	
3094	Baldwin	12/16/1916	Rblt. Style 64 at Dale Street 1/12/1928. Sold for scrap PC c.1/1950.	

Tender Class O-1, Style 60: 13 Tons Coal (Later increased to 15 Tons; some equipped with 4,500 Gallon oil cisterns); 8,000 Gallons; 5½" x 10" Axle Journals. Some rebuilt to **Style 63** (10,000 Gallons) or to **Style 68** (17 Tons Coal; 10,000 Gallons Water; 6" x 11" Axle Journals). Note that some tenders may be been rebuilt to 10,000 Gallons with larger journals but not have had coal capacity increased. Style designation for this is uncertain, but listed as **Style 68** below.

No.	Builder	Date Rcvd.	Disposition	Notes
3095	Baldwin	9/11/1917	Rblt. Style 63 at Superior 9/30/1929. Rblt. Style 68 at Great Falls 9/16/1943. Sold for scrap DI&M 1/14/1955.	
3096	Baldwin	9/11/1917	Rblt. Style 68 at Superior 6/7/1929. Rblt. Style 63, date unknown. Rblt. Style 68 at Superior 1/23/1942. Sold for scrap DI&M 4/23/1952.	
3097	Baldwin	9/14/1917	Rblt. Style 63 at Dale Street 6/22/1927. Sold for scrap PC 5/20/1953.	
3098	Baldwin	9/14/1917	Rblt. Style 63 at Hillyard 8/11/1927. Sold for scrap DI&M 2/12/1955.	
3099	Baldwin	9/19/1917	Rblt. Style 63 at Great Falls 8/24/1929. Reno. X1935(3) (WC) 12/22/1949. Ret. 12/1964.	
3100	Baldwin	10/26/1917	Rblt. Style 63 at Great Falls 8/20/1927. Rblt. Style 68 at Dale Street 10/27/1945. Sold for scrap WEI&M 8/4/1953.	
3101	Baldwin	10/26/1917	Rblt. Style 63 at Great Falls 2/29/1928. Rblt. Style 68 11/1939. Sold for scrap PC 8/1953.	
3102	Baldwin	12/10/1917	Rblt. Style 68 at Superior 5/20/1944. Sold for scrap DI&M 4/18/1952.	
3103	Baldwin	12/20/1918	Rblt. Style 63, date unknown. Sold for scrap PC 12/1949.	207
3104	Baldwin	12/1/1918	Reno. X1968(2) (WC) 8/1933. Reno. X3293 8/13/1943. Off roster between 6/1/1952 and 3/1958 (St. 60).	207
3105	Baldwin	12/20/1918	Rblt. Style 63 10/30/1928 at Great Falls. Rblt. Style 68 9/1940. Sold for scrap PC 8/1953.	207
3106	Baldwin	12/7/1918	Rblt. Style 63, date unknown. Reno. X1953(2) (WC) 3/1933. Reno. X3291 8/14/1943. Off roster between 6/1/1952and 3/1958.	207
3107	Baldwin	6/5/1918	Reno. X2833(2) (WC) at Great Falls 5/16/1940. Reno. X3245 9/2/1943. Ret. 12/1960 (St. 60).	
3108	Baldwin	6/5/1918	Reno. X942 (WC) at Great Falls 8/29/1941. Ret. 5/1959 (St. 60).	
3109	Baldwin	6/1/1918	Reno. X1913(4) (WC) 11/1952. Ret. 2/1960.	375
3110	Baldwin	12/3/1918	Rblt. Style 63 at Dale Street 8/24/1927. Rblt. Style 68 at Dale Street 8/30/1941. Sold for scrap DI&M 5/13/1953.	207
3111	Baldwin	6/22/1918	Rblt. Style 63 at Great Falls 9/6/1927. Rblt. Style 68 7/16/1942. Sold for scrap PC 9/1953.	
3112	Baldwin	6/22/1918	Reno. X2834(2) (WC) at Havre 8/16/1940. Ret. 10/1963 (St. 60).	
3113	Baldwin	6/21/1918	Reno. X2835(2) (WC) at Great Falls 8/6/1940. Ret. 9/1957 (St. 60).	
3114	Baldwin	6/21/1918	Sold for scrap PC 9/27/1952 (Style 60).	
3115	Baldwin	7/4/1918	Reno. X3219 (WC) (coal pit enclosed) at Superior 5/11/1942. Ret. 1/1961.	
3116	Baldwin	7/20/1918	Reno. X1949(3) (WC) 3/1933. Reno. X3290 8/19/1943. Off roster between 6/1/1952 and 3/1958 (St. 60).	
3117	Baldwin	7/20/1918	Sold for scrap PC 4/20/1952.	
3118	Baldwin	7/22/1918	Rblt. Style 63 at Great Falls 5/31/1928. Rblt. Style 68 7/1942. Sold for scrap WEI&M 10/15/1955.	
3119	Baldwin	7/25/1918	Reno. X943(2) (WC) at Great Falls 8/23/1941. Reno. X3238 8/6/1942. Ret. 3/1959 (St. 60).	
3120	Baldwin	7/23/1918	Rblt. Style 63 at Great Falls 11/30/1927. Rblt. Style 68 9/1940. Reno. X1921(4) (WC) 10/1952. Ret. 8/1961.	376
3121	Baldwin	8/4/1918	Sold SP&S (with E3099) 3/1926.	
3122	Baldwin	8/18/1918	Reno. X2837(2) (WC) at Great Falls 5/16/1940. Reno. X3243 3/15/1943. Ret. 4/1984 (St. 60).	377
3123	Baldwin	8/18/1918	Rblt. Style 63 9/29/1928 at Great Falls. Rblt. Style 68 4/1941. Sold for scrap DI&M 8/1953.	
3124	Baldwin	9/3/1918	Scrapped at Superior 10/10/1940.	
3125	Baldwin	8/26/1918	Sold for scrap DI&M 10/1947.	
3126	Baldwin	8/26/1918	Reno. X2838(2) (WC) at Watertown 7/25/1940. Reno. X3296 8/14/1943. Off roster between 6/1/1952 and 3/1958 (St. 60).	
3127	Baldwin	9/20/1918	Rblt. Style 63 at Great Falls 2/11/1928. Rblt. Style 68 9/1937. Sold for scrap PC 6/6/1953.	
3128	Baldwin	9/20/1918	Rblt. WC (coal pit enclosed) 6/1940 at Hillyard. Reno. X1821 (FC) 10/1952. Ret. 4/1985.	378
3129	Baldwin	10/1/1918	Rblt. Style 63 at Great Falls 3/3/1927. Rblt. X1588 (WP) 9/28/1951. Ret. 7/1958.	
3130	Baldwin	10/1/1918	Reno. X2840(2) at Judith Gap 7/19/1940. Rblt. WC at Great Falls 12/11/1941. Reno. X3240 7/13/1943. Ret. 4/1962 (St. 60).	379
3131	Baldwin	10/27/1918	Rblt. Style 68 at Superior 8/12/1943. Sold for scrap DI&M 12/1949.	
3132	Baldwin	10/4/1918	Rblt. Style 63 at Hillyard 2/10/1928. Sold for scrap PC 8/1953.	
3133	Baldwin	10/13/1918	Rblt. Style 68 at Great Falls 5/20/1929. Rblt. Style 63 date unknown. Rblt. Style 68 6/1941. Sold for scrap PC 1/14/1955.	
3134	Baldwin	10/17/1918	Reno. X2841(2) (WC) at Great Falls 7/20/1940. Ret. 12/1956 (St. 60).	
3135	Baldwin	10/17/1918	Rblt. Style 63 at Great Falls 8/31/1927. Rblt. Style 68 2/1939. Ret. 3/1958. Sold for scrap DI&M 12/1962.	
3136	Baldwin	12/7/1918	Rblt. Style 63 at Hillyard 2/16/1927. Rblt. Style 68 at Great Falls 4/28/1945. Sold for scrap PC 6/30/1953.	
3137	Baldwin	12/20/1918	Rblt. WC at Hillyard 10/1/1941. Reno. X1948(3) (WC) 7/1951. Ret. 4/1965 (St. 60).	380
3138	Baldwin	1/21/1919	Rblt. Style 63 at Great Falls 11/10/1926. Rblt. Style 68 at Dale Street 5/28/1943. Ret. 12/1957. Sold for scrap c.1962.	381
3139	Baldwin	2/2/1919	Rblt. Style 63 at Hillyard 7/11/1927. Rblt. Style 68 3/1946. Reno. X1962(3) (WC) 10/1952. Ret. 2/1960.	350
3140	Baldwin	2/14/1919	Rblt. Style 68 at Great Falls 10/20/1942. Sold for scrap PC 11/4/1955.	
3141	Baldwin	2/21/1919	Rblt. Style 68 at Great Falls 4/30/1942. Ret. 4/1955. Sold for scrap WEI&M 6/4/1955.	
3142	Baldwin	2/24/1919	Sold for scrap DI&M 7/18/1953.	
3143	Baldwin	3/11/1919	Rblt. Style 68 at Great Falls 8/10/1942. Sold for scrap DI&M 12/1949.	
3144	Baldwin	3/16/1919	Rblt. Style 68 at Great Falls 6/30/1942. Sold for scrap WEI&M 5/7/1953.	

Tender Class O-3, Style 71: 16 Tons Coal; 10,000 Gallons Water; 6" x 11" Axle Journals

No.	Builder	Date Rcvd.	Disposition
3145	Alco-Schenectady	4/7/1919	Reno. GN 3200 4/16/1919.
3146	Alco-Schenectady	4/7/1919	Reno. GN 3201 4/17/1919.
3147	Alco-Schenectady	4/2/1919	Reno. GN 3202 4/9/1919.
3148	Alco-Schenectady	4/2/1919	Reno. GN 3203 4/22/1919.

Tender Class O-2, Style Unassigned: 9 Tons Coal; 5,000 Gallons Water; 5" x 9" Axle Journals

No.	Builder	Date Built	Original No.	Disposition
3149	Alco-Brooks	10/1915	SDC 18	Sold for scrap DI&M 1932.

Tender Class O-3, Style 71: 16 Tons Coal; 10,000 Gallons Water; 6" x 11" Axle Journals.

No.	Builder	Date Rcvd.	Original No.	Renumbered From	Date	Disposition	Notes
3200	Alco-Schenectady	4/7/1919	GN 3145	GN 3145	4/16/1919	Ret. 4/1955. Sold for scrap PC 6/27/1955.	
3201	Alco-Schenectady	4/7/1919	GN 3146	GN 3146	4/17/1919	Ret. 4/1955. Sold for scrap PC 10/10/1955.	
3202	Alco-Schenectady	4/2/1919	GN 3147	GN 3147	4/9/1919	Ret. 4/1955. Sold for scrap PC 6/10/1955.	
3203	Alco-Schenectady	4/2/1919	GN 3148	GN 3148	4/22/1919	Sold for scrap DI&M 9/8/1952.	
3204	Alco-Brooks	1/1920	EP&SW 390	EP&SW 390	1920	Ret. 8/1955. Sold for scrap PC 10/3/1955.	208
3205	Alco-Brooks	1/1920	EP&SW 391	EP&SW 391	1920	Ret. 4/1955. Sold for scrap DI&M 6/10/1955.	208
3206	Alco-Brooks	1/1920	EP&SW 392	EP&SW 392	1920	Sold for scrap DI&M 5/28/1953.	208
3207	Alco-Brooks	1/1920	EP&SW 393	EP&SW 393	1920	Reno. X3307 (RT) at Hillyard 6/22/1950. Ret. 9/1957.	208
3208	Alco-Brooks	1/1920	EP&SW 394	EP&SW 394	1920	Ret. 8/1955. Sold for scrap PC 9/1955.	208

Tender Class O-4, Style 100: 20 Tons Coal (Some equipped with 5,200 Gallon oil cistern); 10,000 Gallons Water; 6" x 11" Axle Journals

No.	Builder	Date Built	Disposition	Notes
3210	Baldwin	10/1920	Ret. 4/1956. Sold for scrap PC 5/27/1956.	
3211	Baldwin	10/1920	Rblt. X2902(3) (CHEM) (with T3246) at Superior 4/29/1954. Sold Hyman-Michaels 10/1978.	
3212	Baldwin	10/1920	Sold SP&S (with E3211) 4/1950.	
3213	Baldwin	10/1920	Ret. 3/1958. Sold for scrap DI&M 12/6/1962.	
3214	Baldwin	10/1920	Sold for scrap PC 4/11/1952.	
3215	Baldwin	10/1920	Sold SP&S (with E3214) 4/1950.	
3216	Baldwin	10/1920	Ret. 4/1956. Sold for scrap WEI&M 5/27/1956.	
3217	Baldwin	10/1920	Sold for scrap PC 1/21/1955.	
3218	Baldwin	10/1920	Sold for scrap PC 2/18/1956.	
3219	Baldwin	10/1920	Sold for scrap DI&M 9/1/1952.	
3220	Baldwin	10/1920	Ret. 12/1957. Sold for scrap PC 12/1962.	
3221	Baldwin	11/1920	Sold for scrap DI&M 5/5/1953.	
3222	Baldwin	11/1920	Sold for scrap PC 1/8/1955.	
3223	Baldwin	11/1920	Ret. 12/1957. Sold for scrap c.1962.	
3224	Baldwin	11/1920	Sold for scrap DI&M c.1/1950.	
3225	Baldwin	11/1920	Sold for scrap PC 1/15/1955.	
3226	Baldwin	11/1920	Rblt. X2900(3) (CHEM) (with T3229) 7/1953. Ret. 11/1967.	382
3227	Baldwin	11/1920	Sold for scrap PC 5/15/1953.	
3228	Baldwin	11/1920	Sold for scrap PC 3/29/1952.	
3229	Baldwin	11/1920	Rblt. X2900(3) (CHEM) (with T3226) 7/1953. Ret. 11/1967.	382, 383
3230	Baldwin	11/1920	Ret. 12/1957. Sold for scrap c.1962.	
3231	Baldwin	11/1920	Ret. 12/1957. Placed on public exhibition at GN Depot, Williston, ND, (with E3059) 8/2/1958.	
3232	Baldwin	11/1920	Ret. 4/1955. Sold for scrap PC 6/10/1955.	
3233	Baldwin	11/1920	Sold for scrap DI&M 8/10/1953.	
3234	Baldwin	11/1920	Ret. 4/1955. Sold for scrap PC 5/18/1955.	
3235	Baldwin	11/1920	Ret. 4/1955. Sold for scrap PC 5/18/1955.	
3236	Baldwin	11/1920	Ret. 12/1957. Sold for scrap c.1962.	
3237	Baldwin	11/1920	Reno. X6704 4/1956. Ret. 10/1967.	
3238	Baldwin	11/1920	Donated to Seattle Board of Park Commissioners (with E1246). Placed on exhibition at Seattle, Woodland Park, WA, 7/18/1953.	
3239	Baldwin	11/1920	Sold for scrap WEI&M 4/19/1956.	
3240	Baldwin	11/1920	Sold for scrap PC 6/1962.	
3241	Baldwin	9/1920	Ret. 4/1955. Sold for scrap PC 6/27/1955.	
3242	Baldwin	9/1920	Ret. 4/1955. Sold for scrap PC 6/4/1955.	
3243	Baldwin	9/1920	Rblt. X2901(3) (CHEM) (with T3250) 12/1953. Ret. 8/1983. Sold G.W. Rockeries 2/4/1984.	382, 383
3244	Baldwin	9/1920	Sold for scrap PC 8/1953.	
3245	Baldwin	9/1920	Sold for scrap PC 8/16/1956.	
3246	Baldwin	9/1920	Rblt. X2902(3) (CHEM) (with T3211) at Superior 4/29/1954. Sold Hyman-Michaels 10/1978.	
3247	Baldwin	9/1920	Sold for scrap DI&M c.1/1950.	
3248	Baldwin	9/1920	Ret. 9/1953. Sold for scrap PC 5/18/1955.	
3249	Baldwin	9/1920	Ret. 4/1955. Sold for scrap PC 6/10/1955.	
3250	Baldwin	9/1920	Rblt. X2901(3) (CHEM) (with T3243) 12/1953. Ret. 8/1983. Sold G.W. Rockeries 2/4/1984.	383
3251	Baldwin	9/1920	Ret. 12/1957. Sold for scrap c.1962.	
3252	Baldwin	9/1920	Sold for scrap PC 5/1/1952.	
3253	Baldwin	9/1920	Ret. 4/1955. Sold for scrap PC 5/28/1955.	
3254	Baldwin	9/1920	Sold for scrap DI&M 1/15/1955.	298

Tender Class O-5, Style 73: 12 Tons Coal (some equipped with 4,500 Gallon oil cistern); 8,000 Gallons Water; 5½" x 10" Axle Journals. Some rebuilt to **Style 74** (15 Tons Coal; 6" x 11" Axle Journals). Some rebuilt to **Style 75** (10,000 Gallons Water; 6" x 11" Axle Journals). Some rebuilt to **Style 76** (15 Tons Coal; 10,000 Gallons Water; 6" x 11" Axle Journals). Some rebuilt to **Style 77** (10,000 Gallons Water).

No.	Builder	Date Rcvd.	Renumbered From L-2 No.	Disposition	Notes
3300	Baldwin	3/25/1908	GN 1802(2)	Reno. X1987(4) (WC) 5/15/1950. Ret. 12/1958.	173
3301	Baldwin	4/14/1908	GN 1844	Sold Midland Railway Company of Manitoba 8/1951.	188
3302	Baldwin	5/17/1907	GN 1806	Sold for scrap PC 1947.	175
3303	Baldwin	3/31/1908	GN 1835	Reno. X1971(3) (WC) 9/1949. Ret. 3/1957 (St. 73).	
3304	Baldwin	3/25/1908	GN 1801(2)	Reno. X6901 12/1956. Ret. 9/1958.	173
3305	Baldwin	4/3/1908	GN 1838	Sold for scrap PC 8/1953.	
3306	Baldwin	6/9/1907	GN 1819	Rblt. Style 76 at Delta 1/30/1929. Rblt. Style 77, date unknown. Rblt. Style 76 at Hillyard 10/14/1941. Reno. X1993(3) (WC) 2/1950. Ret. 12/1956.	178
3307	Baldwin	5/20/1907	GN 1808	Reno. X1907(2) (WC) at Hillyard 4/30/1947. Ret. 1/1959 (St. 73).	176
3308	Baldwin	5/20/1907	GN 1809	Rblt. Style 77 at Delta 5/10/1928. Sold for scrap PC 9/1953.	176
3309	Baldwin	5/22/1907	GN 1810	Rblt. Style 77 at Delta 12/7/1927. Rblt. Style 76 at Hillyard 1/11/1944. Sold SP&S (with E3122) 1/1944.	

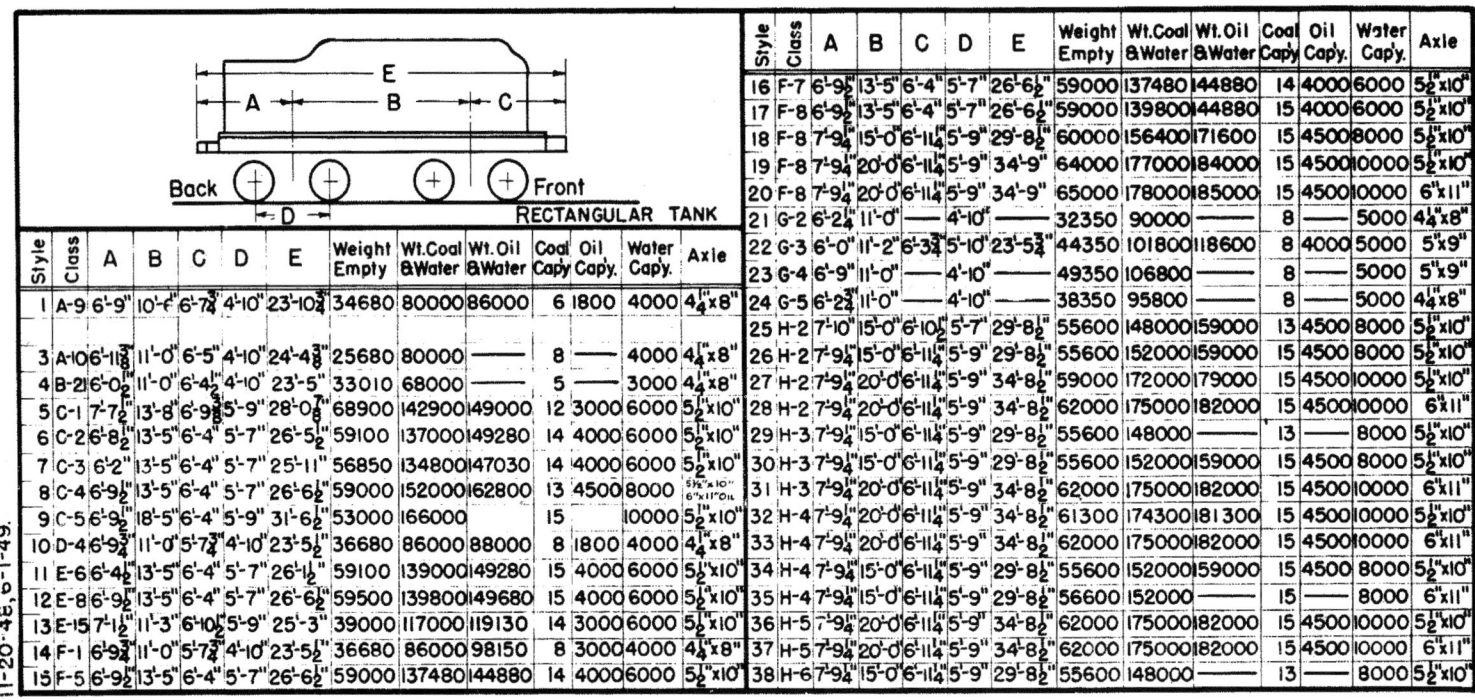

Appendix - Page Nº. ii

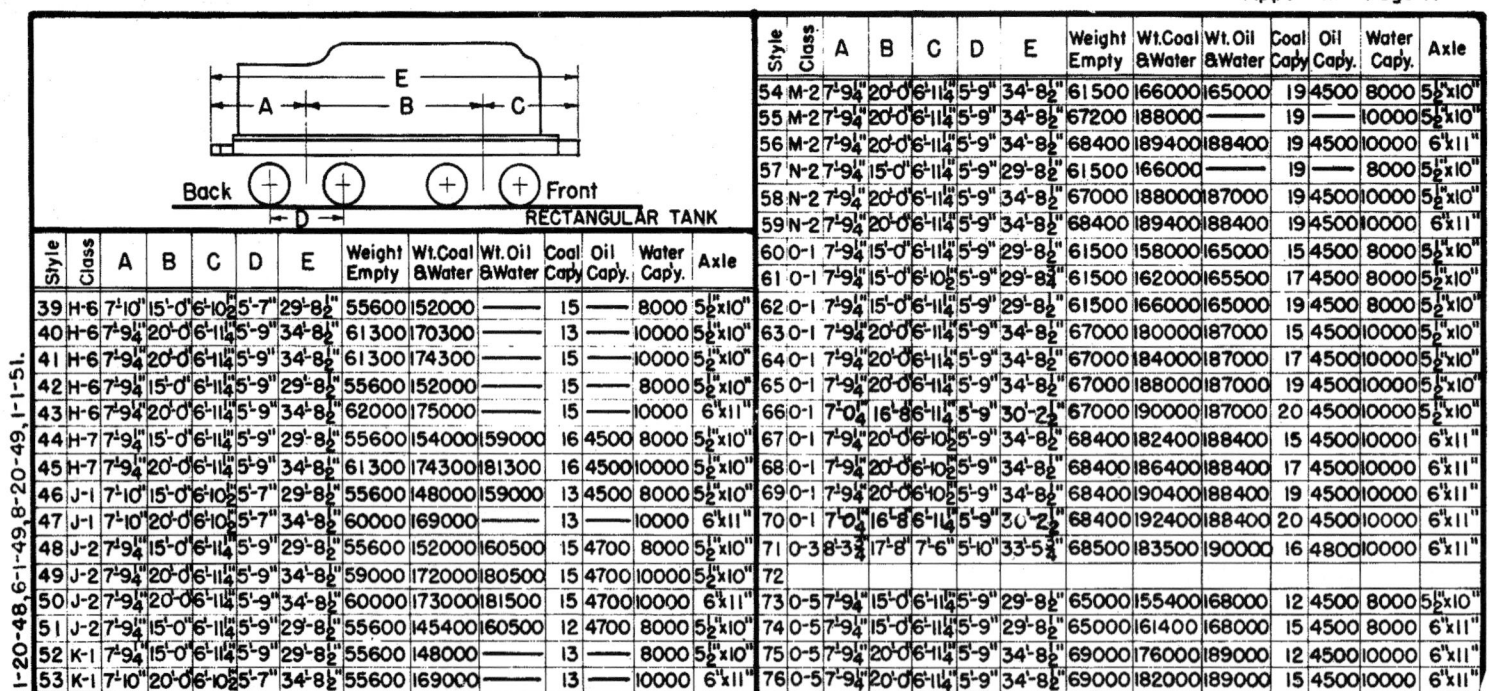

Appendix - Page Nº. iii

3310	Baldwin	3/31/1908	GN 1836	Wrecked at Wenatchee, WA, 3/7/1943. Dismantled at Hillyard 4/1943.	
3311	Baldwin	3/25/1908	GN 1831	Sold for scrap WEI&M c.6/1948.	186
3312	Baldwin	7/30/1907	GN 1828	Reno. X2843(2) (WC) at Yarnell 6/21/1940. Ret. 5/1959 (St. 73).	
3313	Baldwin	3/27/1908	GN 1834	Reno. X2846(2) (WC) at Whitefish 7/3/1940. Ret. 1/1956 (St. 73).	
3314	Baldwin	6/30/1907	GN 1822	Reno. X3207 (WC) at St.Cloud 2/12/1942. Ret. 6/1968.	181
3315	Baldwin	8/6/1907	GN 1829	Ret. 5/1958.	185
3316	Baldwin	4/7/1908	GN 1840	Reno. X2848(2) (WC) at Great Falls 9/27/1940. Lost car 3/30/1989 (St. 73).	
3317	Baldwin	6/30/1907	GN 1823	Reno. X3248 (WC) at Great Falls 10/24/1941. Ret. 5/1959.	181
3318	Baldwin	3/25/1908	GN 1804(2)	Reno. X3203 (WC) at St.Cloud 3/19/1942. Ret. 7/1959 (St. 73).	174
3319	Baldwin	6/2/1907	GN 1812	Ret. 1/1948. Reno. X809 (WC) 3/1948. Ret. 12/1962 (St. 73).	177
3320	Baldwin	8/11/1907	GN 1824	Ret. 9/1947. Reno. X811(2) (WC) 11/1947. Ret. 3/1968 (St. 73).	337
3321	Baldwin	3/27/1908	GN 1833	Reno. X2819(1) (WC) at Grand Forks 10/10/1941. Reno. X3227 at Grand Forks 4/20/1942. Ret. 10/1959 (St. 73).	
3322	Baldwin	3/31/1908	GN 1832	Reno. X3341 (FO) 8/1948. Ret. 5/1962 (St. 73).	
3323	Baldwin	4/3/1908	GN 1837	Sold for scrap PC 6/9/1952.	
3324	Baldwin	6/6/1907	GN 1816	Sold for scrap DI&M 7/1932.	178
3325	Baldwin	7/6/1907	GN 1825	Reno. X2854(3) (WC) at Great Falls 7/20/1940. Reno. X939(4) 1/1947. Ret. 8/1958.	182
3326	Baldwin	4/7/1908	GN 1842	Sold for scrap PC 10/18/1951.	
3327	Baldwin	7/21/1907	GN 1826	Reno. X2863(3) (WC) at Minot 9/18/1940. Reno. X3360 10/19/1942. Ret. 9/1966 (St. 73).	183
3328	Baldwin	6/5/1907	GN 1817	Ret. 1/1948. Reno. X3345 (WC) 3/1948. Ret. 5/1962 (St. 73).	178
3329	Baldwin	6/5/1907	GN 1818	Rblt. Style 77 at Hillyard 8/30/1926. Sold for scrap PC 2/24/1947.	178
3330	Baldwin	5/17/1907	GN 1807	Reno. X1981(2) (WC) at Superior 12/28/1941. Reno. X3233 at Minot 5/8/1942. Ret. 1/1961 (St. 73).	175
3331	Baldwin	4/7/1908	GN 1841	Rblt. Style 77 (15 Tons Coal) at Dale Street 9/26/1927. Rblt. Style 76 11/14/1942. Sold for scrap DI&M 8/10/1953.	188
3332	Baldwin	4/3/1908	GN 1839	Rblt. Style 77 (16 Tons Coal) at Great Falls 5/21/1927. Sold for scrap WEI&M 3/29/1952.	187
3333	Baldwin	6/25/1907	GN 1821	Reno. X2820(1) (WC) at Grand Forks 11/1/1941. Reno. X3228 at Grand Forks 4/23/1942. Off roster between 8/1/1950 and 6/1/1952 (St. 73).	180
3334	Baldwin	5/28/1907	GN 1813	Reno. X2821(1) (WC) at Grand Forks 11/26/1941. Reno. X3229 at Grand Forks 4/22/1942. Reno. BN 973057 11/1972. Sold Earl Goldsberry 7/1978 (St. 73).	177
3335	Baldwin	5/22/1907	GN 1811	Rblt. Style 77 at Hillyard 3/1/1927. Reno. X6702 3/1955. Ret. 9/1962.	
3336	Baldwin	5/28/1907	GN 1815	Reno. X1931(2) (WC) 3/1933. Ret. 4/1958 (St. 73).	177
3337	Baldwin	3/27/1908	GN 1803(2)	Sold for scrap PC 10/10/1952 (St. 73).	
3338	Baldwin	9/24/1907	GN 1814	Reno. X3210 (WC) (coal pit enclosed) at St.Cloud 3/21/1942. Off roster between 6/1/1952 and 11/1958 (St. 73).	177
3339	Baldwin	6/26/1907	GN 1820	Reno. X2866(3) (WC) at Yarnell 6/21/1940. Ret. 6/1967 (St. 73).	179
3340	Baldwin	7/28/1907	GN 1827	Reno. X1974(3) (WC) 8/1933. Reno. X3212 3/2/1942. Ret. 12/1964 (St. 73).	184
3341	Baldwin	4/7/1908	GN 1843	Sold for scrap (apparently without tank) DI&M 6/1948. Rblt. X3305 (40FWC) 5/1949. Ret. 12/1956.	188
3342	Baldwin	5/17/1907	GN 1805	Reno. X2870(3) (WC) at St.Cloud 5/25/1940. Reno. X3298 8/27/1943. Off roster between 8/1/1950 and 6/1/1952 (St. 73).	
3343	Baldwin	3/25/1908	GN 1830	Ret. 1/1948. Reno. X833(2) (WC) 3/1948. Ret. 5/1959 (St. 73).	186
3344	Baldwin	3/25/1908	GN 1800(2)	Reno. X1977(2) (WC) 12/1949. Ret. 6/1958 (St. 73).	173

Appendix - Page Nº.iv.

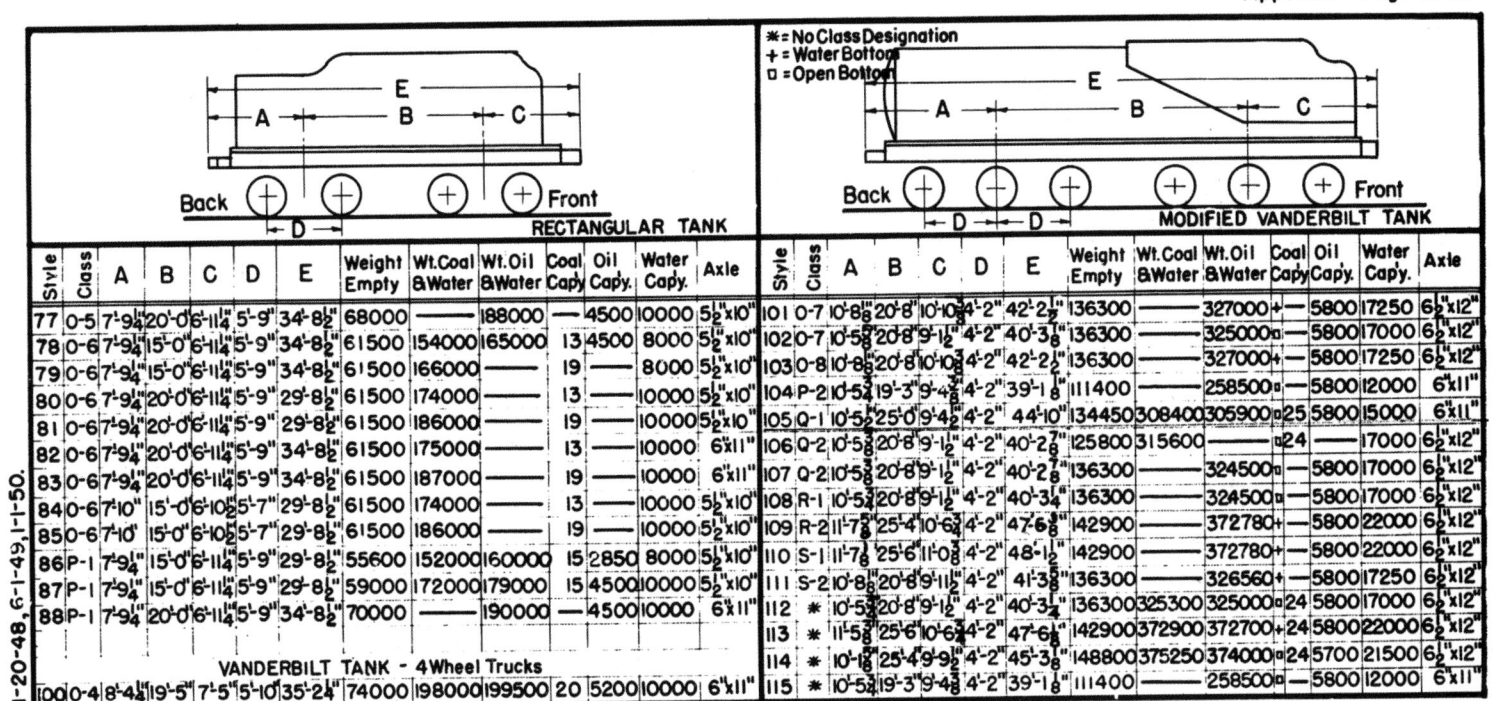

Tender Class O-6, Style 78: 13 Tons Coal (some with 4,500 Gallon oil cistern); 8,000 Gallons Water; 5½" x 10" Axle Journals. Some rebuilt to **Style 79** (19 Tons Coal). Some rebuilt to **Style 80** or **Style 84** (10,000 Gallons Water). Some rebuilt to **Style 81** or **Style 85** (19 Tons Coal; 10,000 Gallons Water). Some rebuilt to **Style 82** (10,000 Gallons Water; 6" x 11" Axle Journals). Some rebuilt to **Style 83** (19 Tons Coal; 10,000 Gallons Water; 6" x 11" Axle Journals).

No.	Builder	Date Rcvd.	Renumbered From L-1 No.	Disposition	Notes
3350	Baldwin	4/27/1908	GN 1910	Reno. X3236 (WC) at Great Falls 6/8/1942. Ret. 6/1962 (St. 79).	191
3351	Baldwin	4/27/1908	GN 1913	Sold for scrap PC 6/1951 (St. 79).	191
3352	Baldwin	5/9/1908	GN 1919	Reno. X1938(4) (WC) 7/1949. Ret. 4/1960 (St. 78).	
3353	Baldwin	5/12/1908	GN 1920	Sold for scrap DI&M c.1/1950.	189
3354	Baldwin	9/11/1906	GN 1901	Sold for scrap DI&M 5/14/1947.	172
3355	Baldwin	4/27/1908	GN 1911	Rblt. Style 82 or 83 at Dale Street 7/12/1928. Sold for scrap DI&M 4/20/1952.	191
3356	Baldwin	4/17/1908	GN 1908	Reno. X1973(2) (WC) 6/1950. Ret. 3/1970 (St. 79).	190
3357	Baldwin	9/6/1906	GN 1900	Sold for scrap PC 11/27/1928.	172
3358	Baldwin	9/30/1906	GN 1903	Sold for scrap PC 8/22/1941.	172
3359	Baldwin	9/22/1906	GN 1902	Sold for scrap 5/1940.	
3360	Baldwin	5/9/1908	GN 1918	Disposition unknown.	
3361	Baldwin	5/4/1908	GN 1916	Rblt. Style 82 (16 Tons Coal) at Dale Street 10/13/1927. Rblt. Style 80 or 84 date unknown. Rblt. Style 82 at Dale Street 5/7/1942. Sold for scrap PC 3/8/1949.	192
3362	Baldwin	10/22/1906	GN 1904	Rblt. WC at Grand Forks 11/20/1934. Reno. X2871(3) (WC) at Grand Forks 7/29/1940. Reno. X3298 8/27/1943. Off roster between 8/1/1950 and 6/1/1952 (St. 78).	
3363	Baldwin	5/16/1908	GN 1906(2)	Reno. X804(2) (WC) 11/1947. Ret. 9/1957 (St. 78).	189, 337
3364	Baldwin	4/27/1908	GN 1912	Sold for scrap DI&M 9/1953 (St. 78).	191
3365	Baldwin	5/4/1908	GN 1917	Rblt. Style 82 at Superior 6/21/1928. Sold for scrap PC 1/21/1965.	192
3366	Baldwin	5/25/1908	GN 1907(2)	Reno. X2876(3) (WC) at Great Falls 5/24/1940. Ret. 2/1955 (St. 78).	189, 384
3367	Baldwin	5/1/1908	GN 1915	Reno. X2877(3) (WC) at Havre 8/2/1940. Ret. 5/1957 (St. 78).	385
3368	Baldwin	5/1/1908	GN 1914	Disposition unknown.	
3369	Baldwin	5/12/1908	GN 1905(2)	Ret. 8/1955. Sold for scrap DI&M 9/7/1955.	189
3370	Baldwin	4/17/1908	GN 1909	Sold for scrap WEI&M 3/29/1952.	190
3371	Baldwin	5/16/1908	GN 1921	Ret. 5/1958.	189

Tender Class O-7, Style 101: 5,800 Gallons Oil; 17,250 Gallons Water; 6½" x 12" Axle Journals. Four tenders had water capacity of only 17,000 Gallons and were considered **Style 102**.

No.	Builder	Date	Disposition
3375	GN (Hillyard)	2/21/1930	[Style 102] (Reno. from T2190 10/27/1930) Ret. 4/1956. Sold for scrap PC 5/13/1956.
3376		1930	Ret. 3/1958. Sold for scrap PC 2/1963.
3377		1930	[Style 102] Ret. 12/1957. Sold for scrap c.1962.
3378		1930	[Style 102] Ret. 12/1957. Sold for scrap c.1962.
3379		1930	Ret. 3/1958. Sold for scrap PC 2/1963.
3380		1930	Ret. 5/1958. Sold for scrap PC (with E2042) 3/1962.
3381		1930	Ret. 5/1958. Sold for scrap WEI&M (with E3390) 10/1963.
3382		1930	Ret. 5/1958. Sold for scrap DI&M 5/1962.
3383		1930	[Style 102] Ret. 8/1956. Sold for scrap PC 9/6/1956.
3384		1930	Ret. 12/1957. Sold for scrap PC 10/1963.
3385		1930	Ret. 5/1958. Sold for scrap PC 3/1962.
3386		1930	Ret. 5/1958. Sold for scrap PC (with E3386) 12/1963.
3387		1931	Ret. 3/1958. Sold for scrap PC 3/1962.
3388		1931	Disposition unknown.
3389		1931	Ret. 5/1958. Sold for scrap DI&M (with E3389) 10/1963.
3390		1931	Ret. 5/1958. Sold for scrap PC (with E3387) 4/1963.
3391		1931	Ret. 3/1958.
3392		1931	Ret. 5/1958. Sold for scrap DI&M (with E3377) 10/1963.
3393		1932	Ret. 12/1957. Sold for scrap c.1962.
3394		1931	Ret. 5/1958. Sold for scrap PC (with E2040) 3/1962.
3395		1932	Ret. 3/1958. Sold for scrap PC 3/1962.
3396		1932	Ret. 5/1958. Sold for scrap PC (with E2120) 5/1962.

Tender Class O-8, Style 103: 5,800 Gallons Oil; 17,250 Gallons Water; 6½" x 12" Axle Journals

No.	Builder	Date	Disposition
3397		1932	Ret. 3/1958. Sold for scrap PC 5/1962.
3398		1932	Ret. 5/1958. Sold for scrap DI&M (with E3394) 12/1963.
3399		1932	Ret. 12/1957. Sold for scrap PC 11/1963.

Tender Class Z-6, Style Unassigned: 6,000 Gallons Oil; 20,000 Gallons Water; 6¾" Axle Journals

No.	Builder	Date Built	Original No.	Renumbered From	Date	Disposition	Notes
4000	Alco-Schenectady	5/1937	SP&S 903	SP&S 903	1/25/1940	Sold SP&S (No. 903) (with E4000) 4/27/1950.	216
4001	Alco-Schenectady	5/1937	SP&S 904	SP&S 904	1/18/1940	Sold SP&S (No. 904) (with E4001) 7/1/1946.	216

Class H-5 engine 1355 was photographed at Kelly Lake, MN, on September 6, 1953. It has been equipped with a slant-front cab, electric train indicators and a foot board pilot. This engine is now preserved at Sioux City, IA. Collection of Stan Kistler.

Chapter 33

Great Northern Steam Locomotive Roster Notes

NOTE 1: DS&WT 1 and 2 are shown by Lambert M. Baker as being Brooks C/N 3297 and 3298 in one location and C/N 3301 and 3302 in another. The latter two numbers are confirmed by the Brooks order list. HCR Vol. 40 (NE5) confirms that GN 56(2) and 57(2) were renumbered to ABD 1 and 2, respectively, in 1909.

NOTE 2: C&RM 9 was delivered by Baldwin as RM 9, but was jointly owned by the RM and C&RM until the sale of the C&RM to GN in 1907 according to Poor's Manuals of Railroads. HCR Vol. 41 (NE6) shows this locomotive as SF&N 9. URPC indicates that even after the sale of the C&RM to GN, the locomotive remained half owned by the RM until 1/1922, when the RM half was purchased by the GN under AFE 21131.

NOTE 3: MH&O 26-30 became DSS&SA locomotives when the MH&O merged with other roads to become the DSS&A in 1887. These locomotives were acquired by the D&W c.1890 from the DSS&A. One of these locomotives was moved to the D&W on 5/24/1890 (Aurele A. Durocher, personal communication to Robert C. Post, 1/20/1981). Individual locomotive renumberings may not have been exactly as shown.

NOTE 4: DMR&N 1 and 2 were purchased from Wells-Stone Company (Frank A. King, 1981. *Minnesota Logging Railroads*, Golden West Books, San Marino, CA.).

NOTE 5: "List of DS&W engines and equipment turned over to the E. Ry. of Minnesota, June 23rd, 1898" (Minnesota Historical Society GN/DS&W Files, Box 22.C.11.3B) has DS&W 1 and 2 typed on page, but the numbers have been changed to 102 and 103 by hand. This document shows DS&W 2, 3, 101 and 104 as fit only for scrap.

NOTE 6: While the major locomotive renumbering of StPM&M to GN locomotives took place in 1899, some evidence (e.g. the Lambert M. Baker roster and the few renumbering dates known for certain) indicate that some of the EM and MC to GN renumberings may not have taken place until 1900. All EM locomotives still on the roster were leased to GN on 5/1/1902, and sold to GN on 7/1/1907. All MC locomotives still on the roster were sold to GN on 7/1/1907.

NOTE 7: Some confusion exists in the records regarding the engine which was originally StP&P 28. HER information shows the engine sold to DL&N 9/14/1902 or 10/1902, and reno. FG&S 1. Steam locomotive notes of Norman C. Keyes, Jr., indicate this engine was renumbered 6/1913, and then sold A. Guthrie & Co. at some time after that date. However, it is likely that the engine was renumbered in 1902 as that is the date of incorporation of FG&S. The engine which was originally StP&P 27 was also sold to A. Guthrie & Co., and HER indicates this occurred in 6/1913. It is likely that both locomotives were sold at the same time.

NOTE 8: Walter F. Becker ("Iron Brothers – The Crooks and the Rice", Railway and Locomotive Historical Society Bulletin No. 107, October 1962) states that the *William Crooks* and the *Edmund Rice* were probably identical when built. *The Report of the First Division of the St. Paul and Pacific Railroad*, for the six months ending May 31, 1867, shows the engines were not the same in 1867 and that the *Edmund Rice* was "thoroughly repaired" in 1865. It is possible, but not confirmed, that this repair could have changed the dimensions and weight of the engine.

NOTE 9: GN 364(1) was sold to BA&P on 11/30/1893 (1880 HER), and was renumbered as BA&P 31(1) on that date [HCR Vol. 36 (NE1)]. BA&P 31(1) was renumbered BA&P 10(1) in 1898. BA&P 10(1) was sold to Columbia & Southern (No. 10) before 1906. Columbia & Southern No. 10 was sold to the Oregon Railway & Navigation Co. (No. 10) on 7/1/1906. OR&N No. 10 was sold to the Oregon-Washington Railway & Navigation Co. (No. 10) on 12/23/1910. OWR&N 10 was assigned Union Pacific No. 4209 on 9/1/1915, but was sold to Montana Western (No. 10) in, 5/1916, before renumbering had taken place (information probably from W. Kratville and H.E. Ranks, *Motive Power of the Union Pacific*, Barnhart Press, Omaha, NE, 1959, per personal communication from Norman C. Keyes, Jr., to Kenneth R. Middleton dated 2/9/1980).

NOTE 10: Information sent by George Sittig to Norman C. Keyes, Jr., believed to be derived from the Baldwin builder's list, shows N&FS Nos. 7 and 8 built in 10/1893. John Fahey (1965, *Inland Empire, D.C. Corbin and Spokane*. University of Washington Press, Seattle, WA., p. 139) indicates that the two N&FS locomotives were purchased in 1894. However, a contract between the N&FS and Burnham, Williams & Co., proprietors of the Baldwin Locomotive Works, for the lease and purchase of two locomotives (Minnesota Historical Society GN 22.C.127B.F3) has been found. The contract was dated 2/28/1894, but was effective 2/1/1894. This indicates that perhaps these locomotives were built for stock, and not delivered to the N&FS until 2/1894. It also provides confirmation that these locomotives were owned by the N&FS. They were, however, apparently transferred to the SF&N fairly soon, since they are listed under SF&N ownership by Poor's Manual of Railroads in 1899 (the C&RM locomotive is listed as separate ownership until 1908).

NOTE 11: StP&P 4 was purchased used from Dayton & Union, received 1/31/1865 (Norman C. Keyes, Jr. Personal communication to Kenneth R. Middleton dated 11/22/1979). Date built is unknown.

NOTE 12: *The Report of the First Division of the St. Paul and Pacific Railroad* for the six months ending May 31, 1867 and the 1880 HER confirm engines StP&P 3, 6, and 7 were built by Norris despite an entry in the StPM&M records (MHS Acc 3419) listing some engines as having come from R. Morris & Son.

NOTE 13: George Sittig indicated that StP&P 8 and 9 had dimensions of 14x22-60. The Lambert M. Baker roster shows 15x24-49. The 1891 and 1892 Annual Reports of the Machinery Department show StP&P 8 as having 14"x22" cylinders and 56" drivers, with StP&P 9 having 15" x 24" cylinders and 56 3/8" driver centers, respectively. This probably indicates a 63" driver diameter over the tires. 1880 HER indicates tires of StP&P 8 were turned down to 61 3/4" on 4/9/1881, and that StP&P 9 received new 62 3/4" tires on 6/24/1882, probably confirming 63".

NOTE 14: George Sittig lists StP&P 10 as having dimensions of 14x22-60. The Lambert M. Baker roster shows 16x24-49. The 1891 and 1892 Annual Reports of the Machinery Department show this engine as having 15"x22" cylinders and 56" driver centers, probably indicating a 63" driver diameter over the tires. 1880 HER shows tires turned down to 62" on 11/21/1880, probably confirming this.

NOTE 15: George Sitting lists StP&P 11 as having 60" drivers. The 1891 Annual Report of the Machinery Department shows this engine to have 56 3/8" driver centers , probably indicating a 63" driver diameter over the tires. Sittig also shows this engine built in 6/1869. HER shows 4/1869, and MHS Acc. 3419 shows this engine received 5/1869.

NOTE 16: Robert Sloan (personal communication to Kenneth R. Middleton, 5/1976) indicated that Northern Pacific 20(1)-23(1) were sold to StP&P (20-23) in 12/1871, which MHS Acc. 3419 indicates as their date of delivery. George Sittig (personal communication to Norman C. Keyes, Jr., dated 10/10/1968) stated that on a visit to Baldwin Locomotive works in 1906 or 1907, he had been told that these locomotives were ordered by the Northern Pacific, but delivered as StP&P locomotives. Sittig showed Nos. 20 and 21 as having been constructed in 11/1871.

NOTE 17: StPM&M 47-50 were ordered as StP&P 47-50 but were not delivered until after the StPM&M had purchased the StP&P. MHS Acc. 3419 shows the delivery date of these four locomotives as 11/1879, while the 1891 and 1892 Annual Reports of the Machinery Department show the date as 12/1879. There is also a discrepancy in driver size. The 1880 HER shows these engines as having 5 foot (60-inch) drivers. The 1891 and 1892 Annual Reports of the Machinery Department show them to have 56-inch driver centers, which would normally result in a 63-inch driver diameter. Locomotive diagrams from 1900 and c.1918 also show these locomotives to have 63-inch drivers. A further discrepancy exists in the disposition of GN 251(2), delivered as StPM&M 49. Lambert M. Baker shows this engine as leaving the roster in 1901, while Robert Graham shows it as retired in 1902. Walter F. Becker only comments that the records are not complete.

NOTE 18: 1880 HER shows StPM&M 69 received 9/1/1880 on page 69, and 8/25/1880 on page 461.

NOTE 19: 1880 HER shows StPM&M 88 received 4/9/1881 on page 88, and 4/2/1881 on page 461.

NOTE 20: 1880 HER indicates that StPM&M 6 had 16"x24" cylinders, and that StPM&M 7 had 16"x22" cylinders.

NOTE 21: MHS Acc. 3419 shows StPM&M 90 received 4/13/1882. 1880 HER shows 4/12/1882.

NOTE 22: StP&D 16(2) and 17(2) were built in 2/1882 according to the Rogers Locomotive Works order list. Larry P. Schrenk (personal communication to Kenneth R. Middleton dated 12/30/1977) indicates Northern Pacific records show these as sold to StPM&M 4/4/1882.

NOTE 23: 1880 HER shows StPM&M 96(1) and 97(1) received 5/28/1882. MHS Acc. 3419 shows 5/29/1882.

NOTE 24: 1880 HER shows StPM&M 184-186 received 4/7/1883. MHS Acc. 3419 shows 3/28/1883, 3/29/1883, and 3/30/1883, respectively.

NOTE 25: 1880 HER shows StPM&M 198 received 1/30/1883. MHS Acc. 3419 shows 1/31/1883.

NOTE 26: A previous locomotive numbered 199 had been received (perhaps in error) by StPM&M on 12/9/1882, and was readied for service on 12/11/1882, but was then turned over to the CStPM&O in 12/1882 according to 1880 HER. The locomotive which became StPM&M 199 was then received 2/5/1883 according to 1880 HER (MHS Acc. 3419 shows received 2/6/1883).

NOTE 27: 1880 HER shows StPM&M 200, 201 and 202 received on 12/28/1882, 2/5/1883, and 2/5/1883, respectively. MHS Acc. 3419 shows these locomotives received 12/29/1882, 2/6/1883, and 2/9/1883, respectively.

NOTE 28: 1880 HER entry for GN 203 indicates "RPL&V letters changed to GN on 11/5/1890".

NOTE 29: Though builder's records show these locomotives as sold to GN, and though they were in fact operated by GN from the time of their delivery, GN 371 was received with "StPM&M" lettered on the tender (photograph from Harold K. Vollrath). The later engines were delivered with "G.N. Ry." lettered on their tenders (Norman C. Keyes, Jr., personal communication to Kenneth R. Middleton dated 7/25/1976). Since these engines were never operated by the StPM&M they are listed in the GN section of the roster.

NOTE 30: Builder's photos indicate that GN 450(1) was delivered with "StPM&M" lettered on the tender (i.e. as StPM&M 450). The last of this series (GN 499) was received with "G.N. Ry." lettered on the tender (Norman C. Keyes, Jr., personal communication to Kenneth R. Middleton dated 7/25/1976), indicating that some time in 1892 those locomotives on the roster which were owned by the StPM&M were considered to be "Great Northern" locomotives. These locomotives are listed in the roster as GN 450(1)-480(1) and 481-499.

NOTE 31: New York Locomotive Works order list shows S&N 1 and 2 as being C/N 627 and 629, respectively. However, information derived from Historical Engine Record shows S&N 2 as C/N 627 (no reference is made to S&N 1 in this document since this locomotive was not acquired by GN). However, personal communication from Gerald M. Best (2/22/1980), who researched these locomotives for his book, *Ships and Narrow Gauge Rails, the Story of the Pacific Coast Company*, confirms S&N 2 as C/N 627, indicates that S&N 1(2) was C/N 628, and that C/N 629 was Port Townsend Southern 2, later C&PS 9, scrapped in 1910. Lambert M. Baker also shows the locomotive [as GN 139(2)] to be C/N 627.

NOTE 32: S&N 1(2) was originally Port Townsend Southern 1 and was sold to the Columbia & Puget Sound Railroad Company [No. 5(1)] in 1897. C&PS 5(1) was traded to the S&N [No. 1(2)] c.1897 in exchange for S&N 1(1) (Gerald M. Best. Personal communication to Kenneth R. Middleton, dated 2/22/1980).

NOTE 33: Great Northern Railway Company Historic Car Records Volume 94 (Historical Record of S.C. and N. and Sioux City and Western, January 1, 1900) (Minnesota Historical Society) shows SC&N 9 received 7/11/1890. This seems somewhat unlikely since the Rogers order list shows this engine constructed 3/1891.

NOTE 34: While it is not absolutely certain that Sioux City & Northern No. 11 was in fact Pittsburgh C/N 168, SC&N records indicate that SC&N No. 11 was purchased from the Chicago, St.Paul, Minneapolis & Omaha for $900 about 1890. Roy W. Carlson [Chicago, St.Paul, Minneapolis & Omaha roster. *Midwest Railroader, the Complete Roster Journal*, No. 41 (March, 1964)], lists this locomotive only as being dropped from the roster about 1890, the only locomotive so listed. The rather indefinite disposition of this locomotive from the CStPM&O makes this locomotive the most likely candidate for having become SC&N No. 11. SC&StP 4(1) was built in 11/1871 and became StP&SC 20, date unknown. StP&SC 20 was sold to CStPM&O (No. 220) on 5/9/1881 (per Carlson). CStPM&O 220 was sold to SC&N (No. 11) in 1890.

NOTE 35: SC&StP 1 was built 5/1871, and became StP&SC 21, date unknown. StP&SC 21 was sold to CStPM&O (No. 221) on 5/9/1881. CStPM&O 221 was sold to SC&N (No. 12) in 1890 [Roy W. Carlson. Chicago, St.Paul, Minneapolis & Omaha roster. *Midwest Railroader, the Complete Roster Journal, No. 41* (March, 1964)]. The dimensions shown are from the 1880 HER. The Taunton Locomotive Works Order List shows this locomotive as having 14"x24" cylinders, 54" drivers, and a weight of 57,230 lb.

NOTE 36: MCCo 131(1) and 132(1) were apparently diverted to the Wyoming Pacific Improvement Company by Rhode Island Locomotive Works, and were delivered new to the Pacific Short Line. This is supported by the fact that locomotives intended to be MCCo 131(2) and 132(2) (Rhode Island C/N 2359 and 2360) were built in 6/1890, per the Rhode Island Locomotive Works order list. Builders photos of these locomotives supposedly exist showing them lettered for "Pacific Short Line". These locomotives were likely numbered 10 and 11 since the next similar locomotive purchased received number 12, and the three received numbers 16-18 when purchased by the SCO&W.

NOTE 37: The only known reference to this locomotive is a letter, dated 11/5/1893, from T. Roope, SCO&W Master Mechanic, to Ed Haakinson, Vice President of the SCO&W, containing an inventory of SCO&W locomotives. The engine is listed as "in poor condition not fit for service." Since no other references have been found to this locomotive, it was presumably sold or scrapped shortly thereafter.

NOTE 38: URPC shows GN 142 sold for scrap to Pacific Coast Steel. AFE 31257 shows NSRM.

NOTE 39: SDC 11 was purchased used, date of purchase and original owner unknown according to George Sittig (personal communication to Norman C. Keyes, Jr.). Sittig indicated that this locomotive was built in 1902, which agrees with the Lambert M. Baker roster and with information derived from Historical Engine Record. The builder is listed here as Alco-Schenectady since the Schenectady order list indicates that all 2-6-0's built in 1902 were constructed after Schenectady became part of Alco. The HER information shows this locomotive renumbered to GN 430 on 9/19/1921, while the CNRA shows 5/17/1922.

NOTE 40: SDC 12 was probably purchased used, date of purchase and original owner unknown according to George Sittig (personal communication to Norman C. Keyes, Jr.). Sittig indicated that this locomotive was built in 1906, which agrees with the Lambert M. Baker roster and with information derived from Historical Engine Record. The HER information shows this locomotive renumbered to GN 431 on 8/1/1921, while the CNRA shows 4/15/1922.

NOTE 41: K&M 279 was renumbered to K&M 540 (date unknown) (George Sittig, Great Northern steam locomotive roster information sent to Norman C. Keyes, Jr.), and was then sold to SDC between 1908 and 1911 (William D. Edson, personal communication to Kenneth R. Middleton and Norman C. Keyes, Jr., c.1979.). Information derived from Historical Engine Record shows this locomotive renumbered to GN 432 on 7/11/1921, while the CNRA shows 4/1/1922.

NOTE 42: George Sittig indicated that SDC 14 (Brooks C/N 52834) was built for the Tennessee, Alabama & Georgia Railway in 4/1913, and sold to the SDC 8/1914. This is somewhat confirmed by the Brooks order list, which shows this engine as SDC 14 with an 8/1914 date. However, a footnote confirms that the engine was built for the TA&G, the C/N fits into a 1913 sequence, and a locomotive produced under the same order number was constructed in 4/1913. George Sittig stated that the locomotive was originally TA&G 322, while George Weir has annotated the Lambert M. Baker roster with a note that says the American Locomotive Company records indicate that it was TA&G 321.

NOTE 43: A letter from the General Manager of Somers Lumber Company (signature illegible) to W.B. Irwin, dated September 11, 1937, indicates that GN 60(2) was sold to Somers Lumber Company in March 1930. URPC indicates February 1930.

NOTE 44: John Fahey (1965, *Inland Empire, D.C. Corbin and Spokane*. University of Washington Press, Seattle, WA.) indicates that the first two SF&N locomotives were received in Spokane Falls on 5/23/1889, and at that time were numbered 310 and 311. No additional evidence of these numbers or a renumbering date has been found. Personal communication from Fahey to Kenneth R. Middleton, dated 1/22/1977, reported that this information was from Baldwin Locomotive Works records.

NOTE 45: V&S 3 was originally built for NP and was sold to the Victoria Lumber and Manufacturing Company (No.1) in 1899. It was acquired by V&S from the Victoria Lumber and Manufacturing Company in 6/1902 (Darryl E. Muralt, 1993. *The Victoria and Sidney Railway 1892-1919*. British Columbia Railway Historical Association, Victoria, BC.)

NOTE 46: V&S 2 was originally built as the Canadian Locomotive Company's entry at the American Centennial Exhibition in 1876 at Philadelphia. On its return from exhibition, it is believed to have been sold to the Kingston & Pembroke Railway, and then possibly was used on the Canadian Pacific Railway prior to coming to the V&S [George Hearn and David Wilkie, 1973. *The Cordwood Limited*. The British Columbia Railway Historical Association, Victoria, BC (4th Ed.)].

NOTE 47: GN Vice-President Operating File 39-01, Sale of Equipment (Minnesota Historical Society) shows GN 2 sold for scrap PC 2/21/1934. AFE 47969 shows 6/11/1934. The sale order was apparently issued 2/21/1934, but the locomotive was not actually delivered to PC until 6/11/1934.

NOTE 48: Walter F. Becker shows GN 13(2) sold Kettle River Quarries 5/1917. URPC indicates ret. 2/1918.

NOTE 49: Harold L. Goldsmith (personal communication to Robert Post, dated 12/28/1980) indicated that GN 17(3) was sold U.S. Army 9/22/1938. URPC shows retired 12/1938.

NOTE 50: GN 30(3) and 31(3) were acquired from GNIOP in 9/1917. GN 30(3) was purchased from Grant Iron Mining Company (No. 203). GN 31(3) was purchased from Arthur Iron Mining Co. (No. 204) [HCR Vol. 43 (NE8)]. These locomotives were part of an order of 8 locomotives (GNIOP 201-208) produced by Lima (C/N 5133-5140) (information provided by George Sittig to Norman C. Keyes, Jr.). The other locomotives were never incorporated into the GN roster, and disposition is unknown.

NOTE 51: Walter F. Becker shows GN 34(2) sold Great Lakes Coal & Dock Co. 12/1921. URPC indicates retired 11/1921. Index entry for AFE 19215 shows sold 11/21/1921.

NOTE 52: Walter F. Becker shows GN 37(2), 39(2) and 40(2) sold John Cox 2/1923. URPC shows ret. 3/1923. AFE 23375 shows these engines retired 3/1923 through sale to John Cox.

NOTE 53: Information derived from Historical Engine Record indicates GN 32(3) and 33(3) were converted to A-5(2) from D-5's in 1926 and on 2/19/1926, respectively. GN Locomotive Diagram dated 1/1/1926 shows these locomotives rebuilt 2/16/1925. URPC shows 2/26 for 33(3). AFE 30741 indicates that 32(3) was rebuilt in 1925, and that 33(3) was rebuilt 2/19/1926. This seems the most likely in view of other records.

NOTE 54: GN Locomotive Diagram dated 1/1/1926 shows D-5 GN 457 rebuilt to A- 5(2) GN 34(3) at Delta 1/1926. Walter F. Becker states "there are indications that 457 about 1925 temporarily had its pilot wheels removed, similar to 455 and 458, and given No. 34(2), and later returned to its former status as No. 457." There is no evidence of the 457 to 34(3) rebuild in URPC. In view of the fact that the diagram is dated on the first day of the year, it is questionable whether this rebuild actually took place.

NOTE 55:   Walter F. Becker shows GN 47(2) sold National Surface Guard Co. 1/1918. URPC indicates retired 3/1918.

NOTE 56:   Walter F. Becker indicated GN 48(2) scrapped 4/1918. URPC shows 5/1918.

NOTE 57:   Walter F. Becker shows GN 52(2) scrapped 1937. URPC shows retired 1/1938.

NOTE 58:   Walter F. Becker shows GN 58(2) scrapped 9/1926. URPC shows retired 12/1926. AFE 31608 shows sold for scrap DI&M 12/1926.

NOTE 59:   Walter F. Becker shows GN 62(2) scrapped 9/1929. URPC shows retired 10/1929. AFE 41601 shows sold for scrap DI&M 10/1929.

NOTE 60:   GN 258(1), 351(1), 410(2), 515, and 650 were exhibited at the Columbian Exposition prior to their delivery to the GN (Norman C. Keyes, Jr., personal communication to Kenneth R. Middleton dated 2/2/1980).

NOTE 61:   Secondary sources from GN records (Walter F. Becker and Lambert M. Baker) and URPC show GN 65(2) sold Great Lakes Coal & Dock Co. 9/1927. William D. Edson shows 9/1937. However, the engine was sold under AFE 35221, which was dated 9/20/1927.

NOTE 62:   AFE 42724 shows GN 69(2) sold for scrap DI&M 7/21/1932 (but not under this AFE). AFE 47969 shows GN 69(2) retired under this AFE and sold for scrap DI&M 3/18/1934. URPC confirms the 3/1934 date.

NOTE 63:   HCR Vol. 38 (NE3) indicates GN 73(2)-82(2) were originally placed in Old Class 7A.

NOTE 64:   Walter F. Becker shows 96(2), 97(2), 98, and 99(2) scrapped 1937. URPC shows retired 1/1938.

NOTE 65:   George Sittig indicated GN 103 received new boiler 1908. Information derived from Historical Engine Record shows 1/1910.

NOTE 66:   Some previous rosters (e.g. Walter F. Becker) have grouped these three locomotives (StPM&M 115, 116, and 117) with the Old Class 24 locomotives which later became Class B-13. However, the locomotive dimensions as given in the 1891 and 1892 Annual Reports of the Machinery Department are the same as those engines (StPM&M 118-124) which later became Class B-14. The Annual Reports group these three with those engines, as has been done in this roster.

NOTE 67:   Walter F. Becker and Lambert M. Baker show GN 130, 131, and 132 retired 1937. URPC shows retired 1/1938.

NOTE 68:   Information derived from Historical Engine Record shows GN 136 scrapped 10/26/1918. URPC shows retired 12/1918. AFE 9328 shows 10/16/1918.

NOTE 69:   AFE 31608 shows GN 141 sold NSRM 3/1926. URPC shows sold to Ike Statman 3/1926.

NOTE 70:   GN Locomotive Diagram dated 6/1/1923 indicates GN 147 received new boiler in 1906. Information derived from Historical Engine Record indicates 9/1907.

NOTE 71:   Information derived from Historical Engine Record shows GN 172, 177, and 182 scrapped on 11/6/1918, 11/18/1918 and 11/18/1918, respectively. URPC indicates retired 12/1918.

NOTE 72:   AFE 31608 shows GN 173 sold to NSRM in one location and Pacific Coast Steel in another.

NOTE 73:   URPC shows GN 175 sold for scrap DI&M 6/1926. AFE 33767 shows 2/1927.

NOTE 74:   Information derived from Historical Engine Record and Walter F. Becker show GN 178 sold for scrap 12/1926 and scrapped 12/1926, respectively. URPC and AFE 33769 show retired 2/1927.

NOTE 75:   Walter F. Becker shows GN 185 scrapped 1937. URPC shows retired 1/1938.

NOTE 76:   Lambert M. Baker indicates GN 150 was scrapped in 1916. However, a letter from William Kelly to C.O. Jenks, dated 12/24/1934, indicates this engine was sold in 1908.

NOTE 77:   Information derived from Historical Engine Record shows GN 205 sold for scrap 12/1926. URPC shows retired 1/1927.

NOTE 78:   Information derived from Historical Engine Record shows GN 213 sold for scrap 11/1928. URPC shows retired 12/1928.

NOTE 79:   Information derived from Historical Engine Record shows GN 217 sold for scrap 3/23/1928. URPC shows retired 4/1928. AFE 35872 shows sold for scrap DI&M 4/1928. Lambert M. Baker and "List of Engines Disposed of During Years 1920 to 1931 Inclusive" (Minnesota Historical Society GN VP-Operating File #39-31, 21.F.5.6F) show 1927 as the disposition date.

NOTE 80:   Information derived from Historical Engine Record shows GN 222 and 224 sold for scrap DI&M 10/9/1929. AFE 41601 shows 11/1929.

NOTE 81:   Information derived from Historical Engine Record shows GN 225 sold for scrap DI&M 8/28/1928. AFE 37274 shows dismantled at Superior 8/29/1928.

NOTE 82:   Information derived from Historical Engine Record shows GN 227 sold for scrap 11/25/1925. URPC shows retired 12/1925.

NOTE 83:   Information derived from Historical Engine Record shows GN 228(2) scrapped 1937. URPC shows retired 1/1938.

NOTE 84:   Information derived from Historical Engine Record shows GN 231(2) sold for scrap NSRM 6/1926. URPC and AFE 41601 show retired 3/1926, sold for scrap to Ike Statman. AFE 41601 shows that a sale order was written to NSRM, but cancelled.

NOTE 85:   On page 50, 1880 HER appears to have an entry for GN 50 that says "Sold 5/16/01" (hard to read). There is also an entry indicating GN 50 [by that time renumbered 252(2)] was outshopped on that date. Since GN 252(2) was on the roster much longer than that (sold for scrap to PC 3/1926 under AFE 31608), it is possible this was an entry error and that the locomotive sold on 5/16/1901 was GN 251(2) (ex 49). The 1901 sale date for 251(2) agrees with Lambert M. Baker's roster.

NOTE 86:   NE1 shows GN 253 and 254 received 1/6/1893. 1880 HER shows 1/7/1893.

NOTE 87:   Norman C. Keyes, Jr., information in steam locomotive notes (probably from CNRA) shows GN 289 sold for scrap 9/11/1929. URPC and AFE 41601 show 10/1929.

NOTE 88:   Information derived from Historical Engine Record shows GN 292 received a new boiler in 1906. GN Locomotive Diagram dated 7/1/1925 shows 1905.

NOTE 89:   URPC shows GN 292 and 293 retired 11/1927. AFE 35186 shows engines delivered DI&M 8/3/1927.

NOTE 90:   Norman C. Keyes, Jr., (personal communication to Kenneth R. Middleton dated 10/9/1977) indicated GN 295 was scrapped 10/2/1900. 1880 HER shows "10/2", which if interpreted as 10/1902 agrees with the 1902 date shown in the Lambert M. Baker roster.

NOTE 91:   The return of FG&S 4 to GN as 341(2) was proposed (as indicated by an undated diagram), but the locomotive was sold before this occurred.

NOTE 92:   NE1 shows GN 351(1) received 11/15/1893. 1880 HER shows originally received 1/1/1893, and received from the "World Fair" 11/16/1893. URPC shows the same locomotive as GN 400(2) sold for scrap 3/1926. AFE 31037 indicates that the date of sale was 2/1926, with retirement 3/1926.

NOTE 93:   1880 HER shows GN 359 received 8/26/1893. NE1 shows 8/28/1893.

NOTE 94:   1880 HER shows GN 362 and 363(1) received 11/22/1893. NE1 shows 11/21/1893.

NOTE 95:   1880 HER shows GN 364(1) and 365(1) received 11/28/1893. NE1 shows 11/27/1893.

NOTE 96:   Information derived from Historical Engine Record shows GN 402(2) sold for scrap Pacific Coast Steel. URPC and AFE 31608 show NSRM.

NOTE 97:   Information derived from Historical Engine Record shows GN 413(2) sold for scrap 8/5/1927. URPC shows retired 9/1927. AFE 35186 shows sold for scrap DI&M 9/1927.

NOTE 98:   Information derived from Historical Engine Record shows GN 417 dismantled 3/24/1925. URPC shows retired 6/1925.

NOTE 99:   Norman C. Keyes, Jr. indicated GN 420 sold SP&S 10/1924, and also 10/24/1922 (the latter date from SP&S records of Bob Johnston). Information derived from Historical Engine Record shows 7/14/1925. URPC shows a disposition date of 6/1925. AFE 24548, under which the locomotive was sold, is dated 10/10/1923.

NOTE 100: Information derived from Historical Engine Record shows GN 425 and 426 sold for scrap 9/1926. URPC and AFE 31608 show 12/1926.

NOTE 101: Information derived from Historical Engine Record shows GN 401(2), 405(2), 408(2), 409(2), 410(3), 412(2), 414(2), 415, 418 and 421 sold for scrap 6/1926. AFE 31608 shows 4/1926.

NOTE 102: Information derived from Historical Engine Record shows GN 402(2), 468(2) and 471(2) sold for scrap Pacific Coast Steel. AFE 31608 and URPC indicate this sale was cancelled and the engines sold NSRM.

NOTE 103: Information derived from Historical Engine Record shows GN 403(2), 404(2), 411(2), 419, 423, 451(2) and 469(2) sold for scrap 6/1926. AFE 31608 and URPC show 4/1926.

NOTE 104: Information derived from Historical Engine Record shows GN 424 sold for scrap 6/1926. URPC shows 3/1926, and AFE 31608 shows 5/1926.

NOTE 105: Information derived from Historical Engine Record shows GN 413(2) sold for scrap 8/5/1927. AFE 35186 shows 9/1927.

NOTE 106: The return of FG&S 3 to GN as 430(2) was proposed (as indicated by an undated diagram), but the locomotive was sold for scrap DI&M in 1927 (prior to return) according to AFE 35186.

NOTE 107: GN 499 was originally delivered as a tandem compound with dimensions of 13&22x26-55-180-147,000-130,000- ?   (Norman C. Keyes, Jr., personal communication to Kenneth R. Middleton dated 1/25/1981). It was rebuilt about 1901 to a simple engine with the same dimensions as the rest of the class (work to simple the engine was approved under AFE 4342, approved 6/25/1901).

NOTE 108: 1880 HER shows GN 452(1) and 453(1) received 6/20/1892. NE1 shows 6/19/1892.

NOTE 109: 1880 HER shows GN 456(1)-459(1) received 6/27/1892. NE1 shows 6/28/1892.

NOTE 110: Information derived from Historical Engine Record shows GN 468(2) and 471(2) sold for scrap Pacific Coast Steel. URPC and AFE 31608 show NSRM.

NOTE 111: Information derived from Historical Engine Record shows GN 460(2) sold Midland of Manitoba 1926. AFE 31608 shows this engine sold for scrap DI&M 6/1926.

NOTE 112: Norman C. Keyes, Jr., (steam locomotive notes) indicated GN 525 was repurchased from Somers Lumber Co. c.1925. Walter F. Becker says scrapped in 6/1928, renumbered to X1969 in 12/1931 (the renumbering pertains to the tender only). Walter F. Becker then gives a scrap date of 11/1951 for a GN 525(2), but cannot determine the origin of this 525(2). AFE 29868, for the return of this engine from Somers, was dated 8/28/1925, and covered the repurchase of this locomotive as well as the sale to Somers of GN 342. URPC indicates a sale date of 10/1925 for GN 342, so it is reasonable to suspect that this was the return date for GN 525(2). The source or meaning for the 6/1928 date is unknown, but the 11/1951 scrap date applies to GN 525 as indicated by AFE 81610.

NOTE 113: Norman C. Keyes, Jr., and Robert Graham indicate these engines were owned by EM, but no evidence has been found in GN records. Their receipt was cataloged in NE1 (EM equipment was not normally included in GN New Equipment Registers). The builder's photo shows a small "G.N. Ry" on the tender rather than "E.M.". Also, the 1900 diagram book shows that these engines were owned by GN rather than EM.

NOTE 114: Norman C. Keyes, Jr. steam locomotive notes indicate that GN 601 was sold PC 11/1928. URPC indicates scrapped 12/1928.

NOTE 115: George Sittig indicated that GN 605 was sold DI&M 11/29/1928. URPC indicates scrapped 12/1928.

NOTE 116: George Sittig indicated GN 607 was sold 10/1941. URPC shows wrecked 12/1941.

NOTE 117: Information derived from Historical Engine Record shows GN 742 receiving a boiler from GN 755 in 1/1911 in one location and on 11/21/1908 in another location. The 1911 date is more likely correct since GN 755 did not receive the boiler from GN 767 until 3/25/1909 or 8/1910 (two dates are shown here also).

NOTE 118: Information derived from Historical Engine Record indicated GN 742 sold for scrap 3/26/1948. URPC shows retired 5/1948.

NOTE 119: Information derived from Historical Engine Record and AFE 74045 indicate GN 747 sold for scrap 4/30/1947. URPC shows retired 5/1947.

NOTE 120: Information derived from Historical Engine Record indicated GN 748 sold for scrap 4/21/1953. URPC shows retired 5/1953, and AFE 83761 shows 5/16/1953..

NOTE 121: Information derived from Historical Engine Record indicated GN 749 sold for scrap 8/5/1949. URPC shows retired 11/1949.

NOTE 122: Information derived from Historical Engine Record shows that GN 755 received the boiler from GN 767 in 8/1910 in one location and on 3/25/1909 in another location.

NOTE 123: Information derived from Historical Engine Record indicated GN 756 and GN 759 sold for scrap 3/20/1948. URPC shows retired 5/1948.

NOTE 124: Information derived from Historical Engine Record indicated GN 757 sold 9/17/1944. URPC shows 10/1944.

NOTE 125: Information derived from Historical Engine Record indicated GN 758 sold for scrap 2/1941. URPC shows retired 3/1941.

NOTE 126: Information derived from Historical Engine Record indicated GN 763 sold for scrap 4/16/1948. URPC shows retired 6/1948.

NOTE 127: Information derived from Historical Engine Record indicated GN 764 sold for scrap 8/28/1950. URPC shows retired 10/1950.

NOTE 128: Information derived from Historical Engine Record shows GN 852 sold for scrap 4/14/1948. URPC shows retired 6/1948. CNRA shows the rebuild to GN 852 was finished 5/29/1925, and AFE 29152 shows 10/30/1925.

NOTE 129: CNRA shows GN 853 completed 11/7/1925. AFE 29152 shows 10/19/1925.

NOTE 130: CNRA shows GN 858 completed 7/27/1926. AFE 30741 shows 7/28/1926.

NOTE 131: Information derived from Historical Engine Record shows GN 861 sold for scrap 4/21/1953. URPC shows retired 5/1953. AFE 83761 shows sold for scrap 5/7/1953.

NOTE 132: Information derived from Historical Engine Record and AFE 74045 show GN 866 sold for scrap 4/28/1947. URPC shows retired 5/1947.

NOTE 133: Information derived from Historical Engine Record shows GN 869 sold for scrap 3/26/1948. URPC shows retired 5/1948.

NOTE 134: Information derived from Historical Engine Record shows GN 873 scrapped at Seattle 9/1939. AFE 57443 shows this engine retired 9/1939, and sold for scrap Bethlehem Steel c.10/1939.

NOTE 135: Information derived from Historical Engine Record shows GN 878 and GN 879 sold for scrap 4/21/1953. AFE 83761 shows 5/5/1953. The letter from the General Superintendent of Motive Power asking for the locomotives to be shipped to Superior was dated 4/21/1953 (AFE 83761).

NOTE 136: Lambert M. Baker shows that GN 1308 was rebuilt to C-3 899, and then renumbered to GN 883(2). However, AFE 32972 indicates that GN 1308 was rebuilt directly to GN 883(2) on 12/7/1926. Walter F. Becker also could not confirm that this engine ever carried No. 899.

NOTE 137: Information derived from Historical Engine Record shows GN 883(2) and 890 sold for scrap PC 10/3/1952. AFE 82873 shows 10/2/1952.

NOTE 138: Information derived from Historical Engine Record shows W&SF 16 renumbered GN 910 8/11/1921. CNRA shows 4/10/1922.

NOTE 139: Information derived from Historical Engine Record shows W&SF 17 renumbered GN 911 7/14/1921. CNRA shows 5/12/1922.

NOTE 140: Information derived from Historical Engine Record shows GN 927 sold for scrap 10/10/1950. URPC shows retired 11/1950.

NOTE 141: AFE 62055 shows GN 928 sold for scrap 8/8/1941. URPC shows retired 9/1941.

NOTE 142: Information derived from Historical Engine Record shows GN 931 sold for scrap 4/14/1948. URPC shows retired 6/1948.

NOTE 143: AFE 74045 shows GN 932 sold for scrap 3/28/1947. URPC shows retired 4/1947.

NOTE 144: Information derived from Historical Engine Record shows GN 937 and GN 938 sold for scrap 4/16/1948. URPC shows retired 6/1948.

NOTE 145: URPC shows GN 1007 superheated 8/1918. AFE 21168 shows 10/1918.

NOTE 146: GN 1008-1032 were delivered lettered as Class E-13 [as shown in builder's photographs and indicated in HCR Vol. 40 (NE5)], but were changed to E-14 almost immediately after delivery.

NOTE 147: HCR Vol. 38 (NE3) shows GN 1069 received 3/31/1905, but shipped from builder 4/12/1903 (which may be a clerical error since the engines with preceding numbers were shipped in 1904). It is uncertain why this locomotive took so long to be received, as most were received within about two weeks after shipment.

NOTE 148: GN 1160(1)-1164(1) may have been renumbered directly to GN 1095-1099 in 1902, though HCR Vol. 99 (GN Subsidiary Renumberings Book) indicates that they were renumbered GN 1195(1)-1199(1) in 1902, and then renumbered GN 1095-1099 in 1903.

NOTE 149: Walter F. Becker shows GN 1099 scrapped 1937. URPC shows retired 1/1938.

NOTE 150: Information derived from Historical Engine Record shows GN 1103 sold for scrap 10/4/1948. URPC shows retired 11/1948.

NOTE 151: Walter F. Becker shows GN 1145, GN 1200, GN 1205, GN 1211, and GN 1214 scrapped 1937. URPC shows retired 1/1938.

NOTE 152: Walter F. Becker indicates that GN 1207 may have been rebuilt to C-4 791, but this rebuild probably did not occur. URPC shows the locomotive was scrapped as 1207.

NOTE 153: BA&P 26 and 27 were purchased by GN in 2/1917 (George Sittig, Great Northern steam locomotive roster information sent to Norman C. Keyes, Jr.). BA&P 26 was renumbered GN 1326 at Havre 5/24/1917. BA&P 27 was renumbered GN 1327 at Butte 3/17/1917.

NOTE 154: Walter F. Becker shows GN 1378 sold SP&S 11/1944. URPC and AFE 69574 (under which the sale was made) show 10/1944. AFE 30176 shows GN 1378 was equipped with a booster as it was rebuilt to an H-7. URPC shows the booster applied 5/1930 under AFE 41721.

NOTE 155: AFE 47774 shows GN 1406 sold for scrap PC in one location and DI&M in another.

NOTE 156: Walter F. Becker and Lambert M. Baker show GN 1414 scrapped 1937. URPC shows retired 1/1938.

NOTE 157: A memo from William Kelly to W.R. Wood, dated 3/18/1921, states that GN Nos. 1421, 1425, 1428, 1430 and 1433 had been converted to H-3 (by the addition of piston valves) as of that date. AFE 16496, while not clear as to actual dates of conversion, was dated 1/12/1921, and was written for these locomotives, implying that the conversion took place in early 1921.

NOTE 158: GN 1425 was delivered with a Baldwin superheater [based upon diagrams and an article in the 10/26/1906 issue of *The Railroad Gazette* (Vol. 41, No.7)], and for this reason was transferred at some time prior to 1910 to Class H-3(1).

NOTE 159: Norman C. Keyes, Jr., research on the date of rebuilding of GN 1426 to H-3 found that the GN Equipment List of January 1942 showed the engine as an H-2, while the list of September 1947 showed the engine as an H-3, indicating that the rebuild occurred in between (personal communication to Kenneth R. Middleton dated 5/3/1975). However, a diagram dated 7/12/1940 already shows this engine as an H-3.

NOTE 160: GN 1549 was delivered with a Baldwin superheater [based upon diagrams and an article in the 10/26/1906 issue of *The Railroad Gazette* (Vol. 41, No.7)], and for this reason was transferred at some time prior to 1910 to Class J-3. It was returned to Class J-1S with the installation of a Schmidt superheater on 1/5/1914 (as indicated by diagram).

NOTE 161: HCR Vol. 39 (NE4) shows GN 1608 and 1609 received 5/28/1907. HER shows 5/27/1907.

NOTE 162: HCR Vol. 39 (NE4) shows GN 1628 and 1629 received 6/16/1907. HER shows 6/14/1907.

NOTE 163: HCR Vol. 39 (NE4) shows GN 1638 received 7/2/1907. HER shows 6/30/1907.

NOTE 164: HCR Vol. 39 (NE4) shows GN 1704, 1705, 1706 and 1707 received 6/6/1906. HER shows 6/7/1906.

NOTE 165: HER shows GN 1706 sold for scrap 9/9/1941. AFE 62055 shows 9/8/1941.

NOTE 166: HCR Vol. 39 (NE4) shows GN 1708 and 1709 received 6/26/1906. HER shows 6/28/1906.

NOTE 167: A number of locomotives are listed in HER as being sold 4/19/1956 under AFE 87722. Dates of Sale Orders under this AFE were 4/11/1956, and actual delivery dates to scrappers are shown in the AFE. These delivery dates are used in the roster since BN officials have indicated that the actual delivery dates are considered the official sale dates.

NOTE 168: A number of locomotives are listed in HER as being sold 4/21/1953 under AFE 83761. This may have been the date of the Sale Orders under this AFE, and was the date of the memo from the General Superintendent of Motive Power requesting shipment of the engines to Superior. Actual delivery dates to scrappers are shown in the AFE. These delivery dates are used in the roster since BN officials have indicated that the actual delivery dates are considered the official sale dates.

NOTE 169: A number of locomotives are listed in HER as being sold 12/28/1954 and 5/9/1955 under AFE 85072. This was the date of the Sale Orders under this AFE. Actual delivery dates to scrappers are shown in the AFE. These delivery dates are used in the roster since BN officials have indicated that the actual delivery dates are considered the official sale dates.

NOTE 170: A number of locomotives are listed in HER as being sold 8/16/1956 under AFE 87970. This was the date of the Sale Orders under this AFE. Actual delivery dates to scrappers are used in the roster (when available) since BN officials have indicated that the actual delivery dates are considered the official sale dates.

NOTE 171:   A number of locomotives are listed in HER as being sold 7/16/1953 under AFE 84143. This was the date of the Sale Orders under this AFE. Actual delivery dates to scrappers are used in the roster (when available) since BN officials have indicated that the actual delivery dates are considered the official sale dates.

NOTE 172:   HCR Vol. 39 (NE4) shows GN 1800(1), 1801(1) and 1803(1) received on 9/6/1906, 9/11/1906, and 9/30/1906, respectively. HER shows 9/7/1906, 9/13/1906, and 10/1/1906.

NOTE 173:   HCR Vol. 40 (NE5) shows GN 1800(2)-1802(2) received 3/25/1908. HER shows 3/26/1908.

NOTE 174:   HCR Vol. 39 (NE4) shows GN 1804(2) received 3/25/1908. HER shows 3/27/1908.

NOTE 175:   HCR Vol. 39 (NE4) shows GN 1806 and 1807 received 5/17/1907. HER shows 5/16/1907.

NOTE 176:   HCR Vol. 39 (NE4) shows GN 1808 and 1809 received 5/20/1907. HER shows 5/19/1907.

NOTE 177:   HCR Vol. 39 (NE4) shows GN 1812-1815 received 6/2/1907, 5/28/1907, 9/24/1907, and 5/28/1907, respectively. HER shows 5/29/1907 for all.

NOTE 178:   HCR Vol. 39 (NE4) shows GN 1816-1819 received 6/6/1907, 6/5/1907, 6/5/1907, and 6/9/1907, respectively. HER shows 5/6/1907 for all.

NOTE 179:   HCR Vol. 39 (NE4) shows GN 1820 received 6/26/1907. HER shows 6/25/1907.

NOTE 180:   HCR Vol. 39 (NE4) shows GN 1821 received 6/25/1907. HER shows 5/25/1907.

NOTE 181:   HCR Vol. 39 (NE4) shows GN 1822 and 1823 received 6/30/1907. HER shows 5/30/1907.

NOTE 182:   HCR Vol. 39 (NE4) shows GN 1825 received 7/6/1907. HER shows 7/7/1907.

NOTE 183:   HCR Vol. 39 (NE4) shows GN 1826 received 7/21/1907. HER shows 7/22/1907.

NOTE 184:   HCR Vol. 39 (NE4) shows GN 1827 received 7/28/1907. HER shows 7/29/1907.

NOTE 185:   HCR Vol. 39 (NE4) shows GN 1829 received 8/6/1907. HER shows 8/5/1907.

NOTE 186:   HCR Vol. 39 (NE4) shows GN 1830 and 1831 received 3/25/1908. HER shows 3/26/1907.

NOTE 187:   HCR Vol. 39 (NE4) shows GN 1839 received 4/3/1908. HER shows 4/5/1908.

NOTE 188:   HCR Vol. 39 (NE4) shows GN 1841, 1843 and 1844 received 4/7/1908, 4/7/1908 and 4/14/1908, respectively. HER shows 4/8/1908 for all.

NOTE 189:   HCR Vol. 40 (NE5) shows GN 1920-1924 received 5/12/1908, 5/16/1908, 5/12/1908, 5/16/1908 and 5/25/1908, respectively. HER shows 5/13/1908, 5/17/1908, 5/13/1908, 5/17/1908, and 5/24/1908.

NOTE 190:   HCR Vol. 40 (NE5) shows GN 1908 and 1909 received 4/17/1908. HER shows 4/18/1908.

NOTE 191:   HCR Vol. 40 (NE5) shows GN 1910-1913 received 4/27/1908. HER shows 1910 and 1911 received 4/29/1908, and 1912 and 1913 received 4/28/1908.

NOTE 192:   HCR Vol. 40 (NE5) shows GN 1916 and 1917 received 5/4/1908. HER shows 5/1/1908.

NOTE 193:   HCR Vol. 40 (NE5), HCR Vol. 41 (NE6) and builder's photos indicate that GN 1950-1959 were received as Class L-3 and that GN 1960-1984 were received as Class M-2, but both groups were apparently considered to be Class M-1 almost immediately after delivery (i.e. the L-3 and M-2 designations were never actually used in practice).

NOTE 194:   HCR Vol. 40 (NE5) shows GN 1950-1955 received 3/7/1910, 1/19/1910, 1/17/1910, 1/19/1910, 1/23/1910 and 2/5/1910, respectively. HER shows 3/11/1910, 1/20/1910, 1/18/1910, 1/20/1910, 1/24/1910, and 2/6/1910.

NOTE 195:   HCR Vol. 40 (NE5) shows GN 1959 received 3/7/1910. HER shows 3/8/1910.

NOTE 196:   HCR Vol. 41 (NE6) shows GN 1962 and 1966 received 7/23/1910. HER shows 7/24/1910.

NOTE 197:   HCR Vol. 41 (NE6) shows GN 1977 received 9/5/1910. HER shows 9/6/1910.

NOTE 198:   HCR Vol. 41 (NE6) shows GN 1984 received 10/10/1910. HER shows 10/11/1910.

NOTE 199:   It is impossible to tell from HER exactly when GN 2021 was simpled (i.e. rebuilt to N-2). However, the engine received exhaust piping from the back cylinders to the feedwater heater in 3/1926 under AFE 30186 according to URPC. This was one of the AFE's authorizing simpling of the locomotives (27634, 30186, 30616 and 31179), which probably indicates the simpling was completed in 3/1926. Since the locomotive was in the Superior shops from 12/11/1925 through 3/31/1926, this appears to be the likely date of conversion to N-2.

NOTE 200:   A number of locomotives are listed in HER as being sold 8/16/1956 under AFE 87970. This was the date of the Sale Orders under this AFE. Actual delivery dates to scrappers are used in the roster (when available) since BN officials have indicated that the actual delivery dates are considered the official sale dates.

NOTE 201:   A number of locomotives are listed in HER as being sold 5/9/1955 under AFE 85072. This was the date of some of the Sale Orders under this AFE. Actual delivery dates to scrappers are shown in the AFE. These delivery dates are used in the roster since BN officials have indicated that the actual delivery dates are considered the official sale dates.

NOTE 202:   Construction Numbers given for GN 2034-2059 are boiler numbers. Boilers were supplied to GN by Puget Sound Machinery Depot.

NOTE 203:   HER shows the new boiler of GN 2047 to be 46208-1. Lambert M. Baker shows 46208-2, and that 46208-1 was assigned to GN 2054. Since the entire sequence of new boiler numbers was obtained from L.M. Baker, 46208-2 is believed to be correct.

NOTE 204:   HER shows GN 2122 sold for scrap 4/19/1956, but URPC indicates this engine was not retired until 12/1957, and shows 2121 retired 4/1956. It appears probable that the retirement information was written onto the wrong page in HER.

NOTE 205:   Norman C. Keyes, Jr., shows all of the Q-2 class which were retired in 1957 and 1958 as being scrapped in 1963. Since the only 1960's date for which information is available in the AFE's corresponds with George Sittig's dates, these have been used in the roster.

NOTE 206:   GN 2550-2555 received an unclassified shopping at Dale Street on 5/22/1929, 5/24/1929, 6/6/1929, 6/6/1929, 6/7/1929 and 6/7/1929, respectively. It is possible that these are dates received.

NOTE 207:   HCR Vol. 43 (NE8) shows that GN 3103, 3104, 3105, 3106 and 3110 were shipped in May and June, 1918, but were consigned to the Regional Director of Eastern Railroads (presumably of the United States Railroad Administration), care of the Wheeling and Lake Erie Railroad at Canton, OH. Since these engines were not received by GN until 12/1918, it appears likely that they were used for a time on the W&LE.

NOTE 208:   GN 3204-3208 had been assigned to the El Paso & Southwestern by the USRA. They were built in 11/1918 (per George Sittig) and purchased by GN in 1/1920 (AFE 14003).

NOTE 209: Information derived from Historical Engine Record shows GN 3300 sold for scrap 7/6/1948. AFE 76560 shows 5/7/1948, but this may be the date of the Sale Order rather than the delivery date.

NOTE 210: Information derived from Historical Engine Record shows GN 3311 completed 5/28/1923. AFE 21009 shows 5/29/1923.

NOTE 211: Information derived·from Historical Engine Record shows GN 3313 completed 5/31/1923. AFE 21009 shows 6/2/1923.

NOTE 212: Information derived from Historical Engine Record shows GN 3324 sold for scrap DI&M 9/30/1949. AFE 42724 indicates this engine was sold for scrap DI&M 7/21/1932, but AFE 78418 and URPC confirm the 9/1949 date. Also, the locomotive appears on a GN diagram dated 1/30/1947.

NOTE 213: Information derived from Historical Engine Record show GN 3327 sold for scrap PC 9/27/1941. AFE 62055 shows 9/8/1941.

NOTE 214: Information derived from Historical Engine Record shows GN 3331 sold for scrap 2/7/1947. AFE 74045 shows 2/17/1947.

NOTE 215: Information derived from Historical Engine Record shows GN 3342 sold for scrap 9/15/1941. AFE 62055 shows 10/14/1941, and confirms this as the delivery date.

NOTE 216: CNRA shows GN 4000 and 4001 purchased from SP&S 7/1939, but Norman C. Keyes, Jr., indicated the engines were actually received 1/25/1940 and 1/18/1940, respectively. Norman C. Keyes, Jr., shows these engines sold back to SP&S on 3/27/1950 and 7/1/1946, respectively, but CNRA shows them as retired 4/1950 and 11/1946. AFE 79433 contains a copy of the Sale Order for GN 4000, which is dated 4/27/1950. Information derived from Historical Engine Record shows GN 4001 delivered to SP&S 10/21/1946.

NOTE 217: Steam Motor No. 6000 is listed in GN diagrams as rebuilt by GN in 1908, but is listed in HER as having been received at St.Paul 1/9/1909 and at Delta 7/27/1909. Actual date of acquisition from the CB&Q is unknown.

NOTE 218: HER shows that construction of Q-2 2187 was initiated on 7/31/1928 in one entry and on 8/1/1928 in another.

NOTE 219: No reference has been found for the date of renumbering of GN 11(2) to GN 244(2). The date of 1907 has been used since it would have been necessary to clear the number at that time for A-9 11(3) which was received in 1907.

NOTE 220: URPC shows GN 32(3) sold 10/1929. AFE 41470 indicates the locomotive was actually delivered 9/24/1929, but not retired until 10/1929.

NOTE 221: The 1900 locomotive diagram book shows GN 88(2) and 89(2) in Old Class 8. However, the index of the locomotive diagram book dating from c.1915 shows them as having been in Old Class 8A prior to being assigned to Class A-10. While no records have been located to indicate the date when these locomotives were renumbered to GN 98 and 99, it was probably done in 1905 to clear the numbers for A-9 locomotive 98, delivered in that year. This is probably corroborated by the Baker roster, which shows GN 85(2)-87(2) renumbered as 95(2)-97(2) in 1905, no doubt for the same reason.

NOTE 222: Information derived from Historical Engine Record shows GN 159 and 163 received new Baldwin-built boilers in 8/1908. Lambert M. Baker shows the boilers as built by GN.

NOTE 223: The disposition date of GN 261 (originally StP&P 33) is uncertain. The Lambert M. Baker roster and steam locomotive notes of Norman C. Keyes, Jr., indicate that the locomotive was scrapped in 1901. Information obtained by Norman F. Priebe (based on the HER) indicate the locomotive was scrapped in 1899. The 1880 HER shows only "Scrapped AFE 3957" with no date given.

NOTE 224: GN 515 was originally delivered as a tandem compound with dimensions of 13&22x26-55-180-147,000-130,000- ?   (Norman C. Keyes, Jr., personal communication to Kenneth R. Middleton dated 1/25/1981). It was rebuilt about 1900 to a simple engine with the same dimensions as the rest of the class (work to simple the engine was approved under AFE 3391, approved 11/17/1900, with a notation that work had already been completed).

NOTE 225: William D. Edson's notes on the Charles E. Fisher locomotive roster indicate that GN 701 was rebuilt from a 4-8-0 to a 2-8-0 in 1902. This rebuilding was conducted under AFE 4621, approved on 8/6/1901. According to this AFE the locomotive was badly wrecked on the Cascade Division by "running into a push car loaded with dynamite." The decision was made to repair it as a Consolidation rather than a Mastodon to increase the weight on the driving wheels. The date of completion is not given in the AFE, so the work could have taken until 1902 to be completed.

NOTE 226: URPC shows GN 954 and 967 scrapped 3/1926 and 5/1926, respectively. AFE 31037 shows both of these locomotives sold for scrap 2/1926, with retirement not occurring until the dates indicated by URPC.

NOTE 227: URPC shows that GN 1073 was retired under AFE 45259 in 6/1930. While this locomotive is listed in AFE 45259 (approved 1/13/1932), no disposition is shown. It only states that the locomotive is being held at Great Falls for disposition. However, a notation in AFE 42724 (approved 6/6/1930) states that the locomotive left Great Falls for DI&M on 6/20/1932.

NOTE 228: URPC shows GN 1074, 1075 and 1076 sold in 6/1925 under AFE 24548. AFE 24548 (approved 10/20/1923) was written for the sale of six locomotives to SP&S, but these three are not listed. The locomotives listed in the AFE were 951, 966, 967, 1506, 1532 and 1641. Apparently the locomotives originally intended for sale to SP&S were refused or considered unacceptable, and these three were substituted, but no documentation exists in the AFE. George Sittig (Great Northern steam locomotive roster information sent to Norman C. Keyes, Jr.) indicated that these locomotives were sold to SP&S in 3/1924.

NOTE 229: Based upon the Lambert M. Baker roster, Great Northern records show GN 1078 to be Baldwin C/N 34904. William D. Edson (personal communication to Norman C. Keyes, Jr., 1979) stated that the Baldwin builders list shows GN 1078 as C/N 34903. However, Ron Nixon, who had a photo of the locomotive, examined the negative with a magnifier and found that the builder's plate on the locomotive showed C/N 34904 (Norman C. Keyes, Jr., personal communication to Kenneth R. Middleton dated 2/2/1980).

NOTE 230: AFE 12447 shows in one location that GN 1409 received Heron valves on 8/2/1919, and in another location 9/2/1919.

NOTE 231: AFE 12447 shows that GN 1414, 1419, 1423 and 1424 received Heron valves on 3/6/1919, 3/28/1919, 9/25/1918, and 6/15/1918, respectively. URPC shows 5/1919 for all of these locomotives.

NOTE 232: A number of locomotives are listed in HER as being sold 1/6/1955, 4/26/1955, and 5/9/1955 under AFE 86021. Those were the date of the Sale Orders under this AFE. Actual delivery dates to scrappers are shown in the AFE. These delivery dates are used in the roster since BN officials have indicated that the actual delivery dates are considered the official sale dates.

NOTE 233: A number of locomotives are listed in HER as being sold 10/7/1955 under AFE 87055. This was the date of the Sale Orders under this AFE. Actual delivery dates to scrappers are shown in the AFE. These delivery dates are used in the roster since BN officials have indicated that the actual delivery dates are considered the official sale dates.

NOTE 234: A number of locomotives are listed in HER as being sold 8/25/1955 under AFE 86830. This was the date of the Sale Orders under this AFE. Actual delivery dates to scrappers are shown in the AFE. These delivery dates are used in the roster since BN officials have indicated that the actual delivery dates are considered the official sale dates.

NOTE 235: AFE 1661 was approved on March 9, 1916, for the construction of a "Q-1" 2-6-2 + 0-6-2 locomotive from two J-1 2-6-2's. The rear engine was to be located under the tender tank. A diagram was prepared, the number 1998 was assigned, and most of the required castings were completed by June 1917. However, by July 1917 it had become apparent that the delivery of the O-1 2-8-2's had eliminated the need for such a locomotive, and the AFE was closed some time later.

NOTE 236: AFE 81696 shows the booster removed from GN 2102 in 10/1951 in one location and 12/1951 in another.

NOTE 237: The deduction that the original driver size for Class 2(2) was 51 inches is based on the fact that the 1891 Machinery Department Annual Report shows the drivers having 44 inch centers, and the 1880 HER shows 3 5/8 inch tires.

NOTE 238: StPM&M 400-409 were probably rebuilt with larger cylinders and moved from Class 37(1) to Class 38 about 1892 or 1893. Evidence for this is that Class 37 was reused for GN 2-6-0's 351-365 received in 1893.

NOTE 239: URPC shows T7(2) scrapped 5/1949. AFE 74189 shows this tender sold for scrap DI&M 2/25/1947.

NOTE 240: URPC shows T8(3) dismantled 5/1926. AFE 31037 shows sold for scrap Pacific Coast Steel 2/1926, but not officially retired until 5/1926.

NOTE 241: URPC shows T18(3) sold for scrap 10/1928. AFE 38218 shows dismantled at Great Falls 10/12/1928.

NOTE 242: Another T26 is shown as retired 4/1918 (Tender only in Engineer's Report in URPC).

NOTE 243: Walter F. Becker shows E37, E39 and E40 sold to John Cox 2/1923. AFE 23375 shows E37 and T21, and E40 and T37, retired 3/1923 through sale to John Cox.

NOTE 244: Walter F. Becker shows GN 34(2) sold Great Lakes Coal & Dock Co. 12/1921. URPC indicates ret. 11/1921. Index entry for AFE 19215 shows sold 11/21/1921.

NOTE 245: URPC shows T32 scrapped 10/1928. AFE 37274 shows dismantled at Dale Street 8/4/1928. AFE 38281 shows sold for scrap PC 8/1928.

NOTE 246: URPC shows T47(2) retired as GN 42.

NOTE 247: URPC shows T59(2) sold for scrap 10/1941. AFE 62055 shows sold for scrap DI&M 8/27/1941.

NOTE 248: Another T128 is shown as retired 5/1918 (AFE 7369). The Valuation Engineering Report confirms the duplicate numbers as of 6/30/1915.

NOTE 249: Another T129 is shown as retired 6/1916. The Valuation Engineering Report confirms the duplicate numbers as of 6/30/1915.

NOTE 250: URPC shows T138 sold for scrap DI&M 3/1926. AFE 30624 shows 2/1926, but not officially retired until 3/1926.

NOTE 251: URPC shows T142 sold for scrap DI&M 6/1927. AFE 34441 shows 1/1927.

NOTE 252: AFE 69899 shows GN X900(2) completed on 6/29/1946 in one location and on 6/30/1946 in another.

NOTE 253: CNRA Account 57 shows T144 renumbered X951(1) 1/1927, then renumbered X1946(1) 5/1927, and retired 6/1927. AFE 33767 shows T144 sold for scrap DI&M 3/1927.

NOTE 254: CNRA Account 57 shows T150 reno. X1916(1) in 6/1927. URPC shows T151 reno. X1916(1) in 6/1927. T151 is confirmed by AFE 34696.

NOTE 255: CNRA Account 57 shows T152 renumbered X1946(2) 6/1928. AFE 36713 shows retired 2/1928.

NOTE 256: URPC shows T159 sold for scrap 5/1926. AFE 31037 shows 2/1926, but not officially retired until 5/1926.

NOTE 257: URPC shows T164 sold for scrap 10/1928. AFE 37274 shows dismantled at Dale Street 8/31/1928. AFE 38281 shows sold for scrap PC 8/1928.

NOTE 258: URPC shows T168 sold for scrap 2/1930. AFE 43690 shows retired 12/1930, and dismantled at Dale Street 3/3/1931.

NOTE 259: URPC shows T179 sold for scrap 1/1929. AFE 39040 shows sold for scrap DI&M 12/1928.

NOTE 260: URPC shows T184 sold for scrap Pacific Coast Steel 3/1927. AFE 33767 shows DI&M.

NOTE 261: AFE 45259 shows X1935(1) [formerly T188(2)] retired on 8/12/1932, and sold DI&M 9/1932. However, the sale apparently did not occur, as X1935(1) was again retired in 3/1934 and sold DI&M 3/29/1934 under AFE 47969.

NOTE 262: URPC shows T198 sold for scrap 3/1926. AFE 30624 shows 2/1926, but not officially retired until 3/1926.

NOTE 263: URPC shows T210 scrapped 10/1928. AFE 38218 shows sold for scrap DI&M 9/25/1928.

NOTE 264: CNRA Account 57 shows X1508 [previously numbered T255(2), 296093, and T95008] renumbered X1983 in 7/1927 and retired 2/1957. AFE 37520 shows T221 to X1983 8/1928, but it is possible this was just a replacement of the tank. AFE 47969 shows X1983 sold for scrap PC 6/11/1934. AFE 66666 then shows T1515 renumbered X1983 7/1943, for which there is no entry in CNRA Account 57. AFE 73476 shows this car sold for scrap DI&M 5/7/1947.

NOTE 265: URPC shows T237 sold for scrap 11/1927. AFE 35895 shows 12/18/1927.

NOTE 266: URPC and AFE 57837 also show a T241 scrapped 5/1940 (in addition to dismantled 2/1921).

NOTE 267: AFE 31806 shows T258(2) sold to Pacific Coast Steel in 12/1926. AFE 34696 shows this car renumbered as X1907(1) in 6/1927.

NOTE 268: URPC shows T271 sold for scrap DI&M 2/1928. CNRA Account 57 shows reno. X1985(2) in 6/1928. CNRA Account 57 shows this car retired 8/1932. AFE 45840 shows this car retired 11/1928 and stripped at Superior 8/8/1932. AFE 46484 shows it sold DI&M 10/1932.

NOTE 269: AFE 31608 shows T287 sold 12/1926, while AFE 33767 and URPC show 1/1927.

NOTE 270: AFE 37274 shows T293 dismantled at Dale Street 8/31/1928. AFE 38218 shows sold for scrap PC 8/1928.

NOTE 271: AFE 37274 shows T306 dismantled at Dale Street 8/20/1928. AFE 38218 shows sold for scrap PC 8/1928.

NOTE 272: CNRA Account 57 shows T308 renumbered X1913(2) 2/2/1929. AFE 30189 shows this car renumbered 296091 10/1925. Since no disposition has been found for 296091, it is probable the renumbering sequence was from T308 to 296091, then to X1913(2).

NOTE 273: URPC shows T318 scrapped 10/1928. AFE 38218 shows sold for scrap DI&M 8/1928.

NOTE 274: AFE 31608 shows X940 (formerly T339) sold for scrap Pacific Coast Steel 12/1926. AFE 33739 shows 1/1927, which agrees with the CNRA Account 57 retirement date of 1/8/1927.

NOTE 275: URPC shows T348 sold for scrap to DI&M in 11/1927. AFE 35895 shows 9/2/1927.

NOTE 276: URPC shows T389(2) scrapped 9/1931. AFE 44517 shows 11/6/1931.

NOTE 277: CNRA Account 57 shows T403(2) and boxcar 34744 rebuilt to X951(3) in 10/1947. AFE 69899 shows 3/31/1947.

NOTE 278: CNRA Account 57 shows T407(2) renumbered X1999(1). URPC and AFE 30829 show sold for scrap DI&M 5/1926.

NOTE 279: CNRA Account 57 shows that X835(2), which was built from automobile boxcar 36631 and X1906(3), formerly T412(2), was later renumbered as X3693. A diagram dated 6/1/1952 indicates that X3693 was a material car, and the diagram shows the appearance of a house car.

NOTE 280:   Norman C. Keyes, Jr., indicated GN 420 sold SP&S 10/1924, and also 10/24/1922 (the latter date from SP&S records of Bob Johnston). Norman F. Priebe found that information derived from the Historical Engine Record shows 7/14/1925. URPC shows a disposition date of 6/1925. AFE 24548, under which the locomotive was sold, is dated 10/10/1923.

NOTE 281:   URPC shows T422 sold for scrap 5/1926. AFE 31037 shows sold for scrap 2/1926, but not officially retired until 5/1926.

NOTE 282:   CNRA Account 57 shows T459(2) renumbered as X2853(2) in 8/1931. AFE 44856 shows 9/1931. CNRA Account 57 shows X2853(2) retired 8/1934. AFE 42724 shows that it was dismantled at Superior 8/19/1932.

NOTE 283:   AFE 37274 shows T460(2) and T476(2) dismantled at Dale Street on dates shown. AFE 38218 shows these tenders sold for scrap PC 8/1928 and DI&M 9/12/1928, respectively.

NOTE 284:   URPC shows T469(2), T474(2) and T502(2) scrapped 10/1928. AFE 38218 shows these tenders as sold for scrap DI&M 9/25/1928, 9/21/1928, and 9/25/1928, respectively.

NOTE 285:   The AFE Index shows that T477(2) was retired under AFE 34692 (dated 6/10/1927) in order to be renumbered as X1999. However, CNRA Account 57 shows no evidence of this renumbering, and no useful information was found in the AFE itself.

NOTE 286:   CNRA Account 57 shows T479(2) renumbered as X1994(2) in 2/1940. AFE 57793 shows 11/1939.

NOTE 287:   CNRA Account 57 shows T505 renumbered X2823 12/30/1940. AFE 58595 shows 11/11/1940.

NOTE 288:   URPC shows T510 sold for scrap 4/1932. AFE 45303 shows dismantled at Delta 4/14/1932.

NOTE 289:   AFE 45840 shows X1932(1) (formerly T515) as retired in 11/28, and being shipped from Havre to Superior on 8/27/1932. AFE 47969 shows this car retired 3/1934 (which agrees with CNRA Account 57), and sold for scrap to DI&M on 3/29/1934.

NOTE 290:   AFE 42724 shows X1954(2) (formerly T519) dismantled at Superior 8/19/1932. CNRA Account 57 does not show this car as being retired until 8/1934.

NOTE 291:   CNRA Account 57 shows T531, T598, and T772 reno. X3347, X3348, and X3349, respectively, on 10/26/1942. URPC shows 1/1943.

NOTE 292:   URPC shows T541 sold for scrap 1/1929. AFE 39040 shows sold for scrap 11/1928.

NOTE 293:   The records in CNRA Account 57 are somewhat confusing for cars numbered as X1945. The first entry in this number was renumbered from X950 (formerly T550) on 6/1/1927. This car is then shown as retired in 9/1932. AFE 45840 shows that this car was stripped at Superior on 8/19/1932. Another car (T1354) was renumbered as X1945(2) in 3/1933. This car is shown as being moved to Account 51 in 11/1943, which is consistent with AFE's 67645, 68036 and 68037 which show that X1945(2) was retired from Account 51 in 11/1943, and renumbered as X3252 in 1/1944. However, an entry under X906(2) indicates that it was built from X1945 and Boxcar 14688 in 10/1946. It seems possible that this may have been the tank from X1945(1), which may have been salvaged during the stripping operation.

NOTE 294:   URPC shows T609 scrapped 1/1929. AFE 39040 shows sold for scrap 10/18/1928.

NOTE 295:   URPC shows T701 scrapped 10/1928. AFE 38218 shows sold for scrap 8/1928.

NOTE 296:   T749(2) was originally T736 [renumbered 4/7/1910 per HCR Vol. 41 (NE6)].

NOTE 297:   CNRA Account 57 shows T755 and boxcar 36280 rebuilt to X952(3) in 10/1947. AFE 69899 shows 3/31/1947.

NOTE 298:   CNRA Account 57 shows T3254 renumbered as X1949(4) in 7/1951. AFE 81400 shows T3254 renumbered as X1949 in 5/1951, and X3254 (formerly T757) renumbered as X1949 in 2/1953. AFE 69899 shows X3254 renumbered as X1949(4) on 5/27/1945. A diagram dated 6/1/1952 does show X1949 as being a Style 100 (Class O-4) tender. However, AFE 85072 shows T3254 sold for scrap DI&M 1/15/1955. It seems most likely that this is an error in record keeping, and that it was in fact X3254 that became X1949(4), with the diagram being lettered in error as a result.

NOTE 299:   URPC and CNRA Account 57 show T781 renumbered X2830(1) 6/1934. CNRA Account 57 also shows T781 renumbered X2864(2) 9/1931. AFE 44857 agrees with the latter information.

NOTE 300:   CNRA Account 57 shows X946(1) (former T788) as having been renumbered to X1941(1) on 5/26/1927 in one location and in 6/1927 in another location.

NOTE 301:   URPC shows T803 sold for scrap 8/1936. AFE 51290 shows 7/27/1936.

NOTE 302:   URPC shows T807 scrapped 10/1928. AFE 38218 shows sold for scrap 8/1928.

NOTE 303:   CNRA Account 57 shows T857 and boxcar 23268 rebuilt to X822(2) on 10/14/1947. AFE 69899 shows 5/8/1947.

NOTE 304:   CNRA Account 57 shows GN X959(2) rebuilt as X933(3) on 10/25/1943 in one location and 10/25/1945 in another.

NOTE 305:   URPC shows T875 scrapped 10/1928. AFE 38218 shows sold for scrap 9/12/1928.

NOTE 306:   CNRA Account 57 shows T889 renumbered as X1960(3) in 7/1947. AFE 69899 shows 1/1945, and AFE 75252 shows 5/1947.

NOTE 307:   URPC shows T897 dismantled 11/1947. CNRA Account 57 then shows the cistern going to X3301 in 5/1948. AFE 74857 shows both of these events occurring on 12/18/1947.

NOTE 308:   URPC shows T952 retired 10/1928. AFE 38218 shows sold for scrap 8/28/1928.

NOTE 309:   AFE 45259 shows X1929(1) (formerly T959) sold to DI&M in 9/1932. AFE 47969 and CNRA Account 57 show this car as being retired 7/1934.

NOTE 310:   URPC shows T962 scrapped 1/1929. AFE 39040 shows sold for scrap 11/30/1928.

NOTE 311:   CNRA Account 57 shows X2870(2) (formerly T968) retired 3/1934. AFE 47969 shows the car as being retired 6/1934 (when it was sold to PC).

NOTE 312:   AFE 35148 shows X1974(1) (formerly T992) as sold DI&M 8/25/1927. CNRA Account 57 shows this car as retired 9/1927.

NOTE 313:   AFE 37274 shows T1004 dismantled at Dale Street 8/20/1928. AFE 38218 shows sold for scrap PC 8/1928.

NOTE 314:   AFE 32296 shows T1017 rebuilt to 10,000 gallon capacity at Havre 1/15/1927. AFE 35769 shows rebuilt to 10,000 gallon capacity at Delta 10/23/1928 (after renumbering to T1372).

NOTE 315:   AFE 58595 shows T1069 renumbered as X1935(1) on 5/28/1940. CNRA Account 57 shows 7/2/1940.

NOTE 316:   CNRA Account 57 shows T1066 renumbered as X946(3) in 12/1946. AFE 74094 shows 11/1946.

NOTE 317:   URPC shows T1070 scrapped 9/1931. AFE 44517 shows 12/1931.

NOTE 318:   CNRA Account 57 shows T1073 and boxcar 35597 rebuilt to X849 on 10/14/1947. AFE 69888 shows 5/8/1947.

NOTE 319:   URPC shows T1083 retired 9/1941. AFE 62177 indicates that this tender was actually placed behind Montana Western locomotive No. 10 on 3/8/1941. The sale order was not issued until 10/22/1941.

NOTE 320: AFE 35148 shows X2843(1) (formerly T1098) as sold Dulien Steel Products 8/1939. CNRA Account 57 shows this car as retired 9/1939.

NOTE 321: CNRA Acct. 57 shows T1104 renumbered as X961(1) in 6/1938. AFE 54901 shows that this car was not retired from Account 51 until 10/1938.

NOTE 322: CNRA Acct. 57 shows T1136 renumbered as X962(1) in 8/1938. AFE 54901 shows that this car was not retired from Account 51 until 9/1938.

NOTE 323: CNRA Account 57 shows T1140 renumbered as X1941(3) in 9/1950. AFE 80500 shows 10/1950.

NOTE 324: AFE 37274 shows T1172 and T1173 dismantled at Dale Street 8/27/1928. AFE 38218 shows these tenders sold for scrap PC 8/1928.

NOTE 325: AFE 54901 and URPC show T1187 retired from Account 51 in 10/1938. However, CNRA Acct. 57 shows this car renumbered as X963(1) in 8/1935.

NOTE 326: CNRA Account 57 shows T1195(2) renumbered X3346 10/26/1942. URPC shows 1/1943. AFE 83761 shows sold for scrap PC 5/16/1953. URPC shows T1195 renumbered X1500, and CNRA Account 57 shows X1975 as having been renumbered from X1500 5/26/1927, with this car being renumbered T1195 7/24/1943.

NOTE 327: CNRA Account 57 shows T1204 renumbered as X948(4) in 7/1947. AFE 75252 shows 5/1947.

NOTE 328: X3258 was probably either T1233(2) or T1250, for which no dispositions are known. T1250 may be the more likely candidate since it is known to have been rebuilt to Style 19.

NOTE 329: AFE 68037 shows X3272 (formerly T1239) as retired 11/1943. However, AFE 68036 indicates that this was actually a transfer from Account 57 (work equipment) to Account 51 (steam locomotives) since the car had been permanently fitted up as an auxiliary tender. This car is listed in the work equipment diagram book (page dated 6/1/1952), but was no longer on the roster when the auxiliary tenders in Account 51 were transferred back to Account 57 in 3/1958.

NOTE 330: CNRA Account 57 shows T1240(2) renumbered as X949(3) in 10/1947. AFE 75252 shows 5/1947.

NOTE 331: URPC shows T1304 renumbered T895, which would be expected from the engine renumbering. However, AFE 32972 shows T1304 renumbered T885 6/1927. Since E1307 became E885 6/1927, it is more likely that T1304 became T895, as indicated by URPC.

NOTE 332: CNRA Account 57 shows T1359 and T1984 renumbered X1997(3) and X2849(2), respectively, in 12/1949. AFE 78935 shows 8/1949.

NOTE 333: AFE 84771 shows T1365 scrapped at St.Cloud 5/1955. AFE 85072 shows 6/1954.

NOTE 334: CNRA Account 57 shows T1366 renumbered as X1945(4) in 7/1951. AFE 81400 shows 5/1951.

NOTE 335: CNRA Account 57 shows T1370 renumbered X2832(2) 5/1956. AFE 85336 shows 5/1954.

NOTE 336: CNRA Account 57 shows T1375 renumbered as X2830(3) in 12/1946. AFE 74094 shows 11/1946.

NOTE 337: CNRA Account 57 shows T1378, T3320, and T3363 renumbered X2820(2), X811(2), and X804(2), respectively, 11/1947. AFE 75848 shows 9/1947.

NOTE 338: CNRA Account 57 shows T1382 renumbered X1947(3) 10/1952. AFE 83323 shows 9/1952.

NOTE 339: CNRA Account 57 shows T1384 renumbered X 1913(3) 4/1933. AFE 46654 shows 2/1933.

NOTE 340: CNRA Account 57 shows T1407 renumbered X967(1) 11/1937. AFE 54901 shows 11/1938.

NOTE 341: CNRA Account 57 shows T1424 renumbered X2824 2/20/1941. AFE 58595 shows 11/22/1940.

NOTE 342: CNRA Account 57 shows T1432 renumbered X945(2) 9/1947. AFE 63969 shows T1432 renumbered X3217 4/22/1942.

NOTE 343: X3260 was probably T1445, the only H-4 tender for which no disposition is known.

NOTE 344: CNRA Account 57 shows T1542 renumbered as X937(3) 8/27/1941. AFE 61390 shows 8/25/1941.

NOTE 345: CNRA Account 57 shows T1550 renumbered as X1982(2) on 7/24/1940. AFE 58595 shows 7/20/1940.

NOTE 346: CNRA Account 57 shows T1605 renumbered as X1916(2) in 4/1933. AFE 46654 shows 2/1933.

NOTE 347: CNRA Account 57 shows T1622 renumbered X1917(2) 4/1933. AFE 46654 shows 2/1933.

NOTE 348: CNRA Account 57 shows T1625 renumbered X938(3) 8/20/1941. AFE 61390 shows 8/30/1941.

NOTE 349: AFE 32229 shows T1631 rebuilt to Style 49 7/2/1926. AFE 53722 shows it rebuilt to Style 50 11/1939. AFE 38082 shows it rebuilt to Style 49 at Hillyard 3/6/1929, and rebuilt to Style 50 at Delta 5/21/1929.

NOTE 350: CNRA Account 57 shows T1637 and T3139 renumbered X1959(3) and X1962(3), respectively, 10/1952. AFE 83323 shows 9/1952.

NOTE 351: CNRA Account 57 shows T1648 renumbered X1986(2) 7/5/1940. AFE 58595 shows 7/22/1940.

NOTE 352: CNRA Account 57 shows T1703 renumbered X1988(2) 8/12/1940 and retired 6/1948. AFE 58595 shows renumbered 2/6/1941. AFE 76560 shows retired 5/29/1948.

NOTE 353: CNRA Account 57 shows T1704 renumbered X1989(2) 8/12/1940. AFE 58595 shows 7/12/1940.

NOTE 354: GN locomotive diagrams show T1755 as Style 88. GN maintenance equipment diagrams show X939(3) as Style 86.

NOTE 355: CNRA Account 57 shows T1951 renumbered as X3340 in 8/1948. AFE 77523 shows 9/1948.

NOTE 356: URPC shows T1955 retired 1951, but AFE 81610 indicates T1617 was substituted on the sale. CNRA Account 57 indicates T1955 renumbered X1989(3) 7/1952.

NOTE 357: X3255 was probably T1426, the only H-2/H-3 tender for which no disposition is known.

NOTE 358: CNRA Account 57 shows T1956 renumbered X1995(2) 7/14/1940. AFE 58595 shows 7/4/1940.

NOTE 359: CNRA Account 57 shows T1959 renumbered as X1908(4) in 12/1957. AFE 74857 shows 10/15/1947, and AFE 76119 shows 11/1947.

NOTE 360: AFE 74857 shows T1972 renumbered as X1916(3) on 3/4/1948. AFE 76632 shows 5/1948.

NOTE 361: X1988(3) is assumed to be former T2001 since dispositions for all other N-2 class tenders are known. A diagram dated 6/1/1952 indicates that X1988(3) was Style 57.

NOTE 362: CNRA Account 57 shows T2031 renumbered X1940(5) 6/1950. AFE 79719 shows T2031 renumbered X3343 6/15/1950, and then renumbered X1940(5) 8/24/1950.

NOTE 363: AFE 89606 shows T2082 sold for scrap in 11/1962. AFE 89913 shows 12/3/1962.

NOTE 364: AFE 85072 shows T2107 sold Erie Mining Co. (with E2114) 12/13/1954. AFE 87722 shows this tender retired 4/1956 and sold for scrap PC 6/27/1956.

NOTE 365:   CNRA Account 57 shows T2204 renumbered as X1939(3) in 4/1950. AFE 79634 shows 2/1950.

NOTE 366:   Walter F. Becker shows GN 1378 sold SP&S 11/1944. URPC shows 10/1944.

NOTE 367:   CNRA Account 57 shows T3010 renumbered as X1991(2) in 6/1953. AFE 83215 shows this tender renumbered as X1921 in 8/1952.

NOTE 368:   CNRA Account 57 shows T3012 renumbered X1998(3) 9/18/1940. AFE 58595 shows 4/13/1940.

NOTE 369:   CNRA Account 57 shows T3019 renumbered as X800(2) in 11/1948. AFE 77523 shows 9/1948.

NOTE 370:   CNRA Account 57 shows T3023 renumbered X941(3) 8/15/1941. AFE 61390 shows 8/25/1941.

NOTE 371:   AFE 78867 shows T3024 renumbered as X1933(3) on 12/22/1949. CNRA Account 57 shows 11/1950.

NOTE 372:   CNRA Account 57 shows T3026 renumbered X2825(2) 9/17/1940. AFE 58595 shows 4/13/1940.

NOTE 373:   AFE 74857 shows T3032 renumbered as X1918(3) on 3/4/1948. AFE 76632 shows 5/1948.

NOTE 374:   CNRA Account 57 shows T3084 rebuilt to X1586 2/1951. AFE 86021 shows that T3084 was sold for scrap DI&M 5/28/1955.

NOTE 375:   CNRA Account 57 shows T3109 renumbered X1913(4) 11/1952. AFE 83332 shows 10/1952.

NOTE 376:   CNRA Account 57 shows T3120 and T2018 renumbered X1921(4) and X1930(3), respectively, in 10/1952. AFE 83323 shows 9/1952.

NOTE 377:   CNRA Account 57 shows T3122 renumbered X2837(2) 9/15/1940. AFE 58595 shows 5/16/1940.

NOTE 378:   CNRA Account 57 shows T3128 renumbered as X1821 in 10/1952. AFE 83215 shows 8/1952.

NOTE 379:   CNRA Account 57 shows T3130 renumbered X2840(2) 7/14/1943. AFE 58595 shows 7/19/1940.

NOTE 380:   CNRA Account 57 shows T3137 renumbered as X1948(3) in 7/1951. AFE 81400 shows 5/1951.

NOTE 381:   URPC shows T3138 rebuilt to Style 68 3/1946. AFE 67377 shows 5/28/1943.

NOTE 382:   CNRA Account 57 shows X2900(3) rebuilt from T3243 and T3226. AFE 84381 shows this car rebuilt from T3226 and T3229.

NOTE 383:   CNRA Account 57 shows X2901(3) rebuilt 10/1953 from T3229 and T3250. AFE 84799 shows this car rebuilt 12/1953 from T3243 and T3250.

NOTE 384:   CNRA Account 57 shows T3366 renumbered X2876(3) 8/2/1940. AFE 58595 shows 5/24/1940.

NOTE 385:   CNRA Account 57 shows T3367 renumbered X2877(3) 9/12/1940. AFE 58595 shows 8/2/1940.

NOTE 386:   URPC shows T223 scrapped 1/1929. AFE 38218 shows sold for scrap DI&M 12/1928.

NOTE 387:   CNRA Account 57 shows X938(1) (formerly T320) reno. X1936(1) in 11/1927 in one location and 5/26/1927 in another location.

NOTE 388:   CNRA Account 57 shows T1092 renumbered X1912(2) 10/1932. AFE 46654 shows 2/1933.

Engine 3100, a member of the 1917 order of O-1's, is shown being serviced at Hillyard in 1935. It still has its original smokebox front, tall stack and square cab, but has been equipped to burn oil and also has a booster and a Sellers exhaust steam injector. Maynard Rikerd photograph from the GNRHS collection.

This photograph shows how the GN changed tenders between coal and oil carrying capability.
It was taken at Minot, ND, in autumn of 1945. Photograph by W. J. Pontin (RPS).

Chapter 34

Known Tender Assignments

Class A-9 0-6-0

Engine Number	1937-1939 Style	1937-1939 Class	1937-1939 Number	1940 Style	1940 Class	1940 Number	October 1943 Style	October 1943 Class	October 1943 Number	July 1947 Style	July 1947 Class	July 1947 Number	June 1949 Style	June 1949 Class	June 1949 Number
5(3)	1	A-9	53										1	A-9	53
6(2)													1	A-9	
7(2)	1	A-9													
8(3)				1	A-9					1	A-9				
9(3)	1	A-9	4										1	A-9	4
10(3)	1	A-9													
12(3)													1	A-9	6
14(3)				1	A-9										
15(3)							1	A-9	15	1	A-9	15	1	A-9	15
16(3)													14	F-1	508
18(3)													1	A-9	3
19(3)													8	C-4	778
23(3)													1	A-9	80
53(2)													1	A-9	9
54(2)													17	F-8	1196
55(2)				1	A-9										
57(2)													10	D-4	413
86(3)													22	G-3	761
89(3)													17	F-8	1203
384(2)													17	F-8	1165
385(2)													24	G-5	800
386(2)													1	A-9	397
388(2)	1	A-9											10	D-4	402
389(2)													1	A-9	12
390(2)													6	C-2	863
394													6	C-2	851
395				1	A-9								17	F-8	1152
396													22	G-3	724
397(1)													1	A-9	92

Class F-1 2-8-0

Engine Number	1934-1939			April 1943			June 1945			June 1949			1950-1951		
	Style	Class	Number	Style	Class	Number	Style	Class	Number	Style	Class	Number	Style	Class	Number
508				12	E-8	1061	12	E-8	1061	12	E-8	1061	12	E-8	1061
511	13	E-15	1087	13	E-15	1087	13	E-15	1087	13	E-15	1087			
512				16	F-7	1135	16	F-7	1135						
519	12	E-8													
521				34	H-4	1473									
525(1)				22	G-3	749	22	G-3	749	34	H-4	1473	12	E-8	1058
527				17	F-8	1200	17	F-8	1200						
540							11	E-6	934						
544										13	E-15	1078	13	E-15	1078

Class G-1 4-8-0

Engine Number	April 1943		
	Style	Class	Number
603	48	J-2	1551
606	86	P-1	1759
612		F-8	1252

Class G-3 4-8-0

Engine Number	April 1943			June 1949			December 1951		
	Style	Class	Number	Style	Class	Number	Style	Class	Number
721	18	F-8	1240						
722	13	E-15	1081						
723	8	C-4	786	8	C-4	786	8	C-4	786
724	62	O-1	3022						
725		H-7	1378	54	M-2	1984			
726		O-6	3354	60	O-1	3103			
728	46	J-1	1531	79	O-6	3356			
729		M-2	1974						
730		J-1	1505						
731	54	M-2	1957						
732	78	O-6	3368	78	O-6	3368			
733		J-1	1518						
734	46	J-1							
735	18	F-8	1224						
737	18	F-8	1232						
739		N-2	2006	62	O-1	3011			
742	49	J-2	1635						
743	62	O-1	3032	42	H-6	1724	48	J-2	1613
744	46	J-1	1524						
745	54	M-2	1972	35	H-4	1484			
746	35	H-4	1483						
747		O-1	3103						
748	12	E-8	1057	17	F-8	1195	17	F-8	1195
749		M-2	1952						
751	62	O-1	3009						
752	62	O-1	3025	62	O-1	3025			
753	62	O-1	3008	62	O-1	3008			
754		J-1	1504						
756	61	O-1	3074						
759	79	O-6	3356						
760		J-2	1621	73	O-5	3326			
761		N-2	2004						
763	54	M-2	1980						
764	17	F-8	1140	17	F-8	1140			
765		J-2	1639						
767		O-1	3006						
768		J-1	1535						
769	54	M-2	1959	32	H-4	1460			

Class C-4 0-8-0

Engine Number	January 1930 Style	Class	Number	March 1933 Style	Class	Number	December 1938 Style	Class	Number	April 1943 Style	Class	Number	June 1949 Style	Class	Number
780				18	F-8					18	F-8				
781	17	F-8								17	F-8				
782	17	F-8								17	F-8				
783	17	F-8	1137	17	F-8	1137	17	F-8	1137	17	F-8	1137	17	F-8	1209
784							17	F-8	1150	17	F-8	1150	17	F-8	1150
785	17	F-8	1213	17	F-8	1213	17	F-8	1213	17	F-8	1213	17	F-8	1213
786							17	F-8	1169	17	F-8	1169	17	F-8	1169
787							18	F-8		18	F-8				
788							17	F-8		17	F-8				
789							17	F-8							
790							18	F-8							

Class C-2 0-8-0

Engine Number	October 1947 Style	Class	Number	June 1949 Style	Class	Number	March 1952 Style	Class	Number
852	17	F-8	1175						
854				18	F-8	1222			
855				17	F-8	1177			
856				17	F-8	1181			
859				15	F-5	1096			
861				11	E-6	933	17	F-8	1213
863				17	F-8	1191			
864				17	F-8	1160			

Class C-5 0-8-0

Engine Number	April 1940 Style	Class	Number	April 1943 Style	Class	Number	November 1948 Style	Class	Number
871	15	F-5		15	F-5				
872	15	F-5		15	F-5		11	E-6	928

Class C-3 0-8-0

Engine Number	1925-1926 Style	Class	Number	June 1949 Style	Class	Number	December 1951 Style	Class	Number
876	7	C-3	882	48	J-2	1557	48	J-2	1557
878				15	F-5	1101	15	F-5	1101
879	15	F-5	1105	11	E-6	930	11	E-6	930
880				16	F-7	1138			
881	7	C-3	877	7	C-3	879			
883(2)				44	H-7	1376	44	H-7	1376
884	7	C-3	883	15	F-5	1109			
886				15	F-5	1103			
887				16	F-7	1133			
888				12	E-8	1053			
890				12	E-8	1062	12	E-8	1062
891				7	C-3	885			
893				7	C-3	896			
894				17	F-8	1159			
896				7	C-3	887			

Class E-2(2) 4-6-0

Engine Number	1938 Style	Class	Number	April 1943 Style	Class	Number	October 1947 Style	Class	Number
910	13	E-15	1086	13	E-15	1086	13	E-15	1086
911				13	E-15	1077	13	E-15	1077

Class E-6 4-6-0

Engine Number	1934 Style	Class	Number	April 1943 Style	Class	Number	January 1947 Style	Class	Number	June 1949 Style	Class	Number	January 1950 Style	Class	Number
925				13	E-15	1075	13	E-15	1075						
926					O-1	3090		O-1	3090						
927				62	O-1	3039	62	O-1	3039	62	O-1	3039	62	O-1	3039
929				25	H-3	1408	25	H-3	1408	25	H-3	1408			
930	18	F-8	1233	18	F-8	1233	18	F-8	1233						
931				18	F-8	1227	18	F-8	1227						
932					J-2	1586									
933					H-4	1480		H-4	1480						
935				13	E-15	1073	13	E-15	1073						
936					O-1	3109		O-1	3109						
939				22	G-3	764	22	G-3	764						

Class E-15 4-6-0

Engine Number	November 1948		
	Style	Class	Number
1090	36	H-5	1365

Class F-5 2-8-0

Engine Number	June 1949		
	Style	Class	Number
1100	88	P-1	1760
1107	27	H-2	1429

Class F-7 2-8-0

Engine Number	April 1943			June 1949			January 1950			January 1951		
	Style	Class	Number	Style	Class	Number	Style	Class	Number	Style	Class	Number
1130	88	P-1	1757	88	P-1	1757	88	P-1	1757			
1131	46	J-1	1526	54	M-2	1957	54	M-2	1957			
1132	26	H-2	1426									
1135				48	J-2	1599	48	J-2	1599	48	J-2	1599
1136	18	F-8	1231	34	H-4	1483	34	H-4	1483			
1137				18	F-8	1217	18	F-8	1217	18	F-8	1217
1138	88	P-1	1751	88	P-1	1751	88	P-1	1751			

Class F-8 2-8-0

Engine Number	January 1930 to May 1941			April 1943			June 1949			1951			March 1952		
	Style	Class	Number	Style	Class	Number	Style	Class	Number	Style	Class	Number	Style	Class	Number
1141					O-5	3302	37	H-5	1373						
1142					H-6	1713	18	F-8	1231	58	N-2	2023			
1144				31	H-3	1430	49	J-2	1628	49	J-2	1628			
1146				54	M-2	1964	78	O-6	3369				37	H-5	1373
1147				36	H-5	1359	36	H-5	1361	36	H-5	1361	36	H-5	1361
1148				18	F-8	1250	73	O-5	3337	73	O-5	3337	73	O-5	3337
1149					N-2	2020									
1150				58	N-2	2022	62	O-1	3020						
1152				18	F-8	1246	18	F-8	1246	18	F-8	1246			
1153				86	P-1	1750	86	P-1	1750						
1154				55	M-2	1967									
1156				73	O-5	3337									
1158				12	E-8	1066									
1159				39	H-6	1712									
1163				36	H-5	1361	32	H-4	1461	32	H-4	1461	32	H-4	1461
1165					H-4	1484	58	N-2	2022						
1168				68	O-1	3127	68	O-1	3127	68	O-1	3127	68	O-1	3127
1170				62	O-1	3028	62	O-1	3028	62	O-1	3028	62	O-1	3028
1171	13	E-15	1077	79	O-6	3370	79	O-6	3370						
1172				73	O-5	3307	48	J-2							
1173				29	H-3	1425	29	H-3	1425	29	H-3	1425			
1176				18	F-8	1244									
1177				42	H-6	1724	42	H-6	1724				62	O-1	3020
1178				78	O-6	3363									
1179					J-2	1627									
1180				54	M-2	1984									
1181					H-2	1406									
1182				49	J-2	1556									
1183				77	O-5	3335	77	O-5	3335	77	O-5	3335	77	O-5	3335
1184				17	F-8	1186									
1186					O-6	3369									
1187				62	O-1	3024									
1188					H-2	1417									
1189	15	F-5	1106		H-7	1381	54	M-2	1950						
1190					O-1	3125	61	O-1	3006	61	O-1	3006	61	O-1	3006
1192					M-2	1951	6	C-2	868				54	M-2	1950
1193				89	F-12	1326	57	N-2	2022				39	H-6	1712
1195				18	F-8	1220	18	F-8	1220				66	O-1	3050
1196				49	J-2	1626	49	J-2	1626	49	J-2	1626	49	J-2	1626
1197				54	M-2	1981	17	F-8	1156	17	F-8	1156			
1202				46	J-1	1520	46	J-1	1520	46	J-1	1520			
1203					O-5	3301									
1206				15	F-5	1097	15	F-5	1097						
1209				18	F-8	1219									
1210				89	F-12	1327	89	F-12	1327						
1216				12	E-8	1060	62	O-1	3027						
1218				62	O-1	3000	54	M-2	1960						
1219					H-2	1420									
1220				18	F-8		55	M-2	1967						
1221				46	J-1	1534	6	C-2	860						
1222				17	F-8	1153	48	J-2	1606						

Engine Number	January 1930 to May 1941 Style	Class	Number	April 1943 Style	Class	Number	June 1949 Style	Class	Number	1951 Style	Class	Number
1224					O-5	3326						
1226					O-1	3011						
1227				54	M-2	1968						
1230				17	F-8	1156	54	M-2	1981	54	M-2	1981
1231				57	N-2	2002	57	N-2	2002	57	N-2	2002
1233				17	F-8	1155	79	O-6	3351			
1236					J-1	1515	48	J-2	1647			
1239				54	M-2	1960						
1243				48	J-2	1606	17	F-8	1174			
1244				58	N-2	2023	58	N-2	2023			
1245					J-2	1599	54	M-2	1962			
1246					O-5	3310						
1250					M-2	1966	48	J-2	1615			
1252				12	E-8	1058						

Class F-12 2-8-0

Engine Number	May 1932 Style	Class	Number	April 1943 Style	Class	Number	June 1949 Style	Class	Number
1326	89	F-12		48	J-2	1588	48	J-2	1588
1327	89	F-12			J-2	1615			

Class H-5 4-6-2

Engine Number	May 1941 Style	Class	Number	April 1943 Style	Class	Number	June 1949 Style	Class	Number	December 1951 Style	Class	Number	March 1952 Style	Class	Number
1350	115	–	2597	20	F-8	1225	20	F-8	1225	20	F-8	1225			
1352	66	O-1	3054	66	O-1	3054	104	P-2	2512						
1353		O-1	3059	70	O-1	3057	70	O-1	3057	70	O-1	3057	70	O-1	3057
1354	70	O-1	3060	59	N-2	2016	59	N-2	2016						
1355	70	O-1	3052	33	H-4	1451	33	H-4	1451	33	H-4	1451	33	H-4	1451
1356	56	M-2	1983	56	M-2	1983	56	M-2	1983	56	M-2	1983	56	M-2	1983
1357	69	O-1	3015	69	O-1	3015	69	O-1	3015	69	O-1	3015	69	O-1	3015
1358	70	O-1	3061	66	O-1	3050	66	O-1	3050						
1359	70	O-1	3048	70	O-1	3048	50	J-2	1578	50	J-2	1578			
1360				70	O-1	3051	63	O-1	3105	63	O-1	3105			
1361				70	O-1	3061	69	O-1	3034	31	H-3	1436			
1362	104	P-2	2513	104	P-2	2513	104	P-2	2513						
1363	104	P-2	2512	66	O-1	3054	70	O-1	3061	70	O-1	3061			
1364				59	N-2	2011	59	N-2	2011	59	N-2	2011			
1365	70	O-1	3055	70	O-1	3055	70	O-1	3055	70	O-1	3055			
1366				70	O-1	3056				100	O-4	3246			
1367				66	O-1	3046	58	N-2	2008						
1368	70	O-1	3069	70	O-1	3069	32	H-4	1472						
1369				104	P-2	2515	104	P-2	2515	104	P-2	2515			
1370				104	P-2	2509	104	P-2	2509	104	P-2	2509			
1371				50	J-2	1578	69	O-1	3034	69	O-1	3034			
1372					M-2	1963	104	P-2	2505	104	P-2	2505			
1373				70	O-1	3045	70	O-1	3045	70	O-1	3045			
1374				70	O-1	3052	70	O-1	3052	70	O-1	3052			

Class H-7 4-6-2

Engine Number	April 1943 Style	Class	Number	January 1949 Style	Class	Number	July 1953 Style	Class	Number
1375	104	P-2	2525	104	P-2	2525	104	P-2	2525
1376	104	P-2	2511	104	P-2	2511	104	P-2	2511
1377	104	P-2	2518	104	P-2	2518	104	P-2	2518
1378	104	P-2	2508						
1379	104	P-2	2503						
1380	104	P-2	2510	104	P-2	2510	104	P-2	2510
1381	115	–	2596	115	–	2596	115	–	2596
1382	104	P-2	2502	104	P-2	2502	104	P-2	2502
1383	115	–	2597	115	–	2597	115	–	2597
1384	115	–	2599	115	–	2599	115	–	2599

Class H-2 4-6-2

Engine Number	March 1933 Style	Class	Number	May 1941 Style	Class	Number	April 1943 Style	Class	Number	June 1949 Style	Class	Number
1407				54	M-2	1960						
1409					M-2	1966						
1413				54	M-2	1973	62	O-1	3038	62	O-1	3038
1418					O-1	3031						
1429										62	O-1	3036
1438	54	M-2	1958	54	M-2	1958	54	M-2	1958	54	M-2	1958
1439	54	M-2	1969	54	M-2	1969						

Class H-3 4-6-2

Engine Number	May 1941 Style	Class	Number	April 1943 Style	Class	Number	June 1949 Style	Class	Number
1412		P-1	1756		O-6	3365	54	M-2	1982
1421	54	M-2	1956						
1423							50	J-2	1594
1425							54	M-2	1969
1426					O-6	3355			
1428					O-1	3018			
1430							18	F-8	1244
1431	18	F-8	1249						
1436	62	O-1	3005		M-2	1961	62	O-1	3033

Class H-4 4-6-2

Engine Number	March 1933 Style	Class	Number	May 1941 Style	Class	Number	April 1943 Style	Class	Number	June 1949 Style	Class	Number	March 1952 Style	Class	Number
1441				70	O-1	3047	70	O-1	3047	70	O-1	3047	70	O-1	3047
1442							70	O-1	3059	70	O-1	3059			
1443							70	O-1	3064	70	O-1	3064	70	O-1	3064
1444	31	H-3	1436				50	J-2	1594						
1445							62	O-1	3017	62	O-1	3017	62	O-1	3017
1446	50	J-2	1594												
1448				54	M-2	1960	54	M-2	1971	54	M-2	1971			
1449										78	O-6	3364	78	O-6	3364
1450							31	H-3	1428	33	H-4	1453	33	H-4	1453
1452								J-2	1647	34	H-4	1481			
1453							36	H-5	1369	36	H-5	1369	36	H-5	1369
1454					M-2	1963				54	M-2	1953			
1455							70	O-1	3065	31	H-3	1428	31	H-3	1428
1456				59	N-2	2011		N-2	2012	57	N-2	2018			
1457							33	H-4	1453	38	H-5	1350			
1458							70	O-1	3066	70	O-1	3068	70	O-1	3068
1459								H-5	1350	70	O-1	3066	70	O-1	3066
1461							62	O-1	3001	62	O-1	3001			
1462							54	M-2	1975	54	M-2	1975			
1463							62	O-1	3002	62	O-1	3002			
1464							25	H-2	1413	25	H-2	1413			
1465								M-2	1965						
1467							62	O-1	3010	62	O-1	3010			
1469							54	M-2	1982	83	O-6	3365			
1470							54	M-2	1979	54	M-2	1979			
1471	57	N-2	2009	57	N-2	2009	57	N-2	2009	57	N-2	2009	57	N-2	2009
1473							60	O-1	3114	60	O-1	3114	60	O-1	3114
1474							62	O-1	3029	62	O-1	3029			
1475							54	M-2	1955	54	M-2	1955			
1476							79	O-6	3353	79	O-6	3353			
1477	54	M-2	1982	54	M-2	1982	8	C-4	785	8	C-4	785			
1479							54	M-2	1950	79	O-6	3355			
1480							44	H-7	1376						
1482	88	P-1	1753	88	P-1	1753									
1483								H-7	1383						
1484							62	O-1	3033	62	O-1	3033			
1485							48	J-2	1557						

Class K-1 4-4-2

Engine Number	July 1940 Style	Class	Number	April 1943 Style	Class	Number
1702	60	O-1	3124			
1704	62	O-1	3029			
1709					H-6	1719

Class H-6 4-6-2

Engine Number	March 1933 Style	March 1933 Class	March 1933 Number	February 1938 Style	February 1938 Class	February 1938 Number	April 1943 Style	April 1943 Class	April 1943 Number	June 1949 Style	June 1949 Class	June 1949 Number	January 1951 Style	January 1951 Class	January 1951 Number
1710					N-2	2003	88	P-1	1758	88	P-1	1758	88	P-1	1758
1711					M-2	1976		M-2	1976	60	O-1	3144	60	O-1	3144
1712	104	P-2	2507				104	P-2	2507	69	O-1	3042	69	O-1	3042
1713				50	J-2	1574	50	J-2	1574	50	J-2	1574	50	J-2	1574
1714					O-1	3014	70	O-1	3068	88	P-1	1753	88	P-1	1753
1715								H-4	1481	28	H-2	1439	28	H-2	1439
1716	115	–	2598	115	–	2598	115	–	2598	115	–	2598	115	–	2598
1717	104	P-2	2506	104	P-2	2506	104	P-2	2506	104	P-2	2506	104	P-2	2506
1718		P-1	1755					J-2	1563	78	O-5	3300	78	O-5	3300
1719	62	O-1	3017				70	O-1	3062	70	O-1	3062	70	O-1	3062
1720	83	O-6	3365				83	O-6	3365	60	O-1	3141	60	O-1	3141
1721		O-1	3049		O-1	3049		O-1	3049						
1722				70	O-1	3067	70	O-1	3067	70	O-1	3067	70	O-1	3067
1723				69	O-1	3042	69	O-1	3034	50	J-2	1578	63	O-1	3132
1724				88	P-1	1758	88	P-1	1753	70	O-1	3065	70	O-1	3065

Class P-1 4-8-2

Engine Number	1915-1920 Class	1915-1920 Number	Engine Number	1915-1920 Class	1915-1920 Number	Engine Number	1915-1920 Class	1915-1920 Number
1751	H-4	1442	1754	E-14	1011	1757	L-2	1838
1752	E-14	1017	1755	F-8	1216	1758	J-2	1645
1753	H-4	1441	1756	H-4	1477	1759	H-4	1459

Class L-2 2-6-6-2

Engine Number	1915-1920 Class	1915-1920 Number	Engine Number	1915-1920 Class	1915-1920 Number	Engine Number	1915-1920 Class	1915-1920 Number
1800	L-2	1824	1821	L-2	1801	1830	L-2	1803
1804	J-2	1648	1822	L-2	1831	1832	J-2	1639
1805	J-2	1641	1823	L-2	1836	1837	L-2	1837
1807	L-2	1843	1824	L-2	1804	1840	L-2	1835
1812	J-2	1644	1825	J-2	1640	1841	L-2	1839
1814	L-2	1829	1829	L-2	1842			

Class M-1 2-6-8-0

Engine Number	1915-1920 Class	1915-1920 Number	Engine Number	1915-1920 Class	1915-1920 Number	Engine Number	1915-1920 Class	1915-1920 Number
1950	H-4	1447	1962	J-2	1573	1974	F-8	1223
1951	H-4	1469	1963	H-4	1475	1975	J-2	1614
1952	J-2	1631	1964	L-2	1808	1976	H-4	1474
1953	J-2	1609	1965	H-4	1466	1977	J-2	1612
1954	M-1	1972	1966	H-4	1485	1978	H-4	1478
1955	H-4	1461	1967	F-8	1226	1979	H-4	1463
1956	J-2	1632	1968	H-4	1465	1980	H-2	1439
1957	–	785	1969	M-1	1984	1981	J-1	1541
1958	F-8	1227	1970	–	784	1982	H-4	1454
1959	J-2	1560	1971	F-8	1242	1983	H-4	1464
1960	F-8	1238	1972	M-1	1978	1984	H-4	1472
1961	H-4	1462	1973	–	786			

Class M-2 2-6-8-0

Engine Number	1932-1933 Style	1932-1933 Class	1932-1933 Number	April 1943 Style	April 1943 Class	April 1943 Number	June 1949 Style	June 1949 Class	June 1949 Number	January 1950 Style	January 1950 Class	January 1950 Number	December 1951 Style	December 1951 Class	December 1951 Number
1951	112	–	2097	77	O-5	3306	77	O-5	3306						
1963	112	–	2069	100	O-4	3247	100	O-4	3247						
1965	112	–	2076	36	H-5	1351	36	H-5	1351	36	H-5	1351	36	H-5	1351
1967	108	R-1	2043	105	Q-1	2124	70	O-1	3051	70	O-1	3051	70	O-1	3051
1968	112	–	2063	105	Q-1	2122	32	H-4	1471	32	H-4	1471	32	H-4	1471
1972	32	H-4	1462	19	F-8	1238	19	F-8	1238	19	F-8	1238			
1973	32	H-4	1475	32	H-4	1471	104	P-2	2500				104	P-2	2500
1974	36	H-5	1351	32	H-4	1462	32	H-4	1462	32	H-4	1462			
1977	112	–	2077	49	J-2	1611	49	J-2	1611	49	J-2	1611	49	J-2	1611
1980	63	O-1	3133	112	–	2094	100	O-4	3229	100	O-4	3229			
1981	19	F-8	1238	112		2067	70	O-1	3069	70	O-1	3069	70	O-1	3069
1983	112	–	2094	63	O-1	3133	63	O-1	3133	63	O-1	3133	63	O-1	3133
1984	48	J-2	1573	34	H-4	1476									

Class N-1 2-8-8-0

Engine Number	Class	1915-1920 Number	Engine Number	Class	1915-1920 Number	Engine Number	Class	1915-1920 Number
2000	O-1	3059	2007	O-1	3060	2014	O-1	3046
2001	O-1	3051	2008	O-1	3052	2015	O-1	3064
2002	O-1	3066	2010	O-1	3061	2016	O-1	3055
2003	O-1	3047	2011	O-1	3058	2019	O-1	3046
2004	O-1	3050	2012	O-1	3054	2021	O-1	3069
2005	O-1	3057	2013	O-1	3045	2024	O-1	3063
2006	O-1	3056						

Class N-2 2-8-8-0   Class N-3 2-8-8-0

Engine Number	March 1933 Style	Class	Number	April 1943 Style	Class	Number	January 1946 Style	Class	Number	June 1949 Style	Class	Number	December 1951 Style	Class	Number
2000				113	–	2195	113	–	2195	113	–	2195	113	–	2195
2001	114	–	2210	114	–	2216				114	–	2210	114	–	2210
2002				114	–	2210				114	–	2216	114	–	2216
2003				113	–	2206	113	–	2206	113	–	2206	113	–	2206
2004				114	–	2226	114	–	2226	114	–	2226	114	–	2226
2005				113	–	2194	113	–	2194	113	–	2194	113	–	2194
2006				114	–	2218	114	–	2218	114	–	2218	114	–	2218
2007				114	–	2213	114	–	2213	114	–	2213	114	–	2213
2008				113	–	2196	113	–	2196	113	–	2196	113	–	2196
2009				113	–	2209	113	–	2209	113	–	2209	113	–	2209
2010				113	–	2198	113	–	2198	113	–	2198	113	–	2198
2011				114	–	2215	114	–	2215	114	–	2215	114	–	2215
2012				114	–	2220	114	–	2220	114	–	2220	114	–	2220
2013				113	–	2201	113	–	2201	113	–	2201	113	–	2201
2014				114	–	2222	114	–	2222	114	–	2222	114	–	2222
2015				114	–	2211	114	–	2211	114	–	2211	114	–	2211
2016	114	–	2224	114	–	2224				114	–	2221	114	–	2221
2017				113	–	2197	113	–	2197	113	–	2197	113	–	2197
2018				114	–	2223	114	–	2223	114	–	2223	114	–	2223
2019				114	–	2212	114	–	2212	114	–	2212	114	–	2212
2020				114	–	2225	114	–	2225	114	–	2225	114	–	2225
2021				114	–	2217	114	–	2217	114	–	2217	114	–	2217
2022				114	–	2221	114	–	2221	114	–	2224	114	–	2224
2023				114	–	2219	114	–	2219	114	–	2219	114	–	2219
2024				114	–	2214	114	–	2214	114	–	2214	114	–	2214

Locomotives in helper service usually had a pilot at the rear of the tender for protection while operating in reverse. This one is on the Q-1 class tender assigned to No. 2113 at Havre in the 1930's. George Wier photograph from the collection of Norman F. Priebe.

Class R-1 2-8-8-2

Engine Number	March 1933			April 1943			June 1949		
	Style	Class	Number	Style	Class	Number	Style	Class	Number
2030							108	R-1	2033
2031							108	R-1	2041
2032							112	–	2066
2033							112	–	2078
2034							108	R-1	2030
2035							102	O-7	3378
2036							108	R-1	2034
2037							108	R-1	2032
2038							102	O-7	3377
2039				112	–	2070	103	O-8	3399
2040							102	O-7	3383
2041	113	–	2202				109	R-2	2044
2042	109	R-2	2050	108	R-1	2038	108	R-1	2038
2043	109	R-2	2054				112	–	2070

Class R-2 2-8-8-2

Engine Number	June 1949		
	Style	Class	Number
2044	109	R-2	2057
2045	109	R-2	2047
2046	109	R-2	2053
2047	109	R-2	2045
2048	109	R-2	2052
2049	113	–	2207
2050	109	R-2	2050
2051	109	R-2	2055
2052	109	R-2	2058
2053	109	R-2	2059
2054	113	–	2205
2055	109	R-2	2049
2056	109	R-2	2050
2057	113	–	2200
2058	109	R-2	2046
2059	109	R-2	2048

The R-1 Style 108 tenders had a rivet line running along the side of the tank. It was at about the same level as the bottom of the coal bunker. GN-built R-1 2042 was at Minot, ND, in September 1952. Stan F. Styles collection of GTC Collectibles.

Class Q-1 2-10-2

Engine Number	April 1943			June 1945			June 1949			December 1951		
	Style	Class	Number	Style	Class	Number	Style	Class	Number	Style	Class	Number
2100	108	R-1	2035	108	R-1	2035	108	R-1	2035			
2101	105	Q-1	2102	105	Q-1	2102	105	Q-1	2102			
2102	105	Q-1	2105	105	Q-1	2105	112	–	2095	108	R-1	2043
2103	112	–	2067	112	–	2067	112	–	2067	112	–	2067
2104	105	Q-1	2104	105	Q-1	2104	105	Q-1	2104			
2105	108	R-1	2034	108	R-1	2034	112	–	2077	112	–	2077
2106	105	Q-1	2114	105	Q-1	2114	105	Q-1	2114			
2107	105	Q-1	2107	105	Q-1	2107	105	Q-1	2107			
2108	108	R-1	2042	112	–	2097	108	R-1	2042			
2109	105	Q-1	2109	105	Q-1	2109	112	–	2069	112	–	2069
2110	105	Q-1	2100	105	Q-1	2100	112	–	2081	112	–	2081
2111	105	Q-1	2111	105	Q-1	2111	105	Q-1	2111			
2112	112	–	2097	112	–	2099	112	–	2099			
2113	105	Q-1	2108	105	Q-1	2108	105	Q-1	2108			
2114							105	Q-1	2117			
2115	113	–	2202				112	–	2093	112	–	2097
2116	112	–	2073	112	–	2073	112	–	2073	112	–	2073
2117	112	–	2065	112	–	2065	108	R-1	2043	112	–	2095
2118	105	Q-1	2118	105	Q-1	2118	112	–	2090			
2119	113	–	2204				112	–	2065	112	–	2063
2120	105	Q-1	2120	105	Q-1	2120	108	R-1	2031			
2121	102	O-7	3375	102	O-7	3375	102	O-7	3375	102	O-7	3375
2122	112	–	2063	112	–	2063	112	–	2063	112	–	2065
2123	112	–	2092	112	–	2092	112	–	2092	112	–	2092
2124	108	R-1	2043	108	R-1	2043	112	–	2094	112	–	2094
2125	105	Q-1	2123	105	Q-1	2123	113	–	2204	108	R-1	2042
2126	108	R-1	2036	108	R-1	2036	108	R-1	2036	108	R-1	2036
2127	112	–	2074	112	–	2074	112	–	2074	112	–	2074
2128	112	–	2068	112	–	2068	113	–	2202	113	–	2202
2129	112	–	2077	112	–	2077	112	–	2068			

Class Q-2 2-10-2

Engine Number	April 1943 Style	April 1943 Class	April 1943 Number	June 1949 Style	June 1949 Class	June 1949 Number	December 1951 Style	December 1951 Class	December 1951 Number
2175	106	Q-2	2175	106	Q-2	2175	106	Q-2	2175
2176	107	Q-2	2176	107	Q-2	2176	107	Q-2	2176
2177	112	–	2071	112	–	2071	112	–	2071
2178	106	Q-2	2178	106	Q-2	2178	106	Q-2	2178
2179	107	Q-2	2179	107	Q-2	2179	107	Q-2	2179
2180	106	Q-2	2180	106	Q-2	2180	106	Q-2	2180
2181	106	Q-2	2181	106	Q-2	2181	112	–	2066
2182	112	–	2080	112	–	2080	112	–	2080
2183	107	Q-2	2183	107	Q-2	2183	107	Q-2	2183
2184	106	Q-2	2187	106	Q-2	2187	112	–	2068
2185	107	Q-2	2185	107	Q-2	2185	107	Q-2	2185
2186	112	–	2083	112	–	2083	112	–	2083
2187	106	Q-2	2184	106	Q-2	2184	112	–	2090
2188	112	–	2088	112	–	2088	112	–	2088
2189	106	Q-2	2182	106	Q-2	2182	108	R-1	2035

Class P-2 4-8-2

Engine Number	April 1943 Style	April 1943 Class	April 1943 Number	June 1949 Style	June 1949 Class	June 1949 Number	December 1951 Style	December 1951 Class	December 1951 Number
2500	105	Q-1	2124	104	P-2	2522	104	P-2	2522
2501	105	Q-1	2122	105	Q-1	2127	105	Q-1	2122
2502	105	Q-1	2115	104	P-2		105	Q-1	2124
2503	105	Q-1	2128	105	Q-1	2122	105	Q-1	2127
2504	105	Q-1	2127	105	Q-1	2128	105	Q-1	2128
2505	105	Q-1	2112	105	Q-1	2110	105	Q-1	2110
2506	105	Q-1	2129	105	Q-1	2129	105	Q-1	2129
2507	105	Q-1	2116	105	Q-1	2105	105	Q-1	2105
2508	105	Q-1	2119	105	Q-1	2119	105	Q-1	2119
2509	104	P-2	2521	105	Q-1	2124	104	P-2	2526
2510	105	Q-1	2125	105	Q-1	2125	105	Q-1	2125
2511	105	Q-1	2110	105	Q-1	2112	105	Q-1	2112
2512	105	Q-1	2126	105	Q-1	2126	105	Q-1	2126
2513	104	P-2	2526	104	P-2		105	Q-1	2100
2514	105	Q-1	2106	104	P-2	2527	104	P-2	2527
2515	104	P-2	2514	104	P-2	2514	104	P-2	2514
2516	104	P-2	2516	104	P-2	2516	104	P-2	2516
2517	105	Q-1	2101	105	Q-1	2118	105	Q-1	2118
2518	105	Q-1	2113	105	Q-1	2113	105	Q-1	2113
2519	104	P-2	2505	111	S-2	2585	111	S-2	2585
2520	104	P-2	2527	105	Q-1	2106	105	Q-1	2106
2521	105	Q-1	2121	105	Q-1	2121	105	Q-1	2121
2522	104	P-2	2522	105	Q-1	2103	105	Q-1	2103
2523	105	Q-1	2103	105	Q-1	2115	105	Q-1	2115
2524	104	P-2	2519	104	P-2	2519	105	Q-1	2111
2525	104	P-2	2523	105	Q-1	2101	105	Q-1	2101
2526	104	P-2	2524	105	Q-1	2123	105	Q-1	2123
2527	104	P-2	2517	104	P-2	2523	104	P-2	2523

Class S-1 4-8-4

Engine Number	June 1949 Style	June 1949 Class	June 1949 Number
2550	110	S-1	2550
2551	110	S-1	2551
2552	110	S-1	2552
2553	110	S-1	2554
2554	110	S-1	2555
2555	110	S-1	2553

Class S-2 4-8-4

Engine Number	June 1949 Style	June 1949 Class	June 1949 Number
2575	111	S-2	2575
2576	111	S-2	2576
2577	111	S-2	2577
2578	111	S-2	2578
2579	111	S-2	2579
2580	111	S-2	2580
2582	111	S-2	2582
2583	111	S-2	2581
2584	111	S-2	2584
2585	111	S-2	2581
2586	111	S-2	2587
2587	111	S-2	2588
2588	111	S-2	2586

One of the very last steam moves from Sioux City, IA to Willmar, MN was in June 1953 following the bad flood at Sioux City. All steam fueling facilities and most of the water tanks en route had already been removed. The result was the need for a lash-up of multiple auxiliary tenders to make the trip. The locomotive is No. 3215, shown at Marshall, MN, while returning a work train to Willmar. Great Northern diagrams list X3257 as a Style 22 G-3 tender, but this looks unlikely in the photograph, as this tender looks much larger than the G-3's 5,000 gallon water capacity. GN X3212 was originally L-2 tender 1827, renumbered to 3340 when its engine was rebuilt to an O-5 Mikado. Diagrams indicate that it was a Style 73 8,000 gallon tender. Photograph by Norman F. Priebe.

Class O-1 2-8-2

Engine Number	1915-1920			Engine Number	1915-1920			Engine Number	1915-1920	
	Class	Number			Class	Number			Class	Number
3000	H-4	1458		3025	L-1	1916		3048	O-1	3055
3001	F-8	1240		3026	J-2	1623		3049	F-8	1244
3002	J-2	1604		3027	N-1	2002		3050	N-1	2000
3003	O-1	3006		3028	H-4	1445		3051	J-2	1598
3004	O-1	3004		3029	H-4	1444		3052	N-1	2006
3005	J-2	1559		3030	H-4	1470		3053	N-1	2010
3006	J-2	1576		3031	J-2	1611		3054	F-8	1217
3007	H-4	1476		3032	J-2	1558		3055	O-1	3040
3008	F-8	1253		3033	L-2	1840		3056	H-4	1471
3009	H-2	1427		3034	O-1	3022		3057	N-1	2012
3010	H-4	1457		3035	O-1	3035		3058	E-14	1041
3011	E-14	1018		3036	F-8	1239		3059	L-2	1822
3012	F-8	1241		3037	N-1	2014		3060	N-1	2015
3013	O-1	3049		3038	E-14	1019		3061	N-1	2013
3014	J-2	1580		3039	L-2	1828		3062	F-8	1224
3015	M-2(1)	1999		3040	O-1	3037		3063	H-4	1448
3016	J-2	1564		3041	L-2	1823		3064	N-1	2004
3017	J-2	1572		3042	J-2	1590		3065	H-4	1479
3018	F-8	1229		3043	J-2	1566		3066	O-1	3053
3019	H-2	1427		3044	H-4	1483		3067	J-2	1606
3022	J-2	1608		3045	N-1	2007		3068	J-2	1561
3023	H-4	1440		3046	N-1	2008		3069	M-1	1974
3024	F-8	1235		3047	H-4	1453				

Engine Number	March 1933			April 1943			June 1949			December 1951			March 1952		
	Style	Class	Number	Style	Class	Number	Style	Class	Number	Style	Class	Number	Style	Class	Number
3000	49	J-2	1604	100	O-4	3226	100	O-4	3226	66	O-1	3046			
3001	49	J-2	1596	107	Q-2	2188	100	O-4	3227	100	O-4	3227			
3002	36	H-5	1360	65	O-1	3021	68	O-1	3102						
3003	61	O-1	3006	58	N-2	2018	58	N-2	2018						
3004	82	O-6	3361	82	O-6	3361	60	O-1	3117						
3005	60	O-1	3133	36	H-5	1352									
3006		J-2	1580		J-2	1580	58	N-2	2013	58	N-2	2013	58	N-2	2013
3007	79	O-5	3332	79	O-5	3332	79	O-5	3332						
3008	112	–	2079	32	H-4	1479	70	O-1	3058						
3009	66	O-1	3063	66	O-1	3063	9	C-5	870						
3010	19	F-8	1229	19	F-8	1229									
3011	112	–	2084	49	J-2	1596	49	J-2	1596						
3012	65	O-1	3021	77	O-5	3331	36	H-5	1360	36	H-5	1360			
3013	49	J-2	1614	49	J-2	1614	49	J-2	1614	49	J-2	1614	49	J-2	1614
3014	9	C-5	870	9	C-5	870	70	O-1	3046						
3015	107	Q-2	2188	100	O-4	3224	64	O-1	3071						
3016	112	–	2082	112	–	2029	100	O-4	3250						
3017	32	H-4	1443	32	H-4	1443	19	F-8	1242	19	F-8	1242			
3018	107	Q-2	2177	107	Q-2	2189	100	O-4	3243						
3019	106	Q-2	2186	63	O-1	3098	71	O-3	3203	71	O-3	3203	71	O-3	3203
3020	19	F-8	1253	19	F-8	1253	66	O-1	3054	66	O-1	3054	66	O-1	3054
3021	32	H-4	1479		O-1	3117	68	O-1	3086				100	O-4	3224
3022	63	O-1	3120	112	–	2084	100	O-4	3219	100	O-4	3219	100	O-4	3219
3025	61	O-1	3081	32	H-4	1442	32	H-4	1442	32	H-4	1442	32	H-4	1442
3027	57	N-2	2012	32	H-4	1485	32	H-4	1485	32	H-4	1485	32	H-4	1485
3030	49	J-2	1576	64	O-1	3078	64	O-1	3078	64	O-1	3078	64	O-1	3078
3031	112	–	2086	100	O-4	3214	100	O-4	3214						
3032	112	–	2087	32	H-4	1478	32	H-4	1478						
3033	58	N-2	2010	58	N-2	2010	58	N-2	2010	32	H-4	1463			
3034	69	O-1	3004	62	O-1	3016	62	O-1	3016	62	O-1	3016			
3035	107	Q-2	2189	100	O-4	3243	100	O-4	3243	65	O-1	3037			
3036	19	F-8	1226	19	F-8	1226	19	F-8	1226	19	F-8	1226	19	F-8	1226
3037				58	N-2	2014	58	N-2	2014	32	H-4	1475			
3038				49	J-2	1609	49	J-2	1609	49	J-2	1609	49	J-2	1609
3040	65	O-1	3037	41	H-6	1716	41	H-6	1716	58	N-2	2007			
3041	48	J-2	1640	48	J-2	1640	48	J-2	1640	48	J-2	1640			
3042	48	J-2	1590	64	O-1	3085	64	O-1	3085	64	O-1	3085			
3044	49	J-2	1564	49	J-2	1564	32	H-4	1465	32	H-4	1465			
3045	58	N-2	2007	61	O-1	3080	61	O-1	3080	61	O-1	3080			
3046	59	N-2	2008	59	N-2	2008	66	O-1	3063						
3047	63	O-1	3096	63	O-1	3096	63	O-1	3096						
3048	58	N-2	2015	63	O-1	3120	63	O-1	3120						
3049	87	P-1	1763	87	P-1	1763									

Class O-1 2-8-2: Continued

Engine Number	March 1933 Style	Class	Number	April 1943 Style	Class	Number	June 1949 Style	Class	Number	December 1951 Style	Class	Number	March 1952 Style	Class	Number
3050	57	N-2	2000	19	F-8	1242	32	H-4	1443	32	H-4	1443			
3051	45	H-7	1377	77	O-5	3308	77	O-5	3308	77	O-5	3308			
3052	36	H-5	1370	36	H-5	1370	36	H-5	1370	36	H-5	1370	36	H-5	1370
3053	65	O-1	3040	65	O-1	3040	65	O-1	3040	65	O-1	3040	65	O-1	3040
3054	63	O-1	3095	63	O-1	3095	63	O-1	3095	63	O-1	3095	63	O-1	3095
3055				61	O-1	3088	61	O-1	3088	61	O-1	3088			
3056	19	F-8	1223	19	F-8	1223	19	F-8	1223	19	F-8	1223	19	F-8	1223
3057	41	H-6	1710	41	H-6	1710	41	H-6	1710	41	H-6	1710			
3058	49	J-2	1558	49	J-2	1558	65	O-1	3021	65	O-1	3021	65	O-1	3021
3059	32	H-4	1465	32	H-4	1465	32	H-4	1465	19	F-8	1251			
3060	19	F-8	1237	69	O-1	3004	69	O-1	3004						
3061	58	N-2	2013	58	N-2	2013	56	M-2	1954						
3062	36	H-5	1352	68	O-1	3131	63	O-1	3098	63	O-1	3098	63	O-1	3098
3063	34	H-4	1448	34	H-4	1448	49	J-2	1645	49	J-2	1645	49	J-2	1645
3064	19	F-8	1242	64	O-1	3077									
3065	32	H-4	1458	32	H-4	1458	49	J-2	1645	49	J-2	1645	49	J-2	1645
3066	32	H-4	1485	70	O-1	3060	70	O-1	3060	70	O-1	3060			
3067	32	H-4	1442	53	K-1	1709	45	H-7	1380	45	H-7	1380	45	H-7	1380
3068				49	J-2	1561	49	J-2	1561	49	J-2	1561	49	J-2	1561
3069	32	H-4	1477	64	O-1	3087	64	O-1	3087	64	O-1	3087			
3070	49	J-2	1637	49	J-2	1637	49	J-2	1637						
3071	64	O-1	3071	64	O-1	3071	112	–	2061	100	O-4	3254			
3072				69	O-1	3037	69	O-1	3037						
3073				56	M-2	1954	56	M-2	1954	32	H-4	1477			
3074				58	N-2	2007	58	N-2	2007						
3075				49	J-2	1576	49	J-2	1576	49	J-2	1576			
3076				64	O-1	3084	64	O-1	3084	64	O-1	3084			
3077				64	O-1	3083	32	H-4	1479	32	H-4	1479			
3078				64	O-1	3123	64	O-1	3123	64	O-1	3123			
3079				64	O-1	3070	64	O-1	3070						
3080				64	O-1	3092	64	O-1	3092				49	J-2	1564
3081				34	H-4	1474	34	H-4	1474	34	H-4	1474			
3082				64	O-1	3082	64	O-1	3082	64	O-1	3082	64	O-1	3082
3083				19	F-8	1237	19	F-8	1237	19	F-8	1237	19	F-8	1237
3084				64	O-1	3053	64	O-1	3053						
3085				63	O-1	3101	63	O-1	3101	63	O-1	3101			
3086	64	O-1	3086	64	O-1	3086									
3087				36	H-5	1360	77	O-5	3331	77	O-5	3331			
3088				64	O-1	3079	64	O-1	3079				63	O-1	3120
3089				64	O-1	3089	64	O-1	3089	64	O-1	3089	64	O-1	3089
3090				59	N-2	2015	59	N-2	2015				104	P-2	2519
3091				64	O-1	3091	64	O-1	3091						
3092				32	H-4	1477									
3093				64	O-1	3093	64	O-1	3093						
3094				64	O-1	3094	64	O-1	3094						
3095	32	H-4	1454	32	H-4	1454	32	H-4	1454	33	H-4	1469			
3096				49	J-2	1645	34	H-4	1448	34	H-4	1448	34	H-4	1448
3097				63	O-1	3097	63	O-1	3097	63	O-1	3097	63	O-1	3097
3098	112	–	2029	63	O-1	3129	63	O-1	3129						
3100	69	O-1	3042	69	O-1	3042	104	P-2	2507	104	P-2	2504			
3101				63	O-1	3135	63	O-1	3135	63	O-1	3135			
3102				68	O-1	3102	49	J-2	1558	49	J-2	1558			
3103				26	H-2	1438	26	H-2	1438				66	O-1	3063
3104				100	O-4	3228	100	O-4	3228						
3105				49	J-2	1604	49	J-2	1604						
3106	63	O-1	3098	63	O-1	3100	63	O-1	3100						
3107				63	O-1	3099									
3108				36	H-5	1362									
3109	45	H-7	1382	45	H-7	1382	45	H-7	1382	45	H-7	1382	45	H-7	1382
3110				63	O-1	3110	63	O-1	3110	63	O-1	3110	63	O-1	3110
3111				63	O-1	3111									
3112				87	P-1	1764	87	P-1	1764	87	P-1	1764			
3113				19	F-8	1248									
3114	32	H-4	1468	32	H-4	1468	32	H-4	1468	32	H-4	1468			
3115				63	O-1	3118	63	O-1	3118	63	O-1	3118			
3116	32	H-4	1441	32	H-4	1441	32	H-4	1441	32	H-4	1441			
3117				19	F-8	1216	19	F-8	1216	19	F-8	1216			
3118				45	H-7	1380	45	H-7	1380	63	O-1	3111			
3119				58	N-2	2017	19	F-8	1218	19	F-8	1218			

Engine Number	March 1933			April 1943			June 1949			December 1951			March 1952		
	Style	Class	Number	Style	Class	Number	Style	Class	Number	Style	Class	Number	Style	Class	Number
3120				32	H-4	1455	32	H-4	1455	32	H-4	1455			
3121				49	J-2	1560									
3122				77	O-5	3309									
3123	68	O-1	3127	87	P-1	1761	87	P-1	1761	87	P-1	1761			
3124				32	H-4	1459	32	H-4	1459	32	H-4	1459			
3125				50	J-2	1617	50	J-2	1617	50	J-2	1617			
3126				50	J-2	1632	50	J-2	1632	50	J-2	1632			
3127				49	J-2	1631	49	J-2	1631	49	J-2	1631			
3128				36	H-5	1358	36	H-5	1358						
3129				49	J-2	1584	49	J-2	1584	49	J-2	1584			
3130				87	P-1	1762	87	P-1	1762	87	P-1	1762			
3131		O-1	3099	63	O-1	3139	63	O-1	3139						
3132				49	J-2	1641	49	J-2	1641	49	J-2	1641	49	J-2	1641
3133				32	H-4	1463	32	H-4	1463				70	O-1	3058
3134				19	F-8	1243									
3135		O-1	3129	112	–	2082	100	O-4	3220						
3136					O-1	3142	49	J-2	1610	49	J-2	1610			
3137	63	O-1	3105	63	O-1	3105	104	P-2	2520						
3138	32	H-4	1478	63	O-1	3138	63	O-1	3138						
3139				63	O-1	3132	63	O-1	3132	70	O-1	3065			
3140				60	O-1	3140	60	O-1	3140	60	O-1	3140			
3141				60	O-1	3136	60	O-1	3136	70	O-1	3048			
3142				35	H-4	1481	104	P-2	2504						
3143				68	O-1	3143									
3144				104	P-2	2504	104	P-2	2501						

Class O-2 2-8-2

Engine Number	January 1930			April 1943		
	Style	Class	Number	Style	Class	Number
3149		O-2	3149	34	H-4	1457

Engine 3042 has been equipped with a Worthington BL-2 feedwater heater and slant front cab, but still appears to have its original smokebox front. It has also been converted to an oil-burner. The tender behind it is 3085, a Style 64 O-1 tender. This tender originally looked more like the tenders behind engines 3030 and 3042, shown in Chapter 20. However, perhaps because of its conversion to oil, the odd curved coal bunker sides and bracing have been removed, and it now looks like a rather plain straight-sided tender. It was photographed at Fort Wright, WA, in 1945. George Corey (RPS) photograph from the collection of Norman F. Priebe.

Class O-3 2-8-2

Engine Number	January 1930			April 1943			June 1949			December 1951		
	Style	Class	Number	Style	Class	Number	Style	Class	Number	Style	Class	Number
3200	71	O-3	3208	71	O-3	3208	71	O-3	3208	71	O-3	3208
3201	71	O-3	3205	71	O-3	3205	71	O-3	3205	71	O-3	3205
3202	71	O-3	3201	71	O-3	3201	71	O-3	3201			
3203	71	O-3	3204	71	O-3	3204	71	O-3	3204	71	O-3	3204
3204	71	O-3	3200	71	O-3	3200	71	O-3	3200	71	O-3	3200
3205	71	O-3	3207	71	O-3	3207	71	O-3	3207			
3206	71	O-3	3203	71	O-3	3203						
3207	71	O-3	3206	71	O-3	3206	71	O-3	3206	71	O-3	3206
3208	71	O-3	3202	71	O-3	3202	71	O-3	3202	71	O-3	3202

Class O-4 2-8-2

Engine Number	April 1943			June 1949			December 1951		
	Style	Class	Number	Style	Class	Number	Style	Class	Number
3210	100	O-4	3216	100	O-4	3233	100	O-4	3211
3211	100	O-4	3212	100	O-4	3212			
3212	100	O-4	3218	100	O-4	3248	100	O-4	3240
3213	100	O-4	3211	100	O-4	3213	100	O-4	3238
3214	100	O-4	3213	100	O-4	3215			
3215	100	O-4	3217	100	O-4	3216			
3216	100	O-4	3215	100	O-4	3233			
3217	100	O-4	3251	100	O-4	3246	106	Q-2	2182
3218	107	Q-2	2177	107	Q-2	2177	107	Q-2	2177
3219	100	O-4	3219	112	–	2084	112	–	2084
3220	100	O-4	3220	112	–	2082	112	–	2082
3221	100	O-4	3221	107	Q-2	2189	107	Q-2	2189
3222	100	O-4	3223	100	O-4	3223	100	O-4	3223
3223	100	O-4	3222	100	O-4	3231			
3224	112	–	2087	112	–	2087	112	–	2087
3225	112	–	2086	112	–	2086	112	–	2086
3226	112	–	2079	112	–	2079	112	–	2079
3227	100	O-4	3225	100	O-4	3225	100	O-4	3225
3228	106	Q-2	2186	106	Q-2	2186	106	Q-2	2186
3229	112	–	2094	105	Q-1	2109	105	Q-1	2109
3230	100	O-4	3230	100	O-4	3230	100	O-4	3230
3231	100	O-4	3231	100	O-4	3222	105	Q-1	2107
3232	100	O-4	3232	100	O-4	3232	100	O-4	3232
3233	100	O-4	3237	100	O-4	3237	100	O-4	3237
3234	100	O-4	3234	100	O-4	3234	100	O-4	3234
3235	100	O-4	3235	100	O-4	3251	100	O-4	3251
3236	100	O-4	3236	100	O-4	3236	100	O-4	3236
3237	100	O-4	3233	100	O-4	3210	100	O-4	3210
3238	100	O-4	3238	100	O-4	3235	100	O-4	3235
3239	100	O-4	3239	100	O-4	3239	100	O-4	3239
3240	100	O-4	3240	100	O-4	3217	100	O-4	3217
3241	100	O-4	3241	100	O-4	3241	100	O-4	3241
3242	100	O-4	3242	100	O-4	3242	100	O-4	3242
3243	100	O-4	3227	107	Q-2	2188	107	Q-2	2188
3244	100	O-4	3244	100	O-4	3244	100	O-4	3244
3245	100	O-4	3245	100	O-4	3245	100	O-4	3245
3246	100	O-4	3246	100	O-4	3218	100	O-4	3218
3247	112	–	2069	105	Q-1	2120	105	Q-1	2120
3248	100	O-4	3248	100	O-4	3248	100	O-4	3248
3249	100	O-4	3249	100	O-4	3249	100	O-4	3249
3250	100	O-4	3250	112	–	2029	112	–	2029
3251	100	O-4	3210	100	O-4	3240	100	O-4	3213
3252	100	O-4	3252	100	O-4	3221	112	–	2076
3253	100	O-4	3253	100	O-4	3253	100	O-4	3253
3254	100	O-4	3254	100	O-4	3254	112	–	2061

Class O-5 2-8-2

Engine Number	April 1938 Style	Class	Number	April 1943 Style	Class	Number	June 1949 Style	Class	Number
3300				28	H-2	1437			
3301				27	H-2	1434			
3302				49	J-2	1620			
3303	49	J-2	1556						
3304	36	H-5	1361						
3306	58	N-2	2022						
3307	36	H-5	1372						
3308				32	H-4	1447			
3309				19	F-8	1218			
3310	58	N-2	2017	48	J-2	1613			
3312				36	H-5	1373			
3313				49	J-2	1628			
3314				61	O-1	3076			
3315				73	O-5	3322			
3316	32	H-4	1475						
3318				73	O-5	3319			
3319					O-5	3315			
3320				73	O-5	3320			
3323				73	O-5	3343			
3324				73	O-5	3344			
3325				41	H-6	1723			
3326				33	H-4	1469			
3328				73	O-5	3328			
3329					O-5	3341			
3331	76	O-5	3331	61	O-1	3075			
3334	77	O-5	3308	19	F-8	1234			
3335				49	J-2	1610	60	O-1	3142
3338					O-5	3323			
3341					O-5	3300			
3344					M-2	1978			

Class O-6 2-8-2

Engine Number	March 1933 Style	Class	Number	April 1943 Style	Class	Number	June 1945 Style	Class	Number	June 1949 Style	Class	Number	March 1952 Style	Class	Number
3350	49	J-2	1628	112	–	2085	112	–	2085	112	–	2085	112	–	2085
3351	112	–	2090	112	–	2081	112	–	2097	112	–	2097	112	–	2097
3352	77	O-5	3335	112	–	2095	112	–	2095	104	P-2	2521	108	R-1	2041
3353	28	H-2	1437	101	O-7	3393	101	O-7	3393	101	O-7	3393	101	O-7	3393
3354	37	H-5	1373	112	–	2098	112	–	2098	112	–	2096	112	–	2096
3355	69	O-1	3042	112	–	2062	112	–	2062	112	–	2062	112	–	2062
3356	32	H-4	1460	112	–	2090	112	–	2090	104	P-2	2517	112	–	2069
3357	45	H-7	1380	112	–	2061	112	–	2061						
3358	108	R-1	2040	112	–	2091	112	–	2091	112	–	2091	112	–	2091
3359	19	F-8	1248	32	H-4	1472				112	–	2076	112	–	2076
3360	112	–	2093	112	–	2093	112	–	2093	32	H-4	1447	106	Q-2	2187
3361	36	H-5	1360	112	–	2099	112	–	2099	104	P-2	2524	108	R-1	2033
3362	108	R-1	2031	112	–	2089	112	–	2089	112	–	2089	112	–	2089
3363	112	–	2096	112	–	2096	112	–	2096	112	–	2098	108	R-1	2037
3364	112	–	2063	112	–	2075	112	–	2075	112	–	2075	112	–	2075
3365	108	R-1	2043	33	H-4	1460									
3366	112	–	2091	49	J-2	1571	49	J-2	1571	49	J-2	1571	106	Q-2	2181
3367	49	J-2	1620	108	R-1	2040	108	R-1	2040	108	R-1	2040	108	R-1	2040
3368	112	–	2089	108	R-1	2037	108	R-1	2037	108	R-1	2037	112	–	2098
3369	108	R-1	2032	112	–	2064	112	–	2064	112	–	2064	112	–	2064
3370	108	R-1	2039	108	R-1	2039	108	R-1	2039	108	R-1	2039	108	R-1	2039
3371	112	–	2062	77	O-5	3329									

Class O-7 2-8-2 / Class O-8 2-8-2

Engine Number	March 1933			April 1943			August 1945			December 1951		
	Style	Class	Number	Style	Class	Number	Style	Class	Number	Style	Class	Number
3375	112	–	2072	112	–	2072				101	O-7	3387
3376	101	O-7	3394	101	O-7	3394	101	O-7	3394	101	O-7	3394
3377	101	O-7	3392	101	O-7	3392	101	O-7	3392	101	O-7	3392
3378	101	O-7	3376	101	O-7	3376	101	O-7	3376	101	O-7	3376
3379	103	O-8	3397	103	O-8	3397				103	O-8	3397
3380				101	O-7	3379				112	–	2072
3381	101	O-7	3381	101	O-7	3381				101	O-7	3379
3382				101	O-7	3382	101	O-7	3382	101	O-7	3382
3383				101	O-7	3383	101	O-7	3383	109	R-2	2054
3384				101	O-7	3384	101	O-7	3384	101	O-7	3384
3385				101	O-7	3385	101	O-7	3385	101	O-7	3385
3386				101	O-7	3386	101	O-7	3386	101	O-7	3386
3387				101	O-7	3390				101	O-7	3390
3388				101	O-7	3388				101	O-7	3388
3389				101	O-7	3389				101	O-7	3389
3390				101	O-7	3387				101	O-7	3381
3391				101	O-7	3396				101	O-7	3396
3392				101	O-7	3380	101	O-7	3380	101	O-7	3380
3393				101	O-7	3391	101	O-7	3391	101	O-7	3391
3394				103	O-8	3398	103	O-8	3398	103	O-8	3398
3395				101	O-7	3395	101	O-7	3395	101	O-7	3395
3396				103	O-8	3399				109	R-2	2056

Class O-8 2-8-2

Engine Number	March 1933			April 1943			December 1951		
	Style	Class	Number	Style	Class	Number	Style	Class	Number
3397	113	–	2203	113	–	2203	113	–	2203
3398				113	–	2199	113	–	2199
3399	113	–	2208	113	–	2208	113	–	2208

Class Z-6 4-6-6-4

Engine Number	June 1949		
	Style	Class	Number
4000	–	Z-6	4000

Class O-1 engine 3056 has received a short stack, but still has a square cab and the original smokebox front. The tender is probably Class F-8 Style 19 No. 1223. This was originally T1259, but was renumbered after its engine was sold to the SP&S. It has been stretched five feet to increase water capacity to 10,000 gallons. This tender is quite typical of the "stretched version" of the 8,000 gallon tenders delivered with rounded coal bunker sides. These tenders came from the E-14's, Baldwin F-8's, most of the early H-class engines, the J-class engines and the first order of L-2's. The photograph was taken at Minneapolis, MN, before World War II. R. J. Foster photograph from the collection of William Raia.

This photograph of Class H-5 1367 shows the engineer's side view of the streamlined cab with which a few H-5's were equipped. The engine has been equipped with a Sellers exhaust steam injector and a power reverse. Note the boxy enclosed turret in front of the cab. The engine is shown at Winnipeg, MB, in August 1946. Stan F. Styles collection of GTC Collectibles.

Chapter 35
References For The Rosters

Author unknown (General Manager of Somers Lumber Company – signature illegible). Letter to W.B. Irwin, September 11, 1937.

Lambert M. Baker. Locomotives of St. Paul & Pacific Railway, St. Paul, Minneapolis & Manitoba Ry., 1st Div. St. Paul & Pacific Ry., Great Northern Railway, 1953. (locomotive roster annotated by George Wier).

Lambert M. Baker, The *St. Paul and Pacific Railroad*, a Minnesota Pioneer, unpublished manuscript dated 1967.

W.W. Baldwin. Corporate History of the Chicago, Burlington & Quincy Railroad Company and Affiliated Companies (As of date June 30, 1917), p. 405ff (Nebraska Historical Society).

W.R. Ballard (General Manager of Somers Lumber Co.). Request for AFE to dismantle engine 342, dated January 20, 1930.

Walter F. Becker. "Iron Brothers--the Crooks and the Rice." Railway and Locomotive Historical Society Bulletin, No. 107, p. 11 (October, 1962).

Walter F. Becker. Great Northern Railway Company Steam Locomotive Dispositions, 1965.

Gerald M. Best. Personal communication to Kenneth R. Middleton, February 22, 1980.

Roy W. Carlson (ed.). Chicago, St. Paul, Minneapolis & Omaha roster. *Midwest Railroader, the Complete Roster Journal*, No. 41 (March, 1964).

Paul Allen Copeland. Personal communication to Robert C. Post, January 14, 1981.

Joseph R. Douda. Personal communication to Bernard G. Corbin, February 1, 1977.

F.E. Draper. Memo to F.E. Ward, describing the sale of GN 101 to VW&Y, January 5, 1904. (Minnesota Historical Society GN Files).

H.A. Durfy. *Pacific Coast R.R. Co.* Prepared for the Membership of the PNR-NMRA, September 13, 1958.

Aurele A. Durocher. Personal communication to Robert C. Post concerning the ancestry of the Duluth & Winnipeg Dickson locomotives, January 20, 1981.

Larry Easton. Personal communication to Kenneth R. Middleton, January 5, 1981.

William D. Edson. Personal communication to Kenneth R. Middleton and Norman C. Keyes, Jr., c.1979.

Henry Elwood. *Somers, Montana.* Thomas Printing, Inc., Kalispell, MT, 1990.

John Fahey. *Inland Empire, D.C. Corbin and Spokane.* University of Washington Press, Seattle, WA, 1965.

Charles E. Fisher. Great Northern Railway steam locomotive roster, Railway & Locomotive Historical Society (R&LHS).

Harold G. Goldsmith. Personal communication to Robert C. Post, December 28, 1980.

Robert Graham. Great Northern Railway Company steam locomotive roster, 1977.

John Baskin Harper. Personal communication to Norman C. Keyes, Jr., regarding disposition of GN 991, July 15, 1981.

George Hearn and David Wilkie. *The Cordwood Limited.* The British Columbia Railway Historical Association, Victoria, BC (4th Ed.), 1973.

Willis C. Hendrick. Personal communication to Norman C. Keyes, Jr.

Jerrold F. Hilton. "Somers Lumber Company." *Pacific News*, p. 3 (May 1971).

Jerrold F. Hilton. "The Strange Saga of the Pacific Short Line." National Railway Historical Society *Central Region Limited*, 1980

William Kelly. Memo to W.R. Wood noting which engines were Class H-3, March 18, 1921, (Minnesota Historical Society GN Files).

William Kelly. Memo to C.O. Jenks providing locomotive dispositions for Walter F. Becker, December 24, 1934, (Minnesota Historical Society GN Files).

Norman C. Keyes, Jr. Personal communication to Kenneth R. Middleton (various dates from February 2, 1975, through March 29, 1990).

Norman C. Keyes, Jr. R&LHS Butte, Anaconda & Pacific Roster Information.

Norman C. Keyes, Jr. Steam locomotive notes.

Frank A. King. *Minnesota Logging Railroads*. Golden West Books, San Marino, CA, 1981.

Michael Koch. *The Shay Locomotive, Titan of the Timber*. World Press, Inc., Denver, CO, 1971.

Darryl E. Muralt. *The Victoria and Sidney Railway 1892-1919*. British Columbia Railway Historical Association, Victoria, BC, 1993.

Neal Null. Personal communication to Norman C. Keyes, Jr., October 21, 1979.

Norman F. Priebe. "The World's Greatest Mikado." *Trains*, Vol. 29, No. 3, p. 38 (January, 1969).

Michael Richeson. "An old friend returns." *Daily Interlake* (Kalispell, MT), March 29, 2008.

T. Roope. Letter to Ed Haakinson, November 5, 1893 (Minnesota Historical Society GN/SCO&W Files

Larry P. Schrenk. Personal communication to Kenneth R. Middleton, December 30, 1977.

George Sittig. Great Northern steam locomotive roster information sent to Norman C. Keyes, Jr., apparently beginning on August 23, 1966, and extending over an unknown period of time, but at least through October 10, 1968.

Robert Sloan. Personal communication to Kenneth R. Middleton, May 1976.

Paul T. Warner, 1925. "The Great Northern Railway and Its Locomotives." *Baldwin Locomotives*, January, 1925.

Ty Wilson. Personal communication to Kenneth R. Middleton, April 24, 2008.

Charles and Dorothy Wood. *Spokane, Portland and Seattle Ry., the Northwest's Own Railway*. Superior Publishing Company, Seattle, WA, 1974.

Brooks Locomotive Works Order List, Alco Historic Photos, Schenectady, NY.

Contract between the Nelson & Fort Sheppard Railway Company and Burnham, Williams & Co., for the lease and purchase of two locomotives, dated February 28, 1894, and effective February 1, 1894 (Minnesota Historical Society GN Files).

Correspondence concerning GN Motor Car 6000 (Minnesota Historical Society GN Files).

Decisions of the Interstate Commerce Commission of the United States (Valuation Reports), Report of the Commission, U.S. Government Printing Office, Washington, DC, Volume 133 (July-November, 1927). Submitted October 23, 1925 and 'decided' July 11, 1927, covering the valuation of the Great Northern Railway Company as of June 30, 1915.

Great Northern Railway Company Change Number Record Accounts (valuation information), abbreviated "CNRA."

Great Northern Histories and Corporate Records (Minnesota Historical Society GN Files).

Great Northern Railway Company Annual Report No. 34 (December 31, 1922).

Great Northern Railway Company Annual Report No. 40 (December 31, 1928).

Great Northern Railway Company Chart of Corporate History, January 1, 1956.

Great Northern Railway Annual Report, Machinery Department, 1891 and 1892 (Minnesota Historical Society, GN Presidents' Subject Files).

Great Northern Railway Company 1880-1900 Historical Engine Record (abbreviated "1880 HER").

Great Northern Railway Company Authorities for Expenditure.

Great Northern Railway Company Authorities for Expenditure Index.

Great Northern Railway Company Equipment Completion Report and Unit Record of Property Changes - Equipment. While some modifications as early as 1916 are included, locomotives which disappeared from the roster as of November, 1918, are not included. Changes from December, 1918, onward are included (abbreviated "URPC").

Great Northern Railway Company Historic Car Records Volumes 36-43 (New Equipment Registers 1-8) (Minnesota Historical Society).

Great Northern Railway Company Historic Car Records Volume 94 (Historical Record of S.C. and N. and Sioux City and Western, January 1, 1900) (Minnesota Historical Society).

Great Northern Railway Company Historic Car Records Vol. 99 (Great Northern Subsidiary Renumberings) (Minnesota Historical Society).

Great Northern Railway Company Historical Engine Record (abbreviated "HER") modern (post 1900) volumes.

Great Northern Railway Company Locomotive Diagrams, 1900 - 1952.

Great Northern Railway Company Vice-President Operating Files (Minnesota Historical Society).

Interstate Commerce Commission Valuation Engineering Report, Set No. S-66 (Minneapolis Western), June 30, 1915.

Inventory of equipment acquired by the StPM&M from the StP&P, and dates of receipt of StPM&M equipment (Minnesota Historical Society GN Files).

"List of DS&W engines and equipment turned over the E. Ry. of Minnesota, June 23rd, 1898" (Minnesota Historical Society GN/DS&W Files).

"List of Engines Disposed of During Years 1920 to 1931 Inclusive." (Minnesota Historical Society GN VP-Operating Files).

New York Locomotive Works Order List (obtained from Norman C. Keyes, Jr.).

Order information for Class 51 locomotives (GN 1150-1154). (Minnesota Historical Society GN VP Operating Files).

Pittsburgh Locomotive and Car Works Order List, Alco Historic Photos, Schenectady, NY.

Poor's Manuals of Railroads.

The Railroad Gazette, Volume 5, p. 55 (February 8, 1873).

The Railroad Gazette, Vol. 20, p. 597 (September 7, 1888).

The Railroad Gazette, Vol. 22, p. 348 (May 16, 1890).

The Railroad Gazette, Vol. 22, p. 611 (August 29, 1890).

The Railroad Gazette, Vol. 22, p. 849 (December 5, 1890).

The Railroad Gazette, Vol. 22, p. 904 (December 26, 1890).

The Railroad Gazette, Vol. 24, p. 378 (May 20, 1892) and Vol. 23, p. 359 (May 22, 1891).

Rhode Island Locomotive Works Order List, Alco Historic Photos, Schenectady, NY.

Rogers Locomotive Works Order List, Alco Historic Photos, Schenectady, NY.

Schenectady Locomotive Works Order List, Alco Historic Photos, Schenectady, NY.

Table of steam locomotive rebuilding locations, dated December 28, 1925.

Taunton Locomotive Works Order List.

Class P-2 No. 2514, a 4-8-2, is shown departing St. Paul Union Depot with Train No. 1, the Empire Builder. The date is 1937 or later, since a Luxury coach shows up as the third car. A Great Northern Railway photograph, from the Jerrold F. Hilton collection.

Bibliography

Alfred W. Bruce. *The Steam Locomotive in America*, Bonanza Books, New York, 1952.

Anthony Clegg and Ray Corley. *Canadian National Steam Power*, Railfare Enterprises (Trains and Trolleys), Montreal, 1969.

Henry Elwood (Ed.). *Somers, Montana, The Company Town*. Thomas Printing, Inc., Kalispell, MT, 1976.

Jack W. Farrell and Mike Pearsall, *The Mountains*, Pacific Fast Mail, Edmonds, WA, 1977.

Jack W. Farrell and Mike Pearsall, *The Northerns*, Pacific Fast Mail, Edmunds, WA 1975.

S. Kip Farrington. *Railroading Coast to Coast*, Hastings House, New York, 1976.

Robert L. Frey and Lorenz P. Schrenk, *Northern Pacific Railway Supersteam Era*, Golden West Books, San Marino, CA, 1985.

Ralph P. Johnson. *The Steam Locomotive*, Simmons-Boardman Publishing Corporation, New York, NY, 1942.

William Kratville and Harold E. Ranks, *Motive Power of the Union Pacific*, Barnhart Press, Omaha, NE, 1959.

Thomas R. Lee, *Turbines Westward*, Lee Publications, 1975, as quoted in Wikipedia.

Robert LeMassena, *Articulated Steam Locomotives of North America*, Vol. 1 and 2, Sundance Books, 1979 and 1991.

Llewellyn V. Ludy. Locomotive Boilers and Engines, American Technical Society, Chicago, 1920. (On line at San Diego Railroad Museum website: <http://www.sdrm.org/faqs/boiler/title.html>)

David Plowden. *A Time of Trains*, W. W. Norton, New York, 1987.

Poor's Manuals of Railroads.

Angus Sinclair. *Development of the Locomotive Engine*, Annotated edition by John H. White, Jr., M.I.T. Press, Cambridge, 1970.

Linn H. Westcott (Ed.). *Model Railroader Cyclopedia Volume 1 – Steam Locomotives*. Kalmbach Publishing Company, Milwaukee, 1960.

Charles R. Wood, *Lines West* (p. 110), Superior Publishing Co. Seattle, 1967 (1st Ed.).

Roy V. Wright (Ed.). *Locomotive Cyclopedia of American Practice*, Simmons-Boardman Publishing Company, New York (6th Ed.), 1922. RailDriver digital reprint, 2002.

Roy V. Wright (Ed.). *Locomotive Cyclopedia of American Practice*, Simmons-Boardman Publishing Company, New York (9th Ed.), 1930.

Roy V. Wright (Ed.). *Locomotive Cyclopedia of American Practice*. Simmons-Boardman Publishing Company, New York (11th Ed.), 1941.

Duane Amdahl, Myron Gilbertson, Charles F. Martin, W. A. McGinley, Kenneth R. Middleton, Michael D. Oltman and John M. Wickre. Great Northern Class O-1, 2-8-2 Part II. Fraternal Order of Empire Builders Reference Sheet 22, July 1976.

Duane C. Amdahl, Norman C. Keyes, Jr., Kenneth R. Middleton, W. A. McGinley, Michael D. Oltman and the Minnesota Historical Society. Great Northern Class K-1, 4-4-2. Fraternal Order of Empire Builders Reference Sheet 33, June 1977.

Douglas C. Bemrich. "Great Northern Steam Locomotives Class H-5", Great Northern Railway Historical Society Reference Sheet 170, September 1990.

Raymond W. Brown. "The Great Northern's Super Mikados", *Locomotive Quarterly*, Vol. 4, Number 4, Summer 1981.

Robert Bye and James Larson. "Rear-end Collision – Two Passenger Trains, Michigan, North Dakota – August 9, 1945," Great Northern Railway Historical Society Reference Sheet No. 152, September 1989.

Neil L. Carlson. "Simple Articulateds", *Trains Magazine*, January 2002.

Robert W. Downing, "The SP&S, the GN and the NP," GNRHS Reference Sheet No. 240, March 1996.

Theodore F. Doyle, "The Great Northern Flyer," GNRHS Reference Sheet 290, December 2000.

Cyril Durrenberger. "Great Northern's Class O-3 Mikados", *Prototype Modeler*, July-August 1983, p. 32.

William D. Edson and John H. White, "Lima Locomotive Works," The Railway and Locomotive Historical Society Bulletin No. 123, pp. 81-102, October 1970.

Martin Evoy III, Norman C. Keyes, Jr., W.A. McGinley, Wolfgang F. Weber and the Minnesota Historical Society. "Great Northern Equipment Color Schemes." Fraternal Order of Empire Builders Reference Sheet No. 28, 1977.

Jerrold F. Hilton. "Somers Lumber Company," *Pacific News*, May 1971, p. 3.

Jerrold F. Hilton. "Steam Lives on the Burlington Northern," *Model Railroader*, October 1975, p. 78.

Kenneth G. Johnson. "Burlington Northern Steam in 1977," *Pacific News*, February 1977, p. 18.

Norman C. Keyes, Jr., Charles F. Martin, W. A. McGinley, Kenneth R. Middleton, Michael D. Oltman and John Wickre. Great Northern Class O-1, 2-8-2. Fraternal Order of Empire Builders Reference Sheet 12, October 1975.

Norman C. Keyes, Jr., Kenneth R. Middleton, W. A. McGinley, Michael D. Oltman, Norman F. Priebe and the Minnesota Historical Society. Great Northern Class S-2, 4-8-4. Fraternal Order of Empire Builders Reference Sheet 40, May 1978.

Norman C. Keyes, Jr., Charles F. Martin, W. A. McGinley, Kenneth R. Middleton, Michael D. Oltman and the Minnesota Historical Society. "Great Northern N-Class Locomotives, 2-8-8-0," Fraternal Order of Empire Builders Reference Sheet 29, January 1977.

Don Leach. "Counterbalancing 10-Coupled Power," *R&LHS Newsletter*, Vol.24, No.3 (Summer 2004).

Brian Lerohl. "Crown Sheet Failure – Locomotive 2581, Crary, North Dakota – January 9, 1947," Great Northern Railway Historical Society Reference Sheet No. 161, March 1990.

Kenneth R. Middleton, W. A. McGinley, Michael Oltman and the Minnesota

Historical Society. "Great Northern Class E-6, 4-6-0," Fraternal Order of Empire Builders Reference Sheet 26, November 1976.

Kenneth R. Middleton. "Great Northern Steam Locomotives Class J, 2-6-2," Great Northern Railway Historical Society Reference Sheet No. 93, September 1984.

Kenneth R. Middleton. "Great Northern Steam Locomotives Class O-6, 2-8-2," Great Northern Railway Historical Society Reference Sheet No. 137, September 1988.

Kenneth R. Middleton. "Great Northern Steam Locomotive Cab Side Data," Great Northern Railway Historical Society Reference Sheet 334, June 2006.

Gordon Odegard. "Great Northern 1893 Tandem Compound Consolidation," *Model Railroader*, June 1987.

Pennsylvania Railroad. "Report of Great Northern No. 1950", February 16, 1910. Harrisburg PA Archives, sent by Dick Adams to Russ Wilcox, February 20, 2000

Fr. Dale Peterka. "Great Northern Steam Locomotives Class F-8 2-8-0", Great Northern Railway Historical Society Reference Sheet 131, March 1988.

Fr. Dale Peterka. "Great Northern Steam Locomotives Classes P-1 and P-2," Great Northern Railway Historical Society Reference Sheet 174, March 1991.

Fr. Dale Peterka. "Early Steam Developments on the GN," Great Northern Railway Historical Society Reference Sheet 224, December 1994.

Fr. Dale Peterka. "Great Northern's Home-Brew Mallet," Great Northern Railway Historical Society Reference Sheet No. 297, September 2001.

Fr. Dale Peterka. "The GN L-Class Mallets," Great Northern Historical Society Reference Sheet 332,.December 2005.

Norman F. Priebe. "The World's Greatest Mikado," *Trains Magazine*, January 1969, p. 38.

Norman F. Priebe. "Great Northern Steam Locomotives, Class O-8, 2-8-2," Great Northern Railway Historical Society Reference Sheet No. 98, June 1985.

Norman F. Priebe. "Steam's Last Days on the Great Northern," Great Northern Railway Historical Society Reference Sheet No. 124, September 1987.

Norman F. Priebe. "The Z-6 Challenger on the Great Northern," Great Northern Railway Historical Society Reference Sheet No. 262, June 1998.

Norman F. Priebe. "Jackson Street: Stable for GN's Finest," *Minnegazette*, MTM, St. Paul, Vol. 39 No. 2, Spring 2007, P. 15.

Robert H. Shober. "Silk Trains and Other Commerce on Hill's Road," Great Northern Railway Historical Society Reference Sheet 264, September 1998.

Great Northern Railway Historical Society Steam Locomotive Technical Committee. "Great Northern Steam Locomotives, Class O-5, 2-8-2," Great Northern Railway Historical Society Reference Sheet No. 118, March 1987.

Arthur D. Taylor. "Great Northern Class H-6 Pacific," Great Northern Railway Historical Society Reference Sheet 233, September 1995.

Samuel Vauclain, "What Size Drivers," *Baldwin Locomotives*, April-July 1934.

Paul T. Warner, "The Great Northern Railway and its Locomotives," *Baldwin Locomotives*, January 1925 (Also reprinted in *Pacific Railway Journal*, Summer 1956; and by the Fraternal Order of Empire Builders, February 1978.)

"Baldwin Locomotives on the Great Northern Railway," *Baldwin Locomotives*, February 1939.

"2-8-8-2 Type Locomotives for the Great Northern Railway," *Railway and Locomotive Engineering*, p. 223, August 1925.

"Mallet Articulated Locomotives for the Great Northern Ry.," *The Railway and Engineering Review*, Vol. 50, No. 13, p. 306 (March 26, 1910).

"Brooks Freight Locomotive for the Great Northern," *The Railroad Gazette*, Vol. 28 (October 23, 1896).

"Heavy 12-Wheel Locomotives for the Great Northern," *The Railroad Gazette*, Vol. 30, No. 1, p. 3 (January 7, 1898).

"Ten-Wheel Passenger Locomotives for the Great Northern Railway," *The Railroad Gazette*, Vol. 30, No. 40, p. 719 (October 7, 1898).

"Tests of the New 10-Wheel Locomotives of the Great Northern," *The Railroad Gazette*, Vol. 30, No. 41, p. 735 (October 14, 1898).

"Mallet Compound Locomotive for the Great Northern," *The Railroad Gazette*, Volume 41, Number 7, p. 148 (August 17, 1906).

"Mallet Compound Locomotive for the Great Northern," *The Railroad Gazette*, Volume 41, Number 15, p. 315 (October 12, 1906).

"New Locomotives for the Great Northern," *The Railroad Gazette*, Vol. 41, No. 17, p. 371 (October 26, 1906).

"The Mallet Compound Locomotives on the Great Northern," *The Railroad Gazette*, Vol. 42, No. 20, p. 684 (May 17, 1907).

"The Converted Mallet Locomotive," *Railroad Age Gazette*, Vol. 47, No. 23, p. 1046 (December 3, 1909).

"Converted Mallet Locomotive for the Great Northern." *Railroad Age Gazette*, Vol. 47, No. 25, p. 1185 (December 17, 1909).

"Mountain Type Locomotive for Great Northern," *Railway Age*, Vol. 75, No. 23, p. 1065, (Dec. 8, 1923).

"2-10-2 Type Replace Mallets on Great Northern," *Railway Age*, Vol. 76, No. 8, p. 459 (February 23, 1924).

"Great Northern Acquires Mallet Locomotives," *Railway Age*, Vol. 79, No. 8, p. 359 (August 22, 1925).

"Service of Simple Mallets," *Railway Age*, Vol. 80, No. 31, p. 1673 (June 12, 1926).

"Great Northern Buys Six 4-8-4 Type Passenger Locomotives," *Railway Age*, Vol. 87, No. 19, p. 1097 (November 9, 1929).

"Great Northern Adds to 2-8-8-2 Type Motive Power," *Railway Age*, Vol. 87, No. 26, p. 1477 (December 28, 1929).

"4-8-4 Type Locomotives for Passenger Service," *Railway Age*, Vol. 88, No. 17, p. 965 (April 26, 1930).

"Handling Fourteen Thousand Ton Trains," *Railway Age*, Vol. 89, No. 13, p. 609 (September 27, 1930).

"Mikado Locomotives for the Great Northern," *Railway Age Gazette*, Vol. 51, No. 24, p.1214 (December 15, 1911).

"Mallet Locomotives for the Great Northern," *Railway Age Gazette*, Vol. 53, No. 13, p.572, September 27, 1912.

"Passenger Locomotives for the Great Northern," *Railway Age Gazette*, Vol. 57, No. 23, p. 1047 (December 14, 1914).

"Mallet Articulated Locomotives for the Great Northern Ry.", *The Railway and Engineering Review*, Vol. 50, No. 13, p. 306 (March 26, 1910).

"Mikado Type Locomotives for the Great Northern Ry.", *Railway Review*, Vol. 60, No. 1, p. 3 (January 6, 1917).

"Mikado Type Locomotives on The Great Northern", *Railway Review*, Vol. 68, No. 11, p. 405 (March 12, 1921).

"Simple Articulated Locomotives for G. N. Ry.," *Railway Review*, Vol. 77, No. 17, p. 629 (October 24, 1925).

"An Unusual Locomotive Performance," *Railway Review*, Vol. 78, No. 13, p. 598 (March 26, 1926).

M. C. Anderson. Letter to A. F. Kummer (Brotherhood of Locomotive Engineers, St. Paul, MN), February 9, 1946, File E-1(j).

Lambert M. Baker, quoted in correspondence from Frank Perrin to Norman F. Priebe, July 13, 1967.

Alex Colville. Shop Foreman's Notebook, undated.

Robert Downing. Personal communication to Norman F. Priebe, January 14, 1998.

Robert Downing. Speech before the Great Northern Railway Historical Society Grand Forks Convention, July 12, 1999

Joseph R. Douda. Personal communication to Kenneth R. Middleton, February 18, 2008.

Albert Farrow. Telephone conversation with Norman F. Priebe, November 1997.

George E. Fischer. Personal communication to N. F. Priebe, January 16, 1974.

M. L. Glover (Vice Chairman of the Brotherhood of Locomotive Engineers, Burlington Northern, St. Paul, MN). Personal communication to Norman F. Priebe, 1982.

Lawrence Hargis (Porter historian). Personal communication to Norman Priebe, October 17, 2008.

R. E. Johnson. Personal communication to Norman F. Priebe, September 8.

R. E. Johnson and George Wier. Personal communications to Norman F. Priebe.

F. R. Roach (The Standard Stoker Company). Letter to F. I. Plechner, November 21, 1930. Valuation Department Correspondence File, No. 125. Author's collection.

Donald R. Sease. Personal communication to R. E. Johnson relating memories of steam from the 1940's, October 21,1961.

L. V. Stevens (Locomotive Stoker Co.). Letter to W. R. Wood, November 20, 1924. Valuation Dept. Correspondence File, No. 125. Author's collection.

Walter Thayer. Personal communication to Norman F. Priebe

George T. Wier. Personal communication to Norman F. Priebe, November 26, 1973.

Mark S. Wilkouski (Santa Fe Historical Society). Personal communication to Norman F. Priebe, September 27, 2007.

Baldwin Locomotive Company Builders Card for Class N-1 2-8-8-0.

Chicago & Northwestern Railway Company, *Steam Locomotive Profiles*, reprint, Northwood Chapter N.R.H.S. Undated.

Engine Hours and Mileage, attached to a memo from J. F. Pratt to G. H. Emerson, May 7, 1913.

Great Northern Railway Company Annual Report No. 34 (December 31, 1922).

Great Northern Railway Company Annual Report No. 40 (December 31, 1928).

Great Northern Railway Company Annual Report, Machinery Department, 1891 and 1892 (Minnesota Historical Society).

Great Northern Railway Company Authorities for Expenditure (GNRHS).

Great Northern Railway Company Authorities for Expenditure Index.

Great Northern Railway Company Change Number Record Accounts (valuation information).

Great Northern Railway Company Chart of Corporate History, January 1, 1956.

Great Northern Railway Company CMO-office, Statement, *Painting of Steam Locomotives*, March 30, 1964

Great Northern Railway Company Dakota Division Dispatcher Logs, 1956.

Great Northern Railway Company Equipment Completion Report and Unit Record of Property Changes - Equipment. Account No. 51, Steam Locomotives (abbreviated "URPC"). While some modifications as early as 1916 are included, locomotives which had disappeared from the roster as of November, 1918, are not included. Changes from December 1918, onward are included. Portions obtained from various sources.

Great Northern Railway Company Historic Car Records Volumes 36-43 (New Equipment Registers 1-8) (Minnesota Historical Society).

Great Northern Railway Company Historic Car Records Volume 94 (Historical Record of S.C. and N. and Sioux City and Western, January 1, 1900) (Minnesota Historical Society).

Great Northern Railway Company Historic Car Records Vol. 99 (Great Northern Subsidiary Renumberings) (Minnesota Historical Society).

Great Northern Railway Company 1880-1900 Historical Engine Record.

Great Northern Railway Company Historical Engine Record modern (post 1900) volumes.

Great Northern Railway Company Histories and Corporate Records (Minnesota Historical Society).

Great Northern Railway Company List of Equipment 1923-1956.

Great Northern Railway Company Locomotive Assignment Rosters. Published by Fraternal Order of Empire Builders as Reference Sheet 4, July 1954 (Fall, 1974); Reference Sheet 15, December 1936 (January 1976); Reference Sheet 19, March 1942 (April 1976); and Reference Sheet 23, July 1949 (July 1976).

Great Northern Railway Company Locomotive Diagrams, 1900-1952.

Great Northern Railway Company Office General Superintendent Motive Power, Comparison Tonnage That Santa Fe and O-4 Class Engines Can Handle over Same Ruling Grades…, February 21 1921 (Minnesota Historical Society).

Great Northern Railway Company Passenger Timetables, July 1905 through November 1956.

Great Northern Railway Company Statement No. AD–7.1, Performance of Locomotives and Motor Cars, Ten Months Ending October 1954.

Great Northern Railway Company "The Official List of Officers, Stations and Agents" (Minnesota Historical Society).

Great Northern Railway Company Valuation Department Correspondence File No.7, New boilers for Locomotives.

Great Northern Railway Company Valuation Department Correspondence File No. 81, Map showing Locomotives Operating on Various Branch and Main Lines – Year 1915.

Great Northern Railway Company Valuation Department Correspondence File No. 125, Locomotives Equipped with Stokers.

Great Northern Railway Company Valuation Department Correspondence File No. 202, Roller Bearings Applied to Locomotives.

Great Northern Railway Company Vice-President Operating Files (Minnesota Historical Society).

The First Division of the St. Paul and Pacific Rail-Road Company, Report, May 31st, 1867. Anson Herrick & Sons, Printers, New York. (New York City Public Library, Manhattan.)

Interstate Commerce Commission Valuation Report Great Northern Ry. Co. [Decisions of the Interstate Commerce Commission of the United States (Valuation Reports), Report of the Commission, U.S. Government Printing Office, Washington, DC, Volume 133 (July-November, 1927). It was submitted October 23, 1925 and 'decided' July 11, 1927. It covers the valuation of the Great Northern Railway Company as of June 30, 1915.], p. 255.

Interstate Commerce Commission Valuation Engineering Report, Set No. S-66 (Minneapolis Western), June 30, 1915.

New York Locomotive Works Order List (obtained from Norman C. Keyes, Jr.). Author's collection.

Pittsburgh Locomotive and Car Works Order List, Alco Historic Photos, Schenectady, NY.

NISTIR 88-3099, National Technical Information Service, Springfield, VA 22161.

Rhode Island Locomotive Works Order List, Alco Historic Photos, Schenectady, NY.

Rogers Locomotive Works Order List, Alco Historic Photos, Schenectady, NY.

Schenectady Locomotive Works Order List, Alco Historic Photos, Schenectady, NY.

Special Library, University of Minnesota web page: special.lib.umn.edu/findaid/html/mss/nwaa0107.html

Taunton Locomotive Works Order List.

(Engine 60,000) Extract of test taken from Baldwin Locomotives, undated, provided by Robert LeMassena. The complete history of this engine is now available on the Internet at www.cwrr.com/Lounge/Reference/baldwin/baldwin.html

Numerous individual memos between GN personnel, from the files at the Minnesota Historical Society, St. Paul, MN, or associated with Authorities for Expenditure in the files of the Great Northern Railway Historical Society, Jackson Street Roundhouse, St. Paul, MN. These are listed in the End Notes of the chapters where they were cited.

Locomotive Photograph Index

The asterisk indicates the engine is stenciled with a different number than that shown in the index.

Wheel	Number	Page
0-4-0	51	79
	89	80
	191	81
	192	81
0-4-0 Steam Motor	1	363
	6000	364
0-4-0 Dinkey	4175	367
	6715	367
	6927	367
0-4-0 Fireless	S1	365
	S2	365
Shay	1	366
	2	366
0-6-0	S4	48
	1	51
	5	52
	8	48
	14	407
	15	52
	27	54
	28	51
	29	45
	30	44, 54
	31	55
	58	46
	59	47
	65	48
	71	49
	72	49
	78	51
	98	46, 54
	385	52
	386	53
	395	53
0-8-0	780	92
	781	430
	787	82
	789	82
	792	93
	813	83
	814	87
	815	85
	820	84
	825	84
	826	86
	828	85
	829	86
	836	86
	854	87
	856	89
	863	89
	864	89

Wheel	Number	Page
	871	94
	872	94
	876	90
	879	91
	883	82
	886	91
2-6-0	10	101
	300	97
	324	97
	345	98
	351	100
	357	98
	364*	101
	371	102
	400	100
	408	101
	450	102
	452	104
	453	103
	461	103
	478	76
2-6-2	1506	188
	1514	189
	1520	188
	1524	191, 193
	1531	192
	1532	189
	1613	192
	1624	193
	1626	194
	1637	187
	1647	193
2-8-0	15	148
	450	131
	508	133
	511	132, 134
	515	132
	521	133
	531	9
	537	133
	591*	148
	598	135
	701	135
	806	148
	1098	138
	1100	139
	1103	136
	1106	137
	1107	138
	1122	139
	1130	140
	1136	141
	1137	141
	1143	143
	1178	143
	1188	143
	1192	460
	1196	144

Wheel	Number	Page
	1201	144
	1216	144
	1220	145
	1221	145
	1323	147
	1326	149, 150
	1327	150
2-8-2	18	267
	3000	249, 250
	3001	250
	3002	252
	3004	251
	3006	251
	3009	250
	3010	252
	3013	253
	3019	251
	3021	254
	3022	266
	3025	255
	3030	254
	3031	255
	3033	32, 33
	3034	256
	3042	256, 262, 454, 581
	3046	255
	3051	256
	3052	29
	3056	534
	3065	257
	3071	32, 259
	3073	257
	3077	258
	3078	260
	3080	258
	3081	258
	3082	259
	3087	257
	3098	261
	3100	261, 518
	3106	29
	3107	264
	3108	261
	3122	27
	3125	264, 265
	3131	265
	3133	262
	3135	266
	3137	265
	3140	36
	3142	266
	3149	268
	3200	269, 271
	3201	271
	3202	271
	3203	272
	3204	272
	3205	270
	3207	273
	3215	528

Wheel	Number	Page
	3217	275
	3220	275, 280
	3224	276
	3226	276
	3228	274
	3235	277
	3239	274
	3244	277
	3246	272
	3250	278
	3252	280
	3253	274
	3254	278
	3300	281, 285, 286
	3306	283
	3309	284
	3323	284, 285
	3338	286
	3350	289
	3351	289
	3353	289, 290
	3356	292
	3357	288
	3359	287
	3363	290
	3364	290
	3369	288, 291
	3370	293
	3371	293
	3375	296, 299, 302, 309
	3377	307
	3378	297, 307
	3379	41, 297
	3380	303
	3386	298, 304
	3387	298
	3390	294, 295, 299, 309
	3391	297
	3394	307
	3395	299
	3396	307, 308
	3397	300, 306, 308
	3398	301
	3399	301, 309
2-10-2	2100	328
	2102	333
	2103	327
	2105	32
	2106	329
	2113	333
	2114	330
	2117	329
	2119	331
	2122	330
	2124	31
	2127	31, 330
	2129	332
	2175	338
	2177	334, 335, 339
	2178	337

Wheel	Number	Page
	2180	337
	2181	337
	2182	336
	2186	336
	2189	336
4-4-0	1	57, 58
	2	58
	4	59
	5	59
	7	77
	23	63
	35	63
	38	63
	103	69, 70
	105	75
	125	68
	139	76
	148	71
	162	71
	185	412
	186	406
	192	67
	193	67
	199	72
	202	73
	208	397
	209	73
	216	74
	219	381
	226	75, 421
	228	75
	232	78
	241	61, 62
	263*	63
	290	66
4-4-2	1700	195, 198
	1702	197
	1703	199
	1704	197, 198
	1705	196
	1706	199
	1707	200
4-6-0	2	112
	9	105
	16	108
	150	122
	299	113
	600	121
	650	117
	654	117
	901	110
	903	110
	904	111
	906	110
	907	111
	910	108, 109
	911	109
	925	114
	926	114, 115
	927	115
	932	115, 116
	933	116
	935	116
	948	123, 124
	960	118

Wheel	Number	Page
	965	118
	970	124
	991*	105
	999	121
	1000	122
	1010	126
	1012	126
	1027	126
	1028	127
	1032	127
	1033	128
	1042	128
	1053	119, 120
	1054	120
	1059	119
	1078	129
	1081	129
	1082	130
	1089	132
	1092	128
4-6-2	1350	25
	1355	507
	1357	172
	1359	173
	1360	171
	1361	173
	1363	173, 174
	1365	174
	1367	535
	1369	174
	1371	175
	1372	175, 176
	1375	180, 181, 182, 185
	1376	184
	1380	182
	1381	182, 183
	1383	183
	1384	184
	1402	160
	1404	160
	1406	161
	1413	19, 163
	1417	162
	1423	164
	1425	163
	1434	163
	1436	165
	1438	161
	1441	460
	1445	165
	1448	165, 166
	1450	166
	1452	167
	1458	159
	1459	167
	1462	168
	1470	169
	1473	169
	1477	170
	1482	170
	1486	172
	1710	176
	1711	177
	1714	178
	1716	179

Wheel	Number	Page
	1721	447
	1722	180
	1724	27
4-8-0	100	158
	302	153
	400	151
	405	152
	601	152
	607	153
	713	154
	722	156
	723	156
	726	154
	768	155
	769	155
	770	157
	772	156
	807	158
4-8-2	1752	311
	1754	313
	1755	312
	1757	313
	2501	319
	2502	323
	2505	314, 317
	2508	310
	2510	315, 321
	2511	323
	2512	30
	2513	27, 319, 320
	2514	30, 324, 537
	2515	31
	2517	316, 317
	2519	324
	2521	322
	2523	326
	2524	325
	2525	318, 322
	2527	317
4-8-4	2550	343, 347
	2551	343, 344
	2552	341, 343, 344, 347
	2553	345
	2554	346
	2555	345, 346
	2575	350, 354
	2576	358
	2577	348, 356
	2578	352, 353, 356
	2579	353, 357
	2580	340, 351, 357
	2582	354, 355
	2583	355
	2584	358
	2586	350
	2588	352, 353
2-6-6-2	1800	201
	1804	204, 208
	1805	204
	1806	23
	1810	203
	1818	208
	1900	206

Wheel	Number	Page
	1901	207
	1903	205
	1907	202, 203
	1912	206
	1916	207
2-6-8-0	1953	211
	1959	209
	1963	215
	1965	213
	1967	214
	1968	216
	1972	216
	1973	210, 214, 217
	1974	215
	1977	22, 217
	1981	215, 218
	1983	218
	2000	212
2-8-8-0	2000	225
	2001	39, 241
	2002	219
	2003	226, 227
	2004	220
	2005	243
	2006	224
	2008	246, 377
	2009	221
	2013	242
	2014	246
	2017	224
	2018	225, 240
	2020	221, 222
	2022	222, 226, 241
	2023	242
	2024	28, 225
2-8-8-2	2030	227
	2031	228, 229
	2035	230
	2037	230
	2039	231
	2041	231
	2042	527
	2043	232, 233
	2045	244
	2047	234, 235
	2048	238
	2049	235, 245
	2050	239
	2053	257
	2055	236, 246
	2056	236
	2058	236
2-8-8-4 DM&IR	222	368
	223	368
4-6-6-4	4000	360, 361
	4001	359, 361
Turbine	GE 1 & 2	369
	GE 2	376
Diesel, FT		
	5900	352

Subject Index

B

Baker, Lambert M., 303, 309
Barnesville, 8, 79, 180, 340
Belpaire (firebox), 25, 38, 151, 152
Bieber, 91, 227, 246, 258, 292
Breckenridge, 7, 8, 166, 220, 292, 303, 308, 316, 318, 323, 326, 333, 339
Brotherhood of Locomotive Engineers (BLE), 41, 42, 306
Budd, Ralph, 248, 272, 358, 376, 464
Butte, 9, 149, 150, 210, 214, 215
Butte Division, 64, 90, 113, 129, 130, 140, 145, 150, 164, 168, 177, 196, 200, 215, 216, 223, 227, 242, 275, 292, 298, 299, 308, 327, 328, 351, 354, 356

C

Cascade Division, 37, 135, 177, 185, 201, 202, 203, 223, 236, 239, 247, 260, 265, 287, 292, 322, 332, 334
Cascade Tunnel, 9, 137, 206, 316, 318, 363, 368
Clark, T. J., 40, 318
Coal (principal fuel), 25
Columbia Falls, 9, 120, 311, 364, 365
Colville, Alex, 40, 248, 301, 309, 326, 362, 376
Compound
  Balanced, 195
  Vauclain, 119, 121, 131, 195
Crowley, M. B., 40
Cut Bank, 168, 203, 228, 311, 312, 314

D

Dakota Division, 66, 78, 120, 151, 154, 155, 158, 177, 184, 185, 186, 208, 248, 256, 275, 287, 298, 316, 320, 324, 339, 346, 354, 356, 454, 462
Dale Street Shops (St. Paul), 35, 39, 50, 80, 88, 147, 171, 180, 190, 204, 213, 228, 281, 318, 363
Delta Shops, 39, 40, 205, 208, 281, 287
Deverell, A. C., 40, 167, 280, 376
Devils Lake, 9, 111, 144, 180
Dowling, J. J., 40
Downing, Robert, 248

E

Elsner, William H., 300
Embrittlement, 220, 221, 233, 245, 247, 356
Emerson, George H., 35, 40, 166, 168, 209, 213, 223, 248, 249, 254,

326, 368, 369, 376
Everett, 9, 40, 66, 73, 136, 208, 281, 312, 370

F

Fargo, 9, 30, 53, 156, 186, 198, 275, 285, 287, 324, 335, 339, 346, 356, 358
Fergus Falls, 74, 286, 287, 335, 397
Fort Wright, 359, 369, 531

G

Glasgow, 298, 304
Grand Forks, 9, 61, 62, 67, 78, 85, 104, 128, 135, 248, 324, 335, 336, 339, 346, 347, 356
Great Falls (and shops), 9, 39, 40, 80, 84, 88, 98, 119, 129, 130, 134, 155, 210, 214, 215, 216, 264, 295, 296, 304, 309, 335, 407

H

Havre, 9, 40, 58, 196, 274, 292, 295, 296, 298, 304, 308, 312, 342, 351, 356, 526
Hawkins, R. D., 40, 368, 376
Heron, J. C., 35, 376
Heron, J. H., 40
Hill, James J., 7, 8, 9, 11, 19, 58, 72, 95, 201, 219, 377
Hill, Louis W., 166, 170
Hillyard (and shops), 36, 37, 38, 39, 69, 70, 84, 88, 91, 94, 123, 124, 129, 138, 154, 156, 162, 170, 174, 213, 220, 221, 228, 231, 232, 234, 235, 236, 242, 243, 245, 248, 262, 264, 281, 284, 287, 288, 295, 297, 300, 301, 309, 321, 326, 332, 335, 342, 344, 346, 350, 359, 360, 362, 367, 368, 369, 376, 381
Hogeland, A. H., 223, 248, 280
Hurley, J. M., 40, 248, 301

I

Inaugural, *Empire Builder*, 318

J

Jackson Street (St. Paul), 45, 75, 200, 318, 320, 376
Jenks, C. O., 83, 150, 185, 223, 238, 242, 248, 272, 280, 303, 309, 311, 326, 342, 348, 358, 359, 362, 376
Johnson, R. E., 40, 304, 309, 362

K

Kalispell, 9, 311, 364, 365
Kalispell Division, 37, 72, 90, 119, 120, 122, 136, 140, 185, 203, 216, 219, 223, 227, 228, 238, 242, 243,

245, 265, 275, 287, 292, 293, 301, 316, 328, 334, 342, 351, 356, 372
Kelly, William, 26, 40, 83, 150, 170, 185, 238, 242, 248, 280, 300, 303, 309, 342, 348, 358, 376
Kelly Lake, 176
Kerr, D. A., 227, 248
King Street Station, 82, 191, 351
Klamath Division, 37, 227, 242, 246, 247, 292, 334, 368
Klamath Falls, 31, 37, 91, 138, 139, 179, 214, 288, 362

L

Lengby, J. A., 227, 248
Lidgerwood method, 329
Locomotive Accessories, See Ch. 3
Locomotive Assignments, See respective chapter

Locomotive Builders

A

ALCO, 50, 55, 56, 104, 108, 139, 144, 147, 150, 159, 224, 238, 241, 267, 269, 280, 303, 304, 359, 362, 380

B

Baldwin, 30, 34, 39, 50, 53, 55, 57, 61, 63, 64, 66, 78, 83, 95, 98, 99, 119, 121, 122, 125, 129, 130, 131, 136, 139, 140, 144, 145, 159, 162, 164, 165, 168, 170, 171, 187, 195, 201, 202, 204, 209, 212, 213, 219, 221, 224, 227, 228, 229, 230, 234, 238, 248, 249, 263, 272, 280, 292, 295, 301, 304, 314, 318, 320, 321, 324, 326, 327, 342, 348, 356, 369, 370, 372, 380
Brooks, 25, 45, 47, 48, 56, 57, 72, 79, 80, 81, 99, 102, 104, 105, 107, 108, 122, 131, 137, 139, 147, 150, 151, 158, 267, 269, 380

C

Cooke, 137, 280, 380

D

Danforth, 20, 57, 59, 60, 380
Davenport, 367

G

General Electric, 376
General Motors (EMC, EMD), 55, 56, 72, 238, 352
General Steel Castings, 302, 304
Grant, 57, 72, 380

H

Hinkley, 19, 21, 43, 380,

L

Lima, 39, 56, 168, 169, 170, 311, 365, 366, 367, 369, 380

M

Mason, 20, 59, 60, 380

N

New York, 57, 78, 380
Norris, 19, 20, 58, 59, 380

P

Pittsburgh, 57, 380
Porter, 104, 364, 365, 367, 380
Puget Sound Machinery Depot, 228, 234, 248, 380

R

Rhode Island, 57, 67, 72, 78, 95, 105, 113, 380
Rogers, 20, 43, 44, 46, 50, 57, 78, 79, 95, 105, 111, 113, 119, 136, 139, 143, 144, 154, 159, 160, 380

S

Schenectady, 57, 66, 104, 112, 269, 359, 360, 380
Shay, see Lima
Smith and Jackson, 19, 20, 380
Souther, 20, 59, 380

T

Taunton, 22, 64, 66, 380

L (continued)

Locomotive Components See Ch. 3
Locomotive Names (St.P&P), 58-62, 389-391
Locomotive Paint schemes, See Ch. 3
Locomotive Tenders, See Ch. 32 & 34

M

Marathon, 316
Marias Pass, 9, 287, 327, 328
Mesabi Division, 37, 107, 119, 139, 150, 158, 176, 185, 216, 218, 223, 227, 242, 245, 247, 248, 275, 334, 339, 346
Meyers, R. T., 303
Miller, H. W., 240, 300, 303
Miller, J. S., 362
Minneapolis, 7, 8, 9, 200, 241, 242, 246, 282, 292, 293, 308, 324, 333, 339, 342, 346, 350, 355, 356, 363, 370
Minot, 9, 166, 170, 241, 244, 246, 248, 287, 301, 308, 318, 324, 335, 339, 346, 368, 370, 372
Minot Division, 64, 72, 88, 111, 170, 223, 238, 247, 292, 296, 297, 298, 301, 308, 316, 317, 320, 324, 327, 328, 334, 335, 339, 344, 346, 351
Montana Division, 196, 350
Moorhead, 9

N
New Rockford, 287, 308

O
Oil (principal fuel), 25

P
Pasco, 326, 361
Pattee, J. O., 40
Pool, Ira G., 40, 86, 88, 233, 248,
   303, 309, 324, 326

R
Railroads
A
   Atchison, Topeka and Santa Fe
      (a.k.a. Santa Fe), 264, 327
B
   Baltimore and Ohio, 36, 64, 201,
      309, 326, 380
   Butte, Anaconda and Pacific, 47,
      67, 99, 101, 380
C
   Chesapeake and Ohio, 237, 306,
      311
   Chicago, Burlington and Quincy
      (a.k.a. Burlington), 10, 11, 41, 78,
      95, 105, 202, 262, 348, 363, 380
   Chicago, Milwaukee, St. Paul and
      Pacific (a.k.a. Milwaukee Road),
      372
   Chicago, St. Paul, Minneapolis and
      Omaha, 78, 380
   Columbia and Red Mountain, 10,
      136, 380
D
   Duluth, Missabi and Iron Range, 237,
      368
   Duluth, Mississippi River and
      Northern, 9, 104, 105, 380
   Duluth, Superior and Western, 9, 45,
      98, 380
E
   Eastern Railway Company of
      Minnesota, 9, 11, 72, 380
   Erie, 306
F
   Fairhaven and Southern, 10, 22, 112,
      380

G
   Great Northern Railway, 9, 10, 11,
      26, 380

K
   Kanawha and Michigan, 99, 380
L
   Lake Superior and Southwestern, 9
   Lake Superior Terminal and Transfer,
      380
   Louisville and Nashville, 306
M
   Minneapolis and St. Cloud Railroad,
      9, 11
   Minneapolis Western, 44, 79, 380
   Minnesota and Pacific, 7, 58, 380
   Montana Central, 9, 11, 45, 47, 56,
      73, 95, 99, 122, 151, 158, 380
N
   Nelson and Fort Sheppard Railway,
      10, 78, 122, 380
   New York Central, 348
   Nickel Plate, 306
   Northern Pacific, 8, 10, 11, 26, 39,
      59, 272, 359, 380
O
   Oregon, California and Eastern, 218
P
   Pacific Short Line, 78, 95, 105, 113,
      380
   Pennsylvania, 25, 223, 264, 342,
      370
   Red Mountain, 10, 136, 380
   Red River and Manitoba, 8
   Red River Valley Railroad Company,
      8, 9
S
   St. Paul and Pacific, 7, 8, 19, 58,
      380
   St. Paul, Minneapolis and Manitoba,
      8, 9, 11, 19, 21, 38, 43, 57, 48, 363,
      380
   Seattle and Montana, 10, 11, 78,
      112, 380
   Seattle and Northern, 10, 78, 380
   Sioux City and Northern, 10, 78,
      105, 380
   Sioux City and St. Paul, 78, 380
   Sioux City and Western, 10, 78, 105,
      380
   Sioux Falls Terminal Railroad, 10
   Sioux Falls, Yankton and
      Southwestern, 10
   Somers Lumber Co., 363-367
   Spokane Falls and Northern, 10, 11,
      78, 95, 122, 136, 380

   Spokane, Portland and Seattle
      (SP&S), 11, 37, 39, 99, 113, 125,
      129, 131, 139, 177, 185, 187, 188,
      190, 194, 264, 275, 292, 326,
      359–362, 380
   Superior Belt Line and Terminal, 10
   Swan River Logging Company, 10
U
   Union Pacific, 237, 282, 314, 359,
      376
V
   Vancouver, Victoria and Eastern Ry.
      and Nav. Co., 10
   Virginian, 221, 306
W
   Washington and Great Northern, 10
   Watertown and Sioux Falls, 99, 107,
      150, 268, 380
   Western Pacific, 237
   Willmar and Sioux Falls, 10, 78, 105,
      113, 380
   Wheeling and Lake Erie, 254

R (continued)
Rexford (hill), 245, 301
Robson, John L., 40, 362

S
St. Cloud, 7, 8, 11, 185, 292, 318,
   326, 339, 346, 356
St. Paul, 7, 8, 39, 45, 50, 168, 281,
   306, 316, 318, 346, 351, 354, 363,
   364
St. Paul Union Depot, 185, 200
Seattle, 176, 180, 194, 312, 316, 318,
   322, 334, 341, 351, 367
Shelby, 292
Silk Trains, 316
Silver, H. S., 35, 240, 241, 303
Sioux City, 10, 95, 105, 113
Sioux Falls, 10, 267
Smith, A. H., 254
Smith, J. B., 358
Smith, R. A., 40
Somers, 364, 365
Spokane, 10, 39
Spokane Division, 67, 90. 102, 113,
   122, 129, 131, 139, 151, 154, 170,
   216, 223, 238, 247, 339, 356, 462
Superintendents, Motive Power, 40
Superior (and Shops), 37, 39, 83,
   159, 200, 242, 245, 292, 295, 335,
   339, 370

T
Toltz, Max, 40, 363

Trains
   Alexandrian, 198, 199, 200
   Badger, 197, 198, 199, 200
   Cascadian, 356
   Dakotan, 354
   Empire Builder, 170, 281, 310, 318,
      319, 329, 341, 342, 343, 349, 351,
      352, 353, 354
   Fargo Fast, 293
   Fast Mail, 316, 324, 341, 346, 351,
      354
   G. N. Flyer, 21
   Oriental Limited, 170, 195. 196, 311,
      314, 318, 324, 341, 346, 351, 354
   Puget Sounder, 159
   Western Star, 346
   Winnipeg Limited, 185

T (continued)
Trowbridge, A. J., 303, 309

V
Vauclain, Samuel, 301, 303
Separable boiler, 209, 212

W
Wenatchee, 316, 351, 354, 376
Whitefish, 37, 203, 228, 245, 287,
   301, 311, 312, 318, 335, 342, 351,
   356, 368
Williston, 223, 238, 267, 308, 351,
   354, 372
Willmar Division, 50, 56, 64, 72, 73,
   88, 90, 111, 113, 151, 170, 177, 194,
   200, 264, 267, 275, 282, 292, 298,
   308, 316, 318, 324, 326, 334, 339,
   346, 354, 356
Wishram, 37, 227, 360

Y
Yoerg, Henry, 40, 300